Nineteenth-Century Literature Criticism

Guide to Gale Literary Criticism Series

When you need to review criticism of literary works, these are the Gale series to use:

If the author's death date is:

You should turn to:

After Dec. 31, 1959
(or author is still living)

CONTEMPORARY LITERARY CRITICISM

for example: Jorge Luis Borges, Anthony Burgess,
William Faulkner, Mary Gordon,
Ernest Hemingway, Iris Murdoch

1900 through 1959

TWENTIETH-CENTURY LITERARY CRITICISM

for example: Willa Cather, F. Scott Fitzgerald,
Henry James, Mark Twain, Virginia Woolf

1800 through 1899

NINETEENTH-CENTURY LITERATURE CRITICISM

for example: Fyodor Dostoevsky, Nathaniel Hawthorne,
George Sand, William Wordsworth

1400 through 1799

LITERATURE CRITICISM FROM 1400 TO 1800
(excluding Shakespeare)

for example: Anne Bradstreet, Daniel Defoe,
Alexander Pope, François Rabelais,
Jonathan Swift, Phillis Wheatley

SHAKESPEAREAN CRITICISM

Shakespeare's plays and poetry

Antiquity through 1399

CLASSICAL AND MEDIEVAL LITERATURE CRITICISM

for example: Dante, Homer, Plato, Sophocles, Vergil,
the Beowulf Poet

Gale also publishes related criticism series:

BLACK LITERATURE CRITICISM

This three-volume series presents criticism of works by major
black writers of the past two hundred years.

CHILDREN'S LITERATURE REVIEW

This series covers authors of all eras who have written for the
preschool through high school audience.

DRAMA CRITICISM

This series covers playwrights of all nationalities and periods of
literary history.

POETRY CRITICISM

This series covers poets of all nationalities and periods of literary
history.

SHORT STORY CRITICISM

This series covers the major short fiction writers of all
nationalities and periods of literary history.

ISSN 0732-1864

Volume 37

Nineteenth-Century Literature Criticism

Excerpts from Criticism of the
Works of Novelists, Poets, Playwrights,
Short Story Writers, Philosophers, and Other
Creative Writers Who Died between 1800
and 1899, from the First Published Critical
Appraisals to Current Evaluations

Joann Cerrito
Editor

Tina Grant
Alan Hedblad
Drew Kalasky
Jelena O. Krstović
Lawrence J. Trudeau
Associate Editors

 Gale Research Inc. · DETROIT · WASHINGTON, D.C. · LONDON

Contents

Preface   vii

Acknowledgments   xi

Preface

Since its inception in 1981, *Nineteenth-Century Literature Criticism* has been a valuable resource for students and librarians seeking critical commentary on writers of this transitional period in world history. Designated an "Outstanding Reference Source" by the American Library Association with the publication of its first volume, *NCLC* has since been purchased by over 6,000 school, public, and university libraries. The series has covered more than 300 authors representing 26 nationalities and over 15,000 titles. No other reference source has surveyed the critical reaction to nineteenth-century authors and literature as thoroughly as *NCLC*.

Scope of the Series

NCLC is designed to serve as an introduction for students and advanced readers to the authors of the nineteenth century, and to the most significant interpretations of these authors' works. The great poets, novelists, short story writers, dramatists, and philosophers of this period are frequently studied in high school and college literature courses. By organizing and reprinting the enormous amount of commentary written on these authors, *NCLC* helps students develop valuable insight into literary history, promotes a better understanding of the texts, and sparks ideas for papers and assignments. Each entry in *NCLC* presents a comprehensive survey of an author's career or an individual work of literature and provides the user with a multiplicity of interpretations and assessments. Such variety allows students to pursue their own interests; furthermore, it fosters an awareness that literature is dynamic and responsive to many different opinions.

Every fourth volume of *NCLC* is devoted to literary topics that cannot be covered under the author approach used in the rest of the series. Such topics include literary movements, prominent themes in nineteenth-century literature, literary reaction to political and historical events, significant eras in literary history, prominent literary anniversaries, and the literatures of cultures that are often overlooked by English-speaking readers.

NCLC continues the survey of criticism of world literature begun by Gale's *Contemporary Literary Criticism (CLC)* and *Twentieth-Century Literary Criticism (TCLC)*, both of which excerpt and reprint commentary on authors of the twentieth century. For additional information about *TCLC, CLC,* and Gale's other criticism series, users should consult the Guide to Gale Literary Criticism Series preceding the title page in this volume.

Coverage

Each volume of *NCLC* is carefully compiled to present:

- criticism of authors, or literary topics, representing a variety of genres and nationalities
- both major and lesser-known writers and literary works of the period
- 7-10 authors or 4-6 topics per volume
- individual entries that survey critical response to each author's work or each topic in literary history, including early criticism to reflect initial reactions; later criticism to represent any rise or decline in reputation; and current retrospective analyses.

Organization of This Book

An author entry consists of the following elements: author heading, biographical and critical introduction, list of principal works, excerpts of criticism (each preceded by an annotation and followed by a bibliographic citation), and a bibliography of further reading.

- The **author heading** consists of the name under which the author most commonly wrote, followed by birth and death dates. If an author wrote consistently under a pseudonym, the pseudonym will be listed in the author heading and the real name given in parentheses on the first line of the biographical and critical introduction. Also located at the beginning of the introduction to the author entry are any name variations under which an author wrote, including transliterated forms for authors whose languages use nonroman alphabets.

• The **biographical and critical introduction** outlines the author's life and career, as well as the critical issues surrounding his or her work. References are provided to past volumes of *NCLC*.

• Most *NCLC* entries include **portraits** of the author. Many entries also contain reproductions of materials pertinent to an author's career, including manuscript pages, title pages, dust jackets, letters, and drawings, as well as photographs of important people, places, and events in an author's life.

• The list of **principal works** is chronological by date of first book publication and identifies the genre of each work. In the case of foreign authors with both foreign-language publications and English translations, the title and date of the first English-language edition are given in brackets. Unless otherwise indicated, dramas are dated by first performance, not first publication.

• **Criticism** is arranged chronologically in each author entry to provide a perspective on changes in critical evaluation over the years. All titles of works by the author featured in the entry are printed in boldface type to enable the user to easily locate discussion of particular works. Also for purposes of easier identification, the critic's name and the publication date of the essay are given at the beginning of each piece of criticism. Unsigned criticism is preceded by the title of the journal in which it appeared. Publication information (such as publisher names and book prices) and parenthetical numerical references (such as footnotes or page and line references to specific editions of works) have been deleted at the editors' discretion to provide smoother reading of the text.

• Critical excerpts are prefaced by **annotations** providing the reader with information about both the critic and the criticism that follows. Included are the critic's reputation, individual approach to literary criticism, and particular expertise in an author's works. Also noted are the relative importance of a work of criticism, the scope of the excerpt, and the growth of critical controversy or changes in critical trends regarding an author. In some cases, these annotations cross-reference excerpts by critics who discuss each other's commentary.

• A complete **bibliographic citation** designed to facilitate location of the original essay or book follows each piece of criticism.

• An annotated list of **further reading** appearing at the end of each author entry suggests secondary sources on the author. In some cases it includes essays for which the editors could not obtain reprint rights.

Cumulative Indexes

• Each volume of *NCLC* contains a cumulative **author index** listing all authors who have appeared in Gale's Literary Criticism Series, along with cross-references to such biographical series as *Contemporary Authors* and *Dictionary of Literary Biography*. Useful for locating authors within the various series, this index is particularly valuable for those authors who are identified by a certain period but who, because of their death dates, are placed in another, or for those authors whose careers span two periods. For example, Fyodor Dostoevsky is found in *NCLC*, yet Leo Tolstoy, another major nineteenth-century Russian novelist, is found in *TCLC* because he died after 1899.

• Each *NCLC* volume includes a cumulative **nationality index** which lists all authors who have appeared in *NCLC*, arranged alphabetically under their respective nationalities, as well as Topics volume entries devoted to particular national literatures.

• Each new volume in Gale's Literary Criticism Series includes a cumulative **topic index,** which lists all literary topics treated in *NCLC, TCLC, LC 1400-1800,* and the *CLC* Yearbook.

• Each new volume of *NCLC,* with the exception of the Topics volumes, contains a **title index** listing the titles of all literary works discussed in the volume. The first volume of *NCLC* published each year contains an index listing all titles discussed in the series since its inception. Titles discussed in the Topics volume entries are not included in the *NCLC* cumulative index.

A Note to the Reader

When writing papers, students who quote directly from any volume in Gale's Literary Criticism Series may use the following general forms to footnote reprinted criticism. The first example pertains to material drawn from periodicals, the second to material reprinted from books.

[1] T. S. Eliot, "John Donne," *The Nation and the Athenaeum,* 33 (9 June 1923), 321-32; excerpted and reprinted in *Literature Criticism from 1400 to 1800,* Vol. 10, ed. James E. Person, Jr. (Detroit: Gale Research, 1989), pp. 28-9.

[2] Clara G. Stillman, *Samuel Butler: A Mid-Victorian Modern* (Viking Press, 1932); excerpted and reprinted

in *Twentieth-Century Literary Criticism,* Vol. 33, ed. Paula Kepos (Detroit: Gale Research, 1989), pp. 43-5.

Suggestions Are Welcome

In response to suggestions, several features have been added to *NCLC* since the series began, including annotations to excerpted criticism, a cumulative index to authors in all Gale literary criticism series, entries devoted to criticism on a single work by a major author, more extensive illustrations, and a title index listing all literary works discussed in the series since its inception.

Readers who wish to suggest authors or topics to appear in future volumes, or who have other suggestions, are cordially invited to write the editors.

ACKNOWLEDGMENTS

The editors wish to thank the copyright holders of the excerpted criticism included in this volume, the permissions managers of many book and magazine publishing companies for assisting us in securing reprint rights, and Anthony Bogucki for assistance with copyright research. We are also grateful to the staffs of the Detroit Public Library Complex, and University of Michigan Libraries for making their resources available to us. Following is a list of copyright holders who have granted us permission to reprint material in this volume of *NCLC*. Every effort has been made to trace copyright, but if omissions have been made, please let us know.

COPYRIGHTED EXCERPTS IN *NCLC*, VOLUME 37, WERE REPRINTED FROM THE FOLLOWING PERIODICALS:

American Literary Realism 1870-1910, v. 6, Winter, 1973. Copyright © 1973 by the Department of English, The University of Texas at Arlington. Reprinted by permission of the publisher.—*The American Political Science Review,* v. LV, September, 1961. Copyright, 1961, renewed 1989 by The American Political Science Association. Reprinted by permission of the publisher.—*College Literature,* v. IV, Winter, 1977. Copyright © 1977 by West Chester University. Reprinted by permission of the publisher.—*English Studies,* Netherlands, v. 66, June, 1985. © 1985 by Swets & Zeitlinger B.V. Reprinted by permission of the publisher.—*Forum for Modern Language Studies,* v. VIII, April, 1972 for "Figures of Authority in the Works of Heinrich von Kleist" by J. M. Lindsay. Copyright © 1972 by *Forum for Modern Language Studies* and the author. Reprinted by permission of the publisher and the author.—*The Midwest Quarterly,* v. VII, April, 1966. Copyright, 1966, by *The Midwest Quarterly,* Pittsburg State University. Reprinted by permission of the publisher.—*The Modern Language Review,* v. 80, January, 1985 for "The Limitations of Knowledge: Kleist's 'Über das Marionettentheater' " by G. A. Wells. © Modern Humanities Research Association 1985. Reprinted by permission of the publisher and the author.—*New York Literary Forum,* v. 7, 1980. Copyright © *New York Literary Forum* 1980. All rights reserved. Reprinted by permission of the publisher.—*Nineteenth-Century Fiction,* v. 32, September, 1977 for "G. M. Reynolds, Dickens, and the Mysteries of London" by Richard C. Maxwell. © 1977 by The Regents of the University of California. Reprinted by permission of The Regents and the author.—*Novel: A Forum on Fiction,* v. 9, Spring, 1976. Copyright NOVEL Corp. © 1976. Reprinted with permission.—*Partisan Review,* v. XXV, Spring, 1958. Copyright © 1958, renewed 1986 by *Partisan Review.* Reprinted by permission of the publisher.—*The Review of Politics,* v. II, January, 1949. Copyright, 1949, renewed 1976, University of Notre Dame. Reprinted by permission of the publisher.—*Revue des langues vivantes,* v. XXXIV, 1968 for "Tragedy and Self-Deception in Turgenev's 'Fathers and Sons' " by Charles R. Bachman. Reprinted by permission of the author.—*Seminar,* v. XVII, November, 1981. © The Canadian Association of University Teachers of German 1981. Reprinted by permission of the publisher.—*The Slavonic and East European Review,* v. 64, April, 1986. © School of Slavonic and East European Studies (University of London) 1986. Reprinted by permission of the Editors.—*Studies in Romanticism,* v. VI, Summer, 1967. Copyright 1967 by the Trustees of Boston University. Reprinted by permission of the publisher.—*The Times Literary Supplement,* n. 3994, October 20, 1978. © The Times Supplements Limited 1978. Reproduced from *The Times Literary Supplement* by permission.—*Victorian Periodicals Review,* v. XVI, Fall-Winter, 1983. © *Victorian Periodicals Review* Fall & Winter Issue, January 1984. Reprinted by permission of the publisher.—*The Virginia Quarterly Review,* v. 28, Spring, 1952. Copyright, 1952, renewed 1980 by *The Virginia Quarterly Review,* The University of Virginia. Reprinted by permission of the publisher.—*The Yale Review,* v. LXVII, Spring, 1978. Copyright 1978, by Yale University. Reprinted by permission of the editors.—*The Yearbook of English Studies,* v. 11, 1981. © Modern Humanities Research Association 1981. All rights reserved. Reprinted by permission of the Editor and the Modern Humanities Research Association.

COPYRIGHTED EXCERPTS IN *NCLC*, VOLUME 37, WERE REPRINTED FROM THE FOLLOWING BOOKS:

Ackroyd, Peter. From *Dickens.* Sinclair-Stevenson Limited, 1990. Copyright © 1990 by Peter Ackroyd. All rights reserved. Reprinted by permission of the publisher.—Berlin, Isaiah. From *Fathers and Children: The Romanes Lecture.* Oxford at the Clarendon Press, 1972. © Oxford University Press 1972. Reprinted by permission of the publisher.—Bloom, Harold. From *Blake's Apocalypse: A Study in Poetic Argument.* Doubleday & Company, Inc. 1963. Copyright © 1963 by Harold Bloom. All rights reserved. Used by permission of Doubleday, a division of Bantam Doubleday Dell Publishing Group, Inc.—Bowra, C. M. From *The Romantic Imagination.* Cambridge, Mass.: Harvard University Press, 1949. Copyright 1949 by the President and Fellows of Harvard College. Renewed © 1977 by the Literary Estate of Cecil Maurice Bowra. Excerpted by permission of Harvard University Press and the Literary Estate of Cecil Maurice Bowra.—Boyd, Alexander F. From *Aspects of the Russian Novel.* Chatto & Windus, 1972. © Alexander F. Boyd 1972. Reprinted by permission of the publisher.—Brantlinger, Patrick. From *The Spirit of Reform: British Literature and Politics, 1832-1867.* Cambridge, Mass.: Harvard University Press, 1977. Copyright © 1977 by the President and Fellows of Harvard College. All rights reserved. Excerpted by permission of the publishers and the author.—Colby, Robert A. From *Fiction with a Purpose: Major and Minor Nineteenth-Century Novels.* Indiana University Press, 1967. Copyright © 1967 by Indiana University Press. All rights reserved. Reprinted by permission of the publisher.—Damon, S. Foster. From *A Blake Dictionary: The Ideas and Symbols of William Blake.* Brown University Press, 1965. Copyright © 1965 by Brown University. All rights reserved. Reprinted by permission of University Press of New England.—Dyer, Denys. From *The Stories of Kleist: A Critical Study.* Holmes & Meier Publishers, 1977. © Denys Dyer 1977. All rights reserved. Reprinted by permission of the publisher.—Erdman, David V. From *Blake, Prophet Against Empire: A Poet's Interpretation of the History of His Own Times.* Dover Publications, 1991. Copyright 1954, © 1969, 1977 by Princeton University Press. Copyright © renewed 1982 by David V. Erdman. Reprinted by permission of the publisher.—Feuer, Kathryn. From "High Noon: 'Fathers and Sons', Fathers and Children," in *The Russian Novel from Pushkin to Pasternak.* Edited by John Garrard. Yale University Press, 1983. Copyright © 1983 by Yale University. All rights reserved. Reprinted by permission of the publisher.—Frye, Northrop. From *Fearful Symmetry: A Study of William Blake.* Princeton University Press, 1947. Copyright 1947 by Princeton University Press.—Gearey, John. From *Heinrich von Kleist: A Study in Tragedy and Anxiety.* University of Pennsylvania Press, 1968. Copyright © 1968 by the Trustees of the University of Pennsylvania. Reprinted by permission of the author.—Gifford, Henry. From *The Novel in Russia: From Pushkin to Pasternak.* Hutchinson University Library, 1964. © Henry Gifford 1964. Reprinted by permission of the publisher.—Gillham, D. G. From *Blake's Contrary States: The "Songs of Innocence and of Experience" as Dramatic Poems.* Cambridge at the University Press, 1966. © Cambridge University Press 1966. Reprinted with the permission of the publisher and the Literary Estate of D. G. Gillham.—Guerney, Bernard Guilbert. From a foreword to *Fathers and Sons.* By Ivan S. Turgenev, translated by Bernard Guilbert Guerney. The Modern Library, 1961. © copyright 1961, renewed 1989, by Bernard Guilbert Guerney. All rights reserved. Reprinted by permission of Random House, Inc.—Henry, Peter. From "I. S. Turgenev: 'Fathers and Sons' (1862)," in *The Monster in the Mirror: Studies in Nineteenth-Century Realism.* Edited by D. A. Williams. Oxford University Press, 1978. © University of Hull 1978. All rights reserved. Reprinted by permission of the University of Hull.—Hirsch, E. D., Jr. From *Innocence and Experience: An Introduction to Blake.* Yale University Press, 1964. Copyright © 1964 by Yale University. All rights reserved. Reprinted by permission of the author.—Hollingsworth, Keith. From *The Newgate Novel, 1830-1847: Bulwer, Ainsworth, Dickens, & Thackeray.* Wayne State University Press, 1963. Copyright © 1963 by Wayne State University Press. All rights reserved. Reprinted by permission of the author.—Jackson, Wallace. From *The Probable and the Marvelous: Blake, Wordsworth, and the Eighteenth-Century Critical Tradition.* The University of Georgia Press, 1978. Copyright © 1978 by the University of Georgia Press. All rights reserved. Reprinted by permission of the publisher.—Kettle, Arnold. From *An Introduction to the English Novel, Vol. I.* Second edition. Hutchinson University Library, 1967. Reprinted by permission of the publisher.—Keynes, Sir Geoffrey. From *Songs of Innocence and of Experience: Shewing the Two Contrary States of the Human Soul, 1789-1794.* By William Blake. Commentary by Sir Geoffrey Keynes. Orion Press, 1967. © The Trianon Press 1967. © Oxford University Press 1967. All rights reserved. Reprinted by permission of Oxford University Press.—Kleist, Heinrich von. From a letter in *Kleist: A Biography.* By Joachim Maass, translated by Ralph Manheim. Farrar, Straus and Giroux, 1983. Translation copyright © 1983 by Farrar, Straus and Giroux, Inc. All rights reserved. Reprinted by permission of Farrar, Straus and Giroux, Inc.—Lamport, F. J. From *German Classical Drama: Theatre, Humanity and Nation, 1750-1870.* Cambridge University Press, 1990. © Cambridge University Press 1990. Reprinted with the permission of the publisher and the author.—Leader, Zachary. From *Reading Blake's "Songs".* Routledge & Kegan Paul, 1981. Copyright © Zachary Leader 1981. Reprinted by permission of the publisher.—Lombard, Charles M. From an introduction to *Letters on the Spanish Inquisition.* By Count Joseph de Maistre. Scholars' Facsimiles & Reprints, 1977. © 1977 Scholars' Facsimiles & Reprints, Inc. All rights reserved. Reprinted by permission of the publisher.—Lowe, David. From *Turgenev's "Fathers and Sons."* Ardis, 1983. Copyright © 1983 by Ardis. Reprinted by permission of the publisher.—Matlaw, Ralph E. From "Turgenev's Novels and 'Fathers and Sons'," in *"Fathers and Sons" by Ivan Turgenev: The Author on the Novel, Contemporary Reactions, Essays in Criticism.* Edited and translated by Ralph E. Matlaw. A Norton Critical Edition. Norton, 1966. Copyright © 1966 by W. W. Norton & Company, Inc. Reprinted by permission of the publisher.—McGlathery, James M. From *Desire's Sway: The Plays and Stories of Heinrich von Kleist.* Wayne State University Press, 1983. Copyright © 1983 by Wayne State University Press. All rights reserved. Reprinted by permission of the publisher and the author.—Monod, Sylvére. From *Dickens the Novelist.* University of Oklahoma Press, 1968. Copyright 1968 by the University of Oklahoma Press. Reprinted by permission of the publisher.—Paglia, Camille. From *Sexual Personae: Art and Decadence from Nefertiti to Emily Dickinson.* Yale University Press, 1990. Copyright © 1990 by Yale University. All rights reserved. Reprinted by permission of the publisher.—Pagliaro, Harold. From *Selfhood and Redemption in Blake's "Songs".* The Pennsylvania State University Press, 1987. Copyright © 1987, The Pennsylvania State University Press, University Park, PA. All rights reserved. Reproduced by permission of the publisher.—Prandi, Julie D. From *Spirited Women Heroes: Major Female Characters in the Dramas of Goethe, Schiller and Kleist.* Lang, 1983. © Peter Lang Publishing Inc., 1983. All rights reserved. Reprinted by permission of the publisher.—Pritchett, V. S. From *A Man of Letters: Selected Essays.* Random House, 1985. Copyright © 1985

William Blake

Songs of Innocence and of Experience

English poet.

The following entry presents criticism of Blake's *Songs of Innocence and of Experience* (1794). For discussion of his complete career, see *NCLC,* Volume 13.

INTRODUCTION

A slender collection of illustrated, short lyrical poems that have been praised as models of prosody, *Songs of Innocence and of Experience* is considered a principal composition of the Romantic movement for its artistic championship of individuality and imagination and its concomitant condemnation of rationalist philosophy, social blight, and all forms of orthodoxy. Assuming the style of children's poems, the verses in *Songs* betray their ostensibly straightforward form through the incorporation of irony, symbolism, implied narrators, and other complicating devices. The work is subdivided into "Songs of Innocence" that generally reflect on the beauty of nature and the blithe simplicity associated with childhood and "Songs of Experience" that convey the often stern reality of human existence. The complexity of *Songs* shrouds Blake's ultimate assessment of the two states depicted, but general consensus holds that "The Tyger"—widely perceived as sanctioning the diverse and seemingly contradictory aspects within human nature and the universe—best encapsulates Blake's attitude towards his subject.

Blake was born and raised in eighteenth-century London, a city plagued by the public health threats that accompanied its rapid industrialization and urbanization. Air and water pollution, improperly purified water supplies, and an inadequate drainage system contributed to disease and high death rates in the city, exacerbating troubles caused by an outdated educational system, the exploitation of cheap labor, and growing disfranchisement. In 1784 Blake, with his younger brother Robert and the engraver James Parker, began a printing business in his residence. Historians tentatively assign that year to Blake's dramatic satire *An Island in the Moon,* a fragmentary manuscript that contains the earliest extant drafts of at least three poems later incorporated into "Songs of Innocence": "Holy Thursday," "Nurse's Song," and "The Little Boy Lost." After Robert died and the business failed in 1787, Blake chose to experiment with copperplate etching rather than contract commercial publishers, who practiced the conventional letter-press method of printing. Etching— the discriminating application of a corrosive agent such as nitric acid to the surface of copper plates in order to create reliefs—enabled him to retain complete creative control of his manuscripts, fuse designs and text on a single plate, and avoid the exorbitant costs associated with traditional publishing. Scholars have noted the care required by

Blake's "illuminated printing," which entailed transcribing the text backwards on each plate and rendering designs with implements poorly suited to detailed work; furthermore, the prints were sometimes painted by hand with watercolors, insuring artistic singularity. Blake refined his etching technique in such works as *All Religions Are One* (c. 1788) and *There Is No Natural Religion* (c. 1788), both of which advance the claims of imagination over rationalist philosophy, before creating *Songs of Innocence,* a group of pastoral poems first published in 1789 and reissued in various forms throughout his life.

In 1790 Blake moved to the rural area of Lambeth, where he wrote the solemn, urban-oriented "Experience" section that was published together with *Songs of Innocence* as *Songs of Innocence and of Experience.* Of the poems incorporated in "Songs of Experience," eighteen originally had appeared as drafts in a notebook later known both as *The Note-Book of William Blake* and the "Rossetti Manuscript," while four—"Little Girl Lost," "Little Girl Found," "The Voice of the Ancient Bard," and "The School Boy"—had first been included in *Innocence.* While formulating these lyrics, Blake also composed *The Marriage of Heaven and Hell* (1793), in which he exposes the evils inherent in the orthodox conception of virtue and the virtues inherent in the orthodox conception of evil, and, characteristically, identifies religion with laws that focus on restrictions and divisions rather than on spiritual harmony. Twenty-eight copies of *Songs of Innocence and of Experience* printed by Blake are extant and the order of the poems in each varies; the most common reproduction of *Songs* is the 1955 Blake Trust Facsimile edited by Sir Geoffrey Keynes.

Critical approaches to *Songs of Innocence and of Experience* range from close readings of individual poems as self-sufficient works to analyses informed by historical, biographical, or oeuvre-related issues. Relatively straightforward interpretations include the examination of *Songs* as a retelling of the biblical account of humanity's fall from divine grace. Accordingly, the world depicted in such poems of innocence as "The Laughing Song" and "The Lamb" is analogized with the carefree, harmonious life in the Garden of Eden; the condition observed in such poems of experience as "Holy Thursday" is compared with the hardship encountered by humanity upon expulsion from Eden. Other commentators have argued the relative significance of the states of innocence and of experience, variously contending that experience is the necessarily arduous path to the spiritual goal symbolized by innocence, or that innocence entails immaturity and naivete while experience denotes sagacity. Many, however, insist that Blake employs multiple viewpoints and implied narrators in *Songs*, making interpretation necessarily more complex; for example, readers must account for a persona known as the Piper, who relates the "Introduction" in the "Innocence" section, and a character called the Bard, who recites the "Introduction" in "Songs of Experience." Blake remains ironically detached, advocates of this opinion argue, from the overt judgments expressed in many if not all of the poems. In light of this narrative ambiguity, "Songs of Innocence" and "Songs of Experience" can be perceived as satires of each other: innocence is the unreachable ideal, while experience is the disappointing reality.

The social dimension of *Songs* has been greatly scrutinized, with much discussion revolving around Blake's response to industrialization. One of the most famous poems of the collection, "London" is commonly thought to prophesy the dehumanizing influence of commercial cities and capitalism. The two poems entitled "The Chimney Sweeper" allude to the exploitation of cheap labor and the abuses suffered by children who are forced to work. In a related vein, scholars have perceived *Songs* as a condemnation of the philosophy of rationalism—commonly esteemed in science-based, industrially developed societies—which devalues the spiritual and imaginative components of human nature. Other commentators focus on the social injustice and authoritarianism engendered by the Church in the poems "A Little Boy Lost," "The Little Vagabond," "The Garden of Love," and the "Holy Thursday" of "Songs of Innocence," which also seem to decry the restrictive nature of orthodox religion and moral codes. With regard to personal morality, biographers note the demands that marital fidelity placed upon Blake—who was a freethinker—and perceive the advocacy of uninhibited sexuality in the verses "My Pretty Rose Tree," "The Garden of Love," and "The Sick Rose."

Scholars acknowledge the high artistic merit of the designs framing the text of *Songs of Innocence and of Experience* but disagree about their significance. Numerous critics state that the illustrations are essential to the comprehension of the poems, though others argue that they are merely helpful or simply decorative. The central theme of *Songs,* however, endorses the work's format, which fuses creativity and intellect. As "The Tyger" microcosmically conveys, opposition and division must be overcome through the acceptance and harmonious integration of the diverse elements comprising human nature, such as sensuality and spirituality or imagination and reason.

Songs of Innocence and of Experience received virtually no critical attention for half of a century after initial publication; factors contributing to the lack of appreciation include Blake's reputation as an eccentric, the restricted circulation of the text—each copy required painstaking effort to manufacture and passed in a closed society of friends and connoisseurs—and the lack of serious critical study accorded to works perceived as children's literature. In the twentieth century, the trend has reversed, with commentators focusing so extensively on *Songs* that some scholars allege the work unjustly overshadows Blake's longer poems. Nevertheless, the complexity indicated by the myriad diverse and sometimes conflicting interpretations of *Songs* attests to the richness of the text and designs and the resounding depth of its themes.

Alexander Gilchrist   (essay date 1863)

[*Critics generally agree that significant scholarly interest in and understanding of Blake's thought began with the publication of Gilchrist's* Life of William Blake, "Pictor Ignotus." *Gilchrist died in 1861 without completing his book. The unfinished* Life *was subsequently completed by Anne Gilchrist, Dante Gabriel Rossetti, and William Michael Rossetti and published in 1863. In the following excerpt from that work, Gilchrist praises the lyricism and naturalness of* Songs of Innocence and of Experience.]

First of the Poems [in ***Songs of Innocence***] let me speak, harsh as seems their divorce from the Design which blends with them, forming warp and woof in one texture. It is like pulling up a daisy by the roots from the greensward out of which it springs. To me many years ago, first reading these weird Songs in their appropriate environment of equally spiritual form and hue, the effect was as that of an angelic voice singing to oaten pipe, such as Arcadians tell of; or, as if a spiritual magician were summoning before human eyes, and through a human medium, images and scenes of divine loveliness; and in the pauses of the strain we seem to catch the rustling of angelic wings. The Golden Age independent of Space or Time, object of vague sighs and dreams from many generations of struggling humanity—an Eden such as childhood sees, is brought nearer than ever poet brought it before. For this poet was in assured possession of the Golden Age within the chambers of his own mind. As we read, fugitive glimpses open, clear as brief, of our buried childhood, of an unseen world present, past, to come; we are endowed with new spiritual sight, with unwonted intuitions, bright visitants from finer realms of thought, which ever elude us, ever hover near. We encounter familiar objects, in unfamiliar, transfigured aspects, simple expression and deep meanings, type and antitype. True, there are palpable irregularities, metrical licence, lapse of grammar, and even of orthography; but often the sweetest melody, most daring eloquence of rhythm, and what is more, appropriate rhythm. They are *unfinished* poems: yet would finish have bettered their bold and careless freedom? Would it not have brushed away the delicate bloom? that visible spontaneity, so rare and great a charm, the eloquent attribute of our old English ballads and of the early Songs of all nations. The most deceptively perfect wax-model is no substitute for the living flower. The form is, in these Songs, a transparent medium of the spiritual thought, not an opaque body. 'He has dared to venture,' writes Malkin, not irrelevantly, 'on the ancient simplicity, and feeling it in his own character and manners, has succeeded' better than those who have only seen it through a glass.

There is the same divine *afflatus* as in the *Poetical Sketches,* but fuller: a maturity of expression, despite surviving negligences, and of thought and motive. The 'Child Angel,' as we ventured to call the Poet in earlier years, no longer merely sportive and innocently wanton, wears a brow of thought; a glance of insight has passed into

> A sense sublime
> Of something far more deeply interfused

in Nature, a feeling of 'the burthen of the mystery of things'; though still possessed by widest sympathies with all that is simple and innocent, with echoing laughter, little lamb, a flower's blossom, with 'emmet wildered and forlorn.'

These poems have a unity and mutual relationship, the influence of which is much impaired if they be read otherwise than as a whole. . . . (pp. 71-2)

Who but Blake, with his pure heart, his simple exalted character, could have transfigured a commonplace meeting of Charity Children at St. Paul's, as he has done in the **"Holy Thursday"**? A picture at once tender and grand. The bold images, by a wise instinct resorted to at the close of the first and second stanzas and opening of the third, are in the highest degree imaginative; they are true as only Poetry can be.

How vocal is the poem **"Spring,"** despite imperfect rhymes. From addressing the child, the poet, by a transition not infrequent with him, passes out of himself into the child's person, showing a chameleon sympathy with child-like feelings. Can we not see the little three-year-old prattler stroking the white lamb, her feelings made articulate for her?—Even more remarkable is the poem entitled **"The Lamb,"** sweet hymn of tender infantine sentiment appropriate to that perennial image of meekness; to which the fierce eloquence of **"The Tiger,"** in the *Songs of Experience,* is an antitype. In **"The Lamb"** the poet again changes person to that of a child. Of lyrical beauty, take as a sample **"The Laughing Song,"** with its happy *ring* of

merry innocent voices. This and **"The Nurse's Song"** are more in the style of his early poems, but, as we said, of far maturer execution. I scarcely need call attention to the delicate simplicity of the little pastoral, entitled **"The Shepherd"**: to the picturesqueness in a warmer hue, the delightful domesticity, the expressive melody of **"The Echoing Green"**: or to the lovely sympathy and piety which irradiate the touching **"Cradle Song."** More enchanting still is the stir of fancy and sympathy which animates **"The Dream,"** that

> Did weave a shade o'er my angel-guarded bed;

of an emmet that had

> Lost her way,
> Where on grass methought I lay.

Few are the readers, I should think, who can fail to appreciate the symbolic grandeur of **"The Little Boy Lost"** and **"The Little Boy Found,"** or the enigmatic tenderness of the **"Blossom"** and the **"Divine Image"**; and the verses **"On Another's Sorrow,"** express some of Blake's favourite religious ideas, his abiding notions on the subject of the Godhead, which surely suggest the kernel of Christian feeling. A similar tinge of the divine colours the lines called **"Night,"** with its revelation of angelic guardians, believed in with unquestioning piety by Blake, who makes us in our turn conscious, as we read, of angelic noiseless footsteps. For a nobler depth of religious beauty, with accordant grandeur of sentiment and language, I know no parallel nor hint elsewhere of such a poem as **"The Little Black Boy"**—

> My mother bore me in the southern wild.

We may read these poems again and again, and they continue fresh as at first. There is something unsating in them, a perfume as of a growing violet, which renews itself as fast as it is inhaled.

One poem, **"The Chimney Sweeper,"** still calls for special notice. This and **"Holy Thursday"** are remarkable as an anticipation of the daring choice of homely subject, of the yet more daringly familiar manner, nay, of the very metre and trick of style adopted by Wordsworth in a portion of those memorable 'experiments in poetry,'—the *Lyrical Ballads,*—in *The Reverie of Poor Susan,* for instance (not written till 1797), the *Star Gazers,* and *The Power of Music* (both 1806). The little Sweep's dream has the spiritual touch peculiar to Blake's hand. This poem, I may add, was extracted thirty-five years later in a curious little volume (1824) of James Montgomery's editing, as friend of the then unprotected Climbing Boys. It was entitled, *The Chimney Sweeper's Friend and Climbing Boy's Album;* a miscellany of verse and prose, original and borrowed, with illustrations by Robert Cruikshank. Charles Lamb, one of the living authors applied to by the kind-hearted Sheffield poet, while declining the task of rhyming on such a subject, sent a copy of this poem from the *Songs of Innocence,* communicating it as "from a very rare and curious little work." At line five, 'Little Tom Dacre' is transformed, by a sly blunder of Lamb's, into 'little Tom Toddy.' The poem on the same subject in the *Songs of Experience,* inferior poetically, but in an accordant key of gloom, would have been the more apposite to Montgomery's volume.

The tender loveliness of these poems will hardly reappear in Blake's subsequent writing. Darker phases of feeling, more sombre colours, profounder meanings, ruder eloquence, characterise the *Songs of Experience* of five years later.

In 1789, the year in which Blake's hand engraved the *Songs of Innocence,* Wordsworth was finishing his versified *Evening Walk* on the Goldsmith model; Crabbe ('Pope in worsted stockings,' as Hazlitt christened him), famous six years before by his *Village,* was publishing one of his minor quartos, *The Newspaper;* and Mrs. Charlotte Smith, not undeservedly popular, was accorded a fifth edition within five years, of her *Elegiac Sonnets,* one or two of which still merit the praise of being good sonnets, among the best in a bad time. In these years, Hayley, Mason, Hannah More, Jago, Downman, Helen Maria Williams, were among the active producers of poetry; Cumberland, Holcroft, Inchbald, Burgoyne, of the acting drama of the day; Peter Pindar, and *Pasquin* Williams, of the satire.

The designs, simultaneous offspring with the poems, which in the most literal sense illuminate the *Songs of Innocence,* consist of poetized domestic scenes. The drawing and draperies are grand in style as graceful, though covering few inches' space; the colour pure, delicate, yet in effect rich and full. The mere tinting of the text and of the free ornamental border often makes a refined picture. The costumes of the period are idealized, the landscape given in pastoral and symbolic hints. Sometimes these drawings almost suffer from being looked at as a book and held close, instead of at due distance as pictures, where they become more effective. In composition, colour, pervading feeling, they are lyrical to the eye, as the *Songs* to the ear.

On the whole, the designs to the *Songs of Innocence* are finer as well as more pertinent to the poems; more closely interwoven with them, than those which accompany the *Songs of Experience.* (pp. 72-5)

In the *Songs of Experience,* put forth in 1794, as complement to the *Songs of Innocence* of 1789, we come [on more lucid writing than the prophetic books *The Gates of Paradise, Visions of the Daughters of Albion,* and *America: A Prophecy*],—writing freer from mysticism and abstractions, if partaking of the same colour of thought. *Songs of Innocence and Experience, showing the Two Contrary States of the Human Soul: the author and printer, W. Blake,* is the general title now given. The first series, quite in keeping with its name, had been of far the more heavenly temper. The second, produced during an interval of another five years, bears internal evidence of later origin, though in the same rank as to poetic excellence. As the title fitly shadows, it is of grander, sterner calibre, of gloomier wisdom. Strongly contrasted, but harmonious phases of poetic thought are presented by the two series.

One poem in the *Songs of Experience* happens to have been quoted often enough (first by Allan Cunningham in connection with Blake's name), to have made its strange old Hebrew-like grandeur, its Oriental latitude yet force

of eloquence, comparatively familiar:—**"The Tiger."** To it Charles Lamb refers: 'I have heard of his poems,' writes he, 'but have never seen them. There is one to a tiger, beginning—

> Tiger! tiger! burning bright
> In the forests of the night,

which is glorious!'

Of the prevailing difference of sentiment between these poems and the *Songs of Innocence,* may be singled out as examples **"The Clod and the Pebble,"** and even so slight a piece as **"The Fly"**; and in a more sombre mood, **"The Garden of Love," "The Little Boy Lost," "Holy Thursday"** (antitype to the poem of the same title in *Songs of Innocence*), **"The Angel," "The Human Abstract," "The Poison Tree,"** and above all, **"London."** One poem, **"The Little Girl Lost,"** may startle the literal reader, but has an inverse moral truth and beauty of its own. Another, **"The Little Girl Lost, and Little Girl Found,"** is a daringly emblematic anticipation of some future age of gold, and has the picturesqueness of Spenserian allegory, lit with the more ethereal spiritualism of Blake. Touched by

> The light that never was on sea or shore,

is this story of the carrying off of the sleeping little maid by friendly beasts of prey, who gambol round her as she lies; the kingly lion bowing 'his mane of gold,' and on her neck dropping 'from his eyes of flame, ruby tears;' who, when her parents seek the child, brings them to his cave; and

> They look upon his eyes,
> Filled with deep surprise;
> And wondering behold
> A spirit armed in gold!

Well might Flaxman exclaim, 'Sir, his poems are as grand as his pictures,' Wordsworth read them with delight. . . . Blake himself thought his poems finer than his designs. Hard to say which are the more uncommon in kind. Neither, as I must reiterate, reached his own generation. In Malkin's *Memoirs of a Child,* specimens from the *Poetical Sketches* and *Songs of Innocence and Experience* were given; for these poems struck the well-meaning scholar, into whose hands by chance they fell, as somewhat astonishing; as indeed they struck most who stumbled on them. But Malkin's *Memoirs* was itself a book not destined to circulate very freely; and the poems of Blake, even had they been really known to their generation, were not calculated in their higher qualities to win popular favour,— not if they had been free from technical imperfection. For it was an age of polish, though mostly polish of trifles; not like the present age, with its slovenliness and licence. Deficient finish was never a characteristic of the innovator Wordsworth himself, who started from the basis of Pope and Goldsmith; and whose matter, rather than manner, was obnoxious to critics. Defiant carelessness, though Coleridge in his Juvenile Poems was often guilty of it, did not become a characteristic of English verse, until the advent of Keats and Shelley; poets of imaginative virtue enough to cover a multitude of their own and other people's sins. The length to which it has since run (despite Tennyson), we all know.

Yet in this very inartificiality lies the secret of Blake's rare and wondrous success. Whether in design or in poetry, he does, in very fact, work as a man already practised in one art, beginning anew in another; expressing himself with virgin freshness of mind in each, and in each realizing, by turns, the idea flung out of that prodigal cornucopia of thought and image, **"Pippa Passes"**:—'If there should arise a new painter, will it not be in some such way by a poet, now, or a musician (spirits who have conceived and perfected an ideal through some other channel), transferring it to this, and escaping our conventional roads by pure ignorance of them?' Even Malkin, with real sense, observes of the poet in general,—his mind 'is too often at leisure for the mechanical prettinesses of cadence and epithet, when it ought to be engrossed by higher thoughts. Words and numbers present themselves unbidden when the soul is inspired by sentiment, elevated by enthusiasm, or ravished by devotion.' Yes! ravished by devotion. For in these songs of Blake's occurs devotional poetry, which is real poetry too—a very exceptional thing. Witness that simple and beautiful poem entitled **"The Divine Image,"** or that **"On Another's Sorrow."** *The Songs of Innocence* are in truth animated by a uniform sentiment of deep piety, of reverent feeling, and may be said, in their pervading influence, to be one devout aspiration throughout. *The Songs of Experience* consist rather of earnest, impassioned arguments; in this differing from the simple *affirmations* of the earlier *Songs of Innocence,*—arguments on the loftiest themes of existence.

After the *Songs of Experience,* Blake never again sang to like angelic tunes; nor even with the same approach to technical accuracy. His poetry was the blossom of youth and early manhood. Neither in design did he improve on the tender grace of some of these illustrations; irregularities became as conspicuous in it, as in his verse; though in age he attained to nobler heights of sublimity, as the *Inventions to Job* will exemplify. (pp. 116-19)

> *Alexander Gilchrist, in his* Life of William Blake, Vol. I, *revised edition, Macmillan and Co., 1880, 431 p.*

Algernon Charles Swinburne   (essay date 1906)

[*An English poet, dramatist, and critic, Swinburne was renowned during his lifetime for his skill and technical mastery as a lyric poet and is currently regarded as the embodiment of rebellion against the prevailing moral orientation of Victorian aesthetics. Blake scholars also recognize his contribution as the author of the first full-length critical study of the poet,* William Blake: A Critical Essay *(1867). In the following excerpt from the 1906 edition of that work, Swinburne declares* Songs of Innocence and of Experience *the most accessible of Blake's works, and perceives its central theme to be the championship of human instinct.*]

[In Gilchrist's edition of the *Songs of Innocence and of Experience*] we miss the lovely and luminous setting of designs, which makes the *Songs* precious and pleasurable to those who know or care for little else of [Blake's] doing; the infinite delight of those drawings, sweeter to see than music to hear, where herb and stem break into grace of shape and blossom of form, and the branch-work is full of little flames and flowers, catching as it were from the verse enclosed the fragrant heat and delicate sound they seem to give back; where colour lapses into light and light assumes feature in colour. If elsewhere the artist's strange strength of thought and hand is more visible, nowhere is there such pure sweetness and singleness of design in his work. All the tremulous and tender splendour of spring is mixed into the written word and coloured draught; every page has the smell of April. Over all things given, the sleep of flocks and the growth of leaves, the laughter in dividing lips of flowers and the music at the moulded mouth of the flute-player, there is cast a pure fine veil of light, softer than sleep and keener than sunshine. The sweetness of sky and leaf, of grass and water—the bright light life of bird and child and beast—is so to speak kept fresh by some graver sense of faithful and mysterious love, explained and vivified by a conscience and purpose in the artist's hand and mind. Such a fiery outbreak of spring, such an insurrection of fierce floral life and radiant riot of childish power and pleasure, no poet or painter ever gave before: such lustre of green leaves and flushed limbs, kindled cloud and fervent fleece, was never wrought into speech or shape. Nevertheless this decorative work is after all the mere husk and shell of the *Songs.* These also, we may notice, have to some extent shared the comparative popularity of the designs which serve as framework to them. They have absolutely achieved the dignity of a reprint; have had a chance before now of swimming for life; whereas most of Blake's offspring have been thrown into Lethe bound hand and foot, without hope of ever striking out in one fair effort. Perhaps on some accounts this preference has been not unreasonable. What was written for children can hardly offend men; and the obscurities and audacities of the prophet would here have been clearly out of place. It is indeed some relief to a neophyte serving in the outer courts of such an intricate and cloudy temple, to come upon this little side-chapel set about with the simplest wreaths and smelling of the fields rather than incense, where all the singing is done by clear children's voices to the briefest and least complex tunes. Not at first without a sense of release does the human mind get quit for a little of the clouds of Urizen, the fires of Orc, and all the Titanic apparatus of prophecy. And these poems are really unequalled in their kind. Such verse was never written for children since verse-writing began. Only in a few of those faultless fragments of childish rhyme which float without name or form upon the memories of men shall we find such a pure clear cadence of verse, such rapid ring and flow of lyric laughter, such sweet and direct choice of the just word and figure, such an impeccable simplicity; nowhere but here such a tender wisdom of holiness, such a light and perfume of innocence. Nothing like this was ever written on that text of the lion and the lamb; no such heaven of sinless animal life was ever conceived so intensely and sweetly.

> And there the lion's ruddy eyes
>   Shall flow with tears of gold,
> And pitying the tender cries,
>   And walking round the fold,
> Saying *Wrath by His meekness*
> *And by His health sickness*

Is driven away
From our immortal day.
And now beside thee, bleating lamb,
I can lie down and sleep,
Or think on Him who bore thy name,
Graze after thee, and weep.

The leap and fall of the verse is so perfect as to make it a fit garment and covering for the profound tenderness of faith and soft strength of innocent impulse embodied in it. But the whole of this hymn of **"Night"** is wholly beautiful; being perhaps one of the two poems of loftiest loveliness among all the *Songs of Innocence.* The other is that called **"The Little Black Boy"**; a poem especially exquisite for its noble forbearance from vulgar pathos and achievement of the highest and most poignant sweetness of speech and sense; in which the poet's mysticism is baptized with pure water and taught to speak as from faultless lips of children, to such effect as this.

And we are put on earth a little space
That we may learn to bear the beams of love;
And these black bodies and this sunburnt face
Are like a cloud and like a shady grove.

Other poems of a very perfect beauty are those of **"The Piper," "The Lamb," "The Chimney-sweeper,"** and **"The two-days-old Baby"**; all, for the music in them, more like the notes of birds caught up and given back than the modulated measure of human verse. One cannot say, being so slight and seemingly wrong in metrical form, how they come to be so absolutely right; but right even in point of verses and words they assuredly are. Add fuller formal completion of rhyme and rhythm to that song of **"Infant Joy,"** and you have broken up the soft bird-like perfection of clear light sound which gives it beauty; the little bodily melody of soulless and painless laughter.

Against all articulate authority we do however class several of the *Songs of Experience* higher for the great qualities of verse than anything in the earlier division of these poems. If the *Songs of Innocence* have the shape and smell of leaves or buds, these have in them the light and sound of fire or the sea. Entering among them, a fresher savour and a larger breath strikes one upon the lips and forehead. In the first part we are shown who they are who have or who deserve the gift of spiritual sight: in the second, what things there are for them to see when that gift has been given. Innocence, the quality of beasts and children, has the keenest eyes; and such eyes alone can discern and interpret the actual mysteries of experience. It is natural that this second part, dealing as it does with such things as underlie the outer forms of the first part, should rise higher and dive deeper in point of mere words. These give the distilled perfume and extracted blood of the veins in the rose-leaf, the sharp, liquid, intense spirit crushed out of the broken kernel in the fruit. The last of the *Songs of Innocence* is a prelude to these poems; in it the poet summons to judgment the young and single-spirited, that by right of the natural impulse of delight in them they may give sentence against the preachers of convention and assumption; and in the first poem of the second series he, by the same "voice of the bard," calls upon earth herself, the mother of all these, to arise and become free: since upon her limbs also are bound the fetters, and upon her forehead also has

fallen the shadow, of a jealous law: from which nevertheless, by faithful following of instinct and divine liberal impulse, earth and man shall obtain deliverance.

Hear the voice of the bard!
    Who present, past, and future sees:
Whose ears have heard
The ancient Word
    That walked among the silent trees:
Calling the lapsèd soul
    And weeping in the evening dew;
That might control
The starry pole
    And fallen, fallen light renew!

If they will hear the Word, earth and the dwellers upon earth shall be made again as little children; shall regain the strong simplicity of eye and hand proper to the pure and single of heart; and for them inspiration shall do the work of innocence; let them but once abjure the doctrine by which comes sin and the law by which comes prohibition. Therefore must the appeal be made; that the blind may see and the deaf hear, and the unity of body and spirit be made manifest in perfect freedom: and that to the innocent even the liberty of "sin" may be conceded. For if the soul suffer by the body's doing, are not both degraded? and if the body be oppressed for the soul's sake, are not both the losers?

O Earth, O Earth, return!
    Arise from out the dewy grass!
Night is worn,
And the morn
    Rises from the slumberous mass.
Turn away no more;
    Why wilt thou turn away?
The starry shore,
The watery floor,
    Are given thee till the break of day.

For so long, during the night of law and oppression of material form, the divine evidences hidden under sky and sea are left her; even "till the break of day." Will she not get quit of this spiritual bondage to the heavy body of things, to the encumbrance of deaf clay and blind vegetation, before the light comes that shall redeem and reveal? But the earth, being yet in subjection to the creator of men, the jealous God who divided nature against herself—father of woman and man, legislator of sex and race—makes blind and bitter answer as in sleep, "her locks covered with grey despair."

Prisoned on this watery shore,
    Starry Jealousy does keep my den;
Cold and hoar,
Weeping o'er,
    I hear the father of the ancient men.

Thus, in the poet's mind, Nature and Religion are the two fetters of life, one on the right wrist, the other on the left; an obscure material force on this hand, and on that a mournful imperious law: the law of divine jealousy, the government of a God who weeps over his creature and subject with unprofitable tears, and rules by forbidding and dividing: the "Urizen" of the "Prophetic Books," clothed with the coldness and the grief of remote sky and jealous cloud. Here as always, the cry is as much for light as for licence, the appeal not more against prohibition than against obscurity.

> Can the sower sow by night,
> Or the ploughman in darkness plough?

In the *Songs of Innocence* there is no such glory of metre or sonorous beauty of lyrical work as here. No possible effect of verse can be finer in a great brief way than that given in the second and last stanzas of the first part of this poem. It recalls within one's ear the long relapse of recoiling water and wash of the refluent wave; in the third and fourth lines sinking suppressed as with equal pulses and soft sobbing noise of ebb, to climb again in the fifth line with a rapid clamour of ripples and strong ensuing strain of weightier sound, lifted with the lift of the running and ringing sea.

Here also is that most famous of Blake's lyrics, **"The Tiger"**; a poem beyond praise for its fervent beauty and vigour of music. It appears by the MS. that this was written with some pains; the cancels and various readings bear marks of frequent rehandling. One of the latter is worth transcription for its own excellence and also in proof of the artist's real care for details, which his rapid instinctive way of work has induced some to disbelieve in.

> Burnt in distant deeps or skies
> The cruel fire of thine eyes?
> Could heart descend or wings aspire?
> What the hand dare seize the fire?

Nor has Blake left us anything of more profound and perfect value than **"The Human Abstract"**; a little mythical vision of the growth of error; through soft sophistries of pity and faith, subtle humility of abstinence and fear, under which the pure simple nature lies corrupted and strangled; through selfish loves which prepare a way for cruelty, and cruelty that works by spiritual abasement and awe.

> Soon spreads the dismal shade
> Of Mystery over his head;
> And the caterpillar and fly
> Feed on the Mystery.
>
> And it bears the fruit of Deceit,
> Ruddy and sweet to eat;
> And the raven his nest has made
> In the thickest shade.

Under the shadow of this tree of mystery, rooted in artificial belief, all the meaner kind of devouring things take shelter and eat of the fruit of its branches; the sweet poison of false faith, painted on its outer husk with the likeness of all things noble and desirable; and in the deepest implication of barren branch and deadly leaf, the bird of death, with priests for worshippers ("the priests of the raven of dawn," loud of lip and hoarse of throat until the light of day have risen), finds house and resting-place. Only in the "miscreative brain" of fallen men can such a thing strike its tortuous root and bring forth its fatal flower; nowhere else in all nature can the tyrants of divided matter and moral law, "Gods of the earth and sea," find soil that will bear such fruit.

Nowhere has Blake set forth his spiritual creed more clearly and earnestly than in the last of the *Songs of Experience.* "Tirzah," in his mythology, represents the mere separate and human nature, mother of the perishing body and daughter of the "religion" which occupies itself with laying down laws for the flesh; which, while pretending (and that in all good faith) to despise the body and bring it into subjection as with control of bit and bridle, does implicitly overrate its power upon the soul for evil or good, and thus falls foul of fact on all sides by assuming that spirit and flesh are twain, and that things pleasant and good for the one can properly be loathsome or poisonous to the other. This "religion" or "moral law," the inexplicable prophet [Blake] has chosen to baptize under the singular type of "Rahab"—the "harlot virgin-mother," impure by dint of chastity and forbearance from such things as are pure to the pure of heart: for in this creed the one thing unclean is the belief in uncleanness, the one thing forbidden is to believe in the existence of forbidden things. . . . For the present it will be enough to note how eager and how direct is the appeal here made against any rule or reasoning based on reference to the mere sexual and external nature of man—the nature made for ephemeral life and speedy death, kept alive "to work and weep" only through that mercy which "changed death into sleep;" how intense the reliance on redemption from such a law by the grace of imaginative insight and spiritual freedom, typified in "the death of Jesus." Nor are any of these poems finer in structure or nobler in metrical form. (pp. 123-35)

Before parting from this chief lyrical work of the poet's, we may notice (rather for its convenience as an explanation than its merit as a piece of verse) this projected "Motto to the Songs of Innocence and of Experience," which editors have left hitherto in manuscript:

> The good are attracted by men's perceptions,
>   And think not for themselves
> Till Experience teaches them how to catch
>   And to cage the Fairies and Elves.
>
> And then the Knave begins to snarl,
>   And the Hypocrite to howl;
> And all his good friends show their private ends,
>   And the Eagle is known from the Owl.

Experience must do the work of innocence as soon as conscience begins to take the place of instinct, reflection of perception; but the moment experience begins upon this work, men raise against her the conventional clamour of envy and stupidity. She teaches how to entrap and retain such fugitive delights as children and animals enjoy without seeking to catch or cage them; but this teaching the world calls sin, and the law of material religion condemns: the face of "Tirzah" is set against it, in the "shame and pride" of sex.

> Thou, mother of my mortal part,
> With cruelty didst mould my heart,
> And with false self-deceiving fears
> Didst bind my nostrils, eyes, and ears.

And thus those who live in subjection to the senses would in their turn bring the senses into subjection; unable to see beyond the body, they find it worth while to refuse the body its right to freedom.

In these hurried notes on the *Songs* an effort has been made to get that done which is most absolutely necessary—not that which might have been most facile or most delightful. Analytic remark has been bestowed on those poems only which really cannot dispense with it in the eyes of most men. Many others need no herald or interpreter, demand no usher or outrider: some of these are among Blake's best, some again almost among his worst. Poems in which a doctrine or subject once before nobly stated and illustrated is re-asserted in a shallower way and exemplified in a feebler form, require at our hands no written or spoken signs of either assent or dissent. Such poems . . . have places here among their betters: none of them, it may be added, without some shell of outward beauty or seed of inward value. The simpler poems claim only praise; and of this they cannot fail from any reader whose good word is in the least worth having. Those of a subtler kind (often, as must now be clear enough, the best worth study) claim more than this if they are to have fair play. It is pleasant enough to commend and to enjoy the palpable excellence of Blake's work; but another thing is simply and thoroughly requisite—to understand what the workman was after. First get well hold of the mystic, and you will then at once get a better view and comprehension of the painter and poet. And if through fear of tedium or offence a student refuses to be at such pains, he will find himself, while following Blake's trace as poet or painter, brought up sharply within a very short tether. "It is easy," says Blake himself in the *Jerusalem,* "to acknowledge a man to be great and good while we derogate from him in the trifles and small articles of that goodness; those alone are his friends who admire his minute powers." (pp. 136-40)

Algernon Charles Swinburne, in his William Blake: A Critical Essay, *revised edition, Chatto & Windus, 1906, 340 p.*

Osbert Burdett   (essay date 1926)

[*In the following excerpt, Burdett praises* Songs of Innocence and of Experience *as a celebration of emotion, imagination, and simplicity.*]

[In] 1789 Blake issued the *Songs of Innocence,* his first example of Illuminated Printing. This, like all Blake's books except the earlier *Poetical Sketches,* to be appreciated in all its beauty needs to be read in the original form in which it came from his own hand and press. Since this is not possible except for those who visit museum libraries, the method must be faithfully described. In the words of Mr. John Sampson:

> The text and the surrounding design were written in reverse [a painfully laborious method], in a medium impervious to acid upon small copper plates about 5″ by 3″ which were then etched in a bath of aqua-fortis until the work stood in relief as in a stereotype. From these plates, which to economise copper were, in many cases, engraved upon both sides, impressions were printed, in the ordinary manner, in tints made to harmonise with the colour scheme afterwards applied by the artist.

The text and the illustration are thus interwoven into a harmonious whole, and as the colour can be varied no two copies need be exactly alike. Little but the use of a press distinguishes the books so made from illuminated manuscripts, and the etching in reverse together with the press makes the new method even more laborious than the old. The consequence has been that Blake has had no successors in the art which he invented, nor can his originals be copied without great difficulty and expense. Only those who have compared his originals with the printed pages in which his poems are ordinarily read are fully aware of the loss now suffered by his writings, which require to be read as much by the eye as by the mind on pages suffused with life and colour. Blake evidently adopted the method by preference and artistic choice, and because his hand could not write so much as a word without the impulse to trace designs upon the paper. He wished to indulge both his gifts at the same time, and did not marry them because he desired and could not find a publisher. The printed sheets of the *Poetical Sketches* no doubt seemed the death of form to him, and though he would use texts and phrases to decorate his later designs, it is significant that he would hardly ever write without engraving. He was always indifferent to a strictly intellectual appeal, and his writings invite rather artistic than intellectual criticism.

A necessary effect of the Illuminated Printing was to restrict his readers to the few, in the manner of an artist who displays not books but pictures. Blake often painted in words, and should be judged rather as an artist than an author. Mr. Sampson does not think it probable that "the whole impression of the *Songs* issued by Blake exceeded the twenty-two" that he describes. It is hardly surprising, therefore, that Blake's writings were little known. Absorbed in his invention, however, Blake eventually issued from Lambeth a prospectus defending his method and advertising the *Songs of Innocence* and the *Songs of Experience* at five shillings each: "If a method (he thus wrote in 1793) which combines the Painter and the Poet is a phenomenon worthy of public attention, provided it exceeds in elegance all former methods, the author is sure of his reward". As Mr. Symons has said:

> Had it not been for his lack of a technical knowledge of music, had he been able to write down his inventions in that art also, he would have left us the creation of something like an universal art. That universal art he did, during his lifetime, create; for he sang his songs to his own music; and thus, while he lived, he was the complete realisation of the poet in all his faculties, and the only complete realisation that has ever been known.

His combination of talents is his real defence against particular criticism.

What can be well said of the *Songs of Innocence* that has not been said well by other poets? Till lately only men of genius busied themselves with Blake; theirs is the prerogative of praising, and there is now presumably no reader of poetry who does not know the most exquisite section of his verse. The boy who had written the *Poetical Sketches* was already a precocious artist. The imagination of the man who wrote the *Songs of Innocence* had not outgrown the simplicity of the child. Blake might be an inspired child writing for children, and these songs are nursery rhymes of pure poetry which children and their elders can equally love. Such sources as have been suggested for them, for example the *Divine and Moral Songs for Children* by Dr. Watts, only emphasise the transforming power of Blake's touch. The real excuse for looking for sources is that Blake had an extraordinary temptation to surpass any influence that came his way. Later in life, and much against the grain, he surpassed even Hayley in the art of complimentary letters. It would, then, be a curious paradox if songs that seem the very rill of poetry issuing from the mouth of the Muse herself should have had an accidental origin. It is just possible that the title may have been inspired by a casual memory, but with the verse of the **Poetical Sketches** before us it would be absurd and uncritical to derive them from anywhere but the author of the earliest poems. He had shown that he could rival the Elizabethan lyrists, that he could transmute nature into the spirit of the earth, and from first to last the imagination itself was his principal and characteristic theme. In these songs Blake sings neither of love, nature, religion, nor sorrow, but of the imagination which, to be communicable, sees itself reflected, especially on the faces of children, in experiences such as these. The lamb, the shepherd, the infant, the cradle, the laughter of childish voices at play, are pretexts for a music as fresh, tender, awkward, soothing, merry as their original selves. For the first time in nursery poetry we feel that the grown-ups are listening, and that it is the child who is telling its mother about the lamb and God. The way in which the simplicities of feeling are conveyed and false sentiment avoided is miraculous. There is nothing quite to equal **"Infant Joy"** anywhere:

> "I have no name:
> I am but two days old."
> What shall I call thee?
> "I happy am,
> Joy is my name."
> Sweet joy befall thee!

"The Lamb", the **"Laughing Song"**, the almost monosyllabic lines to **"Spring"**, which seem as if they issued from a cradle, the lovely **"Nurse's Song"**, in which the nurse becomes the eldest of her charges for a moment, and the voice of play seems naturally to sing, are absolutely childlike. All poetry becomes young again in them, and artless utterance for the first and last time finds its proper music. There are others, however, in which the poet allows a glimpse of his hand to appear, as in **"The Divine Image"** and the haunting stanzas to **"Night"**, which Swinburne declared to be of the "loftiest loveliness". There are poems which tell stories and poems which speak of religion, taking a child's feelings about sorrow and pain for their simple lessons. So finely are they adjusted to their end that we hardly know whether the mother or her infant is reflecting, and indeed the second childhood of humanity is the blessing of those who have children of their own and are not strangers to them.

Perhaps only a poet who had read no fine literature but as a child reads could have written such things. There is in them an innocence of heart that is not to be found in Shakespeare. A few have the quality of children's hymns,

in which God appears a really loving Father, and mercy, pity, peace, and love, the virtues of childhood at its rare best, become the lineaments of His "divine image". The occasional moral, as at the end of **"The Chimney Sweeper"**, is transformed by the poetry into an exquisite platitude of the world, as this is represented to children in the school-room. Its presence is an abstraction of nurse and completes the nursery atmosphere. Note, too, that the shepherd, the sheep, the cradle, and the rest are nursery symbols, thus enabling Blake to pass from the lamb to "Him who bore its name" without any change of key. The emotions aroused by this poetry are instinctive and almost as characteristic of animals as of men. Indeed, it celebrates the life, motions, and feelings of all young things, with the apparent artlessness of a lamb's bleat or the cry of a bird, a baby's shout of astonishment or pleasure. By returning to these poetry seems to return to its own infancy, and the language is almost as free from meaning, apart from emotion, as a child's prattle.

Both meaning and observation, even of social life, appear in **Songs of Experience,** the companion volume of 1794, though not the next to be written. These darker songs, sometimes on the same themes, and the group often called *Ideas of Good and Evil,* or the Rossetti MS., are a conve-

The illustrated plate of "The Lamb," from Songs of Innocence and of Experience.

nient bridge between the simple lyric poetry with which Blake began and the complex prophecies that were to follow. The scene tends to shift from the nursery to the school-room, from the green to the church, from the open country to the city. We pass from feeling to observation, and the poems that touch on love reveal its troubles. Jealousy and prohibitions, whether personal or ecclesiastical, are named in them. Mr. Ellis has reconstructed a situation that would explain the references to those who are curious of Blake's erotic life. The famous **"Tiger"** is of course here, and with Mr. Sampson's aid we can trace every variant in its gradual composition. The number of revisions reminds us of the care that Blake would still spend upon his form, and which he claimed to have spent later on his prophecies, where the ending of his lines can, in fact, be shown to depend upon the decoration surrounding them. In his own work poetry was to yield to decoration, and there can be no doubt that design was the principal preoccupation of his mind. The first ecstasy of conscious life is complicated with a growing knowledge of good and evil, and the music of the verse will bear the burden of this trouble without caring to assign a cause. Such lines as:

> Ah, sun-flower! weary of time,
> Who countest the steps of the sun,

are the music of heaviness of heart, as the lines to the lamb and the infant had been the music of gladness. When he observes his fellow-men fallen into the bonds of cold reason and dull experience, he wonders

> How can the bird that is born for joy
> Sit in a cage and sing?

And he finds the explanation not in their circumstances but in themselves:

> In every cry of every Man,
> In every Infant's cry of fear,
> In every voice, in every ban,
> The mind-forg'd manacles I hear.

All forms of external control were to Blake the enemy of imagination, and he was right in so far as the dictates of wisdom even have little use for us until we have made them by personal experience our own. All the rest is morality, which, so long as it remains repressive and external, is always accompanied by secret satisfactions and deceit. In the age of experience, as Swinburne finely puts it, "inspiration shall do the work of innocence", and the **"Introduction"** to the *Songs of Experience* tells us that it is by listening to the Voice of the Bard that innocence can be renewed. It is, in fact, the inspiration to be derived from Blake, and not the particular instructions in which he sometimes phrased the call, that we should take from him. The loved disciple is not he who slavishly mimics any master, but one who by embracing his master's example is inspired to make the most of his own gifts and to follow the way of his own understanding. The best of the second group of songs present us with rudiments of thoughts dissolved in music, and it is the strange magic of this music, by leading us to think for ourselves, that we should carry away from them. Their intellectual fascination consists in suggesting rather than in defining their meaning. They make the intellect a thing of beauty by lending it the twilight that it should not possess, and the commentators like bats awakened by the falling shadows find in the gloaming the opportunity for the most crooked of their flights. Blake loved to put his feelings into intellectual forms, but he is really great when he is content with imaginative images, and can haunt our imaginations with lines like:

> When the stars threw down their spears
> And water'd Heaven with their tears.

> The lost traveller's dream under the hill.

> Nor is it possible to thought
> A greater than itself to know,

or the splendid:

> For a tear is an intellectual thing,
> And a sigh is the sword of an angel king,
> And the bitter groan of a martyr's woe
> Is an arrow from the Almighty's bow.

All Blake's emotions, and many of his images, were "intellectual things" to him, but for the reader who would do the poet justice, it is the poetry and not the cloudy forms in which it is often presented that is the truth of Blake's writings. Here is the vital energy that was the foundation of Blake's creed, and for this essence to be separated and praised in poetry it was indispensable that it should not be limited to the very bonds and definitions that are more coherent than itself. Blake's way of attempting to defend intellectually a vitality that is its own defence has misled his less lyrical readers, who forget his relation to his age and the fact that he was protesting against an overintellectual tradition. Law was his particular enemy, and to apply anything like logic to his lyrics, or to the lyrical prose that was soon to overflow them, is to confuse his tactics with his genius. Blake was to stand or fall by his own inspiration, and there are very blank lines here and there. The reader should not shut his eyes to them, though quotation would be ungracious, for they will lead him to study the almost verbal revisions of the **"Tiger,"** the only example we have of Blake's tireless revision of verse. That this was abundantly rewarded, and that Blake remained still to the end impatient even of self-criticism, shows how much his mind and work suffered from being always in revolt. (pp. 41-9)

When we consider the body of Blake's lyrical poetry, we see that he desired a language that should lie on the further side of meaning, all music, all symbol, with none or the slightest foothold on the earth. Thought and meaning were to become wholly lyrical, and yet to use the language of ideas. So far as his aim was attainable by mortal man, he came nearest to it in the *Songs of Innocence and Experience,* songs which no doubt afterward seemed to him but feathers from the phœnix to be born from the ashes of the prophetic books. (p. 61)

> *Osbert Burdett, in his* William Blake, *The Macmillan Company, 1926, 199 p.*

Joseph H. Wicksteed   (essay date 1928)

[*In the following excerpt, Wicksteed attributes the charm and ostensible simplicity of* Songs of Innocence and of Experience *to Blake's poetic vocabulary, rhyme patterns, and nature symbolism.*]

Blake's vocabulary in the ***Songs of Innocence*** was purposely simple. He aimed at making with his "rural pen" a trickling stream of verse of childlike innocence. And without any radical change of form he succeeds in adapting it to the speed and anger of a torrent passing over the rocks of Experience.

In the whole book there are about 5000 words, including the titles and every repetition. *Innocence* proper contains about 2300 of these: the three songs later transferred to ***Experience*** another 700, and ***Experience*** without these about 2000. The whole vocabulary is almost exactly 1000 words, rather more than a quarter being common to both parts.

More than 80 per cent. of the words in both parts are monosyllables, ***Innocence*** having slightly the larger proportion. The whole of ***Experience*** contains only 33 three-syllabled words: *Innocence* about 27 and the transferred songs about 7. ***Experience*** contains 4 four-syllabled words, "caterpillar," "generation," "invisible," and "humility." **"The Little Girl Lost"** one, "futurity"; and the whole of ***Innocence*** one, "harmonious." But it is interesting that this one occurs in **"Holy Thursday,"** which was the first of all the songs to be written, and contains 9 three-syllabled words and altogether 29 per cent. polysyllables (counting repetitions), a larger percentage than any of the other songs except **"Infant Sorrow,"** which has thirty, and **"The Blossom,"** which is unique, being more than half words of two syllables. Very few of the other songs have a quarter of their words more than one syllable, and one, **"The Angel,"** has less than 7 per cent.

We may take it therefore that Blake wrote **"Holy Thursday"** before he had developed what one may call the technique of Innocence. It is not written with a rural pen, and is in some ways the maturest of the earlier songs.

It is clear, then, that Blake's childlikeness was partly self-imposed, and when he requires—either for his meaning, or his atmosphere, or his song—a word of somewhat rarer character, he shows mastery in finding and in using it. Such phrases as:

> The painted birds laugh in the shade . . .
> Under a cruel eye outworn . . .

are not less masterly than

> harmonious thunderings the seats of heaven among.

The many great expressions in ***Experience,*** such as:

> the charterd Thames . . .
> fed with cold and usurous hand . . .
> could twist the sinews of thy heart . . .
> Dare frame thy fearful symmetry . . .
> the mind-forgd manacles I hear . . .
> that might controll the starry pole . . .
> the pale Virgin shrouded in snow . . .
> her thorns were my only delight . . .
> blights with plagues the marriage-hearse . . .
> till some blind hand shall brush my wing . . .

> but his loving look . . . all her tender limbs with
> terror shook;

and many others are not the work of a mere apprentice. In the MS. book we find:

> And in thy horrid ribs dare steep
> In the well of sanguine woe
> In what clay and in what mould
> Were thine eyes of fury rolld

and, one of Blake's greatest couplets:

> Or shrink at the little blasts of fear
> That the hireling blows into my ear.

One is divided in mind whether to wonder more at the genius that could fashion, or the craftsman who could reject, such phrases when he did not want them, leaving them among the debris of his workshop.

It was this self-imposed limitation that seems accountable for, or at all events connected with, certain interesting features of his muse. He never appears to avoid the obvious. Indeed the words and the very form and content of his verse often seem to be dictated by the jingling rhymes, especially of "Innocence." But just when the jingle begins to cloy, he relieves us either by some magic expression and picture like:

> And sport no more seen
> On the darkening green,

or introduces most characteristically a bad rhyme, or even omits the rhyme altogether as:

> Merrily Merrily to welcome in the Year.

His bad rhymes are as effective as they are characteristic, always carrying on the movement and tune while preventing the verse from becoming sugary.

Thus we have on the one hand the obvious and childlike array of bowers and flowers, beams and streams, boys and joys, mothers and brothers, together with rest and nest, mild and child, voice and rejoice, smiles and beguiles, sleeping and weeping, dies and sighs, all introduced almost as though they were ends in themselves worth adding new verses in order to include; and on the other hand we have every form of bad rhyme, such as thrush and bush, weary and merry, name and am or lamb, live and receive, love and grove, blossom and bosom, robin and sobbing, dark and work, fast and lost, joy and by, shade and spread or head, dear and care, face and dress or kiss, peace and distress, lamb and hand, groves and moves, blessing and ceasing, nest and beast, warm and harm, dreadful and heedful, meekness and sickness, spirit and inherit, girl and small, maid and said, crow and you, lick and neck, shade and bed, hum and home, woe and too, gone and moan; and in ***Experience,*** bard and word, return and worn, stood and viewed, worm and storm, heath and death. Then we have other kinds of imperfect rhyme, such as followed and led, injury and misery, reason and teazing, distress and thankfulness, sky and merrily, fly and mystery, joy and poverty, and repetitions for rhymes, like read and reed, well and well, be and be, Love and Love; while we find the same rhyme, such as snow and woe, repeated in consecutive verses and constant changes of rhyme scheme from verse to verse. We find a verse with no real rhyme except a double one in the last line:

> And I saw it was filled with graves
> And tomb-stones where flowers should be
> And priests in black gowns, were walking their
>   rounds,
> And binding with briars, my joys and desires,

or in the last but one:

> Dear Mother dear Mother the Church is cold
> But the Ale-house is healthy & pleasant & warm
> Besides I can tell where I am used well
> Such usage in heaven will never do well.

He is very fond of introducing the auxiliaries (especially do) when they are not grammatically necessary:

> The Sun does arise . . .
> Old John . . . does laugh . . .
> Cock does crow . . .
> Starry Jealousy does keep my den . . .
> And their sun does never shine . . .
> If her heart does ake . . .
> Near where the charterd Thames does flow . . .
> My wrath did end . . . did grow . . .
> And the Raven his nest has made.

On the other hand he seems to avoid the use of the auxiliary "to be" with the present participle. "The children walking" he says for the children were walking.

Phrases like "have took," "the feet of angels moves," "while o'er thee thy mother weep," are annoying to some readers, but most will feel that he has a nearly infallible ear for the music of his verse and he never spoils great passages of song by inappropriate mannerisms.

Trying to picture the process of creation one cannot resist the impression that it begins with something that is neither sight nor sound, but a kind of inspired flame of emotion quite individual in character and associated with a few significant words, but otherwise undefined. And just as Blake saw mighty forms upon a blank wall, or significant scenes upon a clear sheet of paper, which grew and defined themselves as he gazed or worked at them, so these poetic inspirations came first like beams of sunlight or heavy clouds or blasts of prophecy, each with peculiar and specific character, but without defined content until he had found the words and spread the images that filled them out. Their character thus caught, they became permanent and communicable things, never henceforth to be destroyed.

The Piper tells the same tale. A mood of glee without thought or content becomes in a moment of inspiration associated with the word "Lamb." And the word begins a story that is to end in the reed-written book. (pp. 62-7)

The symbolism of these early works . . . is only a little removed from metaphor. When Blake follows "Piping down the valleys wild" with the image "On a cloud I saw a child" he is using a picture to express the fact of inspiration. In a word, the Child on a cloud is his vision of the Muse in Heaven that evokes his song. Half a lifetime later, when he was completing his greatest work in the "Job" designs, he represents, in the second illustration, Jehovah enthroned on the clouds surrounded by the hosts of heaven.

This figure he calls "The Angel of the Divine Presence." The meaning is similar if not the same: "What is above is Within." The reallest things in life, the things that make or mar our outward lives and inspire our poetry in word and deed, are the inward visions and conceptions which we may symbolise as happenings on or above the clouds. In *Innocence* the image is simplicity itself, apparently a light and passing metaphor; but it was the utterance of so fundamental a feature of Blake's mind that it is still there when nearly forty years later he uses it to convey the whole burden of his matured thought on life. In the fourth verse the child disappears, and this is parallel to the disappearance of God (and Satan too) after the seventeenth illustration of the "Job."

Again the meaning, if lighter, is essentially the same. Vision, without which man is nothing, enters and becomes one with us in the life of artistic labour or Christianity. In a sense it leaves us, with nothing but its afterglow, to work out our salvation in the here and the now. But this "here and now" has itself been for ever changed. We are become one with the life of heaven, whether in the writing of a book of songs for children or in the supreme task of realising the life of God on earth.

Meanwhile the "cloud" has come to be used in a variety of ways. It is something within, but it is something hiding the innermost reality, to be broken through before we gain real vision. The child is not in, but on, the cloud, and we can only see him by seeing beyond it. So we have in **"Infant Sorrow"** of the *Songs of Experience* the "Fiend hid in a cloud," describing the divine spirit cribbed and confined in the flesh. It becomes a fiend because it is hid in the cloud and so cut off from the universal divine, which can only be recovered by vision—vision that pierces the clouds.

But not only do the metaphors develop and shift about a centre, there is a constant tendency in Blake's mind to invert them, as Shelley does in "The Revolt of Islam" where the serpent at the beginning represents innocent goodness and the eagle tyrannous power, and so forth. Thus the things that to common understanding seem solid and substantial like the material world, Blake symbolises as water, dew, mist. For the material world is in perpetual flux. The things that appear abstract like Reason he symbolises as stone, and finally as mountains (imaginative things are sometimes marble) because of their unyielding character.

What we call the animal life, the life of the flesh whether innocent or gross, he calls the vegetable life, because it is concerned only with growth and reproduction. In his verses and illustrations it is continually expressed as trees, grass, reeds, moss, and so forth. This use of the word "vegetable" is by no means peculiar to Blake, and though there may possibly be some slight element of perversity in many of his inverted metaphors, the inversion is mainly due to a passionate impulse to bring out neglected aspects of truth. He deliberately associates the most tremendous realities with the gentle and impotent creatures. God is seen in **"The Lamb,"** and Conscious Existence itself is associated with **"The Fly."** The fierce wild beasts are, it is true, used to symbolise the fierce wildness of the passions, but in **"The Little Girl Lost"** and **"Found"** they symbolise sex-love in its most tender and poetic mood.

Blake's use of Night and Morning is more difficult. It is sometimes as clearly not symbolical as it is other times clearly symbolical. When he says in **"The Angel"**:

> And I wept both night and day
> And he wip'd my tears away
> And I wept both day and night
> And hid from him my hearts delight

he is clearly using the words to signify "all the time." But in the next verse, when he says:

> So he took his wings and fled;
> Then the morn blush'd rosy red;

it clearly marks the sudden psychological change in the heroine.

The wonderful song **"Night"** appears to me to begin definitely in the natural world. But gradually fear creeps into its shadows, and then the hosts of heaven descend to allay them, and we find ourselves in the midst of the battleground of good and evil passions until passionate tears lead us to the "immortal day" of the Lamb and to redemption through the cleansing river of life. Everything in nature has become symbolical and spiritual.

When we come to **"The Little Girl Lost"** and its sequel we find practically the same images used entirely symbolically from the first. Both the child's sleep and the wild beasts that surround her in the night are symbolical of states and emotions. In **"The Tyger"** the "forests of the night" and the "Tyger" himself, beginning probably in the natural world, become finished and perfect symbols though still with roots in nature.

It may be said, then, that most of the *Songs of Innocence* are exactly what they seem—lyrics almost as spontaneous as the songs of the birds, often written originally without any thought (or scarcely any) of ulterior or hidden significance. Others even in *Innocence* and many in *Experience* have scarcely any meaning until we unravel their spiritual meaning. Still more, perhaps, are a harmony in several parts, to hear which is to experience a very exquisite delight. Of none is this more true than of the **"Introduction"** to the *Songs of Innocence.* (pp. 69-72)

> *Joseph H. Wicksteed, in his* Blake's Innocence and Experience: A Study of the Songs and Manuscripts, *J. M. Dent & Sons Ltd., 1928, 301 p.*

Mark Schorer   (essay date 1946)

[*An American novelist, short story writer, and biographer, Schorer was also well known for his literary criticism. His essay "Technique as Discovery" (1947) became a critical hallmark for its claim that fiction deserves the close scrutiny, attention, and consideration that was accorded poetry by the New Critics. In the following excerpt, Schorer interprets* Songs of Innocence and of Experience *as social criticism that condemns the repression of human development and expression.*]

". . . Flowers & Fruits, insects & warbling birds." *Songs of Innocence* seizes these idyllic elements from the *Poetical Sketches,* isolates them from the conditions of humanitarian protest almost completely, and develops them for their sake alone, in a paradisaical scene where only the possibility of the "subtil serpent . . . consuming all" exists. Yet exist it does, although very faintly indeed in the most purely pastoral poems. In the opening song, "Piping down the valleys wild," the child who laughs in the tree and asks the poet to sing a song of a lamb, weeps when he hears it, first simply, and then "with joy." Is it that the "child" knows all too well the first fate of the "lamb," although he knows, too, and can therefore mix joy with his weeping, what lies beyond it? The association of shepherd and lamb, Jesus and child, is clearer in the second song, "How sweet is the Shepherd's sweet lot," in the shepherd whose "tongue" is "filled with praise" of man, and most significantly in the fourth, "Little Lamb, who made thee?" where the connection is not at all submerged but is the point of the poem. The figure of Jesus, whether as lamb or child, carries primary overtones of tragedy, and these are absent from only three songs in the entire group— **"Infant Joy," "Spring,"** and **"Laughing Song,"** the last of which at least is more appropriate to the insouciant *Poetical Sketches.*

These elements should not be stressed, perhaps, since they are significant only in a later context. By and large, the impression left by the *Songs of Innocence* is of a vision of pastoral felicity. . . . Innocence, when one views it thus, is a condition of unimpaired consciousness that makes possible a perception of experience unhampered by schism, or by reason and its products; experience apprehended wholly, with all the faculties as they are given to us, and differing from the normal adult experience in that it is "pure," the *whole* experience. "Unorganiz'd Innocence: An Impossibility," Blake was to say a few years later, and the remark is useful to an understanding of the kind of psychology that he is trying to organize in the *Songs,* a psychology opposed to that of Locke and Hartley, in which mind was made relative to the sensuous experience of the individual, and made more and more relative as he developed more and more complexities of association. Without negating individuality, Blake is yet trying to give us a picture of an entire experience, absolutely perceived, without particularizing shutters. That this picture should be associated with a child's world raises a number of points.

Blake does not explicitly assume a primitive condition of innocence in society at large, but only in the individual life, and only in the life of the child. Yet the furnishings of that life have a real significance in the eighteenth century. Not only are the happy poems consistently rural, but they are more devoid of the ordinary habiliments of rural life than any other pastorals that have ever been written. This is such a complete picture of natural "simplicity" that the poems can hardly be considered of "nature" at all. That they were intended to be so is suggested by the fact that two of the three poems based on real social problems are of the city, and that the poems of social misery in the *Songs of Experience,* if they have an explicit setting, are all of the city, and a city great in wealth and commerce.

The suggestion is that at the back of Blake's mind hovered that bugaboo of the century, "luxury." "Luxury," attacked by all manner of men, arose from an expanded commerce, and in allowing the people of a nation to depart too far from the simplicity of the natural state sapped them of their virtue. At the back of Blake's mind, and in the background of these poems, lie the assumptions, ultimately revolutionary, of Rousseau.

Do they point in any way to the revolutionary future? Again, the imagery itself is suggestive. External nature, as Blake presents it here, is kindly to man and generally it is co-operative within itself, as in the poem of the lost emmet, **"A Dream."**

> Pitying, I drop'd a tear;
> But I saw a glow-worm near,
> Who replied: "What wailing wight
> Calls the watchman of the night?
>
> I am set to light the ground,
> While the beetle goes his round;
> Follow now the beetle's hum;
> Little wanderer, hie thee home."

If, as in **"Night,"** natural creatures do not live in harmony, they yearn to do so, and there is a promise of such a situation, even though it is reserved until "our immortal day." There are two poems of separation in this group, that of the emmet and its young, and that of the father and his lost boy. Separation is the equivalent of experience, as unity is of innocence; both poems end with the reachievement of unity. Another characteristic of these poems is the utter absence of ego, the degree of impersonality. They are poems of joy, but joy that suggests Yeats's distinction, "pleasure which is personal and joy which is impersonal," and the regenerate state as Blake himself later describes it, in which selfishness has given way to brotherhood.

One more point is useful to remember, and that is the distinction Blake had already made between "the innocence of a child" and "the errors of acquired folly." This is the primitivistic strand. The progressivistic is contained in the remark "Innocence dwells with Wisdom, but never with Ignorance." Whatever the felicity of the children in *Songs of Innocence,* they can hardly be described as wise. Something lies between—experience; and it hovers at the edge of all these poems. What is its quality, and what is its value?

In **"The Blossom,"** while the sparrow sleeps the robin unaccountably sobs. When, in **"The Ecchoing Green,"** the sun sets,

> . . . the little ones, weary,
> No more can be merry.

Somewhere on the outskirts of this pastoral area is a "lonely fen," and there the little boy is lost in the mists. Those "virtues of delight," mercy, pity, peace, and love, are opposed to human "distress," out of which men pray. And when the mother sits over the cradle of her sleeping, smiling child, she weeps, as Jesus wept, until she remembers that Jesus "Heaven & Earth to peace beguiles." (Yet the intended counterpart for this poem in Blake's manuscript book, where "infant smiles" became "infant wiles," which creep in the "little heart asleep" and which "Heav-en & Earth *of* peace beguiles," Blake never printed. Nor was this because the grammatical difficulty was unsurmountable; rather because it was a too depraved view of human nature, which he could not publicly admit.)

Then there are the three poems founded on social situations—the song of the chimney sweeper, who weeps while he works and who dreams of resurrection; the children of the charity school in **"Holy Thursday,"** singing in St. Paul's to "aged men, wise guardians of the poor"; and the little black boy, born into slavery, whose sufferings have made him wise. Through experience—or through a particularly degrading social experience—the little black boy has achieved another innocence, which "dwells with Wisdom."

This implication, which lurks mainly in evangelical guise in the *Songs of Innocence,* relates them closely to Blake's developing revolutionary doctrine. They are a more positive expression than *Tiriel* of his belief that evil and the misery it brings with it are a mere incrustation on life and the spirit, a negative. In most of these songs the restraints that create evil do not hamper energy or limitless joy, and man's sympathy with man is praised:

> Then every man, of every clime,
> That prays in his distress,
> Prays to the human form divine,
> Love, Mercy, Pity, Peace.
>
> And all must love the human form,
> In heathen, turk, or jew;
> Where Mercy, Love, & Pity dwell
> There God is dwelling too.

The serenity of this envisioned world Blake fashioned out of the conventional imagery of evangelicism, and it is sung in the voice of the Sunday school. It was only 1789; the thunder was not yet loud, as it is not yet loud in the poems. The irony of Blake's forms has yet to become apparent. So, too, has the overt recommendation of violence against restraint if, indeed, out of experience, we are "to inherit" the promised "New worlds." "Joys impregnate," he was yet to say, but "Sorrows bring forth." (pp. 230-34)

The forms of bondage, especially the bondage of "sexual strife," are the chief ingredients of the *Songs of Experience.* They develop out of the second, the humanitarian, element of the *Poetical Sketches,* but they are expressed now with that intensity which is the particular mark of Blake's genius, and without contradiction.

The children of *Songs of Innocence* have become captives who cry for liberty, and, denied it, suffer a deterioration of natural virtue. The onslaughts of authority and the moral consequence begin at once, in infancy:

> Struggling in my father's hands,
> Striving against my swadling bands,
> Bound and weary I thought best
> To sulk upon my mother's breast.

The onslaughts of authority continue. **"The Schoolboy"** reminds us not only of Blake's resistance to education but of the Godwinian assault on it as the root of prejudice. Religion listens to the little lost boy's intuition that man is godly and that God is human, and burns him as a heretic, which is to say that in experience, dogma destroys intuition. The same child, perhaps, pleads in **"The Little Vagabond"** that the free pleasures of the alehouse are more desirable than the repressions of the Church, which decrees good and evil in its law. The protest in all these poems is against authority because it ignores individuality by restraining natural impulse. The impulse that is most emphatically in Blake's mind becomes evident in the yearnings for liberty of the young man and woman in **"Ah! Sunflower"**:

> . . . the Youth pined away with desire,
> And the pale Virgin shrouded in snow.

The bulk of the poems in *Songs of Experience* are directed against the conventional restraints imposed upon sexuality, and the fact that mistaken attitudes toward sexual love are made the root of all the errors in experience is not surprising when one remembers Blake's remark, possibly startling in the context of 1788, that "the origin of this mistake in Lavater & his contemporaries is, They suppose that Woman's Love is Sin; in consequence all the Loves & Graces with them are Sins." The infant who learns to "sulk" immediately is a creature not out of Lavater's psychology but out of Freud's.

The *Songs of Experience* begin with the poet's cry to the earth, the plea that she renew herself: "O Earth, O Earth, return!" And Earth answers:

> "Prison'd on wat'ry shore,
> Starry Jealousy does keep my den:
> Cold and hoar,
> Weeping o'er,
> I hear the father of the ancient men.
>
> Selfish father of men!
> Cruel, jealous, selfish fear!
> Can delight,
> Chain'd in night,
> The virgins of youth and morning bear?
>
> Does spring hide its joy
> When buds and blossoms grow?
> Does the sower
> Sow by night,
> Or the plowman in darkness plow?
>
> Break this heavy chain
> That does freeze my bones around.
> Selfish! vain!
> Eternal bane!
> That free Love with bondage bound."

Authority, bondage, jealousy—it is to become one of the most familiar couplings in Blake, and with it, a particular image that is worth observing:

> Break this heavy chain
> That does *freeze* my bones around.

The chain grows into the bone, becomes the bone, which is to say that restraint *becomes* the character. It is one of the innumerable changes that Blake rings on the theme of interdependence, the subject of "Auguries of Innocence." It is characteristic, too, that with this image comes that of repressed fruition, in the sower and the plowman.

In a song rejected from the final manuscript, Blake had written:

> Love to faults is always blind,
> Always is to joy inclin'd,
> Lawless, wing'd, & unconfin'd,
> And breaks all chains from every mind.
>
> Deceit to secresy confin'd,
> Lawful, cautious, & refin'd;
> To every thing but interest blind,
> And forges fetters for the mind.

The rejection was probably based on the awareness that this antithesis was too sharp and too simple. In these poems deceit is not the opposite of love, but a portion of it, its inversion. The real difference, that between free love and fettered love, Blake expressed much more adequately in **"The Clod and the Pebble,"** where the familiar "Clay" of *Thel,* the pliable earth capable of fertility and growth, expresses one view—

> "Love seeketh not Itself to please,
> Nor for itself hath any care,
> But for another gives its ease,
> And builds a Heaven in Hell's despair"—

and the hard, rounded "Pebble of the brook," incapable of anything, sterile and without plasticity, "bound," sings:

> "Love seeketh only Self to please,
> To bind another to Its delight,
> Joys in another's loss of ease,
> And builds a Hell in Heaven's despite."

The agents that reduce joy to deceit and love to cunning are the familiar slaves of reason, of the "Selfish father of men"—theologians and philosophers, kings and judges and priests:

> Remove away that black'ning church:
> Remove away that marriage hearse:
> Remove away that place of blood:
> You'll quite remove the ancient curse.

Or again:

> The King & the Priest must be tied in a tether
> Before two virgins can meet together.

These, again, are rejected verses that achieved more exact expression in **"The Garden of Love"**:

> I went to the Garden of Love,
> And saw what I never had seen:
> A Chapel was built in the midst,
> Where I used to play on the green.
>
> And the gates of this Chapel were shut,
> And "Thou shalt not" writ over the door;
> So I turn'd to the Garden of Love
> That so many sweet flowers bore;
>
> And I saw it was filled with graves,
> And tomb-stones where flowers should be;
> And Priests in black gowns were walking their
>   rounds,
> And binding with briars my joys & desires.

It is impossible when reading this poem not to think of another of Blake's rejected poems, and since it has impressive elements in itself, to speculate on the reasons for its rejection.

> I saw a chapel all of gold
> That none did dare to enter in,
> And many weeping stood without,
> Weeping, mourning, worshipping.
>
> I saw a serpent rise between
> The white pillars of the door,
> And he forc'd & forc'd & forc'd,
> Down the golden hinges tore.
>
> And along the pavement sweet,
> Set with pearls & rubies bright,
> All his slimy length he drew,
> Till upon the altar white
>
> Vomiting his poison out
> On the bread & on the wine.
> So I turn'd into a sty
> And laid me down among the swine.

In tone and pattern this is a good *Song of Experience,* but something has gone awry in Blake's meaning. His fascination with ambiguous images has got out of hand, and the poem ends by saying something quite different from what most of his lyrics say. The chapel is probably the same as that of **"The Garden of Love,"** and the "Weeping, mourning, worshipping" people without are the frustrated lovers who in "The Garden" are "graves" and "tomb-stones." Then the "serpent" reared up and "forc'd & forc'd & forc'd," and violated the church; but here Blake has turned round upon himself. For while it is true that thwarted sexuality takes unattractive forms, the thwarting originates with the restraining Church, not vice versa. If this was first thought of as a sequel to **"The Garden of Love,"** and a development of the idea of the interdependence of energy and force, yet for some reason Blake did not use it. It is reasonable to suppose that he found the involutions of his meaning becoming a little too complex for a message that he wished to be direct and forthright. He did not wish to seem to say that the "serpent" was at fault when the fault was with the "priest."

For the same idea and without the extreme ambiguity, he found a more satisfactory image than the "chapel all of gold" in **"The Sick Rose,"** where that thwarted impulse which becomes poisonous deceit and jealousy is "The invisible worm That flies in the night" and eats out the heart of the rose.

That "Love, free love, cannot be bound" without suffering a tragic change is the steadiest proposition throughout these poems. When the initial spontaneity of impulse, or act, is hindered, it turns to calculation, and jealousy is born:

> A flower was offer'd to me,
> Such a flower as May never bore;
> But I said "I've a Pretty Rose-tree,"
> And I passed the sweet flower o'er.
>
> Then I went to my Pretty Rose-tree,
> To tend her by day and by night;
> But my Rose turn'd away with jealousy,
> And her thorns were my only delight.

Lavater had written, "As the shadow follows the body, so

restless subtleness the female knave"; but Blake, who was thinking of the effect of the punishment of "thorns," crossed out "subtleness" and wrote "sullenness" over it. But "subtleness," too, has its part in Blake's text, as in an unpublished poem which also shows that he was not without humor in a matter that ordinarily compelled only his anger:

> I asked a thief to steal me a peach:
> He turned up his eyes.
> I ask'd a lithe lady to lie her down:
> Holy & meek she cries.
>
> As soon as I went an angel came:
> He wink'd at the thief
> And smil'd at the dame,
> And without one word spoke
> Had a peach from the tree,
> And 'twixt earnest & joke
> Enjoy'd the Lady.

The hypocritical "angel" triumphs over the sincere man of open impulse. Sincerity, Godwin's "perfect sincerity," is the great neglected virtue in all these poems. The depraved moral of "Never seek to tell thy love" recommends reservation:

> I told my love, I told my love,
> I told her all my heart,
> Trembling, cold, in ghastly fears—
> Ah, she doth depart.

The tragedy of other relationships, no less than that of love, is the absence of "perfect sincerity":

> I was angry with my friend:
> I told my wrath, my wrath did end.
> I was angry with my foe:
> I told it not, my wrath did grow.

Wrath grows into a tree of dissimulation that bears fruit that finally kills the foe. The tree itself is significant: it is the tree of judgment, of good and evil, of restraint, and it will appear again and again; it is authority, law, and it "grows . . . in the Human Brain." Its causes, hardly those intended by Genesis, have effects no less devastating. Blake does not believe that they need last so long:

> Children of the future Age
> Reading this indignant page,
> Know that in a former time
> Love! sweet Love! was thought a crime.

These lines suggest that later lyric which is often thought to be a reminiscence of Mary Wollstonecraft. The poem opens with a description of Mary's appearance at a ball where her charm and beauty win her instant friends and sympathy. But her doctrine is "sincerity," and she makes an inexcusable faux pas:

> Mary moves in soft beauty & conscious delight
> To augment with sweet smiles all the joys of the
>   Night,
> Nor once blushes to own to the rest of the Fair
> That sweet Love & Beauty are worthy our care.

Next morning she is an outcast (". . . no Friend from henceforward thou, Mary, shalt see"):

Some said she was proud, some call'd her a
    whore,
And some, when she passed by, shut to the door;
A damp cold came o'er her, her blushes all fled;
Her lillies & roses are blighted & shed.

"O, why was I born with a different Face?
Why was I not born like this Envious Race?
Why did Heaven adorn me with bountiful hand,
And then set me down in an envious Land?"

Blake's sympathies are expressed in the concluding comment:

All Faces have Envy, sweet Mary, but thine;

And thine is a Face of sweet Love in despair,
And thine is a Face of mild sorrow & care,
And thine Is a Face of wild terror & fear
That shall never be quiet till laid on its bier.

Mary Wollstonecraft had written of her own situation, "I have . . . considered myself as a particle broken off from the grand mass of mankind;—I was alone."

All of man's energies are defaced when bound. Snakes sprang from Hela's head, and Har piped fatuously within a cage. Tiriel himself expired, and his sons and daughters. There are other miseries than "sexual strife" in *Songs of Experience*: pious humiliation and poverty, cruelty and hatred, kingship and warfare. Where now are those "virtues of delight," mercy, pity, peace, and love? They are here, but in another form, as the virtues of Satan, and it is here that Blake's political judgments stand most clearly opposed to his religious judgments:

Pity would be no more
If we did not make somebody Poor;
And Mercy no more could be
If all were as happy as we.

And mutual fear brings peace,
Till the selfish loves increase:
Then Cruelty knits a snare,
And spreads his baits with care.

The second quatrain is especially compelling, for it seems to be an attack on the depraved Hobbesian view of human nature, in which society arises from man's worst qualities rather than from his best. It is a view that lurks at the bottom of even the more enlightened theories of social contract, and it is a view that Blake, who has already indicated his concept of the state of nature, cannot approve. Because it is a "view," it is no less "real." It is, indeed, the reality of experience as Blake has pictured it. The conception of man as a selfish creature, and the resulting necessity of authority, which passes into the hands of the most selfish, ends in every tragic social paradox Blake pursues. Now the real status of those innocents—parish charges—who sing above the heads of "aged men, wise guardians of the poor," is revealed:

Is this a holy thing to see
In a rich and fruitful land,
Babes reduc'd to misery,
Fed with cold and usurous hand?

Is that trembling cry a song?
Can it be a song of joy?

And so many children poor?
It is a land of poverty!

And now finally, in this poem the genuine irony of Blake's *Songs* becomes clear. Imitations of the "good-Godly" songs of the newly founded Sunday schools, the *Songs of Innocence* appropriate the piety doled out to the underprivileged children of the factory and the mining districts, and then, in the same meters, the *Songs of Experience* shift from the ideal images of shepherds and lambs, flowers and fruits, and retain only those which the children of the poor really knew, the images of poverty, despair, and death:

A little black thing among the snow,
Crying " 'weep! 'weep!" in notes of woe!
"Where are thy father & mother? say?"
"They are both gone up to the church to pray.

Because I was happy upon the heath,
And smil'd among the winter's snow,
They clothed me in the clothes of death,
And taught me to sing the notes of woe.

And because I am happy & dance & sing,
They think they have done me no injury,
And are gone to praise God & his Priest & King,
Who make up a heaven of our misery."

                             (pp. 237-46)

[Blake's] most incisive attack, that which includes his whole catalogue of miseries and includes them most poetically, is in the terrible poem "**London.**" In a rejected version of this poem, he had sung more naïvely, even blithely, and he had looked toward an escape:

Why should I care for the men of thames,
Or the cheating waves of charter'd streams,
Or shrink at the little blasts of fear
That the hireling blows into my ear?

Tho' born on the cheating banks of Thames,
Tho' his waters bathed my infant limbs,
The Ohio shall wash his stains from me:
I was born a slave, but I go to be free.

This was a little too near the mood of rural nostalgia in Samuel Johnson's un-Johnsonian poem of the same title, a poem that Blake may have had in mind as contrast. In another version he wrote of "each dirty street" and of "the dirty Thames," and while the filth of London was a European scandal, these details were inadequate to the basic social fact. Blake then combined his two versions and produced his famous third:

I wander thro' each charter'd street,
Near where the charter'd Thames does flow,
And mark in every face I meet
Marks of weakness, marks of woe.

In every cry of every Man,
In every Infant's cry of fear,
In every voice, in every ban,
The mind-forg'd manacles I hear.

How the Chimney-sweeper's cry
Every black'ning Church appalls;
And the hapless Soldier's sigh
Runs in blood down Palace walls.

> But most thro' midnight streets I hear
> How the youthful Harlot's curse
> Blasts the new born Infant's tear,
> And blights with plagues the Marriage hearse.

The lines echo with Paine on monopoly, Godwin on child labor, Mary Wollstonecraft on marriage; but these echoes fade before the total impact of Blake's own juxtapositions. The poem is as unrelieved as the misery it contemplates, and certainly no other work in English makes such a powerful indictment of authority and social tyranny. Blake seems to be saying to a placid world, "It is very true, what you have said. . . . I am Mad or Else you are so; both of us cannot be in our right senses."

Against this social scene, external nature—or such glimpses of it as we are permitted—is relatively serene. The fly, in the poem of that name, takes a dizzy delight in being precisely itself, and "beasts of prey"—lion, leopards, tigers—show a kindness to the lost little girl that the citizens of London are unable to show to one another:

> And her bosom lick,
> And upon her neck
> From his eyes of flame
> Ruby tears there came.

When her parents found her—"And saw their sleeping child Among tygers wild"—they chose as a home the wilderness, which seems more peaceful:

> To this day they dwell
> In a lonely dell;
> Nor fear the wolvish howl
> Nor the lions' growl.

The choice is metaphorical, suggesting that nature is not necessarily savage. The tree of good and evil is not rooted in the universe:

> The Gods of the earth and sea
> Sought thro' Nature to find this Tree;
> But their search was all in vain:
> There grows one in the Human Brain.

It is in the mind, and not intractably there. The article in the title **"A Divine Image"** is vastly important:

> Cruelty has a Human Heart,
> And Jealousy a Human Face;
> Terror the Human Form Divine,
> And Secrecy the Human Dress.
>
> The Human Dress is forged Iron,
> The Human Form a fiery Forge,
> The Human Face a Furnace seal'd,
> The Human Heart its hungry Gorge.

This is only *a* divine image, drawn after a particular god, the cruel judge and mechanist of Iron, Forge, and Furnace; it is opposed to *the* divine image of the earlier poems, drawn after Jesus, the God-Man, lover of sinners. In the cant of Blake's day, it is the difference between man as he is and man as he is not. The distinction promises everything.

Then who will restore lost pastoral delights, bring back the lamb? The answer is the tiger. **"The Tyger"** can be read in many ways—as the simple opposition of innocence and experience; as the paradox of the creation and of Christianity, the antithesis of spirit and matter, love and wrath, good and evil; as the expression of delight and awe before the magnitude and variety of the creation; even as an embodiment of the Popian proposition that all partial evil is universal good. It can be read in all these ways and give pleasure in each, yet in Blake's context it has a more particular and, for that context, a crucial meaning.

The juxtaposition of lamb and tiger points not merely to the opposition of innocence and experience, but to the resolution of the paradox they present. The innocent impulses of the lamb have been curbed by restraints, and the lamb has turned into something else, indeed into the tiger. Innocence is converted to experience. It does not rest there. Energy can be curbed but it cannot be destroyed, and when it reaches the limits of its endurance, it bursts forth in revolutionary wrath. The crucial quatrain is:

> When the stars threw down their spears,
> And water'd heaven with their tears,
> Did he smile his work to see?
> Did he who made the Lamb make thee?

"Starry Jealousy does keep my den," Earth complained in the second song. Why "starry"? The stars in Blake are the symbols of a dominant reason, the association being that of the mechanistic philosophy of science and eighteenth-century rationalism. And when the stars throw down their spears and weep, they are soldiers abandoning their arms in contrition and a readiness for peace. When reason capitulates before wrathful energy, is the creation satisfied? The tiger is necessary to the renewal of the lamb.

"The Tyger," more than any other single poem in *Songs of Experience,* looks forward to the revolutionary synthesis of *The Marriage of Heaven and Hell.* But there are others, and it is significant that in the first copies both the opening and the closing poems were poems not of despair but of millennial expectation and that at least one poem in the body of the volume looks to "futurity," when "the desart wild" shall "Become a garden mild." In the first poem, **"Introduction,"** the prophetic character, already identified with energy, summons the imprisoned earth:

> Hear the voice of the Bard!
> Who Present, Past, & Future, sees;
> Whose ears have heard
> The Holy Word
> That walk'd among the ancient trees,
>
> Calling the lapsed Soul,
> And weeping in the evening dew;
> That might controll
> The starry pole,
> And fallen, fallen light renew!
>
> "O Earth, O Earth, return!
> Arise from out the dewy grass;
> Night is worn,
> And the morn
> Rises from the slumberous mass.
>
> Turn away no more;
> Why wilt thou turn away?
> The starry floor,
> The wat'ry shore,
> Is giv'n thee till the break of day."

This is a challenge to unregenerate man to enjoy his whole powers in natural harmony. The last poem, **"The Voice of the Ancient Bard,"** repeats the invitation. Again, poetry, the life of intuition and of satisfied impulse, which is the true source of knowledge, is set against the authority of reason and of law, the source of multiplied errors:

> Youth of delight, come hither,
> And see the opening morn,
> Image of truth new born.
> Doubt is fled, & clouds of reason,
> Dark disputes & artful teazing.
> Folly is an endless maze,
> Tangled roots perplex her ways.
> How many have fallen there!
> They stumble all night over the bones of the
>   dead,
> And feel they know not what but care,
> And wish to lead others, when they should be
>   led.

The central lines are echoes of old Elizabethan verses, but the challenge of the whole is new.

It is newer, for example, than Shelley, who twenty years later was to make the same attacks that are made in these songs—on the Church, on the God of law, on priests and kings, on custom, on commerce and finance, on marriage—but who was still to make them in terms of that eighteenth-century rationalism from which he finally had to struggle free if intellectual beauty and an ideal of liberty were to be supported in his verse. Blake's instantaneous rejection of it is perhaps the most amazing of his feats of intellect. Before he could properly use in his poetry the texts of revolutionary social criticism, he had to transform the Lockian psychology and its evaluation of life. The indignation of **Songs of Experience** is founded on the easy delight of the **Songs of Innocence.** (pp. 248-53)

> *Mark Schorer, in his* William Blake: The Politics of Vision, *Henry Holt and Company, 1946, 524p.*

Northrop Frye   (essay date 1947)

[*A Canadian-born critic, Frye exerted tremendous influence in the field of twentieth-century literary scholarship, mainly through his study* Anatomy of Criticism *(1957). In this seminal work, he contended that literary criticism should be an autonomous discipline similar to the sciences. Frye maintained that the structure and components of literature—such as genre, myth, and archetypal symbol—are constant and observable like the laws of nature, and thus subject to regulated, objective study. In the following excerpt, he asserts that* Songs of Innocence *and* Songs of Experience *satirize each other.*]

Childhood to Blake is a state or phase of imaginative existence, the phase in which the world of imagination is still a brave new world and yet reassuring and intelligible. In the protection which the child feels from his parents and his evening prayer against darkness there is the image of a cosmos far more intelligently controlled than ours. The spontaneity of life which such protection makes possible is the liberty of the expanding imagination which has nothing to do but complete its own growth. No one can

watch babies, kittens, puppies or even the first green shoots of plants for very long without beginning to smile; and the smile is a partial vision of the state of existence which this infant life is in. It was to the same vision that Jesus was appealing when he put a child in the midst of his disciples.

However, the course of life in this world indicates that there is a higher world to attain to, and that is the world of the Providence and Father itself, which is looked up to in the infantile state. The dawn of imaginative puberty will make one at once impatient with it: one is then no longer a creature but a creator. At twelve Jesus ran away from home, and though his parents sought him as the searching parents in **"A Little Girl Lost"** do, he was now about his Father's business, ready to become one with his Father. But outgrowing the child's world does not imply abandoning what it stands for. In every attempt of an adult to console a crying child there is a reminder of the fact that as long as a single form of life remains in misery and pain the imagination finds the world not good enough.

The reader needs no commentary to help him understand the terrible indictment of this latter world in the **Songs of Experience.** Contempt and horror have never spoken more clearly in English poetry. But Blake never forgets to see behind all the cruelty of man the fact of his fall. Just as no one can watch a baby without smiling, so no one can see a child tortured for its own "good" or neglected for someone else's: no one can see its parents, blackened and twisted by the St. Anthony's fire of moral virtue, stumbling out of a darkened church and blinking like bats in the sun: no one can see prostitution or war or race hatred or poverty, without groping for some cause of what seems to be utterly pointless evil. The reason can supply irrefutable proofs that in such things the world is behaving illogically and contrary to its own best interests. The reason will not take us far. Only vision helps us here, and vision shows us the tree of mystery and morality growing inside the human skull; it shows us the prophet calling to the earth to redeem herself and earth answering with a groan to be delivered; it shows us our accusing enemy who frightens us out of Paradise behind the menacing blaze of a tiger's eyes.

This is the only world the child can grow into, and yet the child must grow. The **Songs of Experience** are satires, but one of the things that they satirize is the state of innocence. They show us the butcher's knife which is waiting for the unconscious lamb. Conversely, the **Songs of Innocence** satirize the state of experience, as the contrast which they present to it makes its hypocrisies more obviously shameful. Hence the two sets of lyrics show two *contrary* states of the soul, and in their opposition there is a double-edged irony, cutting into both the tragedy and the reality of fallen existence. (pp. 236-37)

The actual makes the ideal look helpless and the ideal makes the actual look absurd. (p. 237)

> *Northrop Frye, in his* Fearful Symmetry: A Study of William Blake, *1947. Reprint by Beacon Press, 1962, 462 p.*

Edward FitzGerald on Blake and *Songs of Innocence*:

I have lately bought a little pamphlet which is very difficult to be got, called *The Songs of Innocence,* written and adorned with drawings by W. Blake (if you know his name) who was quite mad, but of a madness that was really the elements of great genius ill-sorted: in fact, a genius with a screw loose, as we used to say. I shall shew you this book when I see you: to me there is particular interest in this man's writing and drawing, from the strangeness of the constitution of his mind. He was a man that used to see visions: and made drawings and paintings of Alexander the Great, Caesar, etc., who, he declared, stood before him while he drew.

Edward FitzGerald, in a 25 October 1833 letter to W. B. Donne, excerpted in William Blake: The Critical Heritage, *edited by G. E. Bentley, Jr., Routledge & Kegan Paul, 1975.*

C. M. Bowra (essay date 1949)

[*An English critic and literary historian, Bowra was considered among the foremost classical scholars of the first half of the twentieth century. He also wrote extensively on modern literature, particularly modern European poetry, in studies noted for their erudition, lucidity, and straightforward style. In the following essay, Bowra provides an overview of* Songs of Innocence and of Experience, *emphasizing the work's theme of creativity and imagination.*]

In 1789, the year of the French Revolution, William Blake issued his *Songs of Innocence* as the first volume to be produced in his new manner of illuminated printing. In 1794 he reissued it in the same manner, but with the addition of *Songs of Experience* to form a single book. This book is noteworthy among Blake's works because it is the only volume of poems which he himself published. The *Poetical Sketches* of 1783 was published by the Reverend Henry Mathew, no doubt with Blake's approval or acquiescence but not with his own loving care. Blake's other publications were either prophetic books or prose works, not poetry in the strict sense. The fact that Blake published the *Songs* as he did shows what importance he attached to them. There can be no doubt that he intended them to be as good as he could make them both in contents and in appearance. The Rossetti manuscript shows not only what pains he took in revising his texts but what self-denial he exerted in omitting from the book poems which are among the best that he wrote but which for some reason he did not think suitable for publication in it. A book formed with such care deserves special attention. Blake was thirty-seven when he issued it in its complete form, and it represents his mature, considered choice of his own poems. It is perhaps not surprising that in recent years scholars have tended to neglect the *Songs* for the prophetic books; for the *Songs* look limpid and translucent, while the prophetic books are rich in unravelled mysteries and alluring secrets. But the *Songs* deserve special attention if

only because they constitute one of the most remarkable collections of lyrical poems written in English.

Blake made in practice a distinction between poetry and prophecy. In the first place, he recognized and maintained a difference of form. In the *Songs* he uses the traditional metres of English songs and hymns without even repeating the experiment, made in *Poetical Sketches,* of lyrical blank verse; in the prophecies, modelling himself on the Bible and Ossian, he uses what is in fact free verse, and his reasons for this are given in the foreword to *Jerusalem*:

> When this Verse was first dictated to me, I consider'd a Monotonous Cadence, like that used by Milton and Shakespeare and all writers of English Blank Verse, derived from the modern bondage of Rhyming, to be a necessary and indispensible part of Verse. But I soon found that in the mouth of a true Orator such monotony was not only awkward, but as much a bondage as rhyme itself.

In the prophecies Blake speaks as an orator and needs an orator's freedom: in the *Songs* he sings and needs the regular measures of song. In the second place, Blake's purpose differs in the *Songs* and in the prophecies. In the prophecies he had a great message for his generation, an urgent call to awake from its slothful sleep, a summons to activity and to that fuller life which comes from exerting the imagination. At the beginning of *Milton* he displays his purpose:

> Rouze up, O Young Men of the New Age! set your foreheads against the ignorant Hirelings! For we have Hirelings in the Camp, the Court and the University, who would, if they could, for ever depress Mental and prolong Corporeal War.

This is not the spirit in which Blake begins the *Songs of Innocence* with a poem significantly called **"Introduction"**:

> Piping down the valleys wild,
> Piping songs of pleasant glee,
> On a cloud I saw a child,
> And he laughing said to me:
> "Pipe a song about a Lamb!"
> So I piped with merry chear.
> "Piper, pipe that song again;"
> So I piped: he wept to hear.

These are the words of a poet who sings because he must, not of a prophet whose first wish is to summon his generation to a new life.

The differences of form and intention between the *Songs* and the prophetic books are paralleled by comparable differences in the presentation of material. When he completed the *Songs,* Blake had already written some of his prophetic books and begun that remarkable system of myths and symbols which gives them so special a character. In the *Songs* there is almost no trace of Blake's mythical figures. Though he wrote *Tiriel* and *The Book of Thel* at the same time as the *Songs of Innocence,* their characters do not appear in the *Songs.* And this is all the more remarkable since the experience in these prophetic books is ultimately not very dissimilar from that in the *Songs* and belongs to the same important years of Blake's life. In the *Songs* Blake pursued a more traditional and more lyrical art, because some deep need in him called for this kind of expression. It is therefore dangerous to try to explain the *Songs* too exactly by the prophetic books. There are undeniable connections between the two, but the *Songs* go their own way in their own spirit. In them Blake speaks of himself from a purely personal point of view. It is true that he uses his own remarkable symbols, but not quite in the same way as in the prophetic books, and certainly not with the same desire for a new mythology to supplement or correct that of the Bible.

It is possible to read the *Songs* and to be so enchanted by them that we do not stop to ask what in fact they mean. Such a procedure has the formidable approval of A. E. Housman, who says of them [in his *Name and Nature of Poetry*] that "the meaning is a poor foolish disappointing thing in comparison with the verses themselves." This is of course true. The mere meaning, extracted from the poems and paraphrased in lifeless prose, is indeed a poor thing in comparison with what Blake wrote. The poems succeed through the magnificence of their poetry, and no analysis can take its place. At the same time, it is almost impossible to read and enjoy poetry without knowing what it means, for the good reason that the meaning is an essential part of the whole and makes an essential contribution to the delight which the poems give. To acquiesce in ignorance of the meaning is more than can reasonably be asked of us. Human curiosity and the desire to gain as much as possible from a work of art reject this limited approach and force us to ask what the subjects of the poems are. Nor does this destroy our pleasure in them. When we know what Blake means, we appreciate more fully his capacity for transforming complex states of mind into pure song and for giving to his most unusual thoughts an appeal which is somehow both intimate and rapturously exciting.

That Blake intended his readers to understand what he said and to pay an intelligent attention to it is clear from his title-page, which describes the songs as "showing the two contrary states of the human soul." Blake groups his verses under two main headings, and there is plainly a great difference of character between the two parts. In so arranging his work, Blake followed his own maxim that "without Contraries is no progression." The contrast meant much to him, and we neglect it at the risk of misunderstanding his intention. So emphatic a division is not to be found in the prophetic books and shows that, when he chose, Blake could impose a fine architectural order on his work. Perhaps he was able to do this because the material and manner of the songs fall more easily into a definite shape than does the various stuff of the prophetic books. In the *Songs* Blake limits himself to a special section of material which is relatively clear in its outlines and limits. He has distilled his thoughts into the shape of song, and his appeal is more direct and more immediate than it can be in the more complicated technique of prophecy.

The two sections of Blake's book, the songs of innocence and the songs of experience, are contrasted elements in a single design. The first part sets out an imaginative vision of the state of innocence: the second shows how life chal-

> **The two sections of Blake's book, the songs of innocence and the songs of experience, are contrasted elements in a single design. The first part sets out an imaginative vision of the state of innocence: the second shows how life challenges and corrupts and destroys it.**
>
> **—C. M. Bowra**

lenges and corrupts and destroys it. What Blake intended by this scheme can be seen from the motto which he wrote for the book but did not include in it:

> The Good are attracted by Men's perceptions,
> And think not for themselves;
> Till Experience teaches them to catch
> And to cage the Fairies and Elves.
>
> And then the Knave begins to snarl
> And the Hypocrite to howl;
> And all his good Friends shew their private ends,
> And the Eagle is known from the Owl.

This little poem shows how the *Songs* are related to some of the most persistent elements in Blake's thought. Since for him the primary reality and the only thing that matters is the active life of the creative imagination, he has nothing but contempt for empiricist philosophers who build their systems on sense-perceptions instead of on vision. Blake believes that the naturally good are deceived by such theories and so corrupted by them that they cease to think for themselves, and restrict those creative forces which he calls "fairies and elves." When this happens, knavery, hypocrisy, and self-seeking enter into the soul, and the state of innocence is lost; but for those who have eyes to see, the free, soaring spirit of the eagle is visible in all its difference from the sleepy, night-ridden owl. This is the main theme of the *Songs*. In the first part Blake shows what innocence means, in the second how it is corrupted and destroyed.

Blake's state of innocence, set forth in symbols of pastoral life akin to those of the Twenty-third Psalm, seems at first sight to have something in common with what Vaughan, Traherne, and Wordsworth say in their different ways about the vision of childhood which is lost in later life, and it is tempting to think that this is what concerns Blake. But he is concerned with the loss not so much of actual childhood as of something wider and less definite. For him childhood is both itself and a symbol of a state of soul which may exist in maturity. His subject is the childlike vision of existence. For him all human beings are in some sense and at some times the children of a divine father, but experience destroys their innocence and makes them follow spectres and illusions. Blake does not write at a distance of time from memories of what childhood once was, but from an insistent, present anguish at the ugly contrasts between the childlike and the experienced conceptions of reality.

> [In Blake's state of innocence,] childhood
> is both itself and a symbol of a state of
> soul which may exist in maturity. His
> subject is the childlike vision of existence.
>
> —*C. M. Bowra*

With a book which deals with so poignant a subject, it is tempting to look in Blake's own life for some event or circumstances which forced this issue so powerfully on him. That he was deeply troubled by it is clear not merely from the agonized poems of *Songs of Experience* but from the prophetic books, *Tiriel* and *The Book of Thel*, which seem to have been written in 1788 and 1789. In Thel Blake presents a symbolical figure who lives in an Arcadian state of innocence but finds herself appalled and helpless before the first appearances of reality; in *Tiriel* he makes his chief figure die when he realizes that he has erred in substituting the deadening rule of law for the free life of the imagination. Both books are, in a sense, concerned with the tragedy of innocence. Just as Thel is unable to endure reality when she sees it and flies back into eternity, so Har and Heva, who represent an innocence which has outlived its real strength, are unable to help Tiriel in his great need. The problems suggested in these two books are not the same as in the *Songs,* but there seems to be a common basis of experience, something which, even when he was writing the *Songs of Innocence,* deeply troubled Blake and forced him to think about this issue in more than one way.

When he composed the *Songs of Experience,* Blake seems to have passed through a spiritual crisis. He, who was in many ways the healthiest of men, wrote in 1793: "I say I shan't live for five years, and if I live one it will be a wonder." Something had shaken his trust in himself and in life. What this was we can only guess, and such clues as are available point to a combination of different causes. The trouble was already there in 1788 when he wrote *Tiriel,* but it seems to have grown and to have preyed more insistently on his mind in the following years. It did not in the least interfere with his creative powers. Indeed, at this time he did an astonishing amount of work both as a poet and as an artist, and most of it is as good as anything that he ever did afterwards. But Blake's genius was not discouraged by trouble and anxiety, and that he had these in full measure is beyond reasonable dispute. In the first place, his rapturous hopes in the French Revolution, expressed in his prophetic book called after it and written in 1791, were soon replaced by the recognition that events were taking a course not to his liking. The English Government was hostile to the Revolution, and Blake's own friends, like Thomas Paine, whom he saved from arrest by a timely warning in 1792, were in danger. What such a disillusionment meant to a visionary like Blake can be seen from his *Visions of the Daughters of Albion,* with its passionate denunciations of oppression and slavery. He was brought down with a terrible shock from his visions of re-

formed humanity to a realization of what political events really were.

In the second place, Blake's domestic life seems at this time to have passed through a strange phase. His excellent wife did not sympathize with his idealistic views of free love and resolutely opposed them. To Blake at first this was an unforeseen denial of the spirit, and it shook him deeply. It seems even for a time to have broken his trust in himself. He found his solution soon enough, and the rest of his life was spent in unclouded happiness with his wife. But what he felt at the moment can be seen from his strange poem **"William Bond,"** and especially from three verses in it:

> He went to Church in a May morning
> Attended by Fairies, one, two and three;
> But the Angels of Providence drove them away,
> And he return'd home in misery.
>
> He went not out to the Field nor Fold,
> He went not out to the Village nor Town,
> But he came home in a black, black cloud,
> And took to his Bed, and there lay down.
>
> And an Angel of Providence at his Feet,
> And an Angel of Providence at his Head,
> And in the midst a Black, Black Cloud,
> And in the midst the Sick Man on his Bed.

Since by "fairies" Blake means the impulses of the creative imagination, it is clear that in this crisis his inner life has received a terrible blow from "Angels of Providence." In his language they are the forces of legality and moralism in which he saw the most sinister enemies of the free life of the imagination. He, who had put all his trust in this free life, found himself frustrated and depressed by the forces which he most condemned. Partly in politics, partly in domestic life, partly no doubt in other matters, Blake seems to have discovered that his central and most cherished beliefs were not shared by others but were the object of hatred and persecution. At some date in these years the common world was revealed to him, and he found it more frightening than he had ever suspected. From this discovery the *Songs* were born.

Blake's crisis takes place in a spiritual order of things and involves spiritual values, and for this reason he has to speak of it in symbols. What he describes are not actual events as ordinary men see and understand them, but spiritual events which have to be stated symbolically in order that they may be intelligible. In the *Songs of Innocence* Blake's symbols are largely drawn from the Bible, and since he makes use of such familiar figures as the Good Shepherd and the Lamb of God, there is not much difficulty in seeing what he means; but in the *Songs of Experience* he often uses symbols of his own making, and his meaning is more elusive. Indeed, some poems in this section are fully understandable only by reference to symbols which Blake uses in his prophetic books; and since the meaning of most symbols tends to be inconstant, there is always a danger that we may make his meaning more emphatic or more exact than it is, especially since, as Blake grew older, he developed his symbols and by placing them in precise contexts gave them a greater definiteness. But in both kinds of song it is clear that Blake anticipates those poets of a hundred years later who forged their own symbols in order to convey what would otherwise be almost inexpressible, since no adequate words exist for the unnamed powers of a supernatural world. Blake's own view of his method can be seen from a letter to Thomas Butts:

> Allegory addressed to the Intellectual powers, while it is altogether hidden from the Corporeal Understanding, is My Definition of the Most Sublime Poetry.

Since by "Corporeal Understanding" Blake means the perception of sense-data, and by "Intellectual powers" the imaginative spirit which is the only reality, it is clear that in his view poetry is concerned with something else than the phenomenal world, and that the only means to speak of it is what he calls "allegory." It is true that elsewhere he sometimes speaks disparagingly of allegory, but that is because he distinguishes between true and false allegory. For him allegory in the good sense is not the kind of "one-one correspondence" which we find in *Pilgrim's Progress,* but a system of symbols which presents events in a spiritual world.

In the **Songs of Innocence** the symbols convey a special kind of existence or state of soul. In this state human be-

The illustrated plate of "London," from Songs of Innocence and of Experience.

ings have the same kind of security and assurance as belongs to lambs under a wise shepherd or to children with loving parents. Nor is it untrue to say that both the shepherd and the father of Blake's poems is God. It is He who is Himself a lamb and becomes a little child, who watches over sleeping children and gives his love to chimney-sweepers and little black boys. In the fatherhood of God, Blake's characters have equal rights and privileges. But by it he means not quite what orthodox Christians do. Blake, despite his deeply religious nature, did not believe that God exists apart from man, but says expressly:

> Man is All Imagination. God is Man and exists in us and we in him . . . Imagination or the Human Eternal Body in Every Man . . . Imagination is the Divine Body in Every Man.

For Blake, God and the imagination are one; that is, God is the creative and spiritual power in man, and apart from man the idea of God has no meaning. When Blake speaks of the divine, it is with reference to this power and not to any external or independent godhead. So when his songs tell of God's love and care, we must think of them as qualities which men themselves display and in so doing realize their full, divine nature. For instance, in **"On Another's Sorrow,"** Blake says:

> Think not thou canst sigh a sigh,
> And thy Maker is not by;
> Think not thou canst weep a tear,
> And thy Maker is not near.
>
> O! He gives to us His joy
> That our grief he may destroy;
> Till our grief is fled and gone
> He doth sit by us and moan.

Blake means that every sigh and every tear evoke a response from our divine nature and through this are cured and turned to joy. Compassion is part of man's imaginative being, and through it he is able to transform existence. For Blake, God is the divine essence which exists potentially in every man and woman.

The power and appeal of this belief appear in **"The Divine Image."** The divine image, of course, is man, but man in part of his complex being and seen from a special point of view. Blake speaks quite literally and means to be taken at his word when he says:

> To Mercy, Pity, Peace, and Love
> All pray in their distress;
> And to these virtues of delight
> Return their thankfulness.
>
> For Mercy, Pity, Peace, and Love
> Is God, our father dear,
> And Mercy, Pity, Peace, and Love
> Is Man, his child and care.
>
> For Mercy has a human heart
> Pity a human face,
> And Love, the human form divine,
> And Peace, the human dress.
>
> Then every man, of every clime,
> That prays in his distress,
> Prays to the human form divine,
> Love, Mercy, Pity, Peace.

> And all must love the human form,
> In heathen, turk, or jew;
> Where Mercy, Love, and Pity dwell
> There God is dwelling too.

The divine qualities which Blake enumerates exist in man and reveal their divine character through him. Though Blake says of man's imagination that "it manifests itself in his Works of Art," he spread his idea of art to include all that he thought most important and most living in conduct. In mercy, pity, peace, and love, he found the creed of brotherhood which is the centre of his gospel. He knew that by itself love may become selfish and possessive and needs to be redeemed by other, generous qualities. It is in the combination of these that man is God. In the state of innocence, life is governed by these powers, and it is they which give to it its completeness and security. That is why Blake calls his *Songs of Innocence* "happy songs" and says that every child will joy to hear them.

In his prophetic books Blake presents something like the state of innocence in what he calls Beulah, a kind of lower paradise, inferior indeed to the highest state of the active imagination which he calls Eden, but superior to the lower states in which reason inhibits and kills the imagination. His Beulah has its own peculiar charm, as of a world of dream:

> There is from Great Eternity a mild and pleasant
>   rest
> Nam'd Beulah, a soft Moony Universe, femi-
>   nine, lovely,
> Pure, mild and Gentle, given in mercy to those
>   who sleep,
> Eternally Created by the Lamb of God around,
> On all sides, within and without the Universal
>   Man.
> The daughters of Beulah follow sleepers in all
>   their dreams,
> Creating spaces, lest they fall into Eternal
>   Death.

When he wrote that, Blake had already decided that Beulah was not the highest state. It is not perfect because there is no effort or struggle in it as there is in Eden, and a full personality can be realized only if men leave Beulah for a state less confined and less secure. There can be little doubt that even when he wrote the *Songs of Innocence,* Blake had formed some of these ideas. He saw that though this state of childlike happiness, which he seems to have enjoyed in his first manhood, is wonderfully charming, it is not everything, and it cannot last. To reach a higher state man must be tested by experience and suffering. This is the link between the two sections of Blake's book. Experience is not only a fact; it is a necessary stage in the cycle of being. It may in many ways be a much lower state than innocence, and this Blake stresses with great power, but it is none the less necessary. The difference between the two states is reflected in the quality of Blake's poetry. Sweet and pure though the *Songs of Innocence* are, they do not possess or need the compelling passion of the *Songs of Experience.* In dealing with innocence Blake seems deliberately to have set his tone in a quiet key to show what innocence really means in his full scheme of spiritual development. He was careful to exclude from the first part

of his book anything which might sound a disturbing note or suggest that innocence is anything but happy. That is why he omitted a striking verse which he wrote in the first version of **"A Cradle Song"**:

> O, the cunning wiles that creep
> In thy little heart asleep.
> When thy little heart does wake,
> Then the dreadful lightnings break.

The illusion of childhood and of the human state which resembles it must be kept free from such intruding suggestions, and there must be no hint that innocence is not complete and secure.

From innocence man passes to experience, and what Blake means by this can be seen from some lines in *The Four Zoas*:

> What is the price of Experience? do men buy it
>   for a song?
> Or wisdom for a dance in the street? No, it is
>   bought with the price
> Of all that a man hath, his house, his wife, his
>   children.
> Wisdom is sold in the desolate market where
>   none come to buy,
> And in the wither'd field where the farmer plows
>   for bread in vain.

Blake knew that experience is bought at a bitter price, not merely in such unimportant things as comfort and peace of mind, but in the highest spiritual values. His *Songs of Experience* are the poetry of this process. They tell how what we accept in childlike innocence is tested and proved feeble by actual events, how much that we have taken for granted is not true of the living world, how every noble desire may be debased and perverted. When he sings of this process, he is no longer the piper of pleasant glee but an angry, passionate rebel. In **"Infant Sorrow"** he provides a counterpart to his **"Introduction"** and shows that even in the very beginnings of childhood there is a spirit of unrest and revolt:

> My mother groan'd! my father wept.
> Into the dangerous world I leapt:
> Helpless, naked, piping loud:
> Like a fiend hid in a cloud.
>
> Struggling in my father's hands,
> Striving against my swadling bands,
> Bound and weary, I thought best
> To sulk upon my mother's breast.

At the start of its existence the human creature feels itself a prisoner and, after its first efforts to resist, angrily gives up the struggle.

When experience destroys the state of childlike innocence, it puts many destructive forces in its place. To show the extent of this destruction Blake places in the *Songs of Experience* certain poems which give poignant contrasts to other poems which appear in the *Songs of Innocence.* For instance, in the first **"Nurse's Song"** he tells how children play and are allowed to go on playing until the light fades and it is time to go to bed. In this Blake symbolizes the care-free play of the imagination when it is not spoiled by senseless restrictions. But in the second **"Nurse's Song"** we hear the other side of the matter, when experience has set to work:

> When the voices of children are heard on the
>   green
> And whisp'rings are heard in the dale,
> When days of my youth rise fresh in my mind,
> My face turns green and pale.
>
> Then come home, my children, the sun is gone
>   down,
> And the dews of night arise;
> Your spring and your day are wasted in play,
> And your winter and night in disguise.

The voice that now speaks is not that of loving care but of sour age, envious of a happiness which it can no longer share and eager to point out the menaces and the dangers of the dark. It sees play as a waste of time and cruelly tells the children that their life is a sham passed in darkness and cold, like one of Blake's terrible prophetic scenes of desolation, as in *The Four Zoas*:

> But from the caves of deepest night, ascending
>   in clouds of mist,
> The winter spread his wide black wings across
>   from pole to pole:
> Grim frost beneath and terrible snow, link'd in
>   a marriage chain,
> Began a dismal dance. The winds around on
>   pointed rocks
> Settled like bats innumerable, ready to fly
>   abroad.

The first and most fearful thing about experience is that it breaks the free life of the imagination and substitutes a dark, cold, imprisoning fear, and the result is a deadly blow to the blithe human spirit.

The fear and denial of life which come with experience breed hypocrisy, and this earns some of Blake's hardest and harshest words. For him hypocrisy is as grave a sin as cruelty because it rises from the same causes, from the refusal to obey the creative spirit of the imagination and from submission to fear and envy. He marks its character by providing an antithesis to **"The Divine Image"** in **"The Human Abstract."** In bitter irony he shows how love, pity, and mercy can be distorted and used as a cover for base or cowardly motives. Speaking through the hypocrite's lips, he goes straight to the heart of the matter by showing how glibly hypocrisy claims to observe these cardinal virtues:

> Pity would be no more
> If we did not make somebody Poor;
> And Mercy no more could be
> If all were as happy as we.

In this corrupt frame of mind, selfishness and cruelty flourish and are dignified under false names. This process wrecks the world. Harsh rules are imposed on life through what Blake calls "Mystery," with its ceremonies and hierarchies and its promise of "an allegorical abode where existence hath never come." It supports those outward forms of religion which Blake regards as the death of the soul:

> Soon spreads the dismal shade

> Of Mystery over his head;
> And the Catterpiller and Fly
> Feed on the Mystery.
>
> And it bears the fruit of Deceit,
> Ruddy and sweet to eat;
> And the Raven his nest has made
> In its thickest shade.
>
> The Gods of the earth and sea
> Sought thro' Nature to find this Tree;
> But their search was all in vain:
> There grows one in the Human Brain.

So Blake re-creates the myth of the Tree of Knowledge or of Life. This tree, which is fashioned by man's reason, gives falsehood instead of truth and death instead of life.

Perhaps the worst thing in experience, as Blake sees it, is that it destroys love and affection. On no point does he speak with more passionate conviction. He who believes that the full life demands not merely tolerance but forgiveness and brotherhood finds that in various ways love is corrupted or condemned. In **"The Clod and the Pebble"** he shows how love naturally seeks not to please itself or have any care for itself, but in the world of experience the heart becomes like "a pebble of the brook" and turns love into a selfish desire for possession:

> Love seeketh only Self to please,
> To bind another to Its delight,
> Joys in another's loss of ease,
> And builds a Hell in Heaven's despite.

The withering of the affections begins early, when their elders repress and frighten children. In **"Holy Thursday"** Blake shows what this means, how in a rich and fruitful land children live in misery:

> And their sun does never shine,
> And their fields are bleak and bare,
> And their ways are fill'd with thorns:
> It is eternal winter there.

The horror of experience is all the greater because of the contrast, explicit or implicit, which Blake suggests between it and innocence. In **"The Echoing Green"** he tells how the children are happy and contented at play, but in **"The Garden of Love,"** to the same rhythm and with the same setting, he presents an ugly antithesis. The green is still there, but on it is a chapel with "Thou shalt not" written over the door, and the garden itself has changed:

> And I saw it was filled with graves,
> And tomb-stones where flowers should be;
> And Priests in black gowns were walking their
>   rounds,
> And binding with briars my joys and desires.

In the state of experience, jealousy, cruelty, and hypocrisy forbid the natural play of the affections and turn joy into misery.

Blake's tragic appreciation of the restrictions which imprison and kill the living spirit was no purely personal thing. It was his criticism of society, of the whole trend of contemporary civilization. His compassionate heart was outraged and wounded by the sufferings which society inflicts on its humbler members and by the waste of human material which seems indispensable to the efficient operation of rules and laws. In **"London"** he gives his own view of that "chartered liberty" on which his countrymen prided themselves, and exposes the indisputable, ugly facts:

> I wander thro' each charter'd street,
> Near where the charter'd Thames does flow,
> And mark in every face I meet
> Marks of weakness, marks of woe.
>
> In every cry of every Man,
> In every Infant's cry of fear,
> In every voice, in every ban,
> The mind-forg'd manacles I hear.
>
> How the Chimney-sweeper's cry
> Every black-ning Church appalls;
> And the hapless Soldier's sigh
> Runs in blood down Palace walls.
>
> But most thro' midnight streets I hear
> How the youthful Harlot's curse
> Blasts the new born Infant's tear,
> And blights with plagues the Marriage hearse.

The child chimney-sweeper, the soldier, and the harlot are Blake's types of the oppressed—characteristic victims of a system based not on brotherhood but on fear. Each in his own way shows up the shams on which society thrives. The chimneysweeper's condemned life is supported by the churches; the soldier's death is demanded by the court; and the harlot's calling is forced on her by the marriage-laws. The contrasts between truth and pretence, between natural happiness and unnatural repression, are stressed by Blake in these three examples, and through them we see the anguish in which he faced the social questions of his time.

The astonishing thing about the *Songs of Experience* is that, though they were inspired by violent emotions and have a merciless satirical temper, they are in the highest degree lyrical. Indeed, no English poet, except Shakespeare, has written songs of such lightness and melody. Yet Blake's subjects are not in the least like Shakespeare's. He writes not about fundamental matters like spring and love and death, but about his own original and complex views on existence; and the miracle is that in presenting themes which might seem to need comment and explanation, he succeeds in creating pure song. His words have an Elizabethan lilt, a music which emphasizes their meaning and conforms exactly to it. Despite his strong emotions and his unfamiliar ideas, Blake keeps his form miraculously limpid and melodious. This success is partly the result of a highly discriminating art. Blake made many changes in his texts before he was satisfied with a final version, and these show how well he knew what he was doing, how clear an idea he had of the result which he wished to reach. But this art was shaped by a creative impulse so powerful that it can only be called inspiration. Blake indeed believed that his words were often dictated to him by some supernatural power. As he wrote to Thomas Butts about a prophetic book, "I may praise it, since I dare not pretend to be any other than the Secretary; the Authors are in Eternity." In the strange workings of the creative mind there is a point at which words come with such force and

intensity that they have a more than human appeal. Though the poet may not receive them all at once but gradually find, as Blake did, the exact words which he needs, yet these songs are miracles because their creation cannot be explained and because with them we feel ourselves in the presence of something beyond the control of man.

Two examples must suffice to illustrate Blake's art of song, and each is equally wonderful. The first is **"The Sick Rose"**:

> O Rose, thou art sick!
> The invisible worm
> That flies in the night,
> In the howling storm,
>
> Has found out thy bed
> Of crimson joy,
> And his dark secret love
> Does thy life destroy.

This illustrates in an astonishing way Blake's gift for distilling a complex imaginative idea into a few marvellously telling words. If we ask what the poem means, we can answer that it means what it says, and that this is perfectly clear. It conjures up the vision of a rose attacked in a stormy night by a destructive worm, and so Blake depicts it in his accompanying illustration. But, as in all symbolical poems, we can read other meanings into it and make its images carry a weight of secondary associations. We may say that it refers to the destruction of love by selfishness, of innocence by experience, of spiritual life by spiritual death. All these meanings it can bear, and it is legitimate to make it do so. But the actual poem presents something which is common and fundamental to all these themes, something which Blake has distilled so finely from many particular cases that it has their common, quintessential character. And this Blake sees with so piercing and so concentrated a vision that the poem has its own independent life and needs nothing to supplement it. If we wish to know more about Blake's views on the issues at which the poem hints, we may find them in his prose works and prophetic books. But here he is a poet, and his thoughts are purified and transfigured in song.

My second example is **"Ah! Sun-flower!"**:

> Ah, Sun-flower! weary of time,
> Who countest the steps of the Sun,
> Seeking after that sweet golden clime
> Where the traveller's journey is done:
>
> Where the Youth pined away with desire,
> And the pale Virgin shrouded in snow
> Arise from their graves, and aspire
> Where my Sun-flower wishes to go.

This raises questions similar to those raised by **"The Sick Rose."** Again a complex thought is distilled into two verses, and again what matters is the imaginative presentation which transports us in intense, excited delight. Here Blake's theme is not quite so single as in **"The Sick Rose."** He has transposed into this song his central ideas and feelings about all young men and young women who are robbed of their full humanity because they are starved of love. Because of this, the youth pines away with desire and the pale virgin is shrouded in snow. It is the pathos of their earthbound state that the song catches and makes significant through Blake's deep compassion. The central spring of the poem is the image of the sun-flower. The flower which turns its head to follow the sun's course and is yet rooted in the earth is Blake's symbol for all men and women whose lives are dominated and spoiled by a longing which they can never hope to satisfy, and who are held down to the earth despite their desire for release into some brighter, freer sphere. In this poem Blake expresses an idea which means a great deal to him, but he does not explain or elaborate it. He assumes that his poem will do its work by itself, and his reward is that **"Ah! Sun-flower"** belongs to that very rare and small class of poems in which inspiration carries words to a final enchantment.

The *Songs of Experience* are more powerful and more magical than the *Songs of Innocence* because they are born of a deep anguish, from a storm in the poet's soul. Blake knows that one kind of existence is bright with joy and harmony, but he sees its place taken by another which is dark and sinister and dead. But Blake was not content simply to complain or to criticize. He sought some ultimate synthesis in which innocence might be wedded to experience, and goodness to knowledge. That such a state is possible he reveals in the first poem of *Songs of Experience,* where he speaks with the voice of the bard and summons the fallen soul of earth to some vast apocalypse:

> O Earth, O Earth, return!
> Arise from out the dewy grass;
> Night is worn,
> And the morn
> Rises from the slumberous mass.
>
> Turn away no more;
> Why wilt thou turn away?
> The starry floor,
> The wat'ry shore,
> Is giv'n thee till the break of day.

The world is still wrapped in darkness, but the stars which pierce the night are a sign of other things to come, and the sea of eternity beats on the narrow shore where mankind lives. The "break of day" is Blake's symbol for the new life in which both innocence and experience are transformed, and the soul passes in its cycle to a fuller, more active life in the creative imagination. As Blake says in a note written on a page of *The Four Zoas*:

> *Unorganiz'd Innocence: An Impossibility.*
> Innocence dwells with Wisdom, but never with Ignorance.

The true innocence is not after all that of the *Songs of Innocence,* but something which has gained knowledge from the ugly lessons of experience and found an expanding strength in the unfettered life of the creative soul. Beyond experience Blake foresees this consummation and hints that it will come, even though he is concerned with the dark hither side of it.

Blake knows well that such a consummation will not come simply from good will or pious aspirations and that the life of the imagination is possible only through passion and power and energy. That is why he sometimes stresses the great forces which lie hidden in man and may be terrifying but are none the less necessary if anything worth while is to happen. He sees that the creative activity of the imagination and the transformation of experience through it are possible only through the release and exercise of awful powers. He chooses his symbols for these powers in violent and destructive things, as when in his **"Proverbs of Hell"** he says, "The wrath of the lion is the wisdom of God," or "The roaring of lions, the howling of wolves, the raging of the stormy sea, and the destructive sword, are portions of eternity, too great for the eye of man." It was in such elemental forces that Blake put his trust for the redemption of mankind, and he contrasted them favourably with the poor efforts of the human intelligence: "The tigers of wrath are wiser than the horses of instruction." The wrath which Blake found in Christ, his symbol of the divine spirit which will not tolerate restrictions but asserts itself against established rules, was the means by which he hoped to unite innocence and experience in some tremendous synthesis.

The poetry of this desire and of what it meant to Blake can be seen in **"The Tyger."** Here, too, enraptured song conveys in essential vision some themes which Blake presents elsewhere in more detail. This is the pure poetry of his trust in cosmic forces. The images of **"The Tyger"** recur in the prophetic books, but in the poem, detached from any very specific context, they have a special strength and freedom. The tiger is Blake's symbol for the fierce forces in the soul which are needed to break the bonds of experience. The "forests of the night," in which the tiger lurks, are ignorance, repression, and superstition. It has been fashioned by unknown, supernatural spirits, like Blake's mythical heroes, Orc and Los, prodigious smiths who beat out living worlds with their hammers; and this happened when "the stars threw down their spears," that is, in some enormous cosmic crisis when the universe turned round in its course and began to move from light to darkness—as Urizen says in *The Four Zoas,* when he finds that passion and natural joy have withered under his rule and the power of the spirit has been weakened:

> I went not forth: I hid myself in black clouds of
>   my wrath;
> I call'd the stars around my feet in the night of
>   councils dark;
> The stars threw down their spears and fled
>   naked away.

If we wish to illustrate **"The Tyger"** from Blake's other works, it is easy to do so, and it adds much to our understanding of its background and its place in Blake's development. But it is first and last a poem. The images are so compelling that for most purposes they explain themselves, and we have an immediate, overwhelming impression of an awful power lurking in the darkness of being and forcing on us questions which pierce to the heart of life:

> Tyger! Tyger! burning bright
> In the forests of the night,
> What immortal hand or eye
> Could frame thy fearful symmetry?
>
> In what distant deeps or skies

Burnt the fire of thine eyes?
On what wings dare he aspire?
What the hand dare sieze the fire?

And what shoulder, and what art,
Could twist the sinews of thy heart?
And when thy heart began to beat,
What dread hand? and what dread feet?

What the hammer? what the chain?
In what furnace was thy brain?
What the anvil? what dread grasp
Dare its deadly terrors clasp?

When the stars threw down their spears,
And water'd heaven with their tears,
Did he smile his work to see?
Did he who made the Lamb make thee?

Tyger! Tyger! burning bright
In the forests of the night,
What immortal hand or eye,
Dare frame thy fearful symmetry?

Just as early in the *Songs of Innocence* Blake sets his poem about the lamb, with its artless question,

Little Lamb, who made thee?
Dost thou know who made thee?

so early in the *Songs of Experience* Blake sets his poem about the tiger with its more frightening and more frightened questions. The lamb and the tiger are symbols for two different states of the human soul. When the lamb is destroyed by experience, the tiger is needed to restore the world.

In the *Songs of Innocence and Experience* there are only hints of the final consummation which shall restore men to the fullness of joy. The poems are concerned with an earlier stage in the struggle and treat of it from a purely poetical standpoint. What Blake gives is the essence of his imaginative thought about this crisis in himself and in all men. When he completed the whole book in its two parts, he knew that the state of innocence is not enough, but he had not found his full answer to his doubts and questions. From this uncertainty he wrote his miraculous poetry. Against the negative powers, which he found so menacingly in the ascendant, he set, both in theory and in practice, his gospel of the imagination. Strange as some of his ideas may be to us, the poetry comes with an unparalleled force because of the prodigious release of creative energy which has gone to its making. The prophet of gigantic catastrophes and celestial reconciliations was also a poet who knew that poetry alone could make others share his central experiences. In the passion and the tenderness of these songs there is something beyond analysis, that living power of the imagination which was the beginning and the end of Blake's activity. In *A Vision of the Last Judgment* he says:

"What," it will be Question'd, "When the Sun rises, do you not see a round "disk of fire somewhat like a Guinea?" O no, no, I see an Innumerable company of the Heavenly host crying, "Holy, Holy, Holy is the Lord God Almighty."

Because Blake pierced beyond the visible world to these eternal powers and made them his daily company, he was

able to give to his poetry the clarity and the brightness of vision. (pp. 25-50)

> C. M. Bowra, "*Songs of Innocence and Experience,*" in his The Romantic Imagination, Cambridge, Mass.: Harvard University Press, 1949, pp. 25-50.

David V. Erdman   (essay date 1954)

[*An American educator and critic, Erdman has edited and written numerous studies of English Romantic poetry, including* Blake: Prophet against Empire. *In the following excerpt from that study, Erdman contends that Blake had an artistic conception of the state of experience even as he created* Songs of Innocence, *and discusses* Songs of Innocence and of Experience *as a work created in reaction to contemporary sociopolitical conditions.*]

Blow, boisterous wind, stern winter frown,
Innocence is a winter's gown;
So clad, we'll abide life's pelting storm
That makes our limbs quake, if our hearts be
    warm.

An alternative to cynicism is the state of mind Blake called organized innocence. His nineteen *Songs of Innocence,* published in 1789 in Illuminated Printing, cannot be understood if we suppose that the author himself is innocent or oblivious of "life's pelting storm." "Innocence dwells with Wisdom," Blake wrote later, "but never with Ignorance." The stanza quoted above, which makes substantially the same point, belongs to a very early Song. The parallel *Songs of Experience* were not published until 1793–1794. But Blake, like Samson, had had experience long before that. And it is misleading to reason that when he etched the *Songs of Innocence* there was "no contrary . . . in his mind." Only a person aware of much amiss and seeking a cloak against ill winds could have made Blake's conscious creative effort to organize a place of shelter for Wisdom and Innocence, lion and lamb, to dwell in together.

It is of course significant that a poet who had written many bitter as well as many sweet songs should choose, in 1789, to publish the sweet ones by themselves. Although the contradictions exposed by the postwar cynicism of *An Island* did not vanish, Blake had, as we shall learn, a strong tendency to suppress prophetic alarm whenever the people were being ruled by covert guile and not open war. Both public and private matters may have encouraged the suppression of Quid the Cynic in favor of the Piper of "happy songs." Wilkism and Reform were asleep; the sharp dramatic conflict of Patriot and Tyrant had subsided. "Tranquillity was diffused" even "over British India," and while the government was taking all the credit for "prosperity," the leaders of the opposition were occupied chiefly in "efforts to amuse and entertain [Robert Bisset, *History of the Reign of George III*].

In such times it was natural to seek the cause and the cure of what was amiss, not in the ambition of tyrants, but in the cold heart of every man, which must be sheltered from wintry weather and warmed from within. The outer world supplied no glowing flames of revolt nor warm rushing together of inhabitants. Blake, coming upon [Swiss poet and mystic John] Lavater's observation that "He, who reforms himself, has done more toward reforming the public than a crowd of noisy, impotent patriots," could write with an exclamation point: "Excellent!" It had not always been his view of patriots, nor would it be. But Blake probably saw more wisdom in [English politician William] Pitt's commercial treaty with France than in the noisy opposition of "Patriots" like [English politician Charles] Fox who in this period "maintained, that France was the inveterate and unalterable enemy of Great Britain" [Bisset]. "Peace," declared Blake as bard of innocence, is "the human dress."

As for private matters, the death of his beloved brother Robert in 1787 produced a kind of sorrow more adequately surmounted by the cultivation of inner warmth than by cynicism, which had required a certain irreverence. The abandonment of the print shop, in the same year, may or may not indicate commercial failure; it may mean that the Blakes had accumulated enough reserve or at least enough confidence to venture independently upon the ocean of business. For their new home, 28 Poland Street, was still a shop. On the one hand the Blakes seem rather plainly not to have come upon halcyon days; on the other hand they must have been warming their hearts with considerable hope as they began to publish works from "Blake's Original Stereotype."

Blakean innocence is more than a cultivated state of inner warmth, however, for the cultivation of innocence is itself a form of social criticism. Blake might have said of his *Songs* what he wrote, at the time of their publication, beside Lavater's 663d aphorism: "Those who are offended with any thing in this book would be offended with the innocence of a child & for the same reason, because it reproaches [them] with the errors of acquired folly." Quid curses and laughs: the happy Piper reproaches. Both express a consciousness of the errors and ironies of a society in which every man's face is a mask. Northrop Frye is exceptional among critics in recognizing [in his *Fearful Symmetry*] that the *Songs of Innocence* "satirize the state of experience" and expose its hypocrisies by contrast. He observes that the "glint in the eye of the poet" who wrote *An Island* never faded out, and that the occurrence of "three of the most delicate and fragile of the *Songs of Innocence*" embedded in the "Gargantuan nightmare" of *An Island* is an indication that Blake's juxtaposition of innocence and experience was "in origin an idea connected with satire."

Before touching the *Songs of Innocence* as published in 1789, let us make use of the excellent opportunity provided by the growth of these fragile songs in a satiric matrix to explore the process whereby organized Innocence *springs out* of Experience. All of the twenty-one poems or parts of poems in *An Island,* sung by nine of the characters, are satiric at least by location. And the subtle matching of song to singer provides a satiric analysis of singer and subject. Three of the songs, sung by Obtuse Angle, Mrs. Nannicantipot, and Quid, are to emerge as *Songs of Innocence.* Two others, **"When old corruption"** and **"Hail**

Matrimony,"** sung by Quid, might have become *Songs of Experience* except that they are not sufficiently *songs.* Seven or eight are versions of popular ballads or street cries, such as Miss Gittipin's **"This frog he would awooing ride"** and Steelyard's **"As I walkd forth one may morning."** Several of these contain a strong element of parody. **"To be or not to be"** and **"This city & this country"** are parodies which also contain ironies not fully apparent to Obtuse Angle and Steelyard, who recite them. Perhaps **"Theres Dr Clash,"** recited by Scopprell, comes into the same group. **"A crowned king,"** recited by the Pythagorean Sipsop, is presumably more consciously satiric. The rest are mainly ribaldry, doggerel, and nonsense verse.

The problem of detecting the degrees of irony in the songs is related to the problem of detecting the degrees of lack of insight in the characters, ranging from the utter fatuity of Scopprell to the overweening suspiciousness of Quid, with the kindly nearsightedness of Obtuse Angle standing as the critical case (which we shall return to in a moment) because it is just the wrong side of being a right angle. This is not to say that the simplest songs are sung by the simplest persons. There are layers of innuendo that reveal themselves only under careful and repeated examination, and the degree of tension between the surface meaning and the satiric implications depends much on the intellectual distance between the singer and the real author, Blake. For example, the satire in Quid's own songs, on Surgery and Matrimony, is direct and of Hogarthian breadth; the meaning cannot be mistaken even by the simple-minded, but only rejected. "Go & be hanged!" is Scopprell's response. Nor are there any two meanings—or even one—in Sipsop's "Italian" song:

> Fa ra so bo ro
> Fa ra bo ra
> Sa ba ra ra ba rare roro, etc.

At the other extreme are the songs of Scopprell and Gittipin. Her **"Leave, O Leave me to my sorrows"** is not funny to her, though Frye is correct in saying that it has a satiric tone midway between **"Ah! Sun-flower,"** a later Song of Experience, and some of Blake's more ribald epigrams. Her garbled rendition of the frog and cock ballad strikes Scopprell as "Truly elegant!" though we, along with Blake, are oppositely impressed. Scopprell's song reducing the Handel Jubilee to a matter of fingers and cash is a statement, at his mind-level, that the Handel concert was elegant and successful. Indirectly it informs us that the young fellow has been impressed by "an empty hubbub," but Scopprell himself is not the satirist.

Between these extremes lie the truly ambiguous songs of Steelyard and Obtuse Angle, reflecting the ambiguous wise blindness or blind wisdom of these friends who are not lumps of ignorance nor yet men of goatish or philosophical vision. Steelyard's song about the good old days of a dateless past when "Good English hospitality . . . did not fail" and when "the Mayor & Aldermen Were fit to give law to the city" is appropriately nostalgic for a man who is worried about reforms that may abolish his parish job. The singer himself does not seem to see anything wrong with a perpetuation of "the hungry poor" as long as they are hospitably invited in to "eat good beef & ale" after the city fathers are through eating "as much as ten." Yet the particulars are as loaded with social comment as are those of Hogarth's picture of *The industrious 'Prentice grown rich, and sheriff of London,* devouring good beef and ale among fat aldermen while the gaunt poor await their leavings.

The songs of Obtuse Angle reflect his character as an amiable pedant who must "empty his pockets of a vast number of papers," close his eyes, and scratch his head before entering the conversation. Both his songs stem from the pendant's kindliness—one lauding a charity school founder, the other blessing the multitudes of charity children in London town. But both also reveal his habit of "shutting his eyes" to the unpleasant and less mathematical aspects of charity. A deleted line indicates that Obtuse Angle is supplying "a Mathematical Song" when he transposes "To be or not to be" into a rimed essay on pragmatism. His hero is Richard Sutton, founder of the Charterhouse or Sutton's Hospital, described in Fuller's *Worthies of England* as "the Master-piece of Protestant English Charity." By worldly standards the Charterhouse in 1784 was a respectable pensioners' home and school for boys. But Blake, as a self-educated person who thanked God he "never was sent to school," saw only social and intellectual stultification in Hospitals (boarding schools) and apparently always considered them "nets & gins & traps to catch the joys of Eternity." If recited by Quid doubtless the hymn to Sutton would have been as cynical as Quid's songs on Surgery and Matrimony. As it is, the cynicism is that of omission.

Our purblind (obtuse) pragmatist concentrates on the building rather than the schooling, on the "great capacity" evident in Sutton's "money in a box" which "he drew out of the Stocks," and on the fervor with which he employed bricklayer and carpenter. According to Fuller, Sutton in his day was charged "with purblindness in his soul, looking too close on earth"; he had accumulated his money by shady and miserly—yet not grasping—practices. Obtuse Angle gives no thought to where the money came from or what may go on behind the "walls of brick & stone." Like Sutton he looks close on earth and is impressed by the "sinks & gutters" and the pavement made "to hinder pestilence."

The practical man, confident of his capacity to hinder pestilence with pavingstones, supposes that the children's happiness follows automatically. But Blake's Schoolboy, in *Songs of Experience,* asks "How can the bird that is born for joy Sit in a cage and sing?" Obtuse Angle in his other song, which turns out to be the "innocent" version of **"Holy Thursday,"** accepts the annual regimented singing of London charity-school children as evidence that the flogged and uniformed boys and girls are angelically happy:

> Upon a holy thursday their innocent faces clean
> The children walking two & two in grey & blue
>   & green
> Grey headed beadles walkd before with wands
>   as white as snow
> Till into the high dome of Pauls they like thames
>   waters flow.

> O what a multitude they seemd, these flowers of
>   London town
> Seated in companies they sit with radiance all
>   their own
> The hum of multitudes were there but multi-
>   tudes of lambs
> Thousands of little girls & boys raising their in-
>   nocent hands.

> Then like a mighty wind they raise to heavn the
>   voice of song
> Or like harmonious thunderings the seats of
>   heavn among
> Beneath them sit the revrent men the guardians
>   of the poor
> Then cherish pity lest you drive an angel from
>   your door.

After this recital the Islanders sit "silent for a quarter of an hour"—not, as some will have it, in admiration of Blake's verse, for it is Obtuse's, drawn from him by Miss Gittipin in a desperate effort to enliven a dull evening at the house of Steelyard.

We can find the story in the newspapers. Every Holy Thursday (Ascension Day) some six thousand uniformed children from all the charity schools of the metropolis would march to St. Paul's to hear a sermon and to sing before their patrons; "though they might not be in perfect musical concord of voice, their little hearts panted with harmony of sentiment, and they felt more than they could express." Sometimes a disturbance was caused by parents or other "improper company" attempting to have a look at the children, some of whom had been benevolently "removed from their wicked parents" and thus "snatched from perdition" to be trained to useful servitude [*The Times* 6 June 1788, 13 Jan. 1789, and 24 April 1789].

Like Obtuse, who thinks only of the pious singing, the scrubbed faces, and the grey-headed beadles, the reporter feels sure that these new services "must raise the mind to sympathy and to brotherly love." He too is uplifted:

> ". . . the glorious sight of 6000 children, reared up under the humane direction of the worthy Patrons, and supported by the public contributions of well disposed persons . . . aiding to the nurture of a future generation to fight his [majesty's] battles—carry forward the commerce and manufactories of Great Britain, and assist in maturing infant arts, to the honour and prosperity of the country.

> "The scene was the most pleasant to be conceived to every friend of Orphan innocence, in seeing so many adopted children of public benevolence brought together, and skreend from the rude hand of misery and shame."

This obtuse, roseate view is refuted point by point when Blake returns to Holy Thursday in the *Songs of Experience*:

> Is this a holy thing to see
> In a rich and fruitful land,
> Babes reduced to misery,
> Fed with cold and usurous hand?

Only the sentimental can call "that trembling cry a song"

or be complacent about the "thousands of little girls & boys" in uniform who are "so many children poor." In a land of true honor and prosperity, babes would "never hunger": "It is a land of poverty!" To deny the latent satire in the first song it is necessary to forget about Quid the Cynic and accept Obtuse Angle as the self-portrait of Blake in 1784.

Following Obtuse Angle's recital and the quarter hour of silence, Mrs. Nannicantipot says, "It puts me in Mind of my mothers song," and proceeds to recite the pastoral stanzas that appear later as **"The Nurse's Song"** in *Songs of Innocence,* beginning:

> When the tongues of children are heard on the
>   green
> And laughing is heard on the hill
> My heart is at rest within my breast
> And every thing else is still.

Mrs. Nannicantipot appears to be a gentle caricature of Mrs. Anna Barbauld, who conducted a boys' school in Suffolk but spent "truly social and lively" holidays in London at Joseph Johnson's and in Birmingham with the Priestleys. The hypothesis is strengthened by evidence that Mrs. Nan's song is a gentle parody of—or at least derives phrasing, images, and mood from—Mrs. Anna's second and fifth *Hymns in Prose for Children* (1781).

Barbauld's two hymns picture the happy play of children and animals in the fields, and then the stillness when the "loud bleating is no more heard among the hills." In her second hymn children sporting on the green with lambs and goslings are glad to be alive to "thank him with our tongues." In the fifth the sun is set, night dews fall, sheep and little birds rest, there is no sound "of voices, or of children at play," and the child sleeps upon its mother's breast until morning. Blake's song interweaves these themes. The little ones playing on the green are called home when the dews of night arise, but because the sheep and little birds are still at play they are allowed to leap and shout till the light fades away, when they must rest till morning; day and night the mother's heart is at rest within her breast.

These and other *Hymns in Prose* are echoed in several of Blake's *Songs.* Especially curious is his use of Barbauld's description of Heaven (Hymn 12) in *both* Holy Thursday poems. First, as Obtuse Angle, Blake draws upon it in good faith, so to speak, comparing the charity children to Barbauld's hymning angels. Later, as bard of Experience, Blake contrasts the actual "eternal winter" of the children's existence with the promissory "eternal spring" of Barbauld's rosy vision, and contradicts her "tree of life" and "flowers that never fade" with his picture of fading and dead "flowers of London town" beneath a leafless tree.

The manuscript of **An Island** shows that Blake's first intention was to follow Mrs. Nannicantipot immediately with Tilly Lally's rough and ready rime about natural children at play—barefoot Bill who "has given me a black eye," Joe who bowls the ball into filth and cleans it "with my handkercher," and the boy telling the story who has "a good mind to go And leave you all." Blake's second thought was to insert between the sentimental and the re-

alistic versions of child-play a note of tragedy, by Quid, who sings of what can happen to a child who is allowed, as in Mrs. Nan's song, to stay out after the night dews fall.

> O father father where are you going
> O do not walk so fast
> O speak father speak to your little boy
> Or else I shall be lost
>
> The night it was dark & no father was there
> And the child was wet with dew
> The mire was deep & the child did weep
> And away the vapour flew

This is the "lost" half of what will become **"The Little Boy Lost"** and **"The Little Boy Found"** in *Songs of Innocence.* The "found" part, written later, implies that the will-o'-the-wisp that has misled the boy is an impersonal God, for only a god in human form—or only a human father—can kiss and save the child.

Quid's song, as a response to Obtuse Angle's, implies that the "holy" atmosphere investing the charity-school beadles does not make up for the children's separation from their real fathers. This dismal ballad sinks the company's spirits for fair, and nobody can sing any longer until Tilly plucks up a spirit and repeats his racy doggerel, after which "a laugh" begins and Miss Gittipin sings two stanzas beginning

> Leave O leave [me] to my sorrows
> Here Ill sit & fade away
> Till Im nothing but a spirit . . .

Her sentimentality carries the will-o'-the-wisp theme to the point of burlesque. It also mocks Barbauld's Hymn 6 in which the "Child of reason" fails to recognize the voice of God in a forest breeze.

Here, then, is the environment in which Blake's "happy songs" of innocence were born. Innocence and Experience as "two contrary states of the human soul" are already present in the songs of Obtuse Angle and Nannicantipot on the one hand and of Tilly Lally and Quid on the other. In context the innocent songs are at least ironic. Yet the same songs, removed from this matrix, illuminated with pictures of carefree babes and birds and put beside **"A Cradle Song," "The Divine Image,"** and **"Night"** in a collection of *Songs of Innocence* announced as "songs of pleasant glee" from the "rural pen" of a Piper piping "with merry chear," are plainly not presented as satire. Their social purpose is larger—to construct one of the foundations of an imaginatively organized and truly happy prosperity. Their author rises a step and sometimes two steps above the Fun of the ignorant philosophers, according to the scale indicated by Blake's "Mirth is better than Fun, & Happiness is better than Mirth. I feel that a Man may be happy in This World."

Perhaps he knew this all along, or it may be that having set out to present the obtuse view as something he could see beyond, he discovered by looking through his own mockery that he could see much *through* the shut eyes of "the Good" who "think not for themselves." As long as his country was at peace he could write without much cynicism:

. . . Mercy has a human heart
Pity, a human face:
And Love, the human form divine,
And Peace, the human dress.

("The Divine Image")

In this spirit he was prone to believe, as he wrote in the margins of John Casper Lavater's *Aphorisms on Man:* "that which [in man] is capable of good is not also capable of evil, but that which is capable of evil is also capable of good." He did not publish his *Songs of Experience* until Britain had once more gone to war and her commercial prosperity had plummeted.

The notes on Lavater, made while Blake was preparing the pages of *Songs of Innocence* for publication, are the nearest thing we have to a commentary on the Songs themselves and are invaluable in that connection. They reveal Blake in a mood in which he loves the obtuse. He will have nothing said against superstition, which is "ignorant honesty . . . beloved of god and man," and he pronounces "heavenly" Lavater's preference for "heroes with infantine simplicity." In Lavater's characterization of the purest religion as "the most refined Epicurism," Blake sees "True Christian philosophy," and he is willing to go much further than Lavater in favor of loving and laughing. "ALL LIFE IS HOLY," Blake declares. He will not accept Lavater's condemnation of *exuberance,* and his strongest disagreement with "Lavater & his contemporaries is, They suppose that Woman's Love is Sin; in consequence all the Loves & Graces with them are Sins." Blake emphasizes the Humanitarian theology, noting that "true worship" is the love of God in men, for "Human nature is the image of God."

All these themes, except Woman's Love, appear in *Songs of Innocence.* Humanitarian Christianity is expressed categorically in **"The Divine Image."** Since the "virtues of delight" are God, and God is Man, "then every man . . . that prays in his distress, Prays to the human form divine":

And all must love the human form,
In heathen, turk or jew,
Where Mercy, Love & Pity dwell
There God is dwelling too.

Addressed to children, the songs assert the joys of sport and laughter and lamb-like behavior and preach the omnipresence of God and guardian angels. Fathers and mothers can "never, never" be indifferent to infant groans and infant fear, and therefore our maker can never, never "Hear the woes that infants bear" without joining in the grief and destroying it with his joy.

There is woe in this world. The robin sobs, the little boy and the emmet get lost, the little black boy is not loved by the "little English boy," the chimney sweeper has been sold to hard labor, and the charity children are poor. And all that the happy Piper can provide for comfort is the inner warmth of faith. The lost are found through the merciful order of God's universe. Angels try to protect the sheep. If the wolves and tygers "rush dreadful," however, the mild spirits of their prey will be transported to a land where the lion's wrath is changed to pity. The black child will receive the white child's love—in heaven. The poor

remain poor, the sweeps have to rise in the dark to work in the soot, but though the morning is cold their cloak of innocence keeps them "happy & warm."

Why do children *weep* "with joy to hear" these songs? Because the message transcends the realities of their condition without changing them. The poet is organizing innocence; weaving a winter's garment of True Christian philosophy. Inadvertently—for it is a lone exception—the admonition, "Then cherish pity," in **"Holy Thursday,"** remains as a word to adults rather than to children; otherwise adults are reproached only indirectly.

In Blake's Lavater notes there are also important themes that belong to the *Songs of Experience,* a further indication that Blake had both contraries in mind all along. The idea that poverty and hunger "appall" the mind of the charity children is elucidated by a note in which Blake speaks of "the omissions of intellect springing from poverty." In modern terms this would amount to an observation that juvenile delinquency is caused by malnutrition and substandard living conditions, for Blake is talking about what is mistakenly "call'd Vice." He accuses Lavater and others of confusing energy, exuberance, and "all the Loves & Graces"—in short "all Act"—with "contrary" behavior such as murder, theft, and backbiting, which is really "the omission of act in self & the hindering of act in another: This is Vice, but all Act is Virtue." "It does not signify what the laws of Kings & Priests have call'd Vice; we who are philosophers ought not to call the Staminal Virtues of Humanity by the same name that we call the omissions of intellect springing from poverty."

In *Songs of Experience* Blake will apply this thesis to the harlots and vagabonds of London. But the *Songs of Innocence* are already permeated with the distinction between virtue as act, and vice as omission of act (or accident). For children they bear the message: laugh and love and play and do your duty, and you will never *feel* harm; you are not vicious for being poor—or for having a black skin, whether by accident of being a Negro or of having been sold apprentice to a sweep. For adults: don't be smug about poverty. Things being what they are, cherish pity, mercy, love, and peace. But do not confuse the accidental features of poverty with the staminal virtues of man's genius. (pp. 105-19)

O Earth O Earth, return!
Arise from out the dewy grass;
Night is worn,
And the morn
Rises from the slumberous mass.

"Introduction," *Songs of Experience*

The Bard who recites the *Songs of Experience,* written in 1792–1793, is capable of seeing "Present, Past, & Future"; yet he must chide Earth's "lapsed Soul" for the tardiness of spring thaw; and **"Earth's Answer"** is really, like the questions of Oothoon, an unanswered appeal for help to "Break this heavy chain That does freeze my bones around." "Cruel jealous selfish fear" (like Fayette's) chains Earth with winter frost; no one can plow or sow; the buds and blossoms are retarded—for Love is held in bondage.

The complaint is essentially that the revolutionary spring torrent, which in 1792 seemed to be "spreading and swelling . . . to fertilize a world, and renovate old earth" (as [English playwright and writer Thomas] Holcroft exclaimed in a prologue in March) is still in England dammed and frozen by cold abstractions and proclamations of "Thou shalt not." The Bard is determined that the spring *shall* come; that Earth from sleep

> Shall arise and seek
> For her maker meek;
> And the desert wild
> Become a garden mild;

and he trusts that his own art has ritual force: "Grave the sentence deep." Yet he laments that a "heavy rain" of cruelty, disguised in the specious abstractions of "Mercy & Pity & Peace," has descended on "the new reap'd grain"; the farmers are "ruin'd & harvest . . . ended." As the times grew worse, Blake added a bitter characterization of the kind of **"Divine Image"** which Cruelty, Jealousy, Terror, and Secrecy were giving to the nation:

> The Human Dress. is forged Iron
> The Human Form. a fiery Forge.
> The Human Face. a Furnace seal'd
> The Human Heart. its hungry Gorge.

Blake retained his sense of balance by engraving together his *Songs of Innocence and of Experience* as "contrary states of the human soul," and his sense of perspective by treating winter as a season and life as an arc of Eternity. "Without contraries is no progression," he still asserts. Yet the peculiar anguish of these songs (and several notebook pieces of the same vintage) derives from the fact that the historical contraries of peace and war, freedom and chains, have come to England in the wrong order. For it is only contrary states of the soul, not of society, that exist in Eternity, and Blake is still firm in the belief that the blighting Code of War & Lust is historically negatable. The earth will "in futurity" be a garden; readers "of the future age" will be shocked to learn "that in a former time, Love! sweet Love! was thought a crime."

Relatively little of the considerable and increasing store of commentary on the *Songs of Experience* deals with their historical matrix; yet it would be pedantic here to . . . go beyond calling attention to the particular setting of some of their major themes. Though immeasurably closer than the prophecies to Blake's ideal of an art that rises above its age "perfect and eternal," these great lyrics soar up from a particular moment of history. The fused brilliance of **"London"** and **"The Tyger,"** the sharp, poignant symbolism of **"The Garden of Love," "Infant Sorrow,"** and many another "indignant page" were forged in the heat of the Year One of Equality (September 1792 to 1793) and tempered in the "grey-brow'd snows" of Antijacobin alarms and proclamations.

The fearful symmetry of the period in its cosmic implications produced Blake's boldest Oothoonian question, **"The Tyger"**. . . . The recurrent negative theme in the *Songs* is the mental bondage of Antijacobinism, manifest not in the windy caves of Parliament or the archetypal howlings of Albion's Guardians but in the lives of children and youth forced into harlotry and soldiery and apprentice slavery by the bone-bending, mind-chaining oppressions of priest and king. In *Europe* and *America* Blake sketches a panoramic view of the youth of England and their parents walking heavy and mustering for slaughter while their minds are choked by volumes of fog which pour down from "Infinite London's awful spires" and from the palace walls and "cast a dreadful cold Even on rational things beneath." In *Songs of Experience* he takes us into the dismal streets and into schoolroom and chapel to see the effects of Empire on the human "flowers of London town." He describes, in **"The Human Abstract,"** the growth of the evil tree which is gallows, cross, and the abstract Mystery that hides the facts of war. The roots of this oak or upas tree of perverted Druidism are watered by the selfish tears of Mercy, Pity, and Peace:

> Pity would be no more,
> If we did not make somebody Poor;
> And Mercy no more could be,
> If all were as happy as we;
>
> And mutual fear brings peace;
> Till the selfish loves increase.

This tree grows "in the Human brain," planted there by priest and king, who use the virtuousness of pity as an excuse for poverty and who define peace as an armistice of fear—and thus "promote war."

It is instructive to note that ideas like these were widely propagated in the latter part of 1792 by an Association for Preserving Liberty and Property against Republicans and Levellers—expressly to persuade "the minds of ignorant men" that all causes of discontent were either inescapable or wholly imaginary, and to prepare these minds for the eventuality of England's being "dragged into a French war" [*Politics . . . Reflections on the Present State of Affairs*, 1792].

These pamphleteers were in favor of the mutual fear and "military policy" that temporarily bring peace and ultimately bring war. And they bluntly defended the inequality that supports pity and mercy. Both the Bible and "experience," they said, tell us that "society cannot exist without a class of poor." Consequently it is our duty to teach the poor that their sufferings are necessary and natural and not to be remedied by laws or constitutional changes—that it is in fact the object of our maligned and "most excellent Government to alleviate poverty" by "poor laws, work-houses and hospitals" [William Vincent, *A Discourse to the People*]. Blake's suspicion that "Churches, Hospitals, Castles, Palaces" are the "nets & gins & traps" of the "Code of War" is confirmed by these anti-levellers:

> Every step . . . which can be taken to bind man
> to man, order to order, the lower to the higher,
> the poor to the rich, is now a more peculiar duty;
> and if there are any means to prevent the spread-
> ing of dangerous and delusive principles, they
> must be sought for in education. [Hence the need
> for] Foundation Schools, Hospitals, Parish
> Schools, and Sunday Schools. [Vincent]

In **"The Schoolboy"** Blake is concerned not simply about

the constraint of the classroom in summer weather but about the moral defeatism forced upon "the little ones" who are compelled to "spend the day In sighing and dismay." And in the poem that follows, Blake's Bard has a contrary educational program:

> Youth of delight, come hither,
> And see the opening morn,
> Image of truth new born.

No use to "stumble all night over bones of the dead."

Blake's counterargument is that if there were not "so many children poor" there would be no need for institutions and moral code—and no ignorant men for sale to the fat fed hireling. Poverty appalls the mind, making youth sufficiently docile to be led "to slaughter houses" and beauty sufficiently desperate to be "bought & sold . . . for a bit of bread." There can be no vital bond of man to man in such "a land of Poverty!" Starvation demonstrates the absurdity of the anti-vice campaign, for the church remains spiritually and physically a cold barn, to which **"The Little Vagabond"** rightly prefers the warm tavern. The harlot's curse will weave Old England's winding sheet, and ultimately the raging desire for bread will undermine the whole misery-built London of spire and palace.

Boston's Angel asked, "What crawling villain preaches abstinence & wraps himself In fat of lambs?" The chimney sweep, a "little black thing among the snow," answers that it is

> God & his Priest & King,
> Who wrap themselves up in our misery [*deleted reading*]
> And because I am happy & dance & sing
> They think they have done me no injury.

King, priest, god, and parents do not reckon the revolutionary potential in the multitude they are stripping naked. Yet even the sheep puts forth "a threat'ning horn" against the tithing priest. As for the chimney sweeper, his father and mother have turned a happy boy into a symbol of death. Once a year he still does dance and sing—on May Day, when London streets are given to the sweeps and milkmaids to perform for alms in grotesque symmetry. *The Chimney Sweeper* is saying to the London citizen: you salve your conscience by handing out a few farthings on May Day, but if you really listened to this bitter cry among the snow you and your icy church would be appalled.

When we turn now to **"London,"** Blake's "mightiest brief poem" [Oliver Elton], our minds ringing with Blakean themes, we come upon infinite curses in a little room, a world at war in a grain of London soot. On the illuminated page a child is leading a bent old man along the cobblestones and a little vagabond is warming his hands at a fire in the open street. But it is Blake who speaks.

"London"

> I wander thro' each charter'd street,
> Near where the charter'd Thames does flow
> And mark in every face I meet
> Marks of weakness, marks of woe.

> In every cry of every Man,
> In every Infants cry of fear
> In every voice, in every ban,
> The mind-forg'd manacles I hear.

> How the Chimney-sweepers cry
> Every blackning Church appalls.
> And the hapless Soldiers sigh
> Runs in blood down Palace walls

> But most thro' midnight streets I hear
> How the youthful Harlots curse
> Blasts the new born Infants tear
> And blights with plagues the Marriage hearse.

In his first draft Blake wrote "dirty street" and "dirty Thames" as plain statement of fact, reversing the sarcastic "golden London" and "silver Thames" of his early parody of [Scottish poet James] Thomson's "Rule Britannia." And the harlot's curse sounded in every "dismal" street. The change to "charter'd" (with an intermediate "cheating") mocks Thomson's boast that "the charter of the land" keeps Britons free, and it suggests agreement with (perhaps was even suggested by) Paine's condemnation of "charters and corporations" in the Second Part of *The Rights of Man,* where Paine argues that all charters are purely negative in effect and that city charters, by annulling the rights of the majority, cheat the inhabitants and destroy the town's prosperity—even London being "capable of bearing up against the political evils of a corporation" only from its advantageous situation on the Thames. Paine's work was circulated by shopkeepers chafing under corporation rule and weary, like Blake, of the "cheating waves of charter'd streams" of monopolized commerce.

In the notebook fragment just quoted Blake speaks of shrinking "at the little blasts of fear That the hireling blows into my ear," thus indicating that when he writes of the "mind-forg'd manacles" in every cry of fear and every ban he is not saying simply that people are voluntarily forging manacles in their own minds. Hireling informers or mercenaries promote the fear; Pitt's proclamations are the bans, linked with an order to dragoons "to assemble on Hounslow Heath" and "be within one hour's march of the metropolis" [*Gazette* 1 Dec. 1792]. A rejected reading, "german forged links," points to several manacles forged ostensibly in the mind of Hanoverian George: the Prussian maneuvres on the heath, the British alliance with Prussia and Austria against France, and the landing of Hessian and Hanoverian mercenaries in England allegedly en route to battlefronts in France.

Blake may have written **"London"** before this last development, but before he completed his publication there was a flurry of alarm among freeborn Englishmen at the presence of German hirelings. "Will you wait till BARRACKS are erected in every village," exclaimed a London Corresponding Society speaker in January 1794, "and till subsidized Hessians and Hanoverians are upon us?" In Parliament Lord Stanhope expressed the hope that honest Britons would meet this Prussian invasion "by OPPOSING FORCE BY FORCE." And the editor of *Politics for the People,* reporting that one Hessian had stabbed an Englishman in a street quarrel, cried that all were brought "to cut the throats of Englishmen." He urged citizens to arm and to fraternize with their fellow countrymen, the British common soldiers.

The latter are Blake's "hapless Soldiers" whose "sigh Runs in blood down Palace walls"—and whose frequently exhibited inclination in 1792-1793 to turn from grumbling to mutiny is not taken into account by those who interpret the blood as the soldier's own and who overlook the potentially forceful meaning of "sigh" in eighteenth century diction. In the structure of the poem the soldier's utterance that puts blood on palace walls is parallel to the harlot's curse that blasts and blights. And Blake would have known that curses were often chalked or painted on the royal walls. In October 1792 Lady Malmesbury's Louisa saw "written upon the Privy Garden-wall, 'No coach-tax; d—Pitt! d—n the Duke of Richmond! *no King!*'"

A number of cognate passages in which Blake mentions blood on palace walls indicate that the blood is an apocalyptic omen of mutiny and civil war involving regicide. In *The French Revolution* people and soldiers fraternize, and when their "murmur" (sigh) reaches the palace, blood runs down the ancient pillars. In *The Four Zoas,* Night I, similar "wailing" affects the people; "But most the polish'd Palaces, dark, silent, bow with dread." "But most" is a phrase straight from **"London."** And in Night IX the people's sighs and cries of fear mount to "furious" rage, apocalyptic blood "pours down incessant," and "Kings in their palaces lie drown'd" in it, torn "limb from limb." In the same passage the marks of weakness and woe of **"London"** are spelled out as "all the marks . . . of the slave's scourge & tyrant's crown." In **"London"** Blake is talking about what he hears in the streets, not about the moral stain of the battlefield sigh of expiring soldiers.

In Blake's notebook the lines called **"An Ancient Proverb"** recapitulate the **"London"** theme in the form of a Bastille Day recipe for freeing Old England from further plagues of tyranny:

> Remove away that blackning church
> Remove away that marriage hearse
> Remove away that—of blood
> You'll quite remove the ancient curse.

Where he might have written "palace" he cautiously writes a dash. Yet despite the occasional shrinking of Blake as citizen, Blake as prophet, from *The French Revolution* to *The Song of Los,* from 1791 to 1795, cleaved to the vision of an imminent spring thaw when the happy earth would "sing in its course" as the fire of Voltaire and Rousseau melted the Alpine or Atlantic snows. In England, nevertheless, the stubborn frost persisted and the wintry dark; and England's crisis and Earth's crisis were threatening to become permanent. (pp. 250-58)

> *David V. Erdman, in his* Blake: Prophet against Empire—A Poet's Interpretation of the History of His Own Times, *Princeton University Press, 1954, 503 p.*

Stanley Gardner   (essay date 1954)

[*In the following excerpt, Gardner discusses Blake's concept of innocence.*]

[In the *Poetical Sketches* Blake was] tied to contemporary poetic fashion, and was repeatedly aware of virtue as a virtue. Even in 'Love and Harmony Combine',

> Innocence and virtue meet,

a meeting impossible in the *Songs of Innocence,* where virtue simply does not exist, since there is no sense of sin. But in the *Poetical Sketches* the young girl is a 'maiden risen like the morn':

> So when she speaks, the voice of Heaven I hear:
> So when we walk, nothing impure comes near;
> Each field seems Eden, and each calm retreat;
> Each village seems the haunt of holy feet.
>
> [from 'Song: Fresh from the Dewy Hill, the Merry year']

There is still 'seeming'—division and comparison. The union of man and nature is still incompletely realized. And it is a measure of the objective achievement in the *Songs of Innocence* that Blake could break from his formal poetic environment, in which Virtue gazed at evil. Already he was criticizing it:

> The languid strings do scarcely move!
> The sound is forc'd, the notes are few.

Innocence is universal reconciliation; mankind with Nature, earth with eternity, infancy with death. Such a reconciliation can only be realized in poetry and only imperfectly expressed in prose. In the latter case it ceases to be Innocence, being viewed from outside, and therefore not universal; and Innocence is by definition universal. The most considerable definition of poetry is that poetry exists as the reconciliation of apparently irreconcilable concepts. The reconciliation implicit in Blake's Innocence *is* the poetry; they are indivisible, and imply no argument outside themselves. To realize Blake's Innocence is to realize his poetry, to which philosophical exposition is not pertinent.

The quality of Innocence becomes apparent in a comparison of the song 'I Love the Jocund Dance', in *Poetical Sketches,* with 'The Echoing Green' in *Songs of Innocence,* two poems which have many points of contact. The former is concerned with things, the latter with relationships. The former is explicit, and the poet is conscious of 'Innocence' apart from other aspects of his theme:

> I love the jocund dance,
> The softly-breathing song,
> Where innocent eyes do glance,
> And where lisps the maiden's tongue.

The result is a pleasant series of verses, without unity—the order of the verses could be changed without detriment to the meaning of the poem. Moreover, the fulcrum of these verses is *Ego,* but no wider implications are poised upon that fulcrum. In the *Songs of Innocence,* on the other hand, when the word 'I' appears, it rarely means Blake; and when it does mean the writer it is not over-weening, but only a point in a range of vision. In 'The Echoing Green'—though this itself lends the poem no special virtue—the word 'I' does not appear. What is potent in the poem is the dramatic unity, compared with the divisible, scenic, nature of 'I Love the Jocund Dance', and the complete identity of Innocence in the action. The poem begins:

The Sun does arise,
And make happy the skies.

It is not a question of seeming or of simile; it is inadequate to attempt a paraphrase, beginning: 'The sun comes up in the morning, and *seems* to make the sky happy just as. . . . ' The word 'seeming' destroys what the poem *is*—an identity. The identity of human joy with the sun and the skies is dissipated once we attempt to fetch a comparison, because a comparison does not exist; the Innocence of the poem is universal. Likewise, when the bells ring their welcome the birds sing louder; *why* is irrelevant. That is the question Experience will ask. And, as the birds sing, the pre-suggestion of the second line of the poem is confirmed, and then the bells, in the epithet 'chearful', are related to skies and sun and the epithet 'happy'. This is not a matter of being analytically subtle; the unity is simply there. And it is a question in the long run of synthesis, not analysis.

The introduction of 'Old John, with white hair' does not lead, as it well might in Wordsworth, to anything extraneous to the poetic meaning. The aged are directly related to the joy which is the unity of the poem, and they recollect their own childhood with complete unregret, laughing with the children,

Till the little ones, weary,
No more can be merry;
The sun does descend,
And our sports have an end.

The joy and the sun are inseparable; the children grow weary and the sun goes down. There is no question of 'when', or 'if', or 'because'. The synthesis between the children, and nature, and the eternal sun is complete and simply stated.

At this point we come to the only simile in the poem, and one of the few in all the *Songs of Innocence,* and its use exemplifies the poetic truth of Blake's writing at its best. The 'sports have an end', and

Round the laps of their mothers
Many sisters and brothers,
Like birds in their nest,
Are ready for rest,
And sport no more seen
On the darkening Green.

The unity of the joy of child and nature dissolves in sleep as the night comes; the separation implicit in a simile marks the end of this unity, as the birds and children go their different ways, and at last a comparison is possible and apposite. And the dramatic unity of the poem is complete; we have moved from sunrise to sunset through a circle of significant action, in no way scenic.

This same simultaneity of joy and daylight is made explicit in the answer of the children to their guardian in **'Nurse's Song'.** The nurse states that peace is supreme when the air from green to hill is full of the sound of children at play; all else is silence, around the heart at rest. We have the familiar Blakean range, from the green, away to the hill, and back to the heart in the human breast. Out of this peace the nurse speaks with the conscience of responsibility:

Then come home, my children, the sun is gone
    down
And the dews of night arise;
Come, come, leave off play, and let us away
Till the morning appears in the skies.

The children's reaction to this argument is not only recognizably natural, but is also directly based on Blake's imagistic philosophy; they cannot (not will not, but cannot) go to sleep, because it is still day, because the birds still fly, and the sheep are still on the hills. Their joy belongs to daylight, their sleep to night. This is a measure of their Innocence, that their joy is simultaneous with the joy of all nature. [Blake uses the symbol of birds] as expressive of the complete joy in the union of two lovers. Later, when Blake comes to set intuitive love in dramatic challenge against marriage and compulsion, we find that he uses, among other symbols, that of the bird and the tree, and that such love is always associated with daylight. The night is for self-consciousness and sin, temptation and compulsion. Thus Blake's later argument develops out of these *Songs,* and from the joy that is here related to the constant symbol for Innocence and humility, the Lamb. This Innocence is inviolable.

The nurse inevitably yields; and

The little ones leaped & shouted & laugh'd
And all the hills ecchoed.

The inviolability of Innocence lies in its universality, and in the complete identity of mankind and living nature—an identity implicit in **'The Blossom'**, a poem in which the synthesis is so complete that paraphrase is impossible.

The birds, sparrow and robin, are identified with a child who seeks his parent. The parent himself—or herself, the sex is irrelevant—is linked with the 'leaves so green'; and the adjective 'happy' makes the blossom part of the universal entity of life in Innocence. The sparrow flies in merriment, 'swift as arrow', with its own impulsive movement into the *cradle* narrow close to the parent bosom; the flight of the bird takes it to the infant cradle, and two apparently irreconcilable ideas are fused. Yet the bird is all the time 'under leaves so green', and these leaves of Springtime green envelop bird and bosom, cradle and blossom in a foliage of Innocence. While the sparrow seeks the cradle in delight, the robin comes to the breast 'under leaves so green' for solace. In joy and sorrow the unity of nature—mankind, leaves, blossom, child, and bird—is unbroken. Experience will break it.

With **'The Blossom'** we may contrast the comparative looseness of **'Holy Thursday'**, a poem which engages matter extraneous to Blake's directly symbolic thinking, and ends in an admonition; a poem which has a purpose outside itself, rather than a relationship outside itself. And we notice that **'Holy Thursday'** is heavy with similes. Once more their incidence is suggestive. Blake uses a simile for the children following the 'grey-headed beadles' into St. Paul's:

Grey-headed beadles walk'd before, with wands
    as white as snow,
Till into the high dome of Paul's they like
    Thames' waters flow.

This is essentially descriptive, and Blake's symbolism breaks into a simile when his theme is dissociate from his poetic thought. Here, moreover, he is seeing the children in subjection to authority, a subjection from which they only escape temporarily in Stanza 2. (This is in direct contrast with **'The Ecchoing Green'**, where the aged are in complete sympathy with youth, and Innocence, and do not seek to govern their actions.) In the second stanza the effect is quite different. Blake's eye is then on the children alone, and they are not *like* flowers, or *like* lambs. The tightening of the poetic grip is at once evident. It is not simply a matter of a change in expression. Now that Blake's mind is totally absorbed with the Innocence of the children, and he is concerned with implicit poetic relationships, rather than extraneous social relationships, a simile is no longer adequate. The identity of the children with 'flowers of London town' (and London itself is an entity here as it never is in *Songs of Experience*) leads to the symbol of the Lamb. The beadles are forgotten, and the children 'sit with radiance *all their own*':

> The hum of multitudes was there, but multi-
> tudes of lambs,
> Thousands of little boys & girls raising their in-
> nocent hands.

The poem began in its opening lines with the *appearance* of Innocence—'innocent faces clean'—supported by the colours of the children's clothes—'red & blue & green'. But the symbol of the Lamb directs the imagination to the *action* of Innocence, and to the limbs—'hands'—and these have nothing to do with mere appearances. The mounting symbolism is matched by dramatic focus, and coincides with a shift from appearance to essential reality.

In the third stanza Blake again becomes conscious of an ulterior purpose; his eye is no longer wholly on the children, and on Innocence, and moves from the specific act of worship to a formal accompaniment of worship. Back come the similes, we are aware of syntax, and the technique shows through in the second line. The poet is engaged with the exigencies of form, rather than with meaning. And even here, in the *Songs of Innocence,* when the children are seen in relation to formal worship, Blake uses the image of 'thunder' for his simile—thunder which is later a constant symbol for repressive religion. It leads here directly to an admonition of no poetic relevance:

> Now like a mighty wind they raise to Heaven the
> voice of song,
> Or like harmonious thunderings the seats of
> Heaven among.
> Beneath them sit the aged men, wise guardians
> of the poor;
> Then cherish pity, lest you drive an angel from
> your door.

So the poetic tension in **'Holy Thursday'** heightens perceptibly when Blake's eye is engaged solely with Innocence, and truth; and the tension slackens when Blake turns from what *is* to what *seems*. The coincidence of complete poetic synthesis with his 'philosophy' of Innocence, and of the break in this synthesis with his introduction of didactic matter, points to the poetic nature of the 'philosophy'. Further suggestions in this direction arise from the stanzas

'Night'. Here, as in **'The Ecchoing Green'**, the stanzas are not interchangeable, and the whole poem has unity. Here, as in **'Holy Thursday'**, religion is involved with Innocence; but, unlike in **'Holy Thursday'**, religion is not imposed upon Innocence from without, by authority, and the aged. The religion here is self-expression, not repression, and instead of appearance and comparison we have, in the poem **'Night'**, reality and symbol. The 'philosophy' is indivisible from the symbol, and the result is a synthesis which becomes closer as the poem develops. At the end we can sense Blake *thinking* in symbols. He starts with night, and a simile; after the going down of the sun,

> The moon like a flower,
> In heaven's high bower,
> With silent delight
> Sits and smiles on the night.

The flower image is caught up in the next stanza in a familiar association; the angels walk where the lambs have been, and

>   pour blessing
> And joy without ceasing,
> On each bud and blossom,
> And each sleeping bosom.

'When wolves and tygers howl for prey', the angels weep in pity—in pity, it appears to me, not only for the children, but for the feral beasts as well; for they seek to turn the 'wolves and tygers' away by removing their lust for the blood of Innocence. This may be over-arguing the point. What at least is certain is that the Angels do not answer aggression against them with aggression; Innocence has not the material frailty to resort to a material defence. Yet the triumph of Angels and Innocence is complete, and involves the transformation of the beast of prey into a creature of Innocence—just as if, in fact, the Angels' pity did extend that far.

When the 'wolves and tygers' attack,

> The angels, most heedful,
> Receive each mild spirit,
> New worlds to inherit.

But this after-life is no allegorical paradise. It is another life of Innocence that is developed from the Innocence that was destroyed by violence on earth; it is an extension of Innocence to include the beasts of prey, who will accept meekness in these new worlds, where

>   the lion's ruddy eyes
> Shall flow with tears of gold,

and the lion, even the Lion of pride, will keep guard over the fold,

> Saying 'Wrath, by his meekness,
> And by his health, sickness
> Is driven away
> From our immortal day.'

The poem, which began in night, ends in the immortal day of Innocence. There is no night of death. And as, in the final stanza, eternity and Innocence meet, and all creation is 'wash'd in life's river', the lion and the Lamb lie down together, and the symbolism heightens. The symbolism is related directly to the intellectual triumph of the angels of meekness, the messengers of the true God, whose humility annihilates wrath. And we may contrast 'His health', one of the weapons of the God of Innocence, with the blight and disease the false god of Experience always brings.

Eternal life and the Innocence of life on earth come to a synthesis in this poem. And, finally, the triumph of Innocence is solely intellectual. As always in the *Songs of Innocence,* the vision expands towards an intellectual significance, from any given, initial poetic situation.

It is from the unassailable Innocence of these *Songs* that Blake launched his onslaught against established religion. The Innocence of the *Songs* is Spring perpetual and joy universal; the child is all creation:

> Sleep, sleep, happy child,
> All creation slept and smil'd.

From this Innocence we move to Experience, which involves an examination of Innocence from a sense of sin. The Springtime is literally gone, as we acknowledge if the two poems, **'A Cradle Song'** and **'The Divine Image'** in the *Songs of Innocence,* are compared with their counterparts in the 'Rossetti Ms.', **'A Cradle Song'** and **'I Heard an Angel Singing."** The season of Spring, invariable throughout the *Songs of Innocence,* is now developed into Autumn; we are aware of conflict in the poems, and the nature of Experience is clear from a comparison with the *Songs of Innocence.* (pp. 23-30)

> *Stanley Gardner, in his* Infinity on the Anvil: A Critical Study of Blake's Poetry, *Basil Blackwell, 1954, 160 p.*

Sir Geoffrey Keynes   (essay date 1955)

[*A noted English biographer, bibliographer, and critic, Keynes was also a Blake scholar who published numerous studies on the poet/artist, as well as a 1955 edition of* Songs of Innocence and of Experience. *In the following excerpt from the commentary in a reprint of that work, Keynes surveys the poems and illustrations. His comments are based on an original now in the Lessing J. Rosenwald collection in the Library of Congress.*]

Below the title [*Songs of Innocence and of Experience: Shewing the Two Contrary States of the Human Soul* on the combined title page] are the figures of fallen Man represented as Adam and Eve. They are girdled with leaves, shewing that they are in a state of Experience. Tongues of flame playing over them indicate their expulsion from Eden, while the bird of Innocence flying overhead has escaped the flames.

The scene [in the frontispiece to *Songs of Innocence*] is a literal illustration of the first poem, entitled **'Introduction'.** The poet is represented as a shepherd with a pipe in his hands looking up at the vision of a child above his head. His sheep are behind him; on either side and in the background are trees, a symbol not mentioned in the poem. Trees of different kinds signified for Blake varying aspects of life on earth; their leaves are in the sky, but their roots are firmly buried in the ground. The twining trunks of the tree on the poet's left symbolize earthly love.

In the decoration [on the title page of *Songs of Innocence*] two children stand at their mother's knee reading a book. Over them arches a broken apple tree bearing a few fruits, with a vine twisting round its trunk—the fruitful symbol of Christianity embracing the tree of sinful life. The letters of the first word are bursting into vegetable growths; among them are small figures and birds, symbols of joy. Leaning against the *I* of *Innocence,* in this copy indistinctly drawn, is a man in a wide hat, such as Blake wore, playing on a pipe. . . . The date 1789, under the right branch of the tree, is also indistinct in this copy.

[In **'Introduction'**, a preliminary poem,] Blake sets the scene for his *Songs,* imagining himself, the poet, as a shepherd wandering in an Arcadian valley and piping to his sheep. With the vision of the child on a cloud he sees himself being directed by the innocent spirit of poetry, and is bidden to pipe a song about a lamb, itself the symbol of innocence. Both child and lamb are symbols, too, of religion in the person of Jesus. The poet is then told to drop his pipe and sing his songs, and finally to write them in a book, using the materials ready to his hand—coloured water with a reed as pen. The last line points to children as his audience, though it is the innocent in heart, whether child or adult, that he means.

The decorations on either side of the text are derived from a mediæval manuscript illustrating the Tree of Jesse, though the tiny figures within each loop are indistinctly drawn.

The second poem [**'The Shepherd'**] is a simple one and needs little comment. The shepherd has now put down his pipe and holds a crook instead, the sign of his calling. The two stanzas express the relationship of the ewes and their lambs with their guardian, the shepherd. All is Arcadian peace and trustfulness. A bird of paradise soars into the sky; on the shepherd's left is a tree with a flowering plant twining up its trunk.

The theme of [**'The Ecchoing Green'**] was anticipated in an earlier 'Song' printed among the *Poetical Sketches* in 1783:

> I love the laughing vale
> I love the ecchoing hill
>
>   . . .
>
> I love the oaken seat
>   Beneath the oaken tree
> Where all the villagers meet
>   And laugh our sports to see.

In **'The Ecchoing Green'** the first stanza assembles all the joyful symbols of the Spring in nature and young humanity. In the second stanza the elder folk, identified as Old John and three motherly women, sit on a bench surrounding an oak tree, while youths and children sport around them. The third stanza is illustrated in the second plate, where Old John is seen leading the tired children home to their rest at sunset.

The oak on the village green is the symbol of strength and security. Later it became connected in Blake's mind with the cruel religion of the Druids, but here it is the guardian of young and old.

The delicately coiling vines in the lower part of the first plate have on the second plate turned into a sturdier growth, perhaps a Tree of Life, with heavy bunches of grapes hanging from its branches. The two boys of the first plate with bat and hoop have become youths plucking the ripe grapes, one of them handing a bunch down to a girl below. They are on the road to Experience, passing from the age of Innocence to that of sexual awareness. The boys on the ground with kite and bat are still in a state of childish innocence.

Rightly regarded as one of Blake's most triumphantly successful poems, ['**The Lamb**'] is also one of his most transparent. The lamb and the child, both symbols of innocence and of religion, converse together, the child properly supplying both question and answer. They are illustrated together in the design, with a cottage to one side and the oak of security in the background. On either side are delicate saplings arching over the scene without any overtones of Experience.

The little black boy sitting at his mother's knee seems in the first stanza [of '**The Little Black Boy**'] to deplore the blackness of his face, since it hides the purity of his soul, whereas the English child is white both inside and out. His mother, looking towards the rising sun, explains how God gives warmth and comfort to all living things by the light of the sun. The boy's black face is but a temporary cloud, a protection, even, from the extreme heat and light of the Sun God. In the penultimate stanza the boy picks up this theme and explains to the English child that they are really both the same, each being clouded by his body until he reaches a spiritual state of joy 'round the tent of God'. He even regards himself as the stronger of the two, acting as guardian and stroking the silver hair of the other until they love one another as equals. In the second illustration the two boys stand before God personified as Christ, the Good Shepherd, with his crook. He sits beside a stream with a willowy tree arching over his haloed head, the water and the vegetation indicating that heaven may be found upon earth.

The poem probably was to some extent inspired by contemporary indignation against slavery and the supposed inferiority of black races, but it also teaches that the creation of the world was an act of divine mercy, by which man might become accustomed to endure the heat of divine love.

[The lovely little poem '**The Blossom**'], at first sight seeming to have but slight meaning, is in truth a poetical expression of the consummation of love by the act of generation. The sparrow 'swift as arrow' is a phallic symbol seeking satisfaction in the blossom of the maiden's bosom. The robin sobs perhaps with the happiness of experience. The cryptic symbolism carries the meaning of the poem with the utmost delicacy, and it is equalled by the beauty of the design. This illustrates the organ of generation both flaccid and erect, with the generative principle breaking from its crest in the form of tiny winged and happy figures. One has found its goal in the maiden's bosom; she sits contentedly among the flying joys, distinguished by her green dress and large angel's wings, since she, with her prospec-

The first of two illustrated plates that comprise "The Little Black Boy" in Songs of Innocence and of Experience.

tive motherhood, is an ideal figure to the male during the act of generation.

The poem '**Infant Joy**' is closely related to '**The Blossom**', though separated from it in this copy of the *Songs* by several other poems.

['**The Chimney Sweeper**', a poem in narrative form,] begins with a line of prose and ends with a seemingly commonplace moral. It is evidently related to the earlier poem, '**The Little Black Boy**', being again inspired by indignation—this time against the shameful use of small boys for sweeping chimneys, the white boy being blackened by the soot of human cruelty. It has been suggested that the name Tom Dacre was formed by transposition of the letters in Tom Dark. The 'weep, weep' of his cry in the street is both a Cockney version of the sweep's profession and a realization of his misery. Many years after its composition Charles Lamb chose this poem as a contribution to James Montgomery's *Chimney Sweeper's Friend and Climbing Boy's Album*, 1824, a book of propaganda against social injustice. In Blake's poem the Angel of Tom's dream unlocks the coffin of his unhappy circumstances and sets his spirit free to float on clouds of the imaginative life. It is perhaps living this life that is the 'duty' of the last line.

The decoration at the bottom of the plate shews the Angel unlocking the coffin and the boys rejoicing in their freedom.

[In **'The Little Boy Lost',** as well as the next poem,] the child represents the human spirit seeking the conventional 'God', or Father, promised to our childish minds, but proving to be non-existent as we flounder in the mire of the material world. The Father is represented in the illustration by a bright Will-o'-the-Wisp misleading the child among the menacing trees of life on earth. The text is surrounded by angelic figures and stars, perhaps representing salvation by the life of the imagination if we can see it.

[**'The Little Boy Found',** a continuation of the preceding verses] shews the child rescued by a person in the image of God leading him out of the forest to his sorrowing mother. She is shewn on the right of the text as a figure with arms stretched out ready to receive him. Both the child and his mother are sanctified by possessing halos; this can only mean that man has been restored to the life of the imagination and thereby saved.

The rescuer's form is ostensibly female, so appearing to be in disagreement with the poem. Probably it is one of Blake's not infrequent androgynous figures, having both mother and father attributes.

The **'Laughing Song'** is simplicity itself, and seems to mean exactly what it says. It is, moreover, literally a song for singing. Blake was said by those who knew him sometimes to sing his poems to tunes of his own composing, and here 'the sweet chorus of Ha, Ha, He' calls for a simple merry tune. The youth standing in the centre of the party seen in the illustration, with his hat and wine-cup held in his hands, is clearly the leader of the chorus.

Blake's **'Cradle Song'** conforms in its simplicity to the general pattern of all lullabies and calls for little comment.

The dreamy tangles of the falling vegetation decorating the margins of the first plate suggest the feeling of the first line:

> Sweet dreams form a shade.

A few indeterminate figures can be made out among the tendrils; one of these near the top on the right, a soft female form hovering with arms stretched out in benison, seems to be suggested by the third and fourth lines of the second verse:

> Sweet sleep Angel mild,
> Hover o'er my happy child.

The illustration on the second plate is uncompromising in the hard outlines of the mother's clumsy chair and the child's wicker cot. Yet a subtle touch is in accord with the transference in the last two verses where the child's image is replaced by that of the infant Jesus—it is surely not by chance that the child's pillow is so arranged as to form a conspicuous halo around its head.

[In **'The Divine Image'**] Blake has expressed one of his most deeply felt themes—the identification of man with God. Many passages can be found throughout his writings illustrating his fundamental belief in the divinity of human nature. God had revealed Himself as a man in the person of Christ, and so a great and good man is to be reverenced as if he were God:

> Human Nature is the image of God (Annotations to Lavater's *Aphorisms, c.*1788). The worship of God is: Honouring his gift in other men . . . those who envy or calumniate great men hate God; for there is no other God (**Marriage of Heaven and Hell,** c.1790). God is Man & exists in us & we in him (Annotations to Berkeley's *Siris, c.*1820)

and so on in many variations. The poem with its steady repetitive beat hammers in the theme that Mercy, Pity, Peace and Love are attributes both human and divine.

Accordingly the decoration is a symbol of human life—a strange flame-like growth, half vegetable and half fire, twined with flowering plants. At its origin below, a Christ-like figure raises man and woman from the earth. At the top small human forms 'pray in their distress', while behind them an angel commits them to the care of Mercy, Pity, Peace and Love, personified as a woman in a green dress.

In **'Holy Thursday'** Blake described an annual event in St. Paul's Cathedral, which he had no doubt witnessed. The poem sounds sentimental, but more probably it was ironic. The 'event' was the marching of some six thousand of the poorest children from the charity schools of London into St. Paul's guided by their Beadles for a compulsory exhibition of their piety and gratitude to their patrons. Blake's true feelings about this were expressed in the corresponding poem in *Songs of Experience,* where the social injustice of poverty and charity is roundly condemned. Only in the last line does more genuine feeling become apparent. Even though the existence of so much poverty was wrong, at least pity was allowable.

The irony (if that is right) is driven home by the regimented and uniformed processions of children depicted at the top and bottom of the plate.

The theme of [**'Night',**] celebrating the gentle delights of a summer's night, was anticipated in a shorter lyric, **'To the Evening Star',** printed in *Poetical Sketches.* In 'Night', where the idea has perhaps become an allegory of death, it is elaborated and given a metrical form of great beauty. In previous poems the cruelty of man was noticed; in this poem the cruelty of Nature is introduced, with promise of its disappearance in another world.

In the decorations, the lion is seen on the right of the first plate, crouching in his den beneath a tree, but a winged figure is poised over him and others have alighted on the upper branches of the tree. Several more extend up the left-hand margin towards the moon. The evening star is shining on the right in some copies of the book, though not in this one. In the second plate five angels with conspicuous halos are walking on the grass ready to receive the 'mild spirits'. Three more are indistinctly seen in the branches of the tree in the left margin. The whole plate has the deep blue colouring of night, with stars shewing through the branches of the tree on the right.

The exquisite texture of ['**Spring'**] defies comment. Its reckless rhymes and half-rhymes run on to end in the refrain of each stanza. Almost without structure, yet the lines express precisely the joyful feeling of spring-time.

The decorative spirals on each plate harbouring small winged figures, with the recurrent conjunction of child and lamb, match perfectly with the simple theme.

The four stanzas of ['**Nurse's Song'**] express with perfect simplicity the happy irresponsibility of childhood. As one critic has said—'few besides Blake could have written such a successful poem on the delight of being allowed to play a little longer until dusk'.

The decoration shows the nurse watching the children dancing merrily in a circle. The weeping willow in the right-hand margin is perhaps a reminder that not all life is fun and games.

The apparent simplicity of [the delicate poem '**Infant Joy'**] and the obvious beauty of the illustration have deceived some critics into taking it at its face value. It has already been mentioned as related to another poem, '**The Blossom'**, regarded as an expression of the consummation of love. '**Infant Joy'**, seemingly so innocent, may be understood to shew the consequences of '**The Blossom'**—the conception of a new life. S. T. Coleridge criticized the poem for its inaccuracy. An infant two days old, he said, cannot smile. But neither can it speak, as it does in the first stanza, so that poetic licence must be given full rein. The illustration reveals the true nature of the verses. The unidentifiable plant has on one stem an unopened bud—an unimpregnated womb. The open flower above is the impregnated womb with the newly conceived infant lying on its mother's lap. Before them stands a winged messenger—the scene is an 'annunciation'; the second stanza may be the words of the mother or of the messenger, or both.

In a very early copy of the ***Songs of Innocence,*** the sepals of the flower have been painted the same colour as the petals. This error has been attributed to Mrs. Blake, though Blake himself was not always an accurate naturalist. In this copy the proper colours give greater beauty to the design as a whole.

[In '**A Dream'**] Blake has composed a simple fable which may perhaps be understood as a statement of the human predicament in terms of the lowest animal creation. The narrator, himself secure and 'Angel-guarded', dreams of an ant lost in the grass and anxious for her children. He is about to bewail her fate with tears when the 'watchman of the night' appears in the shape of a glow-worm and undertakes, with the help of the beetle, to guide her home. Thus the human spirit lost in the 'forests of the night' is portrayed by an allegory of the sorrows besetting the most insignificant of God's creatures. But even the ant is not uncared for and is led to safety by the glow-worm's light, the humble messenger of divine compassion.

The simple decoration includes only one figure—the 'watchman of the night', in the lower right-hand corner.

In '**A Dream'** Blake's narrator was grieving for the sorrows of the ant. The same pity for 'another's woe' is expressed at greater length in the nine stanzas of ['**On Anothers Sorrow',**] human troubles being illustrated by those of small creatures—infants and small birds. Divine compassion and help is promised by the coming of Christ, first as an infant and then as a man of sorrows, who will assuage our sorrows by his own.

The decoration is again simple. On the right is a leafy tree with a vine coiling up its stem; a bird of paradise takes wing from its branches. On the left are vague human figures climbing up to safety.

[The design of the frontispiece to ***Songs of Experience***] is contrasted with the frontispiece to ***Songs of Innocence*** by the different aspect of the youth portrayed. In the first he was the Shepherd in a state of Innocence still in charge of his sheep. In the second he is stepping with his right foot forward to leave his flock behind and advance into the state of Experience. The visionary child of the first picture has now been transformed into a winged cherub invested (in this copy of the book) with a halo and seated on the young man's head. The youth secures the boy's balance by holding his hands with his own. The symbol is not easy to understand, though it seems possible that it originated from *Ezekiel* xxviii.14, where the Prophet likens the King of Tyre to the cherubim seated on the Ark of the Covenant, saying: 'Thou art the anointed cherub that covereth', but adding that the King had sinned because of his great riches. Thus 'the Covering Cherub' came to represent the corruption following Experience. The phrase was often used by Blake in his longer epics to mean the Selfhood, 'that self-seeking, which is the root of all Christian errors' (S. Foster Damon).

The tree trunk on the youth's left has ivy climbing up it, the unpleasant shapes of the leaves indicating the troubles inherent in Experience.

The design on [the title page of ***Songs of Experience***] is conspicuously hard, with the word EXPERIENCE set like a bar across the page. This is accentuated by the formality of the architectural background to the figures below—two young people, arrived at the age of Experience, mourning beside the bodies of the parents whose guidance they have lost. It has been conjectured (by S. Foster Damon) that the arrangement of these figures is intended to suggest a Cross. Between the words SONGS and EXPERIENCE are a naked man and a clothed maiden flying towards one another with arms outstretched in anticipation of the pleasures of love, but between them are ivy leaves, suggesting by their spiky shapes the pains of sex-love and experience.

In his '**Introduction'** to the state of Experience Blake sees himself as the Ancient Bard, the Prophet, who heard Jehovah speaking to Adam in the Garden; he calls the Fallen Man to regain control of the world, lost when he adopted Reason (the 'starry pole') in place of Imagination. Earth is the symbol of the Fallen Man, who is summoned to awake from materialism and to turn again to the free life of the imagination. The 'starry floor' of Reason and the 'wat'ry shore' of the Sea of Time and Space (the edge of materialism) are there only till the break of day if Earth would consent to leave 'the slumberous mass'.

The decoration shews Earth as a female figure reclining on a couch borne on a cloud among a night of stars. In this copy her head is surrounded by a golden circle through which she looks at the Universe.

In the answer to the Bard's call in the 'Introduction' Earth replies [in 'Earth's Answer'] that she is a prisoner of Reason and of the jealous creator of the material world (afterwards named Urizen by Blake). Free love is demanded as typifying the life of freedom lost by the fall of man in Eden.

The decorations are for the most part simple vegetation of the material world. The snake below, perhaps the Serpent of the Garden of Eden, symbolizes for Blake the priesthood with their denial of freedom for natural energies.

[In 'The Clod & the Pebble'] the Clod of Clay, soft and pliable compared with the hard Pebble, sings the song of unselfish love and so of Innocence, thus building a Heaven to the despair of the Hell of selfishness. The Pebble, lying immobile in the waters of materialism, symbolizes the contrary state of Experience, singing the song of selfish love and building a Hell in spite of Heaven. A great deal more can be read into the dialectics of the poem with its obvious reference to the book, *The Marriage of Heaven and Hell,* written earlier than *Songs of Experience.* The Clod of Clay had also appeared in *The Book of Thel,* where it is the lowliest thing in the created world.

The upper illustration shews the sheep of Innocence (though perhaps not now so innocent, since they consist of a ram, two ewes and a lamb) side by side with the heavy bull and cow of Experience drinking the water of materialism. In the lower illustration a duck floats on the water, with frogs and a worm, each in turn preying on the other.

It was suggested that 'Holy Thursday' in *Songs of Innocence* was perhaps a satire on the annual parade of charity children in St. Paul's Cathedral. [In 'Holy Thursday' of *Songs of Experience*] Blake makes a more direct and powerful attack on the shameful presence of so much poverty 'in a rich and fruitful land'. The spiritual state of such a country is eternal winter contrasted with the sunshine enjoyed by a more just society.

The upper illustration shews a mother standing beneath a leafless tree growing on 'the wat'ry shore' of the 'Introduction'; she gazes at the lifeless body of her infant. In the right-hand margin are other scenes of poverty and death.

The two poems of 'The Little Girl Lost' and 'Found', together forming a long ballad of Life and Death, were originally composed by Blake for the *Songs of Innocence.* The first two stanzas shew that the idea of himself as the Prophetic Bard was already in his mind. He predicts that Earth, or mankind, will one day regard death as a release into a pleasant garden in Christ's presence. The human soul is personified as a child named Lyca, living in the sleeping world of Experience. She is found in her sleep by the Lion, here meaning the Angel of Death, who removes her covering of flesh and, with the other animals (none of which, according to a mediæval belief, could harm a virgin), takes her to his cave. Meanwhile Lyca's parents, wandering through the troubles of this life in search of her, themselves meet the Lion, but the Angel of Death is transformed into 'A Spirit arm'd in gold', who leads them to their still sleeping child. They then dwell together in the eternal 'garden mild' of the first stanza.

The decoration on the first plate seems at first to have no relation to the poem until it is noticed that the girl, with her lover, is pointing up to the first prophetic stanzas, whence a bird takes flight. The symbolic serpent turns away on the other side, frustrated by the truth of the Bard's prophecy. In the second plate Lyca is seen about to sleep beneath one of the trees of earthly life. Below, a beast of prey seems to scent his victim. On the third plate children are playing in paradise with the harmless lions beside the twining trees of love. A figure resembling Earth of the 'Introduction' lies unconcernedly beside them.

[In 'The Chimney Sweeper'] in *Songs of Innocence* the little chimney sweep appeared wholly miserable until released by the Angel. In *Experience* the boy is still sometimes happy, but tells of his exploitation by his parents, who imagine they are not wronging him because his spirit is not wholly subdued. The 'holy' parents are in church since the Church condoned the society able to inflict such cruelty on the innocent child.

The illustration is literal, shewing the boy with his bag of soot in the snow.

['Nurses Song'] is a parody of the corresponding poem in *Songs of Innocence.* The difference is emphasized by the form of the title—'NURSES Song' instead of 'Nurse's Song'. In this poem the words are spoken only by the nurse. The children, with their 'whisp'rings in the dale', are no longer real children, but are adolescents aware of sex. The nurse recalls with regret how she wasted her spring-time without real gratification, and tells the 'children' that their winter and night will be spoiled by repression and hypocrisy. Her face turns 'green and pale' because that is traditionally the colour of the sex-starved spinster, sick with longings for experiences which will never be hers.

In the illustration an adolescent boy is allowing his hair to be combed by the nurse; we are to assume his repressed resentment of the woman's power over him and his secret resolution to rebel. His more docile sister sits quietly behind him. The evil of female domination, so destructive of the male personality, already explicit in this poem, was often in Blake's mind, as we know from passages in other writings. The cottage door from which the boy has come is conspicuously wreathed with vines, symbol of the pleasures he will find in life.

['The Sick Rose'] is usually interpreted as an image of the troubles of earthly love. The symbolism of a red rose for corporeal love and of the worm (or the flesh) for the source of the sickness is plain. In the illustration a worm (banded like an earthworm in some copies) is entering the heart of the rose and simultaneously the spirit of joy is extruded. The 'howling storm' in which the worm comes is a symbol of materialism. The bush from which the rose has bent down to the ground presents several other details. On the left is a 'catterpiller' (always spelt thus by Blake) feeding on a leaf, the creature being for him, as for the Bible and the Elizabethan poets, the symbol of the 'pillager' or despoiler. Elsewhere Blake denoted the 'catterpiller' as the chief enemy of the rose, equating it with the priesthood, who lay their curses on the fairest joys. Further down the stems are two figures in attitudes of despair. The menacing thorns scattered along the whole length of the stems emphasize the pains of love on earth.

In the short, flickering lines of ['The Fly'] Blake imitates the flight of an insect darting to and fro. He likens himself to the insect, which chance might destroy at any moment. This is not to say that he, as a man, is unimportant, but that the fly, like any other living creature, has significance, so that Blake himself is like a happy fly, dead or alive.

The design illustrates the cheerful inconsequence of man's life as shewn by children at play, the shuttlecock perhaps being meant to resemble an insect on the wing. Over the group the dead tree of materialism extends its branches.

[In 'The Angel' the poet] imagines himself to be a woman dreaming of love. As a child she had been petted and Angel-guarded. Now she simulates grief to attract pitying attention, and hides her love, so that the Angel flies away. Then her mood changes, and when the Angel returns he finds her hardened by age. Love has come too late and is rejected.

This highly psychological poem is illustrated by a rather ordinary scene of the self-constituted maiden-Queen exacting pity from a winged Cupid for her simulated grief.

In fashioning his poem, **'The Tyger'**, Blake used inspired care in order to attain the effect he wanted to create. His three versions, two in manuscript and one on the etched plate, shew the stages through which his mind worked in achieving one of the finest and most profound poems in the English language. To some readers the result seems to be 'pure poetry', because its superb poetical form conveys no communicable meaning. For others the message must be made clear by picking the symbolism apart until its components appear to form a plain sequence. That this is in fact impossible becomes evident from the various attempts to do so, no one commentator ever agreeing with any other. It seems better, therefore, to let the poem speak for itself, the hammer strokes of the craftsman conveying to each mind some part of his meaning. The poem is deliberately composed of a series of questions, none of which is answered. It contains the riddle of the universe, how to reconcile good with evil. Careful dissection will only spoil its impact as poetry.

Even the illustration of a tiger, supposedly 'the Tyger of Wrath', standing beneath a tree is not as clear as it seems at first. In some copies of the book the animal is a ferocious carnivore painted in lurid colours. In others it appears to smile as if it were a tame cat. Perhaps Blake did not intend to dispel the mystery of his poem by painting an animal of consistent or obvious character.

[The trilogy of short lyrics **'My Pretty Rose Tree'**, **'Ah!**
Sun-Flower', and **'The Lilly'**] resembles musical variations on a theme—different aspects of love. Flowers are time-honoured symbols of love, and the first lyric repeats the symbol of **'The Sick Rose'**. The situation is one that might have occurred between Blake and his wife or any other married couple. Extramarital love is offered to the man. He rejects this by asserting his marital faithfulness, but on returning to his wife is met only with the thorns of reproaches and complaints.

In the second lyric the sun-flower, with its face always turned towards the sun while its roots are planted firmly in the ground, is a natural symbol of man's aspirations. In this context, the youth with his human desires and the maiden shrouded in frigid modesty both turn towards the setting sun where life ends, in the hope that their instincts may find satisfaction in the next world.

In the third lyric the white Lilly, symbol of innocent and honest love, is contrasted with the hypocrisy of the rose with its mock-modesty and the sheep with its simulated courage.

The only decoration is the generally applicable scene of a love-sick youth crouching at the feet of an apparently indifferent maiden.

Flowers being the symbols of love, Blake's thought now turns [in **'The Garden of Love'**] to a garden as the place where love would be naturally found; but the garden where he had played in a state of Innocence is now occupied by the Chapel of negation, surrounded by the graves of the instincts. The priest of organized religion is the agent of repression, and in the illustration he is seen instructing a boy and a girl in his doctrines. Below, the grave-mound of 'joys and desires' is seen bound with briars.

The little vagabond, living in the world of Experience, describes very plainly [in **'The Little Vagabond'**] his naïve notion of an ideal existence with parson and schoolmistress transformed into figures of benevolence. In the circumstances he imagines God as a loving father, and the illustration above is an image of divine forgiveness, the light around the Godhead dispelling the gloom of the forest of materialism and Experience. In the scene below, a family of father, mother and three children are warming themselves at a blazing fire.

In the first typographical edition of the **Songs,** published in 1839, this poem was thought too subversive of authority and was omitted.

The 'mind-forged manacles' of the second stanza [of **'London'**] shew that in this poem Blake is writing of a mental state symbolized by the social injustices seen every day in London. It is a political poem, the term 'charter'd' applied to the streets and the Thames signifying the restricting effects of the charters and corporations of the business world upon the individual. Again, the chimney sweeper's 'weep, weep' is called upon to illustrate social evils condoned by the Church, and the soldier's unhappy lot is invoked as an actual stream of blood running down the walls of the State. Lastly, the manacled mind even converts the marriage bed into a sort of Black Maria, or hearse. This poem is one of Blake's most outspoken protests against the evil effect of industrial civilization upon the life of the individual.

In the illustration a child leads an old man on crutches through the streets. This bearded figure may be the creator, Urizen, himself crippled by the conditions he has created. Below, on the right, another little vagabond is warming himself at a fire.

'The Human Abstract' was named 'The Human Image' in its first form in manuscript. It is therefore the contrary poem to 'The Divine Image' in *Songs of Innocence.* Blake wrote another poem called 'A Divine Image', but its satire was so savage that he did not use it. In the first stanza of 'The Human Abstract' the poet maintains that abstract reasoning is destructive of joy in life, since the attitudes implicit in pity and mercy presuppose the existence of poverty and suffering. The succeeding stanzas shew how false virtues may arise from selfishness, fear and weakness. In the fourth stanza the Tree of Mystery represents the resulting growth of religion, with the priesthood (the Catterpiller and the Fly) feeding on its leaves. The Raven of the fifth stanza is the symbol of the Fear of Death. The last stanza states that Nature does not know of this Tree. It has grown from Experience, or the reasoning powers of the human mind.

The illustration shews Urizen, the creator, himself tangled in the nets of religion. The poem is not, however, to be understood as a denial of all faith. It is a statement of true faith in the divinity of unrepressed human instincts and the holiness of life.

'Infant Joy' in *Innocence* was a statement of the simple joy of a life newly conceived. 'Infant Sorrow' shews the other side of the coin. The newly born infant has been brought forth in pain and sorrow and soon becomes a 'fiend' hidden in a 'cloud' of earthly life and experience. The second stanza expresses the human being's inevitable acceptance of his fate, though he can still shew his feelings by sulking.

The illustration suggests the infant's unwilling surrender to his mother's arms.

In the manuscript version of ['A Poison Tree'] it has the ironic title, 'Christian Forbearance'. It shews how the repression of anger can breed malevolence, so that an artist such as Blake may rejoice in the downfall of a former friend who has stolen his ideas. It is, however, written as a warning, not in exultation. It may be read in conjunction with several of the 'Proverbs of Hell' on the evils of repression in *The Marriage of Heaven and Hell,* and the later couplet addressed to Blake's patron, William Hayley, who had not given him the opportunity to speak his mind:

> Thy Friendship oft has made my heart to ake.
> Do be my Enemy for Friendship's sake.

The design below is a literal illustration of the last stanza.

[In 'A Little Boy Lost'], not in any way contrasted with 'The Little Boy Lost' of *Innocence,* the child is expressing his instinctive attitude to life, self-love being the natural state. By thought a man can only come to venerate an image of the divinity of man in himself. The child likens himself to a little bird picking up crumbs of self-fulfilment dropped from the tables of more experienced people. The natural truth of this infuriates the priest of organized religion and he makes a martyr of the boy, to the admiration of the unthinking onlookers. Naturalism is thus burnt in the boy's person by the fire of religious zeal. In the design below, the boy's parents and family are shewn vainly weeping before the flames. In the right-hand margin are exaggerated sprigs of ivy, the leaves being given a menacing appearance as symbols of vengeance.

In the last line Blake asks, can such things be done in England, his own country? He was himself never 'educated' in a school and would wish that others should not be subjected to the mental deformation caused by interference with the immature mind.

In the introductory stanza Blake addresses ['A Little Girl Lost'] to an idealistic 'future Age', when the hypocrisy of his own time has been shed. Ona, perhaps the feminine form of One, an individual, is personified as a 'little girl', though obviously this is only a poetic conception of the feminine principle. In the six stanzas of the poem proper the story of naturalistic love between the sexes is told as a tragedy. The youthful lovers meet, acknowledge their passion in the morning light, and agree to meet again in the quiet of evening. The girl encounters her father, looking like a 'book', embodying the written laws of forbidden pleasures, and is too terrified to plead her cause. The father is conscious only of outrage, having forgotten in old age the joys of young love.

S. T. Coleridge wished that this poem had been omitted, thinking it could be taken too literally ('not for the want of innocence in the poem, but for the probable want of it in many readers'). Yet it has never been misunderstood in this licentious sense, its meaning in its own context being sufficiently plain.

The decoration is simple, being an innocent-looking tree, with a squirrel and a tiny human figure climbing in the branches. Birds are flying around it at all levels.

[In the obscure poem 'To Tirzah'] Tirzah, perhaps to be pronounced 'Tearzah', is addressed in third stanza as 'Thou Mother of my Mortal part', shewing that she is the maker of the physical body. Blake twice quotes the words of Jesus addressed to his mother in the Temple, 'Then what have I to do with thee?', thus stating the psychological fact that a man is not yet adult until he has thrown off his family ties; not until then is he ready to be freed from earthly generation and to escape to spiritual life. The second stanza relates in four lines the story of the fall of man in Paradise and his condemnation to the sleep of life on earth. In the third and fourth stanzas the poet elaborates the idea of the earthly mother's cruelty in limiting his freedom and imprisoning his senses by material bonds, from which only the death of the Saviour can set him free. The mother's name, Tirzah, is derived from *The Song of Solomon* vi.4, and signifies physical beauty, that is, sex.

In the illustration man's natural body is supported by two women, Mother-love and Sex-love, who failed to save him. At his feet is an aged figure offering him a vessel containing the water of life. On his robe is engraved the second half of St. Paul's sentence, I *Corinthians* xv.44: 'It is sown a natural body; it is raised a spiritual body'.

[The lovely poem 'The School-Boy'] was at first included by Blake among *Songs of Innocence,* and its theme indeed chimes better with these than with *Experience.* It is a sustained protest, registered also in 'A Little Boy Lost', against the destruction of innocence and youthful joy in life by the dreary round in school, where fears and sorrows cause dismay. Self-development had been Blake's own means of education.

In the left-hand margin is an indeterminate plant with a bird taking wing from its summit. On the right are intertwining vines, their loops reminiscent of the decorations on the 'Introduction' to *Innocence.* Three boys are climbing up the stems, and a fourth sits at the top happily reading the book he was unable to enjoy in school. On the ground two boys and a girl are gathering the fruits fallen from the vine.

[The short poem 'The Voice of the Ancient Bard',] at first placed by Blake among *Songs of Innocence,* recalls the prophetic Bard with whom the 'Introduction' to *Experience* opened. Now, at the conclusion of the sometimes terrifying visions of Experience, he seeks to reassure the 'Youth of delight' that the morning of regeneration is at hand, when the doubts and disputes of mortal life will be dispelled, even though many have fallen on the way. The versification is unusual, the first line having no rhyme and the last three breaking into an irregularity expressive of the stumbling steps they describe.

The illustration of the Bard with his harp and listening youths and maidens needs no explanation. (pp. 131-55)

> *Sir Geoffrey Keynes, in* Songs of Innocence and of Experience: Shewing the Two Contrary States of the Human Soul, 1789-1794 *by William Blake, 1967. Reprint by Oxford University Press, 1977, 155 p.*

Robert F. Gleckner   (essay date 1957)

[*Gleckner is an American educator and critic who has written numerous studies on the works of William Blake, including* The Piper & the Bard, *which presents* Songs of Innocence Songs of Experience, *and several works published in the interim, as the key to Blake's literary and philosophic system. In the following essay, Gleckner emphasizes the importance of perspective and context in the comprehension of* Songs of Innocence and of Experience, *demonstrating how the symbols in the poems relate to Blake's philosophic viewpoint.*]

> A flower was offerd to me;
> Such a flower as May never bore.
> But I said I've a Pretty Rose-tree,
> And I passed the sweet flower o'er.
>
> Then I went to my Pretty Rose-tree:
> To tend her by day and by night.
> But my Rose turnd away with jealousy:
> And her thorns were my only delight.

Joseph Wicksteed, the only critic to devote an entire book

to Blake's songs, said this about Blake's poem, **"My Pretty Rose Tree"**: it "shows how virtue itself is rewarded only by suspicion and unkindness." And Thomas Wright, Blake's early biographer, commented on the poem as follows: " 'My Pretty Rose Tree,' Blake's nearest approach to humour, may be paraphrased thus: 'I was much taken with a charming flower (girl), but I said to myself, No, it won't do. Besides, I have an equally pretty wife at home. Then, too, what would the world say? On the whole it would be policy to behave myself.' But his wife takes umbrage all the same. The thorns of her jealousy, however, instead of wounding him give him pleasure, for they excuse his inclination for the flower. Moral: See what comes of being good!"

On the contrary, the moral is that such off-the-mark commentary is what comes of ignoring the context of Blake's songs (that is, whether the poem is a song of innocence or song of experience) and the point of view from which a given poem is written. **"My Pretty Rose Tree"** is not about virtue perversely rewarded, nor does it have to do with "policy" or morality in the ordinary sense of those words. Virtue by itself meant nothing to Blake unless clarified and qualified by context: in the state of innocence it is **"The Divine Image"**; in experience it is perverted to **"A Divine Image"** and **"The Human Abstract."** Real virtue Blake defined in **"The Marriage of Heaven and Hell"**: "No virtue can exist without breaking these ten commandments. Jesus was all virtue, and acted from impulse, not from rules." In **"My Pretty Rose Tree"** the speaker acts from rules when he refuses the offer of the sweet flower. For, as Blake wrote elsewhere,

> He who binds to himself a joy
> Does the winged life destroy;
> But he who kisses the joy as it flies
> Lives in eternity's sun rise.

The speaker in **"My Pretty Rose Tree"** not only has let the moment go, but also has bound to himself a joy. Furthermore, since this is a *Song of Experience,* about the state of experience, the flower offered the speaker is the opportunity for a joy, a love, an ascent to a higher innocence. We recall that it was not just *any* flower, but a superb one, "such a flower as May never bore." Still, the offer is refused—because the speaker already has a rose-tree. Now, conventionally, this is admirable fidelity; for Blake, however, it is enslavement by what he called the marriage ring. The speaker thus passes up the chance of a spiritual joy (sweet flower) to return to the limited joy of an earthly relationship (pretty rose-tree). He is sorely tempted—but his desire has fallen subject to an extrasensual force symbolized by the existence of, and his relationship to, the rose-tree.

The result, of course, is the speaker's retreat from desire to the only substitute for desire in Urizen's world of experience, duty:

> Then I went to my Pretty Rose-tree:
> To tend her by day and by night.

The last two lines of the poem are the crushing commentary on the whole affair. Virtuous in terms of conventional morality, the speaker is rewarded with disdain and jealousy, ironically the same reaction which would have been forthcoming had the speaker taken the offered flower. It is Blake's trenchant way of showing the "rules" to be inane.

How easily, then, in reading Blake's *Songs of Innocence and of Experience* we can ignore Blake's own individual method. Basically that method is simple, its roots lying in his concept of states and their symbols. Like many other artists Blake employed a central group of related symbols to form a dominant symbolic pattern; his are the child, the father, and Christ, representing the states of innocence, experience, and a higher innocence. These *major* symbols provide the context for all the "minor," contributory symbols in the songs; and my purpose here is to suggest a method of approach that is applicable to all of them—and thus to all the songs.

Each of Blake's two song series (or states or major symbols) comprises a number of smaller units (or states or symbols), so that the relationship of each unit to the series as a whole might be stated as a kind of progression: from the states of innocence and experience to the *Songs of Innocence* and *Songs of Experience,* to each individual song within the series, to the symbols within each song, to the words that give the symbols their existence. Conceivably ignorance of or indifference to one word prohibits the imaginative perception and understanding of the whole structure. As Blake wrote in the preface to *Jerusalem,* "Every word and every letter is studied and put into its fit place; the terrific numbers are reserved for the terrific parts, the mild and gentle for the mild and gentle parts, and the prosaic for inferior parts; all are necessary to each other."

For the serious reader of Blake's songs, then, a constant awareness of the context or state in which a poem appears is indispensable; and since each state is made up of many poems, the other poems in that state must be consulted to grasp the full significance of any one poem. Each song out of its context means a great deal less than Blake expected of his total invention, and occasionally it may be taken to mean something quite different from what he intended. Blake created a system of which innocence and experience are vital parts; to deny to the *Songs of Innocence,* then, the very background and basic symbology which it helps to make up is as wrong as reading *The Rape of the Lock* without reference to the epic tradition. Without the system, Blake is the simplest of lyric poets and every child *may* joy to hear the songs. Yet with very little study the child of innocence can be seen to be radically different from the child of experience, and the mother of innocence scarcely recognizable in experience. The states are separate, the two contrary states of the human soul, and the songs were written not merely for our enjoyment, or even for our edification, but for our salvation.

Closely related to the necessity of reading each song in terms of its state is the vital importance of point of view. Often it is unobtrusive, but many times upon a correct determination of speaker and perspective depends a faithful interpretation of the poem. Blake himself suggests this by his organization of the songs into series, *Innocence* introduced and sung by the piper, *Experience* by the Bard. Su-

perficially there seems to be little to distinguish one from the other since the piper clearly exhibits imaginative vision and the Bard "Present, Past, & Future sees." Yet for each, the past, present, and future are different: for the piper the past can only be the primal unity, for the present is innocence and the immediate future is experience; for the Bard the past is innocence, the present experience, the future a higher innocence. It is natural, then, that the piper's point of view is prevailingly happy; he is conscious of the child's essential divinity and assured of his present protection. But into that joyous context the elements of experience constantly insinuate themselves so that the note of sorrow is never completely absent from the piper's pipe. In experience, on the other hand, the Bard's voice is solemn and more deeply resonant, for the high-pitched joy of innocence is now only a memory. Within this gloom, though, lies the ember which can leap into flame at any moment to light the way to the higher innocence. Yet despite this difference in direction of their vision, both singers are imaginative, are what Blake called the poetic or prophetic character. And though one singer uses "mild and gentle numbers" and the other more "terrific" tones, both see the imaginative (and symbolic) significance of all the activity in the songs. The inexplicit, Blake said, "rouzes the faculties to act." The reader of Blake, then, must rouse his faculties to consider this imaginative point of view always no matter who is speaking or seeing or acting in a poem.

Both singers are of course William Blake. And since he, or they, sing all the songs, whether they are identifiable or not with a character in a poem contributes most importantly to the total meaning of the poem. To take an extreme example, in **"The Little Vagabond"** of *Songs of Experience* there are four points of view: that of the mother, who is now out of her element and can no longer protect her child as she did in *Songs of Innocence*; that of the parson, who is a part of the major symbol of experience, father-priest-king; that of the vagabond himself, a child of experience, not the carefree, irresponsible, thoughtless child of innocence; and that of the Bard, through whose vision each of the other points of view can be studied and evaluated. Without an awareness of this complexity in **"The Little Vagabond"** the poem dissipates into sentimental drivel. Another good example is **"Holy Thursday"** of *Songs of Innocence.*

From a conventional point of view it is thoughtful and kind of the "wise guardians of the poor" to run charity schools and to take the children occasionally to St. Paul's to give thanks for all their so-called blessings. But from the piper's point of view (and Blake's of course) the children clearly are disciplined, regimented, marched in formation to church in the uniforms of their respective schools— mainly to advertise the charitable souls of their supposed guardians. The point here (seen only through the piper's vision) is that in the state of innocence there is, or ought to be, no discipline, no regimentation, no marching, no uniforms, and no guardians—merely free, uninhibited, irresponsible, thoughtless play on the echoing green. Accordingly the children in **"Holy Thursday"** assert and preserve their essential innocence, not by going to church, but by freely and spontaneously, "like a mighty wind," raising to "heaven the voice of song." This simple act raises them to a level far above their supposed benefactors, who are without vision, without innocence, without love: "Beneath them sit the aged men, wise guardians of the poor." The irony is severe, but lost upon us unless we are aware of context and point of view.

As a final example consider the **"Introduction"** to *Songs of Experience.* The main difficulty here seems to be Blake's chaotic punctuation and the ambiguity it causes. Stanzas 1, 3, and 4 seem to be an invitation to Earth to arise from the evil darkness and reassume the light of its prelapsarian state. Such an orthodox Christian reading, however, is possible only if we forget (1) that this is a *Song of Experience,* and (2) that the singer of these songs is the Bard, not God or a priest. In similar fashion, while ignoring the context or the point of view, one might quickly point out the obvious reference in stanza 1 to Genesis iii and forget that the speaker in that chapter is the Old Testament God, Jehovah, the cruel law-giver and vengeful tyrant who became in Blake's cosmos the father-priest-king image. And finally, the Holy Word in Genesis walked in the garden not in the "evening dew" but in the "cool of day," not to weep and forgive but to cast out and curse his children, to bind them to the soil, and to place woman in a position of virtual servitude to man. In view of this, if the second stanza is read as a clause modifying "Holy Word," it is either hopelessly contradictory or devastatingly ironic.

Blake himself hints at the correct reading immediately by means of the ambiguity of the first stanza. There are actually two voices in the poem, the Bard's ("Hear the voice of the Bard"), and the Holy-Word's ("Calling the lapsed Soul"); and the second stanza, *because* of its apparently chaotic punctuation, must be read as modifying both voices. The last two stanzas are the words of *both* voices, perfectly in context when the dual purpose of the poem is recognized. Only in this way can the poem be seen for what it is, an introduction to the state and the songs of experience, in which the Holy Word of Jehovah is hypocritical, selfish, and jealous, thinking and acting in terms of the physical phenomena of day and night and the earthly morality of rewards and punishments. The Bard, mortal but prophetically imaginative, thinks and acts by eternal time and according to eternal values.

But how does one discover the all-important point of view in Blake's songs? One way is to observe the reactions of various characters to the same symbolic act, object, or character, for both the characters and the symbols ultimately resolve themselves into aspects of the major symbol governing that particular poem. Thus the mother of *Songs of Innocence* is symbolic in that her protection of the child contributes to the over-all picture of the child as major symbol of the state of innocence. In addition, many of Blake's symbols are recurrent, so that once a symbol's basic significance is revealed in a kind of archetypal context, each successive context adds association to association within the song series. When the beadle's wand appears in the first stanza of **"Holy Thursday"** of *Innocence,* for example, its immediate connotation is authority. But since a *beadle* wields the symbol, it is also religious authority, the organized church, institutionalized religion. It also

represents an act of restraint which forces the children to act according to rule rather than impulse. The wand is "white as snow" to suggest the frigidity of man-made moral purity as opposed to the warmth of young, energetic, exuberant innocence. And finally, it suggests the worldly, non-innocent concept of duty (and its corollary, harm), the duty of worship which clashes with all of Blake's ideas of freedom and spontaneity. But all of this, it will be said, strongly suggests the world of experience, and **"Holy Thursday"** is a *Song of Innocence*; the over-all point of view is the piper's. The point to be made here is simply this. If we do not read the poem as a *Song of Innocence,* about the *state* of innocence and its major symbol, the joyous child, we *can* read it as a rather pleasant picture of nicely dressed charity children being led to church by a gentle beadle to sing hymns; or as a terrible view of unfortunate, exploited charity children under the thumbs of their elders. And we would *not* see that despite outward appearance the children *are* innocent, essentially free and happy, as they spontaneously sing their songs. Without an awareness of context the symbols do not work as Blake intended them to, and the song becomes a fairly inconsequential bit of sentimental social comment.

Considering, then, the care Blake took with point of view, recurring symbols, and symbolic action, we can see that gradually many of Blake's characters merge. The final products of these mergers are what I have called the major symbols. Kindred points of view tend to unite the holders of those points of view; characters who are associated continually with the same or similar symbols tend to melt into one another; and a similar pattern of action reveals a fundamental affinity among the actors. In these ways the significance and value of any one character in any one song are intensified and expanded beyond the immediate context. The physical identity may shift, but the symbolic value remains constant—or better, is constantly enriched. When the beadle's wand in **"Holy Thursday"** is recognized as part of the basic sceptre motif, the beadle's identity, while being retained as representative of church law, merges with that of Tiriel, say, and the father—and ultimately with the "selfish father of men" in **"Earth's Answer,"** the pebble in **"The Clod and the Pebble,"** the "cold and usurous hand" of **"Holy Thursday,"** God in **"The Chimney Sweeper,"** the mother, parson, and "Dame Lurch" in **"The Little Vagabond,"** "Cruelty," "Humility," and the "Human Brain" in **"The Human Abstract,"** and Tirzah in **"To Tirzah."** Within the identity are inherent all the other identities which combine to make up the major symbol of the context. The priests of **"The Garden of Love"** may bind with briars love and desire, but they do so because they are selfish, fatherly, cold and usurous, worldly, cruel, humble, hypocritical, and so forth.

One serious question remains: how does one distinguish among all these characters, or are they all precisely alike and hence redundant? Professor Mark Schorer answers the question this way—I know of none better: "The point is," he says, "that the individuality of these creations lies not in their rich diversity but in the outline that separates them from their backgrounds." That is, each individual identity in its specific context is at once a part of the whole context and the whole of which it is a part. Both the priest of **"The Garden of Love"** and the flower in **"My Pretty Rose Tree"** are self-sufficient for some understanding of these two poems. Blake simply asked his reader to do more than merely understand: that, he said, is a "corporeal" function. He wanted them to imagine as he imagined, to see as he saw, even to re-create as he created. Only then does his method make sense, only then can one see the minor symbols as parts of a major symbol, only then can the individual song take its rightful place as a *Song of Innocence* or *Song of Experience*. (pp. 531-38)

> Robert F. Gleckner, "Point of View and Context in Blake's Songs," in Bulletin of the New York Public Library, *Vol. 61, No. 11, November, 1957, pp. 531-38.*

Harold Bloom   (essay date 1963)

[*Bloom is one of the most prominent American critics and literary theorists. In* The Anxiety of Influence *(1973), he advanced a theory called revisionism that is based on a perceived authorial urge for individuality of literary voice and vision. Bloom claims that in order to overcome the influence of earlier literary figures, each author deliberately revises, or "misreads," texts, imposing interpretations that conform to his or her own personal philosophy. Thus, there is no single reading of any text, but multiple readings by great authors and critics who understand a work only in ways that allow them to assert their own individuality or vision. In the following excerpt from his study* Blake's Apocalypse, *Bloom denies that* Songs of Experience *is a lamentation for lost innocence, asserting that the poems therein subtly call for a holistic integration of the spiritual and mundane components of human existence.*]

Blake wrote the *Songs of Experience* between 1789 and 1794, engraving them in the latter year but probably not often as a separate work. . . . Blake clearly wanted [*Songs of Innocence* and *Songs of Experience*] to be read (and viewed) together. The title of the 1794 engraved work is *Songs of Innocence and of Experience, Shewing the Two Contrary States of the Human Soul,* and the *Songs of Experience* do not in fact exist for us in a single copy without the preceding work. (p. 129)

Magnificent as the best of the *Songs of Experience* are, it is unfortunate that they continue to usurp something of the study that should be given to Blake's more ambitious and greater works. Their relative conventionality of form has made them popular for some of the wrong reasons, and they frequently tend to be misread. It is as though Milton were to be esteemed for *Lycidas* alone, and *Lycidas* to be read as a tormented mystic's outcry against the harshness of an existence that devastates the dreams of childhood. Even learned readers, who can laugh at such a possibility, are willing to see the *Songs of Experience* as Blake's greatest achievement, and to see it also as a lamentation for lost Innocence.

Songs of Experience begins with a powerful **"Introduction"** addressed to Earth by a Bard, and follows with **"Earth's Answer."** This Bard of Experience has considerable capacity for vision, and has much in common with

> **Magnificent as the best of the *Songs of Experience* are, it is unfortunate that they continue to usurp something of the study that should be given to Blake's more ambitious and greater works. Their relative conventionality of form has made them popular for some of the wrong reasons, and they frequently tend to be misread.**
>
> **—Harold Bloom**

Blake, but he is *not* Blake, and his songs are limited by his perspective. They are songs *of* the state of Experience, but Experience is hardly Blake's highest and most desired state of existence.

We can see the distance between the Bard of Experience and Blake in the second stanza of the **"Introduction."** The first stanza tells us that the Bard sees the "Present, Past & Future," but this is not the statement that will be made later in *Jerusalem*: "I see the Past, Present & Future existing all at once Before me." The later statement is true vision, for it makes the prophetic point that compels clock time to become imaginative or human time: If not now, when? The Bard of Experience sees what is, what was, and what is to come, but he does not necessarily see them all as a single mental form, which is the clue to his tragic mental error throughout the **"Introduction."** His ears *have heard* the Holy Word that *walk'd* among the ancient trees, but he does not hear that Word now. This is made altogether clear when he refers to the Soul as having lapsed:

> Calling the lapsed Soul,
> And weeping in the evening dew;
> That might controll
> The starry pole,
> And fallen, fallen light renew!

The Holy Word is God-as-Man, Jesus, who once walked in the Garden of Eden "in the cool of the day." The Word calls and weeps, and if the Word were heeded, the Fall could be undone, for "the lapsed Soul" still has the potential that might control nature. But the Bard, though he sees all this, thinks of man as a "lapsed Soul," and Blake of course does not, as the *Marriage* has shown us. Blake knows that when man is raised, he must be raised as a spiritual body, not as a consciousness excluded from energy and desire.

The Bard's error takes on an added poignancy as he emulates Milton, in deliberately echoing the desperation of the prophet Jeremiah. He tries to tell the very soil itself what her inhabitants are deaf to, urging the Earth to hear the word of the Lord and to return:

> O Earth, O Earth, return!
> Arise from out the dewy grass;
> Night is worn,
> And the morn

Rises from the slumberous mass.

In this precisely worded stanza, Earth is being urged to arise literally out of herself; to abandon her present form for the original she has forsaken. If the morn can rise in its cycle, cannot Earth break the cycle and be herself at last?

> Turn away no more;
> Why wilt thou turn away?
> The starry floor,
> The wat'ry shore,
> Is giv'n thee till the break of day.

What the Bard urges is what ought to be, but Earth can no more arise "from out" the grass than man's "lapsed soul" can rise from the "slumberous mass" of his body. The Bard's dualism, traditional in orthodox Christian accounts of apocalypse, divides still further an already dangerous division. If Earth returns it must be in every blade of grass, even as man must rise in every minute particular of his body. The starry roof of the spatially bound heavens ought to be only the floor of Earth's aspirations, just as the wat'ry shore marking Earth's narrow border upon chaos ought to be a starting point of the natural, and not its end. But it is again a not fully imaginative hope, to believe that a world of matter is given to Earth only until the apocalyptic break of day. Blake's heaven, unlike the Bard's, is a radical renewal of *this* world, an Earth more alive to the awakened senses than the one that so fearfully turns away.

The Bard is neither the prophetic Devil nor the timeserving Angel of the *Marriage,* but the ancestor of and spokesman for a third class of men in Blake, the almost-imaginative, who will later be termed the Redeemed. The parallel names for Devil and Angel will be the Reprobate and the Elect respectively, and clearly all three names are as ironic as Devil and Angel. The Reprobate are the prophets who appear reprobate to society; the Elect are dogmatists of societal values, as self-deluded as the Calvinist chosen; the Redeemed are those capable of imaginative redemption who still stand in need of it. The central irony of the *Songs of Experience* has proved too subtle for most of Blake's readers; the songs sung directly by the Bard are only in the Redeemed, and not the Reprobate category. That is, just as most of the *Songs of Innocence* are trapped in the limitations of that vision, so are many of the *Songs of Experience* caught in the dilemmas implicit in that state. The Bard's songs are, besides the **"Introduction,"** notably **"The Tyger," "A Poison Tree,"** and **"A Little Girl Lost."** Blake's own songs, in which he allows himself a full Reprobate awareness, are **"Holy Thursday," "Ah! Sun-Flower," "London," "The Human Abstract,"** and the defiant **"To Tirzah."** The remaining poems in *Songs of Experience* belong to various other Redeemed speakers.

One of this group is **"Earth's Answer"** to the Bard. A Reprobate prophet would take a tone less optimistic than that of the Bard, and Earth is too experienced to react to optimism with less than an immense bitterness. Earth is exactly like the Earth of Act I of Shelley's *Prometheus Unbound,* dominated by a "stony dread" of what Jupiter or "Starry Jealousy" may yet do to her, though that Nobo-

---

> **[Just] as most of the *Songs of Innocence* are trapped in the limitations of that vision, so are many of the *Songs of Experience* caught in the dilemmas implicit in that state.**
>
> **—*Harold Bloom***

---

daddy has already done his worst [Bloom describes Nobodaddy as the God who is "the nobody's father of Experience," in contrast with the loving father of Innocence; Nobodaddy connotes an association of sexuality and sin]. Grimly, Blake's Earth refers to her jealous jailer as "the Father of the ancient men," a title Blake would never grant him. Earth is in despair, and will not believe that the oppressive sky-god is merely a usurper of power. Even in despair she allies herself to Oothoon's questionings [Blake's Oothoon is the embodiment of desire and the advocate of free love]:

> Selfish father of men!
> Cruel, jealous, selfish fear!
> Can delight,
> Chain'd in night,
> The virgins of youth and morning bear?
>
> Does spring hide its joy
> When buds and blossoms grow?
> Does the sower
> Sow by night?
> Or the plowman in darkness plow?

Blake's most distinguished commentator remarks that "Earth is not saying, as some critics accuse her of saying, that all would be well if lovers would only learn to copulate in the daytime" [W. B. Yeats, "William Blake and the Imagination"]. But one ought not to leave Blake's image too quickly, since it dominates both these stanzas. The contrast to a dark secret love must be a bright open one, and the dark secret love that destroys is destructive because the dark secrecy is psychic rather than just physical; the concealment is being practiced upon elements within the self. To expose love to the light is a combative image, that takes its force from the social association usually made between night or darkness and the sexual act, an association with a tradition of orthodox Christian imagery behind it.

The issue between the Bard and Earth intensifies in Earth's last stanza:

> Break this heavy chain
> That does freeze my bones around.
> Selfish! vain!
> Eternal bane!
> That free Love with bondage bound.

The Bard sought to put the burden upon nature, urging Earth to turn away no more. Earth gives the burden back to whom it belongs: the Bard, and all men, must act to break the freezing weight of Jealousy's chain. If they can free Love, then nature will respond, but the sexual initiative must be taken by and between humans, for they need not be subject to natural limitations.

The themes announced in these two introductory poems are the principal themes of the entire song cycle. **"The Clod & the Pebble"** opposes two loves, the Clod's of total sacrifice, and the Pebble's of total self-appropriation. The irony is that the opposition is a negation, for neither love can lead to the progression of contraries that is a marriage. The Clod joys in its own loss of ease; the Pebble in another's loss, but there is loss in either case. Heaven is being built in Hell's despair, Hell in Heaven's despite. Both Clod and Pebble are caught in the sinister moral dialectic of exploitation that is a mark of Experience, for neither believes that any individuality can gain except at the expense of another.

This dialectic of exploitation expands to social dimensions in **"Holy Thursday,"** which matches the earlier **"Holy Thursday"** of Innocence. But the ambiguity of tone of the earlier song has vanished:

> Is this a holy thing to see
> In a rich and fruitful land,
> Babes reduc'd to misery,
> Fed with cold and usurous hand?
>
> Is that trembling cry a song?
> Can it be a song of joy?
> And so many children poor?
> It is a land of poverty!

Two contrary readings of the first **"Holy Thursday"** [are] equally true, but from the stance of Experience only one reading is possible. This second poem goes so far as to insist that the charity children live in an "eternal winter" without the fostering power of nature's sun and rain, since the dazed mind cannot accept poverty as natural. **"The Chimney Sweeper"** of Experience has the same childlike logic, with the peculiar rhetorical force that "because" takes in this context:

> Because I was happy upon the heath,
> And smil'd among the winter's snow,
> They clothed me in the clothes of death,
> And taught me to sing the notes of woe.

The second **"Nurse's Song"** affords a remarkably instructive contrast to the first. The Nurse of Experience reacts to the sound of children's voices on the green by recalling her earlier vision, and her face "turns green and pale," as well it might, in comparing the two states, for the movement is from:

> Come, come, leave off play, and let us away
> Till the morning appears in the skies.

to:

> Your spring & your day are wasted in play
> And your winter and night in disguise.

This is neither realism nor cynicism replacing Innocence, but an existence both lower and higher, less and more real than the undivided state of consciousness. The morning does not appear again, and so the generous expectations are self-deceptions. But the wisdom of Experience is at its best too much the wisdom of the natural heart, and we cannot altogether accept that the play was wasted. Nor are we meant to forget that the final waste will be in the disguise of death, which is the culmination of the cruder deceptions of Experience.

The subtler deceptions of Experience are presented in **"The Sick Rose,"** one of Blake's gnomic triumphs, a profound irony given to us in the ruthless economy of thirty-four words:

> O rose, thou art sick!
> The invisible worm
> That flies in the night,
> In the howling storm,
>
> Has found out thy bed
> Of crimson joy,
> And his dark secret love
> Does thy life destroy.

The first line expresses a shock of terrible pity, but what follows puts a probable tonal stress on the "art," for the rose is not blameless, and has an inner sickness that helps bring on the outer destructiveness of the worm's "dark secret love." The worm is borne to the hidden rose bed (it must be "found out") by the agency of nature ("the howling storm"), and his phallic passion devours the rose's life. Dark secret love is the jealous lust for possession of the Devourer, the reasonable Selfhood that quests only to appropriate. Yet the worm is scarcely at fault; by his nature he is the negation, not the contrary of the rose. The rose is less Innocent; she enjoys the self-enjoyings of self-denial, an enclosed bower of self-gratification, for her bed is already "of crimson joy" before it is found out. (pp. 129-35)

"The Fly" is a less ferocious emblem-poem, but it also turns upon unexpected ironies. The insect here is probably a common housefly, and the speaker a man awakening to mortality, to the precariousness of human existence in the state of Experience:

> Little Fly,
> Thy summer's play
> My thoughtless hand
> Has brush'd away.
>
> Am not I
> A fly like thee?
> Or art not thou
> A man like me?
>
> For I dance,
> And drink, & sing,
> Till some blind hand
> Shall brush my wing.
>
> If thought is life
> And strength & breath,
> And the want
> Of thought is death;
>
> Then am I
> A happy fly,
> If I live
> Or if I die.

It may be that Blake is recalling *King Lear,* and the frightening reflection that the gods kill us for their sport, even as wanton boys kill flies. If so, Blake uses the recollection to help us realize that we need to free ourselves of those gods. The want of thought is death; the thoughtless hand is therefore murderous. The blind hand of a god will thus be a thoughtless hand when it brushes us away. If Nobodaddy is the deity, then we are at best happy flies (because deluded ones), whether we live or die. To seek a heavenly father beyond the skies is to find a moral chaos, and to abrogate the pragmatic distinction between life and death, and so to dehumanize oneself. What makes **"The Fly"** so effective a poem is that this grim and humanistic sermon is conveyed in a deliberate sing-song, as light and wayward as a fly's movements.

"The Angel," "My Pretty Rose Tree," and **"The Lilly"** are a group of slight but exquisite exercises upon the frustrating theme of natural modesty or female concealment. **"The Lilly"** celebrates that flower's openness to love, in contrast to the thorny Rose Tree, for the sake of which an offering greater than natural, "as May never bore," was unwisely rejected. **"The Angel"** gains in meaning if the reader will remember the kind of orthodox evasion of passion that Blake associates with Angelic mildness.

With the greatest of these poems, **"The Tyger,"** the Bard of Experience returns, in all the baffled wonder of his strong but self-fettered imagination:

> Tyger! Tyger! burning bright,
> In the forests of the night:
> What immortal hand or eye
> Could frame thy fearful symmetry?

Nobody staring at Blake's illustration to this would see its Tyger as anything but a mild and silly, perhaps worried, certainly shabby, little beast. Blake uses the same irony of contrast between text and design that he has in at least one place in *America,* where Orc is being described by Albion's Angel as a fierce monster while two sleeping children are shown nestling against a peaceful ram. The Tyger of the design is not in the forests of the night, but in the open world of clear vision. The forests are "of " the night in belonging to it; the Bard of Experience is in mental darkness. He sees a burning beast against a bordering blackness, and his own mortal eye is framing the Tyger in a double sense: creating it, and surrounding it with an opaque world. But from the start he desires to delude himself; the first of his rhetorical questions insists on a god or demon for its answer.

Blake evidently derived the notion of confronting a mythic beast and having it serve as the text for a series of increasingly rhetorical questions that will help to demonstrate an orthodox theodicy from the Book of Job. The Tyger is a precise parallel to the Behemoth and the Leviathan, emblems of the sanctified tyranny of nature over man. The Bard's Tyger is also "the chief of the ways of God: he that made him can make his sword to approach unto him."

Fearful and awed, the Bard learns the logic of Leviathan: "None is so fierce that dare stir him up: who then is able to stand before me?" Jehovah proudly boasted of Leviathan that he was a king over men, those deluded children of pride. Though he worships in fear, the Bard also is proud to reveal the Tyger's power. Melville's Moby Dick is another Tyger, but Ahab strikes through the mask, and

asserts [Promethean defiance]. The Bard of Experience is confused, because this world in many of its visible aspects seems to have been formed both in love (the Lamb) and fright (the Tyger). The Bard is one of the Redeemed, capable of imaginative salvation, but before the poem ends he has worked his frenzy into the self-enclosure of the Elect Angels, prostrate before a mystery entirely of his own creation.

To trace this process of wilful failure one need only notice the progressive limitation of the poem's questionings. The second stanza asks whether the Tyger was created in some "distant deeps" (Hell) "or skies" (Heaven). If a mortal were the creator in either case he must have been an Icarus ("On what wings dare he aspire?") or a Prometheus ("What the hand dare sieze the fire?"), both punished by the sky-gods for their temerity. Behind the Tyger's presumably lawful creation must be the blacksmith god who serves as a trusty subordinate to the chief sky-god. His furnace, and not the human brain, wrought the Tyger's deadly terrors, including that symmetry so surprisingly fearful. What Blake called "Deism" is entering the poem, but inverted so that an argument from design induces a question that the Bard cannot wish to have answered:

> When the stars threw down their spears
> And water'd heaven with their tears:
> Did he smile his work to see?
> Did he who made the Lamb make thee?

We will come upon this image later in Blake, but its Miltonic background is enough for our understanding. When the fallen Angels were defeated, when their tears and weapons alike came down as so many shooting stars, did the same god, who is now taken to be an answer to the poem's earlier questionings, smile at his victory? And is that god, clearly the creator of the tyrants of Experience, Tyger and Leviathan, also the god of unsundered Innocence, of which the Lamb is emblematic? The Bard abandons the issue and plunges back into the affrighted awe of his first stanza, but with the self-abnegating change of "Could frame thy fearful symmetry" to "Dare frame." I do not think that Blake meant it to remain an open question, but also he clearly did not want a premature answer. All deities, for him, resided within the human breast, and so, necessarily, did all Lambs and Tygers.

The ironies of apprehension mount in the remaining *Songs of Experience.* The reader learns in time that what these poems demand is a heightened awareness of tonal complexities. Here is the limpid **"Ah! Sun-Flower"** so evidently a study of the nostalgias, and yet as cruel a poem as Blake ever wrote:

> Ah, Sun-flower! weary of time,
> Who countest the steps of the Sun,
> Seeking after that sweet golden clime
> Where the traveller's journey is done:
>
> Where the Youth pined away with desire,
> And the pale Virgin shrouded in snow,
> Arise from their graves, and aspire
> Where my Sun-flower wishes to go.

Blake himself speaks here, and is a little weary of his own pity for those who will not learn to free themselves from the ascetic delusion—the dualistic hope that a denial of the body's desires will bring about "that sweet golden clime," a heaven for the soul. The whole meaning of this poem is in another of Blake's descriptions of heaven, as "an allegorical abode where existence hath never come." The Sun-flower is weary of time because of its heliotropic bondage; nature has condemned it to the perpetual cycle of counting the steps of the sun. Each twilight it watches the sunset, and desires to be in that sweet golden clime on the western horizon, where all journeys would seem to be done. It is the next stanza that establishes the little poem's pungency, for the three "where"'s are the same. The Sunflower desires to go where the sun sets; that heaven is where the Youth and Virgin are resurrected to the rewards of their holy chastity. They arise, and they still aspire to go to their heaven, but that is where they already are. They have not escaped nature, by seeking to deny it; they have become monuments to its limitations. To repress energy is to join the sunset, and yet still to aspire after it. The flower is rooted in nature; the Youth and the Virgin were not, but have become so. To aspire only as the vegetative world aspires is to suffer a metamorphosis into the vegetative existence.

"The Garden of Love" offers a simpler and poetically less effective bitterness, so much less so that it seems to me the poorest of the *Songs of Experience,* and might perhaps have been better left in the notebook. "The Little Vagabond," much less famous, is not only a better poem, but spills more of the blood of the oppressive Church. Blake's tone is his most popular, and most bitterly jovial, in the sudden vision of a humanized God replacing Nobodaddy in the last stanza.

> And God, like a father, rejoicing to see
> His children as pleasant and happy as he,
> Would have no more quarrel with the Devil
>   or the barrel,
> But kiss him, & give him both drink and
>   apparel.

Nothing jovial exists in the remaining Songs. "London" is a prophetic cry in which Blake turns upon [English politician William] Pitt's city of oppression as Amos turned upon Uzziah's. The epigraph might well be from Amos: "The Lord hath sworn by the excellency of Jacob, surely I will never forget any of their works." But we mistake the poem if we read it as an attack upon oppression alone. Blake is a poet in whom the larger apocalyptic impulse always contains the political as a single element in a more complex vision. Of the four stanzas of "London" only the third is really about the oppression of man by society. The other three emphasize man's all-too-natural repression of his own freedom. The street is charter'd by society (both bound and, ironically, supposedly granted liberties) but the Thames is bound between its banks as well. There are marks of woe in every face, but marks of weakness are mentioned first. Every voice and every ban (Pitt's bans against the people—but every vow authorized by society including those relating to marriage) has in it the sound of mind-forged manacles, but that mind is every mind, and not just the mind of Pitt. It is because all men make and accept mental chains, that the Chimney-sweeper's cry

(" 'weep! 'weep!' in notes of woe") makes the perpetually blackening Church yet blacker:

> How the Chimney-sweeper's cry
> Every black'ning church appalls;
> And the hapless Soldier's sigh
> Runs in blood down Palace walls.

"Appalls" means "drapes in a pall" here; in its intransitive sense it hints, not that the exploiting Church is at all unhappy about the sweeper's servitude, but that it trembles involuntarily at the accusing prophecy of the cry. The hapless Soldier, enforcing a ban he has not the courage to defy, releases a breath that is a kind of prophetic handwriting on the wall of the Palace, foretelling the King's punishment and the suffering of all society before the storm of revolution and subsequent apocalypse. But most of all, Blake hears the consequences of the societal code that represses sexuality:

> But most thro' midnight streets I hear
> How the youthful Harlot's curse
> Blasts the new-born Infant's tear,
> And blights with plagues the Marriage hearse.

Two readings, at least, are possible here, and may reinforce one another. One is that the blasting of the tear refers to prenatal blindness due to venereal disease, the "plagues" of the poem's last line. A closer reading gives what is at first more surprising and yet finally more characteristic of Blake's individual thinking. Most of "London" is *sounds;* after the first stanza, Blake talks about what he hears as he walks the streets of his city. In the midnight streets of the city, he hears a harlot's curse against the morality of the Bromions, who speak of her with the authority of reason and society and, as they would suppose, of nature. But it is her cry, from street to street that weaves their fate, the winding sheet of their England. They have mistaken her, for she is nature, and her plagues are subtler than those of venereal disease. A shouted curse can *blast* a *tear* in a quite literal way; the released breath can scatter the small body of moisture out of existence. Blake knows his natural facts; he distrusted nature too much not to know them. The tear ducts of a new born infant are closed; its eyes need to be moistened before it can begin to weep. Blake ascribes a natural fact to the Harlot's curse, and so the Harlot is not just an exploited Londoner but nature herself, the Tirzah of the last Song of Experience. In this reading, [the concluding line of "London"] takes a very different and greater emphasis. The curse of nature that blights the marriage coach and turns it into a hearse is venereal infection in the first reading. But Blake is talking about *every* marriage, and he means literally that each rides in a hearse. The plagues are the enormous plagues that come from identifying reason, society, and nature, and the greatest of these plagues is the Jealousy of Experience, the dark secret love of the natural heart.

The heart of Experience is the theme of "The Human Abstract," a matching poem to "The Divine Image" of Innocence. Blake's title is probably not to be understood in terms of the Latin *abstractus* ("separated," "drawn apart"), for the contrast between the two poems is not between the integral and the split human nature, but rather between the equal delusions of Innocence and Experience as to the relationship of the human to the natural. **"The Divine Image,"** as we have seen, is no image at all but a deliberately confused tangle of abstractions, as befits the limitations of the Innocent vision. **"The Human Abstract"** is an image, the organic and terrible image of the Tree of Mystery, growing out of the human brain and darkening vision with thickest shades:

> Pity would be no more
> If we did not make somebody Poor;
> And Mercy no more could be
> If all were as happy as we.
>
> And mutual fear brings peace,
> Till the selfish loves increase:
> Then Cruelty knits a snare,
> And spreads his baits with care.

The virtues of **"The Divine Image"** are exposed as being founded upon the exploiting selfishness of natural man. Not content with this inversion, the death-impulse of Cruelty traps the self-approving heart through the most dangerous of its smugnesses, Humility:

> He sits down with holy fears,
> And waters the ground with tears;
> Then Humility takes its root
> Underneath his foot.

From this root there soon spreads "the dismal shade of Mystery," the projection of Experiential man's fears upon the body of nature, and the subsequent identification of those fears with the Mystery of the Incarnation. The poem climaxes in the Deceit of natural religion, with images drawn from Norse mythology:

> And it bears the fruit of Deceit,
> Ruddy and sweet to eat;
> And the Raven his nest has made
> In its thickest shade.
>
> The Gods of the earth and sea
> Sought thro' Nature to find this Tree;
> But their search was all in vain:
> There grows one in the Human Brain.

Odin, the Norse Nobodaddy, hanged himself upon Yggdrasil, a Tree of Mystery, self-slain as a sacrifice to himself, that he might gain knowledge of the runes, a key to mystery. The fruit of Deceit includes the runes and the apple of Eve's fall, the natural entrance to the negations or moral good and moral evil, [and ethical mazes]. The Raven is Odin's emblem, a Devourer who nests within the tree waiting to consume the Prolific of man's sacrificed desires. The last stanza evidently refers to an adumbration of the Norse myth of Balder's death. The other gods seek vainly for the mistletoe, a branch of which had slain Balder; but the Tree of Death is now not in nature but within the human mind.

Much the same tree appears in the slighter **"A Poison Tree,"** first entitled "Christian Forbearance," a grisly meditation on the natural consequences of repressed anger. **"Infant Sorrow"** and **"A Little Boy Lost"** are less successful, for Blake does little in them to guard himself against his own indignation, against nature in **"Infant Sorrow,"** against priestcraft in **"A Little Boy Lost."** "A Little

Girl Lost" is saved by its simplicity, by the very starkness of its contrast between two kinds of love, that which can "naked in the sunny beams delight" and the jealous paternal "loving look" that strikes terror even as the restrictive Bible of Heaven can.

Perhaps as late as 1805, Blake added a final poem to the *Songs of Experience,* together with an illustration depicting the raising from death of the Spiritual Body. This poem, **"To Tirzah,"** is a condensed summary of the entire cycle of *Songs of Innocence and of Experience.* Tirzah [appears] later in Blake, but all we need to know of her for this poem is in her name. Tirzah was the capital of the kingdom of Israel, the ten lost tribes, and therefore opposed to Jerusalem, capital of Judah, the two redeemed tribes. By 1801, Jerusalem, for Blake, symbolizes Milton's Christian Liberty, the spiritual freedom of man. Tirzah therefore stands for man's bondage to nature:

> Whate'er is Born of Mortal Birth
> Must be consumed with the Earth,
> To rise from Generation free:
> Then what have I to do with thee?

As Jesus denied his mother and so declared his freedom from mortal birth, so Blake now denies the motherhood of Tirzah. Whatever is mortal will be consumed, when the Earth is enabled to heed the opening plea of the Bard of Experience. Consumed by the revelation of the human, with natural disguise fallen away, the generative cycle can cease:

> The Sexes sprung from Shame & Pride,
> Blow'd in the morn; in evening died;
> But Mercy chang'd Death into Sleep;
> The Sexes rose to work and weep.

Blake is not saying that the sexual act sprang from the Fall, but he is insisting that sexual division in its present form must be the result of a "Shame & Pride" that were not originally human. In *The Book of Urizen,* Blake identifies the Fall with the Creation of man and nature in their present forms. They came together in the morn of history and would have died already, but for the Mercy of time's potential, which allows the imagination to convert the deathly nightmare of history into the sweet and bitter sleep of human survival, the generative struggle of sexual labor and lamentation. But that struggle, if it is to turn into a progression, must be freed of its mortal patroness:

> Thou Mother of my Mortal part,
> With cruelty didst mould my Heart,
> And with false self-decieving tears
> Didst bind my Nostrils, Eyes, & Ears;
>
> Didst close my Tongue in senseless clay,
> And me to Mortal Life betray:
> The Death of Jesus set me free:
> Then what have I to do with thee?

Nature restricts the heart and four senses; she cannot bind or close the fifth sense, the specifically sexual sense of touch. The Atonement set Blake free, not from the orthodox notion of original sin, but from the deceits of natural religion. Blake understands the Atonement as the triumph of the imaginative body over the natural body, a triumph *through* touch, an improvement in sensual enjoyment. **"To**

Tirzah" repudiates Innocence and Experience alike, for Tirzah is the goddess of both states, the loving mother of one and the mocking nature of the other. (pp. 136-45)

Harold Bloom, in his Blake's Apocalypse: A Study in Poetic Argument, *Doubleday & Company, Inc., 1963, 454 p.*

John Ruskin, presumably on *Songs of Innocence and of Experience:*

I cannot enough thank you for trusting me with the invaluable little volume which I return to day—nor at all express to you the pleasure I have had in looking it over;—I had, before, the deepest respect for the genius of Blake—yet I was quite ignorant of his fine feeling for colour—which is one of the ruling & lovely qualities of these noble designs—I am afraid—when I was at your house—that you thought me cold to the beauty of its treatment—but in proportion to the real power and rank of any work of art—is the necessity of separate & quiet worship of it—the incapability of tasting it in such accumulation—I saw too much . . . I have been prevented by the severity of the weather from again waiting upon you—but I hope personally to express my thanks to you for this kindness as soon as the 'sun does arise—& make happy the Skies'—

John Ruskin, in an undated letter to Maria Denman (d. 1859), excerpted in William Blake: The Critical Heritage, *edited by G. E. Bentley, Jr., Routledge & Kegan Paul, 1975.*

E. D. Hirsch, Jr.   (essay date 1964)

[*Hirsch is an American critic and educator best known for his* Cultural Literacy: What Every American Needs to Know *(1987), a controversial indictment of the American educational system. In* Cultural Literacy, *he states that the average contemporary student is seriously ill-informed about basic historic and literary concepts, and supplies a list of names and terms that he considers indispensable; critics have variously accused Hirsch of imposing elitist standards and unjustly promoting memorization over reasoning. In the following excerpt, Hirsch explicates the poem "The Tyger" from* Songs of Innocence and of Experience.]

[The] greatest of Blake's poems displays his most distinctive characteristic as a lyric poet: the contrast between his vividly simple language and his immense complexity of meaning. If ["The Tyger"] is a richer poem than "The Lamb," it is not because its language is more difficult. Verbally, the most daring phrase of "The Tyger" is "forests of the night," which is not different in kind from "clothing of delight" in "The Lamb." The great distinguishing mark of "The Tyger" is the *complexity* of its *thought and tone.*

Like "The Lamb," which it satirizes, it begins with a question about the Creator:

Little Lamb, who made thee?	Tyger, Tyger! burning bright
Dost thou know who made thee?	In the forests of the night
Gave thee life, & bid thee feed	What immortal hand or eye
By the stream & o'er the mead?	Could frame they fearful symmetry?

While "The Lamb" answers the questions it poses, "The Tyger" consists entirely of unanswered questions. In this simple fact lodges much of the poem's richness. The questions it asks are ultimate ones, and while the answers are implicit in the poem, they cannot be pat answers because, no matter how the reader construes its implications, the poem remains a series of questions. The way each question is formed makes it also an answer, but still the answer is formed as a question, and neither is resolved into the other. All the complexities of the poem are built on this doubleness in its rhetoric, and every aspect of the poem partakes of this doubleness.

Blake's first intention in forming such a poem was no doubt to satirize the singlemindedness of "The Lamb," a poem which excluded all genuine terror from life and found value only in what is gentle, selfless, pious, and loving. It is true that the *Songs of Innocence* as a whole do not exclude cruelty and terror. In "Night," "wolves and tygers howl for prey," and in other poems there is a sufficiency of pain and tears. But cruelty and terror are presented as aspects of life that are to be finally overcome and therefore have no permanent reality or value. In "Night" the lion is ultimately transformed into a loving guardian; in Eternity he lies down with the lamb. Thus, while *Innocence* acknowledges tigerness, it entertains two reassuring ideas about it: that it is temporary and transcended, and that it is directly opposite to true holiness, which consists entirely of the lamblike virtues of Mercy, Pity, Peace, and Love. These are the two ideas that "The Tyger" satirizes as illusions. To the idea that the terrors of life will be transcended, the poem opposes a tiger that will *never* lie down with the lamb. He is just as fundamental and eternal as the lamb is. To the idea that only lamblike virtues are holy, the poem opposes a God who is just as violent and fiery as the tiger himself. He is not a God whose attributes are the human form divine, but a God who is fiercely indifferent to man. Thus, to the singlemindedness of "The Lamb," "The Tyger" opposes a double perspective that acknowledges both the human values of Mercy, Pity, and Love, and, at the same time, the transhuman values of cruelty, energy, and destructiveness.

For this reason "The Tyger" is not primarily a satirical poem. It submerges its satire beneath its larger concerns. It counters "The Lamb" by embracing both the lamb and the tiger, and it accomplishes this by embracing two attitudes at once. That is the brilliant service performed by the device of the question. The first stanza, for example, really makes two statements at once. The speaker's incredulity when confronted by a tiger who is just as fundamental as a lamb is the incredulity of one who is still close to the standpoint of *Innocence.* Could *God* have made this ferocity? Is there, after all, radical evil in the world? Can it be that the God who made the tiger is a tiger-God? The speaker's astonishment is that of a man who confronts for the first time the possibility that what is divine may not be what is reassuring in terms of human values, may indeed be entirely evil from the exclusively human perspective. All sympathetic readers of the poem have experienced this evocation of an evil that in human terms remains evil. Blake meant us to experience this, as we know from such phrases in the first draft as "cruel fire," "horrid ribs," and "sanguine woe."

Nevertheless, Blake canceled these phrases because they interfered with an equally powerful affirmative motif in the poem. This is easily seen when the moral astonishment of the question is transformed into something quite different by converting the question to a statement:

> Tyger, Tyger burning bright
> In the forests of the night
> None but immortal hand or eye
> Could frame thy fearful symmetry.

That would simplify the poem quite as much as "horrid ribs" and "sanguine woe," but it would also show that the *language* of the poem makes an affirmation that is just as powerful as its horrified confrontation of radical evil.

That is because the tiger is not simply burning; he is burning bright. His ferocity and destructiveness are not diminished by his brightness, but transfigured by it. His world

The illustrated plate of "The Tyger," from Songs of Innocence and of Experience.

is the night—dangerous, and deadly—but "forests," like "bright" transfigures all that dread. Blake's usual word for a tiger's habitat was "desart" (**"The Little Girl Lost"**)and it was the word normally used by Blake's contemporaries, if we may judge from Charles Lamb's misquotation of the line [in a 15 May 1824 letter]: "In the desarts of the night." "Forests," on the other hand, suggests tall straight forms, a world that for all its terror has the orderliness of the tiger's stripes or Blake's perfectly balanced verses. The phrase for such an animal and such a world is "fearful symmetry," and it would be a critical error to give preponderance either to that terror or that beauty.

Nor should we regard the image summoned up by the incantation of the first line as anything less than a symbol of all that is dreadful in the world. For the terror of the vision corresponds to the terror of the created thing itself—the *felis tigris*. No other animal combines so much beauty with so much terror. The symbol of the natural fact is grounded in the natural fact. The speaker's terror thus constitutes an insight that is just as profound as the poet's admiration of the tiger's beauty, and to disregard that terror is to trivialize the poem. **"The Tyger"** is not about two modes of looking at a tiger but about the nature of the creation.

In the **"Proverbs of Hell,"** Blake had celebrated the divinity of natural strife and energy, and in the revision of *There Is No Natural Religion* he had stated quite unambiguously: "He who sees the Infinite in *all* things sees God." There can be no doubt that **"The Tyger"** is, among other things, a poem that celebrates the holiness of tigerness. This aspect of the poem is reminiscent of one of the Proverbs of Hell: "The roaring of lions, the howling of wolves, the raging of the stormy sea, and the destructive sword, are portions of eternity too great for the eye of man." But the poem is a far greater statement of this religious faith than the proverb, because the mere assertion that the terrors of creation have a holiness transcending the human perspective is too complacent to be believed. How can this confident assertion be too great for the eye of man? Though the raging of the sea may be holy, it is merely terrible to the man at sea, unmitigably evil and malignant. Blake's accomplishment in **"The Tyger"** is to preserve the divine perspective without relinquishing the human. The union of terror with admiration makes the general tone of the poem that of religious awe, but this general tone is compounded of two attitudes that never altogether collapse into one another.

In the second stanza, Blake continues to evoke the doubleness of the tiger in images which suggest equally God and the Devil:

> In what distant deeps or skies
> Burnt the fire of thine eyes?

Is the tiger's fire from the deeps of Hell or the heights of Heaven? Whether good or evil, the fire has a provenance beyond the realm where human good or evil have any meaning.

> On what wings dare he aspire?
> What the hand dare seize the fire?

Did the immortal dare to fly like Satan through chaos?

Did he dare like Prometheus to bring the fire from Heaven?

As the God begins to form the tiger, the immensity of his power takes precedence over the daring of his exploit:

> And what shoulder and what art
> Could twist the sinews of thy heart?

The twisting shoulder of the god forms the twisting sinews of the tiger's heart. This imaginative identification of the tiger and the god carries the same kind of double-edged implication as the preceding images. The identification of the tiger and his creator turns the god into a tiger: if that shoulder could make that heart, what must be the heart of the god? The divine artist plays with ferocity out of ferocity. Yet if the god is a tiger, then the tiger is a god. The fire of those eyes is the spark of divinity. As the astonished and uncertain mind of the speaker shifts alternatively from god to tiger he lapses into an incoherent confusion that makes no literal sense (the couplet is an unassimilated vestige from an earlier draft) but makes good dramatic sense:

> And when that heart began to beat
> What dread hand and what dread feet?

Finally, the creation of the tiger is seen not as an act of ruthless physical daring and power but as an act of fiery craftsmanship in a fantastic smithy. This is Blake's favorite image for artistic creation, whether it be the creation of a tiger, a world, a religion, or a poem. The fiery forge is a place where incandescent energy and artistic control meet, just as they meet in the fearful symmetry of the tiger. As the rhythmic pulses of the verse fall like hammer blows, the speaker looks alternatively at the maker and the thing made, in an ecstasy of admiration and empty horror:

> What the hammer? What the chain?

[The hammer is wielded by the god, the chain is beaten by the hammer.]

> In what furnace was thy brain?
> What the anvil? What dread grasp
> Dare its deadly terrors clasp?

The staccato beats of controlled fury are succeeded by a stanza of immense calm that enormously widens the imaginative range of the poem. It is a highly compressed and difficult stanza, but it is perhaps the finest moment in Blake's poetry:

> When the stars threw down their spears,
> And water'd heaven with their tears,
> Did he smile his work to see?
> Did he who made the Lamb make thee?

The effect of the last two lines is to throw into clear relief the unresolved conflict between the divine perspective that has been implied all along in the poem, and the speaker's terrified and morally affronted perspective. The god smiles, the man cowers. (Of course, God smiled, and the answer to both questions is, "Yes!" The entire stanza is formed from traditional biblical and Miltonic imagery, and within that tradition, "God saw everything that he had made and behold it was very good.") But while the man cowers, he has a growing sense of the reason for

God's smile. It could be a satanic and sadistic smile, but it could also be the smile of the artist who has forged the richest and most vital of possible worlds, a world that contains both the tiger and the lamb.

This broader perspective is introduced in the first two, highly compressed, lines of the stanza. "When the stars threw down their spears" is an allusion to the angelic fall as presented by Milton:

> They astonisht all resistance lost,
> All courage, down their weapons dropt.
>   [*Paradise Lost* VII. lines 1838 f.]

The defeat of the rebellious angels is followed by their being cast into Hell, which is followed in turn by the creation of the world. That moment of the angelic defeat is therefore a decisive moment in the divine plan. The fall of the angels is the prelude to the fall of man, and in the tradition it is thus the prelude to the bringing of death into the world and all our woe. This moment begins the catalogue of evil and cruelty that will include the tiger. Yet the angelic fall was also "his work." To smile at that is to smile at the tiger.

But why does Blake call the rebellious angels "stars"? His reason belongs to the central conception of the poem, and it is given in the next line: "And watered heaven with their tears." The defeat of the angels caused them to weep tears, and these tears, left behind as they plummeted to Hell, became what we now call the stars. The angels are named "stars" proleptically to explain the name now given to their tears. The immediate result of the angelic defeat was therefore the creation of the stars, just as its indirect result was the creation of the world. No doubt, the God whose "work" was the angelic fall is a terrible and inscrutable God, but however terrible his work is, it is sanctified by vitality, order, and beauty. The stars of night are part of the same awesome design as the forests of the night and the fearful symmetry of the tiger. When, therefore, the poet repeats the questions of the first stanza, it is with no less terror but with increased awe. The question is no longer how *could* a god—physically and morally—frame such *fearful* symmetry, but how *dare* God frame such *fearful symmetry*. The last line now emphasizes the artistic daring inherent in a creation that is incredibly rich, and terrifyingly beautiful, and is like God himself beyond human good or evil.

While **"The Tyger"** expresses a religious affirmation that is common to all of Blake's poetry in the 90s, it is the most comprehensive poem Blake produced in that period. Philosophically, of course, it is no more inclusive than **"The Clod and the Pebble,"** *The Marriage of Heaven and Hell,* or *The Book of Urizen,* but in tone it is the most inclusive poem Blake ever wrote. It celebrates the divinity and beauty of the creation and its transcendence of human good and evil without relinquishing the Keatsian awareness that "the miseries of the world Are misery." For all its brevity, its spiritual scope is immense. (pp. 244-52)

E. D. Hirsch, Jr., in his Innocence and Experience: An Introduction to Blake, *Yale University Press, 1964, 335 p.*

S. Foster Damon   (essay date 1965)

[*An American poet, critic, and biographer, Damon established himself as the American pioneer of Blake studies with the publication of* William Blake: His Philosophy and Symbols *(1924). In the following excerpt from his later* Blake Dictionary, *he identifies dichotomy as the central underlying structural and thematic principle of* Songs of Innocence and of Experience.]

[*Songs of Innocence and of Experience*:] "Innocence" was the technical word for the state of the unfallen man; "Experience" was used by Blake to indicate man's state after the Fall. The idea of a single work of two contrasting parts was doubtless suggested by Milton's *L'Allegro* and *Il Penseroso*, which together form a single cyclical work: where either ends, the other begins. But where Milton contrasted gaiety and thoughtfulness, Blake contrasted ecstasy and despair; and he anticipated not repetition but progress to a third state.

Blake's obvious parallels are limited to comparatively few of the poems: the two **"Chimney Sweepers,"** the two **"Nurse's Songs,"** the two **"Holy Thursdays"**; there are also contrasting titles: **"Infant Joy"** and **"Infant Sorrow,"** **"The Divine Image"** and **"A Divine Image."** Some parallel titles are not real contrasts, but different subjects: thus **"The Little Girl Lost"** deals with the death of a child, while **"A Little Girl Lost"** describes her first love affair; and **"The Little Boy Lost"** describes the child's agony at being misled, while the second poem with a similar title tells of his martyrdom for having his own ideas.

Other poems are contrasted only by subject. Thus **"The Lamb"** (God's love) is to be paired with **"The Tyger"** (God's wrath); **"The Blossom"** with **"The Sick Rose"**; and probably **"The Ecchoing Green"** with **"The Garden of Love,"** and **"The Shepherd"** with **"London."** Beyond this, the reader may make his own conjectures, because Blake was not mechanically systematic.

The first poem in the book, the **"Introduction"** to the *Songs of Innocence,* indicates the two Contrary States when the piper plays his tune twice: the first time, the child laughs, and the second time, he weeps. But at the third performance (this time with words) the child weeps with joy—the third stage where the contraries are synthesized. The last poem of the book, **"To Tirzah"** (added about 1795), is a fitting conclusion, as it expresses the third stage—revolution. The lad becomes himself by rejecting the maternal authority, using Jesus' own words to Mary: "Woman, what have I to do with thee?" (*John* ii:4). But the sense goes deeper; for in rejecting the mother, the lad also rejects what his mother gave him: his mortal body, with its closed senses and the misery of sex. When that is transcended, "it is Raised a Spiritual Body" (*I Cor* xv:44). (p. 378)

> S. Foster Damon, in his A Blake Dictionary:
> The Ideas and Symbols of William Blake,
> Brown University Press, 1965, 460 p.

D. G. Gillham   (essay date 1966)

[*Gillham is a South African educator and critic. In the*

following excerpt, he contends that Songs of Innocence and of Experience *requires only straightforward, close study of each poem in the context of the work as a whole rather than interpretation informed by historical, biographical, or oeuvre-related issues. He also asserts that Blake maintains detachment from the views advanced in any specific lyric: "Blake's own voice is detected in the purpose that governs the assembly of the* Songs *rather than in any particular utterance."*]

Most Blake studies are based on the assumption that the poet requires allowances to be made for his unusual manner of writing. The ***Songs of Innocence and of Experience*** most decidedly do not require a special critical technique. . . . Blake's intention may best be discovered by a patient reading of the poems themselves without forcing on to them assistance that only a specialized knowledge can give. . . . [The ***Songs of Innocence and of Experience***] explain themselves if they are read together. Each poem must be read for its own sake, but it may most adequately be read by a mind that is informed by the remainder of the poems.

No period of history is very remote when seen through the eyes of a poet, and Blake is very much our contemporary because we are still attempting to come to terms with the rationalism that, by stimulating his antagonism, provoked his complex insight. Though we do not need the help of a special knowledge in order to understand the problems of our poet, [it is useful to note intellectual developments] of Blake's own time. This is not done on the supposition that the poetry can be explained in terms of influences that were brought to bear upon Blake, but in order to remind us of our own problems, and to throw into relief the qualities of Blake's peculiar genius in meeting those problems.

During the twentieth century a great deal has been written about Blake; most commentators have had something to say about the ***Songs,*** but for a number of reasons the commentaries on these short poems have been disappointing. Perhaps Blake is, himself, partly to blame for this. His 'Prophetic Books', by their obscure and involved construction, invite a ponderous and mysterious explanation, and the ***Songs,*** regarded as an adjunct of the 'Prophecies', are crushed beneath the weight of an exegesis they cannot bear. This is true even of Joseph Wicksteed's [*Blake's Innocence and Experience*], which sets out to make a restrained and unpretentious examination of the poems, which succeeds in making many valuable observations, but cannot sustain its moderation. Wicksteed falls often into sentimentality and sometimes overloads the poems with 'symbolic' significances culled from his knowledge of the 'Prophetic Works'.

Since the publication of Wicksteed's book three others have appeared which concentrate their attention on Blake's earlier and shorter writings. Stanley Gardner insists, in his work [*Infinity on the Anvil: A Critical Study of Blake's Poetry*], that 'We cannot find the key to the meaning of the early books by reading the final books'; we must 'interpret the symbolism in its interrelationship, each symbol in its context'. This is a sensible approach, and Gardner's discussion of the ***Songs of Experience*** is particularly valuable. In R. F. Gleckner's work [*The Piper* *and the Bard*] the **Songs** are forced into a rigid framework of 'symbolic' meanings derived from the 'Prophecies', and the analysis distorts the poetry. In the most recent work, [*Innocence and Experience*], E. D. Hirsch discusses the two sets of songs on the assumption that they 'express two distinct outlooks that Blake in each case held with an unqualified vigor and fervor of belief'. This assumption seems wrong, but the critical insights of the writer are good, especially in discussion of *The Songs of Innocence.*

The reader's attention is beckoned away from the **Songs** by Blake's eccentric manner of composing his poetry as well as by the 'mythology' of the 'Prophetic Books'. In putting together his verse he was in the habit of using fragments ('odds and ends', as Eliot calls them) from his wide and unusual reading. Much careful research has gone into tracing the influence on Blake's verse of various philosophers, of writers in the Hermetic tradition, and of the tensions and events of his day. For the reader of the **Songs**, however, the fruits of this research are not very helpful, and may even obscure the poetry by demanding a kind of attention that is not warranted. Blake so radically transformed the material he used, it became so very much subordinated to his own way of looking at things, that a knowledge of its origins usually seems irrelevant.

The complicated 'mythology' of Blake's later works and the idiosyncratic manner in which he chose to write them have both militated against the **Songs** receiving what they most need: a careful appreciation of their tone. Overwhelmed by the apparent need for a special exegetical apparatus, the reader is distracted from applying to the poems the sort of sensitivity that would be given poetry found in a less unusual setting. The **Songs** themselves are not idiosyncratic, but it is supposed that they should be, and the accepted tools of the reader are abandoned. Normally, we realize very soon whether a poet is speaking on his own behalf (through the mouth of an imagined character, perhaps) or is presenting us with a persona (with some character whom we cannot take as being the poet's direct representative). In lyrical poetry, it is true, we may very often take the sentiments offered as being the poet's very own, but this is not always so. In the **Songs** this decidedly cannot be the case, certainly not always—there is too marked a diversity in the attitudes presented.

One would expect the reader of the **Songs,** on making this discovery, to take all the poems with some caution; to wonder, when reading every one of them, if Blake is speaking in his own voice, or if he is presenting a possible attitude for our inspection. The outcome of such an examination should be the realization that none of the **Songs** can be taken simply as a direct personal utterance. Innocence is not self-aware in a way that allows it to describe itself, and the poet must stand outside the state. From the mocking tone of many of the **Songs of Experience** it is clear that the poet does not suffer from the delusions he associates with that condition. Again, the poet stands beyond the state depicted. Blake, in short, is detached from the conditions of awareness imposed on the speakers of his poems.

Blake's critics do not follow the clue given by his tone, however, and, although the best commentaries all have glimpses of the detachment, the insight is sporadic and soon set aside. The poet is identified with one selection from the **Songs** or another, or, in an attempt to make them all emanate from the poet, it is stated that we may take the **Songs of Innocence** to belong to an earlier and hopeful period while the **Songs of Experience** belong to a later condition of disillusionment. The critics have been determined that Blake should commit himself in some part of the **Songs,** and this determination is understandable. The poems are obviously the work of a thinker, and this thinker identifies himself, sometimes, with the prophet, which suggests that he might wish to lay down some definite guide to conduct. The philosopher and the prophet are usually men with a message, are men with formed and finalized ideas, and the poet appears to resemble them, particularly a poet with the decided manner of speaking shown by Blake. Wicksteed, for example, will sometimes find Blake's commitment in such songs as '**London**' or '**The Garden of Love**', which show natural human propensities being smothered by institution. But Blake is too good a thinker to be putting forward the Godwinian idea as an explanation of man, though he does put it forward as being indicative of one of the shoals on which the human vessel may run itself aground. The idea may chart a point in Blake's psychology but it does not define his 'philosophy'. In '**London**' Blake does not express his despair of the human condition, but depicts a condition of despair, not necessarily his own. All the songs depict 'states of the soul', as the title-page tells us, and Blake's own voice is detected in the purpose that governs the assembly of the **Songs** rather than in any particular utterance.

Blake has no message, or 'philosophy', and would not be more worth reading as a poet if he had. He offers something better: a serious and responsible consideration of the ways in which human energy may manifest itself. In the course of his study he touches on various ideas of the nature of man, but not because he regards any of them as absolutely true, as saying the last word on what we are. His concern is a moral one and he makes (or implies) a judgement of the positions he describes, though he does not dispute their truth. Any -ism is true for the person who believes it to be so, though it does not follow that all such truths may be said to reflect a decent condition of the mind. They are to be judged according to the fullness of the life that (it may be inferred) supports them. Although he refers us to various dogmas in his description of the states, Blake subscribes to no one of them, he presents no ultimate truths but leaves us to forge our own. He does attempt to awaken us to the responsibility of becoming alive to the best truths of which we are capable, but the poet detaches himself from the task of saying what those truths should be.

There was a strong tendency during the eighteenth century to view man simply as the outcome of education and conditioning. He was seen as an intelligent animal, but the intelligence itself was conceived as a calculating faculty, enabling him to make use of his experience to civilize himself. There were no fundamental impulses in the individual that could properly be called moral, but men could estimate that it would serve them well to behave according to an accepted morality. In the course of the **Songs of Ex-**

perience Blake often presents us with this conception of human nature, and implies that it may appear true to those who have lost their benign impulses. They need control from without and the restraint of self-interested conformity if they are to behave well. In the ***Songs of Innocence,*** however, Blake presents us with beings who cannot be accounted for on this explanation. These songs do not present us with persons equipped with premeditated or formulated moral notions, it is true, but we are shown individuals with affectionate and sympathetic impulses that dispose them to benign forms of conduct.

In ***The Songs of Experience*** Blake allows some of his characters to affirm the values and theories of rationalism, but he emphasizes that these are valid for the mind working in a superficial way only, and he describes the alternative mentality of Innocence. This alternative is not put forward as an original character or as a stage in the development of man, but as a condition of perfection, a completeness and harmony of being. Because we usually recognize this in children, we associate it with ignorance—the child shows its simple faith and wholehearted vitality because it knows so little, has not entered into the cares of a more responsible time of life. Blake is not setting up an ideal of childishness, however, and his Innocents are not all children. All men have their innocent moments, though what constitutes an innocent poise at one time of life will not be proper at another, and what will indicate perfection of balance for one person will not do so for some other. What is important is that we have known the perfection of Innocence, and though we can no more induce a state of perfection in ourselves than we can return to childhood, we are provided, by this knowledge, with a measure of the success of our more deliberate activities.

The measure is an inarticulate one, is an intuition of the sort of thing we can hope for and not a programme we can follow, but it does provide us with a more fundamental and constant guide than convention or rational argument can offer. One convention can drive out another and arguments are subject to endless amendment, but as they pass into the mind they come under the control of a being who has known affection, sympathy, fascination and delight, and who, therefore, has a touchstone (a sort of conscience) which, without our being able to give a detailed and explicit account of what it is, directs our more articulate and deliberate impulses. By introducing us, in the ***Songs,*** to the concept of Innocence Blake shows a dimension of the mind which the eighteenth century chose to ignore because there was no formula for it. (pp. 1-7)

> *D. G. Gillham, in his* Blake's Contrary States: The "Songs of Innocence and of Experience" as Dramatic Poems, *Cambridge at the University Press, 1966, 258 p.*

Nick Shrimpton   (essay date 1976)

[*In the following essay, Shrimpton examines* Songs of Innocence and of Experience *as a work that arose from an eighteenth-century tradition of children's hymns.*]

Blake's strangeness is of two kinds. There is first the strangeness of creative originality, of genius, a peculiarity which, in Eliot's words, 'is seen to be the peculiarity of all great poetry'. But even after we have made this recognition there remains an oddness. This second, enduring strangeness is one of form. Having come to realize that Blake's literary manner is not merely idiosyncratic and spontaneous we are left with the fact that the public and, in the best sense, conventional forms which he uses are now unfamiliar ones. We can sense the imaginative vitality of ***The Marriage of Heaven and Hell*** without knowing that it is an imitation of a Swedenborgian treatise. We cannot, however, properly understand or enjoy it without realizing that the form is not arbitrary but referential and that such reference is part of its meaning. Similarly our reading of the so-called Prophetic Books depends in important ways upon our appreciation of the extent to which their form is derived from the Ossianic epic or the Bible. As we begin to understand the nature and the contemporary currency of such modes we begin to appreciate how Blake uses them. Most important of all, because it is the least conspicuous and therefore potentially the most deceptive, we are beginning to understand the form of Blake's lyrics. They remain strange poems in my second sense if we come to them with expectations derived only from what the anthologies present as the mainstream of the English lyric. Diverse as that lyric form may be, and broadly as any general tradition must be conceived, the ***Songs of Innocence and of Experience*** still stand outside, still seem different.

The reason for this is simple. They spring from an exceptionally specialized branch of the lyric which happened to be very active in the latter part of the eighteenth century: the children's hymn. The genre can be traced back at least as far as Bunyan, received its greatest impetus from Isaac Watt's *Divine Songs Attempted in easy Language for the use of Children* (1715) and subsequently flourished in the hands of such writers as Charles Wesley (*Hymns for Children,* 1763), Christopher Smart (*Hymns for the Amusement of Children,* 1770), and Mrs Barbauld (*Hymns in Prose for Children,* 1781). One of Blake's very few contemporary reviewers, writing in the *Monthly Review* in October 1806, was, however inept in other respects, at least in no doubt that the literary company in which Blake's ***Songs*** should be set was that of Dr Watts. In terms of quality there is a great gap between Blake and contemporary hymn-writers, but this does not mean that, in so far as our response to the ***Songs of Innocence and Experience*** depends upon a correct sense of form, we can afford to ignore this peculiar tradition. Accordingly there has in recent years been no shortage of work upon this topic of the precise genre of Blake's ***Songs.*** What is curious is that such work has been undertaken in isolation from the very vexed question of the meaning of the ***Songs of Innocence and of Experience,*** a question which depends essentially upon the interpretation of certain of the ***Songs of Innocence*** and the consequent tone of that book. I would like to suggest that a reading of other poems of this particular kind can help us to understand what Blake is saying.

What I have called a tradition is itself twofold. John Holloway [in his *Blake, The Lyric Poetry*] has both paid close attention to Blake's use of hymn metres and usefully extended the comparison beyond the customary authors to the hymns of Philip Doddridge. But he simultaneously reminds us of the importance to Blake's poems of 'the impress of popular verse tradition'. One might add that it is not only Blake who draws on popular literature. All these hymn-writers, particularly when they address children, deliberately exploit a popular medium. General Booth was by no means the first Christian to feel that the devil should not have all the best tunes. In the last decades of the eighteenth century a flourishing popular form was being reorchestrated by the godly with extraordinary energy. In numerical terms the most startling manifestation of this enthusiasm came in 1794 when Hannah More founded the *Cheap Repository Tracts,* with the intention of rescuing the new readers produced by Sunday schools from the vulgarity of popular chapbooks and the subversive influence of cheap editions of Paine. With characteristic thoroughness Miss More assembled a collection of penny literature and imitated the stories and ballads which she found there. She wrote to Zachary Macaulay [in a letter dated 6 January 1795]:

> Vulgar and indecent penny books were always common, but speculative infidelity, brought down to the pockets and capacity of the poor, forms a new aera in our history. This requires strong counteraction.

And to a Mrs Bouverie she explained her methods [in a letter dated 24 January 1795]:

> . . . it has occurred to me to write a variety of things somewhere between vicious papers and hymns, for it is vain to write what people will not read.

Between 1795 and 1798 one hundred and fourteen tracts were published, with phenomenal success. By the March of 1796 over two million copies had been sold. Hannah More had achieved, in material terms at least, the supreme success in a genre which had been active in other hands as well as hers throughout the 1780s and 1790s, an art strenuously devoted to religious and political persuasion and aimed with a significant lack of discrimination at both children and the poor. Whether Blake shared William Cobbett's ungallant opinion of Miss More ('an old bishop in petticoats') we do not know. What is certain, however, is that his decision to write children's hymns was not an eccentric one. It was a decision to participate in what was to be the most prolific and controversial literary form of the decade.

Our knowledge of this form provides an immediate explanation of Blake's choice of topics. The animal poem, the flower poem, and the insect poem were all traditional features of collections of children's verse, in which such objects functioned as moral exempla. Similarly Blake's poems about lost children are using a fairy-tale situation immensely popular in contemporary ballads. Blake is not inventing, he is transforming a convention. And the word 'transforming' is important. He is not like his contemporaries simply exploiting a popular form for didactic purposes. Neither is he merely working in the popular medium. If one wanted a diagram it would have three stages: Blake is parodying the imitation of a popular form. But the parody, which is at the same time both mockingly de-

rivative and seriously original, is a form very much his own. A great virtue of such a mode is that statements do not have to be made directly. Meaning can emerge from what is not said, from the disappointment of expectation, from the ways in which poems significantly do not altogether resemble their models.

A contemporary example can perhaps sharpen our sense of how such a literary stratagem works. In 1973 Charles Causley published [in the *Sunday Times,* 21 October 1973] a poem singularly apposite to the discussion of Blake's *Songs,* entitled *On Being Asked to Write a School Hymn.* It goes, we are told, in a way in which Blake's contemporaries might not have needed telling, to the tune Buckland ('Loving Shepherd of Thy Sheep'). Causley's sheep are in the abattoir:

> On a starless night and still
> Underneath a sleeping hill
> Comes the cry of sheep and kine
> From the slaughter house to mine.

The form refers us to familiar ideas, the statement rejects them. The point that emerges from the specifically parodic aspect of the poem is that while the conventional symbolism of God as a shepherd provides a very effective manifestation of care and compassion it does so only at the cost of seriously distorting the nature of that God's involvement in the world: conventionally, the symbolism is truncated, the shepherd postpones the job of turning his sheep into cutlets. In Causley's poem a God who is present everywhere is present in the slaughterhouse:

> But who wields that knife and gun
> Does not strike the blow alone,
> And there is no place to stand
> Other than at his right hand.

A reader with no experience of English hymn-singing would doubtless find some meaning in the poem, although the verse form and diction might appear eccentric. But such a meaning would be a peculiar and limited one compared with that available to readers who have dutifully sung their way through *Hymns Ancient and Modern.* The situation is precisely analogous to that of Blake's *Songs.* The eighteenth-century children's hymn may now seem a negligible literary fossil, but its presence is essential to the life of Blake's poems.

Parody of this serious kind can work either by inclusion or by omission. Causley's method is inclusion: he puts into his poems facts about the world which more conventional users of the form choose to overlook. Blake's *Songs* use both inclusion of this kind and its reverse: significant omission of conventional details or attitudes. In the *Songs of Experience* Blake's inclusions or additions are obvious. But what are the differences that constitute so large a part of the meaning of the *Songs of Innocence*? On the face of it there has been no shortage of commentary. Vivian de Sola Pinto [in 'William Blake, Isaac Watts, and Mrs. Barbauld' in her *The Divine Vision: Studies in the Poetry and Art of W. Blake*] has set **'A Little Boy Lost'** against Watts's Song XXIII with the suggestion that Blake's poem is surely intended as a reply to the 'fierce Old Testament morality' of this reproach to childish misbehaviour.

D. V. Erdman [in his *Blake, Prophet against Empire*] has compared Mrs Barbauld's *Hymns in Prose* with Blake's poems, suggesting rather unspecifically that Blake echoes them with gently parodic intention. M. W. England has compared Blake and Wesley and in the process has suggested several differences between Blake and other writers ['Wesley's Hymns for Children and Blake's *Songs*' in M. W. England and J. Sparrow, *Hymns Unbidden: Donne, Herbert, Blake, Emily Dickinson and the Hymnographers*]. Bunyan, Watts, and Mrs Barbauld she declares to 'abound in moralistic injunctions'. Watts and Bunyan are preoccupied with instilling a fear of hell. Smart and Mrs Barbauld present a world in which fear has no place at all. 'Blake', she declares, 'offered his little lambs no such bland and Rousseauistic picture of life. Certainly Wesley did not.' There remain, however, differences between Blake and Wesley. John Holloway indicates one of them simply by quoting a stanza from [Hymn C of] Wesley's 'Hymns for the Youngest':

> O Father, I am but a child,
>   My body is made of the earth,
> My nature, alas! is defiled,
>   And a sinner I was from my birth.

An uneasy hesitation between children as a symbol of innocence and a conviction that children's nature 'is defiled' is an integral part of the tradition and is something that Blake's poems conspicuously omit. Holloway's own study of 'considered and intended difference' between Blake's work and that of his predecessors produces two main conclusions. First he argues that while other writers impose an adult morality upon children Blake was writing songs, '. . . such that, in a sense, they could come spontaneously from children'. Secondly he suggests that while Blake retains the 'pastoral and beatific side' of the other writers' religious feelings he 'totally repudiates the sin-and-retribution side'. How can these scattered judgements best be organized? Perhaps the least confusing method is to revert to my two categories of parody. Blake does omit 'sin-and-retribution' or 'fierce Old Testament morality' but it is important to recognize the way in which he does so. He presents pleasure as something self-justifying. There are a number of poems in the *Songs of Innocence,* most notably **'Spring'** and **'Laughing Song'**, about which it is genuinely hard for critics to find anything to say. They seem simply expressions of mood. But in the context of the tradition we can see that to present this mood of pleasure without any attendant moralizing does in itself constitute the expression of a moral attitude. Children's hymns were written to improve children, not to celebrate their instinctive behaviour. Compare Blake's two poems with Watts's Song XX ('Against Idleness and Mischief'):

> In Works of Labour, or of Skill,
>   I would be busy too:
> For *Satan* finds some Mischief still
>   For idle Hands to do.
>
> In Books, or Work, or healthful Play,
>   Let my first years be past,
> That I may give for every Day
>   Some good Account at last.

Even when Watts unbends sufficiently to write a poem supposedly praising play, as in his song 'Innocent Play', he is still essentially preaching. John Holloway suggests that Smart's poem 'Mirth' more nearly approaches Blake's *Songs* than almost anything else in the genre. Yet even here there is an intrusion of a kind which significantly does not occur in **'Spring'** or the **'Laughing Song'**:

> With white and crimson laughs the sky,
>   With birds the hedge-rows ring;
> To give the praise to God most high,
> And all the sulky fiends defy,
>   Is a most joyful thing.

The difference also affects the way in which the traditional *exempla,* especially animals, are used. In most children's hymns animals simply perform ethical object lessons, either of dreadful warning ('Let Dogs delight to bark and bite') or of corrective encouragement like Watts's doves and lambs. Blake's animals do not come from this moral circus ring. The children in the **'Nurse's Song'** of *Songs of Innocence* are not, for once, exhorted to improve themselves on the model of ideal birds and sheep. Rather they themselves use the behaviour of real sheep and real birds as an argument with which to contradict an adult opinion. The sheep endorse the children's instincts. And this omission of preaching involves a preliminary omission of the belief that children are unredeemed sinners. Children's instincts are significantly not reproved. Simultaneously the importance of children is actively heightened. Christ is so much identified with children that adults must feel humble. In **'A Cradle Song'** the mother states:

> Sweet babe, once like thee,
> Thy maker lay and wept for me.

'Wept' not just 'for thee' but 'for *me*'—the detail is minute, but the contrast with, say, Watts's 'A Cradle Hymn' is marked. The lesson is for adults as well as for children.

Omission in fact adds up into an argument. What is more, the argument is one which strikes at the heart of the form in which it is presented. The children's hymn and the moralized ballad for the poor (forms which, as I suggested while discussing Hannah More's tracts, often overlap) were essentially designed to keep children and the poor in their place. The form is characteristically a repressive one. Blake's *Songs* were certainly written for children, though not exclusively so, but like all children's literature they had to be bought by adults who wished to teach or improve. Yet Blake's poems encourage children to believe their own instincts to be superior to any adult instruction. The poems implicitly reject the very act of teaching. A habitual customer of Mrs Barbauld or Miss More who, with educative intention, bought a copy of the *Songs of Innocence* for his children would have been the victim of a gigantic confidence trick, a trick fully worthy of a man who would write a Swedenborgian treatise in refutation of Swedenborg. At the end of that treatise, having already produced the Proverbs of Hell, Blake threatens to give us yet another inversion of a familiar form: 'The Bible of Hell.' It is I think not altogether fanciful to suggest that in the *Songs of Innocence and of Experience* he is, in the same sense, offering us the children's hymns of Hell.

I have not, however, yet mentioned the way in which

Blake's *Songs of Innocence* are parodic by inclusion. The most useful example is the poem **'Night'** and the most relevant comparison is here with Mrs Barbauld. Her *Hymns in Prose for Children* are designed to be devotional rather than doctrinal but that choice of emphasis is no excuse for the fact that when doctrine does emerge, as inevitably it must, it is heavily censored. Her fifth hymn is, like Blake's poem, about night. The difference between the two poems arises when they come to the question of the dangers of the night. Mrs Barbauld, as M. W. England has pointed out, pretends that such dangers do not really exist:

> You may sleep, for he never sleeps: you may close your eyes in safety, for his eye is always open to protect you.

> When the darkness is passed away . . . begin the day with praising God, who hath taken care of you through the night.

In Blake's **'Night'** the angels are equally protective but they are not always successful. As in Charles Causley's poem, suffering and death, which the form habitually ignores, are included. Blake presents, however simply, an unusually full version of one Christian explanation of pain. God does not protect us in this world, his consolation is a posthumous one:

> When wolves and tygers howl for prey,
> They pitying stand and weep;
> Seeking to drive their thirst away,
> And keep them from the sheep;
> But if they rush dreadful,
> The angels, most heedful,
> Recieve each mild spirit,
> New worlds to inherit.

In the *Songs of Experience* Blake is to question the adequacy of this doctrine in **'The Tyger'** and **'Ah! Sun-Flower'**. In the *Songs of Innocence* he simply states the doctrine in full, an activity which seems unspectacular only as long as we are unaware of its literary context. Blake's statement raises questions which children's hymns normally attempt to suppress.

The scale of the questions thus raised brings one necessarily to the problem of the political poems, the poems upon which our conception of the structure and meaning of the *Songs of Innocence and of Experience* ultimately depends. In a sense, such division of Blake's poems by topic is misleading. Fundamentally they cohere around the single theme of protection. Blake's interest is in the relationship between protection and oppression, in asking at what point loving care becomes possession or tyranny. This act of protection underlies many different relationships: parent protects child (the paradigm), ruler protects subject, philanthropist protects pauper, priest protects believer, lover protects lover, God protects his creation. Once the *Songs of Experience* are added to the account the same acts become acts rather of oppression and domination. All Blake's *Songs,* however diverse their immediate topics, address themselves to this problem, with, I think, the single exception of the subsequently added **'To Tirzah'**. None the less the surface topics remain diverse and one is politics, the relationship between ruler and ruled, between employer and employee. And at this point I think I should explain what I meant when I said initially that work on the genre of Blake's *Songs* had been undertaken in isolation from the question of their meaning. In view of my obvious debt to M. W. England and John Holloway in what I have said so far it may well be asked why I should make such a suggestion. The point is that these crucial political poems, above all **'The Chimney Sweeper'** and **'Holy Thursday'**, have not, with the exception of a brief, and I think misleading, note by R. F. Gleckner [in 'Blake and Wesley' in *Notes and Queries* n.s.iii (1956)], been considered in the context of the hymn tradition.

Fundamentally [*Songs of Innocence and of Experience*] cohere around the single theme of protection. Blake's interest is in the relationship between protection and oppression, in asking at what point loving care becomes possession or tyranny.

—*Nick Shrimpton*

A great deal has been written to show, by historical evidence, just how horrific was the treatment of chimney-sweeps and of children in Charity Schools. Such critics have assumed, quite justifiably, that Blake was in the 1780s fully aware of such facts, and they have then gone on to assume, with altogether less justification, that **'The Chimney Sweeper'** and the **'Holy Thursday'** of the *Songs of Innocence* are therefore ironic. How could a man who knew these things, the argument runs, have uttered the pious and contented morals of these poems without ironic intention? The argument is supported by two important pieces of evidence. **'Holy Thursday'** first appeared in the satirical *An Island in the Moon* in the mouth of the ridiculous Mr Obtuse Angle. Secondly, Blake continued for many years after the completion of the joint *Songs of Innocence and of Experience* to issue separate editions of the *Songs of Innocence*; which contradicts suggestions either that Blake simply changed his mind or that he originally wrote the *Songs of Innocence* as a mere target for *Experience.* The objection to these ironic interpretations of the *Songs of Innocence* is essentially a literary one. Why, when you have written a work of subtle and brilliant irony, add a further section saying the same things in a manner which must by comparison seem lumberingly direct and explicit? I do not believe that the two books are merely repetitive. They offer, in Blake's own word, 'contraries'. **'Night'** is not an ironic poem, though it is parodic in the sense that it makes implicit criticism of the inadequacies of conventional versions of what it has to say. Rather it gives a sincere and carefully complete account of what Blake believes to be the Christian position against which are subsequently set the views of **'The Tyger'** and **'Ah! Sun-Flower'**. All the *Songs,* in my opinion, including the political ones, present just such a tension between contradictory but independently coherent views. But what then, the question remains, is the independently coherent view expressed in 'The Chimney Sweeper' and the 'Holy Thursday' of *Innocence*? What makes it possible for Blake to go on issuing, without correction from a 'contrary', these seeming endorsements of a cruel social *status quo*?

D. V. Erdman has offered the most satisfying account of the way in which Blake's two sets of songs interact as 'contraries'. Discussing those Songs of Innocence which first appear in **An Island in the Moon** he observes that,

> . . .the same songs removed from this matrix . . . are plainly not presented as satire. Their social purpose is larger—to construct one of the foundations of an imaginatively organized and truly happy prosperity.

He adds that Blake,

> . . . having set out to present the obtuse view as something he could see beyond . . . discovered through his own mockery that he could see much *through* the shut eyes of 'the Good' who 'think not for themselves'.

He adduces in support of this contention those annotations to Lavater's *Aphorisms on Man* in which Blake calls true superstition 'ignorant honesty . . . beloved of god and man' and praises Lavater's declaration that the saints of humanity are those who practise unconscious goodness, 'heroes with infantine simplicity'. This goes a long way towards providing us with an explanation of **'Holy Thursday'**. The innocent speaker of that poem is certainly simple. Quite apart from any abuses in their management, the Charity Schools were more than a little suspect in their claim to altruism. They were carefully designed not to educate children above their station and thereby provided society with a steady supply of soldiers and domestic servants. Yet Blake can celebrate the instinct of charity which prompts the speaker's delight, however ill-informed that delight may be. The speaker is profoundly wrong in his analysis of what Charity Schools are like. But he is profoundly right in his naive sense of what Charity Schools should be. And the **'Holy Thursday'** of the **Songs of Experience** confirms this reading. For the logical structure of that poem depends at a crucial point upon just such an innocent intimation. The declaration,

> For where-e'er the sun does shine,
> And where-e'er the rain does fall,
> Babe can never hunger there,
> Nor poverty the mind appall,

is not a deduction from experience. On the contrary it flies in the face of observed fact. The moral impulse is an instinctive one and can express itself whether one is making the best or the worst interpretation of an existing institution or doctrine (that being the difference between the two **'Holy Thursday'**s as it is between so many of the directly contrary **Songs**). Yet convincing as Erdman's analysis may be we remain rather unclear as to just what this 'organized innocence' is that the **Songs of Innocence** are so sincerely advocating. In **'Holy Thursday'** it is perhaps a question of the moral instinct. But what about **'The Chimney Sweeper'**? Erdman states merely: '. . . all that the happy piper can provide for comfort is the inner warmth of faith'. What does that mean? In what way can innocence here

hold its own against the acute sociological analysis of *Experience*? It is here I think that the hymn tradition can once again help us.

The only book of Wesley's hymns which we certainly know Blake to have read is *Hymns for the Nation* (1782). His copy survives, autographed and dated: 'W Blake 1790'. But whether or not he ever read Wesley's *Hymns for the use of Families and on Various Occasions* (1767) the book provides us with an illustration of contemporary attitudes which clarifies our understanding of **'The Chimney Sweeper'**. The hymns in this collection which we now find hardest to accept are those designed for a group of people no longer found in the average family, the servants. But in 1767 servants were an inevitable part of a literate household and Wesley's hymnbook reflects the fact. Essentially these hymns suggest that servants are working not for their immediate, earthly master but rather for the God who has called them to their station:

> Come, let us anew
> Our calling pursue,
> Go forth with the sun,
> And rejoice as a giant our circuit to run:
> 　Whom Jesus commands
> 　To work with our hands,
> 　Obeying his word,
> We a service perform to our heavenly Lord.
>
> While we labour for Him
> And each moment redeem,
> His service we own
> Our freedom indeed, and our heaven begun:
> 　If he give us a smile
> 　We are paid for our toil,
> 　If our work He approve,
> 'Tis a work of the Lord, and a labour of love.
> 　　　　　　　　　　[from Hymn CXXXIII]

If that seems startling then its effect is rapidly eclipsed by a subsequent hymn written for the servant who is subject to a tyrannous master:

> Lord, if Thou hast on me bestow'd
> A master, not humane and good,
> 　But froward and severe,
> Assist the servant of thy will
> With grace and wisdom to fulfil
> 　The Christian character.
>
> Trampled as dirt beneath his feet,
> O may I quietly submit
> 　To all his stern decrees,
> Insults and wrongs in silence bear,
> And serve with conscientious care
> 　Whom I can never please.
>
> Under the gauling iron yoke
> To Thee my only Help I look,
> 　To Thee in secret groan:
> I cannot murmur or complain,
> But meekly all my griefs sustain
> 　For thy dear sake alone.
> 　　　　　　　　　　[from Hymn CXLI]

Our most immediate hostility to such writing probably springs from a suspicion that a self-interested upper class is cynically putting words into servants' mouths. Blake attempts to avoid this effect, and thereby to improve upon

Wesley's expression, by making his poem a dramatic incident, a dialogue between chimney-sweeps in which morals are expressed by the class for whom they are intended. But before we simply condemn Wesley's work I would like to quote a single verse of another of the *Family Hymns,* no. LXXXV:

> Welcome incurable disease,
> Whate'er my gracious God decrees
>   My happy choice I make,
> Death's sentence in myself receive,
> Since God a man of griefs did live,
>   And suffer for my sake.

Our first response is probably laughter—it is not an attractive piece of poetry, overstrenuous perhaps and indelicate. But such laughter is largely an effect of shock and cannot long be justified. For if in such a situation this hymn is a comfort, who are we to withhold it? And the same thing can in fact be said of the hymns for servants. It requires an effort of the historical imagination to grasp how comforting a Methodist conversion must have been for an eighteenth-century servant who one week was simply serving 'A master, not humane and good' and the next was, in his sincere belief, serving God. But that effort must I think be made if we wish to understand Blake's 'The Chimney Sweeper'. Of course Blake's poem, with brutal frankness, stresses the importance to such beliefs of reward in an after-life. But Blake is also concerned with the active and present comfort brought by a sense that labour, though arduous, is at least not pointless: in Wesley's words, ' . . . a work of the Lord, and a labour of love'. We cannot, of course, call this a conventional belief, except in the sense that it was part of the hymn convention that Blake inherited. Such Wesleyan convictions were still in the 1780s exceptional rather than customary. Blake is once again choosing the best available defence of the *status quo,* just as he had given the most generous interpretation of Charity Schools in 'Holy Thursday' and the fullest version of one Christian explanation of pain in 'Night'. Radicals, naturally, came to hate such Methodist attempts to make the poor contented even more violently than they hated the merely cynical or expedient defences of the social system (one thinks perhaps of Cobbett's *Sermon to Methodists*) and 'The Chimney Sweeper' of the *Songs of Experience* expresses just this response. But such hatred arises precisely because this is the most adequate defence of the system, the only defence which itself incorporates something humane and vital. With this belief one might well be harmed but in a very real sense one need not, even in the extreme circumstances of being a chimney-sweep, '*fear* harm'. Wesley in the third stanza of Hymn CXXXIII makes the point through paradox:

> . . . . we cannot complain
> Of our daily delight as a wearisome pain.

In this conception harm is a spiritual delight. Certainly this attitude is an acceptance of existing explanations—in the words of the unused 'Motto to the Songs of Innocence & of Experience',

> The Good are attracted by Men's perceptions,
> And Think not for themselves.

But it is also the case that such attitudes when properly and fully articulated, when chosen in their best expression, are a response to the facts not an evasion of them. As Blake put it in that difficult note written in the margin of the manuscript of *The Four Zoas:*

> Innocence dwells with Wisdom, but never with
> Ignorance.

Merely incomplete or evasive explanations of the world do not constitute 'Innocence'. The *Songs of Innocence* discriminate between the good and bad defences of the established order, presenting in their most adequate form those best defences which themselves incorporate something of value in the human spirit.

Blake's book is therefore both parodic and deeply serious. It makes constant reproachful reference to a literary tradition and in so far as it transforms the attitude to children which lies at the heart of that tradition it stands the form on its head. But in another sense Blake's *Songs of Innocence* simply do very well what most children's hymns had done badly. The *Songs* present the best possible defences and interpretations of the act of protection in its familial, religious, and political contexts, providing for example an account of the protection of children which, unusually, allows them free expression of their instincts (a conception much richer than the protective attitude which produces children's hymns). The strength of the arguments is essential to the achievement of a real tension between contraries. Yet I hope it is also now clear why it is that Blake could continue to issue the *Songs of Innocence* independently. Having chosen to work in a form which is characteristically devoted to the maintenance of the *status quo* Blake is in a sense conforming to its bias. But in doing so he is carefully setting very exacting standards for conservative argument. By making the best defences he suggests the inadequacy of the customary defences. We can, for example, accept the employment of children as chimney-sweeps if we, and they, seriously and consistently believe in a sacramental concept of work—but not otherwise. Even before the *Songs of Experience* are added to the debate, the implication that is beginning to emerge, by simple statement rather than by irony, is that if we cannot in fact have protection of this quality then perhaps we should not have 'protection' at all. (pp. 19-35)

Nick Shrimpton, "Hell's Hymnbook: Blake's 'Songs of Innocence and of Experience' and Their Models," in Literature of the Romantic Period, 1750-1850, *edited by R. T. Davies and B. G. Beatty, Barnes & Noble Books, 1976, pp. 19-35.*

Michele Leiss Stepto   (essay date 1978)

[*Stepto is an American critic and educator specializing in children's literature. In the following essay, she explores both the nurturing and stifling roles of parental figures—mothers, fathers, Nature, and God—in* Songs of Innocence.]

The *Songs of Innocence* are, at one level, exactly and unambiguously what they seem, tender evocations of a state of mind as well as a time of life, infancy and childhood, which is pre-social, largely unconscious, and in full harmony with the natural rhythms of physical life—day and night, pleasure and pain, play and rest, birth, growth, and decay. Of this side of Innocence, Jean Hagstrum has written that it "is in every Western man's own personal history—in childhood, in nature, in the innumerable relations of simple faith—as child to parent, man to woman, teacher to pupil, nurse to ward, human being to angel." In the face of such wholehearted evocations of this state as **"Laughing Song," "Spring,"** and **"Infant Joy,"** it may seem perverse to search for signs of the darker vision which fills the *Songs of Experience* and the Prophetic Books; but if we are to understand Blake's later, fully developed creation, the Female Will, this is exactly what we must do, for its roots lie in the gentle mothers and nurses of Innocence and generally in the parental love—typified by mothers but embracing fathers as well—which is the chief subject of these early songs. Although the reader may find that the more glorious side of Blake's Innocence is given somewhat short shrift in what follows, he should not forget—nor, the writer hopes, will she—that it exists always, irradiating these songs and, as Blake tells us, life itself.

The double nature of Innocence is broached in the opening poem of the series, **"Introduction,"** where the auditory richness of pure song is contrasted with the child-angel's injunction to "write / In a book that all may read." In following the commanded progression from wordless tune to organized, verbal art, the poem's speaker deftly hints at the problematical nature of writing itself:

> And I made a rural pen,
> And I stain'd the water clear,
> And I wrote my happy songs
> Every child may joy to hear.

The act of writing, which here receives its full, phallic import as a mechanical process involving pen ("a hollow reed") and ink, would seem to muddy the clarity of initial vision, although with his usual ambivalence toward nature Blake, in his syntax, leaves some doubt as to whether the water is merely "stain'd" or "stain'd . . . clear." As the written word, the poems are offered up to the critical act of reading. Yet they remain, in the ear of childhood, "happy songs," and jockey for a place in our hearing amid all the other sounds they set ringing—the call of birds and bleating lambs, the echoing fields, and, above all, the sounds of children at play. Moreover, they evoke an immediate response, Innocence being preeminently a place where all sounds, whether happy or sad, are heard and answered. The lamb's call in **"The Shepherd"** gains the ewe's "tender reply"; the gentle query in the first stanza of **"The Lamb"** is as gently answered in the second; the sobbing robin of **"The Blossom,"** the lost emmet of **"A Dream"** are each heard and comforted; and, throughout, the land echoes with the sound of children's song and play.

This call-and-response, heard throughout the songs, is the auditory image of life under the guardianship of the Good Mother. As Erich Neumann writes in *The Great Mother*, "To nourish and protect, to keep warm and hold fast— these are the functions in which the elementary character of the feminine operates in relation to the child." The creatures of Blake's Innocence live, protected, in the bosom of

a mothering nature; they grow and flourish in a landscape which is undemanding and gently responsive. Here, human mothers and children take their place alongside the lamb, the robin, and the emmet, barely differentiated by sex or species. It is when the lines of communication are down, when response is wanting, as in **"The Little Boy lost"** and **"The Chimney Sweeper,"** that these cease to be "happy songs" and begin to demand, as written art, a more than auditory attention. The emergence of the written poem is thus coincident with the appearance of a deficiency in nature herself.

The antiphonal music of a land and people at peace is still the predominant theme of **"Laughing Song"** and **"The Ecchoing Green."** In **"Laughing Song,"** all creation sings in simple praise of the riches of the summer season. Blake's poem partakes determinedly of this simplicity; even the line, "When the painted birds laugh in the shade," carries none of the darker meaning it might hold in another context. **"The Ecchoing Green"** is considerably more complex, for here a hierarchy of human and nonhuman elements in the scene is established. The three stanzas, which present the morning, noon, and evening of a day, progressively stress the primacy of the human as opposed to the secondary or "ecchoing" status of nature herself. In the morning or infancy of the day, all nature, human and non-human, is caught up indiscriminately in the antiphonal music of **"Laughing Song."** Sunrise is felt as a ripple of sound throughout the land, shaking into song bells and birds in turn. But even here, as the last lines of the first stanza remind us, nothing occurs except in relation to the human:

> While our sports shall be seen
> On the Ecchoing Green.

Blake's punctuation, which makes this half-sentence a discrete thought, suggests that the human sports are the primary backdrop against which all the other actions of the stanza become audible. The sharp distinction between the "sound" of nature and the "sight" of human activity further emphasizes the contrast.

In the second stanza, the sun would seem to stand high in the sky, for Old John and the other "old folk" have taken refuge in the shade of an oak, where they reminisce about "youth-time," their own time in the sun. With reminiscence come self-consciousness and a faint, though good-natured, alienation. Unlike Blake himself, who once pointed to children at play outside his window and remarked, "That is heaven," the elders here cherish the thought that the children will be old, like themselves, soon enough. Their dark thoughts are echoed in a changed landscape. The semi-refrain, so full of promise and futurity, which closed the first stanza, is now transmuted to nostalgic cliché:

> Such such were the joys.
> When we all girls & boys,
> In our youth-time were seen,
> On the Ecchoing Green.

Here the careless, clucking "Such such" cruelly underlines their alienation from the joy and activity of youth.

The sun drives the elders to seek the shade but shines

harmlessly, it appears, on the children themselves. Only when they have wearied does the sun, in seeming response, leave the sky:

> Till the little ones weary
> No more can be merry
> The sun does descend,
> And our sports have an end.

As the children are gathered into their mothers' laps, "Like birds in their nest," the "Ecchoing Green" becomes the "darkening Green." The children's sunlit play thus stands in sharp contrast to this final, mothering darkness which gathers home at night. Together they form an alternating, diurnal cycle which is one of Blake's chief metaphors of Innocence and which, in *Milton* and *Jerusalem,* will be amplified to express the recurrent passage between Eternity's "Realms of day" and the "moony night" of Beulah. Although the children of Innocence are still in the shadow of the Great Mother, their sunlit play signifies, in nascent form, the joys of Eternity which occur at the expense of the female Emanations. In **"Nurse's Song,"** the contrast between the day of play and the night of rest emerges as a genuine conflict of visions, for while the nurse "sees" night and calls the children home, for them, "it is yet day." When the nurse relents and lets them play longer, the question is resolved, but we are left free to imagine other situations in which this incipient Female Will would insist on obedience.

Of all the relationships in Innocence, that between mother and child is the most prominent and serves as a prototype for the rest. Freudian theory, which finds in the child's first love, the mother, a model for all subsequent loves, provides a relevant psychological basis here, as does the transpersonal or Jungian theory whereby all of the soul's possible relations to the feminine are already present in the child's experience of the mother. There is the threat of a conflict of visions in **"Nurse's Song,"** as we have seen, but by and large it is the Good Mother, fruitful, nurturing, and protective, whose presence we feel in Innocence. Her negative counterpart, the Terrible Mother, who is associated with fixation, ensnarement, devouring, and death, stands fully revealed only in the later Prophetic Books as Tirzah, mother of the mortal body. Blake's fairly untrammeled view of the mother in the *Songs of Innocence* is related to the fact that he never again treated the initial paradise so fully or sympathetically.

The fathers of Innocence present a more complicated picture. Like the father of Freudian and Jungian theory, they intervene between mother and child, but hardly with the same positive results. The earthly fathers of the *Songs*— the few that we can identify—are one and all implicated in the abandonment or victimization of their children, as we shall see. They appear as agents of Experience and are substantially responsible for the bleaker moments in the *Songs.* The divine father who is "ever nigh" and his angelic ministers, similarly omnipresent, are, perhaps by way of compensation, more protective and loving; but even they are unable to either prevent harm coming to their children or lead them up and out of their vulnerable condition. The fact that the angels of **"Night"**

> pour blessing,
> And joy without ceasing,
> On each bud and blossom,
> And each sleeping bosom

suggests that, in their view at least, all life is plant-like and human in equal measure, an ambivalence which Blake would later find intolerable. According to Erich Neumann, this confusion of plant and animal life is particularly associated with life under the guardianship of the Great Mother:

> In this primordial world of vegetation, dependent on it and hidden in it, lives the animal world, bringing danger and salvation. . . . Roaring and hissing, milk-giving and voracious, the animals fill the vegetative world, nestling in it like birds in a tree. . . . But all this destroying, wild, terrifying animal world is overshadowed by the Great Mother as the Great World Tree, which shelters, protects, nourishes this animal world to which man feels he belongs. Mysterious in its truthfulness, the myth makes the vegetative world engender the animal world and also the world of men, which thus appears merely as a part of the World Tree of all living things.

This is the same tree which stands revealed, in the *Songs of Experience,* as the Tree of Mystery, darkening life with its growth of moral law and natural reasoning. Life in Blake's Innocence is life in the Great World Tree, and it should come as no surprise that it is a life heavily "peopled" by birds and vegetation: the children of **"The Ecchoing Green"** are "Like birds in their nest"; the foundlings in **"Holy Thursday"** are "flowers of London town"; the speaker of **"Night"** seeks his nest as day ends. The angels of **"Night"** who watch over the Great World Tree, peering into nests and bringing sleep and unconsciousness, are little more than cooperative male attendants to the maternal goddess of Innocence. Far from partaking of a paternal all-powerfulness, they share with the earthly mothers and fathers of Innocence a helplessness in the face of real danger. When the "wolves and tygers" of Experience "howl for prey,"

> They pitying stand and weep;
> Seeking to drive their thirst away,
> And keep them from the sheep.
> But if they rush dreadful;
> The angels most heedful,
> Recieve each mild spirit,
> New worlds to inherit.

The dire passage from Innocence to Experience, here pictured as a feral thirst to be discouraged in the individual soul, appears to carry a "male" sign, in contrast to the decidedly female contentment with the natural state which is elsewhere the subject of the *Songs.* The fractious spirits are promised an "immortal day" of the biblical variety, in which the lion will lie down with the lamb. But we should note that, at the poem's end, it is still a question of shepherd and fold, of danger and guardianship. The fully armed soul, capable of grasping the "deadly terrors" of Experience, is still submerged in the parental shadow.

The "immortal day" pictured at the close of **"Night,"** however compromised it may be within the nocturnal context of the Great Mother, is still preferable to the fate suffered by other outcast children of Innocence. Four of the *Songs*—**"The Little Boy lost"** and **"The Little Boy Found,"** **"The Chimney Sweeper,"** and **"The Little Black Boy"**—deal specifically with children for whom the bond with their human parents has either ceased to exist or become compromised by the encroaching world of Experience. In **"The Little Boy lost,"** a child is abandoned by his father in a deserted spot. We are free to imagine the circumstances that have brought the father to this act—poverty, imminent starvation—but the suggestion of abandonment, although it is rarely mentioned by critics of this poem, is unmistakable in the child's opening words:

> Father, father, where are you going
> O do not walk so fast.
> Speak father, speak to your little boy
> Or else I shall be lost.

In Innocence, where God is "ever nigh," abandoned children are literally left to heaven. Although "no father was there," God appears to the boy, "like his father in white," and leads him back to his mother. The father's ruse has failed this time, but it is probably only a matter of time before he suggests to his son another walk in the "lonely fen." Unlike Hansel and Gretel, who are victims of a similar scheme, Blake's child hasn't the cunning—or experience—to save himself. Hansel and Gretel know who their enemy is and what she intends; they foil the stepmother's first plot and eventually murder her, in the person of the witch of the gingerbread house, a daring act which not only saves their lives but insures that, in the future, they will have their honest but weak-willed father to themselves. Blake's child, by contrast, is utterly dependent upon a parental presence. When this fails him, he must rely upon a father-like divine presence which, far from lessening his dependence, only serves to emphasize it. The mother of Blake's poem is not a party to the father's act, but, like Hansel and Gretel's father, she appears completely powerless to prevent her child's abandonment. In her welcoming gesture—illustrated in the female spirit with out-raised arms that floats alongside the text—she seems to preside over the second poem as the chief deity in this world of dangerous, childish dependency.

The foundling boys of **"Chimney Sweeper"** follow a similar path from parental abandonment to "salvation" through the fatherly God promised by the angel in Tom Dacre's dream. The mother in this poem is dispensed with in the speaker's first words—"When my mother died"—and he is left to the less tender care of a father who

> sold me while yet my tongue,
> Could scarcely cry weep weep weep weep.
> So your chimneys I sweep & in soot I sleep.

As in **"The Little Boy lost,"** the cry for help brings no response. The communication between creature and nature, child and parent, which is the mark of Innocence, has been broken. Here, too, the responsibilities of parental care—protection, nurturance, and even love—are essentially maternal. The mother is all that stands between the child and abandonment; but mothers can die or otherwise prove incapable of preventing their children being sold or abandoned. Then children are left at the mercy of the harsher world of the father.

The illustrated plate of "The Chimney Sweeper," from the "Innocence" section of Songs of Innocence and of Experience.

Blake's picture of human fathers in these songs is a bleak one. Considering his statement that "All deities reside in the human breast," it is curious that the divine image of the Good Father should persist in the face of these children's experience of their earthly fathers. Although Tom Dacre must return from his dream to the benighted life his father has sold him into, he is "happy and warm," remembering the angel's promise that "if he'd be a good boy, / He'd have God for his father & never want joy." But the heavenly father in this poem is not so very different from the earthly one. He, too, demands that Tom sweep chimneys and sleep in soot—"be a good boy"—in return for a distant, paternal love promised only in dreams. The solace which Tom and the other foundlings gain from his dream is a sign of the limitations of their innocence. Not for these children Blake's proverb, "You never know what is enough unless you know what is more than enough," or the simpler legend over one of Blake's gates of paradise, "I want! I want!" Nor is their seeming grace its own reward. However much it was once the spontaneous image of childhood, the quietist vision they take such joy in has become, with their hard work and meager food, another "gift" of the cold and usurious hand that rules them.

Only in Tom's dream do the sweeps enjoy what is the natural right of happier children in these songs—laughter and play on the green, the cleansing river, sunshine, and maternal care. Without these props of Innocence, the sweeps face the experience of waking life as victims. The terrible irony of their life is expressed in the childish wisdom of the second stanza:

> There's little Tom Dacre, who cried when his
>   head
> That curl'd like a lambs back, was shav'd, so I
>   said.
> Hush Tom never mind it, for when your head's
>   bare,
> You know that the soot cannot spoil your white
>   hair.

The sweeps share with the lamb both his beauty and victimage. As the lamb, of "Softest clothing wooly bright," lives for the shearer's knife, so the soot that befouls their lives and spoils Tom's lamb-like curls is the all too palpable given of the sweeps' existence, their bed and board and eventually their death. Like the gold-tipped horns of the sacrificial animal, Tom's white curls serve to enhance his beauty and assure the worth of his sacrifice.

The little black boy, like the foundling sweeps and the little boy lost, winds up at the knee of a paternal—and paternalistic—divine father. In Africa, he had taken comfort in his mother's fable of the origin of racial differences. Now, separated from mother and motherland, the slave-companion of a bigoted English child, he remembers her teaching:

> Look on the rising sun: there God does live
> And gives his light, and gives his heat away.
> And flowers and trees and beasts and men re-
>   ceive
> Comfort in morning joy in the noon day.

This is the same sun, the natural sun, that drives the elders of **"The Ecchoing Green"** into the shade at midday. As the daily bringer of light, it is the god of "those poor Souls who dwell in Night," and stands in sharp contrast to the visionary planet which shines harmlessly upon the play of children in Innocence. Though necessary to biological life, "flowers and trees and beasts and men," the natural sun burns and blackens, literally turning people into slaves:

> And we are put on earth a little space,
> That we may learn to bear the beams of love,
> And these black bodies and this sun-burnt face
> Is but a cloud, and like a shady grove.

It is thus the perfect, natural symbol of a god who instigates and oversees African slavery, and, in worshipping it, mother and child countenance the very system which has separated and enslaved them. Although they regard the slaver sun as a liberator, it is clear that, like the god of Tom Dacre's dream, theirs demands a life of hard work and bodily mortification. In return, he promises an afterlife of simple, childlike innocence at his fatherly knee:

> For when our souls have learn'd the heat to bear
> The cloud will vanish we shall hear his voice.
> Saying: come out from the grove my love & care,
> And round my golden tent like lambs rejoice.

Only when the human soul has left its body does the sun-god leave his golden tent and assume a human form. But revelations to the dead are not revelations at all. Daniel's companions were preserved bodily in the furnace of Nebuchadnezzar by a god who revealed himself to the living. Likewise, the faithful Job knew that he would see God in his flesh. The god who offers comfort only in the next life is a god of slavery, which comes to signify, in this poem, a system of moral thought which reviles the body and condemns it to a state of joyless servitude.

Although **"The Little Black Boy"** is filled with a sense of maternal solicitude, this does not obscure the fact that the mother of the poem literally hands her son over to a life of slavery. Maternality and slavery are, in fact, connected: her words, which are spoken in the shade of the Tree of Mystery and establish once and for all, in her son's mind, the image of god as a benevolent taskmaster, are twice sealed with a kiss. And these kisses are echoed, in turn, in her son's gentle caress of the English boy at the poem's end:

> I'll shade him from the heat till he can bear,
> To lean in joy upon our fathers knee.
> And then I'll stand and stroke his silver hair,
> And be like him and he will then love me.

Through the veil of sentiment which cloaks this final scene, one glimpses the essential irony of the black boy's existence: deprived of freedom and taught to despise his own person, he is unable to imagine a heaven any different from the hell he already inhabits. Blake's second design for this poem shows the black boy taking a deferential second place, at his father's knee, to the English child, who is smaller in stature than himself. His unconscious grace and hesitant caress form a sharp contrast with the insistent attitude of the English boy, who clasps his hands in prayer before his father's face. Both god and white child are seemingly unaware of the presence of the black boy, who remains, in his own heaven, a servant.

What are we to make of these harsh fathers, human and divine, in Blake's Innocence? Clearly, the sky-god of transpersonal psychology, who leads the individual out of dependency upon the Great Mother into the light of consciousness, is an unsuitable analogue of the father who abandons or sells his child outright to the world of Experience. Nor is Freud's terrible father, whose intervention in the Oedipal relation between mother and son leads to the formation of the "civilizing" super-ego, applicable here. The fact is that Blake had little use for either fathers or mothers. While concerned with the opposition between nature and spirit, the unconscious and consciousness, he did not choose to embody it along traditional, mother-father lines. There is, in his myth, no clear-cut cosmological or psychological distinction between the mother and father; both, as parents, are associated with the state of nature, childhood, and unconsciousness, disparate but nevertheless cooperative deities who shape and prolong the state of infantile helplessness. As Northrop Frye has written (in *Fearful Symmetry*), "The 'sin' in the sex act, then, is not that of love but that of parentage, the bringing of life into time. It is the father and the mother, not the lover and the beloved, who disappear from the highest Paradise." The passage from the maternal nest to the paternal knee does not represent a spiritual advance. The exile from Innocence, whether necessary or not, carries a negative sign insofar as it is accomplished through parental agency—either through a lapse in maternal care or through outright paternal treachery. The presence of the father in the advent of Experience assures that it is a premature event, fixating the outcast in a state of spiritual infancy.

> **Childhood is [in *Songs of Innocence and of Experience*] a perilously vulnerable state which can change at any moment into victimage.**
>
> **—*Michele Leiss Stepto***

Childhood is thus, in Blake's songs, a perilously vulnerable state which can change at any moment into victimage. If Blake's chief complaint against parents—and especially against mothers—is that they seem unable to prevent this happening, it is not as uncharitable as it sounds. Man is born into a state of complete, physical dependency, and very shortly learns to rely upon the great deity of infancy, the mother, for all of his physical and emotional comforts. The visions of this state of mind, which are idealities predicated upon an actual psychological experience—for "All deities reside in the human breast"—are peopled by a mothering nature, human in her lineaments and all-fruitful and protective, and a fathering presence, less physical though decidedly beneficent. But while they are all-powerful, the human parents of whom they are the visionary projections are not. It is logical to assume that the child who suffers abuse or neglect or who comes to harm despite parental care would eventually abandon the parental images in favor of a deity that reflected his own needs for greater mastery and self-sufficiency. Blake would certainly have shared Freud's contempt for the "religious attitude [which] can be traced back in clear outlines as far as the feeling of infantile helplessness." But he would have vehemently objected to the notion that this was the sole religious attitude of which man is capable. In his Jesus, the Divine Humanity, and in his many designs of vigorous youths, of which "Glad Day" is perhaps the most beautiful example, Blake depicted the source of true religion as a god fashioned after man in his greatest strength and competence.

But the grand images of childhood die hard, if at all. Like the state over which they preside, they are eternal, less a product of circumstance than the initial shape of the mind itself. As Blake reveals in *Jerusalem,* resisting them, replacing them with fit images of our own mental and physical competence are tasks requiring unfailing strength and imagination. There is not only our own endemic slavishness of spirit to contend with; society itself has an interest in maintaining in its members the images of an all-powerful and loving mother and father, for the mind in which they continue to reign is a mind which, like the child's, can be easily ruled—and overruled. Nor does biological nature have much use for the mind, independent or otherwise. In Darwin's theory, which would have been anathema to Blake, it and all other "racial improvements" are mere by-products of biological activity. An active mind is likely to be one that isn't serving nature's chief end, the ceaseless propagation of the species. Realizing all this, we may begin to understand the genesis, in Blake's gentle mothers and nurses, of Tirzah, goddess of sexual reproduction, and her association in the fallen world with Satan-Urizen, prince of men and nations.

In this world of danger and guardianship, where humanity is seen as a child and the child as a victim, the typical revelation is of the Lamb of God, touchingly beautiful but unarmed. The foundlings on holiday in **"Holy Thursday"** are "multitudes of lambs" whose voices, in concert, shake the seats of heaven as well as the seats of the "aged men wise guardians of the poor" in the earthly church below. In such numbers, marshalled into church to celebrate the Ascension of their namesake, the foundlings are a discomfiting revelation of Eternity, as Blake reminds us in his final injunction to "cherish pity, lest you drive an angel from your door."

The mother of **"A Cradle Song"** traces in her sleeping child the lineaments of the infant Jesus, weeping for a world of innocents like himself. Like the angels of **"Night,"** she is a guardian of sleep and the unconscious, the land of "happy silent moony beams," where "Contrarieties are equally True" and tears and smiles hopelessly intermixed. The dream her lullaby weaves reveals, not the vigorous Christ of miracle and parable but, as Frye writes, the "helpless victim of circumcision and other parts of the Jewish law, overshadowed by a father and mother."

And finally, **"The Lamb,"** most celebrated of the *Songs of Innocence,* makes explicit the identification of the lamb, type of a sacrificial humanity, with the infant Jesus dear to the Christian church. His fur is "Softest clothing" only in a land which keeps him for his wool; his "tender voice" is as likely to be raised in a cry of fear as of joy. If its companion poem in Experience, **"The Tyger,"** deals with the origin of evil, then **"The Lamb"** deals with the origin of the victims of evil, and tells us that the answer to the question, "Did he who made the Lamb make thee?" must surely be yes, for where there are beasts of prey, there will also be victims. In calling himself by the name of the lamb, Christ claimed kinship with the suffering victim and promised, by his act of self-sacrifice, to banish both tiger and lamb. But the identification with the lamb could not be assumed lightly or thrust upon others. In exalting the Lamb of God as the chief revelation of humanity, the Church institutionalizes a dialectic of cruelty and suffering which Christ meant to obliterate. In such a world, mankind has sore need of the double blessing which closes the poem:

> Little Lamb God bless thee.
> Little Lamb God bless thee.

(pp. 357-70)

Michele Leiss Stepto, "Mothers and Fathers in Blake's 'Songs of Innocence'," in The Yale Review, *Vol. LXVII, No. 3, Spring, 1978, pp. 357-70.*

Allen Ginsberg on setting *Songs* to music:

William Blake (1757-1827), engraved his own picture plates, hand colored, & printed *Songs of Innocence & Experience* (1789-1794), only a couple dozen copies. Thus every word, every picture & every print of the book he made in his life bore the impress of his own intelligent body; there was no robot mechanical repetition in any copy. The title *Songs of Innocence & Experience* is literal: Blake used to sing them unaccompanied at his friends' houses.

The purpose in putting them to music was to articulate the significance of each holy & magic syllable of his poems; as if each syllable had intention. These are perfect verses, with no noise lost or extra accents for nothing. . . .

I hope that musical articulation of Blake's poetry will be heard by the Pop Rock Music Mass Media Electronic Illumination Democratic Ear and provide an Eternal Poesy standard by which to measure sublimity & sincerity in contemporary masters such as Bob Dylan, encouraging all souls to trust their own genius Inspiration.

Allen Ginsberg, in his 1969 liner notes to the album Songs of Innocence and of Experience. *Reprinted in* Sparks of Fire: Blake in a New Age, *North Atlantic Books, 1982.*

Wallace Jackson   (essay date 1978)

[*Jackson is an American educator and critic whose scholarship has focused on eighteenth- and nineteenth-century British literature. In the following excerpt, he warns against imposing systematic readings on* Songs of Innocence.]

It is unfortunate that Blake has been viewed as an especially difficult poet, abstruse and obscure, for the obvious importance of the *Songs of Innocence* resides in its attempt to state the immanent divinity of man in terms of the unfallen imagination and to provide a basis for the reconstructed image of human nature. Yet his poetry has been commonly regarded as highly problematical, so much so that it has led at least one modern scholar to complain of the "substitution of exegesis for criticism which characterises the bulk of critical writing about the work of William Blake," [S. F. Bolt, "The Songs of Innocence," *William Blake: Songs of Innocence and of Experience,* edited by Margaret Bottrall]. Blake therefore has become the kind of poet who inspires critics to offer techniques for the reading of his poems. E. D. Hirsch [in his *Innocence and Experience*] has suggested that the " 'dialectical' meaning of the *Songs of Innocence* . . . exists within the poems themselves; that is why they have their fullest impact when they are properly read—seriatim and as an autonomous whole." In the same vein Robert Gleckner has proposed the necessity to be mindful of symbol and context in the *Songs:* "many of Blake's symbols are recurrent, so that once a symbol's basic significance is revealed in a kind of archetypal context, each successive context adds associ-

ation to association within the song series" ["Point of View and Context in Blake's Songs," Bottrall]. Both Hirsch and Gleckner are fine critics, but both suggestions are wrong and unfortunately misleading; there is in fact no method, either dialectical or archetypal, for the reading of Blake's *Songs of Innocence.* I do not mean to imply by this statement that the *Songs* cannot be read but that there are ways in which they should not be read. Some assumptions need to be put aside.

The first of these is that the songs of *Innocence* are exclusively about the state of innocence. They are not always so and sometimes very importantly not so. Occasionally the songs are about the state of experience. It seems also true that the *Songs of Innocence* is an exploratory volume; that is, composed of poems in which Blake unmethodically explored the state of innocence as he was coming to conceive of it between the years 1784 and 1789. Therefore it is not always easy and not always desirable to find explicit relationships among all the songs. There is good evidence for remaining highly doubtful about any particular order in which *Innocence* is to be found. From 1789 to the last years of Blake's life and through five different editions he continued to change the order of the songs. As David Erdman points out [in *The Prose and Poetry of William Blake,* Erdman, ed.]: "In no two copies of *Innocence* . . . are the plates containing the songs arranged in exactly the same order." These are the obvious difficulties confronting any "seriatim" reading of the *Songs.* While Hirsch resists the tendency to systematize *Innocence,* he nevertheless commits himself to the view that "man's sacramental reenactment of Christ's care for man is one of the two principal themes of the *Songs of Innocence.*" Because of this burden of consistency, Hirsch argues that the narrator of **"The Chimney Sweeper"** of *Innocence* "plays the part of guardian to little Tom Dacre." Consequently, Hirsch reads the last line of the poem—"So if all do their duty, they need not fear harm"—as a "misfortune" which "jars in the poem."

So, too, does Martin Nurmi propose that "doing one's duty here means primarily going up chimneys without having to be forced, and the 'harm' is the very real punishment given boys who would not climb" ["Fact and Symbol in 'The Chimney Sweeper' of Blake's *Songs of Innocence,*" *Bulletin of the New York Public Library* 68 (1964)]. Both critics reveal a degree of desperation before the shifting perspectives of Blake's songs, a shifting perspective that is not solved by Gleckner's proposal of an accretively established symbolic context. Thus of the beadles' wands in **"Holy Thursday"** Gleckner remarks: "The wand is 'white as snow' to suggest the frigidity of man-made moral purity as opposed to the warmth of young, energetic, exuberant innocence." Gleckner is undoubtedly right, but presumably white is a symbol in **"Holy Thursday"** even as "red & blue & green" are symbols of the flower children of innocence. Therefore if we know what *white* means in one context, we will know what it means in another as "each successive context adds association to association within the song series." But Tom Dacre's hair before it was shaved was white, and the little English boy who will come to love the little black boy is white. In no way are these three uses of the word *white* interchangeable, and in only two of the three instances can the word be construed as having a symbolic function at all. The songs do not work in the way Gleckner suggests because point of view is qualified by the perspective of the speaker of each song, and innocence is seen variously by various speakers. One might go so far as to remark that each of Blake's speakers is himself (or herself) in a different relation to innocence, and not all are either within innocence or sympathetic to it. As everything we know about the composition of the *Songs* indicates, between 1784 and 1789 Blake was exploring various relations to innocence within the large-scale context he was unmethodically constructing.

Yet, at the same time, one must attempt definitions—not merely readings of the individual poems but a conception of what the songs are about. The most immediate form of innocence is that state of complete containment and contentment within a joyfully animated nature in which human and divine, animal and vegetable, are correspondent parts of an undivided vision. But such a definition is emphatically not pertinent to all the actors within *Innocence.* Hirsch's view that the last line of **"The Chimney Sweeper"** is a "misfortune" is itself unfortunate, since it is apparent that the speaker of the poem is himself unhappily corrupted and therefore speaks from the perspective that experience necessarily takes upon innocence. The autobiographical data of the first stanza is not a gratuity in the poem:

> When my mother died I was very young,
> And my father sold me while yet my tongue,
> Could scarcely cry weep weep weep weep,
> So your chimneys I sweep & in soot I sleep.

Rather, such information supplies us with what we must know of the speaker. The guardian mother of innocence has died; the cruel father has sold him into slavery. It is inevitable therefore that he speaks with the rationalizing voice of experience—"Hush Tom never mind it, for when your head's bare, / You know that the soot cannot spoil your white hair"—and offers the hypocritical moral enforcing the idea of "duty" at the end of the poem. Tom's vision, however, has nothing to do with duty; it has everything to do with the vision of innocence that lives within the child, which sustains itself if only one is faithful to its own terms.

The apparent companion poem to **"The Chimney Sweeper"** is **"Holy Thursday"** of *Innocence.* Like the speaker of the first poem, the speaker of **"Holy Thursday"** preaches the moral of his own corrupted vision in which "pity" is the rigorous and stony-eyed truth of an abstract morality. In both poems the speakers are in effect the real victims of the morality they acknowledge, as the children of **"Holy Thursday"** cannot be and as Tom Dacre obviously is not. In relation to both poems, one must read **"The Divine Image"** as setting out imagistically the true conditions of compassion. **"The Divine Image"** is not founded on an abstract morality, but it is clearly located in those human virtues which are, finally, "virtues of delight."

It is almost axiomatic in the *Songs of Innocence* that any specific divorce between morality and the human image is suspect, as any separation between human and divine is suspect, as any alienation of human from animal life is equally suspect. There cannot be an image which is too anthropomorphic in the *Songs of Innocence* because an innocent world is an extension of the child; the father in heaven is not a remote deity, but the child's imagined form of the adult as, for that matter, the lamb is the imagined form of Christ who "became a little child." Earth is beneficent because to the child it is the incarnate form of God, as the creatures are the separate and collective manifestations of that God. Thus Harold Bloom's suggestion [in his *Blake's Apocalypse*] that the "human child of *Songs of Innocence* is a changeling, reared by a foster nurse who cannot recognize his divinity, and whose ministrations entrap him in a universe of death" cannot be more in error. To make the statement is to read the *Songs of Innocence* from the perspective of **"The Mental Traveller,"** but not from those perspectives which the songs themselves provide on their context. Bloom remarks on **"The Divine Image"** that "until its matching contrary comes to it in *Songs of Experience,* the poem's prime characteristic is its deliberate incompleteness." There is, however, nothing incomplete about **"The Divine Image"** within the context of the *Songs of Innocence*; because of its presence one understands the false witness borne by the speakers of **"The Chimney Sweeper"** and **"Holy Thursday."** The presence within the collection of **"The Divine Image"** steadies our comprehension of the songs and lends surety to our readings of other poems within *Innocence.* The important point to bear in mind about the *Songs of Innocence* is that innocence is always innocent, but not all the figures in *Innocence* are innocent.

The poems vary widely from the immediate conditions of the protective and protected world, in which immanent delight is the wholly governing virtue of that world, to such a poem as **"The Little Black Boy,"** in which the mother's understanding is qualified and defeated by the child's invulnerable innocence. Poems of the first sort, however, would include **"Spring," "Laughing Song,"** and **"Infant Joy,"** all characterized by the pervasiveness of an unreflective delight, an immediate apprehension of song or laughter or joy as the primary principle of life in the world. But this condition is not always sustained in the songs if only because the character of the speaker changes from poem to poem. **"A Cradle Song"** and **"A Dream"** are both songs about innocence, but they are spoken by speakers not themselves within the context of innocence. In both poems a pitying protective figure mourns the imminence of experience, but, like the nurse of the **"Nurse's Song"** or the speaker of **"The Ecchoing Green,"** can do nothing about the inevitable oncoming of experience which only he or she perceives. Such poems are prophetic of experience, aware, that is, of the lengthening shadows cast over the garden. The perspective of the speaker communicates the fact that the tenure of innocence is indefinite, that as a state of the soul it is subject to time and circumstance and therefore perishable.

While the fall from innocence is inevitable, there is also evidence that even as early as 1784-1789 Blake recognized such a fall as desirable. There is for one thing the evidence of the two poems, **"The Little Girl Lost"** and **"The Little Girl Found"** (later transferred to *Experience*), in which

Lyca willingly submits to the descent into experience, a descent largely realized imagistically through the implicit sexual encounter that governs her submission. There is also the evidence of *Thel,* composed at approximately the same time, in which protracted innocence results in the rationalizing morality apparent in Thel's motto.

But the earliest versions of the *Songs of Innocence* suggest a wide-ranging conception of innocence, from the child's complete identity with the natural and created world to the willing farewell to innocence of the Lyca poems. In between there are such important poems as **"The Chimney Sweeper," "Holy Thursday," "The Divine Image,"** and **"The Little Black Boy."** Bloom says that the last is "the best poem in the series." It is surely one of the more interesting in that the protective guardian figure of the mother is troubled by the necessity to account for the difference between black and white skins. In order to do so she develops, inadvertently perhaps, a myth of the Fall based on the conception of Original Sin and the complementary myth of Redemption based on trial and endurance. To this myth the child, speaking the poem in his own voice (an important consideration), adds his own role as protective guardian of the little white boy. The drama of protected innocence is reenacted by the little black boy who in effect will bear for the little white boy the burden of love that his mother now bears for him.

It is customary to criticize the mother's "confusion" in the poem, but we should remember that she is explaining the occasion of blackness to her son as evidence of the trial that God's love imposes upon us. Those with black bodies have absorbed more of God's love than have those with white bodies. At the least it is a very sweet maternal notion. Bloom states that the child's "urge to work out the consequences of such truth reveals the inadequacy of Innocence, of the natural context to sustain any idealizations whatsoever." However, because the child accepts his mother's teaching as truth, he works out an analogy between the truth which pertains on the level of nature and that which pertains on the level of the divine. The little black boy experiences no sundering of the natural and divine; what is true on one level is true on another. Nothing could be closer to that state of the soul which *Innocence* celebrates than such a mode of reasoning.

While there are some songs of *Innocence* in which the end of innocence is clearly suggested, there are no poems that reflect the inadequacy of innocence, none that reflect merely a sentimental and hence ironic conception of innocence. Even **"Night,"** the poem most susceptible to such interpretation, does not deny the protective guardianship of the angels. Nor is this protective guardianship qualified in any sense by the speaking voice of the poem. Eternity ("immortal day") implies the restoration of innocence. **"Night,"** as the title implies, has for its immediate context the state of experience, but it is at least arguable that **"Night,"** unlike **"The Little Girl Lost"** and **"The Little Girl Found,"** does not present experience as a desirable progression of the soul from one state to another. On the contrary, the lion of the poem is not the symbolically purgative figure of Blake's tiger of *Experience* but the predator who yearns to be released from his wrathful nature and delivered to the mild conditions of the peaceable kingdom.

Of all the songs initially placed by Blake within *Innocence* only **"The Little Girl Lost"** and **"The Little Girl Found"** insist upon the value of the transition from innocence to experience. It is conjectural, but attractive to believe, that Blake came in time to perceive the full implications of a contrary state of the soul, implications which are, however, only occasionally apparent in the earliest versions of the *Songs of Innocence.* It is only therefore from the standpoint of experience that one can talk, as Gleckner does [in his *The Piper and the Bard*], about the "tragedy" of innocence. By definition there can be no tragedy in innocence, and not until Blake composed *Thel* did he perceive clearly that protracted innocence is itself a tragedy.

The poem that most effectively leads the reader from *Innocence* to *Experience* is **"On Another's Sorrow,"** usually printed at the end of the *Songs* and perhaps standing as a conclusion to it. Here, if anywhere in *Innocence,* the affinity of grief for grief suggests an end to innocence. But by the time we have come to **"On Another's Sorrow,"** we have run an extraordinary gamut of possibilities pertinent to innocence, and the state of innocence has been explored from a number of different perspectives. Though none of these effectively challenge that state, some of them communicate how innocence appears from the perspective of experience (**"The Chimney Sweeper"** and **"Holy Thursday"**). At least one song dramatizes the invulnerability of innocence confronted by the facts of experience (**"The Little Black Boy"**). At least two represent the impending end of innocence (**"The Ecchoing Green"** and **"Nurse's Song"**). Four show the restoration of innocence before the imminent and threatening conditions of experience (**"The Little Boy Lost"** and **"The Little Boy Found," "Night,"** and **"A Dream"**). Several make apparent the quality of immanent delight that lies at the heart of innocence (**"Laughing Song," "Spring,"** and **"Infant Joy"**), and some simply reinforce the image of true guardianship through the protective figures of mother or shepherd or vegetable life (**"The Shepherd," "A Cradle Song," "The Blossom,"** and probably **"The Divine Image"**). That Blake should have transferred **"The Little Girl Lost"** and **"The Little Girl Found," "The Voice of the Ancient Bard,"** and **"The School Boy"** from *Innocence* to *Experience* makes perfect sense in the light of the argument I have been presenting. In one way or another (definitely not in the same way), the four transferred poems are songs of experience. Because of the diversity of the *Songs of Innocence,* however, no single ordering principle prevails.

Songs of Innocence is not a long poem; it is a composition of short, experimental lyrics that has no seriatim unity, no accretively established context of symbols, no dialectical relationship among its parts. The direct background for these poems is that of an even more eclectic assortment, the *Poetical Sketches* of 1783, in which one can dimly perceive the early and incipient awareness of both states of the soul developing in Blake's poetry. The song beginning "I love the jocund dance" is a very early version of **"The Ecchoing Green,"** whereas **"Mad Song"** and the two songs, one beginning "Memory, hither come," and the other, "How sweet I roam'd from field to field," are early songs of experience.

But if there is no method as such for reading the *Songs of Innocence,* there are in any event values that remain relatively stable within *Innocence.* These may be listed as follows: (1) delight is a state of the soul entirely consonant with innocence and never rendered ironically; (2) abstract moral propositions are suspect, and the one who voices them speaks from within the context of experience; (3) no two poems have the same speaker or employ identical perspectives on the state of innocence; (4) if we exclude the four songs later transferred to *Experience,* the state of experience is never viewed as advantageous; (5) the maternal guardian is always good, if not always an effective guardian; (6) the paternal guardian is always bad unless specifically associated with God the father; (7) all animal and vegetable life is good. With these seven propositions we can find our way through the songs of *Innocence* recognizing them for what they are: an early assortment of poems variously stating the terms of innocence and organized nonprogressively, nonassociatively, nonlogically. There is no ruling principle of organization—a fact that may explain why Blake could not rest satisfied with any of his various editions. For that matter, there is no fidelity to the conception of the songs as "happy" as stated in the **"Introduction."** (pp. 94-104)

> *Wallace Jackson, "William Blake," in his* The Probable and the Marvelous: Blake, Wordsworth, and the Eighteenth-Century Critical Tradition, *The University of Georgia Press, 1978, pp. 89-121.*

Zachary Leader   (essay date 1981)

[*In the following excerpt, Leader studies Blake's illustrations for* Songs of Innocence and of Experience, *insisting that they are intrinsic to the work and as carefully and thoughtfully executed as the poems.*]

This [essay] begins with a familiar refrain, since critical studies of Blake's verse continue to appear which ignore his visual art, or pay it only lip service: Blake meant the poems and designs of his Illuminated Books to remain together. When picture and poem are separated the result is 'Loss of some of the best things.' The designs, he writes, turning the equation around, 'perfect accompany Poetical Personifications and Acts, without which poems they never could have been Executed.' Nor would he have approved of readers who treat the designs as so much attractive but irrelevant decoration. Painting, he believed, ought to be 'as poetry and music are, elevated to its own proper sphere of invention and visionary conception.' Pictures ought to be studied as closely as poems:

> I intreat that the Spectator will attend to the Hands and Feet the Lineaments of the Countenances they are all descriptive of Character and not a line is drawn without intention and that most discriminate and particular <as Poetry admits not a Letter that is insignificant so Painting admits not a Grain of Sand or a Blade of Grass <insignificant> much less an Insignificant Blur or Mark>.

Explicit statements of this sort are backed by great personal sacrifice. Critics who fail to read the poems in light of the designs forget how high a price Blake paid to create his illuminated pages '—in time, money, patronage, friendship and spiritual energy' [Jean H. Hagstrum, *William Blake: Poet and Painter*]. 'I know myself both Poet and Painter,' Blake insists, defying those (often, as in this case, important patrons) who would prevent his 'more assiduous pursuit of both arts.' Only a few sympathetic contemporaries understood the nature of the designs: Coleridge spoke of 'Blake's poesies, metrical and graphic'; Robinson mentions 'poetic pictures of the highest beauty and sublimity'; the anonymous author of 'The Inventions of W. B., Painter and Poet' (Keynes thinks it C. A. Tulk), finds 'The figures surrounding and enclosing the poems . . . are equally tinged by a poetical idea'; to Allan Cunningham, writing in the same year, 1830, text and design are 'intertwined . . . so closely in his compositions, that they cannot well be separated.'

This [essay] takes as one of its starting points a somewhat more timid version of David Erdman's 'working assumption' [in *The Illuminated Blake*] that 'every graphic image has its seed or root in the poetry': almost every graphic image bears some relation to—colors if it does not, in fact, grow out of—the poetry. It argues that we cannot properly appreciate the larger meaning or 'vision' of *Songs* without a knowledge of the designs, and in a few cases it even questions the extent to which certain poems can stand alone. **'Spring,'** from *Innocence,* provides a case in point. Robert Gleckner complains [in his *The Piper and the Bard*] that in the poem's last stanza 'the "I" is not identified, except possibly as Blake himself, [and] the lamb's appearance is unprepared for.' But in the scene at the bottom of the second plate we are shown a child petting (or 'pulling') the 'soft wool' of a 'little lamb.' We notice lamb and child as soon as we turn the page (before we read the last stanza) and we identify them with similar figures on the first plate. When we turn then to the last stanza we realize at once that the child (not Blake) must be the poem's speaker and that the lamb he refers to is pictured in the designs. Text and design 'cannot well be separated.' Gleckner's complaint disappears when **'Spring'** is returned to its original format.

'The Little Girl Lost' and **'The Little Girl Found'** provide an example of a subtler and more frequently recurring interdependence of text and design. They also bring us closer to understanding the difference between Blake's illuminations and conventional illustration. **'Lost'** tells the story of little Lyca's separation from her parents and her wanderings in 'desart wild.' Exhausted, she lies down beneath a tree, falls asleep, and is soon approached by magical 'beasts of prey' who undress her (while she sleeps) and carry her off to their caves. **'Found'** tells of the wanderings of Lyca's distraught parents. They too encounter a magical beast (a lion who becomes 'a spirit arm'd in gold') who leads them to where Lyca sleeps 'among tygers wild.' In the final stanza the parents are said to 'dwell / in a lonely dell,' no longer fearing wolves and tigers.

A story of this sort, rich in folk and fairy-tale motifs, and 'obviously nonsensical on the level of natural fact' [Kathleen Raine, *Blake and Tradition*], is bound to give rise to elaborate symbolic readings. One of the more plausible of these readings takes **'Lost'** as an allegory of sexual awakening in which Lyca's separation from her family is to be seen as a fall; her wanderings in 'desart wild' as the stirrings of desire; the tree under which she sleeps as a type of the Tree of the Knowledge of Good and Evil; and her eventual abduction by 'beasts of prey' as a symbolic sexual initiation. **'Found'** is then read as Blake's account of the necessary adjustments parents must make when their children grow into experience. A number of suggestive details lend support to the reading: the southern setting (traditionally associated with the passions); our twice being told of Lyca's loveliness; the seductive influence of 'wild birds song'; Lyca's calling out to 'sweet sleep' in the manner of a lover; the lion's licking her neck and bosom; the loosing of Lyca's 'slender dress.'

Those who object to a sexual interpretation of this sort begin with line 13, in which Lyca is said to be 'Seven summers old'—hardly an age of sexual awakening. Details such as the story's setting or the removal of Lyca's 'slender dress' are interpreted along Neoplatonic lines, their sexual overtones ignored or minimized. If the poems are taken in isolation, this approach has some merit. But the designs lend strong support to a sexual reading. On the first plate a couple embraces. We notice them before we turn to the text, and our first impulse is to identify the female in the design with the **'Little Girl'** of the title. Once we begin reading, though, we are forced to retract the identification (Lyca being alone in 'desart wild' and too young to have a lover). When we turn to the second plate, still in search of some connection between the lover's embrace and Lyca's story, our uncertainty deepens. A young woman lies alone in a forest beneath a tree. Again, our immediate impulse is to identify her with Lyca, interpreting the design as an illustration of stanzas 5 through 8. But what of her age? Like the female on the first plate, she wears a gown whose folds reveal a woman's body. We begin to wonder about line 13. Perhaps we were not meant to take Lyca's age literally? Perhaps Blake chose the number seven for its symbolic associations? This is what the design on the third plate seems to imply. Below the text, a naked female lies asleep next to a lioness. A male lion sits off to the right. Three children, two male and one female, caress and play with the lions. To the right of the text two trees entwine, their smooth curves like those of human limbs in embrace. There can be little doubt about the identity of the maiden on this plate. She is Lyca, naked and asleep among beasts of prey. The identification confirms our suspicions about the young women on the previous plates. Once we have overcome our doubts about Lyca's age, we return to the maiden on the first plate and notice that her hair and dress are similar in color to those of the maiden on the second plate, now more confidently identified as Lyca. We return to the problems of the first design: how are we to connect Lyca's story with a lover's embrace?

Questions of this sort—no matter what their answers—affect the way we read the 'Lyca' poems. They direct our attention along specific lines, adding emphasis and point to subtle sexual suggestions in the text. Though we are not confined by the designs to any single level of meaning, they

make it impossible for us to ignore the story's sexual dimension. Like most of Blake's 'illuminations,' the pictures occupy a middle ground between illustration and interpretation. They provide no missing information, as do the designs to **'Spring,'** but they prevent partial or misdirected readings. They also have a larger and more general effect: by taking certain liberties with the text (why lions and not tigers on the third plate?) they encourage a similar freedom in our own interpretations. We find ourselves looking for what Blake calls 'mythological and recondite meaning, where more is meant than meets the eye.'

Designs of a more abstract nature can affect our readings in equally complex and subtle ways. On the first plate of **'A Cradle Song,'** for example, the text (a mother's lullaby to her sleeping child, sung in response to the child's smiles, moans and sighs) is set against a night sky and surrounded by a tangle of flame-like vegetative forms and tiny human figures. Our initial reaction to the design is uncomplicated. The decoration, we feel, neatly captures the poem's dominant note of security and protection. Delicate intimations of identity between mother, child, and all creation are echoed in the swirling continuity of text, vegetation and human form. To Keynes, 'the dreamy tangles of falling vegetation . . . suggest the feeling of the first line: "Sweet dreams form a shade." ' He also points to the 'soft female form with arms stretched out in benison' above and to the right of the second stanza who 'seems suggested by . . . "Sweet sleep Angel mild, / Hover o'er my happy child" ' [Keynes, ed., *Songs of Innocence and of Experience*]. Erdman writes of 'Suggestive, indeterminate vegetable and human forms of dreams, smiles, sweet moans, and sighs which fill the verdure backed by night sky.' When comparing this plate with other examples of flame-plant decoration, continues Erdman, 'we see that the lullaby form of energy and desire thins into "pleasant streams" and "happy silent moony beams." '

But the poem is not all gentle sweetness and content. Its delicate beauty, like that of Coleridge's 'Frost at Midnight,' is faintly disturbing and enigmatic. We wonder, for example, at the ease with which the mother overcomes her sense of Christ's sorrows. 'The tears of the Christ child,' writes Bloom [in his *Blake's Apocalypse: A Study in Poetic Argument*],

> were not an image of infant helplessness, but a lament for all mortality, for the transience of Innocence. Yet the mother singing **'A Cradle Song'** will not see this, but converts the infant god of Innocence very rapidly into a father god of the same state, with a supposedly inevitable movement from 'Wept for thee, for me, for all' to 'Smiles on thee, on me, on all.'

The mother's steady, unvarying tone fails to dispel the darker implications of moans, sighs and tears. A gap opens between what we feel and what the mother's tone would make us feel—a gap anticipated in the design on the first plate. What Erdman sees as 'pleasant streams' and 'happy silent moony beams,' others see quite differently. Wagenknecht, for example, writes of the 'terribly twisted and dark vegetation which winds against a dark background like seaweed . . . in one place tinged with red which suggests flesh as well as vegetation' [*Blake's Night:*

William Blake and the Idea of Pastoral]. Vague premonitions of threat and danger soon complicate any initial impression of exuberant organic life. This vegetation, we realize, is thicker, darker and heavier than the light curlicues and intertwinings found elsewhere in *Innocence.* The more we look at its swirling strands, the less likely we are to associate them with the dream-formed 'shade' of line 1. 'The hedging of each stanza,' writes Eben Bass, 'implies protection for the cradled child, but the stanzas are also, in fact, nearly oppressed by the design.' The decoration begins to affect the way we read. Bass wonders if ' "Sweet dreams form a shade" could imply the mother's clouding, as well as protective, influence' ["*Songs of Innocence and of Experience:* The Thrust of Design" in *Blake's Visionary Forms Dramatic,* Erdman and Grant, eds.]. Words like 'hovers' and 'beguiles' take on new and more ambiguous meanings. As the thinning strands of vegetation work their way into the text, tiny ripples of doubt disrupt the reassuring flow of the mother's words. We turn to the second plate secure in our sense of a world bounded and fused by the loving identity of mother and child, but we are also vaguely troubled. The design catches out and alerts us to subtle intimations of threat and danger in the text—even as it sounds the poem's dominant note of protection and contentment. It is like Bellini's *The Madonna of the Meadow* in the National Gallery, in which the Virgin looks down, in prayer, on a naked infant whose pose reminds us of those of the dead Christs of countless Renaissance Pietàs. Here and elsewhere in *Songs* the marginal decoration repays close attention. We must learn to take seriously Blake's claim that 'not a Grain of Sand or a Blade of Grass [is] <insignificant> much less an insignificant Blur or Mark.'

Even when a design seems awkward, crude, or perfunctory we ought not to dismiss the impressions it makes upon us. The second plate of **'A Cradle Song'** provides a convenient example. Our first impulse is to seek some extra-literary excuse for its unpleasant appearance. Damon speaks [in his *William Blake: His Philosophy and Symbols*] of 'a sort of Raphaelesque hardness, which in these days is not pleasant' (but refers to it nowhere else in *Innocence*); Keynes calls the second plate 'uncomprising in the hard outlines of the mother's clumsy chair and the child's wicker cot,' leaving us with the impression (since he gives no reasons for its oddly 'uncompromising' character) that Blake himself has been clumsy or careless in execution. Erdman's off-hand reference to 'the thickly wrapped, perhaps even threateningly swaddled, infant,' is equally puzzling. Though he is hardly likely to charge Blake with clumsy or careless execution ('A failure to find the textual referent is a failure to find something that is there'), he records no other discrepancies between the poem's designs and its textual lullaby. Why, then, does the child's appearance disturb us?

There is no mistaking the design's unpleasantness. The stark backdrop of dark, draped cloth is like nothing else in *Innocence.* Its strong, straight lines are of a piece with the 'hard outlines' of the chair, the large, hooded cradle, and the folds of the mother's dress. The ground's dark mottled colors suggest a patterned carpet, but the patterns lack definition or outline. Like much else in the design, it

reminds us of a similarly enclosed scene in **'Infant Sorrow,'** a poem about the stifling, oppressive weight of parental influence. The hooded wicker cradle looks coffin-like, in part because of its length. Is this an accident, the wholly fortuitous result of Blake's habitual 'clumsiness' with perspective? And what of the mother? Why does she look so much less attractive and appealing than the mother on the first plate of **'Spring'?** 'Amply, almost redundantly gowned,' [Wagenknecht], with a head-dress like a wimple, she is stiff and awkward as she bends over her child. 'It is surely not by chance,' writes Keynes, 'that the child's pillow is so arranged as to form a conspicuous halo around its head.' But what of more disturbing details? Is it chance that wraps the child's bedclothes around him as tightly as a cocoon? Why not attribute their unpleasant, 'threatening' appearance to the mother, a woman whose own clothing wholly conceals the curves of her body?

'The cradle's hood,' writes Bass, 'and the draped cloth behind are the mother's way of sheltering her child from cold and drafts, but both testify as much to danger and mortality as they do to protection.' Our doubts about the poem's concluding stanzas increase as we look at the second plate. The world, it seems, is not as benevolent as the mother's words would have us believe; protection takes on the appearance of something more threatening. We worry again about 'hovers' and 'beguiles.' Maternal affection is frequently ambiguous in *Innocence*: nurture slides easily into dependency, protection tightens into possessiveness. On **'The Blossom'** plate, for example, a tiny child is almost totally obscured by the embrace of a winged female dressed in green, presumably its mother. She faces *against* the cycle of generation traced by the other figures in the design.

The designs to **'A Cradle Song'** hint at the dangers implicit in the mother's easy passage from tears to smiles. Innocence must be protected, enclosed against an outside world whose threatening harshness is figured in the acanthus-shaped leaves at the top of the second plate or the nightmarish tangles of plate 1. But the domestic scene offers its own dangers. The disturbingly 'uncompromising' nature of the design on the second plate is no accident. Blake was a careful and conscious craftsman with a professional engraver's eye for detail. He thought seriously about technique, and knew how to adapt his style to different moods. No artist who supported himself by illustrating or engraving other men's works could have 'missed' or 'overlooked' the design's want of delicacy. Had he been displeased with the harsh outlines on the original copperplate, Blake could have softened them with color, as he did in earlier copies. When a design seems crude or perfunctory, the impressions it makes upon us ought not to be dismissed too quickly. Blake has flaws, both as poet and as painter—the pictorial language of his designs is, at times, as in the case of *Tiriel,* inappropriate—but his visual art deserves the same respectful scrutiny as his poetry. 'In the art of the late eighteenth century,' writes Robert Rosenblum [in his *Transformations in Late Eighteenth-Century Art*], 'a one-to-one correlation of style and subject was as frequently the exception as the rule'; in Blake's art, it was more often the rule than the exception. 'Not a line is drawn without intention,' he insists, 'and that most discriminate and particular.' We ought to try to take him at his word.

In some plates, though, Blake seems subject to purely technical or formal limitations. The text of 'The Chimney Sweeper' in *Innocence,* for example, fills almost the whole plate. Blake, we feel, has no choice but to squeeze his design into a half-inch strip along the bottom of the plate. As a result, sweep-heaven seems neither airy, light, nor particularly pleasant. But Blake need not have confined himself to a single plate. Had he spread the text over two pages, as he does in 'Spring,' a poem only three lines longer than 'The Chimney Sweeper,' he would have had ample room to depict a heaven every bit as joyous as lines 15 to 18 describe. Plate 1 could have been bleak and dreary, a picture of the sweeps' grinding poverty and oppression, plate 2 bright and energetic. At this point a host of insupportable conjectures suggest themselves. Perhaps Blake was short of copperplate (we know he sometimes used both sides)? Perhaps he had not realized how much room the text would take up? Was he in a hurry that day? Or distracted? (In that case, he must also have had an off day thirty-seven years later when coloring Crabb Robinson's copy.) But no critic can take this sort of speculation seriously. Doubtless Blake fell victim to all sorts of technical difficulties (both as poet and as painter), but these are of no more value to a reading of the designs than they are to a reading of the poems. We must look first to the work itself, and when we do, we shall discover subtle but important reasons for the design's depressing appearance.

As 'The Chimney Sweeper' opens, an older and more experienced sweep, the speaker, comforts a younger sweep ('little' Tom Dacre) against the pain of a newly encountered experience. Little Tom has just had his head shaven, a ritual initiation and subjugation 'like those given in prison or in the army' [Martin K. Nurmi, 'Fact and Symbol in "The Chimney Sweeper" of Blake's *Songs of Innocence,'* in *Blake: A Collection of Critical Essays,* Northrop Frye, ed.]. (Its ostensible purpose was to reduce the risk of hair catching fire from pockets of smoldering soot.) Tom has but newly entered his apprenticeship and cries for the loss of his curly white hair (an echo of 'softest clothing wooly bright' in 'The Lamb').

The speaker's instinctive sympathy and fellow-feeling has a profound effect on young Tom. So, too, his thoughts on 'duty.' Tom's dream ends with an admonition from the liberating angel identical in spirit to that of the poem's last line, and equally disturbing:

> And the Angel told Tom if He'd be a good boy,
> He'd have God for his father and never want joy.

In this case, being a good boy entails doing what one's told, and doing it without complaint. Tom may have picked up such 'advice' from any of several sources: the father who sold him; the master who exploits him; perhaps a priest of the sort we encounter in 'A Little Boy Lost,' or one of the 'Wise guardians of the poor' in the innocent 'Holy Thursday.' But he is also likely to have picked it up from the older sweep, whose experience has no doubt taught him the painful consequences of disobedience. That Tom dreams of the eventual salvation not just of himself but of 'thousands of sweepers Dick, Joe, Ned and Jack,'

suggests that he has also caught something of the speaker's spirit of compassion.

The very existence of the dream seems to owe something to the older sweep's influence. 'It is not for nothing,' writes Wicksteed [in his *Blake's Innocence and Experience*], 'that the child's vision follows immediately after his being given the idea that his "white hair" is potentially "there" just as much when it is shaved off as before.' Like his friend the speaker, Tom builds an imaginary ideal out of the bleakest and most depressing of realities. The 'coffin of black' is an obvious example. 'To wash in a river and shine in the sun,' sporting 'naked and white' in the landscape of innocence, is another. As Martin Nurmi writes:

> Nakedness is not here merely a symbol of innocence. In dreaming of it Tom is making a connection between his dream imagery and his ordinary life. For sweeps often went up chimneys naked. . . . Naked immersion in soot, therefore, is Tom's normal state now, and white naked cleanliness is its natural opposite.

The sweeps' trust in the justice and benevolence of the very world that has injured them is terribly pathetic. We see all too clearly the price they must pay for their few moments of warmth and happiness. Though they still retain some sparks of imaginative life, much has already been lost. Tom learns to submit to the loss of his hair with all the docility of a sheep; the cheerless anapests of the older sweep's matter-of-fact tone, especially in the first stanza, sound only the faintest echoes of the more energetic speech of children in other Songs. The off-hand manner in which he recounts the cruelties of his life ('His mother's death he puts in a dependent clause . . . his being sold by his father . . . he emphasizes less than the fact that he was very young' [E. D. Hirsch, Jr., *Innocence and Experience: An Introduction to Blake*]), suggests a spirit numbed by suffering. Only when recounting the imaginary joys of Tom's dream does the speaker recapture the animated rhythms of childhood. The cold, dark mornings must soon, we sense, take their inevitable toll.

The poem concludes with what Bloom calls 'a new fierceness for Blake.' The sweep lacks sufficient strength or security to question what he has been taught, and his call to duty is without conscious irony. The last line is a brutal indictment of the sorts of traditional pieties we encounter again and again in 'Good Godly' books, or in Watts's *Divine Songs* or Mrs Barbauld's *Hymns in Prose.* Yet the poem belongs in *Innocence* because, unlike its experienced counterpart, it inspires neither outrage nor indignation. Our attention is almost wholly absorbed in the sweeps' last few glimmers of imagination and fellow-feeling.

The scene at the bottom of the plate depicts Tom's heaven. To the far right a robed and haloed figure (presumably the angel with a bright key) reaches down to lift a small boy out of a black coffin. The flowing curves of his gown suggest a figure out of a dream. To the left, eleven sweeps rejoice at their liberation. Those furthest from the coffin run towards a river [tinted blue in this copy]. The sweeps are barely more than stick-figures. Their 'heaven' is compressed into a space too small to provide any visual equivalent for the wide expanse suggested by the line, 'down a green plain leaping laughing they run.' The dark blue-green of the mottled landscape, and the pale yellow wash behind the poem's last stanzas, sound but the faintest echo of 'wash in a river and shine in the sun.' No attempt has been made to capture the airy lightness of 'rise upon clouds and sport in the wind.' The scene lacks the very qualities the sweeps most long for: open spaces, sun, warmth, clear, bright colors. The great block of text presses down upon Tom's dream like a weight, stunting and crushing it much as Innocence itself is ground down by a life of poverty and oppression. That the poem is 'illuminated' by the design's cramped and unpleasant appearance encourages us (here and elsewhere) to take our initial reactions seriously—even when we might plausibly relate them to circumstances beyond Blake's control.

Failed or flawed designs in *Songs* are the product less of carelessness or incompetence than of ambition. Some simply ask too much of us. The oddly inoffensive creature on 'The Tyger' plate provides a notorious case in point. Blake might easily have drawn a fearful or ferocious tiger. 'He had no trouble drawing a fearful were-wolf,' Erdman reminds us [in his *Blake: Prophet against Empire*], 'or for that matter a fearful flea.' And on the sixth page of the Notebook (or 'Rossetti Manuscript'), another page of which contains a draft of the poem, we find two genuinely ferocious beasts, one unmistakably a tiger. Yet in none of the extant copies of *Songs* is there a creature remotely comparable to the picture created by the poem's awe-struck speaker. 'Comical,' 'inquisitive,' 'simpering,' 'quaint,' 'gentle,' 'tame,' 'patient,' 'worried,' 'fatuous,' 'supercilious'—these are the adjectives critics use to describe the visual equivalent of the poem's bright burning beast. Even at its most ferocious, [in one particular copy], the tiger is only 'formidable,' not yet the 'heroic Tyger' Grant ['Mothers and Methodology,' *Blake Newsletter* 2, No. 6 (15 December 1968)] and others seek. Keynes speaks of an unspecified 'ferocious carnivore,' but neither Erdman nor anyone else has seen it.

Once we accept the obvious discrepancy between poem and design, a whole range of possibilities opens: the design is Blake's attempt 'to portray the smile of the Deity on its [the tiger's] lips, and to show the ultimate "humanity divine" of Nature's most terrific beast'; or it is 'a mask, deriding those who expect upon a mortal page the picture of the Deity at work' [Wicksteed]; or a depiction of 'the final tiger, who has attained the state of organized Innocence as have the adjacent lions and tigers of **"The Little Girl Lost"** and **"The Little Girl Found"** ' [Erdman], or a joke, not so much on us as on 'the awestruck questioner, or the Tyger, and perhaps on the Creator himself' [Grant, 'The Art and Argument of the "Tyger",' *Discussions of William Blake,* John E. Grant, ed.].

I tend towards the last of these possibilities. Blake and the poetic voice ought not to be confused, especially in a Song of Experience. Much of what the awestruck questioner says implies a world (and a way of looking at it) that Blake would have found unnecessarily limited and limiting. He might well have sought to undermine the speaker by domesticating or defanging his tiger, just as he cuts Behemoth and Leviathan down to size (Paley [in his *William*

Blake] calls them 'houshold pets') in plate 15 of the *Illustrations to the Book of Job* (figure 4).

But an 'explanation' of this sort makes the design no less jarring or unsatisfactory. Hagstrum is still right, the tiger *is* 'unworthily illustrated,' even if Blake thinks the speaker's celebration of its fierce majesty wrong or misguided. The poem is simply too powerful to be undercut so brutally. We have neither time nor inclination to make the necessary adjustments of perspective the design demands of us.

This is also a common problem for readers of the later prophetic books. Blake's poems and designs suffered increasingly from an absence of public recognition. Lacking informed and sympathetic criticism, he grew less and less inclined to anticipate (or even consider) the needs and expectations of his almost nonexistent audience. At times, in his eagerness to attain the widest and most comprehensive vision, Blake would alter his works substantially, often at the expense of their coherence and our comprehension. The revisions that turned *Vala* into **The Four Zoas,** for example, introduce so many new themes and connections that the original narrative sequence and allegorical pattern become hopelessly confused; those to what was, in effect, its visual counterpart, a huge Last Judgment design, turned one version, according to Cumberland's son, 'black as your hat'—so feverishly was it worked over and elaborated. We can reconstruct Blake's intentions in these cases, and find subtle and complicated justifications for the thematic coherence of much of the additional material, but each new idea makes the poem or the design less accessible and attractive, even to the most learned and partisan of Blake's readers.

The design to **'The Tyger'** is marred by a comparable lack of restraint. Blake is so eager for us to see the whole, so delighted with the ease with which he can expose his speaker, that he momentarily loses his sense of tact. The reader is much too abruptly wrenched out of the mood of the poem. On occasion, abruptness of this sort can produce astonishing effects, as in plate 9 of **Europe,** where all of human history is condensed into three lines:

> Eighteen hundred years, a female dream!
> Shadows of men in fleeting bands upon the wind;
> Divide the heavens of Europe

but here we feel betrayed and bewildered. **'The Tyger,'** though, is an extreme case. More often than not, when a design undercuts a poem's speaker, or adds an unexpected twist, the poem is enriched.

A subtler and more problematic example is provided by **'The Little Boy Found.'** Our difficulties begin with the figure Keynes calls 'a person in the image of God.' If, as the poem tells us, the child's rescuer is 'God ever nigh,' who appears to him 'like his father in white,' why is its form in the design 'ostensibly female, so appearing to be in disagreement with the poem'? Keynes is not alone in thinking this an oddly feminine Savior. Others have made much of the figure's long flowing hair, lack of beard and high-waisted gown, which, in the shading of some copies . . . , suggests a female bosom. Erdman, Grant, and Bindman take a dim view of such speculation. Erdman disdains comment, simply assuming the figure's masculinity; Grant points to nine other unmistakably male figures wearing high-waisted gowns in *Songs,* as well as to numerous depictions of Christ outside the *Songs,* many of which bear a striking resemblance to the figure on this plate; Bindman relegates the controversy to a footnote. We ought not to be bullied. No matter what its appearance in other copies, or how much it resembles Blake's Christs elsewhere, in [the copy under discussion] the little boy's rescuer looks more like a masculine female than a feminine male. Our first impulse is to identify it as the little boy's mother. But the text clearly tells us that 'God ever nigh' (or the 'father') 'by the hand led' the little boy. Besides, what of the smaller female figure in the bottom half of the plate whose arms reach out just below the word 'Found' in the title? Is she not a more plausible mother, as Grant argues? We are soon forced to conclude, with Keynes, that the design's 'God ever nigh' is 'Probably . . . one of Blake's not infrequent androgynous figures, having both mother and father attributes.' Blake may be suggesting that the little boy sees the watchful benevolence of both parents in the divinity of the father. He almost never spoke approvingly of God the Father, and the sexual ambiguity of the little boy's rescuer may well be an attempt to forestall criticism of the child for believing in the wrong kind of Savior.

Yet we remain troubled. Though we can find plausible explanations for the figure's androgyny, our initial confusion is distracting. We are made to move too quickly from problem to problem. The design is another of Blake's attempts to do too much—to make too many points, answer too many questions. As in 'The Tyger' neither carelessness nor incompetence need have anything to do with the design's failings. When 'God the father' looks feminine, as in [the copy under discussion], Blake's ambition has simply got the better of his tact. Though the design may be flawed, we still sense a complex and subtle intelligence at work.

Let us return to 'The Tyger' for a moment, since it provides a convenient opening to larger and more general questions of pictorial style in *Songs.* 'The Tyger' is disappointing, argues Ann Mellor [in her *Blake's Human Form Divine*], because 'Blake was forced to re-use Stothard's illustrative style in the companion volume to *Songs of Innocence.* Stothard's sentimental decorative mode is by 1794 clearly inadequate to Blake's poetic vision.' Stothard, a friend of Blake's from bachelor student days, had already begun to make a name for himself by 1780 as 'a prolific inventor of charming vignettes for the booksellers.' What William Gaunt calls his 'modest faculty for design,' Stothard put to the service of fashionable allegory and *conversazioni.* 'At their worst,' writes Hagstrum, Stothard's illustrations 'place preposterous medieval cavaliers and white-clad society ladies in the wooded parks of English country estates or fill the sky with allegorical heads derived academically from Raphael, Guido Reni, Correggio, or the antique.' Only 'now and then' do they capture 'authentic echoes of the greater tradition from which he and his fellows sprung.'

Until the abrupt and bitter termination of their friendship in 1806, Blake engraved a number of illustrations after Stothard. Bindman thinks he may even have worked in partnership with Stothard, producing, by 1785, as many as thirty-three engravings of the latter's illustrations. While openly admitting the similarity between Stothard's style and that of his own early work, Blake vigorously denies any influence on Stothard's part. 'Heath and Stothard were the awkward imitators at that time,' writes Blake of his early artistic career. Praise for Stothard's draftsmanship, he claims, is almost wholly derived from 'those little prints which I engraved after him five and twenty years ago.' Though Blake's remark about 'awkward imitators' is that of an embittered rival, a friend who thought himself cruelly wronged ('Resentment for Personal Injuries has,' Blake admits, 'had some share in this Public Address'), it points to real, if subtle, differences between his own style in *Songs* and that of more fashionable contemporaries.

Anthony Blunt was among the first of Blake's modern critics to detect Stothard's 'sentimental decorative mode' in the designs for *Innocence,* but even when he thinks Blake most artificial or mannered, as in 'Laughing Song' or 'The Shepherd,' Blunt also notes [in his *The Art of William Blake*] details 'typical of Blake's best illumination.' Though the idiom may be conventional, 'the movement is equally personal.' Mellor notes that, on the whole, Blake's figures are less artificial than Stothard's, their sturdier and more muscular bodies frequently set off by clinging or transparent drapery. (Compare, for example, the child on the cloud in the frontispiece to *Innocence* with what Hagstrum calls the 'simpering cupids' of more fashionable society allegories.)

Blake rings subtle changes on the conventional mode. His pictorial style in *Innocence* is as deceptively familiar as the nursery and lullaby rhythms of the poems. Though at first it reminds us (as it means to) of Stothard and others like him, we soon discover delicate discordances, subtle and unexpected touches (the sharp-pointed fingers of the winged figure in 'Infant Joy,' the 'naive rigidity' [Blunt] of the children's procession in 'Holy Thursday,' the claw-like roots of the tree on the second plate of 'The Little Black Boy') which hint at a deeper and more complex vision. This is even more true in *Experience,* where the poems invariably undercut and overturn the expectations we bring to them from the designs. The text of 'The Angel,' for example, is clearly meant to indict all that the mannered gestures of the figures in its design imply. When Mellor suggests that by 1794 Blake had somehow outgrown the sentimental style of an earlier and more optimistic poetic vision, we should bear in mind Frye's witty reference [in his *Fearful Symmetry*] to the artist of *Experience* as 'no longer a child of thirty-two but a grown man of thirty-seven.'

Of all the designs in *Innocence,* that of 'Laughing Song' owes most to Stothard. The faintly Neoclassical arrangement of figures, the 'rather Roman or Hellenistic chairs' [Erdman], the highly stylized gestures and attitudes of the seated revellers, even the 'fine hat' (with its feather or plume) [Erdman] which the standing youth holds aloft in his left hand—all point to the attenuated pastoralism of Stothard's designs (engraved by Blake in 1783) for Joseph Ritson's *A Select Collection of English Songs.* Nor is this an accident. Blake subtly adapts his pictorial style to the mood and spirit of a text, and if the design to **'Laughing Song'** strikes us as more derivative than others in *Innocence*—more in tune with the fashionable pastoralism of eighteenth-century illustration—so too does the poem. Not only is its world one of 'green woods,' 'dimpling streams,' 'painted birds,' and 'merry wit,' but its speaker closes with the traditional pastoral 'invitation':

> When the painted birds laugh in the shade
> Where our table with cherries and nuts is spread
> Come live and be merry and join with me,
> To sing the sweet chorus of Ha, Ha, He.

The poem's daringly unselfconscious refrain prevents a well-worn pastoral convention from sounding calculated or disingenuous. Though **'Laughing Song'** owes more to the traditions of late eighteenth-century pastoral than any other poem in *Innocence,* its celebration of simple rustic pleasures is natural and unaffected. Blake largely avoids what Hallett Smith calls the 'transparent pretence' of most post-Elizabethan pastoral by making his poem as simple or 'native' as possible. The latinized names of the early manuscript version, for example, become common English names in *Innocence;* 'Mary and Susan and Emily' are substituted for 'Edessa and Lyca and Emilie.' Blake knows and uses the tradition, but carefully adapts it to his needs. So too in the design: the flat outline style, with its minimum of interior modelling, though hardly 'native,' mutes 'transparent pretence'—in this case, that of Stothardian rococo. Spartan Neoclassicism, like that of Flaxman, subtly undercuts what Rosenblum calls the 'Neoclassic Erotic.' Similarly, though the youth in the center holds a plumed hat of a sort that suggests the stylized jauntiness of traditional pastoral illustration (and is unlike any other hat in *Innocence*), neither his unfashionably simple costume nor his sturdy, muscular body are in the least like anything Stothard might have produced. Though Blake may have inherited what Roger Fry [in his *Vision and Design*] calls 'the worn-out rags of an effete classical tradition,' he used them in *Songs*—or at least those of Stothard (there being nothing 'effete' about the monumental Neoclassicism of David, for instance, or of Blake's own early 'Joseph' watercolors (1785) or of the 'Job' and 'Ezekial' prints of the following years)—to piece together the visible garments of a deceptively complex and shifting set of attitudes and themes.

Blake's relation to the several varieties of late eighteenth-century Neoclassical theory and practice is an extremely complex business—almost as complex as late eighteenth-century Neoclassicism itself. One of its smaller mysteries—that of the depiction of facial expression—is worth noting at this point, since it affects the readings that follow. Despite his early approval of Lavater, author of *Physiognomical Fragments* (1775-8), as well as of . . . *Aphorisms on Man* (1788), the Blake of *Songs* belongs, in the matter of physiognomy at least, to the school of Winckelmann (and Lessing and Mengs), which is also that of Fuseli and Reynolds, despite their disapproval of the subtleties of German interpretation.

Though other aspects of Blake's art suggest a belief, with Lavater, that 'Each part of an organized body is an image of the whole, has the character of the whole,' the physiognomy of his figures all too frequently (and sometimes incongruously) suggests 'noble simplicity and sedate grandeur in Gesture and Expression'—Winckelmann's oft-quoted terms of praise for the sculpture of the Greeks. The oddly remote, generalized placidity of the faces of Blake's figures (their bodies are another matter, as capable of violent or passionate distortion, especially in the later Lambeth books, as the figures of Mortimer or Fuseli), when combined with the frequently minute scale in *Songs,* makes interpreting physiognomy (always a tricky business) especially difficult. On the whole, therefore, I try to avoid readings based on facial expression.

Other aspects of Blake's visual art require similar caution. Very little has been written about the formal or compositional aspects—the general geometry—of Blake's pictures; or at least about those of his illuminated books. Aside from sections of W. J. T. Mitchell's *Blake's Composite Art,* and Mellor's book, which makes use of Heinrich Wölfflin's distinction between closed (or 'tectonic') and open (or 'atectonic') composition, we have only Wicksteed's theories [advanced in his *Blake's Vision of the Book of Job*] of right and left (together with subsequent controversy), several brief but interesting essays in *Blake's Visionary Forms Dramatic,* and a dazzling (if somewhat bizarre) essay on *The Marriage of Heaven and Hell* by Morris Eaves.

My [essay] adds little to the little already written about formal or compositional meanings in the designs. Aside from brief remarks in passing, . . . I avoid, on the whole, the study of what Arnheim calls 'elementary form patterns.' My reasons are twofold. First, I lack the training. Second, the meanings yielded by previously published formal analyses of the designs, or at least those with which I am familiar, tend to be large and relatively abstract generalizations, on a level apart from (and of little use in delineating) the subtle variations of tone and point of view so important to a proper understanding of *Songs.* Take, for example, Eben Bass's reading of **'The Divine Image'** in *Blake's Visionary Forms Dramatic.*

'Innocence,' writes Bass, 'is the line of the Piper's instrument in the frontispiece (pl. 2), lower left to upper right. Experience is the line of the flames in the general titlepage (pl. 1) or of the falling snow in **'The Chimney Sweeper'** (pl. 37), upper left to lower right.' The reversed 'S' curve of the flame-plant in **'The Divine Image'** ('which *is* the Divine Image') 'resolves thrust into counterthrust [and] is part of Blake's dramatization of the "Two Contrary States." ' As for the design's tiny human figures, Christ raises up the reclining male and female in the lower right corner, and the four figures at the top of the page represent 'Mercy Pity Peace and Love,' since 'in the sense of composition, four figures are expressive of four virtues.' Though Bass can be a close and perceptive reader of Blake's designs, his preoccupation with formal elements in a passage like this obscures or distracts us from important (if more obvious or specific) connections between poem and picture. The text to **'The Divine Image'** teaches us that God is both immanent and transcendent and that, in Hirsch's words, 'the relationship of the transcendent God (Father-

Christ) to the immanent God (Man-Christ) is the feeling of sameness in difference which is the essence and meaning of love.' The repetition in the second stanza,

> For Mercy Pity Peace and Love,
> Is God our father dear:
> And Mercy Pity Peace and Love,
> Is Man his child and care.

is but one of several ways in which 'sameness in difference' is suggested. The arrangement of the design's human figures is another.

The haloed Christ who stands upon the green earth at the foot of the flame-plant stretches his left arm over two naked human figures in a gesture of blessing or release. He is Hirsch's 'transcendent God (Father-Christ)' come to earth to free us from the 'distress' (line 14) of what in *Europe* Blake calls 'The Night of Nature.' At the same time, in the top left corner of the design, directly above the poem's title, a haloless female, carrying a 'pitcher or cruet' in her left hand, and 'something round under her right arm, possibly a loaf of bread' [Erdman], moves towards two figures at prayer, the 'All' of line 2 who 'pray in their distress.' A second gowned figure, also without a halo, points the way.

Though 'in the sense of composition, four figures are expressive of four virtues,' something subtler and more important is going on at the top of the design. An earthly Savior, Hirsch's 'immanent God (Man-Christ),' brings worldly relief, in the form of food and water (or, perhaps, bread and wine) to those who, with backs turned to human goodness, seek help from above. The scene at the bottom of the plate is balanced by the scene at the top, just as the first two lines of the second stanza are balanced by the second two. Christ walks on the green earth; heaven above is but a world of earthly virtues, of distinctly human figures whose actions realize the divinity of the human image. In this case, at least, Bass's concern with formal or compositional meanings causes him to overlook what is most artful and illuminating about the design.

Much has been written about Blake's use of tradition, both poetic and pictorial. His iconography, drawn from an astonishingly wide range of sources, mixes Christian, Classical and esoteric meanings, sometimes within a single design. In *Songs,* of course, it also draws frequently upon the specific motifs of instructional literature: from the fruit-picking children of Lily's famous Latin Grammar, or the anonymous late eighteenth-century children's book, *Mirth Without Mischief,* so like the youths on plate 2 of 'The Ecchoing Green,' to the countless scenes of maternal instruction on the frontispieces of seventeenth- and eighteenth-century readers and alphabets, obvious analogues to the title-page to *Innocence.* But as even the most dedicated iconologist is quick to admit, Blake's borrowings are peculiarly selective (or 'creative' or 'eccentric'). Tradition, whether 'heterodox' (Yeats's phrase) or established, was for him double-edged. Take, for example, the following confession in his description of *The Last Judgement,* painted in 1810:

> < The Greeks represent Chronos or Time as a
> very Aged Man this is Fable but the Real Vision

of Time is in Eternal Youth I have < however > somewhat accomodated my Figure of Time to < the > common opinion as I myself am also infected with it and my Visions also infected and I see Time Aged alas too much so. >

Though students of Blake's iconography are unlikely to find an annotation of this sort reassuring, tradition is at least upheld. Elsewhere Blake abandons it completely:

> The Ladies will be pleased to see that I have represented the Furies by Three Men and not by three Women It is not because I think the Ancients wrong but they will be pleased to remember that mine is Vision and not Fable The Spectator may suppose them Clergymen in the Pulpit Scourging Sin instead of Forgiving it.

The tone of these passages is as revealing as their iconoclastic content. I belong to that school of readers for whom Blake at his wildest is often Blake at his most ironic or purposefully extravagant. Phrases like the second passage's 'The Ladies will be pleased to note . . . ,' or the 'alas' of the first, suggest gentle mockery rather than other-worldliness; a parody or joke at the expense of the sorts of iconographical explanations or 'programmes' upon which both esoteric and traditional Renaissance (and post-Renaissance) art works were frequently based. Given irreverence of this nature, the source-hunter ought to take care. Of what use is it to the reader of 'The Lilly,' for example, a Song of Experience the meaning of which is much debated, to know that Jacob Boehme associated lilies with 'the Birth of the Life and Love and Joy of God in the lives of men'? Even if one could determine Blake's feelings about Boehme in 1794 and/or 1825 (the coloring of the design is of importance) what would that prove? Similarly, do we really need Swedenborg to tell us that the circle represents harmony, or the stone truth? Would the latter correspondence apply, for instance, to 'The Clod and the Pebble,' or to the dreaded 'Stone of Night' in *Jerusalem*?

The critical commonplace, in other words, is worth repeating: tradition plays its part in a study of Blake's iconography, but context and careful attention to detail are infinitely more important. Many of the plants, flowers, birds and beasts in *Songs* are iconographic in nature, but their meanings, whether traditional or not, change and develop from plate to plate. Even the most famous of Blake's symbols—the giant compasses we associate with Urizen, Newton, and the Ancient of Days—can be utterly transformed, as in *Christ in the Carpenter's Shop* (c.1800) where they find their way into the hands of an heroic, unironized Christ.

This view of the unfixed nature of Blake's symbols, and of their relative freedom from (or rather 'with') tradition, lies at the heart of my interpretation both of *Songs* and of Blake's whole life and career. . . . [Several] traditional misconceptions (or misconceptions about tradition) ought here to be mentioned. It is often assumed that Blake's is a Neoplatonic and/or Kabbalistic philosophy of symbolism. This is true, though, only in a restricted and frequently misunderstood sense. Blake was an inveterate foe of mystery and priesthood: he could not have adhered to . . .

The illustrated plate of "The Chimney Sweeper," from the "Experience" section of Songs of Innocence and of Experience.

[Tradition] plays its part in a study of Blake's iconography, but context and careful attention to detail are infinitely more important. Many of the plants, flowers, birds and beasts in *Songs* are iconographic in nature, but their meanings, whether traditional or not, change and develop from plate to plate.

—Zachary Leader

a philosophy of symbolism the central feature of which was 'The augur interpreting a portent, the mystagogue explaining the divinely ordained ritual, the priest expounding the image in the temple, the Jewish or Christian teacher pondering the meaning of the word of God' [E. H. Gombrich in his *Symbolic Images: Studies in the Art of the Renaissance*]. For Blake, fixed systems were enemies, the creations of a priesthood that 'took advantage of and enslav'd the vulgar by attempting to realize or abstract the mental deities from their objects . . . [c]hoosing forms of worship from poetic tales.'

Blake's symbol system in *Songs,* like Fuseli's, has much close affinities to the rival Aristotelian or analogical tradition exemplified by the emblem books of Ripa, Quarles, and Wither; a tradition in which the icon defines as well as represents the given concept. This is as one would expect, given Blake's training as an engraver (engraving being one of the last fields in which Renaissance iconology survived), and his poetic apprenticeship to the school of Thomson, the Wartons, Collins, Gray, and other admirers of the personified abstraction.

Blake's connection to the Neoplatonic philosophy of symbols lies less in the nature of the images he uses (only rarely of a mysterious or apophatic sort, in which like represents unlike), than in the seriousness with which he takes them; his refusal to treat visual symbols as sophisticated games, clever analogues upon which the full meanings of motifs or whole designs so frequently depend. For Blake, as for the Neoplatonist, the visual symbol was more than a mere sign or metaphor: the Neoplatonist saw his symbols as theophanies, the forms in which God Himself chose to appear to the limited human mind; Blake saw them as no less divine, but only because they were human, an expression of man's god-like creative or poetic faculty, the only true divinity.

The other point of similarity between Blake's use of visual symbols and that of the Neoplatonists is the value he places on their power to communicate on a pre-rational level. For the Blake of *Songs* this power need entail no repudiation of analogy or rational analysis; it is simply another, though at the moment repressed (and *therefore* more important), way of arriving at meaning. Blake's attitude to pre-conscious ways of knowing, and the ease with which it can be misunderstood, is paralleled in the following definition, from E. H. Gombrich, of the Renaissance emblem or *impresa:* 'an image [that] reveals an aspect of the world which would seem to elude the ordered progress of dialectic argument.' We ought to note and emulate Gombrich's care here: 'would seem' not 'does.' With Blake too, it is easy to mistake what seems (a hatred of reason *per se,* and of the analytic habits of the Aristotelian) for what is (hatred of the mis-use of reason, and fear for the dangerous consequences of its abuse). That Blake himself . . . was prone to such mistaking, has much to do with its continued occurrence.

Finally, a brief word about recurring gestures in Blake's designs. Figures who crouch, stride, raise or stretch their arms, cross their legs or clutch their heads, appear so frequently in Blake's art that Laurence Binyon [in his *The Drawings and Engravings of William Blake*] can barely bring himself to forgive what he calls 'the endless repetitions of attitude and gesture.' Many, as Bo Lindberg and others have suggested, are derived from, or subtly allude to, past traditions, others take on uniquely personal meanings. Again, the key to understanding lies in context and careful attention to detail. (pp. 37-59)

Zachary Leader, in his Reading Blake's "Songs", *Routledge & Kegan Paul, 1981, 259 p.*

D. R. M. Wilkinson (essay date 1985)

[*In the following excerpt, Wilkinson examines numerous varying and sometimes contradictory interpretations of* Songs of Innocence and of Experience.]

It is true that today we cannot avoid seeing Blake, even in his **Songs of Innocence and Experience,** in the wider context of his times. We are trained in our reading to draw on, and where relevant to refer to, the historical background, the literary, religious and artistic contexts, contemporary usage of language, and Blake's own unique and complex beliefs and symbols. We are advised to study the significance to the texts of his illustrations, and even to see a unity in his entire oeuvre. This is all very right and good, yet in trying to take stock of the situation, if only in relation to these same **Songs of Innocence and Experience,** one cannot but be disturbed in the first place by the very mass of the Blake industry, and in the second place by the speculative extravagance of much of the commentary and interpretation. It is often difficult these days to remain altogether sane about Blake, particularly when one observes that where the nineteenth century tended to look on him as Blake-the-Child or Blake-the-Madman, we have now come full circle in the twentieth century and have discovered a kind of Henry James-Blake, full of subtle irony and wit, very conscious of point-of-view and tone, and playing with and echoing traditional and inherited art forms and ideas much in the manner of a T. S. Eliot. The sophistication of our reading habits—at any rate of the reading habits of those influenced by the universities—is such that we are in danger often of being quite unable to agree on, or even to decide for ourselves about, what is allowable and what is not allowable in the way of an interpretation even of a fairly simple poem.

As long ago as 1818, Coleridge borrowed a copy of Blake's **Songs** from a friend and then wrote brief verdicts on them (ranging from 'It gave me pleasure in the highest' to 'in the lowest degree') [in a letter to C. A. Tulk in *The Collected Letters of S. T. Coleridge*], some of which strike one as very significant, and some as rather strange. He had them in his keeping for only a week apparently, and maybe what I. A. Richards has said [in *Practical Criticism: A Study of Literary Judgement.*] is true, namely that a week is not long enough for the reading of four poems—so what, we might ask, could even a Coleridge do with 45 in the same period? The most striking fact is that by and large he found the **Songs of Innocence** superior to the **Songs of Experience,** a preference that is reflected also in the comments of Allan Cunningham [in his *The Lives of the Most Eminent British Painters*], Alexander Gilchrist [in *The Life of William Blake,* edited by W. Graham Robertson], and D. G. Rossetti [*Critics on Blake,* edited by Judith O'Neill], to mention three representative nineteenth-century commentators, whereas the twentieth century tends to make much more of the **Songs of Experience.** When Coleridge declares that the two songs of *Innocence,* '**Night**' and '**The Little Black Boy**', are the best Blake

wrote, it would be a bold critic who would maintain it was a judgment based on lack of insight or information, Coleridge being what he was. At the same time it is very difficult to come to terms with his verdict that the innocent '**Holy Thursday**' is to be preferred to '**The Tyger**', '**London**' and '**The Sick Rose**'. No doubt a certain degree of eccentricity must be allowed him, and, by twentieth-century standards, a certain lack of critical sophistication, if that's the right phrase for it, might explain some of his preferences. But if there was a tendency in the nineteenth century to prefer the **Songs of Innocence** to those of **Experience,** it went along with a braver tendency to respond positively to the simple, the beautiful, the pure, the noble and the mystical than the twentieth century can manage. So that it looks as though their values were significantly different, and that we, in taking a less innocent, post Freudian, 'Waste Land' view of things than they, *and* in having an academic industry to keep us up to the mark, are in no position to recover and endorse their apparently less complicated perceptions. We have a library of confusing standpoints in the matter of interpreting Blake's **Songs,** so that there are some grounds for despair among those who find contradictory meanings not altogether acceptable—at least not in all cases.

Yet progress has been made. In this century three basic criteria have altered the approach to these **Songs** quite radically, namely: (a) that Blake's philosophy, his thought, his system, it is claimed, is not only coherent but constant, and that his poems *inevitably* gain in meaning by being interpreted in the light of his philosophy/system: (b) that there is always a sharp distinction between Blake's own voice and that of the speakers of the **Songs;** and (c) that the design or illustration to each poem is essential to the understanding of that poem. Without these criteria, there would have been very much less development in the commentaries on the **Songs;** but on the other hand it is by now very clear that such criteria can also produce their own kind of interpretative chaos. One of the main aims of this [essay] is to inspect certain significantly representative comments on a select number of the **Songs** in order to illustrate the type of chaos. A recent book by Zachary Leader, *Reading Blake's 'Songs'* is very much to the purpose here, for it is most sophisticatedly modern, very thorough and informative, and registers very sensitively both the progress referred to above and some of the chaos. Recourse will be had, of course, to a few other commentators.

'**The Little Black Boy**' is a good poem to begin with since Coleridge waxed lyrical about it, it is also apparently quite simple, and yet it has given rise to some remarkably confusing interpretations even among the most responsible critics. The problem revolves round the question of the speaker's character and point of view. It seems likely that Coleridge took it 'conventionally', as supporting, say, certain views of the *Society for the Abolition of the Slave Trade* (founded in 1787).

The Little Black Boy

My mother bore me in the southern wild,
And I am black, but O! my soul is white;
White as an angel is the English child,

But I am black, as if bereav'd of light.

My mother taught me underneath a tree,
And sitting down before the heat of day,
She took me on her lap and kissed me,
And pointing to the east, began to say:

'Look on the rising sun: there God does live,
'And gives his light, and gives his heat away;
'And flowers and trees and beasts and men re-
    cieve
'Comfort in morning, joy in the noonday.

'And we are put on earth a little space,
'That we may learn to bear the beams of love;
'And these black bodies and this sunburnt face
'Is but a cloud, and like a shady grove.

'For when our souls have learn'd the heat to
    bear,
'The cloud will vanish; we shall hear his voice,
'Saying: "Come out from the grove, my love &
    care,
' "And round my golden tent like lambs re-
    joice".'

Thus did my mother say, and kissed me;
And thus I say to little English boy.
When I from black and he from white cloud free,
And round the tent of God like lambs we joy,

I'll shade him from the heat, till he can bear
To lean in joy upon our father's knee;
And then I'll stand and stroke his silver hair,
And be like him, and he will then love me.

The anxiety of the little black boy, one takes it, about the colour of his skin gives rise to the mother's consoling statement on learning to bear God's love here on earth, with the further implication (as the boy sees it) that ultimately in God's eyes all are equal, so that the white boy may come to love him too. Whether or not Coleridge read it in this way cannot be known, but this is more or less how the poem is often taken. As Martin Nurmi says [in his *William Blake*]: the boy has been taught

> by a visionary mother to see beyond his present state to a time when both he and the English boy, who in the poem represents the dominant white society that instituted slavery, will both stand revealed in their common humanity and play around the tent of God, both of them free of the 'clouds' that now obscure their humanity.

That is probably as central a statement as one can get. But even in a poem as simple as this, one must be ready to take into account certain of Blake's ideas—provided the meaning is thereby significantly affected. A note on Swedenborgian influence tells us, for instance, what we are to understand by those 'clouds' and the 'sun, light and heat'. Swedenborg wrote: 'The Sun of heaven is the Lord, and the light there is Divine Truth, & the heat is Divine Good, and both proceed from the Lord as the Sun' [quoted in *William Blake: Selected Poetry and Letters*, edited by A. S. Crehan]. But this heat and light are difficult to bear, apparently. Even the angels, for protection, 'are veiled in a thin suitable cloud', it appears. If we are left a little uncertain as to why angels should need this kind of protection, it does at least seem likely that Blake would have used

these words with these associations. But this example illustrates in the simplest way that his 'system' was not fixed once and for all, for when he was writing the ***Songs of Innocence*** he had a sympathy for the Swedenborgians which he later relinquished. If it is argued that he merely modified Swedenborg's views later to suit himself, that modification is itself an indication of development and change. What matters more though is that in exploiting these connotations of clouds, sun, light and heat in this poem, Blake has *created* a context that functions poetically even without reference to Swedenborg. A poem is not a piece of philosophy, and can seldom be said simply to enact an idea.

Everyone interested in Blake will know Geoffrey Keynes's edition of the illuminated ***Songs,*** so it will be to the purpose to see his comments on **'The Little Black Boy'** (though his comments on **'The Blossom'** might make one pause). He too affirms that the poem teaches us 'that the creation of the world was an act of divine mercy, by which man might become accustomed to the heat of divine love'. Coleridge might well have gone along with this. He might even have shared Gilchrist's enthusiasm of 1863, namely:

> For a nobler depth of religious beauty, with accordant grandeur of sentiment and language, I know no parallel nor hint elsewhere of such a poem as **"The Little Black Boy"**.

Nobler depth of religious beauty, grandeur of sentiment and language. Coleridge presumably felt something like this. Nobility and grandeur were terms commonly used to endorse Milton's greatness in the nineteenth century—qualities which our self-questioning age can be embarrassed by, though that embarrassment might well prove a handicap in reading Blake.

At all events what Coleridge and Gilchrist would not have been ready to accept is Zachary Leader's account of the poem. Leader finds the mother's attitude towards suffering un-Blakeian and therefore suspect. According to him she says we are put on earth in order to learn to bear the beams of love through *suffering:* 'the teachings of the mother suggest a deeply pessimistic response to life on earth,' and she 'bases her acceptance of loss and limitation on the promise of a heavenly reward'. The idea of suffering in this life and getting a reward hereafter while no doubt conventionally Christian is indeed un-Blakeian, at least in the sense that he can be shown to have expressed the view that this life is what we know of heaven or hell or eternity. Leader goes on to argue that the poem offers a 'powerful but compassionate critique of the mother's teaching' which 'gently discredits those who would have us look for an Eden beyond or outside this world'—a characteristic Blakeian view—Eden is here or nowhere—'the conventional Christian heaven', in other words, 'is a dangerous illusion'. This seems to be sound Blake scholarship, yet it is very difficult to see the poem as it stands as pessimistic: a typical dilemma in Blake criticism, brought about by the reliance on the criterion that requires the poems to be strictly related to what Blake thought and expressed elsewhere. This is not to say that one must not accept this, but that one must not *subordinate* the poem to the idea or the 'system', or to what is presumed to be the author's essential stance.

Leader continues: 'Just as the traditional doctrine does not satisfy Blake, so the mother's explanations do not resolve her son's doubts'. She does not in fact answer his questions, apparently, and as Harold Bloom (quoted in Leader) also claims, the black boy is left confused, only partly reassured, still sensing his inferiority. At this point in the argument, Blake's design, his illustration, is adduced as further evidence that the boy's fears are substantiated. In the design, which follows the last line of the poem, the white boy is *between* Christ and the black boy (who is stiff and separate). 'The drawing is a continuation of the poem', writes Leader, 'it presents a context in which the black boy's doubts and fears are given meaning. It marks the end of the child's innocence'. The poem is thus seen as a typical Blake satire on conventional Christian notions—all in keeping with his expressed views, no doubt; but then it can be argued that the mother is not necessarily talking about a hereafter at all—about a reward in heaven—but about a reward here and now, and this is also very much in keeping with Blake's views—that heaven is here or nowhere. In this case the mother, then, is not pessimistic at all, but loving, and innocently concerned to allay the fears of her child.

And then the further problem—Gilchrist recognised it too: are we to see the designs as *essentially* and *qualifyingly* related to the poems—and always? If so, it must be assumed that Blake was as good an artist as he was a poet, and this is difficult to accept. But even granting that he was, there is good reason to believe that his drawing was not always adequate to his poetry, just as, no doubt, his drawing sometimes may have been superior to his poetry. And this can complicate everything. Those who confidently claim that the designs are not only necessary to but inseparable from the poems seldom seem to take this into account. Just as they do not always take sufficiently into account the fact that the designs are not always coloured the same. For instance Leader argues that the little black boy in the design is darker than, and so will not become like, the little English boy. But this is so only in *most* of the later copies. And so we must take *them* into account and not the earlier ones? Does this mean that Blake only discovered his intention later? And if he did, why did he then not colour all of the later ones darker? Need we assume, furthermore, that the later Blake is the more trustworthy artist—the better artist? We do not simply assume that the later Wordsworth was the better Wordsworth. At the same time it must be admitted that there is a long-established tendency to place considerable emphasis on the significance of the designs, and it would be irresponsible to attempt to reject this. What can be shown, though, is that the *determination* to make the designs bear on the poems in some cases causes more confusion even than the poems themselves do—and this is to multiply problems quite purposelessly.

More importantly it can be said that this reading of Leader's (and it is not entirely new) is based on the even more troublesome assumption that the mother's views differ from Blake's—that the speakers of these *Songs* are often, if not always, putting forward views for emotional and imaginative inspection, for critical questioning by the reader. Point of view has always now to be considered—

even in the most innocent of the *Songs of Innocence.* Again we are faced with: who is the speaker? and how does Blake mean us to take him or her? But if the speaker of the poems, particularly of the poems of *Innocence,* is indeed suspect, is indeed expressing views or sentiments that are mistaken, or even destructive (in Blake's eyes), then one cannot but ask where Innocence ends and where Experience begins? Why the clear division into two types of song? (Of course everyone knows that Blake shifted some of them from one group to the other, but in the whole conception of the two groups this is neither here nor there.) When Blake declares that he is presenting us with the 'Two Contrary States of the Human Soul,' one must presume that he means what he says and that such an express statement of his about innocence and experience should carry more weight than subtle inferences to the contrary, derived from an interpretation of his 'philosophy' or of other poems of his. And if in that most innocent of all *Innocence* poems, **'Infant Joy',** when the mother says to her child (let us assume it is the mother) 'Sweet joy befall thee!'—if in this poem we are meant to believe (as Leader argues) that she says it 'perhaps because she is secretly worried that it may not', then the twentieth century has become too un-Coleridgean, too incapable of responding to nobility, grandeur and, we might add, the holiness of the heart's affections? Blake himself claims in the innocent 'Introduction':

> And I wrote my happy songs
> Every child may joy to hear.

There is a degree of literal acceptation of Blake's words that is indispensable, for if the experiences of the *Innocence* poems are to be read in the deceitful light of the *Experience* poems, then the experiences there recorded can hardly be taken as the true contraries of anything in the *Songs of Experience.*

In the *Experience* poem **'Infant Sorrow'** the child finds the world hostile. The child in **'Infant Joy'** finds the world to be trusted. These are the basic contraries. There should be no question but that the mother's statement 'Sweet joy befall thee!' is a blessing on the child, though not of course a guarantee of any kind. To suggest that it might be a wish reflecting doubt is to attribute the doubts and fears of the twentieth century unnecessarily to Blake. And what is more, it is a failure to see these fears and doubts as emotional and imaginative weakness in a poem boldly enacting the nature of love and trust.

Coleridge, it will be remembered, found another of Blake's *Songs* quite above criticism, namely **'Night'.** In this verdict he might have been surprised to find Leader altogether at one with him: 'One of the most complex and beautiful of Blake's creations', he writes, in a very long and satisfying analysis—he sees the persuasive power of the rhythms and the rich inclusiveness of the night scene uniting, as it were, Death and Eden Garden—that is the sort of thing he is pointing at, and it must be acknowledged that this quality of comment is something we would look for in vain in nineteenth-century criticism.

It is time to look more specifically at certain select comments on the *Experience* poems **'London', 'The Tyger'** and **'The Sick Rose'.** Of **'London',** John Beer says [in *In-*

terpreting Blake, edited by Michael Phillips] quite rightly that it is 'perhaps the least controversial of Blake's works', which makes it all the more curious to discover certain interpretations so controversial that they seem calculated to disconcert.

The two most important critical problems with regard to **'London'** revolve round the meanings of certain key words and the questionable character of the speaker of the poem, it would appear. It might be said that until a reader has established the meanings of 'charter'd', 'mark' and 'ban', for instance, in all their complexities, he cannot qualify as a twentieth-century Blake reader.

LONDON

I wander thro' each charter'd street,
Near where the charter'd Thames does flow,
And mark in every face I meet
Marks of weakness, marks of woe.

In every cry of every Man,
In every Infant's cry of fear,
In every voice, in every ban,
The mind-forg'd manacles I hear.

How the Chimney-sweeper's cry
Every black'ning Church appalls;
And the hapless Soldier's sigh
Runs in blood down Palace walls.

But most thro' midnight streets I hear
How the youthful Harlot's curse
Blasts the new born Infant's tear,
And blights with plagues the Marriage hearse.

The fullest recent explanation of 'charter' is Thompson's [in his essay 'London' in *Interpreting Blake*] where he shows that for Blake's contemporaries, Burke and Paine, the word had opposite connotations. For Burke it was a good word, a charter gives rights, it involves a 'heritable set of liberties and privileges', while for Paine it was a bad word, involving not freedom but monopoly; it implied exclusion and limitation. Blake is obviously using the word in Paine's sense, where 'the adjectival form—charter'd—enforces the direct commercial allusion: "the organisation of a city in terms of trade" '. It is the sort of information that places Blake historically and politically, but it is in no sense a new placing. It is relevant and confirmatory information, but it hardly affects one's reading of the poem at all, for the *created* significance is already there.

The word 'mark' only became a real subject of debate in 1978 where Thompson and Glen [in her 'Blake's Criticism of Moral Thinking in *Songs of Innocence and Songs of Experience*' in *Interpreting Blake*] offered alternative biblical origins for Blake's usage. Thompson falls back on the 'mark of the beast' from *Rev.* iii, 16-17, but rejects, it seems rightly, Glen's citing of *Ezekiel,* ix, 3 & 4. The mark of the beast, Thompson argues, 'would seem, like "charter'd", to have something to do with the buying and selling of human values', but it is not clear what. And he is forced to conclude rather limply that this 'question is incapable of final proof' as though it were a theorem. Thompson does not altogether sacrifice good sense to sophistication, but his arguments exemplify certain weaknesses of those with a *special thesis.* He wishes to establish that 'the sym-

bolic organisation' of the poem 'is within the clearly conceived and developing logic of market relations'. The word 'charter'd' had set him going, and from there onwards he sees all the imagery as market orientated, which is simply to omit certain very important connotations. If we look at the poem without axes to grind, we might say that the first seven lines are monotonously simple, the insistent repetition—'charter'd, charter'd, mark, marks, marks, every cry, every . . . cry, every, every'—emphasising the drabness and the constricting sameness of the city; and then the abrupt change in the eighth line:

The mind-forg'd manacles I hear.

In the interests of sanity, if of nothing else, it must be asserted that those manacles are hardly market matters—they are *mind-forg'd.* It is the central experience of the poem—it is at once the experience, the analysis, the explanation and the protest. It is the mind that is responsible, one would say, for this horror, this mental Urizenic horror. What follow—the telling images of chimney sweeper, soldier, harlot and marriage hearse—are supporting objective illustrations of the basic experience. Those final 'blasts' and 'blights' are not market words either, though they do relate to the harvest. One recalls 'the blasted ear of corn' mentioned three times in *Genesis* xli, and here so finely (and unconsciously?) transmuted into 'tear'; and 'blasts' carried over into 'blights' with cumulative emphasis, withering all that is natural (the 'tear') along with that restrictive institution of marriage.

All the apparent certainties of this last paragraph, however, will be challenged when we look at the questionable character of the speaker of the poem. Before doing so, there is one more key word to be held up for inspection, viz. 'ban'. Thompson refutes the commentator who maintained that 'ban' only meant 'curse'—which was a common meaning of the word in those days—and adds that one 'must be prepared for 17 types of ambiguity in Blake'. Which is to say we have now made a William Empson-Blake of him—one step further into the twentieth century than our Henry James-Blake. Instead of 'curse', Thompson offers some old and some new meanings: prohibition, banns before marriage, and even the 'bans of Church and State against the publications . . . of the followers of Tom Paine'. Ransacking the dictionary, or history, can make a problem of any word where there need be little to query. The word here is no doubt complex, but one cannot do without the central connotation of 'curse'. The word appears in a stanza in which we get 'In every *cry* . . . / In every Infant's *cry* / In every *voice*'—a sequence of sounds, noises, street noises even, as Thompson himself later points out, ending with 'ban'. In the final stanza, too, we have the 'Harlot's curse' harking back to 'ban'. There will have to be far more convincing reasons for dropping this central connotation, however many others are adduced as well.

While uncertainty about the meanings of words can prove a very real difficulty in reading Blake, the questioning of the speaker's character and role can do more, it can alter one's reading altogether. Coleridge would no doubt have been ready to accept the speaker often as no other than the author. After all, Coleridge was often so himself in his poems. But it is otherwise with Blake. He seems to have been, in T. S. Eliot's sense, one of the most impersonal of poets, seldom speaking in his own voice. As regards '**London**', it was Heather Glen who put the most extreme case—in her 1978 essay—making him a tainted speaker who is offering to judge the external rottenness of society. And to judge in such a society is seen as a deeply ambiguous act. He can really only 'mark' and not teach anything—'a paralysing mental activity'. Acutely self-aware, he is nevertheless 'trapped within the world he is trying to judge'. The speaker is exposed in the poem quite as much as the society he is judging.

In 1981 Leader partly endorsed this view of Glen's. The speaker, he says, 'like so many others in *Experience,* is himself a victim to the evils he so brilliantly exposes and analyses', and refers in his footnote to Thompson, Glen and others. He makes quite clear that we must 'distinguish between Blake's vision and that of his speaker'.

In her new book of 1983 [*Vision and Disenchantment: Blake's Songs and Wordsworth's Lyrical Ballads*], however, Glen revises her position. She has dropped *Ezekiel,* for one. The problem of the speaker is still central to her lengthy and fascinating interpretation, but there is a great gain in the ambivalence with which he is treated. He is the observer, still 'fatally linked to the way in which' he sees the world. He is 'trapped within the world on which he is trying to comment', but he is only a 'thinly present I' now. From here it is a brief step to: ' "**London**" seems much closer to Blake's own voice than do many others of the *Songs of Experience:* most obviously, this is because of the way in which it pushes beyond exposure of its speaker's limitations . . . into a more apocalyptic mode'. This is a pretty considerable qualification, even though it does not colour her whole argument. In the world of this London 'there is no sense of human potentiality, and no creative change'. . . . 'People have become objects. . . . Yet the effect is not one of defeat'. This is a most welcome development in commentary on the *Songs,* for although Glen still seems to imply that the speaker in *Experience* is *by definition* suspect, in the case of '**London**' she allows for an ambivalence that tests such an assumption fruitfully. It is worth recording, too, that in her view the speakers of *Innocence* are granted full innocent status.

If one had any doubts about whether the design was always indispensable to a reading of one of the *Songs,* the design to '**London**' should clinch the matter, for it produces only confusing interpretations. It is of an old man being led by a boy, and as Leader rightly states: 'the design's weakness detracts—or rather distracts us—from the poem's greatness'. We get told that the old man is perhaps the Creator Urizen [Keynes], that he is just an old man, blind like the speaker [Glen], that he is probably the Bard, but may be the City of London [Leader], for Blake himself in *Jerusalem* writes: 'I see London blind and age-bent begging thro the streets of Babylon, led by a child. His tears run down his beard'. One might have expected this last interpretation, what with Blake's own supporting comment, to have been made more of, but in the general debate this is relegated to a footnote. Commentators are almost inevitably selective in engaging Blake's expressed support

where the problems begin to appear insuperable. But it is clear that in this case a satisfactory interpretation has not been found, and until it has, generalisations about the relevance of the design should be avoided.

And the same can be said about the much more notorious design to '**The Tyger**'. 'In none of the extant copies of *Songs*', writes Leader, 'is there a creature remotely comparable to the picture created by the poem's awestruck speaker'. There for him is the problem. It is known that Blake could depict ferocious animals, yet this tiger is a domestic tabby-cat. The redoubtable John E. Grant, quoted in Leader, has gone so far as to suggest that it could be seen as a joke, 'a joke, not so much on us as on the awestruck questioner, or the Tyger, and perhaps on the Creater himself'. But this is neither sophisticated nor sensible. Some years later he proposed another reading [in *Blake Newsletter* V, No. 3 (1967)], namely that it was an intentional irony of Blake's to make the two tigers contrast so sharply. Blake, he argues, 'is always trying to elicit or provoke a determinate response from his audience, rather than incoherent evidence that they have been moved'. But if it was an intentional irony, one can still be baffled that that was all Blake meant. The case of the '**Tyger**' almost emboldens one to affirm that one cannot claim that the designs are indispensable. But no doubt absolutes and finalities should be avoided in criticism.

Leader at all events is subtler:

> Much of what the awestruck questioner says implies a world (and a way of looking at it) that Blake would have found unnecessarily limited and limiting. Blake might well have sought to undermine the speaker by domesticating or defanging his tiger.

How else, one might argue, can one justify the design? But it is such phrases as 'Blake would have found' and 'Blake would have thought', that must give one pause. Such suppositions can only be tentative. At best they can be taken as the scientist takes hypotheses—to see if they work. And maybe one ought not to forget that Blake once wrote in reply to a critic, the Rev. Dr. Trusler (granted—in irritation), that that 'which can be made explicit to the idiot is not worth my care' [*The Complete Writings of William Blake,* edited by Geoffrey Keynes], and he may have overestimated us.

In turning to '**The Sick Rose**' we have another poem of Blake's that is commonly accepted as one of his greatest, but there the agreement ends. Keynes largely neglects the problems with the following rather vague gesture: 'This poem is usually interpreted as an image of the troubles of earthly love'. More significantly, critics have explored most sophisticatedly the conflicting connotations of the 'rose' and the 'worm' symbols in this poem, have discovered explicit moral significance in such words as 'crimson' and 'dark secret', and have given them a marked *Experience* twist by balancing them against the *Innocent* phrasing of '**The Blossom**' (a poem which is much less clear than '**The Sick Rose**'). In this case it is not the speaker who becomes suspect, but the 'rose'—thus a variant of the rule.

In 1964 two commentators put forward more or less the same view, namely that the poem is a sort of satire on the rose-figure, depicted as a woman who is hypocritical about her acceptance of love. If **'The Blossom'** was innocent, the **'Rose'** must be corrupt.

The Sick Rose

O Rose, thou art sick!
The invisible worm
That flies in the night,
In the howling storm,

Has found out thy bed
Of crimson joy:
And his dark secret love
Does thy life destroy.

The one commentator, Martin Price, argues [in his *Blake: Vision and Satire*] that ' "crimson joy" suggests the rose's complicity both in passion and in secrecy, disguise destroys from within'. The other, E. D. Hirsch [in his *Innocence and Experience: An Introduction to Blake*], maintains that 'the idea of sickness like syphilis [the modern touch], is the internal result of love enjoyed secretly and illicitly instead of purely and openly . . . the rose is the type of female who, enjoying the outward show of modesty promotes the repressive and hypocritical customs of the "Father of Jealousy" '. This is to see the poem as a moral analysis of the 'main character', rather than as a clash of opposing forces. And this is to leave out of account the rich vitality of the rose. It is difficult to believe that the rose's sickness is 'the internal result of love enjoyed secretly and illicitly' when it is the *worm* that is the active one: it is the *worm* that has 'found out thy bed / Of crimson joy', and it is *his* 'dark secret love' that 'Does *thy* life destroy' (italics mine). As for the complicity of the rose, one must look elsewhere for that. One must either deduce it theoretically from the purity of **'The Blossom'** or one must assume a kind of sympathetic condescension in the words 'O Rose, thou art sick!' The first is to go unnecessarily outside the poem (which is sufficiently an *Experience* poem without doing so), and the second is difficult to reconcile with what follows.

But it is not difficult to register the tremendous clash between what is essentially life-giving in the poem (the rose and the bed of crimson joy) and the powerfully destructive (the worm, the howling storm and the dark secret love), between the opulent vitality of life, of love, and what is destructively possessive. The following comment by F. R. Leavis [in *Scrutiny* XIII (1945-46)] captures something of the essence of the poem. In evoking the significance of the words, he explores poetic resonances in a spirit quite other than that of the *Blake Dictionary*:

> 'Rose' as developed by 'thy bed of crimson joy' evokes rich passion, sensuality at once glowing, delicate and fragrant, and exquisite health. 'Bed of crimson joy' is voluptuously tactual in suggestion . . . and there is also a suggestion of a secret heart ('found out'), the focus of life, down there at the core of the closely clustered and enclosing petals.

The invisible worm
That flies in the night,

In the howling storm,

> offering its shock of contrast to the warm security of love . . . conveys the ungovernable otherness of the dark forces of the psyche when they manifest themselves in disharmonies.

At all events, to make the rose in some sense suspect is to put theory before poetry—is to make **'The Sick Rose'** fit a satiric and negative *system* of *Experience,* rather than to see the essential clash rendered here in great poetry. Maybe it solves nothing to say that commentary is in the case of this poem irrelevant, and I am glad it was Northrop Frye and not myself who said [in 'Blake After Two Centuries', reprinted in **William Blake: Songs of Innocence and of Experience,** ed. Margaret Bottrall] that the poem speaks 'with the unanswerable authority of poetry itself', but that is more useful than to read it as a satire.

It should by now be clear that this [essay] is not intended simply to be dismissive towards the main body of twentieth-century commentary on Blake's **Songs.** Much progress, useful progress, has obviously been made. Such stock-taking as can be managed within the length of an [essay] must necessarily be limited to significant examples. A book would be too short to cover the material; but it would also be too long. There has been too much written, and interpretation has become both complex and contradictory. If it was for the twentieth century to elicit multiple readings from Blake's **Songs,** then that may well be to the credit of the twentieth century. Should a contemporary reader find that the holding of a multiplicity of interpretations simultaneously in his mind and heart is an impossible task, it is possible that he ought to leave Blake to others—at least as far as the debate about meanings is concerned. But at the same time there is a point at which a multiplicity of interpretation not only befogs the issue, but has unfortunately become something of an academic requirement. Where that point is, I have here and there tentatively tried to suggest in particular instances. But there can be no useful general line of demarcation prescribed. Three tentative rules can, however, be proposed though, namely: that we should not be ready to take on trust (i) that each of Blake's **Songs** must of necessity be seen to be related to other songs of his or to his system or ideas recorded elsewhere; (ii) that there is *necessarily* a sharp distinction between his own voice and the voices of the speakers of both **Innocence** and **Experience;** and lastly, (iii) that the design is, in each case, proven to be necessarily of direct value in appreciating the **Songs.** We are in duty bound not to make Blake more confusing than is absolutely necessary! And this means, too, that we must be more cautious than hitherto about accepting all these that offer over-all explanations. Though in this matter, Heather Glen's thesis whereby she makes a virtue of Blake's 'disconcerting inconclusiveness' would seem to be something of an exception. In her case the real progress in recent Blake criticism is very evident in her allowing for Blake's **Songs** as 'foregrounding and exploring the problematic nature of that process by which men seek to categorize and label experience'. Ambiguity and open-endedness can in this way come to be seen as basic strategies for Blake in his efforts to challenge the conventions of his time. It is not altogether new in Blake criticism, but the emphases given are. It is a welcome development, and may reduce the confusion in the matter of interpretation. Though considering the industry it may not.

At all events we have the poet/painter's word for it that we are on the right path:

> I intreat, then, that the Spectator will attend to the Hands & Feet, to the Lineaments of the Countenances: they are all descriptive of Character, & not a line is drawn without intention, & that most discriminate and particular. As Poetry admits not a Letter that is Insignificant, so Painting admits not a Grain of Sand or a Blade of Grass Insignificant—much less an Insignificant Blur or Mark.

We are on the right path, no doubt, but there are a number of learned signposts inviting us in more than one direction at a time these days. (pp. 227-40)

> D. R. M. Wilkinson, "Blake's 'Songs': Taking Stock, 1984," in English Studies, *Netherlands, Vol. 66, No. 3, June, 1985, pp. 227-40.*

Harold Pagliaro   (essay date 1987)

[*In the following excerpt from his* Selfhood and Redemption in Blake's "Songs," *Pagliaro asserts that in* Songs of Innocence and of Experience *Blake proposes a psychology that enables reconciliation with adversity.*]

If one reads each poem in **Songs of Innocence and of Experience** for evidence of the chief character's functioning psychology in the world of the poem, one finds that a pattern of redemption emerges for the **Songs** as a whole. Though such critics as Frye [in "Blake's Introduction to Experience," in *Blake: A Collection of Critical Essays,* edited by Frye], Gleckner [in his *The Piper and the Bard*], and Bloom [in his *Blake's Apocalypse*] are aware of a gradual progress in the **Songs** from Innocence to Experience, and with the ideal of organized Innocence beyond, they rely on a knowledge of Blake's redemptive process as it is identified in the prophecies and other works for crucial elements of their critical structure of the **Songs.** In this method, Blake's universe is identified in fairly large terms derived from all of his poetry and prose, and then the **Songs** are analyzed with fairly extensive reference to that rich and suggestive context of meaning. I doubt that anyone who has read all of Blake can avoid being affected by a sense for the whole as he reads the **Songs,** and I am not about to recommend an exclusive address to the **Songs.** Nor do I wish to suggest that the readings produced by Frye, Gleckner, Bloom, and others, along with readings that adduce a special context in which to consider the **Songs**—the idea of pastoral, or the eighteenth-century debate about education and childhood—are not accurate and extremely useful to students of Blake. I wish only to claim that reading the **Songs** from the "inside," to a much greater extent than has been usual, with an eye to the functioning psychology of the chief characters, will yield evidence for defining not only various states of Innocence and states of Experience the **Songs** have been shown to represent but also the psychology underlying the passage from one to the other and beyond. Though it is a commonplace for criticism about the **Songs** to say that a character is in this or that degree of Innocence or Experience, no study has concerned itself with the psychological process *as* process, of movement from one state to another, a process I believe to be evidenced in the **Songs.**

The comprehensiveness of religious archetypal structures to which Blake's works have been convincingly referred, in terms so full and adequate it seems impossible to enlarge the territories of Blake's meaning, has proved a blessing. The works of Damon, Frye, Frosch, Fox, and Gallant come most immediately to mind. But the very excellence of this scholarship, which has guided us all, may obscure a crucial issue and mislead us to a doubtful conclusion. I believe it may be too generally assumed that the paradigm of redemption in Blake's work—Selfhood formed, Selfhood examined, Selfhood annihilated—is amply understood. But the combination of Hebrew prophetic, Christian, and psychological terms used to discuss the paradigm, though identifying it well enough, has not articulated it in terms most likely to move us so that we may be said to share in its operation rather than to observe it. I believe such terms are available and that they derive from the psychology out of which states and changing states of characters in the **Songs** are generated.

It was not until Blake wrote **Milton** that he used the terms "Selfhood," "Self-examination," "Self-annihilation." By that time he had very clear notions about the redemptive process these terms represent, notions heavily qualified by his sense for the difficulty of its success. He knew the mind to be a complex instrument, so profoundly and unconsciously committed to saving the life of the body in which it was located that its other love, eternity, seemed remote. Blake's poetical development from the **Songs** to the long poems, by way of the shorter prophecies, seems to be in part the record of his earlier recognition of this dark complexity at the same time that it is a new means of giving it shape. In the prophecies he works to characterize redemption in universal terms, making use of characters bigger than life. We understand the general psychology of their spiritual quest, but so far, at least, we understand much more abstractly than we would wish to. This is not the place to argue the precise reasons for Blake's change of poetic mode. Indeed there is probably no very solid evidence on which to base such an argument. The relevant fact for my present purpose is that his epic poems, which presumably give an appropriate magnitude to his perennial concern—humanity's redemption—also remove it from the world of the **Songs,** in which we encounter characters who may help us to recognize it immediately. Almost as complicated as **Milton** in their totality, the **Songs** are nevertheless made up of separated elements, the individual poems, which we may at a first level regard discretely. Each one with its illustration treats a psychological state that both masks and reveals the mind passing through that state or arrested by it. Each one provides us with an opportunity for seeing such operations as the formation of Selfhood, the function of Selfhood, the reflexive regard of Selfhood, the failed attempt to circumvent Selfhood, the partial or momentary dissolution of Selfhood, the vision beyond Selfhood. The many studies of the **Songs,** accurate though they may be in their readings of individual poems, treat them with what may be too heavy an emphasis on their representation of divided entities in want of an act of union—the marriage of child and adult, lamb and tiger, world and otherworld, day and night. There can be no doubt that the *Songs* imply such unions through the juxtaposition of these and other polarities, which are essential to our understanding them. But underlying the poles of thought or being, and their implicit marriages, is a psychological continuum, important elements of which have yet to be identified. Psychologically considered, the *Songs* include their own act of union.

Though it is the readings that will show the limits of value of this view of the *Songs,* I believe the accidents of my own mental life which brought me to the view may have their interest too. Such attempts at revelation have their own limits and dangers, of course. But my reader may judge. What follows is a highly schematized history of my response to Blake's work, especially the *Songs.*

At the heart of my feelings about Blake's poetry is a sense for his frequent presentation of minds utterly exposed to experience—bare, sensitized minds, highly vulnerable to the people and things around them, and yet somehow not aware of what they endure. At the same time, I am also affected by a sense of Blake's power to imply or show that the uncompromised regard of this exposure to pain is possible, even necessary. His way of treasuring vulnerable characters, often ignorant of their own psychological state, is to regard them steadily. Though all poets make deep life stand still, no poet reaches deeper into life or arrests it more significantly for our scrutiny.

Closely allied is my strong sense that Blake's metaphors very often turn on the idea of death. It is the subject on which he draws to identify the basis of human vulnerability. In Blake's world it is death that limits us to mortality, death that requires us to accommodate ourselves to the natural world or perish, death that defines the natural world in which we live. When I first read the *Songs,* I had just been exposed to the risk of death in war for some months, and though I had no doubt that Blake understood death's ubiquitous presence in many disguises—the garden of love is filled with graves; chimney sweepers are locked in black coffins; the Raven of death nests in the man-made tree of holy Mystery; the cycle of life in London begins in the marriage Hearse; man and fly are married in death; the Little Black Boy anticipates deliverance from social prejudice by leaving forever his unalterable black body; some nameless power dared to clasp the Tyger's deadly terrors—I thought I might be overreading its force for him. But as time passed, several strands of evidence served to reinforce rather than to diminish my first powerful impression.

At Thel's grave plot, the vision of life as hostile and deadly seemed to me like much of Blake's poetry, from the *Songs* through the prophecies, to combine human vulnerability and the steady regard of threatening forces. Though the two functions are often divided, so that, for example, **"London's"** young Harlot is vulnerable, while **"London's"** speaker (in some sense vulnerable himself) looks steadily at her vulnerability, Thel experiences both functions in full measure. True, she is enabled by her creator, Blake,

to flee the world in which death figures prominently, but until she does, she sees death everywhere, and it promises to define the life she contemplates. Neither blaming Thel for giving up the chance for a life of natural experience nor congratulating her for turning away very sensibly from a bad scene seemed to me a reasonable way of handling her vision of things. Blake's treatment of death, viewed with an eye to her psychology, left me feeling that there was no simple resolution of the dilemma the poem represents. It also made me think of Blake's Self-examination and Self-annihilation, and of his Jesus, whose sacrificial death sets us free and yet leaves each of us struggling individually for redemption, and of Albion's repeated dying in *Jerusalem.* Obviously much in Blake's work turned on death and the perceptions of life it begets and on death and our ways of responding to it imaginatively. These conclusions were not new in Blake studies, but they seemed to me to occupy a place of much greater significance than the amount of time spent on them in the criticism implies they might have.

The very first sentences of David Erdman's Preface to [*A Concordance to the Writings of William Blake*] gave a certain palpable support to my view that the poet's interest in death was marked, and they also offered presumptive evidence for my belief that Blake's readers make less of the fact than they might reasonably do. Erdman begins:

> Each new concordance brings its particular surprises, those most immediately accessible being some of the words that come out at the top of the frequency count—or at the bottom. We may have expected to find MAN, LOVE, ETERNAL, and EARTH among Blake's most used words, but not DEATH so near the top or NIGHT so far ahead of DAY.

In fact, the only words that occur more frequently than "death" in the poetry are "all," "O," "upon," "Los," "like," "as," "Albion," and "man." In short, the only words that might be reckoned words of substance ahead of "death" in frequency are "all," "Los," "Albion," and "man," and two of them are proper nouns. But how he uses the word (and those closely related to it) is the important thing. A psychologist perhaps unique in the combination of his great sensitivity and great detachment, Blake almost never uses it to refer to physical death. Without morbidity, he associates "death," "dead," and their proxies with the fallen world that imposes itself on us—the world through which we move as we live our lives, stumbling "all night over bones of the dead." They help to characterize our natural and our social context. Or he uses them to suggest a sense of ourselves or a point of view we have adopted, often unconsciously, as a result of being imposed upon by the world of death around us: "They clothed me in the clothes of death." One way or another, Blake lets us know that death does not simply mark the human terminus we cannot avoid, the time and place of our dissolution, though it is precisely the fear that it may do so, he understands, that gives death its power over us. Aware that we are unconsciously intimidated by it, he treats death dynamically, as a conditioning force variously disguised in the world around us, and as a force we incorporate into our unconscious life as we accommodate ourselves to the threats it poses in natural life, in order that we may survive.

I knew Blake was not alone in his sensitivity to death as a proximate force in our daily lives. Many of his predecessors for a hundred and fifty years or more before the publication of the *Songs* had left evidence of their preoccupation with the subject, which roughly parallels the emergence of highly individualized Protestant sects and the philosophical regard of the New Science. This long-lived and complicated interest in death may be said to have been brought to resolution in a not entirely satisfactory way with the posthumous publication of Hume's *Essays on Suicide, and the Immortality of the Soul* in 1783. There Hume argues that we have only that control over life and death represented by our power to do away with ourselves, a power he believes we have every right to exercise. But he discounts the possibility of an afterlife, as if to settle the disturbing matter once and for all. Most others who wrote on the subject were either personally moved to reveal their sense of loneliness and uncertainty in the face of death— John Donne, Jonathan Swift, Samuel Johnson, and hundreds more. Or they sought to control death by incorporating it into a system of things that reduced its power to harass the imagination. Often, existing religious systems that had grown powerless to help the anxiety of doubt were modified to accomplish this reduction of death's disturbing presence. Or entirely secular activities, from the institution of charity hospitals and soup kitchens to the resuscitation of the apparently dead by scientific means, were undertaken to hold death back.

It seemed apparent that despite Blake's interest in social reform and his invention of a psycho-Christianity (both were hallmarks of the response to death among his predecessors and contemporaries), he was decidely unlike the others. Certainly he shared with them an inescapable heritage. Protestant man, though not every Protestant, by the logic of his religious position, might very well suppose himself individually responsible for arranging the terms of his own covenant with God—a lonely job, full of doubt. And the heirs of the New Science, unless they had religious faith, found themselves without the sure means of appraising the nature of their relationship to the physical universe they occupied. It seemed to operate in accordance with immutable mechanistic laws requiring neither God nor man for their continuance, a world of dead ratios without human meaning. Without meaning, life is uncertainty, anxiety, the threat of nonentity, death. It was in this context that Cambridge Platonism, Christian mortalism, and Humean skepticism were formulated, along with many other religious and secular structures, the net effect of each being to reduce death's power to give pain. Sensitive and introspective as he was, Blake could no more have escaped this heritage than he could have chosen to be born in a different age, or, like Thel, chosen to remove himself from the grave plot to a different place, where there was no death. But instead of locating death reductively in a new or resurrected system, or, like Hume, naturalizing the idea of death by relentlessly identifying human limitations, Blake made its effects on our mental life the chief object of his regard. As sensitive as Thel to death's disguised presences, he was also able to do what she could

only avoid—to look at it steadily, without loss of sensitivity and without loss of detachment. (pp. 1-7)

[Death is indeed a very important subject for Blake, who] treats it not morbidly but as a conditioning force in the world around us and as a force we incorporate so that it defines us no less than the world in which we live. . . . Instead of representing death primarily as the frightening power that dissolves life, Blake sees its functions and transformations at work in the minds of his characters. Death becomes the variably disguised object of his scrutiny, out of which he generates a psychology of redemption. But in keeping with the dynamic power of death and the range of meanings it may imply, Blake's redemption is not a system one may adopt "philosophically." It is rather a process one may try to make a part of one's imaginative life, a process that makes use of a disciplined introspection, working at often hidden feelings. (p. 7)

[I read] the *Songs* with three ideas in mind. For the moment, it will be useful to anticipate these ideas in isolation. First, as I have stressed now in various ways, Blake often talks about both the natural and the human-made worlds in the terms of death and its hold on the imagination. Second, Blake may be said to prefer over his other characters those who have come to understand that death fills the world in many shapes (as social evil, as formal religion, as parents' education of children), who are sensitive enough to see that in their earlier lives they have been coerced by its threatening presences, and who are brave (detached) enough to survive the emotional consequences to themselves of such disturbing recognitions. And third, taken as a whole, *Songs of Innocence and of Experience* is primarily a record of the coercion of mental life, covering both the psychological consequences of such coercion and the possibility of getting past it.

It would be hard to overemphasize the seriousness and intensity of Blake's concern, directly expressed in **"To Tirzah,"** that all of us have been conditioned by a threatening environment or by one of its representatives; we have been "moulded" by the Mother of our "Mortal Part," so that our "Nostrils Eyes & Ears" are bound, our senses and our beings limited. The threatening world around us determines what we see, what we feel, and what we become, a mere function of mortality's requirements for survival; but we scarcely know at all that it is so. If we did, there would be no moments of discovery of the sort we find in the speaker's obviously new recognition of his mortal mother's hold on him in **"To Tirzah."** We do not know that we yield to coercion, necessarily yield, it turns out, and yet yield at great cost. And we are not in a position to know what we become as a result of our unconscious yielding, nor by what process we have been made what we are.

It is this threatening aspect of our earthly predicament that Thel identifies in her vision of the grave. Blake's poetry argues as if we are all controlled unconsciously by such a view of things, unless we can somehow discover our confinement of vision and accept the conscious threat of death such recognition includes. Imagine that Thel had accommodated herself to her own vision of the grave by rationalizing its deadly qualities into something more benign, that she had learned to live in that falsely benign context and had *become* what she had learned. What would it take for her to change? As it is, Thel escapes the threatening predicament by refusing to join life. Like the speaker of **"To Tirzah,"** the rest of us have no such option. To survive in the world Thel sees, which is the world we see, our minds distort the terrible truth to make it bearable, as Blake implies in several of the *Songs*. Here it may be enough to point out that the emblem of humanity's need to rationalize its predicament is that shortly after the Fall "Mercy changed Death into Sleep." Death threatens, and to flee its presence nonphysically (we do not have Thel's choice, after all) our minds distort its grim reality into something we can bear. As a result, we see with blinders on, and we become what we behold. The life-preserving mechanism paradoxically reduces life.

It is generally acknowledged that very few of the *Songs of Innocence* present characters unaffected by physical and emotional dangers in the natural world. The child in the **"Introduction"** and in **"The Lamb"** are among the few persons in these poems to feel an unqualified sense of union with the world around them. They are in the blessed state in which people and forces outside them seem "continuous" with, not inimical to, themselves, as Robert F. Gleckner, John Holloway [in his *Blake: The Lyric Poetry*], David Erdman [in his *The Illuminated Blake*], and others have in different ways shown. On a cloud, the child of the **"Introduction"** expresses a series of unself-conscious commands that are obeyed, the result being the Piper's songs that are presumably to unite all children in joy. And the child-speaker of **"The Lamb"** is seen to be "identical" with the lamb and with Christ—"I a child & thou a lamb, / We are called by [Christ's] name." It is worth observing that in these poems, when a wish is immediately fulfilled, the wisher feels the continuity of events outside him with himself; what is inside his mind is given shape in his environment, which for the occasion, at least, appears absolutely congenial. Similarly, when one observes others with whom one feels identical, the world of persons besides oneself appears entirely congenial. **"Laughing Song,"** like the **"Introduction"** and **"The Lamb,"** celebrates this affinity of inside with outside and of one with another. There, laughter and song are one; so are the children and the speaker; and so are the human voices and the voices of woods, stream, air, hill, meadow, and grasshopper.

Understood from the children's point of view, and not from Blake's or the Piper's or our own, Innocence is a condition of unself-conscious indentification with the world and the people outside one. Such unself-consciousness might be defined negatively as a failure on the part of the child to perceive inimical elements in the world. It has seen nothing that requires it to protect the organism that is itself, and so it has no sense of itself as a separate entity. Quite the contrary, it feels or thinks in terms of its continuity with persons, objects, and events around it. Few readers, of course, can join this world of unity, even when invited to do so by an unself-conscious speaker who lives there, as is the case in **"Laughing Song"**: "Come live & be merry and join with me, / To sing the sweet chorus of Ha, Ha, He." Self-consciousness, or the knowledge that the world is not a unity, restrains us in some degree from

membership in joy's coherence. And this restraint may be said to represent part of the meaning of the poem. But we may also be able to imagine the unity, even recollect its qualities, by the exercise of selective memory from our own pasts. Certainly we can do more than simply distinguish the children of unity from ourselves; we can appreciate something of the nature of their way of seeing and being. We can both be "ourselves" and in some sense be them. Awareness of this capacity is important for an understanding of the *Songs*.

What about the other *Songs of Innocence*? Do they not, as various critics observe, register a world of sorrow and disillusion? The answer depends on whose point of view one takes. The reader may see in them a world of sorrow. Obviously the Chimney Sweeper and the Little Black Boy are both children driven very hard by a cruel society. Or Blake the man may be thought of as using irony in order to express his anger at society's treatment of the boys. The last line of **"The Little Black Boy"** and the last of **"The Chimney Sweeper"** both undercut the palliating vision earlier presented by the child of the poem. "So if all do their duty, they need not fear harm" may of course be read as Blake's ironic way of rendering illusory the comfort of Tom Dacre's dream. "And be like him and he will then love me" may be Blake's ironic way of rendering illusory the comfort of the Black mother's lesson; if the Black Boy would rather be loved by the white than to accept his mother's view of him as especially benefited by experience, what good is her lesson, after all? But for the moment consider these *Songs of Innocence* from the point of view of the children who experience their action rather than from the point of view of the reader or Blake. It is the children, finally, who dwell in Innocence or leave that state, and not we or Blake. It is their point of view, in and out of Innocence, that provides a means of understanding their psychology. Let us assume both the Chimney Sweeper and the Little Black Boy to be consistent in their attitudes from first to last. The reader then would have to conclude that "So if all do their duty, they need not fear harm" was literally intended by the speaker. And it would follow that he was taken in by Tom Dacre's dream. That is, one would understand that the speaker accepts the rationalization the dream amounts to, masking and transforming as it does the deadly social present of the chimney sweepers with a promise of heavenly protection. . . . (pp.7-10)

Read with the same expectations for consistency, the Little Black Boy's "And be like him and he will then love me" underscores a similar presentation of social evil and the speaker's psychological escape from that evil. What is most important about the last line of **"The Little Black Boy"** is that it permits the reader to see the mind of the child working at two levels, quite self-deceivingly. At one level the boy accepts his mother's lesson so thoroughly that he recounts the occasion of its delivery to him with unself-conscious pleasure—"She took me on her lap and kissed me" —and then he repeats the lesson verbatim, surely an act of faith in its efficacy. But at another level, it turns out, he makes it something very different from what it claims to be, namely, the promise of a future state in which his spiritual superiority (which his mother tries to get him to realize he enjoys in the *present* life) will enable him to help the English boy. Instead, he finds in it a reason for believing he can become enough like the white boy for the white boy to love him. In effect, the Black Boy has both accepted his mother's lesson and repudiated it, by using it, inappropriately, to cope with the problem it was intended to transcend.

If the children of other *Songs of Innocence* are similarly moved to rationalize their early recognitions of danger to themselves, their first apprehensions of mortality, then it may be appropriate to redefine Innocence so that it includes, in addition to the child's sense of unself-conscious identification with the world and the people outside him, his unself-conscious will to prolong that sense in the face of evidence that might be expected to displace it. It is precisely the weight of such evidence that has encouraged readers to see disillusion in *Songs of Innocence,* or to see Blake's irony working to undercut the children's improbable willingness to maintain their faith, though that willingness seems not to have been well identified or understood. But the weight of evidence ought not to obscure the fact that these children *know not what they do.* Read with the child's point of view in mind, the poems reveal two crucial facts about the departure from Innocence. First, it is a departure reluctantly undertaken, and second, the forces initiating that departure seem to precipitate unconscious mental operations, ultimately self-deceiving or defensive in nature.

All of the other *Songs of Innocence* do not as explicitly support the thesis I have proposed as do the two I have so far considered. But the others fall readily into one of the two categories I have identified, or they include elements of both in a special equilibrium. That is, they present characters who feel unself-consciously united with the world, or characters who unself-consciously prolong that feeling in the face of adverse evidence, or they join the two. Along with the **"Introduction," "The Lamb,"** and **"Laughing Song,"** the first group includes **"The Shepherd," "Spring,"** and **"Infant Joy."** In addition to **"The Little Black Boy"** and **"The Chimney Sweeper,"** the second includes **"A Cradle Song," "Night," "A Dream," "The Little Boy Lost"** and **"The Little Boy Found"** considered as a unified pair, and **"On Anothers Sorrow." "The Ecchoing Green"** and **"Nurses Song,"** both of which include grown-ups sympathetic to innocents who feel unself-consciously at home in the world, but grown-ups who do not unself-consciously share the innocents' vision, provide a psychological bridge to the third group, in which a firm and realistic adult view seems to correct the vision of congenial innocence or to admonish adults who may misunderstand that innocence—**"The Blossom," "Holy Thursday,"** and **"The Divine Image."**

These three last-named poems are themselves a bridge to *Songs of Experience,* which present characters who of their own accord address or who are made to address the forces of death in the world outside them. Self-conscious of danger, or somehow urged or otherwise moved to become conscious of it, they confront their trouble or they feel the pain of it. If they try to rationalize or otherwise dispose of their difficulties, as in different ways Ona and the Sick Rose seem to do, they are brought up short by editorial indictment or in a confrontation with another character, so that, unlike the Little Black Boy or The Chimney Sweeper of Innocence, no comfort is available to them. Psychologically the "obverse" of his counterpart in Innocence, the Chimney Sweeper of Experience knows he has been imposed upon, and he resents it: "because I am happy, & dance & sing, / They think they have done me no injury." His words make it clear that he has an unvarnished view of his own predicament, but they also reveal that he has begun to appraise the mental operations of his mother and father, who, as he sees it, are able to believe, somehow, that they have done him no harm, when of course they have "clothed [him] in the clothes of death." And beyond that knowledge, he shows a further psychological sophistication by associating his parents with other creators of a false heaven: "God & his Priest & King / Who make up a heaven of our misery." Though the Sweeper's association has social and religious levels of meaning, I wish here to stress only the acute psychological consciousness with which it shows this child of Experience to be endowed. Unlike the Chimney Sweeper of Innocence, he is fooled neither by himself nor by others, at one level of consciousness, at least. Somehow he has begun to see things "for what they are." What he sees is only a beginning, of course, but it marks a crucial difference between the children of Innocence and of Experience.

Among the other characters in *Songs of Experience* who see into their manipulation by persons, ideas, and institutions that make up their world, or who see into the manipulation of others, are the Little Vagabond, the School Boy, Lyca, and the speakers of **"The Clod & the Pebble," "Holy Thursday," "The Little Girl Lost," "The Little Girl Found," "The Sick Rose," "The Angel," "My Pretty Rose Tree," "Ah! Sun-Flower," "The Garden of Love," "London," "The Human Abstract," "A Poison Tree," "A Little Girl Lost," "A Little Boy Lost,"** and **"To Tirzah."** In fact, the discovery of destructive psychological coercion to oneself is the chief subject of *Songs of Experience,* though needless to say the subject has many facets and gradations. It brings some of the characters in the poems to the threshold of control over their own lives through a new consciousness of their predicament, or it reveals through the speakers' observations to the reader the heavy failure of such visionary control.

As close readings of the *Songs* . . . make clear, the roots of psychological coercion run deep. For example, the parents who join God, Priest, and King in delivering their own son to the deadly life of a chimney sweeper, along with Ona's and Lyca's parents and with Tirzah, are themselves unconscious agents of institutions and attitudes long since invented to protect life against dangers that life fears without understanding. It would be simple indeed to think that Ona's complex guilt, related as it is in a dozen ways to the expectations for civilized living buried in the mind of a whole society, could be remedied by an enlightened father. Though it is true that things might have been better at home for Ona—Lyca's parents are "better" in the matter of coercive conditioning, it seems; Tirzah is worse—no simple solution is available for her, any more than for her father, who is a product, with his daughter, of the same deadly heritage. His mother was a Tirzah of some sort, too.

Other *Songs of Experience,* by their very subject and tone, imply both a complexity of cautionary restraint in the mind's contours and the mind's occasional releases from such complexity. **"The Fly,"** for all its mischievous paradox, raises clear questions about the uncertainties of the borderline between one being and another, and between one's own species of being and another. The speaker's recognition is not that he has been painfully imposed upon by another person or by some institutional system of things but that his conditioned sense of himself as "finite" and "identifiable" has been put into doubt or nullified. Here he is, and there is the fly, and then suddenly *he* is the fly, or at least he can no longer see a real difference between the fly and himself. Though this self-reflexive behavior may not be referred to the speaker's recognition and overthrow of coercive conditioning, it does mark the overthrow of his conventionally induced perception. He has experienced a minor vision of the truth of things beyond himself and yet including him. For reasons one can only guess at, he treats the vision comically. Similar and yet more portentous for self-discovery is the experience of **"The Tyger's"** speaker, whose vision results in his redefinition of God the Creator, and of his relationship with Him, the lamb, the Tyger, and with himself as well. Among the realizations thrust upon him is this one: that quite beyond what man may do to man, there are natural forces of destruction woven into the very fabric of the physical universe. These forces also need psychological management by those who want to be saved.

A few characters in *Songs of Experience,* far from being on the verge of some productive discovery about themselves or in the midst of discovery, seemed closed off from such a blessing altogether. The Nurse and the Sick Rose are two of these. Their presence in *Songs of Experience* reinforces the idea and the value of Self-examination nevertheless, for both of them are identified dramatically as psychologically wanting. The Nurse, contrasted with the Nurse of Innocence, identifies herself not only as confining in her treatment of the children who are her charges but as defeated in her view of life and of herself. She uses the knowledge that her adulthood is spent in "disguise"—that is, controlled by suppressed desire, which she seems to have no real means of handling—not as the beginning of Self-examination but as a general indictment of life and as a threat about their own adulthoods to the children. The Sick Rose is treated by the speaker as if it were a clinical case in need of diagnosis. Whatever its state may be, the Rose seems incapable of understanding and commenting on its own predicament. The most passive of Blake's characters in Experience (even the Sunflower and the Clod have a point of view), the Sick Rose endures defeat through an incapacity to engage life reciprocally. For the moment it will be enough to say that both of these characters, Nurse and Sick Rose, face serious unpleasantness, but unlike those on hard times in Innocence, they do not promote a happy delusion about their bad predicaments, and unlike most characters in Experience, their speech or other responsive behavior implies no constructive course

of action. Their pasts control them. Indeed, they are their pasts.

It may be important to ask whether the voices of speakers, which I have understood to represent "characters," are not after all disembodied, so that I have invented an implausible critical fiction. I think the answer to the question is not to be found in a completely characterized mind available through any single voice in the *Songs*—no such completeness obtains. Nor is it to be found in a simple compositing of all the voices to build the "one mind" of the *Songs.* The voices vary enormously in emotional strength, intelligence, sensitivity, and temperament. But they all collect to suggest a continuing mental process, which, if not complete, is certainly full. It seems reasonable, finally, to think of the voices as speaking for characters, because so viewed, they contribute to a full sense of Blake's vision of the human predicament. And its representation, dynamic as it is, invites us as much to participate in the process it identifies as to consider it analytically.

Innocence and Experience, as I have so far treated them, imply a transition between the one and the other, during which the reluctance to acknowledge threats to life in Innocence (The Chimney Sweeper's rationalization, for example) gives way to the willingness to admit that something is very wrong, and perhaps to indict and correct the trouble. In fact, the *Songs* may be thought of as representing a continuous psychological process, an inevitable movement from the state of Innocence, in which (from the child's point of view) one enjoys an unself-conscious unity with one's surroundings, to an encounter with evidence that threatens life, such evidence being for a time displaced by rationalization, but later intruding into the conscious mind. At this point the mind may be thought of as in Experience by virtue of its inability to rationalize the threatening evidence (the Nurse), or a distinctly different matter, by virtue of its willingness to accept it (the second Chimney Sweeper). Where the mind can no longer rationalize the evidence and yet cannot deal with the problem it represents, the evidence is likely to register as fear, pain, or the sense of defeat. Where the mind receives the evidence with knowledge enough to give it "meaning," the evidence becomes a problem that is understood to need a solution or a problem for which a solution is sought and sometimes found. For example, the speaker of **"To Tirzah"** believes he can explain the reasons for his circumscribed perception and the way to escape domination by his mother.

As I have already indicated, one ought probably to avoid expecting the "mind" of the foregoing model to reveal itself throughout the poems as a single human psychology or as consistently intelligent or consistently sensitive. Lyca seems to be healthy, whereas the Sick Rose is not; the speaker of **"The Fly"** is a metaphysician who makes and breaks analogies, whereas Ona seems hardly to know the most obvious implications of her actions; the speaker of **"The Tyger"** is struck deep by an aspect of creation, whereas the Sun-flower is weary of time. Individual though they are, these characters help to illuminate the psychological process that is the movement from Innocence through Experience, control of which is ultimately required by Blake's Self-annihilation, his remedy for death in the world and for the vision it generates. The alternative to such emotional "dying" into new life is to survive behind a wall of self-delusion, narrowly defined by the very threats to life one refuses unconsciously to acknowledge and to assimillate.

In the *Songs,* Blake tells us a good deal about the formation of the vision of death, the Selfhood that needs annihilation. Unless this accumulation of largely unconscious experience is recognized in some detail, the process of redemption—one's liberation from that accumulation—is likely to be understood more as an idea than as a deeply felt realization. It seems obviously in the spirit of Blake's way of writing and thinking to prefer the second to the first (pp. 10-15)

Blake's insistent treatment of redemption throughout his work results in the close reader's increasing sense of enrichment and complexity. But certain difficulties stand in the way of our appreciating this accretion. In the *Songs of Innocence and of Experience* the psychology of redemption is detailed. Yet, as I have said, no single mind is a vehicle for its entire display. We see bits and pieces of the process implied by a wide range of quite different kinds of characters in various predicaments, though of course the broad outlines of the process are implied by the psychological principle distinguishing (and uniting) the two sets of *Songs.* In the major prophecies, single characters do in fact annihilate the Selfhood, but it is not easy to infer in very full detail the psychology that sponsors the redemption. Certainly more evidence is given to use there than we can handle critically. At times the Self-annihilation seems an act of individual will and at times a gift of grace. In one sense these redemptions are individual; in another, universal. They may be understood to take place over great stretches of time and space, and yet they may be accomplished very locally, in a single pulsation of the artery. And finally, Blake's practical expectations for himself and others who attempt such redemption seem complicated. To leave off is to die; on the other hand, it seems there is no completing the process. According to Henry Crabb Robinson, Blake said as late as February 1826, "Every man has a Devil in himself, and the conflict between his *Self* and God is perpetually going on" [*Nineteenth-Century Accounts of William Blake*]. Blake also tells us in the late Inscription in the Autograph Album of William Upcott (1826) that he was "Born 28 Novr 1757 in London and has died several times since" [Erdman, *The Complete Poetry and Prose of William Blake*]. Apparently he realized in looking at himself that no complete annihilation of the Selfhood is possible. The mind is far too complicated for one to search deep enough into its dark pits and turns, or always to hold on to the burst or flicker of new vision one may experience there. Perhaps no consciousness is so penetrant as to keep the mind from protecting itself from more life than it can bear. (pp. 15-16)

Harold Pagliaro, in his Selfhood and Redemption in Blake's "Songs," *The Pennsylvania State University Press, 1987, 161 p.*

Camille Paglia   (essay date 1990)

[*Paglia is an American critic and the author of* Sexual Personae: Art and Decadence from Nefertiti to Emily Dickinson *(1990), a critical history of Western art and culture from ancient Egypt to the nineteenth century. This study intends, in Paglia's words, "to demonstrate the unity and continuity of Western culture" in opposition to "the modernist idea that culture has collapsed into meaningless fragments." In the following excerpt from* Sexual Personae, *Paglia asserts that the removal of social and moral restraints, which* Songs of Innocence and of Experience *presents as stifling, introduces violence and peril into society.*]

Prophet and radical, Blake denounces all social forms. He takes Rousseau's hostility to civilization farther than Rousseau himself. For Blake, sexual personae, which belong to the social realm of role-playing, are artificial and false. He differs from the other English Romantics on several points. All believe love is primal energy. But Blake is the only one to oppose androgyny as a solution to rigid sex roles. Blake condemns androgyny as solipsism. His hermaphrodites are monstrous. Romantic solipsism, a self-communing and self-fructification, becomes sterile in Blake. Why? Because Blake, though he follows and extends Rousseau's politics, sees nature with Sade's eyes. In Blake, Rousseau's tender nature mother makes a fin-de-siècle leap into daemonic monumentality. Brother to Sade, whom he could not have known or read, Blake revives the bloodthirsty goddess of ancient mystery religion, sensational with Asiatic barbarism. He longs to defeat her. But by attacking her, he creates her and confirms her power. Ironically, he becomes her slave and emissary, a voice crying in the wilderness. Nowhere else in literature is the Great Mother [of chthonian nature] as massively, violently eloquent as she is in Blake.

Blake, following Spenser, constructs a complex symbolic psychology not yet fully understood. One of Blake's basic patterns is that of warring contraries through which spiritual progress is pursued, as in *The Faerie Queene.* As his poetry develops, Blake's principal combat is between male and female, metaphors for the tension between humanity and nature. In the early *Songs of Innocence* (1789), sex was is not yet an issue, but it is prefigured in the theme of tyrannical power relations, toward which Blake takes Rousseau's view but Sade's tone. Blake is interested in coercion, repetition-compulsion, spiritual rape. He sees sadism and vampirism in male authority figures. The child speakers of **"The Chimney Sweeper"** and **"The Little Black Boy"** are physically exploited and psychologically manipulated. They are the invisible slaves or houris of a corrupt new industrial society. Their minds have been invaded by a daemonic compact of church and state. "So if all do their duty, they need not fear harm": adult voices come from their mouths in evil ventriloquism. The sexual element in this brainwashing is evident in **"Holy Thursday,"** where grey-haired beadles with "wands as white as snow" herd a stream of children into St. Paul's Cathedral. The wands are Spenser's phallic white rods, here symbolizing wintry devitalization. The beadles are perverts, voyeurs, decadents. They freeze the children's river of life.

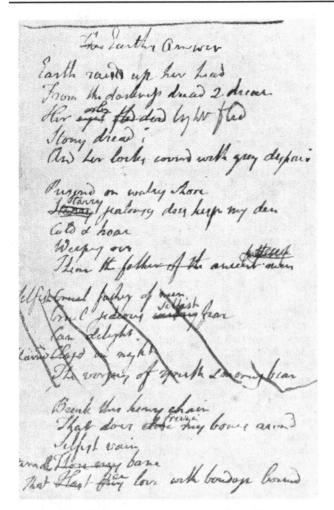

The Poem "The Earth's Answer," from Songs of Innocence and of Experience, *as it appears in the Rossetti Manuscript.*

In *Songs of Innocence* white is the color of desexing. The white hair of the lamblike chimney sweep, little Tom Dacre, expresses his premature adult experience. The child-slaves advance from childhood to old age without passing through adult virility. As in the penalty card of capitalist Monopoly: "Go directly to Jail. Do not pass Go. Do not collect $200." Elsewhere in Blake, sexual jealousy cripples human energy. In *Songs of Innocence,* male authority is an impotent Herod, massacring the innocents while ravishing them with eye and mind. Society operates by vicious pederasty. In 1789, both sexes still powdered their hair or wore wigs. The eighteenth century honored age and tradition, overthrown by Romanticism in its youth-cult. Blake's white-haired chimney sweep is ritual victim of an unnatural regime. The high stylization of eighteenth-century wigs—we hear of women unable to pass through doorways, of towering arrangements of fruit, foliage, and birds' nests—was a symptom of decadence. Powdered hair is a perverse fantasy of frost and angel dust, worldliness masquerading as innocence. Blake's artificially whitened children are overexperienced and knowledgeable. An unsettling analogy can be found in a Roman imperial sarcophagus decorated with leering obese putti,

fetid with adult sensuality. Blake's cherubs are depraved by adult tyranny. Henry James takes up Blake's theme in *The Turn of the Screw,* where an obsessed hierarch, the governess, projects sexual sophistication upon a boy who dies an exhausted prisoner of her febrile imagination. Blake's white-haired chimney sweep represents the class of all exploited persons. The white hair is sexually universalizing, because the exploited are humiliatingly feminized by amoral political power. Erich Fromm says [in his *Escape from Freedom*], "For the authoritarian character there exist, so to speak, two sexes: the powerful ones and the powerless ones." Sexual personae in *Songs of Innocence* are imagined as generations cannibalizing each other. Blake's innocent children are precursors of his male victims emasculated by cruel women.

"Infant Joy" is Blake's most neglected major poem. Harold Bloom devotes one sentence to it in his book on Blake, and he and Lionel Trilling omit it from the *Oxford Anthology* of Romantic literature. **"Infant Joy"** has a deceptive simplicity:

> I have no name
> I am but two days old.—
> What shall I call thee?
> I happy am
> Joy is my name,—
> Sweet joy befall thee!
> Pretty joy!
> Sweet joy but two days old.
> Sweet joy I call thee:
> Thou dost smile.
> I sing the while
> Sweet joy befall thee.

We have regressed to the infancy of consciousness. We see Rousseau's saintly child as it crosses the border into being. What do we find there? Tenderness and innocence threatened on all sides. I learned to read poetry from Milton Kessler, whose brilliant remarks on **"Infant Joy"** I reconstruct from my college notes:

> **"Infant Joy"** is a flawless physical caress which induces weeping. The metaphor for this poem is taking the child in one's hands. But an adult taking up a newborn is suddenly, involuntarily conscious of the ease with which he could crush it to pieces. In **"Infant Joy"** there is a sense of the enormous proximity, the closeness and intimacy of the speaker. The child has no voice of its own yet. It is given an identity by some great coercive power. There are certain forms of sadistic tenderness more intimate than the psyche will allow. **"Infant Joy"** is like Theodore Roethke's "Elegy for Jane," where the bearlike poet, with his terrifying and roaring energy, approaches a delicate being in dangerous nearness. The elegy begins: "I remember the neckcurls, limp and damp as tendrils."

"Infant Joy" exposes the authoritarianism in Rousseauist "concern," "caring," and "understanding," today's self-righteous liberal values. In the poem's eerie dialogue I hear George Herbert's homoerotic intensities. In its blank encapsulization I feel claustrophobic Spenserian embowerment. **"Infant Joy"** comes from the rape cycle of *The Faerie Queene.* It is the provocative vulnerability of the fleeing Florimell, the purity that sucks filth into its wake. **"Infant Joy"** is a Rousseauist vacuum into which Sadean nature is about to rush.

Blake's infant has no name, no persona. It is barely individuated. Infant joy is what Blake later calls a "state," a condition of being. We feel rawness, sensitivity, defenseless passivity. Rousseauist childhood is no blessing. Sensory experience is the avenue of sadomasochism. **"Infant Joy"** recreates the dumb muscle state of our physicality, the readiness which converts into sex, or rather the surging power that is sex. George Eliot says [in her novel *Middlemarch*], "If we had a keen vision and feeling of all ordinary human life, it would be like hearing the grass grow and the squirrel's heart beat, and we should die of that roar which lies on the other side of silence. As it is, the quickest of us walk about well wadded with stupidity." **"Infant Joy"** removes the buffering between persons and beings. Eliot imagines a perfect perceptual openness and a sensory flood into a receptacle too small to contain it. The egoless softness of the poem awakes in us Kessler's sensation of overwhelming power, which we unconsciously check. Sharpening the senses inflames them—and here comes sadism. Rousseauist responsiveness and nurturance automatically flip over into their opposites.

"Infant Joy" has the moral emptiness of Spenser's femininity, a space cleared in nature. It is like the still heart of a geode, rimmed with crystalline teeth. In **"Infant Joy"** a devouring presence waits, a Blakean tiger: the reader. This is one of the uncanniest poems in literature. Seemingly so slight and transparent, it harbors something sinister and maniacal. **"Infant Joy"** is strongly ritualistic. Kessler calls it a "caress." The poem's hypnotic repetitions are a series of soothing gestures, like rubbing a lantern to make a genie appear. The poem is a spell materializing a dark power, latent in the reader. **"Infant Joy"** is a daemonizing poem: it daemonizes the reader, drawing him into the rapacious cycle of natural process. By making the reader a sadist, it subverts his complacent trust in his own morality and benevolence. Blake was contemptuous of "Mercy, Pity, Peace." **"Infant Joy"** is a parodistic critique of Rousseauism. As much as Blake's chimney-sweep poems, it indicts the oppressive paternalism of society's self-appointed guardians. Every gesture of love is an assertion of power. There is no selflessness or self-sacrifice, only refinements of domination.

The psychosexual design of **"Infant Joy"** is *hovering*. Hovering is the relation of speaker to infant, reader to poem. The evil droning menace in such proximity is shown in Blake's watercolor, *God Creating Adam*. Winged Urizen, Blake's tyrant Jehovah, hovers with a smothering weight above corpselike Adam, stretched flat as if crucified. God is a vampire snatching back man's Promethean fire. The picture seems to show an unnatural sex act, homosexual and sadomasochistic. Criticism is squeamish about admitting these perversities in Blake. (pp. 270-74)

Blake's **"Infant Joy"** evokes an impulse toward criminal trespass. Reading it, we hover at the edge of a forbidden locus of experience. We hold our breath. We uneasily sense the aesthetic contrast between our adult grossness and the infant's delicacy, eroticized by the poem's implied touching. The infant exists in Blake's Beulah state of blissful passivity, the numb groping of polymorphous perversity. The infant is blind. But we aggressively see. Along the track of our seeing skids our unbrakeable will.

The same dialectic of blind whiteness and aggressive eye occurs in *The Faerie Queene,* where the boisterous cannibals hang over sleeping Serena to study her "dainty flesh," which the poet gives a silky sheen (VI. viii. 36-43). Is this the source of Blake's poem? The violation in **"Infant Joy"** is the exposure of something private, unprotected, quivering, and moist. An infant two days old is barely sexually differentiated. It is still muzzy from the womb. **"Infant Joy"** brings us face to face with the biologically fundamental. The preconscious simplicity of Blake's infant is almost cellular. In fact, the poem *is* a cell, one simple cell of protoplasmic life. **"Infant Joy"** unveils a physiological mystery. We have penetrated into a female realm, as Melville does in *Tartarus of Maids* or Leonardo in his drawing of a fetus. This is proved by Blake's drawing of the poem, where an infant lies in the lap of a hovering mother and both are swallowed up in the flamelike maw of a giant flower, Blake's rapacious nature. Thus the infant's powerlessness is aversion of the chimney sweeps' enslavement. The womblike **"Infant Joy"** is a surgical opening up of a female body, nature's organic machine. **"Infant Joy"** is the secret sex-crime of a ravisher-poet. It looks forward to Blake's overtly sadistic **"Mental Traveller,"** where the "Babe" of humanity is handed over to old mother nature, surgeon and torturer. **"The Mental Traveller"** literalizes the authoritarian manipulations of **"Infant Joy."** Blake corrects Rousseau: man is born into his chains, the mother-born body binding us to creature comfort, sex, and pain.

In *Songs of Experience* (1794), **"Infant Joy"** advances to sexual maturity. Blake's response to **"Infant Joy"** is not **"Infant Sorrow"** but **"The Sick Rose."** Here the Spenserian embowerment of Blake's newborn shifts from Rousseau to Sade:

> O Rose thou art sick.
> The invisible worm,
> That flies in the night
> In the howling storm:
> Has found out thy bed
> Of crimson joy:
> And his dark secret love
> Does thy life destroy.

"The Sick Rose" is Spenser's Bower of Bliss destroyed by sex war. The literary convention of female flight and male pursuit, satirized by Spenser in the ever-fleeing Florimell, reveals its innate hostility. Woman's flirtatious arts of self-concealment mean man's approach must take the form of rape. The phallus becomes the conquerer worm, death's agent. Withdrawal and concealment are always negative in Blake. Here they provoke sadistic attack, partly a hallucination by the reclusive rose. The rose is a narcissistically convoluted psyche. Female genitals are traditionally symbolized by the queen of flowers, from the medieval Mystic Rose of Mary to the rock classic, "Sally, Go Round the Roses." Blake sees solipsism as the danger in female sexuality. The rose's exclusiveness blends fear, shame, and pride. Its layered petals are a form of self-population. That the rose's "bed of crimson joy" suggests masturbatory pleasure is well accepted by critics. For Blake the rose's self-completion is perverse and sterile. The rose is a sexual schismatic, making division where there should be wholeness and unity in nature. It is thus an early version of the solipsistic hermaphrodites of Blake's prophetic books.

Blake's masturbatory rose belongs to the tradition begun in Egypt where autoeroticism is a method of cosmogony. Blake sees a sexually private world as a prison cell. The rose is sick because, she thinks, the communion of sex drains and obliterates her identity. Blake's own ambivalence toward sex produces the cryptic duality of the poem. Male fear of woman's self-containment is written all over mythology and culture. It is male, not female identity that is annihilated in the night-storm of nature. The fascination of woman's autonomy is plain in Ingres' *The Turkish Bath,* a witty parallel to Blake's rose poem. Ingres' painting is oddly round, a rose window or Madonna tondo turned pagan peephole, through which we spy the plump nude bodies of a dozen women amorously entwined, like lesbian flower petals. It is a snaky Medusa head, steamy with Asiatic lewdness. Trying to liberate sex from society, Blake keeps running back into the cul-de-sac of female sexuality. Courtly convention alone did not make woman "the hidden." Nature makes woman's body a cavern of the unseen, divined by sadomasochistic mystery religion.

The ambiguous **"Sick Rose"** qualifies the sexual assertions of Blake's earlier *The Book of Thel* (1789). A cloud tells the virgin Thel she is "the food of worms": "Every thing that lives, / Lives not alone, nor for itself." Nature as harmonious interrelationship: this Buddhist perception is not sustained in Blake, who is too conflicted about the dominance of female nature. In **"The Sick Rose,"** Thel's worms are phallic heavenly messengers, miming the growth cycle. Blake thinks the being living alone and for itself is sick because it rejects the strife of contraries by which energy evolves. Thel's book ends in hysterical retreat, as she jumps from her seat and dashes shrieking back to her native valleys. Blake combines the seat-stuck virgin of Milton's *Comus* with Spenser's fleeing Florimell and Belphoebe, who disappears mid-sentence. Blake regards virginity as a perverse fetish. He wants to believe Thel's rejection of sexuality is childish, a swerve from menarche and fruitfulness. Thus Blake's chastity is diametrically opposite to that of Spenser and Shakespeare, for whom it signifies spiritual integrity and force. Like Sade, Blake sees chastity as unnatural, energy-killing. But in urging Thel, a sick rose, to cure herself by surrendering to communion, Blake is closer to Shakespeare of the comedies, where all are given in marriage, than he is to his fellow Romantic poets, for whom solitude is imaginative perfection. Shakespeare, subordinating sex to society, makes a Renaissance escape from the problem confronting Blake. Trying to eliminate society but redeem sex, Blake keeps finding himself in Leonardo's rockscape. Every inch he saves for sex is lost in the desolate mile of mother nature. (pp. 275-79)

Camille Paglia, "Sex Bound and Unbound: Blake," in her Sexual Personae: Art and Decadence from Nefertiti to Emily Dickinson, *Yale University Press, 1990, pp. 270-99.*

FURTHER READING

Adams, Hazard. *William Blake: A Reading of the Shorter Poems.* Seattle: University of Washington Press, 1963, 337 p.
> Devotes four chapters to a discussion of *Songs of Innocence and of Experience,* analyzing such issues as "the father-mother-child relationship," garden symbolism, and perspective. Adams often explicates the text with the aid of Blake's own terms and mythology.

Bass, Eben. "*Songs of Innocence and of Experience*: The Thrust of Design." In *Blake's Visionary Forms Dramatic,* edited by David V. Erdman and John E. Grant, pp. 196-213. Princeton, N.J.: Princeton University Press, 1970.
> Perceives the movement and flow in the designs of *Songs of Innocence and of Experience* as dramatizing both the "Divine Image"—humankind, created as the earthly image of God—and the contrary states of humanity: innocence and experience.

Bentley, G. E., Jr., ed. *William Blake: The Critical Heritage.* Boston: Routledge & Kegan Paul, 1975, 294 p.
> Contains a section entitled "*Songs of Innocence and of Experience*" that comprises commentaries on *Songs* by Blake's contemporaries, such as William Hazlitt, S. T. Coleridge, and John Ruskin.

Berger, P. "Chronological Survey—Lyrical Poems." In his *William Blake: Poet and Mystic,* translated by Daniel H. Conner, pp. 282-324. New York: E. P. Dutton & Co., 1915.
> Praises *Songs of Innocence* as faithfully depicting the central elements of childhood: "perfect happiness," "perfect innocence," "unhindered communion between the child's own life and that of the animals and things that surround it," and "clear vision of the divine world." Berger finds *Songs of Experience* to be symbolic and prophetic.

Bronowski, J. "Innocence and Experience." In his *William Blake, 1757-1827: A Man without a Mask,* pp. 109-26. 1944. Reprint. New York: Haskell House Publishers, 1967.
> Discusses issues in *Songs of Innocence and of Experience* such as the shortcomings of society, the progression from innocence to experience, and the symbolic significance of children and fathers.

Connolly, Thomas E. " 'Little Girl Lost,' 'Little Girl Found': Blake's Reversal of the Innocence-Experience Pattern." *College Literature* XVI, No. 2 (Spring 1989): 148-66.
> Observing that *Songs of Innocence and of Experience* often present children who become "experienced" through the guidance of adults, Connolly states that the lyrics "Little Girl Lost" and "Little Girl Found" reverse the usual pattern because the child depicted in the two poems reaches maturity unaided, and consequently helps her parents attain a state of innocence.

Cox, Stephen D. "Adventures of 'A Little Boy Lost': Blake and the Process of Interpretation." *Criticism* XXIII, No. 4 (Fall 1981): 301-16.
> Examines the history of critical reaction to "A Little Boy Lost" in *Songs of Experience.* Cox stresses that criticism should account for the literal meaning of a text, examine the likelihood of each interpretation, and ac-

knowledge the problematic and uneven qualities of an author's work.

Damon, S. Foster. "*Songs of Innocence* and *Songs of Experience*." In his *William Blake: His Philosophy and Symbols,* pp. 268-86. 1924. Reprint. Gloucester, Mass.: Peter Smith, 1958.
Includes commentary on each poem and description of the designs.

Davidson, Clifford. "Blake's *Songs of Experience* and 'Rebel Nature'." *Research Studies: Washington State University* 44, No. 1 (March 1976): 35-41.
Claims that in *Songs of Experience* love and sex are not perceived as evil or contemptible, but rather are associated with positive concepts such as imagination and the creative process.

Dyson, A. E., and Lovelock, Julian. "The Road of Excess: Blake's *Songs of Innocence and Experience*." In their *Masterful Images: English Poetry from Metaphysicals to Romantics,* pp. 125-35. New York: Barnes & Noble Books, 1976.
Argues that the ambiguity of Blake's poems in *Songs of Innocence and of Experience* allows diverse and often conflicting interpretations, thereby communicating the complexity and richness of the issues addressed.

Ellis, Edwin John, and Yeats, William Butler. "*Songs of Innocence and of Experience*." In their *The Works of William Blake, Vol. II,* pp. 9-17. 1893. Reprint. New York: AMS Press, 1973.
Explicates *Songs of Innocence and of Experience* within the context of Blake's "symbolic system."

Frye, Northrop. "Blake's Introduction to Experience." *The Huntington Library Quarterly* XXI, No. 1 (November 1957): 57-67.
Studies the "Introduction" from *Songs of Experience* with the aim of demonstrating that the poems comprising this work address many issues examined in Blake's longer poems, which Frye terms "elaborate prophecies."

————, ed. *Blake: A Collection of Critical Essays.* Englewood Cliffs, N.J.: Prentice-Hall, 1966, 183 p.
Includes Robert F. Gleckner's "Point of View and Context in Blake's Songs," as well as discussions focusing on various poems: the "Introduction" to *Songs of Experience,* "The Chimney Sweeper" in *Songs of Innocence,* "The Fly," "Sunflower," and the two poems about "little girls lost."

Gardner, Stanley. *Blake's "Innocence" and "Experience" Retraced.* New York: St. Martin's Press, 1986, 211 p.
Presents historical and biographical circumstances as significantly influencing the creation of *Songs of Innocence and of Experience.*

Glazer-Schotz, Myra, and Norvig, Gerda. "Blake's Book of Changes: On Viewing Three Copies of the *Songs of Innocence and of Experience*." *Blake Studies* 9, Nos. 1-2 (1980): 100-21.
Studies the roles of color and iconography in the viewer's experience of *Songs of Innocence and of Experience.* Glazer-Schotz and Norvig perceive that the coloring contributes to the symbolic meaning of each plate, and suggest that the individually painted copies of *Songs* may thereby each possess a unique meaning.

Gleckner, Robert F. *The Piper & the Bard: A Study of William Blake.* Detroit: Wayne State University Press, 1959, 322 p.

Studies *Songs of Innocence* (1789), *Songs of Experience* (1794), and four works—*Tiriel, The Book of Thel, The Marriage of Heaven and Hell,* and *Visions of the Daughters of Albion*—written in the intervening period. Gleckner states that these works are "the key elements of an organic and ever-developing 'system' that began with the seeds of innocence and resulted finally in the prophetic books."

Gleckner, Robert F., and Greenberg, Mark L., eds. *Approaches to Teaching Blake's "Songs of Innocence and of Experience."* Approaches to Teaching World Literature, edited by Joseph Gibaldi. New York: The Modern Language Association of America, 1989, 162 p.
Sixteen essays by various critics on approaches to teaching *Songs of Innocence and of Experience* in the classroom. The essays are preceded by a discussion of texts, reference materials, critical studies, and visual aids related to *Songs.*

Glen, Heather. "Blake's Criticism of Moral Thinking in *Songs of Innocence and of Experience*." In *Interpreting Blake,* edited by Michael Phillips, pp. 32-69. New York: Cambridge University Press, 1978.
Contends that in *Songs of Innocence and of Experience* Blake condemns moral law as an artificial, repressive code of rational utilitarianism that inhibits spontaneous, intuitive sympathy.

Heffernan, James A. W. "Text and Design in Blake's *Songs of Innocence and of Experience*." In *Imagination on a Long Rein,* edited by Joachim Möller, pp. 94-109. Marburg, Germany: Jonas Verlag, 1988.
Avers that while the designs of *Songs of Innocence and of Experience* are not essential to a basic understanding of the poems, "a continuing concentration on the interplay between text and designs in the *Songs* reveals aspects of their meaning—and of the contrariety between innocence and experience—that we can learn in no other way."

Lindsay, David W. *Blake: Songs of Innocence and Experience.* London: Macmillan Education, 1989, 91 p.
Discusses critical approaches to both *Songs of Innocence* and *Songs of Experience* and, focusing on several poems, examines the development of *Songs of Innocence and of Experience* in the context of Blake's other writings.

Manlove, C. N. "Engineered Innocence: Blake's 'The Little Black Boy' and 'The Fly'." *Essays in Criticism* XXVII, No. 2 (April 1977): 112-21.
Argues that "The Little Black Boy" in *Songs of Innocence* "describes the preservation of innocence by falsification of experience; and . . . in this it is very like one of the *Songs of Experience,* 'The Fly'."

Paley, Morton D., ed. *Twentieth Century Interpretations of "Songs of Innocence and of Experience": A Collection of Critical Essays.* Englewood Cliffs, N.J.: Prentice-Hall, 1969, 115 p.
Contains commentaries by such noted critics as Northrop Frye, Harold Bloom, Mark Schorer, E. D. Hirsch, Jr., and the American pioneer of Blake studies, S. Foster Damon. Some essays focus on particular poems in *Songs of Innocence and of Experience* while others examine large-scale interpretive approaches.

Phillips, Michael. "William Blake's *Songs of Innocence* and

Songs of Experience from Manuscript Draft to Illuminated Plate." *The Book Collector* 28, No. 1 (Spring 1979): 17-59.

    An account of the origin and evolution from 1784 to 1794 of *Songs of Innocence and of Experience.*

Wilkie, Brian. "Blake's *Innocence and Experience:* An Approach." *Blake Studies* 6, No. 2 (c. 1975): 119-37.

    Regarding perspective in Blake's *Songs of Innocence and of Experience,* Wilkie observes: "The total context provided by the *Songs* is a reliable if not infallible guide to point of view and persona, and in most of the poems there is also enough internal evidence to establish the speaker's identity and characteristics and to reveal his limitations."

Williams, Porter. " 'Duty' in Blake's 'The Chimney Sweeper' of *Songs of Innocence.*" *English Language Notes* XII, No. 2 (December 1974): 92-6.

    Perceives in "The Chimney Sweeper" of *Songs of Innocence* the deliberate use of the term "duty" to imply moral imperative—a contrast to the poem's ostensible concern with vocational obligation.

Charles Farrar Browne

1834-1867

(Wrote under the pseudonym Artemus Ward) American humorist and lecturer.

INTRODUCTION

Browne is best remembered as a humorist, a pioneer in the genre of the comic lecture, and as an important figure in the development of the American popular press. He derived his fame through the creation of the character Artemus Ward, whom he patterned after P. T. Barnum, the celebrated nineteenth-century American showman. Adopting a homespun style noted for its grotesque spellings, distorted dialect, and deliberate violations of grammar, Browne achieved international renown as the outstanding representative of nineteenth-century American humor.

Born in 1834, Browne was reared in a farming community in Waterford, Maine. He received no formal education, and his first contact with literature followed the death of his father in 1847, when he became an apprentice to a printer in Lancaster, New Hampshire. Four years later he began work as a printer and editor of a Boston literary journal, *The Carpet-Bag,* which published his first article, "The Incident," and several other pieces. Over the next few years Browne worked as a printer in various Ohio towns, eventually becoming the editor of the Cleveland *Plain Dealer* in 1857. During this period he published burlesques and other comic works in numerous periodicals. On 30 January 1858, the *Plain Dealer* published his "Letter from a Side-Showman," the piece that introduced the persona of the flamboyant promoter, Artemus Ward, who eventually became identified with the author in the public's mind. Soon afterward Browne began to forge a national reputation for himself. His 1860 "Interview with the Prince of Wales" was a success, and he became a regular contributor to the New York humor magazine, *Vanity Fair,* beginning with his piece, "Artemus Ward Visits Brigham Young." In the early 1860s he capitalized on the growing popularity of the old showman by assuming the character on stage. Browne began a lecture tour of New England in 1860 with "Children in the Wood," which he delivered for the first time in New London, Connecticut, to popular acclaim. He extended the tour into the Midwest and West over the next two years, during which time his articles were collected and published as *Artemus Ward, His Book.* Subsequent tours took him to California, where he befriended the young Mark Twain in 1863, Montreal and New Orleans. In 1865 Browne published *Artemus Ward; His Travels* which contains his most acclaimed piece, "Among the Mormons." He took his tour to London in 1866 and became a weekly contributor to *Punch,* a British literary journal. However, illness forced him to

give up lecturing in January 1867 and he died of tuberculosis two months later in Southampton, at the age of thirty-two. His last work, *Artemus Ward in London, and Other Papers,* was published posthumously later that year.

Browne's literary canon consists of anecdotes, burlesques, and letters. Although he did not consider himself a disciplined writer, his witty observations of human experiences enabled him to build a natural rapport and a common bond with his audience. Seemingly effortless and spontaneous, such anecdotes as "A Little Difficulty in the Way," the story of a traveling salesman's encounter with a cuckolded rail-splitter, reveal his gift for vividly relating ordinary experiences of daily life, and his facility with local color, characterization, and dialect is demonstrated in pieces like "Horace Greeley's Ride to Placerville." In addition to anecdotes, Browne composed at least twelve burlesques. The most famous, "Fourth of July Oration," "The Crisis," "Moses the Sassy," and "Cruise of the Polly Ann," satirized what Browne considered the hypocritical morality of the popular sentimental novels of the period.

The greatest portion of the humorist's output consists of his Artemus Ward letters. The earliest ones were ostensible correspondence from the showman to the editor of the newspaper in which the letters appeared. In time, however, the letters evolved into news reports on the adventures of daily living. Browne employed a variety of literary devices to enhance the humorous elements of the letters, including puns, clichés, and the satiric use of archaic verbs and pronouns. His most salient comic device was the use of misspellings and nonstandard grammatical constructions. Some critics have contended that the verbal gags ridiculed genteel culture, and others have argued that they were intended to indicate the illiteracy of characters and imitate dialect. Works such as "Artemus Ward Visits Abraham Lincoln," "On the Way," and "A War Meeting" reveal the three-part format of the letters: identifying the time and place of an incident, relating the exchange between Artemus Ward and another character, and concluding with philosophical advice. Critics have generally agreed that the popularity of the letters was not so much rooted in their content as in the character of Artemus Ward himself. Shrewd, pragmatic, and something of a rogue, the old showman represented the "common man" of Jacksonian democracy, eminently suited to self-government because he had been endowed with common sense. He reflected the values of the typical American by valorizing the lower classes and scoffing at the pomp and pretentiousness of the upper echelons of society.

As a lecturer, Browne received critical acclaim both at home and abroad, and paved the way for future American humorists by making the comic lecture reputable and lucrative. His discourses were parodies of the more solemn and thought-provoking lecturers of the day like Greeley, Ralph Waldo Emerson, and Henry Ward Beecher. Although the old showman was characterized as ebullient and gregarious, the thin and delicate-looking Browne delivered his orations in a dead-pan manner, seeming to drift confusedly from subject to subject. Browne established an approach in "Children in the Wood" that he followed in subsequent lectures, whereby patent absurdities were uttered with flat expression, slowly building to a climax of a calculated pause, succeeded by a punchline of startling incongruity. His most famous lecture, "Artemus Ward among the Mormons," was first delivered in October 1864 at a time of heightened national interest in the West and Mormonism. This particular oration was notable for its use of a lavish moving panorama, which often depicted comically irrelevant or inappropriate scenes, to the speaker's apparent consternation.

Browne's contemporaries, including Bret Harte and Mark Twain, acknowledged him as an outstanding storyteller and satirist. English critics as well recognized him as a perceptive and original commentator on American culture. Browne was a favorite of Abraham Lincoln during the Civil Ward period, and the President reportedly read "High-Handed Outrage at Utica" to his cabinet before presenting them with the Emancipation Proclamation, stating, "With the fearful strain that is upon me night and day, if I did not laugh I should die, and you need this medicine as much as I do." Criticism in the early twentieth century focused on the literary relationship between Browne and Twain. Most scholars of this period agreed that Twain far surpassed Browne as a comic narrative writer but pointed out that Twain was greatly indebted as

a lecturer to his predecessor, both for material and comedic style. Recent critics have devoted much attention to Browne as a social commentator, noting that he directly addressed complicated issues such as prohibition, feminism, and slavery, but always from a moderate viewpoint, cautious to avoid extremism. Although his works are little read today, historians value them for the picture they provide of nineteenth-century America. As John Q. Reed has asserted, Browne "was in almost complete rapport with the majority of his contemporaries. . . . As a newspaperman, magazine editor, and comic lecturer, he played an important role as an observer and critic of his society."

PRINCIPAL WORKS

Artemus Ward, His Book (prose) 1862
Artemus Ward; His Travels (prose) 1865; also published as *Artemus Ward (His Travels) among the Mormons* [enlarged edition] 1865
Artemus Ward in London, and Other Papers (prose) 1867
Artemus Ward's Lecture (As Delivered at the Egyptian Hall, London) (prose) 1869; also published as *Artemus Ward's Panorama (As Exhibited at the Egyptian Hall London)* 1869
The Complete Works of Charles F. Browne, Better Known as "Artemus Ward" (prose) 1870; also published as *The Complete Works of Artemus Ward (Charles Farrar Browne)* [revised edition] 1898
Selected Works of Artemus Ward (prose) 1924

Bret Harte   (essay date 1863)

[*Harte was a prominent nineteenth-century American short story writer and lecturer. As a young man he traveled to California and used his experiences to weave such colorful tales of the American West as "The Outcasts of Poker Flat" and "The Luck of Roaring Camp." In the following excerpt taken from an article originally published in the 27 December 1863 edition of the* Golden Era, *a California newspaper, he judges Browne a quintessentially American humorist whose exaggeration of ordinary experiences captures the essence of national life.*]

Artemus Ward has gone. The Showman has folded his exhibition tent like the Arab and silently stolen away. But like the Arab, Artemus has been accused of certain Bedouin-like qualities, and has been viewed by some interior critics as a literary raider—scouring the face of the land and skimming the fatness thereof. Others have thought themselves humbugged at his lectures and openly assert that his "Babes" are stuffed with sawdust—the sawdust of old circus arenas at that.

Of course this sort of thing is new to Californians. They are by nature excessively cautious. They never invest money in doubtful speculations. They are never carried away by excitements, and it is clear that if Artemus has issued stock at a dollar a share and people consider it don't pay, the imposition is altogether unprecedented and worthy of reprehension.

But has it been an imposition? Did Artemus by implication or reputation profess more than he has accomplished?

He came to us as the author of an admirable series of sketches which exhibit a special type of humor. It is not exactly the highest nor the most ennobling type. Artemus is not the greatest American humorist, nor does he himself profess to be, but he deserves the credit of combining certain qualities which make him the representative of a kind of humor that has more of a national characteristic than the higher and more artistic standard. His strength does not lie simply in grotesque spelling—that is a mechanical trick suggested by his education as a printer—and those who have gone to hear him in this expectation have been properly punished—but it is the humor of audacious exaggeration—of perfect lawlessness; a humor that belongs to the country of boundless prairies, limitless rivers, and stupendous cataracts. In this respect Mr. Ward is the American humorist, *par excellence,* and "his book" is the essence of that fun which overlies the surface of our national life, which is met in the stage, rail-car, canal and flat boat, which bursts out over camp-fires and around bar-room stoves—a humor that has more or less local coloring, that takes kindly to, and half elevates, slang, that is of to-day and full of present application. The Showman has no purpose to subserve beyond the present laugh. He has no wrongs to redress in particular, no especial abuse to attack with ridicule, no moral to point. He does not portray the Yankee side of our national character as did Sam Slick, partly because there is a practical gravity and shrewdness below the clockmaker's fun—but chiefly because it is local rather than national. He has not the satirical power of Orpheus C. Kerr.

Of such quality was Artemus Ward's literary reputation as received by us. And yet some people are surprised and indignant that his late lectures exhibited this lawless construction—that he gave us fun without application. This is a pretty hard criticism from people who are content to go night after night to the Minstrels and listen to the pointless repetition of an inferior quality of this humor. But it affords a key to their criticism. Let the Minstrel wash his face—and remove his exaggerated shirt-collar—and how long will they stand his nonsense? When a keen-looking, fashionably-dressed young fellow mounts the stage and begins to joke with us in this fashion without the accessories of paint or costume, we feel uneasy. Had Artemus appeared habited as the Showman, surrounded by a few wax figures, even the most captious critic would have been satisfied.

Artemus Ward's career in California has been a pecuniary success. The people have paid liberally to see the Showman, and he has reaped a benefit greater than he might have made from the sale of his works. It was a testimonial to the man's talent, which is not objectionable *per se*—though better judgment might have kept the subscription paper out of his own hand. It is a success that will enable him for some time to live independent of mere popularity—to indulge his good taste and prepare something more enduring for the future. In the mean time no one enjoying

the pleasure of a personal acquaintance with his frank, genial nature; none who have observed his modest and appreciative disposition, or the perfect health and vigor that pervades his talent, will grudge him that success. (pp. 126-28)

> *Bret Harte, "Artemus Ward," in his* Stories and Poems and Other Uncollected Writings, *edited by Charles Meeker Kozlay, Houghton Mifflin Company, 1914, pp. 126-28.*

Mark Twain on Browne's comedic technique:

To string incongruities and absurdities together in a wandering and sometimes purposeless way, and seem innocently unaware that they are absurdities, is the basis of the American art. . . . Another feature is the slurring of the point. A third is the dropping of a studied remark apparently without knowing it, as if one were thinking aloud. The fourth and last is the pause.

Artemus Ward dealt in numbers three and four a good deal. He would begin to tell with great animation something which he seemed to think was wonderful; then lose confidence, and after an apparently absent-minded pause add an incongruous remark in a soliloquizing way; and that was the remark intended to explode the mine—and it did.

For instance, he would say eagerly, excitedly, "I once knew a man in New Zealand who hadn't a tooth in his head"—here his animation would die out; a silent, reflective pause would follow, then he would say dreamily, and as if to himself, "and yet that man could beat a drum better than any man I ever saw."

> *Mark Twain, in his* How to Tell a Story and Other Essays, *Harper and Brothers, 1905.*

Arthur George Sedgwick   (essay date 1866)

[*Sedgwick was a conservative literary critic who strove in his writing to counteract what he perceived to be a loosening of the prescribed rules of taste and decorum. In the following excerpt, he acknowledges Browne as a "genuine humorist" in his satires of American life, but a "genuine buffoon" in his unconventional use of language.*]

Artemus Ward's popularity, having extended itself over America, has reached England, and now promises to become as great there as here. Whatever may be the subtile causes which of late have brought so many American books into repute on the other side of the water, on this side at least it is easy to account for the favor with which he has been received; in the first place he is a genuine humorist, in the second, he is a genuine buffoon. Had he been a wit, nine tenths of his present readers might never have known him. But he has a capacity for seizing the unformed jest of the hour and vivifying it, letting it go shaped and perfect. When we were all laughing at the final disguise of Jefferson Davis, Artemus Ward wrote a letter in seeming confusion as to the ex-President's sex, speaking "of him as a her as frekent as otherwise," and guessing that "he feels so hisself." The love of the Union at the South he succeeded in hitting off in the same letter by introducing a Southerner, who tells him that there had been a tremendous Union feeling in Richmond from the first, but that the inhabitants had been kept down by a reign of terror, and who asks him in conclusion whether he has a daguerreotype of Wendell Phillips about him, and whether he can lend him four dollars "till we air once more a happy and united people." He once represented himself as making a speech at a war-meeting, in which he said that not only had the crisis come itself, but had brought all its relations; that Washington would be safe if the Federal army succeeded in taking it. Again, "I return to the Atlantic States after a absence of ten months; and what State do I find the country in? Why I don't know what State I find it in. Suffice it to say, that I do not find it in the State of New Jersey." These instances are sufficient illustrations of the tone and calibre of Artemus Ward's humor; a humor of low purpose, indeed, for his satire is not directed against the idols which society sets up and holds in honor, but simply uses as its butt the laughing-stock that society already ridicules. Thus a distinction is continually presenting itself between his humor and its object; the one original, racy, and strong, the other borrowed, and sometimes unpleasantly coarse.

But something more than this is required to account for Artemus Ward's popularity, and this something is buffoonery, that appeal to the love of the absurd, those capers and tumbles and contortions of mind or body, which from the days of court jesters to those of the circus clown have drawn admiring crowds. Artemus Ward has played the part of the literary clown with such success, that what he is now best known by is not the quaint oddity of his jests, but the slang which he adopted and introduced, his tone of impudent familiarity in speaking of distinguished persons, the twisting of his words, and the nonsensical form of his sentences. This has tickled the fancy of such as are content to be amused cheaply with ungrammatical phrases, burlesque words, and silly impertinence. The great test of the genuine buffoon is that he makes you laugh, and he must have no object but laughter; if he has an end in view, he loses his character,—for the buffoon, as buffoon, is always shallow. Humor would have you laugh with, buffoonery at, itself. The buffoon's want of self-respect is painfully noticeable in Artemus Ward. To the natural love of buffoonery, then, and, worse, to that taste for levity in our society, which, however natural as the opposite of an unnatural extreme, is still itself extreme,—a levity that pastes bills on monuments, and makes natural scenery an advertising agent for quack medicines,—Artemus Ward has pandered.

To grin through a literary horse-collar of slang and bad spelling,—to be a negro minstrel among authors,—with such a station he was content for a long time; but at length, desirous of achieving a more creditable reputation, he attempted to get it by abandoning cap and bells, and he now appears before the world, in the last part of these *Travels,* no longer as Artemus Ward, the showman, but in his own character as the humorist, Mr. Browne. Alas! the two veins of humor and buffoonery which we might have sup-

posed accidentally combined, and separable, he now proves to be mingled in grain. The attempt was praiseworthy; but when he gave up the motley with which his humor had been clothed, it died of the exposure. With Artemus Ward laughter was too often the end, not the means; with Mr. Browne, in his commendable but fatal attempt at high comedy, the only end which it seems possible he can propose either to his readers or himself is that of his book.

In presenting himself as the author of a book Mr. Browne, indeed, subjected his powers to a hard test, for the articles of which his volume is made up are in their nature ephemeral, and belong properly to the weekly papers in which they first appeared. The genius of such writers as Artemus Ward, Petroleum V. Nasby, Orpheus C. Kerr, Josh. Billings, and Francis Bret Harte is specially appropriate to the flying pages of the comic journal. We may hope that at some day all these—Nasby, with his rich vein of political satire, which so delighted Mr. Lincoln that he said he had offered to change places with him; Orpheus C. Kerr, liberal in politics, a good parodist, a capital writer of burlesque; Harte, a parodist of such genius that he seems a mirror into which novelists may look and be warned; and Josh. Billings, with his wise saws and modern instances—will, instead of letting their humor ooze out of the soil at unexpected times and places, send it forth from one great fountain-head, to flow over and enrich the thirsty land. (pp. 586-88)

Arthur George Sedgwick, in an originally unsigned essay titled "Artemus Ward's Travels," in The North American Review, *Vol. CII, No. 211, April, 1866, pp. 586-92.*

Matthew Freke Turner   (essay date 1876)

[*In the following excerpt, Turner, a British critic, attempts to account for Browne's greater acceptance among foreign audiences than American.*]

There are, as is well known, individuals of the human race so luckless as to have been born without any perception of certain mental sensations which constitute very important sources of pleasurable emotion to their fellow-men. The curious phenomena of colour blindness have only recently been established, and the fact incontestably proved that there are unfortunate persons to whom the blue sea, the green trees, and the tints of the sky at sunrise and sunset, show uniformly grey and sombre, to whom a photograph seems a perfect representation of the most gorgeous landscape, and an engraving in black and white no better and no worse a thing than the finest picture by Titian or Giorgione. A commoner incapacity is music deafness, where the actual hearing is acute enough, but the sensibility to musical notes is wanting. A man so *non-possessed* shall hear with equal satisfaction the strains of the finest organ and the shooting of stones from a cart, and think a strathspey on a Scotch bagpipe as enjoyable as a well-rendered symphony of Beethoven.

Pitiable as such cases are, it may be doubted whether the patients are in so deplorable a case as those unhappy men who are born destitute of any sense of humour, and who live long lives and go to melancholy graves without having once laughed at a joke, or enjoyed the keener delight of a witticism. To be indifferent to the harmonies of sweet sounds or fine colour is but to have one avenue to the senses closed; but to be insensible to wit, and unassailable by humour, is surely a more grievous misfortune. It is to have "wisdom at one entrance quite shut out;" for, as philosophers tell us, these things are but *modes of wisdom.* Such persons are condemned, not only to melancholy, but to stupidity.

Let those who feel themselves to belong to the unhappy category I have described read no further, lest they conceive I depart from the dignity of literature when I mention, and dwell on admiringly, and largely quote from, a humourist who will assuredly hold a place with posterity in the famous line which begins with Rabelais and ends with Charles Dickens.

Among the developments of modern literature, few are more curious than the sudden and unexpected rise, on the other side of the Atlantic, of a school of writers of a quite peculiar kind. There have already appeared, in the somewhat scanty field of American literature, authors who deserve to be classed as humourists in the sense in which Thackeray used the word; but not one of these writers can be allowed a high place in the world of letters, either on account of originality or eminence. Among them, Washington Irving has the highest place, but he has little claim to be considered an original writer. Addison and Steele were conspicuously the models of this charming writer, in humour and in manner, and he has not disdained to borrow literary graces from Goldsmith and from Lamb. Lowell, the author of the "Biglow Papers," and Wendell Holmes, both excellent writers, are hardly acknowledged as humourists in Europe; and the reputation of Hawthorne, deservedly high as it stands, owes hardly any of its eminence to his fame as a humourist.

It was at so recent a period as the commencement of the American Civil War that a school of writers sprang up, whose works, redolent of American soil and racy of American manner, began to make themselves welcome, not to American readers only, but to speakers of the English tongue all the world over. So sudden and widespread a popularity as was attained by works of so seemingly local and ephemeral a character was, no doubt, due to the great interest awakened in things American by the great Civil War; but something—even a good deal—was owing to the excellence, and the vigour, and the originality of the works themselves.

Hardly less singular than the writings of these men was the mode in which they reached the reading public.

The cupidity of New York and Boston publishers, the desire of one part of the American reading public to buy the brain-coinings of Transatlantic authors under cost price, and the somewhat strangely unpatriotic neglect, by the people of the United States, of the just claims of native American literature—all these various causes have joined to make it almost impossible for an American author to appear in the native book market against competitors whose productions can so easily undersell him. Thus it came to be that an American author was hopelessly over-

weighted in the great literary handicap, and American literature suffered, and, indeed—the cause continuing—does still suffer.

It was in consequence of these depressing influences that Mr. Charles Brown—the head, the founder, and still incomparably the foremost of the new school of writers—never wrote a book at all till his literary reputation was attained and was well established, and when he could appeal to a widening circle of readers outside his own country. Even then his name was hardly known beyond the circle of his private friends.

It was not long before the breaking out of the war, that short paragraphs began to go the round of the American papers, under the signature of *Artemus Ward;* and in a very short time the utterances of this personage were more familiar to the great reading public of the United States than those of any writer who had ever addressed them on any subject not distinctly connected with either religion or politics. Mr. Brown had given this name to a pure creation of his own, an old Yankee showman—a shrewd, vulgar, unprincipled, ignorant vagabond—and from the point of view of the said Artemus Ward, without for a moment speaking out of character, he addressed the American public upon the topics of the day. One of the characteristics of the showman's communications is his brevity. Mr. Brown would fill one side of a piece of his note paper, sign it *Artemus Ward,* send it to the *Cleveland Plain Dealer,* or the "New York Vanity Fair," and in a week his paper would be repeated by every journal from Boston to San Francisco, and a circulation obtained such as no author could look for by any ordinary mode of publication.

It is to be presumed that literary labours, of whose results it was open to all the world to avail itself, could not have been profitable in a pecuniary sense, and this it obviously was which induced Mr. Brown to turn lecturer. I am not particularly concerned with his proceedings as a lecturer, except incidentally, and so far as they affect his character as an author. When so well-known a writer announced his intention to appear before an audience, his success was certain beforehand, and crowds flocked to the lecture-room prepared to find themselves addressed by the personification of the character of the old rowdy showman with whom they were so familiar. Their disappointment is described as almost ludicrous when they saw before them a quiet, decorous, somewhat delicate-looking young man of less than twenty-five, with a good deal of the dress, the manners, and the enunciation of a gentleman.

Mr. Charles Farrer Brown, whose brief literary career lasted but five or six years, and ended, with his life, in 1866, at the early age of thirty, was of a respectable family in New England. He had got an education a little better than usually falls to the lot of a boy of the middle classes in America—that is, a very much higher one than would fall to the lot of a lad of similar position in this country—but his relations were poor, and he began his struggle with existence some way down in the social scale. Like his countryman, Franklin, he was apprenticed to a printer, and learned to be skilful with the composing-stick before he had taught himself to make any profitable use of the pen. As a youth, he wandered from city to city of New England, finally settling in Boston, where it was, I believe, that he first began to contribute short tales and essays to the newspapers. It was in the columns of "Vanity Fair"—a sort of New York "Punch"—that he first wrote the famous *Artemus Ward* papers.

There was this in Mr. Brown, which distinguishes him from most other humourists—that he was a dramatic artist of decidedly great power. His conception and delineation of the character of the Showman, quite apart from the jests which he makes him utter, come very near to true genius. Setting aside the conceptions of Dickens—the Gamps, the Wellers, and the Pecksniffs—we greatly doubt if this century has produced any character of greater comic power, any that will float longer down the stream of time, than the Artemus Ward of Mr. Charles Brown.

He never speaks but in character, and the reader gets almost, at last, to believe in his "three moral bares," his "kangaroo," his "snaix," "wax figgers of G. Washington, and General Tayler, &c., besides several miscellanyus moral wax statoots of celebrated piruts and murderers," and so forth. The characteristic spelling of the illiterate old vagabond has been criticized as but a mechanical mode of getting a laugh; but it is surely legitimate enough, seeing that a writer has no other means of rendering characteristics of manner, while the actor has the resource of voice and manner. In Mr. Brown's case, indeed, mis-spelling is almost abused; but the abuse itself is a source of fun, so bold, and so utterly unlooked for are some of his phonetic renderings.

The Showman has a keen eye to his own interests, a shameless disregard of all sort of honesty and truth in the pursuit of those interests, and a strong conviction that most orders of men are neither better nor worse than himself. Herein lies the humourist's mode of attack. He abandons his creation from the first, shows him up unreservedly, that he may bring him in as king's evidence against his accomplices.

Here is a letter to a country editor, headed, **"One of Mr. Ward's Business Letters"**:—

> I shall hav my handbills dun at your offiss. Depend upon it. I want you should git my handbills up in flamin stile. Also git up a tremenjus excitemunt in yr paper 'bowt my onparaleld Show. We must fetch the public sumhow. We must wurk on their feelins. Cum the moral on 'em strong. If it's a temprance community, tell 'em I sined the pledge fifteen minits arter Ise born; but on the contery ef your peple take their tods, say Mr. Ward is as Jenial a feller as we ever met, full of conwiviality, & the life an Sole of the Soshul Bored. If you say anythin abowt my show, say my snaiks is as harmliss as the new born Babe. What a interestin study it is to see a zewological animil like a snaik under perfeck subjecshun! My kangaroo is the most larfable little cuss I ever saw. All for 15 cents. I am anxyus to skewer your infloounce. I repeet in regard to them handbills that I shall git 'em struck orf up to your printin offiss. My perlitercal sentiments agree with yourn exackly. I know they do, becawz I never saw a man whoos didn't.

Respectively yures,
A. WARD.

Respectively yures,
A. WARD.

The Artemus Ward literature—it is still scattered, and the task of collecting it in a single volume from the columns of contemporary newspapers, and arranging it intelligently and according to date, is still to be performed—consists of letters to the editors of various newspapers on the political and social topics of the day, and to his strong-minded, middle-aged wife. As the fictitious showman grows into fame, he thinks it due to the public to give "sum leadin incidents" of his life.

"I hav no doubt," he writes to a newspaper editor,

> that a article onto my life, grammattycally jerked and properly punktooated, would be a addition to the chois literatoor of the day.

> To the yooth of Ameriky it would be vallyble as showin how high a pinnykle of fame a man can reach who commenst his career with a small canvas tent and a pea-green ox, which he rubbed it off while scratchin hisself agin the center pole, causin' in Rahway, N. J., a discriminatin' mob to say humbugs would not go down in their village. The ox resoomed agricultooral pursoots shortly afterwards.

> I next tried my hand at givin Blind-man concerts, appearin as the poor blind-man myself. But the infamus cuss who I hired to lead me round towns in the daytime to excite simpathy drank freely of spiritoous licker unbeknowns to me one day, and while under their inflooance he led me into the canal. I had either to tear the green bandige from my eyes or be drownded. I tho't I'd restore my eyesight.

> In writin about these things, Mr. Editer, kinder smooth 'em over. Speak of 'em as eccentrissities of gen'us. . . .

> If you see fit to kriticise my Show, speak your mind freely. I do not object to kriticism. Tell the public, in a candid and graceful article, that my show abounds in moral and startlin cooriosities, any one of whom is wuth dubble the price of admission.

> I hav thus far spoke of myself excloosivly as a exhibiter.

> I was borne in the State of Maine of parents. As a infant I attracted a great deal of attention. The nabers would stand over my cradle for hours and say, "How bright that little face looks! How much it nose!" . . .

> I have allers sustained a good moral character. I was never a Railroad director in my life.

> I am a early riser. . . . I may add that I am also bald-heded. I keep two cows.

> I am 56 (56) years of age. Time, with its relentless scythe, is ever busy. The Old Sexton gathers them in, he gathers them in! I keep a pig this year.

> Trooly yours,
> ARTEMUS WARD.

The showman has an overweening and ludicrous sense of his own importance, and of the value of his smallest utterance on "affairs and things."

"The stoodent and connyseer," he writes,

msut have noticed and admired, in varis parts of the United States of America, large yeller hand-bills, which not only air gems of art in theirselves, but they troothfully sit forth the attractions of my show—a show, let me here observe, that contains many livin' wild animals, every one of which has got a Beautiful Moral.

Them handbills is sculpt in New York, & I annoolly repair here to git some more on 'em.

& bein here I tho't I'd issoo a Address to the public on matters and things.

Since last I meyandered these streets, I have bin all over the Pacific Slopes and Utah. I cum back now with my virtoo unimpared, but I've got to git some new clothes.

Many changes has taken place, even durin' my short absence, & sum on 'em is sollum to contempulate. The house in Varwich Street, where I used to Board, is bein torn down. That house, which was rendered memoriable by my livin' into it, is "parsin' away! parsin' away!" But some of the timbers will be made into canes, which will be sold to my admirers at the low price of one dollar each. Thus is changes goin' on continerly. In the New World it is war—in the Old World Empires is totterin' and Dysentaries is crumblin'. These canes is cheap at a dollar.

As his wandering avocations lead him into various parts of the country, his letters are filled with his impressions of what he sees:—

DEAR BETSY—I write you this from Boston, "the modern Atkins," as it is denomyunated, altho' I skurcely know what those air. I'll giv you a kursoory view of this city. I'll klassify the paragrafs under seprit headins, arter the stile of those Emblems of Trooth and Poority, the Washington correspongdents.

Spread-eagleism, bunkum, and all the varieties of sham and vulgar patriotism are abominations to Mr. Brown, and he never loses a chance of ridiculing them.

I went over to Lexington yes'd'y. My Boosum hove with sollum emotions. "& this," I said to a man who was drivin' a yoke of oxen, "this is where our revolutionary forefathers asserted their independence and spilt their Blud. Classic ground!"

"Wall," the man said, "it's good for white beans and potatoes, but as regards raisin' wheat, 't'ain't worth a dam!"

At the close of the American war, a great deal of nonsense was being talked of Union sentiment in the beaten South, and of the lofty consciousness of their new-got freedom entertained by the emancipated negroes. He writes from Richmond:

The old man finds hisself once more in a Sunny

climb. I am here a few days after the city catter-pillertulated.

My naburs seemed surprised & astonisht at this darin' bravery onto the part of a man at my time of life, but our family was never know'd to quale in danger's stormy hour. My father was a sutler in the Revolootion War. . . .

"My brother," he says to the negro hotel waiter, "air you aware that you've bin 'mancipated? Do you realise how glorus it is to be free? Tell me, my dear brother, does it not seem like some dream, or do you realise the great fact in all its livin' and holy magnitood?"

He sed he would take some gin.

He exposes the true causes of the professed loyalty to the Union in the South:—

There is raly a great deal of Union sentiment in this city. I see it on ev'ry hand. I met a man to-day—I am not at liberty to tell his name, but he is a old and inflooentooial citizen of Richmond—and sez he, "Why! we've bin fightin' agin the Old Flag! Lor' bless me, how sing'lar!" He then borrer'd five dollars of me, and bust into a flood of tears.

Sed another (a man of standin', and formerly a bitter rebuel), "Let us at once stop this effooshun of Blud! The Old Flag is good enuff for me. Sir," he added, "you air from the North! Have you a doughnut or a piece of custard pie about you?"

Our extracts have been chosen rather to give some general idea of Mr. Brown's great personification than to produce any evidence of his powers as a humourist. The delineation of the showman's character, his shrewdness and his ignorance, his weaknesses, his vanity, his combination of selfishness and geniality, his own exaggeration of every prevailing national absurdity—all this is brought out by innumerable little touches of quite inimitable art. The humour is broad—too broad, perhaps, for some refined readers. There is absolutely no "culture" at all, or pretence to it, about Artemus Ward's "perlite literatoor." I have made my extracts with all due deference to the purists, and have chosen with a view not to shock them, but even as it is, I fear many persons of elevated literary tastes will have read my quotations with feelings of sickly disgust. It is perhaps because Mr. Brown somewhat disregarded the voices of such people that his reputation is not so high with ordinary readers as with those whose critical judgment has ceased to be on trial, and need not fear to pass a bold opinion. It takes more than a commonplace critic to see genius in a literary work where every ordinary rule of grammar and orthography and style is disregarded. The mass of common-place readers laugh at Mr. Brown's jests, but fail to see the art that underlies them.

In this country it was, among the higher classes of literary men, that the young American was first recognized as a true genius. His reception by such men in London was remarkable. It was due, in the first place, entirely to his intrinsic merits, and only afterwards was it enhanced and extended by the man's own genial nature and charm of manner. Even our philosophers delighted in his freshness and originality, and Mr. Carlyle himself has been heard to speak of him emphatically as the "divine Artemus."

This high opinion of Mr. Brown does not extend to his own country. He has no great honour among the more cultivated classes of his countrymen. I have heard him spoken of by Americans as quite a low writer, dealing in gross, vulgar jests and feeble puns. The truth is that there is a cause for this, over and above any literary shortcomings on the author's part. In politics he was on the losing side. He was unable to rise to the level of that earnest spirit of antagonism to Southern pretensions and Southern ideas which has made the Civil War of America, in the eyes of many politicians on both sides of the Atlantic, one of the grandest spectacles of this century. He was blind to the great principle which underlay the struggle, though he could see with unequalled clearness all those petty meannesses which come to the surface in the course of such great national movements. He was keenly sensible of the baseness of much pretended patriotic valour and devotion, the corruption of the great army contractors, the various shifts and hypocrisies of indolence and cowardice, and he made exquisite fun of all this.

It was not for us—a foreign nation with our then very imperfect knowledge of American affairs—to arrive all at once at a right judgment. We took something of Mr. Brown's view of the matter: we could see, as he saw, the straws and the dust caught and twisted in the side eddies, but we many of us neither knew the direction nor guessed the strength of the great main current of wind. Much that the humourist laughed at richly deserved derision, but when he involved in his ridicule principles that were and are sacred in the breasts of most Americans, he jarred against the feelings of his countrymen. So it is, as I believe, that a people gifted with a very strong sense of humour, and possessing a very true literary judgment, have failed to appreciate a writer who in breadth, in insight, in perception and in expression is pre-eminent, and who is a true master of all that goes to make a great humourist. (pp. 198-207)

Matthew Freke Turner, "Artemus Ward and the Humourists of America," in New Quarterly Magazine, *Vol. VI, April-July, 1876, pp. 198-220.*

M. A. DeWolfe Howe   (essay date 1898)

[*Howe was an author of numerous biographies and non-fiction accounts of New England life. In 1924, he was awarded the Pulitzer Prize for his biography* Barrett Wendell and His Letters. *In the following excerpt, he extols Browne's unique style and concludes that the humorist represented a class of writers, devoid of literary pretensions, which cannot be overlooked in any general survey of American literature.*]

According to a reported declaration of Artemus Ward, Major Jack Downing was his pattern. It is not difficult of belief, for in the use to which they put the Yankee vernacular, in their assumed familiarity with conspicuous persons, and in the "free-born-American-citizen" attitude of each writer there is much that suggests a family relation-

ship. Artemus Ward—as the man whose real name was Charles Farrar Browne is more familiarly called—may be regarded as typical of the entire class of humourous journalists and speakers who have followed him. Certainly he has not been denied the homage of imitation, and certainly the writings he has left behind him are enough more than mere "comic copy" to give him his place as a representative figure. Lowell told the truth about one of the humourous methods in which Artemus Ward excelled when he said: "There is no fun in bad spelling of itself, but only where the misspelling suggests something else that is droll *per se.*" It is the merit of Artemus Ward's verbal vagaries—for example, when a friend sends him a copy of "Chawcer's poems," and he says, "Mr. C. had talent, but he could n't spel"—that the droll personality of Charles Farrar Browne's creation is always realised more clearly by reason of what may be called his mental dialect.

If Artemus Ward's descent as a humourist is to be traced from Major Jack Downing, it is thus that he accounts from the Browns, as the family name was written before he himself adopted the final *e:* "I should think we came from Jerusalem, for my father's name was Levi, and we had a Nathan and a Moses in the family. But my poor brother's name was Cyrus, so perhaps that makes us Persians." As a matter of fact, the Browns came to Maine from Massachusetts in 1783, and on April 26, 1834, the humourist was born in the village of Waterford. He was one of four children, and, unlike many men who have made a mark in the world, could not have regarded his mother as the source of his peculiar distinction. She is described as the fondest of parents, but a person entirely lacking in humour and the sense of it. It is related that when she first heard her son lecture in Boston, she was startled and irritated exceedingly by hearing him vouch for one of his statements by the use of a real name and a real formula which had frequently fallen from her own lips, and was introduced into the lecture entirely for her benefit: "I know it's true, for my Uncle Ransford Bates said so." The youthful antics ascribed to her son must have been equally trying to the good woman, and yet the devotion which he cherished for her through life helps one to realise what it must have meant to her to let the boy, only thirteen years old when his father died, go out into the world almost immediately to make his living in printing-offices. He was but fifteen when, after four experiments under country editors in New Hampshire and Maine, he found himself in the Boston printing house from which B. P. Shillaber's (Mrs. Partington's) comic paper, *The Carpet Bag,* was issued. Setting up the type of Mrs. Partington's paragraphs and of J. G. Saxe's witty verses, he ventured to write jokes himself, and had the felicity of seeing them printed.

A roving disposition carried him, soon after this humble beginning of a journalistic career, to Tiffin, Ohio. This was in 1856, and before 1860 he had won his spurs in Toledo and Cleveland, where the editor of the *Plain Dealer,* hearing the fame of his wit, secured him as local editor at the salary of twelve, afterward advanced to fifteen dollars a week. At this post he remained three years. His Cleveland associates have since recalled him as a youth of surpassing awkwardness and rusticity at first, but developing by de-

A rendering of the character Artemus Ward.

grees a regard for his personal appearance which brought him later to an ill-advised fondness for diamonds and curled hair. But there is ample evidence in this period also of his more essential graces and virtues. Generous, companionable, and trusting, laughing over his work, serious withal, sometimes to the degree of mental suffering, given to ways eccentric and unconventional, he seems to have fallen in with the mode of journalistic life which needs but does not always receive the help of native qualities like Browne's to make it alluring. There are innumerable stories of his practical jokes, but one will suffice to indicate their audacity. One night with a fellow wag in journalism known as "the Fat Contributor," he went to the hotel where a dramatic reader, who was to give his first entertainment in the place the next day, was stopping. They called him from his bed, told him they were newspaper men, and would ruin his prospects unless he should come with them as he was to the hall near by, and show what he could do as a reader. The poor man protested, but their threats were too much for his courage, and shivering with cold, he went with them to the dreary, unheated hall, and, if the story be true, entertained them for several hours with his selections. "They had always thirsted to hear a dramatic reader in night dress," they told him; and if they

did not commend his more decorous performance in public, their rather heartless idea of humour must have profited the unhappy reader but little.

It was in Cleveland that Browne began signing the name of Artemus Ward to his productions. The most credible theory of the source of this *nom de plume* is that the veritable *nom de guerre* of General Artemas Ward of the Revolutionary army appealed to the humourist, who adopted it with the change of a single letter. By degrees the new Artemus Ward became a definite character, a showman who could write of his equipment:

> My show at present consists of three moral bares, a Kangaroo (a amoozin' little Raskal—'t would make you larf yerself to deth to see the little cuss jump up and squeal), wax figgers of G. Washington, Gen. Tayler, John Bunyan, Capt. Kidd and Dr. Webster in the act of killin' Dr. Parkman, besides several miscellanyus moral wax statoots of celebrated piruts & murderers, &c., ekalled by few & exceld by none.

It was in Cleveland, too, that Browne first conceived the idea of becoming a public lecturer. But that was not to be until after he went, in 1860, to live in New York, as editor of the promising comic journal, *Vanity Fair,* and one of the

Bohemian set which frequented Pfaff's, and presented to Mr. Howells, picking up his first impressions of Eastern writers, a notable contrast to the group of men he had just left in Boston.

On a desperately stormy night, near the end of 1861, Browne first faced a New York audience as a public speaker, and suffered a loss of thirty dollars; but he had already tried his lecture, on "The Babes in the Wood," in Norwich, Connecticut, and other towns. It was a peculiarity of Ward's lectures that they had little or nothing to do with the subject announced. He would begin with a mention of it, then ask the audience to let him tell them a little story, which would wander on into irrelevant witticisms occupying about an hour and a half, when he would take out his watch, appear to be overcome with shame and confusion, and bring his talk to a hurried, apologetic end. In Norwich the good people, who had laughed immoderately at his jokes, crowded around him when the lecture was finished to express sympathy for the nervousness through which, as they supposed, he had failed to say anything at all about the Babes in the Wood. He himself modestly told a different story, at the breakfast-table of James T. Fields, when he said of his first audiences: "I was prepared for a good deal of gloom, but I had no idea they would be *so much* depressed." "Artemus Ward will Speak a Piece" was the sum and substance of the advertising placard which announced his appearance in various places. Even the tickets were whimsical and characteristic. For one of his most popular lectures the card of admission read: "Artemus Ward among the Mormons. Admit the Bearer and One Wife." The programmes were not without their individuality. In London they were enriched with the note, "Mr. ARTEMUS WARD will call on the citizens of London at their residences, and explain any jokes in his narrative which they may not understand." There may have been reason enough in such an offer if John Bright was reported with even an approach to truth in saying: "I must say I can't see what people find to enjoy in this lecture. The information is meagre and is presented in a desultory, disconnected manner. In fact, I can't help seriously questioning some of the statements."

Probably enough has been said to show that Artemus Ward stood entirely alone among the lecturers who galled one another's kibes on the lyceum platforms of his day. Of the sober entertainments which they provided Ward said: "The men go becauz its poplar and the wimin folks to see what other wimin folks have on." To his lectures they went solely to be amused, and as their success became rapidly known, he soon found that he had done well to abandon journalism. East and West his "show" was in demand. A San Francisco manager telegraphed him, "What will you take for forty nights in California?" and his immediate response, "Brandy and water," so tickled the Western humour that when he came to Virginia City the miners took charge of the entertainment, would have no tickets sold, but invited everybody, and collected sixteen hundred dollars in gold for the lecturer by passing round hats, one of which broke with the weight of its contents. Brigham Young received him cordially in Salt Lake City, in spite of the jests he had made and was still to make about the sect of men whose "religion is singular, but their wives are

plural." There was little of appreciation left for him to win from his own countrymen, at least of those who "liked that sort of thing," when in 1866 he determined to try the fortunes of his wit in London.

Mr. Higginson's phrase, "the amazed curiosity of Englishmen," well describes the state of mind which Artemus Ward excited in the mother country. There could not have been many John Brights in the audiences which thronged Egyptian Hall for the six weeks before his failing health made the seventh his last week of public appearance. The abashed manner of the lecturer, his personal peculiarities of which he himself made fun, the difficulties with his panorama, which in general was painted as badly as possible, because excellence was expensive, the eccentricities of the moon and the prairie fires, which would shoot up and flare out at the wrong moments, to the apparent consternation of the lecturer,—all these, to say nothing of the humour of his talks, are reported to have kept his hearers in a frenzy of laughter. Who can wonder that they were quite overcome by the gravity with which he would point to dark regions in his canvas and say: "These are intended for horses; I know they are, because the artist told me so. After two years he came to me one morning and said, 'Mr. Ward, I cannot conceal it from you any longer; they are horses.' " It was in the full tide of success, achieved simply by the exercise of natural gifts, that his career of unique popularity was cut short. His contributions to *Punch* had won him a place on the staff of the paper, and all things indicated the continuance of success. But the cough which had made nearly all his lecturing in London difficult stopped it entirely. His friends took him to the island of Jersey, in the hope that its milder air might restore him. Then they tried to bring him back to London, but he could not bear the journey beyond Southampton, where he died early in 1867, not quite thirty-three years old.

It may be thought that an inordinate space has been devoted to a person who stood related to literature as *bouffe* to grand opera. Yet Artemus Ward represented conspicuously a class of writers which must not be overlooked in any general survey of American letters. (pp. 163-71)

M. A. DeWolfe Howe, "Some Humourists," in his American Bookmen, *Dodd, Mead and Company, 1898, pp. 163-75.*

W. D. Howells (essay date 1912)

[*Howells was the chief progenitor of American Realism and an influential literary critic of the late nineteenth and early twentieth centuries. Popularly lauded as the "Dean of American Letters," he wrote nearly three dozen novels and stands as one of the major literary figures of his era. In the following excerpt taken from his introduction to a collection of Browne's stories, Howells praises the humorist's mirth and keen observation of American life while simultaneously judging him generally inferior to Mark Twain in form and content.*]

In the first place, while the editor of this selection [Clifton Johnson] is still out of hearing, in the next room, I should like to praise the good judgment he has shown in it; and still more I should like to praise the simple manner of the very interesting memoir which he has prefaced it with. Another, myself we will say, might have been tempted to overdo it, by imparting to the droller's life the pathos of his early death, or by exaggerating his importance among the humorists whose humor the world has decided to call distinctively American. But Mr. Johnson has not made either of these mistakes. He has felt what was characteristic in the author's experiences, and he has had the self-restraint to leave time the censor of his qualities.

I wish his forbearance might govern me in what I have to say of the extravaganzas, once the whole English-speaking world's delight, which, after half a century of fitful and not over-vigorous survival, have been selected here for a sort of final appeal. I will own that when I talked his enterprise over with the editor, I began to have my misgivings of it after a first flush of enthusiasm. An examination of the material confirmed me in my doubt; but a renewed acquaintance with it in Mr. Johnson's presentation has brought back much of my old pleasure in it.

My pleasure is very old indeed, for it began with those earliest drolleries which, in the later eighteen-fifties, made Charles F. Browne's pseudonym known in the columns of the Cleveland *Plain Dealer.* He was then the "local editor" of that newspaper, and in the dearth of personal and police items, or any sort of moving accident or human event, he filled his space with any reckless joke, but oftenest with the wild burlesque of an imaginary showman from the imaginary village of Baldinsville, Indiana, whom he called Artemus Ward. How much the fun was helped from one entirely American heart to other entirely American hearts by the showman's bad spelling can never be known. Our exuberant race had long before wreaked its joy in the like; but it must have been something more than the bad spelling which gave Browne's humor a currency beyond that of all other humorists before his time. It was strictly of his time and place, and it was dwarfed and deformed by the popular prejudices, the partisan prejudices. It reflected the dislike of the anti-slavery movement and of the other contemporary reforms; but it did not miss a good chance of hitting those prejudices if it offered. In fact, it is interesting to see how the wit of Browne humanized with the process of comparatively few suns, and passed from derision of the slave and his friends to derision of the slaveholder and his friends. By the time the volunteering for the war against Secession had begun, the Baldinsville showman was as good a patriot as any Home Guard in the land. In his change he shared the change of Browne in his undramatized humor, which dealt with any contemporary aspect or incident in a spirit of frank and ready adaptability.

Certain facts of what seems a very remote time were caught and are held here in the net of that freakish fancy. Men of my age will remember the universal joy in Artemus Ward's fable of his interview with the Prince of Wales, then visiting our States, whom the showman addresses as freely and equally as we would all have liked to have the Prince approached by one of our sovereign people. Some phrases of it were at once on every tongue, as Ward's question how "Wales" liked "bein' a prince as fur as he had got." Mormonism was then a very live, if not lively interest, and we all rejoiced in the satire which Ward

visited upon the Mormons and their "peculiar institution." We were none of us so serious about this as some of us were about the "peculiar institution" of the South; and Browne had not to vary the attitude of his showman to suit it to the swiftly varying popular moods. It never ceased to amuse him, but when he went to lecture in Utah he was able to sober himself to a realization of the local respectability of a patriarchal phase which cannot cease to be abominable elsewhere to all survivors of the patriarchal age. One of those felicities, one of those pieces of good luck remaining from his contact with Mormonism, was the ticket to his later lecture on that imposture which required the gateman to "Admit the Bearer and One Wife."

Mormonism and slavery, then denounced as "twin relics of barbarism," have outlived the date of the general abhorrence which bracketed them together in some condition of polygamy and servitude more tolerable to our present national mood. But two other phases of our civilization, which almost equally shared the humorist's satire, would not claim his attention now in the old proportion. He would not now find spiritualism so interestingly the object of his mockeries as it was in the eighteen-fifties; people are either tired of it, or they have been reconciled by Psychical Research to whatever of importance there is really or imaginarily in it. But it had long been a waning interest while Woman Suffrage, which Artemus Ward found and made so amusing, is now taken seriously by the vast majority of those who do or do not think about it. Both subjects are exhausted as sources of fun; but in his day they seemed inexhaustibly funny.

He was on the safe side regarding them, not necessarily because he was selfish or timid and preferred the majority to the minority for his personal safety, but because he was of the satirist's usual make, skeptical, ironical, pessimistic. He was by no means unkindly; on the contrary, he much preferred making the joke that did not hurt, that did not displease, or wholly displease even the object of it. But it must be owned that he had not Mark Twain's greatness of nature, his generous scope, his actual humanity. Artemus Ward's humanity itself was of a potential sort which oftenest showed itself in some belated occasion; it was opportunist, to say the best of it. He felt bound to make you laugh, first of all; Mark Twain felt bound to make you laugh, too, but not always first of all; he might first wish to make you feel.

This is a main difference between the men; but I would not have it tell too heavily against the blithe spirit who remains here mainly in his fun, and must not be too closely questioned as to anything else. He overjoyed his generation, and that was enough to do, at least enough for him, and there is much in him to overjoy this, if it will not be too exacting with him. It must remember how Lincoln loved him, and sought him in times of trouble, when wiser and better authorities could not have consoled him nearly so much. Browne had already expressed the feeling of far the greatest number of his fellow-Democrats concerning the problems before Lincoln, in Artemus Ward's interview with the President-elect when the showman rescues him for the time from the horde of office-seekers who never ceased to infest him.

" 'How kin I ever repay you, Mr. Ward, for your kindness?' sed old Abe, advancin and shakin me warmly by the hand. 'How kin I ever repay you, sir?'

" 'By givin the whole country a good, sound administration. By porein ile upon the troubled waturs, North and South. By pursooin a patriotic, firm, and just course, and then if any State wants to secede, let 'em Sesesh!' "

If the droller was not of a more telescopic vision than this, it must be considered that he lived in a very myopic time, when many were accustomed to argue that negroes could justly be made slaves because black men had no souls. When science began to question whether white men had them, the balance was more equitably adjusted between the races; but it was too late then to apply a magnanimous agnosticism to the solution of the difficulties involving our whole nation. If Artemus Ward became of a more patriotic mind about secession when the war for the Union actually began, it cannot be claimed that the humor of his inventor was ever a very valuable contribution to pro-Union literature. I can imagine that it was with distinct relief that he turned from the triumphs of Reconstruction, and that he lost whatever ache he had for the sorrows of the Civil War in the immense, the wholly unmeasured acceptance he found in England when our battles were all over and our troubles seemed so provisional, so merely preparatory to the state of lasting political bliss on which we fancied ourselves entering.

The English could enjoy "Artemus the delicious," as Charles Reade called him, with the unstinted delight to which they sometimes like to abandon themselves. They could accept the bad spelling of his school as something peculiar or original with him. They had themselves had the bad spelling of the *Yellowplush Papers,* so much more skilfully and artistically done; but they could not know that there was an American school of it, famed before Browne's time and destined to survive him, though now, at last, it seems extinct. I myself never liked that sort of easy fun, not even when Lowell commended it generally and defended it specifically in the case of his Hosea Bigelow, who, indeed, wrote a dialect rather than misspelled our common parlance. It does make you laugh out of proportion to the means it uses, and perhaps it comes to its highest effect in Artemus Ward; but oftenest, perhaps, the author seems to be overworking himself in it. If it takes the words "out of their dictionary clothes," as Lowell said, it is not always to leave them in a state of nature which appeals to the love of beauty.

Browne was of no such inventive gift as Clemens, and he is at his best in his own character as a shrewd, tolerant, pessimistic Yankee observer of life. His showman was the figment of a fancy working at haphazard in the desperate haste of a "local editor," and it did not gain in character or quality through the greater leisure and experience of its creator. It remains his one invention, and its humor lies rather in the wild impossibility of its relation to the persons and things of its contact, in the delightful, the inviting make-believe of the whole situation. At this the reader may sometimes find himself working as hard as the author; but his sufficient reward will be in the final truth to human nature, either actual or potential, which the joint

supposition evokes. It is such fun to think of Artemus Ward talking to Lincoln or the Prince of Wales on the terms assumed, that you are willing and even glad to think it.

Clemens, in the wide range of his imagination, asks no such help of you. The inventor of the *Connecticut Yankee at King Arthur's Court* is as compellingly and independently creative as the inventor of *Don Quixote de la Mancha;* and the thousand and one slighter figures of his fancy persuade and convince without asking your help. I do not say all, or that our greatest humorist does not sometimes require too much self-devotion from his readers. I wish he never did; but I must own he sometimes does; and I think that whoever renews or makes acquaintance here with the fun of the earlier humorist will be struck with the fact that in some of his beginnings Mark Twain formed himself from, if not on, Artemus Ward. The imitation could not last long; the great master was so immensely the master; but while it lasts it is as undeniable as it is curious, and it by no means impeaches his superiority. I think him incomparably the greater talent, and yet not always. In such a sketch as **"Affairs Around the Village Green,"** where Browne consents to be most himself, there is a sweetness, a gentleness, a fineness in the humor and the quaint unexpectedness of its turns, which is not surpassed by anything that Clemens did.

I do not know whether others will feel the pathetic suggestion of languor and weariness in this most amusing, most charming sketch; but it hints that sort of thing to me. It must have been done in some interval of Browne's New York life, perhaps shortly before or after the comic paper which he edited "got to be a conundrum, and he gave it up"; but when he had yet some half a dozen years to live. He spent them strenuously and adventurously enough in lecturing everywhere in his own country, until his fame took him to England, where probably the happiest years of his short life were spent. The English liked him with that self-abandon which wins the American heart, and made him so wholly at home among them that, after some brief intervals in America, he returned to die in England. He died very young of consumption, and his face was already prophetic of the end when I saw him last, sometime in 1866, at Boston. I have told elsewhere of the double recognition he gave me, one general, as for any member of the public who chose to claim him friend, and another personal, for one who really knew him. I had known him first in Columbus, when he visited the State capital on some newspaper mission from Cleveland, and we had passed the whole time together: a time of laughing and making laugh. Then afterward I had visited him in the office of *Vanity Fair,* where he ineffectively promised me some "ducats," as he called them, for a contribution. I am glad now to think he never was able to pay them, for the contribution was probably not worth any. All my remembrances of him are glad, even to the last in the laugh his double recognition gave us; and in once more renewing our early acquaintance among the merry jests gathered here, I have had the sense of him as one of those living presences which abound for me now more in the past than in the days that are yet to pass. (pp. vii-xvi)

W. D. Howells, in an introduction to Artemus Ward's Best Stories, *edited by Clifton Johnson, Harper & Brothers Publishers, 1912, pp. vii-xvi.*

Albert Jay Nock   (essay date 1924)

[*Nock was a social critic and journalist who wrote numerous articles, essays, and books concerning cultural issues, including education, feminism, and morality. He is also considered to be one of the finest editors of the twentieth century. In the following excerpt from his preface to a selection of Browne's works, Nock extols the writer's "Intelligenz," his ability to perceive things as they really are, and argues that Browne belongs in the company of Rabelais and Cervantes as a social critic.*]

[Clearly] it is not by the power of his humour that Ward has earned his way in the world of letters, but by the power of his criticism. Ward was a first-class critic of society; and he has lived for a century by precisely the same power that gave a more robust longevity to Cervantes and Rabelais. He is no Rabelais or Cervantes, doubtless; no one would pretend that he is; but he is eminently of their glorious company. Certainly Keats was no Shakespeare, but as Matthew Arnold excellently said of him, he is *with* Shakespeare; to his own degree he lives by grace of a classic quality which he shares with Shakespeare; and so also is Ward with Rabelais and Cervantes by grace of his power of criticism.

Let us look into this a little. . . . Ward has become a special property, and . . . he can never again be a popular property, at least until the coming of that millennial time when most of our present dreams of human perfectability are realized. I have no wish to discourage my publishers, but in fairness I have had to remind them that this delectable day seems still, for one reason or another, to be quite a long way off, and that meanwhile they should not put any very extravagant expectations upon the sale of this volume, but content themselves as best they may with the consciousness that they are serving a vital interest, really the ultimate interest, of the saving Remnant. Ward is the property of an order of persons—for order is the proper word, rather than class or group, since they are found quite unassociated in any formal way, living singly or nearly so, and more or less as aliens, in all classes of our society—an order which I have characterized by using the term *intelligence.* If I may substitute the German word *Intelligenz,* it will be seen at once that I have no idea of drawing any supercilious discrimination as between, say, the clever and the stupid, or the educated and the uneducated. *Intelligenz* is the power invariably, in Plato's phrase, to see things as they are, to survey them and one's own relations to them with objective disinterestedness, and to apply one's consciousness to them simply and directly, letting it take its own way over them uncharted by prepossession, unchanneled by prejudice, and above all uncontrolled by routine and formula. Those who have this power are everywhere; everywhere they are not so much resisting as quietly eluding and disregarding all social pressure which tends to mechanize their processes of observation and thought. Rabelais's first words are words of jovial address,

under a ribald figure, to just this order of persons to which he knew he would forever belong, an order characterized by *Intelligenz;* and it is to just this order that Ward belongs.

The critical function which spirits like Ward perform upon this unorganized and alien order of humanity is twofold; it is not only clearing and illuminating, but it is also strengthening, reassuring, even healing and consoling. They have not only the ability but the *temper* which marks the true critic of the first order; for, as we all know, the failure which deforms and weakens so much of the able second-rate critic's work is a failure in temper. Take, for example, by way of a comparative study in social criticism, Rabelais's description of the behaviour of Diogenes at the outbreak of the Corinthian War, and put beside it any piece of anti-militarist literature that you may choose; put beside it the very best that M. Rolland or Mr. Norman Angell or even Count Tolstoy himself can do. How different the effect upon the spirit! Or again, consider . . . the pictures which Ward draws of the village of Baldwinsville under stress of the Civil War. Not one item is missing of all that afflicted the person of *Intelligenz* in every community at some time in the last ten years. Ward puts his finger as firmly as Mr. Bertrand Russell and Mr. H. L. Mencken have put theirs, upon all the meanness, low-mindedness, greed, viciousness, bloodthirstiness and homicidal mania that were rife among us—and upon their exciting causes as well—but the person of *Intelligenz* turns to him, and instead of being further depressed, as Mr. Russell and Mr. Mencken depress him, instead of being further overpowered by a sense that the burdens put upon the spirit of man are greater than it can bear, he is lifted out of his temporary despondency and enervation by a sight of the long stretch of victorious humanity that so immeasureably transcends all these matters of the moment. Such is the calming and persuasive influence of the true critical temper, that one immediately perceives Ward to be regarding all the untowardness of Baldwinsville *sub specie æternitatis,* and one gratefully submits to his guidance towards a like view of one's own circumstances.

The essential humanity of Abraham Lincoln may be largely determined in one's own mind, I think, by the fact that he made just this use of Artemus Ward. Mr. Seitz [in his *Artemus Ward: A. Biography and Bibliography,* 1919] tells us how, in the darkest days of the Civil War, Lincoln read the draft of his Emancipation Proclamation at a special meeting of his Cabinet, and, to the immense scandal and disgust of his associates, prefaced it by reading several pages from Ward. The incident is worth attention for the further establishment of the distinction drawn among men by the quality of *Intelligenz.* Seward, Chase, Stanton, Blair, had ability, they had education; but they had not the free, disinterested play of consciousness upon their environment, they did not instinctively tend to see things as they are, they thought largely by routine and formula, they were pedantic, *unintelligent*—that is precisely the word that Goethe, the greatest of critics, would have applied to them at once. Upon them then, naturally, Lincoln's performance made the impression of mere impudent levity; and thus one is directly led to see great force in Ward's sly suggestion that Lincoln should fill up his

Cabinet with showmen! Alas! how often the civilized spirit is moved to wish that the direction of public affairs might be taken out of the hands of those who in their modesty are fond of calling themselves "practical" men, and given over to the artists, to those who at least have some theoretical conception of a satisfying technique of living, even though actually they may have gone no great way in the mastery of its practice.

In another place Mr. Seitz tells us how the great and good John Bright, the Moses of British political liberalism, attended one of Ward's lectures in London, sat gravely through it, and then observed that "its information was meagre, and presented in a desultory, disconnected manner"! The moment I read that, I laid down the book, saying to myself, *Behold the reason for liberalism's colossal failure!* The primary failure of liberalism is just the failure in *Intelligenz* that we see so amusingly indicated in the case of Mr. Bright; its secondary failure, as we saw in the case of the late Mr. Wilson, for example, is a failure in the high and sound character that depends so largely upon *Intelligenz* for its development. Can one imagine that Ward would be more intelligible to representative British liberals since Bright's day, or that he would make a more serious and salutary impression upon the energumens who in this country are busily galvanizing some of Mr. Wilson's political formulas into a ghastly simulacrum of life, and setting them up as the soul and essence of liberalism—upon ex-Justice Clarke, for example, or ex-Secretary Baker or Mr. George Foster Peabody? One smiles at the thought of it.

Ward said of writers like himself that "they have always done the most toward helping virtue on its pilgrimage, and the truth has found more aid from them than from all the grave polemists and solid writers that have ever spoken or written. . . . They have helped the truth along *without encumbering it with themselves.*" I venture to italicize these remarkable words. How many good causes there are, to be sure, that seem hopelessly condemned and nullified by the personality of those who profess them! One can think of any number of reforms, both social and political, that one might willingly accept if only one need not accept their advocates too. Bigotry, arrogance, intolerance, self-assurance, never ran higher over public affairs than in Ward's day, yet he succeeded in putting upon all public questions the precise critical estimate that one puts upon them now in the perspective of fifty years; its correspondence with the verdict of history is extraordinarily complete. It would be nothing remarkable if one should arrive now at a correct critical estimate of the Negro question, for example, or of the policy of abolition, or of the character and qualities of public men of the day, or of the stock phrases, the catchwords and claptrap that happened for the time being to be the stock-in-trade of demagoguery; but it is highly remarkable that a contemporary should have had a correct critical estimate of them, and that he should have given to it an expression so strong and so consistent, and yet so little *encumbered with himself* as to be wholly acceptable.

Really, there are very few of the characteristic and distinctive qualities of American life that Ward's critical power left untouched. I read somewhere lately—I think in one

of Professor Stuart P. Sherman's deliverances, though I am not quite sure—that Americans are just now very much in the mood of self-examination, and that their serious reading of novelists like Mr. Sinclair Lewis or Mr. Sherwood Anderson, and of essayists like Mr. Ludwig Lewisohn or Mr. Mencken, is proof that they are in that mood. I have great doubts of all this; yet if it be true, I can but the more strongly urge them to re-examine the work of a first-rate critic, who fifty years ago drew a picture of our civilization that in all essential aspects is still accurate. Ward represents the ideal of this civilization as falling in with one only of the several instincts that urge men onward in the quest of perfection, the instinct of expansion. The claim of expansion is abundantly satisfied by Ward's America; the civilization about him is cordial to the instinct of expansion, fosters it, and makes little of the obligation to scrupulousness or delicacy in its exercise. Ward takes due pride in relating himself properly to the predominance of this instinct; he says that by strict attention to business he has "amarsed a handsum Pittance," and that when he has enough to permit him to be pious in good style, like his wealthy neighbours, he intends to join the Baldwinsville church. There is an ideal of civilized life for you, a conception of the progressive humanization of man in society! For the claim of instincts other than the instinct of expansion, Ward's America does nothing. It does nothing for the claim of intellect and knowledge (aside from purely instrumental knowledge) nothing for the claim of beauty and poetry, the claim of morals and religion, the claim of social life and manners.

Our modern school of social critics might therefore conceivably get profit out of studying Ward's view of American life, to see how regularly he represents it, as they do, as manifesting an extremely low type of beauty, a factitious type of morals, a grotesque and repulsive type of religion, a profoundly imperfect type of social life and manners. Baldwinsville is overspread with all the hideousness, the appalling tedium and enervation that afflict the sensitive soul of Mr. Sinclair Lewis. The young showman's courtship of Betsy Jane Peasley exhausts its resources of romance and poetry; its *beau ideal* of domesticity is completely fulfilled in their subsequent life together—a life fruitful indeed in certain wholesome satisfactions, but by no means such as a "well-formed mind would be disposed to relish." On the side of intellect and knowledge, Baldwinsville supports the editor of the *Bugle* as contentedly as New York supports Mr. Ochs and Mr. Munsey, and to quite as good purpose; it listens to the schoolmaster's views on public questions as uncritically as New York listens to Mr. Nicholas Murray Butler's, and to quite as good purpose. Baldwinsville's dominant type of morals is as straitly legalistic, formal and superficial as our own; its dominant type of religion is easily recognizable as the hard, dogged, unintelligent fanaticism with which Zenith confronted Mr. Sinclair Lewis. We easily recognize the "dissidence of Dissent and the protestantism of the Protestant religion," which now inspires the Anti-Saloon League, and which informs and animates the gentle ministrations of the Ku-Klux Klan.

Thus Ward, in his own excellent phrase, powerfully helps along the truth about civilization in the United States; and all the more powerfully in that, unlike Mr. Lewis and Mr. Mencken, he does not so encumber it with himself, so overload it with the dragging weight of his own propensities, exasperations, repugnances, that his criticism, however accurate and interesting, is repellant and in the long run ineffectual. Often, indeed, his most searching criticism is made by indirection, by the turn of some phrase that at first strikes one as quite insignificant, or at least as quite irrelevant to any critical purpose; yet when this phrase once enters the mind it becomes pervasive, and one finds presently that it has coloured all one's cast of thought—and this is an effect which only criticism of the very first order can produce. For instance, consider the first sentence that he writes in a letter to his wife from the Athens of America:

> Dear Betsy: I write you this from Boston, 'the Modern Atkins' as it is denomyunated, altho I skurcely know what those air.

Nothing but that. Yet somehow when that little piece of exquisite raillery sinks in, it at once begins to put one into just the frame of mind and temper to meet properly the gentle, self-contained provincialism at which it was directed. Let the reader experiment for himself. Let him first recall the fearfully hard sledding he had on his way through, say, Mr. Barrett Wendell's "History of American Literature," or the recent volume of Mrs. Field's reminiscences; let him remember the groan of distress that now and then escaped him while reading Mr. Howells's really excellent novel, "The Rise of Silas Lapham." Then with this sentence in mind, let him try reading any one of the three books again, and see how differently it will impress him.

After the same fashion one may make quite good headway with Mr. Villard's biography of John Brown if one's spirit is cleared and steadied by Ward's inimitable critique of **"Ossawatomie Brown, or, the Hero of Harper's Ferry."** Amidst the squalor of our popular plays and popular literature, one preserves a decent equanimity by perusing Ward's reviews of East Side theatricals and of Forrest's "Othello," and his parodies of the cheap and lurid romances of his day. Our popular magazines take on a less repellant aspect when one remembers how, after three drinks of New England rum, Ward "knockt a small boy down, pickt his pocket of a New York *Ledger,* and wildly commenced readin Sylvanus Kobb's last Tail." No better criticism of our ludicrous and distressing perversion of the religious instinct can be found than in his account of his visit to the Shakers, the Free Lovers and the Spiritualists. Never was the depth and quality of routine patriotism more accurately measured than by this, from the account of his visit to Richmond after the surrender:

> I met a man today—I am not at liberty to tell his name, but he is an old and inflooential citizen of Richmond, and sez he, "Why! we've bin fightin agin the Old Flag! Lor bless me, how sing'lar!" He then borrer'd five dollars of me and bust into a flood of tears.

Again, how effective is Ward's criticism of the mischievous and chlorotic sentimentalism to which Americans seem invariably to give their first allegiance! During the Civil War the popular regard for motherhood was exploited as viciously as during the last war, or probably in all wars, and Ward's occasional reflections upon this peculiarly contemptible routine-process of militarism are more effective than any indignant fulminations of outraged common sense; as when he suggests, for instance, that "the song writers air doin' the Mother bisness rayther too muchly," or as when in another place he remarks that it seems about time somebody began to be a little sorry for the old man. He touches another fond topic of sentimentalism in his story, which I must quote, of leaving home as a boy to embark in the show business. Where can better criticism than this be found?

> You know, Betsy, that when I first commenced my career as a moral exhibitor with a six-legged cat and a Bass drum, I was only a simple peasant child—skurce 15 summers had flow'd over my yoothful hed. But I had sum mind of my own. My father understood this. "Go," he said, "Go, my son, and hog the public!" (he ment "knock 'em," but the old man was allus a little given to slang). He put his withered han' tremblingly onto my hed, and went sadly into the house. I thought I saw tears tricklin down his venerable chin, but it might hav' been tobacker juice. He chaw'd.

But I must end these illustrations, which I have been tempted perhaps unduly to multiply and enlarge upon because their author has never yet, as far as I am aware, been brought to the attention of modern readers in the one capacity wherein he appears to me to maintain an open communication with the future—the capacity of critic. In conclusion I cannot forbear remarking the spring, the abounding vitality and gusto, that pervades Ward's work, and pointing out that here too he is with Rabelais and Cervantes. The true critic is aware, with George Sand, that for life to be fruitful, life must be felt as a *joy;* that it is by the bond of *joy,* not of happiness or pleasure, not of duty or responsibility, that the called and chosen spirits are kept together in this world. There was little enough of joy going in the society that surrounded Ward; the sky over his head was of iron and brass; and there is even perhaps less joy current in American society now. But the true critic has his resources of joy within himself, and the motion of his joy is self-sprung. There may be ever so little hope of the human race, but that is the moralist's affair, not the critic's. The true critic takes no account of optimism or pessimism; they are both quite outside his purview; his affair is one only of joyful appraisal, assessment and representation.

Epitaphs are notably exuberant, but the simple line carved upon Ward's tombstone presents with a most felicitous precision and completeness, I think, the final word upon him. "His name will live as a sweet and unfading recollection." Yes, just that is his fate, and there is none other so desirable. *Mansueti possidebunt terram,* said the Psalmist, the *amiable* shall possess the earth; and so, in the long run, they do. Insight and wisdom, shrewdness and penetration—for a critic these are great gifts, indispensable gifts, and the public has regard for their exercise, it gives gratitude for the benefits that they confer; but they are not enough of themselves to invest a critic's name with the quality of a sweet and unfading recollection. To do this they must communicate themselves through the medium of a temper, a prepossessing and persuasive amiability. Wordsworth showed himself a great critic when he said of his own poems that "they will co-operate with the benign tendencies in human nature and society, and will in their degree be efficacious in making men wiser, better and happier"; and it is just because of their unvarying co-operation with the benign tendencies in human nature and society that Ward's writings have made him in the deepest sense a possession, a cherished and ennobling possession, of those who know him. (pp. 12-25)

> *Albert Jay Nock, in a preface to* Selected Works of Artemus Ward, *edited by Albert Jay Nock, 1924. Reprint by AMS Press Inc., 1972, pp. 7-26.*

An excerpt from "Interview with President Lincoln"

"How kin I ever repay you, Mr. Ward, for your kindness?" sed Old Abe, advancin and shakin me warmly by the hand. "How kin I ever repay you, sir?"

"By givin the whole country a good, sound administration. By poerin ile upon the troubled waturs, North and South. By pursooin' a patriotic, firm, and just course, and then if any State wants to secede, let 'em Sesesh!"

"How 'bout my Cabinit, Mister, Ward?" sed Abe.

"Fill it up with Showmen sir! Showmen is devoid of politics. They hain't got any principles! They know how to cater for the public. They know what the public wants, North & South. Showmen, sir, is honest men. Ef you doubt their literary ability, look at their posters, and see small bills! Ef you want a Cabinit as is a Cabinit fill it up with showmen, but don't call on me. The moral wax figger perfeshun musn't be permitted to go down while there's a drop of blood in these vains! A. Linkin, I wish you well! Ef Powers or Walcutt wus to pick out a model for a beautiful man, I scarcely think they'd sculp you; but ef you do the fair thing by your country you'll make as putty a angel as any of us! A. Linkin, use the talents which Nature has put into you judishusly and firmly, and all will be well! A. Linkin, adoo!"

He shook me cordyully by the hand—we exchanged picters, so we could gaze upon each others' liniments when far away from one another—he at the hellum of the ship of State, and I at the hellum of the show bizniss—admittance only 15 cents.

> Charles Farrar Browne, in his *Artemus Ward, His Book,* Carleton, 1862.

Van Wyck Brooks (essay date 1947)

[*An American critic and biographer, Brooks is noted chiefly for his biographical and critical studies of Mark Twain, Henry James, and Ralph Waldo Emerson, and for his influential commentary on the history of American literature. Contending that America's past was unique and artistically valuable, he was consistently concerned with the reciprocal relationship between the writer and society. In the following excerpt, he credits Browne with effectively deflating the pompous and trite in his works, which helped produce a more natural style in American journalism and on the stage.*]

As for Artemus Ward himself, with his melancholy air on the platform and his great nose that resembled the beak of the macaw, he concocted burlesques in *Vanity Fair* of the high-flown French romances that were so popular especially in the New York of the time. In fact, he was largely effective in changing the tone of thought and speech in more than one respect during [the 1850s], deflating the bombast that throve on the stage with the "world-renowned tragedians," in Congress, in thousands of orations on the Fourth of July. He made it impossible henceforth to take their pomposity seriously, for he had a sharp eye for the flatulent, the pretentious and the trite, and the change to a more natural style that followed in the press and the theatre alike was due in some measure at least to Artemus Ward. He was one of many influences that marked the end of a romantic age, foreshadowing a realistic future, for his mind was dry, conservative and matter-of-fact; surrounded by optimists, he was a pessimist, a Yankee Sancho Panza abounding in the practical wisdom of the common people, a sceptic and a counterpoise to the indiscriminate quixotism, the sometimes flighty idealism of the pre-war years. He was opposed to the "long-haired reformers" for whom the world was out of joint, while he thought it needed only a little greasing, to the agitators for women's rights, temperance, free love, the "affinity business," the spirit-rappers, John Brown, abolition. He spoke for the cautious majority, incredulous, wary, cool and shrewd, that always mingled policy with its kindness; yet his sweetness of spirit was singularly winning and his humour, never pert or smart, spontaneously expressed a nature that was friendly and genial. His mind seemed to float along a current of ideas in which the most natural of all was the topsy-turvy, a novel and delightful confusion of the true and the absurd. (pp. 212-13)

> *Van Wyck Brooks, "The Bohemians," in his* The Times of Melville and Whitman, *E. P. Dutton & Co., Inc., 1947, pp. 192-216.*

Stanley T. Williams (essay date 1952)

[*Williams was a scholar, editor, and author of several books on British and American literature. In the following excerpt, he analyzes the technical aspects of Browne's humor and observes that the writer was a keen observer of society, able to address difficult issues of his day in an honest and rational manner.*]

As a born antiquarian rather than as a professional student of American literature I have long been interested in the changing fashions in American prose. I like, for example, to examine the stately periods of Hawthorne and then the clipped, tense sentences of Ernest Hemingway. Much in the history of the republic lies behind this astonishing change; these styles reflect not merely the authors but their respective epochs; Hawthorne's was born of an incredibly different America. And never do the changes seem so arresting as when we contemplate the humor of yesterday. The passage below (in which the italics are mine) was in its day a classic by a humorist regarded by his contemporaries as a shade less immortal than Rabelais and Cervantes and more entertaining than Mark Twain. Today we read it with misgivings. Was this the best he could do, this "Artemus the Delicious," as our fathers affectionately christened him?

> Some years ago I pitched my tent and onfurled my banner to the breeze in Berlin Hites, Ohio. I had hearn that Berlin Hites was ockepied by a extensive seck called Free Lovers, who beleeved in affinertys and sich, goin back on their domestic ties without no hesitation whatsomever. *They was* likewise spirit rappers and highpresher reformers on gineral principles. If I can improve these 'ere misgided peple by *showin* them my onparalleld show at the usual low price of admitants, methunk, I shall not hav lived in vane! But bitterly did I cuss the day I ever sot foot in the retchid place. I sot up my tent in a field near the Love Cure, as they called it, and bimeby the free lovers begun for to congregate around the door. A ornreer set I have never *sawn*. . . .

> Presently a perfeckly orful lookin female presented herself at the door. Her *gownd* was *skanderlusly* short and her trowsis was shameful to behold.

> She eyed me over very sharp, and then startin back she *sed,* in a wild voice:

> "Ah, can it be?"

> "Which?" sed I.

> "Yes, 'tis troo, O 'tis troo!"

> "15 cents, marm," I anserd.

> She bust out a cryin & sed:

> "And so I hav found you at larst—at larst, O at larst!"

> "Yes," I anserd, "you have found me at larst, and you would hav found me at *fust,* if you had *cum* sooner."

> She grabd me vilently by the coat collar, and brandishin her umbreller wildly round, exclaimed:

> "*Air* you a man?"

> *Sez* I, "I think I air, but if you doubt it, you can address Mrs. A. Ward, Baldinsville, Injianny, postage pade, & she will probly giv you the desired *informashun.*"

> "Then thou ist what the cold world calls marrid?"

> "Madam, I istest!"

> The exsentric female then clutched me franticly by the arm and hollered:

> "You air mine, O you air mine!"

> "Scacely," I sed, endeverin to git loose from her. But she clung to me and sed:

> "You air my Affinerty!"

> "What upon arth is that?" I shouted. . . .

> I was very mutch riled, and *fortifyin* myself with a spare tent stake, I addrest them as follers: You *pussylanermus* critters, go way from me and take this retchid woman with you. I'm a law-abidin man, and beleeve in good, old-fashioned institutions. I am marrid & my orfsprings resemble me, if I am a showman! I think your Affinity bizniss is cussed noncents, besides bein outrajusly wicked. . . . You *wimin* folks, go back to your lawful husbands if you've got any, and take orf them skanderlous *gownds* and *trowsis,* and dress respectful, like other *wimin.* You men folks, cut orf them pirattercal whiskers, burn up them infurnel pamplits, put sum weskuts on, go to work choppin wood, splittin fence rales, or tillin the sile." I pored *4th* my indigna*shun* in this way till I got out of breth, when I stopt. I shant go to Berlin Hites agin, not if I live to be as old as Methooseler.

So this was it? Just tell the "goak," says Artemus Ward, "laffin one of his silvery larfs." Everyone quoted his sayings, such as this, with his characteristic whip of the unexpected: "Chaucer was a great poet, but he couldn't spell"; or of Jeff Davis: "It would have been better than ten dollars in his pocket if he had never been born." These will do well enough even now, and even if they have a flavor of the archaic they set us off on that engaging topic, the history and nature of American humor. On this subject flourish many learned works, besides Constance Rourke's brilliant monograph. But I am still mystified. (pp. 214-16)

From about 1850 until 1880 . . . Western humorists formed a kind of guild, convulsing America with mirth. They do not convulse us; dust has settled on most of their jests. Yet we must remember that these guffaws and horse-laughs were for men still building the Republic. The audiences of Mark Twain and Artemus Ward were men living and fighting on the frontier; men mining for gold; men building cities, railways, ships, and Atlantic cables. These robust jests were not for white-collar gentry planning socialized medicine, and hysterical over the infiltration of spies or trials for perjury. In reading this exuberant humor we are reminded of the sign in the Western saloon: "If your steak is too tough, walk out quietly. This is no place for weaklings." Their laughter seems to belong to another, bolder, freer world.

Indeed, none of these stalwart humorists was a weakling. They were not what Walt Whitman called contemptuously "collegers," although "Josh Billings" did finally complete his freshman year at Hamilton College. They were wanderers through their vast country. They were wanderers through their vast country. They were newspapermen, businessmen, easy-going characters, very much at home in the rough-and-tumble America so vividly described by Mrs. Trollope in 1832 in her "Domestic Manners of the Americans." Artemus Ward, for instance, was a traveling printer; Josh BillinArtemus Ward, for instance, was a traveling printer; Josh Billings's occupations included those of real estate agent, farmer, coal operator, and auctioneer. The point is this: all these "funny men" resemble each other in their vital participation in the life of their times, in their fearless criticism of the society in which they lived, in their techniques, and even in their use of pseudonyms. Samuel Clemens was "Mark Twain"; Henry W. Shaw was "Josh Billings"; David R. Locke was "Petroleum Vesuvius Nasby"; Robert H. Newell was "Orpheus C. Kerr"; and Charles Farrar Browne was "Artemus Ward." We cannot designate this one of the great movements of thought in American history, and its esthetic and literary values are peripheral, but it is a lively eddy in the roaring stream of American life about a century ago. Though I shall speak presently of individual differences, we must think of all of these humorists as part of one basic pattern. Thus Josh Billings says in his "Essa on the Muel":

> The mule is haf hoss and haf Jackass, and then cums to a full stop, natur diskovering her mistake. Tha weigh more, akordin tu their heft than enny other kreetur, except a crowbar.

In the same hilarious mood Artemus replied to the telegram inviting him to lecture in California: "What will you take for forty nights in California?" He answered instantly: "Brandy and Water."

The biographies of all these humorists are engaging, but none is more fascinating than that of our Artemus, and with that for a moment we shall be concerned. His life is an amazing mixture of the picturesque and of the romantic and of the witty and the wise—yes, of the wise, for he fulfilled the truth of Josh Billings's epigram: "yu hav tew be wise before yu can be witty."

Born in Waterford, Maine, one hundred and eighteen years ago, he began, like Mark Twain, as an incorrigible, red-headed printer's devil. We hear of him before he was fifteen years old at work for various New England newspapers, among them the Skowhegan *Clarion.* Next we learn that he lived in Ohio, and when, in 1857, at the age of twenty-three, he became the city editor of the Cleveland *Plain Dealer,* already a distinguished Democratic newspaper, he had been a professional journalist for almost a decade.

We may pause, for now occurred the emergence of something from the chrysalis, not exactly a butterfly but certainly, as he himself would have said, an unusual "critter." In other words, he had his transforming idea; Charles Farrar Browne suddenly became Artemus Ward. In January 27, 1858, with all the cacography and some of the other fantastic antics which he perfected later, he wrote the following letter from Pittsburgh:

The Plane Dealer

Sir:

I write to no how about the show bisnis in Cleeveland i have a show consisting in part of a Calforny bare two snakes tame foxies Xc also waxworks my waxworks is hard to beat, all say they is life . . . now mr. Editor scratch off few lines and tell me how is the show bisnis in your good city i shall have hanbills printed at your offis you scratch my back and i will scratch your back, also git up a grate blow in the paper about my show don't forgit the waxworks.

yours truly
Artemus Ward
Pitsburg Penny

p S pitsburg is a 1 horse town A. W.

In this absurd epistle lay concealed the wealth and fame of its writer and the inextinguishable laughter of millions of Americans and Englishmen. From now on the "Showman" moved throughout the United States, in Virginia, in California, in the great cities, in the tiny villages, and always in the country's eccentric corners. We see him exhibiting his "waxworks" against such odd backgrounds as the Free Love Colony in Berlin, Ohio, in the Shaker settlements, or among the Mormons of Utah. In 1860 his prestige as a humorist brought him to New York as an editor of *Vanity Fair,* and in May of the following year he was this magazine's editor-in-chief. All during the war he laughed with and at America, lecturing from coast to coast, and plying his unique trade among Mexicans, Indians, gamblers, or within the cult of his hero, Brigham Young. It is not surprising that Abraham Lincoln kept halting the deliberations of his cabinet to tell a "little story" from Artemus, for on one side of his nature honest Abe was of the blood of the pioneer humorist, Artemus.

This is, indeed, a brilliant, if homespun, version of the American success story, but probably Artemus Ward's most spectacular triumph occurred in his prolonged visit to London in 1866. While the condescending British still denied the validity of an American literature and ignored the writings of such contemporaries of Ward's as Emerson, Thoreau, Hawthorne, Poe, Melville, and Mark Twain, they flocked to hear Artemus and subjected his humor to solemn British analysis in their most solemn periodicals. Here in London, night after night, Artemus appeared. Surprisingly enough, he turned out to be a gentlemanly young man in correct evening clothes, with a quiet, mournful demeanor. With a hesitant, somewhat befuddled manner he pointed out on a huge canvas a panorama of life among the Mormons while a pianist played soft music during what he described as pathetic episodes. One of his accessories was an artificial moon illuminating the Great Salt Desert. The machinery of this contraption always gave way, and the lecturer would then inquire hopefully, "Is there a good moonist in the audience?" Perhaps, after all, the sad manner was not without proleptic pathos, for Artemus Ward died in the next year, leaving behind him his world-wide fame. This fame, this cornucopia of mirth and happiness—for it was really this—was suddenly checked by his death at the age of thirty-two.

Why did everyone laugh? The illustrative passage is "dated" (1862), but the crafts of the "Genial Showman's" art are worth studying briefly if only to understand better his influence upon at least two generations of Americans. The most obvious characteristic of the excerpt is, of course, the cacography, a device scorned by Mark Twain in favor of the cadences of the human voice, but employed by these Western humorists. In "Huckleberry Finn" Mark Twain uses no less than seven different dialects, but he misspells only to recreate these accurately and never to attain bizarre effects. But Artemus delights in outrageous orthography. At first his typographical oddities seem utterly hit-or-miss. We observe, for example, that the final "g's" are dropped; that the gender and the functions of pronouns are confused; that there are antics like the intrusion of numerals and the ampersand; and, in general, that there seems to be a wild saturnalia of misspelling without any principle whatever.

No supposition could be more inaccurate than this. For Artemus deliberately developed his queer means of communication with a singular precision and with an almost complete consistency in the forms of language. Even in this short selection we perceive that the words "gownd" (gown) or "trowsis" (trousers) or "wimen" (women) or the second personal singular "air" (are) or the suffixes in such words as "informa*shun*" (information) or "indigna*shun*" (indignation) conform to rules as inevitable as those of an Oxford or Texas accent. When the word is repeated, so is the peculiarity, and within the crazy spelling function inviolable laws. Having determined upon the representation of a sound, Artemus usually represents it on its recurrence in the same way. Among his scores of neologies (or word corruptions) which are thus seemingly based on principle, we may detect three or four methods guiding him in this ruthless rape of the English language.

The first of these is an austere economy. All the simplest words, the commonest verbs, the pronouns or the nouns, the words which we cannot open our lips without using, are stripped to their naked phonetic base. In the passage, "said" has become "sed"; "says" has become "sez"; "come" is "cum." Throughout the collected writings we encounter "sum," "bin," "hav," "hed," "deth," and so on, all reduced to the most frugal representation of their sounds. Secondly, we perceive something which is not evident in these simple words whose pronunciation remains unharmed by corrupt spelling; we see that many words represent exactly the natural pronunciation of Artemus's fellow countrymen. We have all heard these pronunciations, from the lips of a backwoods farmer, a Maine guide, or a Cape Cod fisherman. Such words are the salt of American speech, and Artemus Ward loves their earthy quality: "putty" (pretty); "wuss" (worse); "orter" (ought to); "fust" (first); "riz" (rose); "hull" (whole); "hoss" (horse); "hearn" (heard); "bust" (burst); "tuk" (took); "axed" (asked); "hist" (hoist). This is, indeed, a language itself, with its own integrity, and hostile to variations from its heterodox norm. And finally, there are the polysyllabic words which at first seem merely farfetched but which are also based on phonetics. These are faithful sound recordings of what Browne heard on his rounds. It is clear that the narrator, the speaker whom Artemus has in mind, makes a tolerable showing in recording "sed" or "hoss" but is defeated by words which he has heard, blown down, as it were, from the learned to the illiterate, such as "skanderlusly" or "pussylanermous." Thus the Showman writes for *veracity,* "verrasserty," and for *et cetera,* "etsettery"; completely baffled by past participles or preterits, he writes (as he has heard the words) "sawn" for *seen* and for *glided* "glode"!

And what is the purpose of all this? Not merely to amuse, surely. Why is this language so consistent, so phonetically true to the experience of our own ears even now? Why this careful avoidance of all the tricks of dialect (as in Lowell's artificial "Biglow Papers")? Here is no use of antonyms, like those of Shakespeare's Dogberry: "You will be condemned into everlasting *redemption* for this." Here are no malapropisms, such as "an allegory on the banks of the Nile." Instead, there is a new language, within its limits logical, clear, and forceful. The answer to the question is self-evident. Ward is recreating a particular individual. This individual is the run-of-the-mill American of a century ago. Before the days of compulsory education, before the state universities, this "language" (with some exaggeration) was what Browne heard. Not without caricature, this language suggests how the American talked; that is, the American whom Walt Whitman thought the spine of the republic, the person whom he called somewhat ambiguously the "powerful uneducated" man. Let us momentarily shut our eyes to this carnival of misspelling. Let us forget our own irreproachable, twentieth-century education. Let us read these phrases aloud. We hear clearly the American "Democrat" of a century ago.

One fact is certain. No matter how much we deplore the "Genial Showman's" illiteracy, the portrait he draws of himself (and so of this typed American of 1860) is amazingly distinct. Thus this American estimates shrewdly one problem of his country:

> Feller Sitterzens [he says] the Afrikan may be Our Brother. Several hily respectyble gentlemen, and sum talentid females, tell us so. . . . I don't beleeve it my self. But the Afrikan . . . isn't our grandfather and our grate grandfather, and our Aunt in the Country. Scacely. . . . But we've got the Afrikan, or ruther he's got us, & now what air we going to do about it? He's a orful noosance.

He is equally percipient on the draft, on war, on Brigham Young, or on bogus patriotism. After the surrender of the Confederates, he remarked:

> I met a man today—I am not at liberty to tell his name but he is an old and inflooential citizen of Richmond, and sez he "Why! we've bin fightin agin the Old Flag! Lor bless me, how sing'lar." He then borrer'd five dollars of me and bust into a flood of tears.

The "Showman" is both astute and kindly but obviously a little flustered by all the conflicting opinions and elements which toss him about in his democracy: The Shakers, the Quakers, the Mormons, the Spiritualists, Harvard College, the Atlantic Monthly, or the tragedies of Shakespeare on the New York stage. It is seldom defensible to identify the opinions of a fictitious character, whether Hamlet or an "exsentric female," with those of his creator, the author, but it is easy to believe that this "figger" of the American reflects the actual convictions of this Maine Yankee, with his brilliant mind and his impressive intimacy with the common life of the republic. How often his admiring contemporaries were wont to preface an earnest judgment on a political or social problem with the words, "As Artemus Ward says. . . ." To all intents and purposes what comes from the lips of Artemus Ward belongs to the thoughtful mind of Charles Farrar Browne.

Viewed in this light, it seems certain that behind his jester's mask Browne had something to say, and I am not sure that what he says has not some pertinence now in the America which he would never recognize. Or would he? Some hints exist, I think, that he foresaw its tragic, regimented future. But omitting the multifarious opinions on American life which delight us even now for their own uproarious sake, we are struck by the persistence in all his thinking of two points of view (closely allied) which water the roots of all his kindliness and optimism. The first is that inevitably a truly free society breeds extremisms; that the excesses of individualism lead to fanaticism. In this sense every little essay of Browne's, so deceptively good-humored (the Shakers, the Fenians, the jingos, the Mormons, Ossawatomie Brown, the "moral lecturers" of his day, the abolitionists, the secessionists, the sentimentalists) is an appeal for reason, for balance, for common sense. Browne knew that the act of laughter was an act of criticism and he used his wit as a weapon of satire. Perhaps his conception of the satirist, of the loyal democrat standing apart and laughing at the faults of the democracy he loved, was the most valuable contribution of his realistic transcripts of America. If the issues which he assailed seem far away to us, this is not true of the temper of his mind, so sharp, so honest, so courageous.

For it is evident that Browne thought of himself as a free man. He conceived of the individual citizen as endowed with a free, ranging consciousness. He regarded it as axiomatic that this citizen should apply this consciousness directly without fear to the problems of his personal and public life. He had not heard of loyalty oaths, of societies on internal security, of federal bureaus of investigation. He could speak without misinterpretation of the policies of Lincoln, of copperheads, of Southern chivalry, of the evils of the draft, of hysterical religious movements. Writing of a war meeting, he said:

> It was largely attended. The editor of the Bugle arose and got up, and said the fact could no longer be disguised that we were involved in a war.

How natural it sounds! But Browne was not denounced as a warmonger.

> Human gore [he went on] is flowin. All able-bodied men should seize a musket and march to the tented field. I repeat it, sir,—to the tented field.
>
> A voice—"Why don't you go yourself, you old blowhard?"

Yet for this bit of satire no one called Browne a defeatist, an isolationist, a retreatist. It makes one a little wistful for an America that seems to have passed into history. It would be easy to imagine chapters from Browne's pen on the Communist front societies, on social security, on the income tax, on foreign policy in Asia, on the present Congress. If he were writing of these problems (instead of abolition or Mormonism) I do not think he would flinch from his deep, inborn consciousness of what true freedom is, and I think that in his rôle of critic of our troubled times he would still be "Artemus the Delicious." (pp. 219-27)

Stanley T. Williams, "Artemus the Delicious," in *The Virginia Quarterly Review, Vol. 28, No. 2, Spring, 1952, pp. 214-27.*

John Q. Reed   (essay date 1958)

[*In the following excerpt, Reed presents Browne as a social commentator on such issues as women's rights, the temperance movement, economics, and abolition, suggesting that the humorist was moderate and always approached controversial subjects with common sense.*]

Charles F. Browne, creator of Artemus Ward, was much more than a mere entertainer; he was also a searching critic of the society in which he lived. The decades of the 1850's and 1860's constituted a period of change and conflict, and they presented numerous incongruities and contradictions. Clear-sighted criticism of American society was badly needed, and there is every evidence that Ward realized this and that he took seriously his role as a critic of the American scene. Although it cannot be denied that his criticism occasionally displayed bigotry and Philistinism, it is also indisputable that he was often able to reveal issues in their true perspective during a period of intense ferment and confusion.

One of the most frequent objects of Ward's satire was the general reform movement which was so prominent a feature of mid-nineteenth century America. The following paragraph, which appeared in his column in 1859 under the heading **"Why?",** states clearly his general attitude toward the wave of reform which was sweeping the northern and middle states in the 1850's.

> We can see no possible use for the numerous long-haired men and disagreeable he-women that are scattered over this Great Republic, and think they had better die as soon as possible. They profess to be in the Reform business but they are decided loafers. They toil not, neither do they spin. They are unmitigated sponges [Cleveland *Plain Dealer,* 26 March 1859].

The social consciousness and the humane spirit which were characteristic of the intellectual climate of the period found overt expression in such remedial enterprises as the temperance and abolition movements, campaigns for economic reform, and the crusade for women's rights. Firm in their belief that both men and institutions could and should be improved, and buttressed by nineteenth century pietism, the leaders of these movements were preoccupied with the idea of doing good and worked at it with a religious fervor. Merle Curti says [in his *The Growth of American Thought,* 1943] that the complex forces behind the general reform movement of the period include the Enlightenment, romanticism, Utilitarianism, Christianity, democracy, and the social and economic tensions of the time. Its close relationship to the religious fervor of the age can be seen clearly in the career of Charles G. Finney, a very successful revivalist in the 1820's, who later became a leader of the abolition movement in the West.

One reform movement which caught Ward's attention was the campaign for women's rights. Led by such women as Lucretia Mott, Susan Anthony, Elizabeth Stanton, Elizabeth Smith, and Sara Josepha Hale, this movement was very strong during the 1850's and '60's. The organization of women in their own cause may be said to have begun in August, 1848, when a women's rights meeting was held in Rochester, New York. In 1850 the first national convention was held, and within a decade the movement had spread throughout all of the northern states and to the west as far as Wisconsin and Kansas. Elizabeth Smith, wife of Seba Smith who wrote the Jack Downing papers, lectured on the question of women's rights, and Sara Josepha Hale carried on a campaign for equal rights for women in *Godey's Lady's Book* for years. Although the struggle to obtain equal opportunities for women in education, in the professions, in the business world, and before the law, had made considerable headway by 1860, the accomplishments were made in the face of formidable opposition. Artemus Ward, who ridiculed the movement, was certainly not alone in his views. In 1849, for example, Richard Henry Dana had delivered a lecture throughout the country in which he ridiculed the demands of women for equal rights and privileges.

Two of Ward's letters deal in a humorous and disparaging manner with the question of women's rights. In the first letter, which appeared in *Vanity Fair* under the heading **"Artemus Ward on His Travels,"** the old showman tells of his meeting a determined and outspoken advocate of women's rights while traveling on a train westward from Detroit. The hard-headed showman was not impressed by the harangue of this woman about women's "spears."

> On the cars was a he-lookin' female, with a green-cotton umbreller in one hand and a handful of Reform tracks in the other. She sed every woman should have a Spear. Them as didn't demand their Spears, didn't know what was good for them. "What is my Spear?" she axed, addressin the peple in the cars . . . "Is it to stay to home & darn stockins & be the *serlave* of a domineerin man? Or is it my Spear to vote & speak & show myself ekal of man? Is there a sister in these keers that has her proper Spear?" Sayin which the eccentric female whirled her umbreller round several times, & finally jabbed me in the weskit with it.

> "I have no objecshuns to your goin into the Spear bizniss," sez I, "but you'll please remember I ain't a pickeril. Don't Spear me agin if you please." She sot down.

The showman's second experience with fanatical advocates of women's rights occurs one night while he is presenting his show in "Injianny." As he is standing outside his tent collecting admission fees, a group of women who claim to be members of the "Bunkumville Female Moral Reformin & Women's Rites associashun" ask him if they can see the show without buying tickets. When the showman refuses, one of the group delivers a spirited discourse on the rights of women. The showman finally loses his patience when the women tell him that he is a "crooil, crooil man" and expresses in a formal and heartfelt manner his views on women's rights.

> "O, woman, woman!" I cried, my feelins worked up to a poetick pitch, "you air a angle when you behave yourself; but when you take off your

proper appairel & (mettyforically speaken)—get into pantyloons—when you desert your firesides, & with your heds full of wimin's rites noshuns go round like roarin lyons, seekin whom you may devour somebody—in short, when you undertake to play the man, you play the devil and air an emfatic noosance [*Artemus Ward; His Book*]

In **"Artemus Ward on His Travels"** the showman, in addition to encountering the militant advocate of women's rights is also forced to cope with a very aggressive temperance lecturer. Although the temperance movement was not as strong in the 1850's as it had been during the two previous decades, it still displayed considerable vitality. The Order of the Sons of Temperance, the best known of the temperance organizations, could boast in the 1850's of thirty-six grand divisions, nearly six thousand subordinate units, and a quarter of a million paying members. A very active unit of this organization was functioning in Cleveland during Ward's tenure on the *Plain Dealer,* and be reported on many of its meetings in his column. In the late 1850's a new national organization called the Band of Hope was organized, and it flourished widely for a few years. During the fifties the classic temperance novel, Timothy Shay Arthur's *Ten Nights in a Bar-Room and What I Saw There* was a best seller, and *Godey's Lady's Book* was an active instrument of the Temperance Movement. Despite the fact that his father had been active in the Temperance Movement of the 1840's, Ward apparently found the endless temperance meetings and lectures wearisome affairs.

The showman's encounter with a temperance lecturer occurs on the train when he is seized with a sudden faintness, real or imaginary, and orders a drink of whiskey. Just as he is about to swallow the spirits, however, a pale-faced man wearing gold spectacles lays a hand on his shoulder and says very solemnly, "Look not upon the vine when it is red." Although Artemus protests that he is drinking rye, not wine, the reformer continues to needle him until the showman loses his temper and tells him to mind his own business. This is the only criticism of the Temperance Movement to be found in Ward's writings, and it is a fairly mild one. Perhaps he felt that since the movement was so popular at the time, a stronger attack might alienate a number of his readers, and it is possible, too, that his fondness for liquor influenced his attitude.

Abolitionism was another reform movement about which Ward had much to say. In fact, the most vitriolic satire to be found in his writings was aimed at the abolitionists. Since I analyzed in detail in an earlier article his comments on this issue [in *Civil War History* II, September 1956], I will limit myself here to a summary account of them.

Ward's first attacks on abolitionism were aimed at Oberlin College. In August, 1858, he denounced the policy of the college of admitting Negro students. Then in the fall of the same year he reported the freeing by a mob of John Price, a fugitive slave, and the subsequent arrest of fifteen members of the mob, It was during the trial of these men the following April that the now famous **"Oberlin Letter"** appeared. In it he attacks Henry Peck and Charles G. Finney, both leaders of the abolitionist group at the college. He also denounces bitterly the policy of giving Negro students the same privileges as those granted to white students.

In April, 1860, Ward again attacked the Abolitionists in a letter entitled **"Artemus Ward Encounters the Octoroon."** In this letter the showman relates in an amusing fashion his being duped on a railway train by a white man and a mulatto who poses as a freed slave from Mississippi. The two plead with the showman to give them money to help free the woman's eighty-seven-year-old mother from slavery. After he has good-naturedly given them fifty dollars, he learns that they are swindlers who prey on the sympathies of gullible people. The inference is, of course, that most abolitionists are innocent people who are being gulled by the Negro slaves in the South.

On the subject of economic reform Ward was virtually silent. The industrial revolution which was spreading rapidly over the northern states during his lifetime brought new wealth and economic independence to the common man, but it was also the cause of serious social and economic problems which baffled the best thinkers of the age. Mushroom-like, cities to house workers sprang up around the new industrial plants in a haphazard fashion. As new immigrants, willing to work for appallingly low wages, crowded into the United States, native industrial workers became restless. Working hours were long, working conditions unhealthful and dangerous, and living conditions crowded and unsanitary; but since a philosophy of *laissez faire* dominated the economic thinking of the time, industry went uncontrolled until after the Civil War. Reformers of the period attacked every phase of the factory system as well as the prevailing economic philosophy. Some Transcendentalists took a firm stand against industry and the capitalistic system, and the collectivistic communities stood for radical economic reform. Trade unions were also revived in the early fifties, and labor leaders protested vehemently against the special privileges of business. There was little agreement, however, as to how the economic and resultant social problems were to be solved, and few reforms were actually effected.

Cleveland, because of its advantageous location, was growing rapidly during Ward's stay there. New industries employing from ten to one hundred men were constantly springing up in the city, and many immigrants, chiefly German, were being drawn to Cleveland by them. Ward's reports of court proceedings show vividly that the city faced serious social problems arising directly or indirectly from industrial expansion. Daily, cases of prostitution, rape, incest, drunkenness, assault, murder, robbery, and arson were tried in the police court or in the court of common pleas. Although Ward was most certainly aware of the underlying economic causes of many of these ugly problems, he did not take a firm stand against the prevailing *laissez faire* economic philosophy nor against the commercialism of the times. Albert J. Nock, in an article written some years ago [in the *Atlantic Monthly* CLIV, September 1934], contends that Ward did adopt such a position in his writings. Nock writes, "As Ward saw America, its god was Good Business; its monotheism was impregna-

ble. Of man's fundamental social instincts only one, the instinct of expansion, had free play, and its range was limitless." Nock presents, however, scanty evidence to support this viewpoint, and a close perusal of Ward's writings will show that there is meagre proof to substantiate it. It is true that the business ethics of the old showman are not of the highest calibre; he does advise the editor to whom he addresses **"One of Mr. Ward's Business Letters"** to "cum the moral on 'em strong" and he solemnly promises, "You scratch my back & Ile scratch your back." But economic protest is not a prevailing theme in his writings. In his comments on the Shakers, for example, he neither praises nor condemns their practice of communism. The only other article in addition to the one mentioned above which contains statements that might be interpreted as indictments of the inequalities of the economic system is contained in a review of a book by William Sanger entitled *The History of Prostitution*. In his review of the book, he says,

> We hear something, now and then about the "clanking" of Negroes' chains in the South. A vast deal has been said about the evils of intemperance. Eminently respectable sums of money have been contributed by eminently respectable churches to convey the gospel across the seas to howling, dirty savages. But we never heard of missionaries being sent among the factory workers of New England, to tell them that their reeking-hot, sickly and deathly mills were supplying the New York houses of prostitution with the larger part of their fresh victims—for such is the plain truth [*Plain Dealer,* 13 November 1858].

Ward neither eulogizes industrial expansion, business ethics, and the *laissez faire* economic philosophy of the time, nor does he oppose contemporary economic reformers; but silence does not imply assent in either case. Perhaps as the local editor of an important newspaper in a city which was intoxicated with the idea of expansion, he did not dare to dissent openly. Advertisers also had to be taken into consideration. At any rate, in view of the scanty evidence available in his works, Ward can be safely classified neither as an economic reformer nor as an outspoken enemy of economic reform.

In conclusion, it should be remembered that Ward, in registering his opposition to most reformers and reform movements was not presenting a minority report. Many reformers were unstable individuals who over-simplified the solutions to very complex social problems, and many reformers themselves spoke out sharply against overzealousness. Curti states that the majority of Americans were either "indifferent or hostile to the reform movements." Mildly conservative in most things Ward directed his satire largely at the "lunatic fringe" in the reform groups. His norm is usually sanity and good sense. The one outstanding exception to this, his extreme antipathy to abolitionism, is to be explained, first by his deepseated prejudice against the Negro race, and secondly, by his strong political convictions. (pp. 20-6)

John Q. Reed, "Artemus Ward on Reform and Reformers," in The Educational Leader, *Vol. XXII, No. 1, July, 1958, pp. 20-6.*

Charles Farrar Browne the lecturer.

John Q. Reed (essay date 1966)

[*In the following excerpt, Reed examines Browne's relationship to nineteenth-century culture, asserting that in order to properly evaluate the humorist's place in American literature, it is necessary to understand the social context in which he wrote and lectured.*]

When literature used in American Studies is not subjected to rigorous literary analysis, two dangers immediately present themselves: first, underestimating the contribution of the major writer to the study of culture; second, its converse, overrating the contribution of the minor writer. [Arlin] Turner accurately outlines the nature of the second hazard: "Lesser writers, the producers of our minor literature, often seem more usable in American Studies because they are more likely to belong more wholly to their times and reproduce their world more literally in their works" ("Nathaniel Hawthorne in American Studies," *College English,* XXVI). To illustrate this proposition, let us consider the case of a minor writer: Charles Farrar Browne, better known as Artemus Ward, the old showman. Extremely popular in his own day as a journalist, author, and lecturer, Browne presently occupies a modest but apparently secure niche in American literature. Selections from his writings appear in most anthologies of American literature and American humor, and he is included in many survey courses in American literature.

Since the social and historical approach is both helpful and appropriate in studying Browne's work, let us first briefly examine his humor in its relationships to the milieu in which it was written. Browne, like most humorists and satirists, was closely attuned to contemporary culture, and his work reveals a great deal about the social, political, and economic climate of the 1850's and 1860's. Conversely, a thorough understanding of the culture, the leaders, and the events of that period is essential if one is to understand fully his humor and satire. A native of New England, he lived and worked as a journalist in Toledo, Cleveland, and New York, and he lectured extensively throughout the United States. He not only took the materials and techniques of his humor from nineteenth century culture, but he also commented imaginatively and perceptively on numerous facets of that culture. Far from being alienated, he was in almost complete rapport with the majority of his contemporaries and was lionized by the popular audiences of his time. As a newspaperman, magazine editor, and comic lecturer, he played an important role as observer and critic of his society. Some of his observations and criticism may seem unimaginative to the liberal mind of today, but if Browne was often wrong, then so was the majority of his contemporaries. A moderate and a defender of the status quo, he usually presented a majority report.

Browne's most extensive body of writing appears in the daily column which he wrote for the Cleveland *Plain Dealer* between 1857 and 1860. Except for the Artemus Ward letters which appeared in his column, it must be classified as journalism rather than as literature, but it does present a literal and detailed account of social disorganization in a young, raw, and growing Middle Western city. His Artemus Ward letters generally treat national issues and national figures. Adopting his "old showman's" point of view, he propounded in the letters his humorous and satirical comments on the contemporary scene.

Reformers and cultists, a prominent feature of mid-nineteenth century America, caught Browne's attention early in his career, and he directed some of his most pungent satire at the fanatics among them. Like Emerson, he was convinced that the only lasting and effective kind of reform was self-reform. He attacked the militant feminists in **"Women's Rights,"** the zealous temperance advocates in **"Artemus Ward on His Travels,"** the Shakers in a letter entitled **"The Shakers,"** the Mormons in **"Artemus Ward Visits Brigham Young,"** the Spiritualists in **"Artemus Ward Among the Spirits"** and the proponents of free love in **"Artemus Ward Among the Free Lovers."** But he reserved his biggest guns for the Abolitionists. In his famous **"Oberlin Letter"** he began an attack on Abolitionism which did not cease until slavery was a dead issue.

A strong Northern Democrat, Browne also commented extensively on the subject of national politics. During the presidential campaign of 1860 he unwaveringly supported Stephen A. Douglas and opposed Abraham Lincoln. Never virulent in his opposition to Lincoln, he confined himself to making fun of the campaign image of Honest Abe, the rustic rail-splitter from Illinois. This he did effectively in **"How Old Abe Received the News of His Nomi-**

nation." After Lincoln's election Browne announced his willingness to support him, and like most Northern Democrats he was loyal to him until his assassination. Browne left the *Plain Dealer* late in 1860 and joined the staff of *Vanity Fair* early in 1861; most of his comments on the Civil War appeared in *Vanity Fair*. Although he attacked the Southern Confederacy in **"The Show is Confiscated"** and **"Thrilling Scenes in Dixie,"** most of his satire written during the war was directed at the inept handling of the war effort in the North rather than at the South. He severely attacked Congress in **"Things in New York,"** the Union Army and its generals in **"The Showman at Home,"** draft dodgers in **"The Draft in Baldinsville,"** and pseudo-patriots in **"A War Meeting."** Browne was not a vindictive man, however, and after Appomattox he took a conciliatory attitude toward the South. In **"Artemus Ward in Richmond,"** for example, he tells a young Southerner that the North and South must reconcile their differences and make the Union even stronger than it was before the War. He was much more willing to let bygones be bygones than were many Northerners.

Throughout his career Browne also expressed in numerous articles his socio-economic views, views which were in general those of the Democratic Party. He was consistently critical of questionable business practices, the mania for making money, speculation, and the excesses of capitalism in general, but perhaps most of all he attacked the false ideals of his age. The blind nationalism and shallow patriotism so characteristic of his era he ridiculed again and again. His famous **"Weathersfield Oration"** is a telling burlesque of the essential falseness and emptiness of the spread-eagle oration, and **"Boston"** is a humorous but biting attack on the exaggerated respect which many of his contemporaries had for national monuments. In a number of burlesques of the popular romance he attacked the questionable ethics and superficial moralism which characterized that genre. In **"Woshy-Boshy"** he burlesqued the romance of the noble red man, in **"The Fair Inez,"** the romance of adventure on the high seas, and in **"A Romance: William Barker,"** the rags-to-riches story. In all of his burlesques of popular literature he pleaded for genuine emotional content, realistic plot, convincing dialogue, and above all for a right sense of values and a more realistic view of life.

In his newspaper column and elsewhere Browne also commented on major writers like Poe, Melville, and Emerson; on current plays and players; on operas and opera singers, on lyceum lectures, and on many other aspects of his era. In fact, few facets of mid-nineteenth century American culture are not effectively reflected somewhere in his writing.

In addition to his great success as a humorous writer, Browne also holds the distinction of being the first American humorist to achieve great popularity as a comic lecturer. Although his lectures can be analyzed as examples of oral humor or public address, they were essentially pure entertainment calculated to please a mass audience, and they can best be understood from a cultural viewpoint. Basically, of course, his comic lectures were burlesques of the serious lyceum lecture and, since the lyceum enjoyed much widespread popularity, they were also good-natured attacks on public taste. His skill on the lecture platform is attested to by the fact that he could appear on lecture series with men like Wendell Phillips and Bayard Taylor, burlesque the type of lectures which they presented, and captivate the very audience whose taste he was ridiculing. By careful planning and cautious experimentation he succeeded in appealing to a large segment of the American people, and by making comic lecturing both respectable and profitable he paved the way for Mark Twain and the many other literary comedians who followed him. Any study of popular entertainment in the nineteenth century can hardly ignore Browne's comic lectures.

For almost two decades, then, as national jester and oracle, Browne held the attention, affection, and respect of most Americans, including President Lincoln, who was one of his greatest admirers. Pleading for sanity, common sense, and moderation, he helped to shape public opinion during a most critical period in American history. He did, without doubt, have considerable insight into the culture of the age as well as some influence on it.

The foregoing discussion has demonstrated that the cultural approach is very useful in analyzing and evaluating a popular writer and entertainer like Browne. But a major danger in using this method exclusively is that of losing perspective on him as a writer. The social scientist or historian can no doubt explain why he used literary forms like the anecdote, the letter to the editor, and burlesques, since these forms did have their roots deep in American culture, but only the literary critic can make a disciplined analysis of his writing and arrive at a valid estimate of the skill with which he used these literary forms. The cultural historian can demonstrate that Artemus Ward, like Jack Downing and Sam Slick, is a reflection of the Jacksonian revolution and the triumph of popular democracy, but only the literary critic can evaluate the vitality, the consistency, and the credibility of the characterization, and only a linguist is equipped to investigate the dialect which he speaks. The analysis and evaluation of the techniques of humor and satire which Browne employed are *exclusively* problems for the literary critic, since neither a knowledge of the culture nor an awareness of what is being satirized will help one recognize satirical devices, let alone evaluate the skill with which they are used.

Although the scope of this essay does not permit a detailed investigation of Browne's literary artistry, I shall attempt a summary evaluation of his art, discussing very briefly his use of literary forms, his handling of humorous and satirical techniques, his skill in characterization, and finally, his stature in American literature.

Browne used skillfully most of the literary forms which he attempted. If he did not rise above mediocrity in his use of the anecdote, he assuredly did excel in his letters written from the old showman's point of view. Carefully planned and deliberately written, his letters are unified, well organized, and economical. Although some of his burlesques fail because he did not consistently satirize style or subject, he had an instinctive feeling for the genre, and most of his burlesques are artistically successful. His lectures he constructed painstakingly, using a chain of association or primitive stream-of-consciousness technique, and he subjected them to continuous revision. It is fair to say, however, that despite their humor and originality, they have limited value as literature. The literary forms which Browne used, then, were rudimentary rather than mature, and as a result his humor is fragmentary and his criticism incomplete. Although his onslaught on decadent romanticism helped to prepare the way for the rise of realism in American fiction, he made no major contribution to realistic fiction as Mark Twain did.

Close examination of Browne's writing reveals that he had mastered most of the standard techniques of humor and satire. He had a keen sense of the incongruities which abounded in his culture, and he excelled in understatement and logical confusion. His use of overstatement, anticlimax, comic tautology, puns, irony, and paradox, if not outstanding, is more than competent. Although he is condemned by many critics today for his comic misspelling, a careful analysis of his work will reveal that his use of this humorous device is decidedly more effective than that of any of his imitators. Browne's best humor, however, is not the result of a mastery of superficial humorous devices; it is good because the humor is inherent in the situation depicted, the language used, and the character portrayed.

Browne's outstanding literary achievement is, without doubt, the creation of Artemus Ward. Firmly conceived and convincingly portrayed, he is a representative American as well as an individual. He is shrewd, pragmatic, and expedient, but he is also moderate, sane, humane, and self-reliant. The vernacular which he uses is appropriate to his character, and it is also accurate and amusing. Considering the fact that Browne employed the old showman as an *alter ego* over a period of about eight years in numerous letters and burlesques, the consistency of his character is amazing. A substantial literary achievement, he is a generic American who constantly verges on the mythical, and he has become an enduring character in American literature.

Browne, then, was much more than a popular writer. He had a natural and genuine artistic sense, and his work is superior to that of all earlier and contemporary American humorists except Mark Twain. Despite the enduring qualities of his humor and satire, however, he produced no literary monuments, and consequently he is not a major American writer. (pp. 243-50)

> *John Q. Reed, "Artemus Ward: The Minor Writer in American Studies," in* The Midwest Quarterly, *Vol. VII, No. 3, April, 1966, pp. 241-51.*

Robert Rowlette (essay date 1973)

[*In the following excerpt, Rowlette compares the literary styles of Twain and Browne, concluding that Twain paraphrased the basic detail and structure of Browne's writings and lectures.*]

Although scholars have long agreed that Mark Twain learned much about humorous lecturing from Charles

Charles Farrar Browne.

Farrar Browne, better known as Artemus Ward, they have disagreed sharply on the corresponding question of a literary indebtedness. From the early years of Twain's writing career critics regularly linked their names in tacit attribution of influence. Two years after Twain's death William Dean Howells [in his Introduction to *Artemus Ward's Best Stories*, edited by Clifton Johnson, 1912] wrote that "in some of his beginnings Mark Twain formed himself from, if not on, Artemus Ward. The imitation could not last long; the great master was so immensely the master; but while it lasts it is as undeniable as it is curious." Twenty-five years later the relationship was still mentioned often enough for Walter Blair to remark [in his *Native American Humor*, 1937] that it had become "conventional to suggest that Mark learned from Ward not only the way to speak but also the way to write humorously." Others have since asserted Ward's tutorship.

The only serious challenge to this convention was issued forty years ago by Bernard DeVoto in the monumental but pontifical *Mark Twain's America*. Scorning the widespread belief among academicians "that Mark Twain's humor developed in imitation of . . . Artemus Ward," he produced from "conscientious study" of their works nine parallels which, with discounted but unspecified similarities in their treatment of a common theme, the Mormons, "compose the sum of Mark Twain's indebtedness to Artemus Ward." That indebtedness, he concluded, is "almost wholly verbal—fifty words in the collected works. Their minds were disparate, their intentions antagonistic, their methods incommensurable. They were humorists and in the production of humor Artemus Ward was chronologically the first. That is all." DeVoto's pronouncements have won adherents, but neither side in the controversy has investigated further; the question remains an untidy loose end in Twainian criticism.

The convention that links Twain and Ward began with their bibulous acquaintance in December 1863 in Virginia City, Nevada, where Twain was a reporter for the *Territorial Enterprise*. Ward, arriving from San Francisco for a few days of lecturing in Virginia City and neighboring towns, found Twain and his *Enterprise* cronies so congenial that, his lecturing done, he lingered a few more days to play. For Twain, with his still regional reputation and outlook as a journalist and with only an amateur's standing as a local speaker, Ward's visit was propitious. Only a year the elder, Ward was already famous as a lecturer and as the author of newspaper sketches and the cacographic letters from the itinerant showman bearing his pseudonym, all collected in *Artemus Ward, His Book* the year before. Quite probably he became Twain's early standard of success as an author and his model as a humorous lecturer. Certainly he recognized Twain's gift for humorous writing and encouraged him to contribute to prestigious Eastern journals; his "powerfully convincing" note to the *Sunday Mercury* was followed shortly by the appearance in its pages of two of Twain's articles; and Twain's "Jumping Frog," which brought his first fame in the East, was intended for inclusion in Ward's second book, *Artemus Ward, His Travels* (1865), but arrived after the publisher's deadline.

Ward's death in England in 1867 and the tearful response in that country and his own may have prompted Twain in the next few years to capitalize on his knowledge of both the man and his material. Besides his use of Ward in his first books, to be taken up presently, he recorded some of his impressions of the humorist's piquant personality in "First Interview With Artemus Ward" (1867). More particularly, in his lecture tour of 1871-1872 he presented, several times a week for about seven weeks, a talk on Artemus Ward, probably because of the subject's presumed sure-fire appeal. The lecture "embodied biographical data of dubious accuracy," says [Paul Fatout, in his *Mark Twain on the Lecture Circuit*, 1960], which "served only as pegs on which to hang jokes by Ward and by Mark Twain so well mixed that he once introduced himself as 'Charles F. Clemens' . . . and led one reporter to call the mixture 'Mark Ward on Artemus Twain.' " Some of these jokes, with other items, had already been transferred to Twain's pages; others were to follow.

Seldom after that did Twain acknowledge Ward. One cannot be sure that the inclusion of nine items from Ward in *Mark Twain's Library Of Humor*, planned in 1880 and finally published in 1888, indicates that Twain had carefully re-read the other's work or even that he himself made the selections. Although Twain was officially the compiler of

the anthology, Howells and Charles Hopkins Clark, the associate editors, did most of the work. Howells wrote the graceful introduction, and one scholar believes the volume should have been entitled "The Howells Library of Humor," since he selected the contents. Even though Twain had earlier borrowed heavily from one of the Ward items, **"A Visit to Brigham Young,"** and had echoed two others, **"Artemus Ward and the Prince of Wales"** and **"Interview with Lincoln,"** the question of selection is largely academic since his use of Ward was by this time negligible. In "How to Tell a Story" (1895), however, the acknowledgment is explicit and important. Here, Twain indicates how closely he had studied Ward's lecturing techniques—some of which doubled as comic-writing techniques—citing especially Ward's skillful use of the nub, the apparently casually dropped studied remark, and above all the pause. Finally, in 1896 Twain's mind turned back to the beginning; his "At Home" readings for friends that winter sometimes featured his account of how Artemus Ward, internationally renowned humorist, had befuddled with meaningless plausibilities the young *Enterprise* reporter who interviewed him on his arrival in Virginia City thirty-three years before.

In denying Ward any influence on Twain, DeVoto challenged the doubtful to examine a theme they shared, the Mormons. For some years the Mormons, particularly with their "peculiar institution" of polygamy, had been exciting an extraordinary curiosity, here and abroad, which writers humorous and humorless alike tried to satisfy. Ward had catered to this curiosity in 1860 with **"A Visit to Brigham Young,"** a humorous account of a fictitious interview with the Mormon leader four years before he visited Salt Lake City in January 1864; in *Artemus Ward, His Travels* he devoted ten chapters to the Mormon segment of his Western journey. Twain had spent two days in the Mormon city in early August 1861 while enroute with his brother Orion to Nevada; he did not, however, turn the Mormon material to literary purposes until the composition of *Roughing It* a decade later. Several passages from *Roughing It* suggest that he may have found Ward's account useful to jog his memory or to provide ideas; they manifestly resemble some from Ward in more than subject matter. Compare these two descriptions of Salt Lake City . . . :

> The population of Great Salt Lake City is 20,000.—The streets are eight rods—and are neither flagged nor paved. A stream of pure mountain water courses through each street—and is conducted into the gardens of the Mormons. The houses are mostly of adobe—or sundried brick—and present a neat and comfortable appearance . . . no house [do you see] that is dirty, shabby, and dilapidated. . . . Every Mormon has a tidy dooryard. Neatness is a great characteristic of the Mormons. [*The Complete Works of Artemus Ward*]

> Next day we strolled about everywhere through the broad, straight, level streets . . . of a city of fifteen thousand inhabitants. . . . A limpid stream rippling and dancing through every street . . . block after block of trim dwellings,

built of "frame" and sunburned brick.—A great thriving orchard and garden behind every one of them, apparently—branched from the street stream winding and sparkling among the garden beds and fruit trees—and a grand general air of neatness, repair, thrift, and comfort around and about and over the whole. [*Roughing It*]

While Twain needed no help for his descriptions, especially such a routine one as this, he often needed it for his memory. Both writers see what any traveler would see and many had already described; but Twain's passage seems to paraphrase Ward's, following its basic details and their order and emphasis too closely for mere coincidence. Only the population figures vary significantly. Twain's figure could easily come from his memory; more likely it comes from a memorandum he had recently received from Orion.

From Ward almost certainly comes the mandatory joke about polygamy:

I had a man pointed out to me who married an entire family. He had originally intended to marry Jane, but Jane did not want to leave her widowed mother. The other three sisters were not in the matrimonial market for the same reason; so this gallant man married the whole family, including the girl's grandmother, who had lost all her teeth, and had to be fed with a spoon. [**His Travels**]

The next most interesting thing is to sit and listen to these Gentiles talk about polygamy; and how some portly old frog of an elder, or a bishop marries a girl—likes her, marries her sister—likes her, marries another sister—likes her, takes another—likes her, marries her mother, likes her, marries her father, grandfather, great grandfather, and then comes back hungry and asks for more. [*Roughing It*]

Twain's insatiable polygamist, like Ward's less earthy one, marries four sisters and their mother, then, with no grandmother to wed, improves on Ward's and on the peculiarity of the institution by marrying all the sisters' male ancestors as well. Probably Twain supplied the three generations of males when he noticed the burlesque possibilities of having his old frog literally marry a whole family of both sexes—an opportunity Ward's gallant man did not have.

Each author offers an anecdote about the ruler of Utah and his unruly wives; Ward's is from **"A Visit to Brigham Young"**:

His wives air very expensiv. Thay allers want suthin & ef he don't buy it for um thay set the

house in a uproar. He sez he don't have a minit's peace. His wives fite amung theirselves so much that he has bilt a fittin room for thare speshul beneift, & when too of 'em get into a row he has em turned loose into that place, whare the dispoot is settled accordin to the rules of the London prize ring. Sumtimes thay abooze hisself individooally. Thay hev pulled the most of his hair out at the roots & he wares meny a horrible scar upon his body, inflicted with mop-handles, broom sticks and sich. Occashunly they git mad & scald him with bilin water. When he got eny waze cranky thay'd shut him up in a dark closit, previsly whippin him arter the stile of muthers when thare orfsprings git onruly. Sumtimes when he went in swimmin thay'd go to the banks of the Lake & steal all his close, thereby compellin him to sneek home by a circootious rowt, drest in the Skanderlus stile of the Greek Slaiv. "I find that the keers of a marrid life way hevy onto me," sed the Profit, "& sumtimes I wish I'd remaned singel." [**His Book**]

And Mr. Johnson said that while he and Mr. Young were pleasantly conversing in private, one of the Mrs. Youngs came in and demanded a breast-pin, remarking that she had found out that he had been giving a breast-pin to No. 6, and *she,* for one, did not propose to let this partiality go on without making a satisfactory amount of trouble about it. Mr. Young reminded her that there was a stranger present. Mrs. Young said that if the state of things inside the house was not agreeable to the stranger, he could find room outside. Mr. Young promised the breast-pin, and she went away. But in a minute or two another Mrs. Young came in and demanded a breast-pin. Mr. Young began a remonstrance, but Mrs. Young cut him short. She said No. 6 had got one, and No. 11 was promised one, and it was "no use for him to try to impose on her—she knew her rights." He gave his promise and she went. And presently three Mrs. Youngs entered in a body and opened on their husband a tempest of tears, abuse, and entreaty. They had heard all about No. 6, No. 11, and No. 14. Three more breast-pins were promised, and the weird sisters filed out again. And in came eleven more, weeping and wailing and gnashing their teeth. Eleven promised breast-pins purchased peace once more.

Young explained to his guest that before the farce were ended, "No. 6's breast-pin will cost me twenty-five hundred dollars before I see the end of it. And those creatures will compare those pins together, and if one is a shade finer than the rest, they will all be thrown on my hands, and I will have to order a new lot to keep order in the family." [*Roughing It*]

In each case expensive and abusive wives mar the domestic peace of the hen-pecked sovereign. The abuse is physical in Ward but verbal in Twain, whose anecdote elaborates the first three sentences of Ward's and particularizes both the item provoking the tempest and the cost. On the lecture platform in 1868 Twain's first version of this yarn starred the unhappy Sultan of Turkey and his 900 wives; it was closer in some respects to Ward's, especially in the humor of hair-pulling fights among the wives.

Nearly as troublesome as the prophet's wives were his ubiquitous children. Says Ward, again in **"A Visit to Brigham Young"**:

> He don't pretend to know his children, thare is so many of um, tho they all know him. He sez about every child he meats calls him Par, & he takes it for grantid it is so. (***His Book***)

And Twain:

> Along with each wife were her children—fifty altogether. . . . He said that Mr. Young told him several smart sayings of certain of his "two year olds" . . . and then wanted to show Mr. Johnson one of the pets that had said the last good thing but he could not find the child. He searched the faces of the children in detail but could not decide which one it was. (*Roughing It*)

He amplifies further with Young's anecdote:

> Why, sir, a woman came here once with a child of a curious lifeless sort of complexion (and so had the woman), and swore that the child was mine and she my wife. . . . Well, sir, she called my attention to the fact that the child looked like me, and really it did seem to resemble me—a common thing in the territory—and, to cut the story short, I put it in my nursery, and she left. And . . . when they came to wash the paint off that child it was an Injun! (*Roughing It*)

In such a way Twain seems repeatedly to build on suggestions from Ward. Brigham Young continues to interest them most. Both, for example, describe him as a shrewd man of extraordinary administrative ability; Ward illustrates by showing Young using "revelation" to persuade the faithful to shingle his huge dwelling free of charge, and Twain by showing him enforcing contractural procedure among his followers against their own business interests (***His Travels***; *Roughing It*). Both observe his command presence and gentle eye; report his cordiality (Ward had been understandably apprehensive because of his burlesque treatment of him in **"A Visit . . ."**), his sovereign power, his people's unquestioning devotion to him, his immense wealth; and joke about his seventy or eighty wives in Salt Lake City as well as others "sealed" to him throughout the Territory. Other aspects of Mormon culture elicit comparable comment from both. They report that the Mormon women are neither ugly nor lovely and speculate whether they are happy, and comment on the girls' being intensely trained from childhood to approve plurality. Finally, both read or began to read the Book of Mormon and pronounced it tedious, tiresome, or worse. Ward then padded out his book by quoting (in the last chapter) sixteen pages from Joseph Smith's revelations and Twain his by quoting the Mormon Bible intermittently for nine pages (interspersing his own biting commentary), then adding an appendix of twenty-three pages more.

These things, the padding aside, were inherent in the "Mormon question," and the reading public would expect them to be treated. Yet quite as much as the proliferation of common topics, the order of their occurence and the similarity of treatment and attitude suggest that Ward's material on the Mormons was one source of Twain's.

Roughing It contains one additional passage not on the Mormon theme that requires notice. Ward had written a long account of Horace Greeley's wild forty-mile dash, in a coach driven by Hank Monk, from Carson City to Placerville where he was to be feted at seven o'clock. They started late, but Monk, oblivious to rock-strewn roads, to Greeley's head going up and down through the roof of the coach and his broken pleas to slow down, and mindful only of his orders to get his passenger there on time, careened into Placerville with the gasping Greeley promptly at seven (***His Travels***). Twain reports the story as being maddeningly and unvarying inflicted on him by successive fellow-passengers late in his stage-journey to Nevada, and concluding always with Monk's tiresome refrain: "Keep your seat, Horace, and I'll get you there on time!"

Parallels with Ward occur sporadically in Twain's other early work. Some, as in *Roughing It,* consist chiefly of ideas or situations adopted and adapted. Compare these experiences with foreign tongues, Ward's at a Chinese theater in San Francisco, Twain's in the Sandwich Islands:

> The Chinaman at the door takes my ticket with the remark, "Ki hi hi ki! Shoolah!"

> And I tell him that on the whole I think he is right. . . . As my time is limited, I go away at the close of the second act. . . . The doorkeeper again says, "Ki hi-hi ki! Shoolah!" adding this time, however, "Chow-wow." I agree with him in regard to the ki hi and the hi ki, but tell him I don't feel altogether certain about the chow-wow. [*His Travels*]

> "Fine day, John."

> "Aole iki."

> [I took that to mean, "I don't know."]

> "Sorter sultry, though."

> "Aole iki."

> "You're right—at least I'll let it go at that, any way. It makes you sweat considerably, don't it?"

> "Aole iki."

> "Right again, likely. . . . " [*Letters from the Sandwich Islands*]

Situations, remarks, and responses are closely similar; so are the reactions in these scenes showing male honor supposedly threatened by strange women:

> *Ward was discussing women's rights with a woman who grabbed him by the collar.* "I hope, marm," sez I, starting back, "that your intentions is honorable? I'm a lone man hear in a strange place." [*His Book*].

> *Twain was in a bath-tub in Milan when his room was invaded by a maid whom he admonished:* "Beware, woman! . . . I am an unprotected

male, but I will preserve my honor at the peril of my life." [*The Innocents Abroad*]

Twain may have found one of Ward's "Original Programmes" announcing his lecture useful for a description of art in *Innocents Abroad*:

> *The program announced:* THE APPEARANCE OF ARTEMUS WARD. Who will be greeted by applause. . . . When quiet has been restored, the lecturer will present a rather frisky prologue, of about ten minutes in length, and of nearly the same width. It perhaps isn't necessary to speak of the depth. [*Complete Works*]

> *Twain enlivened an account of art in Rome:* The colors are fresh and rich, the "expression," I am told, is fine, the "feeling" is lively, the "tone" is good, the "depth" is profound, and the width is about four and a half feet, I should judge. [*Innocents Abroad*]

Each piece depends upon incongruous use of dimensions—width in both cases, width and depth in Ward's—for its effect. Incongruity in another of Ward's programs must also have appealed to Twain:

> Artemus Ward as speaks at Dodsworth Hall, and shows his Paintings the Evening of Every Day at 8 o'clock. Opening his portals at 7 1/2 o'clock. [*Complete Works*]

> *Twain remembered the advertisement announcing his first lecture to have read:* Doors open at 7 1/2. Trouble begins at 8. [*Roughing It*]

Souvenir hunters on old battlefields figure in these parallel sketches of the rapacious exploiting the gullible:

> On the Plains of Abraham there was once some tall fitin, and ever since then there has been a great demand for the bones of the slew'd on that there occasion. But the real ginooine bones was long ago carried off, and now the boys make a hansum thing by cartin the bones of hosses and sheep out there, and sellin' 'em to intelligent American towerists. [*His Travels*]

> There was nothing else to do, and so everybody went to hunting relics. . . . Some . . . brought bones . . . and were grieved to hear the surgeon pronounce them only bones of mules and oxen. Blucher . . . brought a sack full . . . and is labeling his trophies now. I picked one up . . . and found it marked "Fragment of a Russian General." I carried it out to get a better light upon it—it was nothing but . . . a jawbone of a horse. [*Innocents Abroad*]

One battlefield is replenished with the bones of sheep and horses when the human supply runs out, the other with bones of mules, oxen, and horses; Twain again adds an improving touch of particularity.

DeVoto cites Twain's "General Washington's Negro Body-Servant" as a possible reminiscence of the Revolutionary Soldier in Ward's **"Affairs Round the Village Green."** Ward remembered reading an account of "Another Revolutionary Soldier Gone," then visited with one who still lived; this old veteran still

distinctly remembers Washington, of course; they all do. But what I wish to call special attention to, is the fact that this Revolutionary soldier is one hundred years old, that his eyes are so good that he can read fine print without spectacles—he never used them by the way—and his mind is perfectly clear. [*His Travels*]

> George, the favorite body-servant of the lamented Washington, died in Richmond, Va., last Tuesday, at the ripe age of 95 years. His intellect was unimpaired, and his memory tenacious, up to within a few minutes of his decease. He was present at the second installation of Washington as President, and also at his funeral, and distinctly remembered all the prominent incidents connected with those notable events. [*Sketches New and Old*]

Three close correspondences—the distinct remembrance of Washington, the advanced age, and the unimpaired faculties of each—make the case for a reminiscence. DeVoto overlooked in the same sketch by Ward the probable source of another Twain "reminiscence" in *Life on the Mississippi*. Ward surveyed in retrospect the careers of nine of his boyhood companions, noting sadly that most of them had not done well in life—the good little boy, for example, who was "in the penitentiary for putting his uncle's autograph to a financial document." Twain questioned an old resident of Hannibal in "My Boyhood Home" about a larger number of his boyhood friends and learned that many of them, too, had been defeated by life. Each inquired especially about the town dullard who, by contrast and to the surprise of all, turned out well:

> Hubertson, the utterly stupid boy—the lunkhead who never had his lesson—he's about the ablest lawyer a sister State can boast. [*His Travels*]

> "Well now, his case *is* curious! There wasn't a human being in this town but knew that that boy was a perfect chucklehead; perfect dummy; just a stupid ass, as you may say. Everybody knew it, and everybody said it. Well, if that very boy isn't the first lawyer in the state of Missouri today, I'm a Democrat!" [*Life on the Mississippi*]

Twain, unrecognized by his former fellow townsman and using an assumed name, then inquired about Sam Clemens. Ward in another sketch (**"To Reese River"**) had earlier used the device of concealing his identity to discover what another thought of him:

> Mr. Ryder knows me only as "Mr. Brown," and he refreshes me during the journey by quotations from my books and lectures.

> "Never seen Ward?" he said.

> "Oh no."

> "Ward says he likes little girls, but he likes large girls just as well. Haw, haw, haw! I should like to see the d——d fool."

> He referred to me. [*His Travels*]

> "Oh, he succeeded well enough—another case of

a d——d fool. If they'd sent him to St. Louis, he'd have succeeded sooner."

It was with much satisfaction that I recognized the wisdom of having told this candid gentleman, in the beginning, that my name was Smith. [*Life on the Mississippi*]

Additional correspondences, strictly verbal in nature, flicker through the two writers' pages. Predominantly catch-phrases or punch-lines, many were shared with others of the comic-writing tribe, but a few appear to originate with Ward. DeVoto cites one of the more familiar examples—Ward's "My wife says so, too," which Twain echoes with Huck's "Tom Sawyer, he says the same"— and one of the least—Ward's "I was 96 minits passin a given point," which Twain uses several times. Several times also he borrowed and varied Ward's question to the Prince of Wales—how did he like "bein a prince as fur as he had got?" Ward's response to the telegram from the manager of the San Francisco Opera House asking what he'd take for forty nights in California became famous. He said, "Brandy and water." And Twain, calling on the Secretary of the Treasury, was asked, "What will you have?" He said, "Rum punch."

More memorably, the nub climaxes a longer passage. Ward's painful experience with a mustard plaster leads in to a humorously intended misapplication of Scripture:

I lay there in this wild, broiling way for nearly two weeks, when one morning I woke up with my head clear and an immense plaster on my stomache. The plaster had *operated.* I was so raw that I could by no means say to Dr. Williamson, "*Well done,* thou good and faithful servant." [*His Travels*]

Twain writes of a much more severe case of burning flesh:

He said there was no joke about this matter—for the house was full of smoke—he had heard dreadful screams—he recognized the odor of burning flesh. We soon found out that he was right. A poor old negro woman, a servant in the next house, had fallen on the stove and burned herself so badly that she soon died. It was a sad case . . . all spoke gloomily of the disaster. . . . In a grave voice and without even a shadow of a smile, Riley said: —"WELL DONE, good and faithful servant."

Finally, Ward's "most notable contribution" to Twain, as DeVoto says, is the punch-line in the best-known passage in *Innocents Abroad* and one of the best-known in Twain's entire canon. At an inn in London Ward asks the innkeeper to attend a seance with him. It is to be conducted by a "Trans-Mejim" who says "the sperrits of departed great men talk through him. He says that tonight sev'ril em'nent persons will speak through him —among others, Cromwell." The landlord hesitates. "And this Mr. Cromwell— is he dead?" In Genoa Twain and his traveling companion, the doctor, harass their current guide by affecting a stupid indifference to the grandest wonders he can show. Before the bust of Columbus and before the Egyptian mummy the doctor, his eyeglass relentlessly in place, produces not the expected gratifying burst of admiration but a series of imbecilic questions ending with the solemn and unsettling, "Is—is he dead?"

Collectively, these parallels show that Twain borrowed considerably from Ward, far more than DeVoto would allow. Mostly he borrowed the staples of the comic-writers' trade—jokes, anecdotes, catch-phrases, snappers, one-liners—for use in his Sandwich Island letters, *The Innocents Abroad, Life on the Mississippi,* and several sketches; he borrowed more of these as well as details for development and factual material, and probably the idea of padding with appendices, for more extensive use in *Roughing It,* where Ward's influence on several chapters has gone largely unnoticed. The borrowing did not continue for long. After *Roughing It,* except for striking correspondences in *Life on the Mississippi,* it virtually ceased.

This sudden decline probably owes much to Twain's strong resentment at being unfavorably compared with Ward, whose popularity was still greater than his own. His high opinion of Ward's platform artistry was matched by a low opinion of his literary artistry. Early in 1866 he was thankful that the "Jumping Frog" had not appeared in the "wretchedly poor" *His Travels;* and the truth of Edgar M. Branch's remark [in his "My Voice is still for Setchell," *PMLA* 82, December 1967] that "the genius of the 'Jumping Frog' dwarfs Ward's talent" was doubtless apparent to Twain long before he turned to Ward's book for his own purposes in *Roughing It.* He came to resent Ward especially for the charge of imitation, a charge, ironically, that he himself, more with his "Artemus Ward" lectures on the tour of 1871-1872 than with his books, did most to encourage. On the platform that winter, says Fatout, he soured unbecomingly when audiences and newspaper reporters made damaging comparisons of his and Ward's rendering of the same jokes. Rankled, he alluded rather gracelessly to Ward's alleged coarseness and unpolished wit. At times he went so far as to imply "that the illiterate showman of the badly-spelled sketches was only the alter ego of Ward himself." After that, he was not likely, in his lectures or his writing, to encourage the comparison again. (pp. 13-21)

> *Robert Rowlette, " 'Mark Ward on Artemus Twain': Twain's Literary Debt to Ward," in* American Literary Realism 1870-1910, *Vol. 6, No. 1, Winter, 1973, pp. 13-25.*

David E. E. Sloane (essay date 1979)

[*In the following excerpt, Sloane examines the ethical content of Browne's letters and comic pieces.*]

Artemus Ward was the outstanding literary comedian of the 1860s, and his reputation lasted well beyond his death in 1867. [Petroleum Vesuvius] Nasby's political power and [Orpheus C.] Kerr's literary consciousness were fused in his expressions of middle-class northern sentiment. He was pragmatic, humorously vulgar, intolerant of radical fringe groups only insofar as they were harmful extremists; he was concerned with maintaining his own income; he saw the Constitution as superior to the issue of abolition on either side, a stance very close to Lincoln's. He was moderate, and his humor endorsed moderation and personal integrity. . . . In pose, too, he attained flexibility which Nasby merely breached and Kerr never attempted. Although he disavowed outright didacticism, he took humor to be moral and serious, consistent with the qualities of a "man" as previously defined [a person with values and beliefs]; he wanted his voice to be meaningful.

Most of Ward's letters have an ethical dimension. Public figures should have enlightened concern; his showman, a transparent fraud to a skeptical public, is nonetheless capable of detecting other falsifications by virtue of his own skepticism. So he interviews Brigham Young on polygamy and burlesques the free lovers, Shakers, and other enthusiasts. His comment on the Shakers is characteristic: "Shakers was all goin kerslap to the Promist Land, and nobody want goin to stand at the gate to bar 'em out, if they did they'd git run over." Ward responds to their physical denial by advising that their daughters marry manly young suitors—a practical and conventional suggestion that stresses natural intimacy between individuals.

As Walter Blair notes, in *Horse Sense in American Humor,* the practical showman who appears so eager to gain patrons actually drives the free lovers at Oberlin away with a sermon, and Ward elsewhere delivers moralistic rebukes to spiritualists, women's rights fanatics, and the spoilmen surrounding Lincoln; he forthrightly advises the Prince of Wales and Prince Napoleon and stands uncompromisingly by the threatened flag, both in Dixie and in Baldinsville: "The country may go to the devil, but I won't!" Lincoln loved Ward's humor for this reason. Lincoln too had to reject extremist political and moral issues in attempting to sustain the Constitution, as he rejected Horace Greeley's demands for abolition in 1862. Lincoln and Ward are united in their political idealism; and when Ward depicted his visit to Lincoln, his most prominent statement is "I have no politics." Ward does not come to collect political debts. An outsider to political spoils, he attacks the officeseekers who, in the burlesque, are even sliding down on Old Abe through the chimney. Much of Ward's humor is maintained within this ideological framework; if "refined" northeasterners missed the ideology, Confederates and their Bill Arp bitterly recognized it.

Ward's comments are really universal, going beyond the Civil War in philosophy if not in subject matter. The naïve materialist is a moralist who confronts high-principled neighbors with low-principled humanity: "Sez Perfesser Peck, "Mister Ward, I don't know 'bout this bizness. What air your sentiments?' Siz I, 'I hain't got any.' " Ward adds: "The pint is, can I hav your Hall by payin a fair price? You air full of sentiments. That's your lay, while I'm a exhibiter of startlin curiosities." The cacography works innocently and perfectly ("air full" of sentiments), while the polarity between worldly work and moral rigidity is only superficially negative, since a higher order of liberalism is involved and "fair" is the point of negotiation.

Ward's interview with the Prince of Wales was an instant national success. Appearing in September, 1860, just before he moved to New York to work for *Vanity Fair,* it made Ward nationally known. William Dean Howells, the arbiter of American literary realism in the later nineteenth century, remembered the "universal joy" with which the piece was greeted [in his introduction to *Artemus Ward's Best Stories,* 1912]. Although using contemporary news as its subject matter, the burlesque was directed at formal conventions in international politics:

> We sot & tawked there sum time abowt matters & things, & bimeby I axed him how he liked bein Prince as fur as he'd got. "To speak plain, Mister Ward," he sed, "I don't much like it. I'm sick of all this bowin & scrapin & crawlin & hurrain over a boy like me. I would rather go through the country quietly & enjoy myself in my own way, with the other boys, & not be made a Show of to be garped at by everybody. When the *people* cheer me I feel pleased, fur I know they mean it, but if these one-horse offishuls coold know how I see threw all their moves & understan exackly what they air after, & knowd how I larft at 'em in private, theyd stop kissin my hands & fawnin over me as they now do."

In answer to the Prince's democratic spirit, with its emphasis on "the *people,*" Ward makes a burlesque affirmation of the Prince's humanity which corresponds to the idea of manliness characteristic of the literary comedians: "Albert Edard, I must go, but previs to doin so I will obsarve that you soot me. Yure a good feller, Albert Edard, & tho I'm agin Princes as a gineral thing, I must say I like the cut of your Gib. When you git to be King try and be as good a man as yure muther has bin! Be just & be Jenerus, espeshully to showmen." Several analogues come to mind for this brief exchange. The Prince's conversation with Ward suggests the plot that Twain was to develop in *The Prince and the Pauper,* an appealingly democratic viewpoint toward commonplace experience. The showman's response re-echoes Dickens' showman Sleary in *Hard Times,* and Ward digresses even further as that figure would have. Most important, however, is the continued emphasis, in burlesque, on "being a man," and the sketch makes clear that Ward understands and admires this trait and that he will even accept a monarch who has it. Both the Prince and Ward hold "objective" viewpoints, a fictional equivalent of the deadpan; they are "good fellers" distinguished from a procession of "noosenses" trying to start a religious war and from the venal politicians already described. The sentiment is northern; although it may be "conservative," it is genteelly idealistic; it is democratic: a social viewpoint is dramatized in a partly real but mostly fictional format.

Reality and the detachment from reality form the major component of Ward's comic vision, separating him from the ferociously attached Nasby and the ironically aloof Kerr. Describing the war fever in Baldinsville, he declared, "If I'm drafted I shall resign . . . everywheres I've bin inrold." The naif withdraws himself from enthusiasm, as with moderates everywhere, but without withdrawing himself from his basic ethical position. His promoral but seemingly antiwar statements are thus as consistent with his pro-Union sentiments as Lincoln's pro-Union and antislavery beliefs proved to be during the course of the Civil War. The excesses of the opposition provide the antagonist to the objective humanitarian. Ward depicted them in burlesque as nuisances; Twain was later to melodramatize them as the political and religious fomenters of atrocities. (pp. 25-8)

> *David E. E. Sloane, "Literary Comedy," in his* Mark Twain as a Literary Comedian, *Louisiana State University Press, 1979, pp. 13-28.*

FURTHER READING

Austin, James C. *Artemus Ward.* New York: Twayne Publishers, 1964, 141 p.
Biographical and critical overview.

Cracroft, Richard H. "Distorting Polygamy for Fun and Profit: Artemus Ward and Mark Twain among the Mormons." *Brigham Young University Studies* 14, No. 2 (Winter 1974): 272-88.
Compares Browne's and Twain's humorous use of the Mormon culture in their lectures and writings. Cracroft concludes that Browne was a "brilliant and imaginative humorist who not only showed Mark Twain some of the tricks of the writing and lecturing game, but on occasion even bested him."

Dahl, Curtis. "Artemus Ward: Comic Panoramist." *The New England Quarterly* XXXII, No. 4 (December 1959): 476-85.
Outlines Browne's tour of the West in 1863. Dahl examines the humorist's employment and satiric treatment of a moving panorama in his lectures.

Devoto, Bernard. "The Critics of Mark Twain." In his *Mark Twain's America and Mark Twain at Work,* pp. 217-39. Boston: Houghton Mifflin Company, 1932.
Refutes the argument that Mark Twain was an imitator of Browne and asserts that there is little, if any, commonality between the two authors.

Hingston, Edward P. *The Genial Showman: Being Reminiscences of the Life of Artemus Ward and Pictures of a Showman's Career in the Western World.* 2 vols. London: John Camden Hotten, 1870.
An account of Hingston's days as Browne's manager.

Johnson, Clifton. "Recollections of Artemus Ward." *The Overland Monthly* LXVII, No. 1 (January 1916): 28-33.
Examines Browne's childhood environment and its subsequent influence on his writing.

Lorch, Fred W. "Mark Twain's 'Artemus Ward' Lecture on the Tour of 1871-1872." *The New England Quarterly* XXV, No. 3 (September 1952): 327-43.
Recounts Twain's 1871 lecture tour of which Browne was the subject. Lorch includes a composite text of the lecture, derived from newspaper accounts.

Lucas, E. V. "Three American Humorists." In his *Only the Other Day: A Volume of Essays,* pp. 95-105. Philadelphia: J. B. Lippincott Company, 1936.
Explores the emergence of a distinctive American humor. Lucas singles out Browne as the first American to gain international recognition for his comic works.

McKee, Irving. "Artemus Ward in California and Nevada, 1863-1864." *Pacific Historical Review* XX, No. 1 (February 1951): 11-23.
Discusses the western lecture tour of 1863, providing humorous anecdotes of the trip.

Mott, Frank Luther. "The Beginnings of Artemus Ward." *Journalism Quarterly* 18, No. 2 (June 1941): 146-52.
Probes Browne's early career, especially his tenure as editor of the Cleveland *Plain Dealer.* Mott maintains that due to childhood influences the humorist never viewed journalism as a reporting of facts, but as a form of entertainment.

Myers, J. Arthur. "Artemus Ward." In his *Fighters of Fate,* pp. 151-73. Baltimore: Williams and Wilkins Company, 1927.
Biographical portrait of the humorist's life and career.

Nock, Albert Jay. "Artemus Ward's America." *The Atlantic Monthly* 154, No. 3 (September 1934): 273-81.
Praises Browne as the first great critic of American society.

Pullen, John J. *Comic Relief: The Life and Laughter of Artemus Ward, 1834-1867.* Hamden, Conn.: Archon Books, 1983, 202 p.
Biography of the humorist with entertaining anecdotes and thorough bibliographical notes.

Reed, John Q. "Civil War Humor: Artemus Ward." *Civil War History* II, No. III (September 1956): 87-101.
Analyzes Browne's works as diversions for the American people during the Civil War. Reed praises the humorist's ability to give perspective to the highly charged issues of the day.

Richmond, Robert W. "Humorist on Tour: Artemus Ward in Mid-America, 1864." *The Kansas Historical Quarterly* XXXIII, No. 4 (Winter 1967): 470-80.
Outlines Browne's lecture tour of the Missouri Valley, assembling numerous newspaper accounts to document audience reception of his performances.

Rodgers, Paul C., Jr. "Artemus Ward and Mark Twain's 'Jumping Frog'." *Nineteenth-Century Fiction* 28, No. 3 (December 1973): 273-86.
Discusses Browne's influence on Twain's first published sketch. Rodgers contends that there is similarity in style, pace, and characterization between the two writers and that Twain deliberately modeled Browne's success as an American humorist.

Ruthrauff, C. C. "Artemus Ward at Cleveland." *Scribner's Monthly* XVI, No. 6 (October 1878): 785-91.
Originally unsigned survey of Browne's journalism career offering insight into the humorist's personality.

Seitz, Donald C. *Artemus Ward.* New York: Harper and Brothers, 1919, 338 p.
Seminal biographical portrait of Browne with extensive bibliography.

Tandy, Jennette. "The Funny Men: Artemus Ward and Josh Billings." In her *Crackerbox Philosophers in American Humor and Satire,* pp. 132-157. Port Washington, N. Y.: Kennikat Press, 1925.
Traces Browne's professional career and includes anecdotes from the humorist's life.

"Artemus Ward." *The Times Literary Supplement,* No. 1682 (26 April 1934): 289-90.

Commemorates the one hundredth anniversary of Browne's birth. The critic particularly admires the humorist's originality, describing him as the "earliest missionary" of American humor.

Additional coverage of Browne's life and career is contained in the following source published by Gale Research: *Dictionary of Literary Biography,* Vol. 11.

Charles Dickens

Oliver Twist

(Also wrote under the pseudonym Boz) English novelist, short story writer, dramatist, poet, and essayist.

The following entry presents criticism of Dickens's novel *Oliver Twist* (1838). For discussion of Dickens's complete career, see *NCLC,* Volume 3. For criticism focusing on Dickens's novels *Bleak House* (1853), *The Mystery of Edwin Drood* (1870), and *Great Expectations* (1861), see *NCLC,* Volumes 8, 18, and 26, respectively.

INTRODUCTION

One of Dickens's most popular and best-known works, *Oliver Twist; or, The Parish Boy's Progress* traces an orphaned boy's ascent from destitution to middle-class comfort. Featuring a stinging attack on laws concerning the treatment of the poor in England as well as vivid depictions of murder, poverty, and prostitution in London, *Oliver Twist* repelled some Victorian critics, who objected to the novel on moral grounds. Most readers, however, responded favorably to the novel's sensational plot and sentimental characterizations, prompting pirated versions of the work and numerous stage adaptations.

Late in 1836 Dickens signed an agreement with Richard Bentley to edit and contribute fiction to *Bentley's Miscellany,* a periodical scheduled to begin publication in 1837; *Oliver Twist* was introduced to readers in the journal's second monthly installment. Written under the pseudonym Boz, the novel was Dickens's second, differing significantly in tone and content from the comic *Pickwick Papers* that preceded it. According to biographer Peter Ackroyd, *Oliver Twist*'s "appearance in a magazine format gave [Dickens] both the context and the licence to introduce more overtly propagandistic elements" in his fiction; as a result, the novel was more controversial than *Pickwick Papers.*

Oliver Twist opens with Oliver's birth in a workhouse, often referred to as a "debtor's prison." The identity of Oliver's father is unknown, and, upon the death of his mother, the boy endures maltreatment at an orphanage before returning to the workhouse at age nine. There Oliver is again treated inhumanely; his request for more gruel, perhaps the best-known episode of the novel, leads to his expulsion from the institution. After an unhappy apprenticeship to an undertaker, Oliver flees to London, where he meets John Dawkins, the Artful Dodger. Dawkins leads the boy to Fagin, the ringleader of a gang of young thieves. Attempting to initiate Oliver into a life of crime, Fagin sends him with Dawkins on a criminal assignment, during which he is captured and charged with a robbery actually committed by Dawkins. Exonerated by the testimony of an eyewitness, Oliver finds refuge in the home of the vic-

tim, Mr. Brownlow, who, it is revealed, was a friend of Oliver's father. Kidnapped a second time by Fagin's gang, Oliver is sent with the ruthless felon Bill Sikes to burglarize a home. Oliver is shot during this robbery and, abandoned by Sikes, is taken in and nursed to health by the Maylie family, victims of the attempted burglary. Subsequently, the Maylies reunite Oliver with Brownlow, while the character Monks is introduced as a stranger inquiring into Oliver's parentage. Monks consults with Fagin and the two plan to recover the boy from the Maylie household. Later, Sikes's mistress, the prostitute Nancy, discloses to Rose Maylie that Monks is Oliver's half-brother who, seeking to prevent Oliver from receiving any of their father's inheritance, has plotted with Fagin to corrupt the boy. Although Sikes murders Nancy for her betrayal, the novel ends happily for Oliver, who receives the inheritance and is adopted by Brownlow.

Published in book form in November 1838, *Oliver Twist* angered many early reviewers, including the novelist William Thackeray, who accused Dickens of writing a "Newgate" novel. Referring to London's notorious Newgate prison, this type of fiction consisted of romanticized crime stories that many felt inadvertently encouraged vice.

Richard Ford, reviewing the novel for the *Quarterly Review* in 1839, expressed the concerns of many of his contemporaries, asserting: "We object *in toto* to the staple of *Oliver Twist*—a series of representations which must familiarize the rising generation with the haunts, deeds, language, and characters of the very dregs of the community. . . . It is a hazardous experiment to exhibit to the young these enormities, even on the Helot principle of inspiring disgust." Dickens responded to his detractors in the preface to the 1841 edition of the novel, insisting that he was offering a "service to society" with his forthright depiction of the "miserable reality" of criminal life. Dickens added: "I wished to show in little Oliver the principle of Good surviving through every adverse circumstance and triumphing at last, and when I considered among what companions I could try him best . . . I bethought myself of those who figure in these volumes."

Most of the evils that Oliver overcomes in the novel are directly related to England's 1834 Poor Law Amendment Act inspired by the political philosophies of Jeremy Bentham and Thomas Malthus. The Act was intended to discourage pauperism and curb procreation among the lower classes by instituting workhouses in which men and women were separated and where measures were taken to make residence as distasteful as possible. The increase in crime that followed the passage of the Act was viewed by Dickens and many of his contemporaries as testimony to the deplorable conditions of workhouse life. Through his use of a child protagonist Dickens melodramatically exposed the abuses of this institution, prompting G. K. Chesterton's remark that *Oliver Twist* "attacks the modern workhouse with a sort of inspired simplicity as of a boy in a fairy tale who had wandered about, sword in hand, looking for ogres and who had found an indisputable ogre."

Many critics have contended that improbabilities in plot and characterization undermine the effectiveness of Dickens's social protest. Denouncing the seemingly absurd coincidences which propel the novel toward its happy conclusion, these commentators similarly object to what they consider an unrealistic portrayal of its eponymous hero. Despite an environment of deprivation and cruelty, Oliver remains, as Humphry House has noted, a "paragon of sweet gratitude and the tenderest right feeling," a weak central figure who "is so much the mere embodiment of the idea of a lonely ill-used child that he is scarcely granted character enough to be anything else." By contrast, the criminals in the novel appear vibrant and fascinating, prompting some critics to question, as did many of Dickens's contemporaries, the author's moral intentions. In a seminal discussion of *Oliver Twist*, Graham Greene suggested that the vividness of Dickens's evil characters, when contrasted with such "inadequate ghosts of goodness" as Brownlow, indicates that Dickens sought to represent a Manichaean struggle between good and evil in the novel.

Many critics refute the idea that plot and characterization are inferior in *Oliver Twist*. Such critics argue that Dickens's use of coincidence to ensure that "the principle of Good" would survive in Oliver demonstrates his belief in providence while accentuating the drama of the innocent orphan's plight. In this manner, according to Edward Le Comte, *Oliver Twist* may be viewed as "a backward glance at Bunyan," whose *Pilgrim's Progress* is reflected both in the subtitle and in the fairy-tale aspects of Dickens's novel. Similarly, many commentators emphasize the effectiveness of fantasy and nightmare in *Oliver Twist*. Summarizing this view, John Bayley has written that with *Oliver Twist* Dickens achieved a feat "surely unique in the history of the novel" by "combining the genre of Gothic nightmare with that of social denunciation, so that each enhances the other." *Oliver Twist* has consequently been widely praised as an imaginative and effective attack on social oppression.

The Spectator (essay date 1838)

[*In the following excerpt from a review of* Oliver Twist, *the critic considers the novel's plot unrealistic and ill-conceived, attributing the work's popularity to its engaging descriptions and dialogue.*]

The story of **Oliver Twist** is altogether improbable. The events are unlike the general course of human affairs either now or at any other period; and the actor who sets the whole in motion is an unnatural character—his motives are insufficient, his conduct is inconsistent. A parish foundling, such as Oliver Twist appears at the opening, running away from his master and falling among thieves, is nothing very extraordinary. It is not *very* extraordinary, perhaps, for a benevolent old gentleman to patronize an innocent child, whom he was the cause of wrongfully bringing before a police magistrate; nor for a Jew receiver of stolen goods to be anxious to get back an unwilling pupil, lest he should inform against him. Even Oliver's second escape from the gang, in the burglarious expedition, might be granted to the necessities of fiction. But all beyond this in the tale is a violation of nature and probability. Mr. Monks pursuing his illegitimate brother Oliver without motive or object—hunting after a portrait and wedding ring of no use to anybody—making an extravagant bargain for them in a dismal room over a roaring river by the solitary dip in a lantern, and then theatrically dropping them through a trapdoor into the stream—together with all his wanderings in town and out of town in mysterious masquerade, looking the hero of Minor melodrama—are a bad imitation of bad romances. Whilst the connexion of the benevolent old gentleman and the benevolent young lady with Oliver Twist, one by blood and the other by a family friendship, if in less bad taste, is equally improbable and clumsy.

The defects here indicated are not only faults in themselves, but lead to one of a deeper kind, and injurious to the permanent standing of the work. The want of truth in the story, leaves all the crime and rascality of the book without a general moral lesson. True, indeed, all the guilty die: the wretched girl, attached to the ruffian Sikes, is murdered by him for holding a communication with the benevolent old gentleman, touching Monks and Oliver;

Sikes, after being tormented by his fears, accidentally hangs himself whilst endeavouring to escape from the officers; and the Jew, being taken, is left to the law, as an accessory before the fact. But their punishment is not the direct and necessary consequence of their life of crime: it flows from the fortunes of Oliver and the intrigues of Mr. Monks; both of which are so extraordinary that no general lesson can be deduced from them.

So much for the structure and conduct of the story. As a whole, it is exceedingly readable, though not enchaining. Sections once begun, we wish to finish; but this desire does not extend to the whole story. Part of the want of continuous attraction is, no doubt, attributable to the structural defect, that visible, even when its operation is unseen; some of it to the necessities of periodical publication, where a certain effect was to be produced in a given space, without regard to the coming or the past. But there are other drawbacks. Boz is not happy in pure narrative; he is *magazinishly* diffuse, as if spinning paragraphs: instead of shortening by concentration, he endeavours to make the road pleasant by reflections which are sometimes feeble, and by witticisms often flat. His knowledge of life seems mostly limited to the middling and lower class of Cocknies; hence, except his Londoners, and persons with peculiarities and oddities that are *sui generis,* his characters are either imitations of other authors, or the fictions of his fancy. Such, in the work before us, are Mrs. Maylie the benevolent old lady, Miss Maylie, the benevolent young lady, and her lover young Maylie: each of them merely agreeable figures, without substance or individuality. The benevolent old gentleman has more of strength and elaboration than these, but not much more of general nature; and his friend Mr. Grimwig is a useless bore. A portion of the something which at certain stages of the book almost reaches an indifference to go on, may also arise from the nature of the subject. We are not of those who would banish all that is vulgar and low from the materials of fiction; for wherever action, passion, and character exist, there are elements of interest—unless physical suffering and gross crimes sink every other feeling in disgust. At the same time, such materials should never be made the staple of a long story: because our sympathies can only occasionally be excited for the actors, and because, though the higher will always yield moral instruction to the lower, the lower will more rarely yield it to the higher: the ambition of Macbeth, the jealousy of Othello, the solitary fidelity of Abdiel, conveys a lesson which the humblest may apply: but no one can profit much from the fate of a thief save thieves themselves. In short, the remark of MILTON on satire may have a qualified application to fiction—that it should "not creep into every blind tap-house, that fears a constable more than a satire."

The numerous readers who have been moved to laughter or to sadness, led to grave reflection, or excited to horror, by some of the passages in **Oliver Twist,** may naturally ask why they and criticism so differ? The answer will be, that they have been moved by *parts:* we are speaking of the work considered as *a whole,* and testing it by a reference to time, and those models of enduring art with which certain over-zealous *clacqueurs* have challenged comparison. Quitting these larger views, we will go a long way with Boz's admiring readers, and endeavour to point out the sources of their admiration, and the reasons of their idol's success. The *Quarterly Review,* about a year ago, resolved the popularity of Mr. DICKENS into his "being the first to turn to account the rich and varied stores of wit and humour discoverable amongst the lower classes of the Metropolis, whose language has been hitherto condemned as a poor, bald, dispirited, unadorned, and nearly unintelligible slang, utterly destitute of feeling, fancy, or force." That this author exhibits genius in embodying London character, and very remarkable skill in making use of peculiarities of expression, even to the current phrases of the day, is undoubtedly true; but he has higher merits, and other elements of success. His powers of pathos, sadly touching rather than tearful, are great; he has a hearty sympathy with humanity, however degraded by vice or disguised by circumstances, and a quick perception to detect the existence of the good, however overlaid; his truth and nature in dialogue are conspicuous to all; he has the great art of bringing his actors and incidents before the reader by a few effective strokes; though deficient in *narrative,* his *description* is sometimes nicely true, and often powerful; and his command of language considerable, without his style ever appearing forced. In addition to these qualities, he has a manly self-reliance—above all pretence, and all conventional servilities of classes and coteries; nor does he ever, with a sickly vanity, obtrude *himself* upon the reader's attention. Above all, he has genius to vivify his observation. Three novelists of the present day have, more or less, chosen somewhat similar subjects; and it is only necessary to compare Boz with his competitors to see at once his preeminence. The personages of HOOK are ill-natured and farcical exaggerations of some prevalent weakness, often mere general abstractions without marks of individuality: the robbers of AINSWORTH are dashing, roystering, high-spirited blades, with sufficient coarseness, but are drawn rather from imagination and the poetry of the "road" than actual life—they are the romance of thievery: BULWER's "family men" in *Pelham* and *Paul Clifford* are only disguised dandies, with sentiments drawn from fancy and words from the flash dictionary. But the thieves, their comates, and the Londoners of Boz, are flesh and blood— living creatures.

Besides the extrinsic circumstances which we pointed out formerly as contributing to the immediate success of this writer, a few others may be named. Appearing in parts, each of which contained something striking and readable for all ranks, his works were the very thing for "the press" to fasten upon, as furnishing a ready means of filling up blank space, without any trouble on the part of the journalist, beyond a hearty panegyric on the writer who had occupied the "abhorred vacuum;" so that his production really gets a score of "notices," where others, however *taking,* only receive one . . . .

The earlier workhouse scenes in **Oliver Twist,** with the hard-hearted indifference of the parochial authorities, the scanty allowance of the paupers, and the brutal insolence of office in the beadle, were intended to chime in with the popular clamour against the New Poor-law: but Boz has combined the severity of the new system with the individual tyranny of the old,—forgetting that responsibility amongst subordinate parish-officers and regularity of management came in with the Commissioners. The scenes of pauper misery, whilst Oliver on hiking with the parish undertaker, appear to have been suggested by some inquests: and there are points thrown out by the Jew to flatter the opponents of capital punishment,—although the tendency of the work is to show that nature and habit cannot be eradicated by a sentimentality which contents itself with substituting a penitentiary for a gallows. These things tell with many readers, but they must detract from the permanence of the writer who freely uses them. (pp. 1114-15)

"Boz's Oliver Twist," in The Spectator, *Vol. 11, No. 509, March 31, 1838, pp. 1114-16.*

Richard Ford   (essay date 1839)

[*Ford was an English essayist and critic. In the following excerpt, he assesses the strengths and weaknesses of* Oliver Twist.]

[The] strength of Boz consists in his originality, in his observation of character, his humour—on which he never dwells. He leaves a good thing alone like Curaçao, and does not dilute it; wit, which is not taught in Gower street, drops out of his mouth as naturally as pearls and diamonds in the fairy tale; the vein is rich, racy, sparkling, and good-natured—never savage, sarcastic, malevolent, nor misanthropic; always well placed and directed against the odious, against purse-proud insolence, and the abuse of brief authority. Boz never ridicules the poor, the humble, the ill-used; he spares to real sorrow 'the bitterest insult of a scornful jest;' his sympathies are on the right side and carry his readers with him. Though dealing with the dregs of society, he is never indelicate, indecent, nor irreligious; he never approves nor countenances the gross, the immoral, or offensive; he but holds these vices up in a pillory, as a warning of the disgrace of criminal excess. Boz, like the bee, buzzes amid honey without clogging his wings; he handles pitch charmingly; the tips of the thumb and fore-finger of the cigaresque señoras of Paraguay are infinitely more discoloured. He tells a tale of real crushing misery in plain, and therefore most effective, language; he never *then* indulges in false sentimentality, or mawkish, far-fetched verbiage. Fagin, Sikes, and the dog especially, are always in their proper and natural places, always speaking, barking, and acting exactly as they ought to have done, and as far as we are able to judge, with every appearance of truth. Boz sketches localities, particularly in London, with marvellous effect; he concentrates with the power of a camera lucida. Born with an organic bump for distinct observation of men and things, he sees with the eye, and writes with the pen of an artist—we mean with artistical skill, and not as artists write. He translates nature and life. The identical landscape or occurrence, when reduced on one sheet, will interest and astonish those who had before seen with eyes that saw not, and heard with ears that heard not, on whom previously the general incident had produced no definite effect. Boz sets before us in a strong light the water-standing orphan's eye, the condemned prisoner, the iron entering into his soul. This individuality arrests, for our feelings for human suffering in the aggregate are vague, erratic, and undefined. He collects them into one burning focus; a practical oppression is perfectly understood by the mass, even by the irrational 'masses,' however they may be ignorant of the real causes and appropriate remedies. A general wrong, a poll-tax, will be borne without resistance, while a particular outrage shown to the daughter of Wat Tyler came home to the clenched fists of a million fathers; for private feelings pave the way to public outbreaks. Death, again, as an abstract idea, is a thing for declamation. Boz gives the newly-dug grave, the rope grating when withdrawn from under the lowered coffin, and the hollow sound from the shovelful of earth thrown in. The nearer we approach to the corpse, the more appalling is death. The circumstantiality of the murder of Nancy is more harrowing than the bulletin of 50,000 men killed at Borodino. Bloodshed in midday comes home to our peaceful threshold, it shocks the order of things; it occurs amid life. Wholesale carnage, battle's own daughter, is what we expect, and is gilded with glory and victory, not visited by shame and punishment.

Boz fails whenever he attempts to write for effect; his descriptions of rural felicity and country scenery, of which he clearly knows much less than of London, where he is quite at home and wide awake, are, except when comical, over-laboured and out of nature. His 'gentle and genteel folks' are unendurable; they are devoid of the grace, repose, and ease of good society; a something between Cheltenham and New York. They and their extreme propriety of ill-bred good-breeding are (at least we hope so) altogether the misconceptions of our author's uninitiated imagination, mystified by the inanities of the kid-glove Novelists. Boz is, nevertheless, never vulgar when treating on subjects which are avowedly vulgar. He deals truly with human nature, which never can degrade; he takes up everything, good, bad, or indifferent, which he works up into a rich alluvial deposit. He is natural, and that never can be ridiculous. He is never guilty of the two common extremes of second-rate authors—the one a pretension of intimate acquaintance with the inner life of Grosvenor Square—the other an affected ignorance of the doings, and a sneering at the bad dinners, of Bloomsbury—he leaves that for people to whom such dinners would be an unusual feast. We are bound to admit that Boz's young ladies are awful—Kate Nickleby is the best of them—but they are all bad enough; but we must also admit that, both in fiction and reality, these bread-and-butter budding beauties are most difficult to deal with, except we are in love with them. They are neither fish, flesh, nor fowl, and as Falstaff says of Dame Quickly, no man knows where to have them.

Boz is regius professor of slang, that expression of the mother-wit, the low humour of the lower classes, their Sanscrit, their hitherto unknown tongue, which, in the present phasis of society and politics, seems likely to become the idiom of England. Where drabs, house-breakers, and tavern-spouting patriots play the first fiddle, they can only speak the language which expresses their ideas and habits. In order fully to enjoy their force, we must know the conventional value of these symbols of ideas, although we do not understand the lingo like Boz, who has it at his fingers' ends. We are amused with the comicality, in spite of our repugnance that the decent veil over human guilt and infirmities should be withdrawn; we grieve that the deformity of nakedness should not only be exhibited to the rising generation, but rendered agreeable by the undeniable drollery; a coarse transcript would not be tolerated. This is the great objection which we feel towards Oliver Twist. It deals with the outcasts of humanity, who do their dirty work in work, pot, and watch houses, to finish on the Newgate drop. Alas! for the Horatian precept, 'Virginibus puerisque canto.' The happy ignorance of innocence is disregarded. Our youth should not even suspect the possibility of such hidden depths of guilt, for their tender memories are wax to receive and marble to retain. These infamies feed the innate evil principle which luxuriates in the supernatural and horrid, the dread and delight of our childhood, which is never shaken off, for no man entirely outlives the nursery. We object to the familiarising our ingenuous youth with 'slang;' it is based in travestie of better things. Noble and generous ideas, when expressed in low and mean terms, become ludicrous from the contrast and incongruity; 'du sublime au ridicule il n'y a qu'un pas.' But the base vehicle conveys too frequently opinions and sentiments which could thus alone gain admission. The jests and jeers of the 'slangers' leave a sting behind them. They corrupt pure taste and pervert morality, for vice loses shame when treated as a fool-born joke, and those who are not ashamed to talk of a thing will not be long ashamed to put it into practice. These Dodgers and Sikes break into our Johnsons, rob the queen's lawful current English; they, at least, are unfettered by grammar. They speak the energetic tone of this era of popular outbreaks—*potus et ex lex.* The classics, like other dogs, have had their day. Fagin, reasoning well, votes Plato a bore. Can Cicero sharpen the 'artful Dodger,' or Euclid enlighten the speculative Mr. Sikes? 'D—Homo!'—these 'ancients,' dead and buried, can't go the railroad pace of 'them lifers.' Boz is no reader of Aristotle—

> Laws his Pindaric parents minded not,
> For *Boz* was tragi-comically got.

[His plot] is devoid of art. This, a fault in comedy, is pardonable in tragedy—where persons, not events, excite. We foresee the thunder-cloud over Œdipus and the Master of Ravenswood without decrease of interest, which is not diminished even on reperusal, by our perfect knowledge of the catastrophe; but Boz must remember that he is not in the high tragedy line, which deals more in expression of elevated persons and thoughts, in an elevated manner, than in the mere contrast of situations and events; and make a better story next time. He should also avoid, in future, all attempts at pure pathos,—on which he never ventures without reminding us of Sterne and his inferiority to that master. Let him stick to his native vein of the *serio-comic,* and blend humour with pathos. He shines in this; his fun sets off his horror as effectually as a Frenchman's gravity in a quadrille does his levity in an *emeute,* or a massacre.

He appears to propose to himself in all his works some definite abuse to be assailed. Thus Pickwick, the investigator of 'tittle-bats,' sallying forth with his disciples on knight-erratic discoveries, conveys a good-humoured satire on the meetings of those peripatetic philosophers who star, sectionise, and eat turtle in the commercial towns, making

fools of themselves, throwing a ridicule over science, and unsettling country gentlemen from their legitimate studies of poor, poachers, and turnpikes. Buzfuz and tomata-sauce are a fair exposition of the browbeating system of our courts of injustice; the verdict does honour to trial by jury. Nickleby is aimed, primarily, at those cheap seminaries where starvation is taught gratis, and which we fear were too common throughout England; and we rejoice to hear that the exposure has already put down many infant bastilles. We fear, however, that no Nickleby will reform the weak, vacillating Verisophts, or the griping, spider-like pettifoggers; for where there is carrion there will be kites. The poor-creature tribe of dandies (of which Boz has a most imperfect and conventional idea) would otherwise have been created in vain. The destiny of rivers, according to Brindley, was to feed navigable canals; that of the harmless exquisites is to eat Crocky's *entrées,* and to be eaten up by blacklegs, Opera-dancers, their own conceit, their valets, and usurious attorneys.

Oliver Twist, again, is directed against the poor-law and work-house system, and in our opinion with much unfairness. The abuses which he ridicules are not only exaggerated, but in nineteen cases out of twenty do not at all exist. Boz so rarely mixes up politics, or panders to vulgar prejudices about serious things, that we regret to see him joining in an outcry which is partly factious, partly sentimental, partly interested. The besetting sin of 'white-waistcoated' guardians is profusion, not parsimony; and this always must be the case where persons have to be charitable out of funds to which individually they are small contributors. After all, the proof of the pudding is in the eating: one week's poorhouse pot-luck fattens a pauper brat up to such a sucking-pig nicety, that its own parent, like Saturn, longs to eat it up with more than kisses. The real danger to the poor will commence when these 'white-waistcoats' have got tired of their present hobby-horse of guardianising, and commit those whose crime is poverty to the tender mercies,—the 'dura messorum ilia,'—of farmers, bowelless men of horny hearts and hands.

We shall say very little more about this book, which we presume all our readers have read. The plot, if it be not an abuse of terms to use such an expression, turns on the early misfortunes, persecutions, and final prosperity of Mr. Oliver Twist. His mother, immediately after having given him birth, expires in a workhouse—under circumstances of wretchedness and destitution, which are graphically detailed. Oliver, as we collect from some unravellings and discoveries, which form a considerable and certainly the most tiresome part of the concluding volume, is the natural son of a gentleman, who, having separated from his wife by whom he has one son, connects himself with the daughter of an officer; she is left, from a concurrence of unforeseen events, to perish amid strangers and paupers, while her seducer dies abroad; the widow perpetuates on the child of her rival her hatred to his father, which she instils into her son; this man, who goes by the name of Monks, appears at every important crisis, unexpectedly and mysteriously, like Zamiel, or some evil demon in a melodrame; willing to kill and yet afraid to strike, he seeks to work out the ruin of his younger brother through the agency of others. It appears that their common father, in his will, had attached a conditional forfeiture of a bequest to the unborn Oliver, in case he should ever be convicted of any disgraceful or felonious crime; and the object of Mr. Monks' whole existence is to give effect to this proviso by corrupting the child—though why we hardly understand, since the will has been suppressed by himself and his mother. Monks employs a Jew named Fagin, over whom he has some unexplained influence, to instil into the lad's mind the mysteries of 'prigging fogles and tickers, and cracking,' that is, the gentle craft of picking pockets and house-breaking. Fagin is a 'fence,' a receiver of stolen goods, and moreover a schoolmaster at home. This 'merry old gentleman' is a professor of rigmarole and of 'useful and entertaining knowledge,' a modern sophist, whose trade is to make mankind wise, by teaching them the utilitarian principle of Mr. Jeremy Bentham—*alias,* the golden rule of *number one* of Mr. Jeremy Diddler.

It is obvious that Master Oliver would have a tendency, under the finish of this London university, to turn out a complete master of arts and practical philosophy. Born of a mother 'without a wedding-ring,' in a workhouse—cradled in ignominy—clad in the livery of misery—ill-fed, scorned, and buffeted—the world his enemy—his susceptible youth was educated in unmitigated vice, unchecked—unredeemed by any single religious or social corrective: he is apprenticed to a low undertaker, and made acquainted with death under every form of horror, misery, and disgust, to which familiarity had long rendered his master callous. Oliver at last runs away, to escape from the ill-usage of a co-apprentice—Noah Claypole—who, born and bred under similar circumstances, grew up naturally to be unprincipled, cowardly, cruel, selfish, greedy, cunning, and a compound of all the lowest and meanest forms of vice—a liar, and not even a *good* thief. Oliver arrives in London, and the first person he meets (as was particularly likely) is an emissary of Fagin's, to whose den he is consigned, and there initiated into the gin, blasphemy, tricks, and crimes of the deepest depths of St. Giles's, Billingsgate, and the Old Bailey. After some preparatory tuition, Master Oliver is taken between Charles Bates and the Artful Dodger, two tame elephants, to try his hand at earning an honest livelihood; the Dodger picks the pocket of a respectable old gentleman, who is absorbed at a stall of books, *et totus in illis.* He is observed, and makes off; Oliver is caught by the police, and had up: he escapes through the acquitting testimony of the bookseller, and is taken home by the book-collector, Mr. Brownlow, who (singularly enough) happens to have been his father's best friend, and in whose house Oliver sees (quite by accident) the portrait of his mother, with which (as she died in child-bed, and nobody in the house knew that he was her son) it was highly probable that he should be instantaneously affected. Oliver, after a time, goes out on a message, and by another accident, is met by another of Fagin's emissaries, by whom he is taken back to his studies. His next essay is in a house-breaking adventure, in which he is wounded by the servants—and *again* adopted by the masters; Miss Maylie, the companion of the mistress, happening to be the sister of Oliver's mother, though nobody knew it. In a word, each crime he witnesses is the making of him, and all robbed by his companions

of the Clan Fagin, are the only people connected with his past history and future fortunes.

The whole tale rivals in improbabilities those stories in which the hero at his birth is cursed by a wicked fairy and protected by a good one; but Oliver himself, to whom all these improbabilities happen, is the most improbable of all. He is represented to be a pattern of modern excellence, guileless himself, and measuring others by his own innocence; delicate and high-minded, affectionate, noble, brave, generous, with the manners of a son of a most distinguished gentleman, not only uncorrupted but incorruptible; less absurd would it be to expect to gather grapes on thorns, to find pearls in dunghills, violets in Drury Lane, or make silk purses of sows' ears. Boz, in his accurate representation of Noah Claypole, shows that he knows how much easier the evil principle is developed than the good. He draws the certain effects of certain causes. Workhouse boys are not born with original virtue; nor was any one except Daniel exposed to wild beasts without being eaten up. We are not afraid that the rational portion of Boz's readers may be misled by examples which they know never did and never can exist in reality, and which they presume were invented in order to exaggerate the pathos, and throw by contrast an additional horror on vice; yet the numerical majority of the young, and of the lower orders—(for whom books in shilling Numbers have the *appearance* of being mainly designed)—judge from feelings, and are fascinated by the brilliant fallacies which reach the head through the heart. We trust that Boz is happily unacquainted with the modern and execrable school of French drama and romance; we acquit him entirely of any fellow-feeling in those pollutions of palled imaginations, of which the works of some of our own living novelists and play-wrights are the mere superfetation;—mountebanks, who minister to the worst and most diseased appetites—whose trashy false taste is alike untrue to human nature and common honesty—whose object is the destruction of all the barriers between vice and virtue, honour and profligacy, by suggesting to the minds of the young and inexperienced the possibility first—and then the probability!—that the thoughts, feelings, sentiments, hitherto ascribed to the good, to the virtuously and religiously educated, may inhabit the foul bosoms of murderers and Messalinas. These corruptions of literature, blinded by personal vanity, living in a fool's paradise of self-satisfied ignorance, rather cultivate, we understand, the notion that in their vicious pictures they have bared their own distempered hearts—which, of course, are supposed (by them and their dupes) to be redeemed by some 'romantic' quality—*alias,* the nauseous outpourings of the Rousseau confessional. Gladly, we repeat, acquitting Boz (who in a thousand places betrays that his heart is as sound as his head) of any participation in the cool *schemes* of these charlatans, we are obliged to tell him that we fear he is running some risk of helping them by the misdirection of energies with which theirs can sustain no comparison. Our apprehension is that, in spite of honest intentions, he may be found practically a co-operator with those whose aim is to degrade the national mind—well knowing that in a pure and healthy atmosphere of opinion their own gaudy fictions must wither as soon as blown. His *implied* negation of the inevitable results of evil training has a tendency to countenance their studied sentimentalization of the genus *scamp*. But we object *in toto* to the staple of **Oliver Twist**— a series of representations which must familiarize the rising generation with the haunts, deeds, language, and characters of the very dregs of the community; 'where ignorance is bliss, 'tis folly to be wise.' It is a hazardous experiment to exhibit to the young these enormities, even on the Helot principle of inspiring disgust. This perversion of education deadens and extinguishes those pure feelings which form the best guides through life; this early initiation into an acquaintance with the deepest details of crime reverses the order of nature; it strips youth of its happy, confiding credulity—the imputation of no wrong, the heart pure as a pearl. It inspires the caution and distrust which are, alas! natural to age and experience, but out of place and unamiable in the morning of our day.

The certainty, however, of our reaping as we sow is so self-evident, that we may spare our *prose*—and pass on to the heroine, Nancy, a character which all will admit is delineated with great power, however they may differ in regard to its propriety and truth. Nancy was ushered into this world, according to her own words, 'with the alley and gutter for her cradle, and to be her death-bed'—with 'no certain roof but the coffin.' The brothel and gin-shop were her school. She comes upon the scene the mistress of Bill Sikes, a ferocious, consummate villain. She is an instrument by which Oliver is inveigled—sent out with 'a key of a house-door and a basket, to look respectable.' She is the *Mrs. Masham* of these thimbleriggers. When Fagin is in despair that the poor little child should have slipped a moment out of his clutches, Nancy comes like the deliveress of the pious Æneas, recognised by her balmy breath (of Geneva) and her grace of (street) walking—*et vera ingressu patuit dea*. She is the decoy duck by which he is taken as an accomplice to the housebreaking: yet, having done all this, without any apparent reason, she at once sacrifices her companions in order to save the very victim whom she had entrapped, and that with so much art, that Mr. Sikes, who was not prodigal of commendation, had affirmed her 'to be an *honour* to her sex.' Nancy now exhibits the greatest courage and single-hearted disinterestedness: she returns money from Miss Maylie; she rejects a proffered home, the loss of which she knew so well; she declines the means of repentance, for which she yearned at moments of the hauntings of the good spirit. This and more she renounces in order to cling to her *lover!*—a nasty, brutal scoundrel, who beats and kicks her, even after her tenderest watchfulness over his sick bed, and who ends by cutting her throat. While the romantic approve, and metaphysicians speculate on the abstract possibility of this union of virtue and vice, we all sympathise with Nancy's melancholy fate: her death is drawn with a force which quite appals. This devotedness to her unworthy companion, to whom, notwithstanding her early history, she is clearly constant, forms her redeeming point. Woman's love, like the deep-rooted trees on the tomb of Geryon, cannot be plucked out without blood. Nancy is described as aware of her degraded situation: she felt the awe of the undefiledness of virtue, at which vice stands abashed; yet, when Miss Maylie, who, seeing only the horror and guilt, calmly reasons, and attempts to save her

from Sikes, Nancy, who loves, is faithful and unmoved. We may indeed *speculate* whether such metal, had it been cast in a better mould, would not have run true and clear. We can only *reason* on what of necessity must have been the result of the influences to which she had been exposed from her birth downwards. Notwithstanding that the greater tendency in woman towards the gentler affections renders a Nancy somewhat less improbable than an Oliver, we fear that both characters must be considered contrary to the laws of human nature and experience everywhere, and particularly in England. Here, a woman once lost descends instantaneously, as through a trap-door, into unknown depths, to be heard of no more. There is no climbing up again, none to forgive, none to say 'sin no more;' all throw the first stone, all press on the bruised reed,—and her own sex the heaviest: not only those who are themselves unscathed, merely because they have never known want, misery, or temptation; but even the wise, the thoughtful, the experienced, the truly and intrinsically pure,—even they can pardon every crime and cover every shame save that of an erring sister.

The character of Bill Sikes, the housebreaker and murderer, is drawn, we conceive, with equal power and accuracy: he is a thorough miscreant, of that coarse, bulldog grossness, which is peculiar to this country, like his legs, which are of that kind that seem incomplete without fetters. He is unredeemed by any single merit; he cannot feel even for Nancy, whose affection and tears he calls 'whining;' when she faints at his ill-usage, he 'tries a little blasphemy,'—which one of the heroes of the Rolliad administered to Lord Chancellor Thurlow, with his best Burgundy, *to put him in good humour*. This energy, this 'shotting his gun,' forms part of the $\eta\theta o\delta$ of Mr. Sikes: it partakes of that tendency which, according to Professor Keble, is akin to poetry, that seeking an animated outbreak, as a safety-valve for inner feelings and excitement. Mr. Sikes, like Mount Vesuvius in an eruption, shoots forth his 'words that burn,' either in reference to that locality of which fire and sulphur form the staple, or by invoking condemnation on his own and other people's visual organs,—with a liberality of anathema which, if realized, would render ophthalmia less uncommon than the measles. Boz, however, has a curious felicity in wrapping up this hero—brimstone in silver-paper; he rectifies the above-proof drams by the dilution of humorous periphrases. The account of the behaviour of the murderer after the deed is done is of first-rate excellence: he is traced step by step, where an inferior writer would have generalized. The attempt to drown the dog, and the dialogue while the mail-coach stops, are perfect.—Those matter-of-fact, every-day occurrences, which the conscience-haunted outcast applies to self-accusation, heighten the truth of the picture, and evince that close observation of incidents and perception of character and professions so remarkable in our author.

As the tale proceeds, the bad characters are duly made examples of, while Oliver, with the posse comitatus of old ladies and gentlemen, young bride and bridegroom, footmen, apothecary, and so on, all settle down in a country village in one lot, being, we infer, unable to do without each other. The Fagin cabinet is broken up; the pleasant premier is executed at Newgate, although it would puzzle most Old Bailey lawyers to explain why. He certainly *deserved* to be hung; that, however, was *primâ facie* in favour of his acquittal; inasmuch as, not being hampered by having justice on his side, he had all the chances of all the crotchets of judges, and twelve honest and true men, to say nothing of the characteristic absurdity of English prosecutors and people, whose eagerness to catch a thief and to bring him to trial is only equalled by their morbid anxiety, when conviction has taken place, for cheating the gallows and Jack Ketch of their just perquisites: Fagin, however, not having even the excuse of fourteen children, nor the benefit of a mercy-mongering Mulgrave, is 'launched into eternity.' Nancy, as we have already seen, is murdered by Sikes. This prime supporter of the Fagin administration, the burly and bandy-legged ruffian of the gang, the head of the cursers, hangs himself, by accident, in an attempt to escape with a rope from the roof of a house: his unintentional self-destruction presents an apt illustration of the political truth, that unprincipled, incompetent bunglers will put an end to their own existence, if only let alone and supplied with rope enough. The minor tail get off better than their leaders. Noah Claypole takes to the trade of an informer, the Artful Dodger is transported a 'lifer,' while Charley Bates reforms, cuts the concern, and becomes a respectable dealer in bullocks in one of the midland counties.

We have introduced our readers neither to the lovers and 'genteel' folks above stairs, nor to the maids and footmen below: they are all birds of the same feather, and in whom we take no interest. Mr. Bumble, the beadle, and Mrs. Corney, the work-house matron, are infinitely better company: their lives and loves are interwoven in the tale like shotted silk. Mr. Bumble is one of that numerous tribe of poor creatures who are puffed out with insolence of office, the pride of brief authority, and with whom we have been too long familiar:—mean and cowardly in heart, craven to his superiors, insulting where insult is safe, a true redtapist pauper bully. Power has a natural tendency to corpulency, which becomes a beadle; moreover he is full of admiration of the outward and visible signs of his dignity, his cocked hat especially, which silences the poor-house and churchyard. In that he is true to 'human natur.' 'L'habit ne fait pas le moine' may be true of French monks, but is false as regards English Beadles, Speakers, and Chancellors. Mr. Bumble, when turned out, deplores the loss of his respect-inspiring costume: shorn of his strength, like Samson, he tastes the misery of an ex-Right-Honourable cit, subsiding pinmaker into the Minories, from the glories of recording angels, turtles, and 'your lordship' of the Mansion-house. The relinquishment by our bench of bishops of their powdered bird-nest wigs preceded the heavy and serious blow dealt to the establishment by the cathedral-destruction commission.

Mr. Bumble, while in office, is fully sensible of the envy which frowns at authority. Like all small people in great place, he endeavours to disarm the fructification of the evil eye by lamenting that 'a parochial life is not a bed of roses.' His visit to Mrs. Corney is admirable. Boz paints to the life the ceremonious, courteous dignity of the beadle, who, notwithstanding, keeps a sharp look-out at her 'real silver spoons,' and their number; the 'how much has she' principle of more interested than interesting silver-forkers. Mrs. Corney, although matron of a work-house, had a heart, and could feel for—a beadle: she sighs to exchange the solitary grandeur of power for the long-missed, never-forgotten endearments of marital bliss. If ever a beadle looked tender ours did, and the widow is won. Once become one, Mr. and Mrs. Bumble soon find out that, after pearls and diamonds, the next rare thing is the union of power and rank with connubial felicity, which, as we observed in the case of Ferdinand and Isabella of Spain, thrives best in the unseen joys of private intimacies. Beadles are but men. Mahomet failed in convincing his wife of his supernatural powers. Mrs. Bumble turns out to be a virago of the true grey mare, the Xantippe breed . . . : the pitch of her character has a constant tendency to boil over, which she at last exemplifies by throwing the soap-suds over her lord and master, thereby upsetting all St. Paul's decisions respecting weaker vessels. 'It is sometimes,' says Quevedo, 'better to buy a quart of milk than to keep a cow.'

But we are getting tedious—so one word of farewell to our pleasant Boz. 'Macte novâ virtute puer'—we warn him like the weïrd sisters—beware of the worst cockneyism—that of Mayfair: eschew mawkish, unmanly sentimentalism: beware of pseudo-Byrons, of men without cravats or principles, whose rude, false, sensual, ungenerous hearts are poorly concealed beneath golden chains and speckled waistcoats, men more truly vulgar than any Bates or Dodger. If Boz values his fair fame more than Mr. Bentley's ducats—if he aspires to something better than being made a show of for a season or two—let him alike shun Mr. Sikes and his gin-bottle, Miss Nancy and my Lady Matilda's syllabubs. The world is wide enough without them; nor is there any lack in London of witty men and pretty women, of decent books and cooks, wherewith to sharpen his intellect and refine his taste. If Boz neglects these hints, and is besirened by the 'tanti palpiti' of the Mulgravian hurdy-gurdies, then, as Sam Slick says, 'He don't know the valy of his diamond.' (pp. 50-6)

Richard Ford, in an originally unsigned review of "Oliver Twist," in The London Quarterly Review, *No. CXXVII, June, 1839, pp. 46-56.*

Charles Dickens   (essay date 1841)

[*In the following essay, presented as a preface to an 1841 edition of* Oliver Twist, *Dickens defends the novel's moral purpose.*]

The greater part of [*Oliver Twist*] was originally published in a magazine. When I completed it, and put it forth in its present form three years ago, I full expected it would be objected to on some very high moral grounds in some very high moral quarters. The result did not fail to prove the justice of my anticipations.

I embrace the present opportunity of saying a few words in explanation of my aim and object in its production. It is in some sort a duty with me to do so, in gratitude to those who sympathized with me and divined my purpose at the time, and who, perhaps, will not be sorry to have their impression confirmed under my own hand.

It is, it seems, a very coarse and shocking circumstance that some of the characters in these pages are chosen from the most criminal and degraded of London's population, that Sikes is a thief and Fagin a receiver of stolen goods, that the boys are pick-pockets and the girl is a prostitute.

I confess I have yet to learn that a lesson of the purest good may not be drawn from the vilest evil. I have always believed this to be a recognized and established truth, laid down by the greatest men the world has ever seen, constantly acted upon by the best and wisest natures, and confirmed by the reason and experience of every thinking mind. I saw no reason, when I wrote this book, why the very dregs of life, so long as their speech did not offend the ear, should not serve the purpose of a moral at least as well as its froth and cream. Nor did I doubt that there lay festering in Saint Giles's as good materials towards the truth as any flaunting in Saint James's.

In this spirit, when I wished to show in little Oliver the principle of Good surviving through every adverse circumstance and triumphing at last, and when I considered among what companions I could try him best—having regard to that kind of men into whose hands he would most naturally fall—I bethought myself of those who figure in these volumes. When I came to discuss the subject more maturely with myself, I saw many strong reasons for pursuing the course to which I was inclined. I had read of thieves by scores—seductive fellows (amiable for the most part), faultless in dress, plump in pocket, choice in horse-flesh, bold in bearing, fortunate in gallantry, great at a song, a bottle, pack of cards or dice-box, and fit companions for the bravest. But I had never met (except in Hogarth) with the miserable reality. It appeared to me that to draw a knot of such associates in crime as really do exist; to paint them in all their deformity, in all their wretchedness, in all the squalid poverty of their lives; to show them as they really are, for ever skulking uneasily through the dirtiest paths of life, with the great, black, ghastly gallows closing up their prospects, turn them where they may—it appeared to me that to do this would be to attempt a something which was greatly needed and which would be a service to society. And therefore I did it as I best could.

In every book I know, where such characters are treated of at all, certain allurements and fascinations are thrown around them. Even in the *Beggar's Opera,* the thieves are represented as leading a life which is rather to be envied than otherwise; while Macheath, with all the captivations of command, and the devotion of the most beautiful girl and only pure character in the piece, is as much to be admired and emulated by weak beholders as any fine gentleman in a red coat who has purchased, as Voltaire says, the right to command a couple of thousand men or so and to affront death at their head. Johnson's question, whether any man will turn thief because Macheath is reprieved, seems to me beside the matter. I ask myself whether any man will be deterred from turning thief because of his being sentenced to death and because of the existence of Peachum and Lockit; and remembering the captain's roar-

ing life, great appearance, vast success, and strong advantages, I feel assured that nobody having a bent that way will take any warning from him, or will see anything in the play but a very flowery and pleasant road, conducting an honourable ambition, in course of time, to Tyburn Tree.

In fact, Gay's witty satire on society had a general object which made him careless of example in this respect and gave him other, wider, and higher aims. The same may be said of Sir Edward Bulwer's admirable and most powerful novel of Paul Clifford, which cannot be fairly considered as having, or being intended to have, any bearing on this part of the subject, one way or other.

What manner of life is that which is described in these pages, as the everyday existence of a Thief ? What charms has it for the young and ill-disposed, what allurements for the most jolter-headed of juveniles? Here are no canterings upon moonlit heaths, no merrymakings in the snuggest of all possible caverns, none of the attractions of dress, no embroidery, no lace, no jack-boots, no crimson coats and ruffles, none of the dash and freedom with which "the road" has been time out of mind invested. The cold, wet, shelterless midnight streets of London; the foul and frowsy dens, where vice is closely packed and lacks the room to turn; the haunts of hunger and disease, the shabby rags that scarcely hold together—where are the attractions of these things? Have they no lesson, and do they not whisper something beyond the little-regarded warning of a moral precept?

But there are people of so refined and delicate a nature that they cannot bear the contemplation of these horrors. Not that they turn instinctively from crime, but that criminal characters, to suit them, must be, like their meat, in delicate disguise. A Massaroni in green velvet is quite an enchanting creature, but a Sikes in fustian is unsupportable. A Mrs. Massaroni, being a lady in short petticoats and a fancy dress, is a thing to imitate in tableaux and have in lithograph on pretty songs; but a Nancy, being a creature in a cotton gown and cheap shawl, is not to be thought of. It is wonderful how Virtue turns from dirty stockings, and how Vice, married to ribbons and a little gay attire, changes her name, as wedded ladies do, and becomes Romance.

Now, as the stern and plain truth, even in the dress of this (in novels) much exalted race, was a part of the purpose of this book, I will not, for these readers, abate one hole in the Dodger's coat or one scrap of curlpaper in the girl's dishevelled hair. I have no faith in the delicacy which cannot bear to look upon them. I have no desire to make proselytes among such people. I have no respect for their opinion, good or bad, do not covet their approval, and do not write for their amusement. I venture to say this without reserve; for I am not aware of any writer in our language having a respect for himself, or held in any respect by his posterity, who ever has descended to the taste of this fastidious class.

On the other hand, if I look for examples and for precedents, I find them in the noblest range of English literature. Fielding, Defoe, Goldsmith, Smollett, Richardson, Mackenzie—all these for wise purposes, and especially the two first, brought upon the scene the very scum and refuse of the land. Hogarth, the moralist, and censor of his age—in whose great works the times in which he lived and the characters of every time will never cease to be reflected—did the like, without the compromise of a hair's breadth, with a power and depth of thought which belonged to few men before him and will probably appertain to fewer still in time to come. Where does this giant stand now in the estimation of his countrymen? And yet, if I turn back to the days in which he or any of these men flourished, I find the same reproach levelled against them every one, each in his turn, by the insects of the hour, who raised their little hum and died and were forgotten.

Cervantes laughed Spain's chivalry away by showing Spain its impossible and wild absurdity. It was my attempt, in my humble and far-distant sphere, to dim the false glitter surrounding something which really did exist by showing it in its unattractive and repulsive truth. No less consulting my own taste than the manners of the age, I endeavoured; while I painted it in all its fallen and degraded aspects, to banish from the lips of the lowest character I introduced, any expression that could by possibility offend, and rather to lead to the unavoidable inference that its existence was of the most debased and vicious kind than to prove it elaborately by words and deeds. In the case of the girl in particular I kept this intention constantly in view. Whether it is apparent in the narrative, and how it is executed, I leave my readers to determine.

It has been observed of this girl that her devotion to the brutal housebreaker does not seem natural, and it has been objected to Sikes in the same breath—with some inconsistency, as I venture to think—that he is surely overdrawn, because in him there would appear to be none of those redeeming traits which are objected to as unnatural in his mistress. Of the latter objection I will merely say that I fear there are in the world some insensible and callous natures that do become, at last, utterly and irredeemably bad. But whether this be so or not, of one thing I am certain: that there are such men as Sikes, who, being closely followed through the same space of time and through the same current of circumstances, would not give, by one look or action of a moment, the faintest indication of a better nature. Whether every gentler human feeling is dead within such bosoms, or the proper chord to strike has rusted and is hard to find, I do not know; but that the fact is so, I am sure.

It is useless to discuss whether the conduct and character of the girl seems natural or unnatural, probable or improbable, right or wrong. It is true. Every man who has watched these melancholy shades of life knows it to be so. Suggested to my mind long ago—long before I dealt in fiction—by what I often saw and read of in actual life around me, I have for years tracked it through many profligate and noisome ways, and found it still the same. From the first introduction of that poor wretch to her laying her bloody head upon the robber's breast, there is not one word exaggerated or over-wrought. It is emphatically God's truth, for it is the truth He leaves in such depraved and miserable breasts, the hope yet lingering behind, the last fair drop of water at the bottom of the dried-up weed-

choked well. It involves the best and worst shades of our common nature, much of its ugliest hues and something of its most beautiful; it is a contradiction, an anomaly, an apparent impossibility, but it is a truth. I am glad to have had it doubted, for in that circumstance I find a sufficient assurance that it needed to be told. (pp. v-x)

Charles Dickens, in a preface to his Oliver Twist, *The New American Library of World Literature, Inc., 1961, 496 p.*

George Gissing   (essay date 1900)

[*Gissing is best known as a novelist whose* New Grub Street *(1891) and* Born in Exile *(1892) are characterized by the harsh, disillusioned realism typical of much English fiction written during the late Victorian era. An astute critic, he is also highly regarded for his critical studies of the works of Dickens; his* Charles Dickens: A Critical Study *(1898) is widely recognized as one of the earliest and most comprehensive analyses of Dickens's writings. In the following essay, originally published as an introduction to the Rochester Edition of* Oliver Twist *(1900), Gissing offers an overview of the novel.*]

It was a proof of Dickens's force and originality that, whilst still engaged upon *Pickwick,* with the laughter of a multitude flattering his joyous and eager temper, he chose for his new book such a subject as that of *Oliver Twist.* The profound seriousness of his genius, already suggesting itself in the course of Mr. Pickwick's adventures, was fully declared in "The Parish Boy's Progress." Doubts might well have been entertained as to the reception by the public of this squalid chronicle, this story of the workhouse, the thieves' den, and the condemned cell; as a matter of fact, voices were soon raised in protest, and many of *Pickwick*'s admirers turned away in disgust. When the complete novel appeared, a *Quarterly* reviewer attacked it vigorously, declaring the picture injurious to public morals, and the author's satire upon public institutions mere splenetic extravagance. For all this Dickens was prepared. Consciously, deliberately, he had begun the great work of his life, and he had strength to carry with him the vast majority of English readers. His mistakes were those of a generous purpose. When criticism had said its say, the world did homage to a genial moralist, a keen satirist, and a leader in literature.

In January, 1837, appeared the first number of a magazine called *Bentley's Miscellany,* with Dickens for editor, and in its second number began *Oliver Twist,* which ran from month to month until March of 1839. Long before the conclusion of the story as a serial, it appeared (October, 1838) in three volumes, illustrated by Cruikshank. Some of these illustrations were admirable, some very poor, and one was so bad that Dickens caused it to be removed before many copies of the book had been issued. Years after, Cruikshank seems to have hinted that his etchings were the origin of *Oliver Twist,* Dickens having previously seen them and founded his story upon them. The claim was baseless, and it is not worth while discussing how Cruikshank came to imagine such a thing.

There had fallen upon Dickens the first penalty of success;

he was tempted to undertake more work than he could possibly do, and at the same time was worried by discontent with the pecuniary results of his hasty agreements. During the composition of **Oliver** he wrote the latter portion of **Pickwick** and the early chapters of **Nickleby;** moreover, he compiled an anonymous life of the clown Grimaldi, and did other things which can only be considered hack-work. That he had not also to work at **Barnaby Rudge,** and thus be carrying on three novels at the same time, was only due to his resolve to repudiate an impossible engagement. Complications such as these were inevitable at the opening of the most brilliant literary career in the Victorian time.

How keenly Dickens felt the hardship of his position, toiling for the benefit of a publisher, is shown in Chapter XIV, where Oliver is summoned to Mr. Brownlow's study, and, gazing about him in wonder at the laden shelves, is asked by his benefactor whether he would like to be a writer of books. "Oliver considered a little while and at last said he should think it would be a much better thing to be a bookseller; upon which the old gentleman laughed heartily and declared he had said a very good thing."—"Don't be afraid," added Mr. Brownlow, "we won't make an author of you whilst there's an honest trade to be learnt, or brickmaking to turn to." An amusing passage, in the light of Dickens's position only a year or two after it was written.

Oliver Twist had a twofold moral purpose: to exhibit the evil working of the Poor Law Act, and to give a faithful picture of the life of thieves in London. The motives hung well together, for in Dickens's view the pauper system was directly responsible for a great deal of crime. It must be remembered that, by the new Act of 1834, outdoor sustenance was as much as possible done away with, paupers being henceforth relieved only on condition of their entering a workhouse, while the workhouse life was made thoroughly uninviting, among other things by the separation of husbands and wives, and parents and children. Against this seemingly harsh treatment of a helpless class Dickens is very bitter; he regards such legislation as the outcome of cold-blooded theory, evolved by well-to-do persons of the privileged caste, who neither perceive nor care about the result of their system in individual suffering.

> I wish some well-fed philosopher, whose meat and drink turn to gall within him; whose blood is ice, whose heart is iron, could have seen Oliver Twist clutching at the dainty viands that the dog had neglected. . . . There is only one thing I should like better, and that would be to see the philosopher making the same sort of meal himself, with the same relish. (Chapter IV.)

By "philosopher" Dickens meant a political-economist; he uses the word frequently in this book, and always in the spirit which moved Carlyle when speaking of "the dismal science." He is the thorough-going advocate of the poor, the uncompromising Radical. Speaking with irony of the vices nourished in Noah Claypole by vicious training, he bids us note "how impartially the same amiable qualities are developed in the finest lord and the dirtiest charity boy." This partisanship lay in his genius; it was one of the sources of his strength; its entire sincerity enabled him to carry out the great task set before him, that of sweetening

in some measure the Augean stable of English social life in the early half of our century.

That he was in error on the point immediately at issue mattered little. The horrible condition of the poor which so exasperated him resulted (in so far as it was due to any particular legislation) from the old Poor Law, which, by its system of granting relief in aid of insufficient wages had gone far towards pauperizing the whole of agricultural England. Not in a year or two could this evil be remedied. Dickens, seeing only the hardship of the inevitable reform, visited upon the authors of that reform indignation merited by the sluggishness and selfishness which had made it necessary. In good time the new Act justified itself; it helped to bring about increase of wages and to awaken self-respect, so far as self-respect is possible in the toilers perforce living from hand to mouth. But Dickens's quarrel with the "guardians of the poor" lay far too deep to be affected by such small changes; his demand was for justice and for mercy, in the largest sense, for a new spirit in social life. Now that his work is done, with that of Carlyle and Ruskin to aid its purpose, a later generation applauds him for throwing scorn upon mechanical "philosophy." Constitutional persons, such as Macaulay, might declare his views on social government beneath contempt; but those views have largely prevailed, and we see their influence ever extending. Readers of *Oliver Twist,* nowadays, do not concern themselves with the technical question; Oliver "asks for more," and has all our sympathies; be the law old or new, we are made to perceive that, more often than not, "the law is an ass," and its proceedings invalid in the court of conscience.

In a preface to **Oliver** (written in 1841) Dickens spoke at length of its second purpose, and defended himself against critics who had objected to his dealing with the lives of pickpockets and burglars. His aim, he tells us, was to discredit a school of fiction then popular, which glorified the thief in the guise of a gallant highwayman; the real thief, he declared, he had nowhere found portrayed, save in Hogarth, and his own intention was to show the real creature, vile and miserable, "for ever skulking uneasily through the dirtiest paths of life." From the category of evil examples in fiction of the day, he excepts "Sir Edward Bulwer's admirable and powerful novel of Paul Clifford," having for that author a singular weakness not easily explained. His own scenes lie in "the cold, wet, shelterless midnight streets of London," in "foul and frowsy dens," in "haunts of hunger and disease"; and "where"—he asks—"are the attractions of these things?"

This defence, no doubt, had in view (amongst other things) the censure upon **Oliver Twist** contained in Thackeray's story of *Catherine,* which was published in *Fraser's Magazine,* 1839-40, under the signature of "Ikey Solomons jun." Thackeray at this time was not the great novelist whom we know; seven years had still to elapse before the publication of *Vanity Fair.* His *Catherine* is a stinging satire upon the same popular fiction that Dickens had in view, but he throws a wider net, attacking with scornful vigour *Paul Clifford* and *Ernest Maltravers,* together with the Jack Sheppards and Dick Turpins and Duvals, and, in two instances, speaking contemptuously of

Oliver asking for more. Illustration by George Cruikshank.

Oliver itself. "To tread in the footsteps of the immortal Fagin requires a genius of inordinate stride," and he cannot present his readers with any "white-washed saints," like poor "Biss Dadsy" in *Oliver Twist.* Still, says the author, he has taken pains to choose a subject "agreeably low, delightfully disgusting, and at the same time eminently pleasing and pathetic." His heroine is a real person, one Catherine Hayes, whose history can be read in the Newgate Calendar; she was brought up in the workhouses, apprenticed to the landlady of a village inn, and, in the year 1726, was burned at Tyburn for the murder of her husband. Thackeray uses his lash on all novelists who show themselves indulgent to evil-doers. "Let your rogues act like rogues, and your honest men like honest men; don't let us have any juggling and thimblerigging with virtue and vice." In short, he writes very angrily, having, it is plain, Dickens often in mind. Nor is it hard to see the cause of this feeling. Thackeray was impatient with the current pictures of rascaldom simply because he was aware of his own supreme power to depict the rascal world; what thoughts may we surmise in the creator of Barry Lyndon when he read the novels of Bulwer and of Ainsworth, or the new production of the author of *Pickwick*? Only three years more, and we find him writing a heartfelt eulogy of the *Christmas Carol,* praise which proves him thoroughly to have appreciated the best of Dickens. But it must be avowed that very much of *Oliver* is far from Dickens's best, and Thackeray, with his native scorn of the untrue and the feeble, would often enough have his teeth set on edge as he perused those pages. *Cath-*

erine itself, flung off in disdainful haste, is evidence of its author's peculiar power; it has dialogues, scenes, glimpses of character beyond the reach of any other English novelist. In certain directions Thackeray may be held the greatest "realist" who ever penned fiction. There is nothing to wonder at in his scoff at Fagin and Nancy; but we are glad of the speedy change to a friendlier point of view.

It was undoubtedly Dickens's conviction that, within limits imposed by decency, he had told the truth, and nothing but the truth, about his sordid and criminal characters. Imagine his preface to have been written fifty years later, and it would be all but appropriate to some representative of a daring school of "naturalism," asserting his right to deal with the most painful facts of life. "I will not abate one hole in the Dodger's coat, or one scrap of curl-paper in the girl's dishevelled hair." True, he feels obliged so to manipulate the speech of these persons that it shall not "offend the ear," but that seemed to him a matter of course. He appeals to the example of the eighteenth-century novelists, who were unembarrassed in their choice of subjects. He will stand or fall by his claim to have made a true picture. The little hero of the book is as real to him as Bill Sikes. "I wished to show, in little Oliver, the principle of good surviving through every adverse circumstance, and triumphing at last." Think what we may of his perfectly sincere claim, the important thing, in our retrospect, is the spirit in which he made it. After a long interval during which English fiction was represented by the tawdry unreal or the high imaginative (I do not forget the homely side of Scott, but herein Scott stood alone), a new writer demands attention for stories of obscure lives, and tells his tale so attractively that high and low give ear. It is a step in social and political history; it declares the democratic tendency of the new age. Here is the significance of Dickens's early success, and we do not at all understand his place in English literature if we lose sight of this historic point of view.

By comparison with the book which preceded it, *Oliver Twist* seems immature. Putting aside the first chapter or two, *Pickwick* is an astonishingly ripe production, marvellous as the work of a man of five and twenty, who had previously published only a few haphazard sketches of contemporary life. *Oliver,* on the other hand, might well pass for a first effort. Attempting a continued story, the author shows at once his weakest side, the defect which he will never outgrow. There is no coherency in the structure of the thing; the plotting is utterly without ingenuity, the mysteries are so artificial as to be altogether uninteresting. Again, we must remember the time at which Dickens was writing. Our modern laws of fiction did not exist; a story was a story, not to be judged by the standard of actual experience. Moreover, it had always to be borne in mind how greatly Dickens was under the influence of the stage, which at one time he had seriously studied with a view to becoming an actor; all through his books the theatrical tendency is manifest, not a little to their detriment. Obviously he saw a good deal of *Oliver Twist* as if from before the footlights, and even in the language of his characters the traditional note of melodrama is occasionally sounded. When, long years after, he horrified a public audience by his "reading" of the murder of Nancy, it was a singular realization of hopes cherished in his early manhood. Not content with his fame as an author, he delighted in giving proof that he possessed in a high degree the actor's talent. In our own day the popularity of the stage is again exerting an influence on the methods of fiction; such intermingling of two very different arts must always be detrimental to both.

Put aside the two blemishes of the book—on the one hand, Monks with his insufferable (often ludicrous) rant, and his absurd machinations; on the other, the feeble idyllicism of the Maylie group—and there remains a very impressive picture of the wretched and the horrible. Oliver's childish miseries show well against a background of hopeless pauperdom; having regard to his origin, we grant the "gentle, attached, affectionate creature," who is so unlike a typical workhouse child, and are made to feel his sufferings among people who may be called inhuman, but who in truth are human enough, the circumstances considered. Be it noted that, whereas even Mr. Bumble is at moments touched by natural sympathy, and Mr. Sowerberry would be not unkind if he had his way, the women of this world—Mrs. Corney, Mrs. Sowerberry, and the workhouse hags—are fiercely cruel; in them, as in many future instances, Dickens draws strictly from his observation, giving us the very truth in despite of sentiment. Passing from the shadow of the workhouse to that of criminal London, we submit to the effect which Dickens alone can produce; London as a place of squalid mystery and terror, of the grimly grotesque, of labyrinthine obscurity and lurid fascination, is Dickens's own; he taught people a certain way of regarding the huge city, and to this day how common it is to see London with Dickens's eyes. The vile streets, accurately described and named; the bare, filthy rooms inhabited by Fagin and Sikes and the rest of them; the hideous public-house to which thieves resort are before us with a haunting reality. Innumerable scarcely noticed touches heighten the impression; we know, for instance, exactly what these people eat and drink, and can smell the dish of sheep's head, flanked with porter, which Nancy sets before her brutal companion. Fagin is as visible as Shylock; we hear the very voices of the Artful Dodger and of Charley Bates, whose characters are so admirably unlike in similarity; Nancy herself becomes credible by force of her surroundings and in certain scenes (for instance, that of her hysterical fury in Chapter XVI) is life itself. The culminating horrors have a wild picturesqueness unlike anything achieved by other novelists; one never forgets Sikes's wanderings after the murder (with that scene in the inn with the pedlar), nor his death in Jacob's Island, nor Fagin in the condemned cell. These things could not be more vividly presented. The novelist's first duty is to make us see what he has seen himself, whether with the actual eye or with that of imagination, and no one ever did this more successfully than Dickens in his best moments.

His allusion (in the Preface) to Hogarth suggests a comparison of these two great artists, each of whom did such noteworthy work in the same field. On the whole, one observes more of contrast than of likeness in the impressions they severally leave upon us; the men differed widely in their ways of regarding life and were subjected to very different influences. But the life of the English poor as seen by Dickens in his youth had undergone little outward change from that which was familiar to Hogarth, and it is *Oliver Twist* especially that reminds us of the other's stern moralities in black-and-white. Not improbably they influenced the young writer's treatment of his subject. He never again deals in such unsoftened horrors as those death-scenes in the workhouse, or draws a figure so peculiarly base as that of Noah Claypole; his humour at moments is grim, harsh, unlike the ordinary Dickens note, and sometimes seems resolved to show human nature at its worst, as in the passage when Oliver runs after the coach, induced by promise of a half penny, only to be scoffed at when he falls back in weariness and pain (Chapter VIII). Dickens is, as a rule, on better terms with his rascals and villains; they generally furnish matter for a laugh; but half-a-dozen faces in *Oliver* have the very Hogarth stamp, the lines of bestial ugliness which disgust and repel.

One is often inclined to marvel that, with such a world to draw upon for his material, the world of the lower classes in the England of sixty years ago, he was able to tone his work with so genial a humanity. The features of that time, as they impress our imagination, are for the most part either ignoble or hideous, and a Hogarth in literature would seem a more natural outcome of such conditions than the author of *Pickwick* and the *Christmas Carol*. Dickens's service to civilization by the liberality of his thought cannot be too much insisted upon. The atmosphere of that age was a stifling Puritanism. "I have been very happy for some years," says Mrs. Maylie; "too happy, perhaps, It may be time that I should meet with some misfortune." (Chapter XXXIII.) Against the state of mind declared in this amazing utterance, Dickens instinctively rebelled; he believed in happiness, in its moral effect, and in the right of all to have their share in it. Forced into contemplation of the gloomiest aspects of human existence, his buoyant spirit would not be held in darkness; as his art progressed, it dealt more gently with oppressive themes. Take, for instance, the mortuary topic, which has so large a place in the life of the poor, and compare Mr. Sowerberry's business, squalid and ghastly, with that of Mr. Mould in *Chuzzlewit,* where humour prevails over the repulsive, and that again with the picture of Messrs. Omer and Joram in *Copperfield,* which touches mortality with the homeliest kindness. The circumstances, to be sure, are very different, but their choice indicates the movement of the author's mind. It was by virtue of his ever-hopeful outlook that Dickens became such a force for good.

Disposing of those of his characters who remain alive at the end, he assures us, as in a fairy tale, that the good people lived happily ever after, and we are quite ready to believe it. Among the evildoers he distinguishes, Mr. Bumble falls to his appropriate doom; Noah Claypole disappears in the grime which is his native element—severity, in his case unmitigated by the reflection that he, too, was a parish-boy and a creature of circumstances. Charley Bates it is impossible to condemn; his jollity is after Dickens's own heart, and, as there is always hope for the boy who can laugh, one feels it natural enough that he is last heard of as "the merriest young grazier in all Northamptonshire." But what of his companion, Mr. Dawkins, the Dodger? Voices pleaded for him; the author was besought to give him a chance; but of the Dodger we have no word. His last appearance is in Chapter XLIII, perhaps the best in the book. We know how Dickens must have enjoyed the writing of that chapter; Mr. Dawkins before the Bench is a triumph of his most characteristic humour. What more is to be told of the Dodger after that?

We take philosophic leave of him, assured that he is "doing full justice to his bringing-up, and establishing for himself a glorious reputation." (pp. 63-87)

> *George Gissing, "Oliver Twist," in his* The Immortal Dickens, 1925. *Reprint by Kraus Reprint Co., 1969, pp. 63-87.*

G. K. Chesterton   (essay date 1907)

[*Regarded as one of England's premier literary critics during the first half of the twentieth century, Chesterton was a colorful bon vivant, a witty essayist, and creator of the Father Brown mysteries and the fantasy* The Man Who Was Thursday (1908). *In the following essay, originally published as an introduction to the Everyman Edition of* Oliver Twist *in 1907, he regards Dickens's fascination with the macabre and his attack on social oppression as the two salient features of the novel.*]

In considering Dickens, as we almost always must consider him, as a man of rich originality, we may possibly miss the forces from which he drew even his original energy. It is not well for man to be alone. We, in the modern world, are ready enough to admit that when it is applied to some problem of monasticism or of an ecstatic life. But we will not admit that our modern artistic claim to absolute originality is really a claim to absolute unsociability; a claim to absolute loneliness. The anarchist is at least as solitary as the ascetic. And the men of very vivid vigour in literature, the men such as Dickens, have generally displayed a large sociability towards the society of letters, always expressed in the happy pursuit of pre-existent themes, sometimes expressed, as in the case of Molière or Sterne, in downright plagiarism. For even theft is a confession of our dependence on society. In Dickens, however, this element of the original foundations on which he worked is quite especially difficult to determine. This is partly due to the fact that for the present reading public he is practically the only one of his long line that is read at all. He sums up Smollett and Goldsmith, but he also destroys them. This one giant, being closest to us, cuts off from our view even the giants that begat him. But much more is this difficulty due to the fact that Dickens mixed up with the old material, materials so subtly modern, so made of the French Revolution, that the whole is transformed. If we want the best example of this, the best example is *Oliver Twist.*

Relatively to the other works of Dickens *Oliver Twist* is not of great value, but it is of great importance. Some parts of it are so crude and of so clumsy a melodrama, that one is almost tempted to say that Dickens would have been greater without it. But even if he had been greater without it he would still have been incomplete without it. With the exception of some gorgeous passages, both of humour and horror, the interest of the book lies not so much in its revelation of Dickens's literary genius as in its revelation of those moral, personal, and political instincts which were the make-up of his character and the permanent support

---

An excerpt from *Oliver Twist*

Oliver Twist and his companions suffered the tortures of slow starvation for three months: at last they got so voracious and wild with hunger, that one boy, who was tall for his age, and hadn't been used to that sort of thing (for his father had kept a small cookshop), hinted darkly to his companions, that unless he had another basin of gruel *per diem*, he was afraid he might some night happen to eat the boy who slept next him, who happened to be a weakly youth of tender age. He had a wild, hungry eye; and they implicitly believed him. A council was held; lots were cast who should walk up to the master after supper that evening, and ask for more; and it fell to Oliver Twist.

The evening arrived; the boys took their places. The master, in his cook's uniform, stationed himself at the copper; his pauper assistants ranged themselves behind him; the gruel was served out; and a long grace was said over the short commons. The gruel disappeared; the boys whispered each other, and winked at Oliver; while his next neighbours nudged him. Child as he was, he was desperate with hunger, and reckless with misery. He rose from the table; and advancing to the master, basin and spoon in hand, said: somewhat alarmed at his own temerity:

'Please, sir, I want some more.'

The master was a fat, healthy man; but he turned very pale. He gazed in stupefied astonishment on the small rebel for some seconds, and then clung for support to the copper. The assistants were paralysed with wonder; the boys with fear.

'What!' said the master at length, in a faint voice.

'Please, sir,' replied Oliver, 'I want some more.'

The master aimed a blow at Oliver's head with the ladle; pinioned him in his arms; and shrieked aloud for the beadle.

The board were sitting in solemn conclave, when Mr. Bumble rushed into the room in great excitement, and addressing the gentleman in the high chair, said,

'Mr. Limbkins, I beg your pardon, sir! Oliver Twist has asked for more!'

There was a general start. Horror was depicted on every countenance.

'For *more!*' said Mr. Limbkins. 'Compose yourself, Bumble, and answer me distinctly. Do I understand that he asked for more, after he had eaten the supper allotted by the dietary?'

'He did, sir,' replied Bumble.

'That boy will be hung,' said the gentleman in the white waistcoat. 'I know that boy will be hung.'

> *Charles Dickens, in his* The Adventures of Oliver Twist, *Oxford University Press, 1949.*

of that literary genius. It is by far the most depressing of all his books; it is in some ways the most irritating; yet its ugliness gives the last touch of honesty to all that spontaneous and splendid output. Without this one discordant note all his merriment might have seemed like levity.

Dickens had just appeared upon the stage and set the whole world laughing with his first great story *Pickwick. Oliver Twist* was his encore. It was the second opportunity given to him by those who had rolled about with laughter over Tupman and Jingle, Weller and Dowler. Under such circumstances a stagey reciter will sometimes take care to give a pathetic piece after his humorous one; and with all his many moral merits, there was much that was stagey about Dickens. But this explanation alone is altogether inadequate and unworthy. There was in Dickens this other kind of energy, horrible, uncanny, barbaric, capable in another age of coarseness, greedy for the emblems of established ugliness, the coffin, the gibbet, the bones, the bloody knife. Dickens liked these things and he was all the more of a man for liking them; especially he was all the more of a boy. We can all recall with pleasure that fact that Miss Petowker (afterwards Mrs. Lillyvick) was in the habit of reciting a poem called "The Blood Drinker's Burial." I cannot express my regret that the words of this poem are not given; for Dickens would have been quite as capable of writing "The Blood Drinker's Burial" as Miss Petowker was of reciting it. This strain existed in Dickens alongside of his happy laughter; both were allied to the same robust romance. Here as elsewhere Dickens is close to all the permanent human things. He is close to religion, which has never allowed the thousand devils on its churches to stop the dancing of its bells. He is allied to the people, to the real poor, who love nothing so much as to take a cheerful glass and to talk about funerals. The extremes of his gloom and gaiety are the mark of religion and democracy; they mark him off from the moderate happiness of philosophers, and from that stoicism which is the virtue and the creed of aristocrats. There is nothing odd in the fact that the same man who conceived the humane hospitalities of Pickwick should also have imagined the inhuman laughter of Fagin's den. They are both genuine and they are both exaggerated. And the whole human tradition has tied up together in a strange knot these strands of festivity and fear. It is over the cups of Christmas Eve that men have always competed in telling ghost stories.

This first element was present in Dickens, and it is very powerfully present in *Oliver Twist.* It had not been present with sufficient consistency or continuity in *Pickwick* to make it remain on the reader's memory at all, for the tale of "Gabriel Grubb" is grotesque rather than horrible, and the two gloomy stories of the "Madman" and the "Queer Client" are so utterly irrelevant to the tale, that even if the reader remember them he probably does not remember that they occur in *Pickwick.* Critics have complained of Shakespeare and others for putting comic episodes into a tragedy. It required a man with the courage and coarseness of Dickens actually to put tragic episodes into a farce. But they are not caught up into the story at all. In *Oliver Twist,* however, the thing broke out with an almost brutal inspiration, and those who had fallen in love

with Dickens for his generous buffoonery may very likely have been startled at receiving such very different fare at the next helping. When you have bought a man's book because you like his writing about Mr. Wardle's punch-bowl and Mr. Winkle's skates, it may very well be surprising to open it and read about the sickening thuds that beat out the life of Nancy, or that mysterious villain whose face was blasted with disease.

As a nightmare, the work is really admirable. Characters which are not very clearly conceived as regards their own psychology are yet, at certain moments, managed so as to shake to its foundations our own psychology. Bill Sikes is not exactly a real man, but for all that he is a real murderer. Nancy is not really impressive as a living woman; but (as the phrase goes) she makes a lovely corpse. Something quite childish and eternal in us, something which is shocked with the mere simplicity of death, quivers when we read of those repeated blows or see Sikes cursing the tell-tale cur who will follow his bloody foot-prints. And this strange, sublime, vulgar melodrama, which is melodrama and yet is painfully real, reaches its hideous height in that fine scene of the death of Sikes, the besieged house, the boy screaming within, the crowd screaming without, the murderer turned almost a maniac and dragging his victim uselessly up and down the room, the escape over the roof, the rope swiftly running taut, and death sudden, startling and symbolic; a man hanged. There is in this and similar scenes something of the quality of Hogarth and many other English moralists of the early eighteenth century. It is not easy to define this Hogarthian quality in words, beyond saying that it is a sort of alphabetical realism, like the cruel candour of children. But it has about it these two special principles which separate it from all that we call realism in our time. First, that with us a moral story means a story about moral people; with them a moral story meant more often a story about immoral people. Second, that with us realism is always associated with some subtle view of morals; with them realism was always associated with some simple view of morals. The end of Bill Sikes exactly in the way that the law would have killed him—this is a Hogarthian incident; it carries on that tradition of startling and shocking platitude.

All this element in the book was a sincere thing in the author, but none the less it came from old soils, from the graveyard and the gallows, and the lane where the ghost walked. Dickens was always attracted to such things, and (as Forster says with inimitable simplicity) "but for his strong sense might have fallen into the follies of spiritualism." As a matter of fact, like most of the men of strong sense in his tradition, Dickens was left with a half belief in spirits which became in practice a belief in bad spirits. The great disadvantage of those who have too much strong sense to believe in supernaturalism is that they keep last the low and little forms of the supernatural, such as omens, curses, spectres, and retributions, but find a high and happy supernaturalism quite incredible. Thus the Puritans denied the sacraments, but went on burning witches. This shadow does rest, to some extent, upon the rational English writers like Dickens; supernaturalism was dying, but its ugliest roots died last. Dickens would have found it easier to believe in a ghost than in a vision of the

Virgin with angels. There, for good or evil, however, was the root of the old *diablerie* in Dickens, and there it is in *Oliver Twist.* But this was only the first of the new Dickens elements, which must have surprised those Dickensians who eagerly bought his second book. The second of the new Dickens elements is equally indisputable and separate. It swelled afterwards to enormous proportions in Dickens's work; but it really has its rise here. Again, as in the case of the element of *diablerie,* it would be possible to make technical exceptions in favour of *Pickwick.* Just as there were quite inappropriate scraps of the gruesome element in *Pickwick,* so there are quite inappropriate allusions to this other topic in *Pickwick.* But nobody by merely reading *Pickwick* would even remember this topic; no one by merely reading *Pickwick* would know what this topic is; this third great subject of Dickens; this second great subject of the Dickens of *Oliver Twist.*

This subject is social oppression. It is surely fair to say that no one could have gathered from *Pickwick* how this question boiled in the blood of the author of *Pickwick.* There are, indeed, passages, particularly in connection with Mr. Pickwick in the debtor's prison, which prove to us, looking back on a whole public career, that Dickens had been from the beginning bitter and inquisitive about the problem of our civilisation. No one could have imagined at the time that this bitterness ran in an unbroken river under all the surges of that superb gaiety and exuberance. With *Oliver Twist* this sterner side of Dickens was suddenly revealed. For the very first pages of *Oliver Twist* are stern even when they are funny. They amuse, but they cannot be enjoyed, as can the passages about the follies of Mr. Snodgrass or the humiliations of Mr. Winkle. The difference between the old easy humour and this new harsh humour is a difference not of degree but of kind. Dickens makes game of Mr. Bumble because he wants to kill Mr. Bumble; he made game of Mr. Winkle because he wanted him to live for ever. Dickens has taken the sword in hand; against what is he declaring war?

It is just here that the greatness of Dickens comes in; it is just here that the difference lies between the pedant and the poet. Dickens enters the social and political war, and the first stroke he deals is not only significant but even startling. Fully to see this we must appreciate the national situation. It was an age of reform, and even of radical reform; the world was full of radicals and reformers; but only too many of them took the line of attacking everything and anything that was opposed to some particular theory among the many political theories that possessed the end of the eighteenth century. Some had so much perfected the perfect theory of republicanism that they almost lay awake at night because Queen Victoria had a crown on her head. Others were so certain that mankind had hitherto been merely strangled in the bonds of the State that they saw truth only in the destruction of tariffs or of by-laws. The greater part of that generation held that clearness, economy, and a hard common-sense, would soon destroy the errors that had been erected by the superstitions and sentimentalities of the past. In pursuance of this idea many of the new men of the new century, quite confident that they were invigorating the new age, sought to destroy the old sentimental clericalism, the old senti-

mental feudalism, the old-world belief in priests, the old-world belief in patrons, and among other things the old-world belief in beggars. They sought among other things to clear away the old visionary kindliness on the subject of vagrants. Hence those reformers enacted not only a new reform bill but also a new poor law. In creating many other modern things they created the modern workhouse, and when Dickens came out to fight it was the first thing that he broke with his battle-axe.

This is where Dickens's social revolt is of more value than mere politics and avoids the vulgarity of the novel with a purpose. His revolt is not a revolt of the commercialist against the fedualist, of the Nonconformist against the Churchman, of the Free-trader against the Protectionist, of the Liberal against the Tory. If he were among us now his revolt would not be the revolt of the Socialist against the Individualist, or of the Anarchist against the Socialist. His revolt was simply and solely the eternal revolt; it was the revolt of the weak against the strong. He did not dislike this or that argument for oppression; he disliked oppression. He disliked a certain look on the face of a man when he looks down on another man. And that look on the face is, indeed, the only thing in the world that we have really to fight between here and the fires of Hell. That which pedants of that time and this time would have called the sentimentalism of Dickens was really simply the detached sanity of Dickens. He cared nothing for the fugitive explanations of the Constitutional Conservatives; he cared nothing for the fugitive explanations of the Manchester School. He would have cared quite as little for the fugitive explanations of the Fabian Society or of the modern scientific Socialist. He saw that under many forms there was one fact, the tyranny of man over man; and he struck at it when he saw it, whether it was old or new. When he found that footmen and rustics were too much afraid of Sir Leicester Dedlock, he attacked Sir Leicester Dedlock; he did not care whether Sir Leicester Dedlock said he was attacking England or whether Mr. Rouncewell, the Ironmaster, said he was attacking an effete oligarchy. In that case he pleased Mr. Rouncewell, the Ironmaster, and displeased Sir Leicester Dedlock, the Aristocrat. But when he found that Mr. Rouncewell's workmen were much too frightened of Mr. Rouncewell, then he displeased Mr. Rouncewell in turn; he displeased Mr. Rouncewell very much by calling him Mr. Bounderby. When he imagined himself to be fighting old laws he gave a sort of vague and general approval to new laws. But when he came to the new laws they had a bad time. When Dickens found that after a hundred economic arguments and granting a hundred economic considerations, the fact remained that paupers in modern workhouses were much too afraid of the beadle, just as vassals in ancient castles were much too afraid of the Dedlocks, then he struck suddenly and at once. This is what makes the opening chapters of *Oliver Twist* so curious and important. The very fact of Dickens's distance from, and independence of, the elaborate financial arguments of his time, makes more definite and dazzling his sudden assertion that he sees the old human tyranny in front of him as plain as the sun at noonday. Dickens attacks the modern workhouse with a sort of inspired simplicity as of a boy in a fairy tale who had wandered about, sword in hand, looking for ogres and who had found an indisputable ogre. All the other people of his time are attacking things because they are bad economics or because they are bad politics, or because they are bad science; he alone is attacking things because they are bad. All the others are Radicals with a large R; he alone is radical with a small one. He encounters evil with that beautiful surprise which, as it is the beginning of all real pleasure, is also the beginning of all righteous indignation. He enters the workhouse just as Oliver Twist enters it, as a little child.

This is the real power and pathos of that celebrated passage in the book which has passed into a proverb; but which has not lost its terrible humour even in being hackneyed. I mean, of course, the everlasting quotation about Oliver Twist asking for more. The real poignancy that there is in this idea is a very good study in that strong school of social criticism which Dickens represented. A modern realist describing the dreary workhouse would have made all the children utterly crushed, not daring to speak at all, not expecting anything, not hoping anything, past all possibility of affording even an ironical contrast or a protest of despair. A modern, in short, would have made all the boys in the workhouse pathetic by making them all pessimists. But Oliver Twist is not pathetic because he is a pessimist. Oliver Twist is pathetic because he is an optimist. The whole tragedy of that incident is in the fact that he does expect the universe to be kind to him, that he does believe that he is living in a just world. He comes before the Guardians as the ragged peasants of the French Revolution came before the Kings and Parliaments of Europe. That is to say, he comes, indeed, with gloomy experiences, but he comes with a happy philosophy. He knows that there are wrongs of man to be reviled; but he believes also that there are rights of man to be demanded. It has often been remarked as a singular fact that the French poor, who stand in historic tradition as typical of all the desperate men who have dragged down tyranny, were, as a matter of fact, by no means worse off than the poor of many other European countries before the Revolution. The truth is that the French were tragic because they were better off. The others had known the sorrowful experiences; but they alone had known the splendid expectation and the original claims. It was just here that Dickens was so true a child of them and of that happy theory so bitterly applied. They were the one oppressed people that simply asked for justice; they were the one Parish Boy who innocently asked for more. (pp. 38-49)

> *G. K. Chesterton, in his* Appreciations and Criticisms of the Works of Charles Dickens, *1911. Reprint by Kennikat Press, 1966, 243 p.*

Humphry House (essay date 1949)

[*A respected English scholar and lecturer, House is best known for his seminal work of Dickens criticism,* The Dickens World *(1941). In the following essay, originally published as an introduction to the 1949 Oxford edition of* Oliver Twist, *House comments on the textual history of the novel as well as the work's significance as social criticism.*]

Dickens began *Oliver Twist* as a serial in *Bentley's Miscellany,* of which he had just become editor, in February 1837. He was a young man of twenty-five, full of confidence and energy, who had suddenly found himself famous and was very pleased about it. *Pickwick* was not yet even finished; but, so far from trying to repeat his success as a popular humorist, he began "The Parish Boy's Progress". Some of his public, wanting more Pickwicks, protested; but they still read. Dickens, trained as a journalist, responded most readily to an outside stimulus; he breathed the air and smelt what was wanted. The declared subject was intensely topical and, by chance, the course of events made it more so as the publication proceeded. The controversies, alarms, hardships, and bitternesses which attended the introduction of the new Poor Law in 1834 may now seem remote; but *Oliver Twist* cannot be fully understood without remembering that it was planned and begun in an atmosphere of heightened public interest and of anxiety which deepened as the story ran.

It was Dickens's first attempt at a novel proper. The sequence of the external events which befall Oliver and form the framework of the book, though improbable, is at least straightforward, organised, and fairly well proportioned; but all the subordinate matter designed to explain and account for these events is at once complicated and careless. It has often been remarked that many features of the plot have a strong likeness to the melodrama of the time. Many conundrums are solved "off", and are then expounded to the audience in hurried, uneasy dialogue. The coincidence by which Oliver is made to break into the home of his unknown aunt Rose is not more startling than that, for instance, by which Jane Eyre, exhausted and starving, collapses on the doorstep of her cousins. Such things were then part of the idiom of storytelling. But in *Oliver* the disproportion and lack of continuity or development, in many subordinate parts of the story, are not even in that way idiomatic. The past history of the Leefords and their connection with Mr Brownlow and the Maylies is treated almost contemptuously. Monks is at first a most promising villain and appears in an air of genuine mystery and terror; but he collapses in ridiculous ruin, as if his creator had lost interest or not given himself time to do better—there may be something in both these explanations.

Dickens was in fact doing more work than even he could altogether cope with. The last number of *Pickwick* did not come out till November 1837, when *Oliver* had already been running for ten months: the first monthly part of *Nicholas Nickleby* appeared in April 1838 when *Oliver* was still a long way from being finished. Simultaneously, Dickens was editing the *Miscellany* and contributing occasional papers of his own. On top of this he took on the editing of Egerton Wilks's *Memoirs of Grimaldi* which needed much rearrangement and a good deal of rewriting. Such furious work was characteristic of his temperament. He plainly could give himself little leisure for thought; and cool thinking was no part of his method. Under pressure he speeded things up rather than postponed them. The story of *Oliver* was in fact finished and published in three volumes in November 1838, before the serial publication was complete.

He was then living at 48 Doughty Street, and his brother-in-law, Henry Burnett, described an evening there:

> One night in Doughty Street, Mrs Charles Dickens, my wife and myself were sitting round the fire, cosily enjoying a chat, when Dickens, for some purpose, came suddenly from his study into the room. "What, you here!" he exclaimed; "I'll bring down my work." It was his monthly portion of *Oliver Twist* for *Bentley's*. In a few minutes he returned, manuscript in hand, and while he was pleasantly discoursing he employed himself in carrying to a corner of the room a little table, at which he seated himself and recommenced his writing. We, at his bidding, went on talking our "little nothings",—he, every now and then (the feather of his pen still moving rapidly from side to side), put in a cheerful interlude. It was interesting to watch, upon the sly, the mind and the muscles working (or, if you please, *playing*) in company, as new thoughts were being dropped upon the paper. And to note the working brow, the set of mouth, with the tongue tightly pressed against the closed lips, as was his habit.

And Forster records that he "never knew him to work so frequently after dinner, or to such late hours (a practice he afterwards abhorred), as during the final months of this task".

On top of this appalling pressure of work the book was interrupted by the sudden death of Dickens's sister-in-law, Mary Hogarth, a girl of seventeen who lived with him and his wife. Dickens had for her an intense romantic affection; she died in his arms. He was so prostrate with grief that he could not work, and missed one monthly instalment of *Pickwick* and one of *Oliver Twist.* The character of Rose Maylie became an idealised portrait of Mary, and Dickens externalised his sorrow in Rose's otherwise irrelevant illness, only at the last minute reprieving her from death.

The unity of the book derives from impulse and from the energy of its imagination, not from its construction.

Superficially the impulse would appear mainly didactic and moral; and it was this aspect of the story that Dickens himself emphasised in the Preface which he first wrote for the edition of 1841. In that Preface he concentrated on his portraiture of thieves and murderers and prostitutes "as they really are, for ever skulking uneasily through the dirtiest paths of life, with the great, black, ghastly gallows closing up their prospect". He suggested that such realism in itself would perform a "service to society". He was then answering critics, like Richard Ford in the *Quarterly Review;* who said "we object *in toto* to the staple of *Oliver Twist*—a series of representations which must familiarize the rising generation with the haunts, deeds, language, and characters of the very dregs of the community. . . . It is a hazardous experiment to exhibit to the young these enormities, even on the Helot principle of inspiring disgust."

Dickens's answer was, in effect, a plea for broadening the whole scope of prose fiction, for the abandonment of false attitudes. Low life and criminal life exist, he argues, and nothing but a healthier frame of mind can follow from the knowledge of them. The technique and tone of what came to be called realism vary from generation to generation; speech tabus are inconstant; even the forms in which moral purpose is expressed are largely a matter of fashion. Allowing for such changes in custom, we must recognise in *Oliver,* besides its own inherent qualities, a novel which permanently affected the range, status, and potentialities of fiction. Even Ford admitted as much when he wrote:

> Life in London, as revealed in the pages of Boz, opens a new world to thousands bred and born in the same city, whose palaces overshadow their cellars—for the one half of mankind lives without knowing how the other half dies: in fact, the regions about Saffron Hill are less known to our great world than the Oxford Tracts; the inhabitants are still less.

The "revelations" in the novel were not in themselves by any means new: Dickens was not in that way a pioneer: he used material that was fairly well known, and ready to hand. The Saffron Hill district was notorious, among those who were inquisitive or needed to know, as the haunt of pickpockets and thieves: the two eldest Trollope boys, for instance, went there and found that

> Saffron Hill was a world of pocket-handkerchiefs. From every window and on lines stretched across the narrow street they fluttered in all the colours of the rainbow, and of all sizes and qualities. The whole lane was a long vista of pennon-like pocket-handkerchiefs!

The appalling filth of the slums in that area had been familiar in the cholera epidemic of 1832. The Jew fence was not merely a London character: he was known all over the country:

> A Jew seldom thieves, but is worse than a thief; he encourages others to thieve. In every town there is a Jew, either resident or tramping; sure to be a Jew within forty-eight hours in the town, somehow or other. If a robbery is effected, the property is hid till a Jew is found, and a bargain is then made ["Report of the Society for the Suppression of Mendicity," *Quarterly Review* (LXIV)].

It was also common knowledge that young recruits for gangs of thieves were most commonly enticed by girls of the Nancy type, who haunted lodging-houses and pubs like The Three Cripples. In his knowledge of such things Dickens was by no means unique; but using it in a novel, with all the heightened interest of a vivid story, he brought it home to the drawing-rooms and studies and boudoirs where ignorance, blissful and delicate, might be touched. In *The Newcomes* Thackeray made Lady Walham take *Oliver Twist* secretively to her bedroom.

Some vague stirring in the intelligence or conscience was indeed all that the novel could be expected to achieve; for a serious, considered moral lesson is very hard to find. If the purpose were to show that the starvation and cruel ill-treatment of children in baby-farms and workhouses produced ghastly effects on their characters and in society, then Oliver should have turned out a monster or a wretch, a boy who did very well at Fagin's school. Instead of this he remained always a paragon of sweet gratitude and the tenderest right feeling: at school he was distinguished for invincible greenness and showed no skill or even promise in bringing back fogles and tickers. When it has finally been disclosed that Oliver's parents were an unhappy gentleman of means and the daughter of a naval officer, are we to conclude that Dickens's main lesson was that a good heredity can overcome anything, and that in some cases environment counts for nothing at all? He probably never even asked himself the question in that form; from his other work—more perhaps from his journalism and speeches than from his novels—we know that all his emphasis was on the physical environment generally; but Oliver and Nancy teach the opposite; it was a dilemma he never fully faced and certainly never solved.

But Dickens's most revealing comment on *Oliver* was not in his Preface. For four years in the prime of his life he practically abandoned writing, gave rein to his exhibitionism, his histrionic and mesmeric powers, and poured his prodigious energies into public readings from his own works. The effect was that of a complete, competent, highly emotional, theatrical performance. As time went on he developed an increasing desire to read "The Murder of Nancy" from *Oliver Twist*. "I have no doubt", he wrote, "that I could perfectly petrify an audience by carrying out the notion I have of the way of rendering it." He had known for thirty years that the whole episode was charged with emotional dynamite; for he had reported to Forster just after he had finished writing it: "Hard at work still. Nancy is no more. I showed what I have done to Kate last night, who was in an unspeakable '*state*': from which and my own impression I augur well."

He overrode all objections and began the public readings of the "Murder" early in 1869. At Clifton in January he gave "by far the best murder yet done", and wrote of the performance: "We had a contagion of fainting. And yet the place was not hot. I should think we had from a dozen to twenty ladies borne out, stiff and rigid, at various times!" At Cheltenham old Macready said the murder was "two Macbeths". Milling crowds, more or less hysterical, were common. The performance got such a hold on Dickens that he gave the murder at three readings out of four, and sometimes four nights in a single week. His doctors noticed that, though his pulse rose with all the public readings, it rose far higher—dangerously high—when he read the "Murder". This was in fact a main cause of his death, and during the period of obsessive passion for this reading he said he walked the streets as if he himself were wanted by the police.

How utterly remote are these scenes and this state of mind from the earnest moralities of the Preface! To understand the conjunction of such different moods and qualities in a single man is the beginning of serious criticism of Dickens. The theme of murder, and still more of the murderer being hunted and haunted after his crime, treated not as a detective story, but as a statement of human behaviour, recurs several times in his major work. Both Sikes and Jonas Chuzzlewit are transfigured by the act of murder.

The psychological condition of a rebel-reformer is in many ways similar to that of a criminal, and may have the same origins. A feeling of being outside the ordinary organisation of group life; a feeling of being an outcast, a misfit or a victim of circumstance; a feeling of bitter loneliness, isolation, ostracism or irrevocable disgrace—any one or any combination of such feelings may turn a man against organised society, and his opposition may express itself in what is technically crime or what is technically politics: treason, sedition, and armed rebellion manage to be both. Dickens's childhood had been such that all these feelings, at different times in different degrees, had been his: he knew no security and no tenderness: the family home was for a time the Marshalsea prison, and for six months Dickens himself was a wretched drudge in a blacking-factory. These two experiences, and others similar, lie behind the loneliness, disgrace and outlawry which pervade all his novels. These were always his leading psychological themes. *Oliver Twist* reveals them in an early stage, not fully developed, certainly not analysed, but very clear. Oliver himself is so much the mere embodiment of the idea of a lonely ill-used child that he is scarcely granted character enough to be anything else. Noah Claypole is a second, and far more convincing, example of what may happen to a boy branded by society. The workhouse is merely the extreme form of the debtors' prison. The Fagin-Sikes group are both outlaws and social outcasts: it is curious to find even Swinburne, whose panegyric on Dickens is not generally remarkable for social or psychological insight, calling Fagin and Sikes "victims of circumstance and society".

It is not merely true that Fagin, Sikes, Nancy, and even the Dodger, are treated with more intelligence and interest in the novel than any other characters; they are also treated, in the deepest sense, with more sympathy. Dickens is prepared to take infinite pains to follow the working of their minds, to clarify their policies and motives, to give their personalities scope in the descriptions of all that they do or suffer. The absence of this sort of sympathy in the treatment of Monks, whose melodramatic and inefficient malignity is contemptuously devised to supply the mechanism of the tale, brings out the point by contrast. Fagin and Sikes are never despised, even though what they do is despicable. The cringing meanness of the one and the unmitigated coarse brutality of the other are treated with immense and serious respect: Dickens lives into these characters as they grow. At the crisis in the life of each there is no question of moralising or preaching: Dickens identifies himself with them; he himself is the lonely outcast capable of crime. Fagin in the dock, when "the court was paved, from floor to roof, with human faces", when "in no one face—not even among the women, of whom there were many there—could be read the faintest sympathy with himself", is a figure of the most terrifying loneliness; and the jumping of his mind from detail to detail—one man's clothes, another man's dinner, the broken spike—is the psychological counterpart of Sikes's haunted wandering in the country north of London. In Sikes the criminal impulse is cruder and more violent: but Dickens's understanding is not less. The atmosphere of horror is achieved just because of his fear that he might do exactly such a murder as Sikes did. During the famous readings he used to speak jokingly of giving way to his "murderous instincts"; but it was no joke.

The lasting impression left by this novel is one of macabre horror. For us there appears to be little connection between the mood and incidents of the later chapters, and those of the earlier. We begin to wonder whether perhaps, as the Fagin-Sikes themes took hold upon him, Dickens was liable to forget his sub-title, "The Parish Boy's Progress". But to an alert reader in 1837-9 the factual and emotional connection between the beginning and the end would have seemed far stronger: the mood of the book was topical.

The "philosophers", with blood of ice and hearts of iron, on whom Dickens pours his sarcasm in the early chapters, were the Malthusians and economists, whose theory of population underlay the new Poor Law of 1834. Their doctrine briefly was that, however much the general wealth of the country grew, there would always be a section of the population below subsistence level, because of an inevitable natural tendency of population to increase faster than the means of subsistence. Vice and misery were the two first checks on the multiplication of unwanted mouths; the only third possible check was moral or prudential restraint, which meant the prevention, by one means or another, of breeding in the poorest classes. All forms of dole, charity or relief to a man unable to maintain himself or his family were suspect, because they were a direct inducement to breed in idleness, and thus aided the dismal course of nature. If the preaching of thrift and continence failed, the only acceptable policy was to give relief in the most unattractive form, under conditions which made breeding impossible.

By the Act of 1834 the Parish remained the primary unit of administration, and relief depended on a parish "settlement". For Poor Law purposes parishes were formed into "Unions"; each Union had its Workhouse, and a Board of Guardians to administer relief. But, as far as possible, relief was to be given only in the "house". Conditions there were deliberately made hard: the diet was sparse; husbands were separated from wives; a special uniform was worn, and so on. The "Workhouse-test" was intended as a deterrent. Dickens does not discuss the rightness or wrongness of the basic theory, nor the evils of subsidising wages from the rates which its application was largely designed to cure. He directs his angry sarcasm only to some of the human consequences of what was done.

The original Poor Law Commissioners, on whose findings the Act was drafted, had quite rightly urged that different classes of pauper needed different treatment. The old, the infirm, the insane, the diseased, unable to earn their own living, were a charge upon the community of a different kind from the able-bodied unemployed or the "sturdy beggar". Children in particular, and orphan children most of all, were plainly in a separate category, and no workhouse-test could be held to apply to them. But, through inefficiencies and difficulties in the practical application of the Act, these proper distinctions did not generally lead to differences of treatment. The workhouse tended to remain the "general-mixed" institution which had been such a scandal in the earlier days; people of both sexes, of all ages, all physical and moral conditions, were herded indiscriminately together, and treated like recalcitrant idlers, all equally kept on low diet: the deterrent system, meant only for the able-bodied, in practice put the screw on all alike. The children obviously suffered worst.

Oliver was born in a workhouse of the old law; when he came back from Mrs Mann's, the new law had just come in and "the Board" had just been set up. Dickens seems to have imagined the actual workhouse building unaltered, for the new "Bastilles" were not built in a hurry; Bumble was probably meant to be a "parochial officer" taken over from the old system: in these respects Dickens was attacking abuses allowed to continue. But the low diet was the one outstanding typical feature of the new system. Dickens's "three meals of thin gruel a day, with an onion twice a week, and half a roll on Sundays" was a telling caricature of the Commissioners' recommended dietaries. To a modern reader, after the rationing of two wars, these dietaries do not, on paper, seem quite so terrible: but it is hard to say how they worked out in practice. Certainly they were very ill-balanced and dull. In the No. 1 Dietary for an able-bodied man, published in 1836, there was meat on only three days of a week, and 1 ½ pints of gruel every day. Women were to have less, and children over nine the same as women; children under nine were to be dieted "at discretion". Contemporary opinion can be judged by the fact that in March 1838 the Guardians of the Dudley Union presented a petition to the House of Lords complaining that the diets recommended by the Commissioners were not enough to feed the paupers: and then already half the country was laughing or weeping over Oliver, who "asked for more". It also happened that in the third year of the new law there was a very severe winter; in the fourth a trade depression; and that the fifth was a year of scarce food and high prices. With these causes of hardship the unpopularity of the law grew, and *Oliver Twist* appeared to be not merely topical but prophetic.

Through administrative muddles and false economy, through conflicts between the central and local authorities, through jealousy of the central power, and most of all through the impotent fears engendered by Malthusian orthodoxy, the condition of pauper children remained appalling for many years after *Oliver Twist* was written. Dickens did not forget the image of the Good Samaritan on Bumble's buttons. As a journalist and editor he published many articles on the subject, the gist of which was summed up in *Household Words* in 1850:

> Ought the misdeeds of the parents to be visited on their innocent children? Should pauper and outcast infants be neglected so as to become pests to Society . . . ? Common sense asks, does the State desire good citizens or bad?

Oliver Twist had been written in a period when the possibility of armed revolution was constantly before men's minds—there was in fact an abortive rising in 1839; and in that atmosphere the problems of the Poor Law had an urgency and horror which they lost in the relative security and peace of the mid-Victorian age. When Dickens came back to the book and gave the readings of the "Murder", he had thirty years of burning life and imagination behind him: the obsessive interest in violent crime, registered on his pulse, was linked in memory both to the early Chartists and the lynchings by Rebecca and her Daughters, and also to the terrors and rebelliousness of a lonely outcast child, of whom the wretched Oliver himself was but a very pale and ineffectual reflection. (pp. 190-200)

> *Humphry House, "An Introduction to 'Oliver Twist',"* in his *All in Due Time: The Collected Essays and Broadcast Talks of Humphry House,* Rupert Hart-Davis, 1955, pp. 190-200.

An excerpt from *Oliver Twist*

When the breakfast was cleared away, the merry old gentleman and the two boys played at a very curious and uncommon game, which was performed in this way. The merry old gentleman, placing a snuff-box in one pocket of his trousers, a note-case in the other, and a watch in his waistcoat pocket, with a guard-chain round his neck, and sticking a mock diamond pin in his shirt: buttoned his coat tight round him, and putting his spectacle-case and handkerchief in his pockets, trotted up and down the room with a stick, in imitation of the manner in which old gentlemen walk about the streets any hour in the day. Sometimes he stopped at the fire-place, and sometimes at the door, making believe that he was staring with all his might into shop-windows. At such times, he would look constantly round him, for fear of thieves, and would keep slapping all his pockets in turn, to see that he hadn't lost anything, in such a very funny and natural manner, that Oliver laughed till the tears ran down his face. All this time, the two boys followed him closely about: getting out of his sight, so nimbly, every time he turned round, that it was impossible to follow their motions. At last, the Dodger trod upon his toes, or ran upon his boot accidentally, while Charley Bates stumbled up against him behind; and in that one moment they took from him, with the most extraordinary rapidity, snuff-box, note-case, watch-guard, chain, shirt-pin, pocket-handkerchief, even the spectacle-case. If the old gentleman felt a hand in any one of his pockets, he cried out where it was; and then the game began all over again.

> *Charles Dickens, in his* The Adventures of Oliver Twist, *Chapman and Hall, 1910.*

Graham Greene   (essay date 1950)

[*Greene is considered one of the most important novelists in modern English literature and is also esteemed as a biographer and film and literature critic. In the following essay, originally published as an introduction to a 1950 edition of* Oliver Twist, *he rejects interpretations of the novel as social realism, contending that its strength lies in its "Manichaean" emphasis on darkness and evil.*]

A critic must try to avoid being a prisoner of his time, and if we are to appreciate *Oliver Twist* at its full value we must forget that long shelf-load of books, all the stifling importance of a great author, the scandals and the controversies of the private life; it would be well too if we could forget the Phiz and the Cruikshank illustrations that have frozen the excited, excitable world of Dickens into a hall of waxworks, where Mr Mantalini's whiskers have always

the same trim, where Mr Pickwick perpetually turns up the tails of his coat, and in the Chamber of Horrors Fagin crouches over an undying fire. His illustrators, brilliant craftsmen though they were, did Dickens a disservice, for no character any more will walk for the first time into our memory as we ourselves imagine him and *our* imagination after all has just as much claim to truth as Cruikshank's.

Nevertheless the effort to go back is well worth while. The journey is only a little more than a hundred years long, and at the other end of the road is a young author whose sole claim to renown in 1836 had been the publication of some journalistic sketches and a number of comic operettas: *The Strange Gentleman, The Village Coquette, Is She His Wife?* I doubt whether any literary Cortez at that date would have yet stood them upon his shelves. Then suddenly with *The Pickwick Papers* came popularity and fame. Fame falls like a dead hand on an author's shoulder, and it is well for him when it falls only in later life. How many in Dickens's place would have withstood what James called 'the great corrupting contact of the public', the popularity founded, as it almost always is, on the weakness and not the strength of an author?

The young Dickens, at the age of twenty-five, had hit on a mine that paid him a tremendous dividend. Fielding and Smollett, tidied and refined for the new industrial bourgeoisie, had both salted it; Goldsmith had contributed sentimentality and Monk Lewis horror. The book was enormous, shapeless, familiar (that important recipe for popularity). What Henry James wrote of a long-forgotten French critic applies well to the young Dickens: 'He is homely, familiar and colloquial; he leans his elbows on his desk and does up his weekly budget into a parcel the reverse of compact. You can fancy him a grocer retailing tapioca and hominy full weight for the price; his style seems a sort of integument of brown paper.'

This is, of course, unfair to *The Pickwick Papers.* The driest critic could not have quite blinkered his eyes to those sudden wide illuminations of comic genius that flap across the waste of words like sheet lightning, but could he have foreseen the second novel, not a repetition of this great loose popular holdall, but a short melodrama, tight in construction, almost entirely lacking in broad comedy, and possessing only the sad twisted humour of the orphan's asylum?

> "You'll make your fortune, Mr Sowerberry," said the beadle, as he thrust his thumb and forefinger into the proffered snuff-box of the undertaker: which was an ingenious little model of a patent coffin.

Such a development was as inconceivable as the gradual transformation of that thick boggy prose into the delicate and exact poetic cadences, the music of memory, that so influenced Proust.

We are too inclined to take Dickens as a whole and to treat his juvenilia with the same kindness or harshness as his later work. *Oliver Twist* is still juvenilia—magnificent juvenilia: it is the first step on the road that led from *Pickwick* to *Great Expectations,* and we condone the faults of taste in the early book the more readily if we recognize the distance Dickens had to travel. These two typical didactic passages can act as the first two milestones at the opening of the journey, the first from *Pickwick,* the second from *Oliver Twist.*

> And numerous indeed are the hearts to which Christmas brings a brief season of happiness and enjoyment. How many families, whose members have been dispersed and scattered far and wide, in the restless struggles of life, are then reunited, and meet once again in that happy state of companionship and mutual goodwill, which is a source of such pure and unalloyed delight, and one so incompatible with the cares and sorrows of the world, that the religious belief of the most civilized nations, and the rude traditions of the roughest savages, alike number it among the first joys of a future condition of existence, provided for the blest and happy.

> The boy stirred and smiled in his sleep, as though these marks of pity and compassion had awakened some pleasant dream of a love and affection he had never known. Thus, a strain of gentle music, or the rippling of water in a silent place, or the odour of a flower, or the mention of a familiar word, will sometimes call up sudden dim remembrances of scenes that never were, in this life; which vanish like a breath; which some brief memory of a happier existence, long gone by, would seem to have awakened; which no voluntary exertion of the mind can ever recall.

The first is certainly brown paper: what it wraps has been chosen by the grocer to suit his clients' tastes, but cannot we detect already in the second passage the tone of Dickens's secret prose, that sense of a mind speaking to itself with no one there to listen, as we find it in *Great Expectations*?

> It was fine summer weather again, and, as I walked along, the times when I was a little helpless creature, and my sister did not spare me, vividly returned. But they returned with a gentle tone upon them that softened even the edge of Tickler. For now, the very breath of the beans and clover whispered to my heart that the day must come when it would be well for my memory that others walking in the sunshine should be softened as they thought of me.

It is a mistake to think of *Oliver Twist* as a realistic story: only late in his career did Dickens learn to write realistically of human beings; at the beginning he invented life and we no more believe in the temporal existence of Fagin or Bill Sikes than we believe in the existence of that Giant whom Jack slew as he bellowed his Fee Fi Fo Fum. There were real Fagins and Bill Sikes and real Bumbles in the England of his day, but he had not drawn them, as he was later to draw the convict Magwitch; these characters in *Oliver Twist* are simply parts of one huge invented scene, what Dickens in his own preface called 'the cold wet shelterless midnight streets of London'. How the phrase goes echoing on through the books of Dickens until we meet it again so many years later in 'the weary western streets of London on a cold dusty spring night' which were so melancholy to Pip. But Pip was to be as real as the weary streets, while Oliver was as unrealistic as the cold wet midnight of which he formed a part.

This is not to criticize the book so much as to describe it. For what an imagination this youth of twenty-six had that he could invent so monstrous and complete a legend! We are not lost with Oliver Twist round Saffron Hill: we are lost in the interstices of one young, angry, gloomy brain, and the oppressive images stand out along the track like the lit figures in a Ghost Train tunnel.

> Against the wall were ranged, in regular array, a long row of elm boards cut into the same shape, looking in the dim light, like high shouldered ghosts with their hands in their breeches pockets.

We have most of us seen those nineteenth-century prints where the bodies of naked women form the face of a character, the Diplomat, the Miser, and the like. So the crouching figure of Fagin seems to form the mouth, Sikes with his bludgeon the jutting features, and the sad lost Oliver the eyes of one man as lost as Oliver.

Chesterton, in a fine imaginative passage, has described the mystery behind Dickens's plots, the sense that even the author was unaware of what was really going on, so that when the explanations come and we reach, huddled into the last pages of *Oliver Twist,* a naked complex narrative of illegitimacy and burnt wills and destroyed evidence, we simply do not believe. 'The secrecy is sensational; the secret is tame. The surface of the thing seems more awful than the core of it. It seems almost as if these grisly figures, Mrs Chadband and Mrs Clennam, Miss Havisham and Miss Flite, Nemo and Sally Brass, were keeping something back from the author as well as from the reader. When the book closes we do not know their real secret. They soothed the optimistic Dickens with something less terrible than the truth.'

What strikes the attention most in this closed Fagin universe are the different levels of unreality. If, as one is inclined to believe, the creative writer perceives his world once and for all in childhood and adolescence, and his whole career is an effort to illustrate his private world in terms of the great public world we all share, we can understand why Fagin and Sikes in their most extreme exaggerations move us more than the benevolence of Mr Brownlow or the sweetness of Mrs Maylie—they touch with fear as the others never really touch with love. It was not that the unhappy child, with his hurt pride and his sense of hopeless insecurity, had not encountered human goodness—he had simply failed to recognize it in those streets between Gadshill and Hungerford Market which had been as narrowly enclosed as Oliver Twist's. When Dickens at this early period tried to describe goodness he seems to have remembered the small stationers' shops on the way to the blacking factory with their coloured paper scraps of angels and virgins, or perhaps the face of some old gentleman who had spoken kindly to him outside Warren's factory. He had swum up towards goodness from the deepest world of his experience, and on this shallow level the conscious brain has taken a hand, trying to construct characters to represent virtue and, because his age demanded it, triumphant virtue, but all he can produce are

The artful Dodger introduces Oliver to Fagin. Illustration by George Cruikshank.

powdered wigs and gleaming spectacles and a lot of bustle with bowls of broth and a pale angelic face. Compare the way in which we first meet evil with his introduction of goodness.

> The walls and ceiling of the room were perfectly black with age and dirt. There was a deal table before the fire: upon which were a candle, stuck in a ginger-beer bottle, two or three pewter pots, a loaf and butter, and a plate. In a frying pan, which was on the fire, and which was secured to the mantel-shelf by a string, some sausages were cooking; and standing over them, with a toasting-fork in his hand, was a very old shrivelled Jew, whose villainous-looking and repulsive face was obscured by a quantity of matted red hair. He was dressed in a greasy flannel gown, with his throat bare . . . "This is him, Fagin," said Jack Dawkins: "my friend Oliver Twist." The Jew grinned; and, making a low obeisance to Oliver, took him by the hand, and hoped he should have the honour of his intimate acquaintance.

Fagin has always about him this quality of darkness and nightmare. He never appears on the daylight streets. Even when we see him last in the condemned cell, it is in the hours before the dawn. In the Fagin darkness Dickens's hand seldom fumbles. Hear him turning the screw of horror when Nancy speaks of the thoughts of death that have haunted her:

> "Imagination," said the gentleman, soothing her.
>
> "No imagination," replied the girl in a hoarse voice. "I'll swear I saw 'coffin' written in every

page of the book in large black letters,—aye, and they carried one close to me, in the streets to-night."

> "There is nothing unusual in that," said the gentleman. "They have passed me often."

> "Real ones," rejoined the girl. "This was not."

Now turn to the daylight world and our first sight of Rose:

> The younger lady was in the lovely bloom and springtime of womanhood; at that age, when, if ever angels be for God's good purposes enthroned in mortal forms, they may be, without impiety, supposed to abide in such as hers. She was not past seventeen. Cast in so slight and exquisite a mould; so mild and gentle; so pure and beautiful; that earth seemed not her element, nor its rough creatures her fit companions.

Or Mr Brownlow as he first appeared to Oliver:

> Now, the old gentleman came in as brisk as need be; but he had no sooner raised his spectacles on his forehead, and thrust his hands behind the skirts of his dressing-gown to take a good long look at Oliver, than his countenance underwent a very great variety of odd contortions . . . The fact is, if the truth must be told, that Mr Brownlow's heart, being large enough for any six ordinary old gentlemen of humane disposition, forced a supply of tears into his eyes by some hydraulic process which we are not sufficiently philosophical to be in a condition to explain.

How can we really believe that these inadequate ghosts of goodness can triumph over Fagin, Monks, and Sikes? And the answer, of course, is that they never could have triumphed without the elaborate machinery of the plot disclosed in the last pages. This world of Dickens is a world without God; and as a substitute for the power and the glory of the omnipotent and omniscient are a few sentimental references to heaven, angels, the sweet faces of the dead, and Oliver saying, 'Heaven is a long way off, and they are too happy there to come down to the bedside of a poor boy.' In this Manichaean world we can believe in evil-doing, but goodness wilts into philanthropy, kindness, and those strange vague sicknesses into which Dickens's young women so frequently fall and which seem in his eyes a kind of badge of virtue, as though there were a merit in death.

But how instinctively Dickens's genius recognized the flaw and made a virtue out of it. We cannot believe in the power of Mr Brownlow, but nor did Dickens, and from his inability to believe in his own good character springs the real tension of his novel. The boy Oliver may not lodge in our brain like David Copperfield, and though many of Mr Bumble's phrases have become and deserve to have become familiar quotations we can feel he was manufactured: he never breathes like Mr Dorrit; yet Oliver's predicament, the nightmare fight between the darkness, where the demons walk, and the sunlight, where ineffective goodness makes its last stand in a condemned world, will remain part of our imaginations forever. We read of the defeat of Monks, and of Fagin screaming in the condemned cell, and of Sikes dangling from his self-made noose, but we don't believe. We have witnessed Oliver's temporary escapes too often and his inevitable recapture: *there* is the truth and the creative experience. We know that when Oliver leaves Mr Brownlow's house to walk a few hundred yards to the bookseller, his friends will wait in vain for his return. All London outside the quiet shady street in Pentonville belongs to his pursuers; and when he escapes again into the house of Mrs Maylie in the fields beyond Shepperton, we know his security is false. The seasons may pass, but safety depends not on time but on daylight. As children we all knew that: how all day we could forget the dark and the journey to bed. It is with a sense of relief that at last in twilight we see the faces of the Jew and Monks peer into the cottage window between the sprays of jessamine. At that moment we realize how the whole world, and not London only, belongs to these two after dark. Dickens, dealing out his happy endings and his unreal retributions, can never ruin the validity and dignity of that moment. 'They had recognized him, and he them; and their look was as firmly impressed upon his memory, as if it had been deeply carved in stone, and set before him from his birth.'

'From his birth'—Dickens may have intended that phrase to refer to the complicated imbroglios of the plot that lie outside the novel, 'something less terrible than the truth'. As for the truth, is it too fantastic to imagine that in this novel, as in many of his later books, creeps in, unrecognized by the author, the eternal and alluring taint of the Manichee, with its simple and terrible explanation of our plight, how the world was made by Satan and not by God, lulling us with the music of despair? (pp. 101-10)

> *Graham Greene, "The Young Dickens," in his* Collected Essays, *The Bodley Head, 1969, pp. 101-10.*

V. S. Pritchett   (essay date 1950)

[*Pritchett is a highly esteemed English novelist, short story writer, and critic. A twentieth-century successor to such early nineteenth-century commentators as William Hazlitt and Charles Lamb, Pritchett employs much the same critical method: his own experience, judgment, and sense of literary art are emphasized, rather than a codified critical doctrine derived from a school of psychological or philosophical speculation. In the following essay, written in 1950 as a response to Graham Greene's introductory assessment of* Oliver Twist, *Pritchett rejects Greene's suggestion that the novel bears the influence of Manichaeism, noting instead its emphasis on virtue and justice.*]

Oliver Twist is the second novel of Charles Dickens. It was begun before *Pickwick* was finished when he was twenty-six and in the full conceit and harassing of sudden fame; and *Barnaby Rudge* was started before he got Nancy murdered and before Bill Sikes slipped by accident off the wall on Jacob's Island into his own noose. It is a novel speckled with good London observation, but the critics agree that the book which gave the word Bumbledom to the language is a gloomy and inferior work, stretched out on an incredible plot, blatant with false characters and false speech and wrecked by that stageyness

which Dickens was never long to resist. The story is a film scenario full of tears and 'ham', an efficacious splurge of Cockney self-pity. On the other hand, the reader must protest that all this is no drawback to his excitement. The popular thriller is generally based on the abstraction of sinister human wishes from the common reality of life; and, willingly suspending disbelief, we can eagerly accept Fagin, even Bill Sikes and Mr Brownlow, even Nancy and Rose Maylie, as permitted fantasies. Is it because of the hypnotic fame of Dickens or because he is completely responsive to the popular taste for uninspected myth, that all his characters stay in the mind? Only the neurotic Monks and the creaking, sceptical Grimwig, have one false foot in the world of our experience.

A new edition of *Oliver Twist* has the advantage of a really brilliant, melancholy and subtle appreciation by Mr Graham Greene, himself a thorough initiate in the art of writing thrillers. It is one of those uncommon prefaces that expertly test the technical merits of a book and enlarge its suggestion. Before turning to his main points, there are two obvious yet easily forgotten virtues in *Oliver Twist* which put what might have been a total failure on its feet. For there is no doubt that *Oliver Twist* 'comes off'. In the first place it is a literary novel, nourished by Dickens's early reading. The echoes from Monk Lewis, the touches from *Jonathan Wild* in the framing of the portraits of Mr Bumble or the Artful Dodger, the preface which curiously boasts that at last we are to be given real criminals—except in the matter of bad language—and not romantic ones, are all touching and agreeable glances from a spruce young author towards his tradition. (And, as Mr Greene shows, we certainly get real thieves' kitchens and the sour poverty of criminal life, the background but not the foreground.) In the second place, the book is given a kind of authority by the frank copying of Fielding's mock heroic and disquisitional moralising. By this Fielding displayed the assurance of his sensible morality, and it is true that Dickens debases the manner by turning it into something journalistic, sprightly and even facetious; nevertheless, the manner enabled him to assume a central place in the tale, from which he could exploit, without confusion, the variety of its moods.

It was Edmund Wilson who first saw the biographical importance of the melodramatic and criminal episodes in Dickens's work. They are for the most part the least successful as literature. They are commonly over-acted and, indeed, too much stress on these and the didactic side of Dickens, is likely to take us away from his greatness. It is all very well for modern critics to neglect the comic Dickens for there, as a writer, he was completely realised. On the other hand, the impurity of Dickens as a creator is an important fact; in his confusions and concealings, strange psychological shapes are disclosed. His relation was with the public which he bowed to and upon whose not always reputable feelings he played. Upon them, as upon an analyst, he enacted a transference. Mr Graham Greene's main point is, in a sense, an extension of Edmund Wilson's into the field of religion. He suggests the religious cast of Dickens's imagination:

> How can we really believe that these inadequate ghosts of goodness [Mr Brownlow and Rose

Maylie] can triumph over Fagin, Monks and Sikes? And the answer is, of course, that they never could have triumphed without the elaborate machinery of the plot disclosed in the last pages. The world of Dickens is a world without God; and as a substitute for the power and the glory of the omnipotent and omniscient are a few sentimental references to heaven, angels, the sweet faces of the dead, and Oliver saying, 'Heaven is a long way off, and they are too happy there to come down to the bedside of a poor boy!' In this Manichaean world we can believe in evil-doing but goodness melts into philanthropy and kindness. . . .

And Mr Greene ends with this paragraph:

> . . . Is it too fantastic to imagine that in this novel, as in many of his later books, creeps in, unrecognised by the author, the eternal and alluring taint of the Manichee, with its simple and terrible explanation of our plight, how the world was made by Satan and not by God, lulling us with the music of despair?

That *is* too fantastic, of course, as a description even of Dickens's demonic imagination, of his unconscious as distinct from his conscious, orthodox religion. The terror of *Oliver Twist* is the acted terror inherited from literature and married to personal hysteria. The Manichee is good theatre. But the suggestion is an interesting one and if we follow its lead, we must be struck by the flashes of contact between *Oliver Twist* and the Manichaean myth. The child of light is lost in the world of darkness—the terrors of childhood are the primitive terrors of the dark—from which the far-away Elect will save him. When he is saved, the end of the world of darkness is brought about—Nancy is murdered, Sikes and Fagin are hanged. We might grope farther along the strange tunnels of the Manichaean allegory and discover there a suggestion upon which the Freudian analyst of the tale of ghosts or terror will immediately pounce. These tales are now held to be artistic transpositions of the fear of castration and when one turns (as an ignorant reviewer so often must) to the authority of the *Encyclopaedia Britannica,* one indeed finds that the thriller writers have pious if tainted progenitors in the fourth century. In their belief 'primal man descends into the abyss and prevents the further increase of the generations of darkness by cutting off their roots.' What is notable (one reflects) is that the enormous preoccupation of Victorian literature for murderous melodrama—and we remember the horrifying success of Dickens in his public readings of murderous scenes—goes with an extreme sexual prudery in literature. Murder—as the saying is—is 'cleaner' than sex. We seem to see a violent age seeking a compensation for its losses.

Whether or not the imaginative world of *Oliver Twist* is without God in the Christian sense we must leave to the theologians; the interest of Mr Greene's suggestion is the inevitable implication that the emissaries of light, the Elect, are the middle classes. It is Mr Brownlow and Miss Maylie who come down, to the tune of the ineffable music of the Three Per Cents. Only by sitting at the throne of Grace could they face the abyss of darkness in which the industrial poor, the everlastingly guilty were damned and

lived waiting for their doom. Only by making Rose Maylie an angel could the existence of Nancy be assimilated; only by making kindness old-fashioned and respectable, could Sikes be faced as a modern, sullen and temperamental brute. It does not follow, as Mr Graham Greene suggests, that the evil represented is stronger than the good, in the imaginative effect; the balance between these cardboard unrealities is perfect and a thieves' kitchen always sounds more dramatic and 'strong' than a drawing-room. And so, too, on a more reputable plane: against the half-dreamed figures of Monks and Fagin at the window that seemed like the imprint of a primitive memory, must be placed those other half-waking intimations Oliver had of some happiness in a far-away past never known. What we are convinced of, even though by the long arm of coincidence, is the long arm of humanity and justice.

Oliver Twist is a literary novel. Magnificent juvenilia is Mr Graham Greene's just phrase. The plots of Dickens were to improve and one does not know whether to put down their tedious elaboration to Mr Chesterton's belief that they were an attempt to set out 'something less terrible than the truth'. That looks like a Chestertonian attempt to put down something more eccentric than a fact. Perhaps Dickens in his exhibitionism wanted to put down something *more* terrible than the truth. Either explanation sharply applies to the disastrous passion for plot general to the Victorian novel. It is a fact that Dickens had the greatest difficulty in inventing probabilities and that may be related to the fantastic turn of his mind.

All the main strains of his genius are crudely foreshadowed in *Oliver Twist.* There is the wonderful clean snap of scene and episode; nearly everything is 'realised'. Mr Greene has perceived one of those reflective passages, memory evoking or regarding its own act, which Proust admired, and there are occasional phrases—the absurd servant's face 'pale and *polite* with fear'—or touches of detail that show the hand of the master. We recall things like the wisp of human hair on Sikes's club, that sizzled for a second when he threw it in the fire; the notices in the country village warning vagrants to keep out. Sikes's speech is ludicrous—' "Wolves tear your throats," muttered Sikes'—but his death is wonderful; one remembers the boy at the window taken by surprise when the hanged body drops and shuts off his view and how he pushes it aside. The crude London scenes have the rattle of the streets in them; it is a novel of street journeys.

Mr Bumble's proposal of marriage and all the sour and tippling termagants which foretell Dickens's long gallery of patchy and disgruntled women, have the incalculable quality of nature. Dickens (and Forster supported him) believed Oliver to be real; and indeed he sometimes is. He is hardly the evacuee of our time; a hundred years had to pass before the happy English middle classes were to discover what a child from the industrial slums could be like. Oliver is simply 'one of Lord Shaftesbury's little victims'. But the misery and the fear of Oliver are very real, his leaning to virtue (now so unfashionable) profoundly convincing. Why should we complain if Vice is over-exposed and Virtue over-exalted; the convention has the authority of Hogarth, and belongs to the eighteenth century, the morality of pre-industrial England. Hence—we may be tempted to think—not the absence of God or the taint of the Manichee, but the author's lingering assumption that the belief in justice, the knowledge of retribution and of the passion of mercy are self-evident in human nature, and that a good dose of terror and a long tangled plot of ill-chance and malignance will bring them out. Dickens was not the first or the last novelist to find virtue more difficult to portray than the wish for it. (pp. 69-73)

V. S. Pritchett, "Oliver Twist," in his A Man of Letters: Selected Essays, *Random House, 1985, pp. 69-73.*

Arnold Kettle   (essay date 1951)

[*Kettle was an English educator, editor, and critic, as well as an influential member of Britain's Communist Party who wrote and edited numerous works on Communist history and theory. Regarded as one of Europe's foremost Marxist literary critics, Kettle is best known for his two-volume study* An Introduction to the English Novel. *In the following excerpt from the second edition of that work, he analyzes* Oliver Twist *as a symbolic struggle of the poor against the oppression of the bourgeois state.*]

In the twelfth chapter of *Oliver Twist,* Oliver, carried insensible by Mr Brownlow from the magistrate's court, wakes up to find himself in a comfortable bed:

> Weak, and thin, and pallid, he awoke at last from what seemed to have been a long and troubled dream. Feebly raising himself in the bed, with his head resting on his trembling arm, he looked anxiously round.
>
> 'What room is this? Where have I been brought to?' said Oliver. 'This is not the place I went to sleep in.'
>
> He uttered these words in a feeble voice, being very faint and weak, but they were overheard at once; for the curtain at the bed's head was hastily drawn back, and a motherly old lady, very neatly and precisely dressed, rose as she withdrew it from an armchair close by, in which she had been sitting at needlework.
>
> 'Hush, my dear,' said the old lady softly. 'You must be very quiet, or you will be ill again; and you have been very bad—as bad as bad could be, pretty nigh. Lie down again; there's a dear!' With these words, the old lady very gently placed Oliver's head upon the pillow, and, smoothing back his hair from his forehead, looked so kindly and lovingly in his face, that he could not help placing his little withered hand in hers, and drawing it round his neck.
>
> 'Save us!' said the old lady, with tears in her eyes, 'what a grateful little dear it is! Pretty creature! What would his mother feel if she had sat by him as I have, and could see him now?'

It is a central situation in the book—this emergence out of squalor into comfort and kindliness—and it is repeated later in the story when once again Oliver, after the robbery

in which he has been wounded, wakes to find himself cared for and defended by the Maylies. There is more than mere chance in the repetition and we meet here, indeed, a pattern recurring throughout Dickens's novels. It is worth while examining it more closely.

The first eleven chapters of *Oliver Twist* are an evocation of misery and horror. We have been drawn straight with the first sentence (of which workhouse is the key word) into a world of the most appalling poverty and ugliness, a world of brutality and violence in which life is cheap, suffering general and death welcome. That the evocation is crude, that it is marred by moments of false feeling and by a heavy-handed irony which weakens all it comments on, is not for the moment the consideration. By and large, the effect is of extraordinary power. . . . It is an effect which is, in the precise sense of a hackneyed word, unforgettable. The workhouse, the parochial baby-farm, Mr Sowerberry's shop, the funeral, the Artful Dodger, Fagin's lair: they have the haunting quality, but nothing of the unreality, of a nightmare. It is a curious comment on Victorian civilisation that this was considered suitable reading for children.

What is the secret of the power? Is it merely the objective existence of the horror, the fact that such things were, that strikes at our minds? Fairly obviously not or we should be moved in just the same way by a social history. There is a particularity about this world which is not the effect of even a well-documented history. It is not just any evocation of the life of the poor after the Industrial Revolution; when we read the Hammonds' *Town Labourer* or Engels's *Condition of the Working Class in England in 1844* our reaction may not be less profound than our reaction to *Oliver Twist,* but it is different, more generalised, less vivid, less intense.

The most obvious difference between *Oliver Twist* and a social history is, of course, that it deals with actual characters whose personalities we envisage, whose careers we follow, and whose feelings we share. But this difference is not, I think, quite so important as we might assume. For in fact we do not become involved in the world of *Oliver Twist* in the way we become involved in the world of *Emma.* We do not really know very much about any of these characters, even Oliver himself, or participate very closely in their motives and reactions. We are sorry for Oliver; we are on his side; but our feeling for him is not very different from our feeling for any child we see ill-treated in the street. We are outraged and our sense of outrage no doubt comes, ultimately, from a feeling of common humanity, a kind of identification of ourselves with the child in his misery and struggles; but our entanglement in his situation is not really very deep.

In the famous scene when Oliver asks for more it is not the precise sense of Oliver's feelings and reactions that grips us; we do not feel what he is feeling in the way we share Miss Bates's emotion on Box Hill, and in this sense Oliver is less close to us and matters to us less than Miss Bates and Emma. But in another way Oliver matters to us a great deal more. For when he walks up to the master of the workhouse and asks for more gruel, issues are at stake which make the whole world of Jane Austen tremble. We care, we are involved, not because it is Oliver and we are close to Oliver (though that of course enters into it), but because every starved orphan in the world, and indeed everyone who is poor and oppressed and hungry is involved, and the master of the workhouse (his name has not been revealed) is not anyone in particular but every agent of an oppressive system everywhere. And that, incidentally, is why millions of people all over the world (including many who have never read a page of Dickens) can tell you what happened in Oliver Twist's workhouse, while comparatively few can tell you what happened on Box Hill.

That this episode from *Oliver Twist* should have become a myth, a part of the cultural consciousness of the people, is due not merely to its subject-matter but to the kind of novel Dickens wrote. He is dealing not, like Jane Austen, with personal relationships, not with the quality of feelings involved in detailed living, but with something which can without fatuity be called Life. What we get from *Oliver Twist* is not a greater precision of sensitiveness about the day-to-day problems of human behaviour but a sharpened sense of the large movement of life within which particular problems arise. It is pointless to argue whether the way Dickens tackles life is better or worse than the way Jane Austen tackles it. One might just as well argue whether it is better to earn one's living or to get married. Not merely are the two issues not exclusive, they are indissolubly bound up. In a sense they are the same problem— how best to live in society—but, for all their interdependence, one does not tackle them in precisely the same way.

What distinguishes the opening chapters of *Oliver Twist* from, on the one side, a social history and, on the other side, *Emma,* is that they are symbolic. It is not a sense of participation in the personal emotions of any of the characters that engages our imagination but a sense of participation in a world that is strikingly, appallingly relevant to our world.

The *Oliver Twist* world is a world of poverty, oppression and death. The poverty is complete, utterly degrading and utterly realistic.

> The houses on either side were high and large, but very old and tenanted by people of the poorest class: as their neglected appearance would have sufficiently denoted, without the concurrent testimony afforded by the squalid looks of the few men and women who, with folded arms and bodies half-doubled, occasionally skulked along. A great many of the tenements had shop fronts; but these were fast closed, and mouldering away, only the upper rooms being inhabited. Some houses which had become insecure from age and decay were prevented from falling into the street, by huge beams of wood reared against the walls, and firmly planted in the road; but even these crazy dens seemed to have been selected as the nightly haunts of some houseless wretches, for many of the rough boards, which supplied the place of door and window, were wrenched from their positions, to afford an aperture wide enough for the passage of a human body. The kennel was stagnant and filthy. The

very rats, which here and there lay putrefying in its rottenness, were hideous with famine.

The oppression stems from the 'board'—eight or ten fat gentlemen sitting round a table—and particularly (the image is repeated) from a fat gentleman in a white waistcoat; but its agents are the (under) paid officers of the state: beadle, matron, etc., corrupt, pompous, cruel. The methods of oppression are simple: violence and starvation. The workhouse is a symbol of the oppression but by no means its limit. Outside, the world is a vast workhouse with the 'parish' run by the same gentleman in a white waistcoat, assisted by magistrates fatuous or inhuman, by clergymen who can scarcely be bothered to bury the dead, by Mr Bumble. London is no different from the parish, only bigger.

The oppressed are degraded and corrupted by their life (plus a little gin) and either become themselves oppressors or else criminals or corpses. Of all the recurring themes and images of these opening chapters that of death is the most insistent. Oliver's mother dies. ' "It's all over, Mrs Thingummy," said the surgeon. . . .' The note of impersonal and irresponsible horror is immediately struck. It is not fortuitous that Mr Sowerberry should be an undertaker, presiding over an unending funeral. Oliver and Dick long for death. Fagin gives a twist of new and dreadful cynicism to the theme: ' "What a fine thing capital punishment is! Dead men never repent; dead men never bring awkward stories to light." ' The ultimate sanction of the oppressive state becomes the ultimate weapon of its degraded creatures in their struggles against one another.

The strength of these opening chapters lies in the power and justice of the symbols, through which is achieved an objective picture arousing our compassion not through any extraneous comment but through its own validity. The weakness lies in Dickens's conscious attitudes, his attempts to comment on the situation. These attempts are at best (the ironical) inadequate, at worst (the sentimental) nauseating.

> Although I am not disposed to maintain that the being born in a workhouse is in itself the most fortunate and enviable circumstance that can possibly befall a human being. . . .

The heaviness of the prose reflects the stodginess and unsubtlety of the thought. So does the reiteration of the 'kind old gentleman' as a description of Fagin. (The less satisfactory side of Dickens's treatment of the thieves obviously comes direct from *Jonathan Wild;* the same irony—even to the very words—is used, but because it is not based on Fielding's secure moral preoccupation it becomes tedious far more quickly.) The incursions of 'sentiment' (i.e. every reference to motherhood, the little scene between Oliver and Dick) are even more unsatisfactory. After Dickens has tried to wring an easy tear by playing on responses which he has done nothing to satisfy, we begin to be suspicious of the moments when we really *are* moved, fearing a facile trick.

But the weaknesses—which may be summed up as the inadequacy of Dickens's conscious view of life—are in the first eleven chapters of *Oliver Twist* almost obliterated by the strength. The subjective inadequacy is obscured by the objective profundity. Again and again Dickens leaves behind his heavy humour, forgets that he ought to be trying to copy Fielding or vindicating our faith in the beauty of motherhood, and achieves a moment of drama or insight which burns into the imagination by its truth and vividness. We have already noticed the surgeon's comment on Oliver's mother's death. Most of the Mr Bumble-Mrs Mann conversations, the whole of the undertaker section, the meeting with the Artful Dodger, the first description of the thieves' kitchen are on the same level of achievement. So is the moment when Oliver asks for more and the passage when Oliver and Sowerberry go to visit the corpse of a dead woman.

> The terrified children cried bitterly; but the old woman, who had hitherto remained as quiet as if she had been wholly deaf to all that passed, menaced them into silence. Having unloosed the cravat of the man, who still remained extended on the ground, she tottered towards the undertaker.
>
> 'She was my daughter,' said the old woman, nodding her head in the direction of the corpse; and speaking with an idiotic leer, more ghastly than even the presence of death in such a place. 'Lord, Lord! Well, it *is* strange that I who gave birth to her, and was a woman then, should be alive and merry now, and she lying there, so cold and stiff! Lord, Lord!—to think of it; it's as good as a play—as good as a play!'
>
> As the wretched creature mumbled and chuckled in her hideous merriment, the undertaker turned to go away.
>
> 'Stop, stop!' said the old woman in a loud whisper. 'Will she be buried tomorrow, or next day, or tonight? I laid her out and I must walk, you know. Send me a large cloak—a good warm one, for it is bitter cold. We should have cake and wine, too, before we go! Never mind; send some bread—only a loaf of bread and a cup of water. Shall we have some bread, dear?' she said eagerly, catching at the undertaker's coat, as he once more moved towards the door.
>
> 'Yes, yes,' said the undertaker, 'of course. Anything, everything.' He disengaged himself from the old woman's grasp, and, drawing Oliver after him, hurried away.

There is no sentimentality here, only horror, and with something of the quality which one associates particularly with Dostoievsky, the strengthening of realism by the moment of fantasy, the blurring of the line between reality and nightmare, a stretching to the ultimate of the capacity of the mind to deal with the world it has inherited.

And then from the desperate horror of the nightmare world Oliver awakes, lying in a comfortable bed, surrounded by kindly middle-class people. He has become all of a sudden a pretty creature, a grateful little dear. And from that moment the plot of the novel becomes important.

It is generally agreed that the plots of Dickens's novels are their weakest feature but it is not always understood why this should be so. The plot of *Oliver Twist* is very complicated and very unsatisfactory. It is a conventional plot about a wronged woman, an illegitimate baby, a destroyed will, a death-bed secret, a locket thrown into the river, a wicked elder brother and the restoration to the hero of name and property. That it should depend on a number of extraordinary coincidences (the only two robberies in which Oliver is called upon to participate are perpetrated, fortuitously, on his father's best friend and his mother's sister's guardian!) is the least of its shortcomings. Literal probability is not an essential quality of an adequate plot. Nor is it a damning criticism that Dickens should have used his plot for the purposes of serial-publication, i.e. to provide a climax at the end of each instalment and the necessary twists and manœuvres which popular serialisation invited. (It is not a fault in a dramatist that he should provide a climax to each act of his play, and the serial instalment is no more or less artificial a convention than the act of a play.) What we may legitimately object to in the plot of *Oliver Twist* is the very substance of that plot in its relation to the essential pattern of the novel.

The conflict in the plot is the struggle between the innocent Oliver, aided by his friends at Pentonville and Chertsey, against the machinations of those who are conspiring from self-interest to do him out of his fortune. These latter stem from and centre in his half-brother Monks. It is not, even by its own standards, a good plot. Oliver is too passive a hero to win our very lively sympathy and Monks is a rather unconvincing villain who is, anyway, outshone in interest by his agents. The good characters are, by and large, too good and the bad too bad. If the centre of interest of the novel were indeed the plot then the conventional assessment of a Dickens novel—a poor story enlivened by magnificent though irrelevant 'characters'—would be fair enough. But in fact the centre of interest, the essential pattern of the novel, is not its plot, and it is the major fault of the plot that it does not correspond with this central interest.

The core of the novel, and what gives it value, is its consideration of the plight of the poor. Its pattern is the contrasted relation of two worlds—the underworld of the workhouse, the funeral, the thieves' kitchen, and the comfortable world of the Brownlows and Maylies. It is this pattern that stamps the novel on our minds. We do not remember, when we think back on it, the intricacies of the plot; we are not interested in the affairs of Rose and Harry Maylie; we do not care who Oliver's father was and, though we sympathise with Oliver's struggles, we do not mind whether or not he gets his fortune. What we do remember is that vision of the underworld of the first eleven chapters, the horror of Fagin, the fate of Mr Bumble, the trial of the Artful Dodger, the murder of Nancy, the end of Sikes. What engages our sympathy is not Oliver's feeling for the mother he never saw, but his struggle against his oppressors of which the famous gruel scene is indeed a central and adequate symbol.

The contrast of the two worlds is at the very heart of the book, so that we see a total picture of contrasted darkness and light. Often the two are explicitly contrasted in divided chapters. The two worlds are so utterly separate that

Oliver's two metamorphoses from one to the other must inevitably take the form of an awakening to a new existence and the root of the weakness as 'characters' of both Oliver and Monks is that they are not fully absorbed in either world. Oliver is rather a thin hero because, though he is called upon to play a hero's part, he never becomes identified with the heroic forces of the book; while Monks's stature as the fountainhead of evil is wrecked by his parentage; how can he compete with Sikes and Fagin when he is to be allowed, because he is a gentleman, to escape his just deserts?

The power of the book, then, proceeds from the wonderful evocation of the underworld and the engagement of our sympathy on behalf of the inhabitants of that world. Its weakness lies in Dickens's failure to develop and carry through the pattern so powerfully presented in the first quarter of the novel. It is by no means a complete failure; on the contrary, there are passages in the latter part of the book quite as successful as the early scenes: and in the final impression of the novel the sense of the two worlds is, as has been suggested, the dominant factor. But the failure is, nevertheless, sufficiently striking to be worth consideration.

It is not by chance that the plot and Mr Brownlow emerge in the novel at the same moment, for their purpose is identical. It is they who are to rescue Oliver from the underworld and establish him as a respectable member of society. It is not through his own efforts that the metamorphosis takes place and indeed it cannot be. For if the whole first section of the novel has convinced us of anything at all it is that against the whole apparatus set in motion by the gentleman in the white waistcoat the Oliver Twists of that world could stand no possible chance.

The introduction of the plot, then, savours from the very first of a trick. It is only by reducing the whole of Oliver's experiences up till now to the status of 'a long and troubled dream' that he can be saved for the plot. But we know perfectly well that these experiences are not a dream; they have a reality for us which the nice houses in Pentonville and Chertsey never achieve. Indeed, as far as the imaginative impact of the novel is concerned, it is the Brownlow-Maylie world that is the dream, a dream-world into which Oliver is lucky enough to be transported by the plot but which all the real and vital people of the book never even glimpse. The Brownlow-Maylie world is indeed no world at all; it is merely the romantic escape-world of the lost wills and dispossessed foundlings and idiotic coincidences which make up the paraphernalia of the conventional romantic plot.

The plot makes impossible the realisation of the living pattern and conflict of the book. This conflict—symbolised, as we have seen, by the gruel scene—is the struggle of the poor against the bourgeois state, the whole army of greater and lesser Bumbles whom the gentleman in the white waistcoat employs to maintain morality (all the members of the board are 'philosophers') and the *status quo*. The appalling difficulties of this struggle are impressed on our minds and it is because Oliver, however unwillingly, becomes an actor in it that he takes on a certain symbolic significance and wins more than our casual pity.

It is notable that Dickens makes no serious effort to present Oliver with any psychological realism: his reactions are not, for the most part, the reactions of any child of nine or ten years old; he is not surprised by what would surprise a child and his moral attitudes are those of an adult. And yet something of the quality of precocious suffering, of childish terror, is somehow achieved, partly by the means by which other characters are presented, with a kind of exaggerated, almost grotesque simplicity, and partly through the very fact that Oliver is—we are persuaded—a figure of symbolic significance. Because he is *all* workhouse orphans the lack of a convincing individual psychology does not matter; it is Oliver's situation rather than himself that moves us and the situation is presented with all of Dickens's dramatic symbolic power.

Once he becomes involved in the plot the entire symbolic significance of Oliver changes. Until he wakes up in Mr Brownlow's house he is a poor boy struggling against the inhumanity of the state. After he has slept himself into the Brownlow world he is a young bourgeois who has been done out of his property. A complete transformation has taken place in the organisation of the novel. The state, which in the pattern of the book is the organ of oppression of the poor and therefore of Oliver, now becomes the servant of Oliver. The oppressed are now divided (through the working of the plot) into the good and deserving poor who help Oliver win his rights and the bad and criminal poor who help Monks and must be eliminated. It is a conception which makes a mockery of the opening chapters of the book, where poverty has been revealed to us in a light which makes the facile terms of good and bad irrelevant.

By the end of the book Nancy can be pigeon-holed as good, Sikes as bad. But who can say whether the starving creatures of the opening chapters are good or bad? It is for this kind of reason that the plot of ***Oliver Twist*** has so disastrous an effect on the novel. Not merely is it silly and mechanical and troublesome, but it expresses an interpretation of life infinitely less profound and honest than the novel itself reveals.

The disaster, happily, is not complete. For one thing, the plot does not immediately, with the entrance of Mr Brownlow, gain entire ascendancy. The kidnapping of Oliver by Nancy and Sikes and his return to the thieves gives the novel a reprieve. The robbery episode is excellently done. But in this section (chs. XII to XXIX) the plot is beginning to seep into the underworld. Monks appears. And the reintroduction of the workhouse (the death of old Sally, the marriage of Mr Bumble), despite some delicious moments ('It's all U.P. here, Mrs Corney'; Noah and Charlotte eating oysters; 'Won't you tell your own B?'), too obviously serves the contrivances of the plot.

Once, however, the robbery is done with and Oliver awakes for a second time in the respectable world, the plot completely reasserts itself. The third quarter of the book (chs. XXIX to XXXIX) is its weakest section. Oliver is here entirely at the mercy of the Maylies and the plot. Monks bobs up all over the place. And our interest is held (if at all) only by the Bumble passages, now completely involved in the plot, and the incidental 'characters', Giles and Brittles, Blathers and Duff. And because these characters have no part in the underlying pattern of the book and are therefore, unlike Bumble and Fagin and the Artful Dodger and Noah Claypole, without symbolic significance, they are merely eccentrics, comic relief, with all the limitations the phrase implies.

The basic conflict of the novel is brought, in this quarter, almost to a standstill; the people who have captured our imagination scarcely appear at all. The world of the opening chapters has been replaced by another world in which kindly old doctors like Losberne and crusty but amiable eccentrics like Grimwig are in control of the situation. But after what we have already experienced, we simply cannot believe in this world in the way we believed in the other.

In the final quarter of the book (ch. XXXIX onwards) plot and pattern, artifice and truth, struggle in a last, violent encounter. The plot wins the first round by extracting Nancy from the clutches of the pattern. The girl's genuine humanity, revealed earlier in the novel by the simple moving language of her moment of compassion for the suffering wretches within the walls of the jail, is debased by the plot into the conventional clichés of cheap melodrama. But Nancy's abduction is countered almost at once by one of the great episodes of the novel, the trial of the Artful Dodger. This scene is irrelevant to the plot except in so far as the Dodger has to be got out of the way before the final dispensing of reward and punishment. It is an interesting instance of the power of Dickens's genius that he should have realised that in the Dodger he had created a figure which the plot was quite incapable either of absorbing or obliterating. And so he is obliged to give the irrepressible boy his final fling, a fling which again raises the book into serious art and plays an essential part in its (by this time) almost forgotten pattern.

The trial of the Artful Dodger (it is a greater because emotionally and morally a profounder scene than Jonathan Wild's dance without music) re-states in an astonishing form the central theme of *Oliver Twist:* what are the poor to do against the oppressive state? The Dodger throughout the book is magnificently done: his precosity, the laboured irony of his conversation (which becomes involuntarily a comment on the quality of Dickens's own irony), his shrewdness, his grotesque urbanity, his resourcefulness (gloriously at variance with his appearance), his tremendous vitality, all are revealed without false pathos but with an effect of great profundity.

For what is so important about the Artful Dodger is not his oddity but his normality, not his inability to cope with the world but his very ability to cope with it on its own terms. Oliver is afraid of the world, the Dodger defies it; it has made him what he is and he will give back as good as he got. His trial contrasts in the novel with all the other trials. He turns up with all his guns loaded and fires broadside after broadside which for all their fantastic unexpectedness and apparent inappropriateness have an irony beyond any other statements in the novel.

> It was indeed Mr Dawkins, who, shuffling into the office with the big coat-sleeves tucked up as usual, his left hand in his pocket, and his hat in his right hand, preceded the jailer, with a rolling

gait altogether indescribable, and, taking his place in the dock, requested in an audible voice to know what he was placed in that 'ere disgraceful sitivation for.

'Hold your tongue, will you?' said the jailer.

'I'm an Englishman, ain't I?' rejoined the Dodger; 'where are my priwileges?'

'You'll get your privileges soon enough,' retorted the jailer, 'and pepper with 'em.'

'We'll see wot the Secretary of State for the Home Affairs has got to say to the beaks, if I don't,' replied Mr Dawkins. 'Now then! Wot is this here business? I shall thank the madg'strates to dispose of this here little affair, and not to keep me while they read the paper for I've got an appointment with a genelman in the city, and as I'm a man of my word and very punctual in business matters, he'll go away if I ain't there to my time, and then pr'aps there won't be an action for damage against them as kept me away. Oh, no, certainly not!'

At this point the Dodger, with a show of being very particular with a view to proceedings to be had thereafter, desired the jailer to communicate 'the names of them two files as was on the bench', which so tickled the spectators, that they laughed almost as heartily as Master Bates could have done if he had heard the request.

'Silence there!' cried the jailer.

'What is this?' inquired one of the magistrates.

'A pick-pocketing case, your worship.'

'Has the boy ever been here before?'

'He ought to have been, a many times,' replied the jailer. 'He has been pretty well everywhere else. I know him well, your worship.'

'Oh! you know me, do you?' cried the Artful, making a note of the statement. 'Wery good. That's a case of deformation of character anyway.'

Here there was another laugh, and another cry of silence.

'Now then, where are the witnesses?' said the clerk.

'Ah! that's right,' added the Dodger. 'Where are they? I should like to see 'em.'

This wish was immediately gratified, for a policeman stepped forward who had seen the prisoner attempt the pocket of an unknown gentleman in a crowd, and indeed take a handkerchief therefrom, which, being a very old one, he deliberately put back again, after trying it on his own countenance. For this reason, he took the Dodger into custody as soon as he could get near him, and the said Dodger being searched, had upon his person a silver snuff-box, with the owner's name engraved upon the lid. This gentleman had been discovered on reference to the Court Guide, and being then and there present, swore that the snuff-box was his, and that he had missed it on the previous day, the moment he had disengaged himself from the crowd before referred to. He had also remarked a young gentleman in the throng particularly active in making his way about, and that young gentleman was the prisoner before him.

'Have you anything to ask this witness, boy?' said the magistrate.

'I wouldn't abase myself by descending to hold no conversation with him,' replied the Dodger.

'Have you anything to say at all?'

'Do you hear his worship ask if you have anything to say?' inquired the jailer, nudging the silent Dodger with his elbow.

'I beg your pardon,' said the Dodger, looking up with an air of abstraction. 'Did you redress yourself to me, my man?'

'I never see such an out-and-out young wagabond, your worship,' observed the officer with a grin. 'Do you mean to say anything, you young shaver?'

'No,' replied the Dodger, 'not here, for this ain't the shop for justice. . . .'

(pp. 115-27)

Now the point about the Dodger's defiance which is apt to escape our notice, so fantastic and uproarious is the scene and so used are we to regarding a Dickens novel simply in terms of a display of eccentric 'character', is the actual substance of his comments. Yet in fact, if we recall the court in which Mr Fang had heard Oliver's case, we must realise the justice of the Dodger's complaints, which strike at the very heart of the judicial system that is doing its worst on him. Where *are* the Englishman's privileges? Where *is* the law that allows the jailer to say what he does? What, in sober fact, *are* these magistrates? What comment could be more relevant than the contemptuous 'this ain't the shop for justice'? The importance of the Artful Dodger in the pattern of the novel is that he, almost alone of the characters of the underworld, does stick up for himself, does continue and develop the conflict that Oliver had begun when he asked for more.

The final section of the book (the murder of Nancy, the flight and end of Sikes, the death of Fagin and the tying-up of the plot) is an extraordinary mixture of the genuine and the bogus. The violence which has run right through the novel reaches its climax with the murder of Nancy; and the sense of terror is remarkably well sustained right up to the death of Sikes.

Here again Dickens's instinct for the symbolic background is what grips our imagination. The atmosphere of squalid London, powerfully present in so much of the novel, is here immensely effective, especially the description of Folly Ditch and Jacob's Island, sombre and decayed, 'crazy wooden galleries common to the backs of half a dozen houses, with holes from which to look upon the slime beneath; windows broken and patched, with poles thrust out on which to dry the linen that is never

there . . . chimneys half crushed, half hesitating to fall. . . . ' The scene itself ceases to be a mere backcloth and becomes a sculptured mass making an integral part of the novel's pattern. So that in the end it is not Sikes's conscience that we remember but a black picture of human squalor and desolation. Sikes is gathered into the world that has begotten him and the image of that world makes us understand him and even pity him, not with an easy sentimentality, but through a sense of all the hideous forces that have made him what he is.

The end of Fagin is a different matter. It is sensational in the worst sense, with a *News of the World* interest which touches nothing adequately and is worse than inadequate because it actually coarsens our perceptions. It is conceived entirely within the terms of the plot (Oliver is taken—in the name of morality—to the condemned cell to find out where the missing papers are hidden) and the whole debasing effect of the plot on the novel is immediately illustrated; for it is because he is working within the moral framework of the plot—in which the only standards are those of the sanctity of property and complacent respectability—that Dickens *cannot* offer us any valuable human insights, *cannot* give his characters freedom to live as human beings.

That is why the struggle throughout ***Oliver Twist*** between the plot and the pattern is indeed a life and death struggle, a struggle as to whether the novel shall live or not. And in so far as the plot succeeds in twisting and negating the pattern the value of the novel is in fact weakened. To a considerable degree the novel *is* thus ruined; the loss of tension in the third quarter and the dubious close are the testimony. But the total effect is not one of disaster. The truth and depth of the central vision are such that a vitality is generated which struggles against and survives the plot. Oliver himself does not survive; but the force he has set in motion does. This force—let us call it the sense of the doom and aspirations of the oppressed—is too strong to be satisfied with the dream-solution of Oliver's metamorphosis, too enduring to let us forget the fat gentleman in the white waistcoat who has so conveniently faded from the picture till he is recalled by the Artful Dodger. Confused, uneven, topsy-turvy as the effect of the novel is we would yet be doing it great injustice to discuss it, as it is often discussed, simply in terms of random moments and exuberant caricature. There is pattern behind that power, art behind the vitality, and if we recognise this in *Oliver Twist* we shall not come unarmed to Dickens's later, more mature and greater books: *Bleak House, Little Dorrit, Great Expectations, Our Mutual Friend.* (pp. 127-29)

> Arnold Kettle, "Dickens: Oliver Twist," in his An Introduction to the English Novel, Vol. I, *second edition, Hutchinson University Library, 1967, pp. 115-29.*

Kathleen Tillotson   (essay date 1959)

[*In the following essay, Tillotson discusses Dickens's plans for the structure of* Oliver Twist.]

There has been no lack of discussion of *Oliver Twist* in either Dickens's century or our own, but some aspects of the novel have not been sufficiently considered in the light of his own intentions and attitude, known and inferred. This I am attempting here. My approach is not another examination of 'Dickens at work', for which the relevant material is at once too voluminous and too incomplete for condensed discussion, but the complicated history of publication must be borne in mind and will be conveniently summarized first.

Oliver Twist lies outside Dickens's usual pattern, for it appeared in a monthly magazine (*Bentley's Miscellany*) in instalments of irregular length, and was also published in three volumes some months before its serial conclusion. The whole course of its publication was bedevilled by Dickens's arguments with Richard Bentley, both over his contracts and his status as editor; the actual writing, apparently done between January 1837 and early September 1838, was attended by many other difficulties, notably the overlap with the last ten numbers of *Pickwick* (to November 1838) and the first six of *Nickleby* (from April 1838). As often, he was also under the pressure of many other activities, such as editing, play-and sketch-writing, and of many domestic troubles—the lasting grief of Mary Hogarth's sudden death, the temporary exactions of Catherine Dickens's confinements, and of house-hunting and travel. Cruikshank, the illustrator, sometimes had to receive the 'slips' of manuscript in instalments; and Forster says he never knew Dickens to 'work so frequently after dinner, or to such late hours'. In mid-July 1838 he had written only two-thirds of the novel and then believed it 'indispensably necessary' that the whole should be *published* in September; no wonder he felt 'sadly harassed'. (He did in fact finish the writing early in September, but the final illustrations delayed publication until 9 November.) Not only composition engaged him; collation shows that he also revised the earlier chapters of the *Bentley's* version. And he continued to revise at intervals, in at least three subsequent editions up to the collected edition of 1867-8; the total revision is much more extensive than for any other novel.

Even in 1868 he had not finished with it; in the last year

of his life he made his final version of chapters XLV-XLVIII, when he devised the most famous of his public readings, *Sikes and Nancy*. And when in 1869 he said farewell to the 'garish lights' under which he had 'petrified' audiences with this performance, he turned to the writing of a novel not greatly dissimilar in shape and colouring: another short novel, another tale of mystery and crime, an exploration of guilt and fear, designed to close with a scene in the condemned cell. The difference in social setting, the greater introspectiveness and the less specific social content, do not disguise the dark affinities of *Edwin Drood* and *Oliver Twist.*

In one sense then *Oliver Twist* extends over the whole of Dickens's working life. His first thoughts of it go back, I believe, to the end of 1833; when his first story had just appeared 'in all the glory of print', he wrote to his friend Kolle ablaze with future projects:

> I am in treaty with them [the *Monthly Magazine*] . . . and if we close, my next paper will be Private Theatricals, and my next London by Night. I shall then, please God, commence a series of papers (the materials for which I have been noting down for some time past) called The Parish. Should they be successful . . . I shall cut up my proposed novel into little magazine sketches.

No other novel is so closely allied to the early sketches as *Oliver Twist,* and none before *David Copperfield* so deeply rooted in Dickens's own childhood and youth. His confidence in undertaking to write it while still committed to several other publications, his passionately defensive prefaces and his solicitude over revision, all suggest that among his early works this was a 'favourite child'. Though the writing was a feverish race against clock and calendar, the design was surely of early and slow growth.

There are several arguments for this. First, for good or ill, this novel, unlike *Pickwick,* has a constructed plot. Dickens was fully aware of the contrast; he said in the 1837 Preface to *Pickwick* that in such a work 'no artfully interwoven or ingeniously complicated plot can with reason be expected'; yet he had no hesitation in almost simultaneously elaborating, also for serial publication, the plot of *Oliver Twist,* even boasting that 'the story, unlike that of *Pickwick Papers,* is an involved and complicated one'. This was no 'monthly something', no periodical miscellany, with Dickens initially an executant and collaborator in a plan formed by others; he was independent, and could return to 'my proposed novel', working out in advance the situation which he believed could best express his moral and social intentions. He was probably not ironical even when referring to 'my long-considered intentions and plans regarding this prose epic'. His ambitions may be imperfectly fulfilled, but their very presence, and the whole weight of conscious intention behind the novel, makes it a different kind of work from *Pickwick;* a difference which has of course generally been felt, but too loosely defined.

In more than one way Dickens had been for some years preparing himself to write *Oliver Twist;* many of the sketches, and one or two of the tales, of 1834-6 show him exploring the same areas of experience. This is not simply a matter of anticipation of maturer work, such as Forster remarked when he said 'Mr. Bumble is in the parish sketches, and Mr. Dawkins the Dodger in the Old Bailey scenes'. A number of the sketches have what is essentially the same background material, presented in a way that shows Dickens's long and close familiarity with it. To read, for example, the first part of 'The Streets—Morning', the whole of 'Seven Dials', 'The Pawnbroker's Shop', and 'The Prisoner's Van' and especially 'Criminal Courts', 'A Visit to Newgate', and 'The Hospital Patient' is to enter the London of Fagin and Sikes, and the similarity is emphasized by Cruikshank's illustrations to both sketches and novel. In his own observations Dickens is sometimes more cautious, assuming the detached and urbane attitude of a spectator, as befitted the editorial 'we'; but at times there appears the same kind of sarcastic comment as in the novel. He refers to 'that enlightened, eloquent, sage and profound body, the Magistracy of London' or says that the sight of a poor man 'will make your heart ache,—always supposing you are neither a philosopher nor a political economist'. The device of mock elevation is already a favourite; just as Fagin is a 'merry old gentleman', and Nancy and Bet 'a couple of young ladies', so, in the *Sketches,* two slum women fighting in 'Seven Dials' are a 'couple of ladies' who have 'differed on some point of domestic arrangement'; in the debauched horseplay at Greenwich Fair he has 'the ladies, in the height of their innocent association, dancing in the gentlemen's hats'; the homes of the old-clothes-dealers show 'that neglect of personal comfort so common among people who are constantly immersed in profound speculations'. Again as in *Oliver Twist,* this elevation is set against moderately realistic dialogue (including a number of imprecations which he later found it necessary to soften or remove); and his descriptions of the slums are frank enough. The account of the St. Giles's rookery in 'Gin-shops' is more succinct but hardly less squalid than that of Jacob's Island, and is similarly introduced to the sheltered reader—'the filthy and miserable appearance of this part of London can hardly be imagined by those (and there are many such) who have not witnessed it'. The *Sketches* were not objected to in early reviews for their 'lowness', and this may have emboldened Dickens to go further in the same direction in his novel; but there he had more complex motives, as well as a deliberate plan, a principle of unity.

This plan is defined very clearly and simply in the first preface, added in 1841. The centre of the design was little Oliver, in whom was to be shown 'the principle of Good surviving through every adverse circumstance, and triumphing at last'. That is, Dickens set out to write a moral fairytale in contemporary terms. It is often said that he erred in failing to see that his picture of unconquerable virtue in Oliver made his social protest less effective, that if he was attacking the system in which pauper children were reared he should have emphasized its corrupting effect on character. Dickens was not blind to such effects, and provided an example in Noah Claypole, the charity-boy (as later, in the less irreclaimable Rob the Grinder); but Oliver was the necessary embodiment of his moral optimism—and, less consciously, of his impulse towards fairytale and romance in his heroes and heroines: Oliver is the dispossessed heir, the child of noble birth. Occasion-

ally this is rationalized: 'nature or inheritance had implanted a good sturdy spirit in Oliver's breast'. We are not told what implanted the religious spirit. As an idea it was more acceptable then, and had a few much later defenders, such as Swinburne:

> The heredity of heroism and spiritual refinement in an outcast child may seem less natural to the literary patients of Dr. Ibsen than the heredity of contagious debasement and degradation by disease: to others it may seem not less credible and very much more amenable to other than medical treatment.

The burden of representing the principle of Good may seem to hamper the development of individual character in Oliver (and still more, of natural boyishness—as Swinburne goes on to admit), and for much of the time he is simply acted upon; but Dickens wisely allowed him, early in the story, two 'heroic' actions, both of which help to propel the narrative—the famous 'asking for more' in Chapter II, and the fight with Noah Claypole in defence of his mother's name, which starts him on his flight to London. He also showed him as at least open to temptation, when Fagin has him for the second time and sets out not merely to train him in the technique of theft but to corrupt his mind:

> the old man would tell them stories of robberies he had committed in his younger days: mixed up with so much that was droll and curious, that Oliver could not help laughing heartily, and showing that he was amused in spite of all his better feelings.

> In short, the wily old Jew had the boy in his toils. Having prepared his mind, by solitude and gloom, to prefer any society to the companionship of his own sad thoughts in such a dreary place, he was now slowly instilling into his soul the poison which he hoped would blacken it, and change its hue for ever.

Fagin, diabolic in appearance and behaviour, is the main representative of the evil forces battling for Oliver's soul, and is given an extra motive, in terms of plot, by becoming the ally and agent of Monks, Oliver's half-brother and implacable foe; but this, for greater suspense, is kept in the background. (Sikes's question is pointed—'wot makes you take so much pains about one chalk-faced kid?') The far-fetched coincidences by which Oliver's first adventure in crime leads him unwittingly to his father's old friend Mr. Brownlow, and his second to his mother's sister Rose Maylie, are designed by Dickens precisely to illustrate the power of the principle of Good; Mr. Brownlow says it was a 'stronger hand than chance' that brought Oliver to his door, and the sophisticated reader is not meant to add that the stronger hand was the author's. Such a scene as the climax of Fagin's attempt at corruption should also be judged in the light of this intention; in revulsion against the evil world opened to him by reading stories of criminals, Oliver falls to praying and is so found by Nancy:

> 'God forgive me! . . . I never thought of this'.

She has already manifested a 'soul of goodness in things evil' in her instinctive defence of him against brutal blows;

henceforth there is an Abdiel among the powers of darkness, and their defeat as well as her own death arises directly from her perilous confidence in Rose. But the triumph of Good is also brought about by means that are convincing enough on a simply realistic level; we have already been shown the weakness inherent in the conspiracy of evil—mutual fear, distrust and double-crossing. The alliance of the conspirators is uneasy and gallows-haunted. The elaborate manœuvring of Fagin, Monks, Bill Sikes, and even Bumble and Mrs. Corney, weaves their own destruction; and the increasing power of the later chapters arises partly from Dickens's concentration on the defeat of evil by evil, which is equally part of his moral.

Humphry House's statement [in his introduction to *Oliver Twist,* 1949] that 'the unity of the book derives from impulse and from the energy of its imagination, not from its construction' needs some modification. The plot has been much censured (in early reviews as well as later criticism) but as an expression of the simple moral that Dickens had in mind, it is designed with some aptness, and also with economy and concentration; in contrast to many of Dickens's novels, there are no side-issues, no mere episodes or interpolated tales (unless we count the story of Conkey Chickweed), but each character and incident carries its moral and narrative weight in the whole. The weakness lies rather in the way the 'mystery-plot' is disclosed. Nothing is too melodramatic for Dickens to *present* with some conviction, but he cannot give life to a retrospective summary of events.

The other obvious failure is Rose Maylie, over whom he was pathetically painstaking, evidently in an attempt to make Mary Hogarth live again (he was writing Chapter XXXIII around the time of the first anniversary of her death); if so, it is an extreme instance of the wisdom of Henry James's austere prohibition that 'with a relation *not* imaginative to his material the story-teller has nothing whatever to do'. Rose's theatrical sententiousness infects other characters, especially Nancy; the sudden development of literacy in a girl who had been in Fagin's gang since the age of five strains credulity much more than her 'soul of goodness'.

Many critics have found the same kind of sentimentalism in the character of Oliver himself, and have looked no further. Yet in his very haplessness there is a curiously magnetic power, inviting emotional identification. Chesterton acutely says that

> characters which are not very clearly conceived as regards their own psychology are yet at certain moments managed so as to shake to its foundations our own psychology.

He is speaking, aptly enough, of Sikes and Nancy as murderer and victim, but what he says can be applied to Oliver at many 'moments' in the first half of the book. Elsewhere Dickens has 'shaken' our psychology to its foundations by engaging us in the sufferings of children, especially as inflicted by unloving parents or substitute-parents; but Oliver alone is in the situation most deeply dreaded by any child, of having no adult who cares about him at all, no one who is on his side, and discovering in each potential protector—Bumble, Gamfield, Mrs. Sowerberry, Fagin,

and Mr. Fang—the overpowering harshness and evil of the adult world, yet never quite losing hope and faith. 'Oliver Twist is pathetic because he is an optimist . . . he does believe he is living in a just world'. After those first eleven chapters, Mr. Brownlow's benevolence seems no sentimental fancy, but salvation; and no one who first read *Oliver Twist* at Oliver's own age will ever forget the sense of horrified despair when Oliver is recaptured and returned to Fagin's world, or of renewed hope when Nancy appears to be on his side after all.

The innocence of Oliver is also technically valuable as a passport to the reader entering the unfamiliar underworld of thieves. The traditional device of the 'innocent at large' becomes almost a Dickensian formula (more subtly and satirically used a little later for Mr. Pickwick in the Fleet); but it begins when Dickens, with some daring, lets us see Oliver from the Dodger's point of view: 'He is so jolly green'. Readers of 1837 were also tinged with green when it came to meeting the pickpockets of Saffron Hill in a magazine on their drawing-room tables.

For this was a novelty in fiction, and to introduce it was, as Dickens also makes clear in his Preface, an important part of his purpose. The link between his moral and his socio-literary purpose was indeed explicit:

> I wished to show, in little Oliver, the principle of Good surviving through every adverse circumstance, and triumphing at last; and when I considered among what companions I could try him best, having regard to that kind of men into

Oliver's shock upon first viewing the Dodger's handiwork. Illustration by George Cruikshank.

whose hands he would most naturally fall; I bethought myself of those who figure in these volumes. When I came to discuss the subject more maturely with myself, I saw many strong reasons for pursuing the course to which I was inclined.

Chief of these 'strong reasons' was Dickens's dissatisfaction with the sham romantic glamour with which thieves in action had been surrounded—'seductive fellows (amiable for the most part) faultless in dress . . . bold in bearing, fortunate in gallantry'. In place of these, and with Hogarth as his exemplar, he offered thieves 'as they really are'; not 'cantering on moonlit heaths' but in the 'cold, wet, shelterless midnight streets of London'. He had anticipated that such characters would be objected to on 'very high moral grounds', and so it fell out; it was thought 'a very coarse and shocking circumstance' that 'Sikes is a thief, and Fagin a receiver of stolen goods; that the boys are pick-pockets, and the girl is a prostitute'. As so often in his early work, he took his stand on eighteenth-century precedent—Defoe, Fielding, Smollett; and he chose as epigraph a quotation from *Tom Jones:*

> Some of the author's friends cried, 'Lookee, gentlemen, the man is a villain; but it is Nature for all that'; and the young critics of the age, the clerks, apprentices, etc., called it low, and fell a groaning.

He concluded with an earlier parallel:

> Cervantes laughed Spain's chivalry away. . . . It was my attempt in my humble . . . sphere, to dim the false glitter surrounding something which really did exist, by showing it in its unattractive and repulsive truth.

The Cervantes reference is a quotation, or rather misquotation, from Byron's *Don Juan;* and it had been used before him, with the same substitution of 'laughed' for 'smiled', by Ainsworth in *Rookwood.* Dickens must have had Ainsworth in mind as one of the glamorisers of thieves; but he was discreet in not naming him, for he used more than one hint from *Rookwood,* such as the comic use of 'flash' language (Jerry Juniper) and the description of Conkey Jem's hut in Thorne Waste where Turpin takes refuge. These borrowings, though superficial, complicate Dickens's picture of himself as a reformer, and gave an edge to some of the attacks on him, as we shall see. Nevertheless the general contrast with the 'heroes' of both Ainsworth and Bulwer is emphatic; Dickens's thieves are contemporary not historical, 'low' not aristocratic, their surroundings are squalid and their end miserable. He insisted, and rightly, that this 'lowness' was justified both by its truth and its morality. Unfortunately the contrast with Ainsworth's next novel, *Jack Sheppard* (1839-40), was less obvious; its appearance in *Bentley's* and the Cruikshank illustrations associated them in the public mind as 'Newgate novels', and in the moralists' attacks on 'the Jack Sheppard mania' which developed (largely from the numerous dramatic versions) Dickens felt he was in danger of being unfairly tarred with the same brush. He complained of being 'by some jolter-headed enemies most unjustly and untruly charged with having written a book after Mr. Ainsworth's fashion . . . I shall take an early

opportunity of replying'. The reply is probably the 1841 Preface.

But by 1841 he had been attacked also from the other side, not for being 'coarse and shocking' in his endeavour at realism, but for being half-hearted and sentimental in that endeavour. Thackeray in particular saw Dickens as himself tainted with the sham romance that he claimed to be reacting against. It was an exasperating position for the realist-reformer, to be classed with Bulwer and Ainsworth, and reacted against in his turn. Thackeray's chief ground of complaint was the sentimentalizing of Nancy; and it is clearly to the contemptuous references in *Catherine* and *'Going to see a Man Hanged'* that Dickens is replying when, with passionate conviction breaking into capitals, he writes:

> It is useless to discuss whether the conduct and character of the girl seems natural or unnatural, probable or improbable, right or wrong. IT IS TRUE. . . . Suggested to my mind long ago—long before I dealt in fiction—by what I often saw and read of, in actual life around me, I have, for years, tracked it through many profligate and noisome ways, and found it still the same:

a passage fortunately overlooked by Dickens's modern biographers. The impression, like others in the novel, is said to have been formed 'long ago'; and there is evidence that the topic was in his mind in 1835 in the incident at the close of 'The Pawnbroker's Shop', where the prostitute breaks 'into an agony of tears' and Dickens notes how 'strange chords in the human heart . . . will lie dormant through years of depravity'.

This may indeed have been 'true'; if not necessarily therefore convincing; but Dickens does not and could not answer Thackeray's objection that it makes an unbalanced picture, since so much of the rest of the truth about a prostitute's feelings was necessarily suppressed. 'Not being able to paint the whole portrait, he has no right to present one or two favourable points as characterizing the whole'.

This is partly, though not only, a matter of language, and here it is modern critics who have especially censured Dickens's omissions. The violence of imprecation is merely suggested, the inevitable obscenity not even hinted. Here Dickens's concessions were enforced, and conscious: in the Preface he makes a virtue of having 'endeavoured . . . to banish . . . any expression that could by possibility offend'. He was more aware of the problem than this suggests, and employs various circuitous methods of indicating 'low' speech. The thieves' speech is at least differentiated by their use of cant and slang (already popularized by *Rookwood*), but better assimilated for the polite reader by Dickens, who works his footnotes into the text, either implying the meaning through context, or having the terms translated as a concession to Oliver's simplicity: the Dodger explains that a beak is not a bird's mouth but a magistrate. He also uses the device of general statement, common in nineteenth-century books for boys (no one complains of it in *Treasure Island*): 'threatening him with horrid imprecations', 'cant terms . . . which would be quite unintelligible if recorded here'; and, less acceptably, substitutes locutions that are morally inoffensive but theatrically violent, such as 'Wolves tear your throats!' 'Grind him to ashes!' 'Burn my body!'. But his favourite method is the humorous circumlocution (what the *Quarterly* called 'brimstone in silver paper'), which is essentially realistic because immediately translatable, but skilfully puts the narrator at a sophisticated remove from the fact, as here:

> a very common imprecation concerning the most beautiful of human features: which, if it were heard above, only once out of every fifty thousand times that it is uttered below, would render blindness a disorder as common as measles.

Even so, the problem of low language haunted him in his revisions, here as in the *Sketches.* In another place, Sikes did actually say 'D— your eyes!'; but only up to 1841. As the reading public became progressively more fastidious, Dickens panted after it, removing more Damn's in every edition; even the phrase 'uttering a savage oath' and Monks's 'Wither his flesh!' and 'Fire the sound!' survive only to 1846; in 1867 Sikes's 'Damnation!' (before 'How the boy bleeds!') is finally dropped, and in the reading version a 'Damme' becomes 'Hallo'. but the process evidently began in proof, and probably under the guidance of Forster; several 'damns', a 'cursed', and a 'God' are in the manuscript but not in *Bentley's.* In Chapter XIII Fagin's 'Where's Oliver, you young devils?' becomes first 'Where's Oliver, you young hounds?' and finally 'Where's Oliver?'.

Nancy's language is generally purer than that of her male associates ('in the case of the girl . . . I kept this intention constantly in view') but this also was progressively refined, along with slight but steady recolouring of her whole behaviour. It was mistaken; violence, moodiness, and hysterics are consistent with her defence of Oliver and her attachment to Sikes, and Dickens had surely no need to alter her 'jiggered' to 'blessed', 'bawled Nancy' to 'said Nancy', or to omit her beating of her feet on the ground and her fit of loud laughter after her 'God forgive me!' at seeing Oliver praying. And one would think this circumlocution for the insensitive 'gallows' in Chapter XIX was discreet enough:

> Miss Nancy prefixed to the word 'cold' another adjective, derived from the name of an unpleasant instrument of death, which, as the word is seldom mentioned to ears polite in any other form than as a substantive, I have omitted in this chronicle.

So in *Bentley's;* but the whole passage disappears as early as 1838, no doubt because Dickens's view of Nancy changed when he had written the later chapters. One suspects that Dickens would have changed Nancy's appearance had he not been committed by Cruikshank's illustrations; but he does not alter the scenes between her and Sikes, and it was Mr. Podsnap's young person rather than a change of view that enforced the omission of 'the girl is a prostitute' from the Preface of 1867. With all Dickens's omissions and small later refinements, Nancy remains a much more truthful portrait of her type than Alice Marwood in *Dombey and Son* or Martha Endell in *David Copperfield.*

The 1841 Preface says nothing about the more specific social and political purposes of the novel, and this perhaps suggests that Dickens felt them relatively incidental and temporary. In the 1850 Preface, where one would expect him to follow his usual practice in the cheap edition and emphasize his attacks on abuses, he concentrates on sanitary reform, in counterblast to Sir Peter Laurie, who had called Jacob's Island fictitious. The exposure of workhouse conditions clearly subserves Dickens's main ends, being another aspect of his 'indignant pity' for the oppressed, and also increases the sense of reality, by making the action specifically recent in time as well as, in the London scenes, precisely localized. Most critics of *Oliver Twist* have been aware of its status as a piece of radical journalism, attacking the Commisioners of the New Poor Law of 1834 and the 'philosophers' generally, and the inefficiency and savagery of Laing, the Hatton Garden magistrate; and some, such as House (who gives the best and fullest account of its contemporary relevance) have also emphasized its more general relation to the revolutionary mood of the 1830s. Dickens's attack has been criticized in some particulars; but his fundamental justification is seen in a contemporary defence of the new law [*London and Westminster Review* (January 1837)], which takes the high ground that 'laws cannot be made to suit individual cases'.

Dickens's dislike of the 'philosophers' may have begun when he reported the Poor Law debates in 1834; but any study of the press of 1835-6 shows that (as so often later in his career) he was joining an existing outcry rather than initiating one. Yet although protests against the harsh operation of the new law were widespread he ran some risk of alienating influential readers. Not surprisingly, the *Quarterly* objected to his 'unfairness' and complained that the general protest was 'partly factious, partly sentimental, partly interested'; but there were also objections from nearer home. Forster [in the *Examiner* (10 September 1837)] thought that 'an unwarrantable and unworthy use is made of certain bugbears of popular prejudice'; Barham, another contributor to the *Miscellany* and a friend of Bentley, wrote in April:

> By the way, there is a sort of Radicalish tone about *Oliver Twist* which I don't altogether like. I think it will not be long before it is remedied, for Bentley is loyal to the backbone himself.

If Barham is right, this difference of opinion may have further exacerbated relations between proprietor and editor. Moreover, the magazine had been projected and advertised as primarily humorous—'the new comic Miscellany', 'the Wits' Miscellany'; and Boz himself, in the second number, speaks of his 'sincere anxiety for the amusement and lightheartedness of the community'. This might seem inconsistent with the opening numbers of *Oliver Twist.* But Dickens early became aware of his double responsibility as protester and entertainer; 'having an audience', he 'resolved' to attack social corruption, but 'I have kept down the strong truth and thrown as much comicality over it as I could' [preface to *Nicholas Nickleby*]. One danger is obvious; the comicality may obscure the strong truth and even endear it to us, and some readers may feel that this happens at times with Bumble and Mrs. Corney, and perhaps with the Artful Dodger. But Dickens was at least unusually successful in this novel in keeping his comedy integral to plot and theme. In the early chapters especially he must have surprised readers by the contrast to *Pickwick;* the only 'comicality' is in the narrator's tone, sarcastically presenting officialdom in its own terms. And even later, the comedy never takes the form of mere interludes. Dickens does not court a *tu quoque* when he notes in Chapter XVII the way melodramas 'present the tragic and comic scenes, in a regular alternation, as the layers of red and white in a side of streaky bacon'. In *Pickwick,* the layer of 'red' in the inset tales was crude enough; now, Dickens mingles humour and horror in the same scene, producing (often abetted by Cruikshank) the grotesque and macabre rather than the 'outrageous and preposterous', carrying a bitter irony even into the climactic scene of Sikes's death on the rope by which he hopes to escape.

It had been Dickens's purpose, according to his Preface, to show his criminals,

> for ever skulking uneasily through the dirtiest paths of life, with the great, black, ghastly gallows closing up their prospect, turn them where they may.

The 'strong truth' of the gallows haunts, even obsesses, this novel from beginning to end. ' "That boy will be hung," said the gentleman in the white waistcoat.' Fagin's treachery is hinted early ('Ah, it's a fine thing for the trade! Five of 'em strung up in a row!'), and he and Sikes often converse in covert allusions to their ultimate power over each other:

> Mr. Sikes contented himself with tying an imaginary knot under his left ear, and jerking his head over on the right shoulder; a piece of dumb show which the Jew appeared to understand perfectly.

The Dodger glosses the word 'scragged' for Oliver's (and the reader's) benefit by 'a lively pantomimic representation' with a handkerchief, amid much laughter. Against this grim jocularity stands the incident where Nancy and Sikes cross Smithfield as the church-bell strikes eight:

> 'Poor fellows!' said Nancy, who still had her face turned towards the quarter in which the bell had sounded. 'Oh, Bill, such fine young chaps as them!'
>
> 'Yes; that's all you women think of,' answered Sikes. 'Fine young chaps! Well, they're as good as dead, so it don't much matter.'

Finally, in Chapter LII, 'The Jew's [altered to 'Fagin's' in 1867] Last Night Alive' Dickens imaginatively enters the consciousness of Fagin and gives us directly what in 'A Visit to Newgate' three years before he had observed and reconstructed, the hour-to-hour fears of a criminal tried, condemned, and awaiting execution. The chapter ends with the onlooker's view:

> A great multitude had already assembled; the windows were filled with people, smoking and playing cards to beguile the time; the crowd were pushing, quarrelling, joking. Everything told of life and animation, but one dark cluster of objects in the centre of all—the black stage, the cross-beam, the rope, and all the hideous apparatus of death.

A scene to which many Londoners in the 1830s were habituated, or avoided merely because it was 'low'; but not Dickens. He perceived and penetrated, both in Sikes and Fagin, the 'strong truth' of the horrible, deserved yet pitiable, isolation of the criminal; and indeed this was the natural fulfilment of his intention to show criminals 'as they really are'.

When at last 'the . . . gallows clos < es > up their prospect, turn them where they may', and we see Sikes in his blood-haunted flight and at bay in the black squalor of Jacob's Island, and Fagin, mauled by the mob, in the Court 'paved with human faces', there is added to the reality of their evil natures, brutish and violent, mean and cringing, the reality of the lonely and terrified human being. The imaginative force with which Dickens conveys that loneliness and terror, in compelling detail, is ill interpreted if it is seen as a shift of moral sympathy or in any way divergent from his stated purpose. His imagination was more strongly stimulated by the 'dregs of life' and by 'adverse circumstance' than by the triumphing 'principle of Good'; in this he resembles other great writers. Dickens concluded his retrospect of how his aim 'appeared' to him with the simple words 'And therefore I did it as I best could'; the ring of satisfaction is surely justified. (pp. 87-105)

Kathleen Tillotson, "Oliver Twist," in Essays and Studies, *n.s. Vol. 12, 1959, pp. 87-105.*

John Bayley　(essay date 1962)

[*Bayley is an English novelist and critic who has written extensively on nineteenth-century authors and their works. In the following essay, he maintains that* Oliver Twist *contains an imaginative synthesis of social criticism and elements of Gothic nightmare.*]

Oliver Twist is a modern novel. It has the perennially modern pretension of rejecting the unreality of a previous mode, of setting out to show us 'things as they really are'. But its modernity is more radical and more unsettling than this pretension implies; it can still touch us—as few novels out of the past can—on a raw nerve; it can still upset and discountenance us. *Pickwick* is not modern. It is a brilliant and successful recreation of the English novel's atmospheres and personalities; but Dickens, like Kipling, had a bargain with his daemon not to repeat a success. It was not *Pickwick* that made Thackeray ruefully praise Dickens's perpetual modernity, or Chesterton announce that Dickens had remained modern while Thackeray had become a classic.

Oliver Twist lacks only one attribute of the modern novel—complete self-consciousness. No novelist has profited more richly than Dickens from not examining what went on in his own mind. His genius avoids itself like a sleep-walker avoiding an open window. Chesterton says what a good thing it is we are not shown Pecksniff's thoughts—they would be too horrible—but the point about Pecksniff is that he has no thoughts: he is as much of a sleep-walker as Dickens: he is the perfect hypocrite because he does not know what he is like. Dickens recoiled from what he called 'dissective' art, and if he had been able and willing to analyse the relation between our inner and outer selves he could never have created the rhetoric that so marvellously ignores the distinction between them. Unlike us, he had no diagrammatic view of mind, no constricting terminology for the psyche. The being of Bumble, Pecksniff, Mrs. Gamp is not compartmented: their inner being *is* their outer self. When Mrs. Gamp says: 'We never know what's hidden in each other's hearts; and if we had glass windows there, we'd need to keep the shutters up, some of us, I do assure you'—she is saying something that will be true of John Jasper and Bradley Headstone, but the great early characters are in fact windowed and shutterless. Noah Claypole carousing with Charlotte over the oysters, a *mass* of bread and butter in his hand; Bumble announcing the cause of Oliver's rebellion to Mrs. Sowerberry—' "It's not madness, Ma'am, it's meat", said the beadle after a few moments of deep meditation'—their monstrosity luxuriates without depth or concealment. When Proust sets out to 'overgo' the Dickensian monster with his Charlus and Françoise, the ebullience and energy are seen to proceed from a creative centre which is meticulous, reflective, and the reverse of energetic: the peculiar Victorian harmony of created and creating energy is lost.

Their wholeness and harmony have a curious effect on the evil of Dickens's monsters: it sterilizes it in performance but increases it in idea. The energy of Fagin or Quilp seems neutral; there is not enough gap between calculation and action for it to proceed to convincingly evil works. By contrast, Iago and Verhovensky are monsters because they know what they are doing; their actions let us loathe them and recoil from them into freedom, but we cannot recoil from Dickens's villains: they are the more frightening and haunting because we cannot expel them for what they do; they have the unexpungable nature of our own nightmares and our own consciousness.

We cannot recoil—that is the point. For in spite of the apparent openness of its energy and indignation *Oliver Twist* is in fact the kind of novel in which we are continually oppressed by the disingenuousness of our own impulses and fantasies, the kind of novel in which the heroine, say, is immured in a brothel, and in which we, like her, both shrink from the fate and desire it. *Clarissa* is in the background. 'Richardson', says Diderot in a famous passage, 'first carried the lantern into the depths of that cavern . . . he breathes on the agreeable form at the entrance and the hideous Moor behind it is revealed.' The lantern has been carried pretty often into the cave since then, and the hideous Moor has become a familiar enough figure: we are introduced in many a modern fiction to our hypothetical sadomasochistic interiors. But whereas a novel like *Death in Venice,* or *Les Caves du Vatican,* divides one aspect of the self from another with all the dramatic cunning and the nice impassivity of art—the author being perfectly aware what he is up to—Dickens presents the nightmare of what we are and what we want in its most elemental and undifferentiated form. All unknowing, he does not let us escape from the ignominy of our fascinations, because he does not try to escape from them himself.

Oliver Twist is not a satisfying novel—it does not liberate us. In achieving what might be called the honesty of the dream world it has to stay in prison. The sense of complete reality in fiction can perhaps only be achieved by the author's possessing, and persuading his reader to share, a sense of different worlds, different and indeed almost incompatible modes of feeling and being. The awareness of difference is the awareness of freedom, and it is, moreover, the knowledge of reality we normally experience in life. But in *Oliver Twist* there are no such contrasts, no such different worlds. Even the apparent contrast between Fagin's world and that of Rose Maylie and Mr. Brownlow is not a real one, and this is not because the happy Brownlow world is rendered sentimentally and unconvincingly by Dickens, but because the two do in fact co-exist in consciousness: they are twin sides of the same coin of fantasy, not two real places that exist separately in life. And there is no true activity in the two worlds, only the guilty or desperately innocent daydreams of our double nature.

The superior power and terror of the unreal is continually harped on. Nancy tells Mr. Brownlow that she can think of nothing but coffins and had just seen one carried past her in the street.

> 'There is nothing unusual in that. They have passed me often.' *'Real ones,'* rejoined the girl. 'This was not.' (Ch. 46.)

Where the reality of action is concerned, Fagin's world has the technical advantage over the Maylie one of *reporting*—as in the dialogue of the thieves' kitchen and the boys going out with Oliver to pick pockets—but it is significant that the long burglary sequence, when Sikes takes Oliver down to Chertsey to crack the Maylie house and the two worlds collide at last, is one of the most dreamlike in the novel. Dreamlike too is a later collision, the meeting of Nancy and Rose Maylie in the hotel bedroom: another novelist would make such a confrontation of worlds the most reality-enhancing note in his tale, but in *Oliver Twist* they only confirm the dream atmosphere. Even when he is firmly inside the Maylie world, Oliver can, so to speak, deprive another character of reality by compelling him to act out Oliver's fantasy of what life in such a world is like. Oliver goes out to gather flowers every morning, and when Henry Maylie returns home 'he was seized with such a passion for flowers, and displayed such a taste in their arrangement, as left his young companion far behind'.

As we shall see, Dickens frequently defends himself against the charge of using literary devices and conventions by pointing out their similarity to real life, and he seems to imply that he is using the dream atmosphere as a kind of convention in this spirit. He gives two accounts of the nature of waking dreams, the first at Fagin's, and the second when just after the flower episode Oliver sees Fagin and Monks at the window of the Maylie's parlour and their eyes meet. 'There is a kind of sleep that steals upon us sometimes which, while it holds the body prisoner, does not free the mind from a sense of things about it, and enables it to ramble at its pleasure.' (Ch. 34.) So similar are the two accounts of this state that it seems likely Dickens repeated himself accidentally in the hurry of composition (for the second half of the novel was written under great pressure), but the effect is none the less potent for that. It is a dream from which Oliver awakes to find it true, even though no footprints of the pair can be found. It recalls the earlier waking dream, when he lay watching Fagin sorting his stolen goods, and we realize it is not physical distance that keeps him from Fagin's house, a house which had once belonged to respectable people like the Maylies, and in which the mirrors of the unused rooms where Fagin and Monks confer now only reflect the dusty floor and the slimy track of the snail.

That the two worlds are one in the mind appears even in Cruickshank's drawings, where Oliver often has a distinct look of Fagin. Henry James remarked that as a child the pictures of the good places and people frightened him more than the bad! It is often said, and with some justice, that Dickens muddles the message of his novel by making Oliver immune to an environment which is denounced as necessarily corrupting. But Oliver is not psychologically immune, nor is Dickens, nor are we. It is true that Dickens cheerfully adopts a vaguely Rousseauesque notion of the innocent warped and made evil by institutions—('what human nature may be made to be') and also seems to adopt with equal readiness the tory doctrine that birth and breeding will win through in the end. But however muddled as propaganda—indeed perhaps because they are muddled—these contradictions are entirely resolved in the imaginative certainty of the novel. Dickens might well proclaim, as he did to critics who found Nancy's love for Sikes implausible—that IT IS TRUE! His imagination makes nonsense, just as life does, of theories of how human beings will or will not behave in a given environment. Notwithstanding the claustrophobic nature of the book, and its heavy dream atmosphere, Dickens's triumph is to have made Oliver—and Charley Bates and Nancy too—free of all human possibility, free in spirit and impulse against all physical and factual likelihood. The world of the novel may be a prison but they are not finally enclosed in it. And he has made this ultimate freedom seem true.

Still, Fagin's wish to incriminate Oliver, and hence confine him for ever in the evil world, is an objective and social terror as well as a psychological one. There remains the plain and sickening fact that Fagin's school and all it stands for extinguishes the hope and chance of better things, though not necessarily the capacity for them: of his pupils, Oliver escapes by the needs of the plot, Charley Bates by the death of Sikes and Fagin, and Nancy not at all. Dickens himself had been at Fagin's school—the blacking factory—and the boy who chiefly befriended him there was actually called Fagin. No wonder Fagin the criminal is such an ambivalent figure when the real Fagin's kindness had, so to speak, threatened to inure Dickens to the hopeless routine of the wage-slave. So passionate was the young Dickens's desire for the station in life to which he felt entitled, and so terrifying his sense that it was being denied him, that he must have hated the real Fagin for the virtue which he could not bear to accept or recognize in that nightmare world, because it might help to subdue him into it. The real Fagin's kindness becomes the criminal Fagin's villainy.

Like Oliver reading the tales of crime in Fagin's den, Dickens 'prayed heaven to spare him from such deeds'. He came later, at the time of his readings from *Oliver Twist,* to have a clear and horrifying awareness of his split personality: he dreaded himself, and the possibility that he might be exiled by his own doing into the world of the murderer and the social outcast. The premise of *Oliver Twist* is the gnostic one of Melville's poem:

> Indolence is heaven's ally here
> And energy the child of hell . . .

Dickens feared the surrender to the demon of energy which his nature continually imposed on him. One of the many biographical glosses on the novel is the idyll which in the summer of 1849 he claimed to be enjoying with his family in the Isle of Wight, an idyll rudely interrupted when Dickens could stand it no longer and hurried them all away again from the picnics, the charades, and the flower gathering.

The power of *Oliver Twist* depends more than any other of Dickens's novels on his personality and background—that is why one has to insist on them so much. Everything in the novel means something else; it is shot through and through with involuntary symbolism, with that peculiar egocentric modernity which Edmund Wilson tells us to be fiction's discovery of its true self. Except possibly for Giles the butler, nobody and nothing exists merely in itself. Even the famous 'household' passages, like Oliver asking for more, do not have the legendary authority of an epic moment but make a piercing appeal to something private and vulnerable in the memory of the reader. 'Things as they really are' turn out to be things as the fantasy fears, and feared in childhood, that they may be. In *David Copperfield* childhood fantasy is also dominant, but in the objective setting of true existences, David's mother, Peggotty, Betsy Trotwood, and Barkis—there is the breadth and solidity of epic. In *Oliver Twist* the child is *right:* there is no suggestion that his vision of monsters is illusory or incomplete, and the social shock to us is that the child here is right to see things thus—the system is monstrous because he finds it to be so. His vision is the lens to focus Dickens's *saeva indignatio.* The grotesque conversation between Noah, Bumble, and the gentleman in the white waistcoat, about what is to be done with Oliver, is true because it is just how Oliver would imagine it. But in *Copperfield* the child may be wrong; he only partially apprehends the existences around him, and Murdstone, for instance, is more arresting and intriguing than anyone in *Oliver Twist* because there is no assumption that David really knows what he is like.

Dickens's crusading purpose underwrites Oliver's view of things and creates a powerful satiric method at the cost of losing the actual child's involuntary existence. Indeed it is the loss of the mere condition of childishness, as an abused animal or bird loses its natural status, which is so heart-rending—Oliver is never allowed to *be* what he is, and when liberated he has to act the part, a fact unconsciously recognized by Cruickshank in drawings which have the look of a twenty-year old actor playing a schoolboy. Oliver has been cheated of childhood like his friend Dick, whose limbs are 'like those of an old man'. Acting, indeed, as Dickens implies in his facetious but revealing preamble to Chapter 17, is the clue to the mode by which we are to be moved by the persona and events of the story. We must put ourselves in their place and act as they are acting. We must be like the crazy old woman for whom her daughter's death was 'as good as a play'.

> It is the custom on the stage, in all good murderous melodramas, to present the tragic and comic scenes in . . . regular alternation. . . . We behold, with throbbing bosoms, the heroine in the grasp of a proud and ruthless baron: her virtue and her life alike in danger, drawing forth her dagger to preserve the one at the cost of the other; and just as our expectations are wrought up to the highest pitch, a whistle is heard, and we are straightway transported to the great hall of the castle: where a grey-headed seneschal sings a funny chorus.
>
> Such changes appear absurd: but they are not so unnatural as they would seem at first sight. The transitions in real life from well-spread boards to death-beds, and from mourning weeds to holiday garments, are not a whit less startling; only, there, we are busy actors, instead of passive lookers-on, which makes a vast difference. The actors in the mimic life of the theatre, are blind to violent transitions and abrupt impulses of passion or feeling, which, presented before the eyes of mere spectators, are at once condemned as outrageous and preposterous.

It is a brilliant apologia for his whole creative method. He implies that it is *because* Oliver is an actor that the spectator should not withhold sympathy if the tale seems artificial and implausible, thus ingeniously confounding the stage actor with the actor in real life and claiming that in both cases the only true view is the participant's: we must ourselves participate in order to feel the truth of the thing, and not merely appraise it from outside.

In seeking to disarm criticism by drawing his readers into a hypnotic unity with the tale and the author, Dickens relies heavily on convention to increase both the shared hypnosis and the emotion of truth. As Forster tells us, he delighted in coincidence and in pointing out how common it was in life. And in *Oliver Twist* he positively takes refuge in melodramatic ceremonial: it would be a disaster if the taste of the age had allowed him to describe what must have been the continual and brutish sexual activity in Fagin's hole—(*Jonathan Wild,* and *The Beggar's Opera,* which Dickens protests is unrealistic, are much franker about this)—or to have rendered the actual oaths of Sikes instead of giving him grotesquely and perhaps deliberately exaggerated euphemisms like 'Wolves tear your throats!' . . . Though he may not have been conscious of it, Dickens knew that such disguises and prevarications are indeed the truth of the fantasy. And he enhances their effect by putting them beside facts of a neutral and professional kind, like his catalogue of the districts—Exmouth Street, Hockley in the Hole, Little Saffron Hill, etc.—through which Oliver is led by the Artful Dodger, and through which Sikes wanders after the murder. The setting in which Noah eavesdrops on the meeting between

Nancy and the Maylies is detailed with the offhand expertise of Kipling:

> These stairs are a part of the bridge; they consist of three flights. Just below the end of the second, going down, the stone wall on the left terminates in an ornamental pilaster facing towards the Thames. At this point the lower steps widen: so that a person turning that angle of the wall, is necessarily unseen by any others on the stairs who chance to be above him, if only a step. (Ch. 46.)

The old device of the eavesdropper has never been more effectively localized. But reality depends on the convention. Dickens was the first to protest against the new French 'realism', because he felt it might discredit his mystery. He has often been blamed for giving the happy ending to *Great Expectations,* in deference to Bulwer Lytton, but he has there a sure sense, as in *Oliver Twist,* not of what the *donnée* demanded, but of upholding the kinds of agreement he had made with the reader. The artistic rigour of a Flaubert alienates, and Dickens is faithful only to what he and his audience can make of the thing together.

Yet in his last novels he is beginning to hold the reader off. It is extremely illuminating to compare *Oliver Twist* with *Edwin Drood,* because we are not required to participate in the exquisitely murderous atmosphere of the last novel. We can stand back, and watch the familiar two worlds—the world of goodness and innocence and the world of murder and hallucination—conjured into a real and objective existence. Canon Crisparkle and his mother, the Virginia creeper, and the home-made wines and jellies, are solid and reassuring presences: they have strength as well as gentleness. Rosa Budd and Helena Landless, 'a beautiful barbaric captive brought from some wild tropical dominion', are as meticulously alive as Jasper, raising his high voice in the shadowy choir and hating the rôle he has made for himself. Dickens has adopted the principle of depth; hypocrisy is real at last. Instead of the divided nature being flat and two-dimensional as a Rorschach inkblot, spreading over the whole of life, it now exists in and perceives an upper and lower world. At the cost of transforming his social earnestness into an earnestness of craftsmanship Dickens keeps his imagination working at full pressure, but in a new sphere of complication and plurality. His vision proves to be as fecund as Shakespeare's, and to have the same power of continued transformation. It was transforming itself afresh when he died.

So far I have stressed the waking nightmare which is the imaginative principle of *Oliver Twist,* and the way it dispels any true distinction between the world of darkness which Oliver is in, and the world of light which he longs for. None the less the impressive power of the novel does depend upon a most effective distinction, of quite another kind, and of the force of which Dickens seems equally unaware. It is the distinction between crime and murder.

We are apt to forget how early-Victorian society, the society of laissez-faire, took for granted individual conditions of privacy and isolation. It was a society where each unit, each family and household, led their secret lives with an almost neurotic antipathy to external interference. It was the age of the private gentleman who wanted nothing but to be left alone. He could ignore politics, the Press, the beggar who happened to be dying of hunger in the coach-house; he need feel no pressure of social or national existence. Noah Claypole provides an ironic gloss when he says about Oliver: 'let him alone! Why, everyone lets him pretty much alone!' And the poor had the same instincts as their betters. At the time of the Crimea, when a suggestion of conscription was raised, labourers and miners said they would take to the woods or go underground rather than be caught for it. There has probably never been a time when England was—in the sociological phrase—less integrated.

Dickens has a most disturbing feeling for this. Like most Victorians his sense of other things, other places and people, was founded on fear and distrust. The Boz of the Sketches seems to hate and fear almost everything, even though it fascinates him. For unlike other people he had no home to go to, no hole in which he could feel secure. Normal living and the life of crime are almost indistinguishable in *Oliver Twist,* for both are based on the burrow. Both Jacob's Island and the town where Oliver is born consist largely of derelict houses which are not owned or occupied in the normal way but taken possession of as burrows, or 'kens', with an 'aperture made into them wide enough for the passage of a human body'. Fagin, who when out of doors is compared to a reptile 'looking for a meal of some rich offal', has his den on Saffron Hill; when he first enters the district Oliver sees that from several of these holes 'great ill-looking fellows were cautiously emerging, bound, to all appearance, on no very well-disposed or harmless errands'. The stiltedness of the writing here somehow emphasizes the effect of evening beasts coming out on their normal business. Mr. Brownlow (whose name oddly suggests a fox) and Mr. Grimwig are holed up in Clerkenwell; Mrs. Corney has her snug corner in the workhouse; the Maylies live behind the walls of their Chertsey house as if it were in the Congo. The house to which Oliver is taken before the abortive 'crack', and which he afterwards identifies, is found then to have some quite different tenant, an evil creature who is hastily left to his own devices. A man on the run makes the round of the kens and finds them already full, as if they were shells tenanted by crabs.

All these people have the same outlook and the same philosophy of life, a philosophy which that private gentleman, Fagin, sums up as 'looking after No. 1'. As one would expect, Dickens can see nothing in the idea of 'private vices, public virtues' except a degradingly mutual kind of blackmail. In presenting his characters as animals, purposeful, amoral, and solitary in their separate colonies, with no true gregariousness or power of cohesion, he draws a terrifying imaginative indictment of what private life may be like in an open society, in his age or in our own.

Murder transforms all this. Like a magic wand it changes the animals back into men again: what we think of as 'human nature' returns with a rush. And it is an extraordinary and sinister irony that makes murder the only imaginative vindication in the book of human stature and human meaningfulness. Though Dickens may not have bargained for the effect it is the crowning stroke in the satirical violence of his novel. Just as murder, in the Victorian literary mythology, was cleaner than sex, so in Dickens's vision is it more human than crime and the inhumanity of social institutions, for crime is the most characteristic aspect of the social order. Bumble, Fagin and the rest are evil beings because they are not human beings; they are doing the best they can for themselves in their business, and Sikes was similarly an animal in the business—'the mere hound of a day' as Fagin says—until murder turns him into a kind of man. Thereupon, too, society develops the cohesion and point that it had lacked before—indeed this, like so much else in the book, is grotesquely though effectively overdone. Nancy's murder assumes the proportions of a national crisis, 'Spies', we hear, 'are hovering about in every direction'. Significantly, until the murder no one seems to take notice of Fagin—he is engrossed in his repellent business like any other citizen—but after it he is nearly lynched. Crime is like animal or mechanical society, cold, separated, and professional, but murder is like the warmth and conviviality which Dickens always praises—a great uniter.

Undoubtedly Dickens is saying something here about society which has lost none of its potency. With a shudder we realize what we are still like. Of course, Dickens had a perfectly 'healthy' interest in murder and hanging, just as he took a normal English pleasure in illness, funerals, and ballads like 'the blood-drinker's burial'; but murder in *Oliver Twist* has a more metaphysical status, is less literary and less purely morbid and professional, than any other in Dickens. His later murders, beautifully done as they are, have by comparison a dilettante flavour. In *Our Mutual Friend* and *Drood* other characters mime the murderous atmosphere in proleptic touches that are almost Shakespearian. Lammle wrenches the stopper off a siphon 'as if he wanted to pour its blood down his throat'. At the end of term celebrations in the dormitory of Miss Twinkleton's seminary, one of the young ladies 'gives a sprightly solo on the comb and curl-paper until suffocated in her own pillow by two flowing-haired executioners'. But murder in *Oliver Twist* is definitely not considered as one of the fine arts. It is not an aesthetic matter sealed off in its artifice and our satisfaction, but a moral act which for that reason penetrates not only the life of the novel but our own lives as well.

Dostoevsky, a great admirer of *Oliver Twist,* also makes murder a kind of social revelation. Writers who learn from Dickens usually develop explicitly an effect which is implicit in their source, and Dostoevsky makes Roskolnikov a rebel who murders the old moneylender out of frustration, as a kind of thwarted substitute for idealist terrorism. We know from his diary that Dostoevsky was bothered by Roskolnikov's lack of an obvious motive—he realized that the significance with which the author endowed the crime was showing too clearly through the story. But Sikes's motive is brutally simple and straightforward. Nancy must be got rid of because she has betrayed the gang: the whole burrow principle of looking after No. 1 demands her instant elimination. None the less, it is a duty, and duty is a human and not an animal concept.

Without once turning his head to the right or left, or raising his eyes to the sky, or lowering them to the ground, but looking straight before him with savage resolution: his teeth so tightly compressed that the strained jaw seemed starting through his skin; the robber held on his headlong course, nor uttered a word, nor relaxed a muscle, until he reached his own door. (Ch. 47.)

Like Macbeth, Sikes 'bends up each corporal agent to this terrible feat'. An animal kills naturally, like a cat killing a bird; and in Dickens's other murders the murderer's animality is increased by the deed. Jonas Chuzzlewit skulks like a beast out of the wood where his victim lies; Rogue Riderhood lives by furtive killing, and Dickens suggests his nature in two brilliant images—the fur cap, 'like some small drowned animal', which he always wears, and the shapeless holes he leaves in the snow, 'as if the very fashion of humanity had departed from his feet'. Headstone's course is the exact opposite of Sikes's: the lust to kill strips the veneer of decency and laboriously acquired culture from him, and turns him into the terrifying creature who grinds his fist against the church wall until the blood comes. Like Chuzzlewit he feels no remorse, only the murderer's *esprit de l'escalier*—he cannot stop thinking how much more ingeniously the deed might have been done. Reduced to the animal status of Riderhood, he loses even his own name, his last link with humanity, when at Riderhood's bidding he writes it on the school blackboard and then rubs it out.

But Sikes finds his name. It is on every tongue in the metropolis. Other murderers become conscienceless animals, but he acquires the form and conscience of a man, almost indeed of a spirit. 'Blanched face, sunken eyes, hollow cheeks . . . it was the very ghost of Sikes.' And as his killing of Nancy makes him a man, so her love for him transforms her into a woman. 'Pity us', she says to Rose Maylie, 'for setting our rotten hearts on a man. Pity us for having only one feeling of the woman left, and that turned into a new means of violence and suffering.' The act she puts on when she enquires for Oliver at the police station, and helps to recapture him in the street, is a nightmare parody of social pretences and what they conceal, a sort of analogue to the pomposities of Bumble and the realities of the workhouse. Her revulsion when Oliver is brought back to Fagin's den is one of the most moving things in the book, but its denizens suppose she is still keeping up the part ('You're acting beautiful,' says Fagin) and they eye her ensuing rage and despair with bestial incomprehension. 'Burn my body,' growls Sikes, 'do you know what you are?', and Fagin tells her 'It's your living.'

> 'Aye, it is!' returned the girl; not speaking, but pouring out the words in one continuous and vehement scream. 'It is my living and the cold wet dirty streets are my home; and you're the wretch that drove me to them long ago, and that'll keep me there, day and night, night and day, till I die!' (Ch. 16.)

Nancy's living is the living of England, a nightmare society in which drudgery is endless and stupefying, in which the natural affections are warped, and the dignity of man appears only in resolution and violence. It is a more disquieting picture than the carefully and methodically symbolized social panoramas of *Bleak House, Little Dorrit,* and *Our Mutual Friend.* It is as raw and extemporized as Nancy's outburst. *Oliver Twist* quite lacks the overbearing pretension of the later novels, a pretension which Edmund Wilson defers to rather too solemnly when he tells us that Dickens in *Our Mutual Friend* 'had come to despair utterly of the prospering middle class'. It is the same pretension which G. K. Chesterton notes apropos of Riah, the good Jewish money-lender introduced because of complaints from Jewish correspondents about Fagin: 'It pleased Dickens to be mistaken for a public arbiter: it pleased him to be asked (in a double sense) to judge Israel'.

Oliver is not in a position to despair of the middle class, or anything else, and the humility of this is communicated in some way to the author and moves us more than all his later stridency. Oliver is a true everyman: he does not, like David Copperfield or D. H. Lawrence, shriek at us incredulously—'They did this to *me!*' It is logical that he has no character, because he has no physical individuality—he is the child element in a nightmare which is otherwise peopled by animals, and precariously by men. Child, beast, and man indeed merge and change places phantasmagorically throughout the book. Oliver is sometimes adult, almost middle-aged, and sometimes like an animal himself, as when his eyes glisten at the sight of the scraps of meat in Mrs. Sowerberry's kitchen—one of the few really physical intimations of him we have. After the murder the lesser criminals are as lost and bewildered as children, and the hardened Kags begs for a candle, saying 'Don't leave me in the dark'. Sikes and Nancy, as hero and heroine, have their transformation from beast to man: only Fagin remains a reptile throughout and to the end, losing at last even his human powers of speech and intellect and crouching in the dock like something snared, his glittering eyes 'looking on when an artist broke his pencil point and made another with his knife, as any idle spectator might have done.' He has the animal victim's unnerving air of detachment from his own predicament, and the butchery of one kind of beast by another is the final horror of his execution. 'Are you a man, Fagin?' asks the gaoler.

> 'I shan't be one long,' he replied, looking up with a face containing no human expression but rage and terror. 'Strike them all dead! What right have they to butcher me?'

It is a horribly penetrating appeal, when we think of society as *Oliver Twist* presents it. And in contrast to the almost heroic death of Sikes, Fagin will lose even his animal identity at the very end, and revert to a dreadful human simulacrum, 'a dangling heap of clothes'.

'To be thoroughly earnest is everything, and to be anything short of it is nothing.' Dickens's credo about novel-writing is certainly true of *Oliver Twist,* but whereas in the later novels this seriousness extends to the technique which fashions symbols and symbolic atmospheres—the famous fogs, prison, dust, etc.—he does not insist on, or even seem aware of, the animal symbolism here: it hits the reader like a sleepwalker's blow, involuntarily administered. It seems a natural product of the imagination, like that of Shakespeare and Hardy; though Dickens's later symbolic technique is closer to Lawrence's, purposeful and claustrophobic, the meaning too unified to expand into an ordinary human range of possibility. Character remains imprisoned in the author's will and we are uneasily aware of the life that has been left out. The Dickens of **Hard Times,** whom Dr. Leavis admires, manipulates symbolic meaning in a manner that reaches its apotheosis with Clifford Chatterley sitting in his motor-chair. Nor do his 'straight' characters always escape the same fate. It is with some complacency that he reports how his mother, his model for Mrs. Nickleby, protested that there could not be such a woman. One sympathizes with her, and one is inclined to think she was right. Her son was rather too confident that his imagination could give another being its real life, and that what Mrs. Nickleby (or Mrs. Dickens) felt themselves to be was nothing in comparison with what Dickens saw them to be.

It is the more remarkable, therefore, that Sikes and Nancy have such a range. His intentions about them are overt enough. He says he is not going to abate one growl of Sikes or 'one scrap of curl-paper in Nancy's dishevelled hair'. This confidence of the realist is hardly very encouraging. The description of the Bow Street officers, based on a 'Wanted' notice, 'reveals them', says Dickens, 'for what they are'; and we are not allowed to forget Cratchit's shawl-pattern waistcoat or the humorous overcoat sported by the Dodger. Sikes himself

> was a stoutly-built fellow of about five and thirty, in a black velveteen coat, very soiled drab breeches, lace-up half boots, and grey cotton stockings, which enclosed a bulky pair of legs, with large swelling calves—the kind of legs, which in such costume, always look in an unfinished and incomplete state without a set of fetters to garnish them. (Ch. 13.)

The bit about fetters gives the game away, and shows that for all his protestations of realism Dickens is really drawing on Gay and Hogarth. But what brings Sikes and Nancy to life is the gap between what they look like and what they are like, between their appearance as Dickens insists we shall have it, and the speech and manner with which another convention requires him to endow them. They rise, as it were, between two stools; they achieve their real selves by being divided between two modes of artifice. Nancy looks like the slattern in curl-papers lifting the gin bottle and exclaiming 'Never say die'! but inside there is the desperate being who confronts Fagin and bitterly describes herself to Rose Maylie. The Sikes in grey cotton stockings is the same man who goes to murder like Macbeth.

In asserting an apparent realism, Dickens actually achieves a striking balance—very rare in his characterization—between the outward and inward selves that make up a whole person. The nonsense talked by Bumble, Pecksniff, or Squeers, their total lack of the responsibilities of intercourse, mark Dickens's most contemptuous, though most inspired, refusal to recognize an inner self in such persons. But Sikes and Nancy have an eloquence, a brutal and urgent power of communication, that shows how seriously Dickens takes them, and how seriously they are

compelled to take themselves. The dimension of these two is the triumph of the novel, and it closely corresponds to the main feat—surely unique in the history of the novel—which Dickens has achieved in combining the genre of Gothic nightmare with that of social denunciation, so that each enhances the other. (pp. 49-64)

> *John Bayley, "Oliver Twist: 'Things As They Really Are'," in Dickens and the Twentieth Century, edited by John Gross and Gabriel Pearson, University of Toronto Press, 1962, pp. 49-64.*

Keith Hollingsworth   (essay date 1963)

[*In the following excerpt, Hollingsworth discusses* Oliver Twist *as a Newgate novel in which Dickens draws on current events and literature in his portrayal of criminal activity in London.*]

Although Dickens' interest in crime and criminals was lifelong, it was the early novel, **Oliver Twist,** which for a time placed him among the Newgate novelists. Its "low" material was disliked by a few readers even to the beginning of the twentieth century. (George Saintsbury, who had a favorite joke about "grime" novels, wrote deprecatingly of it in 1917, in the *Cambridge History of English Literature.*) **Oliver Twist** was attached to the contemporary scene in a fashion not equalled in the other Newgate novels. It reflected the prevalence of juvenile crime; the recent development of the trade in stolen goods, which seemed in the twenties almost to be keeping pace with legitimate commerce; and the general attention to crime and punishment. (p. 111)

Besides observing the streets of London, Dickens must have read what came to hand about youthful criminals, and he probably sought out more. The newspapers of any year of the period show the kind of notice given to young thieves: when they were brought before a magistrate there was little opportunity for discrimination between the novice and the professional criminal. Judges had certain discretionary powers, but the jury, deciding between guilty and not guilty, knew that the penalty of imprisonment or transportation or indeed death was as applicable to the boy of ten or twelve as to the man of thirty. The attitude of the judge did of course make a great difference in the handling of an individual case. Real innocence might receive pity, but the system and the minds which carried it on were not constituted to deal with boys who were still at the beginning of a criminal career.

The newspapers had made Dickens' readers equally well prepared to accept Fagin. Isaac or Ikey Solomon, whose name (with *s* added) Thackeray was to take as a burlesque pseudonym for *Catherine,* had become known as the most successful and elusive of London fences, and his activities had been extensively reported. Dickens' receiver is not shown to have so large a business as Solomon's nor does his character parallel Solomon's in detail, but the notoriety of the actual person was such that every adult reader must have thought of him. The case had been closed, so far as the English courts were concerned, when Solomon was transported to Australia in 1831, but references to him were frequent for years thereafter. Born in 1785, he was first a peddler, a passer of bad coins, and a pickpocket. He learned to deal in stolen goods and made enormous profits. For many years the police knew of his operations, but the requirements of the law for identifying stolen goods were so stringent that a conviction was hard to obtain. No great ingenuity seems to have been matched against Solomon's, but the accounts do not suggest that he paid for immunity. In making the traffic of a fence into a well-organized business, Solomon was extremely careful to see that identifying marks on all objects were removed before the goods came to rest in his house. It was a precaution which no one had applied so consistently before. (Dickens' Fagin sets Oliver Twist at removing the marks from handkerchiefs.) One writer has it that as Solomon advanced in his career he dealt only in big lots; he advised the thieves who supplied him not to take continual risks on small jobs but to live better by carrying off one or two well-planned large operations in a year.

He was a successful dealer in stolen notes of the Bank of England; he had agents outside London who sent the notes (as well as other goods) to the Continent, whence they returned to the bank through legitimate channels of trade. (Fagin remarks of a stolen note that it will have to be sent out of the country.) Property in Solomon's house at the time of his arrest was supposed to be worth £20,000. He was tried at last on July 9, 1830, and transported the next May. In the course of his career, he had become legendary—a modern businessman who made Jonathan Wild seem a crude amateur.

Oliver Twist reflects also the parliamentary attention given to revision of the criminal law, an attention nearly constant between 1833 and 1837. For observing the social and political legislation of a great period of change, Dickens had experience unparalleled by that of other novelists, for he began a four-year period of parliamentary reporting in the reform year, 1832. He was twenty years old when he first entered the reporters' gallery of the House of Commons. After or concurrently with work on another paper, he was employed by the *Mirror of Parliament,* a journal which emulated the completeness of *Hansard;* he was with the *Mirror* for two sessions. By August 1834, he had achieved a coveted position with the *Morning Chronicle,* which he resigned two years later, at the close of the session in August 1836. His work for the *Chronicle* kept him chiefly in the Commons, but on numerous occasions he was sent to cover important parliamentary elections in the towns. Such absences were of short duration, a few days at a time. He must surely have been aware of every important measure which the House of Commons dealt with between March 1832 and August 1836.

Although Dickens was no longer a reporter in this conclusive year, 1837, there is every reason to suppose that he followed the course of the pending legislation. Bills proposed by the Royal Commission were introduced in the Commons in March and passed without difficulty; they were delayed in the Lords, where the second reading did not occur until July 4, after which they had to return to the Commons in their amended form. The completed acts, which received the royal assent at the close of the session on July 17, were certainly among the principal achievements of that parliament.

The dates are interesting. It cannot have been by accident that Dickens inserted an argument against capital punishment into *Oliver Twist* while the long-awaited measures were at the obstacle of the House of Lords. Fagin, the vicious exploiter of other men's theft, looks over his treasures and mutters to himself:

> What a fine thing capital punishment is! Dead men never repent; dead men never bring awkward stories to light. Ah, it's a fine thing for the trade! Five of 'em strung up in a row, and none left to play booty, or turn white-livered!

Nothing could have been more topical and current at the beginning of July 1837, when this came to the readers of *Bentley's Miscellany.*

If certain features of *Oliver Twist* came to it directly from the contemporary scene, others came by way of Dickens' earlier work. What signs of Dickens' interest in criminals and their milieu preceded *Oliver Twist*? The two sets of *Sketches by Boz,* which contain thematic indications for so many of the novels, show the subjects of his observation, the aspect of London which his criminal novel was to use, and a few very specific anticipations of the characters in it.

Among the frankly fictional items, there is some indication of Dickens' special interest in "The Black Veil," in which a physician is engaged in advance to try to resuscitate a hanged man, and "The Drunkard's Death," the chronicle of an evil wretch responsible for the deaths of his daughter and his son. The reporting pieces begin to show us the parts of London we might expect. As a boy of nine or ten, Dickens had been fascinated by walking through Seven Dials, and this locality served for one of the street scenes. The sketches "Gin-Shops" and "The Pawnbroker's Shop" contain further observation of poor neighborhoods.

Others draw much closer to the scenes and characters of *Oliver Twist.* "Criminal Courts," published in the *Morning Chronicle,* October 23, 1834, describes a visit to the Old Bailey, newsworthy because the recent act of parliament had reorganized it as the Central Criminal Court. From a scene in the New Court there, he recorded some words from an ingenious young offender like Jack Dawkins. "The Prisoners' Van" tells of two young girls being taken away from the Bow Street police office; one is a novice, the other still in the first steps of a life of vice and crime. "A Visit to Newgate" gives an account of what was apparently Dickens' first experience of the interior of the prison. Dickens noticed that the women in Newgate had needlework to do, whereas the men had no employment. The relics of famous criminals—Sheppard, Turpin, and the recent Bishop and Williams—were for him incidental; he had come to record the human reality of the present.

The sketch most closely connected with *Oliver Twist* is "The Hospital Patient." In the police-office Dickens heard a young man charged with having beaten a woman, and he accompanied the magistrates when they found it necessary to confront the accused with the victim in the hospital where she was confined. She was a girl of twenty-two or twenty-three, badly beaten, who cried and covered her bruised face when she at length recognized the handcuffed man before her. She was sworn, that her testimony might be taken. The man looked anxious, but said nothing.

> "Oh, no, gentlemen," said the girl, raising herself once more, and folding her hands together; "no, gentlemen, for God's sake! I did it myself—it was nobody's fault—it was an accident. He didn't hurt me; he wouldn't for all the world. Jack, dear Jack, you know you wouldn't!"
>
> Her sight was fast failing her, and her hand groped over the bedclothes in search of his. Brute as the man was, he was not prepared for this. He turned his face from the bed, and sobbed. The girl's color changed, and her breathing grew more difficult. She was evidently dying.
>
> "We respect the feelings which prompt you to this," said the gentleman who had spoken first, "but let me warn you, not to persist in what you know to be untrue, until it is too late. It cannot save him."
>
> "Jack," murmured the girl, laying her hand upon his arm, "they shall not persuade me to swear your life away. He didn't do it, gentlemen. He never hurt me." She grasped his arm tightly, and added, in a broken whisper, "I hope God Almighty will forgive me all the wrong I have done, and the life I have led. God bless you, Jack. Some kind gentleman take my love to my poor old father. Five years ago, he said he wished I had died a child. Oh, I wish I had! I wish I had!"
>
> The nurse bent over the girl for a few seconds, and then drew the sheet over her face. It covered a corpse.

Bill Sikes and Nancy are here, and Nancy's unshakable devotion, her repentance, and her murder. Dickens states that the incident happened "a twelvemonth ago," thus placing it approximately in the summer of 1835. Whether fact or fiction, this may be called the tangible beginning of *Oliver Twist.* The tale is turned too neatly to be unadulterated fact, but Dickens may well have seen the essence of it. His later preface to *Oliver Twist* is vehement in its assertion that Nancy's devotion to Sikes "IS TRUE." In the novel itself, the scene seems to be alluded to in Nancy's words to Rose Maylie: persons like herself have "no friend in sickness or death but the hospital nurse."

The subjects of the sketches were Dickens' own—it was not assignments from editors which took him to police court and prison. The localities he sought out were not unnatural for an enterprising reporter, who wanted salable feature materials, but the subjects do betray an individual and special interest.

This concern with the prison may also be seen in *Pickwick Papers.* Full of laughter though it was, it was written by the author of the sketches, the same author who was to begin *Oliver Twist* before *Pickwick* was ended. The prison

there was the Fleet. It had not the same kind of associations as Newgate, nor had the Marshalsea, where Dickens' father was; but all were prisons. Any prison might extend itself broadly to an imaginative boy, as a symbol of authority and law; he might transfer easily and without volition his experience of rebellious fear to his images of other persons confined by the law and find himself readily provided with a fund of sympathy for outcasts. The prison went with Dickens all his life. Edmund Wilson, in "Dickens: the Two Scrooges," pointed out the thematic relation of parts of *Pickwick* to Dickens' obsession with crime; and Lionel Trilling, in a more recent discussion of *Little Dorrit,* remarked that "The prison obsession was due not only to the Marshalsea but also to Dickens' consciousness of the force and scope of his will." All this, however, is the study of modern critics. To Dickens' contemporaries, the debtors' prison, which was no new thing in literature, was pathetic or sometimes funny, but not completely outside the range of ordinary life. *Pickwick Papers* did not prepare them for *Oliver Twist.*

The underworld part of the second novel, drawing upon the social scene and upon Dickens' earlier work, was also touched by certain literary influences. E. A. Baker sees one of them as Marryat. *Snarleyyow, or the Dog Fiend* (1837) had appeared serially in the *Metropolitan Magazine.* Baker calls Smallbones, in that novel, the prototype of Dickens' friendless boys, and has it that Dickens copied Nancy Corbett, the prostitute who has become an honest wife. There seems no reason to doubt that she contributed something, but in view of the scene in "The Hospital Patient" one hesitates to say that it was much more than her first name. Incidentally, Mr. Bumble's method of naming foundlings may owe something to the similar comic naming in *Japhet in Search of a Father,* the Marryat novel which preceded *Snarleyyow.*

Victor Hugo's *Le Dernier jour d'un condamné,* had been mentioned by a reviewer of *Sketches by Boz.* The circumstance may well have sent Dickens to Hugo, if he did not already know the little book. Elizabeth Barrett, reading *Le Dernier jour* later, was convinced that Hugo, whom she thought more powerful than the author of *Oliver Twist,* had had a strong influence upon him: "In his serious powerful Jew-trial scenes, he has followed Hugo closely, and never scarcely looked away from 'Les Trois Jours d'un Condamné'." She may well be right, although there are few specific likenesses between the two books. One of them must be responsible for the way she remembered Hugo's title: the greater part of *Le Dernier jour* deals with the last three days of the man's life, and Dickens' chapter, "Fagin's Last Night Alive," containing the trial scene, also covers Fagin's last three days. Hugo's work offered an example persuasive in two respects: it had a criminal in a contemporary setting, and it employed psychological realism with an unprecedented acuteness of detail. Dickens, like Hugo, presents moments of sharp attention alternating with uncontrolled trivial reverie.

Other contemporary influences involved close personal relationships. It would be surprising if Dickens, ambitious as he was, had not paid attention to the most popular books of the early thirties; and his association with their authors, Ainsworth and Bulwer, forms part of the background of Newgate novel controversy. The relations of the three, or four when we include Forster, may be followed in Dickens' letters and in the several biographies. At some time in 1834, Dickens met Ainsworth; he was one of Ainsworth's numerous guests in 1834 and 1835. Ainsworth then was a literary lion, Dickens still a reporter. Through Ainsworth he met in 1836 John Forster, literary editor of the *Examiner,* who was to be his lifelong friend and his biographer; probably through Ainsworth he met Bulwer. After he met Forster, the relation between the two grew faster than the friendship of either with Ainsworth; but both were, for the next two years and more, increasingly associated with Ainsworth. They rode together, dined together, and called themselves the Trio. Ainsworth and Dickens talked of collaborating on a book. During January and February 1839, Dickens was effecting his separation from his publisher, Bentley. He was not sorry to have Ainsworth replace him as editor of *Bentley's Miscellany,* though Ainsworth may have been hoping for that outcome. A breach came, however, when Dickens was led to suspect that Ainsworth had misrepresented Forster's part in the negotiations. After Dickens' letter of protest, March 26, 1839, the familiar letters and the trio dinners ceased. Forster's attitude will be spoken of in connection with *Jack Sheppard.* The friendship of Dickens and Ainsworth, despite some later exchanges of dinners, was not on its old footing, and by 1845 even their meetings were rare accidents. A small residue of the association with Ainsworth remains in the name of Sikes, in *Oliver Twist;* a James Sykes figures in the historical accounts of Jack Sheppard. Perhaps there is another in Fagin's giving Oliver a *Newgate Calendar* to read.

Bulwer's literary influence must have been more substantial; he had shown a boy in miserable surroundings turned into a thief by bad companions. *Paul Clifford,* later mentioned in the preface to the third edition of *Oliver Twist,* was certainly one of the books Dickens set out to surpass with his realistic story of a workhouse boy. But neither Paul nor any other boy in a book (such as Humphry Clinker) can have been as important for the making of Oliver as the boy Charles Dickens. Bulwer's books were a stimulus of importance, but in some respects Dickens saw in them what to avoid. Though the two authors shared the same view of the criminal law and also an interest in criminals, one cannot say that either learned from the other a manner of handling such themes. Between the men themselves, there was no intimacy but a kind of reciprocal appreciation. Already having met, perhaps in 1835, they were on terms of mutual respect from the time when Dickens emerged as a writer. John Forster, friend of Bulwer and close friend of Dickens, knew both of them better than they knew each other. (pp. 112-19)

Oliver Twist has great vitality and a large measure of realism in its Newgate furnishings. There is force in the workhouse scenes; there is psychological conviction in the crisis of the murderer and the condemned man. "Fagin's Last Night Alive" employs essentially the method that was to be rediscovered later and named internal monologue or stream of consciousness. To enjoy the story, however, one must set no limit on coincidence, and be ready to accept

a birth-mystery for the hero, with another added for good measure. This staple of fiction, unknown parentage—the use of which weakens the logic of the humanitarian sermon—was quite in harmony with Dickens' predilections; as a child he had noticed a handsome little chimney sweep and had been sure the boy was the lost heir of some illustrious man. The sweep "believed he'd been born in the Vurkis, but he'd never know'd his father." Oliver, unfortunately, has no substance as a character.

Dickens makes an effort to have his several classes of characters speak appropriately, though Oliver has the improbable language and deportment of a little gentleman. There is a limited amount of underworld slang, introduced so carefully that the genteel reader need never be at a loss for the meaning. One gets the impression that Dickens had indeed heard the thieves' language in idiomatic context—but that his acquaintance with it was not extended or familiar. If it had been, he would not have been able, even in censoring them, to let his low characters relapse into the stately literary rhythms they sometimes use. George Gissing, quoting Sikes's exclamation, "Wolves tear your throats!" pointed out that the influence of contemporary melodrama reached beyond Dickens' plot to his very language. The words of Toby Crackit, telling Fagin about the unsuccessful robbery, illustrate the author's divergencies. "The crack failed," Toby says in words of one syllable; but a little later, with an original nautical phrase, he says that Bill Sikes "scudded like the wind."

Both language and action are cleansed for presentation to the family circle. In the preface to the third edition Nancy is called a prostitute; she is never so named in the story, and her occupation is most delicately suggested, chiefly

The Burglary. Illustration by George Cruikshank.

through her protestations of guilt. Dickens wishes to show repulsive truth, but—

> No less consulting my own taste, than the manners of the age, I endeavoured, while I painted it in all its fallen and degraded aspects, to banish from the lips of the lowest character I introduced, any expression that could by possibility offend; and rather to lead to the unavoidable inference that its existence was of the most debased and vicious kind, than to prove it elaborately by words and deeds. In the case of the girl, in particular, I kept this intention constantly in view.

Much of Dickens' writing is affected by this practice of leading to "unavoidable inference"; he is thoroughly conscious of the method, but its application seems almost automatic. Humphry House comments that the atmosphere Oliver was plunged into in London would have been "drenched in sex." Dickens could, it is true, have made Nancy more realistic if he had been willing to do so, but he would have had to heap disgust upon her, and he was sensitive to popular taste. His reticence, though, does not seem merely calculated. The whole conception of Nancy is sympathetic: one feels it to have been quite as important that Charles Dickens should be fond of her as that readers should not protest. For this, she had, while remaining a prostitute, to take on, in Mr. Brownlow's words, "the courage and almost the attributes of virtue."

Nancy's original, as we have seen, was the girl in the hospital. The development of the character, however, has another involvement, Nancy's association with Rose Maylie. Rose is the first of the several girl characters in the novels drawn, one feels sure, from Mary Hogarth, the young sister-in-law who lived with Dickens and his wife. Seventeen years old, Mary died of a sudden illness in May 1837, when Dickens had been married a little more than a year. His diary and his letters at the time show a sorrow patterned by convention but as deep and as devastating as any tragedy of young love and death in romantic literature. The heightened quality of his feeling for her is hard to explain. He wrote in *Bentley's* (to account for the omission of the installment of *Oliver Twist* which he had been unable to work on) that the editor was mourning "the death of a very dear young relative . . . whose society has been for a long time the chief solace of his labours." Almost five years later he wrote to Forster, at the time of another death in the Hogarth family:

> The desire to be buried next her is as strong upon me now, as it was five years ago; and I *know* (for I don't think there ever was love like that I bear her) that it will never diminish. . . . I cannot bear the thought of being excluded from her dust. . . . I shall drive over there, please God, on Thursday morning, before they get there; and look at her coffin.

The fictional Rose Maylie is, to take the words of Dickens' epitaph for Mary Hogarth, "young, beautiful, and good." Near to the first anniversary of Mary's death, in the June 1838 installment of *Oliver Twist,* he gave Rose a severe illness, though he stopped short of making it a fatal one.

Nancy, who was to be so much criticized, is the counterpart, among the low characters, of Rose Maylie. Rose is "not past seventeen"; neither is Nancy, although her original, the hospital patient, was five or six years older. Both girls are kind to the boy hero, with whose unhappy life Dickens had reason to feel a close identification. A penitent sinner, Nancy arouses pity for her ruined youth when she is brought face to face with the girl of sheltered virtue. If Rose and other innocent young in girls in Dickens are astral bodies emanating from Mary Hogarth, surely Nancy may be regarded as another, whose creation likewise afforded him satisfaction. The sentiment he lavished upon her thus becomes understandable, as well as his later warmth in her defense.

Dickens wrote no death scene for Rose Maylie—he allowed her to recover. In effect, Nancy dies in her place. When the time comes for the murder of Nancy, the event is given special fury and pathos. A degree of identification of the two girls' characters has been achieved. Nancy's good impulses have made her appealing, and she has become pure in heart through her contact with Oliver and Rose; her final supplication to Sikes is that he go away with her so that they may "far apart lead better lives, and forget how we have lived, except in prayers, and never see each other more." Unmoved, Sikes brutally kills her. In a sense, then, Dickens wrote the death scene after all. In emotional terms, he created and defended Nancy as the unadmitted sexual aspect of Mary Hogarth—and then expiated his sin with Nancy's death.

Oliver Twist was the more Newgate novel because of the author's fascination with crimes of violence, although his treatment of them brought him considerable praise and almost no specific blame. When Dickens was to do a murder he set himself to wring the most from it. In the famous scene of the killing of Nancy he unfortunately tries for a stagey pathos before she dies, and so falsifies his conception, but the occasion has impressive moments. A little after her death, the morning sun lights the room; Sikes, in a daze, makes pointless efforts to remove, not the body, but the blood and the weapon, in a kind of unreasoned ritual:

> He struck a light, kindled a fire, and thrust the club into it. There was hair upon the end, which blazed and shrunk into a light cinder, and, caught by air, whirled up the chimney. Even that frightened him, sturdy as he was; but he held the weapon till it broke, and then piled it on the coals to burn away, and smoulder into ashes. He washed himself, and rubbed his clothes; there were spots that would not be removed, but he cut the pieces out, and burnt them. How those stains were dispersed about the room! The very feet of the dog were bloody.

In following the behavior of Sikes after the murder, Dickens maintains urgency and tension to a high degree; and in the few minutes which Sikes spends with the boys of the gang in their last hiding place, he makes both boys and man conscious of the murderer's isolation from mankind. Such parts of the story are impressive.

The murder is by no means a necessity of the plot. Indeed, it is forced. Nancy has been portrayed as deeply attached and Sikes as violent by nature, but there has been nothing to show that his feeling for her could be attended by murderous passion at a supposed betrayal. Evil-tempered as he is, he might be expected to clout her on the head and then to leave London till the trouble should blow over. Or, since he has had a hanging look from the beginning, he might have gone to the gallows; but Dickens found himself writing his way toward a murder, and Sikes must do it.

Whatever the Newgate novel owes, then, to social circumstances or literary fashion, it owes something more to the arrival, in the eighteen-thirties, of a writer who had a deep personal interest in crime. Edmund Wilson, in "Dickens: the Two Scrooges," points out the rebellion which compelled Dickens to an identification with murderers. He finds its origin in the psychic trauma of Dickens' childhood despair:

> He identified himself readily with the thief and even more readily with the murderer. The man of powerful will who finds himself opposed to society must, if he cannot upset it or if his impulse to do so is blocked, feel a compulsion to commit what society regards as one of the capital crimes against itself. With the antisocial heroes of Dostoevsky, this crime is usually murder or rape; with Dickens it is usually murder. . . . In Dickens' novels, this theme recurs with a probing of the psychology of the murderer, which becomes ever more convincing and intimate.

The obsession with murderers can also be traced, outside the novels, in the interests which Dickens frequently displayed to the end of his life. The death of Nancy was the most exciting of the dramatic readings in his last platform appearances; no one can fail to be impressed by his determination, against all advice, to include it and by his extraordinary satisfaction in the performance. "In deciding to add the murder of Nancy to his repertory," says Edgar Johnson, "he was sentencing himself to death." He would not give up, and the murder scene was in the renewed series of readings that began six months before he died. (pp. 121-25)

Oliver Twist was reviewed in general quite favorably. It was not immediately described as another Newgate novel; that accusation came chiefly from Thackeray a little later. While it was still young in *Bentley's,* the *Westminster Review* spoke of it as fine but almost too painful; the *Quarterly*'s first review of Dickens' work, though favorable, objected that he was writing too much and too fast. *Oliver Twist* was said to show improvement.

The *Edinburgh Review* dealt with all his works when the magazine serial was two-thirds done, shortly before the book itself appeared; it gave the most confident praise which had come from the important periodicals. It compared him to Smollett, Fielding, and Washington Irving, but chiefly to Hogarth. (Hogarth was frequently used as a standard of comparison for the Newgate writers.) Admiring particularly the arraignment of evils, the tendency to "make us practically benevolent," the review found no evil in the book. On the contrary, Dickens

> never endeavours to mislead our sympathies—to pervert plain notions of right and wrong—to

make vice interesting in our eyes. . . . His vicious characters are just what experience shows the average to be. . . . We find no monsters of unmitigated and unredeemable villany; no creatures blending with their crimes the most incongruous and romantic virtues.

Though Bulwer was not named, no doubt a contrast with him was intended in those phrases.

The *Monthly Review,* crediting the author of *Oliver Twist* with a moral aim, objected only to too much "muscular agony"; the *Athenaeum* raised no objection; and of course the *Examiner* praised. The *Spectator* had a few compliments but a larger bulk of dispassionate objections.

In June 1839, the *Quarterly* built on *Oliver Twist* a substantial article, the writing of which Lockhart assigned to Richard Ford. It is an excellent article, still thoroughly interesting, with verve and an allusive style not usually to be found in the solid reviews. It sets out to place Dickens in the literary currents of the time, holding that the search for excitement in contemporary novels is a reaction against the dominion of the fashionable school and against the increasing seriousness of everyday life. The March of Intellect sobers everything, and highwaymen became the delight of fiction when they had disappeared. Dickens is the voice of a new class in a new age:

> Life in London, as revealed in the pages of Boz, opens a new world to thousands bred and born in the same city, whose palaces overshadow their cellars—for the one half of mankind lives without knowing how the other half dies; in fact, the regions about Saffron Hill are less known in our great world than the Oxford Tracts: the inhabitants still less. . . .

With the slight condescension which flavors the article throughout, he says that the upper classes enjoy Boz; the *centre gauche* fear to demean themselves with his low book. Dickens' gentle and genteel people are "unendurable" and his young ladies "awful," but he is not vulgar when he deals with vulgar subjects: "He is natural, and that can never be ridiculous." Is this entirely a compliment?

The reviewer (or perhaps reviewers—for the humorist of the first pages becomes a serious-minded critic after a time, and one does not know how much of Lockhart's work to find in Ford's article) puts himself to some trouble to praise Dickens' fidelity and his delicacy and yet to complain of the material of his book. *Oliver Twist* brings to light evil that should not be made known: "Our youth should not even suspect the possibility of such hidden depths of guilt." The author must "shun Mr. Sikes and his gin-bottle."

The first distinct review of Dickens' work in *Fraser's* came a year and a half after the publication of *Oliver Twist.* The verdict is generally favorable, but the tone is cool. Cruikshank is praised to the point of detraction from Dickens, though chiefly for his work in the *Sketches.* And the *Fraser's* reviewer holds that Fagin's hanging is hardly legal: because Fagin was not present at the murder of Nancy he could not be called an accessory before the fact. (This same point, in a wittier form, is attributed to G. S. Venables, who was a practising lawyer: "Dickens hanged Fagin for being the villain of a novel".) The whole review gathers up a variety of objections—but immorality and a Newgate tendency are not among them.

The next mention of *Oliver Twist* appeared in *Fraser's* in August 1840, not in a review but in the essay, "Going to See a Man Hanged." Thackeray went to see the execution of Benjamin Courvoisier, on July 6, and reported his observations, ending with a fervent prayer that these public spectacles should cease. He watched the crowd attentively, not accustomed to seeing such people as he mingled with that day. Amid much else, he noticed girls of sixteen or seventeen, and one who might have been a study for Nancy:

> The girl was a young thief's mistress evidently; if attacked, ready to reply without a particle of modesty; could give as good ribaldry as she got; made no secret (and there were several inquiries) as to her profession and means of livelihood. But with all this there was something good about the girl; a sort of devil-may-care candor and simplicity that one could not fail to see. Her answers to some of the coarse questions put to her, were very ready and good-humoured. . . . Her friend could not be more than fifteen. They were not in rags, but had greasy cotton shawls, and old, faded, ragshop bonnets. I was curious to look at them, having, in late fashionable novels, read many accounts of such personages. Bah! what figments these novelists tell us! Boz, who knows life well, knows that his Miss Nancy is the most unreal fantastical personage possible; no more like a thief's mistress than one of Gessner's shepherdesses resembles a real country wench. He dare not tell the truth concerning such young ladies. They have, no doubt, virtues like other human creatures; nay, their position engenders virtues that are not called into exercise among other women. But on these an honest painter of human nature has no right to dwell; not being able to paint the whole portrait, he has no right to present one or two favorable points as characterizing the whole: and therefore, in fact, had better leave the picture alone altogether.

The moral objection is here stated in critical terms, more persuasively than Thackeray usually took the trouble to state it. He presses Dickens closely on the point, but, as in the *Pendennis* preface later, he thinks it unnecessary to defend the first assumption—that the "whole portrait" cannot be painted.

One can imagine Dickens' objections, on several grounds, to being classified as a writer of the Newgate school, though he did not express them publicly for more than two years. His attitude is to be seen in a letter to R. H. Horne, written near the end of 1839, when Thackeray's *Catherine* and Ainsworth's *Sheppard* were still running their courses:

> I am by some jolter-headed enemies most unjustly and untruly charged with having written a book after Mr. Ainsworth's fashion. Unto these jolter-heads and their intensely concentrated humbug I shall take an early opportunity of tem-

perately replying. If this opportunity had presented itself and I had made this vindication, I could have no objection to set my hand to what I know to be true concerning the late lamented John Sheppard, but I feel a great repugnance to do so now, lest it should seem an ungenerous and unmanly way of disavowing any sympathy with that school, and a means of shielding myself.

Dickens' delicacy does him credit, especially since this was during the time of his definite estrangement from Ainsworth. There would have been a certain embarrassment, too, in joining with Thackeray against Ainsworth, when Thackeray had already tarred Dickens and Bulwer with the same brush.

The temperate reply which Dickens planned was written in April 1841, as a preface to the third edition of *Oliver Twist,* and most of it has been retained in later ones. Dickens withdrew nothing and defended himself with vigor.

> It is, it seems, a very coarse and shocking circumstance, that some of the characters in these pages are chosen from the most criminal and degraded of London's population; that Sikes is a thief, and Fagin a receiver of stolen goods; that the boys are pickpockets, and the girl is a prostitute.
>
> I confess I have yet to learn that a lesson of the purest good may not be drawn from the vilest evil.

He is answering, with the conviction of an evangelist, the satire of Thackeray, the chidings of reviewers, and most recently, the jesting of Bon Gaultier, in *Tait's Magazine.* He dissociates himself from the merely entertaining Newgate writers—even little Oliver represents "the principle of Good"—and asserts his reforming aim. He has read of scores of gallant seductive thieves, "great at a song" (*Rookwood* was full of songs): "But I had never met (except in Hogarth) with the miserable reality. It appeared to me that to draw a knot of such associates in crime as really do exist . . . would be a service to society." Dickens points out that his book offers no enticement "for the most jolter-headed of juveniles." Since he specifically exempts from censure *The Beggar's Opera* and *Paul Clifford,* this preface includes a pointed refusal to sanction Ainsworth publicly. It must have been interpreted so by Dickens' former friend, who in 1836 had praised Dickens in the preface to a new edition of *Rookwood.* The two prefaces, five years apart, compose an irony of time and change. The forceful effort which Dickens makes to separate himself from Ainsworth and assert his own purposes shows how strongly he felt the criticism. Thackeray's article, in particular, roused him to a vehement reply. The preface closes with a defiant word against hypocritical refinement ("It is wonderful how Virtue turns from dirty stockings") and an eloquent defense of the truth of Nancy:

> It is useless to discuss whether the conduct and character of the girl seems natural or unnatural, probable or improbable, right or wrong. It is true. Every man who has watched these melancholy shades of life knows it to be so. Suggested to my mind long ago—long before I dealt in fiction—by what I often saw and read of, in actual

life around me, I have, for years, tracked it through many profligate and noisome ways, and found it still the same. From the first introduction of that poor wretch, to her laying her bloody head upon the robber's breast, there is not one word exaggerated or over-wrought. It is emphatically God's truth. . . . It involves the best and worst shades of our common nature . . . it is a contradiction, an anomaly, an apparent impossibility, but it is a truth.

This last paragraph must surely have been written for Thackeray.

An excerpt from *Oliver Twist*

It was Sunday night, and the bell of the nearest church struck the hour. Sikes and the Jew were talking, but they paused to listen. The girl looked up from the low seat on which she crouched, and listened too. Eleven.

"An hour this side of midnight," said Sikes, raising the blind to look out and returning to his seat. "Dark and heavy it is too. A good night for business this."

"Ah!" replied Fagin. "What a pity, Bill, my dear, that there's none quite ready to be done."

"You're right for once," replied Sikes gruffly. "It is a pity, for I'm in the humour too."

Fagin sighed, and shook his head despondingly.

"We must make up for lost time when we've got things into a good train. That's all I know," said Sikes.

"That's the way to talk, my dear," replied Fagin, venturing to pat him on the shoulder. "It does me good to hear you."

"Does you good does it!" cried Sikes. "Well, so be it."

"Ha! ha! ha!" laughed Fagin, as if he were relieved by even this concession. "You're like yourself to-night, Bill! Quite like yourself."

"I don't feel like myself when you lay that withered old claw on my shoulder, so take it away," said Sikes, casting off the Jew's hand.

"It makes you nervous, Bill,—reminds you of being nabbed, does it?" said Fagin, determined not to be offended. "Reminds me of being nabbed by the devil." returned Sikes. "There never was another man with such a face as yours, unless it was your father, and I suppose *he* is singeing his grizzled red beard by this time, unless you came straight from the old 'un without any father at all betwixt you; which I shouldn't wonder at, a bit."

Fagin offered no reply to this compliment; but, pulling Sikes by the sleeve, pointed his finger towards Nancy, who had taken advantage of the foregoing conversation to put on her bonnet, and was now leaving the room.

Charles Dickens, in his The Adventures of Oliver Twist, *Chapman and Hall, 1910.*

In 1844, R. H. Horne published his *New Spirit of the Age,* which contains echoes of the controversy. Although the author assumes a wide public appreciation of Dickens, he defends Dickens as a moralist, and the first book he undertakes to praise is not **Pickwick** but **Oliver Twist.** Though it is "the work which is most open to animadversion," it has a beneficial moral tendency. Of Dickens' defence in the 1841 preface, he says, "It is unanswerable, but ought not to have been needed." (pp. 126-31)

> *Keith Hollingsworth, "The Newgate Novel and the Moral Argument, 1837-40," in his* The Newgate Novel, 1830-1847: Bulwer, Ainsworth, Dickens, & Thackeray, *Wayne State University Press, 1963, pp. 111-66.*

Robert A. Colby   (essay date 1967)

[*Colby is an American educator and critic specializing in the study of Victorian literature. In the following excerpt, he surveys literary influences on* Oliver Twist.]

Oliver Twist announces his entrance into life with a lusty cry. As Dickens says, had little Oliver known what awaited him, he would have cried louder. Without the social status of Edward Waverley, or the family connections of Fanny Price, "he was badged and ticketed, and fell into his place at once—a parish child—the orphan of a workhouse—the humble, half-starved drudge—to be cuffed and buffeted through the world—despised by all, and pitied by none." Despite his low status, however, he is subjected no less than Fanny Price to educational schemes: "a systematic course of treachery and deception" at the parish workhouse, the "parental superintendance" of that efficient domestic economist Mrs. Mann; the "experimental philosophy" tried out by the board of the "brick and mortar elysium" which serves Oliver, for lack of better, as his nursery and elementary school. Because of Oliver's peculiar circumstances, his formal education is brief, perfunctory, and rather hit-or-miss, but he somehow manages to acquire perfect manners and faultless grammar.

In Jane Austen's time . . . bluestockings like Hannah More, Laetitia Matilda Hawkins, and Elizabeth Hamilton dedicated their pens to the cause of the education of the poor, but by the 1830's the issue was being debated in the halls of Parliament. The New Poor Law, a familiar part of the background of **Oliver Twist,** raised the nagging problem of the schooling of workhouse wards. By now the need for educating the children of paupers and abandoned or orphaned children was widely recognized, but there was no agreement as to who was responsible for it. The farming-out system employed for Little Oliver and his fellow inmates was certainly obsolete by this time. Dickens, a legislative reporter, was undoubtedly aware of the bill proposed by John Arthur Roebuck in 1833 calling for the establishment of an infant school in every parish. But this was before the concept of state education had taken root, and Roebuck's scheme came to naught. In May 1835 Lord Brougham, addressing the House of Lords, declared it inexpedient to establish parish schools; he suggested instead "voluntary effort" by the philanthropic and civic-minded. It may have been he whom Dickens lampooned a few years later in a sketch ["The Political Young Gentleman," in his *Sketches of Young Gentlemen,* 1838] as "the Radical . . . of the utilitarian school . . . having many ingenious remarks to offer upon the voluntary principle and various cheerful disquisitions connected with the population of the country." Most of Dickens' examples of volunteer educators in *Oliver Twist,* at any rate, are far from heartening. Mrs. Mann is one. Fagin is another, offering to Oliver the seminary for youth where he is such an inept pupil. Oliver eventually proves more fortunate than Fagin's other pupils by falling in with Mr. Brownlow, who furnishes the home-school so congenial to Dickens' ideals of education. But first he—and the reader—undergo the rigorous regimen of the streets.

Oliver Twist is not only tossed between the Old Poor Law and the New Poor Law, but bandied about from guardian to guardian. Nor does there seem to have been much agreement as to what waifs thrown on "the tender mercies of churchwardens and overseers" were supposed to learn. The red-faced "philosopher" in the white waistcoat who interviews Oliver in the workhouse assumes that he is to be "taught a useful trade," but depends on unsupervised volunteers to carry out the program. Evidence from other sources indicates that vigorous efforts were being made during these years to protect helpless boys from the real-life Gamfields and Sowerberrys. Barbara Hofland, a popular children's writer, pointed to her native Sheffield as a model for the administration of poor relief. In this large manufacturing town, she proudly proclaimed [in the preface to her *Elizabeth and Her Three Beggar Boys,* 1830], even though the poor are numerous, funds are ample and the overseers are "men of property and benevolence, alike liberal and conscientious"—more like Mr. Brownlow, one supposes, than Mr. Bumble. She contrasts the wealthy city with "petty villages" where "the poor are at the mercy of the mean and tyrannical who conceive that they oblige their neighbours by curtailing the comforts of the poor." Among Oliver Twist's misfortunes is being born in the "petty village" of Mudfog.

Bill Sikes, of all people, is our source of information about another institution that was trying to ease the "parish boy's progress." The master thief complains that the Juvenile Delinquent Society is encroaching on his "occupation" when it takes a vagrant boy in hand, "teaches him to read and write, and in time makes a 'prentice of him." But things could be worse. "If they'd got money enough (which it's a Providence they have not), we shouldn't have half a dozen boys left in the whole trade, in a year or two" (CH. XIX). That threat seems indefinitely averted. Dickens had, however, a more encouraging example before him in the Foundling Hospital, located in Great Coram Field near Doughty Street, where he lived while he was writing *Oliver Twist.* He took an active interest in this institution, regularly attending chapel there during the few years that he lived in the neighborhood, and in this connection became acquainted with a namesake of Oliver's benefactor—John Brownlow. At the time when Dickens met him, Brownlow was in charge of the placement of boys and had succeeded in reforming the policy of the Foundling Hospital with regard to apprenticeship after bringing to light cases of cruelty by masters. In other respects too Brownlow showed up the "experimental philosophers" of Mud-

fog, effecting improvements in the physical care and the diet of the inmates of the Foundling Hospital. Brownlow himself was living proof of the benefits of this institution; he had originally entered it himself as a charity boy. As will be shown later, Dickens' association with this asylum, rooted in eighteenth-century paternalism and hallowed by missionary zeal, is closely linked to the theme and tone of *Oliver Twist.*

To its first readers, *Oliver Twist* had the glare of an exposé. Serial publication allied it with topical journalism; Cruikshank's illustrations made the characters leer, simper, glower, and beam right out of its pages. In the playbill of a "serio-comic burletta" hacked out of the tale while the press ink was hardly dry, the author was applauded for " 'Holding the mirror up to nature' albeit in its worst light." Dickens, according to this playsmith, was "opening one of the darkest volumes of life, and revealing facts that must startle the more strongly, from the previous total ignorance of their existence, even by those persons residing in the very heart of the scenes in which they are daily and nightly passing." Dickens was not, of course, introducing his readers to the seamy side of London life for the first time. Some of the *Sketches by Boz Illustrative of Every-Day Life and Every-Day People,* which first appeared in newspapers, germinated characters and episodes in *Oliver Twist.* The first of the sketches, "The Parish," begins ominously: "How much is conveyed in those two short words—'The Parish.' And with how many tales of distress and misery, of broken fortune, and ruined hopes, too often of unrelieved wretchedness and successful knavery are they associated." Bumble is anticipated in the portrait that follows of the Beadle "in his state-coat and cocked hat with a large-headed staff for show in his left hand, and a small cane for use in his right" officiously marshaling the urchins in his charge. The master of the workhouse and the parish schoolmaster are among others sketched. "A Visit to Newgate" takes in juvenile delinquents and a school for pickpockets. Among the "Scenes" transferred in part to *Oliver Twist* are "The Streets—Morning," "The Streets—Night," "Gin-Shops," "Criminal Courts," "The Prisoners' Van," and "The Drunkard's Death." In Dickens' first book, parish boys, charity schools, apprenticeship, and crime are brought together between covers but not yet amalgamated into a novel.

In the Preface to the Second Edition of the *Sketches,* the youthful "Boz," pleased with the success of his "pilot balloon," promises his faithful readers "fresh sketches, and even connected works of fiction of a higher grade, [for which] they have only themselves to blame." Connection, indeed, is what he particularly insists upon in many of the chapter headings of his first plotted novel: "Treats of a very poor Subject. But is a short one; and may be found of some Importance in this History" (CH. XXIV—the death of the hag who stole the locket from Oliver's mother); "In which a mysterious Character [Monks] appears upon the Scene; and many things inseparable from this History are done and performed" (CH. XXVI); "Is a very short one, and may appear of no great importance in its Place, but it should be read notwithstanding, as a Sequel to the last, and a Key to one that will follow when its Time arrives" (CH. XXXVI—the parting of Rose Maylie and

Harry). His description of his new book as a "history" in itself stresses causal sequence. Dickens was struggling against the serial publication of the story, its picaresque tendency and particularly the association of his name in readers' minds with trivial comedies and ephemeral journalism. His problem was complicated by the concurrent appearance of **Pickwick Papers** and the reissue of **Sketches by Boz** in monthly parts. Probably, however, Dickens was most concerned about his reputation with critics who had questioned his ability to sustain a long narrative and were already predicting the exhaustion of his sparkling vein. The highly cultivated style of the book, which contributes to its satirical effect, also indicates, together with his self-conscious exposure of his artistry, that he was trying to convince the snobbish gentlemen of the press that he was something more than "the literary Teniers of the metropolis" [so called by the critic for the *London and Westminster Review* (July 1837)].

Dickens, moreover, was making a bid for consideration as an interpreter of life, not merely a reporter of it. The playbill of the burletta that was the first of numerous efforts to extend his message to the semiliterate who attended the theatre hailed the author of **Oliver Twist** as a "Hogarth [who] has raised a beacon on the basis of truth to warn the erring, guide the inexperienced, instruct the ignorant to avoid the shoals by which they are surrounded." Dickens' tale was reduced here to "a great moral lesson" proving that vice is eventually punished and virtue rewarded. Dickens himself, though disavowing this dramatization, echoed its program note in his first public pronouncement on his first novel, the Preface to the Third Edition of 1841, where he invoked the spirit of Hogarth, "the moralist and censor of his age." Too many readers, to Dickens' annoyance, had become so engrossed in the low life of his novel that they had missed its high purpose. The Princess Victoria for one [according to Elizabeth Longford in her *Queen Victoria: Born to Succeed,* 1964], reading it in *Bentley's Miscellany,* confided to her mother that she found it "too interesting" and was promptly scolded for indulging in light literature. Thackeray, his greatest rival, while ridiculing **Oliver Twist** in his mock-novel *Catherine,* admitted that "the reader at once becomes [Dickens'] captive, and must follow him whithersoever he leads." But Thackeray did not like where he was being led. Against critics who had condemned **Oliver Twist** as salacious and immoral, Dickens felt compelled to defend his choice of characters, "from the most criminal and degraded of London's population." "I have yet to learn," he continues, "that a lesson of the purest good may not be drawn from the vilest evil." Out of Oliver's adventures in the underworld he extracted a fable of incorruptible innocence, as wholesome as *Sandford and Merton* or *The Shepherd of Salisbury Plain:* "The principle of Good surviving through every adverse circumstance, and triumphing at last."

The serial publication of **Oliver Twist** tended to leave the outcome of "the principle of Good" in suspense as Oliver was shunted between malefactors and benefactors. The three-volume publication, which antedated the conclusion of the serial, also left the survival of innocence in doubt, since the first volume ended with Fagin's turning over Oliver to Bill Sikes, and the second with the rendezvous between Oliver's evil half-brother Monks and the corruptible Bumble. But Dickens' intention was finally fixed indelibly in the readers' minds with the edition in numbers which, contrary to normal practice, came out five years after the three-decker. Here the front wrapper designed by Cruikshank sets out in a series of panels Dickens' conception of Oliver's "progress" as a modern morality—at the top Oliver embracing a benign lady inside a cottage, at the bottom Fagin shivering in his cell, while flanked on the right and left between "heaven and hell" are Oliver's tormentors and tempters. To us, the survival of Good "through every adverse circumstance" seems a matter of Oliver's being in the right place at the right time, but we need to put ourselves in the frame of mind of Dickens' generation, who more readily assumed that God helps the helpless. Many years later, in a letter to Wilkie Collins, Dickens expressed his own conviction as to "the ways of Providence, of which all art is but a little imitation."

In his 1841 Preface Dickens emphasizes the pathos of his tale, for the benefit of children and his more delicate adult readers. A careful reading of his pronouncement prepares one for the full blend of sensation, satire, and sentiment that he was working up into his formula, but he shrewdly understates the first two elements. During the serial publication of **Oliver Twist** and afterward, he was plagued by invidious comparisons with the so-called "Newgate" school of fiction. The coupling of his novel with *Jack Sheppard* was inevitable, since the Ainsworth melodrama also appeared in *Bentley's Miscellany* (under Dickens' editorship) and was illustrated by Cruikshank. A reviewer of *Jack Sheppard* recognized the essential moral seriousness of Dickens' story but candidly added, "We are certain that it is far less the under-current of philosophy which has sold his book, than the strong flavour of the medium, in which he has disguised the bitterness of its taste" [*Athenaeum* (26 October 1839)]. Thackeray, despite a "sneaking kindness" for the book, lumped it—largely on the basis of the sentimental treatment of Nancy—with Ainsworth's stories and with Bulwer's *Paul Clifford* and *Eugene Aram* in his parody *Catherine,* where he denounced the glorifying of crime. Dickens does his best to dissociate himself from this company, writing in the Preface: "Here are no canterings on moonlit heaths, no merrymakings in the snuggest of all possible caverns, none of the attractions of dress, no embroidery, no lace, no jack-boots, no crimson coats and ruffles, none of the dash and freedom with which 'the road' has been, time out of mind, invested." Instead, like Cervantes, he attempts "to dim the false glitter surrounding something which really did exist, by showing it in its unattractive and repulsive truth." So his criminals are city thieves and murderers, not glamorous highwaymen, wear greasy flannel, frayed velveteen, soiled breeches, and disport themselves in dark, filthy taverns. Little Oliver, no more attracted by crime in literature than in life, flings away the lurid history of the lives and trials of great criminals that Fagin gives him, just as readers are supposed to do.

The pumped-up Gothic atmosphere of some scenes in **Oliver Twist** suggests a lingering memory of Dickens' childhood reading in other crime fiction. Old Sally, the midwife who attends Oliver's mother, is a stereotype of the literary witch: "Her body was bent by age, her limbs trembled with palsy, and her face distorted into a mumbling leer" (CH. XXIV). As Dickens admits, she "resembled more the grotesque shaping of some wild pencil than the work of Nature's hand," perhaps a concession that he got her out of an illustration from a penny dreadful. Oliver's elder brother, with his "dark figure," "trembling hands," "grim laughs," "excited imagination," and obsession with demons is straight out of the literature of "the awful and the terrific." The nocturnal meeting between this villain and the Bumbles takes place in a noisome swamp near the river, amidst a cluster of abandoned huts and a dilapidated old factory where they are interrupted occasionally, and predictably, by peals of thunder and flashes of lightning. Here Dickens transforms the props of the Gothic romances—ruined castles, abbeys, murky tarns, and crashing storms—to suit a modern urban setting. His giving the nickname Monks to his malevolent schemer is a lame joke that has generally gone unappreciated.

His true wit comes out in his handling of a more contemporaneous realistic genre. A contemporary of Dickens, accounting for the success of **Oliver Twist,** recalled that "he arose at a time when the novels of England were both vicious and snobbish, when one set of writers was producing the Satanic school of literature, and another, like those poor things whom we name to forget, the Countess of Blessington and Lady Charlotte Bury, was cultivating what was appropriately called the silver-fork school" [J. Hain Friswell, "Mr. Charles Dickens," *Modern Men of Letters Honestly Criticised,* 1870]. In "London Recreations," one of the **Sketches by Boz,** Dickens pokes gentle fun at "the small gentility—the would be aristocrats—of the middle classes, . . . tradesmen and clerks, with fashionable, novel reading families." One of the early reviewers of **Oliver Twist** was pleased that its author took the novel out of the drawing room into the streets. Dickens' popularity, he observes [*Quarterly Review* (October 1837)], "has been fairly earned without resorting to any of the means by which most other writers have succeeded in attracting the attention of their contemporaries. He has flattered no popular prejudices and profited by no passing folly; he has attempted no caricature sketches of the manners or conversation of the aristocracy; and there are few political or personal allusions in his works." Dickens himself declared in his 1841 Preface:

> I saw no reason, when I wrote this book, why the dregs of life, so long as their speech did not offend the ear, should not serve the purpose of a moral, at least as well as its froth and cream. Nor did I doubt that there lay festering in Saint Giles's as good materials towards the truth as any to be found in Saint James's.

These words have usually been taken at their face value, but the alert reader can catch the sly author winking between the lines. Such a reader is best able to savor the irony of Dickens' description of the infant Oliver in his swaddling clothes: "What an excellent example of the power of dress, young Oliver Twist was! Wrapped in the blanket which had hitherto formed his only covering, he might have been the child of a nobleman or a beggar; it would have been hard for the haughtiest stranger to have

assigned him his proper station in society" (CH. I). Dickens does not mean here merely to anticipate Oliver's refined parentage. The barbed chapter headings scattered through the novel suggest that, but for the grace of God, Oliver "might have been" the hero of a "Silver Fork" novel. His apprenticeship in particular suggests an unlike likeness with the career of the dandy. Chapter III, which introduces Gamfield, "Relates How Oliver Twist was very near getting a Place, which would not have been a Sinecure"—like a seat in the House of Lords or a commission. Oliver's situation at this point could also have been contrasted with that of the hero of another Bentley novel advertised in the first edition—*Melton de Mowbray; or, The Banker's Son.* The next chapter, where Oliver meets Sowerberry, headed "Oliver, being offered another Place, makes his first Entry into public Life," suggests the fortunes of Disraeli's Young Duke. This vein is sustained by ambiguous chapter summaries that ape the *ton:* "How Oliver passed his Time in the improving Society of his reputable Friends" [Jack Dawkins and Charlie Bates]; "Atones for the Unpoliteness of a former Chapter; which deserted a Lady [Mrs. Corney] most unceremoniously"; "An old acquaintance of Oliver's [Noah Claypole], exhibiting decided Marks of Genius, becomes a public Character in the Metropolis"; "Comprehending a Proposal of Marriage [Harry and Rose Maylie] with no Word of Settlement or Pin-money."

Through Noah Claypole in particular Dickens parodies the peacocks who strut through *Almacks* and *The Exclusives.* As a charity-boy, Noah is one rung up the social ladder from Oliver, a mere workhouse orphan: "No chance-child was he, for he could trace his genealogy all the way back to his parents, who lived hard by; his mother being a washerwoman, and his father a drunken soldier." Noah, himself derided by the shop-boys, follows the pecking order by abusing Oliver, "now that fortune had cast in his way a nameless orphan, at whom the meanest could point the finger of scorn." Among other things, Dickens is writing the poor man's *Book of Snobs.* As he observes of the relationship between Noah and Oliver: "It shows us what a beautiful thing human nature is, and how impartially the same amiable qualities are developed in the finest lord and the dirtiest charity-boy" (CH. V).

Bill Sikes, hiding out in a dingy tenement after an unsuccessful "expedition" to Chertsey, bears a faint resemblance to Beau Brummell: "The house-breaker was lying on the bed, wrapped in his white greatcoat by way of a dressing gown"; "Nor were there wanting other indications of the good gentleman's having gone down in the world of late, for a great scarcity of furniture, and total absence of comfort, together with the disappearance of all such small movables as spare clothes and linen, bespoke a state of extreme poverty" (CH. XXXIX). Bill's overdressed accomplice Toby Crackit, with his "smartly cut snuff-coloured coat, with large brass buttons; an orange neckerchief," and his red-dyed hair "tortured into long corkscrew curls," is a grotesque version of a Regency fop, and at the same time neatly hits off Bulwer's gentleman thieves (CH. XXII). His speech also is pseudo-Holland House: "I can't talk about business till I've eat and drank; so produce the sustenance, and let's have a quiet fill-out for the first time these three days!" (CH. XXV). Dickens has indeed kept his promise to his readers not to "offend the ear." Crackit is ashamed to be seen playing cribbage with Tom Chitling, "a gentleman so much his inferior in station and mental endowments," but is pleased to take the easy money. Chitling is too much dazzled by Crackit's gentility to care about his loss. Their creator cannot help interposing that "there are a great number of spirited young bloods upon town who pay a much higher price than Mr. Chitling for being seen in good society, and a great number of fine gentlemen (composing the good society aforesaid) who establish their reputation upon very much the same footing as flash Toby Crackit" (CH. XXXIX). He depicts two such, Lord Frederick Verisopht and Sir Mulberry Hawk, in his next novel, *Nicholas Nickleby.*

In "London Recreations" Dickens had observed: "The wish of persons in the humbler classes of life to ape the manner and customs of those whom fortune has placed above them is often the subject of remark, and most frequently of complaint." He furnishes plenty of examples among Oliver's "improving friends." The Artful Dodger, Jack Dawkins, a "young gentleman," introduces Oliver to Fagin, a " 'spectable old gentleman." Fagin lives up to the role. When Oliver first meets him, "the Jew grinned; and making a low obeisance . . . took him by the hand, and hoped he should have the honour of his intimate acquaintance" (CH. VIII). Everybody to him is "my dear"; Oliver is taught manners ("Make 'em your models, my dear—make 'em your models . . . do everything they bid you, and take their advice in all matters—especially the Dodger's, my dear. He'll be a great man himself, and will make you one, if you take pattern by him"); he is avuncular toward Nancy ("Why . . . you're more clever than ever tonight. Ha! Ha! my dear, you are acting beautifully [giving her a basket]. Carry that in one hand, it looks more respectable, my dear"); he attempts to polish her uncouth companion ("Come, come, Sikes . . . we must have civil words—civil words, Bill."). Bill proves somewhat refractory, but Nancy knows how to lay out "tea things" in the garret after he has finished a bout of debauchery, and Oliver takes time out for "making his toilet" before accompanying him on a pre-dawn burglary expedition.

But Dickens' satire is double-edged. Most of the episodes involving Fagin, Bill Sikes, their "associates" and their "protégés" have their counterparts in the "Exclusivism, fashionable novelism, Nashism, and fifty other fribbleisms of the West-end" recalled by one of Mrs. Gore's retired gentlemen [in her *Cecil the Peer*]. For the schools of deportment and the dancing academies, substitute the public house in Saffron Hill where Fagin puts his "dear boys" through their paces. For the faro and gaming tables, substitute the whist matches of the Artful Dodger, Toby, and Tom. In Fagin's household the magazine is not the *Journal des Modes* but the *Hue and Cry*. In place of the elegant shopping districts of Bond Street and Regent Street, readers are escorted to Field Lane, the "dismal alley" leading to Saffron Hill, in whose "filthy shops are exposed for sale huge bunches of second-hand silk handkerchiefs, of all sizes and patterns; for here reside the traders who purchase them from pickpockets," and are invited to peer inside warehouses where "stores of old iron and bones, and heaps of mildewy fragments of woollen-stuff and linen, rust and rot in the grimy cellars" (CH. XXVI).

Among their other "London Recreations" Dickens' would-be aristocrats of the lower classes like to "get up tavern assemblies in humble imitation of Almack's and promenade the dingy 'large room' of some second-rate hotel with as much complacency as the enviable few who are privileged to exhibit their magnificence in that exclusive haunt of fashion and foolery." Peer, parvenu, and poor come together in that low-life Almack's, the Three Cripples Inn. This euphemistically styled, smoke-laden "establishment" has its "chairman with a hammer of office in his hand" and its exclusive membership like "a professional gentleman, with a bluish nose and his face tied up for the benefit of the toothache, [who] presided at a jingling piano in a remote corner." Soon the distinguished company join voices in a ribald ballad. A few years earlier, Bulwer had proclaimed proudly in *England and the English* that the clubs which "form a main feature of the social system of the richer classes of the metropolis" were no longer "merely the resort of gamblers, politicians or bon vivants." He ventured to predict, completely without tongue in cheek, that these institutions would infiltrate the lower levels of society, for their atmosphere of "moral dignity" and "intellectual relaxation" "contain the germ of a mighty improvement in the condition of the humbler classes." This improvement obviously has not reached that hideout, the Three Cripples, to judge by the music of the establishment and the conversation, which turns mainly on such topics of the day as police news and the affairs of Fagin, Sikes, and Company. The membership as a whole has reached this stage of enlightenment: "Cunning, ferocity and drunkenness in all its stages were there, in their strongest aspects . . . presenting but one loathsome blank of profligacy and crime."

One has the feeling that in this Hogarthian scene Dickens was not merely exposing his more privileged readers to the cesspools of London but showing them their own reflections there. Certainly the society mirrored in some of the novels of the day was not the shining example visualized by Bulwer. The hero of the anonymous *Russell; or, The Reign of Fashion* shuns "that too numerous class of idle, useless, worthless fools of fashions, whose studies and anxieties are devoted to cravat-tying, whisker-pruning, opera-lounging, actress-hunting, dinner-eating, tobacco-smoking, prize-fighting, billiard-playing." Another disenchanted member of the Silver-Fork set recalls a Grosvenor Street soirée where "I, of course, met with some of my Oxford contemporaries, of whom I recognized some dandies and dissipated idlers transformed into legislators and official personages; others sustaining their original characters, and matured into gamblers, jockeys, patrons of tailors, and opera-girls—in a word, men of fashion" [W. Massie, *Sydenham; or, Memoirs of a Man of the World*]. Dickens, it appears, had not really separated the "dregs" of society from its "froth and cream," but homogenized them. His fictitious inhabitants of St. Giles could just as well be the inhabitants of St. James in masquerade. When all is said and done, both groups are engaged in the same occupations—drinking, gambling, idling, and whoring. Presumably the criminal poor of *Oliver Twist* are no more parasitic either than the wastrels of high society. Of all the early reviews of *Oliver Twist,* the youthful Dickens must have been particularly gratified by one which compared it with *The Beggar's Opera* and *Jonathan Wild* for "the boldness with which the writers have stripped society of its disguises, and exhibited the shallowness of those conventionalities which varnish the vices of fashionable life, the falsehood of its pretences, the hypocrisy of its assumptions of decency and propriety" [*Athenaeum* (26 October 1839)].

A modern reader of *Oliver Twist* might prefer the bitter without the sweet, but the story was undoubtedly most palatable to its first audience as the *Parish Boy's Progress,* promised by its original label. The universal appeal of the orphan in fiction, the topicality of the workhouse and private charity, along with Dickens' own identification with the plight of oppressed children—these suggested to him the foundling story as a vehicle for his parable of society. The tradition of the orphan eventually rescued from poverty by revelation of his respectable birth extends well back into the eighteenth century. Its central theme is announced in the title of Eliza Haywood's once popular *The Fortunate Foundlings* (1744). Literary historians customarily trace Oliver Twist back to *Tom Jones* and *Humphry Clinker,* which are among the books read by young David Copperfield. However, waifs and strays abounded in the early nineteenth century—Charlotte Brooke's *Emma; or, The Foundling of the Wood* (1803); the anonymous *Amasina; or, The American Foundling* (1804); Elizabeth Somerville's *Aurora and Maria; or, The Advantages of Adversity* (1809); Mary Pilkington's *Sinclair; or, The Mysterious Orphan* (1809); Charles Lucas' *Gwelygordd; or, The Child of Sin* (1820); Dorothy Kilner's *Edward Neville; or, The Memoirs of an Orphan* (1823); and the perennial and much pirated *Fatherless Fanny; or, A Young Lady's First Entrance into Life.*

A foundling story in vogue during Dickens' childhood, Agnes Maria Bennett's frequently reprinted *The Beggar Girl and Her Benefactors* (1797), may be taken as seminal in its mixture of philanthropy with picaresque adventure. Mrs. Bennett apologizes, exactly forty years before Dickens, to her "polite readers, supposing she should be honoured with any such," for "the vulgar people and low scenes to which perforce the memoirs of a beggar must introduce them" (I, CH. VI). With gentle mockery she twists humility into subtle indignation:

> But notwithstanding no creature living has a more due and profound respect for the higher order of society which all ranks know they merit . . . yet, as, to the eternal disgrace of the police, which, to be sure, should order these things better, there are such things as little folk, who have the presumption to breathe the same atmosphere with the greatest of the great, and by the up and down jumble of chance, not only mingle their paltry interests in the grand movement of high life, but sometimes actually swim on the surface, like common oil on the richest wines. . . .

Presumably, the fact that Mrs. Bennett's beggar girl Rosa Wilkins turns out, like Oliver Twist, to be derived from

rich wine rather than common oil does not negate her egalitarian philosophy.

The Beggar Girl and Her Benefactors probably did much to fix in the minds of early nineteenth-century readers the stereotypes of the outcast waif and benevolent gentleman. The ingredients of Dickens' fable are laid out here: the specter of the parish workhouse (Rosa is rescued from its jaws by the wealthy Colonel Buhanun, who takes her to live with him), the career of persecution and exploitation, the flight to the city, the long-delayed reunion (Rosa proves to be not the daughter of a prostitute, as was supposed, but the natural daughter of her benefactor). There is also satire, if somewhat crude, of the world of fashion through such figures as Mrs. Modely, Lady Gauntley, and Mrs. Wouldby, with whom little Rosa gets involved during her London adventures.

The prestige of a commendation from Coleridge in one of his rare remarks on the fiction of his times has kept the name of Mrs. Bennett flickeringly alive. "*The Beggar Girl* is the best novel, *me judice,* since Fielding," he scribbled on the flyleaf of one of his books. "I should like, therefore, to read the others." At a time when the ranks of female novelists were headed not by Jane Austen but by Jane West, such a remark may not have seemed outlandish. Agnes Maria Bennett might be described as a self-taught writer, but she schooled herself in masters. Such figures as the semiliterate maid Betty Brown, whom Coleridge enjoyed, the tenderhearted hypochondriac Colonel Buhanun, and the scoundrelly Sir Solomon Mushroom bear the stamp of Smollett; elsewhere she echoes Fielding's banter. Her loosely woven tale is eked out with much padding (she was paid by the volume and had a large family to support by her pen), but its good spirits and warm humanity carry one over dull stretches. Whether Dickens knew it directly or not is uncertain, but he was acquainted with many a tale influenced by it. In "Astley's," one of the *Sketches by Boz,* he chafes at the popularity of estranged fathers and children in the theatre:

> By the way, talking of fathers, we should very much like to see some piece in which all the dramatis personae were orphans. Fathers are invariably great nuisances on the stage, and always have to give the hero or heroine a long explanation of what was done before the curtain rose . . . Or else they have to discover, all of a sudden, that somebody whom they have been in constant communication with, during three long acts, without the slightest suspicion, is their own child, in which case they exclaim, "Ah! What do I see! This bracelet! That smile! These documents! Those eyes! Can I believe my senses?—It must be!—Yes—it is—it is—my child!" "My father!" exclaims the child, and they fall into each other's arms, and look over each other's shoulders, and the audience give three rounds of applause.

He followed through with a piece in which virtually "all the dramatis personae were orphans," but he was not above bringing in his own variant of a stage father to effect a happy ending.

The 1830's in particular saw a proliferation of orphan

tales, bounded at one end of the decade by *Elizabeth and Her Three Beggar Boys* and *The Stolen Boy; An Indian Tale,* at the other by *Oliver Twiss,* a parody-sequel of Dickens' novel by a hack named Thomas P. Prest, who signed himself "Bos." In the year when **Oliver Twist** was being serialized in *Bentley's Miscellany,* there appeared one of the numerous reprints of *Fatherless Fanny.* Again, that enterprising hawker of literary wares, Newman, points to an important vogue. It is significant that after 1820, "Minerva Press," with which he had long been associated from his partnership with William Lane, was dropped from his imprints and his catalogues began to feature very prominently "Juvenile and Prize Books." Some of these were of the fanciful and pretty sort, such as *Angelina; or, Conversations of a Little Girl with her Doll* and Miss Selwyn's *Fairy Tales,* but his staple was the true adventure story. Superseding the romantic, didactic fables of the last century—such as Fénelon's *Télémaque,* Lucy Peacock's *The Adventures of the Six Princesses of Babylon in Their Travel to the Temple of Virtue,* and the twice-told ancient legends that were supposed to edify *Sandford and Merton*—were the pious, polemical tales of the times toward which Hannah More had led the way. One of the most popular and fertile producers of this "improving" fiction for youth during the 1820's and 1830's, and one of Newman's stars, was the "amiable and ingenious writer of tales for young and old alike," Mrs. Barbara Hofland. Her titles bristle with the moral virtues—*Decision, Energy, Self-Denial, Fortitude, Patience,* and virtually all of them, like *Young Crusoe; or, The Shipwrecked Boy,* follow the tribulations of young vagabonds whose characters are strengthened rather than toughened by the buffets of the cruel world.

One of Mrs Hofland's fiction-sermons, *Elizabeth and Her Three Beggar Boys* (ca. 1830), adapted from her earlier *Tales of the Priory* (1820), attaches the foundling tale to the social agitation that preceded the enactment of the New Poor Law. Like many of Mrs. Hofland's books, this is a "Tale Founded on Fact." It concerns the progress of a parish boy, William Warren, from rags to riches, as he passes from the workhouse into the rough hands of a cruel farmer, thence into the kinder hands of a religious farmer's wife. She has him apprenticed to a pottery manufacturer, who makes him a partner. The fact is based on the career of the charitable Elizabeth Linley, a cottager's wife from Wakefield, who, despite her poverty, devoted her life to the care of homeless children. The purpose is made explicit in the preface:

> To shew the poor, that even in their poverty they may do much good, and to prove to the rich, that the poor are capable of displaying those virtues which circumstances render extremely difficult, and thus to bring both parties into that contact which their common nature admits, and the religion they alike profess insists upon, wherever faith or morals are concerned, is the especial object of the writer. In her own opinion she has never offered to the world a narrative more true to nature, or better calculated to move the rich to benevolence, and the poor to exertion; and this belief must be her apology for rewriting and re-offering to the young and amiable a "twice-told tale."

Mrs. Hofland defines here the role of emissary of good will among the classes that was being assumed by some of the more social-minded writers at this time. The humbler format of this new condensed version of her tale is an emblem of her humanitarianism—stately half-calf giving way to paper wrappers in order to insure it wider circulation. She reaches simultaneously up and down, involving high and low in a sense of mutual obligation, anticipating Dickens' moral scheme in **Oliver Twist.** In other ways too Mrs. Hofland's tale for her times prepares us for Dickens' fable. Both their parish boys are miraculously preserved from sickness and starvation, despite the workhouse, are saved from criminal careers, are brought up on the New Testament, *The Pilgrim's Progress,* and hymn books. With Mrs. Hofland, as with Dickens, Good Works is the hero and Public Charity the villain. With both authors the pastoral scene is sentimentalized and sacramentalized. Oliver inherits wealth, unlike William Warren, but like William he becomes the benefactor of the next generation of poor. Sympathy and benevolence lubricate the wheels of society.

Another tale of the day, although it is placed in the previous century, is *Hans Sloane: A Tale Illustrating the History of the Foundling Hospital* (1831), written by Dickens' friend John Brownlow. Brownlow's sole venture into fiction rather awkwardly interweaves a rudimentary tale of a fortunate foundling with a memorial to Captain Coram, the founder of the hospital that employed Brownlow. *Hans Sloane* went generally unnoticed in its time, but there is every evidence that Dickens was familiar with it. Brownlow's story, with its lurid intrigue joined to sentimental humanitarianism, seems to have influenced **Oliver Twist** even more than his real-life career.

Hans Sloane begins in the summer of 1740, about a year after Captain Coram's establishment of the Foundling Hospital. The young hero is legitimate and of a well-to-do family, but becoming orphaned at birth, he falls into the hands of an unscrupulous uncle. The uncle, now sole heir to the strictly entailed family estate, is worried about the eventual claim of his brother's surviving child. He refuses to adopt the infant, as his wife wishes. Refraining from murdering him only out of fear of the law, he orders his wife to leave the child at the newly established Foundling Hospital, where it can be brought up in ignorance of its birth. Reluctantly she brings the infant to the home in the dead of night, concealing her own identity. But, contrary to her husband's instructions, she ties around the baby's neck an amulet containing a miniature portrait of his mother. Here is the germ of the much deplored Monks' plot of **Oliver Twist,** which Dickens complicated by making his infant illegitimate, the villainous relative a half-brother instead of an uncle (though preserving his motivation), and by having him seek out the child and rather implausibly plan its moral destruction. Above all, Dickens conceals the whole relationship from the reader until the end to invest the story with an air of mystery.

To return to the misadventures of little Hans Sloane—he is named by the nurses at the hospital after one of its great benefactors, the distinguished Chelsea doctor who also endowed the British Museum. After baptism, little Hans is sent out to be reared by cottagers and then comes back to

Oliver at Mrs. Maylie's door. Illustration by George Cruikshank.

the hospital, where he spends his childhood. Despite the constricted spiritual and physical fare of this institution, Hans, like Oliver, grows into a sprightly, alert lad. He is, however, spared one of Oliver's ordeals. As a "private" child he remains up to the age of twelve under the protection of the hospital instead of being sent out to work. It is then his good fortune to be adopted by a kindly childless couple, the Reverend Mr. Humphries and his wife. By a contrived quirk of destiny the miniature portrait around his neck is recognized by Mrs. Humphries as that of her dead sister. All comes to light when Mr. Humphries attends the death bed of a strange woman at an inn; she proves, of course, to be Hans' aunt, who had deposited him at the Foundling Hospital years before. Upon seeing the amulet she confesses all and dies; and the unscrupulous uncle, his treachery now discovered, commits suicide, leaving the family estate clear for Hans. The Humphries feel thankful "for the miraculous interposition by which they were restored to a relative of whom they had every reason to be proud," and young Hans is determined to use his new-found wealth for the benefit of less fortunate orphans.

Allowing for additional complications introduced by Dickens to unravel his more whorled plot, the conclusion of this crude fable anticipates the dénouement of *Oliver Twist,* with the function of Mr. and Mrs. Humphries dispersed among Mr. Brownlow, Dr. Losberne, Rose Maylie, and her adopted mother. *Hans Sloane* is basically a prose hymn of praise to the Foundling Hospital and to its bene-

factors. In *Oliver Twist* Dickens retains the eighteenth-century moral atmosphere—faith in human benevolence and divine providence (the key, probably, to his much denounced sentimentalism and "outrageous" use of coincidence), along with the assumption of the original virtue and innocence of children. But he updates his story to bring it into line with then current interests in the New Poor Law and juvenile crime.

The historical essays and lay sermons that interlard Brownlow's desultory tale concern perils that Little Hans escapes, but to which Little Oliver is exposed. The initial situation of *Oliver Twist,* for example, may well have been suggested by the account of Captain Coram's encounter with a victim of seduction who had abandoned her infant, an experience which led him to establish the hospital. Brownlow's animadversions on the education of foundlings in the last century prefigure, in turn, the "school" for thieves. He relates that Doctor Johnson, horrified during a visit to the Foundling Hospital to discover that the inmates were not receiving religious instruction, exclaimed: "To breed children in this manner is to rescue them from an early grave, that they may find employment for the gibbet; from dying in innocence that they may perish by their crimes." With his particular interest in apprenticeship, Brownlow denounces the bonus system introduced by Parliament during Captain Coram's time to induce employers to take on homeless boys and relieve the towns of the burden of rearing them. He cites good as well as bad examples, but leaves the impression that Gamfield and Sowerberry were more typical than the unnamed farmer who supervises the regeneration of Charley Bates. All of these issues are revived by Dickens in contemporary settings. The Reverend Mr. Growler, the cynical friend of Mr. Humphries, who predicts a bad end for little Hans, has his counterpart in Mr. Grimwig, the friend of Oliver's benefactor, Mr. Brownlow. Another parallel is Paul Pipkin, an unscrupulous tavern keeper of Eastcheap, whom Bill Sikes resembles.

Dickens' imagination seems particularly to have been stirred by one of Brownlow's moral digressions in which he pleads for sympathy for the unwed mother, urging his readers to abandon their smugness in favor of "a compassionate estimate of the weaknesses of humanity, and a just measure of relief to voluntary repentance":

> This lesson of mercy was eminently taught by the Founder of Christianity Himself, when he bade the Jew who was without sin cast the first stone at the repentant adulteress, and then calmly dismissed her with the charge to *sin no more.* It was not that her crime was venial, but He who desired not the death of a sinner, but rather that she should repent and live, saw perhaps in this wretched criminal sufficient of remorse to be the object of a lesson to mankind,—that the rigour of human law should not be exercised without a human regard to the circumstances under which the crime may have been committed, and the sincerity which may have followed. (CH. X)

For the character of Fagin, Dickens is now believed to have drawn upon a notorious Jew named Ikey Solomon, a fence and a seducer of boys into crime. His "fallen woman," Nancy, presumably could have been based on numerous Cheapside prostitutes. But Brownlow's allusion suggests the biblical analogy that Dickens intended the Fagin-Nancy relationship to convey. Fagin, forgetting that he is responsible for her downfall, flings stones at Nancy for her profession, as the unenlightened reader might also be disposed to do. Dickens' frequent reference to Fagin by the generic term "the Jew" indicates that he may have conceived him in the image of the sanctimonious Pharisee of the New Testament. Certainly Nancy is a modern incarnation of the penitent Magdalen, the aspect of her character that Dickens emphasizes in her meeting with the innocent Rose Maylie (CH. XL), and reiterates with scriptural eloquence in his preface to the 1841 edition, where he felt called upon to defend her portrayal:

> IT IS TRUE. Every man who has watched these melancholy shades of life, knows it to be so. . . . It is emphatically God's truth, for it is the truth He leaves in such depraved and miserable breasts; the hope yet lingering behind; the last fair drop of water at the bottom of the dried up, weed-choked well. It involves the best and worst shades of our common nature; much of its ugliest hues, and something of its most beautiful; it is a contradiction, an anomaly, an apparent impossibility; but it is a truth.

In naming Oliver's benefactor Mr. Brownlow, Dickens seems to have been paying an early tribute to one of the most dedicated social servants of his age. John Brownlow must be counted among Dickens' unsung progenitors, but it is probable that a far more distinguished foundling than Hans Sloane is to be included among Oliver's literary brothers—Professor Diogenes Teufelsdröckh. Among the first critics of *Oliver Twist,* the young George Henry Lewes was virtually alone in noting [*National Magazine* (December 1837)] that Dickens' works "are volumes of human nature, that have a deep and subtle philosophy in them, which those who read only to laugh may not discover." As early as *Oliver Twist* we may discern the allegorizing tendency of Dickens' imagination, particularly in his attempts to invest his sordid characters with moral—even biblical—significance. But the moral that draws together all his characters—genteel and pseudo-genteel—grows out of the initial episode where Little Oliver, "enveloped in the old calico robes which had grown yellow in the same service . . . was badged and ticketed, and fell into his place at once—a parish child. . . ." The whole novel, as well as Oliver himself, is "an excellent example of the power of dress." Incongruities of wearing apparel, as we have seen, figure in the satire of the book—Fagin in his greasy coat teaching his ragamuffins how to filch silk handkerchiefs, the elaborate getup of the housebreaker Toby Crackit, Nancy's passing herself off as Oliver's mother by means of a shawl and basket. Dickens also uses the device seriously to connote character. Bill Sikes' "black velveteen coat, very soiled drab breeches . . . dirty belcher handkerchief around his neck" are the fitting garments of his obscene soul, just as the "powdered head and gold spectacles . . . bottle-green coat with a black velvet collar, . . . white trousers, and . . . smart bamboo cane" appropriately deck out Mr. Brownlow's fairy-godfather elegance of character.

However, the idea Dickens wished to convey in his novel was that clothes do not really make the man except in the eyes of the beholder. So he hints in his pointed Preface of 1841, when he defends his choice of characters from St. Giles to his more squeamish readers:

> But there are people of so refined and delicate a nature, that they cannot bear the contemplation of these horrors. Not that they turn instinctively from crime; but that criminal characters, to suit them, must be, like their meat, in delicate disguise. A Massaroni in green velvet is an enchanting creature; but a Sikes in fustian is insupportable. A Mrs. Massaroni, being a lady in short petticoats and a fancy dress, is a thing to imitate in tableaux and have in lithograph on pretty songs; but a Nancy, being a creature in a cotton gown and cheap shawl, is not to be thought of. It is wonderful how Virtue turns from dirty stockings; and how Vice, married to ribbons and a little gay attire, changes her name, as wedded ladies do, and becomes Romance.

Accordingly, in the novel itself he scrambles clothes and characters to illustrate the arbitrariness of distinctions based on dress. Rags cover Nancy as well as Bill Sikes and Fagin. Bill Sikes and Mr. Brownlow both wear black velvet. To outward seeming, Monks and Mr. Brownlow are both gentlemen. Oliver changes clothes as he moves from thieves' den to country cottage and back again, but he does not change character. A facetious illustration of the accidents of attire is Bumble's fall from beadledom after his marriage to Mrs. Corney:

> The laced coat, and the cocked hat, where were they? He still wore knee-breeches, and dark cotton stockings on his nether limbs; but they were not *the* breeches. The coat was wide-skirted, and in that respect like *the* coat; but, oh, how different! The mighty cocked-hat was replaced by a modest round one. Mr. Bumble was no longer a beadle.

Bumble's downfall leads Dickens to philosophize on mankind in general:

> There are some promotions in life, which, independent of the more substantial rewards they offer, acquire peculiar value and dignity from the coats and waistcoats connected with them. A field-marshal has his uniform, a bishop his silk apron, a counsellor his silk gown, a beadle his cocked hat. Strip the bishop of his apron, or the beadle of his hat and lace; what are they? Men. Mere Men. Dignity, and even holiness, too, sometimes, are more questions of coat and waistcoat than some people imagine. (CH. XXXVII)

These observations were not new. A few years before, some, at least, of the first readers of *Oliver Twist* had been startled also by passages like:

> Has not your Red hanging-individual a horsehair wig, squirrel-skins, and a plush-gown; whereby all mortals know that he is a JUDGE?— Society, which the more I think of it astonishes me the more, is founded upon Cloth.

> Aprons are Defences; against injury to cleanli-

ness, to safety, to modesty, sometimes to roguery. . . . How much has been concealed, how much has been defended in Aprons! Nay, rightly considered, what is your whole Military and Police Establishment, charged at uncalculated millions, but a huge scarlet-coloured, iron-fastened Apron, wherein Society works (uneasily enough). . . . But of all Aprons the most puzzling to me hitherto has been the Episcopal or Cassock. Wherein consists the usefulness of this Apron? The Overseer (*Episcopus*) of Souls, I notice, has tucked-in the corner of it, as if his day's work were done: what does he shadow forth thereby?

Lives the man that can figure a naked Duke of Windlestraw addressing a naked House of Lords? Imagination, choked as in mephitic air, recoils on itself, and will not forward with the picture. The Woolsack, the Ministerial, the Opposition Benches?—*infandum! infandum!* And yet why is the thing impossible? Was not every soul, or rather every body, of these Guardians of our Liberties, naked, or nearly so, last night; 'a forked Radish with a Head fantastically carved'? And why might he not, did our stern fate so order it, walk out to St. Stephens's, as well into bed in that no-fashion; and there, with other similar Radishes, hold a Bed of Justice?

Thomas Carlyle's Professor Diogenes Teufelsdröckh was, of course, after bigger game than parish beadles, but his caustic wisdom encompasses Mudfog. The life and opinions of this abandoned waif, who grew up to occupy the Chair of Things-in-General at the University of Weissnichtwo, appeared in book form in 1838, while *Oliver Twist* was still running serially, but they had burst forth five years earlier in the pages of *Fraser's Magazine*. Dickens' long-lived (and generally unrequited) adulation of Carlyle's writings apparently began even earlier than *The French Revolution. Oliver Twist* takes over from *Sartor Resartus* not only Professor Teufelsdröckh's Philosophy of Clothes, but his scorn for the dismal science of political economy as well. Herr Teufelsdröckh's "Liberals, Economists, Utilitarians . . . European Mechinisers" are Dickens' "experimenters" and "well-fed philosophers" anonymously and mysteriously responsible for Oliver's plight. Carlyle, in addition, overtly denounces what Dickens implicitly parodies—the "buck, or Blood, or Macaroni, or Incroyable, or Dandy."

Of all Dickens' immediate contemporaries it was Carlyle who raised the orphan tale to the level of metaphysical and moral fantasy. *Oliver Twist* echoes the transcendentalism as well as the satire of *Sartor Resartus*. Entepfühl embraces Eastcheap, particularly in Teufelsdröckh's recollection of his obscure origins, as recorded in the chapter pointedly entitled "Genesis":

> Ever, in my distresses and my loneliness, has Fantasy turned, full of longing, to that unknown Father, who perhaps far from me, perhaps near, either way invisible, might have taken me to his paternal bosom, there to lie screened from many a woe. . . .
>
> And yet, O Man born of Woman . . . wherein is my case peculiar? . . . The Andreas and Gret-

chen, or the Adam and Eve, who led thee into Life, and for a time suckled and pap-fed thee there, whom thou namest Father and Mother; these were, like mine, but thy nursing-father and nursing-mother; thy true Beginning and Father is in Heaven, whom with the bodily eye thou shalt never behold, but only with the spiritual.

So Dickens reminds us about his orphan hero. In one of the more sentimental episodes he shows us Little Oliver, after suffering in silence from the corporal punishment of Mr. Sowerberry and the brutal taunts of Noah, finally giving vent to his repressed emotion: "But now when there were none to see or hear him, he fell upon his knees on the floor, and hiding his face in his hands, wept such tears as, God send for the credit of our nature, few so young may ever have cause to pour out before Him!" (CH. VII). This cloys because we feel removed from the situation and flatter ourselves that we don't need to be reminded, as Dickens assumed that his first readers needed to be, that the high and the humble have a common origin. Oliver's angelic appearance, his preternatural virtue and piety, his general aura of "clouds of glory" are all intended to recall his eternal home.

At a remove of more than a century we are especially likely to squirm over Oliver's farewell to the dying orphan Dick:

> "Yes, yes, I will [stop] to say good-bye to you," replied Oliver. "I shall see you again, Dick, I know I shall! You will be well and happy!"
>
> "I hope so," replied the child. "After I am dead, but not before. I know the doctor must be right, Oliver, because I dream so much of Heaven, and Angels, and kind faces that I never see when I am awake. Kiss me," said the child, climbing up the low gate, and flinging his arms round Oliver's neck. "Good-bye, dear! God bless you!"
>
> The blessing was from a young child's lips, but it was the first that Oliver had ever heard invoked upon his head; and through the struggles and sufferings and troubles and changes of his after life, he never once forgot it. (CH. VII)

But no reader of Wordsworth had difficulty believing in children who see angels. A reader of Carlyle besides, like Dickens, could see the orphan as representative of man's estrangement from his creator—Diogenes Teufelsdröckh's vision of the human condition. Little Oliver and Little Dick are best regarded not as real children but as symbolic children moving in a world that seems real but is reality transfigured.

Dickens provided a kind of postscript to *Oliver Twist* in his letter, "Crime and Education," contributed to the *Daily News* [4 February 1846] several years after the novel was first published. Here he comments on the Ragged Schools he had visited, charity schools where overworked volunteers attempted to teach the poor, children and adults, "and show them some sympathy and stretch a hand out, which is not the iron hand of Law, for their correction." He conveys a lesson he carried away from a fetid classroom in Saffron Hill, where *Oliver Twist* takes place:

> This, Reader, was one room as full as it could

hold; but these were only grains in sample of a Multitude that are perpetually sifting through these schools; in sample of a Multitude who had within them once, and perhaps have now, the elements of men as good as you or I, and maybe infinitely better; in sample of a Multitude among whose doomed and sinful ranks (oh, think of this, and think of them!) the child of any man upon this earth, however lofty his degree, must, as by Destiny and Fate, be found, if, at its birth, it were consigned to such an infancy and nurture, as these fallen creatures had!

Such a "fallen creature" is Oliver Twist, who "might have been the child of a nobleman or a beggar." Unlike Nancy and Little Dick, he is rescued from this multitude because Dickens has singled him out for a special mission. Dickens was critical of the Ragged Schools, particularly of their overemphasis on religious mysteries beyond the comprehension of their pupils, but he urges his readers to support them. He would especially like to see funds that have been contributed by the wealthy toward the building of new churches diverted to these impoverished classrooms, "as an appropriate means of illustrating the Christian Religion." He suggests, moreover, that they do not remain aloof, but "go themselves into the Prisons and the Ragged Schools, and form their own conclusions." Through Oliver Twist, in effect, he enables his readers to be reborn. With Oliver they live among the "doomed and sinful ranks," the Ragged Schools writ large in the dens of Eastcheap. They even descend with him into the cells of the condemned. What we might have expected to be a shattering, traumatic experience for Little Oliver—his witnessing of Fagin's last night alive—instead brings out the depth of his human sympathy. "Oh! God forgive this wretched man!" are his words as his most fiendish tormentor is led to the gallows. So high and low, old and young, virtuous and villainous, are brought together in a common bond.

Sensationalism, satire, and sentiment—those disparate and sometimes discordant elements of Dickens' genius—tend toward the same goal—to make humanity recognize what they have in common. Depending on Dickens' mood, all men are criminals, fops, or angels. As early as *Oliver Twist* we recognize a tension between the tender-minded and the tough-minded Dickens. "Men who look on nature, and their fellow men, and cry that all is dark and gloomy, are in the right," he observes halfway through his story, "but the sombre colours are reflections from their own jaundiced eyes and hearts. The real hues are delicate and need a clearer vision" (CH. XXXIV). To us he seems to see more powerfully out of his "jaundiced eyes" than with his "clearer vision." In *Oliver Twist* his "sombre colours," the murky city scenes, somehow impress themselves on our memory, while the "delicate hues," the idyllic country scenes, remain a roseate blur. The vividness that Dickens gives to the world of darkness has led Graham Greene mistakenly to call him a Manichean. Dickens really means for "the principle of Good" to survive, but the principle of Evil engaged both his imagination and his sense of humor more. Whereas his irony and caustic wit come into play in his treatment of the thieves, he leaned on stock associations of the good, the beautiful, and the pathetic in representing Rose Maylie

and her family. His own representation of humanity, therefore, may seem out of focus; but a balanced picture, he reiterates in his various prefaces to *Oliver Twist,* includes "the best and worst shades of our nature; much of its ugliest hues, and something of its most beautiful."

Although we tend to think of *Oliver Twist* as a novel about the poor, it really contains in essence the novel of society that Dickens developed with greater amplitude in *Bleak House, Little Dorrit,* and *Our Mutual Friend,* where all classes are reciprocally involved not merely symbolically but literally. The pattern of the well-born descending to the lower depths tends to reverse itself in the mature novels, with the low-born moving up and discovering their new-found wealth to be a curse rather than a blessing. With his growing cynicism Dickens also was to stress the acquisitiveness rather than the kindliness of the wealthy. But he continued to lodge his faith in the hearts of men rather than in institutions. The motiveless benignity of a Mr. Brownlow and the Cheeryble Brothers counted for more than a parish workhouse, a Bible Institute, or organized philanthropy as represented by Mrs. Jellyby and Mrs. Pardiggle. If distrust of institutions accounts for some of his most effective satire, trust in man accounts for some of his most mawkish sentimentality. At the beginning of his career he could glance back nostalgically at an ideal eighteenth-century vision of the benevolent gentleman carrying on God's work in the world. This is the tradition inherited by Oliver Twist and Rose Maylie, who—temporarily fallen from their true places—are restored to them; "tried by adversity, [they] remembered its lessons in mercy to others, and mutual love and fervent thanks to Him who had protected and preserved them." Humanity is joined in a circle of empathy and an apostolic succession of benevolence.

Of all the popular types of fiction that Dickens wove into this children's story for adults, he had a special affinity, in these early years, for the foundling tale. A true story that his first readers did not know—as remarkable in its way as the Parish Boy's Progress—was his own progress from Baynham Street and Camden Town to Regent's Park. *Oliver Twist* was the first of what was to be a series of projections of his own situation as the *arriviste.* It is not a mere accidental detail, surely, that Oliver sees his gentleman-savior for the first time in front of a bookstall. It was, after all, to literature that Dickens owed his own "rescue" from obscurity. Mr. Brownlow's library plays as important a part in Oliver's rehabilitation as the village church. Oliver rejects the crime thrillers of Fagin in favor of the Bible, *The Pilgrim's Progress,* and those numerous unnamed books given him by Mr. Brownlow, at the time when Dickens was leaving behind mere amusement and entertainment and dedicating himself to "improving" literature. Mr. Brownlow, in a way, stands for the reading public that made possible Dickens' rise from reporter to novelist-prince. This public Dickens was later to visualize as Abel Magwitch, in terms of Frankenstein's monster pursuing his creator—but that, of course, is another story. (pp. 105-36)

Robert A. Colby, " 'Oliver Twist': The Fortunate Foundling," in his Fiction with a Purpose: Major and Minor Nineteenth-Century

Novels, *Indiana University Press, 1967, pp. 105-37.*

Sylvère Monod (essay date 1968)

[*Monod is a French educator, critic, and translator who has written numerous critical studies of Dickens's fiction. In the following excerpt from his* Dickens the Novelist, *he examines the compositional technique of* Oliver Twist, *regarding the novel as unique among Dickens's early works.*]

[*Oliver Twist* is] a novel composed and published in small fragments over many months and subjected to many vicissitudes and accidents. No one should be surprised at finding weak points in its structure. Dickens makes a larger use than in his other works of digressions. However poorly constructed *Pickwick* had been, it had contained no digressions; true, one can digress only from a straight line, while the outline of *Pickwick* had been so broken and zigzagging that there was no knowing when the author went away from it. In *Oliver Twist,* whose story is more consecutive and closely knit, many digressive passages stand out: Oliver's conversation with Mr. Brownlow about books and the writer's profession is as superfluous as it is improbable; yet its conclusion, as Mr. Brownlow tells Oliver—"We won't make an author of you, while there's an honest trade to be learnt, or brick-making to turn to,"— shows it to have been but a fresh example of the author's youthfulness; dazzled at finding himself in the position of a professional and prosperous novelist at the age of twenty-five, he relishes such ironical and conventional allusions to his craft. And there are in *Oliver Twist* other digressions as well as other kinds of unnecessary elements: a long and commonplace description—as commonplace as most of Dickens' general remarks are at the time—of rustic pleasures; a too detailed presentation of a huckster whose part is at best episodic, during Sikes' flight; or again, the unduly developed description of "Jacob's Island." Some of those fragments may possibly have been added or expanded at proof stage in order to fill up deficient installments. Yet their more obvious purpose generally appears to be an attempt at smoothing the passage from one chapter or one scene to another. Dickens, as a youthful novelist, has not yet mastered the art of securing an easy transition between two incidents, or the greater art of linking incident to incident solidly enough to be able to dispense with a transition altogether. Transitions in *Oliver Twist* are often ponderous and artificial. Here, as in *Pickwick,* a great display of ingenuity betrays the author's uncertain hand; thus, when Dickens declares, at the end of Chapter XXVII, "With these words, the beadle strode . . . from the undertaker's premises. And now that we have accompanied him so far on his road home . . . let us set on foot a few enquiries after young Oliver, and ascertain whether he be still lying in the ditch where Toby Crackit left him," his hesitation might have been less glaring if he had contented himself with closing the chapter after the first of the above-quoted sentences, and beginning the next chapter without a preamble. A similar feeling is elicited by several passages of the book; two additional examples may be given: "Talking all the way, he followed Mr. Giles up stairs; and while he is going up stairs, the reader may be informed, that Mr. Losberne, a surgeon in the neighborhood . . . "; "Upon the very same night when Nancy . . . hurried on her self-imposed mission . . . there advanced towards London . . . two persons, upon whom it is expedient that this history should bestow some attention." Such phrases, involving active interference of author, reader, or more or less personified "history," are the hallmark of immature technique, of a narrative method still in need of external aids to insure its progress.

Side by side with those unquestionable weaknesses can however be observed in *Oliver* evidence of the author's earliest conscious artistic attempt; its result will be better understood when its purpose and other peculiarities have been defined. *Oliver Twist* is no isolated production; the book belongs to what Thackeray called "The Newgate School of Fiction," a series, very popular in the eighteen-thirties, of novels whose heroes are great criminals. This kind of literature, whose origins are very remote, had been very fashionable in the eighteenth century, with the works of Defoe (*Moll Flanders*) and Fielding (*Jonathan Wild*) among others; yet the criminal ideal had again flourished more recently thanks to Byron, whose *Lara* appeared in 1814. Bulwer Lytton, ever ready and eager to adapt himself to the passing taste, wrote two "Newgate Novels" (*Paul Clifford* in 1834, and *Jack Sheppard,* which succeeded *Oliver* in *Bentley's Miscellany* in 1839); Charles Whitehead, the writer who had recommended Boz to Chapman and Hall, published *The Autobiography of Jack Ketch* in 1834. In that field, then, Dickens was by no means a pioneer, and was in fact rather fighting a rearguard action, since *Oliver Twist* came out shortly before the reaction set in against the "Newgate Novels"; the reaction was led mainly by Thackeray, who wrote no fewer than three parodies of the genre: *Catherine* in 1839-40, *Barry Lyndon* in 1844, and *George de Barnwell* in 1847. At the end of *Catherine,* when he was about to introduce the most violent and sanguinary scene, the author exclaimed:

> We are now prepared, O candid and discerning reader, who are sick of the hideous scenes of brutal bloodshed which have of late come forth from the pens of certain eminent wits, to give to the world a scene infinitely more brutal and bloody than even the murder of Miss Nancy . . . if you turn away disgusted from the book, remember that this passage has not been written for you, who have taste to know and hate the style in which it has been composed; but for the public, which has no such taste. . . . Stretch your throats, sweet ones—for our god, the public, is thirsty, and must have blood.

"And there was the body—mere flesh and blood, no more—but such flesh, and so much blood!" Dickens had been writing in *Oliver Twist.* If the public was as bloodthirsty as Thackeray believed it to be, Dickens was ready to slake its thirst. He was ready to cater to its taste for every kind of sensation—for violence, mystery, emotion and horror: the death of Old Sally, just as she seemed about to reveal the identity of Oliver's mother; the mysterious apparitions, in various places, and the hideous disease and general aspect of Monks; the harmony between the storm, the surroundings, and the broken speech of the characters during his interview with the Bumbles; the secret kinships suddenly disclosed and other sensational identifications; the past events revealed in theatrical style, as " . . . in the West Indies—whither, as you well know, you retired upon your mother's death"; the fantastic form in which had been couched a will which has been destroyed but remains compelling; and the no less fantastic entanglement of secret relationships—such that, in the final scene, "a father, sister, and mother, were gained, and lost, in that one moment"—all those incidents which, nowadays, do little, if anything, for the success of the book, were introduced by Dickens for the purpose of pleasing the contemporary popular taste, and can be looked upon as so many effects of his careful and complex, though slightly mistaken, technical labor.

The quest for sensational effects is favored by the alternation of comical with tragical scenes. The procedure is first criticized in the digressive introduction to Chapter XVII, in a style characteristic of Dickens' imagery: "It is the custom on the stage, in all good murderous melodramas, to present the tragic and comic scenes, in as regular alternation, as the layers of red and white in a side of streaky bacon." If the novelist's terms are correct, then *Oliver Twist* undoubtedly is "a good murderous melodrama," for the tendency to a change of atmosphere after the more dramatic passages is clearly marked, as if to relieve the tension. In general, Dickens relinquishes his London characters and takes us to see some incident in Bumble's life. He does so in Chapter XVII, after the great quarrel in the thieves' den following Oliver's return there; in Chapter XXIV, while Oliver lies, wounded, in a ditch; in Chapter XXVII, after the mysterious interview between Monks and Fagin has come to a close; in Chapter XXXVII, after the separation between the quaint lovers, Harry and Rose Maylie. All of these changes do not merely modify and relax the atmosphere of the narrative; they also result in a change of scene. Thus the composition of *Oliver* is more complex than that of *Pickwick,* which had been founded on a mobile group of characters, ever escorted by the narrator; in *Oliver,* on the contrary, two, then three groups of characters evolve in separate areas, but find themselves linked together by increasingly manifold bonds. In spite of the ironical tone of the statements on the subject also to be found at the beginning of Chapter XVII ("sudden shiftings of the scene and rapid changes of time and place, are not only sanctioned in books by long usage, but are by many considered as the great art of authorship"), it is clear that Dickens is obeying the impulse to display his technical skill. The result is on the whole creditable: some of the shiftings from one scene to another are either too abrupt or too labored, but the sequence of incidents is controlled with a certain cleverness and appears methodically organized. This is mostly the case from the moment Oliver has been admitted into the home of the Maylies—his second benefactors. There are then three series of scenes providing information about Oliver's progress and the Maylies family life, about the uncertainties and anxieties of the Fagin gang, and about the evolution of affairs in the Bumbles' small anonymous town. The scenes are superficially independent, but the reader is made to feel their increasing unity. Oliver himself is a permanent link: he had been born

in an unknown town, and it is the mystery of his birth that is looked for there; among the thieves, it is his disappearance that causes alarm, and a good deal of plotting against him is constantly going on; Monks, Oliver's half-brother, is first seen in connection with Fagin's gang; then Oliver himself catches sight of him; finally he shows himself to Bumble. A fresh link is created and the triangle becomes complete when Nancy, the thieves' accomplice, has an interview with Rose Maylie.

Through the firmness of its plot, then, *Oliver Twist* is a work superior, not only to *Pickwick,* but also to *Nickleby,* and indeed to all the other novels of Dickens' first period; it has better construction; indeed, it has *more* construction than the others. Traces of inexperience can still be discerned in it, however, for, while the outline of the narrative is coherent, the machinery is still somewhat artificial. There was not enough organization in *Pickwick,* but there is rather too much of it in *Oliver,* and the result is the same in both cases: the passage from one incident to the next is jerky, and occasionally forced; the use of coincidence is just as lavish as in the preceding book, and the whole plot rests on a twofold monumental coincidence; Oliver is twice made to work for the thieves: the first time, he is present when the victim of a robbery happens to be Mr. Brownlow, his father's oldest friend, and the second time, the boy is constrained to take part in the burglarizing of a house where his aunt happens to be living. The fact that the first link was no afterthought with Dickens is proved by the existence in Mr. Brownlow's house of a portrait of Oliver's mother, to which the reader's attention is drawn as early as Chapter XII, and even earlier, when Mr. Brownlow finds something familiar to him in Oliver's countenance.

Several minor coincidences could be listed; those above mentioned will suffice to show what an important part that convenient procedure is called upon to play in the book. Its value is indeed openly proclaimed, both by virtuous characters who see in it the action of divine providence, like Mr. Brownlow, when he says to Monks: "Your brother . . . was cast on my way by a stronger hand than chance," and by evil-doers, who see in it Satan's influence, like Monks, when he says to Bumble, with theatrical cynicism: "I came down to this place to-day, to find you out; and, by one of those chances which the devil throws in the way of his friends sometimes, you walked into the very room I was sitting in."

Through its accidental encounters, *Oliver Twist,* in spite of its uniqueness among Dickens' works, has something in common with most of them. The ending of the novel is equally characteristic of the usual Dickensian manner. Like all Dickens' early novels, *Oliver Twist* is crowned by what Forster calls "the quiet closing chapter," in which, within four pages, the reader is informed of the fate of some twelve characters.

"And now the hand that traces these words falters, as it approaches the conclusion of its task; and would weave, for a little longer space, the thread of these adventures"—thus Dickens wrote in his concluding chapter. Forster has fortunately described the mirthful evening in the course of which those melancholy lines were penned, when the owner of the faltering hand did not conceal his joy at having done with Oliver for good and all.

Our perception of the differences and resemblances between the composition of *Pickwick* and that of *Oliver Twist* should not be taken to mean that there has been an evolution from one to the other of two works which were in great part contemporaneous, but rather that two distinct efforts coexisted in the early experimental phase of Dickens' career, from 1836 to 1839; he was only gradually finding himself, through trial and error as well as through trial and triumph. As far as style is concerned, his search is less hesitant already. As a considerable portion of the manuscript of *Oliver* has been preserved, it is possible to form an idea of his purpose by looking at the way in which he corrected himself.

In the first place, the vocabulary employed by Dickens in *Oliver Twist* shows a greater tendency to archaism—not without a touch of pedantry—than is often believed. As in the *Sketches,* "sundry" and "divers" are often used where "some" or "several" would have done just as well, and Dickens introduces dubious refinements, such as calling Fagin's abject gang "that respectable coterie"—or unusual grammatical forms: "nor stopped they once to breathe." But, side by side with such poorly written passages, there are others in *Oliver Twist* of higher quality. Dickens, at some apparently inspired moments, seems to rise almost to a kind of poetry; for instance, in three paragraphs of Chapter X (each beginning with the cry, "Stop thief !"), through the incantatory iteration of those two words, as well as through cumulative, intensifying, and quickening effects, the style of the passage becomes exalted. This again occurs in the tragic episode of the murder; it would seem that Dickens, while writing that portion of his narrative, had been obsessed by the remembrance of Shakespeare, and particularly of *Macbeth,* in which are also to be found the preparation of a crime and the hauntings of remorse; the words in which Fagin greets Sikes emulate Shakespearean syntax through the omission of the relative pronoun, and might, *mutatis mutandis,* have been used by Lady Macbeth to salute her husband: "I've got that to tell you, Bill, will make you worse than me." Likewise, the admirable chapter describing the criminal's flight, begins in solemn, quasi-inspired style: "Of all bad deeds, that under cover of the darkness . . . that was the worst," in which the very use of the word "deed" to mean "murder" is once more reminiscent of *Macbeth*—"I have done the deed"—as is, throughout the passage, the obsessive presence of blood-stains; "There were spots that would not be removed. How those stains were dispersed about the room!"

Apart from the most mediocre and the most felicitously written passages that have just been mentioned, Dickens' use of language in *Oliver Twist* already illustrates some of his more permanent characteristics, such as the sentimental coloring that has often been noticed in his works. One word that was to play a great part in Dickens' style, the adjective "old," already appears here with its most idiosyncratic connotation: to a novelist who is deeply attached to whatever in the past is personal, anything that belongs to former days, anything familiar, tends to be treated as touching and moving. Such is the value assumed by "old" in phrases like "faces that the grave had changed and closed upon, but which the mind . . . still dressed in their old freshness and beauty . . . "; the association of "old" with "freshness" is at first sight paradoxical; it is less so, of course, when one thinks of the adverbial form "of old"; and in any case, it is the direct outcome of Dickens' sentimental vision of the past, so that his use of "old" is always one of the most easily identifiable leitmotivs of his work. Sentimentality is frequently allied with intensity of expression; Dickens constantly reinforces his assertions by means of such adverbs as "quite" and "indeed," such forceful adjectives as "great," and any number of superlatives; in one page of *Oliver* will be found the following expressions: "the most eager desire . . . the greatest caution and most circumspect behavior . . . great politeness . . . great benevolence . . . great crash . . . the most unmitigated wonder"; whenever Dickens is powerfully taken by his theme, and participates in the emotions he is describing, such expressions inevitably crop up in his writing.

An examination of the manuscript reveals that *Oliver Twist* was written with uneven ease; the number of corrections varies greatly from page to page. The general aspect of the manuscript, if compared to those of later works, affords an impression of more flowing inspiration or less careful labor. The handwriting is broad and swift; the cancelled words are at first crossed with one horizontal line that leaves them comparatively legible; then, half way through Chapter XIII, the straight line is given up in favor of a series of close loops which are thereafter Dickens' single system of self-correction and make his other manuscripts much harder to interpret. On the whole, there are few corrections in *Oliver Twist;* occasionally, two whole paragraphs occur in succession without a single change being made; and when there are extensive changes, the cause is easy enough to guess. As often as not, it is due to some peculiar difficulty experienced by the author. When composing some pseudo-philosophical digression on a general theme, Dickens was less sure of his ground than in narrative or dialogue; in Chapter XII, for instance (called Chapter XIII on the manuscript), he canceled, after much hesitation, a whole sentence: "In proof of which proposition I need hardly [refer] appeal to everybody's experience of every day and every school," which may, understandably, have struck him on second or third thoughts, as rather too commonplace and vague [in a footnote the critic adds: "In every quotation from Dickens' MSS, the words in square brackets are those he had himself crossed out "]. In the same chapter one gesture was added—perhaps as he reread his page—in order to increase the shock of Sikes's brutality; after " 'She's a honour to her sex,' said Mr. Sikes, filling his glass," he inserted, above the line, "and striking the table with his enormous fist." That is on the occasion of Sikes's first appearance, and Sikes is one of the book's most sensational figures; the writer cannot spare his most vivid colors. Similarly, the first time we see—or rather hear—Rose Maylie, a girl of ideal sweetness, the manuscript discloses a great deal of effort and hesitation between such words as "light," "soft," "gentle," "musical," and "tripping," before Dickens could satisfy himself that he had conveyed the right impression. The description of a dilapidated house which he wished to render impressive—for it is there that the momentous interview between Monks and the Bumbles will take place—apparently occasioned him the same kind of problem.

In the final section of the book, Dickens apparently sought to tone down, rather than enhance, the impressions of brutality and coarseness. That, at least, appears to be the cause of corrections of the following kind: "Let me get off this [thundering] [cursed bed] thundering bed anyhow." A little later, after "Sikes struck her" (Nancy), the author cancels "in the face." Sikes shouts to Nancy: "bustle about, or I'll beat it out of you" ("it" being "your foolery"), but the end of the sentence is turned into the much tamer "and don't come over me with your woman's nonsense." Fagin, who had been called at first "false-hearted old swine," is reduced to being termed merely a "false-hearted wagabond." A few chapters earlier there had already occurred the following extenuation, whose involuntary humor need not be pointed out: Fagin asks Nancy, " 'And where should you think Bill was now, my dear, eh?' ['In Hell, for anything I know,' the girl replied without raising her face.] The girl moaned out [that she could] some scarcely intelligible reply."

But, however interesting a study of Dickens' manuscript, apart from the general impression that the writer did his job seriously and conscientiously enough, it is difficult to gain from his corrections any clear idea of his stylistic principles.

Any survey of style in *Oliver Twist* would be grievously incomplete if it did not refer to the way in which Dickens handles one word which must have been originally meant to belong to the book's main theme. The complete title of the novel is *Oliver Twist, or the Parish Boy's Progress.* The word "progress" immediately calls to mind Hogarth—who is incidentally mentioned by Dickens in the preface, as an artist whose unique realism he wishes to emulate—and his famous *Rake's Progress,* while the alliteration in *Parish . . . Progress* is yet more markedly reminiscent of Bunyan's *Pilgrim's Progress.* The title thus stresses the fact that Oliver is a parish-boy, a boy raised, that is, since there is little or no ecclesiastical connotation attaching to the word "parish," as a pauper, at the expense of the community. It will be observed that the word "parish," together with its derivatives "parishioner," "parochial," and Bumble's delightful variant of the latter, "porochial," are used some thirty times in the course of the first four chapters, and keep recurring to the end of the book. With two other terms—"workhouse" and "pauper"—equally evocative of the idea of administrative, impersonal, inhuman charity, the word "parish" is thus closely linked with the purpose of the narrative, as an attack launched against the New Poor Law of 1834 and its rigid parochial organization of spurious official philanthropy. The method—perhaps only half consciously adopted in *Oliver*—which consists in bestowing permanent prominence on one idea through the constant iteration of the same word or words, was used again and systematically enlarged in later novels.

Thus we find more unity in the style and composition of *Oliver Twist* than in those of *Pickwick.* (pp. 120-30)

There are clearly three distinct categories of characters in *Oliver Twist:* the comic figures who are fully alive, the melodramatic villains, and the angels. The comic figures are the most characteristically Dickensian creations. There are many, especially in the small anonymous city of Oliver's birth; they are true photographic reproductions of living beings, treated in unquestionably realistic style; such as Mrs. Mann, Mrs. Corney—though she tends to join the second category once she has degenerated into Mrs. Bumble—the two Sowerberrys, and the immortal Bumble.

The melodramatic villains also reappear in Dickens' later works. "I fear there are in the world some insensible and callous natures, that do become, at last, utterly and irredeemably bad," the novelist wrote in his preface to *Oliver.* Such malevolent beings, who do evil for evil's sake, are a great resource of Dickensian plots; they create any number of difficulties and obstacles to the happiness of the heroes and heroines, and the annihilation of these evil-doers tends to become the ultimate purpose of the plot. These dark figures never completely disappear from Dickens' work, but their psychology becomes increasingly complex and flexible. There are plenty of characters of this class among the thieves, and they are not all contemptible creations; if Monks may be thought too purely spectacular, too inhuman, with his hideous disease and almost gratuitous malevolence, Sikes on the contrary is a well-drawn figure of a brute, and his flight and remorse are convincingly described. As for Fagin, he is vigorously depicted and comes to life with his perpetual greed, but also with his disquieting mirth and scathing irony; he can even be regarded as one of Dickens' few truly great villains.

Finally, there are in *Oliver Twist* a number of angelic figures meant to arouse our admiration and touch our hearts; yet they are drawn in a way that is not likely to convince the modern reader. To that group belong chiefly Oliver himself, Rose Maylie, and Nancy from the time of her conversion. Oliver totally lacks the naturalness that gives such appeal to other Dickensian children, like David Copperfield or Pip. He is too uniformly pure and pious. It may seem unpleasant to criticize a literary creation inspired by such a noble ideal; yet Oliver is an almost perfect illustration of André Gide's dictum that bad literature is produced by worthy feelings; the noblest ideal cannot become art without a modicum of truth and life, and this is conspicuously lacking in the portrait of Oliver. Several critics have rightly protested against the purity of both language and feeling which Oliver simply could not have acquired in the workhouse, where religion and morals were not taught, and where the only kind of language spoken was that of Bumble, superbly picturesque and entertaining, but fundamentally ungrammatical and corrupted. Yet the young hero, under the most stupendous circumstances, will more than once preach and pray in impeccable English. "For the love of all the bright angels that rest in Heaven!" he tells the two robbers who are taking him along on their expedition, "have mercy upon me!"; and in Fagin's condemned cell, Oliver is not yet twelve when he holds forth thus: "Let me say a prayer. Do! Let me say one prayer. Say only one, upon your knees, with me, and we will talk till morning." Such an attempt ought perhaps to be touching; but it could hardly be more glaringly unreal; and the Merry Old Gentleman would lose much of his convincing force if he could comply with such an edifying invitation; however, in addition to not being a Christian, he has other views of the least intolerable way of spending one's last few hours on earth.

In the character of Nancy is to be seen another new and interesting effort on Dickens' part. She is not all of a piece, being neither uniformly good like Oliver or Rose, nor uniformly bad like Sikes or Fagin. Dickens was thoroughly convinced of her being true to life, and in fact she has many real traits. The appearance in the midst of the dishonest gang of a child who wishes to keep himself pure awakens in her some feelings of motherly tenderness. Such an evolution can be justified. What is less defensible is the kind of language she uses once she has been redeemed. Admittedly Dickens was hampered by the Grundyism of his time. He could not say outright that Nancy was a prostitute. He had to content himself with referring to "that particular species of humanity to which Nancy belonged"; the word "prostitute" was to appear only three years later, in the 1841 preface. Therefore, when she becomes repentant, she is unable to let the reader know, except in the form of the vaguest allusions, what faults she is repenting. This modesty after the event makes her language sound extremely artificial and unconvincing. Thackeray's comment concerning prostitutes seems appropriate: "as no writer can or dare tell the *whole* truth concerning them, and faithfully explain their vices, there is no need to give *ex parte* statements of their virtue." Dickens' acceptance of the rigid rules of Victorian discretion did make it impossible for him to produce any satisfactory and balanced portraiture in this field.

Rose Maylie's case is different. The history of that character is closely linked with the remembrance Dickens preserved and cherished of his young sister-in-law's death. Her psychological or aesthetic interest is practically nonexistent. Her significance for an understanding of Dickens' art is immense.

It is curious to find how Rose Maylie, meant to embody purity, innocence, beauty, and joy, is constantly associated with the theme of death. Even before the terrible occurrence of May 7, 1837, the theme of youth and death had already inspired the author of **Oliver Twist** with at least one passage whose pathos will nowadays sound very thin and unreal; Dick, the consumptive orphan boy, is speaking: "I heard the doctor tell them I was dying. . . . I know the doctor must be right, Oliver, because I dream so much of Heaven, and Angels, and kind faces I never see when I am awake." After Mary's death, Dickens' allusions to the same theme become more frequent and sound more sincere and moving; in Chapter XII, written immediately after May, 1837, Oliver is speaking of his mother, who had died in childbirth, and says: "If she had seen me hurt, it would have made her sorrowful; and her face has always looked sweet and happy, when I have dreamed of her." At the beginning of Chapter XXIV, there is a description of human faces in death, which opens with the words, "It is a common thing for the countenances of the dead . . . "; in spite of the generalization, this deserves

to be read with some respect, for it is doubtless a description of Mary's countenance, "so calm, so peaceful." When Rose Maylie plays her part, and especially, of course, when she is dangerously ill, there are recognizable allusions in increasing number: "The memories which peaceful country scenes call up, are not of this world"; "I have seen enough . . . to know that it is not always the youngest and best who are spared to those that love them"; "Oh! the suspense, the fearful, acute suspense, of standing idly by while the life of one we dearly love is trembling in the balance!"; "We need be careful with those about us, when every death carries to some small circle of survivors, thoughts of so much omitted, and so little done!"

Still more significant and moving than the preceding allusions are those which Dickens canceled before publication and which remained unreproduced for more than a century. While describing Oliver's return to consciousness at Mr. Brownlow's after his fever, Dickens had first thought of evoking the remembrance of his sister-in-law's recent, fatal illness, and saying that, after a troubled dream, the boy "awoke with an effort so strong and painful that it seemed as if death would have been easier and sweeter than life," but he crossed out this sentence on rereading Chapter XII. And on the occasion of Rose's first appearance, he had intended to use the sadly personal exclamation: "Oh! where are the hearts [that] which, following some halting description of youth and beauty, do not recall a loved original that [Death] Time has sadly changed, or Death resolved to Dust."

Vivid personal emotion cannot produce felicitous artistic results with such a sentimental novelist as Dickens was in those days, and Rose Maylie is not a success. She can touch us only through the evocation of Dickens' sincere grief, not through her own intrinsic merits as a characterization. There is no more to be said of her: she is perfect, and perfectly vague, as must inevitably be the idealized remembrance of some dear departed being. Besides, she is called upon to play in the novel an awkward part. The author needed a pair of lovers; they are supplied by Rose and her pseudo cousin Harry Maylie. In other words, he needed a love story, some obstacle to be surmounted before marriage became possible. The obstacle is but a shadow: it consists of Rose's ill-defined scruples. Thus the love scenes in which the heroine takes part, and in which she ought to display her full charm, like Dora later, and to a lesser extent Agnes also, in **Copperfield,** are slow, solemn, turgid, and grandiloquent. The reader cannot be overjoyed when the happy ending looms in sight, since it has been both too laboriously delayed, and too easily foreseeable. Harry Maylie evinces some clear-sightedness only when he defines the victory he has gained: "to level all fancied barriers between you and me."

The final happiness, rustic, frugal, seraphic, of the whole large family of characters in the novel is of the kind which Dickens himself criticized later, when referring to some edifying pictures: "Have [the authors] considered the awful consequences likely to flow from their representations of virtue? . . . When they were leaning against a post," he says of the characters thus represented, "drunk and reckless, with surpassingly bad hats on . . . they were rather picturesque, and looked as if they might be agree-able men. . . . But, when they had got over their bad pro-pensities, and when, as a consequence . . . their hair had got so curly that it lifted their blown-out cheeks up . . . and their eyes were so wide open that they never could do any sleep, they presented a spectacle calculated to plunge a timid nature into the depths of infamy."

Colored by the author's obsessive grief and somewhat weakened by a multiplicity of social and moral purposes, *Oliver Twist* is not, like *Pickwick,* an essentially comic book. The young hero, Oliver, does not make the reader laugh even once. An examination of the comic elements in this book can be conducted rapidly. There is Jack Dawkins, the "Artful Dodger," a near relation of Sam Weller through his gusto, aplomb, and popular gift of gab. There are a few eccentrics, like Grimwig, ceaselessly offer-ing to eat his own head, and Brittles the footman, who is still being treated as a small boy though he is over thirty. The case of these two is significant in that it illustrates a mistake made by Dickens. Although as a rule he had a re-markably accurate perception of public taste, he would oc-casionally make a serious mistake. The most monumental was to be the creation of *Master Humphrey.* Among the minor errors are a number of eccentrics characterized by a single trait, often very unnatural—such as Grimwig's baroque threat or the confusion as to Brittles' age. Because that trait seemed to him irresistibly droll, Dickens fancied, not only that the reader could not fail to share in his amusement, but also that he would never tire of seeing it reiterated. Thus does Grimwig tirelessly repeat his offer. Thus is Brittles' name constantly followed by the word "boy," until in the final chapter "the last-named boy" is said to be "quite grey."

Yet the most important comic figure is Bumble, who em-bodies the parochial theme of the novel, and thus possess-es a far richer kind of comic force. He thinks only of the parish, lives but for and by the parish, speaks of nothing else. He is a sincere believer in his own supreme impor-tance and dignity. Of the parish, in fact, he embodies every fault: its cruel hardness and spurious amiability, its affec-tation of paternal kindness, and its fundamental indiffer-ence to the sufferings of the poor.

At the beginning of the novel, an attempt is made to ex-ploit the themes of macabre humor, almost always present in Dickens' fiction and embodied here by Mr. Sowerberry, the undertaker, with his coffin-shaped snuff-box, who is "rather given to professional jocosity." It is only natural that, after Mary's death, after his painful contact with the realities of the Sowerberrys' trade, Dickens should have momentarily refrained from deriving comic effects from it.

In *Oliver* once more, as in the *Sketches* and *Pickwick,* there is a considerable display of ironical epithets, with a more aggressive intent than formerly; Mrs. Mann, the su-perintendent of the country branch of the workhouse, is described as Oliver's "benevolent protectress"; Mr. Brownlow is introduced "into the imposing presence of the renowned Mr. Fang"; Dawkins has a smile "on his in-tellectual countenance"; mature, hard-boiled Mrs. Corney is "the bashful beauty," and so on.

In spite of all this, however, the reader can hardly forget the central interest of the book, the cruelty of the parochi-al system and the shadow of the gallows in which the malefactors live. *Oliver Twist* is an admirable rendering of an atmosphere, and the atmosphere is not a mirthful one.

Dickens' earliest preface for *Oliver* was written as late as 1841. As usual, it was devoted to a justification of the work against certain criticisms that had been made on its publi-cation. Against those who reproached him with excessive realism and the choice of low types, he invoked in succes-sion the authority and example of Fielding, Hogarth, Cer-vantes, Defoe, Goldsmith, Smollett, Richardson, and Mackenzie. Thus the preface to *Oliver* is the most literary preface ever written by Dickens. To those who thought the character of Nancy improbable, he replied: "It is useless to discuss whether the conduct and character of the girl seem natural or unnatural, probable or improbable, right or wrong. IT IS TRUE." Among the charges that had been made one was not mentioned by the author. The preface does not refer to the construction of the novel; yet the re-viewer of the *Dublin University Magazine* [December 1838] had written: "It is a jumble of striking scenes . . . carelessly thrown together, and obviously framed with lit-tle regard to mutual dependence or sequence, one upon the other," and the critic of the *Monthly Review* [January 1839]: "It is a mere string of sketches that might be carried to any length, or if cut short at any part, a chapter might wind up the indefinite thread." Such strictures would have been fair enough, if applied to *Pickwick,* and they can only be accounted for by a superficial examination of *Oliver,* under the vague impression that it must resemble its im-mediate predecessor. Dickens could easily have shown that such an impression was unfounded. But . . . he ig-nored all undeserved reproaches and put up a defense only when confronted by justified attacks. His attitude was not ignoble; whenever the work was sufficiently demonstra-tive, he would let it take care of itself; on the other hand, he was thus led to defend only the indefensible. He might have gloried in the characters and in the comedy of *Pick-wick* instead of justifying its plot. He might have drawn attention to the plot of *Oliver* instead of endeavoring to demonstrate the genuineness of its psychology.

In fact, through its comparatively elaborate composition, *Oliver Twist* occupies a unique place in Dickens' work. No other novel, at least in the first period, again achieved comparable precision and solidity of structure. But what makes the original strength of this first novel also makes its weakness, for technical ingenuity and the quest for the sensational are pursued at the expense of naturalness, spontaneity, verve—at the expense, in short, of the kind of pleasure normally expected from a book by Dickens. The composition of *Oliver Twist* is as isolated in the histo-ry of Dickens' technique as Chapter III is in Oliver's story. Just as the boy narrowly escaped being taken into the ser-vice of Gamfield the chimney-sweep, Dickens narrowly escaped joining the sensational school of novelists. This chapter might have been entitled, in a slightly modified form of the heading to Chapter III in the novel itself: "Re-lates how Charles was very near getting a technique, which would not have been a sinecure." Fortunately, in both cases, the danger is avoided, the parenthesis is closed, and the hero's career is more happily launched in the very next chapter. (pp. 132-39)

> *Sylvère Monod, in his* Dickens the Novelist, *University of Oklahoma Press, 1968, 512 p.*

Angus Wilson (essay date 1970)

[*One of the most important English novelists of the post-World War II era, Wilson is also an esteemed critic of English literature who has written extensively on Dickens. In the following excerpt from his* The World of Charles Dickens, *originally published in 1970, he discusses the popular appeal of* Oliver Twist.]

Oliver Twist is surely one of the great popular works of art of all time—rightly seized upon by film, stage and television producers, rightly made the prey of pop composers. It is two novels which Dickens, without the technical powers needed, attempts but fails to join together by a preposterous plot of coincidence and improvised mystery. The first part lies nearer to his journalism; but in its assured, controlled and concise language (even when it is most sentimental) it is journalism of genius. The story of Oliver, the illegitimate orphan, first at the baby-farmer's, then at the workhouse, and finally in the wider world apprenticed to the undertaker, is a story of the routine cruelty exercised upon the nameless, almost faceless submerged of Victorian society by a system, which would be harsh if efficient, and, given the built-in inefficiency of human beings, is deadly. That it was an attack upon the ideas of serious, intelligent, educated and well-intentioned men presented with an intractable social problem, is not relevant to modern readers, nor even that Dickens in his often wrongheaded attack upon them largely saw the truth instead of the statistics which obsessed the legislators. What matters is that it is one of the most successful social satires, which, in great degree, deals not in personalities but in human anonymity, in the 'crowd', in 'society'. To my own taste, the achievement is made at the cost of Dickens's greatest gifts of dialogue and characterization; it is also done by a profuse use of that heavy irony which marks all his novels down to *Dombey and Son.*

It is unlikely however that I should entirely favour this first part, for I am entirely seduced by the second—the strange evil world which encloses the ridiculous melodrama of little Oliver fallen among thieves. This part has many more glaring faults than the first: an army of good, genteel characters, all finally by far-fetched explanations to prove related to the little boy they have befriended, an army which is totally vapid when it is not mawkish or playfully whimsical; a long, irrelevant illness given to the heroine, Rose Maylie, simply as a result of the impact of Mary Hogarth's death upon the author; and even among the glamorous, gamey, stinking set of petty thieves and brutal robbers a key character, the prostitute Nancy, who, to my thinking, has only the shadowiest existence. Fagin, Sikes, Charley Bates, Noah Claypole and above all, the Artful Dodger (Sam Weller gone downhill from his unfurnished lodgings underneath the arches to pit all his Cockney liveliness against Mr Pickwick's decency instead of on its behalf)—these are superb individual characters; but they are also a superb gang, perhaps the first and the best of all the thousands of fictional gangs to follow them, because the gaiety, the high spirits of desperation never conceal for a moment the total brutality and treachery of these men and boys, for whom the Golden Rule is the reverse of the Sermon on the Mount, 'Look after Number One'. But a collection of characters, even a gang, cannot account for the extraordinary effect of the second part of this novel. This comes from the masterly incorporation of the human characters into their physical setting—a gang constantly on the move, slithering, squeaking and scuttling from one unoccupied, rat-ridden old London house to another, like the vermin themselves.

The rodent criminal world, indeed, is unnoticed by the indifferent crowd until the cry of murder goes up. Then a bloodthirsty rat-hunt is immediately on, with all the world ready to lynch Sikes or Fagin; the indifferent, everyday workpeople of society have turned avenging mob. The picture is stylized, an injection of real delight into mythic story, but it has an extraordinary surrealist, nightmare conviction.

These two parts *are* joined; not by the plot, but by the figure of little Oliver, the orphan boy fallen among thieves, who speaks and behaves with absolute gentility. Oliver is a vacuum. But so he has to be. All through his life Dickens hammered home the point that crime was the result of the terrible Poverty and Ignorance in Victorian society. He worked hard on society's compassion in order to diminish the poverty and the ignorance; but with minor exceptions he did not wish to rouse its compassion for the criminals whom he declared to be the result of these evils. He was concerned for justice, and believed, as he says in the preface to this very novel, 'I fear there are in the world some insensible and callous natures, that do become utterly and incurably bad.' And, as we see from his gloomy account of young delinquents in the 'Newgate' piece of *Sketches by Boz,* he saw total corruption taking over at a very early age in the criminal mind.

There is a gulf between the corrupting causes of crime and the absolutely evil nature of most criminals, a gulf that cannot easily be crossed. For this reason it is as well that Oliver, who is intended to act as the bridge, should have no reality, should be merely an image of humanity worked upon by external forces. He rouses in the first part our hatred of a system which is cruel, which exploits poverty and ignorance; he rouses in the second part our fear of those people who fight that system by means of the evil, violence, and brutality within themselves—the criminal gang.

But the good, genteel people in the second part—Oliver's friends—belong, whether Dickens likes it or not, to the anonymous society that exploits the poor and ignorant in the first part—that is perhaps why they are so null and void, these sweet Rose Maylies and jolly old Mr Brownlows, that they are almost anonymous too. Mr Brownlow, the kind old gentleman who befriends Oliver, is only another mask for the gentleman in the white waistcoat on the board of guardians, who in the first part fails to realize that Oliver is human. Inevitably, then, although Dickens by the force of his powers of rhetoric and narrative can rouse us to join the rat hunt against Fagin and Sikes after the murder is known, for the most part we find ourselves, however we shrink from their brutality, treachery and filth, living the second half of the novel *with* the gang, for they alone are alive, they alone share the author's power of laughter, however devilishly. And we cannot but suspect that, somewhere in himself, though Dickens feared them and implacably condemned them, he participates with the villains of the second part (Fagin, Dodger & Co.) in their fight against the villains of the first part (the gentlemen who run society for their own well-being).

The book is in two parts, in fact, because the problem of crime as a social waste cannot be reconciled with crime as a deadly poison. And this surely, apart from the wonderful characterization and atmosphere, is why *Oliver Twist* is a great 'pop' novel, for the public at large (we, that is) by instinct want to feel compassion for the exploited, but does not want to face the difficult problem of exploring the results in detail. It wants to pity Oliver, but he must not be real, for then he might be corrupted and brutalized into Fagin, whom it must loathe. The public wants, also, to join in the hue and cry against the gang when the moment comes to hunt them out; yet in its imagination it wants to share in the gang's violence and glamour (however squalid, perhaps nowadays the more squalid the better) and feverish, doomed fun. (pp. 124-32)

> *Angus Wilson, in his* The World of Charles Dickens, *1970. Reprint by Penguin Books, 1972, 302 p.*

Patrick Brantlinger   (essay date 1977)

[*In the following excerpt from a discussion of "Benthamite" fiction of the nineteenth century, Brantlinger considers* Oliver Twist *in relation to the utilitarian reformist philosophy of Jeremy Bentham.*]

In his treatise on *Popular Government,* the great legal historian Sir Henry Maine writes, "It does not seem to me a fantastic assertion that the ideas of one of the great novelists of the last generation may be traced to Bentham." This is a puzzling judgment, since in *Oliver Twist,* the Christmas stories, and *Hard Times,* Dickens places himself in conscious opposition to Benthamism and political economy. But Dickens's attacks on official institutions and the delays of the law are at least as important and certainly more frequent than his attacks on Benthamism, which are never very logical or thorough.

It has been well-said that Benthamism emphasizes the "getting" of early industrial capitalism more than the "spending." Without questioning other aspects of it on any very fundamental level, Dickens reverses its empahsis by insisting upon spending in all the areas where utilitarian political economy preaches thrift, hard work, and prudence. In terms of money, Dickens calls for the spending involved in charity, generosity, and public good works. In terms of time, he calls for the spending of it in the pursuit of jolly good fun rather than in work, self-improvement, or rigorous Sunday observances. And in terms of the private lives of workers and of "ordinary people" like himself, Dickens calls for a kind of emotional spending—not just the rejection of "cash-nexus" calculation in the name of brotherly love, but also the rejection of the Malthusian calculation that would raise wages by, apparently, inhibiting love and marriage among the working class.

But important as the emphasis on benevolent generosity is in Dickens, Sir Henry Maine is still able to find much to connect him with Benthamism: "Dickens, who spent his early manhood among the politicans of 1832 trained in Bentham's school, hardly ever wrote a novel without attacking an abuse. The procedure of the Court of Chancery and of the Ecclesiastical Courts, the delays of the Public Offices, the costliness of divorce, the state of the dwellings of the poor, and the condition of the cheap schools in the North of England, furnished him with what he seemed to consider, in all sincerity, the true moral of a series of fictions." Of course what Dickens learned as a parliamentary reporter did not make him a Benthamite in any strict sense of that term. Whatever new attitudes he acquired by listening to reform-minded radicals in Parliament (like Daniel O'Connell, whose speech on the disturbances in Ireland in 1832 reduced him to tears) were fueled by the deep distrust of existing institutions which he had learned in the Marshalsea and the blacking warehouse. It was a distrust that he could apply to new Benthamite institutions just as easily as he could to ones that, like Chancery, were a snarled heritage from "the Good Old Days." And this is what happens in *Oliver Twist:* it is a reformist novel attacking an abuse, only the abuse happens to have originated in a Benthamite reform.

In several ways *Oliver Twist* is a fuller expression of the broadly Benthamite, reformist culture of the 1830s than either *Paul Clifford* or *Illustrations of Political Economy.* For one thing, Bulwer and Mattineau were not "Philosophic Radicals" in any strict sense either. Bulwer shed his rather shallow Benthamism after *Paul Clifford* and adopted a Tory-radicalism close to Disraeli's. His historical and occultist novels of the 1840s, like *Zanoni* and *The Last of the Barons,* he conceived as reactions against the democratic goals of the French Revolution and Chartism. And R. K. Webb says that Martineau was never an orthodox Benthamite, partly because she was too "doctrinaire, utopian, and woolly" to be a reformer by the patient application of the "Felicific Calculus." In any case, in *Paul Clifford,* Bulwer tries to adapt an old literary form— eighteenth-century moral satire—to the new issues of social reform in the 1830s, and runs into contradictions. And Martineau's "improving" tales, which share more traits with religious tracts than with Dickens's novels, are meant to serve the cause of self-reform or self-help more clearly than the reform of laws and institutions. With *Oliver Twist,* Dickens achieves a synthesis of appropriate form with new content that gives full and energetic expression to a middle-class, radical, reformist viewpoint—one that Bulwer and Martineau reflect only imperfectly or in fragments.

Plenty of novels in the 1830s and 1840s attacked abuses, but many of these could not be called Benthamite by any stretch of logic. Factory reform novels like Mrs. Tonna's *Helen Fleetwood* and Mrs. Trollope's *Michael Armstrong* (an imitation of *Oliver Twist*) express a Tory and Christian reaction against utilitarianism, political economy, and, indeed, against liberalism and industrialism in general. Despite much urging, Dickens did not chime in with the Ten Hours Movement that Mrs. Trollope was writing to support. And he would never have agreed with Mrs. Tonna that the factory system was the work of the devil; he was much more inclined to believe that her brand of religion was the work of the devil, as per the Rev. Mr. Stiggins and the Murdstones. But Sir Henry Maine emphasizes that Dickens "in all sincerity" found "the true moral" of his novels in the reform of particular social evils and that he was therefore doing something original in fiction. Dickens's lessons are to be applied not just to changing individuals in the manner of Scrooge but to effecting improvements in the structure of society as well. This is true also of Bulwer in *Paul Clifford,* but more superficially. Bulwer's treatment of the theme of environmental causation does not clearly shift the burden of moral agency away from individuals, as he says it does. But Dickens is able to dramatize the ruinous effects of bad environment—and, therefore, the responsibility of society for crime—in the boldest, most terrifying fashion. *Oliver Twist* is melodrama, true—but one that rises to the level of a powerful social nightmare by asking us to look on as the workhouse and the demonic world of the thieves crush their innocent victim. Oliver's escape does not offset either the terror or the reality of the dangers that assail him. And even the fact that he is not transformed into a thief like Paul Clifford is no contradiction. Dickens understands the nightmares and the longings of childhood and could never have written, as Bulwer does in skipping over the life of his hero until he is twelve, that "there is little to interest in a narrative of early childhood, unless, indeed, one were writing on education." Such an assertion prompts one to wonder what Bulwer thinks he is writing about, if not education?

Oliver is the archetypal hero of melodrama and also of countless folktales and fairy tales, the sacrificial lamb snatched just at the right moment from the jaws of hell. To make him develop—to make him grow or regress either one—would rather spoil the effect than aid it. In fact, it is his very unchanging helplessness that makes him appear to be the pawn of environment. To show him growing more like the thieves would both diminish our sympathy for him and, paradoxically, give us a sense of his independence. The Artful Dodger does not represent the final stage of "the parish boy's progress" that threatens Oliver, because the Dodger knows how to help himself. If he is a product of his environment, he is also a highly independent, impudent entrepreneur, albeit on the small scale of watch chains and pocket handkerchiefs. It is not adaptation to environment that Dickens wants to show, but a failure to adapt, and the annihilation of a life which that failure threatens.

Oliver is a symbolic version of the Lockean tabula rasa. He is the white paper of innocence upon which anything may be written by "circumstances" or environment: "In short, the wily old Jew had the boy in his toils. Having prepared his mind, by solitude and gloom, to prefer any society to the companionship of his own sad thoughts in such a dreary place, he was now slowly instilling into his soul the poison which he hoped would blacken it, and change its hue for ever." Again, it is true that Fagin does not poison Oliver's soul, but the danger is meant to be and felt to be real. As Dickens said of his own childhood experience in the blacking warehouse and on the streets of London, "I know that, but for the mercy of God, I might easily have been, for any care that was taken for me, a little robber or a little vagabond." How did Dickens escape that fate? Apparently, in much the same nearly miraculous way that Oliver escapes: so he must have felt after his father quarreled by letter with James Lamert, and he was sent home "with a relief so strange that it was like oppression." At any rate, Oliver's innocence is not of a positive, assertive kind—he is not the saintly prig he is sometimes made out to be—but of a negative, passive kind. Dickens wants us to believe in his malleability at the same time that he wants to preserve him unscathed for the world of Mr. Brownlow and Rose Maylie, and into that world of middle-class sweetness and light Oliver eventually ascends, as by a miracle. But because we also know that miracles are infrequent, we remain aware that others—Nancy, Charlie Bates, the Dodger, and even Fagin and Sikes—are not so fortunate. Although it is easier to think of children and women as the victims of circumstance, towards the end of the novel, after Oliver is safe, Fagin and Sikes become caught up in powerful undercurrents of sympathy. As Arnold Kettle puts it, "Sikes is gathered into the world that has begotten him and the image of that world makes us understand him and even pity him, not with an easy sentimentality, but through a sense of all the hideous forces that have made him what he is."

The novel that commences with the helpless orphan trapped in the workhouse ends with the helpless villain trapped in the condemned call. Workhouse and prison frame the story, with Saffron Hill in between. It is as fitting a symbolic expression as one can find in the 1830s of the Benthamite theory that institutions determine conduct, and that to change conduct one must first change the institutions. That theory is one of the reasons why the problem of crime and punishment is as central to Bentham's thinking as it is to Dickens's. Both make penology their constant study. At the same time, at least one major difference separates them. For Dickens, prison is the symbol for all that is wrong with society, and utopia for him would be a place without prisons because without the injustices that breed crime. But Bentham is that contradictory monster, a utopian penologist. He spent much time and (rational) zeal in designing his ideal prison, the Panopticon. And his emphasis on crime and punishment comes about in designing the future, or the ideal constitutional and legal code, rather than in worrying about crime and injustice in actual society. Crime occupies such a large portion of Bentham's thinking because it is almost the only thing that legislators and judges will have to deal with in the ideal state. Bentham's ideal governors will have very little to do except to design appropriate punishments to curtail the various mischiefs that men will, in their blindness to general utility, continue to perpetrate:

> It remains to be considered, what the exciting causes are with which the legislator has to do. These may . . . be any whatsoever: but those

Dickens's home at 48 Doughty Street, where he wrote Oliver Twist.

which he has principally to do [with] are those of the painful or afflictive kind. With pleasurable ones he has little to do, except now and then by accident . . . The exciting causes with which he has principally to do, are, on the one hand, the mischievous acts, which it is his business to prevent; on the other hand, the punishments, by the terror of which it is his endeavour to prevent them.

Bentham, in short, emphasizes crime because he is an incurable optimist. Everything else in a rational society— everything "pleasurable"—can take care of itself without the interference of government. But Dickens emphasizes crime because his vision is rooted in actual society and in its great distance from the ideals of justice and equality. Although a believer in industrial and democratic progress, he is no utopian. In his depictions of social evils is always a sad sense of their great stubbornness, their resistance to change, which makes his prisons loom all the darker and colder in the midst of his fictions. Although he took a keen interest in prison reform and design, he could not be called a utopian penologist in any sense.

Dickens's attack upon the New Poor Law workhouse comes at the start of the novel and seems logically disconnected from the rest of what happens, despite the rather awkward transitions back to Mr. Bumble's love life. But the underlying feeling is that everything terrible that happens—the entire demonic world of the London slums— flows directly out of the workhouse. It is the primum mobile of Oliver's life, at once his birthplace and the adumbration of his death. After Oliver's daring raid on the kettle of gruel, one of the Poor Law guardians prophesies with an ironic truth that he will be hanged. The workhouse keeps the hangman busy, and a direct route leads from it to prison even for such an innocent child as Oliver. Between the supposedly benevolent institution and the penal one there is little to choose. And they do not merely frame the story. In an important way they form, along with the London slums, the main elements of the environment that is always closing in on Oliver, always threatening to destroy him, claustrophobically cutting off the air and the light of middle-class freedom and virtue, like one of Mr. Sowerberry's coffins or like the dark coal bin in which Oliver is shut after his combat with Noah Claypole. As in his later novels, Dickens is concerned to show the symbiotic relationship between the world of official institutions and the world of poverty and crime: workhouse and prison help to cause the conditions which they are meant to correct.

But in a sense the workhouse seems merely tacked on, not an integral part of what happens in the rest of the story. As with Yorkshire schools in *Nicholas Nickleby,* or with Chancery in *Bleak House,* or with divorce law or industrial pollution in *Hard Times,* the workhouse in *Oliver Twist* seems to be a merely local evil, a wen on the body politic that can be easily cut away, at the same time that it is a center from which enormous and nearly all-engulfing evil spreads. So Benthamite optimism seems to clash with a deeper pessimism. The reformer must always feel the urge to make a specific evil seem important, dangerous, universally threatening, and he must always feel the contrary urge as well—to make it seem inorganic, unnecessary, and correctible by obvious, practical measures. Dickens portrays whatever abuse he takes in hand as larger than life, give it universal and almost (as with Fagin's diabolism) supernatural properties, so that it becomes a symbol of all of the abuses and injustices in the world. And on the other hand, he circumscribes the abuse, makes it appear to be the work of a few selfish individuals, or suggests that it is a minor and temporary ailment that can be cured by some Morrison's Pill or other. (Dickens never shared Carlyle's rejection of politics but rather was a strenuous advocate of Morrison's Pills of all sorts, especially in *Household Words* and *All the Year Round.* What he did share with Carlyle was a healthy distrust in the ability of "the National Dustheap" of Parliament and of other official institutions to effect needed reforms.) In one direction, Dickens is led almost to the denial of the possibility of social progress; in the other, he is led to the rosy belief that the evils which he depicts are minor and temporary and can be corrected by a little good will applied in the right ways, either through private charity or through benevolent legislation.

This dialectic of reform, corresponding to class structure, is the main source of the polarized quality of Oliver's experience. Just as social evil in the form of Fagin and Sikes is about to extinguish all hope of freedom, Oliver is whisked off to the middle-class world of Mr. Brownlow and the Maylies. Terror and certain destruction are canceled by easy rescues and by the untangling of the history of Monks and Oliver or of the conventional inheritance plot, which seems like such an unnecessary excrescence on an otherwise powerful story. Moreover, as the world of the thieves is likened to hell, so the world of Mr. Brownlow is likened to heaven—it is the apotheosis of middle-class comfort and benevolence: "They were happy days, those of Oliver's recovery. Everything was so quiet, and neat, and orderly; everybody was kind and gentle; that after the noise and turbulence in the midst of which he had always lived, it seemed like Heaven itself." In the middle-class world, everything is easy and orderly; in the slums, everything is difficult, terrifying, turbulent. These values are implicit in the idea of reform itself: against terrific social evils are ranged the means to correct them, easy, obvious, and readily available to benevolent members of the middle class. Fundamental changes in economic or even political structure are unnecessary, if only the middle class would get about the business of reform. These attitudes are underlying assumptions throughout Dickens's early fiction, and in the literature of reform in general.

But despite the falseness of the plot that converts a pauper boy into a respectable young bourgeois, there is no falseness about what Brownlow means to Dickens. Benevolent middle-class individualism is quite simply the only solution that Dickens sees to the social problems that he raises. It is the one institution—if it can be called that—which is incorruptible. Certainly no solution is going to come from the world of official institutions in the novel—the courts, the lawyers, and perhaps even Blathers and Duff are, like workhouse and prison, sources of evil or at least of incompetent bungling rather than of social improvement—and that leaves only Mr. Brownlow, Mr. Losberne, and their like to rescue the Olivers of the world through their private initiatives. Brownlow's importance in the novel, then, comes as much from Dickens's having nowhere else to turn to for social improvement as from his desire to celebrate the bourgeois virtues à la Podsnap. All the same, as Brownlow sets about single-handedly to undo Monks and Fagin and magically to transform Oliver's future from workhouse and prison to middle-class freedom, Dickens expresses his faith in the ability of middle-class individualism to banish evil and darkness from the world and to remodel it in its own image. The characterization of Brownlow is related to the novel's narrative structure: he is the type of Dickens's ideal reader—a member of the honest, hard-working middle class in whom alone in the 1830s history seemed to have invested the power of social redemption.

The sharp antithesis that the novel effects between what Brownlow represents and what Fagin represents is not entirely reducible either to the categories of class difference or to the categories of good and evil. The novel from beginning to end is about the glaring contrast between rich and poor, but Fagin does not stand for the deserving poor and Brownlow does not stand for the oppressing rich. On the contrary, Oliver is the chief representative of the deserving poor, and the Poor Law guardians are perhaps the

clearest representatives of the oppressing rich. And although the bourgeois world of Brownlow is heaven to Fagin's underworld, a direct translation of these metaphors into moral terms is not possible either, because of the feeling that Fagin himself is not a free agent but a dehumanized creature of the slum world he inhabits: "As he glided stealthily along, creeping beneath the shelter of the walls and doorways, the hideous old man seemed like some loathsome reptile, engendered in the slime and darkness through which he moved: crawling forth, by night, in search of some rich offal for a meal." While Fagin is never openly an object of pity, and Oliver's forgiveness of him at the end of the novel therefore rings false, he is what he would make Oliver, a creature "of slime and darkness." The price of a life of crime is imprisonment and the gallows; but more than these, it is the loss of freedom and of the possibility of fulfillment outside of prison as well. Dickens divides experience into two irreconcilable categories, not based directly upon good and evil but upon freedom (identified with middle-class benevolence and respectability) and upon grinding necessity and death (identified with the lives of the poor, the outcast, and the "criminal refuse" of London).

The contradictory results of the antithesis between freedom and necessity can be seen perhaps most clearly in Nancy. Fagin and Sikes have made a complete forfeit of their humanity and, hence, of their free will. But Nancy, like Oliver, is somehow resistant to the corrosive effects of environment. "The girl's life had been squandered in the streets, and among the most noisome of the stews and dens of London, but there was something of the woman's original nature left in her still." Despite being "the fallen outcast of low haunts," says Dickens, Nancy still retains "a feeble gleam of the womanly feeling . . . which alone connected her with that humanity, of which her wasting life had obliterated so many, many traces when a very child." Nancy, however, disagrees with this favorable assessment of herself, and, when Mr. Losberne tries to persuade her to reject her old life in favor of a life of middle-class freedom and virtue, she says she is "past all hope."

> "You put yourself beyond its pale," said the gentleman. "The past has been a dreary waste with you, of youthful energies mis-spent, and such priceless treasures lavished, as the Creator bestows but once and never grants again, but, for the future, you may hope. I do not say that it is in our power to offer you peace of heart and mind, for that must come as you seek it; but a quiet asylum, either in England, or, if you fear to remain here, in some foreign country, it is not only within the compass of our ability but our most anxious wish to secure you . . . Come! I would not have you go back to exchange one word with any old companion, or take one look at any old haunt, or breathe the very air which is pestilence and death to you. Quit them all, while there is time and opportunity!"

One hears in Mr. Losberne's language the echo of countless scenes of "social reclamation" that took place during the nineteenth century (Gladstone's nocturnal perambulations come immediately to mind). There is enough false sentiment in Dickens's characterization of Nancy and of "fallen women" in other novels to swamp the works of lesser writers. But to his credit, Nancy is not "reclaimed." Although as a creature of environment she should not be capable of exercising free choice, she chooses—apparently freely—to stick with Bill and the "wasting life" she has always known. At the same time, the inconsistent characterization of Nancy reveals a greater inconsistency: Dickens's treatment of the effect of environment on character is operative only part of the time, through one half of the social experience that he depicts, and the division follows class lines. The poor, it seems, are always in danger of ceasing to be human—but by becoming victims of their environment. The point at which they become morally culpable is also the point at which they cease to be morally culpable.

The division between freedom and necessity that marks Oliver's experience is basic to the middle-class consciousness that created the literature of reform. It is as much a feature of utilitarian radicalism as of Dickens's "sentimental radicalism" and is implicit in Bentham's "doctrine of circumstances." For example, both Mr. Losberne's language to Nancy and James Mill's essay on "Education" (1818) are governed by the same antithesis. Mill writes:

> It is now almost universally acknowledged that on all conceivable accounts it is desirable that the great body of the people should not be wretchedly poor; that when the people are wretchedly poor, all classes are vicious, all are hateful, and all are unhappy. If so far raised above wretched poverty as to be capable of being virtuous, though it is still necessary for them to earn their bread by the sweat of their brow, they are not bound down to such incessant toil as to have no time for the acquisition of knowledge and the exercise of intellect.

Vice and poverty are linked, although poverty makes vice involuntary. There is a kind of double robbery of "the poor" in Mill's language, well-intended though it is, that makes them incapable of being virtuous and also incapable of free moral choice. At the same time, the path upward to freedom from the bondage of environment, or of necessity and vice, lies through an education that would give to "the poor" the middle-class virtues of industry and self-reliance, but without making them middle class. It is obviously not an argument for equality. Godwin and Paine remained far in advance of Bentham and James Mill on the issue of economic equality, and middle-class political theory in the Victorian years did not recapture their ground until the 1870s and 1880s. (pp. 43-52)

> *Patrick Brantlinger, "Benthamite and Anti-Benthamite Fiction," in his* The Spirit of Reform: British Literature and Politics, 1832-1867, *Cambridge, Mass.: Harvard University Press, 1977, pp. 35-59.*

Irving Howe   (essay date 1981)

[*A longtime editor of the magazine* Dissent *and a regular contributor to* The New Republic, *Howe is one of America's most highly respected literary critics and social historians. In the following essay, he offers a favor-* *able assessment of* Oliver Twist, *focusing on Dickens's characterizations of Oliver and Fagin and addressing allegations of anti-Semitism in the novel.*]

With the opening chapters of **Oliver Twist** Dickens made his way, forever, into world literature. His place in the English tradition was already secure: he had written **The Pickwick Papers,** a work of spectacular comic gifts, marred, it's true, by sentimentalism but lovely as an idyll of gentlemanly-Christian innocence. **The Pickwick Papers** seems utterly English, a fiction attuned to the idiosyncrasies of its own culture. **Oliver Twist,** however, can attract and hold almost every kind of imagination, since its main figures—the defenseless waif, the devilish fence, the unctuous beadle—speak a language of gesture and symbol that quite transcends national cultures. Drawn with those expressionist stabs of language that would become one of Dickens's major resources, **Oliver Twist** anticipates such later, greater novels as **Bleak House** and **Little Dorrit.** True, it lacks the compositional richness and maturity of feeling we find in Dickens's culminating work; but in its opening chapters, where Oliver is coldly brutalized by agents of English society, and in the sequence where Oliver is kidnapped and taken by Bill Sikes on a housebreaking expedition, we can recognize the Dickens who belongs in the company of Gogol, Balzac, and Dostoevsky.

It has been customary in recent decades to speak of at least two Dickenses, the first an exuberant performer of comedy and the second a mordant social critic increasingly expert in the uses of symbolic grotesquerie. Modern literary criticism has understandably focused on the second, the dark and serious Dickens, but it's only in analysis that the two Dickenses can be separated. In the strongest novels, entertainer and moralist come to seem shadows of one another—finally two voices out of the same mouth.

The entertainer takes over now and again in **Oliver Twist.** He is splendidly busy in the chapter where Bumble courts Mrs. Corney, with one hand round her waist and both eyes on her silver, while expressing—definitively, for all the ages—"the great principle of out-of-door relief," which is "to give the paupers exactly what they don't want, and then they get tired of coming." Entertainer and moralist are not always at ease with one another; they tend at some points to go about their business separately; and that's one reason we find it unprofitable to keep **Oliver Twist** neatly placed in a categorical bin—is the book a crime story, a fairy tale, a novel of education, a social melodrama? The only sensible answer is that it is all of these together, mixed up with Dickens's usual disregard for the boundaries of genre.

For all our pleasure in its comic play, **Oliver Twist** finally grips us as a story of moral rage. The opening chapters may seem a little too declamatory, even strident—some of Dickens's furious interjections might well have been cut. But remember, this is a young man's book, full of anger and mistakes; and one's deepest response to the "overture" of the first few chapters isn't critical at all, it is a blend of astonishment and admiration. Oliver begging, "I want more"; the horrible chimney-sweep Gamfield explaining that "boys is very obstinit, and very lazy, and there's nothingk like a good hot blaze to make 'em come down [from chimneys] with a run"; Bumble growing warm over the ingratitude of the poor ("It's meat," he opines, that has made Oliver so refractory); Dickens sputtering on his own that he wishes he could see "the Philosopher" (read, Economist) "making the same sort of meal himself, with the same relish" that Oliver has just made—such bits of incident must survive in collective memory as long as the world knows the bitter taste of the insolence of office.

Some decades ago critics were inclined to "place" *Oliver Twist* historically, which often meant to take the sting out of the book. They explained that Dickens had as one of his targets the English Poor Law of 1834, which he regarded as inhumane; that paupers had indeed been treated brutally in England, though not quite so brutally as Dickens imagined; and that the passage of time has improved the conditions of the poor, so that it would be an error to take literally Dickens's version of the poorhouse. Now, all this is true enough, yet by one of those turns of history that make a joke out of all historical schemas, the social outlook Dickens was attacking has again come to seem familiar. No one talks about "welfare chiselers" in *Oliver Twist,* perhaps because Bumble and Mrs. Corney were born a little too soon; but that apart, we have no difficulty in aligning Dickens's caricature with our own familiar reality.

In these opening chapters, then, the twenty-five-year-old Dickens found his voice and his subject. Through the year 1837 *Oliver Twist* appeared serially in a London magazine, overlapping with *The Pickwick Papers:* it would be hard to imagine a more remarkable literary debut. Many writers take years to find their true voice and inescapable subject; some never do. Perhaps it would be better to say that Dickens's subject found him, laying rough hands on his throat, never to let go. The remembered humiliations of childhood, when his father had been taken to debtors' prison and he had been sent to labor in a blacking factory, seethed in his imagination from the start of his career to the finish. Whether it is really true, as Graham Greene once said, that all writers form their picture of the world in the years of childhood, I do not know; but it certainly was true for Dickens.

Later on he would often misuse his gifts; sometimes as the result of sheer exuberance, sometimes through a retreat from the fearful conclusions to which his imagination kept driving him—for how could the most popular novelist of Victorian England acknowledge to himself that his strongest books formed a scathing condemnation of early industrial capitalism? Often there is a deep split between what Dickens the writer shows and what his mind imposes on his books in their concluding pages. But finally, his imagination could never really be tamed, it could only be diverted—and even then it would break out again in spontaneous fury. Dickens had a passion for seeing things as they are.

A little boy creeps through this book, an orphan, a waif, an outcast. He is a puling, teary little fellow, never rebellious for more than a few minutes, and seldom even angry. He is a perfect little gentleman who has managed somehow to come into the world, and the novel, with a finished

code of morality. The wickedness of the world never stains him. Through all his wanderings in "foul and frowzy dens, where vice is closely packed"—as Dickens puts it in his preface to the novel's third edition—Oliver maintains a sublime loyalty to English grammar. Starved, beaten, terrorized, kidnapped, he is nevertheless unwilling to resort to the foul language or gutter slang it may be reasonable to suppose he has heard in the slums of London.

To some readers this represents a strain on their credulity, and so indeed it would be if Oliver were conceived by Dickens as an ordinary realistic figure, just another boy thrust into "the cold, wet, shelterless midnight streets of London." But it would be a mistake to see Oliver in that way. Dickens himself tells us, again in the preface to the third edition, that "I wished to show, in little Oliver, the *principle* of Good surviving through every adverse circumstance and triumphing at last." I stress the word "principle" in order to suggest that more is at stake here than the life of an individual character.

For Oliver is one in a series of recurrent figures in the Dickens world, slightly anticipated in *Pickwick* but more fully realized in *Little Dorrit.* Oliver is emblematic of "the principle of Good" sent into the world on a journey of suffering. This journey, which has some points of similarity to that of Christian's in Bunyan's *Pilgrim's Progress,* Oliver undertakes with no armor other than a blessed helplessness. Oliver is not expected to overcome the evil of the world, nor to struggle vigorously against it, nor even to learn much from his suffering. He is not a figure of strong imposing will—on the contrary, he is usually ready to accept whatever burdens the world imposes on him. He acts only to refuse evil, never to combat it. Yet, as if by some miracle of grace, this journeyer emerges from his experience morally immaculate, quite like the hero of a Western movie who after gunfights and killings doesn't even need to straighten his hat. Everywhere about Oliver evil thrives, but at the end he is as pure as at the start.

This celebration of the passive hero is sometimes related to primitive Christianity, though perhaps what we really mean is that it forms an historical residue of Christianity, clung to by those who can no longer believe God is omnipotent or even attentive, and who must consequently make of passivity a substitute for active moral engagement. The modern sensibility finds this view of things very hard to accept, even though it is a view that keeps recurring, as a benefit of desperation, in modern literature.

Yet in his very powerlessness Oliver reveals an enormous power: the world cannot destroy him. It is as if he had received, from whom we can hardly say, the blessing that mother Rebecca schemed so hard to get for her son Jacob. Clearly, no one in this world has blessed Oliver, his blessing must have come from another world; and if so, all it can do for him, through the main stretch of the book, is to protect without rescuing him. It's as if God had given Oliver all that He can—which in the world of Dickens's London is not enough.

Such feelings about "the principle of Good" are by no means unique to Dickens: they are to be found among many sincere Christians. Dostoevsky called Dickens "that great Christian" and saw in Pickwick "a positively good man," perhaps a faint emblem of Christ. The creator of Myshkin would have understood why Dickens located "the principle of Good" in a completely helpless little boy.

To gather Dickens's intentions regarding Oliver is not, however, to find his treatment entirely satisfying. Most readers learn to brush past Oliver, seeing him as a (slightly inconvenient) convenience of the plot. We care about what happens to him, but hardly suppose anything much is happening within him. Still, it's worth asking why Dickens's effort to realize "the principle of Good"—always very difficult for a novelist—seems shaky in *Oliver Twist* and relatively successful in *Little Dorrit.* A plausible answer might be that Oliver, no matter how extreme his suffering, never gets past the conventions of middle-class behavior. One of his few signs of spontaneous life is the burst of laughter with which he watches Fagin and the boys pantomime the picking of a gentleman's pocket; but whenever Oliver is with Mr. Brownlow, Rose Maylie, and the other paragons of middle-class virtue, he serves mostly as their parrot. Such a goody goody doesn't make a persuasive agent of "the principle of Good," if only because he seems so inert before the temptations of the Bad. Little Dorrit, by contrast, cares nothing about status or respectability; she neither accepts nor rejects the standards of the world; she is beyond their reach, a selfless creature forever assuaging, healing, and loving those near her. It took Dickens the better part of a lifetime to discover what "the principle of Good" really is.

Fleeing poorhouse and apprenticeship, Oliver makes his way to the big city: there is no place else to go. His entry into London, stylishly eased by the Artful Dodger, forms a critical moment in the history of nineteenth-century literature—one of the first encounters with the modern city as physical presence, emblem of excitement, social specter, locus of myth. The early Dickens is still vibrantly responsive to whatever seems fresh in the world, he takes an eager pleasure in the discovery of streets. For him the city is a place of virtuosity, where men can perform with freedom and abandonment: London as the glass enlarging upon the antics of Sam Weller, Sairey Gamp, and a bit later, Micawber. But London—this note is first struck in *Oliver Twist*—is also pesthole and madhouse, a place of terror from which the child-hero must be rescued periodically through a convalescence in the countryside.

Now it is the mixture of these contradictory feelings about the city that helps give the novel its distinctive tone of diffuse anxiety. The contradictory feelings about the city interweave, clash, and run along uneasy parallels, and from the tension they generate Dickens makes his drama. The darkening vision that will overwhelm Dickens's later novels is already present, shadowlike, in *Oliver Twist*—that vision which will prompt him to write in *Our Mutual Friend* that London is "a hopeless city, with no rent in the leaden canopy of its sky. . . ." Yet in *Oliver Twist* London is also the home of spectacle, lurid and grotesque, and one of Dickens's narrative purposes—slyly helped along by the sequence that starts with the Artful Dodger discovering the hungry Oliver and ends when the boy is brought to Fagin's den—is to involve us in Oliver's excitements of

discovery. But more than involve: it is a saving characteristic of this novel that we are never limited to Oliver's milky perceptions.

Fagin's den, one of those spittled gray-and-black hovels in which he hides out, is reached by a labyrinth of stairs, eerie and dark. "The walls and ceilings . . . were perfectly black with age and dirt," but, it's important to note, there is a fire in the den before which "a very old shrivelled Jew, whose villainous-looking and repulsive face was obscured by a quantity of matted red hair," stands roasting some meat. Here Dickens's ambivalence about the city—which finally is to say, about English society—reaches a high point: this London hovel is hell yet also a wretched sort of home, these are thieves and murderers yet also lively figures who have made for themselves a perverse sort of community.

The point is well elaborated by J. Hillis Miller: "Fagin's den is both a dungeon and a place of refuge. It is . . . absolutely shut off from the outside world, but it is also a parody, at least, of a home, that place where one lives safely . . . Fagin's den [says Dickens] is a 'snug retreat,' and inside its walls we find a society leagued for common protection against the hostility of the outside world."

Those of us who have but little taste for a romantic glorification of criminality will resist the temptation to see Dickens as totally caught up with the world of Fagin and Sikes—though the accounts we have of Dickens's public readings from *Oliver Twist,* in which he impersonated its characters with a terrifying vividness, suggest that part of him must have felt a subterranean kinship with these outlaws. (Less, I think, with their criminal deeds than with their experience as outsiders.) We are surely meant by Dickens to deplore the thieves and murderers, to feel disgust and fright before them. Yet their enormous vitality and articulateness of feeling put them in the sharpest contrast to the blandness of the "good" characters. Fagin and his gang talk like recognizable human beings, Mr. Brownlow and the Maylies, as if they had stepped out of a copybook. And when the Artful Dodger, in one of Dickens's most brilliant set-pieces, is dragged into court, he sounds like a comic echo of Julien Sorel at the end of *The Red and the Black.* "Gentlemen, I have not the honor to belong to your class," Julien tells his jurors. "This ain't the shop for justice," the Artful Dodger tells his judges.

The living core of the novel is neither the story of Oliver nor the depiction of his protectors; it is primarily those segments of narrative devoted to Fagin and his gang. Just as Dostoevsky often yielded himself to the sinners he was determined finally to make suffer, so Dickens yielded himself to the criminals he knew had to be brought to a relentless punishment. We are talking here not about conscious intent but about those energies of the unconscious which, in every true writer, shape his values.

Fagin is the strongest figure in the book—certainly the most troubling. He is more figure than character, and more force than figure. He barely exists as an individual—barely needs to. We learn nothing about his interior life, we are not invited to see him as "three dimensional," except, minimally, in the glittering chapter toward the end, where he sits in prison waiting to be hanged and suffers that terror of death which finally makes him one of us. Nor is Fagin given the sort of great redeeming speech that Shakespeare gives Shylock. Fagin does cry out before his death, "What right have they to butcher me?" but this has little of the generalizing moral resonance of Shylock's "Hath not a Jew eyes?" Clever and cunning, with a talent for mimicking the moral axioms of the respectable world, Fagin is all of a piece, monolithic, a creature of myth. He never rises to Shylock's tragic height, he never so much as becomes a character at all. Fagin is an emanation of historical myth, generic, emblematic, immensely powerful. Having so created him—or better yet, having so dredged him up out of the folk imagination—Dickens had no need to worry about nuances of depiction.

And Fagin, we cannot forget, is "the Jew." Throughout the novel he is called "the Jew," though in revising for a later edition, especially in the chapter devoted to Fagin's last night, Dickens tried to soften the impact by substituting "Fagin" for "the Jew." It did not help or matter very much: Fagin remains "the Jew" and whoever wants to confront this novel honestly must confront the substratum of feeling that becomes visible through Dickens's obsessive repetition of "the Jew." The film adaptation made several decades ago in England did precisely that. Alec Guinness impersonated Fagin with brilliant, indeed, frightening effect, putting heavy stress on the idea of an archetypal Jewish villain, as well as a secondary stress on the homosexual component of Fagin's gang that Dickens could only hint at.

Most critics have been skittish about Fagin. They have either ignored Dickens's fixed epithet, "the Jew," as if there were nothing problematic or disconcerting about it, or they have tried to blunt the meaning of Dickens's usage by "explaining" Fagin historically. There is, of course, something to explain. Dickens himself, in a letter to a Jewish woman who had protested the stereotypical treatment of Fagin, sought to reduce the problem to one of contemporary verisimilitude. "Fagin," he wrote, "is a Jew because it unfortunately was true, of the time to which the story refers, that that class of criminal almost invariably was a Jew." Whether this was "almost invariably" so is a question, but that some fences were Jewish is certainly true. One of these, Ikey Solomons, had been tried and sentenced in a spectacular trial only a few years before Dickens wrote *Oliver Twist,* and it seems likely that Dickens, with his keen reportorial scent, drew upon this case.

I am convinced that, despite some conventionally nasty phrases about Jews in his letters, Dickens was not an anti-Semite—he had neither conscious nor programmatic intent to harm Jews. Indeed, a writer with such intent could probably not have created so "primitive" and therefore haunting a figure as Fagin. For, if the fascination with criminal life that's evident in *Oliver Twist* derives in some twisted way from Dickens's childhood traumas, the representative or mythic strength of Fagin comes, I believe, from somewhere else: it comes from the collective folklore, the sentiments and biases habitual to Western culture, as these have fixed the Jew in the role of villain: thief, fence, corrupter of the young, surrogate of Satan, legatee

of Judas. With Fagin, as Edgar Rosenberg says, "we are . . . thrown back to that anonymous crowd of grinning devils who, in the religious drama of the 14th century, danced foully around the Cross and who, in mythology, functioned as bugaboos to frighten little boys . . . [Dickens] has come up with some prehistoric fiend, an aging Lucifer whose depravity explains him wholly."

The spectral image of "the Jew" may indeed be "prehistoric" in the sense that it abides in the timeless space of myth, but it is also very much part of a continuous Western history. The image of the fiendish Jew has survived with remarkable persistence through the Christian centuries. Like Judas, Fagin has red hair, and like Satan, he is compared to a serpent. "As Fagin glided stealthily along, creeping beneath the shelter of the walls and doorways, the hideous old man seemed like some loathsome reptile, engendered in the slime and darkness through which he moved: crawling forth, by night, in search of some rich offal for a meal." Whenever we encounter such overripe language, Fagin expands into a figure other than human: he becomes a monster drawn from the bad dreams of Christianity.

Novels are composed by individual writers, but in some sense they also derive from the cultures in which these writers live. Collective sentiments, collective stories, enter the most individual of fictions. Imagining a world, the writer must draw on the substance of his culture, and thereby, so to say, the culture speaks through and past him. All great writers are in part ventriloquists of myth—some inferior writers, nothing else. Fagin the individual figure was conceived by Dickens, but Fagin the archetype comes out of centuries of myth, centuries, too, of hatred and fear.

The power of Fagin is a collective, an anonymous power. Once we realize this, the question of what "to do" about Fagin comes to seem hopelessly complicated—as if there were something one could "do" to expunge the record of the deepest biases of Western culture! as if one could somehow cancel out the shadowy grotesques of Satan and Judas, Shylock and the Wandering Jew! There is nothing to "do" but confront the historical realities of our culture, and all that it has thrown up from its unsavory depths. That this can lead to reflections exceedingly somber, I would be the last to deny.

The ending of *Oliver Twist,* like the ending of that far greater book *The Adventures of Huckleberry Finn,* is a mess. Theme and plot, uneasily stitched together for the bulk of the novel, are ripped apart at the end. Dickens rushes his plot to a neat conclusion that lifts Oliver to suburban security while, in effect, abandoning the theme of the book—which is simply the condition of all the Olivers.

Mark Twain, having launched his adolescent hero on a journey that washes away, in the sublime waters of the Mississippi, all signs of race and caste, has no plausible resolution for his story. For the idyll of Jim and Huck cannot last, the problems they have "transcended" on the raft persist on shore. Dickens, having launched his child-hero on a terrifying journey through the city, keeps accumulating social difficulties and contradictions that his plot cannot cope with. "Until Oliver wakes up in Mr. Brownlow's house," remarks Arnold Kettle, "he is a poor boy struggling against the inhumanity of the state. After he has slept himself into the Brownlow world he is a young bourgeois who has been done out of his property." Oliver's troubles are miraculously disposed of, through the generosity of Mr. Brownlow—a convenience for the plot and a disaster for the theme. But no serious reader is likely to be satisfied, for the difficulty is not just that the issues cast up by Oliver's story are left hanging in the air, it is that even if we confine ourselves to the narrow boundaries of Dickens's plot, the ending must seem weak and willed. Falling back on Mr. Brownlow, that is, on the individual benevolence of a kindly gentleman, Dickens could not confront the obvious truth that a Mr. Brownlow is utterly unequipped to deal with the problem of Oliver. Nor could Dickens confront the truth already prefigured in Blake's lines:

> Pity would be no more,
> If we did not make somebody Poor:
> And Mercy could no more be,
> If all were as happy as we . . .

Dickens's imagination had led him to a point where his mind could not follow. Endings are always a problem for novelists, and the problem for the young Dickens wasn't simply that he lacked the courage to see his story through to its bitter end, it was that he didn't really know what that bitter end might be. So he wound up, in the person of Mr. Brownlow, with that "Pity" and "Mercy" about which Blake had written so scornfully.

Even writers determined to show things as they really are, often have no choice but to leave us anxious and uncertain. Why should we expect "solutions" in their books to problems we cannot manage in our lives? Whatever is vibrant and real in *Oliver Twist,* every reader will recognize; the rest is the filler of literary convention, here a sign of the evasions a writer must turn to when his imagination, over-extended, is finally balked. (pp. ix-xix)

> *Irving Howe, in an introduction to* Oliver Twist *by Charles Dickens, Bantam Books, 1981, 419 p.*

Peter Ackroyd (essay date 1990)

[*Ackroyd is an English novelist and biographer who has written acclaimed studies of the lives of T. S. Eliot and Charles Dickens. In the following excerpt from his* Dickens, *he examines biographical influences on the style and content of* Oliver Twist.]

There is some dispute about the origin of *Oliver Twist,* largely engineered by George Cruikshank who many years later (and after the novelist's death) insisted that he had been the principal begetter of young Oliver and of his sad history. On the face of it this is unlikely—Dickens was not the kind of writer or person who acquiesced in the ideas of others—but it is at least possible that Cruikshank suggested the notion of writing something like an Hogarthian poor boy's "progress" through poverty and misery. In any case Cruikshank and Dickens shared many of the same preoccupations; they were both fascinated by London,

particularly in its more squalid and darker aspects, and by images of prison or punishment. There is no doubt, for example, that Cruikshank had sketched the "condemned cell" of Newgate long before he made Fagin its occupant. This proves nothing about *Oliver Twist* itself, only the fact that author and illustrator were eminently well suited to work together upon this saga of London "low life".

What *is* clear is that as soon as Dickens had hit upon his "capital notion" of the deprived and abused child, the whole conception caught fire in his imagination. It is even possible that this was in essence the "proposed Novel" which he had been contemplating ever since he began seriously to write, and it has been said, rightly, that *Oliver Twist* is the first novel in the English language which takes a child as its central character or hero; a revolution, perhaps, although not one which was widely noticed at the time. This is largely because factual "orphan tales" were actually quite common in the period, and Dickens himself had often read autobiographies which emphasise the miseries and privations of childhood: even Johnson's life of Richard Savage has a long passage on the horrors of his infancy. There was also an ancient but still healthy tradition of "rogue literature", which in part chronicled the dramas of lost or abandoned children. So the theme of *Oliver Twist* was not in that respect new. Nevertheless it was one that directly appealed to Dickens's own sense of himself and his past, and was therefore one in which all the resources of his imagination could be poured. In the original sketch Oliver was born in Mudfog or Chatham, the site of Dickens's own infancy, and the figure of the parish boy's "progress" was one that at once attracted a cluster of childhood feelings and associations. Oliver Twist's forced association with Fagin, which seems like a savage reprise of the young Dickens's companionship with Bob Fagin in the blacking factory; Oliver's flight towards respectability; his journey from dirt to cleanliness and gentility. Thus does Dickens seem able to work through his own childhood in disguised form, both in its troubled reality and in its disturbed fantasies of escape. The life of Warren's, the foul streets of London, the sheer helplessness of the lost child resound through a narrative which becomes the echo chamber of Dickens's own childhood. In the March number of *The Pickwick Papers* Tony Weller had mentioned "Warrens's blackin'" and in the following month's episode of *Oliver Twist* a "blackin' bottle" is mentioned by the notorious beadle. The associations come flooding back as Dickens writes.

But his childhood does not pass untrammelled into his fiction; that is one reason why he was an artist and not a memoirist. And that is also why it is important to realise that he was working on *The Pickwick Papers* and *Oliver Twist* at the same time—in fact he was writing the opening chapters of the poor boy's progress, filled as they are with suffering and abandonment, at precisely the time he was also writing some of the most comic passages in *The Pickwick Papers* concerning as they do the misadventures of Bob Sawyer and the skating party at Dingley Dell. In fact Dickens soon adopted the characteristic rhythm of writing *Oliver* first, and *Pickwick* after, and it could plausibly be maintained that as a result *The Pickwick Papers* assumes a more buoyant form, as if much of the pathos which he had once introduced into the comic narrative has now been transferred to the monthly serial in *Bentley's Miscellany*. But the relationship between the novels cannot be taken too far since they have quite different forms. For one thing *Oliver Twist* is much shorter, with some nine thousand words in each episode compared to *Pickwick's* eighteen or nineteen thousand; in addition, the publication of a narrative in monthly parts was quite a different undertaking, with quite different rules, from that of publishing a monthly serial in a magazine. *Oliver Twist* was surrounded by other fiction (although it was always placed *first* in *Bentley's Miscellany*) and those who came to read it would approach it with habitual assumptions about the kind of "adventure" it was likely to provide: monthly magazine serials were commonly of the adventure or mystery sort, and relied to a large extent upon formal devices of suspense and plot to maintain that mood. In that sense, it could not be said that *Oliver Twist* disappointed them. It conformed to type even as it transcended that type, and in the brilliant exploitation of familiar material part of Dickens's genius is to be found.

There were other differences between Dickens's first two novels. It is quite clear, for example, that from the beginning he had decided to give a polemical air to *Oliver Twist* which had not been present in *The Pickwick Papers.* Presumably this is because *Oliver Twist*'s appearance in a magazine format gave him both the context and the licence to introduce more overtly propagandistic elements within it, but it is equally likely that Dickens was already aware that his range was being artificially restricted while he remained a "comic" novelist. Indeed the imperatives of his own childhood suffering must have led him ineluctably forward to the more sharply "up to date" tone of the first chapters of *Oliver Twist.* The point is that these early chapters were aimed at the workings of the New Poor Law—not so much a Law as a series of measures introduced three years before, which were only now attracting public attention because of the abuses which were arising from their provisions. In the early months of 1837 a Select Committee of Parliament had been examining the working of the Law, and it was also in this period that its principles were first introduced into the metropolis. That *Oliver Twist* was part of the contumely directed against the New Poor Law is not in doubt—*The Times,* which attacked the "BENTHAMITE cant" involved in these rationalised administrative measures, printed sections of the novel as it appeared, and Dickens himself believed that he was directing a blow against it. It meant that he was also ranging himself against some of his more radical friends, who would have approved of the measures precisely because they were "Benthamite" in character; the idea, after all, was to cut down on the cost of the poor by precluding the able-bodied pauper from relief and by making the life of the workhouse distinctly unpalatable. But Dickens's distaste for these measures was instinctive and immediate. What, after all, was the New Poor Law doing? It was tearing families apart, by consigning sexes to different quarters within the same workhouse and, with the abolition of the "search for the father" clause (which meant it was no longer required that the fathers of illegitimate children should be traced), it constituted a total disregard of the need for family life among the poor and needy. Together

with the new dietary provisions, which were satirised by Dickens precisely in Oliver's asking for " . . . some more", it is possible to see why the New Poor Law provoked in Dickens angry memories of his own deprivation, of his own separation from his family, and his own obsessive comparison of the need for food with the need for love. So when he began work upon the novel his own childhood experiences merged ineluctably with the national experience; Dickens was detailing the miseries of the poor and of those being crushed by "the system", as the new workhouse regulations were already being called, even as he recalled the phantoms of his own childhood.

Everything was close to him again. In fact, as he wrote the scenes within Fagin's lair in Field Lane, and as he described the squalid alleys and ditches around it, we do well to remember that he was himself living almost beside them; Field Lane itself was no more than a minute or two from Furnival's Inn or from Doughty Street (where he was soon to move). Given the fact that the twin preoccupations of the urban middle-class were the fear of disease and the fear of theft, and that both of these were thought literally to spread in a miasma from the rookeries and courts of the poor, it is important to note that Dickens was living alongside one of the most squalid areas in the whole metropolis. A short stroll would have taken him to Saffron Hill, and the neighbourhood of Field Lane where "excrement was thrown into a little back yard where it was allowed to accumulate for months together"; and there, beside it, Fleet Ditch, which was no more than an open sewer of fetid water. He knew of what he wrote, and it is a tribute to the power of his imagination that even those desperate elements of urban life, physically so close to him, are transposed by the power of his imagination into a larger theme. Never before had a novelist so closely aligned his narrative with topical and familiar events. Never before had the roles of novelist and journalist been so cunningly combined. So for his audience there was a double fascination—as the *Spectator* said in a review which criticised Dickens's use in fiction of the "popular clamour against the New Poor Law", the author nevertheless possessed "remarkable skill in making use of peculiarities of expression, even to the current phrase of the day". It was a kind of genius, the instantaneous transformation of the speech and events and locales of the moment, and it is one which his contemporaries were quick to recognise.

And Dickens was doing it quite instinctively, making it up literally as he went along. Apparently the name of Oliver had come from an omnibus conductor's conversation which Dickens overheard; he had seen a pauper's funeral at Cooling Church (how often that church upon the marshes is connected in Dickens's mind with death) and transposed it to the novel; he knew of a magistrate, Mr Laing of Hatton Garden, whom he went to see before turning him into Mr Fang of *Oliver Twist;* an enquiry was being conducted into the deaths of workhouse children who had been "farmed out" (that is, adults were paid to take care of them in private houses), and he used *that* too. At first he had difficulties with the length—the first instalment was too short—but within a matter of weeks he was getting into his stride. There had been nothing quite like it before—*The Pickwick Papers* and *Oliver Twist* running together, two serials of quite different types appearing simultaneously. What was admired then, and what one admires still, is the sheer fluency and easy flow of these narratives; the humour itself lies almost as much in Dickens's unflagging invention as in the scenes themselves, since it is the laughter and gaiety of human creativity. For Dickens is enjoying it, too; never can a writer so young have had such easy access to all the resources of the language, effortlessly wielding what was for him an instrument of power, the only instrument of power he had ever possessed. (pp. 216-20)

. . . . .

On 7 May, 1837, [Dickens's sister-in-law] Mary Hogarth died at the age of seventeen. She had been the previous night with Dickens and [his wife] Catherine to see a performance of his farce *Is She His Wife?* at the St James's Theatre. They had returned home to Doughty Street at about one in the morning; Mary went to her room but, before she could undress, gave a cry and collapsed (the doctors were to diagnose her condition as one of heart failure). Mary's mother, Mrs Hogarth, was called, and in her grief became insensible; Catherine and Dickens stayed with Mary as she lay in her bed in the little back room, but she never recovered. At three o'clock the following afternoon she died in Dickens's arms. Or, rather, it seems that she was dead for some time before he fully appreciated the fact. An undertaker was summoned—in an essay many years later he recalled "the one appalling, never-to-be-forgotten undertaker's knock" on the door—and she was placed in a coffin which remained in the bedroom overlooking the garden of 48 Doughty Street. She was buried six days later. Mrs Hogarth became hysterical after her collapse and had to be kept from the bedroom by force, while Catherine on the other hand showed surprising and what seemed to Dickens almost excessive calmness and strength. But, in this situation, clearly it was she who had to remain strong.

For the effect upon her husband was of the most extraordinary kind. His grief was so intense, in fact, that it represented the most powerful sense of loss and pain he was ever to experience. The deaths of his own parents and children were not to affect him half so much and in his mood of obsessive pain, amounting almost to hysteria, one senses the essential strangeness of the man. He cut off a lock of Mary Hogarth's hair and kept it in a special case; he took a ring off her finger, and put it on his own. These are all very natural reactions but, more eccentrically, he kept all of her clothes and two years later was still on occasions taking them out to look at them—"They will moulder away in their secret places," he said. He also continually expressed a wish to be buried with her in the same grave. To keep the clothes of a seventeen-year-old girl, and to desire to be buried with her, are, even in the context of early nineteenth-century enthusiasm, unusual sentiments.

It has been surmised that all along Dickens had felt a passionate attachment for her and that her death seemed to him some form of retribution for his unannounced sexual desire—that he had, in a sense, killed her. The fact that she died immediately after seeing his farce upon the problems of married life has added fuel to these speculations.

But all this is unproven and unprovable. Far more likely, in fact, that he kept her clothes, and that he expressed the wish to be buried with her, because in a sense he identified himself with her—"Thank God she died in my arms," he said just after her death, "and the very last words she whispered were of me." That sounds like the most unfortunate kind of self-obsession, but it is not so; it is an indication of the fact that he imagined some form of union between them. For the next nine months he dreamed of her every night—he called these nocturnal phantoms "visions" of Mary—and in addition he used to say that her image haunted him by day. So what precisely *was* the significance of Mary to him, apart from being his companion during the first happy months of his marriage? In his public remarks he describes himself as having a "father's pride" in her, and his descriptions of her suggest something like paternal closeness: "From the day of our marriage," he wrote, "the dear girl had been the grace and life of our home, our constant companion, and the sharer of all our little pleasures." In an announcement to the readers of *Oliver Twist* he went even further, in words that could not have been entirely acceptable to Catherine since he describes Mary as one " . . . whose society had been for a long time the chief solace of his labours". But the death of even such a close companion cannot explain the depth of Dickens's grief, and it seems likely that there were other forces at work which compounded his misery. Particularly after Catherine became pregnant, it is to be expected that he would draw close to his seventeen-year-old sister-in-law: he had a deep desire to retain certain elements of his childhood (as in his singing of the old songs) and it is more than likely that, whereas Catherine now represented the adult world of responsibility and work, Mary for him was still a child with whom he could recapture the world of his own happy childhood. She became another sister, like the sister he had known at Chatham. So it is not surprising that all the qualities he wished to retain from childhood—principal among them that passivity and gentleness which he had already celebrated elsewhere—were precisely the ones which he believed her to have possessed, and which he mourned in her passing. It ought to be remembered that, in the melodrama of the period, the good were passive and the bad essentially thrusting and aggressive; all the experiences of Dickens's own life would lead him to trust that sense of life, and in his novels the good characters would follow the same pattern of helpless passivity and gentleness. In that sense he identified his own best self with Mary Hogarth, the gentle and innocent girl. But there is also an important chronological point. Her death led once more to the destruction of his childhood at precisely the time when, in the early episodes of *Oliver Twist,* he was also exploring the death of innocence in the life of the parish boy. Everything came together, and the death of Mary merely intensified the autobiographical anguish which he was transposing to his fiction. That is why all his early sorrow and loneliness come back in his distraught letters after her death, and why once again he experiences the savage pain in his side which had disabled him in the blacking factory. Dickens's mood was ostensibly one of adult grief and even prostration, but there would also have been moments of desolation, moments when in this new separation from a loved one he felt again all the anguish and fear of his infancy. For his evident happiness during the time at Furnival's Inn—the only time in his life when it can be said that he was truly happy—was due as much to the presence of Mary Hogarth as to that of his wife. Both the passionate and sexual aspects of his nature were then being assuaged (or perhaps we can say both his infantile and adult aspirations). After Mary Hogarth's death there came once more that emptiness, that ache, that yearning perpetually renewed, always fresh and yet always the same, which by his own account became one of the guiding aspects of his life. (pp. 225-27)

Much critical acumen has been expended in trying to locate the time when Dickens first decided that [*Oliver Twist*] should take on the definite shape of a novel and not be simply a parish boy's "progress" in the conventional sense—when in other words he provided a circular rather than simple linear shape to the narrative, and began to tie up all the loose ends which previously he had been happy to leave trailing on the ground. But there is another change which has been less widely noticed since it is in the episode after the death of Mary Hogarth, and in those that follow, that Dickens begins to lose interest in the topical and polemical intent of the first chapters. The suppressed poetry of the narrative begins more clearly to emerge as a result, and what had been in part a series of sharp satirical sketches turns into a narrative at once more romantic and more mysterious. It may be unwise to suggest a firm connection between this transition and the death of Mary, but her presence does also become visible in certain direct ways. So it is that he now creates Rose Maylie, a young girl of seventeen " . . . so mild and gentle; so pure and beautiful; that earth seemed not her element . . . "; and so it is that she passes through a perilous illness, comes close to death, but then miraculously recovers. He raises Mary Hogarth in his words, and the theme of loss and return is one that becomes central to the story as Dickens now begins to develop it.

The experience of the death of Mary Hogarth enters the novel in other ways, also. It occurs in the words of Mr Brownlow, the kind gentleman who has rescued Oliver from a life of degradation—"The persons on whom I have bestowed my dearest love, lie deep in their graves . . . "—no less than in the account of Oliver watching over the bedside of the languishing Rose Maylie. "The suspense, the fearful, acute suspense, of standing idly by while the life of one we dearly love, is trembling in the balance; the racking thoughts that crowd upon the mind, and make the heart beat violently, and the breath come thick . . . the desperate anxiety *to be doing something* to relieve the pain . . . what tortures can equal these . . . " And there in the italicised words one captures something of Dickens's own agony as he watched by the bedside of the dying girl. Since Mary's death also aroused in Dickens his old, one might even say primal, fears of abandonment, it is perhaps not surprising that after her death the portrait of London in *Oliver Twist* should once more take the shape of that dark, threatening and contaminated city which he had experienced as a child, a city in which it seems that Oliver is "languishing in a wretched prison". It may be significant, too, that the chapters of *The Pickwick Papers* which Dickens wrote immediately after

Mary's death concern Mr Pickwick's own entry into the Fleet prison. The image of prison rises up before him once again; in his desolation of spirit it is always the one which returns.

This is not to suggest that such chapters or passages are uniquely determined by Dickens's experience of Mary Hogarth's death—the pull of the narrative comes from sources deeper and darker than even the most appalling of recent events—but rather that certain aspects of Dickens's creative imagination were thereby strengthened or aroused. That is why there now develops in *Oliver Twist* a constant sense of the need for sleep, for forgetfulness, for that blessed slumber "which ease from recent suffering alone imparts"; and there are episodes in the book now where Oliver hovers between sleep and wakefulness, in which suspended state he experiences what Dickens calls "visions"—visions in which "reality and imagination become so strangely blended that it is afterwards almost a matter of impossibility to separate the two". Was it in that state that he had his own "visions" of Mary? Yet it is also appropriate to the nature of the novel itself. It is on one level a realistic tale in which the Artful Dodger is arraigned for pick-pocketing and calls out " . . . this ain't the shop for justice", in which Fagin, about to be condemned to death, gazes idly over the spectators at his trial and notices that "some of the people were eating, and some fanning themselves with handkerchiefs; for the crowded place was very hot. There was one young man sketching his face in a little note-book. He wondered whether it was like, and looked on when the artist broke his pencil-point, and made another with his knife, as any idle spectator might have done." These scenes could have come straight from Dickens's own days as a reporter but then, beside them, are the other elements in this tale—the resurrection of Rose Maylie, the magical restoration of Oliver himself to gentility, the terrible flight of Bill Sikes from the phantoms of his own making. These scenes belong to another order of reality, and suggest how it is that dream and actuality, fantasy and observation, mingle within the narrative quite freely. Dickens's imagination burns, and the reality wavers above it as it does above a fire—for was not Dickens himself at the time in that state of sleeping wakefulness, of respite stolen from suffering, where reality and imagination are in his words "so strangely blended"?

All that strangeness coming also from Dickens's own state now, as the early fame and success and ambition are so cruelly undermined by the death of his sister-in-law. But in that fall from youthful insouciance and brilliance Dickens himself is broken open and the style that emerges after these events is one which will pervade the rest of his writing. For what are the essential themes brought to life in *Oliver Twist* as he now continued it? Home. Death. Childhood. All of them so curiously blended in the wish to revert to some primal place, some Eden of remembrance, some innocent state, " . . . some pleasant dream of a love and affection he had never known; as a strain of gentle music, or the rippling of water in a silent place, or the odour of a flower, or even the mention of a familiar word, will sometimes call up sudden dim remembrances of scenes that never were, in this life; which vanish like a breath; and which some brief memory of a happier existence, long gone by, would seem to have awakened . . . " And here we glimpse all the memories of Dickens himself—his memory of early infancy when nothing could separate him from his mother, his memory of the life before the blacking factory, his memory of the life he thought that he had led with the blessed companionship of Mary Hogarth—all these things utterly torn from him but returning now, returning in his memory, returning in his fiction as the parish boy himself wakes to find himself saved. Once again Charles Dickens is propelled towards some quite exceptional achievement in *Oliver Twist,* as if it were his fate that all the blessings and miseries of his life were to be transformed into words.

There is a poetry in this novel which is quite unlike anything which is to be seen in previous fiction, a poetry of barely whispered notes that sets up a deep refrain within the text, for it was Dickens's great achievement to bring the language of the "Romantic" period into the area of prose narrative. He was the first novelist really to possess the "sympathetic imagination" of his great poetic predecessors, through which he was able to grasp and integrate an entire world. So, when we come to consider the inconsistencies and difficulties of his view of the world, perhaps we ought to remember Sir Henry Taylor's contemporaneous remarks on the Romantic poets themselves: "A feeling came more easily to them than a reflection, and an image was always at hand when a thought was not forthcoming." These remarks might well be applied to the novelist, too, but it is not enough to say that he inherited the imaginative dispensation of the Romantic poets. Even in *Oliver Twist* itself we see another poetry, the poetry which appears in certain Gothic novels and which in Dickens's writing becomes the poetry of London, the poetry of darkness and isolation, the poetry which Bulwer-Lytton described only a few years later as "the vast and dark Poetry around us—the Poetry of Modern Civilisation and Daily Existence . . . He who would arrive at the Fairy Land must face the Phantoms". The poetry of Civilisation. The poetry of Daily Existence. The poetry of urban suffering. This is the new poetry of the novel. That is why there are times when the world becomes for Dickens one vast orphanage or one echoing blacking factory.

But then one cannot forget in *Oliver Twist* the hysterical humour, the vamping, the mimicry, the farce, the broad comedy. The words of the Artful Dodger defending himself in court: "Oh! You know me, do you? . . . Wery good. That's a case of deformation of character, any way." The remarks of Mr Bumble in sententious mood,

> 'If you had kept the boy on gruel, ma'am, this would never have happened.'
>
> 'Dear dear!' ejaculated Mrs Sowerberry, piously raising her eyes to the kitchen ceiling, 'this comes of being liberal!'

Humour; poetry; declamation; melodrama. All of these elements are here, as they will be in every one of Dickens's novels. But in that variegated mixture do we not also glimpse something of the mercurial character of the author himself as it will slowly be revealed to us—the sudden gaiety and the equally sudden withdrawal within himself,

the seriousness and the mimicry, the high spirits and the anger? There is a deep resemblance always between a writer and his work, but it has nothing to do with his expressed opinions or sentiments; it is rather that the form of his work embodies the form of his personality. But it is important to note, also, that if we can in some sense describe the books as general representations of Charles Dickens—his presence in language as related to his presence in the world—it is also true that the books in turn managed to change and even to "rewrite" him. It can be argued that the books helped to create Dickens's mature personality, strengthening and deepening its possibilities as he came to recognise what each time he had achieved. (pp. 229-32)

Peter Ackroyd, in his Dickens, *1990. Reprint by HarperCollins Publishers, 1990, 1195 p.*

FURTHER READING

Bibliography

Paroissien, David. *Oliver Twist: An Annotated Bibliography.* New York: Garland Publishing, Inc., 1986, 313 p.
  Provides detailed annotations of essays and whole books on *Oliver Twist* dating from 1837—the year of the novel's initial publication—through 1983. Paroissien also cites media adaptations of the novel and related writings.

Criticism

Anderson, Roland F. "Structure, Myth, and Rite in *Oliver Twist.*" *Studies in the Novel* XVIII, No. 3 (Fall 1986): 238-57.
  Argues that the narrative of *Oliver Twist* is shaped by Dickens's incorporation of events and characterizations from mythology and archaic ritual.

Axton, William F. "*Oliver Twist* and Grotesquerie." In his *Circle of Fire: Dickens' Vision and Style and The Popular Victorian Theater,* pp. 84-109. Lexington: University of Kentucky Press, 1966.
  Analyzes the theatrical aspects of *Oliver Twist.*

Cockshut, A. O. J. "The Expanding Prison." In his *The Imagination of Charles Dickens,* pp. 26-49. New York: New York University Press, 1962.
  Focuses on Dickens's preoccupation with prison imagery. Cockshut argues that the prison's meaning as a symbol varies in Dickens's novels, functioning in *Oliver Twist* as an institution "necessary for the control of vermin."

Collins, Philip. "Murder: From Bill Sikes to Bradley Headstone." In his *Dickens and Crime,* pp. 256-89. London: Macmillan and Co., 1964.
  Discusses Dickens's treatment of crime and criminals in *Oliver Twist* and provides a detailed account of Dickens's public readings of Nancy's murder scene.

Connor, Steven. " 'They're All in One Story': Public and Private Narratives in *Oliver Twist.*" *The Dickensian* 85, No. 417, Part 1 (Spring 1989): 3-16.

Examines Dickens's concern with narrative form in *Oliver Twist.*

Crotch, W. Walter. "The Criminals." In his *The Pageant of Dickens,* pp. 85-105. London: Chapman & Hall, 1915.
Includes discussion of Bill Sikes and Fagin as "two of the most vivid types of Dickens's criminal characters."

Daleski, H. M. *"Oliver Twist."* In his *Dickens and the Art of Analogy,* pp. 49-78. New York: Schocken Books, 1970.
Detailed analysis of *Oliver Twist* as a novel representing the earliest phase of Dickens's literary career.

Dickens Quarterly 4, No. 2 (June 1987): 45-127.
Commemorates the 150th anniversary of *Oliver Twist* with a collection of essays which demonstrate the wide variety of interpretations gleaned from a single work. Contributors include Robert Colby and K. J. Fielding.

Eoff, Sherman. *"Oliver Twist* and the Spanish Picaresque Novel." *Studies in Philology* LIV, No. 3 (July 1957): 440-47.
Describes ways in which *Oliver Twist* is informed by Spanish picaresque tales of the sixteenth and seventeenth centuries.

Ferns, John. "Oliver Twist: Destruction of Love." *Queen's Quarterly* LXXIX, No. 1 (Spring 1972): 87-92.
Asserts that *Oliver Twist* is Dickens's vision of the destruction by "rampant materialism" of "a community based upon love."

Fielding, K. J. *"Oliver Twist."* In his *Charles Dickens: A Critical Introduction,* pp. 32-46. Boston: Houghton Mifflin Co., 1965.
Discusses the circumstances surrounding the composition of *Oliver Twist.*

Frederick, Kenneth C. "The Cold, Cold Hearth: Domestic Strife in *Oliver Twist." College English* 27, No. 6 (March 1966): 465-70.
Asserts that, in spite of the apparently positive ending, the forces of evil in *Oliver Twist* leave a stronger impression on the reader because evil is portrayed more vividly than goodness.

Ginsburg, Michal Peled. "Truth and Persuasion: The Language of Realism and of Ideology in *Oliver Twist." Novel* 20, No. 3 (Spring 1987): 220-36.
Examines the narrative voice and characters' speech in *Oliver Twist* to explore what Ginsburg considers Dickens's contradictory aims of depicting criminals in a realistic way and of validating middle-class ideology.

Gold, Joseph. " 'An Item of Mortality': *Oliver Twist."* In his *Charles Dickens: Radical Moralist,* pp. 25-65. Minneapolis: University of Minnesota Press, 1972.
A thorough examination of Dickens's psychological insight. Gold characterizes *Oliver Twist* as an "Anatomy of Society"—an analysis of a hostile, unjust society into which individuals must integrate—in which Dickens criticizes the Poor Law and middle-class attitudes toward the poor.

Johnson, Edgar. "The Thieves' Den and the World." In his *Charles Dickens: His Tragedy and Triumph,* Vol. I, pp. 273-91. New York: Simon and Schuster, 1952.
Discusses *Oliver Twist* as an occasionally implausible but nonetheless powerful novel.

Kincaid, James R. *"Oliver Twist:* Laughter and the Rhetoric of Attack." In his *Dickens and the Rhetoric of Laughter,* pp. 50-75. London: Oxford University Press, 1971.
Examines instances of humor in *Oliver Twist,* averring that "Dickens uses laughter . . . to subvert our conventional reactions and to emphasize more dramatically the isolation of his young hero."

Lankford, William T. " 'The Parish Boy's Progress': The Evolving Form of *Oliver Twist." PMLA* 93, No. 1 (January 1978): 20-32.
Focuses on inconsistencies and contradictions in the novel, which Lankford suggests stem from Dickens's attempt to reconcile "the compulsions of his imagination and the truth about his society."

Le Comte, Edward. Afterword to *Oliver Twist,* by Charles Dickens, pp. 482-94. New York: New American Library, Signet, 1961.
Addresses Dickens's juxtaposition of comedy and melodrama in *Oliver Twist,* concluding that the novel contains the basic elements of a fairy tale.

Lucas, Alec. "Oliver Twist and the Newgate Novel." *The Dalhousie Review* 34, No. 1 (Spring 1954): 381-87.
Describes *Oliver Twist* in the context of the Newgate novel, a genre depicting the London crime world.

Lucas, John. *"Oliver Twist."* In his *The Melancholy Man: A Study of Dickens's Novels,* second ed., pp. 21-54. Sussex, England: The Harvester Press Limited, 1980.
Discusses *Oliver Twist* as a realistic novel in which Dickens presents an authentic portrait of the criminal underworld and forces his middle-class audience to confront and vicariously experience this aspect of their society.

McMaster, Juliet. "Diabolic Trinity in *Oliver Twist." Dalhousie Review* 61, No. 2 (Summer 1981): 263-77.
Analyzes the characters Fagin, Bill Sikes, and Monks, suggesting that they represent "a diabolic inversion of divine knowledge, power, and love."

Miller, J. Hillis. *"Oliver Twist."* In his *Charles Dickens: The World of His Novels,* pp. 36-84. Cambridge, Mass.: Harvard University Press, 1958.
Describes Dickens's imaginative vision and worldview as expressed in *Oliver Twist.*

Patten, Robert L. "Capitalism and Compassion in *Oliver Twist." Studies in the Novel* I, No. 2 (Summer 1969): 207-21.
Outlines the conflict in *Oliver Twist* between calculated self-interest, as represented by both respectable citizens and the gang of thieves, and the instinctive compassion of Mr. Brownlow.

Pugh, Edwin. "Oliver Twist." In his *Charles Dickens: The Apostle of the People,* 89-103. 1908. Reprint. New York: Haskell House Publishers, 1971.
Maintains that Dickens's graphic depiction of crime and corruption reflects a sympathy for socialism and an impassioned attempt to reform society.

Romano, John. "The Sentimental Criticism of Philosophy in *Oliver Twist."* In his *Dickens and Reality,* pp. 117-40. New York: Columbia University Press, 1978.
Discusses Dickens's use of sentimentality in the novel to disprove the arguments of the philosophical radicals of his day. Romano characterizes Nancy as the "sentimental hero of the novel," noting her selflessness in helping Oliver.

Sawicki, Joseph. "Oliver (Un)Twisted: Narrative Strategies in *Oliver Twist.*" *The Victorian Newsletter* 73 (Spring 1988): 23-27.

Addresses the novel's dualities, examining in particular the relationship between London's middle-class society and that of its criminal underworld.

Tick, Stanley. "*Oliver Twist:* 'A Stronger Hand than Chance'." *Renascence* XXXIII, No. 4 (Summer 1981): 225-39.

Discusses the autobiographical elements of the novel, concluding that *Oliver Twist* "is the first original expression of the authentic Charles Dickens."

Tracy, Robert. " 'The Old Story' and Inside Stories: Modish Fiction and Fictional Modes in *Oliver Twist.*" *Dickens Studies Annual,* pp. 1-33. New York: AMS Press, Inc., 1988.

Suggests that in *Oliver Twist* Dickens does not satisfy his readers' expectations because the character of Oliver does not develop and the plot does not progress. Tracy concludes that "Dickens has made his subject the processes and the metaphysic of fiction itself. The subject of *Oliver Twist* is the writing of Oliver Twist."

Walder, Dennis. "*Oliver Twist* and Charity." In his *Dickens and Religion,* pp. 42-65. London: George Allen & Unwin, 1981.

Maintains that the central theme of *Oliver Twist* is that evil can be overcome by charity.

West, Nancy M. "Order in Disorder: Surrealism and *Oliver Twist.*" *South Atlantic Review* 54, No. 2 (May 1989): 41-58.

Explores similarities between *Oliver Twist* and the later surrealist movement in art and literature, emphasizing the novel's pictorial nature and Dickens's fascination with the unconscious mind.

Westburg, Barry. "*Oliver Twist:* A Predevelopmental Fiction." In his *The Confessional Fictions of Charles Dickens,* pp. 1-31. Dekalb: Northern Illinois University Press, 1977.

Suggests that in *Oliver Twist* Dickens formulated his theory of time and psychological development, which he further explored in *Great Expectations* and *David Copperfield.* Westburg refers to these three novels as Dickens's "Confessional Trilogy," noting their similar function as "pseudo-autobiographical narratives of personal development."

Wheeler, Burton M. "The Text and Plan of *Oliver Twist.*" *Dickens Studies Annual,* pp. 41-61. New York: AMS Press, 1983.

Detailed examination of the plot and structure of *Oliver Twist.*

Williamson, Colin. "Two Missing Links in *Oliver Twist.*" *Nineteenth-Century Fiction* 22, No. 3 (December 1962): 225-34.

Analyzes two scenes in *Oliver Twist* that seem to be "loose ends." Williamson asserts that such scenes, which "jut out awkwardly from their surroundings," can provide clues to the writer's subconscious mind.

Additional coverage of Dickens's life and career is contained in the following sources published by Gale Research: *Dictionary of Literary Biography,* Vols. 21, 55, 70; *Nineteenth-Century Literature Criticism,* Vols. 3, 8, 18, 26; and *Something About the Author,* Vol. 15.

Heinrich von Kleist

1777-1811

German dramatist, short story writer, essayist, and journalist. For additional information on Kleist's career, see *NCLC*, Volume 2.

INTRODUCTION

Unappreciated in his own time, Kleist is now considered one of the greatest German dramatists, and his work is favorably compared to that of Johann Wolfgang von Goethe and Friedrich Schiller. In addition to tragedies, a comedy, and historical dramas, Kleist wrote numerous short stories and political essays in which he expressed his ardent patriotism. The extreme stylization and frank sexuality of his works shocked his contemporaries, denying him the public and critical acclaim he coveted; however, these very propensities have ensured continuing interest in his work during the twentieth century, and he is now particularly praised for his acute psychological insight and honest depiction of sexuality.

Kleist was born in Frankfurt an der Oder to a military family that had provided Prussia with eighteen generals. He was educated privately until the age of eleven, when he went to the French Gymnasium in Berlin. He joined the army at the age of fifteen and participated in the 1793 Rhine campaign against the French, but, to the disappointment of his family, left the army in 1799 with no definite plans. Kleist attended the university in his native city for one year, while also working as a tutor to Wilhelmine von Zenge, the daughter of a family friend. Kleist fell in love with Zenge, and their betrothal necessitated that he secure a financially stable position. He found employment in the civil service, but soon left on a long journey through Europe, the true purpose of which has never been discovered. In his letters to Zenge, he refers vaguely to a medical condition for which he is seeking treatment and to a secret mission investigating industries outside Prussia. Scholars note the importance of this trip in Kleist's development; it was in his letters to Zenge that he first expressed his desire to pursue a literary career. Another key event in Kleist's education was his reading in 1801 of Immanuel Kant's *The Critique of Pure Reason* (1788). Kleist's rationalistic belief in human perfectibility and immortality was challenged by Kant's ideas about the inability of reason to discern the truth behind appearances, and he entered a period of despondency that scholars commonly call his "Kant crisis." Critics note that Kleist's reaction to Kant set the tone for the metaphysical background of his creative work, in which he despaired over the impossiblility of epistemological certainty. Financial constraints eventually required Kleist to return to the civil service, but in 1801 he again gave up his position and moved to Paris with his half-sister Ulrike. However, life in France did not

please Kleist, and, influenced by his study of the works of Jean-Jacques Rousseau, he became determined to lead a simple, natural life. Later that year, he retreated to Switzerland and asked Zenge to join him there in an idyllic retreat. She refused but explained in a letter that she understood his need to satisfy his literary ambitions before returning to Germany. Kleist did return to Prussia in 1804 to assume another minor civil service post in Potsdam.

Kleist wrote all of his major works between 1804 and 1810 and, with the German economist Adam Müller, started the literary journal *Phöbus* as a vehicle for his stories. Lack of financial support caused the journal's early demise; this disappointment was compounded by the failure of Goethe's 1808 production of Kleist's play *Der zerbrochene Krug* (*The Broken Jug*). In 1810 the first volume of Kleist's *Erzhälungen,* a collection of stories and novellas which included *Michael Kohlhaas,* "Die Marquise von O . . . ," and "Das Erdbeben in Chile," was published. At this time he also started a political periodical, *Die Berliner Abendblätter,* in which he published anti-Napoleonic articles, but lack of popular support resulted in the closure of the paper after six months. Financial pressures forced him to attempt to regain a position in the civil service, but his request was refused. Throughout his life, Kleist had expressed a wish to die and had frequently asked friends to commit suicide with him. In 1811, he befriended Henriette Vogel, a well-known actress dying of cancer who agreed to a suicide pact. They traveled together to an inn near Potsdam, and on November 21, Kleist shot Vogel and then himself.

Kleist's dramas are written in blank verse rather than the smooth, classical verse used by Schiller and Goethe, and his style is characterized by frequent enjambments, caesuras, and abrupt changes of speaker. Scholars also note that his work is informed with an existential vision emphasizing human frailty. Kleist's plays and stories depict uncontrolled erotic passion, mental confusion, and violent emotional outbursts that offended contemporary notions of propriety and good taste. His exploration of the limits of language and perception and his linking of violence and passion have led critics to characterize Kleist as a peculiarly modern writer. His concern with uncontrolled passion and violence is evident in his first play, *Die Familie Schroffenstein (The Feud of the Schroffensteins)*, a tragedy incorporating a plot similar to Shakespeare's *Romeo and Juliet* in which the feuding fathers kill their own children to prevent their love affair. *Robert Guiscard*, of which only a fragment remains, examines the plight of a dying army commander of Promethean ambition who ultimately comes to despair at his inability to realize his goals. Critics believe that this drama reflects Kleist's own feelings, for although he struggled to complete the play, working on it for three years according to his own account, he was finally dissatisfied and destroyed the manuscript. Kleist's tragedy *Penthesilea*, rejected by Goethe as unplayable, is now regarded as his most powerful portrayal of erotic passion. The play focuses on the love between Achilles and the Amazon queen Penthesilea and revolves around a series of misunderstandings and deceptions which end with Penthesilea's murder and mutilation of Achilles followed by her rejection of Amazonian violence and her suicide. *Das Käthchen von Heilbronn (Kate of Heilbronn)* features a heroine whom Kleist once described as the polar opposite of Penthesilea; critics often interpret Käthchen as the ideal, passive woman Kleist failed to find in his own life. Against a romantic medieval background, she fights with a wicked enchantress for the hero's love; the forces of good are vindicated and the play ends with Käthchen's marriage. Although critics judge this as the most superficial of Kleist's plays, it has been one of the most popular and successful on the stage. *The Broken Jug*, commonly regarded as one of the few great German comedies, is noted for its witty dialogue and memorable central character; like Kleist's other plays, it raises the issue of the imperfection of social institutions—in this case the legal system—and the nature of both truth and reality. Kleist also wrote historical dramas that reflect his fierce nationalism and anti-imperialism, both responses to Napoleon's control of Prussia. In *Die Hermannsschlacht (The Battle of Arminius)* and *Prinz Friedrich von Homburg*, neither of which was published or performed during Kleist's lifetime, he praises dedication to the German nation, advocating absolute surrender of the individual to the cause of national freedom.

Kleist's short works, which similarly address issues of erotic passion and emotional confusion and often mix political history and romance, are typically set in an environment where normal routine is disturbed by disaster. The characters are confronted with situations over which they have no control and in which their usual responses are inadequate. In Kleist's novella *Michael Kohlhaas*, the protagonist pursues justice so vehemently that he unwittingly commits a crime and is sentenced to death. And in "Die Marquise von O . . . ," a respectable woman discovers that she is pregnant, but does not know the circumstances of the conception or the father's identity. Critics note that in his works Kleist often undermined conventional codes of behavior and the values represented by social institutions, with the result that religion, law, and the family are often revealed as false and hypocritical. Scholars trace this concern with the discrepancy between appearances and reality to Kleist's interest in Kantian philosophy and his concern regarding the apprehensibility of truth. In his analysis of Kleist's short fiction, Denys Dyer suggests that the chaos depicted in the stories also mirrors the upheaval in Europe caused by the French Revolution and the Napoleonic Wars.

Kleist's potential genius was acknowledged by such leading German literary figures of his time as Christoph Martin Wieland and Goethe, though most considered his work eccentric and problematical. The critics, too, rejected Kleist's works, and only three were performed during his life: *The Broken Jug, The Feud of the Schroffensteins,* and *Kate of Heilbronn*. Since his death, speculation about the cause and meaning of Kleist's suicide has been an integral part of most interpretations of his works. Nineteenth-century critics searched Kleist's works for evidence of mental illness, focusing on the extreme and eccentric nature of his characters. In the early twentieth century, scholars influenced by Arthur Schopenhauer and Friedrich Nietzsche regarded Kleist's suicide in a more positive light, elevating him as an example of Nietzsche's tragic artist. Others saw Kleist, in the words of Julius Petersen, as the "classic of Expressionism," interpreting his works as a quest for philosophical certainty. German Nationalist critics in the period of Adolf Hitler's rule cited Kleist's suicide as the ultimate sacrifice of an individual for his country and praised his works, especially *Prinz Friedrich von Homburg* and *The Battle of Arminius,* for their glorification of individual commitment to the German nation. In the later twentieth century, critics influenced by existentialist philosophy saw Kleist's suicide as the normal response to the tragic nature of human existence, and they praised his artistic obsession with the human struggle to make sense of an incomprehensible universe. For example, Swana L. Hardy, who interprets Kleist's work as the "allegory" of his life, suggests in her essay "Heinrich von Kleist: Portrait of a Mannerist" that one can "perceive in Kleist and his work the paradigm of the existentialist interpretation of man." It was not until Marxist critics expressed an interest in the political and historical aspects of Kleist's works that literary interpretation was separated from biographical concerns. Many Marxist scholars believe that Kleist's primary concern was the relation of man to society under capitalism, though they debate whether Kleist condoned middle-class values or supported a rebellion against authority. Despite such uncertainty, critics have praised Kleist's perception and honesty and have acknowledged the power and emotional intensity of his dramas.

PRINCIPAL WORKS

Die Familie Schroffenstein (drama) 1804
  [*The Feud of the Schroffensteins,* 1916]
Amphitryon: Ein Lustspiel nach Molière [adaptor; from the drama *Amphitryon* by Molière] (drama) 1807
  [*Amphitryon: A Comedy,* 1962]
Penthesilea: Ein Trauerspiel (drama) 1808
  [*Penthesilea* published in *The Classic Theatre,* Vol. II, edited by Eric Bentley, 1959]
Der zerbrochene Krug: Ein Lustspiel (drama) 1808
  [*The Broken Jug: A Comedy,* 1939]
Das Käthchen von Heilbronn oder Die Feuerprobe: Eins großes historisches Ritterschauspiel (drama) 1810
  [*Kate of Heilbronn* published in *Illustrations of German Poetry,* 1841]
Erzählungen. 2 vols. (short stories and novellas) 1810-11
Die Hermannsschlacht (drama) 1821
Prinz Friedrich von Homburg (drama) 1821
  [*Prince Frederick of Homburg* published in *Prussia's Representative Man,* 1875]

*This is the date of first publication rather than first performance.

Walter Silz   (essay date 1923)

[*In the following excerpt, Silz discusses Kleist's crisis following his reading of Kant and its impact on his work.*]

It is characteristic of Kleist, as of many another German poet, that a philosophical experience of the most profound and enduring significance should have come at the beginning of his adult life, preceding all his poetic production and leaving an indelible impression upon it. As a youth he had, in the spirit of eighteenth-century rationalism, elaborated a personal philosophy capable, in his opinion, of explaining the universe and of assuring success and happiness to any one who lived according to its precepts. Then in his twenty-fourth year he happened upon the philosophy of Kant. The effect of this contact was nothing short of a catastrophe: Kleist realized that his own philosophy had no true basis, and that reason is as such inadequate to interpret the phenomena of existence. The discovery drove him frantic, and he fully recovered his composure only towards the end of his life.

All his poetic works show traces of the rude disillusionment which had overwhelmed him. But he gradually emancipates himself; and as he successively undertakes to treat the tragedy of other lives, there is, in his conception of that tragedy, an increasing tendency to look for it, not in the unreliability of a theory of knowledge, but in the antinomies of ethics. In other words, Kleist, who has failed

to establish for the individual a place in the universe, endeavors to find for him at least a place in human society; and the individuals who claim his attention become more and more clearly those whose problems arise from relationships with their fellow men.

This is not all the case in the first group of plays (*Die Familie Schroffenstein, Guiskard, Amphitryon*), which emerge from the wreck of his shattered confidence. They exhibit the individual in conflict with other powers than those of man or society. There is undeniably a pathetic appeal in the suffering of these characters, baffled and destroyed by forces which they neither understand nor are fit to cope with; but theirs is not that genuine tragedy in which the will is self-determining and character has a right to be what it is.

The works of the second group (**"Die Marquise von O . . . "**, *Penthesilea, Das Käthchen von Heilbronn*) prepare for the conception of the individual as a member of society, in that they leave the realm of the superhuman for the realm of humanity. The tragedy of the inability of reason to comprehend the world is still poignant, but we have in **Penthesilea** to some extent a tragedy of character. **Käthchen,** for special reasons, is a deviation from the direct sequence of development.

In the third and final group the organic conception is that of the state, which in the three works of this group (**Michael Kohlhaas, Die Hermannsschlacht, Prinz Friedrich von Homburg**) gains an ever loftier position. The idea of the state affords Kleist the possibility of a new rational relationship to a world which the study of Kant had deprived of order and meaning. In no poet is there a closer articulation of life and work, and **Prinz Friedrich von Homburg,** which marks the culmination of Kleist's poetic and tragic art, records also a final development in the poet's soul. For Kleist as for his hero, the conception of the individual life in terms of society and of the state is the ultimate salvation from meaningless and self-consuming tragedy. The circle is completed: the effects of the philosophical catastrophe are overcome, and the poet is prepared to go on with a new and finer form of dramatic poetry to lengths which we now can only divine.

The transition from an individualistic to a collectivistic conception of life was by no means peculiar to Kleist. It was shared by a whole generation of men at the beginning of the nineteenth century, a generation nurtured in the optimistic rationalism inherited from Leibniz and Wolff, and engrossed in the pursuit of an individual culture of which the finest flower is Goethe. Under the stress of national calamity, this generation found a new, patriotic faith; it rediscovered the state as a moral institution.

Kleist participated in this national movement. A poet, however secluded his mode of life, is of necessity a sharer in the intellectual history of his time. (pp. 1-2)

But to Kleist this new evaluation of the state denoted more than a heightened patriotism; it denoted also a means of overcoming a personal tragedy. For the possibility of such a catastrophe as we have mentioned was inherent in his character; it could not have come with such disastrous force to one who did not combine in so fatal a duality the heart of a poet and the mind of a philosopher. The discovery of a new relation to society, however, gave him assurance of a reasonable and productive life. The destruction of that relationship in 1811 was the chief cause of his untimely death.

. . . . .

It is somewhat surprising that a poet who first and last lays so much stress on feeling, was as a young man a devout worshipper of reason; even as a lover Kleist was a rationalist. His first considerable production in prose, which he entitled **"Aufsatz, den sichern Weg des Glücks zu finden, und ungestört, auch unter den grössten Drangsalen des Lebens, ihn zu geniessen!,"** betrays in its very title the optimistic simplicity of faith which is characteristic of all pure rationalism. The prime object in life, the author asserts, is the attainment of happiness. The desire for happiness is innate within us; it speaks out of every fibre and nerve of our being; it is a wish implicit in the first dim imaginings of the child, a wish that the aged take with them into the grave.

The desire for happiness has been implanted in our souls by God. God is good and will not deceive us, but will show us the way to happiness, which lies through virtue: happiness is the "full and rapturous joy" which we gain from the contemplation of our own moral perfection. . . . (p. 3)

Be it noticed, for comparison with Kleist's later views, that God is . . . not only good, but comprehensible, showing man the way he ought to go. Kleist arrives at his sureness of happiness by a process of pure reasoning: God is good, therefore He cannot disappoint man's thirst for happiness, with which He himself has endowed His human creatures. God is good, therefore He must make equally accessible to all men a happiness to which all have equal claim. Hence happiness cannot be dependent on outer circumstances, but is the result of our inner consciousness of virtue. All this is as logical as a demonstration in geometry. Virtue makes the virtuous happy even in adversity. There is a universal law, to which prince and beggar alike are subject: virtue is rewarded and vice is punished.

Virtue, and hence happiness, is an achievement of pure reason, of clear seeing, of correct judging. This thought leads Kleist to a tragic hybris. . . .

For the unhappiness of man is due to a defect of reason: he ascribes impossible effects to things, or draws erroneous conclusions from circumstances, and hence finds his expectations disappointed. But we, illuminated by reason, shall penetrate the secrets of the physical and the moral world, and what our keen reason expects of Nature she will surely do. Through reason it is even possible to direct Fate. Thus can the wise man suck honey from every flower, for he *understands* the working of the universe. How clear, harmonious and friendly does this reasoning make the world; how indubitably does it seem to ensure a happiness which Kleist was fated never to enjoy! This eighteenth-century rationalism, which considered itself sceptically empirical, was in truth as helplessly ideological and vulnerable as the purest metaphysics.

An essay which Kleist wrote at this time in the form of a long letter to his former tutor, Martini, contains similar ideas and shows in many instances verbal coincidences with the preceding essay. Here is the same naïve faith in the power of reason alone to regulate the affairs of life, the same quest for happiness as the ultimate goal of existence. Here too virtue is the royal road to happiness, and reason is the guide to virtue. The belief in an inexorable moral law which punishes the guilty and rewards the virtuous; the confident hope that the continued and diligent development of rational qualities is a guarantee against future misfortune, are the same here as in the Essay on Happiness. A righteous God who recognizes our desire for happiness shows us also the means of attaining it.

But Kleist's chief endeavor is to justify his resolution to leave military service. This resolution is not the result of impulse, nor of humanitarian considerations, but is a reasonable and deliberate step toward the execution of a "Lebensplan" of rational character and wide scope. It follows inevitably from a view which regards happiness as the fruit of ever-increasing rational comprehension of the world, that it is the duty of the individual to acquire the greatest and most persistent possible training of the mind. Kleist is leaving the army to devote himself to the study of sciences, with an intellectual omnivorousness that is truly Faustian. He sees in the military profession a condition of life incongruous with his nature; he means to avoid the psychologically unwholesome effects of conflict between his duties as a man and as an officer. He is in effect putting vigorously aside what does not fit into his rationally excogitated "Plan of Life", what does not contribute to his self-culture ("Ausbildung") and hence to his happiness. It is extremely touching to observe the self-confidence, the placid assurance with which his "Plan of Life" inspires him.

He weighs critically the adverse opinions of others, or declines them in advance. "Denken", "an meiner Bildung arbeiten" are his watchwords, "Erkenntnis" is his salvation. He doubts whether he will ever take a government office, for that might mean sacrificing his "golden dependence on the rule of reason". He does not fear misfortune, for even in it there may be culture ("Bildung") of the highest kind, and misfortune shall not turn him from his purpose, which is motivated by "superior reason". There is in all this no hint of the cosmic disorder which baffled and dismayed the poet in his post-Kantian period; here everything is clear and consistent and serene and comforting.

It is proof not only of a didactic strain in Kleist's character, but of his essential unselfishness, that he should wish others to share the happiness to which he has found so sure an access. In a letter of May, 1799, to his sister Ulrike he adjures her to formulate a Plan of Life for herself. He depicts for her the ideal rationalist, the man who governs his own life and is superior to Fate. . . .

All the actions of such a man show a beautiful consistency and appropriateness; all that he thinks, feels, wills, has relation to one only aim; he has "reasonable grounds" for all he does. On the other hand those who have no such clear plan of life remain for ever minors, puppets in the hand of Fate; such a condition is despicable and unworthy of a thinking man, and death is preferable to it.

And then Kleist epitomizes the whole placidity and harmony of soul which, in spite of occasional disturbances (such as the trip to Würzburg), characterize this rationalistic epoch in his life.

> Ja, es ist mir so unbegreiflich, wie ein Mensch ohne Lebensplan leben könne, und ich fühle, an der Sicherheit, mit welcher ich die Gegenwart benutze, an der Ruhe, mit welcher ich in die Zukunft blicke, so innig, welch' ein unschätzbares Glück mir mein Lebensplan gewährt.

Much has been said and written concerning the relation of Heinrich von Kleist and his fiancée, Wilhelmine von Zenge, but no one has yet given this relation its merited interpretation in terms of the rationalism which dominates this period of Kleist's life. When reason has become a passion of such primal urgency, love can hardly be expected to escape its influence. In Kleist's estimation, love, whatever else it does, must contribute to the culture which his Plan of Life imperatively demands. "Edler und besser sollen wir durch die Liebe werden", he writes to Wilhelmine, and underscores, and then goes on to expound his meaning: they are to watch over each other's conduct and improve and educate themselves mutually. Kleist quite expressly puts his love in a subordinate relation to his plan of life. (pp. 4-7)

"Liebe" and "Bildung" are all but synonymous terms for him. Culture and self-culture are to be for both of them the ladder to heaven: "*Dich,* mein geliebtes Mädchen, *ausbilden,* ist das nicht etwas Vortreffliches? Und dann, *mich selbst* auf eine Stufe *näher der Gottheit* zu stellen!*". The ideal wife and mother of his children is to be "erleuchtet, aufgeklärt, vorurteilslos". The height of enlightenment for a woman is the ability to "reflect rationally on her earthly destiny".

Only in relation to this plan of life, in which untiring self-improvement is the price of happiness, does the unparalleled pedantry of his love-letters, do his ***Fragen zu Denkübungen für Wilhelmine,*** do the hair-splitting subtleties of his long epistolary essays acquire meaning, and from this point of view it is tremendously touching to observe with what singleness, honesty and perseverance Kleist pursues an end once fixed upon, with what devotion he labors to ensure the participation of his beloved in this inexhaustible felicity.

Even the terms "heart" and "feeling", so important in Kleist's plays, do not have, when they occur—rarely enough—in the letters of this period, a genuine emotional and imaginative value, but take a rationalistic tinge from their context. The heart does not appear as the seat of elemental passion, as it did to the poet of ***Guiskard*** and ***Penthesilea;*** it has merely a moralistic connotation within a rationalistic scheme of life; it is a salutary counterbalance to the mind—not a surprising view in an age whose poetic theory still held "aut prodesse volunt aut delectare poetae".

As late as November, 1800, in a letter to Wilhelmine, the young rationalist reiterates his belief that imperfections of reason are responsible for much of the tragedy of our existence: our whole view of nature and of life, he asserts, depends on how perfectly the mirror of our souls is polished by culture, and how clearly it therefore reflects the visible world. Many a man would cease to regard the world as evil or tragic if he but improved the mirror of his soul, i.e., if his reason were rendered capable of understanding what it encountered.

On his trip to Würzburg in 1800 Kleist comes for the first time into contact with the Roman Catholic religion, and he regards it, as might be expected, from a coldly rationalistic point of view. He seems to object to its ritual on the ground that it appeals to the mind rather than to the heart, but if we read the passage at all scrupulously, we find that his objections themselves are of a purely rationalistic stamp, as are the very words he uses ("sinnend", "begreifen", "Gedanken", "verstehen", "vernünftigen Gedanken"). He scoffs like a true apostle of Enlightenment at miracles, and likens the ringing of church bells to the clanking of a prisoner's chains. We shall see how differently he judged of Catholicism after his heart-rending experience with Kant.

We have thus surveyed the first period of Kleist's life in a detail warranted only by the new emphasis which our interpretation places upon the tragedy of misunderstanding as an element in Kleist's conception of the tragic. We find that this first period is colored and impregnated with a rationalistic philosophy of life on this earth and beyond. For, as Kleist states in a letter which is soon to occupy our attention, his belief was that after death we should, on another planet, continue our development from the point of perfection which we had attained on this; and that the store of knowledge which we gather here would accompany us into the next existence. Thus rationalism becomes for him a religion, and its commandments, "Wahrheit" and "Bildung", must be obeyed with holy zeal. In return this rationalistic religion brings to its believer serenity and composure amid the vicissitudes of life, a mind single to its purpose, peaceful and unperturbed.

As a stone, dropping suddenly into a pool, breaks up its quiet surface into agitated circles and waves that are long in coming to rest, so there comes upon Kleist, abruptly and without warning, a recognition which destroys forever the premature placidity of his rationalistic system and plunges him into profound distress. This recognition, derived from the study of the Kantian philosophy, constitutes the great and determinative tragedy of his life as a man and as a poet.

Although he must have known and read Kant's philosophy as an officer at Potsdam and as a student at Frankfurt a. O., it is fairly certain that Kleist did not become acquainted with Kant's theoretical doctrines, with the *Kritik der reinen Vernunft,* until the winter of 1800—1801. Then he threw himself into this study with all the dangerous ardor and immoderation of his radical nature. I believe there is a precursor of the coming storm in this passage in a letter to Ulrike of February 5, 1801:

> Liebe Ulrike, es ist ein bekannter Gemeinplatz, dass das Leben ein schweres Spiel sei; und warum ist es schwer? Weil man beständig und

immer von Neuem eine Karte ziehen soll und doch nicht weiss, was Trumpf ist; ich meine darum, weil man beständig und immer von Neuem handeln soll und doch nicht weiss, was recht ist.

Then comes the letter of March 22, 1801, to Wilhelmine, an overwhelming document of the effect of a purely mental experience on a person of absolute intellectual honesty, a person whose nature made compromise impossible and concealment out of the question. Kleist reviews the significance for him of his previous rationalistic plan of life, the details of which we have surveyed above. Then, cautiously, as if he were handling a terrific explosive, he imparts to his fiancée the full scope and import of his grievous misfortune:

> Wenn alle Menschen statt der Augen grüne Gläser Hätten, so würden sie urteilen müssen, die Gegenstände, welche sie dadurch erblicken, *sind* grün—und nie würden sie entscheiden können, ob ihr Auge ihnen die Dinge zeigt, wie sie sind, oder ob es nicht etwas zu ihnen hinzutut, was nicht ihnen, sondern dem Auge gehört. So ist es mit dem Verstande. Wir können nicht entscheiden, ob das, was wir Wahrheit nennen, wahrhaft Wahrheit ist, oder ob es uns nur so scheint. Ist das letzte, so ist die Wahrheit, die wir hier sammeln, nach dem Tode nicht mehr—und alles Bestreben, ein Eigentum sich zu erwerben, das uns auch in das Grab folgt, ist vergeblich—

> Ach, Wilhelmine, wenn die Spitze dieses Gedankens Dein Herz nicht trifft, so lächle nicht über einen Andern, der sich tief in seinem heiligsten Innern davon verwundet fühlt. Mein einziges, mein höchstes Ziel ist gesunken, und ich habe nun keines mehr—

> Seit diese Überzeugung, nämlich, dass hienieden keine Wahrheit zu finden ist, vor meine Seele trat, habe ich nicht wieder ein Buch angerührt. Ich bin untätig in meinem Zimmer umhergegangen, ich habe mich an das offne Fenster gesetzt, ich bin hinausgelaufen ins Freie, eine innerliche Unruhe trieb mich zuletzt in Tabagien und Kaffeehäuser, ich habe Schauspiele und Konzerte besucht, um mich zu zerstreuen, ich habe sogar, um mich zu betäuben, eine Torheit begangen . . . und dennoch war der einzige Gedanke, den meine Seele in diesem äussern Tumulte mit glühender Angst bearbeitete, immer nur dieser: dein *einziges,* dein *höchstes* Ziel ist gesunken—.

It is the Faustian outcry: "Und sehe, dass wir nichts wissen können!" But it means much more than that: it means to Kleist a negation of his whole previous existence, of his present endeavor, of his hope in the life to come. For all these things had received meaning and sanction from his rationalism; it was his way of organizing the world, his formula of life, his religion. And now all that is gone in one tremendous cataclysm; all things are relative, there is no longer any absolute Truth, the world has lost its meaning.

When the first fevered anguish of this recognition is over, there comes a dull sense of blindness to the one who before saw so clearly: "Ach, dunkel, dunkel ist alles". He sees hope of relief only in distraction; he resolves to leave the country and go on a long journey. But by a sinister concatenation of circumstances, he, who had wished to travel alone, finds himself accompanied by his sister; he, who is filled with a profound abhorrence of all science, finds himself on the way to Paris, the stronghold of rationalism, his pass reading for study as the object of his visit, and in his pockets letters of introduction to the very circles he wishes most to avoid. No wonder that he cries out: "Ach, Wilhelmine, wir dünken uns frei, und der Zufall führt uns allgewaltig an tausend feingesponnenen Fäden fort".

The superb order of his universe is gone; there remains only the blind arbitrariness of an inscrutable Fate: "Wer kann die Wendungen des Schicksals erraten?" "O wie unbegreiflich ist der Wille, der über die Menschengattung waltet!" One day, while their carriage is standing before an inn, the horses, frightened by the braying of a train of donkeys, run away; the carriage is overturned, and Kleist and his sister barely escape with their lives. Again he is confronted with the baffling fortuitousness of existence. . . . (pp. 7-11)

A storm which they encounter on the Rhine again puts their lives in jeopardy, and Kleist himself experiences the fear of death which plays such an important part in his ***Prince of Homburg***. . . .

There is nothing absolute; all things, right or wrong, are relative; man is irresponsible, God is incomprehensible. . . . (p. 11)

The experience which dethrones reason as the guide and arbiter of life turns Kleist with the energy of a drowning man to that other organ of the soul, the heart, the seat of feeling. On his first visit to Dresden, en route to Würzburg in September, 1800, he had surveyed the art-gallery with cool appraising reason, he had stared, as he himself says, like a child at a doll. Now, in April, 1801, he perceives these same pictures through the senses and the feeling:

> Alles waren Gegenstände bei deren Genuss man den Verstand nicht braucht, die nur allein auf Sinn und Herz wirken. Mir war so wohl bei diesem ersten Eintritt in diese für mich ganz neue Welt voll Schönheit.

"Rest, rest!" is the cry of his soul; "ach, ich sehne mich unaussprechlich nach Ruhe!" In the turmoil and agony of his distracted mind he yearns for that harmony and confident calm of which he has been so incomprehensibly deprived. He pictures to himself and to his beloved a peaceful green house, the little hut of a fisherman or peasant tucked away in the shelter of a protecting rock, compassed about with the joys of idyllic peace and tranquillity.

He, who in Würzburg in 1800 had only criticism and disdain for the ceremonies of the Roman Catholic church, now longs with a parched soul for the placidity of unquestioning faith; he is stirred by the grandeur of church music; he envies a common man whom he sees on the altar-steps lost in fervent prayer. . . . (pp. 11-12)

Yet I venture to assert that this catastrophe over Kant, harrowing though it was, constituted a necessary step in the development of Kleist as a poet. It is supremely tragic that such a poignant experience should have been needed to recall him from a fruitless endeavor. But what would he have become had he continued undiverted in the rationalistic-scientific direction of his youth? Certainly no dramatist, no tragic poet. No one to whom the world presented itself, as to the pre-Kantian Kleist, so clear-cut and logical, so explicable and unified and free from contradiction, so much the work of a fine reasonableness, could have written great tragedy. For tragedy requires conflict and opposition; it is coeternal with the human race and human sense for the sad disparity between things as they are and as they should be. This sense the Kantian catastrophe awakened in Kleist. And it gave him also a feeling, awesome, but indispensable in a poet, for the infinite, the shadowy and mysterious, for that great submerged nine-tenths of the universe whither the prophetic poet alone can be our guide. . . . (pp. 12-13)

> *Walter Silz, in his* Heinrich von Kleist's Conception of the Tragic, *Vandenhoeck & Ruprecht, 1923, 95 p.*

John C. Blankenagel   (essay date 1931)

[*In the following excerpt, Blankenagel praises Kleist's dramatic achievement, noting that Kleist significantly expanded the range of drama in his time.*]

No German dramatist of note has been considered quite so enigmatic as Heinrich von Kleist. Attempt after attempt has been made to fix him in a definite category and to explain and interpret him and his works from a single viewpoint. The very diversity of these analyses points toward the unsatisfactoriness of such an undertaking. A strictly rationalistic approach to him at any period of his life inevitably results in failure because he was at no time temperamentally a thoroughgoing rationalist. Even in the period prior to his disillusionment by Kantian philosophy Kleist was by no means the rationalist that he temporarily fancied himself and for which he has so frequently been taken. The very enthusiasm, fervor, and ardor with which he approached the philosophy of enlightenment betokens a profoundly emotional nature and precludes the possibility of the sway of cold, mathematical, impersonal, logical abstraction. This passing enthusiasm for a rationalistic conception of life and of the universe sprang largely from his youthful desire for happiness and from his ethical idealism. Aware only too early of the contradictoriness of life, of the waywardness of fortune, and of the instability born of his highly emotional, imaginative temperament, Kleist vainly searched for a stabilizing force without which human existence seemed too uncertain and too terrifying. Stimulated by his readings, the youth began a veritable worship of the life of reason based upon a carefully wrought plan for his future development. Desirous of being serenely happy, Kleist regarded the triumphant sway of reason as the best protection from the insecurity and changefulness of existence and consequently as the safest guarantee of contentment.

The optimistic period in which Kleist firmly believed that happiness can be attained under the guidance of reason is the one which gave rise to most of his extant letters. Their comparative bulk and their impressive insistence on a single point of view have misled many critics into an overemphasis of his alleged rationalistic propensities. Logically minded and desirous of achieving unity, they have frequently yielded to the temptation of reasoning away all contradictory aspects of his nature and writings. In their endeavor to harmonize, they have lost sight of imponderables and of the complexities underlying a personality of profoundly emotional temper. The desire to reduce all reactions and manifestations of the individual to a single formula has caused rationally minded scholars to overlook the fact that sensitively organized beings defy such processes of simplification, which do violence to them by stripping them of much of their individuality. Kleist is too complex to permit of classification as a classicist, a romanticist, or even as a romanticist with certain reservations. And the attempt to account for certain peculiarities in Kleist and his characters by such superficial designations as abnormal, pathologic, morbid, and neurotic, merely obscures and distorts. The fact is that his personality, like that of some of his characters, defies rationalistic analysis because it is essentially emotional.

Among the limitations of the human mind must be included its inability to analyze and comprehend emotion. Conduct which defies logical interpretation and seems to fly in the very face of reason is frequently pronounced unreasonable, quixotic, capricious, or whimsical. Yet such designation does not serve to define or explain the nature, causation, and origin of unreasoned conduct. Since many human acts are imponderable, unreasoned, and unpredictable, and since many run counter to all logical expectations, why should not a dramatist portray such aspects of human life by the side of others? Why not widen the scope of dramatic literature by presenting imponderables as such? Why not stage quixotic acts and caprices as such? If these aspects of man's behavior are an undeniable part of life, why not depart from hoary, logical tradition as well as from dramatic and theatrical convention and simply stage occasional unreasoned acts of emotional personages without attempting complete, exhaustive, logical motivation and explanation of that which defies analysis? This is what Kleist has repeatedly done; he has portrayed the contradictoriness and the inconsistency in human conduct which he observed in himself as well as in others. In such presentation he made no attempt to avoid extremes. In fact, emotional instability seemed all the more impressive and none the less true to life because of its eruptive, violent excesses.

Under the influence of a rationalistic tradition, careful dramatists prior to Kleist had meticulously motivated the acts of characters who themselves were the conceptions of a rationalistic mind. Their actions had to be logical, in keeping with their nature, and hence predictable. Lessing, for example, held that on the stage the public is to learn what every man of a given character will do under given circumstances. And in keeping with such a viewpoint heroes and heroines were so portrayed that their acts were the inevitable, consistent outcome of their reasoned nature. The ideal dramatic problem as based upon character was one of mathematical exactness in which two and two were bound to make four. This well-nigh sacred convention manifested itself clearly in the monologue in which the dramatist demonstrated to the audience the exactness of his skillful calculations. The old stilted monologue reflected the conviction that acts must not only be in harmony with character but must be clearly intelligible as such. The serious business of drama was to create personages of a definite stripe and to present their deeds as the obviously natural consequence of their nature. And to make doubly sure that no one should fail to comprehend, the hero explained in monologues what he was doing, and why he was doing it, and that his conduct was just what one had a right to expect of him.

Now one interesting aspect of life is its uncertainty and its unpredictability. And it is unpredictability in the reactions and acts of persons which, within certain limits, lends them fascination. In fact, it is just this element, based upon emotion and subjective preference, which tends to differentiate the individual from the type. The difficulty lies in presenting a character of this unusual nature in such a manner that his conduct may not seem strained, absurd, or freakish. Consequently the dramatist is not freed from the necessity of careful characterization. It must be borne in mind that even people whose conduct almost invariably seems based on careful analysis of situations occasionally fly impulsively in the face of all logic and make a choice based entirely upon subjective preference. Obviously enough, the individual whose nature is fundamentally emotional is given to acts which, because they defy analysis, seem unreasonable and capricious to his logically minded fellows. What type of dramatist is likely to create characters of this kind? In all probability, the poet of just such temperament will express these eruptive, volcanic tendencies in the persons he creates. And in the case of Heinrich von Kleist we have to do with a man whose conduct was based to a remarkable degree upon feeling, emotion, and intuition. The objection may be raised that impulsive, capricious acts require no motivation in character and that consequently it would have been quite unnecessary for Kleist to portray personages as carefully as he did. But it must not be overlooked that it is only an occasional unreasoned act which makes its appearance in personages like Penthesilea, Strahl, Thusnelda, and Homburg. And even here Kleist sometimes gives a clue as to what may be expected. Of himself he once said that the only constant thing about him was his inconstancy. Similarly, in the case of Penthesilea he prepares the reader or spectator for the incommensurable and imponderable element in her nature through the words of Prothoe who asserts that the queen's soul is incalculable.

Kleist well realized how inconsistent he was inclined to be and how illogical his conduct seemed to others. Endowed, like Homburg, with a vivid imagination, inordinate ambition, and powerful, violent emotion, he was doomed to ups and downs; periods of exultation and high expectancy alternated with deep despair. He was fully aware that unbridled emotion might lead to catastrophe and tragedy; it was this realization that lent terror to life and filled him repeatedly with a nervous, haunting fear and with nameless dread. In such moments he longed for death and yet trem-

> **Kleist is too complex to permit of classification as a classicist, a romanticist, or even as a romanticist with certain reservations. And the attempt to account for certain peculiarities in Kleist and his characters by such superficial designations as abnormal, pathologic, morbid, and neurotic, merely obscures and distorts.**
>
> —*John C. Blankenagel*

bled at the thought of annihilation. Consequently he aimed in one way or another to fortify himself against shocks to his emotions from the vicissitudes of life. His youthful rationalistic plan of life grew out of his instinctive realization of the need for some dominant motive coming from without, which might transcend his existence and fortify him against adversity. When, owing to the inadequacy of its foundations, his early philosophy of life based upon the idea of human perfectibility crumbled, life seemed a hopeless maze, devoid of any stabilizing force. Human existence appeared devoid of sense and the world a madhouse peopled by bewildered, helpless humanity. His first drama was born of such a pessimistic outlook.

If reason fails to function when man is blinded by towering passions, if its conclusions are not to be trusted, then some other stabilizing force must be sought in a seemingly indifferent or even malevolent world. And once more begins a search—a frantic, despondent search—for an anchor in a storm-tossed existence. Naturally enough, this quest is reflected in Kleist's dramas. His characters struggle for poise; they are fearful of anything which may confuse them and undermine their calm. It is strange that Goethe, who strove to attain an Olympian serenity and who carefully endeavored to keep disturbing influences out of his life, should have misjudged Kleist's characters, who, though buffeted about, strive to gain and maintain poise. Kleist was not, as Goethe asserted, everywhere intent upon undermining the stability arising from trusting to feeling and intuition. Although the fortitude of his heroes and heroines is sorely tried, he is much more concerned with ascertaining some means of stabilizing them than with undermining their security. They reflect the storminess of life as he himself experienced it. Painfully reminded of his own youthful struggles, Goethe sensed a Wertherian morbidity in the young dramatist, shrank from the turbulent emotions portrayed in his works, and was unable to judge him with detachment. Consequently he misunderstood Kleist's intention in portraying the rude tests to which mankind is exposed.

It is a commonplace that the emotional element is outstanding in many of Kleist's dramatic personages. He had lost confidence in reason as a reliable guide to thought and action. Knowledge, as such, lost its charm for him when he arrived at the conclusion that it held no absolute truths of universal validity. Characteristically enough, he looked to the opposite pole for salvation and pinned his faith to feeling and intuitive judgment. Deeds, he now maintained, were superior to knowledge, and since the heart prompted spontaneous acts, its voice was to be heeded. He concluded that, because of its tendency to weigh and balance, reason merely made for indecision, and thereby paralyzed initiative. Great creative deeds seemed born of impulse, of trusting to the heart and yielding to its dictates. Hence there arises Kleist's insistence upon obeying the first impulse of one's heart and upon following one's intuitive feeling through which God points to what is right. And since unity and harmony result from absolute reliance upon innate feeling, Kleist's characters endeavor to avoid anything which may render them at variance with themselves. They sense danger in the opposition of the mind to the heart, in doubt, and in the conflict of emotions. Moreover, even tremendously intense emotions may surge back and forth, thereby perturbing the individual. With nothing outside himself to transcend subjective desire, man may become a prey to the instability of changing emotions, no matter how powerful their momentary sway may be. And just this is true of Kleist's characters; unless fortified by some other agency they come to grief in moments of doubt, stress, and strain. Tragedy and catastrophe exist where confusion prevails. These may be averted and security and poise may be obtained by placing one's self in the service of an ideal which transcends the individual. Such a conception of life makes for serenity even under the most untoward circumstances. Having arrived at this conclusion, Kleist turned from tragedy to drama of a more optimistic, conciliatory nature in which man is able to regain composure even after having been severely tried and temporarily worsted in the struggle of life. The most important single motif running through Kleist's dramatic works lies in the effort of his characters to maintain or regain serenity in the face of adversity.

In *Die Familie Schroffenstein* human reason proves inadequate to prevent disaster because madly raging passion obscures it, renders its exercise impossible, and leads to illogical acts of eruptive violence. Blinded by suspicion, jealousy, hatred, and the desire for revenge, man is unable to make an active stand against the destruction growing out of these baser passions. Here man is like a plaything tossed hither and thither by powerful but turbulent and turgid emotions. Yet even in this gloomy tragedy there is a ray of light. In the minds and hearts of Agnes and Ottokar, unselfish, sacrificing love makes for momentary tranquillity, harmony, and peace even though the lovers are beset by murder. The unwavering devotion which Kleist demands of love manifests itself in Ottokar, who gives his life in the hope of saving Agnes. But his efforts are made futile by the inability of others to stifle the vengeful hatred that clouds their reason. Passion, vengeance and murder triumph, but the emotion of self-sacrificing love enjoys a brief moment of happiness even in the face of death.

In *Robert Guiskard* the hero has a definite goal as contrasted with the aimlessness which is so marked in Kleist's first tragedy. Guiskard wages a courageous battle with forces which block his way to the successful achievement of his plans of gigantic conquest; here there is concerted action, struggle, and combat, all of which were substantially lacking in *Die Familie Schroffenstein.* This repre-

sents progress in dramatic concepts and values. Relying upon himself alone, the hero copes valiantly with superhuman odds by asserting a will which hitherto has triumphed over all obstacles. Here Kleist portrays an attempt to secure mastery and stability in a hostile world by the assertion of the human will. Yet the crowning achievement of a great adventurous career remains unrealized because man's will does not suffice to triumph over bodily infirmity. The outcome of this tragic conflict is failure, and is born of a continued pessimistic conception of life. Yet struggle there is, and heroic struggle; Guiskard succumbs while grandly asserting himself.

In *Die Familie Schroffenstein* reason was darkened by base passions, was unable to cope with them, and left man without any stabilizing force to ward off disaster. In *Robert Guiskard* the human will failed to overcome the frailties of the flesh, and once more man was a victim to the vicissitudes of life. In the former, aimlessness; in the latter, a purposeful aim which was defeated. In *Penthesilea* the motive force which impels the heroine is powerful emotion undisciplined by reason or will. Here Kleist portrays the violent extremes to which outraged sensibilities may lead. The queen forgets all obligations to the Amazon tribe, becomes oblivious to the laws of her state, is swept into a fury of temporary insanity and rends and tears the body of her lover who, she fancies, has spurned and humiliated her. Powerful, primitive emotions; but, devoid of stability, they run riot and drive the heroine to a mad act of violence. But in this tensely emotional nature of Penthesilea lies the power of self-annihilation as well. On realizing that she has slain Achilles, she needs no weapon to end her life; her emotions suffice. Kleist, who repeatedly thought of death as the sole escape from an intolerable existence, must frequently have yearned for the strength of emotion of Penthesilea which enabled her to triumph over matter by ending her life without the need of murderous weapons. Out of the depth of her feelings she summons death.

In three tragedies Kleist presented the failure of reason, will, and instinctive obedience to feeling to serve as man's guides or to enable him to triumph over adversity. His other dramas reflect a different conception of life. He writes one comedy fraught with serious elements, one out-and-out comedy, a romantic fairy drama with a holiday mood, and a brace of dramas in which a mature, optimistic view of life predominates. Alkmene is fortified by a profound conviction of the fundamental innocence of her intent; Eve's sacrificial love for Ruprecht and the consciousness of her innocence enable her to endure misrepresentation, slander, abuse, and accusations challenging her honor. But in Käthchen utter devotion and self-sacrificing love celebrate their greatest triumphs as the source of serenity and happiness. Living, as she does, for love and its ultimate realization, she has no doubts and no uneasiness. Unlike Penthesilea, she is a naïve, untroubled child of nature, under no compulsion to be anything other than herself. Her one concern is to be in the presence of the man she loves; having no designs, she remains untroubled at heart, even when repulsed. No reflection undermines the harmony of her being, no doubts arise, and no other emotion wars with her love, which is deep enough to fortify her in her faith in the ultimate goodness of things.

Finally, in his two patriotic dramas, Kleist set forth the stability which may be gained by devotion to a great cause. Hermann's intense patriotism and thirst for freedom lend him a singleness of purpose that triumphs over the waywardness of feeling; he knows no vacillation because individual desire and self-aggrandizement have been submerged in the service of a transcending ideal. Likewise, the Great Elector is calm and self-contained because he subordinates himself to the welfare of the fatherland. By placing themselves in the service of an ideal, Hermann and the elector have risen above the petty, disturbing incidents of human existence and live in a higher sphere. In these two personages Kleist portrayed the harmony and poise which were denied him in his struggles to rise above confusion and chaos. His final "plan of life" points to the whole-souled service of an ideal which absorbs the full depth and strength of man's emotions, determination, and energies. The ultimate tragedy of Kleist's career lies in the fact that conditions in his country made active surrender to a program of this kind impossible at the very time when he longed to embrace such an opportunity. Denied this opportunity for service, he was forced to present it merely as a compensatory ideal; he found nothing else to make existence tolerable, and ended his life. Had the war of liberation come earlier, Kleist could have translated his ideal into action. And so one reason for his untimely, tragic end lies in the fact that he was denied the privilege of serving his country actively at the most critical moment of his life.

In view of the significance he attaches to emotion, the question arises as to Kleist's relation to the romanticist's insistence on feeling. Kleist's emphasis is not upon vapid emotional states as such nor upon the hazy expression of a vague mood that longs for a narcotic atmosphere into which it may be dissipated. He regards feeling as the powerful, energizing, impelling factor in human conduct and not as a vapid state of self-intoxication in which the individual is merged into a dreamy, cosmic whole. He treats emotion as the fundamental, dynamic quality of the individual; the best, most reliable judgments are intuitive; and feelings, rather than the iron logic of the situation, are the best guides to action. He delights in the portrayal of eruptive emotions which at times burst forth into acts of extreme violence. This predilection for emotion leading to deeds differentiates Kleist from the sentimental, more listless treatment of emotion by certain romanticists.

Kleist's sense of form in drama differs from the lyrical undisciplined drama of romanticism. Yet with all his discipline in matters of dramatic form and structure he is a pronounced individualist in the liberties he takes with all formalistic elements. And he is a realist in his refusal to sidestep extreme manifestations of human conduct. In his presentations of emotional excesses he is unconcerned with the resulting violence of behavior. Unhesitatingly he sacrifices esthetic qualities in favor of vraisemblance. The individualization of his more sharply defined personages removes them from the classicistic tendency to typify. Moreover, his presentations of emotional outbursts of a volcanic nature are foreign to the measured calm and repose of classicism. Although his characters strive for poise, their path is likely to lead through excruciating anguish. His curtailment of the monologue as undramatic, his particu-

larization of character, and his emphasis upon the psychological element in the motivation of conduct are realistic tendencies. On the whole, Kleist may be regarded as a bridge leading from classicism and romanticism to modern psychological realism.

Whoever sees beauty and artistry only in classical repose, in Olympian calm, in restraint and moderation, in the even cadence of smooth rhythm, in regularity and harmony, will fail to appreciate Heinrich von Kleist as a dramatist. His uneven periods, irregular, choppy meter, broken lines and jerky, abrupt tempo are an expression of the nervous torment of his life, of sweeping, cataclysmic change, of demoniacal unrest, and of pent-up emotion which finally bursts forth uncontrollably. But whoever is interested in the manifold manifestations of surging, throbbing, straining life, and considers that they, too, deserve to be reproduced in art, will find in Kleist a significant widening of the boundaries of the drama of his time. (pp. 234-46)

> *John C. Blankenagel, in his* The Dramas of Heinrich von Kleist: A Biographical and Critical Study, *The University of North Carolina Press, 1931, 261 p.*

J. M. Lindsay on communication in Kleist's works:

In almost every work which Kleist wrote the idea of communication plays a quite important part. As a rule his works reflect a strong feeling that perfect communication seldom occurs in this world. On the whole, obstacles to communication fall into two categories, those imposed from outside and those which arise from within the characters of his personages. Sometimes it is not easy to distinguish these categories clearly. Perhaps one could go so far as to say that Kleist simply believes that the very fact of being in the world means that one cannot communicate fully or satisfactorily with other people. Now and again this frightful and impossible world seems to recede, and we have momentary glimpses of a better state of affairs, in which immediate, direct and full communication occurs, in which love prevails between human beings, in which eternal and absolute values are not unattainable ideals but the normal conditions of living. Kleist suffered more than most men from his acute awareness of the contrast between the ideal and the actual, and in his representation of communication between man and man we become aware how the unsatisfactory nature of human life is particularly reflected in this aspect of existence. For Kleist communication seems to possess an absolute value. It is an aspect of the divine, perhaps, which is placed out of reach of most of us most of the time, but not so far out of reach that we are unaware of it. Indeed, the torment of being almost but not quite able to achieve it contributed in no small measure to Kleist's feeling that the conditions of life in this world were insupportable.

> *J. M. Lindsay, "Faulty Communication in the works of Kleist," in* German Life and Letters *(October 1977).*

E. L. Stahl   (essay date 1948)

[*In the following excerpt, Stahl analyzes Kleist's plays as reflections of his emotional and philosophical crises and surveys his development as a dramatist.*]

In his essay **"Über die allmähliche Verfertigung der Gedanken beim Reden"** Kleist propounded an interesting theory. He believed that there are two methods of expressing ideas, one of finding suitable words for an idea that had been thought out beforehand, the other of finding the idea in the act of speaking, i.e. of expressing nascent thought. 'Der Franzose sagt' he wrote 'l'appétit vient en mangeant, und dieser Erfahrungssatz bleibt wahr, wenn man ihn parodiert, und sagt, l'idée vient en parlant." A confused expression, he maintained, does not necessarily indicate confused thinking: 'Wenn daher eine Vorstellung verworren ausgedrückt wird, so folgt der Schluss noch gar nicht, dass sie auch verworren gedacht worden sei'. He quotes instances where embarrassment was the cause of faulty expression and arrives at the provocative conclusion: 'Nicht wir wissen, es ist allererst ein gewisser Zustand unsrer, welcher weiss.'

Kleist has described his own method of composition in this essay. He did not work out his plots carefully before proceeding to elaborate them in detail, as Schiller and Lessing usually did. After receiving the initial impetus, Kleist allowed himself to be carried along by the current of his imagination. Hence there are many unexpected developments in his dramas, many apparent inconsistencies and incongruities. He did not always succeed in expressing his ideas, although he may have known what he wanted to say. The ideas may have been definite enough, but they remained at the back of his mind, because he was not capable of expressing them fully. Such an idea is his conception of God. Despite his passion for veracity and his resolution to follow the voice of his heart 'ganz und gar, wo es mich hinführt,' he had his inhibitions. To say outright what he secretly thought would have conflicted with his 'inward satisfaction'. It is difficult to escape the impression that in his pessimistic period Kleist identified God with Fate or Chance, those features of life that filled him with the deepest despair. But neither in his letters nor in his dramas does he explicitly formulate this identification, and yet only when we assume that it, in fact, existed in his own mind, do his tragedies make sense. Viewing together *Die Familie Schroffenstein, Amphitryon* and *Penthesilea* we arrive at the conclusion that the ultimate, if unacknowledged source of his pessimism, and thus the core of the motivation in his tragedies, is his conception of the attitude of God to man. An examination of these plays will show that in them God, or else the representative of the divine power (Jupiter in *Amphitryon,* Mars in *Penthesilea*) is either indifferent to human suffering, or intervenes in human affairs to produce suffering.

However, in *Penthesilea,* Kleist does not use this theme for the motivation of the whole tragedy as he did in earlier dramas, and indeed after completing this work he abandoned the writing of tragedies. His last three plays exhibit a more hopeful attitude to life. He never achieved a stable relationship with his fellow-men, but his distrust of human nature and of the powers that rule man's existence became less pronounced and gave way to a more optimistic outlook. There is, accordingly, a change in his treatment of the themes that he had dealt with in his tragedies. These themes do not disappear entirely from his work, but they were given a new direction and they express a new purpose.

In his last plays, however, Kleist does not so much solve the tragic problems of his earlier dramas, as override them. Kant's philosophy had thrown him into despair. Now he has found a way out, but his new creed is not a logical answer to his earlier doubts. The grounds of his optimism cannot be correlated with the reasons for his pessimism. He had written to Wilhelmine von Zenge on March 28, 1801: 'Der Irrtum liegt nicht im Herzen, er liegt im Verstande und nur der Verstand kann ihn heben'. He did not obey his own principle. Against his earlier fears there now stand his hopes. The outlook of the later dramas is simply the reversal of that displayed in the tragedies, and although Kleist's work as a whole possesses unity, it does not possess the logical unity of Schiller's work or the organic unity of Goethe's.

Nor do the elements of his later belief form a consistent whole. The positive attitude to life revealed in *Käthchen von Heilbronn* is different from that displayed in *Die Hermannsschlacht* and both differ from *Prinz Friedrich von Homburg.* In the first play we observe a new attitude to the problem of the relation of God to man, hence a new estimate of human relationships, in the second drama Kleist's patriotic beliefs are expressed, in the last work we have a portrayal of human relationships without reference to the overruling problem of the nature of God and man. As a drama *Prinz Friedrich von Homburg* is Kleist's most satisfying production because before writing it his metaphysical questionings have patently come to rest. *Die Hermannsschlacht,* too, is a product of his purely human interests, but its dramatic values are inferior to those of his last play. *Käthchen von Heilbronn* is the least valuable of his dramas, considered aesthetically, but it is a significant work, since it reveals most clearly the change from pessimism to optimism so characteristic of Kleist's mature outlook. Just as the origins of his pessimism are laid bare in his study of Kant and a knowledge of this source facilitates the understanding of his tragedies, so one basis of his optimism can be uncovered and will assist us in the interpretation of his last plays.

When he was in Dresden in 1807, Kleist attended Schubert's lectures on *Ansichten von der Nachtseite der Naturwissenschaften.* Some of the theories put forward by Schubert confirmed him in his efforts to overcome his metaphysical pessimism. On August 31, 1806 he had written to his friend Rühle von Lilienstern: 'Es kann kein böser Geist sein, der an der Spitze der Welt steht, es ist ein bloss unbegriffener!' In this letter there is no trace of his former despair. At that time he was composing his *Penthesilea* and the ambiguities contained in this work can only be explained if we assume that he was changing his views about the relation of God and man at the time when he was writing the play. This tragedy reveals elements of his new faith, while it also exhibits features of his earlier dramas.

Kleist has himself emphasized the close relationship between *Penthesilea* and his next work, *Käthchen von Heilbronn.* He described the heroine of the latter work as the 'obverse of Penthesilea' and wrote, in a letter to Collin on December 8, 1808: 'Denn wer das Käthchen liebt, dem kann die Penthesilea nicht ganz unbegreiflich sein, sie gehören ja wie das + und das—der Algebra zusammen, und sind Ein und dasselbe Wesen, nur unter entgegengesetzten Beziehungen gedacht.' His revaluation of life, which is so strikingly manifested in *Käthchen* began in 1807 when he composed *Penthesilea.*

The letter to Rühle, written in that year, hints at the new direction of his thought. 'Jede erste Bewegung' Kleist says 'alles Unwillkürliche ist schön; und schief und verschroben Alles, so bald es sich selbst begreift. O der Verstand! Der unglückselige Verstand!' The new element that we find in Kleist's thought is contained in the phrase 'alles Unwillkürliche ist schön.' Kleist's distrust of the intellect persists, but now he laments not so much the fact that the mind is incapable of grasping the truth, as the fact that it distorts the beauty of involuntary action. The intellect, too, now represents for him the power of self-comprehension, not, as earlier, the faculty directed towards the understanding of external reality. Clearly, Kleist is under the influence of a new set of philosophical propositions. They are, to a large extent, of his own making, but he also appears to have derived much benefit from his association with Romantic writers, notably with Adam Müller and Schubert.

It would be an over-simplification to call Kleist's thought in his later work 'Romantic'. Just as he had developed his own peculiar view of life from a cursory acquaintance with Kant's philosophy, so he conceived his new ideas without adopting the most characteristic theories of the Romantics. But he was also indebted to Adam Müller's lectures on German science, literature and art held in Dresden in 1806, and to Schubert's lectures on the 'night-side of natural science' of the same year. The result of thse contacts is seen in Kleist's profound and suggestive essay 'Über das Marionettentheater', as well as in *Käthchen von Heilbronn.* An equally important influence on these works appears to have been Schiller's *Über Anmut und Würde,* although again Kleist's remarkable originality must be emphasized. (pp. 31-5)

In his essay **'Über das Marionettentheater'**, Kleist puts forward the view that the puppet possesses [the true expression of grace] in the highest degree and that 'es dem Menschen schlechthin unmöglich wäre, den Gliedermann darin auch nur zu erreichen.' The puppet, he says, is infinitely graceful because it has no will of its own, since it is completely obedient to the superior will that rules it, and because it is 'antigrav', i.e. because it is not tied to earth by the force of gravity—'weil die Kraft, die sie in die Lüfte erhebt, grösser ist, als jene, die sie an die Erde fesselt.' Man's nature is the antithesis of that of the marionette; his body is ruled by the law of gravity and his will obstructs the higher will, the will of God. After reference has been made to the third chapter of the Book of Genesis, Kleist continues: 'Ich sagte, dass ich gar wohl wüsste, welche Unordnungen, in der natürlichen Grazie des Menschen, das Bewusstsein anrichtet'. It is the mind of man, his

knowledge and his will, that disturb the beauty and harmony of his being: 'Wir sehen, dass in dem Masse, als, in der organischen Welt, die Reflexion dunkler und schwächer wird, die Grazie darin immer strahlender und herrschender hervortritt.'

The faculty that produces the highest form of grace for Schiller is just that which obstructs it for Kleist. Since human knowledge, Kleist believed, was imperfect, it disturbed the harmony of man's being, so that, if the integrity of man's character is to be restored, the human race must progress to the achievement of the only true knowledge, which is that of God, or rule it out entirely and so attain to the state of the puppet: 'So findet sich auch, wenn die Erkenntnis gleichsam durch ein Unendliches gegangen ist, die Grazie wieder ein; so, dass sie, zu gleicher Zeit, in demjenigen menschlichen Körperbau am reinsten erscheint, der entweder gar keins, oder ein unendliches Bewusstsein hat, d.h. in dem Gliedermann, oder in dem Gott.—Mithin, sagte ich ein wenig zerstreut, müssten wir wieder von dem Baum der Erkenntnis essen, um in den Stand der Unschuld zurückzufallen?—Allerdings, antwortete er, das ist das letzte Kapitel von der Geschichte der Welt.'

This suggestive conversation, so remarkable for its light and almost ironic treatment of the most profound ideas, gives a good indication of the new direction of Kleist's thought. It reveals that his ideal is now not sublimity, but beauty. The acceptance of the ideal of beauty and of grace presumes a belief in universal harmony and with Kleist it suggests a return to the creed of his youth, the belief in a benevolent Deity ruling the life of man. After completing his tragedies he arrived at the conclusion, as Schiller did, that the highest aim of the dramatist could be achieved 'wenn selbst diese Unzufriedenheit mit dem Schicksal hinwegfällt und sich in die Ahnung oder lieber in ein deutliches Bewusstsein einer teleologischen Verknüpfung der Dinge, einer erhabenen Ordnung, eines gütigen Willens verliert.' Upon the basis of a similar belief Kleist constructed his drama *Käthchen von Heilbronn.*

While Wetter vom Strahl possesses a will of his own and thus obstructs the divine will, Käthchen is a puppet without 'Bewusstsein'. The only character in Kleist's earlier dramas with whom we can compare her in this respect is Agnes in *Die Familie Schroffenstein,* whose trust in the goodness of human beings gives her the beauty that Käthchen possesses by virtue of her naïveté. The difference between Kleist's earlier and his later works lies in the fact that Agnes becomes a tragic victim of circumstances, while Käthchen achieves happiness. The ultimate reason for this difference is the effective intervention of God in the lives of the principal characters, whereas in *Die Familie Schroffenstein* God is silent and even appears to will the tragic catastrophe. Kleist's reassessment of values is seen in his revaluation of the relation between God and man.

When Kleist wrote *Käthchen von Heilbronn* he had also revised his views on human nature. He was no longer obsessed with the frailty of the human intellect and the tragedy of human error. A treatment of these themes is still to be found in the drama, but they do not dominate the mind of the author as they had done in the tragedies, and even in the comedy *Der zerbrochene Krug.* The insistence on

A scene from Prinz Friedrich von Homburg.

human error is now overshadowed by the proof of human strength and certainty. The mind of Wetter vom Strahl is incapable of solving the riddles besetting the characters in this play, but Käthchen's instinct is a safe guide towards happiness. When Kleist wrote his tragedies, he regarded both reason and passion as unreliable faculties. Now he emphasized that man's instinct was unerring and infallible. This is the point where he agreed with the Romantics, above all with Novalis, who had said: 'Mit Instinkt hat der Mensch angefangen, mit Instinkt soll der Mensch endigen. Instinkt ist das Genie im Paradiese, vor der Periode der Selbstabsonderung (Selbsterkenntnis).' This statement recalls to mind the argument in **'Über das Marionettentheater'** and illuminates its meaning.

For this view of the value of instinct Kleist may also have been indebted to Schubert. There has been much discussion of the possible influence of his *Ansichten von der Nachtseite der Naturwissenschaften* on Kleist's later thought, and it has yielded little positive result. It can be said that Schubert's views on somnambulism are unimportant in this connection, since he discussed its pathological nature and treated somnambulists as hypnotic media, aspects which are not to be found in Kleist's use of the phenomenon in **Käthchen von Heilbronn** and **Prinz Friedrich**

von Homburg. It is probable that his knowledge of somnambulism was more immediately personal and that it can be traced to his own experiences and to those of Zschokke, with whom he was associated in Switzerland.

There are other elements in Schubert's work which may have influenced Kleist more strongly and more positively, or, at any rate, may have assisted him in his search for new beliefs. It was Schubert's purpose, in his lectures, to trace 'das älteste Verhältnis des Menschen zu der Natur, die lebendige Harmonie des Einzelnen mit dem Ganzen'. This view, as we have seen, is the basis of Kleist's revived optimism. Furthermore, Schubert discussed the faculties of instinct and will. The latter, he said, developed later in man than the former, and instinct, he asserted, was a safer guide than the other faculty: 'Wir finden selten, dass der natürliche Trieb Täuschungen oder Missgriffen ausgesetzt sei, wohl aber ist dieses in gewisser Hinsicht der Wille'. From the testimony of the **'Marionettentheater'** and of **Käthchen von Heilbronn** we are able to conclude that it was this aspect of Schubert's work which Kleist absorbed, that it was linked in his mind with the conception of a benevolent Deity and that by means of a fusion of these ideas he was able to overcome the pessimism of his youth.

The fundamental unity of Kleist's work, however, is revealed by the fact that this valuation of instinct does not appear for the first time in his later work. It is an essential feature of his tragic representations no less than the cardinal principle of his romantic drama. In his earlier plays it may be discovered in his assessment of 'Gefühl' which signified for him the possession of a profound inward certainty—a faculty as different from passion as it is from the intellect. 'Folge nie,' he wrote in a letter dated January 11-12, 1801, 'dem dunklen Triebe (i.e. passion), der immer zu dem Gemeinen führt . . . Was dein erstes Gefühl Dir antwortet, das tue.' In another letter (January 31, 1801) he wrote: 'Immer nannte er (Brockes) den Verstand kalt und nur das Herz wirkend und schaffend . . . Immer seiner ersten Regung gab er sich ganz hin, das nannte er seinen Gefühlsblick, und ich selbst habe nie gefunden, dass dieser ihn getäuscht habe.' Fundamentally this feeling is the instinctive knowledge of what is right and proper, a 'Rechtsgefühl' as Kleist uses this term. It appears in those of Kleist's characters who reveal the positive aspects of his belief—in Eustache, Sylvester, Agnes and Alkmene. This feeling may become confused, but it suffers confusion only when passion triumphs over it (as in Sylvester) or when the appearances of external reality prove overwhelming (as in Alkmene). In itself it is for Kleist, in his tragic period, the only source of truth. His tragedies depict the contamination of this source by the intervention of a malicious power and by the triumph of suspicion and hatred over love. In *Käthchen von Heilbronn,* on the other hand, the source remains pure because it is protected by a benevolent Deity.

Kleist's fundamentally critical temperament, however, did not allow him to base his philosophy of life permanently on the acceptance of a belief in the miraculous order of things. A more stable affirmation of the values of life is found only in *Prinz Friedrich von Homburg,* where the problem is no longer the relation between God and man, but that between the individual and the State. Here, too, Kleist gives an original presentation of the problem and its solution and neither Adam Müller nor any other thinker of the Romantic era supplied him with ideas or formulae. In this drama, as in his other work, it is Kleist's 'innerstes Wesen' that is the true source of his inspiration. 'Es ist wahr, mein innerstes Wesen liegt darin' he wrote of *Penthesilea* in a letter to Henriette Hendel-Schütz (?) in 1807 and no less is true of his last play. Here Kleist reveals an astonishing sense of balance, in his psychological emphases as well as in his use of formal values. The metaphysical disorders of his youth reverberate only as faint echoes and the fanciful constructions of *Käthchen von Heilbronn* have been put aside. Those 'Romantic' fancies had their educative value for Kleist, for, once achieved they made all further speculation on the subject of the ultimate nature of life unnecessary. Kleist was free to consider life in its practical issues, which the Napoleonic Wars made imperative. This task he performed savagely in *Die Hermannsschlacht* and nobly in *Prinz Friedrich von Homburg.* These two plays, whatever the differences between their moral and their artistic values may be, represent the culmination of Kleist's achievement, the resolution of his life's disharmonies. (pp. 35-9)

E. L. Stahl, in his Heinrich von Kleist's Dramas, *Basil Blackwell, 1948, 144 p.*

Ralph Tymms   (essay date 1955)

[*In the following excerpt, Tymms examines Kleist's link with Romanticism.*]

Heinrich von Kleist's relationship with romanticism is unique. . . . He was not a member of any of the romantic groups, though he was in personal touch with the *Christlich-Deutsche Tischgesellschaft,* a patriotic Prussian club founded in 1811 by Arnim and Adam Müller (the romantic political economist), to which other romantic writers also belonged: but it was probably the militant Junker spirit of the club which most appealed to him. He knew Tieck, and he had collaborated, even before the *Tischgesellschaft,* with Adam Müller in editing periodicals. But most important of his connections with the romantics and their prophets was his acquaintance with G. H. Schubert, whose popular exposition of the wonders of 'animal magnetism' introduced to Kleist the possibility of an emergent second self freed from the substrata of consciousness by the impact of a major emotional crisis. From Schubert too he learned of the sinister relationship between love and cruelty—what Schubert calls 'the long-since acknowledged relationship between sexual desire and murderous desire'. This sensualist-sadistic interpretation of love evidently appealed to his deepest instincts, and colour his dramatic interpretation of the sexual relationship.

His individualistic—indeed, idiosyncratic—attitude to the drama and the problems of characterization had many quite unromantic results, but in itself this individualism might be said to corroborate the romantics' insistence on the artist's arbitrary creative rights. Yet, to the romantics, his laconic but urgent and architectonically deliberate dramatic composition was distasteful—the very opposite to their own formless, drifting, digressive, polymetrical, 'ironical' drama. Nor was there any sign in his work of their favourite motif of Christian (or other) asceticism (which prevails in Tieck's *Genoveva* and almost all of Werner's plays) and he only draws on the resources of the *Märchenwelt* in *Das Käthchen von Heilbronn,* which is his weakest play structurally, and perhaps in other ways, too. Like Werner he does, it is true, project a visionary world unfamiliar to ordinary experience, but, unlike Werner's, his visionary world is an extension of reality, and not its negation, so that it is not unrealistic, but 'super-realistic'. His characters are obsessed, but not by the outside, elemental dark powers which invade man's mind in Tieck's and Hoffmann's tales or in Werner's plays—the demons who possess the Prussians in *Das Kreuz an der Ostsee,* for instance, or Hildegunde, in *Attila*—it is a complex of impulses hitherto latent in their own subconscious minds which takes possession of Kleist's characters.

Kleist was unromantic—and unclassicist, too, for that matter!—in that he was usually untendentious: there is political didacticism in *Die Hermannsschlacht* and, to some extent, in *Prinz Friedrich von Homburg,* but otherwise there is no pragmatism—ethical, æsthetic or philosophical; as a writer he appears indifferent to the acquisition and propagation of *Bildung,* though as a man he thirsted for it—veering, as auto-didacts often do, from one imperfectly understood political or philosophical enthusiasm to its opposite: from the *Aufklärung* rationalism of Wolff to Roman Catholicism, and from a Rousseauesque cult of 'natural' freedom to subservience to the Prussian god-State. But though the lack of pragmatism in his work is unromantic, he is unmistakably romantic in his concern with the play of nerves, the instinctive reactions to an emotional impasse, the disintegration of the poised conscious personality of his characters—in this he is Hoffmann's predecessor—and to display this he devises dramatic situations in which an emotional crisis releases unexpected and discordant aspects of the personality from the substrata of consciousness. The conflicts he presents are in fact predominantly those fought out between the warring 'selves'—the conscious and unconscious 'selves'—within the mind of the same person; and on the result of that struggle depends the outcome of the external conflict, which is really an extension of the inner conflict. This obsession with the involuntary emergence of a 'second self' from the subsconscious is likely to appeal to modern readers of the post-Freudian age more directly than it did to Kleist's contemporaries: today one may feel that this aggression by the subconscious 'second self', and the subordination to it of the normal personality, have a convincing potential realism. Because the normal consciousness is not ordinarily set aside in this way, according to one's common experience, it does not mean that the extreme, the exceptional, case can never happen, especially in the exceptional circumstances which Kleist premises: his innovation is to bring into the purview of poetic drama precisely these states of consciousness in which the normal censorship of the waking mind seems to be in abeyance—in dreams and somnambulistic or hypnotic trances. Automatically the 'noble' code of behaviour enjoined by classicist tragedy is suspended at these times, and the dramatist is concerned, not with the triumph of consciously exerted will-power (as in Corneille's drama, or that of the German baroque dramatist Gryphius) but with the triumph of the emergent personality-traits from the dark cellars of the mind, the submerged regions of the consciousness; they may well be ignoble, as in the case of Friedrich of Homburg, or maniacally horrible exaggerations of sadistic impulses, as in *Penthesilea.* But the main point is that Kleist, by showing the play of involuntary impulses taking precedence over conscious decisions, is not contradicting reality, but revealing it, though in a heightened, even exaggerated form: his dramas are certainly not fantastic visions without a basis of reality, as Werner's are. That Kleist himself knew perfectly well what he was doing appears from the letter he wrote to Goethe when he sent him *Penthesilea*—quite the least suitable of all his plays for the purpose of winning over the *Dichterfürst,* since it culminates in an outbreak of maniacal fury. The operative sentence in the letter is the one in which he speaks of the situation in the play as a conceivable projection of reality: 'As it stands here, one will perhaps feel obliged to acknowledge the premises as possible, and subsequently not start back in alarm when the conclusion is drawn.'

For our present purposes we need concern ourselves only with those among Kleist's plays in which this theme of 'subconscious aggression' is clearly presented, since it has such relevance to romantic practice, especially in the fiction of Hoffmann, who also interested himself (as Kleist did in a much more desultory way) in 'animal magnetism'. Kleist's first play, *Familie Schroffenstein* (written 1801, published 1803), is not one of these 'subconscious' plays: in fact it is in every sense a minor one, an horrific variation on the Romeo and Juliet theme, originally given a Spanish setting—obviously appropriate for the theme of revenge—which was then changed by a friend, with Kleist's consent, into a Tieckian Old-German milieu by the simple expedient of altering the names. Abruptly, with his second play, **Robert Guiskard** (written 1802-3, destroyed 1803, partly rewritten 1808), or what exists of it, Kleist emerges as a great dramatist. Even the ten scenes of the existing fragment present an action of stupendous force and tension, and of extraordinary simplicity. This in itself is not typical of Kleist's technique: there is no suggestion here of the hero's normal heroic personality being overthrown by subconscious impulses: and perhaps it was for this very reason, because its simplicity was too much out of keeping with the dramatist's own complicated nature, that he destroyed the first version. Far from being overwhelmed by involuntary motives, the Norman Duke, who is the hero of the play, enjoys perfect conscious mastery over himself and over his people: not until the last scene of the fragment does he appear from his tent, but from the first moment he has dominated the play in the imagination of the crowd, who have come, like the crowd in the opening scene of Sophocles' *Oedipus Tyrannus,* to bewail to their prince the pestilence that has been visited upon their people. The parallel with Oedipus is stressed—Guiskard is a 'Titan of will-power', with much of the classical, or classicist (Corneillean!) demigod about him, whereas the main characters in his other plays are, on the contrary, 'romantics', the creatures of involuntary impulse and mood, who may cede the proud classicist mastery over themselves.

Nor is Kleist's comedy **Der zerbrochene Krug** (written 1803 and, after a long interruption, 1806) one of the 'romantic' plays in this sense: for one thing it was written to order, and lacks the spontaneity which is an agreeable feature of so much romantic writing. It is a phenomenally ingenious play, which shows to perfection Kleist's genius for retardation and complication, but without losing his grip on the compactly developing plot: the vital piece of information which must bring the play to a close as soon as it is divulged is most ingeniously, though with apparent inevitability, held back by the circumstance that of the five main characters, two conceal the truth for opposite reasons, and the three others, who try to discover it, also do so for opposite reasons: the result is that the same clues in this 'detective-comedy' (set in seventeenth-century Holland) are interpreted differently by everyone concerned.

Kleist's version of the old classical dramatic theme of Amphitryon (1807) gives him the opportunity of prying into the hearts of the three main characters in the traditional imbroglio: he observes their reactions to the respective psychological calamities which befall each one. The god Jupiter visits Amphitryon's wife Alkmene in her husband's form: she is deceived by the imposture. Amphityron's calamity is evident, and for modern taste his plight is not suited for comedy, since he is too noble a man to play the role of comic cuckold. Alkmene's calamity is much more subtle and *'interessant'*: her situation resembles that of Kleist's psychologically overwhelmed, hypnotized, or somnambulistic characters in other plays, since she has committed adultery unwittingly, and with no sense of guilt, as if in a trance; her gradual awareness of what has happened wakens her, as she might be wakened from a dream, while the shattering truth is divulged little by little, with Kleist's usual cruel delaying technique. Even the god is changed from the light-hearted libertine of the legend into a complicated, rather neurotic personage, with much of the German romantic in his temperament: his calamity is the discovery that the deceived husband has triumphed in the end, since in her heart Alkmene was faithful to Amphitryon even when, unconsciously, she committed adultery; the god is left to bewail his loneliness, the prisoner of his own divinity and power.

Before going on to the one pronouncedly political play, and the three in which the distinctively Kleistian emergence of the subconscious secondary personality plays the main part, it may be remarked that the only other literary genre which Kleist used was the *Novelle* (the short story form in which a remarkable event is told with at least apparent objectivity, and in which characterization and editorial comments are alike neglected, or implied only). Kleist shows in the *Novelle* very much the same qualities as he does in the dramas: immensely dramatic, terrifying situations arise, in which the normal personality may be thrown out of its normal balance. In **Michael Kohlhaas** (printed as a fragment in 1808, then completely in a collected volume, 1810) the normally amenable characteristics of a simple peasant horse-dealer are overwhelmed by violent and ferocious traits, evoked by the series of injustices he suffers at the hands of a local squire: he loses his sense of proportion, and his indignation culminates in the furious conviction that justice is dead in the world, and that it is his divine mission to avenge it with fire and sword. Consequently he sets himself up as a self-styled vice-regent of God on earth, or avenging archangel; but he becomes progressively 'possessed' by the obsessive instincts of revenge: instead of controlling them, he becomes their slave and is borne along by seemingly impersonal forces (though in fact of course they emanate all too clearly from his own mind), and he is swept to his doom, the victim of his own disintegrated nature. A second *Novelle*, **'Die Marquise von O. . . . '** *(1808)*, reverts to the situation in which Alkmene found herself when she was gradually awakened from her trance-like unawareness of guilt to the hideous realization of the truth: but in this case the heroine has literally been in a trance when raped by a man whose identity she cannot for a time discover; the realization of her plight and of the man's identity are, of course, the secrets which Kleist divulges only with agonizing deliberation and hesitations.

The first of Kleist's final group of four dramas is **Penthesilea** *(1808)*, based on an Ancient Greek subject. It culminates in the appalling scene in which the heroine, an Amazonian queen, joins with her hounds in tearing her lover, the young Greek hero Achilles, in pieces: the purpose of the preceding action is to show how this monstrous conclusion comes about. Kleist shows the accumulative exacerbation of conflicting impulses within her mind, as passionate love for Achilles overwhelms her mind when she first catches sight of him, and comes into violent conflict with the acquired characteristics of her Amazonian self, her duties as a vestal warrior-queen. Now the authority of her conscious mind is shattered by the surge of instinctive desire for the godlike youth who (as her reason tells her) is her bitterest foe. The insoluble problem has no conciliatory, other-worldly outcome, as it has in the almost identical situation of Werner's play *Wanda:* no compromise between love and hate is possible here; instead they alternate, as Penthesilea's conscious and subconscious 'selves' take it in turns to be in control. Finally she is carried away by the maniacal turbulence of her instinctive self to slay her lover with bloodthirsty fury; then, when she awakes from her access of blood-lust to learn what she has done under the domination of the frantic 'other self' of her dark impulses, she kills herself, but as if for the crime of another person, for which she is not responsible. Achilles, for his part, even before the ghastly culminating attack, has to play the part of the suppliant lover, humouring the distracted woman, as she goes through the preliminary stages of alternating violent love and more violent hate, related in a sinister fashion, as alternative aspects of her emotional reaction to him.

This bizarre situation is reversed in Kleist's next drama: **Das Käthchen von Heilbronn** (published in part 1808, wholly 1810), for here the man is the active party in the almost equally strange and sinister love-play: the woman's contribution is a dog-like self-abasement as morbid as Penthesilea's sadistic ferocity, though not as destructive—she is the negative to Penthesilea's positive character, and her love expresses itself masochistically. But as a play **Käthchen** lacks the dramatic urgency of **Penthesilea:** for one thing the author blurs the main outlines of its plot by introducing meretricious romantic *Märchen*-themes—prophetic dreams, a cherub, and (in the original version) a malicious water-sprite—to eke out the primary subject. The result is that the play is artistically a hybrid affair, part-Kleistian drama, part-*Märchen,* and part-*Ritterstück* (it has a romantic-medieval setting, complete with a session of the *Vehmgericht,* the secret society which meted out justice, by the Emperor's authorization). Precisely because of this largely irrelevant *Märchen-* and romantic-medieval material, and the spectacular effects, the play was the most popular with his contemporaries of anything Kleist wrote. But the strange relationship between the hero, the young knight Wetter vom Strahl, and the girl Käthchen is not, for the most part, to be explained by *Märchen*-enchantments, though she does undoubtedly behave as if he had bewitched her, and he has to defend himself against the accusation; it is an hypnotic—or (to use the romantic word) 'magnetic'—correspondence which subordinates her mind to his, and he is unaware of the power he subconsciously exerts over her until she instinctively answers his cross-examination while she lies in a trance-like state of apparent sleep—a condition in which, as experimental psychologists of the romantic age asserted, the magnetic subject is aware of everything the hypnotist does and says. The telepathic correspondence of dreams which—as her answers now reveal to his conscious awareness—had brought them together before their first actual meeting, also probably belongs to the wonders of 'magnetism' rather than to those of the *Märchen.*

Romantic patriotism and the apotheosis of the 'Old Germany' of the Middle Ages are extended in *Die Hermannsschlacht* (written 1808, published 1821) to the subject of Arminius and his victory over the Roman legions in A.D. 9: the play is a monument to a phase of political enthusiasm in Kleist's life, and he is chiefly concerned with an anachronistic parallel to events of his own day, and with arousing positive action among the Germans against the Napoleonic hegemony; love appears only as a marginal theme. Kleist's efforts to preach a holy war against the French had no practical result, for—by an irony of fate—this *Tendenzdrama* was not performed until more than half a century later (1863, or possibly slightly before).

Kleist did not live to see the fall of Napoleon: he committed suicide in 1811; but in his last (and most mature) play, *Prinz Friedrich von Homburg* (written 1808, published 1821), he turned, as a last resort, to an optimistic vision of the eventual triumph of the Hohenzollerns' military state, to be brought about by the virtues of the traditional Prussian cult of obedience and duty. There is less ferocity here than in his other great dramas, and a more reasonable and conciliatory spirit is shown in the relationship between the erring subject and the monarch (who is also his military commander) than might have been thought conceivable from the author of *Penthesilea.* Yet there is the same surrender to involuntary impulses as in other plays: Homburg commits his crime against the State and his own duty because he had been in a semi-somnambulistic condition when he received his orders, and his mind was still obsessed by the visions—half-real and half-imaginary—of his preceding, wholly somnambulistic condition (in which he is discovered when the play opens). The reason for this somnambulism is not clear: perhaps the effect of love on a hypersensitive mind; but there is no ambiguity about the effect of the sentence of death passed on him for disobeying his orders (even though this leads to victory!). He is dealt a shattering blow, which completes the disintegration of his personality, and he vacillates hopelessly and abjectly between instinctive fear of death and obedience to the code of behaviour in which he has been brought up as a Junker officer; only the appeal to his own voluntary sense of right and honour makes it possible for his normal personality-traits to resume control, after the painful tug-of-war between the rival tyrannies of his 'outer' and 'inner' natures (to use G. H. Schubert's phrases, in his disquisition on the 'shadow-self' which emerges from man's 'lower', or involuntary centres of his nature). Once the conflict within Homburg's mind is decided, and he accepts the justice of his sentence, the outer conflict automatically finds its outcome, too, and the Elector of Brandenburg, who has passed the sentence of death, can now set it aside—though with a characteristically Kleistian refinement of cruelty, even in this moment of clemency!

The conciliatory ending to *Homburg* was not to correspond to the close of Kleist's life: his death by his own hand was the climax to a—brief—life-time's abrupt reverses of opinion, it was the tragic solution to the otherwise apparently insoluble problem of his tormented personality. Practically unknown to his contemporaries, he died one of the very greatest of all German dramatists, showing promise of even greater achievements in the new phase which seemed to open with *Homburg.* (pp. 315-24)

> *Ralph Tymms, "The Drama in the Romantic Period: Zacharias Werner and Heinrich von Kleist," in his German Romantic Literature, Methuen & Co. Ltd., 1955, pp. 298-324.*

Swana L. Hardy (essay date 1967)

[*In the following essay, Hardy discusses Kleist's conversion of personal experience into art and suggests that in his work he presents "the paradigm of the existentialist interpretation of man."*]

In the preface to the collected works of Heinrich von Kleist, published in 1826, Ludwig Tieck recommends the enigmatic figure of the author in the following words: "Wenn er auch nicht von der freiesten Höhe die Kunst übersah und beherrschte, . . . so war er doch auf eine Weise, die zu loben ist, ein grossartiger Manierist."

The formulation of mannerism, by Ernst Robert Curtius [in "Manierismus," in *Europäische Literatur und lateinisches Mittelalter,* 1954] and his school, as a recurring constant in the history of European thought, and its relevance to the critical recognition of the major trends in our present era have sharpened our ear for the apparently contradictory way in which Tieck applies this term to Kleist— "ein grossartiger Manierist." Curtius, it seems, has not been the first to free the concept of mannerism from its exclusive application to a certain period in the history of art, nor from its more popular use as a disparaging attribute of an artificial pseudo-art. Whilst an authoritative study has not yet been made of the history of the words "Manier," "Manierist," "Manierismus," there is evidence— and not just in Tieck alone—that with the romantics *Manier* becomes a descriptive, nonevaluating category of style. It moves into the critical proximity of words such as "allegory," "irony," "conceit," "Witz," "Absicht," and "Modernität," parallel to its original use by Vasari as *maniera nuova.* It is, however, surprising that amongst the more recent contributions pleading the case of mannerism as an anticlassical art style in its own right—as in the study *Romantik und Manierismus* by Marianne Thalmann—little attention has been paid to Kleist, who stands as a key witness in the case. I should like therefore to single out those areas in Kleist's work which most clearly bear the imprint of a mannerist style and process of creation—above all his imagery, his relationship to nature and the world of objects, and the function of language. Before doing so, however, I have to recall those features in Kleist's life and experience which lend the stamp of legitimate necessity to his idiosyncratic use of literary forms— which, in short, make his mannerist traits more than just an artificial extravagance.

The picture which we have of him, even if it were supported by more than that single authentic miniature, comprises features of puzzling contradiction. He is described as childlike, companionable, and gay, yet subject to sudden fits of withdrawal. His simplicity and modesty arouse compassion in some, while his impatience, intolerance, and haughtiness exasperate others. He deliberately ignores the present possibilities of the theater, yet he complains at the total lack of recognition encountered amongst his fellows and—worse still—the rejection of his efforts by the papal authority of Weimar. His demands on love and friendship are absolute, yet he is unable to give himself; he flees from final commitment. Strange and lonely, he travels constantly all over Europe. Although in this incessant *Wanderschaft* we recognize a basic symbol of the romantic form of life, it is not a happy pilgrimage, confident of its goal. It is the lonely trail of a man without a home, a man cast out by his own sentence. The springs of these discrepancies lie, I suggest, in the unconditional claims of an existence for which the dictates of what Kleist ambiguously calls *Gefühl* is the only confirmation of the self. Neither society, which had lost its organic structure, nor nature, which the city dweller did not know intimately any longer, could provide secure scaffolding to build his life. It is the portrait of a man who tries to draw an ultimate certainty out of the unconscious and the unconscionable, who is prepared to approach the problem of his own existence as others have approached that of their art—as a deliberate act and a bid for self-realization in an incoherent universe. To determine his own life—that is the extent of the freedom which Kleist sought to realize and the cause wherein Brentano, and many others, detected his boundless vanity, *grenzenlose Eitelkeit.*

It was a vanity without blindness: a lonely, heroic, and vulnerable attempt to write the book of his own life, to formulate what was unutterable—*den unaussprechlichen Menschen*—in a world of obstacles and disconnected hazards where such endeavor is put endlessly on trial. This is the basic theme, the *Generalbass,* of all his works. Kleist's vanity lies deeper than self-deception and goes further than the baroque conceit of the world's *vanitas* which had its counterpoint in the assurance of God's eternity. Kleist's vanity is the infinitely painful, infinitely glorious freedom of the prisoner.

Under this perspective the labyrinthine chart of his life acquires meaning. How deeply his imprisonment in Fort Joux and Chalons in 1807, where he was suspected of espionage by an arbitrary decree, symbolizes the reality of his situation may be read from the fact that in eight of his sixteen dramas and *Novellen* imprisonment forms a critical motive of the work. In the same way Kleist compared the subjection of Prussia under a foreign tyranny with that of the German tribes under Roman rule, in **Die Hermannsschlacht,** and identified both with the essential human situation.

Kleist's suicide must therefore be seen as the extreme and final step in the attempt to realize his own life. "Eine Tat wie diese, steigt, wenn wir sie vernehmen, mit einem heiligen Erschrecken in unsre Seele," says Tieck. In his death Kleist is finally "making" his life, in the original meaning of the poetic act. Arthur Henkel points out [in "Nachwort," in *Heinrich von Kleist, Penthesilea, Prinz Friedrich*

> **Kleist's work stands as the most revealing allegory of his own existence.**
>
> —*Swana L. Hardy*

---

von Homburg, 1961] that the figure of the mediator, who stands in the very center of the Christian process of redemption, is always missing in Kleist's significantly Biblical imagery. Kleist places his trust in man's own power, more precisely in the poet's own power, to reconcile the dictates of emotion with the challenge of consciousness—a second eating from the tree of knowledge in an effort to regain the paradise of grace.

In the image of flight Kleist describes the serenity of his ultimate decision: "Da unsere Seelen sich, wie zwei fröhliche Luftschiffer, über die Welt erheben," he writes in his farewell to Sophie Haza-Müller. Yet when in his dramas man achieves the rare and final reconciliation, whether in dream or death, the same imagery of weightless movement, of wing and sail, is used to describe the beatitude of free existence. Even Achilles is granted the dignity of that freedom when Penthesilea says: "Frei wie ein Vogel geht er von mir weg" (l. 2918). Just as the prisoner stands for captive life, the Cherub, foreshadowing Rilke's angel, Trakl's *Vogelzug,* becomes Kleist's symbol of freedom. "Mein Cherubim und Seraph, wie lieb ich Dich!"—these words end that baroque cumulation of metaphors written to Henriette Vogel in the last days of their life. Did Kleist ever ponder the significance of the name of his death companion? He had found in her "eine Freundin . . . deren Seele wie ein junger Adler fliegt, . . . die meine Traurigkeit als eine höhere, festgewurzelte und unheilbare begreift." The brilliantly winged Cherub who directs Käthchen's destiny is the guardian angel of a heart that, though questioned and challenged from all sides, is without self-consciousness—*selig in sich selbst.* The image of angelic flight is again evoked in the last monologue of the **Prinz von Homburg**—"Es wachsen Flügel mir an beiden Schultern, / Durch stille Ätherräume schwingt mein Geist" (ll. 1833-34)—and conceptually merged with the image of the ship slipping from its moorings—"Und wie ein Schiff, vom Hauch des Winds entführt, / Die muntre Hafenstadt versinken sieht, / So geht mir dämmernd alles Leben unter" (ll. 1835-37). In the moment when life can be thrown off—"leicht und freudig weggeworfen"—existence is confirmed of its immorality: "Nun, o Unsterblichkeit, bist du ganz mein" (l. 1830). The Prince achieves the state of serene equilibrium in the gesture of abandoning the web in which he is tied through love, fame, ambition, and vitality; he swims "silbern, leicht, ein Fisch" into the realm of infinite freedom. What else but "boundless vanity" to determine his own death, what else but suicide as the ultimate act of freedom makes the Prince choose death when the freedom of decision is tossed back to him?

Kleist's work stands as the most revealing allegory of his own existence. One might say that basic experience is the initial impetus of all art, even where the author assiduously seeks to eliminate every trace of his personal experience. Yet it is the stigma of the mannerist that his work is related to nothing but his own *Grunderfahrung,* that it is self-formulation in the face of the impossible and the absurd. The paradoxical attempt becomes the prerequisite of life. In converting his individual experience into the *Gestalt* of art, Kleist becomes the representative of modern man and the observer of his condition at the same time. It remains to show the manner in which the *Kunstgestalt* realizes such a claim.

Kleist's imagery does not evoke the richness of "world"; it is never the spontaneous response to a singular and natural impulse. [Friedrich Gundolf in *Heinrich von Kleist,* 1922] was the first to observe that Kleist's images are not primarily symbols nor carriers of definite meanings; they are associations freed from their natural context and forced into artificial, even monstrous compounds. The function of imagery is a purely dynamic one: to swell, to heighten, and to exaggerate. Kleist, the mannerist, prefers the intelligible allusion to the immediacy of perception. Angel and prisoner, the two examples which I have chosen above, are related topics of allegorical significance. His Cherub has little in common with the Christian, not even necessarily religious concept. The mannerist "borrows" his imagery in order to reinterpret the natural context in the light of a new and often artificial relation. Beside Bible and Christian theology it is mythology and history that invite such topical reinterpretation. The subjective arbitrariness of an almost sacrilegious choice—as in the essay on the **"Marionettentheater,"** or in the overtones of Christian passion in the *Prinz von Homburg,* and of Christian redemption in the last scene of *Amphitryon*—such choice and the intellectual exercise which it involves have often provoked an indignant rejection of mannerist art. For Kleist, however, the subjective relevance is all important, since the external world is blind to the individual.

A similar principle of selection may be detected in the choice of subjects. All of Kleist's works were conceived through contact with a problem which had already been formed: *Der zerbrochene Krug* was stimulated by a painting and a drama of antiquity, *Amphitryon* by Molière's comedy, his *Novellen* and *Anekdoten* by chronicles, police reports, newspapers, and, most of all, by literary history. The fascination and value of the literary allusion lies in the possibility of retaining enough substance of the original in order to add an antithetic counterpoint to the variation of the theme. As a result the image or topic becomes ambiguous and enigmatic, becomes a conceit the meaning of which cannot be perceived without intellectual effort. If, for example, through the choice of words Achilles in *Penthesilea* acquires the characteristics of the eighteenth-century gallant in addition to the features of the heroic ascendancy of Hellenic man, the thematic conclusiveness is by no means impaired by the anachronism.

A further example of Kleist's functional integration of the literary allusion into the drama comes to mind: the monologue in the mountain cave by Graf Wetter vom Strahl in *Käthchen von Heilbronn* (II, 1). The Count recognizes his love for Käthchen after being acquitted by the secret court. Yet, what should be the unmediated language of the heart which is alone with itself becomes an exercise in rhetoric: "Nun will ich hier wie ein Schäfer liegen und klagen . . . " (l. 660). The Count forces his imagination to build a pastoral scene for his feelings, staffed with the cheap accessories of literary convention: rocks, goats, sheep, white linen, red ribbons, sighs, and Zephyr. He wishes to read the chapter on Emotions in the book of his mother tongue; he indulges in a poor rhyme: "Käthchen, Mädchen, Käthchen." We know that Kleist was able to write the pure language of the heart with unerring mastership. Did taste and talent fail him in this scene? Or does the formal discord convey a message of dramatic significance? Are the Count's feelings perhaps as uncertain and "borrowed" as the images he finds for them? At the end of his monologue the Count reflects the superiority of his social status and ancestry over the supposed daughter of the simple craftsman in Heilbronn. He would not make her his wife, though her qualities would remain the guiding star in his search for his wife and mother of future generations. As he deceives himself in the borrowed cloak of a literary cliché he will later deceive himself in the choice of Kunigunde for his wife. Where he suffers from the impersonal character of the language which seems so far from the truth of his feelings, we hear through the baroque cascade the note of reservation, of withdrawal from final commitment, of uncertainty of emotion.

In this formal use of images the quality of the things themselves is reduced and their natural environment ignored. Significantly [as noted by Marianne Thelmenn in *Romzatik und Manierismus* (1963) and Heinz Ide in *Der junge Kleist* (1961)] we rarely find an immediate impression of nature in Kleist's letters, nor does it ever stimulate his writing. Like many romantics Kleist was a man of the city, of pavement, office, and rooms. His poetry does not contain the smallest element which falls within Emil Staiger's definition [in *Grundbegriffe der Poetik,* 1963] of *das Lyrische.* Kleist has no eyes for locality, for natural environment, for life as it is lived around him. In dramas and *Novellen* the objects of nature are transformed into significant images of merely emblematic character. Thus the trees, under which heroes and lovers dream, and the mountain cave, where the secret designs of love or hatred are revealed, form a recurrent pattern throughout Kleist's writings, resembling the topical localities of the baroque. Light and darkness are perhaps the most persistently used phenomena of nature, yet they never carry a mere atmospheric function: the sun over the battlefield of Fehrbellin becomes the symbol of the brilliance of Homburg's destination; here his life stands at its zenith, whereas the torches had cast a deceptive light over the scene of his dream. When this dream is reconciled with reality in one festive moment, the palace illuminates itself in all its windows.

The objects of the world have lost their original function in Kleist's work; they exist for man only in their fateful significance. At best, they are indifferent, at their worst, threatening and challenging the innermost certainty of man—as evidenced by the ring which compromises Littegarde, or by the golden initial in the diadem of Labdakus, Amphitryon's gift to Alkmene. Artificial and intellectual relations are superimposed on the natural function of objects, which no longer consists of representing the world as a coherent and intelligible entity. Things become ciphers, and man is called upon to acknowledge and read their message in order to confirm his own existence in the face of the ambiguous evidence—like chain, glove, and wreath, the insignia of honor, love, and fame as well as of the changing favors of kings and princes; ambiguous evidence—like the secret message Kohlhaas triumphantly destroys before the eyes of the *Kurfürst* of Saxonia.

Kleist's dramatic form similarly ignores the given code. Its structure is symbolically related to the demands of the individual. The atectonic composition of his dramas reflects its intrinsic necessity perhaps most clearly in **Penthesilea**: the drama precipitates towards its end without the halting structure of acts; however, this cataract from scene to scene is counteracted by the slow and laborious investigation into the riddle of the heart. Max Kommerell recognized in this investigation the basic dramatic situation into which Kleist casts his characters—if we can speak of characters. The questioning, the trial, forms the most persistent formal motive in Kleist's work. His drama is therefore eminently the drama of language. This does not mean that Kleist's dramas are *Lesedramen* and unsuitable for the stage. It literally means the drama of language. Man is challenged to formulate himself without knowing the vocabulary. Speech, the instrument of language, is accompanied by the either confirming or contradictory language of gestures. The daring with which Kleist imposes a highly subjective form on the given instrument has been investigated in many studies [such as Karl Ludwig Schneider's "Heinrich von Kleist. Über ein Ausdrucksprinzip seines Stils," in *Vier Reden*]. The "innere Form des Deutschen" truly becomes the inner form of Kleist. Outstanding amongst these studies is Max Kommerell's essay "Die Sprache und das Unaussprechliche" [in *Geist und Buchstabe der Dichtung*, 1956] where he analyzes the two levels of language which man achieves in Kleist's work: on the one hand the tortured elliptical and disjunctive language of a consciousness that cannot reconcile "das Gefühl, das in deiner Brust lebt" with the paradox of the logic of facts; on the other hand the immediate simplicity of self-expression in the proximity of love, dream, and death when innermost certainty finds a momentary and incorruptible realization in language. Käthchen speaks it in the dream dialogue under the elder tree, Alkmene in her trusting revelation to Jupiter, Penthesilea when she confides her heart and motive to Achilles. In these rare moments the schism between man and world, the schism in man himself is healed. The magnificent Pomegranate whose wandering shadow counts the time for Jeronimo and Josephe, grows for the lovers in a valley of Eden.

Language, where it is not the normative instrument of intellectual security but the continuous process of self-formulation in the face of a discordant world, acquires features of what the age of the baroque called Gongorism. The communicative value shrinks with the coherence of structure while the figures of speech gain a life of their own to such a degree that they border on chaos. [As Wolfgang Kayser has noted in *Das sprachliche Kunstwerk* (1951), we] discover in Kleist's hypotactical style the rhetoric figures favored by baroque writers. Syntactically most dis-

tinctive are hyperbaton and antithesis; we find asyndetic progressions, and in the use of the oxymoron a daring crossing of metaphors. In its open and dynamically interlocked character Kleist's language achieves an extraordinary degree of intellectual tension and thereby of dramatic relevance. Here again the artifact is preferred to the natural. The inclusion of grotesque distortion, of outrage and horror, of ugliness, is common to all mannerist art. Deliberately language is pushed to its limits and often beyond.

The mannerist imposes his law on chaos because he does not know of any other law. He perceives himself as thrown into consciousness without support from a meaningless, absurd, and hostile world. Yet this world paradoxically becomes the very prerequisite of his existence. [According to Gustav René Hocke in "Über Manierismus in Tradition und Moderne," *Merkur* X (April 1956), it] is this paradox which creates the mannerist style. Man as his own creator—that glorious attempt becomes the prophetic role of the artist who realizes himself in his language. This kind of monstrous narcissism—as Emil Staiger notes [in *Vier Reden*]—does not only characterize Kleist; it is a reflection in which we recognize the features of our own age. Language in Kleist's work becomes the gesture of man who is unable to define his existence in terms of a given natural or metaphysical order, yet who in rare moments achieves the expression of pure and weightless grace.

If we are able to perceive in Kleist and his work the para-

Robert E. Glenny on Kleist's characters:

None of Kleist's characters is solipsistic. Rather, they seem to be possessed by a painful and even pathological sensitivity to the power which resides in the very subjectivity of others. The battle goes beyond the compulsive need to control one's own experience; the battle extends further, from the need to control the content and the knowledge of others to the need to control the experience of others as well. It is apparent in Kleist's works that the interaction between two individuals is not only a social encounter but frequently also an existential confrontation . . . Others are the entire significant environment of Kleist's individuals. The jockeying for control of what is, is at times on such a basic level as to be equated with a battle for existence of the self, certainly a battle for sanity. For Kleist, the distinction between sanity and existence is often a useless one to make, because many of his characters are fragile enough to have not only their sanity shaken when their experience and ordering of the world is called into question; their whole sense of who they are is threatened at the same time. . . . Kleist's characters seem to feel that they are entirely too vulnerable in their own experience and identity. The victories that his characters seek are not moral victories but rather the successful defense of fragile experience or the successful manipulation of the experience of others. The problems which confront Kleist's characters are never solely the result of internal conflicts. This is the battle by characters to control their own experience by controlling the experience of others.

Robert E. Glenny, in his The Manipulation of Reality in Works by Heinrich von Kleist, *Peter Lang, 1987.*

digm of the existentialist interpretation of man—which seems indeed a second eating from the tree of knowledge—our understanding of Kleist as a mannerist will come to a full comprehension. This view is justified by the fact that our own century has defined its artistic expression as mannerist in style, whilst its philosophical basis is existentialism—in whatever school of thought. The rejection by Goethe—from which Kleist suffered so much, since his writing had become the condition of his life—this rejection was without doubt prompted by Goethe's shocked recognition that in Kleist the myth of man's own creativity, which Goethe himself had youthfully helped to create, had led to an image of man whose existence defined itself as a free, unlimited consciousness imprisoned in an indifferent and discordant world. (pp. 203-13)

> Swana L. Hardy, "Heinrich von Kleist: Portrait of a Mannerist," in Studies in Romanticism, Vol. VI, No. 4, Summer, 1967, pp. 203-13.

John Gearey (essay date 1968)

[*In the following excerpt, Gearey suggests that Kleist's acceptance of Kant's philosophy brought "no new and less anxious sense of reality, . . . but the same pattern of relentless frustration and opposition."*]

[It] is true that the ideas Kleist found in Kant destroyed many of his strongest beliefs, but not quite in the way that his own account of the crisis in his thought would imply. The *Critique of Pure Reason* did not, as Kleist seems to suggest, break down a door behind which he was innocently standing, rather it opened a door against which he was heavily leaning. The essay on happiness ["**Aufsatz, den sichern Weg des Glücks zu finden**"] leaves no doubt that learning, knowledge, and reason, besides their positive value as guides to truth, served Kleist also as preventive measures against error and disappointment. To quote . . . from that work: "Wie oft gründet sich das Unglück eines Menschen bloß darin, daß er den Dingen unmögliche Wirkungen zuschrieb, oder aus Verhältnissen falsche Resultate zog, und sich darinnen in seinen Erwartungen betrog. Wir werden uns seltner irren, mein Freund, wir durchschauen' dann die Geheimnisse der physischen wie der moralischen Welt, bis' dahin, versteht sich, wo der ewige Schleier über sie waltet." With guidance from reason, the individual could formerly avoid drawing false conclusions or attributing impossible effects to things. Now, after the Kant crisis and the fall of Reason, he was almost bound to err in his judgments, unless he refrained completely from making judgments, which in reality is virtually impossible, or relied solely on chance, which is highly precarious.

But the fact that the human mind was unable to penetrate beyond appearances was not in itself a problem, at least not at the immediate level. It was not one for Kant himself. What made it an acute problem for Kleist, however, was the initial assumption that the world of appearances was somehow an opposing force against which the individual required security and protection. If Kant could read his own works, as it were, and remain undisturbed by their

implications, it was not simply because, with the exact logic of the philosopher, he was able to keep separate in his mind the practical and the metaphysical applications of his theories but also because, born into the relatively ordered world of the early eighteenth century, it would matter little if he did or not. He could afford to prove that man was incapable of grasping the true nature of the things around him, for these things, if incomprehensible in themselves, would nevertheless seem to the rational mind in a stable environment to be ordered and meaningful in appearance, and it could be assumed that they were likewise so in essence. Nothing had really changed. But order and purpose were the very things which Kleist did *not* see or sense in the world about him. To have it proved to his mind and in his new day that the external world reflects the absolute plan in creation would have been, not a saving factor, as it was for Kant, but an additional recognition more confusing than the first. If his own world of appearances was any indication of the world of essences, then Kleist would have had to conclude that there was no plan or meaning at all in creation. He did not take this most modern of metaphysical steps, although some of his dramas and stories show him tottering on the verge of doing so. Rather he left the question open and regarded the world around him, if not as a meaningless, certainly as a strange design, and hoped for a better existence on another star.

And if it seems strange that the *Critique of Pure Reason* could be read as a critique of practical understanding, in the case of Kleist it really is not strange. And perhaps the best way to illustrate the point is to bring up another aspect of the problem that is even more surprising—namely, why he should have experienced the contact with Kant as a clash or crisis in the first place, either on the absolute *or* the immediate level. Though he himself claimed that the new critical philosophy had suddenly broken in and upset the security of his moral and intellectual life, in reality his position had not been entirely secure, for he had harbored some doubts, nor was the crisis so abrupt, for he had anticipated to some extent the arguments that were to cause it. There are two letters which suggest this quite clearly. In the one, dated February 5, 1801, he confesses to his sister that his interest in learning and knowledge has waned, and since the letter was written some time before the crisis, it would stand in contrast to his claim that truth had always and constantly been his only and highest goal. He admits in this letter that he finds life a difficult game, for, as he says, man is called upon again and again to draw a card and yet does not know what trump is. "Selbst die Säule, an welcher ich mich sonst in dem Strudel des Lebens hielt, wankt—Ich meine, die Liebe zu' den Wissenschaften . . . es ist ein bekannter Gemeinplatz, daß das Leben ein schweres Spiel sei; und warum ist es schwer? Weil man beständig und immer von neuem eine Karte ziehen soll und doch nicht weiß, was Trumpf ist; ich meine darum, weil man beständig und immer von neuem handeln soll und doch nicht weiß, was recht ist." And in the other letter, written September 15, 1800, more than a year before the crisis, he actually dismisses the concept of perfectibility—supposedly the basis of his philosophy—as unimportant. It is fruitless, he says, to ponder the destiny of our eternal existence, to attempt to discover whether the enjoyment of happiness, as Epicurus said, or the attainment of perfection, as Leibnitz believed, or the fulfillment of our duty, as Kant assures us, is the ultimate goal of man: "Über den Zweck unseres *ewigen* Daseins nachzudenken . . . das ist selbst für Männer unfruchtbar und oft verderblich." Yet when shown that he could not know this destiny, he felt profoundly disturbed.

This is not to accuse Kleist of self-contradiction or faulty logic. What it does show, however, is that the Kant crisis itself, its very pattern, was influenced by those same emotional factors which were at work in his early thinking. He had emphasized the threat of opposition, of unforeseen circumstances, so strongly in his view of life that, almost instinctively, he would regard the conflict with Kant as a sudden stroke of fate, whereas in fact the breaking-down was a gradual process. The whole matter was a dramatization of reality, but, what is much more important, it was the kind of dramatization that perfectly suited his manner of thinking. In the deepest sense, the content of the crisis was virtually irrelevant. Any event that would have proved to Kleist that his beliefs were not infallible—even a physical mishap, let us say, entering his world which allowed for no mishaps—might have had much the same effect. For the crisis did not create his tragic view of life, it merely released it and exemplified it. This becomes clear from his subsequent correspondence. What concerns him in the aftermath of the crisis is not simply a troubled reassessment of the powers of reason, or a new and disquieting skepticism toward truth and the purpose of existence, all of which we might expect of a young rationalist lately confronted with the critical theories of Kant, but also a problem more central in his development and clearly of his own making. We find him reverting, that is, to his intuitive sense of reality as opposition, and indulging that sense with the same compulsion with which formerly he had attempted to constrain it, as if he felt free now for the first time to think openly what he had always known in secret to be true. Not that Kant did not play an important part in this complete revolution in his thought. Reason had almost literally held the world together for Kleist in the early period, and as it was affected, so too were his own views. But for every letter following the crisis that may be cited as evidence of his new concern with the dark and puzzling questions of existence, there is another letter that shows him involved in the more psychological or personal problem of simply keeping his balance amid the confusing events which, now that Reason, his buffer against the external world, had been removed, he saw descending upon him from every side. Fate and chance begin to haunt him. There is even a suggestion of protestation in his continual reference to their presence and pervasive influence in life. "Ich will Dir erzählen, wie in diesen Tagen das Schicksal' mit mir gespielt hat"—"Doch höre wie das blinde Verhängnis' mit mir spielte"—"Ach, Wilhelmine, wir dünken uns frei, und' der Zufall führt uns allgewaltig an tausend feingesponnenen Fäden fort." These remarks appear in the opening pages of a single letter of April 9, 1801, and they show that, though we have changed philosophies, we have not changed poets. The sense of anxiety remains; whether expressed intellectually, as when Kleist will write with passion of the intricate and twisted design in the universe; or casually, as when he will remark in passing on a minor reversal of fortune and yet see in it the workings of a higher force; or dejectedly and bitterly, as when for example on July 28, 1801, he curses the fates that make man the despicable thing he is: "Wir sinken und sinken, bis wir so niedrig stehen, wie die andern, und das Schicksal *zwingt* uns, so zu sein, wie die, die wir verachten." So completely, in fact, has the idea of fate engrossed his mind that we would be quite surprised to find him blaming himself rather than an external power for some sudden change in purpose or in the course of his life. "Wundere Dich nicht, diesmal ist das Schicksal wankelmütig, nicht ich," he writes to his sister on February 19, 1802, providing us with what is perhaps the only allusion in his whole correspondence of the time to the role of character in determining fate, and that allusion is at best oblique. That it is also in utter contrast to his former beliefs hardly needs mention at this point. His defences are clearly down.

We could go on in this vein. There seems no end to the anxiety Kleist feels as he confronts a world he both fears, as he had always instinctively done, and in addition no longer understands. The twofold purpose of his earlier philosophy—to clarify the universe and to serve as protection against opposition in life—had emerged from the ruins of the Kant crisis as a twofold problem, as the dilemma of man fighting fate in the dark. (pp. 8-13)

Almost immediately after the crisis in his thought, after some months of uneasy travel, Kleist turned seriously to writing, and what he wrote comes as no surprise. Any of the works could serve as illustration, but we may take the one closest to hand, his first drama, **Die Familie Schroffenstein.** His purpose in this tragedy of errors was to state the human dilemma and expose the comfortable but blind assumption that life provides a way for man to a true and just existence. He makes his point rather drastically by allowing deceptive appearances (the influence of Kant is obvious) to lead the characters, despite their righteous intentions, into grotesque error and crime. In the quarrel between the two Schroffenstein families of Rossitz and Warwand, in which each family accuses the other of murder, both with apparent justification and both in the firm belief that they are acting in the name of justice—in this quarrel, not only does the head of the one family, who believes that obvious facts cannot lie, mistakenly kill his own son, who at the moment is masked in the clothing of the enemy, and not only does the head of the other family, who trusts in an inner sense of righteousness as a guide to just behavior, mistakenly kill his own daughter, but the deception goes even deeper. The whole affair, it is eventually disclosed, had itself been based on an illusion. Neither family was guilty of murder, it merely *seemed* so, and the consequent hate, passion, confusion, and crime were utterly meaningless and unwarranted.

Any of the works, we said, could serve as illustration. But perhaps the most striking example—striking because it appears where least expected—is provided by **Die Hermannsschlacht.** This drama, since it has strong political tendencies and was written in fact for a definite political purpose, should, we would assume, form an exception to the other works. Yet it does not. The pattern is merely reversed. Deceptive appearances, which generally play the role of the opposition to the hero, are shifted in this play to the hero's side, and work in his favor—indeed, it is he who manufactures them. Illusions and deceptions help the individual to his goal; they do not, as in the other works, keep him from it. The tragedy occurs on the other side of the fence. Not Hermann but the Roman general, Varus, and his ambassador, Ventidius, are tricked by appearances into a catastrophe; and had Kleist written the play from the point of view of the Roman rather than the German camp, the result would have been a tragedy not unlike *Die Familie Schroffenstein.* If we compare the last lines of the earlier drama with the words that Varus speaks when he discovers that he had been deceived by Hermann, we find an interesting resemblance. The former ends with the words: "Geh, alte Hexe, geh. Du spielst gut aus der Tasche, / Ich bin zufrieden mit dem Kunststück. Geh." Varus' words are: "Da sinkt die große Weltherrschaft von Rom / Vor eines Wilden Witz zusammen, / Und kommt, die Wahrheit zu gestehen, / Mir wie ein dummer Streich der Knaben vor!" (lines 2464-7). In keeping with the political intent of the play, the Romans' tragedy is purposely minimized. But Kleist did not ignore it completely, as he might have, for it struck too close to home.

Even *Das Käthchen von Heilbronn,* a drama which seems to bear little resemblance to Kleist's other writings, is actually not unrelated to them. Again the pattern is inverted. In *Käthchen* what seems false proves true, while in the other works what seems true proves false. This inversion leads, of course, to a complete change in the outcome of the action. The illusion, when dispelled, exposes not the sad reality of a disordered world but the shining "reality" of a fairy-tale-like universe. The play *is* a fairy tale: the girl of common birth proves in the end to be a princess, and she marries the hero with the blessings of the emperor. There is even a "witch," who parades in the form of a beautiful woman and attempts to poison the princess and win the hero for herself. In other words, with its motif of illusion and deception, the play reflects a form similar to that of the other dramas, and though its final implications are much different—if we can speak at all of the "implications" of a fairy tale—the mold in which they are cast is the mold we find throughout Kleist's thinking and writing. The opposition between the individual and illusions or appearances seems to have been uppermost in his mind or, which is probaby saying the same thing, deeply rooted in his thought. Almost every theme he treats, he arranges in this pattern, or he chooses the theme because it already implies the pattern, as in *Amphitryon,* or because it lends itself to it, as in "Die Marquise von O . . . " and "Der Zweikampf," both of which are based on anecdotes. In *Käthchen* a dream (that she will marry the Count) seems at first to be a mere illusion but proves true; in *Penthesilea* a prophecy (that she will crown Achilles with a garland) proves literally true but actually false; in *Prinz Friedrich von Homburg* an illusion (that he will receive the laurels of victory from the hand of the Princess) seems at the outset true, then false, then eventually, but hardly in the way he had imagined, becomes reality. Even the short idyllic poem "Der Schrecken im Bade" deals with deceptive appearances, as do many of the articles which Kleist wrote for the *Berliner Abendblätter,* such as "Unwahrscheinliche Wahrhaftigkeiten" or "Sonderbarer Rechtsfall," the titles

of which speak for themselves. And on the basis of the comedy *Der zerbrochne Krug,* we might also conclude that the humor of this troubled poet, as well as his gravity and fantasy, expresses itself in the form of things not being what they seem.

But it is not only in the extent of his concern with the problem of illusion and reality that we recognize a distinguishing mark of Kleist. There is also an emotional intensity in that concern which is equally characteristic of the man and ultimately more telling in his art. His insight into the fatefully disjointed nature of the human condition, though it continued to occupy and frustrate him throughout his life, was never in fact the mainspring of his poetic urge, nor the starting point in his tragic view of the world. If this thought was uppermost, as we said, in his mind, it held that position only because of another idea that underlay it—less conscious, even partly misguided perhaps, but nevertheless effective in everything he thought and wrote. It was the idea we have found in Kleist from the very beginning, that deeply human, almost primitive sense of the inherent antagonism in things. And it emerges in his art, though more through its form than in its content. A rhythm of opposing factors and forces insinuates itself into the pages of his works with a persistence that suggests compulsion rather than intent, and with a spontaneity at times that brings us as close perhaps as we can come to the innermost workings of an artistic mind. There is hardly a paragraph in Kleist that ends on a note of hope which is not immediately followed by one that points toward despair; hardly a scene in his dramas that creates a feeling of security which is not soon negated; hardly a movement in thought or action which is not somehow aborted, frustrated, or brashly extended to an extreme and then dramatically destroyed. It is almost as if we were observing in this fictional world the physical phenomenon of forces exerted in one direction automatically producing their equal and opposite force. One thinks immediately in this regard of the fate of Alkmene in *Amphitryon,* but the phenomenon is everywhere. One need not read far in "Das Erdbeben in Chili," a story less patently concerned with the machinations of an elusive and deceptive reality, to find the same contrariness of action, but now in a purely physical guise. Where the heroine in *Amphitryon* was only spiritually frustrated, the hero in this story of violence in nature and in man is literally stopped, started, and turned around in every move he attempts to make. "Kaum befand er sich im Freien, als die ganze, schon erschütterte Straße auf eine zweite Bewegung der Erde völlig zusammenfiel. . . . Hier stürzte noch ein Haus zusammen, und jagte ihn, die Trümmer weit umherschleudernd, in eine Nebenstraße; hier leckte die Flamme schon, in Dampfwolken blitzend, aus allen Giebeln, und trieb ihn schreckenvoll in eine andere; hier wälzte sich, aus seinem Gestade gehoben, der Mapochofluß an ihn heran, und riß ihn brüllend in eine dritte. Hier lag ein Haufen Erschlagener, hier ächzte noch eine Stimme unter dem Schutte, hier . . . hier . . ." This horror has less to do with Kant and the problem of understanding than it does with Kleist and his sense of a world almost bent on destroying whatever man attempts to build. For not only do his characters *live* in a universe of reversed logic and seem inevitably to meet the opposite of what they expect at the point where they could least expect it, on occasion they even *die* as if by the same peculiar design. At the beginning of **"Der Zweikampf,"** for example, Kleist seems to go out of his way to make the victim of a murder meet his death, not in a neutral state of mind, as it were, but at a moment in his life when, "happier than ever," he is looking forward to the future. The positive seems of itself to evoke the negative: "Freudiger, als während des ganzen Laufs seiner Regierung in die Zukunft blickend, hatte er schon den Park, der hinter seinem Schlosse lag, erreicht: als plötzlich ein Pfeilschuß aus dem Dunkel der Gebüsche hervorbrach, und ihm . . . den Leib durchborte." Note the caesura marking the catastrophic effect of the change. Indeed, in this particular case the motif has no obvious purpose, for it neither furthers the action, since the victim is dead and, for the story, done with, nor relates to the character or intent of the murderer, since it is without knowledge of the state of mind of the victim that the crime is committed. This tragedy in miniature is of Kleist and not of his story, and in that sense might even be regarded as an artistic failing. But the point is that it serves as a good illustration of the instinctive creative process in the writings of an author who experienced life as a series of unexpected dramatic changes. Whatever happens in his world happens with thrust and recoil.

Yet there are inconsistencies in Kleist. There are abrupt and drastic changes in attitude and obvious contradictions in thought. His view of life changed markedly in the various stages of his development, tending at one point toward pessimism and a distrust of all beliefs, at another toward individualism and a reliance on intuitive principles, and finally, at the end of his career, toward absolute patriotism—an opponent in thought to all that had gone before. And were it not for the unity and consistency we find otherwise in the man and his works, we might long ago have dismissed him as a confused and confusing poet. But such a unity is there, and so obviously that we even wonder whether what appears contradictory and problematic in Kleist is not itself an indication of a deeper unity, as though the more often he changed his mind the more consistent in effect he became.

Our analysis of the early letters and essays suggests that the thought is worth pursuing. We need only make the distinction once again between the conscious and the instinctive elements in his thinking to sense that each newly professed belief, whatever form it may have taken outwardly, was inwardly only a repeated attempt to escape an original dilemma. There is no reason to assume that the later positive attitudes, just because they came later, were more truly a part of his basic sense of life than those he had adopted at the outset of his career with equal resolution and confidence. There is even less reason. For whereas in describing the defensive aspect of his thought in the early period we were forced to read between the lines of his occasional pronouncements of belief and single out the scattered, unguarded remarks, now in interpreting his later views we have as a means of measure the whole world of the drama or story in which these views appear. And what is reflected in that world in the later works is no new and less anxious sense of reality, no change in the temper of fate, no saving grace or basis for hope, but the same pattern of relentless frustration and opposition which Kleist had initially designed to do violence to all forms of rationality or faith. To state a positive principle in such a context is to say in words what in fact is being denied. The absolute trust in intuitive feeling which triumphs in **"Der Zweikampf,"** for example, or the patriotic ideal which is proferred as a final solution in *Prinz Friedrich von Homburg*, or any of the positive motifs which appear intermittently in his works, seem hardly secure or real in the all too perturbing and unabsolute world in which they supposedly have their being. In the case of **"Der Zweikampf "** we have reservations even without reference to the context. Some of the key speeches of the hero betray simply through their tone and manner the same kind of frantic wish to suppress doubt and maintain faith that we have seen so often before. In essence, Kleist does not change. And it is sadly fitting that even in the exaltation which he apparently experienced during the last hours of his life, and which he himself described as the "triumph of my soul," a close friend should have heard yet another artificial or false note. On December 30, 1811, one month after Kleist's death, Ernst von Pfuel wrote to Caroline von Fouqué: " . . . so wie ich Kleist kenne, war hier eine falsch erkünstelte Exaltation"; and somewhat later: " . . . daß Kleist sich überhaupt den Tod gab, habe ich nichts, gar nichts, er war so gequält und zerrüttet, daß er den Tod mehr lieben mußte als das Leben . . . nur so mußte er nicht sterben, so in unechter Exaltation versunken, oder doch versunken scheinend."

But if we are suspicious of Kleist in this regard, if we have turned his hopeful words inside out to find the despairing thoughts behind them, if, in a sense, we have been harsh, it is only in order ultimately to be kind. For in tracing the contradictions in his thought to an inveterate and less than "enlightened" mode of thinking, we gain for him as a writer much more than what little he might thereby lose as a man. The emphasis is now shifted away from his tentative and ambivalent attempts at a solution to a universal problem and back to the problem itself: to the question of the apparently senseless adversity and oppoosition in human experience for which no thinker so far has found a lasting answer. And Kleist explored that problem as few tragic poets before or since. He explored it, not so much because he set himself the task—his conscious concern seems generally to have been with solutions—as because he knew no world or life without it. (pp. 13-19)

> John Gearey, in his Heinrich von Kleist: A Study in Tragedy and Anxiety, *University of Pennsylvania Press, 1968, 202 p.*

J. M. Lindsay   (essay date 1972)

[In the following excerpt, Lindsay analyzes the subject of distrust of authority figures in Kleist's plays and short stories.]

Heinrich von Kleist loved to depict influential and authoritative figures in his plays and stories. If we survey his works rapidly, we see their number and variety. Among them are kings, princes and emperors, priests, priestesses and other ecclesiastical leaders, an abbess or two, a judge and a traveling Commissioner of Justice, to say nothing of people whose seniority and personal standing in the world might be said to give them a certain authority. There are colonels and generals, fathers and uncles, there is even Jupiter, the father of gods and men. Of course, certain works by Kleist are far richer in such persons than others, but Kleist was undoubtedly throughout his career much preoccupied with the fact of authority and the people who exercise it. (p. 107)

In *Amphitryon* there is one figure of authority, Jupiter himself. The father of gods and men enjoys blessed immunity from many of the restrictions that limit human beings. Not only does he live for ever and transport himself with divine ease from one place to another, but he can without penalty exercise sovereign control over all creation. Sometimes this power is exercised with wisdom, temperance and restraint; there are occasions, however, when the supreme power appears to be exercised with wanton irresponsibility. The king of the heavens may, for instance, decide in a fit of mingled curiosity and lustfulness that he would like to spend a night with Alkmene, the chaste wife of the Theban general, Amphitryon, and he is immediately able to indulge this caprice. Nothing is against the rules for Jupiter. He assumes the form of Amphitryon, has his will of Alkmene, gives her, again proving his divine superiority, more pleasure from his embrace than she had known before from Amphitryon, and even complains rather petulantly about the limitations of being omnipotent. Sometimes—but not often—he has inescapable responsibilities:

> Leb wohl, mich ruft die Pflicht.
>
> (Act I, Sc. 4)

The point has been made repeatedly in the Kleist-literature that Jupiter embodies in the most startling and extreme way Kleist's worst fears and misgivings about God. In other works, such as **"Das Erdbeben in Chili,"** we are puzzled by the inexplicable see-sawing of the favours and blows of Fate or God, but are left feeling that Kleist himself has not been able to make up his mind about the spirit that rules the world. The ambivalence of the works reflects Kleist's own uncertainty about the role of the Creator vis-à-vis his creation. In *Amphitryon* the supreme divinity could scarcely behave worse. Alkmene and Amphitryon are devoted to one another and perform their duties to the best of their ability. Neither of them would dream of cheating anyone, let alone deceiving one another, they are both virtuous and straightforward people, bound up in one another, but not to the exclusion of their proper outside obligations. Apart from these basic virtues they both show during the drama qualities of taste and tact which render them intensely sympathetic. They both, in fact, behave at least correctly and generally gracefully, as long as their minds are not clouded and their feelings misled by Jupiter's nefarious manipulations. In a very real sense, Kleist's *Amphitryon* is disturbing, not only because of the distress caused to Alkmene by her unwitting mistake, but because of the nature of Jupiter. If God is both all-powerful and completely irresponsible, capable of trifling like a destructive child with our most intimate and (to our thinking) proper feelings, mankind is in the wretched state of not being able to feel that a benevolent power rules the universe.

Through the whole of *Amphitryon* one realises Kleist's sense of outrage that the world should be so unstable and unpredictable. The inspiration underlying this work closely resembles that underlying **"Das Erdbeben,"** the feeling that the world and God's attitude towards it is indeed hard to understand. However, in *Amphitryon* Kleist renders explicit the feeling which is expressed by implication in **"Das Erdbeben,"** his basic doubt concerning the governance of the universe. He represents with dramatic force his feeling that even the best and most deserving human beings may on occasion be deceived, exploited and ill-used by the very God whom they are trying to serve according to their best lights. In **"Das Erdbeben,"** God is in the background, an unfathomable power which affects man in incomprehensible ways, but which may even, despite appearances to the contrary, mean well towards him. *Amphitryon* reflects a mood in which Kleist clearly does not even give God the benefit of the doubt.

Der zerbrochene Krug is of all Kleist's works that in which he deals in the most thorough-going manner with men in authority. The two such persons in the comedy could not be more different. The contrast between Adam and Walter is brought out by every means at the poet's disposal. Each is firmly delineated as a character in his own right, but they also serve as most effective foils to one another. Adam's conduct towards Eva and Ruprecht would be thoroughly reprehensible even if Walter were not there, but Walter's superior intelligence and absolute integrity are precisely the qualities which most effectively show up Adam's utter inadequacy and unsuitability for the role in which he is cast. Kleist tends to think in terms of pairs of opposites. Nowhere in his works does he use contrasting human personalities to better effect.

The microcosm of Huisum is ruled and administered by the village judge Adam. We do not learn anything to speak of about Adam's past, but we see him in action in the present, and this gives us an abundance of material to form a judgment about him. Adam has always devoted his life to the satisfaction of his appetites. Somehow he has managed to have himself appointed to the position of a small town magistrate, which he clearly uses to his own advantage and no one else's. Huisum—which may indeed be regarded as a symbol of the whole world—is thoroughly maladministered by a person who is not so much malevolent as thoroughly selfish and amoral. He is also coarse, vulgar, completely lacking in consideration for others and any true self-respect. When Walter comes to inspect the administration of justice in Huisum, Adam, being a completely carnal man and altogether without imagination, immediately supposes that the most appropriate way of treating the eminent visitor is to offer him an abundance of food and drink. He judges everyone by the standards he knows, which are of course completely inappropriate in this case. His grossness is funny, partly because it is without malice or evil intent. Adam simply cultivates the satisfaction of his appetites with a total lack of scruple and an almost incredible single-mindedness. He cannot help having a club-foot, but in other respects his ugliness is very

A scene from Der zerbrochene Krug.

largely the result of his lack of restraint at table and his indifference to the kind of figure he cuts.

If Adam were any ordinary petty bourgeois figure in a play with a Dutch setting, it might be possible to regard him as simply funny for the reasons above outlined. However, his function as a judge makes the matter more serious. A judge should be a person of total integrity, who is above suspicion or reproach. It is hard to believe that a person like Adam could hold any important public office without attracting unfavourable publicity. The Huisum public would have to be extraordinarily short-sighted not to recognise that their judge is a far from exemplary human being. And of course it is not simply a matter of bad publicity. A place in which the supreme secular authority were exercised by a man like Adam would be a potential hell upon earth; any imaginable injustice could befall the inhabitants of Huisum, and not merely because the judge was not always able to put injustices right. He is even, as we realise in the play, the initiator of the most scandalous injustices. Indeed, the world in which Eva must live is a very unsatisfactory world; her parents and her fiancé are lacking in understanding and will not show the unqualified confidence in her which Kleist obviously thinks she deserves; the other inhabitants of Huisum naturally follow the lead of those nearest and dearest to her and consider her to be worse than she is; but worst of all for Eva, and for any other man or woman of integrity and goodwill in Kleist, they live in a world where nobody will be fair to them, where their closest relatives misunderstand them, and where even before the seat of judgment they can be wronged, not by accident but by design, by the very person through whom they should be able to seek justice.

It is in this very unpromising situation that Walter's arrival turns out to be so opportune. Attention has been drawn by more than one commentator to the significance of his name. He is indeed the person who rules over all, who puts things to rights. He is free from the slavery to appetite that characterises Adam. He approaches the whole matter of the administration of justice as a serious task which must be given maximum priority in the court-room. Not only must the task be properly performed without avoidable delays, but the correct forms must also be observed. The judge must be properly dressed, and he must begin the proceedings promptly. He applies all his considerable intelligence and legal acumen to the seemingly difficult task of finding out who the culprit is. He must be prepared to follow his instinctive hunch that Eva is innocent despite all evidence to the contrary, and probe the affair until the truth is revealed. The attractive collation provided for him by Adam in an attempt to curry favour with superior authority is impatiently waved aside, although when the proceedings have lasted for some time and Walter has become hungry and thirsty he does agree to take some modest refreshment. In all this he shows himself to be a temperate and moderate man, whose most significant characteristic is the intelligent and conscientious performance of his duty.

The reader or spectator may say at this point: It is good that Kleist sees the wickedness and slackness of those in charge in this world as overruled by superior authority. Adam does not have the last word, but Walter. The ultimate authority in the play is not gluttonous or lecherous but sober, industrious, clever, wise and full of goodwill towards the simple people of Huisum. How reassuring that at precisely the right moment the inspector of courts should turn up and set matters to rights. But this is precisely the point. There is no real reason why Walter should appear at that moment; he might equally well have come a day sooner or later, and not chosen the day when Adam was planning to do great injustice to Eva and Ruprecht. Indeed, one must think of all the other days, on which Adam has been able to wreak considerable harm unimpeded. By the purest coincidence, Eva has escaped with her virtue and her reputation and Ruprecht has not been unjustly punished, but the odds really were that things should have turned out differently. A world in which the right thing happens only occasionally, by chance as it were, is a highly unsatisfactory world. The happy ending of *Der zerbrochene Krug* does not invalidate the general contention that Kleist does not like the way in which authority is wielded in this world. Of course, Walter clears up the mess created by Adam very efficiently when he sees it, but how can one be sure that he will see it? The comedy of the *Krug* hinges completely on the outside chance that Walter should turn up in Huisum on the right day. In more general terms the play suggests simply that in this world you cannot expect justice to be done, or authority to be conscientiously wielded—now and again this may happen by accident, and then one can afford to smile, but as a rule the world is most cruel to those who least deserve it. I see Walter as personifying justice, kindliness, conscience and perspicacity; as far as I can detect, he never fails or falters during the action of the play. However, he is human, and therefore by definition imperfect, and he cannot in any case be there all the time. When he is not there, Eva is at the mercy not only of Adam, who has sexual designs on her, but owing to his misrepresentation of the course of events, of the malice and misunderstanding of her mother and Ruprecht. Adam is not malevolently disposed towards Eva or anyone else; he is merely completely selfish and greedy. (pp. 107-11)

Kleist's last completed drama *Prinz Friedrich von Homburg,* like so many of his earlier works is largely concerned with the representation of authority. It is clear that Kleist leaves deliberate ambiguities here. On a superficial consideration it may seem that the Elector is a representative of authority and justice. However, a man who condemns another to death for pursuing an ambition, which has been half-deliberately implanted in his mind during a highly suggestible somnabulant state, must be regarded as an unsatisfactory representative of authority. It is true that the Elector is able to arouse doubts in Friedrich's mind about the propriety of his conduct, and, thanks in part at least to the authority of his office, to make him sufficiently conscience-stricken to alter his view of his conduct during the battle. He even brings him round from his simple terror of death to a state of courage and self-condemnation. By the exercise of the moral authority inherent in his position, the Elector can make Homburg overcome his natural fear of death and agree that the breaking of military orders should properly be punished with death.

However, one must regard the Elector's decision to *pardon* Homburg as a fickle use of authority. No significant additional evidence has come to light to justify the sudden decision not only not to hang Homburg, but to reward him with the hand of Natalie. If it be objected that the Elector changes his mind after hearing Hohenzollern's account of the glove incident in Act V Sc. 5, one can only say that this is at best a mitigating circumstance, not by any means an exoneration from guilt. If Homburg ever deserved the death sentence, he still deserves it. The elaborate charade at the end of the work, when Homburg is led out blindfold as if to his execution, (to which he still fully assents) and then discovers that his fate is not to be put to death but to marry Natalie, is hard to take. Of course we are pleased that this eager, impulsive and probably slightly psychologically abnormal young man is to be allowed to live. We had scarcely assented to his death even if we felt that the Elector needed to make a gesture against his irresponsibility. Still less easily can we assent to the Elector's sudden change of heart, which in a matter of this magnitude must seem not only unmotivated but also frivolous. Of course, Friedrich von Homburg has himself acted without compunction against a military inferior who had not carried out his orders; perhaps this incident is introduced merely to convey the general ethos of that military society, in which every lapse is severely punishable. It is easier to accept that this should be so than that the situation may change from one day to the next, which is what happens in the case of Prinz Friedrich. We can only conclude that Kleist wishes us to see the Elector as a ruler over a life and death issue who does not know his own mind, who yields readily to the promptings of his own soft heart, especially when they are reinforced by the entreaties of his womenfolk and when he is afraid disaffection may be spreading in his army.

One can rejoice in the outcome of *Prinz Friedrich von Homburg* and still think that authority is just as badly handled in it as in *Der zerbrochene Krug.* It is no wonder that the Prussian aristocracy and military disliked the play; by any reasonable reckoning a national leader who behaves like the Kurfürst inspires no sort of admiration or liking. That the right thing happens to the Prince reminds us of what happens to Eva in the *Krug;* it is a happy accident, not the logical result of justice being well administered or authority correctly wielded.

Michael Kohlhaas is entirely concerned with the hero's sufferings at the hands of various worldly authorities. Kleist describes his hero's *experiences* with minor feudal authority, then with the lower reaches of the law. From these he graduates to dealings with his major feudal superiors, his case comes to the attention of a great clerical leader, and finally the matter comes to the notice of the Emperor himself. In the course of these encounters Kohlhaas discovers that life is barely livable or enjoyable for the ordinary, well-disposed human being, who, going about his business in a perfectly honest, straightforward and harmless way, is liable to be molested and wronged by any or all of the agencies just mentioned. Sometimes it looks as though Kohlhaas were on the point of achieving a breakthrough, even obtaining justice, but then it emerges that he was being over-optimistic and that justice is one value which he can never obtain. The Junker von Tronka commits a comparatively minor offence against Kohlhaas in the first instance. However, this offence represents an evident misuse of authority. When Kohlhaas' lawyer tells him that he ought to drop the proceedings against Tronka, he is in effect conniving at the injustice done to his client. The men who refuse to allow Kohlhaas' case to be heard by the Saxon Electors are even more at fault, and so, of course, are the legal authorities in Saxony who have failed to arrange matters so that straightforward legal complaints such as that of Kohlhaas against Tronka can be attended to. From the lawyers and the agents of government, after vain attempts to be heard by the Saxon Elector, Kohlhaas turns to Luther, who seems for a time to be both aware of the wrong done to Kohlhaas and prepared to do something about it. However, it soon appears that this spiritual authority is also defective, at any rate when regarded in terms of the ordinary man's natural desire for justice within this world. Luther is in reality far more anxious to put an end to the carnage and destruction caused by Kohlhaas and his associates than he is to procure justice for Kohlhaas. The deal arranged by Luther with the Saxon authorities works out to Kohlhaas' disadvantage; Kohlhaas finds himself betrayed and imprisoned. No serious attempt has been made by the competent authorities to inform themselves about the reasons for Kohlhaas' unlawful activities, far less to set matters to rights. It is manifest that the Saxon Elector has had no interest in securing justice for Kohlhaas, but even the Elector of Brandenburg, who espouses Kohlhaas' cause, is not capable of arresting the course of injustice. The situation at the end of the work, where Kohlhaas pays with his life for disturbing the Emperor's peace, although he gets back his horses in good fettle, may be a solution acceptable to Kleist, who for much of his adult life suffered from suicidal impulses, but the ordinary reader must find it difficult to share Kohlhaas' conviction that at last he is getting a square deal from those in authority over him. As far as Kohlhaas is concerned life is over, and he has found it impossible to obtain justice during his lifetime. A good man has had his character perverted and has lost all that made life worth living because of the shortcomings of those who claim to look after the legitimate interests of ordinary people. At the best these people do an incomplete job—at the worst they actually commit or actively connive at major injustices. The story of Kohlhaas records a man's suffering at the hands of worldly authority on various levels, and the one fact about which no doubt exists is that he must suffer. The Saxon Elector is the only important person who positively wishes to deny Kohlhaas justice, but no-one else, not even Luther, is prepared actively to take up the cudgels on his behalf.

At the beginning of **"Das Erdbeben von Chili"** it appears as if, as far as Jeronimo and Josepha are concerned, the wrongs committed against the two lovers, who are being condemned to death for what is at most a trivial offence, are going to be put right. It is true that the earthquake, attended as it is by so much loss of life, may seem a rather drastic way of putting right a purely personal wrong, but God moves in a mysterious way, and at the beginning of the story the reader is inclined to give Him the benefit of the doubt. The reader may well feel genuinely moved—he is certainly meant to be—when the first reaction of the young lovers after the joy of being reunited is to wish to give thanks to Heaven for their deliverance. We accompany them in all naivety to the great church in Santiago, where they wish to record their gratitude to the Almighty for sparing them and their child from destruction against all the odds. In charge of this act of worship is a priest, a person in religious authority, who quickly proceeds to show that the lovers' belief that the nature of the world

has changed is quite erroneous. In fact, just as Richter Adam had seemed to be the last person in the world to be in charge of a court of justice, so the priest in the cathedral at Santiago appears utterly unworthy of being in charge of any Christian act of worship. We remember the forbearance exercised by Jesus towards those who found it difficult to obey the laws of matrimony, and ask ourselves by what right a Christian priest could possibly be so uncharitable and intolerant towards Jeronimo and Josepha. The church becomes the scene of diabolical intolerance, and the priest of God, who should preach love and forbearance, turns out to be an apostle of hatred and inciter to violence. Certainly, Meister Pedrillo soon assumes the role of the devil's agent in the House of God, but he does this in the spirit of the priest. In the early part of the story man's inhumanity to man had seemingly provoked a dramatic divine intervention in human affairs; now, when such an intervention was at least equally necessary, it did not occur. We may well ask ourselves, did the first salvation of the lovers mean anything? Were they saved only in order that they might be more thoroughly doomed on the later occasion? Indeed, the real question which **"Das Erdbeben"** forces us to ask ourselves is not about the nature of the priest, or the parents, or any other purely human figure of authority in the story, but about God Himself, who seems to intervene so dramatically on one occasion, and then to take such a different attitude to the sufferings of the very people whom He has just saved from the jaws of death. We recall the way in which the Kurfürst behaves towards Friedrich von Homburg, high-handedly, cruelly, arbitrarily, inconsistently, and we realise that the fate of Jeronimo and Josepha embraces similarly indefensible arbitrary deeds on the part of their Maker. We may well ask ourselves whether the story represents Kleist's final reflection on the subject of human destiny; it is clear at any rate, that it is at least the product of a mood in which Kleist found it hard to accept the strange and seemingly incomprehensible vagaries of human destiny, in which it could well seem that the very people who had one moment seemingly been singled out specially for divine favour became the next moment the specially chosen victims of particularly grim disaster. Also, the circumstances of Jeronimo's and Josepha's death could scarcely have been more cunningly devised to demonstrate the enigma of the divine nature. What can one think, when the evidence is so contradictory? On the one hand, the Almighty can step in, even cause an earthquake to secure the release of two of his creatures from captivity and certain death; only half a day after the lovers have been rescued, and while their hearts are full of pious thanks for their unexpected deliverance, it turns out not only that their persecution is continuing but that the priest of God is its instigator. Kleist obviously finds a world in which such things can happen very puzzling. A closer look at this story will soon persuade us that it is one of those in which Kleist's lyrical qualities become apparent; the reader who naively supposes on reading the garden-of-Eden-like idyll following the escape of the lovers from death that there has been a permanent and all-determining divine intervention is making an understandable mistake; however, the horror and violence with which he is disabused must come as a shock even to those accustomed to Kleist's sudden changes of mood. It is as if heaven and hell were represented before our eyes with visionary intensity in very rapid succession. These sudden and extreme changes not only of atmosphere but in the writer's whole manner of looking at the world occur frequently in Kleist's works; they are the result not so much of intellectual uncertainty concerning the authority of God in the world, but rather of a basic insecurity of soul and of Kleist's deepest emotional attitudes. He seems desperately to seek an authoritative father-figure, whether he be judge, father, king, priest or emperor; always and ever anew the persons on whom Kleist's characters had placed their hopes turn out to be idols with feet of clay. The paradisal joys of the hours following the great cataclysm of the earthquake yield soon to the man-made horrors of the thanksgiving service; that occasion, on which grateful human beings spontaneously gathered to render thanks for deliverance from mortal peril to their Creator, turns out to be like so many eagerly awaited human experiences, not only a disappointment but the very negation of everything that the participants had promised themselves from it.

In *Amphitryon,* despite the description *Ein Lustspiel nach Molière,* and despite the lighter moments one feels that Kleist is primarily concerned with the representation of divine authority as arbitrary and hard to acknowledge. The interpretation of Alkmene's final "Ach;" will always be in doubt, yet I think many people will always regard this monosyllable as expressing the distress and puzzlement of a sincere human being whose emotional life has been subjected to unwelcome interference by Jupiter's intervention and who perhaps remains human enough to wonder whether being Hercules' mother is adequate consolation to her and her husband for the confusion and humiliation they have suffered. I do not really see how Alkmene, being the women she is, could feel happy at the end of the play, and her weary, sad cry expresses the disillusionment of an idealist who is being forced to come to terms with a life that falls short of her simple intention of loving Amphitryon all her days with all her heart. Even the love of a god makes an indifferent substitute to her for the love of Amphitryon.

In *Der zerbrochene Krug* unworthy authority is flouted by the opportune arrival and intervention of Walter. It is highly satisfactory for author and audience (or readers) that this should happen, and to watch the successive stages of Adam's exposure and incrimination, despite his resourceful but unavailing efforts to shove his guilt on someone else, is highly entertaining. Basically the difference in mood between this play and Kleist's other comedy is engendered by the knowledge that on this occasion an exception occurs to the general rule that in this world authority is badly exercised. And so the comic side of Adam, his grossness, his libidinousness, his determination to escape exposure can be appreciated by spectator or reader without the guilty feeling that, however funny Adam may be in himself, he is doing damage to innocent people every day. Thus he is amusingly rather than horrifyingly grotesque and Eva's escape from his clutches suggests that we need not altogether abandon hope for the world after all.

In the *Prinz Friedrich von Homburg* authority is again

misused but without tragic consequences. Here the use of authority is revealed as a life and death issue in certain circumstances. *Prinz Friedrich von Homburg* is a serious drama, which shows how arbitrarily and harshly even a well-intentioned man can behave towards another. Prinz Friedrich even finds himself condemned to death for an offence committed indirectly at his monarch's instigation. The tone of the drama is serious but not tragic and it is shown how life can sometimes be illogical. Friedrich's survival is an improbable enough circumstance but it happens. He survives because the Elector wills it, although the Elector has not really any good or sufficient reason for pardoning him. As an illustration of how life can be both cruel and kind in a seemingly irrational and unpredictable way, *Prinz Friedrich von Homburg* makes its point effectively. The Elector possesses by virtue of his position both de facto authority and the moral authority of the feudal superior, but he does not possess it by any logical or intrinsic rightness of thinking or judgment. The play simply illustrates how little connexion there may well be in life between man's conduct and its consequences; Friedrich's (admittedly rather foolhardy) courage brings him a death sentence, and his cowardice (reinforced by emotional pleas from his women well-wishers and the army) leads not only to his pardon but to his being generously rewarded. The tone of the play is sober and quiet; it shows, without fuss or indignation, what Kleist felt often occurs in life. The right thing may well happen for the wrong reason and we may rejoice so much over the outcome that we show less than due concern for the stages by which that outcome is reached.

Michael Kohlhaas is a tragic story, even though its hero carries his point at the end of the day and gets his horses back in good health through the Imperial Court of Justice. The price of obtaining justice for Kohlhaas has been life itself and it has proved impossible for him to go on living and have his wrongs put right. Although there are moments of hectic excitement on the way, the tone at the end of this story is measured and sober. Kleist is not here concerned to make any great emotional plea to have an unsatisfactory state of affairs put right, he merely wishes to show the likely consequences of a conflict between an uncompromising idealist (Kohlhaas) and a world where at the best justice can scarcely be obtained and never in full measure.

The **"Erdbeben"** presents a grotesque picture of the way in which authority is wielded in Chili. The priest in the cathedral and Don Pedrillo behave in a monstrous way and the whole final episode of the work forms a Goya-like vision of horrible inhumanity. There is no question of restraint being observed here in the portrayal of authority; one might rather suppose that Kleist is seeking for images horrible enough to express his feelings about the worst aspects of human authority. And of course it is clear to us that the heinous crimes perpetrated against the young lovers, Don Fernando and his family are committed in all good faith by men who believe they are carrying out the will of God fully and unconditionally. If God were irrational, cruel, arbitrary and monstrous, the priest might well represent His wishes perfectly; if God is love and that love is given equally to all men, then the priest cannot be a worthy spokesman for the divine will. The priest does harm to other men which Adam is prevented from doing by the timely intervention of Walter—in the one case we have a comic drama, because of the thwarting of evil authority by a superior, good authority, in the other the evil use of authority proceeds unrestrained to the dire disadvantage of its victims.

It would not be hard to show, by further references to Kleist's plays and stories, that he was always preoccupied with and worried by the question of authority in the world, and in particular by the chameleon-like changes in the behaviour of those who wield authority. The last story we have considered represents only one of the most extreme examples of a phenomenon which one finds again and again in Kleist. Just as Penthesilea's love for Achilles can change in a moment to a perverted lust for his living flesh and blood, so the God who had only hours before been prepared to turn his world upside down to organise the rescue of two of His children from disaster and had improbably enough disposed the hearts of all mankind to charity, had proved incapable of sustaining His effort for long enough for the safety of Jeronimo and Josepha, or had possibly just changed His mind about what their fate should be. It seems more likely, from the way in which Kleist describes the scene in the church and the following events, that he not only did not feel persuaded of the goodness of God, but positively believed that the world is ruled by a malevolent spirit.

Kleist obviously feels concern at the unsatisfactory way in which authority is wielded in the world. Again and again, in one work after the other we find him looking for absolute values in which to believe; truth, justice, love, kingship, priesthood, other forms of worldly authority from fatherhood to social superiority are all carefully regarded and found wanting. Sometimes the shortcomings of those in authority are obvious and emerge quickly; sometimes we become aware of a contrast between appearance and reality, but of one thing we can be sure: in this world authority belongs to those who are not worthy to exercise it. Kleist would positively like to be able wholeheartedly and unreservedly to believe in some divine or human authority, but all the evidence suggests that the incumbents of the highest positions are thoroughly fallible, and that even God Himself may take a perverse delight in playing with, tormenting and misleading His creatures. As I suggested before, this is more of an emotional attitude than an intellectual position. Clearly, it is the kind of emotional attitude which makes life difficult and even unendurable; it cannot be a matter for surprise that Kleist felt while still a young man that he could endure it no longer. We should not, however, be so simple-minded as to suppose that the Kurfürst in *Prinz Friedrich von Homburg* behaves like a perfect ruler any more than Prince Friedrich behaves like a perfect subject or military commander. The Elector behaves very badly, measured by normal human standards. In a rather odd and curiously life-like fashion Friedrich survives his exposure to the Kurfürst's irresponsible behavior and subsequent rigid attitudes, and the Kurfürst's authority over his subjects survives their natural and proper rejection of his proposed cruelty towards Friedrich. There is no logical reason for the "happy ending" of *Prinz*

Friedrich von Homburg, at least not in the arguments advanced by the protagonists. If the "right thing" happens in *Prinz Friedrich* it happens by happy accident, just as the happy ending of *Der zerbrochene Krug* occurs by happy accident, in that Walter happens to be in court to see that justice is done. As far as Kleist is concerned this is the best that can ever be hoped for in this imperfect world, and the best is just not good enough. (pp. 112-19)

> *J. M. Lindsay, "Figures of Authority in the Works of Heinrich von Kleist," in* Forum for Modern Language Studies, *Vol. VIII, No. 2, April, 1972, pp. 107-19.*

Denys Dyer   (essay date 1977)

[*In the following excerpt, Dyer provides an in-depth analysis of Kleist's technique in his short stories.*]

Kleist's *Erzählungen* take place in a world of upheaval and chaos. In every one of them the settled order of things, the normal routine, is disturbed by some disaster or unforeseen event that makes a mockery of conventional human responses and places men and women in situations alien to their normal range of experience. These situations are 'unerhört' in every sense of the word and amply bring out the novel element implied in the word Novelle. Blacks murder whites, an earthquake reduces a city to ruins, the plague infects the members of a Roman family, a citadel is stormed and a woman raped, a marquis sets fire to his castle, a horse-dealer sets himself up as the representative of the Archangel Michael, and in a single moment of time four men are condemned to an existence of grotesque insanity for the rest of their lives. Characters are caught up in situations over which they have no control, things happen to them and they must face the impact of unexpected events as best they can. The motivating force behind all this is chance. Things happen out of the blue, an earthquake, a drenching shower of rain, the sudden return of a Negro leader, a midnight assault on a fortress, and it is impossible to plan ahead to meet possible contingencies. It is impossible, because there is a complete breakdown in the rational world. Characters may deliberate, meetings may be held and courses of action debated, but all is subject to the unpredictable see-saw of events. This is brought out in what might be called Kleist's 'aber wer . . . ' 'but who' technique, the astonishment of a person at an unexpected sudden turn of fortune following hard on what had appeared to be a settled state of affairs. What is certain, and here one can almost speak of a pattern, is that if events appear to be tending in a particular direction they will then suddenly veer in the opposite direction. All is subject to chance and fate is always waiting to strike down the unwary; indeed Kleist seems to revel in laconic descriptions of how they are struck down.

The breakdown in the rational world and the fortuitousness of events help to undermine the reality of things and to ensure that, however solidly based they may appear to be, an element of nightmare and unreality surrounds them. The predominance of chance opens the door to an irrational world and this combines with Kleist's tendency to polarise problems and conflicts and to project them on to a higher plane, in which the forces of heaven and hell, however symbolically understood, are involved; chance is mirrored in the emergence of the miraculous. These irrational forces can be positive or negative as they affect human beings who find themselves caught up in situations that reflect the contradictory nature of the universe itself. One test Kleist imposes on his characters is how they react to such situations.

Under the impact of the extraordinary situations created by Kleist human institutions are frequently found wanting. Organised religion, the operation of the law, social values and family ties, all these are subjected to scrutiny and found deficient. If the upheaval and chaos in the stories to some extent mirrors the upheaval in Europe created by the French Revolution and the Napoleonic Wars, the critical view of human institutions taken in them may be a reflection of the post-Jena depression in Prussia after 1806. Time and time again Kleist shows how officialdom and the establishment, whether represented by venal officials or corrupt priests, defend a scale of values often either obtuse or callously hypocritical ('steinigt sie! steinigt sie! die ganze im Tempel Jesu versammelte Christenheit!' **'Erdbeben'**). As the stories gather momentum accepted values may be unmasked as false, whether through the idyllic picture of one big human family that has survived the earthquake or in the words of an otherwise conforming mother ('ich will keine andre Ehre mehr, als deine Schande' **'Marquise'**). A second test Kleist imposes on his characters is how they react to conventional codes of behaviour and the values represented by social institutions when they find themselves caught up in unexpected situations.

Kleist often starts his stories with a baffling situation, a problem to be solved, a secret to be uncovered. Throughout the *Erzählungen* there runs the theme of truth and knowledge, the deceptive nature of appearances and the reality that may underlie them. His stories are constant variations on this theme, his characters have continually to grope their way through a confusing tangle of misleading appearances, finding out in the process that they are unable to trust the evidence of their senses and unable to rely on the operation of their rational faculties to provide answers to the riddles with which they are so unexpectedly faced. A third test imposed by Kleist on his characters is how they stand up to the conflicting nature of appearances and the contrast between what things appear to be ('Schein') and what they may eventually turn out to be ('Sein').

Not only appearances deceive; characters too deceive one another and themselves. Kleist weaves a web of misunderstanding, error and deceit in all his stories and his characters are enmeshed in it, consciously and unconsciously. Noticeable in this network of deception and self-deception is the breakdown in communication between human beings and the growing isolation of the individual. No speech passes between Toni and Gustav, as he awakes to find himself apparently betrayed and reacting blindly kills her; the 'Wer da?' of the Marquis echoes unanswered in the haunted room in the castle near Locarno before he sets fire to it and despairingly puts an end to his existence; the four

brothers sit in silent adoration of the Cross, isolated from the community of men, and only break their silence at midnight to break out in fearful discordant chanting of the *Gloria;* in isolated seclusion a married woman adores the portrait of a dead lover; a prosperous Roman merchant is strung up in a deserted public square, refusing to surrender his soul to the protective ministrations of Mother Church; characters sit in solitary confinement and are trapped in the prison walls of their windowless individual lives. A fourth test imposed on Kleist's characters is how they react to the web of deceit and self-deceit, and the encompassing isolation in which they are entrapped.

These characters may turn out to be very different from what at first they appeared to be. Kleist delights in showing how apparently normal characters tend to extremes of conduct when jolted out of their routine existence by the intrusion of something alien—an earthquake, a Russian storming a fortress at night, a Swiss seeking sanctuary on an island where blacks are murdering whites, an old crone haunting a castle, the shattering impact of ethereal music. Against a background of chaos and a crumbling social framework the behaviour of characters is polarised and they become angelic knights in armour or satanic monsters of revenge. Initially 'neutral', to use the terminology of the *Allerneuester Erziehungsplan,* they then become charged with positive or negative qualities as they struggle to adjust to unexpectedly changed circumstances. The tensions in them erupt like the gases in a 'Kleistische Flasche'. Once normality is re-established and a valid social framework reasserts itself again, they then revert to their former 'neutrality'. In the course of depicting such characters Kleist is able to indulge in psychological portrayal of a high order. But essentially he is not concerned with characters as total human beings, but rather his business is with how they react to particular situations, the circumstances of which he has carefully engineered to pinpoint this or that problematic aspect of human existence. Yet another test imposed by Kleist on his characters is to what extent they preserve their individuality and integrity when suddenly pitchforked into the jungle of human emotions and made for the first time aware of the contradictory plus and minus of the human personality.

Kleist's world would appear to be a tragic one, and certainly [**'Das Erdbeben in Chili'**, **'Die Verlobung in St. Domingo'** and **'Der Findling'**] offer a picture of the world almost unrelievedly bleak and cheerless. Other stories, however, have non-tragic endings. It is essential to realise that Kleist is always at pains to show that there are two sides to everything. An old crone can exert a baleful ('Bettelweib') or a benevolent *(Kohlhaas)* influence; organised religion can be repressive and hypocritical (**'Erdbeben'**) or comforting and protective (**'Cäcilie'**); a child may be a vindication of human love (**'Erdbeben'**) or carry within it the seeds of the plague (**'Findling'**). For all that, Kleist does indicate some ways in which human beings can rise superior to the circumstances in which they find themselves and reach a non-tragic solution to the problems with which they are faced. One is through the integrity of human feelings, be it love or selfless concern for others, faith in oneself and complete trust in dealings with others. It is of course true that every positive presupposes a negative:

love can degenerate into lust, trust into mistrust, a belief in justice into a thirst for revenge. But the positive aspect of human emotions is stressed by Kleist and they provide something on which characters can fall back when the world around them is baffling and hostile. Another complementary way in which tragedy can be averted is through self-knowledge and an acceptance of human behaviour and the fallible nature of the world. The Marquise von O. acquires self-knowledge ('mit sich selbst bekannt'), and she accepts the 'Gebrechlichkeit der Welt'. Such self-knowledge and an acceptance of the world, so different from what once it appeared to be, is not easily gained. Kleist exposes his characters to cruel, almost sadistic, tests, bringing them to the abyss of despair, making them, to use the imagery of **'Über das Marionettentheater,'** undertake a journey round the world before enabling them to find a way back into paradise and to become properly integrated, undivided human beings. Nor is there any guarantee that a solution, once reached, will be permanent. The external world is ruled by chance, and who knows what situations characters may find themselves caught up in after the curtain comes down on the particular drama in which they have made their appearance. For all that, the validity of love, trust, self-sacrifice and justice remains unimpaired, however they may be put to the test in the ever-changing world of phenomena.

In his stories Kleist is like some kind of scientific experimenter as he puts different problems of life under the microscope. The ingredients are varied in the different experiments, the organisms in the test tube subjected to different procedures, the terms of the equation re-arranged. It can be a cruel and heartless business, this searching inquiry into the human condition, and the results obtained are rarely clear and unambiguous. What makes the experiments so fascinating to the onlooker is not only the compelling nature of their contents, but also the masterful way in which they are presented.

The opening sentences set the tone of the stories. Time, place, and the name of a main character are stated in them, with an insistence on factual detail that appears to guarantee the realism and accuracy of the story. And in this there is a paradox. For as the plot embarks on its outlandish twists and turns it gradually becomes clear, despite the chronicle approach, that the story is anything but realistic and historical. A background of chaos and upheaval is indicated in the opening sentences in a terse relative clause: blacks are murdering whites, an earthquake is about to break out, iconoclasm is rife in the Netherlands. And an extraordinary situation or remarkable paradox is adumbrated at times almost casually: a man is about to commit suicide when thousands are being killed off like flies; a respectable titled lady advertises for the father of the child she is expecting; a horse-dealer and son of a schoolmaster is both 'rechtschaffen' and 'entsetzlich'. The cool detonation of the opening bombshell, the laconic announcement of an extraordinary paradox, triggers off a story primarily concerned with the exploitation of a baffling situation, a riddle to be solved, a secret to be unmasked. The surprise technique rivets the attention of the reader from the opening lines onwards, as the story plunges *in medias res*. The baffling situation is caused by the unexpected arrival of a stranger or a chance event shattering the calm of an apparently normal state of affairs, and more often than not it happens during the night, thus producing a mood of eerie tension heightening the general bewilderment. The opening situation may appear to be exploited for its purely sensational impact; but it soon becomes clear that it is being used as a springboard for an investigation of issues of far-reaching metaphysical import. As the investigation proceeds Kleist gradually discloses relevant detail, so that the situation is endowed with different layers of meaning, various facets of the problem are revealed, and the whole issue developed with a mounting complexity and intricacy that appears eventually to defy rational analysis, until at last the riddle is solved, the secret revealed and the solution proposed, a solution which is not arrived at by rational means and which is sometimes deliberately incomplete and teasingly ambiguous.

The basic situation may be heightened and diversified in various ways. A flashback technique is used, retracing the steps leading up to the point of time indicated in the opening sentence, filling in details and adding to the general interest, while at the same time varying the treatment of time as the narrator explains the present in terms of the past, and by delving back into the past prepares the ground for future events. The situation is further exploited by a technique of shifting perspectives, being seen from various angles through the eyes of different characters. In addition, by stating a theme and developing it in subsequent variations, as for example in the treatment of the earthquake in **'Das Erdbeben'** or the description of the hauntings in **'Das Bettelweib,'** Kleist heightens the mystery and adds to the possible layers of meaning while himself standing aloof as impersonal narrator, only occasionally by means of a loaded phrase indicating his own standpoint in the matter. The situation is still further complicated by the facets of character revealed as the narrative progresses, with positive or negative qualities being manifested by hitherto 'neutral' persons. Flashbacks and interpolated incidents show the complex personality behind the apparently straightforward facade: Marianne Congreve and a Negress with yellow fever represent attitudes of love and betrayal focussed on the character of Toni, Elvire's midnight rescue from fire and water foreshadows the fixation of her worship of a portrait, a count throws mud at a swan (**'Die Marquise'**), and Trota saves Littegarde from a wild boar (**'Der Zweikampf'**). A mirror technique further diversifies the portrayal of character. The actions of Kohlhaas are mirrored in those of Meister Himboldt and Nagelschmidt; Marianne Congreve dies as a result of Gustav's actions and so does Toni; the shooting of five Russian soldiers who intended to rape the Marquise implicitly condemns the man who actually did rape her; Nicolo is a grotesque distortion of his mirror-image Colino. As if all this were not enough, the basic situation is additionally complicated by the reversals of fortune that overtake characters caught on the see-saw of chance.

A particular device employed by Kleist to bring out the contradictions and contrasts of people and events is that of the double, the Doppelgänger. The Doppelgänger is a useful means of indicating the opposing poles of the human personality and exploiting the angel-devil antithesis, such as in the figures of Colino and Nicolo. It adds to the mystery of a situation, since it defies rational explanation, and it contributes added dimensions of meaning through its evocation of supernatural forces. The interrelation of appearance and reality, and the coexistence of rational and irrational interpretations and aspects of a given situation is brought out by Kleist through his use of the Doppelgänger motif.

The opening sentences give the time and place of the story, together with the name of a leading character, just as the first page of a drama sets the time and location and lists the dramatis personae of the piece that is to be played. Kleist's stories are indeed highly dramatic. Where possible they observe the unities, thereby achieving a concentration and compression that heightens the tension and helps to increase the isolation of the main characters. The action of some stories is spread over months and years; but by concentrating on central scenes in the progress of the narrative Kleist blurs the sense of time and focusses the reader's attention on particular pregnant incidents. Dramatic tension is further developed by the 'Flötenton im Orkan' technique, the device sometimes employed of having an interlude of lyrical sweetness and calm in between two moments of savagery and violence. The basic situation in each story has by virtue of its extraordinary and sensational nature a dramatic quality about it. And this situation is then decked out and embellished with an astonishing variety of scenic detail as Kleist fills out his canvas with parallel scenes, significant gestures, and interpolated incidents. The reader is concerned in the main with the bizarre and paradoxical situations that form the backbone of the stories. But after they have been read there linger in the memory isolated, interpolated details, as for example Graf F. rolling away bombs and barrels of gunpowder from the blazing fortress, Nicolo cracking nuts indifferently while Piachi weeps for his lost son, eager boys perched hat in hand on the walls of the Dominican church in **'Das Erdbeben'** waiting for the Te Deum to begin, and the tear that rolls down Kohlhaas' cheek as he receives the letter from his Dresden lawyer telling him of the failure of his attempt to secure justice. Kleist offers little in the way of scenic description. Landscapes when they occur tend to be bleak, emphasising the isolation of the individuals silhouetted against them. But sometimes, at climactic moments, the stage is filled by a great crowd of spectators like a Greek chorus, the 'unermeßliche Menschenmenge' summoned by Kleist to witness key points in the action.

Kleist constructs his stories carefully, and their formal precision often contrasts sharply with the violence and brutality of the events portrayed. It is not possible, however, to construct an overall blueprint for the *Erzählungen,* and different ones are characterised by a particular mood or atmosphere. The interplay of black and white is the dominant feature of **'Die Verlobung';** the symbolism of the plague runs like a dark thread through **'Der Findling';** the pattern of the quest underlies *Michael Kohlhaas;* and the interaction of 'Scherz' and 'Ernst' sets the mood for **'Die Marquise von O.'** The savagery of the lynch mob in **'Das Erdbeben'** contrasts with the singing of the nuns in **'Die heilige Cäcilie,'** the desolation at the end of **'Der Findling'** stands in sharp contrast to the string of young Russians born to Count F. and his wife the Marquise von O. There is no lack of variety in the *Erzählungen.*

These stories are, then, narrated in a prose style staggering in its originality and quite unique in German literature. Long sentences, with the subject separated from the verb and the verb separated from the object by incapsulated clauses, themselves interrupted in turn by participial and adverbial phrases inserted generously, go on from line to line as the various incidents in the plot and stages in the argument are chronicled with meticulous care by a narrator apparently uninvolved subjectively in what he is recounting. The sentences have a forward dramatic impetus, the frequent use of phrases such as 'dergestalt, daß . . . ' and 'so daß . . . ', 'in such a way, that . . . ' and 'so that . . . ', urging the reader on to the final punchline or dramatic twist. The main elements in the sentences, the subject, main verb and direct object, by virtue of being isolated by all the incapsulations, stand out in greater relief, put under the spotlight as it were amidst the accompanying detail. But the forward impetus of the sentences, reinforced by the paratactic narrative method, is then all but brought to a halt by the plethora of attendant detail packed into them, so that a most curious combination of stationary and non-stationary elements is achieved. The sentences give the overall impression of speed, yet can only be read maddeningly slowly, and frequently have to be re-read if the various parts are to be seen in relation to the whole. Kleist designs his sentences as if they were mathematical equations; the main terms of the equation are stated, and then the various pluses and minuses, bracketed formulae and appended fractions are woven into the main body of the statement. They might equally be compared to the different pieces of a jigsaw puzzle, apparently haphazardly assembled and then fitting each into its allotted place to produce the finished puzzle. There is no padding in these infinitely complex structures, and every phrase has its allotted role within the overall pattern.

These sentences then grow enormously in length because of Kleist's use of what might be called his 'indem' technique, (conjunction = 'whilst', 'while'), whereby gestures accompany speech, subordinate actions fill out the main narrative, a whole wealth of attendant detail is brought in like so many stage directions to swell the basic statement, so that an effect of simultaneity is produced and characters' emotions are expressed through external gesture without any additional comment on the part of the narrator being necessary. Two examples may stand for many. When Kohlhaas returns home after discovering how his horses have been treated at the Tronkenburg he finds out from his wife what has happened to Herse, and as he asks her questions he takes off his coat, loosens his collar, and sits down in his chair (chairs and stools are Kleist's stock stage property), and these accompanying gestures give a good impression of the tension building up in him as he struggles to go through the normal routine of relaxing at home. When he arranges the sale of his house to a neighbour his wife's gestures are carefully noted as she kisses her child, busies herself with increasing urgency about the room, and generally strives to suppress her inner agitation at what her husband is doing. In doing this she does not say a word; her actions express her state of mind and make speech superfluous. There are countless examples of Kleist's 'indem' technique, and the result is to put flesh on the bare bones of the narrative and to add layers of meaning to the bald recital of facts laconically reported by the apparently detached chronicler. Since the narrator does not comment directly on these interpolated clauses it is up to the reader to speculate on their implied significance, and the open-ended nature of some of the interpolations adds to the depth and tension of the sentences. Through its introduction of significant detail and symbolic imagery, as for example that of fire, storms or battle, the 'indem' technique also means that occasionally a gleam of poetry illumines the dry factual prose.

Kleist's sentences, their parts carefully arranged to form an intricate whole, proceed on their way remorselessly and the argument develops with an almost icy logic, as if the inevitable nature of the fate governing the stories were expressed through the pre-ordained sequence of the syntax. And yet this cool and carefully elaborated prose, the intellectual tour-de-force of an apparently detached reporter, is used to describe scenes of savagery and horror and to portray the anguish of soul of characters brought to the brink of despair. Violence and sadism is conveyed tersely in subordinate clauses; Meister Pedrillo clubs down Josephe, Hans von Tronka is hurled across the floor of the Tronkenburg, the brains of Gustav bespatter the walls, and all this is narrated almost *en passant*. Tricks of style reinforce the overall effect. Verbs are generally active and, because of the German characteristic of throwing verbs to the end of dependent clauses, they are stored up by Kleist and then released in batches, like so many bullets out of a machine-gun. One wonders if Kleist's exploitation of the peculiarities of German word-order may not be an unconscious projection of his own nervous stammer. Another trick of his is to repeat a conjunction or adverb many times with cumulative effect, leading up to some telling point, as for example in the passage from **'Das Erdbeben'** quoted earlier. Direct speech may be inserted, often without warning, into the narrative with telling effect, an effect frequently heightened by the deliberate omission of inverted commas. On the other hand indirect speech is often used, partly to report a situation or incident with the greatest possible terseness and compression, partly to achieve on occasion a mood almost of unreality or detached irony. A famous example is the scene in **'Die Marquise von O.'** where the count turns up unexpectedly and asks the Marquise to marry him. There are no fewer than thirty-three clauses beginning with 'daß', and far from being a stylistic blemish this insistence on indirect reporting, with its use of conditional tenses and its evocation of another time sequence, creates an effect of something akin to unreality—the scene is in all conscience fantastic enough—and produces an impression of irony well in accord with the prevailing atmosphere in the story. [Another technique is] Kleist's leitmotif use of words and phrases, repeated several times within a few lines to hammer home a point and to reinforce an irony. . . . [For example,] there is the repetition of the word 'Schweinekoben' as Herse tells Kohlhaas how his horses were cooped up in a pigsty at the Tronkenburg, the ludicrousness of the situation contrasting with the mounting anger of Kohlhaas at what has hap-

pened and anticipating, in the grotesqueness of the contrast, the scene with the knacker from Döbbeln; and there is the repeated use of the word 'Hebamme' as the Marquise von O. protests her innocence to her mother, all this leading up to the glorious paradox of 'eine Hebamme und ein reines Bewußtsein'. Another feature of the style is Kleist's treatment of time. On occasions time is drastically compressed, as in the opening sentences of 'Das Erdbeben,' and this increases the dramatic effect. Switching of tenses from past to present further heightens the drama of a situation. And flashbacks, reverting to the past to explain the present and anticipate the future, introduce different layers of time simultaneously and add to the density of the narrative. A final point to be noted about Kleist's style is the ambiguous impression deliberately produced by the variation in mood. Incidents are recounted directly and factually in a way that creates an overall impression of clarity. But this clarity is then brought into question by the studied use of conditional tenses and qualifying phrases, particularly in the loaded sentences with which the stories open and close. (pp. 151-63)

For all its unique character Kleist's style does not lack variety. It can be dry and factual, like some legal protocol. It can acquire an unreal, almost nightmarish and grotesque flavour, when the speed of the narrative accelerates, as in the lynching scene in **'Das Erdbeben'** and the assault on the Tronkenburg in *Michael Kohlhaas.* It can be coarsely comic, as in the scene with the knacker from Döbbeln, or loaded with subtle irony, as in **'Die Marquise von O.'** It can emphasise auditory elements, as in **'Das Bettelweib,'** or under the influence of painting be full of plastic touches, as in **'Die Verlobung.'** A good example of his style, and one which may help to illustrate some of the points made, is the opening sentence of the passage describing the assault on the Tronkenburg made by Kohlhaas and his small band of followers. It goes as follows:

> Er fiel auch, mit diesem kleinen Haufen, schon, beim Einbruch der dritten Nacht, den Zollwärter und Torwächter, die im Gespräch unter dem Tor standen, niederreitend, in die Burg, und während, unter plötzlicher Aufprasselung aller Baracken im Schloßraum, die sie mit Feuer bewarfen, Herse, über die Windeltreppe, in den Turm der Vogtei eilte, und den Schloßvogt und Verwalter, die, halb entkleidet, beim Spiel saßen, mit Hieben und Stichen überfiel, stürzte Kohlhaas zum Junker Wenzel ins Schloß.

What a sentence! It gives an impression of speed and violent action, but it is so packed with detail that it has to be read more than once before it can be properly understood. Twenty different parts, meticulously marked off with commas, go to form the whole. The backbone of the sentence is the statement 'Er (Kohlhaas) fiel auch in die Burg und stürzte zum Junker Wenzel ins Schloß', dramatic enough in all conscience as Kohlhaas erupts into the castle. But this basic statement is then filled out with subsidiary detail. Kohlhaas and his small band ride down the tollkeeper and gatekeeper, though apparently without premeditated intent. The two men just happen to be standing in the way and are bowled over, almost by oversight, in a subsidiary clause, a drastic example of the operation of chance. While

Kohlhaas plunges into the castle Herse's activities are mentioned as he sets fire to the huts and attacks the castellan and the steward, and the backbone of this subsidiary statement, namely, 'während . . . Herse . . . den Schloßvogt und Verwalter . . . mit Hieben und Stichen überfiel', is similarly broken up and filled out with detail, so that the pattern of the whole sentence is mirrored in its dependent parts. Details, like stage directions, are added both to bring the scene to life and to show how unprepared for the attack the inhabitants of the castle were. The tollkeeper and gatekeeper are chatting together by the main gate, and the castellan and steward are sitting down playing cards in their shirt-sleeves, a splendid realistic touch. The verbs used of these two groups of minor characters—'standen' and 'saßen'—are the only non-active ones in the sentence. Time and place are recorded, carefully marked off by commas. Flames leap up suddenly, a suitable introduction of the fire imagery as the Archangel Michael goes about his business. And the impression of actions simultaneously breaking out all over the place is brought out by the use of the present particle ('niederreitend'), the preposition 'unter' combined with the '-ung' terminal ('unter plötzlicher Aufprasselung'), and the use of the conjunction 'während', its force being emphasised by the fact that it is separated by interpolated clauses from the verb it governs. The sentence shows how Kleist can combine violence of subject matter with a rationally designed framework of form. The whole unit is a brilliant blending of spontaneous actions simultaneously breaking out with a backcloth of vivid detail, the forward impetus of the verbs being checked by the scenic elaboration interspersed between them, the different terms of the equation clearly marked off by commas, and all of it plunging irresistibly on to the punch line 'stürzte Kohlhaas zum Junker Wenzel ins Schloß'. If the Archangel Michael were to appear on earth his actions could hardly be more sudden or dramatic, or catch his victims more unprepared. In this way Kleist launches the attack on the Tronkenburg, and he manages to sustain the same pace and to load his sentences with the same significant detail for pages to come.

The opening sentence of *Michael Kohlhaas* starts with a paradox: Kohlhaas is both 'rechtschaffen' and 'entsetzlich'. The opening sentences of **'Das Erdbeben'** and **'Die Marquise von O.'** both in their different ways present highly paradoxical situations, and both stories end on a paradoxical or ambiguous note. The paradox is Kleist's basic means of expression, it is the form of statement most central to his way of thinking. He sees life, whether it be universal metaphysical problems or the riddle of the human personality, in terms of opposition, of plus and minus, of a 'Polarverhältnis'. These opposites coexist and are presented in the form of a paradox. The stories are riddled with paradoxes. Two emaciated horses almost bring the state of Saxony to its knees (*Michael Kohlhaas*); a mother finds honour in her daughter's shame and the sobs of an army colonel shake the foundations of the house (**'Die Marquise von O.'**); the anger of a lynch mob surpasses the fury of an earthquake (**'Das Erdbeben in Chili'**); a misguided lover shoots the girl who is saving his life and that of his friends (**'Die Verlobung in St. Domingo'**); the ethereal singing of nuns results in the discordant chanting of four deranged brothers for whom insanity is a form of

bliss (**'Die heilige Cäcilie'**). This technique of using paradox to probe into the nature of truth is one that Kleist also uses in many of his critical writings. In **'Von der Überlegung. Eine Paradoxe'** he reverses the normal precept to think first and act afterwards and asserts that it is better to act first and think afterwards. In **'Betrachtungen über den Weltlauf'** he inverts the usual way of looking at the progress of human civilisation by stating that man started in a state of perfection and then through the various stages of culture and civilisation gradually degenerated until finally reaching the stage where he is just plain rotten. In **'Über das Marionettentheater'** the limitations of human consciousness are demonstrated and the thesis, startling at first sight, advanced that the two highest forms of existence are embodied either in the puppet or in God. This playing with paradox, this constant demonstration of how one extreme produces its opposite, of how 'Zufall' operating in one direction inevitably results in a reversal of fortune in the other direction, and of how both extremes are immanent in any human situation, all this represents the central feature of Kleist's attitude to life. The element of paradox is present in almost everything he wrote, in his critical writings, in the situations in his stories and the behaviour of the characters in them, and in the majority of the anecdotes, which revolve around a central paradoxical point, and it is reflected as well in the dialectical nature of his sentence construction. Any interpretation of his works has to take this into account. If they are viewed from one standpoint only, and labelled as 'tragic' or 'existentialist' or whatever designation is currently in vogue, then this can only lead to over-simplification.

The essential nature of a paradox is that it combines two opposing points of view, and in the way it is formulated mirrors the problem of appearance and reality. Kleist is generally careful not to clear up his paradoxes and present a clear statement at the end of each story. Life is too complex for this. This is the reason for the anonymity he preserves in the main as narrator, and it is the reason too for the highly conditional phrasing of some of his sentences. When he says that up to the age of thirty Michael Kohlhaas might have been held to be a model citizen the phrase he uses in 'würde haben gelten können'. When at the end of **'Das Erdbeben'** the reader is told that Don Fernando, comparing Philip with the son he had lost, was almost glad of the exchange, the phrase used is 'so war es ihm fast, als müßt er sich freuen', again highly conditional. Kleist deliberately allows an element of ambiguity to remain, and it is left to the reader to wrestle with the paradoxes that conclude the stories. Real life does not yield its secrets easily, any more than music reveals the mystery of its power through the signs on the printed page. Perhaps, when human reason has done its inadequate best, all that man can hope for is a revelation of truth from some irrational source, be it divine revelation through music, or the sibylline utterances of a gypsy woman, or then, and this is what is afforded in the last story to be examined, **'Der Zweikampf,'** truth as a sign of grace from on high. (pp. 165-69)

Denys Dyer, in his The Stories of Kleist: A Critical Study, *Holmes & Meier Publishers, 1977, 205 p.*

Ilse Graham on Kleist's creative engagement with his works:

Kleist fails us so long as we look to him for large solutions, surmounting the bewildering plurality of opaque particulars by soaring symbolisms. He satisfies us, deeply, in that he patiently and unflinchingly exposed himself to the gravitational stresses of the absolutely real, the inscrutably concrete, without yet ultimately forfeiting coherent structures of integrity and meaningful experience. But such integrity and cohesiveness of experience were bought at prohibitive cost. Never was a poet less sparing in his existential engagement or, dare we say it, more deeply incarnate than was Kleist. With his figures he dwelt in a dark outer space threatening to obliterate him with the blinding onslaught of its visitations, tasting the bitter fruits of his literalmindedness, facing the danger of splintering as artist and man, and transcending it through the strength of his loyalty to an impaired yet glorious self and its vision.

Ilse Graham, in her Heinrich von Kleist: Word into Flesh, A Poet's Quest for the Symbol, *Walter de Gruyter, 1977.*

Gerald Gillespie   (essay date 1981)

[*In the following excerpt, Gillespie analyzes Kleist's preference for subjective discourse rather than traditional rhetoric, suggesting that his characters are blinded by subjectivity.*]

In *A Concise History of Rhetoric* Brian Vickers speaks of 'an almost complete change of direction, one which still affects our conscious and unconscious thinking about literature,' when the Romantic age abandoned rhetoric and the traditional genres in favour of a supergeneric, subjective discourse. In this [essay] I shall look at one intriguing case among the multitude which would have to be investigated in any attempt to demarcate the sinuous Romantic frontier. The case holds some special interest, because scholarship still wrestles with the question whether the artist-speculator Heinrich von Kleist belongs to the main movement or a marginal or in-between category. Although one probe cannot yield a sure answer even to this limited problem, it may illustrate how a large set of such probes into the rejection of traditional rhetoric could serve eventually and cumulatively as a new instrument for distinguishing more accurately the features of the Romantic revolution.

Kleist's major statement on language, the short essay **'Über die allmähliche Verfertigung der Gedanken beim Reden'** of 1805, is better understood against the backdrop of his series of crises in search of philosophic certainty. These trace a curious circle from his first intellectual guide, Martin Wieland, who posited the imperative of self-perfection through education, but viewed the psyche as anchored in sensual reality. In late 1800 and early 1801 Kleist's belief in Wielandian eudaemonistic enlightenment was momentarily superseded by Schillerian idealism. Not only did Kleist now torture himself and his fiancée with unfavourable comparisons to high ideals, but he exhausted his enthusiasm for the natural sciences, a prop after his resignation from the army in 1799. Torn inwardly by anxiety over his true vocation, Kleist was affected by the antirationalistic implications of the new Kantian philosophy—a favourite topic of Kleist research—and began to fear that no one could know the purpose of existence or discriminate good and evil, since reason was imperfect and each individual's inner voice or cultural idea of right seemed to represent merely a subjective choice. (pp. 275-76)

Initially it seemed the eudaemonistic principle of striving for happiness had to be repudiated, because conscience was subjective and susceptible human beings could not, in any case, really know all the consequences of their actions, and their freedom of choice was illusory. But Kleist was led in his own fashion over the issues Wieland had broached in *Agathon* back to a troubled acceptance of living, for which the older term 'eudaemonistic' no longer is adequate. Wieland emphasized how doubt undermined the variant moral concepts of peoples, but nature continued, despite their follies through the ages, and thus a man's duty was simply to live deeply, unifying the heart and reason, and to do good to the extent of his powers. None the less, as we see in many of Kleist's stories and plays, his human beings tragically err in their interpretations of persons and events; blinded by subjectivity, they fail to grasp in due time their own or others' deeper motivation or the forces of natural law.

Suffice it to say—for our context—that, in his own spellbinding manner, Kleist shared with Novalis, Hoffman, and other Romantics in the discovery and exploration of the unconscious, a hidden realm out of which existence fed but to which consciousness could exhibit disturbed relationships. A constant theme in Kleist, completing the anthropological approach of Wieland, in opposition to Rousseau's backward gaze at paradise, is that mankind must go forward to re-attain the lost state of unity with nature; that is, the unconscious must be made visible or expressed fully. Overcoming the departure from the purity of mere physical being and re-endowing consciousness with grace as a second, higher nature is the well-known central idea of Kleist's essay **'Über das Marionettentheater.'** But with few exceptions scholarship has neglected the remarkable essay **'Über die allmähliche Verfertigung der Gedanken beim Reden'** in which Kleist proposes that psychologically truer and rhetorically superior expression occurs in a process of release through acting out impulses that are initially not fully conscious.

Kleist treats language as if it were a heap of fragments, not meaningful in themselves, but raw material wielded by the mind in an initially defensive manner and only eventually nudged into some pattern with some rational supervision.

—Gerald Gillespie

In the first person Kleist advises his friend Rühle von Lilienstern, whom he addresses as 'Du,' that in order to discover knowledge, which Rühle has so far vainly sought in meditation, he must teach himself by talking about things he (apparently) does not yet know. Kleist uses himself as an example, relating how he has solved intractable problems in conversation with his sister. When we consider the obvious biographical fact that Kleist did obsessively explore questions in rather one-sided epistolary dialogue with his sister or fiancée, we recognize that his essay '**Über die allmähliche Verfertigung der Gedanken beim Reden'** addressed to Rühle is just such an instance of acting-out. In an intentional paradox Kleist illustrates the dynamics of this kind of searching discourse and the proposition that 'mancher große Redner, in dem Augenblick, da er den Mund aufmachte, noch nicht wußte, was er sagen würde.' Another example then 'occurs' to Kleist: The unexpected response of Mirabeau provoked by the rhetorical question of Louis XIV's master of ceremonies whether the lingering deputies had heard the king's order to dissolve the Estates General. As if in an unwitting drama this cue triggered a daring and brilliant retort enunciating the concept that the deputies represented the nation—words expressing the turning-point of French history. Kleist compares this stunning discharge to the release of electrical energy from a Leyden jar (which in German just happens to be called a 'Kleistische Flasche') and regards the case to demonstrate 'eine merkwürdige Übereinstimmung zwischen den Erscheinungen der physischen und moralischen Welt'—in line with contemporary speculation about secret invisible forces such as animal magnetism. The fox's crafty reply to the lion on the spur of the moment in La Fontaine's fable 'Les Animaux malades de la peste,' shifting social anger onto the harmless donkey, serves as a further illustration of the flux of psychic activity, speech that is 'ein wahrhaft lautes Denken.' Kleist proceeds to discuss the more complicated rhythms of group conversation when 'eine kontinuierliche Befruchtung der Gemüter mit Ideen im Werk ist.' The play of gestures, even without words, the manner of engaging in or retreating from utterance, the struggle through speed or other means to outdo a rival speaker, the stimulation of another—such features reveal the inner contours of the process of creative discourse in the interaction of psyches. And, Kleist holds, our recognition of the psycholinguistic dimensions of discourse ought to lead us to discover their epistemological and pedagogical implications. His brief illustration is the panic blanking out which often results from the shameful procedure of examining university students by having them memorize and parrot back definitions, rather than encouraging them to develop a topic in their own style and words, to think it through out loud.

Here we get to the core of Kleist's concerns. The job of the educator is 'auf ein menschliches Gemüt zu zielen und ihm seinen eigentümlichen Laut abzulocken.' In the paired infinitive phrases we find two major key terms of German Romanticism: *Gemüt* (the totality of mind and feeling), and *eigentümlich* (the particular, intrinsic, individual, and organically unique). Kleist's rejection of fixed norms, of generic models, of memorized truths is on behalf of creative individual participation in life. The excesses of many Kleistian protagonists can be analysed as attempts to realize one's own or another's identity by approaches constituting variously a subjective or an objective fallacy. Ilse Graham [in *Heinrick von Kleist: Word into Flesh, A Poet's Quest for the Symbol,* 1977] links such craving for 'unmediate rapport' to Kleist's own 'radical distrust of the medium of language.' . . . In his essay in the form of a fictitious '**Brief eines Dichters an einen Anderen'** Kleist goes on to view even controlled poetic means—'Sprache, Rhythmus, Wohlklang usw.'—as a necessary evil. It is not a reformulation of the Horatian ideal of artless art when Kleist says 'die Kunst kann . . . auf nichts gehen, als sie möglichst *verschwinden* zu machen.' The general concern over the inadequacy of language and the rejection of rhetoric or controlled means, have of course persisted into Modernism. A salient illustration for German literature would be Hugo von Hofmannsthal's well-known fictitious 'Brief' (1902) from Lord Chandos to Francis Bacon explaining—most eloquently—why he has abandoned literary art. The troubled young writer Chandos deems the means of 'Rhetorik' to be good 'für Frauen oder für das Haus der Gemeinen,' but its 'von unsrer Zeit so überschätzte Machtmittel' are insufficient, 'ins Innere der Dinge zu dringen.' He contrasts a wholeness that is 'eine Art fieberisches Denken, aber Denken in einem Material, das unmittelbarer, flüssiger, glühender ist als Worte.' When, in the year of Conrad's *Heart of Darkness,* Hofmannsthal dates the Chandos letter as if written almost exactly three centuries earlier, we have a valuable marker by a sensitive poet. He links the Romantic problem of subjectivity to a longer process by which language has been steadily called into question and devalued. Whether or not the late Renaissance intended it so, Modernists saw the post-Romantic crisis of language latent in the age of Shakespeare, Bacon, and Donne.

As Graham points out, certain Kleistian characters such as Penthesilea demonstrate regression from awareness of the symbolical, conceptual status of language to a virtually somatic literalism and pre-symbolic semantic. Metaphors of primitive passion are *enacted,* and it is often as if with the poet we descend and disappear into the physicality of language. Kleist's practice seems often to express the opposite of his Neoplatonic repudiation of the material medium of his art. In Graham's words: 'Indeed, in his ferocious exploration of the syntactical and kinaesthetic potential of his medium, . . . language is stripped down to the skeleton of a soma heavily bespeaking itself; and beyond that again to the point where, in yet another incongruous reversal, naked emotional matter takes over, ineffable in its subjectivity, and speech altogether ceases.' Thus literature reverts to the cane waggle of Sterne's Corporal Trim, to acting-out, to gesture more eloquent than utterance. But in Kleist's works there is no gentle consciousness, no Tristram, possessing and observing all the variety of modes of expression. When Sterne sometimes renders body language and meaningful gesture in a graphic form, we easily shift from language to image within his jocoserious authorial framework. But when Kleistian figures use words as if they are gestures, we sense that it is less important in many cases to read these as written signs in a normative mediational system than to experience them as emotive patterning, an enactment.

Wilhelmine von Zenge.

For the moment let us leave aside any argument as to whether the Romantic age, in general, was mistaken in its assumptions about the role of rhetoric and confused the act of substituting a subjectively grounded discourse in place of older rhetoric as somehow liberating us from the inherited, suprapersonal, collective trammels of language. The epochal reaction against rhetoric as a heritage of fixed devices and memorized formulae assumes a special psychological justification in Kleist. In his essay **'Über die allmähliche Verfertigung der Gedanken beim Reden'** he goes so far as to claim that there is no necessary qualitative correlation between apparent or external clarity and order and the actual clarity and order of thought. . . . (pp. 276-81)

Kleist searches to redefine purposefulness and efficacy on a wholly new basis conforming to psychological truth—which may not always be pleasant matter or matter willingly expressed. Jakob Spälti [in 'Aus den Aufsätzen' in his *Interpretationen zu Heinrich von Kleists Verhältnis zur Sprache*, 1975] distinguishes two main themes in Kleist's essay, the first being that of the excitation or release of thought when it is formed in the interplay with, and in the real or imagined presence of, one or several partners, whether inimical or friendly. The second theme is that of the inadequacy of language as the medium of expression for the human spirit. Whereas Kleist regards thinking to be complex and involved, language appears to be linear and to consist of a series of separate expressions; thus there is no necessary correlation between careful, orderly, extended speech and thought. For Kleist, a rapid, balled, knotty expression is a more likely form corresponding to

an actual thought brought forth. He indicates that the temporal dimension of the whole process—theme 1, the excitement of the mind preparing a thought, and theme 2, the manifested product—should not be confused with the linear order of regulated speech, if the order is merely imposed according to external artificial rules. In the most authentic utterance ('wahrhaft lautes Denken'), there will occur a natural congruence of the two orders—that of thought and that of language: 'Die Reihen der Vorstellungen und ihrer Bezeichnungen gehen nebeneinander fort, und die Gemütsakte für eins und das andere kongruieren.' The sentence employed by Kleist to express this idea seems to exemplify traditional balance and order, in contradiction to his assertion; and we may rightly suspect the impulse to paradox is again at work.

Elsewhere Kleist, referring to his own practice, shapes a sentence in his essay which, in obvious contrast to the above instance, more openly imitates the dynamics of the genuinely searching and creative psyche. Whether we interpret this convoluted sentence as confessional self-typing, and thus deliberately paradoxical, too, because it so obviously exhibits his own habits as well as a more complete model for his theory, we certainly *do* recognize Kleistian style *in nuce:* 'Aber weil ich doch irgendeine dunkle Vorstellung habe, die mit dem, was ich suche, von fern her in einiger Verbindung steht, so prägt, wenn ich nur dreist damit den Anfang mache, das Gemüt, während die Rede fortschreitet, in der Notwendigkeit, dem Anfang nun auch ein Ende zu finden, jene verworrene Vorstellung zur völligen Deutlichkeit aus, dergestalt, daß die Erkenntnis, zu meinem Erstaunen, mit der Periode fertig ist.' The dramatic flourish with which Kleist places the endstop will remind readers of episodes and passages where in single complex sentences or a tumultuous paragraph a character discovers something while engaged in an action and thinking his or her way forward.

But, curiously, in the very next sentence of his essay, Kleist the artist confesses that he consciously uses pieces of language and devices lifted out of older rhetoric to temporize and feel his way subjectively. . . . Speaking or writing thus amounts to acting out and releasing some insight or content which initially is resisted, but eventually thrusts itself into the light. Since what demands release is hidden or at best latent, language is not so much an instrument as a product; the surface features and stress lines of utterance are then left to view as the meaningful accidents brought about by underlying forces, much as a geological formation by volcanic pressures. With inner resistances and spells of unconsciousness—which resemble the jagged turnings in his sentences—Kleistian characters err and struggle against the truth; but it will out. Kleist treats language as if it were a heap of fragments, not meaningful in themselves, but raw material wielded by the mind in an initially defensive manner and only eventually nudged into some pattern with some rational supervision. Natural eloquence exhibits the genuine drama of realization, and accordingly Kleist is suspicious of the Horatian notion of an artless art. He rejects the older ideal of a supreme wilful control over rhetorical elements, even for the purpose of depicting the true course of human passions, on the grounds that human beings appear, in fact, not to be in control of language. They are, rather, sometimes repressed under its cultural or subjective weight, but sometimes in turn the agents liberating knowledge by acting out personal content through the haphazard medium. (pp. 281-82)

Gerald Gillespie, "Kleist's Hypothesis of Affective Expression: Acting-out in Language," in Seminar, *Vol. XVII, No. 4, November, 1981, pp. 275-82.*

James M. McGlathery   (essay date 1983)

[*In the following excerpt, McGlathery discusses the combination of comedy and tragedy in Kleist's works, suggesting that they can be interpreted as romantic comedies.*]

The reader of Heinrich von Kleist's plays and stories will almost immediately be struck by the frequent occurrence of violent outbursts on the part of his principal characters and their tendency to withdraw emotionally or succumb to fainting spells. One perceives that Kleist, like Shakespeare, inclines to the depiction of emotional extremes, of troubled souls, and of near insanity. At the same time, the reader becomes equally aware that the origins and causes of these peculiar emotional states are far more obscure than in Shakespeare's characters. In this regard, Kleist anticipates the more enigmatic portrayal of feeling that has become typical of a number of great authors in our century. Thus the key to understanding his works is in fathoming the unusual psychology operating in his figures—the singular emotional constitution some call "Kleistian man."

A related feature of Kleist's works is his proclivity for portrayals that offend moral and aesthetic sensitivities. We continually encounter scenes that, even today, strike many as shocking and scandalous. In three of his eight stories, for example (***Michael Kohlhaas, "Das Erdbeben in Chili,"*** and ***"Der Findling"***), brains ooze from skulls that have been shattered, and in another (***"Die Verlobung in St. Domingo"***) there is a graphic description of how, in a fit of despair, the central figure blows his brains out with a pistol. This tendency is also apparent in Kleist's plays. In ***Penthesilea,*** the heroine, believing herself spurned, slays her beloved and eats his flesh, while in ***Die Hermannsschlacht,*** her counterpart avenges herself by contriving to have her unfaithful admirer killed by a hungry female bear. Like Edgar Allan Poe, Kleist is a "drastic" author whose works contain much that evokes horror and revulsion. Such episodes are all the more shocking in Kleist because he is equally devoted to depictions of the ideal and sublime, and of the comic as well.

As the examples from the two plays suggest, the violent passions in Kleist's characters and the gruesome deeds they often perform are generally not unrelated to the psychology of desire. Indeed, certain Kleist works have offended some readers with their erotically charged atmosphere. His characters express and occasionally act to fulfill their erotic desires with an intensity and openness that was unique in his day and even in our time continues to fill the reader with surprise and amazement. Unlike other authors who have portrayed intense erotic feeling, Kleist

does not prepare us for these passionate outbursts. On the contrary, his characters are typically devoted to lofty, chaste ideals or preoccupied with other matters or causes.

It is precisely this veiled tension between the characters' conscious dedication to their pursuits and their equally characteristic susceptibility to eruptions of unconscious emotions that suggests a basic affinity of Kleist's plays and stories with the spirit of comedy. There are many views regarding the nature of comedy, but the feature mentioned most consistently is incongruity. In lower forms of comedy the incongruity is usually found between conventional behavior and the foolish, roguish, or outrageous actions of the characters. More sublime comedy, however, generally rests on the incongruity between what the character claims, thinks, or feels about himself and what his words and actions suggest about his character, unconscious motivations, or emotions. In higher comedy the forces at work in the character are usually quite different from what he perceives them to be.

If incongruity is a chief ingredient of comedy, the portrayal of the effects of desire clearly belongs among its subjects. This has been the case, of course, for as long as anyone knows. And if higher comedy concerns the incongruity between a character's perception of his emotional condition and the actual state of his feelings, then unadmitted, unconscious desire surely belongs among its subjects. Romantic comedy of this sort is difficult to perceive as such, because the object of its portrayal is necessarily veiled and only hinted at.

In the case of Kleist's works, perception of the underlying comic incongruity is rendered still more difficult—as it is in the works of his German Romantic contemporaries, Tieck and Hoffmann—by the dead earnest or passionate high-mindedness typical of his characters. Their intense or violent reactions to situations belong equally to the traditions of tragedy. His plays and stories end, as often as not, with the central figures' deaths, madness, or emotional despair or confusion. Even in the comedies, ***Der zerbrochne Krug*** and ***Amphitryon,*** and in the stories that are clearly humorous, ***"Die Marquise von O . . . "*** and ***"Der Zweikampf,"*** one or more of the central figures is left uncertain or insecure at the end. A possible reason for these endings as well as for the tragic, if enigmatic, outcomes in other Kleist works is that the incongruity that underlies and motivates the plot is not explained, resolved, or dissolved. Thus the characters are never enlightened about the tensions motivating their behavior as often happens in tragedy or confronted with their folly as occurs in many forms of comedy.

Like Shakespeare, who was surely chief among his models and sources of poetic inspiration, Kleist mingled the traditions of comedy and of tragedy. ***Der zerbrochne Krug*** and ***Amphitryon*** revolve around psychic conflicts that have greater depth and complexity than one expects in comedy, and his two tragedies, ***Die Familie Schroffenstein*** and ***Penthesilea,*** are difficult to accept as belonging to that genre, considering that their potentially comic elements appear in those scenes that are laden with pathos and are intended to be the most moving. For similar reasons, his other plays ***Das Käthchen von Heilbronn*** and the two "histories" *Die Hermannsschlacht* and *Prinz Friedrich von Homburg* do not entirely belong to the neutral category of "spectacle" (*Schauspiel*), because the psychic states portrayed in them are at the same time too intense and too reminiscent of comedy.

The situation with the stories is much the same. Five of them (*Michael Kohlhaas,* "Das Erdbeben in Chili," "Die Verlobung in St. Domingo," "Das Bettelweib von Locarno," and "Der Findling") end with the deaths of the central figures. Yet the circumstances that produce these fates are sufficiently bizarre and the emotions involved are so ambiguous or incongruous that one cannot speak comfortably of them as tragedies. This is also true of "Die heilige Cäcilie oder die Gewalt der Musik," in which four brothers succumb to what in Kleist's day was called "religious insanity." In this story there is the added complication that our attention becomes focused in the end on the psychic condition of the mother, whose discovery of her sons' fates results in her return to the Catholic faith. The other two stories "Die Marquise von O . . . " and "Der Zweikampf" end with the marriage of the hero and heroine but neither seems to belong to romantic comedy in the usual sense. It remains unclear in these stories what sort of emotional conflict prevented the protagonists from consummating their union earlier and, more important, whether this psychic state has entirely passed or been overcome.

The point seems to be that Kleist's characters resemble those of tragedy in that their suffering is profound. Our identification with them is engendered by elements of the sublime and the mysterious in their emotional responses to their situations. By the same token, his figures resemble those of comedy in that they do not understand their emotions and are not willing to do so. We are unable to perceive any clear development in them toward greater self-awareness or philosophical or psychological insight. The best solution may be to say that Kleist's characters are, on the whole, sublimely comic figures who do not know what to make of themselves (*aus sich selbst nicht klug werden*). Their appearance in our eyes as tragic figures results partly from the fact that we ourselves scarcely know what to think of them.

Under these circumstances, the actions, words, and gestures of Kleist's characters must be more closely examined for clues as to their half-conscious or unconscious motivations than is necessary with many other great authors. The special interest of this study is to show that the psychology of desire is at work in the characters even when their minds are on other matters. Indeed, the machinations of desire are particularly apparent at such moments when the characters are defending themselves against charges of harboring unchaste urges or surrendering to passion or when they are seized by a fanatic dedication to some moral, political, or religious cause. The characters are given to unconscious or suppressed sexual fantasies that occasionally burst into the open. More often, though, these fantasies express themselves through various forms of sublimation such as a devotion to ideals of chastity or, still more commonly, to visions of themselves or their beloveds as angels of rescue or as higher, divinely appointed beings. And his characters' frequent fainting spells, lapses of memory, difficulties in hearing or understanding, irrational replies, curious metaphors, and violent outbursts occur at times when they are under particular stress with regard to their embarrassment and suppression of awareness about the role of desire in their feelings.

Such veiled struggling with, and embarrassment about, suppressed passion is clearly a potentially comic subject; we are dealing here with the most sublime form of lover's folly (*Liebestorheit*). Romantic comedy of this type, which amounts to an almost religious celebration of the power of desire, generally requires heroines of sufficient beauty to awaken uncontrollable passion in the men. She is a Venus- or Diana-figure, the *innamorata* of the commedia dell'arte and its immediate descendants. Kleist follows tradition here; his heroines are perhaps more memorable than his heroes. The heroines in Kleist's plays and stories inspire an almost irresistible desire in virtually all the men around them and awaken in other women a degree of vicarious identification (and, occasionally, bitter envy). His beloveds, though, transcend the limits of traditional comedy. They are not merely the objects of desire, but are bothered by it themselves. More than the men, they are dedicated to ideals of chastity and renunciation and experience embarrassment over suppressed urges that conflict with their images of themselves. This hidden conflict renders his heroines that much more mysterious and charming.

Generally speaking, Kleist's young men, like the *amorosi* of traditional romantic comedy, are hot-blooded and express their desire in language that is at once high-minded and erotic. To this extent, they are pure comic types and relatively uninteresting. Yet Kleist's *amorosi* suffer from the same tension as his heroines. Their suppressed shame over their urges to surrender to desire or jealous passion, however, typically produces more violent reactions. In particular, his young men indulge in erotically charged, sexually explicit metaphors, often with direct reference to physical possession of the beloved.

Older men, as doting fathers, guardians, or admirers, played a central role in romantic comedy, especially in the commedia dell'arte and its derivatives. Here, too, Kleist follows tradition by occasionally including this type among his main characters. With the figure of Judge Adam in *Der zerbrochne Krug,* he resurrects the type of the older man who succumbs to an improper passion for a young maiden whom he attempts to seduce (a role still referred to today as the "comic uncle" or *der komische Onkel*). Otherwise, Kleist's fathers and other older men have themselves under better control and suffer rather from a tension between a conscious devotion to propriety and an unconscious identification with the younger men as objects of the heroines' passion.

As was the case in traditional romantic comedy, older women play a minor though significant role in Kleist's plays and stories. This type, the *ruffiana,* from the commedia dell'arte, takes the form of the older woman as matchmaker or go-between (such as the nurse in Shakespeare's *Romeo and Juliet*). A variation of this type occurs in Kleist (like the count's nurse in *Das Käthchen von Heilbronn*), but his older women are almost always maternal figures. His mothers tend to identify with the heroines, who are typically their daughters, as the objects of the men's passions. Usually this identification is not obvious. Except for Frau Martha in *Der zerbrochne Krug,* they do not indulge in graphic thoughts or descriptions of intercourse, as was conventional for their literary ancestor, the *ruffiana.* Indeed, Kleist's mothers, like his other characters, seem preoccupied with different matters. Even Frau Martha appears more concerned with her complaint about her broken pitcher than with her daughter's compromised reputation. Yet, the mothers' unconscious minds similarly proceed along different lines than do their conscious thoughts, so that one again discovers here that basic ingredient of comedy: incongruity.

If Kleist's constellations of characters reveal survivals or modifications of types familiar from older sexual or romantic comedy, what about his plots? How often does he portray love stories in which desire must overcome obstacles, external or internal, that stand in its path? One finds that over one third of Kleist's plots belong to this type and that several others deal merely with its obverse, romantic tragedy. Desire emerges triumphant in *Der zerbrochne Krug, Das Käthchen von Heilbronn, Prinz Friedrich von Homburg,* "Die Marquise von O . . . ," and "Der Zweikampf," and is cheated of its fulfillment in *Die Familie Schroffenstein, Penthesilea,* and "Die Verlobung in St. Domingo." In four other works—*Amphitryon, Die Hermannsschlacht, Michael Kohlhaas,* and "Der Findling"— blissful, or at least stable, unions are subverted temporarily or irrevocably; in a fifth, "Das Erdbeben in Chili," a young couple, after being joyfully reunited, is slain almost immediately by an angry mob. Love stories are absent only in the two minor tales that are hardly more than anecdotes, "Das Bettelweib von Locarno" and "Die heilige Cäcilie," and in the dramatic fragment *Robert Guiskard.* Thus, to a greater extent than his primary models— Shakespeare, Schiller, and Goethe—Kleist is a poet of love.

There is no denying that Kleist's plays and stories do, at many points, give the appearance of having been written by someone mentally or emotionally unbalanced. On the whole, however, it is clear that he was quite sane in his pursuit of his poetic aims, and that the horrifying level of psychic and physical violence in his works was consciously created for effect. And although many may conclude that his works were inspired by a tragic vision of human destiny, there remains the problem of explaining the predominance of intense erotic feeling in a number of his chief figures and the survival of elements of traditional romantic comedy in his handling of plot and character. We are thus not ill-advised in approaching his works as being conceived by an author possessed of a fine and subtle, if unusual, sense of humor, whose aim was to create a new, sublime form of romance through lighthearted portrayal of the incongruity between conscious dedication to high-minded ideals and unconscious susceptibility to the sway of desire. (pp. 11-17)

The fact that Kleist criticism has been almost always ideologically based is partly responsible for the relative lack of consideration of him as a humorous author. Virtu-

ally no thought has been given to the possibility that he wrote sublime sexual comedy. However, comments have occasionally been heard (sometimes only by way of negative criticism) that Kleist was perhaps not primarily an author of tragedy at all, but incorporated elements of older comic opera and *Lustspiel* in his plays and stories. Indeed, Kleist's first and only significant success with the literary public was his adaptation of Molière's comedy *Amphitryon,* and to the extent that Goethe was able to admire Kleist's poetic genius he appreciated him largely as an author of comedies. In the later nineteenth century, the Wagnerian critic Hans von Wolzogen expressed the tentative opinion that Kleist's *Prinz von Homburg* was "one of our best comedies (*Lustspiele*), in the event that it is a comedy." Most other such references to Kleist as writing in a comic tradition have been disparaging. The naturalist critic Julius Hart complained that Kleist was not above including elements from the plays of the popular actor, director, and *Lustspiel* author Iffland; the idealist author and critic Paul Ernst objected to *Lustspiel* elements in *Homburg;* and the Marxist Lukács contended that "If we take a closer look at . . . the plots, we can observe in all of Kleist's dramas something *Lustspiel*-like in the structure and plotting." Other, more scholarly critics referred to opera and romance as important sources of inspiration for Kleist, although attempts have been made to explain away Kleist's comedy as forced upon him by his sources.

While no concentrated effort has been devoted to understanding Kleist's works in relation to the traditions of older, sexual comedy, somewhat more attention has been directed to the role of humor and irony in his works. The nineteenth-century German literary historian Gervinus paid tribute to Kleist's "thoroughgoing humor and the fine irony of clearest common sense (*des klarsten Verstandes*) which at every moment guarantee for us the sanity of his mind." Much of the older criticism on Kleist up through the turn of the century held the same view. Since then, however, Kleist's humor, when it has been discussed, has generally been denied outright, considered incidental, approached formalistically or interpreted, usually in connection with existential concepts, as exposing that which is metaphysically unessential or spiritually or socially corrupt.

The widespread resistance, especially in the twentieth century, to viewing Kleist as a comic author is more surprising when one considers that almost all critics agree that a major interest, if not the focus of attention, in Kleist's works is a tension between the characters' conscious and unconscious. A character who is unknowingly or half-consciously at odds with himself traditionally belonged to the realm of comedy. Of course, in broader types of comedy there is little difficulty in knowing how to view the characters and what motivates them, but Kleist, as critics have remarked time and again, does not make it easy to judge his characters. He does not bare their souls for us through the use of monologues or other devices. We are left to fathom his characters' half-conscious or unconscious feelings through their situation, their words and actions in response to it, or often only their gestures or their misunderstanding of words addressed to them by the other characters. Comedy in Kleist, therefore, is usually of the higher, subtly ironic variety. A majority of Kleist's plots revolve to a considerable degree around erotically charged encounters between members of the opposite sex, and a love interest, with only one or two exceptions, is present in the other works as well. It seems reasonable to ask whether the emotions Kleist invites us to fathom are not often sexual in nature and whether he was in many instances engaged in portraying the psychology of desire from a sublimely comical, teasingly ironic perspective.

Actually, Kleist's ties to the older traditions of roguish, lighthearted sexual humor—traditions that reached their culmination in what may be called the rococo culture of the French ancien régime—have not entirely been ignored. Attention has been paid to the works of Christoph Martin Wieland, the principal German adapter of this French literary mode, as a model for the eroticism in Kleist's plays and stories. Wieland is generally credited with being the first German author to successfully wean his mid-eighteenth-century aristocratic countrymen from their exclusive interest in fashionable French literary products. Kleist, an aristocrat, likely inherited his class's fondness for Wieland, whose popularity persisted through his youth. The principal subject of the literature Wieland adapted to German tastes was love's all-conquering power or desire's sway. The charm of such portrayals lay in the graceful, comic irony with which the matter was handled. One critic's view of Kleist's debt to Wieland is particularly apt:

> It is well known that Kleist had a special taste for the erotic character of love. The purely physical, the carnal pleasure toward which both sexes involuntarily are steering, plays a great role in his works. Kleist everywhere strove for truth and, not putting blinkers before his eyes, he did not evade the firm commandment of nature which drives the sexes together. Precisely because this sensual passion is so free from metaphysical tinge and concerns itself only with concrete matters, Kleist accords it such an important place. . . . As we know, Wieland was the founder of sensualism in German literature. [Hermann Behme, *Heinrich von Kleist and C. M. Wieland*, 1914]

The reference to Kleist's portrayal of the involuntary nature of sexual passion is especially important. Although Wieland and his French models often exploited this characterization of man as an unwitting prisoner of desire, Kleist went farther to introduce an element of suppression of awareness, thereby enhancing the sublimity of his depictions of the effects of sexual passion. This difference helps explain why the eroticism in Kleist's works seems more chaste and at the same time more demonic than Wieland's and also why, despite some recognition of Kleist's attraction to the culture of the Romantic countries, his inclination to the "jovial sensuality" associated with the comic literature of those lands has largely been overlooked when not denied outright.

Kleist's transferral of much of what had been obvious in earlier erotic comedy to the realm of the mysterious and the unconscious was likely related to the widespread interest of his contemporaries in the darker or hidden side of nature as exemplified by the wave of fascination with mesmerism and also with the development of modern psychiatric theory. There has been considerable discussion as to whether Kleist was influenced by, or anticipated, certain ideas of Gotthilf Heinrich Schubert, a disciple of the romantic mystical philosopher of nature (*Naturphilosoph*) Schelling. Kleist became acquainted with Schubert and his ideas in Dresden in 1807-08, but Kleist's works written before that time show that his interest in portraying the unconscious was present from the start of his literary career. Thus, he shared in the broad European enthusiasm for rediscovering man as a creature of nature, an enthusiasm most often associated with the ideas of Rousseau but which has deeper roots in the evolution of modern natural science since the Renaissance. The birth of modern German literature, especially since the Storm and Stress period of the 1770s, was closely linked with that enthusiasm. The young Goethe and Schiller were referred to by contemporary critics—often disparagingly—as naturalists. And the mature Goethe identified himself for a time with Schelling's *Naturphilosophie* and was an important source of its inspiration.

It was left to the romantics in Kleist's generation to focus upon the unconscious as the chief source of revelation about the human spirit in its relation to the natural universe. Whether or not Kleist may be counted among the romantics has long been debated, and there is indeed a crucial difference between his interest in the unconscious and that of the *Naturphilosophen*. Thinkers such as Schelling and Schubert were intent on finding indications in the unconscious that man's basic yearning and the driving force in all of nature was a longing to return to a primeval universal harmony. They saw the universe as ultimately ruled by spiritual forces. In Kleist's portrayal of the unconscious, however, there is no indication that he shared this view. On the contrary, spiritual yearning of any sort whatsoever appears infrequently in his works and when it does it usually amounts to the sublimation of erotic desire. Sexual passion in his characters, no matter how chastely repressed or unconscious, does not point beyond itself to something else, except perhaps to the older, jovially ironic celebration of desire's all-conquering power (*die Allmacht der Liebe*). The judgment of Julius Hart, one of the naturalists of the post-Darwinian literary movement, was perhaps too piously expressed but is nonetheless of interest in this connection: "Kleist makes no secret that the power of love, as one of the deepest and basic powers of nature, achieves already in sexual love a most exalted and holy revelation."

Aside from Kleist's appreciation of the traditions of sexual comedy and his interest in the psychology of the unconscious, there must have been personal reasons for his becoming a poet of the psychology of desire. Although the poetic urge can only have been innate with him, there is, curiously, no evidence that he gave any thought to that vocation, or had any awareness of it, until his engagement to Wilhelmina von Zenge had reached the point where he was forced to embark on a career in the Prussian civil service or risk losing her. With the issue thus joined, Kleist was compelled to admit to himself that such employment would be unbearable for him, and the dream of living as a free artist gradually took shape in his mind. While it is not clear that between the summer of 1800 and the fall of 1801 Kleist had developed any firm idea as to what his poetic themes would be, his emotional experiences in courting Wilhelmina and his subsequent feelings and fantasies in his role of absent prospective bridegroom likely proved decisive for his development into something approaching a love poet. Of course, Kleist never confined himself solely to that subject, but it is fairly clear that only in his love scenes and his portrayals of sexual psychology did he pour forth his life's blood.

Had Kleist kept a diary (there is no evidence that he did), we might have had some direct information about his experience of love and his fascination with the psychology of sexual passion. Even if his letters, especially those to the women in his life, had survived completely intact, the picture might be clearer. At the time of his suicide, Kleist burned all of his papers still in his possession, among which were, without doubt, manuscripts and some notes that he used or planned to use in his writing. Among the letters that have survived, those to Wilhelmina are by far the most important, because they were written during the period of his one great romantic crisis and of his discovery of himself as a poet. Yet these letters were composed largely to defend or excuse his delay in taking up a career of the sort that would have made the marriage possible. His often criticized posture of schoolmaster, which he adopted toward Wilhelmina in these letters, may have been directed not (as occasionally has been suggested) toward tyrannizing her or even ridding himself of her, but toward preparing her for the shock of his eventual proposal that she—like himself the child of an aristocratic Prussian military family—forsake the security and status of her life and follow him into rustic retreat. Similarly, Kleist's now famous letter to Wilhelmina about his Kant-crisis, which has become widely viewed as holding the key to the nature of his poetic career, is suspect as providing an acceptable pretext (Kleist as one of the many victims of the Kantian philosophy about which she may have heard) for his definitive rejection of prospects for a career in the civil service. It also excuses his need to quit Prussia for other lands where he would not be burdened by his family's name and aristocratic standing and his failure to pursue a promising military career in the royal guard and then a position in the civilian bureaucracy. Thus, considering that Kleist in these letters was not being altogether open and honest with Wilhelmina, his plays and stories themselves remain the best testimony as to why he became a poet, where the focus of his poetic imagination lay, and in what spirit his works were written. (pp. 30-5)

> *James M. McGlathery, in his* Desire's Sway: The Plays and Stories of Heinrich von Kleist, *Wayne State University Press, 1983, 255 p.*

Julie D. Prandi   (essay date 1983)

[*In the following excerpt, Prandi analyzes women characters in Kleist's works, interpreting Penthesilea and Käthchen von Heilbronn as evidence of Kleist's reconciliation of the heroic with the feminine.*]

Das Käthchen von Heilbronn appears to resemble Storm and Stress plays in which a man is caught between a virtuous and an evil woman; but the similarities are rather superficial. The configuration Käthchen/Kunigunde is not the same, for instance, as Sara/Marwood. Strahl is not sexually attracted to Kunigunde as Mellefont was to Marwood, or Weislingen to Adelheid. Strahl courts Kunigunde for the simple reason that he believes her to be the emperor's daughter, and not because of any emotional attachment. His temporary resolve to marry the *Fräulein* is based on his obtuseness in failing to recognize her insincerity, not on her charm. Not one utterance of Strahl's reveals any physical attraction to Kunigunde (although he is impressed by her mock generosity, II, 12).

On the other hand, Strahl is definitely sexually attracted to Käthchen; he expresses this feeling undisguised in his monologue at the beginning of Act II:

> Warum kann ich dich nicht aufheben, und in das duftende Himmelbett tragen . . . ? Käthchen, Käthchen! Du, deren junge Seele, als sie heut nackt vor mir stand, von wollüstiger Schönheit gänzlich triefte.
>
> (ll. 687-92)

There is a second allusion to sexual appetite in the last act:

> Der Hirsch, der von der Mittagsglut gequält,
> Den Grund zerwühlt, mit spitzigem Geweih, Er
> sehnt sich so begierig nicht, Vom Felsen in den
> Walstrom sich zu stürzen, Den reissenden, als
> ich, jetzt, da du mein bist.
>
> (11. 2589-94)

Käthchen has been called a sister of Gretchen [in Goethe's *Faust*] because both are naive girls who devote themselves to a man they love. Undoubtedly Faust finds Gretchen sensually desirable as well as spiritually pure. But unlike Gretchen, Käthchen never falls victim to her own sensuality. In the *Vehmgericht* scene where Theobald accuses Strahl of seducing Käthchen, Kleist goes to considerable trouble to prove Strahl's innocence. It is almost as if Kleist were trying to write an anti-Gretchen in the sense that Strahl is vindicated of the very fault of which Faust was guilty in Gretchen's case. Strahl is, unlike Faust, too virtuous to lead a country girl astray, and Käthchen, unlike Gretchen, is too pristine to indulge.

Whereas Gretchen experiences conflict between her love for Faust and her allegiance to her mother and brother, the conflict typical for Sentimental and Storm and Stress women, Käthchen is never for a moment torn between her duty to Theobald and her love for Strahl. She pities Theobald, but never suffers pangs of conscience for deserting him. After her broken bones are healed, she departs from Heilbronn without a word of explanation to Theobald, refuses to go with him when he comes to pick her up at Schloss Wetterstrahl, and leaves him a third time at the monastery in order to come to Strahl's aid. It is, however, not quite accurate to imply, as some critics have, that Käthchen experiences no conflict whatsoever. In the third act she alludes to her dilemma: "Gott im höchsten Himmel; du vernichtest mich! Du legst mir deine Worte kreuzweis, wie Messer, in die Brust!" (11. 1488-90). She cannot decide whether she should enter the convent or marry her betrothed in Heilbronn.

On what exactly is the conflict based, if not on her duty to Theobald? Wetter von Strahl alone is the catalyst of Käthchen's conflict, for while she has made it a law of her being to dedicate her life to Strahl, he has demanded that she keep away. Although she feels under obligation to obey him, and leave, she cannot because this will keep her from serving him perfectly. Her robust energy while following Strahl on the highway proves how easily she can disregard Theobald; her fainting spells befall her only after Strahl makes her promise not to follow him any more.

Although Käthchen's "hündische Dienstfertigkeit" (1. 1866) may also seem to put worlds between her character and that of more self-assertive characters such as Eugenie or Johanna, Käthchen, like Penthesilea, actually is an active hero. Both she and Penthesilea search out their men rather than waiting to be courted. It would be a mistake however to apply the (male) hero role directly to her since there are so many deviations which she, as a conventional woman, must make. The intention of her quest is not to bring back a boon to society. Thus when one tries to apply, for example, Joseph Campbell's model of the hero to Käthchen, difficulties arise. For it appears that she simultaneously functions as hero and as elixir, i.e., the boon the hero is seeking. The prerequisite in Campbell's model seems to be a male protagonist.

Käthchen does show a good deal more independence in her actions than earlier dramatic women such as Gretchen or Luise Millerin. She leaves Heilbronn to follow Strahl without considering Theobald's opposition. Instead of subordinating herself to a given social order, Käthchen in some ways breaks out of it. She appears to be setting her own standard when she leaves her life in Heilbronn behind her. Rather than conforming to a behavior model that is dictated by the society, she follows an inner conviction based on a dream.

The restriction of Käthchen to the private sphere is so obvious that it barely needs exposition. Her total lack of understanding for anything connected to public affairs is illustrated by her conduct before the *Vehme*. On entering the court, she looks to Strahl as her only possible judge. Kneeling before him she says: "Vor meinem Richter hat man mich gerufen" (1. 364). The count tries to inform her that he is actually the accused, but she pays no attention, continues to resist court procedings, and will answer only the questions Strahl poses. Her calling in life is unambiguous and narrow: to serve Strahl, to love him.

Divine and utopian qualities are attributed to Käthchen just as they were to Iphigenie [in Goethe's *Iphigenie auf Tauris*]. Theobald alludes to his foster daughter's divine origin in the first scene: it is "als ob die Himmel von Schwaben sie erzeugte" (11. 78-79). Strahl imagines her in celestial terms when he exclaims: "als ob sie vom Himmel herabgeschneit wäre!" (1. 252). Alongside of such passages one could place Arkas' description of Iphigenie as "die Milde die herab / In menschlicher Gestalt vom Himmel kommt" (11. 1477-78). What is the function of the perfection male characters attribute to conventional spirited women?

In both cases the supposed divine nature of the women translates into healing power. Käthchen has been called a "vessel of healing" since she is Heilbronn, or fountain of healing. Orestes attributes healing powers to his sister in his final speech, in which he claims he was cured by her touch: "von dir berührt / War ich geheilt" (1. 2119f.). Because healing has been associated with the duties of motherhood, medicinal arts have throughout history often been the prerogative of women. Of course, the healing Käthchen and Iphigenie practice is not meant to cure physical wounds but rather psychological ones: Orestes' guilt and Strahl's aching heart. By curing Orestes, Iphigenie enables him to return to himself and to proceed with those heroic duties and adventure which were interrupted by his matricide and its consequences. When in the last act Orestes draws his sword against Thoas, it is clear that he is cured of his disabling guilt.

Käthchen saves Strahl in two ways: by preventing his marriage to Kunigunde and by satisfying his heart so that he can again devote his full energy to knightly duties and battles. If Strahl had married Kunigunde it would have been politically disastrous, for she would have usurped all of his land. Even if Käthchen is not really the agent of healing, it appears to Strahl that her devotion cured him just as it appears to Orestes that his sister cured him of his infirmity. Both men are enabled to pursue their public roles more effectively: Orestes as a prince and Strahl as a knight.

Kleist makes it clear to the reader that Strahl is deficient (i.e., in need of healing) by recounting the episode when Strahl came to Theobald to have his armor repaired. In the opening scene of the play, Theobald describes his first encounter with the Count at the iron forge. Strahl is covered from head to foot in armor, but he has a loose plate between the shoulder and the breast (1. 129-31), which Theobald is required to fix. Figuratively Strahl is wounded in the heart, the area between the shoulder and the breast. He is handicapped by an unfulfilled heart: for he has not yet found "das Mädchen, das fähig wäre, ihn zu lieben" (1. 1160). The implication is that a woman's love will enable him to be fully iron clad always, that there will be no more chinks in the armor. The following remark, made by Theobald, can be read prophetically and symbolically: "die Schiene ist eingerengt, das Herz wird sie euch nicht mehr zersprengen" (1. 175-76). A future time is predicted when Strahl will be a better fighter because his heart will be satisfied, it will not have cause to burst. Theobald may well have fixed the armor, but it is Käthchen who will actually make the necessary repair to the heart.

Strahl's name is not only, as is frequently noted, a synonym for lightning ("Wetterstrahl"), but also a word rhyming with steel ("Stahl"). The emperor unwittingly brings this connection to mind when he addresses Strahl as follows: "Denn du bist da, mit einem Wort von *Stahl* / Im Zweikampf ihren Anspruch zu beweisen!" (11. 2309-10; emphasis added). The references to Strahl's armor and the "rasselnd" noise it makes are frequent enough to function as a characterization of the Count (11. 139, 716, 2071). It is tempting to compare his iron coating with Penthesilea's. One line of Strahl's is especially reminiscent of Penthesilea:

> On Winfried! Grauer Alter! Ich küsse dir die
> Hand, und danke dir, dass ich bin; doch hättest
> du sie *an die stählerne Brust gedrückt,* du hättest
> ein Geschlecht von Königen erzeugt.
>   (11. 714-17; emphasis added)

In contrast to Strahl, Penthesilea feels her armor a hindrance in love:

> Hier *dieses Eisen* soll, Gefährtinnen,
> Soll mit der sanftesten Umarmung ihn
> (Weil ich mit Eisen ihn unarmen muss!)
> *An meinen Busen schmerzlos niederziehn.*
>   (11. 857-60; emphasis added)

The difference in attitude towards armor can be explained in terms of social norms for the expression of love. As far as conventional norms for men are concerned, there is a clear analogy between armor as an instrument of self-assertion, and love as a self-assertive act. For a woman, on the other hand, the defense armor represents can only obstruct love, since it is a social norm in the *Goethezeit* that she express her love through self-denial.

There are strong similarities between Strahl and Penthesilea, but because one is male and the other female, the value judgments are different. Both vascillate between tenderness and brutality, a fact that has received more attention in Penthesilea's case than in Strahl's. Strahl strums the lute in II, 3, then shouts at Käthchen and takes whip in hand in the following scene; however, after discovering the value of the letter brought by Käthchen he throws the whip out of the window. His next action rebounds back to tenderness; he strokes Käthchen's cheek and cries. If both Strahl and Penthesilea have violent natures with sadistic overtones, the question arises as to why Strahl seems a more virtuous character.

One answer lies in the observation that Penthesilea's impulse to love and her need to fight are incompatible, whereas for Strahl, the two complement one another. Many critics have lamented the fate of Penthesilea, who could not discard her armor and love Achilles properly; but little attention has been paid to the odd behavior Strahl exhibits in a dream. He has no need of shedding his iron covering to love Käthchen. On the contrary, he puts on his fighting suit just for her. He goes to her bed chamber fully clad in armor and sees no contradiction whatsoever: "'Den Helm! Den Harnisch! Das Schwert!'—'Wo willst du hin?' fragt die Mutter. 'Zu ihr,' spricht er, 'zu ihr!'" (11. 1182-83). No regrets are associated with pressing Käthchen "an die stahlerne Brust."

Strahl's inhumanity not only to Käthchen, but also to Freiburg and Gottschalk seems less objectionable than Penthesilea's inhumanity partly because such behavior conforms to social expectations for masculine conduct, whereas it violates the norms for feminine role. Strahl treats his faithful servant Gottschalk consistently poorly—ordering him around peremptorily, calling him an old fool: "Schweig alter Esel, du, sag ich" (1. 1663). Strahl attacks Freiburg recklessly and viciously before he knows that knight's true identity. He regrets his brashness, which could easily have made him Freiburg's murderer, but he does not change his conduct in general.

Käthchen's complete forgiveness and acceptance of Strahl's blindness and meanness calls to mind one of Kleist's sententious lines to Wilhelmine: "keine Tugend ist weiblicher als Duldsamkeit bei den Fehlern anderer" (January 22, 1801).

In fact, Käthchen coincides all too perfectly with the normative ideas Kleist expressed on women in his letters to Wilhelmine and to his sister, Ulrike; for example:

> Die Frau . . . ist mit ihrer ganzen Seele für ihren Mann tätig, sie gehört niemandem an als ihrem Manne, und sie gehört ihm *ganz* an; die Frau empfängt . . . nichts von ihm, als Schutz gegen Angriff auf Ehre und Sicherheit, und Unterhalt für die Bedürfnisse ihres Lebens, der Mann hingegen empfängt, wenn die Frau ihre Hauspflichten erfüllt, die ganze Summe seines irdischen Glücks. . . . Der Mann empfängt also unendlich mehr von seiner Frau, als umgekehrt die Frau von ihrem Mann.
>   (Letter to Wilhelmine, May 30, 1801)

In contrast to Rousseau, who underlined the economic dependence of the wife, Kleist presents the new ethic of the times, which was to become increasingly popular in the nineteenth century: woman as savior of man, woman glorified as the bringer of bliss to the family and to her husband. Her economic dependence is brushed aside.

Käthchen does belong totally and unequivocally to Strahl. She also gives much more than she receives in the course of the play, affirming the imbalance of benefits Kleist refers to: "Der Mann also empfängt unendlich mehr . . ." In that same letter to Wilhelmine, Kleist also specifies the restriction of women to the private sphere, which is so obvious in the play that Käthchen would never think to question it:

> Der Mann ist nicht bloss der Mann seiner Frau, er ist auch Bürger des Staates, die Frau hingegen ist nichts, als die Frau ihres Mannes; der Mann hat nicht bloss Verpflichtungen gegen seine Frau, er hat auch Verpflichtungen gegen sein Vaterland; die Frau hingegen hat keine andern Verpflichtungen, als Verpflichtungen gegen ihren Mann.

In total subordination to the man she loves and in voluntary restriction to the private sphere, Käthchen incarnates not merely Kleist's personal "Traumfrau," but also a feminine ideal that would find applause throughout the nineteenth century.

Several critics have commented on the lack of character development in Käthchen. On these grounds it becomes possible to dismiss her as the hero of the play and instead consider Strahl as the central protagonist. It is indeed difficult to discuss Käthchen as an independent character because in the play her character is determined by Strahl's needs. Thus Strahl, in a state of feverish delerium, wishes for a woman who can love him as he feels he merits. Brigitte, Kunigunde's housekeeper, explains the circumstance of his illness:

> Alles, was in seinem Herzen verschlossen war, lag nun, im Wahnsinn des Fiebers, auf seiner Zunge: er schiede gern, sprach er, von hinnen; das Mädchen, das fähig wäre, ihn zu lieben, sei nicht vorhanden; Leben aber ohne Liebe sei Tod. . . .
>
> (11. 1157-61)

In answer to his subjective need for a woman to love him, he has a dream a few days later in which me meets Käthchen. In contrast Käthchen does not express a wish to marry a handsome knight; it is the maid, Mariane, telling Käthchen's New Year's fortune from melted lead. Käthchen prays that God might show her if this prediction would come true:

> In der Silvesternacht, bat ich zu Gott, Wenns wahr wär, was mir die Mariane sagte, Möcht er den Ritter mir im Traume zeigen.
>
> (11. 2099-2101)

Käthchen's dream confirms another person's prediction rather than revealing any subjective wish she had expressed. In effect, Käthchen is pure wish-fulfillment for Strahl in a way he cannot be for her.

Since the reader experiences Strahl's part of the dream in greater depth and earlier in the play than Käthchen's, she appears more a dream woman designed by Strahl than a self-determining subject. Just as Käthchen is a fulfillment of Strahl's wishes, she could also be viewed by a male audience as the epitome of all they might desire in a woman, as Charlotte Schiller suggests [in *Heinrich von Kleists Lebensspuren,* edited by Helmut Sembdner, 1957] when she notes that many men were delighted with Käthchen "weil es sie wohl freuen möchte, wenn sie solche Käthchen hätten, die ihnen durch Wasser und Feuer folgten."

What is the function of Käthchen's endless patience and self-sacrifice? In the eyes of the audience she exonerates Strahl for his inhumanity by accepting it without question. If after all she had resisted his rude questioning of the "Vehme" or shown surprise at Strahl's rough treatment of Gottschalk, it would be easier for the audience to censure Strahl. Having no antipathy for his armor, Käthchen also supports his knightly ambitions. Strahl describes how he once found Käthchen cleaning the rust from one of his weapons (1. 311f.). Later when the Thurneck castle is under siege, she brings Strahl his sword, shield, and lance: "Ich bringe die Waffen," she says (1. 1786). In polishing his sword and bringing him his weapons, Käthchen contributes to Strahl's success as a knight.

The feminine role in this play is exhausted in supporting the ego of the male. Strahl's potency will need to be proven in further acts of either valor or brutality, for which Käthchen will uncritically bring the armor and polish the sword. Unlike in the Griselda stories, to which ***Käthchen*** has been compared, it is not the husband-to-be who puts the woman through terrible tests of loyalty, but rather the woman here, Käthchen herself, who insists on all the trials. By making Käthchen responsible for the dangers undergone, Kleist falsifies the true origin of this type of feminine role, making it appear as though women choose danger and self-sacrifice as a matter of instinct or of free will. Käthchen's marriage to Strahl cannot be viewed as "die höchste Form der Selbstverwirklichung" because she is complying with Strahl's wishes, not her own, and because she quite obviously has no ego or consciousness of self. Such total subordination is actually self-negation, not self-realization.

But it is the radical internalization of feminine role that makes it appear that Käthchen is realizing her own will, or that gives her the illusion of being a dramatic hero. Although she appears to follow a personal calling, she actually behaves in strict accordance with the new ethic for women, which prescribes absolute loyalty to the husband without regard to father or mother (who were still important in Enlightenment and Storm and Stress plays). (pp. 35-42)

The manner in which Penthesilea and Johanna [in Schiller's *Die Jungfrau von Orleans*] are misunderstood by other characters as well as the women protagonists' false estimation of themselves can be traced directly to the conflict between heroism and the accepted social definition of women. In general, other characters fail to comprehend the Amazon hero because they assume that she will, in a given situation, respond in a way that conforms to the subservient and sentimental definition of women during the *Goethezeit*. In Kleist's play, Achilles underestimates the Amazon tribe and refuses to believe that any of them, including Penthesilea, would be able to kill him or even desire to do so:

> Ich kanns nicht glauben: süss, wie Silberklang,
> Straft eure Stimme eure Reden Lügen.
> Du mit den blauen Augen bist es nicht,
> Die mir die Doggen reissend schickt, noch du,
> Die mit der seidenweichen Locke prangt.
> Seht, wenn, auf euer übereiltes Wort,
> Jetzt heulend die entkoppelten mir nahten,
> So würft ihr noch, mit euren eignen Leibern,
> Euch zwischen sie und mich, dies Männerherz,
> Dies euch in Lieb erglühende, zu schirmen.
>
> (11. 1428-35)

He is unaware that Penthesilea has forbidden her troops to harm him. The women warriors prove their ability to fight successfully against the Greeks by freeing their queen, who for a time had been Achilles' prisoner. Prothoe also puts too much faith in Penthesilea's weakness for Achilles. Since Achilles declares that his intentions are honorable (i.e., that he wants to make Penthesilea his wife), Prothoe naively assumes that matters will turn out for the best. Prothoe thinks that under the right circumstances her mistress will gladly follow Achilles, and her response to Achilles' statement that he will make Penthesilea his queen (1. 1524) is one of great relief and deep gratitiude: "O so lass / Mich deine Füsse küssen, Göttlicher!" (1. 1526f.). Such a reverent attitude toward a man hardly befits an Amazon, but it is quite compatible with women's social role as Kleist envisioned it. (pp. 55-6)

It is Achilles who provides for Penthesilea the epithet that succinctly designates her double identity: she is for him "halb Furie, halb Grazie" (1. 2457). Her war-like pursuit of Achilles and the defiance she flings at the High Priestess and even at Prothoe testify adequately to her heroic or "Furie" nature. . . .

Ostensibly impressed by Penthesilea's prowess on the battlefield, Achilles is almost disappointed when the queen reveals the delicate side of her nature. When she mentions how she wept at her mother's death and with what hesitation she agreed to lead the new campaign of the brides of Mars, Achilles brushes aside her revelation with his remark: "Wehmut um die Verblichne lähmte *flüchtig* / Die Kraft, die deine junge Brust sonst *ziert*" (1. 2170f.; emphasis added). There is the shadow of a taunt in this line, as if Achilles is secretly amused because such anecdotes confirmed his suspicion that these women were like all others. Yet if she were like other women, totally devoid of heroic aspirations, Achilles would most assuredly not be so anxious to have her; there would be no novelty and no challenge in the adventure. Achilles does not at all object to the heroic code of the Amazons (although he does not approve of continued breast amputation). Rather than censuring Tanais for being unladylike, he expresses deep admiration for her:

> Nun denn, beim Zeus, die brauchte keine Brüste!
> Die hätt ein Männervolk beherrschen können
> Und meine ganze Seele beugt sich ihr.
>
> (11. 1991-93)
>
> (p. 57)

Kleist . . . tries to establish Penthesilea's basic femininity so that she will be credible as a woman and that the hopelessness of her heroism can emerge more clearly. Penthesilea's "Grazie" of feminine nature is better understood by Prothoe than by Achilles. The nightingale fluttering about Diana's temple serves as an emblem of the gentle side of the Amazon queen. In Themiscyra, Penthesilea was so delicate and sensitive that she could not bear to trod on the worm beneath her foot, and regretted shooting the arrow that killed the wild boar (1. 2689ff.). Through the exaggerated tenderness in this passage, Kleist illustrates Penthesilea's femininity as he understood it. The ferocity with which she tears into Achilles' flesh in the final encounter illustrates her heroic attitude: her determination to carry out the public task of the Amazons as she interprets it. To submit to Achilles would be the feminine attitude, and so to avenge herself, to conquer the man who has humiliated her is in some sense heroic.

As Johanna loves Lionel, Penthesilea shows tenderness for Achilles when she showers him with roses in scene 15:

> Denn die Gefühle dieser Brust, o Jüngling,
> Wie Hände sind sie, und sie streicheln dich.
> (Sie umschlingt ihn mit Kränzen).
>
> (1. 1771f.)

There is an important distinction, however, between Johanna's and Penthesilea's love. Johanna sins by loving Lionel, whereas Penthesilea's loving behavior towards Achilles does not contradict Amazon law (provided she subdues him in battle first). It is true that the Amazons claim masculine prerogatives by governing themselves, by insisting on dominance over men as a prelude to mating with them, and by maintaining a culture that is both matrilineal and matrilocal. Yet the Amazon state has not completely forfeited feminine behavior. Once the women have captured their men, they are free to be gentle with them and minister to their needs: the High Priestess in fact admonishes her women to do so:

> Wollt ihr das Wort nicht freundlich ihnen
> wagen?
> Nicht hören, was die Schlacht ermüdeten,
> Was sie begehren? Wünschen? Was sie brauchen?
>
> (11. 953-55)

This behavior is strongly reminiscent of the feminine stereotype and may surprise the audience, which was just beginning to grow accustomed to the militance of the women in battle. Yet the change from military aggression to gentle, loving behavior toward the men is a part of Amazon culture and is commemorated by the hymn in which the Amazons call for the war god Mars to depart so that the love god, Hymen, can enter:

Chor der Jungfraun (mit Musik):

> Ares entweicht!
> Seht, wie sein weisses Gespann
> Fernhin dampfend zum Orkus neidereilt!
> Die Eumeniden öffnen, die scheusslichen:
> Sie schliessen die Tore wieder hinter ihm zu.

Eine Jungfrau:

> Hymen! Wo weilst du?
> Zünde die Fackel an, und leuchte! leuchte!

Hymen! Wo weilst du?

(11. 1735-42)

When Penthesilea commands this song to be sung in scene 15, she is only wrong because it is premature (i.e., she has not yet conquered Achilles in battle). The sentiment of the song does not contradict the culture to which Penthesilea belongs. Penthesilea provides still more evidence of feminine sensitivity and emotionality among her people when she reports that many of the women wept out of sadness on sending the men away from Themiscyra after the Festival of the Fruitful Mothers (1. 2084).

It is possible to excoriate the Amazon state for its inhumane use of the men it captures. But in fact, by freeing the men to return to their homelands, the Amazons show a certain measure of respect for them. Achilles knows that he can enjoy the orgies of the temple and in a month be free as a bird:

—Auf einen Mond bloss will ich ihr,
In dem, was sie begehrt, zu Willen sein;
Auf einen oder zwei, mehr nicht: das wird
Euch ja den alten, meerzerfressnen Isthmus
Nicht gleich zusammenstürzen!—Frei bin ich
    dann,
Wie ich aus ihrem eignen Munde weiss,
Wie Wild auf Heiden wieder.

(11. 2474-80)

That situation may be compared to one in which Penthesilea would marry Achilles. According to the marriage mores of the *Goethezeit,* she would be sentenced not to a month but to a whole lifetime of servitude. After acknowledging his victory, Achilles claims to have the right to determine Penthesilea's fate:

Dein Schicksal ist auf ewig abgeschlossen;
Gefangen bist du mir, ein Höllenhund
Bewacht dich minder grimmig, als ich dich.

(11. 2255-57)

As Achilles' prisoner, she would totally lose her old identity, which is grounded in Amazon culture. It is possible to argue, as A. Sieck does [in *Kleists "Penthesilea": Versuch einer reuen Interpretation,* 1974], that the Amazon practice of reducing men to instruments for impregnating women is dehumanizing, yet if Penthesilea had followed Achilles, would he not view her as his instrument for producing offspring? He assures us that this is indeed his attitude: "Du sollst den Gott der Erde *mir* gebären!" (1. 2230; emphasis added). In *Käthchen,* Count Wetter von Strahl has a similar concept of his prospective wife. His desire to wed Kunigunde reflects his concern for the political influence his children will exercise. Even in relation to Käthchen, Strahl's desire to possess her is clothed in a craving for power in posterity: " . . . doch hättest du sie an die stählerne Brust gedrückt, du hättest ein Geschlecht von Königen erzeugt, und Wetter von Strahl hiesse jedes Gebot auf Erden!" (1. 716ff).

Achilles would be degraded to a procreative tool in Themiscyra, but so too would Penthesilea if she were queen in Phtia, Achilles' homeland. For each, the other is a possession. Achilles actually risks less by following Penthesilea than she would by following him.

Achilles and Penthesilea both vascillate between tenderness and viciousness towards the object of their love (as did also Count Strahl). Each view the other as an object to be acquired for the purposes of greater self-aggrandizement. Even though Penthesilea would lose her identity by following Achilles, Achilles stands to lose nothing by indulging in a brief erotic adventure. Because she is a woman, Penthesilea is forced to choose between heroism and femininity, between public role and personal desire; it appears that she cannot remain queen of the Amazons and continue to pursue Achilles in the way she does. Achilles, on the other hand, can enjoy Penthesilea and later return to the Trojan war as a soldier. His adventure need not provoke a total break with Greek society.

There is yet another inequality of risk since Achilles has no qualms about deluding Penthesilea in order to achieve his end. Any trick that can bring the Amazon queen to his bed is for him legitimate. Since it does not occur to Penthesilea to lie or cheat intentionally to maintain or establish political power, she is far more vulnerable than Achilles. Penthesilea bares her soul to Achilles in scene 15 regarding her feelings for him and the customs of her people. In contrast, Achilles avoids giving himself away and at times appears to be snickering behind Penthesilea's back about his successful deception. His final combat challenge is but another ruse which she, in her directness and sincerity, fails to see through. That subterfuge is sometimes a political necessity and as such the province of men is emphasized by Pylades in Goethe's *Iphigenie.* In the final scene of that play, Orestes compares masculine and feminine strategies:

Gewalt und List, der Männer höchster Ruhm
Wird durch die Wahrheit dieser hohen Seele
Beschämt und reines kindliches Vertrauen
Zu einem edeln Manne wird belohnt.

(11. 2142-45)

The Amazon queen has a child-like trust in Achilles that can be compared to Iphigenie's trust in Thoas; only Kleist does not reward Penthesilea for it.

By following Penthesilea, Achilles could retain his individuality and at the same time relinquish his rather egotistical desire to own Penthesilea as a means of (re)production. Whereas Penthesilea suffers a psychological conflict because of her desire both to conquer and to love Achilles, his desire to fight the queen and love her appear eminently compatible. Achilles moves comfortably in the private and public realm and is never forced to choose between them as Penthesilea is. It is the exclusion of women from the public sphere, as practiced in the *Goethezeit,* that sets the stage for Penthesilea's identity problem. (pp. 58-61)

Penthesilea's society provides a maximum of personal autonomy for its women. The Amazon women, like men in other societies, are public personages and relate directly to the state. They are unfettered by the exclusive focus on private relationships with family and husband that tend to absorb all the energy of women protagonists such as Iphigenie and Käthchen. When Penthesilea outlines to Achilles the foundation of the Amazon state, her pride understandably shines forth:

Ein Staat, ein mündiger, sei aufgestellt,
Ein Frauenstaat, den fürder keine andre
Herrschsüchtige Männerstimme mehr durch-
    trotzt,
Der das Gesetz sich würdig selber gebe,
Sich selbst gehorche, selber auch beschütze.

(11. 1957-61)

This is a society that establishes laws for the benefit of its constituency and according to their consent; it organizes for its own defense and is not interested in extending itself geographically by conquering other peoples. Indeed this Amazon state is similar to the one proposed by Rousseau in his *Contract social*. Reason seems to be the anchor of the state, mutual consent of the governed the basis for co-operation. Membership in this state is voluntary, as is apparent in the High Priestess' offer to release Penthesilea: "Frei, in des Volkes Namen, sprech ich dich; / Du kannst den Fuss jetzt wenden, wie du willst" (1. 2329f.). It never occurs to the High Priestess or to any of the other princesses to punish their queen for breaking Amazon law or for murdering Achilles, though the former transgression is a threat to the state and the latter, the Amazons agree, an abhorrent crime. To confirm the uniqueness of such a system, one need only compare it with the government Kleist depicts in the later play ***Prinz Friedrich von Homburg***. The state in that play is militarily aggressive and its laws demand that transgressors be punished. Aggression and coercion are more an integral part of the society of the *Kurfürst* than they are in the Amazon state.

The wars waged by the Amazons do not serve to extend their territorial control or to fill their coffers with rich spoils. They have no intention of killing the men they capture though they could easily do so after the Festival of the Fruitful Mothers.

Penthesilea does not struggle as Eugenie and Johanna must to establish political authority, for she is born the rightful queen and has the fullest support of her people, who in fact had pressured her to accept the crown:

—Lange weint ich,
Durch einen ganzen kummervollen Mond,
An der Verblichnen Grab, die Krone selbst,
Die herrenlos am Rande lag, nicht greifend,
Bis mich zuletzt der wiederholte Ruf
Des Volkes, das den Palast mir ungeduldig,
Bereit zum Kriegeszug, umlagerte,
Gewaltsam auf den Thron riss.

(11. 2150-57)

Though she has inherited the crown, Penthesilea, much as other protagonists like Homburg or Don Carlos, must act to secure her birthright. It is her duty to lead the new war, which will bring mates for the brides of Mars.

However, problems arise because her concept of her mission is strongly biased by private concerns. Instead of serving Mars and her people, Penthesilea dreams of realizing her mother's last wish:

—Mars weniger,
Dem grossen Gott, der mich dahin gerufen,
Als der Otrere Schatten, zu gefallen.

(11. 2167-69)

Her goal of capturing or killing Achilles is also tainted by

personal considerations. The welfare of the Amazons is certainly not uppermost in the queen's mind when she sets out in hot pursuit of Achilles. Prothoe recognizes this problem and draws the reader's attention to it relatively early in the play (scene 5):

Du bist, in Flammen wie du loderst, nicht
Geschickt, den Krieg der Jungfraun fortzu-
    führen
[. . .]
Nicht den Peliden, bei den ewgen Göttern,
Wirst du in dieser Stimmung dir gewinnen:
Vielmehr, noch eh die Sonne sinkt, versprech
    ich,
Die Jünglinge, die unser Arm bezwungen,
So vieler unschätzbaren Mühen Preis,
Uns bloss, in deiner Raserei, verlieren.

(11. 796ff.)

Prothoe's prediction that Penthesilea will be ultimately responsible for the loss of the captives is borne out in scene 19. Penthesilea becomes conscious of her guilt and immediately plunges into a deep depression: "Ich will in ewge Finsternis mich bergen!" (1. 2351). Because her duty to the Amazons, her public identity is just as strong as her feeling for Achilles, she can never simply leave her people and follow him. When the High Priestess gives her blessing to the queen to depart in peace from the Amazon society, Penthesilea does not rejoice at being absolved from state duties, nor does she even consider accepting the offer. She appears rather to have been robbed of something very valuable; she suffers a sort of identity crisis, which is proof of her close identification with her role as Amazon leader.

Although a majority of critics since Hellman (1910) [*Heinrich von Kleist: Das Problem seines Lebens und seiner Dichtung*] and Meyer-Benfey (1911) [*Das Drama Heinrich von Kleists*] have insisted that Penthesilea's love for Achilles, i.e., her private longing, is the center of her being, the text of the play does not bear out this position. In scene 5 Penthesilea declares that fame is the goal; she wants to "catch fame by its golden locks when it flies by" (1. 677f.). In her mind this fame can only be achieved by conquering Achilles. When she believes she has conquered him, she experiences her happiest moments in the play. If conquering him really interfered with her love, she would not appear so joyously triumphant in scene 15.

At first it appears that few, if any, of the character traits or modes of behavior the *Goethezeit* considered feminine are applicable to Penthesilea. She does not restrict herself to the private sphere, does not seem passive regarding her fate, and is not subservient to particular men. She challenges her society in a way comparable to male protagonists of the Storm and Stress period. With this in mind, H. A. Korff [*Geist und Goethezeit*] indeed called the play ***Penthesilea*** "die eigentliche Erfüllung der Sturm und Drang Idee." Still, such a view is not quite correct. Though Penthesilea is heroic and appears to be a rebel because she flagrantly disregards her society's norms, she is feminine like Iphigenie, Maria Stuart, and Käthchen in that her values are in part private: she wants to please her mother, not serve her people; to win Achilles for herself, not in order to promote the general welfare. Strong private motivation distinguishes Penthesilea clearly from Kleist's male protagonists such as Prince Friedrich, Hermann, or Robert Guiscard. From the standpoint of her rebellion against Amazon law, Penthesilea is ostensibly active in the quest for self-realization, for greater freedom; but from the standpoint of women's socially dictated restriction to the private realm, Penthesilea's love for Achilles appears surprisingly conventional.

In her desire to renounce her people and follow the one man she thinks she loves, she has the exact same attitude as Käthchen does towards Strahl. Whereas Penthesilea's Amazon identity gives her a wide range of movement, her bond to Achilles threatens to enslave her in a way similar to Käthchen's bond with the Count. For the queen to forsake her Amazon identity is therefore not automatically a liberating act. Although she frees herself from Amazon restriction, she is after all only free to devote and subordinate herself to Achilles. Actually Penthesilea would best realize her own potential if she could vanquish Achilles and remain Amazon queen, which would explain her jubilance in scene 15 when she is tricked into believing that this is indeed the case. Her personal desire would thus be granted without jeopardizing her Amazon identity and she would fulfill both a political and a personal mission. Her wish to accomplish both simultaneously may properly be called heroic. As a woman, she is not permitted to find satisfaction in both the private and the public sphere, yet she finds it impossible to choose and is torn psychologically.

Some critics have spoken about Penthesilea's drive for self-realization in the play or about her need to determine herself apart from Amazon law ("Selbstbestimmung"). But it is the queen's desire to conquer, not her love for Achilles, that is the self-actualizing force. Her love, which is overlaid with normative characteristics of femininity, cannot be self-affirming because it is masochistic, submissive, and abasing. Criticism often recognizes that a woman's love is supposedly different, but it also insists on valuing this feminine version of love positively. For example, [Friedrich Gundolf in *Heinrich von Kleist*, 1922] maintains that the love Penthesilea is forbidden to enjoy represents "ihr zurückgedämmtes Weibtum, die ganze Lust und Demut der Hingabe," by which he implies that it is "natural" for the woman to show "the humility of submission." With similar logic, [Albrecht Sieck in *Kleists "Penthesilea,"* 1976] condemns Penthesilea for failing to love in a fashion that is sufficiently "hingebend-weiblich." Achilles is not expected to prove his love by acting "hingebend weiblich"; no one expects him to subjugate himself to her. [Helmut Riethmuller in *Wunder und Traum bei Heinrich von Kleist*, 1956] laments however that Penthesilea does not have the opportunity to subjugate herself to Achilles: "Es ist ihr verwehrt, sich aus freiem Willen einem Geliebten zu unterwerfen." In my opinion, love should not be defined differently for men and women.

Because her love for Achilles is self-negating, it should not be considered a vehicle for self-realization. There is on the contrary a tendency for self-realization to involve a confirmation of one person's superiority over others. The actual self-realizing force in Penthesilea is not her wish to abase

herself before Achilles, but rather her drive for fame in her society and for personal mastery over Achilles. Admittedly there is little that is in the end positive about this type of self-realization—it is corrupted by a need for absolute dominance over others. But it is also true that the *Goethezeit* ideal of self-realization cannot easily be separated from the problems of power and its misuse.

Because Penthesilea fails to conquer Achilles, her self-expression is channeled into rabid aggression and self-hate, which drives her finally to take her own life. In her path to glory and satisfaction, Penthesilea tries to become the ultimate individual, totally self-determining and separate from her society. This strategy backfires since her obsession with Achilles robs her of her freedom and undermines the only firm basis of identity she has: her connection to Amazon society. At the end of the play, Penthesilea discards her Amazon self in order to follow Achilles. Since conquering him has become her sole reason and purpose for existing, what can fill the void once he is dead? The queen is cut off from her Amazon identity and without it, her only recourse after Achilles' death is suicide.

A fair evaluation of Kleist's Penthesilea requires that one recognize the exemplary quality the Amazon state is given in the text of the drama. It is a state without imperialistic aspirations and one made up of consenting individuals. To presume that women cannot rule a state because they "by nature" want to be dominated, or that women "need" to be restricted to the private realm for their own good, is to be biased about which roles are proper for men and women in society. This bias does not aid in proper understanding of Amazon protagonists such as Penthesilea.

Penthesilea's tragedy is that while her public goals and private desires carry about equal motivational weight, she is not allowed to realize both because she is female. (pp. 70-4)

> *Julie D. Prandi, "Social Role" and "Identity," in her* Spirited Women Heroes: Major Female Characters in the Dramas of Goethe, Schiller and Kleist, *Peter Lang, 1983, pp. 13-44, 45-84.*

G. A. Wells   (essay date 1985)

[*In the following excerpt, Wells analyzes the theoretical implications of Kleist's essay "Über das Marionettentheater."*]

Kleist is concerned in ['**Über das Marionettentheater**'] with the way in which conflict between different tendencies (or its absence) affects the gracefulness of behaviour. He holds that the puppet's graceful movements depend on their proceeding from its centre of gravity, to which the wire is attached, and on there being no second, competing centre from which movement proceeds. With human beings, however, consciousness can act as such a second centre and so interfere with movements that would be automatic, unhesitating, and perfectly graceful without it. (p. 90)

The examples which Kleist gives to illustrate 'welche Unordnung in der natür-Schen Grazie des Menschen das Bewußstein anrichtet' stress the embarrassment or the affectation ('Ziererei') which often accompanies consciousness of one's states or actions. He refers, for instance, to the third chapter of Genesis, where Adam and Eve, previously unperturbed by their nakedness, become ashamed of it once the fruit of the tree of knowledge has made them aware of it. He adds a story about a handsome youth who puts his foot on a stool to dry it after a bathe, but happened at that moment to see himself in a mirror. Being at an age when vanity had begun to make itself felt, he was reminded of the well-known statue of a youth taking a splinter from his foot. The companion whose attention he then drew to this similarity with the 'Dornauszieher' merely laughed derisively, with the result that the youth was quite unable to repeat the movement.

Commentators point to the obvious parallel with Kleist's statement (in a letter of 31 August 1806): 'Jede erste Bewegung, alles Unwillküliche, ist schön; and schief und verschroben alles, so bald es sich selbst begreift. O der Verstand! Der unglüückselige Verstand.' Kleist here recognizes—what psychologists have since expressly stated—that an 'erste Bewegung' is necessarily 'unwillkür-lich', that consciously controlled behaviour can be based only on preceding spontaneous behaviour: that there can be no will to act in a certain way unless the action has already been experienced. (p. 91)

In his essay Kleist uses the terms 'Erkenntnis' and 'Bewußstein' as if they were interchangeable. The *knowledge* man has acquired from the 'Baum der Erkenntnis' consists of *consciousness* of his own states and actions. At the end of the essay, however, Kleist reaches a generalization 'Erkenntnis' is used in the more usual and wider sense of knowledge of all kinds, for this generalization includes not only the terms 'Erkenntnis' and 'Bewußstein' but also, as a further equivalent, 'Reflexion'. In the context, this latter term does not seem to mean merely reflection on one's own states and actions, but any kind of reflection or thinking. That this is so is suggested by the fact that Kleist is here speaking of the role of reflection in organisms generally, not only in man. He writes:

> In dem Maße als in der organischen Welt die Reflexion dunkler und schwächer wird, tritt die Grazie darin immer strahlender und herrschender hervor . . . [Aber] wenn die Erkenntnis gleischam durch ein Unendliches gegangen ist, findet sich die Grazie wieder ein; so daß sie zu gleicher Zeit in demjenigen menschlichen Köperbau am reinsten erscheint, der entweder gar keins oder ein unendliches Bewußtsein hat, d.h. in dem Gliedermann oder in dem Gott.

Kant had said in a well-known passage (*Prolegomena*, paragraph 22) that 'Denken' consists in combining ideas in a 'Bewußtsein'. The 'unendliches Bewußtsein' of God to which Kleist refers is, then, presumably one which takes in all possible ideas and so provides complete and perfect knowledge of everything: 'die Erkenntnis ist durch ein Unendliches gegangen.' (pp. 91-2)

Kleist, even though he and his contemporaries allowed that some non-human creatures possess 'Verstand', cannot be expected to have appreciated the extent to which their behaviour can be guided by reflection. Indeed, immediately following his example of the youth whose consciousness of his own movements embarrassed him and hindered them, and immediately before the generalization about the inverse relationship between reflection and grace in organisms generally, he tells of a bear who was able effortlessly to parry the thrusts of any human fencing opponent and who (unlike any human fencer) was never deceived by feints. Feints are actions performed on the basis of reflection, and the argument seems to be that the bear is the better fencer because his fencing is never dependent on reflection, because he never draws on memories of past encounters.

This story of the fencing bear shows that Kleist's whole argument is vitiated by his failure to distinguish self-awareness (the point of the preceding story about the youth) from reflection (the theme of the following generalization about how 'Erkenntnis' destroys 'Grazie'). A non-human mammal is much less likely than a man to 'sich zieren' because of self-awareness in the performance of certain acts. But it does not follow that a non-human mammal is much less likely to base its behaviour on ideas.

Kleist stresses (with his reference to 'Grazie' in the passage I have quoted from the end of **'Über das Marionet-tentheater'**) that an action which proceeds from reflection is often less assured than unreflecting behaviour. If it is necessary to review a stock of memories and select one of them on which to act, then there will be an element of hesitation preceding action, and perhaps also in its initial stages. The first steps may be faltering and clumsy. Such hesitation and clumsiness are characteristic of actions with which self-awareness ('Bewußtsein') has come to interfere, and this may well be the reason why Kleist does not distinguish properly between behaviour accompanied by 'Bewußtsein and behaviour dependent on 'Reflexion'. Another reason for confusing them is that incomplete knowledge often has the effect which Kleist expressly ascribes to self-consciousness, namely, that of dividing an animal against itself. A situation interpreted as promising food will lead a hungry animal to approach. But if some details of the situation are reminiscent of danger, this impulse may be checked. In such a case different memories prompt opposed actions, and only complete (what Kleist would call divine) knowledge of what the situation really is can determine whether approach or retreat is appropriate.

That Kleist devotes so much of his essay to the embarrassing effects of self-awareness has obscured the fact that what he is stressing in his final generalization is the many possibilities of error in behaviour orientated towards ideas. The representation of the real world in any mind—other (he suggests in this generalization) than that of God—can be but flimsy compared with the reality. Behaviour based on such an inadequate mental picture may lead the animal into serious error—particularly, one may add, since effective action must be based on confidence. When we have reviewed all our relevant beliefs, and found some favourable and others unfavourable to a course of action, we have to make our choice, and unless we can at this crucial moment suppress all the contrary tendencies, our action will be half-hearted even if it occurs at all. The biologist would note that man is here most at risk, for he exceeds all other creatures in his capacity to build up representations in his brain and orientate his behaviour towards them. How many men, for instance, are prompted to deal with a particular situation facing them by some mental representation of, say, Christianity in the first century or the Russian Revolution in the twentieth—a representation that may correspond only very imperfectly to what actually happened at these past times and remote places?

That Kleist has this inadequacy of human ideas very much in mind in his essay is likely because of the frequency with which this theme occurs in his stories and plays. W. Müller-Seidel's demonstration [in *Versehen und Erkennen: Eine Studie über Heinrich von Kleist,* 1961] that 'alle Figuren Kleists sehen sich einer Not des Erkennens gegenüber' has become a commonplace of Kleist scholarship. In Kleist's very first play [*Die Familie Schroffenstein*] Sylvester more than once declares that he is hampered because his understanding of the situation facing him is based on ideas which fall short of divine perfection. When his wife asks him how he can explain certain facts which appear to suggest that he is guilty of a crime, he replies: 'Bin ich Denn Gott, daB du mich fragst?' Having conceded that evidence which seems to point to Rupert's guilt can equally well be interpreted as pointing to his own, he adds that God is 'ein Rätsel' to him. In Kleist's other tragedy, *Penthesilea,* heroine and hero alike base their behaviour on what they suppose the attitude and intentions of the other party to be, and although these suppositions are erroneous, they are the natural and reasonable ones suggested by the evidence available. Everything in Penthesilea's behaviour towards Achilles in Scene 15 points to the justice of his inference in Scene 21 that she will not harm him. Likewise, her interpretation that he means his challenge to single combat as an opportunity to humiliate her is the obvious inference from the facts as known to her.

The final generalization of Kleist's essay, the deprecation of 'Verstand' in the letter of 1806 . . . , and the emphasis in his fiction and in his plays on the tragic consequences of inevitable imperfections in human knowledge might suggest that, in his view, man would be better served with no knowledge at all. He does not in fact suggest this, either in the letter or in the essay, but complains merely that the advent of 'Verstand' has entailed forfeiture of grace and beauty. However, he had earlier—in the well-known letter of 22 March 1801—voiced a much more despairing attitude. He there says that he had hoped to accumulate a body of absolute truths—truths which he could take with him into an after-life; but that acquaintance with 'die neuere sogenannte Kantische Philosophie' has made him suspect that 'wir können nicht entscheiden, ob das, was wir Wahrheit nennen, wahrhaft Wahrheit ist, oder ob es uns nur so scheint'. If, he adds, the latter is the case, then all endeavour to reach absolute truth ('sich ein Eigentum zu erwerben, das uns auch in das Grab folgt') is vain. As he finds this thought almost unbearably depressing, he implies that anything less than absolute truth is not worth pursuing.

Such an attitude is scarcely reasonable. Lavoisier's views on acids are not absolute truths, but without his theory it would not have been possible to reach one which explains more of the relevant facts. Chemists today know that in time their theories will in turn be antiquated, but they know too that this does not make them worthless. Kleist, however, was (at any rate in 1801) satisfied with nothing less than the kind of truth which will never need revision. In ethics too he wanted not merely what is good, but what is absolutely good. Hence he was depressed to find that neither moral consciousness nor utiliarian calculation can provide moral values that are absolute. Moral consciousness is excluded because 'dieselbe Stimme, die dem Christen zuruft, seinem Feinde zu vergeben, ruft dem Seeländer zu, ihn zu braten, und mit Andacht ißt er ihn auf' (letter of 15 August 1801). As for utility, 'es ist so schwer zu bestimmen, was gut ist, der Wirkung nach' (letter of 10 October 1801). Every action one performs, he wrote two months earlier (15 August), has innumerable consequences, some good and others bad, so if it is judged according to its effects, then it cannot properly be called absolutely good or absolutely bad. This we may grant, but it is hardly a ground for despair, still less for supposing that the distinction we make between good and evil is worthless. Are we to allow plunder and murder, for instance, because some of their remote consequences might be good? To insist on absolutes means to lose sight of the short-term issues on which human behaviour largely depends.

By the time he wrote the essay on the 'Marionettentheater' in 1810, Kleist no longer estimated man's capacities so negatively. He even says, at the very end of the essay, that, in the final chapter of the world's history, man will eat again from the tree of knowledge and thereby achieve God's 'unendliches Bewußtein'. In another essay of this period (**'Von der Überlegung'**) he expressly acknowledges such reflection as man is now capable of to be sometimes valuable. He says there that a wrestler who asked himself, in the midst of a contest, what muscles he needed to tense or what limbs to move would simply inhibit 'die zum Handeln nötige Kraft, die aus dem herrlichen Gefühl quillt'. Nevertheless, he adds, reflection subsequent to one such contest can make the wrestler conscious of what he did wrong on that occasion and so 'das Gefühl für andere künftige Fälle . . . regulieren'.

I have tried to show that, whatever criticism may be made of Kleist's essay on the 'Marionettentheater' as a whole, the psychological statements in it show the insight that one would expect from a writer of psychologically realistic drama and fiction, and also an appraisal of the human condition which correlates well with what this particular dramatist and 'Novellen'-writer offers on that subject in his creative works. (pp. 94-6)

G. A. Wells, "The Limitations of Knowledge: Kleist's 'Über das Marionettentheater'," in The Modern Language Review, *Vol. 80, Part 1, January, 1985, pp. 90-6.*

An excerpt from "Über das Marionettentheater" (1810)

"About three years ago", I said [to my friend], "I happened to be at the baths with a young man who was then remarkably graceful in every respect. He was about fifteen, and one could see in him faintly the first traces of vanity, a product of the favour shown him by women. It so happened that just before that we'd seen in Paris the figure of the boy pulling a thorn out of his foot. The cast of the statue is well known; you can find it in most German collections. He was reminded of this when he looked into a tall mirror just as he was putting his foot on a stool to dry it. He smiled and told me what he had discovered. In fact I'd noticed it too at the same moment, but . . . I don't know if it was to test the quality of his apparent grace or to provide a salutary counter to his vanity. . . . I laughed and said he must be imagining things. He blushed and raised his foot a second time, to show me, but the attempt failed, as anybody could have foreseen. In some confusion he raised his foot a third time, a fourth time, he must have tried it ten times, but in vain; he was quite incapable of reproducing the same movement. What am I saying? The movements he did make were so comical that it was only with difficulty that I managed to keep from laughing.

"From that day, from that very moment, an extraordinary change came over this boy. He began to stand all day in front of the mirror. One after another, his attractions slipped away from him. An invisible and incomprehensible power seemed to settle like a steel net over the free play of his gestures, and after a year nothing remained of the lovely grace which had given pleasure to all who saw him. . . . "

[My friend replied], "We see that in the organic world, as thought grows dimmer and weaker, grace emerges more brilliantly and commandingly. But just as a section drawn through two lines suddenly reappears on the other side after passing through infinity, or as the image in a concave mirror, after dwindling into the distance, turns up again right in front of us, so grace itself returns when knowledge has as it were gone through an infinity. Grace appears most purely in that human form which either has no consciousness or an infinite consciousness; that is, in the puppet or in the god."

"Does that mean", I said in some bewilderment, "we must eat again of the Tree of Knowledge in order to return to our state of innocence?"

"Of course", he said, "but that's the last chapter in the history of the world."

F. J. Lamport (essay date 1990)

[*In the following excerpt, Lamport surveys Kleist's plays and assesses his overall achievement and contribution to German drama.*]

[Kleist was the] one writer of uniquely dramatic genius among Goethe and Schiller's younger contemporaries. He was personally acquainted with some of the Romantics and shared some of their characteristic preoccupations, but in his work as in his life he remained, like Hölderlin, essentially a solitary figure. Today he is regarded as one

of the greatest German dramatists, though in his life-time his work met largely with indifference, incomprehension and hostility. Heinrich von Kleist was born in 1777 into an old aristocratic Pomeranian-Prussian family which for generations had supplied officers to the Prussian army. At least one member of the family had, however, also achieved literary fame, the melancholy soldier-poet Ewald Christian von Kleist, friend of Lessing and part-model for Lessing's Tellheim, who died as a result of wounds received at the battle of Kunersdorf in 1759. Heinrich was also destined for a military career, and entered the army at sixteen; but seven years later he resigned his lieutenant's commission to devote himself to the study of literature, philosophy and science. In 1800–1 he suffered what is commonly referred to as his 'Kant crisis', when his reading of contemporary German philosophy destroyed his belief in the sense and order of the universe, or at any rate in its accessibility to human reason and understanding. The reverberations of this intellectual shock are evident in the plays and short stories which he produced in the remaining few years of his life. In May 1807 Goethe read his comedy **Amphitryon** and described it as 'the strangest of signs of the times, a portentous and displeasing meteor in a new literary heaven'. His dislike of **Amphitryon** notwithstanding, Goethe accepted Kleist's other comedy **Der zerbrochne Krug** (**The Broken Jug**) for performance at Weimar the following year. But the performance was a failure, and Goethe rejected Kleist's tragedy **Penthesilea** as unplayable. Kleist's career was indeed meteoric. In 1811 he made a suicide pact with a young woman suffering from inoperable cancer and, on the shores of the Wannsee just outside Berlin, shot her and himself. He was suffering from no comparable physical malady, but 'the truth was', as he wrote in his last letter of farewell to his half-sister Ulrike, 'that there was no helping me in this world'.

Kleist began his career as a playwright with a bloodthirsty tragedy, **Die Familie Schroffenstein (The Schroffenstein Family,** 1803)—originally conceived with a Spanish setting, perhaps reflecting the general interest in Spanish drama [amongst German writers of] the time, but translated to Swabia in its final published version. Another tragedy, **Robert Guiskard, Herzog der Normänner (Robert Guiscard, Duke of the Normans)**, was apparently completed soon after this, but in October 1803, in one of his many crises of depression and self-doubt, Kleist destroyed the manuscript, though he later rewrote or reconstructed the opening scenes and published them as a fragment. The years 1806-8 saw the completion of no less than five plays, some of which at least must have been germinating in his mind in the intervening period: the two comedies and the tragedy **Penthesilea,** already mentioned, the spectacular medieval extravaganza ('großes historisches Ritterschauspiel' or 'grand historical chivalric play') **Das Käthchen von Heilbronn, oder die Feuerprobe (Kate of Heilbronn, or the Ordeal by Fire)**, and the patriotic drama **Die Hermannsschlacht (The Battle of Hermann)**. His final masterpiece, **Prinz Friedrich von Homburg,** was completed in the year of his death, though with **Die Hermannsschlacht** it had to wait another ten years for publication. The plays have all received a bewildering diversity of interpretations, more violently conflicting than in the case of almost any other playwright: plainly they are exploratory dramatisations of the profound uncertainties and contradictory apprehensions of life experienced by their creator, but they seem to reach no definitive conclusion. Critics have tried to trace a thematic or philosophical development in them, but this seems a doubtful enterprise, particularly since they were all conceived and composed within the same short span of years. Kleist went through no definable stylistic evolution, as did Goethe and Schiller in their separate but parallel developments from 'Sturm und Drang' to classicism; and he seems to have felt little or no need to theorise, as in particular Schiller did, about his dramatic intentions. His work certainly shows an advance in stylistic mastery, but even this is not without its lapses and regressions.

Kleist's 'Kant crisis' was probably no sudden reversal of firmly held beliefs, but the culmination of a process of steadily mounting doubt and despair. His temperament was one of extreme intensity, aggravated by what appears to have been a powerful, but heavily repressed sexuality. He was a man satisfied with nothing but absolutes. Even the outward course of his biography is not without its mysteries, and his inner life is ultimately as inaccessible as that of his most characteristic protagonists. As a Prussian, indeed a member of the Prussian ruling class, he was also more keenly exposed to the turmoil of those 'high, momentous times' than were Goethe and Schiller in provincial Weimar. Schiller's words in the *Wallenstein* Prologue of the crumbling of the old order had proved even truer than he could have anticipated in 1798. The Napoleonic tide flowed over the whole of central Europe and engulfed all the German states. Prussia, chief of the northern states and from the mid-eighteenth century apparently the rising power in Germany, collapsed after the battle of Jena in 1806, to be followed in due course by Austria, the traditional political leader of the 'German nation'. Kleist's world was a world in chaos, both without and within. And philosophy could offer no certainty to counter it. Kant taught that we live in a world of sensory manifestations or 'phenomena' ('Erscheinungen'); our minds impose order on these phenomena and assume behind them a stable world of 'noumena' or things as they 'really' are ('Dinge an sich'), but the latter are and remain of necessity totally inaccessible to us. Kant's 'critical' philosophy aimed to establish the limits of reason in order to put a stop to what he regarded as unprofitable speculation about what lay beyond those limits—the 'illusions of metaphysics', as he called them. But Kleist interpreted this philosophy (or its more radical development in the work of Fichte) as meaning that the phenomenal world accessible to our senses and our understanding is nothing but an illusion ('Schein'), a fabric of essentially misleading appearances behind which lies a reality ('Sein') of a totally different kind. This reality may at any time break in upon our illusory world with irresistible disruptive force.

Schiller had been drawn to Kant's moral and aesthetic philosophy, to his doctrines of the moral autonomy of man, of sublimity, and of the high seriousness of art which mediates between the sensory and the moral world, between the realms of 'nature' and 'freedom'. In his theoretical essays he had worked out his own reformulations of Kantian doctrine, and in his plays he had sought to present, in forms of appropriate dignity and elevation, the struggles of characters faced with momentous moral decisions. Kleist's concerns are more basic and elemental. Rarely do his characters rise above the reality which confronts them: often it is more than they can do merely to understand their own destinies and to come to some kind of terms with the unknown powers which control them. In Schiller as in Kleist we encounter the opposition of 'Schein' and 'Sein', of illusion and reality, but for Schiller as for Kant the nature of reality is, if not indubitable, confidently to be assumed for practical or moral purposes; if his characters are the victims of illusion it is usually because they deceive themselves. Kleist's characters live in a world which is deception itself, and reality is for them radically unknowable. They are beset with riddles and confusions, with misleading evidence, with the shattering of the assumptions upon which their lives are based. Nor can they rise above their circumstances with Schillerian sublimity, for the unknowable powers which rule their lives may always intervene—fate or apparent chance, arbitrary human authorities or mythical gods whose benevolence, unlike that of the gods in *Iphigenie auf Tauris*, cannot be assumed, still less guaranteed. 'It cannot be an evil spirit', Kleist wrote to a friend in August 1806, 'that presides over the world, it is only one we do not comprehend.' But the reassurance rings hollow. More characteristic is the note struck by Sylvester's anguished plea in *Die Familie Schroffenstein:*

> God of justice!
> Speak clear to man, that he may see and know
> What he must do!
>
> (v, i)

Schroffenstein is a family tragedy of intrigue and revenge. With its pervading atmosphere of illusion, deception, suspicion, and hideous retributive violence, it is perhaps the most 'Jacobean' of German tragedies. The two branches of the Schroffenstein family, Rossitz and Warwand, are locked in deadly feud. A gleam of peace and reconciliation appears in the love of Ottokar, son of Rupert of Rossitz, and Agnes, daughter of Sylvester of Warwand; but this love, needless to say, is doomed. In a cave in the forest, Ottokar and Agnes exchange clothes in token of the merging of their identities in love. But they are discovered and killed by their fathers—each killing his own child in mistake for the other's. A blind man, a witch and a madman reveal the truth. In the closing lines of the play, Ottokar's crazy half-brother Johann describes the whole action as a satanic conjuring trick on the part of the witch Ursula:

> Away with you, old witch. You conjure well.
> I'm satisfied with your performance. Go.
>
> (v, i end)

The description is apt: by classical standards *Die Familie Schroffenstein* is not so much a tragedy as a kind of grisly farce. Indeed, it is reported that when Kleist first read the work to a group of friends, he and they alike were seized with hysterical laughter, and the reading had to be abandoned. Some of the crudities may be excused, like those of [Schiller's] *Räuber,* as natural in the work of a young writer who has yet to learn artistic discipline. But very similar elements of violence and excess are apparent in

Kleist's other completed tragedy, **Penthesilea,** together with a similar pattern of oppositions and a plot-mechanism similarly founded upon misunderstanding, deception and illusion—even though all this is here submitted to a rigid classical discipline in external form. The subject-matter is also, of course, classical in provenance, the love of the Greek hero Achilles and the Amazon queen Penthesilea. The vision of ancient Greece which we are offered here is, however, to use the terms later coined by Nietzsche, very much a 'Dionysian' rather than an 'Apolline' one: not the Winckelmannian 'noble simplicity and calm grandeur' of *Iphigenie auf Tauris,* but the dark savagery of Euripides' *Bacchae.*

It is not surprising that Goethe was horrified by it. He may even have thought (for there are obvious echoes of his *Iphigenie* in the work) that Kleist was trying deliberately to 'revoke' his own humanitarian message, rather as the composer Adrian Leverkühn, in Thomas Mann's *Doktor Faustus,* sets out to 'revoke' the humanitarian optimism of Beethoven's Ninth Symphony. At all events, **Penthesilea** (written seventeen years before the Ninth Symphony, and at about the time when Beethoven was working on *Fidelio,* another eloquent celebration of the triumph of humanity) seems to offer little hope or comfort, save the ecstasy of the very passion which proves its own destruction. As in **Die Familie Schroffenstein** Kleist presents two groups of characters in conflict—here, Greeks and Amazons—and two individuals whose love seems to transcend the enmity of their nations. But Achilles and Penthesilea are destroyed not by that national enmity as such, nor by the conflict which arises between the two of them as individuals and their duty to their respective nations, but by the intensity and the paradoxical nature of the irresistible force which draws them together, and in which love and hate, tenderness and extreme violence, the desire to possess and the desire to destroy, are inextricably combined. The battle of the sexes, embodied in the war of Greek against Amazon, serves as background to the inner conflict of sexuality itself. A series of encounters, complicated by deceptions and misunderstandings, reaches a horrific climax when Penthesilea, enraged at her latest supposed humiliation by Achilles, challenges him to single combat, sets her dogs on him and joins them in tearing him limb from limb. (In the myth as usually related, it was Achilles who killed Penthesilea.) When she realises what she has done, she resolves to join him in death: she takes farewell of her people, renouncing the Amazon state and its sacred laws, and, in a conclusion as extraordinary as what has led up to it, kills herself—not with any real weapon, but with a visionary dagger forged, as she describes it, from the hammered passions of her own breast.

Both Kleist's tragedies, despite the violence of their content, are constructed with great formal care and symmetry. We have already observed their similar use of opposed blocks of characters; but this underlying pattern is given totally different scenic form in the two plays. In **Die Familie Schroffenstein** the scene changes frequently between Rossitz, Warwand and the open countryside where the lovers meet, and as in [Schiller's] *Räuber* or *Maria Stuart* the different scenes are associated with different characters. In **Penthesilea** a single, unchanged setting is occupied

by Greeks and Amazons in turn as the tide of battle surges back and forth across the stage, in a kind of Dionysian equivalent of the Apolline choreography of Goethe's *Iphigenie.* **Die Familie Schroffenstein** is divided into the usual five acts; **Penthesilea,** in authentically Greek fashion, has no act-divisions (there are occasional 'choric' effects too, though nothing as systematic or deliberate as in [Schiller's] *Braut von Messina*) and the twenty-four scenes ('Auftritte') are marked only by entrances and exits. Yet it seems intended to be no less spectacular in the theatre than **Schroffenstein.** Though most of the actual battle scenes take place offstage and are reported or narrated to us, Kleist also calls for such striking visual effects as the appearance of Achilles in his chariot with horses, the pursuit of Greeks by Amazons in a hail of arrows, and Penthesilea setting out for her final encounter with Achilles accompanied by dogs, elephants and scythed chariots, with the dogs howling and the thunder rolling in sympathy. Both plays also exhibit a remarkable combination of violence and control in their language. From the beginning Kleist writes in blank verse, but in a verse very different from the polished instruments of the classical Goethe and Schiller. With its roughness, its frequent enjambements, breaks and pauses, and changes of speaker in midline, which seem at times designed purposely to disrupt its verse structure, it is technically speaking more like Lessing's blank verse in *Nathan der Weise,* though the techniques are applied to a totally different expressive purpose. There is also, in **Penthesilea** in particular, a tortuousness of syntax and word-order which seems partly intended actually to imitate the surface structure of ancient Greek, praised by Lessing in *Laokoon* for its expressive superiority to German in this respect. Whether this is so or not, such language is supremely dramatic, or 'gestural' ('gestisch'), to use the word favoured by Brecht. It is also essentially poetic, if rarely (though on occasion) self-consciously lyrical: meaning is sought and grasped *in* language, even at times wrested *from* it, rather than preformed in thought and then expressed *through* language, as is often the case, for example, with the more rhetorical Schiller.

If in the case of **Die Familie Schroffenstein** we may feel inclined to make allowances for a beginner, in **Penthesilea** the polarities have become not less but more exaggerated, the violence even more extreme. It is beyond doubt a *tour de force* of amazing virtuosity, in which Kleist has welded together various stylistic elements, some of ancient Greek and some of more modern provenance, with what often looks like reckless daring. He steers a perilous course between the sublime and the grotesque, between poetic intensity and bathos. Ultimately, as with *Die Räuber,* the sheer power of the work compels us to ignore or to forgive its imperfections.

Savage violence is also present, in what may seem even less readily forgivable form, in the patriotic drama **Die Hermannsschlacht,** in which Kleist strikes again a note both atavistically primitive and (more disturbingly) prophetically modern. We seem here to be even further removed from the triumph of humanity. The work can indeed be seen as deliberately anti-classical in more senses than one. The defeat of the Romans by Hermann (Arminius) in AD

9 had already been dramatised by J. E. Schlegel and by Klopstock, in the course of the eighteenth-century quest for patriotic subject-matter; but once again a historical subject had acquired a new topical urgency, now that Germany was under the domination of Napoleon and the Roman rhetoric of the Revolution was being pressed into the service of the recently proclaimed French Empire. Kleist's play seems to have been intended to appeal directly to a German patriotism of the kind which Goethe (cosmopolitan and admirer of Napoleon) had explicitly repudiated. He hoped to have it performed in Vienna, to encourage the Austrians to stand firm against Napoleon and to assume the leadership of Germany after the collapse of his own native Prussia; but after the Austrian defeat at Wagram in July 1809 all such hopes were dashed. Schlegel and Klopstock in their Hermann dramas had depicted the German tribesmen as 'noble savages' in the eighteenth-century style, exemplars of manly uprightness and simplicity. Kleist's Hermann, however, lures the Romans to their defeat by treachery and deceit, angrily repudiating their claims to superior civilisation, refusing to obey the 'rules' for the proper treatment of prisoners-of-war and hurling them back in the face of his captive Septimius:

> You say you know what right is, cursed villain,
> And came to Germany all unprovoked,
> Here to oppress us?
> —Go, take a club of double weight,
> Beat him to death!
>
> (v, xiii)

The play includes other shock effects, some of them almost anticipating those of Howard Brenton's *Romans in Britain*. Kleist's play is a disturbing document in the evolution of modern nationalism; but if it is itself fiercely, even rabidly nationalistic, it is also (like Brenton's) anti-imperialist—Germany being at the time the victim, and not yet even capable of being the perpetrator, of imperialistic aggression. And perhaps too there is something tragic, or potentially so, about Kleist's Hermann, triumphant though he appears at the end of the play, something in his lonely fanaticism of the 'raging melancholy' of Lessing's Prince Philotas, or of the hubris of the charismatic warlord who dreams of his own imperial mission, like [Schiller's] Wallenstein or like Guiskard, the hero of Kleist's own abandoned tragedy of hubristic ambition. The play has rarely been seen on the German stage since 1945; but Claus Peymann's production at Bochum in 1982 sought to bring out these and other undertones which sound beneath its apparent chauvinism.

Kleist's most superficial and least disciplined play is **Das Käthchen von Heilbronn,** but this romantic fairy-tale has nevertheless been one of his most popular and successful works on the stage. Nor does it lack authentically Kleistian features. Kleist described its heroine as the polar opposite of Penthesilea, related to her as are plus and minus in algebra: a woman who pursues her love in total devotion and submission, even when spurned and threatened with violence. Her rival for the love of the hero, Graf Wetter vom Strahl (Count Storm-and-Lightning) is the wicked Kunigunde, a hideous enchantress disguised by cosmetic witchcraft as a beautiful young woman. On briefly glimpsing Kunigunde unadorned, the hero enquires of her maid,

> Who was that strange lady
> Who passed us now, just like the Tower of Pisa?
>
> (v, v)

But he persists in his misguided affection for Kunigunde until it is revealed that not she but Käthchen is the Emperor's daughter whom he is destined to wed. All this is played out against a colourful romantic medieval background of forests and castles, with secret courts meeting in underground caves, a castle destroyed by fire with the heroine escorted through the flames by an angel, and a dream-vision narrated by Käthchen as she lies asleep beneath an elder-bush. In a spectacular final tableau the mysterious truth is at last revealed, and Wetter and Käthchen are betrothed before the Emperor as music plays, bells ring and Kunigunde impotently swears 'plague, death and revenge'. It is Kleist's most operative work, and seems at times to sound a note almost of self-parody. Goethe is said to have criticised its forced, unnatural character and the 'hypochondria' or pathological streak which it revealed in its creator—qualities which Goethe described as typically 'Nordic'. Again the adjective is for the Goethe of 1810 no longer the term of commendation which it is, for example, in [his] Shakespeare essay of 1771. **Käthchen** is, of course, one of the Romantic progeny of *Götz von Berlichingen,* a progeny which Goethe was in his later years at pains to disown. It can also be seen, like *Götz* itself, as a nostalgic evocation of the vanished order of the medieval German Empire.

All these works in their different ways reveal Kleist's predilection for the extreme and the bizarre. But in his best works extremism yields to a subtle, elusive blend, an often precarious balance of paradoxical elements. Remarkably, though Kleist can perhaps be said to have possessed a more authentically or thoroughgoingly tragic view of life than any of the other [German dramatists of the period], none of his greatest plays (unless we include **Penthesilea**) actually ends tragically. Indeed, apart from the fairy-tale happy ending of **Käthchen** and the dubious nationalistic triumph of **Die Hermannsschlacht,** he wrote two plays which are actually designated comedies, and his final drama ('Schauspiel') **Prinz Friedrich von Homburg** again ends on a note of apparent triumph and apotheosis. All these works do indeed skirt the brink of tragedy, and disturbing questions remain unanswered to darken the optimistic or conciliatory tone of their conclusions. Their avoidance of tragic bloodshed may, however, be considered a sign not only of the range and variety of Kleist's talent, but also of superior artistic self-discipline.

Der zerbrochne Krug is generally regarded as one of the few great or classic German comedies, with witty dialogue, a teasing and amusing basic situation, and a memorable central comic character whom we can laugh both at and with. It is a courtroom drama, set in a humble Dutch milieu which is designed to recall the homely, even earthy realism of Dutch painting. It begins with Licht, the clerk to the village magistrate Adam, finding his master lamenting certain mysterious injuries—a sprained foot and wounds about the head—together with the loss of his wig:

LICHT. Why, what the devil, tell me, Master Adam! What has become of you? How do you look?

ADAM. Yes, look! To stumble, all you need is feet; Here on this plain smooth floor, is there a stump? I stumbled here; for every one of us Bears his own stumbling-block about with him.

LICHT. No, tell me, friend! You say each bears his block—

ADAM. About with him!

LICHT. Be damned!

ADAM. What do you say?

LICHT. You had a wild old ancestor, you know, Who fell like that, when first the world was made, And earned a reputation by his fall; You're sure you've not—?

ADAM. What?

LICHT. Likewise—?

ADAM. I? I tell you—! Believe you me, here was the place I fell.

LICHT. Not figuratively?

ADAM. Figuratively, no. It was no pretty figure that I cut.

(Scene i)

But as the action unfolds from the barbed exchanges of this opening, it soon becomes apparent that the old Adam has been up to no good, and that we are indeed witnessing a kind of burlesque re-enactment of that original Fall, of the temptation of Adam by Eve—or, as it seems here, of the temptation of Eve (daughter of Frau Marthe, owner of the eponymous jug) by Adam. And when Marthe brings a suit before Adam for compensation for the breakage of her jug, the judge is trying a case in which he himself is the guilty party. Adam sets about using the machinery of justice not for its ostensible purpose, to bring the truth to light, but to try to hide it; only the chance intervention of the visiting Judge Walter ensures that Adam's purposes are foiled, his guilt and Eve's innocence established, and Eve and her fiancé Ruprecht reconciled and reunited. At the end only Marthe is left unsatisfied, still bemoaning the loss of her jug: object of sublime beauty, priceless family heirloom, document of Dutch history—

Here, right upon this hole, where now there's nothing,
All the United Provinces were handed down
To Philip, King of Spain. Here in his robes
Of state stood Charles the Fifth, the Emperor;
Now nothing but the legs of him is left.
Here Philip knelt, and took from him the crown;
He's fallen through, except his hinder parts,
And even they have taken quite a knock . . .

(Scene vii)

—symbol of Eve's innocence, or even of a whole shattered Kleistian world—or perhaps at last only a jug after all. Adam dominates the proceedings not only verbally, with his constant stream of lies and blusterings, of threats and ingenious excuses, but also as a physical presence, from his bald head (bereft of the wig which would have given it the semblance of judicial dignity, but which has been left hanging in the bushes outside Eve's window) to the club-foot which recalls not only the devil, but also Oedipus the swollen-footed, another judge who was condemned to preside over the revelation of his own guilt. He is an uncouth and threatening presence, but for all his villainy a richly comic and even sympathetic figure, a veritable Lord of Misrule. Kleist has constructed his play skilfully around this dominating central figure. The play raises familiar Kleistian issues—of truth and illusion, of trust between human beings as their only hope of avoiding error, of the imperfection of human institutions such as the law. The conclusion is not one of unqualified optimism—the reconciliation of the lovers has a bitter taste, Adam may yet return to continue his misdeeds, and the jug is still broken. But for all this, ***Der zerbrochne Krug*** affirms the traditional wisdom of comedy—that to seek perfection in this imperfect world is to invite disaster. It is a highly accomplished dramatic creation; and with its economical composition, its rigorous observance of the unities (like ***Penthesilea,*** it has no act-divisions, but unfolds in a single unbroken sequence of scenes) and its employment of blank verse, Kleist demonstrates that comedy no less than tragedy can aspire to the formal perfection of classical drama.

Kleist's other comedy, ***Amphitryon,*** is doubly classical in intention: not only is the subject taken from Gracco-Romam mythology, but, as the subtitle 'A Comedy after Molière' proclaims, it is closely modelled upon a work by the greatest comic playwright in the European neo-classic tradition. Much of Kleist's play is in fact translated directly from Molière's *Amphitryon* of 1668, though he substitutes the uniform discipline of blank verse throughout for Molière's varied rhyming verse. But he makes a number of significant changes, ranging from slight textual modifications to the insertion of whole new scenes, including a new finale, which shift the emphasis of the work considerably. The subject is one with a long history in dramatic literature, from classical antiquity to the twentieth century, when it has been treated by Jean Giraudoux (*Amphitryon 38,* 1929) and by the East German playwright Peter Hacks (1968). Zeus or Jupiter, king of the gods, takes on the shape of Alkmene's husband Amphitryon and makes love to her, knowing that she is too pure to yield to any temptation of infidelity. If the cuckolding of Amphitryon has comic possibilities, the deception of the virtuous Alkmene is at least potentially tragic; and if Molière stresses the former aspect, Kleist brings out the latter, developing Alkmene's character far more than Molière had done and making the testing of her feelings, of her love and loyalty to her husband, the focus of his play. In doing so he has stretched the limits of comedy much further than in ***Der zerbrochne Krug.***

The plot is, of course, a comedy of errors; and as in Shakespeare's play of that name, we have two pairs of characters of indistinguishable physical appearance, in each case a master and a servant—the 'lower' characters re-enacting the 'serious' plot at a more basic, farcical level. Here we have the added piquancy that the 'double' is in each case a god, deliberately imitating his human counterpart. Jupiter takes on the likeness of Amphitryon, Mercury that of

Amphitryon's servant Sosias. Amusing though this may be for the audience with its detached overview, for the person thus cheated of his identity it is, of course, no joke. Mercury simply forces the wretched Sosias to hand over his identity by threats and violence; Jupiter, more insidiously, not only makes love to Amphitryon's wife, but forces her to choose between him and her husband and to declare, confronted with the two of them, that it is Jupiter who really 'is' Amphitryon. And in doubting her husband's identity, she comes perilously close to losing her own. The problem of identity is one which occurs elsewhere in Kleist's work (notably in some of his short stories, where the motif of the 'Doppelgänger' or double is again employed). Molière treats it in a more straightforwardly comic manner; though here too philosophical undertones have been detected, for his play has been interpreted as a burlesque on the philosophy of Descartes—one of the ancestors of that Kantian theory of knowledge which had so disturbed Kleist. Descartes had taught that in order to attain certain knowledge of the world, we had to assume (though we could not prove) the existence of a truthful God (a 'Dieu véridique') rather than of an evil spirit ('mauvais génie') who deceives our senses with illusory impressions. And Kleist himself had written that 'it cannot be an evil spirit who presides over the world, it is only one we do not comprehend'. But if his Jupiter is not positively malign, his capricious intervention in the lives of his mortal creatures is all the more disturbing because his motives are inscrutable: a mixture, it seems, of genuine love for Alkmene, of jealousy of Amphitryon, and of the desire to show the mortals his omnipotence, to expose the human self-sufficiency of their love as an illusion, and so to teach them a lesson (the phrase may literally imply enlightenment, but also suggests punishment for their presumption). Kleist's most important additions to Molière's play are two scenes of intense cross-examination of Alkmene by Jupiter, in which riddles are answered with riddles as Alkmene struggles to preserve her own integrity in a situation increasingly incomprehensible to her, and the final scene in which she is forced to choose between her husband and the god (in Molière's play, Alcmène does not appear in the last act at all). She chooses the god, as she must; but Amphitryon himself now saves the situation by a moving affirmation of his faith in her absolute purity and fidelity. The god at last reveals his identity and the mortals prostrate themselves before him, before he returns to Olympus and they are left to themselves again; but Alkmene can utter nothing but a sigh ('Ach!'), a brief, mysterious syllable with which the play ends. It has been variously interpreted as an expression of joy, of relief, of bewilderment, of horror, of despair; and Kleist's 'comedy after Molière' has correspondingly been described as 'serious comedy', as tragi-comedy, even as tragedy. It is a rare blend of tenderness and cruelty, of farce, philosophical wit, and profound emotion. The mysterious poignancy of its ending makes all traditional generic labels inadequate.

Kleist's last play, *Prinz Friedrich von Homburg,* is the summation of all his dramatic work, and almost all his favourite themes and motifs are combined in it. As in *Die Familie Schroffenstein,* we witness a complex action with repeated reversals and changes of fortune, in which characters act precipitately upon the flimsiest of evidence. As in *Penthesilea* (and *Guiskard*) the protagonist is a military leader seemingly at odds with the national community whose spirit he nevertheless seems to embody in his own person. As in *Das Käthchen von Heilbronn,* we have a fairy-tale in which dream proves truer than apparent reality; as in *Die Hermannsschlacht,* a patriotic history play which for all its apparent nationalistic fervour goes far beyond this in its deeper meanings; and as in *Amphitryon,* a mysterious relationship between a mortal protagonist (the Prince) and a superior authority (the Elector of Brandenburg) who, if not divine, has a number of divine attributes including a degree (to be paradoxical) of omnipotence. Like *Amphitryon,* the play ends with the protagonist seemingly triumphant, but bewildered and inwardly disoriented. And as in *Der zerbrochne Krug,* the outcome hinges upon a judicial question—though here it is not the judge who is the guilty party, but the guilty one who is made his own judge. All this is presented with extraordinary terseness and economy, for *Homburg* is the shortest of Kleist's completed plays—five acts, with eleven changes of scene, taking up less than 2,000 lines of blank verse, shorter than the one-act *Krug* and not much more than half the length of *Penthesilea.* (It is shorter even than the classically simple *Iphigenie auf Tauris,* and less than half as long as [Schiller's] *Maria Stuart.*)

Kleist takes his subject from another episode in German history when national forces rallied to defeat a foreign invader—the defeat of the Swedes by the 'Great Elector' Frederick William of Brandenburg at the battle of Fehrbellin in 1685. During the battle Prince Frederick of Hessen-Homburg earned the Elector's displeasure by charging without waiting for the order to do so, but was pardoned on account of his patriotic zeal and his contribution to the victory. In Kleist's play, however, the Elector actually has the Prince court-martialled and sentenced to death for insubordination, and only pardons him at the very last minute before execution, after pleas and protests verging upon mutiny from his other officers and from his niece the Princess Natalia—but also after having obtained from the Prince himself the recognition that his condemnation was just. The Prince is portrayed as a visionary, lost to the world in romantic dreams of love and military glory. We see him first in a somnambulistic trance, weaving himself a victor's laurel wreath in the garden of the Elector's palace at night; then preoccupied and absentminded, failing to listen to his orders at the briefing before the battle; dashing into the fight, returning triumphant, then dumbfounded when the Elector orders his arrest; reduced to a pitiful wreck, trembling with physical fear at the prospect of death; then regaining his self-possession and courage, facing his execution with equanimity and even joy, resolved (rather like Melville's Billy Budd) to die for the greater glory of the law, his country and his commander. But if the Prince's progress is clearly charted for us, the role of the Elector is more mysterious. Some interpreters of the play have seen him as an ideal ruler, all-wise and benevolent, systematically educating the headstrong young Prince to a true, almost Kantian, sense of duty, and resolved all along to pardon him in the end. Others, however, have seen him in a more problematic light, as capricious, arbitrary, jealous of the younger man's fame and glory and of the love he sees growing between him and

Princess Natalia; on this reading the play depicts not a process of education but an Oedipal conflict in which the younger man struggles to assert his own autonomy against the jealous anger of the older one, who ultimately gives way only because he is forced to. Kleist probably did see the Elector as the representative of an ideal, whether as ruler or father-figure, but the relationship between him and his subordinates remains ultimately as mysterious as that between Jupiter and the mortals in **Amphitryon.** In the final scene, set like the first in the palace garden at night, the Prince is spared before the very muzzles of the firing-squad; he faints—like Alkmene when Jupiter reveals his identity—and recovers consciousness to a storm of acclamation, with cannon firing a salute, a march playing and the palace, as if by magic, illuminated in the background. He seems bewildered, but his old friend Colonel Kottwitz seeks to reassure him:

> KOTTWITZ. Salute the Prince of Homburg!
>
> THE OFFICER. Hail! Hail! Hail!
>
> ALL. The victor on the field of Fehrbellin!
>
> (*A moment's silence*)
>
> HOMBURG. No, speak, is it a dream?
>
> KOTTWITZ. A dream, what else?
>
> SEVERAL OFFICERS. To battle!
>
> COUNT TRUCHSS. To the field!
>
> FIELD MARSHAL. To victory!
>
> ALL. Death to all enemies of Brandenburg!
>
> (v, xi, end)

The Prince's dream, with which the play began, has, it seems, proved truer than the intervening reality of arrest and condemnation. If the dénouement of **Die Familie Schroffenstein** was a satanic conjuring trick, that of **Prinz Friedrich von Homburg** is a sublime one, even if we remain ultimately unconvinced of the benignity of the magician who performs it. In Peter Stein's production at the Schaubühne in Berlin in 1972, both the intensity and the fragility of the dream-vision were strikingly conveyed. The Prince who was carried off shoulder-high by the officers was only a dummy, and the real Prince was left alone on the stage in a trance, as in the opening scene: we were back, it seemed, exactly where we had started.

The note of patriotism is also, as we see, sounded strongly in the play and echoes loudly at its conclusion. Kleist may well have intended the work principally as a patriotic rallying call, a plea for national reawakening and resistance to the foreign oppressor, even an appeal to the overcautious Prussian king Frederick William III to sever the ties that bound him to Napoleon and to risk the political upheavals that a national uprising might bring in its wake. (Kleist wished to dedicate the play to Princess Amalia of Hessen-Homburg, the King's sister-in-law and a descendant of its hero, but the dedication was refused.) But it has many other layers of meaning—metaphysical, psychological, even autobiographical. In the romantic figure of the Prince—soldier and visionary, whose dreams could perhaps find their ultimate fulfilment only in death—there is

undoubtedly much of Kleist himself. No one had sought more ardently than he to rouse the nation with his art, to win fame and acclamation, to be rewarded with the victor's laurel crown. And in the work's technical mastery, as well as in the numerous unmistakable echoes of the recognised masterpieces of the German drama of its day—of *Egmont* and *Tasso*, of *Wallenstein* and of *Maria Stuart*—and of other models such as *Measure for Measure* or Calderón's *Life is a Dream,* we can see Kleist staking and proving his claim to rank with the acknowledged masters, to rank with Goethe or to take the place which Schiller's death had left vacant beside him.

The play also represents the summation of Kleist's stagecraft. Its concision has already been noted. Within a brief compass Kleist presents a great deal of action, both outward and inward: the battle of Fehrbellin and its aftermath, the inner evolution of the Prince and the unfolding of his relationship with the Elector, the turmoil of the army, the threatened mutiny and its suppression. There is much varied spectacle: the torchlit opening and closing scenes in the garden, the presentation of the captured Swedish standards, the final gathering of the whole court and army. The actual battle takes place offstage, but is vividly re-created for us in the excited commentaries of the watching generals, as well as in the noise and smoke of the artillery. The language encompasses a great variety of tone, and the verse ranges from characteristically Kleistian broken lines and 'gestural' speech to set-pieces of considerable eloquence, including monologues (a rarity in Kleist's work) for both the Prince and the Elector. Full and elaborate stage directions show that Kleist has truly conceived his work in the three dimensions of theatrical space. Even the dialogue has spatial depth: to most remarkable effect in the briefing scene in Act I, with its different groups of characters—the officers taking down their orders, the Elector with his wife and niece preparing for their departure, and the distracted Prince in between—all following their own separate courses, rather like the three simultaneous stage bands in *Don Giovanni*. The rhythm of blank verse is maintained, yet the speech is convincingly colloquial; words and actions, and the interplay between them, convey a great deal of important information; the scene has great tension, but also a strong admixture of comedy. There is nothing more intensely dramatic, or quintessentially theatrical, in all the plays of Goethe or Schiller.

Goethe, however, claimed to find Kleist's work not only displeasing but unplayable. He did make some effort to understand and even to encourage the young rival whose work so plainly represented a new and alien world, in accepting **Der zerbrochne Krug** for performance in Weimar. But the production in March 1808 was a disaster, and this must, it seems, be attributed in considerable measure to Goethe's own lack of sympathy for the play and for its theatrical style, so different from that cultivated in Weimar. Though he had complained that it was a piece of 'invisible theatre', static and lacking in visual interest, these supposed defects can only have been exaggerated by the slow pace of the Weimar production and by Goethe's arbitrary division of Kleist's unbroken sequence of scenes into the three acts traditionally thought proper for comedy. Kleist sent Goethe an extract from **Penthesilea** 'on the knees of my heart', claiming that the play was not written for the stage, that the present circumstances of the German theatre were 'neither before the curtain nor behind it' such as to encourage hopes of a successful production, and that he preferred to wait for the future rather than make concessions to vulgar public taste—but obviously hoping that Goethe would be interested in performing it. But if his remarks were intended to earn Goethe's goodwill, in fact they provided him with the opportunity to deal Kleist a stinging rebuff:

> Allow me also to observe (for if one is not to be frank, it would be better to remain silent) that it never ceases to disturb and distress me to see young men of spirit and talent waiting for a theatre that has yet to appear . . . I believe I could take the plays of Calderón to any country fair, perform them on bare boards nailed on barrels, and give the greatest pleasure both to the educated and to the uneducated members of the public . . .

Goethe's remarks even here are not simply hostile or condescending, but reflect, like those of the Director in the Prelude to *Faust,* years of practical concern with the theatre. But they were still unfair and unjustified, and indicate a profound and possibly wilful incomprehension of Kleist's work. Kleist was deeply wounded. In his journalistic essays of the following years he frequently attacks Goethe in return, sometimes with veiled hints, sometimes with satire of savage directness—as in the essay **'Unmaßgebliche Betrachtung' ('A Casual Observation'),** in which he suggests that the only way to make Goethe's plays theatrically viable would be by some sensational gimmick, such as having all the men's parts played by women and vice versa. But the majority of Kleist's own plays remained unperformed in his life-time. **Die Familie Schroffenstein** and **Das Käthchen von Heilbronn** were both first performed in Austria, the former at Graz as early as 1804, the latter in March 1810 at the Theater an der Wien in Vienna, where its spectacular effects were well calculated to appeal—though Iffland in Berlin had rejected it as unplayable. It was also seen at Graz later in the same year, and at Bamberg in September 1811, not long before Kleist's death. It was even performed in Weimar, in 1822, some years after Goethe's resignation as theatre director. But **Die Hermannsschlacht** and **Prinz Friedrich von Homburg** were not even published until 1821, when Tieck . . . first edited Kleist's posthumous works. **Penthesilea** was not performed on stage until 1876, **Amphitryon** not until 1899. In the twentieth century, however, the plays have established a secure place in the classical German repertory, and some of them have been seen outside Germany too: **Homburg,** which might be thought one of the most intransigently 'German' of plays, was successfully produced in Paris in the 1950s, with Gérard Philipe playing the Prince as a hero in the existentialist mould, and this play has also been seen a number of times in Britain. In Germany in recent years Kleist's work has often received more sympathetic theatrical treatment than that of Goethe and Schiller, no doubt in large measure because of that very modernity which so disturbed Goethe—a tell-

ing instance of the fluctuating and problematic relationship between literary drama and the stage. (pp. 160-80)

F. J. Lamport, "A Prussian Meteor: Heinrich von Kleist," in his German Classical Drama: Theatre, Humanity and Nation, 1750-1870, *Cambridge University Press, 1990, pp. 158-80.*

FURTHER READING

Biography

Cohen, Arthur A. "The Sufferings of Heinrich von Kleist." *The New Criterion* 2, No. 4 (December 1983): 26-34.
  Offers speculative explanations for Kleist's isolation and suicide.

Maass, Joachim. *Kleist: A Biography.* Translated by Ralph Manheim. New York: Farrar, Straus and Giroux, 1983, 313 p.
  A detailed biography that includes excerpts from Kleist's letters to his fiance Wilhelmine von Zenge and his half-sister Ulrike.

Newman, Gail. " 'Du bist nicht anders als ich': Kleist's Correspondence with Wilhelmine von Zenge." *German Life and Letters* XLII, No. 2 (January 1989): 101-12.
  Examines Kleist's efforts to shape Zenge's personality through their letters and his attempts to establish a wall between himself and the world.

Criticism

Calhoon, Kenneth S. "Sacrifice and the Semiotics of Power in *Der zerbrochne Krug.*" *Comparative Literature* 41, No. 3 (Summer 1989): 230-51.
  Examines the role of sacrifice as the connection between Kleist's play and the scenes depicted on the broken pitcher.

Cary, John R. "A Reading of Kleist's *Michael Kohlhaas.*" *PMLA* 85, No. 2 (March 1970): 212-18.
  Suggests that in *Michael Kohlhaas* written laws conflict with transcendent ideals of justice.

Davidson, Margaret F. "The Hand in the Works of Heinrich von Kleist." *Colloquia Germanica* 19, Nos. 3-4 (1986): 228-41.
  Studies Kleist's use of hand gestures as a means of communication and as an indication of a character's psyche.

Demeritt, Linda C. "The Role of Reason in Kleist's *Der Zweikampf.*" *Colloquia Germanica* 20, No. 1 (1987): 38-52.
  Examines the dialectical function of reason in *Der Zweikampf* and Kleist's rejection of a dichotomy between "head and heart."

Ellis, John M. *Heinrich von Kleist: Studies in the Character and Meaning of His Writings.* Chapel Hill: University of North Carolina Press, 1979, 194 p.
  A detailed analysis of what Ellis considers Kleist's mature works: "Der Findling," "Die Marquise von O . . . ," "Das Erdbeben in Chile," *Der Zweikampf, Michael Kohlhaas,* and *Prinz Friedrich von Homburg.*

Furst, Norbert. "The Structure of Kleist's Plays." *The Germanic Review* XVII, No. 1 (February 1942): 48-55.

Discusses the musical structure of Kleist's plays.

Greenberg, Martin. Introduction to *Heinrich von Kleist: Five Plays,* by Heinrich von Kleist, translated by Martin Greenberg, pp. ix-li. New Haven, Conn.: Yale University Press, 1988.

A survey of Kleist's literary career, focusing on the development of his philosophical imagination.

Koelb, Clayton. "Incorporating the Text: Kleist's *Michael Kohlhaas.*" *PMLA* 105, No. 5 (October 1990): 1098-107.

Analyzes the gypsy subplot in *Michael Kohlhaas* as an integral part of the story, suggesting that it changes the meaning of Kleist's narrative.

Paulin, Harry W. " 'Papa hat es nicht gern getan': Kleist and Parental Separation." *Colloquia Germanica* 15, No. 3 (1982): 225-38.

Studies Kleist's representation of parent-child relationships and suggests biographical sources for the dysfunctional relations portrayed in his works.

Paulin, Roger. "Kleist's Metamorphoses: Some Remarks on the Use of Mythology in *Penthesilea.*" *Oxford German Studies* 14 (1983): 35-53.

Examines *Penthesilea* as an adaptation of several different myths.

Reeves, Nigel. "Kleist's Bedlam: Abnormal Psychology and Psychiatry in the Works of Heinrich von Kleist." In *Romanticism and the Sciences,* edited by Andrew Cunningham and Nicholas Jardine, pp. 280-94. Cambridge: Cambridge University Press, 1990.

Studies Kleist's use of abnormal psychology and psychopathology as well as the breakdown of his cosmology following his reading of Kant.

Rushing, James A., Jr. "The Limitations of the Fencing Bear:

Kleist's 'Über das Marionettentheater' as Ironic Fiction." *The German Quarterly* 61, No. 4 (Fall 1988): 528-39.

Suggests that Kleist's essay has been misinterpreted by critics who read it as "a straightforward essay which speaks with a single voice more or less equivalent to that of the author."

Ryder, Frank G. "Kleist's 'Findling': Oedipus *Manqué?*" *MLN* 92, No. 3 (April 1977): 509-24.

Suggests that in "Der Findling" Kleist created "a complex of psychological action the full stature and significance of which is apparent only in its partial conjunction with the myth of Oedipus."

Schütze, Martin. "Studies in the Mind of Romanticism: Romantic Motives of Conduct in Concrete Development." *Modern Philology* 16, Nos. 6, 7 (October 1918; February 1919): 281-96, 505-24; 17, No. 2 (June 1919): 77-103.

Parts one and two of this three-part article summarize Kleist's correspondence with Wilhelmine von Zenge, focusing on his increasing absorption with his own state of mind. Part three examines the "ruling passions" that control his characters' actions.

Smith, John H. "Dialogic Midwifery in Kleist's 'Marquise von O . . . ' and the Hermeneutics of Telling the Untold in Kant and Plato." *PMLA* 100, No. 2 (March 1985): 203-19.

Examines the narrative strategies with which Kleist communicates that which is not directly stated in "Die Marquise von O. . . . "

Thum, Reinhard. "Kleist's Ambivalent Portrayal of Absolutism in *Prinz Friedrich von Homburg.*" *The Germanic Review* LVI, No. 1 (Winter 1981): 1-12.

Interprets *Prinz Friedrich von Homburg* as "the dramatic presentation of a social structure . . . in which individuality, however important, is not the sole basis or frame of explanation."

Joseph de Maistre

1753-1821

French essayist and philosopher.

INTRODUCTION

De Maistre was an important early nineteenth-century Catholic theorist whose philosophical writings championed the authority of a united church and state over democracy. A major proponent of ultramontanism, a doctrine favoring the supremacy of papal over national authority, de Maistre formulated his ideas in reaction to the eighteenth-century Enlightenment and the French Revolution. Many commentators have observed that although de Maistre had little or no formal instruction in theology, he skillfully transmitted his theocratic message through his powerful and articulate use of the French language.

De Maistre was born in Chambéry, Savoy, a province then in the kingdom of Piedmont-Sardinia and now part of France. The eldest son of a prominent magistrate, he was groomed from early childhood for a career in law. De Maistre completed his preliminary education in Chambéry, where he also belonged to a Jesuit confraternity that strongly influenced his religious development. After studying law at the University of Turin, he returned to Chambéry and became a successful magistrate as well as a member of the Senate of Savoy. When French revolutionaries invaded Savoy in 1792, de Maistre refused to swear allegiance to the French Republic out of loyalty to his king. Fearing the consequences of his actions, he fled to Switzerland. While staying in Lausanne, he began to write antirevolutionary propaganda, including the anonymously published *Considérations sur la France* (*Considerations on France*). In the succeeding years, de Maistre traveled to Italy, and then Sardinia, where he was summoned to fill a royal appointment. In 1803 he was sent to St. Petersburg as an ambassador, becoming well-respected by the Russian czar Alexander I and his court and remaining at his post for fourteen years. During this time, de Maistre produced several works, including what many commentators believe to be his masterpiece, *Les soirées de Saint-Pétersbourg* (*The Saint Petersburg Dialogues*). De Maistre's position as an envoy came to an abrupt end in 1817, however, when his suspected involvement with Jesuits who sought to convert members of the Orthodox church—the official Russian religion—to Roman Catholicism led to his expulsion. De Maistre spent his remaining years preparing his works for publication and performing the largely honorary duties of a Sardinian minister of state. He died in 1821 at the age of sixty-seven.

Critics maintain that de Maistre's theocratic philosophy might never have developed had it not been for the French Revolution. His *Considerations on France* represents de Maistre's first concerted attempt to articulate his reaction

to the revolt. In this work, he denounced the Enlightenment as an era of liberal philosophic and scientific thought that ultimately facilitated the political ideology of the Revolution. De Maistre's doctrines reflected his belief that sin was prevalent on earth and that suffering, often by the innocent, was necessary to atone for the evildoings of a guilty world. Based on this belief, he portrayed the French Revolution and the subsequent Reign of Terror as the divinely chosen means by which God punished France for its presumptuousness and moral degeneration that led to the overthrow and execution of its sovereign. According to de Maistre, these events initiated a requisite purgation to prepare for what he prophesied as a counterrevolution and the return of the monarchy. Furthermore, he condemned the democratic ideas embodied in the revolution, especially the notion of composing a written constitution, which he considered a meaningless exercise. In broad historical and philosophical terms, he asserted that since history was determined by divine providence, any attempt to write a constitution would invalidate the legitimate government sanctioned by God. Thus, he concluded, if certain rights for individuals did not organically develop in the course of a nation's history, it would be a violation of providence to manufacture them in a social contract. De

Maistre expanded on these ideas in his *Essai sur le principe générateur des constitutions politiques* (*Essay on the Generative Principle of Political Constitutions*). In this work, he reiterated his analysis of the revolution and outlined his ideology of ultramontanism and its relationship to the divine right of kings.

Among the remainder of de Maistre's major works, *Du Pape* (*The Pope*) and *The Saint Petersburg Dialogues* are the most important and influential. In *The Pope*, de Maistre offers a rationalistic approach to various theological questions and assumptions, the most significant of which concern the primacy and infallibility of the pope. De Maistre judged the uncompromising acceptance of the maxims outlined in his work to be crucial to the foundation of papal authority. According to many critics, one of the most remarkable achievements of *The Pope* is that de Maistre skillfully addressed these religious issues in layman's terms so that they could be comprehended by a popular audience. In his *Saint Petersburg Dialogues*, de Maistre treated other theological subjects, including the struggle between good and evil and the divine reason for war, in the form of a series of discussions between three fictional characters: the Senator, the young French Chevalier, and the Count, a figure based on de Maistre himself. His famous portraits of Voltaire and of the executioner are particularly memorable passages in this work, displaying his virulent dislike for eighteenth-century philosophy and his preoccupation with such violent subjects as capital punishment and war.

Early responses to de Maistre's writings were marked by a polarity reflecting the controversial nature of his position: while fellow royalists and conservatives approved of de Maistre's theocratic doctrines and agreed with his condemnation of the revolution, supporters of the revolt, the Enlightenment, and liberalism disagreed vehemently and sought to discredit both de Maistre and his theories. More recent commentators have stressed the difficulty of assessing de Maistre's ideas, noting that the various issues with which he was concerned are presented in a diffuse manner throughout his numerous works. Nevertheless, a number of critics have observed similarities between de Maistre and the eighteenth-century philosophers he despised. These commentators contend that while de Maistre steadfastly argued against liberal philosophy and democracy in France, he applied the same rationalistic techniques in his writings that the Enlightenment thinkers utilized to overthrow the conservative theocratic worldview of previous eras. Jack Lively has described this paradox of de Maistre: "One of the first, the most influential and the most original of reactionary thinkers, he illustrates also the closeness of the right and the left political extremes in modern political thinking." Other critics have attempted to examine de Maistre's works apart from his reaction to the Enlightenment and the French Revolution, portraying his absolutist policy and his advocacy of capital punishment as possible forerunners of modern fascism. In the words of Isaiah Berlin, de Maistre's "violent hatred of free traffic in ideas, and his contempt for all intellectuals, is not mere conservatism, nor the orthodoxy and loyalty to Church and state in which he was brought up, but something at once much older and much newer—something that at once echoes the

fanatical voices of the Inquisition and sounds what is perhaps the earliest note of the militant antirational fascism of modern times."

PRINCIPAL WORKS

Eloge de Victor-Amédée III   (essay)   1775
Considérations sur la France   (essay)   1796-97
   [*Considerations on France*, 1965]
Essai sur le principe générateur des constitutions politiques et des autres institutions humaines   (essay)   1814
   [*Essay on the Generative Principle of Political Constitutions*, 1847]
Du pape.   2 vols.   (essay)   1819
   [*The Pope*, 1850]
De l'Eglise gallicane   (essay)   1821
Les soirées de Saint-Pétersbourg ou entretiens sur le gouvernement temporel de la Providence.   2 vols.   (essays)   1821
   [*The Saint Petersburg Dialogues*, 1965]
Lettres à un gentilhomme russe sur l'Inquisition espagnole   (letters)   1822
   [*Letters on the Spanish Inquisition*, 1838]
Examen de la philosophie de Bacon où l'on traite différentes questions de philosophie rationnelle   (essay)   1836
   [*Examination of the Philosophy of Bacon*, 1962]
Lettres et opuscules inédits du Comte Joseph de Maistre.   2 vols.   (letters and pamphlets)   1850
Mémoires politiques et correspondance diplomatique de Joseph de Maistre   (letters and essays)   1858
Oeuvres complètes.   14 vols.   (essays and letters)   1884-87
The Works of Joseph de Maistre   (essays)   1965

Joseph de Maistre   (essay date 1816-17)

[*In the following excerpt from his "Preliminary Discourse" to* The Pope *written between 1816 and 1817, de Maistre discusses France in the aftermath of the Revolution and asserts that "without the Sovereign Pontiff there is no real Christianity."*]

It may appear surprising that a man of the world should assume the right to treat of questions, which, until our time, have seemed to belong exclusively to the zeal and science of the sacerdotal order. I trust, nevertheless that, after having weighed the reasons that have determined me to enter the lists in this honourable cause, every candid and well-disposed reader will approve them in his conscience, and absolve me from all baseness of usurpation.

In the first place, as our order was during last century egregiously criminal in regard to religion, I do not see why the same order should not present ecclesiastical writers with some faithful allies, who shall array themselves around the altar to keep at a distance from it every rash assailant, without embarrassing the Levites.

I doubt even whether, in these times, such an alliance has

not become necessary. A thousand causes have weakened the sacerdotal order. The Revolution has plundered, exiled, massacred the priesthood; it has practised every species of cruelty against the natural defenders of the maxims which it held in abhorrence. The ancient warriors of the sacred camp have departed to their rest; young recruits are indeed coming forward to fill their places, but they are still necessarily few in number, the enemy having, by anticipation, cut off their supplies with the most fatal ability. Who knows, besides, if Eliseus, before taking wing for his heavenly country, cast his mantle on the earth, and if the holy garment may have been immediately gathered up? It is, no doubt, probable, that as no human motive could have influenced the determination of the young heroes who have entered their names among the new levies, everything may be expected of their noble resolution. And yet how much time must they not spend in acquiring all the knowledge requisite for the combat which awaits them? And when they shall have become masters of the necessary learning, will they have sufficient leisure to employ it? The most indispensable polemics scarcely belong to any other times than those of profound peace, when labours can be freely distributed according to strength and talents. Huet would not have written his "Démonstration Evangélique" whilst exercising his episcopal functions; and if Bergier had been condemned by circumstances to bear during his whole lifetime, in a country parish, *"the burthen of the day and of the heat,"* he would not have been able to present religion with that multitude of works which have entitled him to rank among the most excellent apologists.

In such laborious occupations, holy, indeed, but overwhelming, are now more or less engaged the clergy of all Europe, but more particularly those of France, who were more directly and more violently struck by the revolutionary tempest. As regards them, all the flowers of the sacred ministry are withered; the thorns alone remain. As regards them, the Church is beginning anew, and by the very nature of things, confessors and martyrs must precede doctors. It is not easy to foresee the moment when, restored to its former tranquillity, and sufficiently numerous to bring into full operation all the resources of its immense ministry, it may yet astonish us by its science, as well as by the sanctity of its morals, the activity of its zeal, and the prodigious success of its apostolic labours.

I see no reason why, during this interval, which in other respects will not be lost to religion, men of the world, who from inclination have applied to serious studies, should not number themselves among the defenders of the most holy of causes. Even although they should only fill up the broken ranks of the army of the Lord, they could not be justly denied at least the merit of those courageous women who have been known sometimes to mount the ramparts of a besieged town, in order, if they could do no more, to strike terror into the enemy.

All science, besides, always owes, but especially at a period like the present, a kind of *tithe* to him from whom it proceeds, for *he is the God of sciences, and for him are all thoughts prepared* [1 Kings, II, 3]. We are approaching the greatest of all religious epochs, in which every man is bound, if it be in his power, to bring a stone for the august edifice, the plans of which are obviously fixed. None ought to be deterred by mediocrity of talents; by this, at least, I have not been dismayed. The poor man, who, in his narrow garden, sows only *mint, anise,* and *cummin* [Matthew, XXIII, 23], may confidently present the first leaf to Heaven, as sure of being accepted as the opulent owner of vast fields, who pours in abundance into the temple of God, *the strength of bread and the blood of the vine* [Psalms, CIV, 16].

Another consideration has tended in no small degree to encourage me. The priest who defends religion does his duty, no doubt, and deserves our highest esteem; but, in the eyes of a multitude of frivolous or preoccupied persons, he appears to defend his own cause; and although his good faith be equal to our own, every observer may have often perceived that the wicked and unbelieving mistrust less the man of the world, and allow themselves to be approached by him, not unfrequently, without the least repugnance. Now, all who have attentively examined this wild and sullen bird, know also that it is incomparably more difficult to approach than to seize him.

May I be permitted to say, moreover, if the man who has employed his attention, all his lifetime, on an important subject, who has devoted to that subject every moment he could dispose of, and directed towards it all his knowledge; if such a man, I say, experiences within himself a certain indefinable power which makes him feel it necessary to communicate his ideas, he ought, no doubt, to be on his guard against the illusions of self-love; but, nevertheless, he is, perhaps, in some degree, entitled to believe that this kind of inspiration is really something, especially if it is not wholly without the approbation of other men.

It is now a long time since *I considered France* [in *Considérations sur la France*], and, if I am not completely blinded by the honourable ambition of pleasing that country, my work, it appears to me, has not been disagreeable to it. Since, in the midst of its most terrible calamities, it listened with kindness to the voice of a friend who belonged to it by religion, by language, and by those hopes of a higher order which always remain, why should it not agree still to favour me with an attentive hearing, now that it has made so great a step towards happiness, and that it has so far recovered tranquillity as to be able to examine itself and judge itself wisely?

Circumstances have, indeed, much changed since the year 1796. At that time all honest men were at liberty to attack the brigands at their own risk and peril. Now that all the powers of Europe are restored, error having divers points of contact with politics, there might happen to the writer who should not be constantly on his guard, the same misfortune which befel Diomedes under the walls of Troy,— that of wounding a divinity, whilst pursuing an enemy.

Happily, there is nothing so evident for conscience as conscience itself. If I were not conscious of being penetrated with universal benevolence, absolutely free from all spirit of contention, and from all polemical anger, even in regard to those men whose systems are most revolting to me, God is my witness, I would throw down the open; and I venture to hope that every sincere man who reads me will have no doubt of my intentions. But this consciousness excludes neither the solemn profession of my belief, nor the distinct and dignified expression of faith, nor the cry of alarm in presence of a known or disguised enemy, nor that honest proselytism, in fine, which proceeds from persuasion.

After a declaration, the sincerity of which will, I trust, be fully justified by every page of my work, I would not experience the least disquietude, even although I should be in direct opposition with other creeds. I know what is due to nations and to those by whom they are governed, but I do not think I derogate from this sentiment by telling them the truth with all due consideration. The first lines of my book make known its object; he who might dread being shocked by it is earnestly entreated not to read it. To me it is demonstrated, and I would most willingly prove the same to other men, *that without the Sovereign Pontiff there is no real Christianity, and that no sincere Christian man, separated from him, will sign upon his honour (provided he be well informed) a clearly defined profession of faith.*

All the nations that have withdrawn from the authority of the Holy Father, no doubt, if taken in the aggregate, possess the right (the learned possess it not) to denounce me as paradoxical, but none are entitled to charge me with insulting them. Every writer who restricts himself to the sphere of a severe logic is wanting to nobody. The only honourable revenge that can be taken on him is, to reason against him, and better than he.

Although in the whole course of my work I have confined myself as much as possible to general ideas, it will, nevertheless, be easily perceived that I have given particular attention to France. Until that country understand how deeply it is in error, there is no safety for it; but if it be yet blind in this respect, Europe is still more so, perhaps, in regard to what it has to expect from France.

There are privileged nations that have a mission in this world. In a former work I endeavoured to explain that of France, which appears to me as visible as the sun. There is in the natural government, and in the national ideas of the French people, a certain theocratic and religious element, which is never lost sight of. The Frenchman stands in need of religion more than any other man. If he wants it, he is not only weakened, but mutilated. Consider his history. To the government of the Druids, which was all-powerful, succeeded that of the bishops, who were constantly, but much more in ancient times than in our days, *the counsellors of the king in all his counsels.* The bishops, and Gibbon remarks it, *made the kingdom of France* [*History of the Decline and Fall,* 1812]. There is nothing more true. The bishops *constructed* this monarchy as bees construct a hive. The councils of the Church in the first ages of the monarchy were really national councils. *The Christian Druids,* if I may use the expression, performed in them the principal part. The forms had changed, but we always find the same nation. The Teutonic blood, sufficiently mingled with it to give a name to France, disappeared almost entirely at the battle of Fontenai, and left only the Gauls. We have the proof of this in the language—for when a people is *one,* their language is *one;* and if it be mixed in The Gallican Church, with its power, its doctrine, its dignity, its language, its proselytism, appeared sometimes to bring the two centres into contact, and confound them in the most magnificent unity.

But, O human weakness! O deplorable blindness! detestable prejudices, which I shall have occasion to speak of more at length in the course of this work, had wholly perverted this admirable order, this sublime relation between the two powers. By means of sophistry and criminal manœuvres, one of the brightest prerogatives of the most Christian king, that of presiding (humanly) over the religious system, and of being the hereditary protector of Catholic unity, was too successfully concealed from him. Constantine, of old, gloried in the title of *temporal bishop.* That of *temporal* Sovereign Pontiff flattered not the ambition of a successor of Charlemagne, and this post offered by Providence was vacant! Ah! if the kings of France had been inclined to lend the strength of their arm to truth, what would they not have accomplished? But what can a king do when *the lights of his people are extinguished?* It must even be said, to the immortal glory of an august house, the royal spirit with which it is animated has frequently and most happily been more learned than the academies, and more just than the tribunals.

Overthrown at last by a preternatural tempest, we have seen this mission, so precious for Europe, restored through a miracle, which promises other miracles, and which ought to inspire all Frenchmen with religious courage; but the height of misfortune for them would be to believe that the revolution is at an end, and that the column is replaced, because it has been raised up anew. It must be believed, on the contrary, that the revolutionary spirit is, beyond comparison, more powerful and more dangerous than it was a few years back. The mighty usurper made use of it only for himself; he knew how to compress it in his iron hand, and reduce it to be only a monopoly for the benefit of his crown. But since *justice and peace have embraced,* the genius of evil has ceased to fear; and, instead of agitating at one point, it has reproduced a general ebullition over an immense surface.

May I be permitted to repeat that the French revolution is not like to anything that was ever witnessed in the world in bygone times. It is essentially *satanical* [**Considérations**]. Never will it be wholly extinguished except by the contrary principle, and never will the French people resume their place until they have acknowledged this truth. The priesthood ought to be the principal object of the sovereign's care. If I had under my eyes the table of ordinations, I might predict great events. The French nobility are now presented with an opportunity of offering to the state a sacrifice worthy of them. Let them, therefore, give their sons to the altar, as in days of old. In these times it will not be said that they covet only the treasures of the sanctuary. The Church, in earlier times, conferred on them riches and honour; let them now make a return for her gifts, by bestowing upon her all they have yet in their power—the influence of their illustrious names, which will maintain the ancient opinion, and determine a multitude of men to follow standards borne by such worthy hands: *time will do the rest.* In thus sustaining the priesthood, the French nobility will pay an immense debt they have contracted towards France, and also perhaps as regards all Europe. The greatest mark of respect and of profound esteem that can be shown them, is to remind them that the French revolution—which they would, no doubt, have redeemed with the last drop of their blood—was, nevertheless, in a great measure their own work. So long as a pure aristocracy (in other words, an aristocracy professing, with enthusiasm, national dogmas) surrounds the throne, it is immoveable, even although it should happen to be filled by weakness or error; but if the *baronage* becomes apostate, there is no longer any safety for the throne, even if it were occupied by a St. Louis or a Charlemagne; and this is more true as regards France than any other country. By their monstrous alliance with the bad principle during last century, the French nobility ruined everything. It is now their duty to repair all the evil they occasioned. Their destiny is certain, provided they be well persuaded of the natural, essential, necessary *French* alliance of the priesthood and the nobility.

At the most disastrous period of the revolution, it was said: "This is for the nobility only a well-deserved eclipse. It will resume its place. It will escape at last, by receiving with a good grace children that had no claim to belong to it."

> Des enfants qu'en son sein elle n'a point portés.
> [*Considérations*]

What was said twenty years ago is now in course of being verified. If the French nobility are under the necessity of recruiting, it lies with them to prevent their renewal from being anywise humbling to the ancient houses. When once they shall have understood why this renewal had become necessary, it can no longer be offensive to them or hurtful; but this remark must only be made, as it were, by the way, and without entering into learned details.

I return to my principal subject, by observing that the anti-religious fury of last century against all Christian truths and institutions, was directed against the Holy See. The conspirators were sufficiently aware—they knew, unfortunately, much better than the multitude of well-intentioned men, that *Christianity is wholly based upon the Sovereign Pontiff.* Against this foundation, therefore, they directed all their efforts. If they had proposed to the Catholic cabinets measures directly anti-christian, fear or shame (in the absence of more noble motives) would have sufficed to repel them; for all the princes, therefore, they laid the most subtle snares.

> The wisest of kings, alas! they contrived to lead
> astray.

They represented to them the Holy See as the natural enemy of all thrones; they environed it with calumnies, made it be mistrusted in every way, and endeavoured to place it in opposition to the welfare of states. In short, they forgot nothing that was calculated to connect the idea of dignity with that of independence. By means of usurpation, violence, chicanery, and encroachments of every kind, they rendered the policy of Rome jealous and slow, and then accused it of deficiencies, which it owed entirely to themselves. In a word, they succeeded to a degree that causes the greatest alarm. The evil is such, that the consid-

eration of certain Catholic countries may have sometimes scandalized parties that were strangers to truth, and averted them from it. Nevertheless, without the Sovereign Pontiff the whole edifice of Christianity is undermined, and only requires, in order to be utterly demolished, the development of certain circumstances, which will be shown in their true light.

Meanwhile, facts are not silent. Were Protestants ever known to amuse themselves writing books against the Greek, Nestorian, or Syriac churches, which profess dogmas that Protestantism abhors? They do no such thing. On the contrary, they protect those churches, they compliment them, and show themselves ready to unite with them, always holding as a true ally every enemy of the Holy See.

The infidel, on the other hand, laughs at all dissenters, and makes use of them *all,* quite sure that *all,* more or less, and each one of them in his way, will forward *his great work,* the destruction of Christianity.

Protestantism, philosophism, and a thousand other sects, more or less perverse or extravagant, having prodigiously *diminished truths among men* [Psalms, XI, 2], it is impossible mankind should continue long in the state they are in at present. They are in agitation and labour, they are ashamed of themselves, and are seeking, with an indescribable convulsive energy, to make head against the torrent of errors, after having abandoned themselves to them with the systematic blindness of pride. It has appeared to me useful, at this memorable time, to set forth in all its fulness a theory no less vast than it is important, and to disencumber it of the obscurities with which men have obstinately persisted in enveloping it for so long a time. Without presuming too much on my endeavours, I trust, however, that they will not be altogether fruitless. A good book is not one which persuades everybody; if so, there would be no good book. It is one which completely satisfies a certain class of readers, to whom it is more particularly addressed, and which, moreover, leaves no doubt in any mind of the perfectly honest purpose of the author, and the indefatigable toil he has subjected himself to, in order to become master of his subject, and even to find for it, if possible, some new points of view. I flatter myself, in all simplicity, that in this respect, every equitable reader will decide that I am not out of order. I am convinced that it was never more necessary to surround with every ray of evidence a truth of the first class, and I also believe that truth stands in need of France. I am not without hope, therefore, that France will read me once more with kindness; and I would consider myself fortunate, above all, if its great personages of every order, reflecting on what I expect of them, should make it a point of conscience to refute me. (pp. xi-xxvii)

> *Joseph de Maistre, "Preliminary Discourse,"
> in his* The Pope, *translated by Rev. Aeneas
> McD. Dawson, C. Dolman, 1850, pp. xi-xxvii.*

Caroline de Peyronnet (essay date 1852)

[*In the following excerpt from an essay published anonymously in the* Edinburgh Review, *de Peyronnet locates de Maistre among his contemporaries and comments on elements of his literary style.*]

It was M. Ballanche, we believe, who, many years ago, first applied to Joseph de Maistre the epithet of 'Prophet of the Past,' and thus embodied in one picturesque sentence the best description of his peculiar mind, style, and character. The expression was deservedly successful,—*fit fortune* as the French say,—and has been extended to a whole group of men who, standing like De Maistre on the confines of the last century, looked out anxiously from the midst of the revolutionary storm in which they were enveloped towards a reparatory and avenging Future. Chateaubriand, Bonald, Lamennais (we mean the Lamennais of former days), were among these. There is a prophetic tint cast over the writings of these men which cannot be entirely overlooked; and some of the pages of Chateaubriand, in particular, are, even in the present day, startling to read, so completely have some of his previsions been verified. But this curious characteristic is equally observable in many of their inferior contemporaries, and may be discerned more or less in all writings that are the offspring of troublous and insecure times. There seems to exist in man an unfortunate restlessness under uncertainty—an insatiable desire to know the end of all things, which, coupled with the fact that nothing ever is completely ended in this world, would suffice to make him wretched if he had not the resource of inventing what he cannot discover. In a word, when men cannot see they foresee, and a clouded political horizon calls forth prophecy as naturally as sleep begets dreams. It is not, therefore, as Prophets, but as Prophets of the Past, that these writers were peculiar, as men who foretold, not coming, but returning things, and whose oracles spoke only of restoration. Considered in that light De Maistre stands foremost of the group for good and evil. More brilliant than Bonald, more consistent than Lamennais, he differed widely in one respect from Chateaubriand. The latter belonged only partly to the past. The author of *Les Martyrs,* and of the *Génie du Christianisme,* may indeed be claimed by the Middle Ages; but the writer in the *Journal des Débats,* and the orator of the Chamber of Peers in 1825, belonged to the nineteenth century. Strangely enough it was in his early days that Chateaubriand indulged in those lingering backward glances which are generally the symptoms of declining faculties, and it was only later in life that he made up his mind to live in his own day. It was in his mature years that—to repeat a remark reproachfully made by one of his ultra-Catholic biographers—'he resolved to cast his talents into the gulph of the age, as the Doges of Venice cast their ring into the sea that they wedded with her tempests, her monsters, and her impurities.' Such a stormy, perfidious, and polluted bride had no charm for De Maistre, and no man can be said to have been less influenced by the spirit of the age he lived in, and the moral atmosphere by which he was surrounded. He was a living anachronism—a man of the sixteenth century born two hundred years too late. In this he resembled Bonald. In all matters of faith and opinion there is scarcely any difference between them; but how diverse was the form in which those opinions were expressed! Joseph de Maistre was fond of pointing out the curious conformity of thought between himself and the frigid and heavy Bonald, and of alluding

to what he called, in theological language, the '*loca parallela,*' to be found in their works; but the most friendly disposition could hardly have made him discover in the writings of his brother theocrat the originality and brilliancy which cause his to be read with pleasure, even now, by a sceptical and unsympathising generation. In both we find the same gratuitous display of almost cynical inhumanity. If M. de Maistre has represented capital punishments as one of the poles on which Society revolves, and the executioner as one of its chief magistrates; M. de Bonald, on the other hand, could boast of having uttered, in the Chamber of Peers, words which, in their bland barbarity, can scarcely be matched in the records of any revolutionary tribunal: 'To condemn a man to death, he said, 'was only to send him before his natural judge!' The same dogmatism, the same pretensions to inspiration, the same confusion betwixt novelty and error, are to be found in both, but in De Maistre alone these were relieved by a play of fancy and felicity of expression, which strangely enough remind one often—with a difference—of Voltaire. He may be said, indeed, to have constantly fought with the arms of his adversaries, and his political co-religionists are, perhaps, so proud of him only because he possessed to a certain degree those qualities which they affect to despise as superficial in their opponents. Wit, for instance, was considered by the men of his party, and, indeed, is considered by many dull people all over the world, as an unworthy auxiliary in a good cause, yet Joseph de Maistre's wit, which was by no means of the first order, is a constant theme of exultation with his admirers. In this matter of wit, indeed, many people hold curious notions touching the fitness, and even the possibility of husbanding it, for certain solemnly-appointed holidays of the mind. Our observations would lead us to establish a rule, which from its simplicity we should be ashamed to transcribe, if we did not see it daily put in doubt. Those who possess wit employ it even on the most every-day occasions, and those who have it not manage to dispense with it even when it would be most seasonable. In the intellectual world prodigality and wealth, economy and poverty, are much oftener synonymous terms than is generally supposed. Wit especially is a form, not a garment of the mind, and cannot be put on or cast off at will. Who has not heard of Beaumarchais's witty memorials to his judges on the most prosaic questions, and who has not read scores of dull epigrams? Every one instinctively and necessarily uses the weapons which Nature has furnished. The loveliest woman in the world must darn her stockings (if she be condemned to that employment) with the help of those same lustrous eyes which could enslave a hero. The nature of the task or the object to be attained have little to do with the means employed, for the first alone are matters of choice. If the latter are more brilliant than the undertaking required, the lookers-on have no right to complain. Some years ago a learned farmer somewhere published the account of an experiment, in which a potatoe-field was fertilised by the application of electricity. We speak in profound agricultural ignorance, but, supposing the thing to be possible, who would regret the offensive compost that our ancestors considered alone in possession of the power to produce potatoes, and who would think that Heaven's lightning had been misapplied? No one, except, perhaps, those who consider eloquence as unbecoming in familiar subjects, and wit as unseemly in serious ones. In literary matters especially the means often ennoble the ends, and a pleasant journey may be performed between two uninteresting points. Since the days of the Druids many a worthless mistletoe has been gathered with a golden hook, and been made sacred in the gathering. Let, then, Liberty—that smooths all difficulties, makes all things easy, and adjusts all differences,—reign supreme in her intellectual domain! Let there be no sumptuary laws in the Republic of Letters! We are far from finding fault with M. de Maistre for having sometimes clothed his thoughts in an unusual garb, and are convinced, on the contrary, that his works will live precisely on account of the contrast between manner and matter that they exhibit. His thorough acquaintance, for instance, with classical and Pagan literature, furnished him with quotations and arguments rarely to be found in theological disquisitions, and which many of his fellow-labourers in the same field would have considered profane. The quotations are, perhaps, too frequent for good taste, and things are often said in Latin which might have been as well expressed in French, for M. de Maistre, like many other writers, seemed to think that truth in a dead language is doubly true; Plato, Cicero, and Seneca are often pressed into strange service; but to these pagan and philosophical predilections he was indebted for a style at once perspicuous, concise, and vigorous, that will not often be equalled, we suspect, by the rising Ultramontane generation, which is to be nurtured exclusively in the Latinity of the early Fathers. Could M. de Maistre witness the dispute concerning the Pagan classics which divides at this moment the Episcopal body in France, there is little doubt that, in spite of his aversion to Gallicans, he would side with them, rather than admit that the Hymns of St. Gregory the Great could be substituted with advantage for the poetry of Virgil, or that the prose of Thomas Aquinas could be studied with impunity instead of the 'Orations of Cicero.' Nor was he content with borrowing from the Ancients; Voltaire, Jean Jacques, and even his enemy Bacon, are all laid under contribution; in a word, he may be said, in the widest sense of the expression, to have followed St. Augustine's advice and example, and to have 'spoiled the Egyptians.'

To all these blemishes, as we said before, we are inclined to be lenient; were M. de Maistre's style more in harmony with his subject, he would be still less to our taste. The real defects in his writings are the arrogance of his tone and his authoritative dogmatism, which seem scarcely consistent with a free exercise of reasoning powers. Before a man argues with others, he has generally, if he is conscientious, argued with himself; but there is not a trace of any such mental process having been gone through in M. de Maistre's case. There are no misgivings on any subject, not even on the most minor points of his doctrine; no remains of vanquished doubts showing that a *bonâ fide* combat had taken place in his mind. Doubt is so essential a part of our frail human nature, that we can scarcely comprehend sincerity without it. We are disposed to believe that Joseph de Maistre was convinced of the truth of all the doctrines he advanced, but the impression conveyed by his writings is that he would have continued to assert them as pertinaciously had he suspected them to be false. It is impossible

to imagine him retracting any opinion, and this robs his perseverance of much of its value. No man carried out more completely the system of mental submission inculcated by the Romish Church, and his faith never allowed him to question even the most trifling points of his belief; his defence of them does not therefore necessarily imply that he had ascertained their truth even satisfactorily for himself. It is difficult to understand how, under these circumstances, modern innovators . . . should ever have associated his name with the idea of a religious reform, or a new Divine Revelation. There is no doubt that a few sentences in the *Soirées de St. Petersbourg* convey in somewhat mystical language the notion of some great approaching event in the Christian world; but we wonder that the indignant shade of De Maistre did not arise to reproach with its presence the audacious commentator who first dared to draw from thence any inference against Rome. He may have fancied that a Hildebrand might arise to remodel the Catholic world, but that was all; and any revolution he could look forward to must have originated with Rome herself.

The last remark we have to make applies not only to M. de Maistre's works, but to those of all men who hold his political opinions. It is difficult to understand why they write at all. The mere fact of publishing a book is a concession to that fatal spirit of inquiry and examination which they affirm has ruined the world. If human reason is so completely impotent to produce any good, why do they appeal to it? Logically, the dogmas of Authority should only be expounded with sword and cannon, and the tenets of Liberty should alone be spread by discussion and writings. But after all, it does come to that; and force, we feel, is at the bottom of the arguments of all such writers. They know, at heart, as well as we do, that reason is not to be argued into an act of suicide, and that the pen is not their proper instrument. The paternal explanations afforded by absolutists, reduced by the rebellious spirit of the world to the humiliating necessity of writing books, always remind us of that last thrilling dialogue between Little Red Riding Hood and the wolf in Grandmama's clothes. Mild and even affectionate replies are vouchsafed to every question, and each member of the monster is in turn declared to have been made for the especial benefit of the innocent inquirer. Grandmama, what a big civil list you've got! and many other doubtful exclamations may be all in turn satisfactorily answered; but let the confiding interlocutor come within reach of the dissembler, and venture that last inevitable inquiry about Grandmama's teeth, and we all know the fatal and conclusive answer. We make no exception to our rule of mistrust in such cases in favour of De Maistre, notwithstanding his apparent toleration and philosophy in argument. Tolerant he no doubt was, as the suspected guest of a schismatic autocrat; and as long as force sought to silence his voice, he only demanded free discussion and a fair philosophical field; but if the government of his hopes had been established, what would have been the change? For our part, we feel not the slightest doubt on the matter, and have a comfortable conviction that, circumstances permitting, the system of which this most Christian philosopher was the advocate would have condemned him to the painful necessity of having us burned as heretics, or, at the very least, hanged as Edinburgh Reviewers. In vain he tells us in his favourite Latin that his rule of conduct is, *tantum contende in republica quantum probari tuis civibus possis,* we cannot be reassured. A certain number of chosen heretics might indeed have been reserved, like intellectual gladiators, for controversial combats, but with the rabble he would evidently not have thought it worth while to parley. Like Ulysses (we beg his Majesty of Ithaca's pardon for mentioning him almost in the same breath with Little Red Riding Hood) when he harangues the Greeks in the second book of the *Iliad,* M. de Maistre might indeed only have used the sceptre of the King of Kings, had it been confided to him, to add authority to his eloquence while addressing his equals; but had any inferior rebel opposed him, we feel convinced that, like Ulysses, he would have felt no scruple in laying about him with his sceptre, and belabouring the audacious rebel with it.

We have attempted to convey some idea of . . . the spirit which pervades [De Maistre's] writings. A more complete analysis of his works would be impossible within the limits of an Article; they treat of almost every subject within the range of theology, philosophy, and politics, and his earnest and elaborate defence of the Papacy might alone furnish matter for volumes of criticism. If, however, the foregoing pages induce some of our readers to study his writings, we shall not consider that our labour has been misspent. Every true lover of liberty and humanity must rise from the task invigorated and refreshed—strengthened in an opposite faith, and proud of those conquests against which even such attacks are impotent. It is no despicable advantage to a liberal mind to meet now and then with a worthy adversary. In the security of undisturbed possession, we are apt to disregard the most valuable blessings; they only become really our own when we have defended and, so to speak, reconquered them. It is good to have to find reasons for opinions which we have inhaled in the moral atmosphere around us rather than acquired by any individual mental process: it is like regaining a family inheritance after a long and arduous suit. In another point of view, too, the works of De Maistre are instructive. On the Continent they are quoted and eulogised daily by men who, without his talents, have inherited all his views, and a numerous tribe of degenerate followers devoutly repeat his fearful paradoxes as though they were oracular truths. It is well that every one should know to what structure these fragments belong, notwithstanding their specious beauty. The spirit of the Middle Ages, under the more plausible name of Reaction, is once more abroad: it may be useful to study its meaning in the works of one of its most explicit and consistent advocates. We may gather a just notion of its baneful influence on the ignorant and the narrow-minded, by seeing to what monstrous paradoxes and wilful blindness it reduced one of the clearest intellects of the age, and to what terrible logical conclusions it conducted one so highly gifted that the negation of Progress seems a blasphemy under his pen, and that his most determined opponents, while detesting his doctrines are tempted to exclaim, Would that he had been one of us! (pp. 322-28)

Caroline de Peyronnet, in an originally unsigned essay titled "Joseph de Maistre," in The

Edinburgh Review, *Vol. XCVI, No. CXCVI, October, 1852, pp. 289-328.*

Lord Acton   (essay date 1863)

[*Acton was an English historian and statesman. A political liberal and Roman Catholic, he equally distrusted authoritarian government, socialism, and democracy, believing that the authority of individual conscience supercedes that of the state. Acton was one of the founders of the* English Historical Review *as well as the editor of the Catholic periodical the* Rambler (*later the* Home and Foreign Review). *His canon primarily consists of essays published in these and other periodicals and of lectures; many of his writings were published in the posthumous collections* Lectures on Modern History *(1906) and* Historical Essays and Studies *(1907). In the following excerpt from an essay originally published in* Home and Foreign Review *in 1863, Acton examines the impact of de Maistre's ultramontane theories on nineteenth-century Catholic thought.*]

During the evil days [of the French Revolution, de Maistre] had made himself a name by two political pamphlets, written with the power, the eloquence and depth of Burke, with more metaphysical ability than Burke possessed, but without his instinct for political truth, or his anxious attention to the voice of history. In these pamphlets he had laid down some of the most important principles of civil government, and had explained with special success the necessity of aristocracy for the establishment of freedom. His writings had displayed extensive knowledge, earnest faith, a pointed wit, and an almost unexampled union of common sense with love of paradox and passion for extremes. After his return from St Petersburg, in the first years of the Restoration, he published several works in rapid succession, which have earned for him perhaps the highest place next to Pascal among laymen who have defended religion without the advantage of a theological education.

Society, said M. de Maistre, has been ruined by the want of faith, or by its equivalent in the civil order, the weakness of authority. It is necessary that mankind should be taught the duty of unconditional obedience, the merit of suffering, the sinfulness of self-assertion, the peril of liberty, and the evil of securities against the abuse of power. Tyranny, poverty and slavery are not the faults of society, but the penalties of sin. Monarchy is the only legitimate form of government, because monarchy alone gives the nations a master, and places the sovereign under the restraint of conscience. It is his duty to promote as well as to preserve religion, to suppress error and sinlike crime, and to defend the faith by prescribing knowledge and encouraging superstition.

In these writings de Maistre unquestionably relinquished or modified some of his earlier opinions. There was no longer that love of freedom which he had opposed to the violence of the Revolution, or that admiration for England with which he had been inspired by her long resistance to Napoleon. His ideal state had become more centralized, his sovereign more absolute, his nobility less independent, his people less free. The dread of revolutionary despotism had given place to a horror of constitutionalism. This was the current of the hour. But it inspired de Maistre with the theory which is the chief cause of his celebrity, a theory new to the Catholic thinkers of his time. Catholicism, he maintained, inculcates the absolute authority of the sovereign, and forbids resistance even to the gravest wrong. This unity and absolutism of authority spring from the very nature of religion, and are not only necessary for the State, but essential to the Church. Civil society cannot subsist without the maxim that the king can do no wrong. The Church requires the same privilege for the Pope. Absolute infallibility in the one is a corollary of despotism in the other. It is also its remedy. Denying to the people any part in the vindication of right, de Maistre transferred to the Pope alone the whole duty of moderating kings. Thus the argument for the Papal power flowed into two streams from one source—the theory of civil absolutism. Reasoning by analogy, the Pope ought to be an arbitrary ruler within the Church; while, by contrast, his power was extended over States, and the security of civil rights was to be sought in the completeness of hierarchical despotism.

Whoever studies the writings of de Maistre will find far more than the memorable theory by which he became the founder of a new school of Ultramontanism. He will find some of the best and wisest things ever written on religion and society—a generous one, an admirable style of discussion, and the Catholic system presented often in the noblest manner. These qualities have exercised a powerful and salutary influence on all the succeeding schools of Catholic thought; and some who differ most widely from de Maistre on the questions which he made more particularly his own owe much to his writings. But it was only in the course of years, as the publication of eight posthumous volumes defined more clearly and more amply the character of his mind, that men learned to separate the man from his peculiar theory. At first, all the merits of his system and his style served but to give attractiveness and splendour to the theory of the Papal power, which became the symbol of a party, and gave the impulse to an important movement. No distinct view had yet been put forward so positively or so brilliantly; and its influence on contemporaries was extraordinary. It appeared to a large class of persons as the only perfect form of Catholicism. Everything that fell short of it seemed to them treason or surrender. To limit the Holy See in Church or State was to attack religion, and open the door to Jansenism, Protestantism, and infidelity. Inasmuch as authority was especially odious to irreligious Catholics, it became the part of good Catholics to vindicate it with at least a corresponding zeal. All qualification was taken to be opposition, and was deemed to imply a secret aversion.

Since the question raised by de Maistre was one of fact, and not of speculation, its solution was to be found not in theory but in history. For, as the standing object of his school was to establish a prejudice favourable to the supreme authority of the Church in every period, their labour would be in vain if it could be shown that the pontifical power had manifested itself in various degrees in various times, or that there had been serious vicissitudes in its spirit. Here an entrance was found for a personal element new to ecclesiastical literature, which caused the discussion of character to become more prominent than the discussion of principle. Those who defended a particular view of canon law, history, or politics with orthodoxy obliged themselves to treat all objections to this view as blasphemies against religious truth; whatever was inconsistent with the theory was regarded as really equivalent to a denial of the continuity of tradition. Large tracts of history which had formally involved no theological interest became the arena of controversy; and their adverse and telling facts were only in the brief to be explained away and amplified respectively. De Maistre had given the example of discussing these questions with the arts of advocacy. His rhetorical dexterity enabled him to put wit in the place of argument, to disconcert adversaries by spirited retaliation, or baffle them by ingenuously dissembling or boldly denying whatever might serve their purpose. (pp. 43-7)

> Lord Acton, "Ultramontanism," in his Essays on Church and State, *edited by Douglas Woodruff, The Viking Press, 1953, pp. 37-85.*

John Morley (essay date 1886)

[*In the following excerpt, Morley assesses de Maistre's reaction to eighteenth-century science and philosophy in* Soirées de Saint-Pétersbourg *and* Examen de la philosophie de Bacon.]

The eighteenth century to men like De Maistre seemed an infamous parenthesis, mysteriously interposed between the glorious age of Bossuet and Fénelon, and that yet brighter era for faith and the Church which was still to come in the good time of Divine Providence. The philosophy of the last century, he says on more than one occasion, will form one of the most shameful epochs of the human mind: it never praised even good men except for what was bad in them. He looked upon the gods whom that century had worshipped as the direct authors of the bloodshed and ruin in which their epoch had closed. The memory of mild and humane philosophers was covered with the kind of black execration that prophets of old had hurled at Baal or Moloch; Locke and Hume, Voltaire and Rousseau, were habitually spoken of as very scourges of God. From this temper two consequences naturally flowed. In the first place, while it lasted there was no hope of an honest philosophic discussion of the great questions which divide speculative minds. Moderation and impartiality were virtues of almost superhuman difficulty for controversialists who had made up their minds that it was their opponents who had erected the guillotine, confiscated the sacred property of the church, slaughtered and banished her children, and filled the land with terror and confusion. It is hard amid the smoking ruins of the homestead to do full justice to the theoretical arguments of the supposed authors of the conflagration. Hence De Maistre, though . . . intimately acquainted with the works of his foes in the letter, was prevented by the vehemence of his antipathy to the effects which he attributed to them, from having any just critical estimate of their value and true spirit. 'I do not know one of these men,' he says of the philosophers of the eighteenth century [in his ***Soirées de Saint Pétersbourg***], 'to whom the sacred title of honest man is quite suitable.' They are all wanting in probity. Their very names *'me déchirent la bouche.'* To admire Voltaire is the sign of a corrupt soul; and if anybody is drawn to the works of Voltaire, then be sure that God does not love such an one. The divine anathema is written on the very face of this arch-blasphemer; on his shameless brow, in the two extinct craters still sparkling with sensuality and hate, in that frightful *rictus* running from ear to ear, in those lips tightened by cruel malice, like a spring ready to fly back and launch forth blasphemy and sarcasm; he plunges into the mud, rolls in it, drinks of it; he surrenders his imagination to the enthusiasm of hell, which lends him all its forces; Paris crowned him, Sodom would have banished him. Locke, again, did not understand himself. His distinguishing characteristics are feebleness and precipitancy of judgment. Vagueness and irresolution reign in his expressions as they do in his thoughts. He constantly exhibits that most decisive sign of mediocrity—he passes close by the greatest questions without perceiving them. In the study of philosophy, contempt for Locke is the beginning of knowledge. Condillac was even more vigilantly than anybody else on his guard against his own conscience. But Hume was perhaps the most dangerous and the most guilty of all those mournful writers who will for ever accuse the last century before posterity—the one who employed the most talent with the most coolness to do most harm. To Bacon De Maistre paid the compliment of composing a long refutation of his main ideas, in which Bacon's blindness, presumption, profanity, and scientific charlatanry are denounced in vehement and almost coarse terms, and treated as the natural outcome of a low morality.

It has long been the inglorious speciality of the theological school to insist in this way upon moral depravity as an antecedent condition of intellectual error. De Maistre in this respect was not unworthy of his fellows. He believed that his opponents were even worse citizens than they were bad philosophers, and it was his horror of them in the former capacity that made him so bitter and resentful against them in the latter. He could think of no more fitting image for opinions that he did not happen to believe than counterfeit money, 'which is struck in the first instance by great criminals, and is afterwards passed on by honest folk who perpetuate the crime without knowing what they do.' A philosopher of the highest class, we may be sure, does not permit himself to be drawn down from the true object of his meditations by these sinister emotions. But De Maistre belonged emphatically to minds of the second order, whose eagerness to find truth is never intense and pure enough to raise them above perturbing antipathies to persons. His whole attitude was fatal to his claim to be heard as a truth-seeker in any right sense of the term. He was not only persuaded of the general justice and inexpugnableness of the orthodox system, but he refused to believe that it was capable of being improved or supplemented by anything which a temperate and fair examination of other doctrines might peradventure be found to yield. With De Maistre there was no peradventure. Again, no speculative mind of the highest order ever mistakes, or ever moves systematically apart from, the main current of the social movement of its time. It is implied in the very definition of a thinker of supreme quality that he should detect, and be in a certain accord with, the most forward and central

of the ruling tendencies of his epoch. Three-quarters of a century have elapsed since De Maistre was driven to attempt to explain the world to himself, and this interval has sufficed to show that the central conditions at that time for the permanent reorganisation of the society which had just been so violently rent in pieces, were assuredly not theological, military, nor ultramontane, but the very opposite of all these.

There was a second consequence of the conditions of the time. The catastrophe of Europe affected the matter as well as the manner of contemporary speculation. The French Revolution has become to us no more than a term, though the strangest term in a historic series. To some of the best of those who were confronted on every side by its tumult and agitation, it was the prevailing of the gates of hell, the moral disruption of the universe, the absolute and total surrender of the world to them that plough iniquity and sow wickedness. Even under ordinary circumstances few men have gone through life without encountering some triumphant iniquity, some gross and prolonged cruelty, which makes them wonder how God should allow such things to be. If we remember the aspect which the Revolution wore in the eyes of those who seeing it yet did not understand, we can imagine what dimensions this eternal enigma must have assumed in their sight. It was inevitable that the first problem to press on men with resistless urgency should be the ancient question of the method of the Creator's temporal government. What is the law of the distribution of good and evil fortune? How can we vindicate with regard to the conditions of this life, the different destinies that fall to men? How can we defend the moral ordering of a world in which the wicked and godless constantly triumph, while the virtuous and upright who retain their integrity are as frequently buffeted and put to shame? (pp. 287-92)

Nothing can be more clearly put than De Maistre's answers to the question which the circumstances of the time placed before him to solve. What is the law of the distribution of good and evil fortune in this life? Is it a moral law? Do prosperity and adversity fall respectively to the just and the unjust, either individually or collectively? Has the ancient covenant been faithfully kept, that whoso hearkens diligently to the divine voice, and observes all the commandments to do them, shall be blessed in his basket and his store and in all the work of his hand? Or is God a God that hideth himself?

De Maistre perceived that the optimistic conception of the deity as benign, merciful, infinitely forgiving, was very far indeed from covering the facts. So he insisted on seeing in human destiny the ever-present hand of a stern and terrible judge, administering a Draconian code with blind and pitiless severity. God created men under conditions which left them free to choose between good and evil. All the physical evil that exists in the world is a penalty for the moral evil that has resulted from the abuse by men of this freedom of choice. For these physical calamities God is only responsible in the way in which a criminal judge is responsible for a hanging. Men cannot blame the judge for the gallows; the fault is their own in committing those offences for which hanging is prescribed beforehand as the penalty. These curses which dominate human life are not the result of the cruelty of the divine ruler, but of the folly and wickedness of mankind, who, seeing the better course, yet deliberately choose the worse. The order of the world is overthrown by the inquities of men; it is we who have provoked the exercise of the divine justice, and called down the tokens of his vengeance. The misery and disaster that surround us like a cloak are the penalty of our crimes and the price of our expiation. As the divine St. Thomas has said: *Deus est auctor mali quod est pœna, non autem mali quod est culpa.* There is a certain quantity of wrong done over the face of the world; therefore the great Judge exacts a proportionate quantity of punishment. The total amount of evil suffered makes nice equation with the total amount of evil done; the extent of human suffering tallies precisely with the extent of human guilt. Of course you must take original sin into account, 'which explains all, and without which you can explain nothing.'

> In virtue of this primitive degradation we are subject to all sorts of physical sufferings *in general;* just as in virtue of this same degradation we are subject to all sorts of vices *in general.* This original malady therefore [which is the correlative of original sin] has no other name. It is only the capacity of suffering all evils, as original sin is only the capacity of committing all crimes. *Soirées*].

Hence all calamity is either the punishment of sins actually committed by the sufferers, or else it is the general penalty exacted for general sinfulness. Sometimes an innocent being is stricken, and a guilty being appears to escape. But is it not the same in the transactions of earthly tribunals? And yet we do not say that they are conducted without regard to justice and righteousness.

> When God punishes any society for the crimes that it has committed, he does justice as we do justice ourselves in these sorts of circumstance. A city revolts; it massacres the representatives of the sovereign; it shuts its gates against him; it defends itself against his arms; it is taken. The prince has it dismantled and deprived of all its privileges; nobody will find fault with this decision on the ground that there are innocent persons shut up in the city. [*Soirées*]

De Maistre's deity is thus a colossal Septembriseur, enthroned high in the peaceful heavens, demanding ever-renewed holocausts in the name of the public safety.

It is true, as a general rule of the human mind, that the objects which men have worshipped have improved in morality and wisdom as men themselves have improved. The quiet gods, without effort of their own, have grown holier and purer by the agitations and toil which civilise their worshippers. In other words, the same influences which elevate and widen our sense of human duty give corresponding height and nobleness to our ideas of the divine character. The history of the civilisation of the earth is the history of the civilisation of Olympus also. It will be seen that the deity whom De Maistre sets up is below the moral level of the time in respect of Punishment. In intellectual matters he vehemently proclaimed the superiority of the tenth or the twelfth over the eighteenth century, but it is

surely carrying admiration for those loyal times indecently far, to seek in the vindictive sackings of revolted towns, and the miscellaneous butcheries of men, women, and babes, which then marked the vengeance of outraged sovereignty, the most apt parallel and analogy for the systematic administration of human society by its Creator. Such punishment can no longer be regarded as moral in any deep or permanent sense; it implies a gross, harsh, and revengeful character in the executioner, that is eminently perplexing and incredible to those who expect to find an idea of justice in the government of the world, at least not materially below what is attained in the clumsy efforts of uninspired publicists.

In mere point of administration, the criminal code which De Maistre put into the hands of the Supreme Being works in a more arbitrary and capricious manner than any device of an Italian Bourbon. As Voltaire asks—

> *Lisbonne, qui n'est plus, eut-elle plus de vices*
> *Que Londres, que Paris, plongés dans les délices?*
> *Lisbonne est abîmée, et l'on danse à Paris.*

Stay, De Maistre replies, look at Paris thirty years later, not dancing, but red with blood. This kind of thing is often said, even now; but it is really time to abandon the prostitution of the name of Justice to a process which brings Lewis XVI. to the block, and consigns De Maistre to poverty and exile, because Lewis XIV., the Regent, and Lewis XV. had been profligate men or injudicious rulers. The reader may remember how the unhappy Emperor Maurice as his five innocent sons were in turn murdered before his eyes, at each stroke piously ejaculated: 'Thou art just, O Lord! and thy judgments are righteous.' Any name would befit this kind of transaction better than that which, in the dealings of men with one another at least, we reserve for the honourable anxiety that he should reap who has sown, that the reward should be to him who has toiled for it, and the pain to him who has deliberately incurred it. What is gained by attributing to the divine government a method tainted with every quality that could vitiate the enactment of penalties by a temporal sovereign? (pp. 293-98)

It will be inferred from De Maistre's general position that he was no friend to physical science. Just as moderns see in the advance of the methods and boundaries of physical knowledge the most direct and sure means of displacing the unfruitful subjective methods of old, and so of renovating the entire field of human thought and activity, so did De Maistre see, as his school has seen since, that here was the stronghold of his foes. 'Ah, how dearly,' he exclaimed [in his *Examen de la Philosophie de Bacon*], 'has man paid for the natural sciences!' Not but that Providence designed that man should know something about them; only it must be in due order. The ancients were not permitted to attain to much or even any sound knowledge of physics, indisputably above us as they were in force of mind, a fact shown by the superiority of their languages which ought to silence for ever the voice of our modern pride. Why did the ancients remain so ignorant of natural science? Because they were not Christian. 'When all Europe was Christian, when the priests were the universal teachers, when all the establishments of Europe were Christianised, when theology had taken its place at the head of all instruction, and the other faculties were ranged around her like maids of honour round their queen, the human race being thus prepared, then the natural sciences were given to it.' Science must be kept in its place, for it resembles fire which, when confined in the grates prepared for it, is the most useful and powerful of man's servants; scattered about anyhow, it is the most terrible of scourges. Whence the marked supremacy of the seventeenth century, especially in France? From the happy accord of religion, science, and chivalry, and from the supremacy conceded to the first. The more perfect theology is in a country the more fruitful it is in true science; and that is why Christian nations have surpassed all others in the sciences, and that is why the Indians and Chinese will never reach us, so long as we remain respectively as we are. The more theology is cultivated, honoured, and supreme, then, other things being equal, the more perfect will human science be: that is to say, it will have the greater force and expansion, and will be the more free from every mischievous and perilous connection.

Little would be gained here by serious criticism of a view of this kind from a positive point. How little, the reader will understand from De Maistre's own explanations of his principles of Proof and Evidence. 'They have called to witness against Moses,' he says,

> history, chronology, astronomy, geology, etc. The objections have disappeared before true science; but those were profoundly wise who despised them before any inquiry, or who only examined them in order to discover a refutation, but without ever doubting that there was one. Even a mathematical objection ought to be despised, for though it may be a demonstrated truth, still you will never be able to demonstrate that it contradicts a truth that has been demonstrated before.

His final formula he boldly announced in these words: '*Que toutes les fois qu'une proposition sera prouvée par le genre de preuve qui lui appartient, l'objection quelconque,* MÊME INSOLUBLE, *ne doit plus être écoutée.*' Suppose, for example, that by a consensus of testimony it were perfectly proved that Archimedes set fire to the fleet of Marcellus by a burning-glass; then all the objections of geometry disappear. Prove if you can, and if you choose, that by certain laws a glass, in order to be capable of setting fire to the Roman fleet, must have been as big as the whole city of Syracuse, and ask me what answer I have to make to that. '*J'ai à vous répondre qu'Archimède brûla la flotte romaine avec un miroir ardent.*'

The interesting thing about such opinions as these is not the exact height and depth of their falseness, but the considerations which could recommend them to a man of so much knowledge, both of books and of the outer facts of life, and of so much natural acuteness as De Maistre. Persons who have accustomed themselves to ascertained methods of proof, are apt to look on a man who vows that if a thing has been declared true by some authority whom he respects, then that constitutes proof to him, as either the victim of a preposterous and barely credible infatuation, or else as a flat impostor. Yet De Maistre was no ig-

norant monk. He had no selfish or official interest in taking away the keys of knowledge, entering not in himself, and them that would enter in hindering. The true reasons for his detestation of the eighteenth-century philosophers, science, and literature, are simple enough. Like every wise man, he felt that the end of all philosophy and science is emphatically social, the construction and maintenance and improvement of a fabric under which the communities of men may find shelter, and may secure all the conditions for living their lives with dignity and service. Then he held that no truth can be harmful to society. If he found any system of opinions, any given attitude of the mind, injurious to tranquillity and the public order, he instantly concluded that, however plausible they might seem when tested by logic and demonstration, they were fundamentally untrue and deceptive. What is logic compared with eternal salvation in the next world, and the practice of virtue in this? The recommendation of such a mind as De Maistre's is the intensity of its appreciation of order and social happiness. The obvious weakness of such a mind, and the curse inherent in its influence, is that it overlooks the prime condition of all; that social order can never be established on a durable basis so long as the discoveries of scientific truth in all its departments are suppressed, or incorrectly appreciated, or socially misapplied. De Maistre did not perceive that the cause which he supported was no longer the cause of peace and tranquillity and right living, but was in a state of absolute and final decomposition, and therefore was the cause of disorder and blind wrong living. (pp. 298-302)

John Morley, "Joseph de Maistre," in his Critical Miscellanies, *Vol. II, Macmillan and Co., Limited, 1886, pp. 257-338.*

T. L. L. Teeling   (essay date 1895)

[*In the following excerpt, Teeling discusses the influence of de Maistre's ultramontane philosophy on subsequent nineteenth-century writers.*]

It would be impossible, within the limits of such a paper as the present one, to give any adequate idea of the importance of de Maistre's teaching and influence. He was, as is insisted upon by contemporary writers of our own day, the founder, with his fellow-writer and correspondent, de Bonald, of the great Catholic movement, the new Ultramontanism, of the present century.

For it was the horror of revolution, the farseeing view of its tendencies, its work, and its consequences, which caused de Maistre, who had passed through the very centre of its whirlwind, to seek an intellectual and logical refuge against its "satanic" influence. It had begun with the spirits of negation and destruction called Voltaire, Hume, Rousseau, Mill, Bentham, and their followers, with Diderot and the Encyclopædists; or, further back, with the mockeries of Erasmus; and now all thinking minds sought a counterpoise, a pillar of refuge, to which they might cling in safety when the storm was upon them. De Maistre claimed to find it in the papacy. "Ultramontanism," as Wilfrid Ward writes, "was to be the principle of order and authority and the principle of unity among Christians, as the revolution was among the representatives of democratic anarchy. . . . the Neo-Ultramontane movement represents the growth of those special relations between the papacy and modern Europe which made Döllinger say in 1855 that its moral power was greater than it had been in the palmy days of Innocent III. or Gregory VII" [*Prayer, Free Will and Miracles*].

If any human writing can be said to preface to prophecy, to prepare the ground for a divine act, so we may say that de Maistre's work, ***Du Pape,*** was the human preface to that divine voice which found utterance in our own day in the Vatican Council, the response of the Holy Ghost to the needs of the world. And de Maistre was a layman; a layman who, as he said himself, "entered the breach" in times when priests were overworked and over-absorbed in the practical work of the Church, to "fill the empty places in the army of the Lord." His influence was widely felt in his own day, and is even more powerful in our own. Lamennais, Montalembert, Lacordaire, Veuillot drew inspiration from his writings; many of their friends were "brought up at his feet," as they phrased it themselves. (Lacordaire even wrote of one of Lamennais's works as "an exaggeration of the views of M. de Maistre.") Perrone in Italy, Donoso Cortez in Spain, Döllinger in Germany, Veuillot and the writers of the "Univers" in France, all owned the influence and developed on their several lines the initiatory thoughts expressed by de Maistre in ***Du Pape.*** In fact, his authority was so largely quoted, even by those who least understood his spirit, that, as Frédèric Ozanam wrote of another modern school of thought, unnecessary to be more plainly referred to here, "This school of writers proposes to place at its head Count de Maistre, whose opinions it exaggerates and denaturalizes. It goes about looking for the boldest paradoxes, the most disputable propositions, provided that they irritate the modern spirit."

One of the greatest English Catholic thinkers and writers of the present day, W. G. Ward, also owed much to de Maistre, with whose writings he was familiar at Oxford, and an interesting parallel is drawn between them by the former's son and biographer, who says:

> The vision of horror which led de Maistre to look to the Roman Pontiff as the one hope for order and peace, was due to personal experience of a life lived through the terror of 1793. And perhaps nothing short of a personal experience could have given so keen an edge and marked a direction to his views. Mr. Ward had also the personal experience of confusion, of anarchy, of destruction. . . . . With Ward, as with de Maistre, what had been was but a symptom and a forewarning of what was impending. . . . . The Pope was needed by de Maistre to keep order in times of revolution or of political crises; by Ward, to keep order in times of intellectual anarchy. 'The great thing we want,' says de Maistre, 'is for the Pope to settle things one way or another.' Mr. Ward wrote an essay called 'Are Infallible Definitions Rare?' with the object of proving them to be very frequent, and maintained that this was a matter of congratulation, as increas-

ing the store of truth infallibly guaranteed. [*W. G. Ward and the Catholic Revival*, 1893]

De Maistre ruled "Point de Christianisme sans le Pape"; Ward believed "that a spirit of increased deference to Rome was the great need of the Church in these latter days," and his pen, like that of de Maistre, bore witness to his belief.

"To understand and appreciate Joseph de Maistre," writes Lescure, one of his biographers, "we must never forget these dates, 1794, '95, '96. We must never forget that Joseph de Maistre was a gentleman, a magistrate, a royalist, and an ardent and sincere Catholic. Without the French Revolution and without Catholicism, Joseph de Maistre, philosophically, politically, and morally, would not have existed."

His Catholicism . . . was the mainspring of his life; so also, in a lesser degree, was his unflinching loyalty to that royal family which too often repaid him but with suspicion and ingratitude. "As long as there is a House of Savoy and it deigns to accept my services, I shall remain as I am," was his proud answer to an inquiry from one who knew how little benefit he was ever likely to reap from his steadfast loyalty.

We must not, however, suppose that de Maistre was, as his enemies called him, "the born enemy of all liberty and of modern society, the apostle of a cruel God, of an unyielding pope, of an absolute monarch, the advocate of all manner of bloody ironies, the teacher of all that can irritate or exasperate our new humanity." On the contrary, he advocated a wise liberty, an enlightened discipline, a government (monarchical, if you will, but unprivileged) founded on religion, morality, and justice. "One must unceasingly preach to the people the benefits of authority, and to kings the benefits of liberty," was his earliest axiom in politics, and what better doctrine could he inculcate? Curiously enough, de Maistre, who, during his lifetime and for some years after his death, was taken as an example of all that is most monarchical and anti-revolutionary in teaching, has lately been cited, and his writings misquoted in support of a very opposite line of argument, by those who were only too glad to shield themselves under the ægis of his great name, much to the righteous indignation of his own family.

De Maistre's latest work, which was given to the world by his son for the first time in 1859, is ***Quatres Chapitres sur la Russie,*** the last of which contains an exhaustive study of the varieties of Illuminism, in his day widely spread and active; some branches more or less inoffensive, others, among which are quoted the Bavarian Lodges, actively hostile to the powers civil and ecclesiastical. "I devoted a considerable length of time to studying these gentlemen (the Illuminati)," writes de Maistre to a friend. "I frequented their meetings, I went to Lyons to see them more closely, I kept up a certain amount of correspondence with some of their principal members. But I have remained in the Catholic, Apostolic and Roman Church, not, however, without having acquired a number of ideas by which I have profited." We are told that he confessed to a certain amount of sympathy for some "tendencies of Russian illuminism, above all for that which according to him should aid the propagation of Catholicism in Russia, and *the re-union of the two Churches, which was one of his dreams.* This remark comes to us with added interest at present, when the Holy Father has so lately held out a conciliatory hand to our separated brethren of the East. Apropos of this hoped-for union, de Maistre relates an appropriate anecdote in one of his letters on Russia. "Some one must yield. But who? and how? A clever Genevan lady addressed the same question to me some years since. I answered her, 'We cannot make one single step toward you, but if you will come to us, we will smooth the road at our expense.' "

An able French Review, *La Quinzaine,* has lately received from one of the philosopher's grandsons, an unpublished fragment on politics from some of de Maistre's papers. Speaking of the abuses resulting from a mercenary spirit in public officers, he makes a curious comment on them, which seems worth reproducing.

> Mercenariness (venality) renders a great public service by placing young men in all kinds of posts. It is a grave error to place exclusive confidence in *old* men. The mission of old men is to hinder evil. That of the young is to do good; and this double destination requires the united action of both states of life. Give the helm to a young man, he will upset everything under the pretext of reforms. Give it to an old man, he will let everything become corrupt for fear of innovation. But as all human institutions hold within themselves the germ of decay, and one must continually repair if one would not see the building fall in ruins it follows that public affairs cannot get on without the activity of youth. Old age learns nothing, corrects nothing, establishes nothing.

The publication, so late as 1851, of his voluminous correspondence by his son, appears to have shown Count de Maistre to the world in a new and more attractive light than before. The well-known critic Sainte-Beuve thus writes of him:

> This writer had been given a reputation for the strictest *absolutism;* and he has been called the executioner's panegyrist, because he maintained that societies which wished to maintain their strength could only do so by means of strong laws. . . . (but). . . . now we learn to revere and enjoy him who has so often hitherto only provoked and angered us. This powerful exciter of political reflexions is actually going to become one of our acquaintances, and even one of our friends! [*Lettres, Sentences et Maxims,* 1900]

We may mention in connection with the above critique, that de Maistre's life and works are coming more prominently before the public at the present time than ever before. Two French current Reviews—at the moment when we write these lines—contain articles on Joseph de Maistre and his works. Lecturers, in public conferences and before—such well-known institutions as the Collége de France, have recently taken him as their subject, volume after volume on his life and writings appears year by year, some quoting him as an "absolutist," others, strangely enough, striving to extract from his multifarious writings

some support to their own liberal theories; and all bearing witness to the enduring importance of his teaching and influence. A not unimportant addition to these will be, when completed, the work now issuing at intervals from the pen of his co-citizen and ardent admirer, M. Descotes, of Chambéry, entitled "Joseph de Maistre avant la Revolution," two volumes only of which are at present published. For in Savoie the *man* is still remembered, while all over France the thinker, the teacher, the "prophet" is quoted and reverenced with increasing approbation. (pp. 834-38)

> *T. L. L. Teeling, "Joseph de Maistre," in* The American Catholic Quarterly Review, *Vol. XX, No. 80, October, 1895, pp. 807-38.*

Arnold comparing de Maistre to Edmund Burke:

Joseph de Maistre is [one] of those men whose word, like that of [Edmund] Burke, has vitality. In imaginative power he is altogether inferior to Burke. On the other hand his thought moves in closer order than Burke's, more rapidly, more directly; he has fewer superfluities. Burke is a great writer, but Joseph de Maistre's use of the French language is more powerful, more thoroughly satisfactory, than Burke's use of the English. It is masterly; it shows us to perfection of what that admirable instrument, the French language, is capable. Finally, Joseph de Maistre is more European than Burke; his place at the great spectacle of the Revolution is more central for seeing; moreover he outlived Burke considerably, and saw how events turned. But the two men are of one family, having in common their high stamp of individuality, and their enduring vitality and instructiveness. They have in common, too, their fundamental ideas. Their sense of the slowness of the natural growth of things, of their gradual evolution out of small beginnings, is perfectly expressed by Joseph de Maistre's maxim: "Aucune grande chose n'eut de grands commencements"— "Nothing great ever began great."

> *Matthew Arnold, in* Essays, Letters, and Reviews by Matthew Arnold, *edited by Fraser Neiman, Harvard University Press, 1960.*

R. F. O'Connor   (essay date 1919)

[*In the following excerpt, O'Connor surveys de Maistre's reaction to the French Revolution and his political philosophy in such works as* Du pape *and* Considérations sur la France.]

One of those great primordial thinkers, one of those philosophical politicians who envisaged *la haute politique* from a loftier standpoint than the ordinary party politician, who if he had not dominated and directed the political thought of his epoch, at least transfused into the moribund society of a degenerate age the vital sap of sound ethical principles, and helped to save from utter extinction, from the corrosive and dissolvent action of triumphant sophistry, some still venerated remnants of the old Christian and Catholic order, the personality of Count Joseph de Maistre looms large and lustrous in the dark and dismal retrospect which, viewed in its religious and moral aspects, the history of the closing years of the eighteenth and the opening of the nineteenth century presents to the contemplation of the thoughtful student of history. Although he never ambitioned founding a school, being wholly divested of that narrow individualism which has dwarfed so many lesser intellects—finding in the Church, with whose Catholic spirit he was essentially and deeply imbued, all that could satisfy his lofty mind and broad sympathies—he may be regarded as one of the highest intellectual types of the Catholic writer or publicist, the exemplar, to a great extent, of those valiant literary combatants who followed in his wake, the De Bonalds, Châteaubriands, Genoudes, Cortés, Veuillots, etc., who seem to have been providentially called to do the work of lay Christian apologists, and in critical times loyally and effectively supplement that official defense of the Church which is the special function of the *Ecclesia docens.* The first lay publicist who ventured to treat questions until then exclusively reserved to ecclesiastics, strong reasons impelled him—one might say *compelled* him, so pressing was the need of such a combatant in the then sadly thinned ranks of the defenders of the Christian constitution of civil society, against which the French Revolution, in its first wild outburst, had hurled all its forces—to enter the polemical lists and grapple with the common foe on the ground of philosophy, true philosophy in opposition to its counterfeit, challenging his opponents to a searching discussion of first principles. (p. 367)

In all Europe there was not a man of genius or a power really devoted to the Church. Everywhere kings and statesmen sought to undermine the sacerdotal order, in the hope of erecting upon the ruins of priestly power a monarchical despotism, menaced in its turn by a worse despotism, that of a mob withdrawn from the restraints and influence of that Church. In France the old athletes of the sacred army had descended into the tomb, and the young recruits, slowly advancing to take their places in the ranks, were necessarily few; the enemy, with fatal forethought, having cut off the supplies.

"During this species of interstice which, in other respects, will not be lost to religion, I do not see," said De Maistre [in his Preface to **Du Pape**], writing at the time and with all the startling evidences of the great fundamental and far-reaching changes wrought by the Revolution before his eyes—

> I do not see why men of the world, drawn by their inclinations to serious studies, should not range themselves alongside the defenders of the holiest of causes. Even if they only served to fill the gaps in the army of the Lord, they could not be fairly denied the merit of those courageous women who have been sometimes seen to mount the ramparts of a besieged city to distract the eyes of the enemy. Another consideration, too, encouraged me not a little. The priest who defends religion no doubt does his duty, and merits our esteem, but to numbers of unreflecting or preoccupied men he seems to be defending his own cause, and although his good faith is equal to ours, every observer must have had a thousand opportunities of perceiving that the unbeliever is less distrustful of the man of the world, and often allows himself to be come at without

the least repugnance. Now, all those who have closely examined this wild and flighty bird know that it is incomparably more difficult to get at him than to seize him. Shall I be permitted to say: If a man who has all his life been occupied with an important subject to which he has devoted every moment he could spare, and who has directed all his knowledge to that end—if this man, I say, feels within him I know not what indefinable force which makes him feel the need of disseminating his ideas—doubtless he ought to distrust the illusions of selfishness, still he has, perhaps, some right to think that there is something in this kind of inspiration, particularly if it is not wholly disapproved of by others?

This conception of the function of the lay Catholic publicist has long ceased to be a novelty, and it is greatly owing to the impulse to this species of propagandism which the encouraging and stimulating example of De Maistre supplied, that we owe the foundation and rapid growth of a school of writers who, thoroughly *en rapport* with Rome, have proved that the Catholic Church is no friend to obscurantism or intellectual stagnation. "I am ever convinced," says an eminent French Bishop [the Bishop of Langres, in a letter to Montalembert], referring to the action of laymen in the Church, "that God more than ever calls them to become not only docile children of His household, but active workers and armed soldiers precisely to baffle the hypocritical manœuvres of that impious system disguised under the name of 'lay State,' 'lay Power,' 'lay society,' which in the minds of its authors would signify the State, Power and society without religion. It is, then, to prove to the world that laicism and religion are in no ways antagonistic, that in our days God has raised up those innumerable armies of pious laymen whom, in almost every country in the Catholic world, and particularly in France, He has made the propagators of faith, the instruments of charity and the auxiliaries of the apostolic ministry." And Monsignor Dupanloup, with that breadth of view so characteristic of him, in the third volume of his great work on higher intellectual education, says: "In the order of truth, as in the order of charity, laymen may lend a valuable concurrence to the Church. Not to speak here of contemporaries, whose names are sufficiently illustrious—Prudentius, St. Prosper, Lactantius, St. Justin, Athenagoras, Aristides and Minutius Felix were laymen. Certainly to fill an honorable place in the ranks of the athletes of religion and devote his life and talents to the defense of great religious truths which are at the same time the highest social truths, cannot be the mission of all, but it is assured by a grand and noble destiny" [*Lettres aux hommes du monde*].

It is strange that a life so full of action and influence as De Maistre's, placed as he was in the forefront rank of the diplomatists and writers of his time, should not have found a competent biographer to give us a faithful picture of the *vie intime* as well as the public career of one who, standing as it were between two eventful periods, between the receding past, bearing away with it the last wrecks of the old feudal system and the nearing future, full of mystery and menace, disclosing dim and uncertain vistas of a new age gradually unfolding, was eye-witness of one of the most extraordinary and momentous events in the world's history. But a modern poet has said: "The world knows nothing of its greatest men," and the saying is in part true of De Maistre, one of those meteoric minds whose transient brilliancy sheds a momentary gleam across some gloomy phase in the history of a people at one of those critical epochs when they seem to have temporarily lost their way in the world's wilderness, diverging from beaten tracts:

> Such souls,
> Whose sudden visitations daze the world,
> Vanish like lightning, but they leave behind
> A voice that in the distance far away
> 'Wakens the slumbering ages.
>
> (pp 369-71)

The most philosophically-minded of all those who have made what Carlyle calls "the crowning phenomenon of our modern time" a life study, De Maistre saw in the French Revolution not a fortuitous, isolated event, not an accidental ebullition of French excitability, but a something abnormal, something out of the common order. "We must courageously confess, madame," he wrote to the Marquise de Costa,

> that for a long time we have not understood the Revolution of which we are witnesses. We have long taken it for an event. We were in error. It is an *epoch;* and woe to the generations who are present at the epochs of the world! A thousand times happy the men who are not called to contemplate in history great revolutions, general wars, public opinion at fever heat, parties infuriated, the clashing of empires and the obsequies of nations! Happy the men who pass through the world in one of those moments of repose, intervals between the convulsions of a condemned and suffering nature!

In the *Considerations* he points out as the most striking characteristic of the Revolution that force of attraction and impulsion which swept away every obstacle that human strength could oppose to it like straws upon the wind, none having crossed its pathway with impunity; its most active spirits having something passive and mechanical about them, as if they were the instruments of a superhuman power, a power that seemed to revel in the destruction of human life, and of all that had been sanctified by religion or tradition. The most remarkable of them only attained to the perilous possession of supreme authority by following the current; as soon as they strove to make headway against it, they were submerged. Robespierre, Collot and Barrère, extremely mediocre men, wielded over a guilty nation the most dreadful despotism recorded in history, but as soon as the measure of their iniquity was filled up a breath overthrew them. A monarchist of the old absolutist school, he failed to discover any traces of real greatness among the republicans. When he heard them talk of "liberty" and "virtue," it suggested to him a faded courtesan with painted prudery affecting the airs of a virgin. He dates from their epoch the greatest crimes that ever dishonored humanity. (pp. 375-76)

De Maistre is alternately pessimistic and optimistic. His pessimism is traceable to the sad scenes which Paris, Lyons and Toulon witnessed during the Reign of Terror; his optimism was rooted in his vivid faith, out of which grew an abiding hope that saved him from utter despondency. The political outlook was too cloudy to enable him to see and realize that the basis of power was shifting or had already shifted the great underlying fact of the Revolution. To him the Republic was anathema, for it sounded the death-knell of the old order, with which his whole diplomatic life had been identified. The death throes of monarchical Europe coincided with the birth of a new age—the Age of Democracy. He could not foresee the inevitable growth of that democracy, then in its infancy. Somewhat tinged with that visionary mysticism, that fatalism which infected French legitimists and was fed up by certain alleged prophecies, foretelling the advent of a great Pope and a great King, who were to restore the old order, he could not foresee that a great Pontiff, one of the greatest who filled the Chair of Peter, Leo XIII., would recognize a French Republic as the reasoned expression of the will of the French people and urge all the Catholics in France to rally loyally to its support, thus affirming with all the weight of his great authority the principle of self-determination and that rulers derive their lawful authority from the consent of the majority of the governed—a principle enunciated, not for the first time, by Rome, which was so far in advance of President Wilson and his famous fourteen points.

In one of his best known works, ***Du Pape,*** in which he stood upon firmer ground and handled a more congenial theme, and wherein he advances strong historical arguments in favor of the temporal power, he lays particular stress upon the fact that it is the sacerdotal character of the Supreme Pontiff—highest visible type of the Eternal Priesthood throughout the Universal Church—that gives to the Pontifical sovereignty that inviolable majesty of which every hostile power, human or diabolical, has failed to divest it; that marvelous ascendancy that stopped Theodosius at the gate of the temple, Attila upon the highroad to Rome, and Louis XIV. Before the holy table. "O Holy Church of Rome!" he exclaims in a passage almost rhythmical in its eloquence,

> as long as I shall have the power of utterance I shall use it to celebrate thee. Immortal mother of knowledge and sanctity, I greet thee—*salve magna parens!* It is thou who sheddest light to the extremities of the earth, wherever blind sovereignties do not stop thy influence, and often even in despite of them. It is thou who causest human sacrifices, barbarous or infamous customs, fatal prejudices, the night of ignorance to cease, and wherever thy envoys cannot penetrate, something is wanting to civilization. The great men belong to thee! . . . The Pontiffs will soon be universally proclaimed the supreme agents, the creators of European monarchy and unity, the preservers of learning and the arts, founders and protectors of civil liberty, destroyers of slavery, enemies of despotism, indefatigable upholders of sovereignty, benefactors of mankind. No throne in the universe ever bore so much wisdom, knowledge and virtue. In the midst of all imaginable overturnings, God has constantly watched over thee, O Eternal City! All that could ruin thee has been leagued against

thee, and thou art standing, and as thou was formerly the centre of error, thou art for eighteen hundred years the centre of truth. The Roman Power made thee the citadel of paganism, apparently invincible in the capital of the known world. All the errors of the universe converged towards thee, and the first of thy Emperors, concentrating them in a single resplendent point, consecrates them all in the Pantheon. The capital of paganism was destined to become that of Christianity, and the temple that in this capital concentrated all the forces of idolatry was to unite all the lights of faith—all the saints in place of all the gods. What an inexhaustible subject of profound philosophical and religious meditation!

De Maistre points to the ecclesiastical sovereignties formerly existing in Germany, whose mild dominion gave rise to the proverb, "It is good to live under the crozier"; to the old French monarchy, which employed a larger number of ecclesiastics in its civil administration than any other kingdom, and when the priesthood was one of the three columns that supported the throne; and to the Papal monarchy, a pure theocracy, of which the sacerdotal spirit was the vital principle, as proof of the benevolent action of the Church, through the priesthood, upon politics, when that action was not impeded or vitiated by local causes.

In close relationship with this phase of the politico-religious question is the relative action of the divine and human principles as the bases of institutions. The spectacle of a society in the abnormal condition in which eighteenth century philosophism had left it—culminating in a frightful social cataclysm, when the fountains of the great deep of human passion, maddened by blood-thirst, were broken up and civilized Europe appeared submerged under a moral deluge—led him to investigate the primary cause of this strange perturbation. In the outraged laws of God and the principles of eternal justice; in the rejection or ignorance of truths long forgotten or contemned in France, and which human societies cannot abjure under pain of social death; in the substitution of the human for the divine principle in the constitution and government of States, he felt convinced he had made the discovery he sought, and placed his hand upon the chief seat of the malady, appealing to reason, revelation and history in support of an argument which is the *fond* or groundwork of most of his writings, but chiefly of the ***Considerations, Essai sur le principe generateur des Institutions Humaines, Du Pape*** and the ***Soirées de St. Petersbourg,*** which turn more or less upon the temporal government of Providence and the reparation due to violated order—an order established by God, and which mankind disturbs at its peril. "Modern philosophy," he observes, "is at once too materialistic and too presumptuous to perceive the real springs of the political world. One of the great errors of this century is to think that the political constitution of peoples is a purely human work—that one can make a constitution as a watchmaker makes a watch. Nothing is more false, and what is still more so is that this great work can be executed by an assembly of men." His reflections led him to the conclusion that no really fundamental constitutional law can be writ-

ten; that the more a constitution is reduced to writing the weaker it becomes; that there never was, never will and never can be a nation constituted *à priori*. He scoffs at the imbecility of those who imagine that the real legislators are men, that laws are paper, and that nations can be constituted with ink. There is something, he avers, in every constitution which cannot be written, and which must be left under a sombre and venerable cloud, under pain of overthrowing the State. This "something" is the divine principle, the recognition of the anterior divine origin of human society, of those eternal laws that presided at the creation, and, as far as this earth is concerned, will only be abrogated when the world shall have finished its course in the fullness of time—laws of which the enactments of legislatures are but the dim reflex or halting expression. Every constitution, properly so called, is a *creation* in the fullest sense of the word, and every creation surpasses the power of man. The written law, therefore, is only the declaration of the anterior, unwritten law, just as a dogmatic definition is posterior to the dogma; so that the pretension to establish a new mode of government is, to his thinking, as extravagant an absurdity as for heresiarchs to create new dogmas. "As nations are born," he says, "governments are literally born with then. When they say a people has given itself a government, it is just as if they said they gave themselves a character and a color. If sometimes we cannot distinguish the bases of a government in its infancy, it does not at all follow that they did not exist. Let us not take developments for creations" [Schérer's *Melanges de Critique religieuse*]. Carlyle says all available authority is mystical in its conditions and comes "by the grace of God." It is singular to find the Catholic publicist and the Protestant writer at one in their appeal to and interpretation of first principles. "Man cannot represent the Creator," says De Maistre, "except by placing himself *en rapport* with Him. Madmen that we are, if we want a mirror to reflect the image of the sun, will we turn it towards the earth?" It is this inversion of first principles, he contends, that has caused the general crumbling of the modern political world.

Once again the world witnesses a great upheaval, a great overturning like that which followed the French Revolution. Cast a rapid glance over the startling record of thrones upset and sceptres broken which contemporary history presents. Look at the number of dethroned or exiled sovereigns, the extinction of ancient dynasties like that of the Hapsburgs; at the frequency and audacity with which assassins have struck at heads of States; at the number of statesmen who have been dismal failures; at the miserable mediocrities posing as such in whom the mere politician or party tactician is revealed; at how little high-thoughted statesmanship remains to guide the destinies of Europe; at the vast schemes of religious, political or social regeneration which promised wonders, but performed nothing; at the legislative experimentalism that on the one hand undertakes the reconstruction of beliefs and makes the government of conscience an affair of police and on the other declares the law to be practically unchristian or atheistic; and then try and persuade yourself that you can discern in all this, like the dreamer of "Locksley Hall" that "one increasing purpose" which traverses the ages, or recognize with De Maistre that it is religion alone—

genuine religion, not sham beliefs—can impart to European polity the creative and regenerative forces it needs; that politics, in the higher and broader sense, and religion rightly understood are inseparable like body and soul, and that their violent disruption means the extinction of the vital principle that was the bond of union and the source of strength and stability. All institutions, this deep thinker concludes, rest upon a religious idea or are only transient. "Faith and patriotism," he says, "are the two great wonder-workers of the world. Both are divine; all their actions are prodigious. Talk not to them of examination, choice, discussion; they only know two words—submission and belief; with these levers they raise the universe. These two offsprings of heaven prove to all observers their origin in creating and conserving; but if they combine, unite their forces and together seize upon a nation, they exalt, they divinize it." [*Melanges*]. Ever since the primitive dispersion of the human race and its division and subdivision into distinctive nationalities, each endowed with a particular genius qualifying it to fulfill its special function in the development of civilization, the nations so constituted have been struggling for self-expression in order to "fill the circle marked by heaven," to work out in detail the divine plan discernible in the order of Providence. It is the national idea which at present is transforming Europe, and any Power that strives to counteract it is putting itself against God and nature, and as it has been said that God and one make a majority, such interference with Providence is sure in the long run to suffer defeat. The late war was ostensibly undertaken to secure this need of self-expression for the lesser nationalities, but so far it only seems to mean the substitution of one form of imperialism for another under transparently specious disguises. One at least of the oldest nationalities in Europe, a nation before the first rude hut was erected on the banks of the Tiber, where Imperial Rome afterwards arose, and when the site of the Athenian Acropolis was a bare, rocky elevation, is denied this right of self-expression and self-development by a Power which puts might above right and holds it in thrall by that very militarism which the war was waged to destroy. We seem to be as far off as ever from that millennium of which Tennyson speaks, "when the war drum throbbed no longer and the battle flag was furled in the Parliament of man, the Federation of the world." It is even doubtful if the League of Nations as conceived in the brain of Woodrow Wilson will emerge from its embryonic state and mature into something better than a combination of the big Powers "to hold a fretful world in awe" and prepare to resist the dreaded on-rush of forces from the far East, should the yellow races threaten to invade the West.

De Maistre, whose style has been compared to that of Bossuet for elevation, Voltaire for sarcasm, and Pascal for depth, touches upon many subjects in his thought-compelling books, interesting and instructive whether you agree with him or not. He has some curious and suggestive reflections upon the co-relation of moral and physical evil, the divine origin of language or speech, the reversibility of merits, the law of the effusion of blood and its expiatory effect, the theory of names and numbers, the relative merits of republicanism and monarchism, the influence of religion upon the duration of dynasties, and other pregnant

themes. Few writers have caused serious abstract thought to be better relished and retained. He felt himself that he was called to place the most arduous questions on a level with all understandings. Lamartine says his style will remain the enduring admiration of all who read for the pleasure of reading [*History of the Restoration of the Monarchy in France,* 1865].

With far too modest self-depreciation he writes to a correspondent:

> I am sure I will be believed, when I protest that I think I am inferior in talents and attainments to most of the writers you have in view at this moment, as much as I surpass them in the truth of the doctrines I profess. I am even pleased to confess this primary superiority, which furnishes me with the subject of a delightful meditation upon the inestimable privilege of truth and the nullity of the talents that venture to separate themselves from it. There is a fine book to be written upon the wrong done to all the productions of genius, and even to the characters of their authors, by the errors they have professed for three centuries. What a subject, if it were well treated! But what conclusion shall we draw from this truth? The legitimate conclusion is, that it is necessary to subordinate all knowledge to religion, to firmly believe that we are studying when we are praying, and particularly when we are occupied with rational philosophy; never to forget that every metaphysical proposition that does not, as it were, spontaneously grow out of a Christian dogma, is only and can only be a culpable extravagance. He who has passed his life without ever having relished divine things, who has narrowed his mind and dried up his heart with sterile speculations that can neither make him better in this life nor prepare him for the other, such a one, I say, will reject these kind of proofs. There are truths that man can only seize with the mind of his heart. When the cleverest man has not the religious sense, not only we cannot convince him, but we have even no means of making ourselves understood by him, which only proves his misfortune.

This is developing a bedrock truth succinctly enunciated by another eminent Catholic writer, Donoso Cortes, who affirmed that if we investigate any political problem, any question concerning the common weal, we are sure to strike upon a Christian dogma.

In his appreciation of De Maistre, Moreau says:

> Rooted in tradition, he derives from thence the unshakable assurance which leaves the mental vision all its lucidity, that power of seeing, which is almost equal to foreseeing and predicting, Catholic Christian, by reason as well as by faith, so to speak—detached from everything and even from himself—the true greatness of his doctrine is that it is not his doctrine. He does not give it as a creation of his thought; it is only a demonstration by history and experience of the truth of Christianity. In the despoiled, humiliated, captive Papacy he never ceased to recognize the divine principle that upholds it, and glorify in it the venerable suzerain of all authority, the eter-

nal protector of all legitimate liberty. Against the conspired forces of philosophism, impious science, and pagan politics, nothing now is really erect but the Christian Capitol. All the power of Catholic unity is only in the prayer of the Priest of Rome; but it is the prayer of him for whom Christ prayed. It was the glory of Fénelon, by having recourse to the Holy See, to remind the Bishops, whose hearts were in the court, that the spiritual sovereign was in Rome, and not in Versailles. He showed them his and their too-long-forgotten judge—the Pope. This glory of Fénelon in the seventeenth century is the glory of De Maistre in our days. He, too, by the influence of his genius, by his masterpiece—that powerful argument drawn from the ruins of our prejudices and errors—was the first to rally the sheep round the great Pastor. [Louis Noreau, *Joseph de Maistre*]

And the compiler of the *Pensées du Comte Joseph de Maistre* says:

> Of all the great names of the century, that of Count Joseph de Maistre oftenest, and as by a secret need, instinctively and without an effort reappears under the pen of every writer engaged in treating any high religious or political question, in solving any philosophical problem. The literary and scientific reviews quote his works. The publicist makes him speak in his writings, quite sure of adding more weight to his considerations under the protection of such a name. The philosopher—I mean the true philosopher— seeks the support of this authority, and thus makes his demonstrations more forcible. The apologist feels firmer in the defensive or offensive, when he sees in his hands the arms of this grand and vigorous athlete of the cause of Christ and His Church. The sacred orator himself is not afraid to utter this name from the elevation of the first pulpit in France. All, in fine, seem to advance with more assurance when they march, sustained by Joseph de Maistre.

Statesmen, worthy of a name often misapplied, politicians who are not mere party hacks, and journalists who are not mere straws upon the surface of public opinion, not mere reflectors of the crude ideas of the man in the street, but original thinkers capable of giving an intelligent direction to movements that make or mar a nation, would do well to read De Maistre thoughtfully. They and those who look to them for light and leading, would equally benefit by the perusal. (pp. 379-86)

> *R. F. O'Connor, "Joseph de Maistre," in* The American Catholic Quarterly Review, *Vol. XLIV, No. 175, July, 1919, pp. 367-86.*

Roger Henry Soltau   (essay date 1931)

[*Soltau was a professor of French and Middle Eastern affairs whose works include* French Political Thought in the 19th Century *and* French Parties and Politics. *In the following excerpt, he maintains that while de Maistre was an ardent supporter of order and tradition, his view of society was unrealistic and romantic.*]

The primacy in the championing of authority undoubtedly belongs to Joseph de Maistre. His political experience, limited as it was, his broad culture, knowledge of history and wide reading, however magnified by his champions, gave his work a breadth of outlook, a solidity, an authority that could not be gainsaid. The thought of Maistre can be summarized as a series of bold and violent negations, accompanied by a series of corresponding affirmations that are bold and violent enough in their way but lack the point and "edge" of the negations. Maistre, like the Voltaire he detests and resembles so much, destroys better than he builds. He deprecates principle and *a priori* reasoning in politics, denies that man can deliberately build anything, denounces change; for these he would substitute experience, natural growth and stability.

It is easy to deduce from these his political creed. Society is born, not made, and is in every way anterior to and above the individual. Man is a social animal by nature; necessity drives him into society and his will has nothing to do with the setting up either of society or of government, both natural facts to be accepted as such. There is nothing moral or just about it; no sane person believes that justice is or can be the law of the universe, so any complaint about things being unfair or wrong is simply irrelevant. As to government, it is by its very nature absolute and unlimited; no king can be bound by any law or promise, nor can he be denied recourse to any methods which circumstances may suggest to him. "There can be no human society without government, no government without sovereignty, no sovereignty without infallibility, and this last privilege is so essential that its existence must be assumed even in temporal sovereignty (where it does not reside in fact) as an essential condition of the maintenance of society" [***Du pape***].

To this unlimited legal sovereignty Maistre places only two limitations—both limitations of fact, not of law. The first is one of common sense: "the sovereign can command with real and durable effect only what is within the boundaries of what is admitted by public opinion, and he does not draw those boundaries" [***Soirées de Saint-Pétersbourg***]; further, there are occasions when a *de facto* power commands allegiance before one *de jure,* and that is when society itself is in danger. Maistre believed that after 1793 the Jacobins should be obeyed as the true rulers of France in the face of the national emergency.

Closely bound up with his view of society was his view of human nature and action. Man acts, he said, not from reason but from emotion, sentiment, prejudice, and our aim should be to found society on right prejudices, to surround man's cradle with dogmas, so that when reason awakens he can find his opinions all ready made, at least on everything that bears on conduct. "Nothing is so important for him as his prejudices."

Reason being helpless, so is will: nothing stable in politics can be achieved by human volition, nothing can be made; this was the cardinal error of the Revolution. That which is written is naught; only the spirit matters. Take the British Constitution (in its unreformed days), for which Maistre entertained an admiration based on profound ignorance and misunderstanding: "it was certainly never made *a priori.* Men never met and said, 'Let us create three powers, balanced in such and such a manner.' Nobody gave it a thought: the constitution was the work of circumstances, and the number of these is infinite. Roman ecclesiastical and feudal laws, Saxon, Norman and Danish customs, privileges, prejudices and claims of all kinds, wars, revolts, revolutions, conquests, crusades, virtues and vices, knowledge and passions of every sort—all these elements working together, mixing together, reacting on each other, formed numberless thousands of combinations which finally produced after several centuries a writing of the most complex character and the finest equilibrium of political forces ever seen in this world" [***Essai sur le principe générateur des constitutions politiques***]; and he says elsewhere in the same pamphlet that the true English Constitution is that magnificent unique and infallible public spirit, which is beyond all praise, which leads everything and saves everything!

It follows from all this that authority is of Divine origin and that the most perfect type of authority, its true norm, is the government of the Church by the Papacy. Small wonder that Maistre devoted a big book to the championship of the most absolute Ultramontane claims of the Pope, and to the violent denunciation of Gallicanism, Jansenism and all their works: "The liberties of the Gallican Church? There are none; all that is concealed under that high-sounding name is a conspiracy of the temporal authority for despoiling the Holy See of its legitimate rights and separating it, in fact, from the Church in France while paying lip-service to its authority" [***De l'Eglise gallicane***]. And as to Port Royal, "everything displeases me about these rebellious divines, even what good things they have written" [***Soirées***]. It is easy from these premises to guess what Maistre's historical and personal judgments will be. That he detests the Revolution goes without saying. That he loathed democracy as a ghastly disease of the body politic is also evident. That he could brook no kind of dissent, political or religious, is no less obvious: *à propos* of the Provinciales and Pascal's attack on Jesuit moral laxity he remarks that the real moral laxness is disobedience to authority, "and as for Protestantism, it was the revolt of individual reason against general reason, and therefore the worst thing imaginable—the essential enemy of all beliefs capable of corporate expression and politically inferior to Islam and to Paganism" [Schérer, *Mélanges de critique religieuse*].

It was, however, for the eighteenth century and its chief representatives that Maistre kept the essence of his vituperation. He rightly saw in the era, and in Voltaire and Rousseau as its spokesmen, the fountain-head of the errors that brought about revolution, democracy and dissent. "To others it has been given to astound virtue but Voltaire astounds even vice," he remarks. "If anyone be attracted by the works of the man from Ferney, let him be assured God does not love him. . . . Voltaire deliberately prostituted a genius created for the praise of God; his conception is absolutely unique and *sui generis;* he was crowned in Paris but would have been banished from Sodom." As to Rousseau: "He is one of the deadliest sophists of his age, and yet the most devoid of true learning, of wisdom and particularly of depth—his apparent depth is only a matter

of words, he does not know how to use philosophical language, defines nothing and misuses abstract terms. As La Harpe says, 'he deceives even when speaking the truth' " [***Soirées***].

As we stated earlier, it is easy to charge your opponent with lack of critical faculties, but it is unwise of Maistre to challenge comparison with Rousseau and Voltaire. The works of a voluminous writer like Maistre must inevitably form a peculiar mixture of good and bad; it was impossible for him to write so many pages without making at times absurd statements and without on other occasions uttering remarks full of common sense and wisdom. As a political prophet the writer who stated that "France would be saved by her aristocracy and her clergy," who profoundly disbelieved in the stability of the American Government and bet 1000 to 1 that either Washington would not be built, or that once built it would not be called Washington, or that no Congress would ever meet there, had best be forgotten. It is difficult to hold as a serious political thinker one who could solve the problem of representation by saying that "it is a fallacy to believe that one can be represented only by a duly mandated person. We daily see in law courts children, lunatics and absentees represented by men who hold their representative mandate from the law only: the people is exactly in the same case, being a perpetual child, a perpetual lunatic, a perpetual absentee. Why then could not its guardians dispense with a mandate?" [***Considérations***]. (To Maistre a nation was "the sovereign joined to the aristocracy.") Few of us can feel much intellectual or moral kinship with one to whom "the executioner is both the terror of human society and that which holds it together. Remove that mysterious power and at the very moment order is superseded by chaos, thrones fall and states disappear. He is the very corner-stone of society." On the other hand, while it is true that, in a frequently quoted phrase, he terms war "divine owing to its consequences of a supernatural order," he finds it "difficult to understand how, given man, his reason, feelings, affections, war is even possible," or to explain why there is a general world-wide agreement that the most honourable thing in the world is to shed innocent blood" [***Soirées***].

Even in politics, in spite of his inveterate playing fast and loose with historical facts and documents, Maistre stands as a champion of Catholic thought, and is usually hailed as such. Surely, it is argued, no one could champion the Church as he does without being a true son of hers; and he has undoubtedly the orthodox Catholic reliance on authority and dogma, even in matters non-religious. "Political theory is to him a religion," says Professor Laski [in his *Studies in the Problem of Sovereignty*]. But to take Maistre as an upholder of orthodox Catholicism is surely to take a very narrow view of what is Catholic orthodoxy; and Faguet is surely right when he points out that Maistre is really utterly irreligious, or at least un-Christian, at heart—"his Christianity," says Faguet [in his *Politiques et moralistes du XIX siécle*], "is basically Pagan—it is, in fact, but a slightly cleaned up Paganism—it lacks all idea of love." It is, as Rocheblave says [in his *Étude sur J. de Maistre*], "terrorist Christianity." Irreligious he was in a number of ways: in his amazing disbelief in morality and justice as laws of life, in his refusal to admit any ethical considerations, in his willingness to sacrifice individuals to "public order"—*i.e.* to the welfare of a governing class—in his identification of Providence with things as they are, in his hard, unloving views of God. It may be that "to be attracted by Voltaire means being unloved by God," but it does not seem to occur to Maistre, or indeed to many divines of his ilk, that some people would rather not be loved by the God of his imagination—or prejudices—who has nothing in common with the God of the Christian Gospels. Far from seeing in Maistre a religious prophet we would rather see in him the forerunner of that irreligious religion, of that atheistic Catholicism, of which Maurras was to be the most conscious and deliberate champion, but of which official Catholicism has never been without some representative, as every Liberal or Democrat has known to his cost. He was the founder of that most un-Christian method of polemics of which Veuillot was to give so deplorable an example: attacks on persons instead of arguments. "You ask me," he wrote to M. de Place in 1818, "to have no mercy on opinions, but to respect individuals; but this is a typically French illusion. Nothing has really been done against an opinion as long as the individual has not been attacked, for it is the authority of individuals that upholds opinions."

Nor is this all. His attack on reason, his insistence on obedience as a matter of sentiment, all this was really verging on the "Fideist" heresy and Maistre was really opening the way for Lamennais. As one of the most illustrious of his indirect disciples, Auguste Comte, pointed out, there was an essential contradiction in his mind: he tries to build up by rational arguments the rejection of reason as the basis of society and of the Church; he makes faith the centre of his system but uses reason to establish faith.

It would be easy to multiply arresting quotations from this sincere and often attractive writer, whose cool taking for granted of what is to many of us the delirious negation of common sense, of history, of experience, of reason, alternately exasperates and amuses the modern reader, but it is time to estimate in conclusion the essential meaning and influence of Maistre's work. Putting aside his hasty generalizations and his naïve prejudices, and leaving to those it may concern his philosophy of authority in the Catholic Church, we may agree with his principal biographer, Cogordan, that the permanent value of his writings lies in a wholesome warning against an optimistic belief in the power of man to improvise anything worth while in matters political and social, in a valuable reminder of the part that must be played by development and growth in human affairs—a lesson which it is ever useful to keep before one's mind.

Further, it is certain that de Maistre's works have played a real part in the revival of Catholic Ultramontanism and in the successful struggle against political and ecclesiastical Liberalism. But in spite of the eulogies and vaunted indebtedness ascribed to him by Maurras and his school we cannot see that his philosophy has really contributed to any appreciable extent to the philosophy of latter-day authoritarianism; the utmost that can be said is that it found in Maistre a useful statement of part of its case, a valuable armoury of pseudo-scientific considerations and arguments and a useful champion of indefensible methods of propaganda.

It is advisedly that we have just used the term "pseudo-scientific." Maistre boasts of being scientific, a "realist," but of scientific method he has not a glimmering idea. Few writers have lacked so utterly the objective detachment which marks the scientist, the capacity for recognizing and pursuing unexpected and unpalatable truth; few on the contrary have more steadfastly taken their imaginations for truth and their desires and prejudices for proved facts. If anyone has equalled Rousseau for sheer subjectivism, that person was Maistre, who "identified a state of society that was but an incident in the life of mankind with a necessary and God-conceived universal order, thus remaining all his life under the spell of those pictures that had chained his childhood and old age" [Cogordan, in his *Vie de J. de Maistre*]. This would-be realist lived in fact in an unreal world of his own conceiving. Not only did the past as he saw it never exist, but it needed, as Rocheblave says, "a singular concourse of special circumstances to enable anyone to misunderstand so completely the world in which he lived; to have been born outside and never to have lived within the country for whose people he wrote; to have had no education outside books and have imbibed as dogmas ideas of tradition, authority, immutability of which no concrete instances could be found, and to spend most of life wandering as an exile away from any normally constituted nation in which he could observe the normal interplay of freedom and authority," and even his admirer and disciple Ballanche admitted that "unable to hear anything but the voice of past centuries, that prophet of the past slept within recollections which he took for anticipations." In fact, this champion of order and of tradition, pursuing the will-o'-the-wisp of a Utopia in which no man would ever wish to be free, remained to his dying day an incorrigible romanticist. (pp. 16-24)

Roger Henry Soltau, "The Dogmas of Authoritarianism," in his French Political Thought in the 19th Century, *1931. Reprint by Russell & Russell, 1959, pp. 15-31.*

Edmund Wilson   (essay date 1932)

[*Wilson is generally considered the foremost American man of letters in the twentieth century. A prolific reviewer, creative writer, and social and literary critic, he exercised his greatest literary influence as the author of* Axel's Castle (1931), *a seminal study of literary symbolism, and as the author of widely read reviews and essays in which he introduced the best works of modern literature to the reading public. In the following excerpt, originally published in the* New Republic *on 24 August 1932, Wilson argues that de Maistre's philosophy is unimaginative and inconsistent.*]

When literary people, hard pressed by the threat of democratic reforms, feel the need for a reactionary authority, they are likely to resort to Joseph de Maistre.

De Maistre was one of the few really distinguished writers who spoke for the Catholic reaction in the period after the French Revolution; and he has always been especially useful to conservative-minded intellectuals, because, in reading or remembering him, they are able to tell themselves that in that era all the brilliant brains were not on the subversive side. I have so often had de Maistre thrown at my head as an antidote to modern radicalism that I recently decided to look into him; and my report is that the "prophet of reaction" is by no means so formidable a thinker as he has sometimes been represented.

There was of course after the French Revolution a role for a critic like de Maistre. By the time the Revolution had run its course, it was not difficult to perceive the extravagance of the eighteenth-century doctrines which had led up to it. Rousseau had said that people were naturally good and that it was only institutions which had perverted them. Well, Robespierre had been Rousseau's disciple, and by the time the Republic had foundered in the blood of its quarrelling leaders and given way to the Emperor Napoleon, it did not look as if the people were so naturally good or so amenable to the reforms of the Goddess of Reason as the Rousseaus and Condorcets had asserted.

De Maistre wrote, in his *Essai sur le Principe Générateur des Constitutions Politiques:* "One of the great errors of a century that confessed all the errors was the belief that a political constitution could be written and created a priori, when reason and experience agree in showing that a constitution is a divine production and that precisely the most fundamental and most essentially constitutional part of a nation's laws is something that can never be written." It was impossible, de Maistre insisted, that the work of the Revolution should last: the new system was a purely theoretical one which had been artificially imposed by cranks. De Maistre makes merry over the efforts of the cranks to dignify their work with classic names. It is use and use alone, he says, that can dignify and fill with meaning the names of places and buildings—the Tuileries, for example—that were originally commonplace. And you cannot prop up something ephemeral by giving it a grandiose name. The Odéon, for example: for all the pretentious Greek label, it couldn't last! And then, the Olympic Games, so presumptuously inaugurated, of which an enthusiastic contemporary had asserted that "the day would come when they would attract the whole of Europe to the Champ de Mars"—how preposterous that was! De Maistre's instances were not well-chosen, and his arguments do not sound so good today as they may have done in 1809. There is something in what he says: you cannot invent a new social system and get people to accept it overnight. But that did not mean that in France the old régime had been preferable or that the new, in spite of Napoleon, had not taken a very strong hold—which were the conclusions de Maistre drew. (pp. 509-10)

What is impressive about Joseph de Maistre is what is impressive about most sincere reactionaries from Dr. Johnson to Dostoevsky: his vision of human sin.

The great radical is likely to be one who either is free from a sense of guilt or has evolved a psychological mechanism which enables him to turn moral judgments against himself into moral judgments against society. A man like Kropotkin is himself so guileless, so benevolently disposed toward his fellow-men, that it is impossible for him to imag-

ine that other people, if left to themselves, may not all be as pure as he. A Rousseau, with the elements much more mixed, was able, at the moment of his revelation, to put off all the humiliating experiences which had hindered him and rankled with him on an iniquitous social system, quite alien to the natural man, from which he could dissociate himself.

The reactionary, on the other hand, is likely to start from a profound conviction of the evil of the natural man. Instead of worrying because people do not get enough freedom, he is obsessed by the need for police—authority, discipline, order. How else can you keep the Devil under control? Dr. Johnson, who would not let Garrick take him behind the scenes of his theater for fear of the demoralizing effect on him of the bare necks and arms of the actresses, was all for Church and King; Dostoevsky, who, when the peasants had murdered his father, felt a kind of common guilt with the murderers and who behaved as if he were expiating in Siberia crimes with which he had never been charged, came back full of loyalty to Church and Tsar. De Maistre, who was able to justify the apparent injustice of the days when he and his wife and children had been exiled, homeless and starving, by the sins he knew his soul must answer for before the tribunal of God, defended the divine right of kings and the infallibility of the Pope; and he thus most commands our respect when he is insisting on the evil of life as something which cannot be avoided, which reason can never abolish or rhetoric conjure away. Injustices, from our human point of view, do certainly occur, he says (in *Les Soirées de Saint-Pétersbourg*); people suffer for crimes that they never committed. But if you take mankind in the gross, as God does, you will see that we all share in human sin. This sin is our common inheritance, our common debt; not one of us is free from it; and we must all of us contribute to paying it. De Maistre repudiates, he tells us, the snobbish point of view of that queen who was supposed to have said, "You may be sure that God thinks twice about damning our sort of people!" No: not one of us is innocent! That Elizabeth of France, the King's sister, should have had to die by the guillotine just as the monster Robespierre did, does not prove that God is unjust: "Every man, in his quality of man, is subject to all the ills of humanity." We are subject to unjust executions just as we are to apoplexy. But if we look at things in the large, we shall see "that the greatest mass of happiness, even temporal happiness, goes, not to the virtuous man, but to virtue." Because, if this were not true, the whole moral order would be wrong—which is absurd.

This leads de Maistre to one of his most famous performances. The whole moral order is *not* wrong, and in reality our human justice is acting in behalf of the divine. The executioner, therefore, in spite of the fact that all the world avoids him, is a man appointed by God, "created like a world" and set apart. How else is it possible to account for him?—how else is it possible to explain that a man can be found to accept the job? Yet the executioner does exist and carries out his terrible orders. De Maistre tells you about it:

> A somber signal is given: an abject minister of justice comes to knock at his [the executioner's] door and let him know that he is needed. He sets

out; he arrives at the public square, which is crowded with an eager excited throng. A prisoner or a murderer or a blasphemer is given over to him. He seizes him and stretches and ties him on a horizontal cross; he lifts his arm and a horrible silence falls. Nothing is heard but the cry of the bones cracking under the heavy rod and the howlings of the victim. Then he unties him and carries him to the wheel; the shattered limbs get twisted in the spokes; the head hangs; the hair stands out; and from the mouth, gaping open like a stove, come only now a few bloody words which at intervals beg for death. Now the executioner has finished: his heart beats, but it is for joy; he applauds himself, he says in his heart: 'Nobody is better at the wheel than I!' He comes down and holds out his bloodstained hand, and the Law throws into it from a distance some gold pieces which he carries away with him through a double hedge of people, who draw away in horror. He sits down to table and eats; then he gets into bed and goes to sleep. When he wakes up the next day, he begins to think about something quite different from the work he has been doing the day before. Is he a man? Yes: God receives him into his temples and allows him to pray. The executioner is not a criminal; yet no tongue is willing to say, for example, that he is 'virtuous,' that he is 'a good fellow,' that he is 'estimable,' etc. No moral commendation fits him, because any such commendation assumes some sort of bond with mankind, and the executioner has none.

And yet all grandeur, all power, all discipline are founded on the executioner. He is the horror of the human association and the tie that holds it together. Take out of the world this incomprehensible agent, and at that instant will order give way to chaos, thrones fall and society vanish. God, who is the source of all sovereignty, is, therefore, the source of all punishment, too.

It has been objected to de Maistre that he is hard. The truth is that he is not hard enough. As he says, a professional executioner is incomprehensible to him. In his earlier days, as a matter of fact, he had resigned from the senate of Savoy, which had judiciary functions, precisely because he could not bring himself to sentence people to death. And, although he was willing to face the fact that everything he valued in the world depended on that horrible wheel, he evaded this uncomfortable situation as much as he possibly could. If, according to the divine arrangement, the virtuous must sometimes suffer, then the innocent must sometimes get tortured. What about Jean Calas, the Protestant merchant who had been persecuted by a Catholic mob for a crime he had perhaps never committed and who had been broken on the wheel?—Calas, whom Voltaire had defended and whose name he had made a symbol for the savagery of religious intolerance? Well, the truth is, de Maistre replies, that Calas was probably guilty. The chief thing that makes de Maistre think so is the flippancy displayed by Voltaire while he was agitating in Calas' defense—this flippancy having been exemplified by a remark in one of Voltaire's letters: "You find my memoir too hot, but I am working on another one for you which is going to be a scorcher." Nothing can be more probable

than that God Himself, in a case like this, makes a point of helping the police so that they won't fail to get the right person; and, besides, there is always the chance that, even if a man is executed for a crime which he did not commit, he may deserve to be punished for something else. And yet, even where the victim is certainly guilty, an execution like that of Calas, by "torture ordinary and extraordinary" and by breaking alive on the wheel, is unquestionably a distasteful affair. Even when we can reconcile ourselves to contemplating the agonies of the wicked, how can we contemplate the state of mind imposed on the executioner? We can get around this haunting difficulty by no less heroic a piece of sophistry than excluding the executioner from the human race! De Maistre has to invent for this man a character as frankly inhuman as that of a goblin or a djinn in a fairy-tale. (One is not even convinced by de Maistre's description that he has ever actually witnessed an execution.) He is obliged to tell himself that Jack Ketch is *not* really a man like himself, that he is a different kind of being altogether from the fellow whose humane sensibilities compelled him to resign from the Senate.

I know of no more striking example of the lengths to which an intelligent man can go to escape the disagreeable implications of a position he has an interest in maintaining. The Boston lawyers who steadily maintained that, though Sacco and Vanzetti might well be innocent, it was necessary to have them executed, in order to uphold the authority of the Massachusetts courts, though they are less sympathetic than Joseph de Maistre, were really arguing more soundly than he, as they were arguing more soundly than the thousands of their respectable and kindly fellow-townsmen who, like de Maistre, did their best to convince themselves that, in spite of the dubious evidence, the accused were very likely guilty, or that, if they didn't deserve death for murder, they did for political heresy.

You find this wanting to have it both ways all through *Les Soirées de Saint-Pétersbourg.* So with those other earthly evils—cancer and war. After describing with some vividness their horrors, he tries to show us they are, after all, not so horrible; religion and self-discipline are stimulated in time of war; and as for cancer, there is a girl in St. Petersburg whom cancer has gradually converted into a model of pious devotion. Even in regard to the Revolution, de Maistre is not really so uncompromising as he is sometimes assumed to be. He could not extirpate his early liberalism, and this weakened his royalist position. He was too serious and too intelligent not to realize and deplore the corruption and incompetence of the old régime. But the Revolution was "a great and terrible sermon which Providence has preached to men—a sermon with two morals. Revolutions are made by abuses: this is the first moral, and it is addressed to sovereigns. Nevertheless, it is infinitely better to have abuses than revolutions: this is the second moral, and it is addressed to peoples." And he accepted the French Republic in so far as he believed it the only thing which could hold France together against her enemies.

Not a very satisfactory position. Knowing well that on that quarrelsome continent, where the nations were well engaged in the path that was to lead to 1914, no sovereign could ever bring unity, he advocated setting up a body which should derive its authority from the Pope and keep peace by imposing its decisions. The truth was that Joseph de Maistre had himself been irremediably influenced by the rationalism and humanitarianism of the bourgeois philosophers he patronized. His class bias was, of course, very strong; we see it even in his attempts at justice. The worst crime that de Maistre could imagine was the guillotining of the King's sister. Calas was far from mattering so much. But why, then, should he have mattered at all? From de Maistre's point of view, he was a heretic in any case. Voltaire, against whom, from the St. Petersburg of Alexander I, de Maistre is always railing, has got him worried about Calas after all. And why bother about the fates of common soldiers? A thoroughly hard-boiled aristocrat ought to have taken all that for granted. But Joseph de Maistre's attitude is never really hard-boiled and realistic, but, on the contrary, sophistical and literary. It is an affair of ingenious reasoning and elegiac rumination in a limbo between two worlds. When de Maistre died, Talleyrand said of him: "The prophet of the past has fallen asleep in the bosom of eternity, with his memories which he takes for premonitions." (pp. 511-17)

> Edmund Wilson, "Joseph de Maistre," in his The Shores of Light: A Literary Chronicle of the Twenties and Thirties, *Farrar, Straus and Giroux, 1952, pp. 509-17.*

John C. Murray (essay date 1949)

[*In the following excerpt, Murray presents a comprehensive examination of de Maistre's political thought in his major works.*]

With the restoration of the Bourbons to the throne of France, there began one of the most intellectually fruitful periods in French history. The French suddenly had a greater freedom than had been enjoyed for some time, and as Lamartine tells us, "scarcely was the Empire overturned, when people began to think, to write, and to sing again in France. . . . All that had been hitherto silent now began to speak" [*History of the Restoration of the Monarchy in France,* 1865]. In politics, all sides had powerful spokesmen. But the old regime, suddenly given a new lease on life, seldom before had been favored with such brilliant apologists as Chateaubriand, Bonald, Lamennais, and Joseph de Maistre, the *prophète du passé.* One thing should be made clear. That Maistre's political thought was superior to that of the others of this school, there can be little doubt. But that Maistre was the chief exponent of the reaction during the Restoration is a fact rather falsely assumed or at least open to exceeding doubt. In reality, it seems quite clear that the influence of Maistre in France during this period was almost negligible. Perhaps one might go so far as to say that his position as chief spokesman of the reaction, rather than having been actually held by him, has been assigned to him by later writers.

Within fifteen short years the Bourbon monarchy was forever doomed. The entire fault lay with the indiscreet politics of the reaction, the politics of the Ultras, led by the near-sighted Comte D'Artois who later abdicated as Charles X. This was the group which "had learned nothing and forgotten nothing." It has been rightly said of this party that to them "all compromise was treason, all opposition was rebellion; a Moderate was a Jacobin in disguise; the King was little better. . . . Villèle describes them as *enragés;* the King dubs them *fous*" [G. L. Dickinson, in his *Revolution and Reaction in Modern France,* 1927]. For several reasons it is difficult to subscribe to an opinion that this party of reaction found its inspiration in Maistre. The White Terror was in absolute contradiction to Maistre's description of the counter-revolution. The desire to reestablish the monarchy exactly as it was remembered in 1789 lacked every insight of Maistre's on the consequence of revolutions.

It has been said of both Maistre and Bonald that "during their lifetime, they were praised more than they were cited" [Charles de Rémusat, "Du Traditionalisme," *Revue des Deux Mondes* 9 (1 May 1857)]. It can be pointed out that in Maistre's case, at least, he was not extensively read until long after his death and long after the expiration of the Bourbon Restoration. Indeed, if Maistre exercised a widespread influence in France, it was probably between the years 1840 and 1880 rather than at any other time. Outside of his *Essai sur le Principe générateur des Constitutions politiques* (1814), Maistre had published nothing between the years 1796 and 1819. His *Considérations sur la France* (1796) was undoubtedly widely read by the *émigrés,* some of whom found themselves sharply criticised therein. But who among the Ultras would have gone so far as to say that France had been saved by Robespierre? Or, that "once the revolutionary movement had been established, France and the monarchy were able to be saved only by Jacobinism?" Maistre's *Du Pape* (1819) was hardly calculated to win friends among the predominantly Gallican ranking clergy, so active in the Ultra cause. A series of letters shows that he was completely disheartened by the silent or critical reception given this work. To Lamennais he expressed a concern over the complaints of the "high clergy of France." To Bonald he fretted over the silence of the journals and spoke of the reaction of the clergy being "as if I had denied the existence of God." Lamennais complimented him on this powerful work, but at the same time had to inform Maistre that some in France were maintaining that there were "at least three or four heresies" in the book. Later, Lamennais tried to console him on the difficulty Rome had in appreciating the book. It is not without significance that among the first answers to Maistre's work, if not the first, was given by the Abbé G. A. R. Baston, whose impressive title was "docteur de Sorbonne, ancien chanoine, grand vicaire et professeur de théologie" [*Réclamation pour l'Église de France et pour la vérité, contre l'ouvrage de M. de Maistre, intitulé: Du Pape,* 1821]. The appearance, in 1821, after the death of Maistre, of *L'Église Gallicane,* with its merciless attack on the Four Articles of 1682 and those theologians regarded as decisive in France, must have certainly completed the alienation of the clergy of rank.

Maistre's literary style has justly won him an enduring place in French letters, but at the same time it tends to discourage the examination and understanding of his political and social thought. Thus, de Rémusat, who prided himself on his scholarly, yet sympathetic consideration of the writings of his opponents, frankly admitted that he "had never read ten pages of Count de Maistre without experiencing a profound joy at not thinking as he" [Rémusat].

Maistre's constant love of the paradoxical, his indiscretion, impertinence, and disrespect, and his frequent violence easily lead to his dismissal as an outrageous reactionary. When he is cited, more likely than not the reference will be from his apology of the executioner. This is an excellent example of the Maistrian technique of forcing a point. Instead of simply saying that the authority in the state demands a punitive power, a hardly contestable doctrine, he presses this conclusion only after an excursion into one of the most revolting aspects of society. The reader is suddenly brought into the midst of a nervous, milling crowd anxiously awaiting the executioner's torturing of a prisoner. With an apparent relish, the whole sordid drama is depicted. Bones crack, the blood-filled mouth of the victim gushes out a few words pleading for the mercy of death. The crowd is horrified at the spectacle, but the heart of the executioner beats faster as he compliments himself on his ability to use the torturing wheel. Justice throws a few coins into the bloodied hands of the executioner, and the crowd shrinks back as he passes out of the gathering. This friendless, solitary creature returns home and forgetting his awful tasks resumes his lonely but otherwise natural life. "Is this a man?" asks Maistre. The answer is intentionally shocking. Yes, he is; and more than that! He is "the bond of human association," the very "keystone of society" [*Les Soirées de Saint-Pétersbourg*]. Faguet has aptly said with respect to this technique of Maistre's, that "le paradoxe est le méchanceté des hommes bons qui ont trop d'esprit" [*Politiques et Moralistes du XIX siècle*, 1891].

Maistre's impertinence reaches classic proportions when he remarks, in a passing glance at the period, that "the history of the ninth thermidor is not long: *Several scoundrels killed several scoundrels*" [*Considérations*].

Working on the principle that criticism is most effective when it is accompanied with arguments *ad hominem,* Maistre constantly abuses the opposition. But, as Dennis Brogan reminds us, "French controversy is not gentle" [*French Personalities and Problems*, 1946]. Thus Voltaire, for whom Maistre had an almost unearthly hatred, is treated severely at every possible opportunity. In the *Soirées,* there are, perhaps unwittingly, three literary portraits, that of the executioner, that of the savage, and that of Voltaire. To Maistre, Voltaire's face was itself the picture of evil, indeed "the Divine anathema was written on his face. . . . Nothing absolves him: his corruption is of a genre particular to himself. . . . The laugh he excites is illegitimate. . . . Other cynics scandalize virtue; Voltaire scandalises vice. . . . Paris crowned him; Sodom would have banished him. . . . The greatest crime of Voltaire is the abuse of his talent and the deliberate prostitution of a genius created to glorify God and Virtue" [*Soirées*].

Others fare a little less harshly. Maistre did not think there was anything "new" about Bacon's *Novum Organum*, in fact he asserted that he "honors the wisdom which proposes a new organ as much as that which would propose a new leg" [*Examen de la Philosophie de Bacon,*] The *Essay on Human Understanding* may have been written with "the eloquence of an almanac." Nevertheless, Locke was an honest man and a man of good sense—even if he did tell us only what was already known [*Soirées*].

In good faith it should be noted that this type of criticism was reserved for those whose motives Maistre doubted. "*A insolent, insolent et demi*" [Saint-Beuve, "Joseph de Maistre," *Les Grands Écrivains Français*, 1930]. Purer souls, like Pascal and Bossuet, were much more cordially treated.

All Maistre's efforts were not, of course, spent in the coining of clever insults. The "Plato of the Alps," as Lamartine called him, struck a telling blow at the sensistic psychology of Locke in pointing out that nothing could be more debasing, more deadly for the human spirit. Through this system, "reason has lost its wings, and slithers as a miry reptile; through it the divine source of poesy and eloquence has been dried up; through it, all the sciences have perished. . . . It is the death of every religion, of every exquisite sentiment, of every sublime impetus" [*Soirées*]. At some place or other Maistre examined almost every problem which has challenged the minds of men. But it is his political thought which has challenged us here, for the reason that it has been generally obscured by that section in *Du Pape* where he suggests a universal order presided over by the Pope. Obviously there is more to Maistre than this segment of *Du Pape.*

Maistre's first political work to reach the general public was *Considérations sur la France,* a powerful polemic against the Revolution. With a bitterness equalled only by Burke, Maistre held that "what distinguishes the French Revolution, and what makes it a unique *event* in history, is that it is radically evil; no element of good relieves the observer's eye: it is the highest degree of known corruption, it is pure impurity. . . . In its cradle it showed everything that it was to be. It was a certain inexplicable delirium, a blind impetuosity, a scandalous contempt of everything respectable among men; an atrocity of a new genus which joked over its heinous crimes; it was especially an impudent prostitution of reasoning and of every word made for the expression of ideas of justice and virtue. . . . Learned barbarity, systematic atrocity, calculated corruption, etc."

This work of Maistre's was intended to offset the harm that might be done by the previously published book [*De la force du government actuel et de la nécessité de s'y rallier*, 1796] of that *petit drôle*, Benjamin Constant (a good part of which was the work of Madame de Stael), which sought to rally the royalists to the Republic in France. Maistre's thesis was that France, which "exercises a veritable magistracy over Europe," had, among other things, sinfully contradicted her vocation through the demoralization of Europe effected by the *philosophes.* The Revolution is an act of Providence, a scourge inflicted upon France as a punishment for her crimes. Its providential character is attested by the fact that, following its own course, the Revolution exceeds all human control. The very men who plan the Revolution are but its simple instruments. The most active among them appear passive and mechanical, for once they seek to oppose or alter the course of the Revolution, they disappear from the scene.

According to Maistre, the Revolution would pass as soon as France was regenerated, and with it would go its *a priori* constitutions and governments. If the third constitution were suitable for France, it would daily find new adherents. Instead, "every minute sees a new deserter of the democracy," and thus it is justly said to be "a republic without republicans." If the government appears strong, that is only because it is violent. It is not a generally desired thing; it is merely tolerated for fear of something worse. Even the friends of the Republic do not attempt to show its values. Rather, they seek only to prove that the greatest of evils would result from a return of the old regime—a point of view vigorously denied by Maistre.

The Revolution, Maistre held, had led France into slavery. If the French desire a salvation, they will not find it in the Republic, but in their ancient constitution. He maintained that if the people of France "are made for a greater degree of liberty than that which they enjoyed seven years ago, which is not at all clear, they have under their hand, in all the monuments of their history and legislation, everything necessary to render them the honor and envy of Europe." The objection that this constitution had not been in effect did not disturb Maistre. If such were the case, in his estimation, only the French themselves deserved blame. The important thing is that this constitution could be put into effect upon the restoration of the king through a counter-revolution.

Maistre's ideas on the counter-revolution show at once a love of France greater than that held by a good many of the *émigrés* and an acute sense of the workings of a revolution. He castigates those nobles who would effect the counter-revolution by a force of arms which could result only in the conquest and division of France, massacres and disorders, "the annihilation of her influence and the debasement of her King." Equally at fault were those who were seeking the aid of foreign princes, thinking that these powers would fight for the throne without demanding some indemnity. The counter-revolution would inevitably come about, "the date alone is doubtful," but it would not be by these means.

Those within France who were arguing that the counter-revolution would involve all the horrors of the Revolution, could not be more wrong. Their error was in thinking that the monarchy "overthrown by monsters, must be reestablished by their equals." The arguments that the people fear, or do not desire, or will never consent to the counter-revolution were regarded by Maistre as a waste of words. His conclusion was that "In revolutions the people are as nothing, or at least they enter only as passive instruments. . . . The people, if the monarchy is reestablished, will no more decree its reestablishment than they decreed its destruction or the establishment of the revolutionary government." Instead, "four or five men will give France a king. Some letters from Paris will announce to the provinces that France has a king, and the provinces will cheer: Vive le roi!" And Paris, awakening one morning to find

that it has a king, will react similarly. All opposition will vanish as officers of the army, seeking honors, rush to the king's side. Likewise, rulers of the cities, also hoping for great honors, will turn their jurisdiction over to the king. Whatever wills might be opposed to the king will be unable to unite among themselves. Once the king himself returns, everything will be in his favor; the royalist movement will be invincible.

Whereas the Revolution aroused every vice, Maistre insisted that the counter-revolution would call forth every virtue. This undoubtedly, like the rest of the program, was a broad lesson aimed at the monarchy. With an insight far greater than the Ultras were later to show, Maistre pointed out that "the French have two infallible guarantees against the pretended vengeances which they have been led to fear, the interest of the king and his impotence." For the king would be foolish indeed if he commenced his reign by abuse; and if he were so foolish, he would never summon the strength to fulfill his desires. Thus, there need be no fear of the counter-revolution, for according to Maistre, "the reestablishment of the monarchy, which is called the counter-revolution, will nowise be a *contrary-revolution,* but the contrary of the revolution."

The *Considérations* may have bolstered the hopes of a good many *émigrés,* but within France it naturally did not find a receptive audience. Yet, in a way, the republicans could have profited a great deal from Maistre's reflections on the course of events. He pointed out a good many of their errors; the over-legislation, the futility of attacks upon those things conducive to a stable society, the foolhardiness in alienating the sympathies of many possible friends. In comparing the equalitarianism of the new regime with the grandeur of the *ancien régime,* he taught the psychological desirability of honorary distinctions in society. Napoleon, who built an empire on the rubble of the Revolution, had learned these valuable lessons.

Although today we scorn many critics of the principles of the Revolution, it seems a bit unfair to heap only contumely on Maistre's ideas of the Revolution. The Revolution in 1796 was not the glorious movement it has come to be. It appears that it was not until the end of the Restoration and during and after the "boring" Bourgeois Monarchy, that the Revolution assumed its mythical proportions. There can be little doubt that Cresson is right in saying that even at the beginning of the Restoration "what is especially remembered of the Revolution . . . is the suffering that it has caused. The Revolution is not at this date a great, living idea" [*Les Courants de la Pensée philosophique française,* 1927]. Maistre was too close to events and suffered too much personally—although without petty complaining over his losses—to find any saving grace in the Revolution.

It should be understood that Maistre's apparently impossible request for the reestablishment of the monarchy was not a request for the monarchy which immediately preceded 1789. He certainly realized, and consistently pointed out, the impossibility of restoring intact the old regime. That the returned monarchy would have to be a reformed monarchy was insisted on in the *Considérations* and reiterated several times thereafter. Thus, in 1810, Maistre wrote that the Revolution could not end with a return to previous conditions. Rather, it must end "by a rectification of the condition to which we have fallen," in very much the same way that "the immense revolution caused by the barbarian invasion of the Roman empire did not end by the expulsion of these barbarians, but by their definite establishment which created the feudal state of Europe" [*Mémoire, 1810*].

As for Maistre's interpretation of the Revolution as the active intervention of Providence, that is a thesis which is beyond the scope of history proper. The submission of Providence to the service of a political or social system, however, can be exceedingly injurious to Providence. In the present case, for instance, it brought forth De Remusat's not unjust criticism that Maistre's interpretation of Providence led to this one point: "Conclusion: la Providence fera la contre-revolution." (pp. 63-72)

The political thought of Joseph de Maistre maintains a marvellous consistency. This is especially true after 1794. Earlier in life, however, he was imbued with the doctrines of the eighteenth century. Surprising as it may seem, not only was he a Gallican during this period, but he was considered a liberal at the court in Turin. For some years he was a freemason, dutifully attended lodge-meetings, and, recognized as a reforming spirit, he rapidly rose to high official positions in the organization. In later life he opposed the unqualified accusations that the Revolution was the work of Masonry. During this same period, the gentle Claude de Saint-Martin, *le Philosophe Inconnu*, and his Illuminism, that school of austere, mystical Christians, made a lasting impression on Maistre.

It was during these early years, in his first public composition, that Maistre, speaking of America, pointed out that "Liberty, insulted in Europe, has winged its flight to another hemisphere" [*Éloge de Victor Amédée III*]. Two years later, in his ***Discours sur la Vertu*** delivered before the Senate of Savoy, the young Maistre pictured the birth of society in excellent Rousseauistic terms. But these thoughts of youth were not to last long; the Revolution altered all these early patterns. Just as it reversed his Gallicanism to an ultra-montanism, so also did it lead to a critical contempt of every doctrine of the *philosophes*.

Having refused to pay the tax levied by the revolutionary conqueror, Maistre, in 1793, began the sad journeying of twenty-four years, fourteen of which were spent in Russia as the envoy of the King of Sardinia to the Court of Alexander I. Reflecting upon the violences and disorders of his time and scanning the records of history, he was led to the conclusion that the "effusion of blood is never suspended in the universe," peace is but a respite between wars, and every period of history may be likened to that of Charles V and Francis I, for "each page of their history is red with human blood" [***Considérations***].

There was not the least doubt in Maistre's mind that man could not radically alter this situation, but he did think that its harshness could be lessened. To this end, two things were necessary in society—unity and authority. And the entire political philosophy of Maistre, "apôtre si

sévère de l'unité et de l'authorité" as he said of himself, is built on these foundations.

The theorists of popular sovereignty were, in his estimation, profoundly in error. He held it to be an illusion for the people to think that they are, or can be sovereign, for it always appears that "the people who command are not the people who obey" [***Étude sur la Souveraineté***]. The same proposition holds for representative governments. Here, the people or the nation may be called sovereign, but this is a "metaphysical sovereignty," because, in truth, the representatives are sovereign. Maistre admitted however, that in a certain sense the people are sovereign, in so far as "it is impossible to imagine a sovereignty without imagining a people who consent to obey." The origin of sovereignty, nevertheless, could not by any stretch of the imagination be located in a contract. Since man is always found in a social state and since the nature of a being is to exist as God willed him to exist, then society is divinely ordained. Likewise, since every society demands that there be a directing authority, a sovereignty, then God has also "willed sovereignty and the laws, without which there is no society."

Every conceivable species of sovereignty is absolute, "for there will always be, in the last analysis, an absolute power which will be capable of doing wrong with impunity, which will be, therefore, *despotic* under this point of view, in all the force of the term, and against which there will be no other rampart but that of insurrection." It should be noted that when Maistre maintains that sovereigns are absolute, he does not mean arbitrary, he means unlimited; thus he specifies, "Quand je dis que *nulle souveraineté n'est limité*, j'entends *dans sou exercice légitime*" [***Du Pape***]. An absolutely sovereign ruler could never exist, for there is always something to limit him, it may be "a law, a custom, conscience, a tiara, or a dagger," but still it will be there. Within the boundaries of its power, however, the sovereign is absolute. In his usually extreme manner, Maistre associates infallibility with the sovereignty by saying:

> There can be no human society without government, no government without sovereignty, no sovereignty without infallibility; and this last privilege is so absolutely necessary, that one is compelled to suppose infallibility, even in the temporal sovereignties (where it is not) under penalty of seeing the society dissolve.

Arguments such as this led to Maistre's being called an *"absolutiste féroce. . . légitimiste intransigeant"* [Faguet]. A more temperate mind might have said, without fear of shocking anyone, that the political stability of a society depends on a general deference to the decision of the sovereign power. Maistre, himself, no doubt realized that his theme of infallibility could create confusion, since he went out of his way to explain that the infallibility so "necessary" to the temporal sovereigns does not involve an inability to err. Rather, it means that sovereigns are infallible "puisque nulle part il n'est permis de dire qu'elles se sont trompées" [***Du Pape***]. Or, to put it another way, "de se tromper sans appel." Thus it is likened to a court of last resort (c'est ainsi qu'un tribunal suprême) whose decision is final. Of course, if this principle is not generally accepted, then one is "under the penalty of seeing the association disolve."

Now Maistre maintained that although all sovereign wills are equally absolute, it does not follow that they are all equally vicious or blind to their proper function, that is, the rendering of justice. This leads to a consideration of his ideas on government. It was Maistre's particular judgment that monarchy is the natural government for man. And, of all monarchies, the French was without a peer. In this respect he agreed with Grotius that the French "is the most beautiful kingdom after that of heaven" [*Considérations*]. Not all monarchies, however, are equally excellent or admirable; for Maistre, as a good Italian, was the implacable foe of the House of Austria, that "great enemy of humankind" [A. Blanc, *Mémoires Politiques et Correspondence Diplomatique de j. de Maistre,* 1858].

Although he may have put all his faith in monarchy, Maistre consistently adhered to a political relativism. In 1794, he wrote that the question of the best form of government is academic, "each form of government is the best in certain cases, and the worst in others" [*Étude sur la Souveraineté*]. Nevertheless, if one were to establish a certain criterion for governments, Maistre maintained that "the best government for each nation is the one which, in the space of the terrain occupied by this nation, is capable of procuring the greatest possible sum of happiness and power, to the greatest possible number of men, during the longest time possible."

Democracy, Maistre thought, was the worst form of government: "of all the monarchs, the harshest, the most despotic, the most intolerable, is the monarchy of the people" (*le monarque-peuple*). Republics are much more desirable, but conditions are seldom favorable for them. At times, a republic may be the best of all governments. Maistre was insistent on this point; he went so far as to say, "let us repeat this, because nothing is truer: nothing equals the halcyon days of republics; but it is only a flash." This he deemed to be always the case because the influence of the wise does not suffice to restrain the disordered actions of the people. Furthermore, the *sine qua non* of a republic is a sensible and virtuous people, a condition seldom found. In this respect England, he believed, was most fortunate; Maistre considered it safe to say that "the true English Constitution is that admirable, unique, and infallible public spirit, beyond all praise, which guides everything and preserves everything" [*Essai sur Le Principe générateur des Constitutions politiques*]. Without such a spirit, and he believed the French did not have it, republics can hardly exist.

The stability, unity, and continuity which Maistre held to be absolutely necessary for a durable society were, in his estimation, precisely those things denied society by the teachings of the *philosophes.* No teaching of this school could be more disruptive of stability than its attack on religion. Not only, he argued, would religion be able to withstand this assault, but the very idea of attempting its destruction evidenced a total lack of political wisdom. For the entire course of history offers striking testimony to the powerful role religion has played in the formation of all institutions "from empires to brotherhoods" [*Considér-*

ations]. The value of religion, Maistre maintained, lay in the positive and the negative influences it exercised over the human mind, the result of which is that religion becomes a fundamental source of strength and durability for institutions. It moves men to marvelous deeds, and at the same time "the religious principle already so strong by what it does, is again infinitely more so by what it prevents, in consequence of the veneration with which it invests everything that it takes under its protection. . . . Would you then *preserve* everything, *dedicate* everything" [*Essai*]. This exceedingly pragmatic evaluation of religion is yet more clearly spelled out when Maistre goes on to say that, "These reflections are addressed to everyone, to the believer as to the sceptic: it is a fact that I advance, and not a thesis. Whether you laugh at religious ideas, or whether you venerate them, it makes no difference: true or false, they form no less the unique base of all durable institutions" [*Considérations*]. History, he points out, gives ample evidence that the most famous and "especially the most serious and wise" nations of the past, "such as the Egyptians, Etruscans, Lacedaemonians, and Romans, had precisely the most religious constitutions" [*Essai*].

Small wonder that Auguste Comte paid tribute to Joseph de Maistre! Maistre's completely historical, sociological, and pragmatic sanction of religion caught Comte's attention. Viscount Morley, while criticising this treatment of religion by Maistre, nevertheless recognized the "urgent social need of such a thing being done" [*Critical Miscellanies,* 1879]. But Comte, completely misled, as were many others, in thinking that Maistre was the official spokesman of the Church, suggested an alliance of the Catholics and the Positivists to produce this stable and durable society. He went so far as to send an emissary to Rome to seek the aid of the Jesuits. Needless to say, the emissary was not warmly received. Maistre's treatment of religion may have been good sociology and good statesmanship, but it was far from being good theology.

The *philosophes* completely disregarded the unity of society in professing a belief that society can be altered at will by the mere writing of a constitution based on *a priori* principles. Contrariwise, Maistre proposed four principles which must govern every consideration of constitutions. At the same time, by drawing on the English Constitution as an example—the very constitution so admired by the *philosophes*—Maistre sought to contradict completely the rationalism of the eighteenth century by establishing on historical grounds that the role of the human will in the formation of constitutions is pretty close to non-existent. With a vexatious use of paradox, Maistre made the following proposals:

1. "That the fundamental principles of political constitutions exist before all written law" [*Essai*]. Was the admirable English Constitution created *a priori?* Maistre asked. Did her statesmen ever sit down and say, "Let us create three powers, balancing them in such a manner, etc? No one ever thought of such a thing." This constitution, instead, was the product of a multiplicity of causes and situations, which Maistre panegyrized.

> The constitution is the work of circumstances, and the number of these is infinite. Roman laws,

ecclesiastical laws, feudal laws; Saxon, Norman, and Danish custom; the privileges, prejudices, and claims of all the orders; wars, revolts, revolutions, the Conquests, Crusades; virtue of every kind, and all vices; knowledge of every sort, and all errors and passions;—all these elements, in short, acting together, and forming, by their admixture and reciprocal action, combinations multiplied by myriads of millions, have produced at length, after many centuries, the most complex unity, and happy equilibrium of political powers that the world has ever seen.

In the course of the evolution of the English Constitution, the individuals who influenced the development were, according to Maistre, totally unaware of the functions they were fulfilling. They did not know what they "had done relative to the whole, nor foreseen what would happen." Another might say that fortuitous circumstances led to the end result; but "the lay apologist of Providence" concluded that everything must have been "guided by an infallible hand, superior to man," guided by Providence.

2. "That a constitutional law is, and can only be, the development or sanction of an unwritten pre-existing right." Maistre pointed out that "the English, doubtless would never have asked for the Great Charter, had not the privileges of the nation been violated; nor would they have asked for it, if these privileges had not existed before the Charter." He maintained that the American example of 1787 did not contradict the principle because the Americans are heirs to the democratic and republican spirit of the parent country, and, furthermore, because they "have built on the plan of the three powers, derived from their ancestors, and have not at all made a *table rase,* as the French" [*Considérations*].

3. That which is most essential, most intrinsically constitutional, and truly fundamental, is never written, and could not be without endangering the state" [*Essai*]. Consider the Habeas Corpus Act. If the "authors of this famous act had undertaken to fix the cases in which it should be suspended, they would *ipso facto* have annihilated it." In our own day Maistre would have found an excellent example in the constitutional law concept of substantive "due process of law."

4. "That the weakness and fragility of a constitution are actually in direct proportion to the multiplicity of written constitutional articles." It took a long time for constitution-makers to learn this lesson. But Maistre realized the difficulty of appreciating the truth in these principles, for, in exasperation, he went on to say " . . . but such is the blindness of men, that if, tomorrow, some constitution-monger should come to organize a people, and to give them a constitution *made with a little black liquid,* the multitude would again hasten to believe in the miracle announced."

The continuity deemed by Maistre so essential for the preservation of a society could best be maintained by indoctrination. That is to say, prejudices are necessary. Burke had argued [in *Reflections on the Revolution in France and Other Essays*] that prejudices were of inestimable value in the English society, and the older they were, the more they were cherished, because "We are afraid to put men to live and trade on his own private stock of reason; because we suspect that this stock in each man is small, and that individuals would do better to avail themselves of the general bank and capital of nations and ages." By prejudices, neither Maistre nor Burke meant really false ideas, but "prejudgments," or as Maistre explained, "following the force of the word, any opinion adopted before all examination" [*Étude*]. In either case, however, we are confronted with the perfect argument of status quoism.

As every political theorist must, Maistre examined the question of liberty versus authority, or man versus the state. His answer to this problem perhaps more than anything else earned for him the title of *prophet of the past,* or "sombre figure du moyen âge." Maistre treats the subject in his **Du Pape,** a work especially contradicting the writings of Voltaire and placing in an entirely different perspective the role of the Papacy in mediaeval history. Plunging right to the heart of the issue, Maistre pointed out that "the greatest European problem is . . . to know: *How the sovereign power is able to be restrained without destroying it.*" It must be restrained, for even though justice is the greatest interest of the sovereign, it is not always the case that the sovereign power acts in conformity with this principle. Maistre rejected revolution as a means of checking sovereigns for it is usually more disastrous than a despotism. The doctrine of the right of resistance he held admirable, but untenable, because it leaves unanswered the questions: at what times, and by what men is resistance to be undertaken. Furthermore, the doctrine of non-resistance and the binding oath of fidelity demand, like every general rule, provision for exceptions, for "whenever there is no dispensation, there is violation." To resolve the conflicts between rulers and the ruled there should be a recognized, removed, and disinterested third party with the power to make the necessary decisions. In Maistre's opinion, this power could best be entrusted to the Pope. This was not simply the proclaiming of the indirect power of the Pope, but, instead, it was an entirely new project, a renovation of the role of the mediaeval Popes, a new means whereby internal crises would be settled by decisions made by the Pope according to set rules which could be established and accommodated to each of the national constitutions.

It has always been astonishing to Maistre's readers that a man so intimate with his times should have proposed such an idea, at such a moment in history. For a long while it was thought that Maistre undertook the writing of **Du Pape** as a sort of expiation for some of his highly critical comments on the Pope's participation in the crowning of Napoleon. The literary historians have sufficiently disproved this thesis. Mandoul has suggested the thesis that Maistre, an ardent Italian, discouraged by the consolidation of the Holy Alliance with Austria in the predominant role, was calling on the Papacy once more to take a leading position in politics for the sake of Italy. Mandoul asks that one recall "what hopes had been born, in Italy, during the first years of the Pontificate of Pius IX" [*Un homme d'étatitalien, Joseph de Maistre, et la politique de la maison de savoi,* 1900]. Regardless of what might have been Maistre's motive in writing **Du Pape,** we know that it was coolly received at Rome. The Papacy was in no mood for such adventures.

If Maistre thought he had found a suitable arrangement for the alleviation of internal disorders, the problem of war could not be surmounted so easily. On his own affirmation, he had given long and serious contemplation to the struggle of nations and its resultant personal misery. His final analysis has earned him the reputation of being an apologist of war, but he certainly was no Machiavelli or Clausewitz. To Maistre, the existence of war in society is inexplicable on rational grounds. Especially is this so, if the contract theory is considered valid. "Why," he asks of the *philosophes,* "have not nations had enough good sense or luck as individuals; and why have they never convened in a general society in order to end their particular quarrels, as individuals have come together in a national sovereignty in order to end their particular quarrels?" [*Soirées*].

There can be but one explanation for war, in Maistre's estimation. It is a startling opinion drawn from one of his typically disturbing paradoxes. In the first place, Maistre says that, "for me it is an incontestable truth (that): 'being given man with his reason, his sentiments and affections, there are no means of explaining how war is humanly possible' " [*Soirées*]. Yet it remains equally true, and history "unhappily proves that war is the habitual state of human beings . . . and that peace for each nation is only a respite" [*Considérations*]. A long series of massacres soils all the pages of history. From the birth of nations even to our day, in states at every stage of advancement, "from the state of barbarism to that of the most refined civilization; always one will find war" [*Considérations*].

War is psychologically repugnant, for "in spite of his immense degradation, there is still in man an element of love which draws him toward his equals: compassion is as natural as respiration" [*Soirées*]. Thus, "by what inconceivable magic is he always ready, at the first roll of the drums, to strip himself of this sacred characteristic, to go forth without resistance, often even with a sense of gladness . . . to cut to pieces, on the field of battle, his brother who has never offended him, and who, in his turn, advances to do likewise, if he is able" [*Soirées*]. Indeed, on the field of battle, the tenderest souls are inflamed with an "enthousiasme du carnage."

Since this is so, Maistre then held that war can be explained only by recognizing a "hidden and terrible law which demands human blood" [*Soirées*]. War is but a chapter of that "general law which burdens the universe," visible everywhere, for

> In the vast domain of living things, there reigns a manifest violence, a species of prescribed rage which arms all beings *in deadly combat:* as soon as you emerge from the insensible kingdom, you find the decree of violent death written on the very frontiers of life. [*Soirées*]

In the vegetable kingdom the law is first discernible; in the animal world this "principle of life by violent means" is appallingly evident. Over both these kingdoms rules man, "roi superbe et terrible." But does this law stop at mankind? No, answers Maistre, the last chapter of this law

charges man to slaughter man! He goes on to say, "But how will he be able to fulfill the law, he who is a moral and merciful being, he who is born to love, he who weeps for others as for himself . . . ? It is war that will fulfill the decrees" [*Soirées*]. Thus is explained why the gentlest soul can, on the field of battle, become an almost possessed being and can "perform with enthusiasm that which he has a horror of." In one of his most doleful yet inspiring passages, Maistre tells us:

> Thus is accomplished without end, from the mite to the man, the great law of the violent destruction of living beings. The earth, continually drenched with blood, is but an immense altar whereon all living beings must be sacrificed without end, without measure, without relaxation, until the consummation of things, until the extinction of evil, until the death of death. [*Soirées*]

All this led Maistre to but one conclusion: "La guerre est donc divine en elle-même, puisque c'est une loi du monde." But why should God create, one asks, and then demand the destruction of his creature? Why does Providence, which directs the course and actions of the universe, allow the existence of such a dreadful law? The answer, Maistre replies, is found in the fall of man. The *philosophes,* with their belief in the essential goodness of everything, were blind in not perceiving that "there is only violence in the universe;" and instead of being good, "in a very true sense, everything is evil" [*Considérations*]. Not without sympathy, Maistre mournfully explains: "Guilty mortals, and unhappy because we are guilty! It is we who render necessary all the physical evils, but especially war" [*Soirées*].

This discourse on war is but one aspect of Maistre's analysis of evil. Some critics have complained of his obsession with this subject, but it is now evident that what still remains attractive to some is his mystical treatment of the evils that mankind seems unable to escape. Evil, everywhere present, is portrayed in all its horrifying forms. Yet Maistre constantly points out its spiritual significance. The guilty seem invariably to prosper while the innocent perpetually suffer. Disturbingly enough, Maistre asks that we reflect for a moment on just who is an innocent man. Regardless, he points out, the trials of the innocent always redound to the advantage of the guilty, just as the offering of the Most Innocent was for the salvation of all the guilty. Man may constantly give evidence of his immense degradation, yet at the same time he has the divine characteristic of perfectibility. Man longs for peace and love, although he alone deprives himself of both. Hopelessly and helplessly man is bound to his nature, yet he constructs in thought ideal worldly societies where men must necessarily be other than they are. With sincere compassion Maistre bemoans the plight of humanity in saying that "All creation groans, and tends with effort and sorrow towards another order of things" [*Considérations*].

One might safely say that, in the future, Maistre will still be referred to as *prophète du passé* and *panegyrists du bourreau,* but one hardly renders him exact justice in holding that "he is like one of those curious instances of atavism for which the science of heredity is so signally unable to account" [H. J. Laski, in his *Studies in the Problem of Sovereignty,* 1917]. On the contrary, the roots of Maistre's political thought reach far back into Western culture, stemming directly from the two historical sources of jurisprudence and theology. Furthermore, Maistre was not so radically different from his contemporaries as one might think. In spite of his constant insistence on realism, throughout all his works there are clear traces of rising Romanticism. And in passing, we might say that the attempt to explain Romanticism as a sort of royalist plot is not only too simple but also absurd. In Maistre we find the usual vaunted admiration of the Middle Ages, the typical melancholy, and the persistent presentation of the occult, the horrifying, and the grotesque. Then, too, historical pessimism was a significant note in the last century, and Maistre was quite in tune with the movement.

Maistre's insistent demand that history be recognized as "experimental politics," and his historical and sociological explanations of institutions were clearly in line with the thought of the century that followed. Of course, one might not like Maistre's history, but at least he had the good sense to realize the profound error in Voltaire's conception that the period between the fall of Rome and that of Louis XIV "no more merited a place in history than the story of bears and wolves" [Cited in F. B. Artz, *France under the Bourbon Restoration,* 1931]. Alphonse Cournot, the mathematician-philosopher, and certainly no adherent of Maistrian doctrines, has rightly pointed out that the contribution of both Maistre and Bonald was their insistence on historical naturalism. They were historical theists, but at the same time naturalists. It would not be going too far to say that if one struck Providence out of Maistre's works, he would have, to a great extent, the system of Comte. Thus Brunetière has pointed out that Comte "laicised" the essential principles of Maistre [*La Grande Encyclopédie,* vol. 22].

The greatest error in Maistre's historical realism was the fact that he refused to recognize any contributions from the eighteenth century. Then again, the type of monarchy tempered with a dutiful nobility which he advocated can hardly be found in history. Maistre constantly reminded the critics of the proposed return of the Bourbons that 'they were men, but do you expect to be governed by angels?' That would be exactly the case if his own semi-mystical monarchy could have been founded. Several writers have pointed out that, shocking though it may seem, Maistre was a liberal. By this it meant that he was a liberal in an older sense of the word. That is to say, he favored a political organization where once again the various orders in society would enjoy their ancient liberties. Again this showed a lack of insight on Maistre's part. He failed to realize that the ascendant bourgeois class had attained sufficient strength to endure no longer the presence of the favored class of nobility.

Maistre has never had a school, so to speak. The theology of "traditionalism" was officially disowned in 1835. The eccentric Barbey d'Aurevilly in the latter half of the century gained a certain renown with a rather grotesque distortion of Maistre. Modern Catholic writers, however, while recognizing the genius of Maistre, as one must, will have

no part of his politics or theology. It is true, of course, that the *Action Française* claimed Maistre as one of its *maîtres.* Undoubtedly, there was much in Maistre which could be exploited by these extremists, who could exploit almost anyone. After all, when the *Action Française* commenced its series of articles entitled *"Nos maitres,"* the first to appear was on Voltaire! What a strange assemblage was soon gathered—Voltaire, Bonald, Pierre Bayle, Renan, Maistre, Proudhon, etc.! On many essential points, however, Maistre contradicts their doctrines. Fundamental in his entire writings is the plea for order and quietism; yet a basic theme of the *Action* was violence and the "coup de force." There is the possibility of forgiving Maistre's desires for the reestablishment, in a Europe filled with Crowns, of the lately fallen French monarchy. But one can hardly find any sanity in a twentieth century demand for an immediate return of the monarchy. It is also vitally important to note that Maistre personally lived out the austere programs he suggested for his fellowmen. But in complete accordance with the principle he so often pointed out: that 'the written word is silent, it cannot answer back,' Maistre was unable to repudiate the scoundrels who were one day to claim him as their master. (pp. 72-86)

> *John C. Murray, "The Political Thought of Joseph De Maistre," in* The Review of Politics, *Vol. II, No. 1, January, 1949, pp. 63-86.*

Cioran on de Maistre's reactionary thought:

Among thinkers—such as Nietzsche or Saint Paul—with the appetite and the genius for provocation, Joseph de Maistre occupies a place anything but negligible. Raising the most trivial problem to the level of paradox and the dignity of scandal, brandishing anathemas with enthusiastic cruelty, he created an oeuvre rich in enormities, a system that unfailingly seduces and exasperates. The scope and eloquence of his umbrage, the passion he devoted to indefensible causes, his tenacity in legitimizing one injustice after another, and his predilection for the deadly epithet make of him that immoderate disputant who, not deigning to persuade the adversary, crushes him with an adjective straight off. His convictions have an appearance of great firmness: he managed to overpower the solicitations of skepticism by the arrogance of his prejudices, by the dogmatic vehemence of his contempt.

> *E. M. Cioran, in his* Anathemas and Admirations, *translated by Richard Howard. Arcade Publishing, 1991.*

John Bowle (essay date 1954)

[*In the following excerpt, Bowle focuses on the major political themes in de Maistre's* Du pape *and* Soirées de Saint-Pétersbourg.]

In the wide range of [de Maistre's] works the ***Considérations sur la France,*** the ***Du Pape,*** and the ***Soirées de St. Pétersbourg*** are the most striking. De Maistre combines an Augustinian conviction of original sin with a Hobbesian political pessimism. He was a writer of brilliant, imaginative and incisive prose. He is the most profound and eloquent of those who despaired of the new secularism and the new democracy. He has even been described as an arch-forerunner of Fascism, but his affinities are more patristic. In asserting that government is a mystery backed by force and faith, in his despair of Constitutionalism, and in his detestation of the mob—(do you want, he asks, 'to unmuzzle the tiger'?)—he has, indeed, affinities with the twentieth century. But his outlook is fundamentally religious; he has far more in common with St. Augustine than with Sorel or Pareto. 'I have never denied the inconveniences of absolute power,' he writes, 'I want to diminish them; but one finds oneself between two abysses.'

Temperamentally at odds with the dominant tendencies of his time, he regarded the rise of science as a monstrous perversion, a falling off from a superior and older wisdom. He denounced fundamental developments of modern culture, and savagely attacked its most characteristic qualities. They could lead, he thought, only to perdition. 'Sous l'habit étriqué du nord, la tête perdue dans les volutes d'une chevelure menteuse, les bras chargés de livres et d'instruments de toute espèce, pâle de veilles et de travaux, elle se traine, souillée d'encre et toute pantelante, sur la route de la vérité. . . . Rien de semblable dans la haute antiquité [*Soirées de Saint-Pétersbourg*].

It was a curious vision of science. He not only dismissed liberal ideas; he was also blind to the development of professional knowledge, the other hopeful aspect of the nineteenth century. For all his eloquence, his learning is amateurish, and his brilliant verve leads to folly. He implicitly believes, for example, in the reality of the Flood—what gigantic sins, he remarks, must have been committed to justify so stupendous a catastrophe! He thought the wisdom of the ancient Egyptians superior to all subsequent knowledge, and from their architecture that the Etruscans had been supermen. All this nonsense emphasizes the gulf between the early nineteenth-century view of science and the professionalized knowledge of the 'sixties and 'seventies. Yet the poetic force of his despair make his writings singularly arresting.

In the immediate field of politics his outlook is responsible but exclusive. He insists that men are led not by calculation but by myth. Of voting, he remarks, 'une addition n'est pas un organisme' [*Soirées*]: contract is an abstraction, and the revolutionaries were planning for '30 million men without ancestors'. Society is, in fact, based, as Burke and Coleridge also maintained, on emotion: 'un sentiment obscur, puissant parce qu'obscur, irréfléchi, spontané, tenant de la foi, tenant de l'instinct héréditaire et mystique, irrational sous toutes ses formes . . .' It is a view typical of the romantic reaction against the eighteenth century, and foreshadowing the psychological outlook of the twentieth.

A professional administrator, de Maistre wished to conserve not the rule of aristocracy, but the rule of kings. He held that the privileges of the old nobility interfered with government; but he wished to hedge about the kingly power with a *noblesse de la robe*. His conception of rule is flexible and humane, if absolute. He thought that the

monolithic sovereignty of the popular state, with rule by demagogues in the name of the people, would be the inevitable result of 'freedom', for the general will was a fraud. Hence, given the nature of men, the need for monarchy administered by a patriciate.

His most closely argued work is the ***Du Pape*** with its onslaught on the French Revolution, though the ***Soirées de St. Pétersbourg*** is the more striking.

The Revolution is something without precedent. It is 'Satanic'. In de Maistre's neo-patristic view, it is the result of cumulative intellectual arrogance, the logical outcome of the teaching of Locke and Voltaire. 'Humanity is struggling against the torrent of errors to which it has abandoned itself . . .' In this crisis, with the foundations of civilization collapsing, de Maistre declares the one remedy—the absolute authority of Rome. For the Pope is the 'grand demiurge de la civilisation universelle'. De Maistre is a good European; his book reflects the ancient unity of the Christian world.

In exercising this authority, the Pope is no mere personal tyrant. He rules as head of a great institution, the symbol of supreme world sovereignty. Such an authority there must be, because, de Maistre declares, like Austin, sovereignty is of its nature absolute. The need for government is primordial. It derives from original sin. 'L'homme, en sa qualité d'être à la fois moral et corrompu, juste dans son intelligence, et pervers dans sa volonté, doit necessairement être gouverné.' Without judgment ('sentence'), there will be 'combat'. There is no choice; no question of contract; 'sovereignty results directly from human nature' [***Du Pape***]. With Burke, he believes that mankind and their rulers are mutually interdependent—'born into society'. 'Sovereigns do not exist by the grace of their peoples, sovereignty being no more the result of their will than the existence of society itself.' The people gain more from this symbiosis than the prince, who is sacrificed to his obligations.

In this organic interdependence most societies have their being. In Europe, alone, the 'audacious tribe of Japhet' has always followed an unusual course. They have attempted to restrain sovereign power. The rest of the world—'the immense posterities of Sem and Cham'—have generally acquiesced in despotism tempered by assassination. 'Do what you like,' they have told their rulers, 'and when we are tired of it we will cut your throats.' Europeans have been more subtle. They have set themselves the great problem—'how to restrain power without destroying it'.

De Maistre considers and rejects Constitutionalism. 'Only England, favoured by the sea . . . and a national character that lends itself to these experiments, has been able to do something in this line.' And already the famous edifice of 1688 seems rocking on its foundations. France, of course, was in worse case. Here the most dangerous remedy has been applied—'la révolte, remède terrible, pire que tous les maux'. Consider the consequences: they have merely, amid the shame of foreign occupation, placed on the throne a 'b italique instead of a B majascule'. It was only to be expected. 'Revolutions started by the wisest men are always finished by madmen.' And they founded their doctrines on sand. For the rights of man give no basis for sovereignty, no basis for the control of power. From Protestantism has come the vain idea of the sovereignty of the people, 'a dogma which has been transferred from religion into politics'. It is worthless, for Sovereignty is a high mystery, 'a sacred thing, an emanation of divine power—of its nature unlimited'. Even in England, where it is said to be limited, they have only diminished the power of the king, which by itself is not supreme. But when the three powers which in England make up the sovereignty are in accord, what can they do? 'Il faut repondre avec Blackston—tout.'

Then what is the answer? Must it be that 'the oath of fidelity exposes men to tyrants; resistance without rules to anarchy?' There can only be one solution. If temporal sovereignty is mysterious, it can be controlled only by another and superior mystery—the supreme authority of the Pope. Thus alone can the problem of freedom and order be solved; not by an assertion of popular rights, not by an appeal to a fictitious contract, but by recognition of one supreme and august authority, the embodiment of civilization itself.

Against these profound considerations, de Maistre continues, Rousseau's facile optimism looks absurd. 'Man was never born free.' Anyone who has studied his 'dismal nature' knows that man in general is far too wicked for freedom. 'La maxime rétentissante l'homme est né libre et partout il est dans les fers, que veut-il-dire? . . .' The opposite to this mad assertion is the truth. In pre-Christian times slavery was the normal condition of the vast majority of mankind. Aristotle's view that some men are slaves by nature was right, and Lucan made the sinister observation, 'humanum paucis vivit genus'. This grim outlook, normal in Antiquity, was only gradually altered by the Christians, who alone could have achieved the change. The profound mistake of modern 'progressive' thinkers is to believe that freedom without Christianity is possible. For such is human wickedness, unredeemed, that it can only be controlled by slavery. This alone diminishes the egotism of an unregenerate world. The alternative can only be Christianity. By a kind of 'spiritual grafting', it diminishes 'natural bitterness of will' and enables men to live peaceably, but in a world of liberal utilitarianism there are too many 'wills loose in the world'. The Supreme Authority must be the Church.

Such, for de Maistre, is the predicament; and such the remedy. He concludes with a panegyric on the Church, an appeal to Anglicans to return to the fold, an attack on the 'vulgar innovations' of Luther and Calvin, and a fine evocation of the splendour of Rome.

Eager to restore Christian unity, de Maistre actually cites Hume and Gibbon on the Antiquity of the Catholic Church. Even these sceptics admit that the Church was prior to 'nearly all political establishments in Europe'; that by the fourth century, doctrine was already defined and that the 'seeds of the Papacy were sown even in the apostles' time'. Is it likely, he demands, that Christianity would have become perverted, as the Protestants maintain, so soon after the Redemption? That would deny the wisdom of God. Here is the supreme Protestant error; we must 'efface this word Protestantism from the European

Dictionary'. For only a united European Church can control the innovating and ungovernable quality of the European mind. Only the Church, which has alone endured for eighteen centuries. 'What hidden force has done this—against all rules of probability?' Only a superhuman institution could have so survived.

De Maistre concludes with a prose-poem on Holy Church. 'Je te salue, mère immortelle de la science et de la sainteté, *salve magna parens*.' The Papacy has been the supreme force of civilization. The citadel of the pagan world was the Pantheon: it was transformed to the stronghold of the Saints. As in Milton's ode to St. Cecilia's Day, the theme of the conquest of the Pagan Gods is sung. St. Peter eclipses Janus; St. Francis, Pluto; the miraculous St. Xavier drives before him Bacchus, the fabulous conqueror of India. 'La Divine Marie monte sur l'autel de Venus Pandemique. Tous les Dieux hommes disparaissent devant L'homme Dieu.'

Here, already, are all de Maistre's outstanding themes. A similar outlook is apparent in the curious *Soirées de St. Pétersbourg.* Here the treatment is different: where the *Du Pape* is forcefully systematic, the *Soirées* are cast in the form of casual conversation. They form a strange and often extraordinary sequence of ideas, profound and eccentric. While the motives implicit in the *Du Pape* are further illuminated, the illumination reveals some dark corners. And the queer supplement, the *Traité sur les Sacrifices,* shows an odd preoccupation with blood.

The opening of the *Soirées de St. Pétersbourg* is singularly attractive. De Maistre and two companions, a Russian Privy Councillor and a spirited young Frenchman, the 'Chevalier de B.', are being rowed on the Neva in the long twilight of a Northern summer. There is a superb sunset, reflected on the clouds and in the flaming windows of the Imperial palace. In the soft air the Tsar's standard hangs drooping from its mast, and across the full flowing river float the songs of the Russian boatmen. The inner harbour is alive with pleasure craft; further out are the big foreign ships, crammed with the exotic merchandise the opulence of Russia can command. The evening deepens into golden twilight, unpaintable and strange. As they drift in the silence, the Chevalier observes that they should have on board one of those political 'monsters who weary the earth'. 'And what would you say to him?' 'I would ask whether he found this sight as lovely as I do.' 'My dear Chevalier,' replies de Maistre, 'lost souls never have good nights or beautiful days.' 'So you really think the wicked unhappy?' 'I wish I could believe it, but I see them flourishing . . . A little account for them in this world would not have spoilt anything.'

So the main theme of the *Soirées,* the question of divine justice and original sin, is introduced. De Maistre proceeds to depict the first tea party in the annals of political thought. They hold a symposium on justice, this time not in the grove of the Academy or on Cicero's estate at Arpinum, but round a tea table on the terrace of the Sardinian Minister's residence in Petersburg. Here they discuss the joys of the wicked and the misfortunes of the just— 'C'est le grand scandale de la raison humaine.' The ways of Providence in the world are examined. What is the explanation of human suffering? It reflects evil which comes not from God but from original sin. Here, again, is an Augustinian view. And what is the explanation? Menu, 'grand legislateur des Indes', declared that Brahma created the genius of pain: he is a demon of black aspect and fiery eyes. His task is to save mankind from sin.

De Maistre proceeds to his well-known *tour de force*—the evocation of the executioner. Who is it that sustains the fabric of society? he asks. Not the king, not the first Minister, not the highest dignitaries of the Church. It is a more humble, a more sinister figure—the *bourreau*. In the human family here is the ultimate authority. A strange being, set apart, he lives in queer solitude, alone with his mate and brood. When the day for duty arrives, the executioner appears before the seething crowd. Some criminal—a poisoner, perhaps—awaits him. He proceeds to break him on the wheel. First he extends the victim; then ties him down. Soon the horrible silence is broken by the crack of bones. As they splinter beneath the iron, come screams of agony. Then the criminal is detached. He is deposited upon the wheel, broken limbs entangled with the spokes. With drooping head, with parched and gaping mouth, with matted hair, the victim can mutter only the bloody words that pray for death.

Before this ghastly spectacle, what are the feelings of the executioner? If he is a good professional, they are exultant. His heart beats high; not with pity, but with pride. No one, he says, can break a man so well as I do—'nul ne roue mieux que moi: I am the best executioner in the world'. And so, passing through the ranks of his shrinking fellows, the *bourreau* collects his pay. Back at home, he sits down to a good meal.

Upon the shoulders of this sinister creature society inevitably rests. He is at once 'L'horreur et le lien de l'association humaine'—the horrible mystery, the inescapable bond. Take him away, at once order gives place to chaos, thrones collapse, society dissolves. For God, the author of sovereignty, is the author of punishment. Sovereign power, with its ultimate and terrible sanction, is the only answer to original sin. Its decisions are in general just; if sometimes the innocent perish, such is the law of life: 'cet un malheur comme un autre'. After this harrowing description, the discussion turns to illness. Physical disorders, de Maistre maintains, are in general the 'suites funestes de la volupté'; ill temper, gourmandizing and incontinence—all have their penalties. Most suffering is deserved. Such is the pessimistic outlook behind de Maistre's political opinions.

The Chevalier begins the next conversation by refusing a second cup of tea, a drink which, as a southern Frenchman, he distrusts. 'Élevé, comme vous savez, dans une province méridionale de la France, où le thé n'etait regardé que comme un remède contre le rhume', he has long lived in circles addicted to its consumption. Good Frenchman that he is, he has never brought himself to like it. Tea may even increase illness. Nonsense, says de Maistre, all illness is really unnecessary. It could be abolished by prayer and the abandonment of sin. The reign of physical evil could be indefinitely restrained by this supernatural means. For illness is caused simply by wickedness, 'le

peché original, qui explique tout', and which, one must remember, is still always going on. A sobering consideration. It is the tragedy of mankind that alone of the animals they are aware of sin. Rousseau—'l'un des plus dangereux sophistes de son siècle . . . avec une profondeur apparente qui est toute dans les mots'—was wrong to speak of noble savages. All savagery results from degeneration. Mankind is not progressing, it is groping back towards lost realms of light. Hence the desire for learning. 'No beaver, no swallow, no bee wants to know more than its forebears.' Hence man's greatness and his sorrow. For his will is broken and divided. Ovid and St. Paul echo one another: . . . *video meliora, proboque, Deteriora sequor;* 'For the good that I would I do not: but the evil that I would not, that I do . . . Oh wretched man that I am who shall deliver me from the body of this death?' [Romans, vii, 19 and 24]. Everywhere and at all times there is a dark inclination to wickedness. This dualist horror of life, expressed by many previous writers, had not before found a romantic expression in political theory.

The second evening is also distinguished by the deployment of de Maistre's curious and often fruitful ideas on the nature of speech. He regards it as an expression of the creative capacity of the human spirit, something which moulds the environment of the race. He comes to examine the genius of language in describing the origins of civilization, and touches on subjects raised by Vico. As in the *Du Pape,* he insists, 'where you see an altar, there you will find civilization'. And like religion, speech is mysterious. It is as 'old as eternity', and 'toute langue particulière naît comme animal'. It is a creative process. Why can primitive peoples create a language while modern philologists fail? Once the process becomes self-conscious, it becomes sterile. Surely, the Chevalier suggests, the origin of speech throws light on the origin of ideas? Here if anywhere, is evidence for creative mind. In an interesting attack on Hobbesian materialist sensationalism, de Maistre appears from an unexpected angle as a defender of Cudworth, of all people. To materialize the origins of ideas is profoundly degrading; 'reason loses its wings and crawls like a reptile'. On the contrary, intellect is not merely passive but creative; since intelligence reasons upon impressions, it has the power to generalize, expressed in words. De Maistre shocks the rationalist Chevalier by vindicating St. Thomas, who, for clarity and precision, he declares, is one of the greatest minds. 'Truth', said St. Thomas, 'is the equation between the affirmation and its object.' Its apprehension is a natural and creative act. Man, de Maistre insists, thus lives by the spirit, and the spirit is thought. This creative power cannot be explained. One cannot analyse the human spirit; one can only observe its operations. A clue to this creative activity may be found in the study of language. Citing Plato and using an Hegelian phrase, de Maistre remarks, 'La pensée est le discours que l'esprit se tient à lui-même.' Now 'la pensée et la parole ne sont que deux magnifiques synonimes', and 'être' is the soul of all verbs. You can affirm anything without its pre-existence.

These are suggestive and original ideas. They are embedded in discursive conversations which extend into a curious analysis of war. The Chevalier has no difficulty in defining war. It is to obey the king's orders, he says with soldierly precision. But why are all the best soldiers so extremely polite? Because, even in the heat of action, they are trained to behave with poise, as virtuous wives, de Maistre points out, are chaste even in the transports of wedded love.

Violent death, he insists, is the law of all life; war is the reflection in human society of an inscrutable decree. It 'is divine in itself, because it is one of the laws of the world'. Like the executioner, it is a 'mystery'. Hence its strange glamour. Though there is nothing apparently so much against nature, there is nothing so attractive. After all, were public opinion sufficiently against it, war would be impossible. Yet it was far more difficult, says the Russian Senator, for Peter the Great to abolish beards than to get cannon fodder, even when he was constantly defeated. And why has war never been suppressed? Why was the scheme of the Abbé de Saint-Pierre received with mockery? Because on this subject the human race is mad. This madness can only be explained through some 'occult and terrible law which demands human blood'. De Maistre quotes La Bruyère with effect. 'If anyone told you that all the cats of a large country assembled on open ground, and after having caterwauled (miaulé) their fill, had flung themselves on one another, tooth and claw, with the utmost ferocity; that after this mêlée the corpses of nine or ten thousand animals had been left on the field to infect the air for ten leagues with their decay, wouldn't you say this was the most atrocious sabbath you had ever heard of? And if the wolves did the same—what howls and butchery! And if both cats and wolves told you that they loved glory, wouldn't you laugh at the ingenuousness of the poor creatures?'

Of course, he again asserts, only original sin can explain human behaviour. 'Observe,' he says, 'that this terrible law of war is only a chapter of the general law that weighs on the Universe.' 'Dans la vaste domaine de la nature vivante, il règne une violence manifeste.' 'The decree of violent death is written on the very frontiers of life.' Species prey on species and man is the worst killer of all. King of the animal creation, he 'stuffs the crocodile, tears the guts from the lamb to make music for his harp . . . and uses whale bone to stiffen the girl's corsage'. His tables are 'covered with corpses'. But what animal exterminates man? Only man himself. Yet, insists the Senator, man is a moral being. To fulfil this law of destruction he must, therefore, periodically become insane. 'Don't you hear the earth crying for blood?' he says. The blood of the animals, of criminals, is not enough to assuage so vast a collective guilt. Wars there must be; so periodically, 'la guerre s'allume'. Nations are seized by a frenzy, something different from anger or hate, and drawn to destruction without knowing whither they are bound. Young men who enlist with alacrity are 'innocent murderers' . . . the 'passive instruments of an irresitible hand'. Thus is accomplished the 'great universal law of the violent destruction of living beings'. It will continue until all evil is redeemed, 'until the death of death'. Meanwhile, 'l'ange exterminateur tourne comme le soleil autour de ce malheureux globe'.

In a strange panegyric on war, de Maistre seems to parody himself. It is a divine enigma, surrounded by mysterious glamour. The protection of Providence is accorded to great generals, who seldom get killed themselves—or only when their 'glory' is at its height and their mission accomplished—for they are the instruments of God's vengeance for accumulated crime. War, too, is incalculable. It is not always the most powerful who win. Indeed, the remark attributed to Turenne, that 'God is on the side of the big battalions' can be misleading. The most mysterious and unexpected results occur, and often the victors are worse off than the vanquished. Sometimes, too, those who win wars suffer greater moral degradation than the defeated. Moreover, war gives rise to remarkable poetry. After this peroration, de Maistre loses himself in another panegyric on the Psalms.

Such is the nightmare envisaged by this sensitive observer. Crazy as much of the argument may be, it is worth pondering in the twentieth century. Like lemmings to the sea, it seems, the human race rushes periodically to perdition. The worst misinterpretations of the Darwinian struggle for existence pale before the visions of this original and tormented mind.

For, here indeed is a Manichaean hatred of the 'flesh'; a psychological repulsion, a projected guilt. What subconscious furies drove de Maistre to this cult? The very tension increased his imaginative power, infused his nervous and brilliant style. Here is no Hobbesian materialism, but something far more sensitive. For de Maistre is at heart a romantic, shuddering at the collapse of the aristocratic order to which he belonged, horrified at the blasphemy of philosophers who believed that man could make himself. Discounting the possibilities of technical progress and the promise of the new science and industry, he despairs of mankind. Though at one with his contemporary, Saint-Simon, in the conviction that society needed religion, his outlook is diametrically opposed to Saint-Simon's acceptance of life. Only by the assertion of a mysterious authority, of the world embracing sovereign power of the Pope, could the natural wickedness of society be controlled. It is a strange kind of Christianity, in which there is little compassion. It belongs rather to the old world of Patristic Theologians and medieval heresy, than to the materialist outlook of the future, when totalitarian Dictators were to regard all truth as relative and ideas as instruments of political warfare. For de Maistre declares human motives wicked and the remedies brutal, but he desires government by an administrative Patriciate, loyal to an hereditary king. His affinities are not so much with the parvenu bureaucracy and purblind manœuvres of the dictators of modern mass society, but rather with a more hoary medieval tradition. Of all the figures who have contributed to the colourful tapestry of political ideas he is one of the most singular. (pp. 78-89)

John Bowle, "The Counter-Revolutionaries: de Maistre, Coleridge, Carlyle," in his Politics and Opinion in the Nineteenth Century: An Historical Introduction, *Oxford University Press, Inc., 1954, pp. 75-100.*

Elisha Greifer   (essay date 1961)

[*In the following excerpt, Greifer traces de Maistre's re-action against eighteenth-century philosophers and the French Revolution and asserts that he was "a philo-sophe in spite of himself, an eighteenth century man."*]

It is a commonplace observation of French politics of the past century that men who started out as radicals turned conservative as they grew older, and that party groups launched with radical names and programs, though they kept the names, swung to the Right with the passage of time. In both cases we explain the transformation, in part at least, as evidence of an increasing satisfaction with the *status quo,* as the political system made room for the new-comer. In Joseph de Maistre we have an example from a somewhat earlier age of a less common phenomenon, the conservative turned reactionary, and impelled, moreover, to develop a systematic justification of his new position. Evidently, no parallel explanation will serve to account for this change, for Maistre, though he found a place for him-self in the public life of his time, grew increasingly dissatis-fied with the trend of events around him. It will not do, either, to dismiss him—in the manner of the orthodox tra-dition in the history of political thought—as an authori-tarian ogre, or an irrationalist, or simply as a confused man, a split personality with humanitarian impulses and reactionary ideas. There was no inconsistency in this com-bination. Rather the explanation must be sought in the po-litical situation of his day as he saw it, and in his concern for the perennial problem of political obligation. The posi-tions that concern led him to take, his rationalizations of them, and the difficulties they landed him in, are the sub-ject of this article. For whatever the merit of treating Ma-istre as the first of a century of romantics, or royalist writ-ers, or of Christian pessimists, the more significant fact is that he saw himself at the end of the eighteenth century and as its critic. No French Revolution, no Maistre.

If a Revolution was necessary to induce Maistre to re-act, Maistre before the Revolution should have been merely conservative, not reactionary. And so he was. It was easy for a magistrate to be a conservative in a Savoy whose *an-cien régime* was more enlightened than France's. During the fifty years before the Revolution reforms were exten-sive and feudal rights were gradually extinguished. Even in this enlightened country, Maistre would seem to have been more enlightened than most. One of his biographers, after studying Maistre's decisions as a magistrate, con-cluded that they showed a marked propensity to resolve doubtful cases dealing with seignorial privilege on the side of liberty.

But one should not conclude hastily from Maistre's patri-cian enlightenment that Masonry and illuminism exerted a great influence on him in his earlier days or that these were the source of a supposed mysticism that is the key to his later writings. Descostes says that Maistre never did more than "trifle" with Freemasonry, and the evidence seems to bear him out. As a matter of fact, one of the au-thors trying to make the most out of such connections has to admit that if Maistre used some of Saint-Martin's no-tions he did so *sans y tomber* and without approving *Mar-tiniste* undertakings [A. Viatte, in his *Les Sources occultes du romantisme,* 1928]. Maistre's own writings, in this peri-od and later, make it difficult to understand how anyone could exaggerate the influence. There is extant a *mémoire* that Maistre wrote his fellow Mason, the Duke of Bruns-wick, in 1782 on the state of the lodge. There is no mysti-cism here. Instead, Maistre typically is concerned with the governance of the lodge, throws out democracy and inter-estingly suggests Papal government as a model. If it is to work, the realistic magistrate adds, there must be hierar-chical order and provision for punishment. His verdict on Masonry thirty-five years later is not inconsistent. He does not deny that there is much in the works of the illuminists that is true, reasonable, and touching, but mixed with it is the false and the dangerous, particularly in their aver-sion to authority and clerical hierarchy. Saint-Martin, he noted, *le plus instruit, le plus sage et le plus élégant des théosophes modernes,* died without wanting to receive a priest and with clear proof in his writings that he did not believe in the legitimacy of the *sacerdoce chrétien.*

There is, then, little evidence that Maistre derived much of a positive nature from Saint-Martin. Perhaps he learned something from Saint-Martin's opposition to the *philo-sophes.* But he certainly learned this elsewhere, too. He was taught by the Jesuits in his youth, and he never tired later of praising their respect for authority. He learned from Burke, of course, but the Enlightenment should not be viewed as devoid of *antiphilosophes* from whom he could have learned earlier. In his various works Maistre cites Nicolas Sylvestre Bergier (1715-1790), who wrote a *Réfutation des principaux articles du dictionnaire philo-sophique* in 1771 and in 1789 a Burkean *Quelle est la source de toute autorité?*—"a wise and profound theolo-gian" who saw that social contract was only a frivolous promise "without the dogma of a divine Legislator" [**Essai sur le principe générateur des constitutions politiques**]. He also cites Bellarmine (on the Papacy, not on the origin of political power in the community); Cardinal Orsi (1692-1721), a Roman ultramontane; Bishop Huet (1630-1721), who wrote a censure of Descartes and a *Traité philo-sophique de la faiblesse humaine;* Francesco Antonio Zac-caria (1714-1795), a Jesuit who defended the Holy See in his *Antifebronio.* It is hard to see how Maistre deserves the title of "the earliest of the theocrats" [H. Michel, in his *L'Idée de l'état* 1896].

Maistre derives then, in no small degree, from orthodox writers of the eighteenth century, a conservative group be-fore the Revolution who may have been, as Palmer once thought, no more fiercely intolerant or less reasonable than the philosophic zealots of the new faith. The later Maistre utilizes this orthodoxy with the fierceness that dis-tinguishes the reactionary from his earlier conservative self. In germ, some of the later ideas are seen in the earlier period. In the pedantic eulogy of his king in 1775 he not only praises monarchy, but also finds the occasion to dis-play what later was characteristic of his treatment of reli-gion, praise for it as "the most powerful means and the true nerve of the state" [*l'Éloge de Victor-Amédée III.*]. It is not merely doctrine, however, but also the mode of its exposition that distinguishes the reactionary from the conservative. As a conservative magistrate before the Revolution, Maistre was in the conservative situation of merely defending an order hardly threatened, and not one of trying to restore an order which had been shattered. It is this simple difference in *situation* which makes his 1784 address to the Savoyard magistracy [*Le caractère extérieur du magistrat*]. so uncharacteristic of his later writings. Here he has only the occasion to exhort his hearers to impeccable public behavior as a way of maintaining public respect for the regime. The events of the Revolution changed this conservative complaceny.

Have you seen *l'admirable Burke?*, Maistre wrote to a friend in 1791. *Pour moi j'en ai été ravi, et je ne saurais vous exprimer combien il a renforcé mes idées anti-démocrates et anti-gallicanes.* But with the Revolution Maistre's situation is no longer Burke's. The French disease was more contagious in Savoy than in England. In January Maistre's poor Chambéry was already well-infected, and by June he was reporting that a revolt was in the offing. The next year he fled before a French invasion. Thus, all his published writings postdate his emigration, and so from the first, but for one exception, he writes as an emigré, defending what had become the *ancien régime,* and awaiting its restoration.

The exception confirms the rule. Maistre's very first published writing, **Lettres d'un Royaliste Savoisien,** written for his Savoyard compatriots in 1793, not long after his removal to Switzerland, has the confident air of the recent emigré who expects to return promptly to his rightful place. Consequently, its outlook is still rather conservative. It defends the old order as enlightened and tranquil, possessing none of the abuses of the French regime, neither pecuniary privileges for the first two orders, nor ministerial depotism, nor venality of civil or military offices. He pauses to question the glib use of the word *abuse,* but he does not make any effort to defend France, for the Savoyard conservative can better make his defense by contrasting the rule of Sardinia with other kingdoms. He denies that the new republic (of Allobroges), instituted with the aid of French arms possesses the support of the people, or of anybody except the "city scum."

But Maistre's situation does not long allow him confidence in a quick Restoration. Thus his scope of attention is soon broadened to France and to government in general, and he is plunged more deeply than Burke into the abstract questions which, like Burke, he deprecates and would avoid. The difference between Maistre and Burke is perhaps best seen here. Like Burke he rails against abstract reason, but he immediately turns to writing an extended analytical *Étude de la souveraineté* which, in spite of its recurrent attacks on the abstract method of Rousseau, Voltaire, Paine and the *philosophes,* is in character only an inverted *Social Contract* or *Second Treatise on Government.* Maistre cannot simply return to an Eighteenth Century that produced the Revolution. He must return to a purer, better version of the past. The rightful essential past must be stripped of its corrupt accidents if the Revolution is not to recur after military defeat. This given in Maistre's situation is implicit in all of his analyses, although he only gradually became conscious of it and made it explicit.

The first strategic object is to establish title to the past. Maistre cannot argue contract in any form, for that has been utilized to legitimize the Revolution. He cannot even argue, as Burke does, a Hobbesian irrevocable contract, for the obvious retort now would be that it has been revoked. On the other hand, he cannot simply argue prescription like Burke. For the new, more recent past has displaced the older prescription. He seizes instead upon the not novel idea of the true and enduring genius of a people and makes it the means of his counterattack for possession of the French past. This is inserted into his treatise on sovereignty, which starts with the well-known refutation of contract. If no man is ever born or ever was born anterior to society, no convention could have set up his society, and hence the origin of society is not the work of men, but of God. All those peoples who have stories of their origin trace it to a divinity. The notion of divine origin is a universal idea; it is more than a fable.

This clears the way for Maistre to introduce sovereignty without risking its becoming the property of the people. Burke managed this by dissipating sovereignty in the English mixed Constitution. Maistre achieves the same end by building sovereignty into the original society. Even the Indian tribes are not without laws and a chief:

> His majesty, the Cacique, is covered with an oily beaver skin instead of a coat lined with Siberian fox; he royally eats his enemy prisoner instead of returning him on his word of honor, as in our degraded Europe. But, in the end, there is among the savages a society, sovereignty, a government of some laws or other. [*Étude*]

And were there not, Maistre adds, a savage is only potentially a man anyway. Sociability is part of human nature. It is thus presented as an original and permanent condition that sovereignty and society are co-existent. It would be just as impossible to imagine it otherwise as to imagine a hive and a swarm of bees without a queen.

A nation, then, has its own God-given social and historical constitution in a rooting even more secure than Burke's legal prescription. Even great legislators have not created this order; they rather gave form to what was already immanent in their people. Nor do they deceive themselves (like the Jacobins) into thinking it is human reason which can build lasting institutions. Institutions last because, created by God, they are both political and religious and accepted as sacred by the people. As in Hobbes, it is stability that counts, and here monarchy shines. It is admitted that in their good days, democracies are brilliant, but they are passing meteors, not capable of counteracting the follies of the people. Athens came to ruin. The Roman Empire was less bloody than the Republic. The English mixed constitution is only a century old and probably will not last. "Republican liberty" usually means the good of a few at the expense of the many and is accompanied by daggers, wars, internal dissension and sedition, whereas the grand monarchies have undertaken great projects, produced the Keplers that led to Newton. If one balances the ups and downs, and averages the reigns of sixty-six French kings, one can see that the most stable rule is clearly paternal hereditary monarchy. One has only to submit to authority.

Maistre, however, still had to remove obvious objections that Louis XIV did not face. Louis XIV could cite the sixty-some kings as the only French past. Writing [*Considérations sur la France*] in 1796-97, Maistre has an additional span of years to explain, a new and alternative past which had the advantage for the moment of being the successful one of the two competitors. Later writers sympathetic to the Revolution would sanctify their past by claiming at least parity for *les deux Frances*. Maistre had to argue that the Revolution was only an interregnum, an aberration, a chastening period of anarchy between two Bourbons; that the Revolution had not produced a durable order, and neither could nor would.

Hence the unflagging argument that the Revolution was ordained by Providence to chasten and regenerate a sinful France. God's ways are mysterious, but one can see that the Terror is swallowing up its own Revolutionary parents. By making a national crime out of the Revolution one might admit and yet reason away its popular sanction. The devil does God's work, an anarchical interregnum serves its purpose in the ordered scheme of things, Jacobinism serves the monarchy unwittingly and Robespierre's infernal genius saves France from dismemberment by the Allies. The clergy is regenerated as a result of its sufferings. All serves a grand plan of restoring peace and royalty which will legitimize France's conquests.

Maistre has been attacked for introducing at this point some gloomy reflections on war and violence, as part of the mysterious and apparently permanent order of human life. The offended critics usually make it sound as if Maistre were the first to say that the wages of sin is death or even that God created a world in which the innocent (by men's standards) suffer. All this is as orthodox as to maintain that secular authority comes from God—although Maistre need not arrogate to himself the application of God's ordinances to human particulars. In any case, he saw a war to the death between Christianity and *philosophisme* and called to the French to take their place at the side of His Most Christian King.

If it is necessary for Maistre to deny respectability to the second and newer Revolutionary past, by explaining it away as an episode in the one legitimate French tradition, it is also necessary to adduce evidence that this alternate past cannot take root. Hence a few interesting remarks on the United States, then a symbol to many Europeans. Comte later recalled how in his youth it seemed that the Americans of the revolutionary generation were surrounded by the august aura of republican Rome. Maistre at first disdains even to consider the upstarts:

> America is cited to us; I don't know anything so impatient as the eulogies bestowed on this child in arms. Let it grow up. [*Considérations*]

Besides, the historic social and institutional characteristics differentiating France from the United States allow him to discount experience in the United States as evidence for the durability of the French Revolution, an argument pursued later by Gentz. For Americans, the king was a distant external power. Almost all the first colonists were republicans who left England during the time of religious and political troubles. The colonists built on these elements and

on the English system of three powers; and unlike the French, they did not wipe the slate clean.

In addition to denying the newer Revolutionary past respectability, it is necessary for Maistre to root it out. This means explaining where things went wrong and finding a formula for avoiding the same errors when the old regime is restored. For Maistre, the theories of the Revolution were nothing but the rigorous logical development of the four articles of the unfortunate Gallican declaration of 1682. But he goes further back to find the source of corruption, and equates all its manifestations: Gallicanism, atheism, Protestantism, illuminism, *philosophisme*, Calvinism, Jansen, Rousseau, the *fronde*, together with Bacon, Locke, Helvétius, Kant, and materialism and sensationalism. Everyone not for us is not only against us, but is related in some secret fashion. This is not something I am imputing to Maistre. He believes in "hidden affinities" in the social world, as in the physical world, which, indeed it is the task of science to discover. Such are the negative beginnings of positive social science—in witch-hunting.

The essence of the enemy is variously distilled. Frequently it is labelled the Eighteenth Century or *philosophisme*. But the Eighteenth Century is nearly as often called the daughter of the sixteenth, with Protestantism its symbol. Protestantism is the enemy of every variety of sovereignty as Catholicism is the most ardent friend, conserver and defender of all legitimate governments. Protestantism is *rebelle par essence*, for it substitutes discussion for authority and individual judgment for the infallibility of those in authority. Protestantism is not favorable to *any* government, but is republican under monarchies and anarchist in republics. It is the *sans-culottisme* of religion. It is responsible for the vices of the present. It was the poison in the Gallican Church, which was "Protestant in the XVIth century, *frondeur* and Jansenist in the XVIIth, and finally *philosophe* and republican in the last years." It was the children of this sect who led Louis XVI to the scaffold; not one Protestant writer defended him.

Maistre designates as the philosophic *Urfeind* first Locke, then Bacon. Locke's principles, nurtured in the warm mud of Paris, produced the revolutionary monster which has devoured Europe. "Contempt for Locke is the beginning of wisdom" [*Les Soirées de Saint-Pétersbourg*]. Because there must be no negotiations about authority, nothing about the social contract can be good, and everything Locke says must be controverted. The individual is not prior to the group, and man's inability to invent language proves it. Because the empiricism of Locke's epistemology also seems interlaced with individualism and social contract, Maistre is willing to go back to innate ideas, even if Aquinas presents an embarrassing degree of empiricism, too. While Locke is the official *bête-noir*, Maistre veered toward elevating Bacon to that position when he discovered that Locke is only Bacon's successor. Locke in turn engenders Helvétius, so that "all the enemies of the human race assembled including Cabanis himself, are descended from Bacon" [*Examen de la philosophic de Bacon*]. Kant is drawn into the net, too. All Kant's career is contained *in ovo* in his inaugural dissertation at Koenigsberg in 1770 (a work on epistemology), for it presumably led him to republican heresies and to his being utilized by theosophists for unorthodox purposes. The rest of the Eighteenth Century is similarly disposed of—Rousseau, Voltaire, etc. *Illuminisme*, for example, is an amalgam of Calvinism and *philosophisme*. The Jews get only a sentence.

We have already seen that to anchor the monarchical past Maistre locates sovereignty and authority in the divine origin of a people. He never tires of pointing out the conservative force of popular belief in such a history. No institution *of any sort* can last if it is not founded on religion. The religious principle is *créateur et conservateur*. The overthrow of the old order becomes, then, "an insurrection against God," something which never occurred before the eighteenth century [*Principe générateur*]. Such a patently instrumental approach to religion has made commentators dubious of Maistre's religious sincerity, commentators who are genuinely distressed or profess to be shocked at Maistre's dating the fourteen centuries of national religion—the basis of French national life—from the Druids! Sainte-Beuve patronizingly conceded that Maistre was religious in the practice of religion, but that there was nothing of devotion in his practice. Faguet accuses him of making religion nothing more than a basis for his politics [*Politiques et moralists du dix-neuvième siècle*, 1890]. While this is certainly exaggerated, the practicing Catholic who was shocked at Saint-Martin for dying without last rites and who had a brother who was a Bishop and a sister who was an Ursuline, himself recognizes in the introduction to the 1820 edition of *Du Pape* that his approach to religion had been criticized for being excessively philosophical. He had overly "humanized" the idea of infallibility, the ultramontanes felt, by basing it only on philosophic considerations, over emphasizing analogue to sovereignty in the temporal order. He protests he is not denying revelation, but the fact remains he has nothing much to say in a traditional religious vein, and volumes to say about the Church as a political institution. Lord Acton puts it more dispassionately: Maistre was the foremost of a group of laymen taking the place of the clergy in literature, "all rather inspired by the lessons of recent history than versed in the older details of theological discussion" [in *Essays on Church and State*, edited by D. Woodruff, 1953].

Avoiding the presumptuous question of personal devotion, let us only note how Maistre's ecclesiastical program serves his politics. "If I were an atheist and sovereign," he wrote to a Papal Nuncio in 1815, "I would declare the Pope infallible by public edict for the establishment and the security of the peace in my realms." Maistre consciously treats religion instrumentally. Let us treat Christianity as only a political institution, he can say. From this point of view—justification in the sight of God apart—Tellier's persecution of the Jansenists was *française et bonne politiquement*. Irreligion is *canaille*. The patrician is a lay priest: the national religion is his prime and most sacred property, for his privilege falls with it. If it were permitted to establish degrees of importance, Maistre would put hierarchy before dogma, he wrote to a Russian Orthodox friend. Before the decision, the question of the procession of the Holy Ghost mattered little; what was of infinite importance was the obligation of Greek to submit to Roman authority, for otherwise there would be neither faith nor Church. The ultramontane formula he offered to one of Louis XVIII's councillors begins with the political:

> Point de morale publique ni de caractère national sans religion, point de réligion Européenne sans le christianisme, point de véritable christianisme sans le catholisme, point de catholisme sans le pape, point de Pape sans le suprématie qui lui appartient.

The Church is part of the European political fabric, and it too must be accounted for if the old order is to be restored.

But the restored Church must be purified of false Gallican principles. The aristocracy lost all by its alliance with Gallicanism. Its destiny is in its natural alliance with the ecclesiastical order. The old order to be restored has an honorable place for the aristocracy. But for this old order to be safely restored, monarchical authority must be absolutely unchallenged, and absolute obedience is only taught by the Church, notably by the Jesuits. It took less than thirty years for the generation raised after the expulsion of the Jesuits, without their moral education, "to overturn the altar and cut the throat of the king of France" [*Cinq Lettres sur l'Éducation Publique en Russie*]. Ignoring Jesuit theorists of the right to resistance, like Suarez and Mariana, Maistre claims that the Church has never employed against a civil authority anything but "*apologies, raisonnements et des miracles*" [*Reflexions*]. Aristocracy and clergy must hence make common cause, not against the monarch as before, when the clergy was Gallican and the nobility infected with *philosophisme*, but to bolster the monarchical principle that is their salvation. If the vigor of the Church itself depends on hierarchy and the principle of sovereignty, then it is necessary to be ultramontane. As Maistre never tired of repeating

> plus de pape, plus de sauverainété; plus de sauverainété, plus d'unité; plus d'unité, plus d'autorité; plus d'autorité, plus de foi. [*Léttre à une Dame Russe*]

And faith teaches obedience. Even if the faith itself is persecuted, popular resistance is not justified. So securely is the restored order to be anchored.

While this extreme view tends to make faith a mere instrument for public order, it should be observed in fairness to Maistre that he is more sensitive to the question of the misuse of power than a more thorough-going absolutist like Hobbes. The only restraint upon the ruler Hobbes recognized was "duty." Maistre likewise cannot permit restraint to be exacted as a matter of political right, for that would destroy the principle of authority and mean the dissolution of society. The monarch can be restrained only by a force that is external and non-political. That is to say, spiritual; hence the Papacy. Starting with a sovereign monarch, Maistre is consistent in going on to assert that every liberty won by the Gallican Church from the Holy See meant the enslavement of the French clergy to the temporal power; that the so-called liberties of the Gallican Church were in fact exercised by civil magistrates in a manner reproved by the clergy: that the popes have fought for the legitimate liberties of men; that it is due to the Church that European monarchy is under law, and is not tyranny; that the clergy employed its influence to try to restrain the wickedness of temporal rulers toward South American Indians and extinguished servitude in Europe; and that, indeed, the Popes were *les instituteurs, les tuteurs, les sauveurs et les véritables genies constituants de l'Europe.* If restraint has to come from somewhere, and Maistre would not deny this, it would be exercised logically only by a spiritual and external power, which is most natural and *least dangerous.* The instrumentality of religion is never far from sight.

When is a revolutionary change irreversible? The fact is that Maistre could see even before the demise of Napoleon that the Restoration would not be an unimpaired restoration of the old regime, let alone the purification of the past he prescribed, and that he would have to lecture Louis XVIII as much as his Bourbon predecessors for their mistakes. Principle would not override compromise. And this is what in fact happened. Maistre was as out of place in 1819 as he had been in 1789. The restored Sovereign could not make use of Maistre's anti-Gallican principles; nor for the moment, could the clergy. Only a few years earlier the Pope could not even acknowledge Maistre's offer to dedicate **Du Pape** to him. The reprint in 1815 of Maistre's **Considérations** made it seem he was not merely against constitutions in general, but *a fortiori* against the Charter of 1814, as he indeed was. It was as liberal a charter as could be hoped for under the circumstance, Louis XVIII having learned a lesson entirely different from Maistre's.

Maistre was consistent with what should have been Bourbon principles, but the Bourbon himself was not. The whole problem of settlement had been wrongly defined. Everyone was concerned to find the means of establishing order by touching the revolutionaries and their acts as little as possible. He would propose the opposite, erasing the revolutionaries and their acts as much as possible without endangering the legitimate Sovereigns. Otherwise, the party of sovereignty was lost. Maistre's last letters and conversation showed him bearing bravely the gloomy knowledge that the Revolution had not, by his pure standards, been defeated:

> La révolution est debout, sans doute, et non seulement elle est debout, mais elle marche, elle court, elle rue.

The only difference between this epoch and that of Robespierre is that then heads fell, now faces change. The nobility and the clergy, he wrote to Bonald, have been reduced to the level of the simple bourgeoisie by a government which boasts of legitimacy. Maistre died foreseeing that things would get worse before they got better, that the revolutionary principle would not accept the fall of Decazes, but would react against the monarchy and chase the royal family from France again.

It is Maistre's stubborn principles in times that are out of joint, and not a desire to shock, which leads him to severe judgments. Much earlier, for example, Maistre in 1793 proudly related how during the wars of religion Savoy had suppressed both innovators and inquisition. Before the Revolution it was in no way necessary for a conservative in France or Savoy to defend the Inquisition. But later, in 1815, his reactionary position brought him around to it.

For if one can see now that to undo the Revolution it is necessary to root out the Revolutionary principle, it also can be seen that the old leniency was wrong. The Inquisition was proper. Spain was fortunate, for through the Inquisition she alone escaped the blood of the religious wars. Heresy is a dangerous crime. And, finally, had France possessed this institution, the Revolution would have been avoided. Again, Maistre had earlier no reason to defend venality of offices. Later he saw it as an integral part of the monarchical system. Again, Maistre earlier could be proud of the liberty and equality in enlightened Savoy. Later, he would warn against the dangers of liberating the serfs in Russia. Such unrelenting consistency is worthy of a *philosophe.*

And this is our conclusion. Maistre is a *philosophe* in spite of himself, an eighteenth century man. To be sure, we can see in him earlier orthodox views that were never fully displaced by the Enlightenment. But Maistre has to recast these earlier views as a result of his situation, since he has the reactionary task of restoring the old regime, and not merely the conservative task of defending it. To restore the old regime, however, requires that he see it as a system, and it is system-building which sets both Maistre and his enemies off from a Louis XIV or a Louis XVIII. A monarch can be pragmatic, even lenient. A monarch*ist* or a *philosophe* cannot. It is Maistre's change of *situation* that requires the easy-going conservative to become a systematic political philosopher of reaction. By not merely reacting against the French Revolution, but by seeking as well to erase the infamous principles which were both its cause and justification, Maistre is almost driven to a philosophy of order. He is almost, but not quite, a latter-day Hobbes. After all, it was the good society he sought, not mere survival. (pp. 591-98)

Elisha Greifer, "Joseph De Maistre and the Reaction Against the Eighteenth Century," in The American Political Science Review, *Vol. LV, No. 3, September, 1961, pp. 591-98.*

Etienne Gilson   (essay date 1962)

[*Gilson was a French literary historian and professor. One of the foremost contemporary scholars of medieval philosophy and of the Christian influence on the development of modern civilization, his works include* La philosophie au moyen âge *(1922) and* L'esprit de la philosophie médiévale *(1931-32). In the following excerpt, originally published in 1962, Gilson discusses de Maistre's role as a Christian apologist.*]

The style of de Maistre . . . is very different from that of [Louis] de Bonald, even as a style of thought. He is less a purely speculative philosopher than an apologist of Christian truth and his personal vocation seems to have been to justify, by essentially rational means, the most unpopular parts of the Christian doctrine. He had a gift for it. Above everything else, de Maistre had an extraordinary aptitude never to let himself be disconcerted by any objection. No objection against a truth can itself be true. In such cases, just face the objection, submit it to the light of reason and you will see it dissolve under your very eyes.

Another distinctive trait of de Maistre is that he was very personal in his attacks against error. Reproached with his taste for attacking persons instead of contenting himself with refuting doctrines, he replied that, indeed, nothing has been done to refute error so long as, behind the erroneous doctrine, criticism has not reached its author. De Maistre always plays the man. His *Examen de la philosophie de Bacon* (*Examination of the Philosophy of Bacon*) (1815) is largely directed against Francis Bacon himself whom he reproaches, among other things, with not having known as much science as his thirteenth-century namesake, the English Franciscan Roger Bacon. It is difficult to say whom he detests the most—Bacon, Locke, or Hume. In point of fact, although he seems to consider Hume the more venomous, his favorite target is Locke, no doubt because of the sort of dictatorship he had exercised over the minds of a whole century. De Maistre protests he has nothing against Locke personally. Everything about him was right, except his philosophy. In this Locke resembled the dancing master of whom Swift once said that he had all the good qualities conceivable, except that he was lame. Even the philosophy of Locke would no doubt be excellent had its principles been true.

Locke embodies for de Maistre the "bad principle" which reigned in Europe ever since the time of the Reformation. It is "the principle that denies everything, shakes everything, *protests* against everything: on its bronze forehead is written, NO! and this is the true title of the book of Locke which, in turn, can be considered as the preface to the whole philosophy of the eighteenth century, itself purely negative and therefore, null" [*Les Soirées de Saint Pétersbourg*].

Still more openly than de Bonald, de Maistre considers "the philosophy of the last century" as a kind of doctrinal whole which "will remain in the sight of posterity as one of the more shameful epochs of the human mind." It had a favorite purpose, not to say a unique one, namely to detach man from God: "All that philosophy was only, in fact, a system of practical atheism; I have given that strange disease a name: I call it *theophobia*" [*Soirées*].

The main symptom of theophobia is a constant and marked tendency to resort to any solution rather than God in answering any problem. The symptom can be observed in all philosophical books of the eighteenth century. They would not frankly say: *There is no God,* for fear of getting in trouble with the law, but they would say: *God is not there.* God is not in man's ideas: they come from sense. God is not in our thoughts: these are but transformed sensations. God is not in the plagues that afflict mankind (for instance, the deluge): these are but physical phenomena like all the others and they can be accounted for by means of well-known laws; God does not think of you, nor, for that matter, of any other man: the world is made for the sake of insects as well as of man; in short *no physical event can have a cause related to God.*

Against that general attitude de Maistre undertakes to show that, on the contrary, the explanations of natural and historical facts by the intervention of a supernatural agent acting in view of supernatural ends are the only satisfactory ones. Nothing is more unlike cheap apologetics than the reasons developed by de Maistre. He has a gift for revealing the presence of the preternatural in familiar historical and social facts such as the striking difference there is between the peculiar condition of the public executioner, the most unglorious of men, and that of the soldier, a killer admired by all. De Maistre shows in original sin the only rational answer to many otherwise unexplainable facts. There is a kind of pre-Chestertonian touch—though of a much heavier kind—in the never flustered assurance with which de Maistre makes reason testify in favor of transcendent and revealed truth.

Among the philosophers whom de Maistre likes are Thomas Aquinas, whom he does not know too well, but to whose authority he resorts in order to maintain against Locke that there are in man innate cognitions. He also admires Malebranche, a great mind which France is unworthy to possess. But the philosopher whom de Maistre calls "the best of his friends" is François de Cambrai, that is, Fénelon.

On the positive side, de Maistre favors a traditionalism grounded less in an oral revelation of truth made to man by God than in an exceptionally high intuitive power granted by God to primitive man, and now well nigh lost. According to his own views, God created man endowed with a learning not only greater than our own, but different in kind. In the beginning, man knew effects in their causes; today, men painfully strive to rise up from effects to causes or, rather, they content themselves with effects; they do not bother any more about causes; they do not even know what a cause is. To the favored eighteenth-century theme of the continuous advancement of learning de Maistre thus opposes the contrary certitude that mankind has unlearned what it first knew and is now engaged in the slow work of recouping part of the loss.

The problem of language is the same as that of knowledge; "language is eternal and every tongue is as old as the people that speaks it." The notion that all languages were poor in their beginnings is only one more gratuitous supposition made by the philosophers. 'Tis true those primitive languages have disappeared, *etiam periere ruinae*, but they did exist, because man cannot have received knowledge without at the same time receiving language. The problem of the "origin of ideas," so dear to philosophers (e.g., Condillac) is therefore absurd: "thought and language are but two magnificent synonyms" [*Soirées*]. Both come to man by way of revelation and rest upon authority.

On the problem of society and its principle, de Maistre was at one with de Bonald, not because he was borrowing anything from him but on account of what he himself considered their quasi-miraculous agreement. Man is not the maker of things; he finds them already made and endowed with natures it is not in his power to change. "Man can modify everything within the sphere of his activity, but he creates nothing; such is his law, in the physical as in the moral realm. Man can of course plant a seedling, grow a tree, and perfect it by grafting and pruning in a hundred ways; but he has never fancied that he has the power of making a tree. How has he come to imagine that he had that of making a constitution?" [*Considérations sur la France*].

For all his rationalism, de Maistre had a soft spot for mystical doctrines related to the notion of divine illumination. The more remarkable feature of his doctrine in this respect was that, as he himself saw it, science was already striving to recall men from matter to spirit. This seemed evident to him when he thought of Newton, whom he absolutely refused to put in the same class with Locke. Only men like Voltaire dare to say: Locke and Newton, as if any comparison were possible between the two names! Scientists are always speaking of "mechanical laws" and of "mechanical principles" while, in fact, there is nothing really mechanical about the notions they have in mind. They are unwilling to acknowledge the fact, but scientists are now behaving like a secret sect enjoying the monopoly of truth and hoarding secrets hidden from the public. They seem to forbid other people to know more things, and to interpret them otherwise than they themselves do.

De Maistre foresees the coming of a new era. Introducing in one of his *Soirées de Saint Petersbourg* (Evenings in St. Petersburg) a curious personage, different from himself, but with whom he obviously feels in sympathy, de Maistre has him announce that the proud science of the day will soon find itself humbled by an *illuminated* posterity which will blame it for its inability to draw from the truths God has given to it consequences more precious for the happiness of man. "The face of the whole science will then be changed; long dethroned and despised spirit will recover its place. It then will be demonstrated that all the ancient traditions are true; that even paganism was only a system of truths corrupted and out of their respective places; that it is enough to clean them up, so to speak, and to restore them to their places in order to see them shine again. . . ." As we said, all of this expressed the position of some illuminists rather than that of de Maistre himself. Yet he never wholly disapproved of them. Disliking as he did their tendency to join secret sects and to separate themselves from the Church, he felt that their minds were moving in the right direction, from a revelation lost by man's rebellion, to a revelation regained, under God's guidance, by the patient effort of human reason. (pp. 214-17)

> Etienne Gilson, "The Christian Reaction," in Recent Philosophy: Hegel to the Present *by Etienne Gilson, Thomas Langan, and Armand A. Maurer, C.S.B., Random House, 1966, pp. 208-31.*

R. V. Sampson   (essay date 1973)

[*In the following excerpt, Sampson provides a comprehensive analysis of de Maistre's theories regarding the nature of power and war.*]

It would not be easy to think of a writer likely to inspire greater distaste in Tolstoy than de Maistre; yet there is a structural resemblance between de Maistre's belief in a divine Providence guiding the general direction of historical events irrespective of the will of individual protagonists whom men regard as all-powerful, and the philosophy of history which Tolstoy espoused at the time of writing *War and Peace*. De Maistre in religious, philosophical and political outlook was everything which Tolstoy was not.

More than any other modern writer he evokes the image of Machiavelli whom he resembled in the single-minded determination with which he pursued diplomatic office. From this vantage point he could observe at first hand the negotiations and intrigues inseparable from political and military power without himself being directly involved at the level of those bearing primary responsibility. As Machiavelli was Secretary to the Council of Ten at Florence for fourteen years from 1498 to 1512, the Comte de Maistre held office at St. Petersburg as ambassador at the court of Alexander for thirteen years from 1803 (appointed 1802) to 1815, when he returned to Savoy. Both share that rare quality of being able and willing to describe truthfully those aspects of reality which by their squalor, degradation, cruelty or horror do not commonly invite close or honest scrutiny except by those anxious to expose the conditions in order to abolish them. Reformers, radicals or revolutionaries, we expect to draw attention to and depict realistically the world's ills; conservatives and defenders of the *status quo* are not commonly quite so eager to draw attention to the abscesses suppurating in the body politic. Yet both Machiavelli and de Maistre do just this.

Machiavelli in particular does it so effectively, laying bare the bone with the precision of a surgeon and with the destructive quality of vitriol, that critics like Rousseau have concluded that he must be considered essentially as a satirist. Similar emotions and doubts arise in us in reading some of the passages in which de Maistre describes for example the phenomenon of war and speculates as to why men do it. But in his case as in that of Machiavelli, the intent is not at all satirical—we are not being invited to the pillory to execrate our morbid pathology—quite the contrary! The acid realism of the description is an antecedent not to denunciation but to approval. What radicals lament and revile, what the majority, busily minding their own business, avoid looking at, the Machiavellis and de Maistres zestfully expose to view in order unabashed to teach us to accept and even revere.

Although de Maistre himself attached great importance to blood and lineage, having exalted notions of his own descent from a Languedoc line, the facts suggest a steady ascent from humble and obscure origins: muleteers, then millers, then drapers, then Joseph's grandfather studied law at Turin and aspired to the magistracy, a coat of arms and a family crest, while Joseph's father rose from membership of the Savoy Senate at Chambéry to the Presidency of that august body, and was finally made a Count. He was described as 'rather surly', a man who 'did not laugh, not even with his children'. Joseph himself described his own childhood approvingly as one that was 'reared in all the ancient severity, immersed from the cradle in serious studies'. The critical note which is markedly absent in the son's account of the father's regimen appears however in a revealing comment by the grandson concerning his father's childhood. 'When the time for study marked the end of recreation, [he] appeared on the step of the garden gate without saying a word and he took pleasure in seeing the toys fall from his son's hands, without allowing him even one last throw of the ball or shuttlecock' [Robert Triomphe, in his *Joseph de Maistre: Étude sur la Vie et sur la Doctrine d'un Matérialiste Mystique,* 1968].

In short, Joseph's father enjoyed his magisterial role, a role he did not confine to the public courts. He was a man who inspired fear in others and in children in particular. Joseph's mother, who was all the more important to him in view of his father's severity, died while still young. A pious woman, who learnt to school her emotions so as not to reveal her feelings, entirely given up to the care of her family, she is said to have evinced for 'Joson', her eldest child, an 'especial friendship', which was reciprocated by Joson in pathetically but understandably hyperbolic terms. Joseph spoke of his 'sublime mother' as 'an angel to whom God had lent a body'. The boy's outstanding characteristic as a child brought up in a severely authoritarian atmosphere was one of obedience, or as his son, Rodolphe, expressed it, 'a loving submission to his parents'. In their absence as well as when they were present, at all times, 'their slightest desire was a law absolutely binding for him'. He cites as a concrete illustration the way in which he remained in parental leading-strings even when departure from home for his education gave him at least physical freedom from the parental yoke. 'During the entire time that the young Joseph spent at Turin following the law course at the University, he never allowed himself to read a book without having written to his father or mother at Chambéry to obtain authorization' [Triomphe].

As a young man we find him under his father's eye delivering speeches of rotund pomposity and unction in praise of the antiquity and grandeur of the judiciary in the presence of the assembled judicature. But although de Maistre was subsequently to express great sympathy for the Jesuits (with whom he was eventually expelled from St. Petersburg for his proselytizing activities), the major influence under which he came in the Savoyard Senate was that of the Jansenists in the writings of De la Rochefoucauld and Pascal. Jansenism (called after Bishop Jansenius, 1558-1638) continued to uphold the Augustinian position in the famous Pelagian controversy, asserting the sufficiency of divine grace as against the belief in salvation by works. It was a religious tradition within the Catholic fold as austere, as pessimistic and as committed to a theology of predestination as the Calvinist sector within Protestantism. The year the French Revolution broke out saw the death

of de Maistre senior, and the son inherited his father's fortune and recently acquired hereditary title. Thus worldly self-interest coincided with his ultramontanist, authoritarian upbringing and severe, not to say gloomy religious nurture to produce the Revolution's proudest and most fanatical foe, defender of tradition, of feudal privilege, of wealth, of the authority of Church and Crown.

There remains however a curious paradox in the man's beliefs and action. Not surprisingly in the light of his religious background, de Maistre attached immense importance to the family as a social institution. His ideological regard for its status is akin to Hegel's notion of the State. He believed it to be a unique moral entity, transcending the individual's responsibility, and shaping a man more decisively than any other agency apart from the nation to which he belonged. Yet he himself of his own free will chose at the age of fifty to abandon his wife and two children in Savoy for twelve years while he occupied his diplomatic post at the Petersburg court. Perhaps, on the principle that the visitation of the sins of the fathers upon the children is a basic illustration of the primacy of the family over the individual, he felt that he was in his own peculiar way paying homage to the sanctity of the *lares et penates* of the domestic hearth.

The majority of men, endowed with conscience as they are, nevertheless seem to experience little difficulty in persuading themselves that the world sanctions a 'healthy' concern for one's own interests. There is, however, ceaseless tension between conscience and self-interest. Thus most men find themselves pulled in opposite directions, with a resultant ambivalence and confused uncertainty in their moral pronouncements. In these circumstances, any man who for whatever reason is not afraid to or is impelled to adopt an evil premise on the basis of which he may reason logically and clearly, free from the temptation to soften in any way the harsh outlines of reality, is in a position to exert great influence over the weak and morally confused. De Maistre was such a man. He reasons vigorously, lucidly, logically in limpid prose; he describes reality truthfully without illusions, but all to evil purpose. He is perverted because of his whole-hearted acceptance of the monstrous proposition that war is divine. Given this premise, offensive to the sensitivities even of the naturally aggressive, he can afford to diagnose its cause quite accurately in a way embarrassing to conservatives, who are not at all anxious to look candidly at the causes of a phenomenon which both common sense and an instinct for what is politic forbid them to label 'divine'. Hence the interest which still attaches to what de Maistre has to say on this vitally important subject, notwithstanding the pernicious content of his advocacy.

What pacifist, for instance, could express as well as de Maistre, in his dialogue between the senator and the knight in the **Soirées de Saint-Petersbourg,** the extraordinariness of the fact that men should with such zest slaughter their own kind?

> There is, however in man, despite his immense degradation, an element of love which draws him towards his own kind: compassion is as natural to him as breathing. By what inscrutable

sorcery is he always ready, at the first sound of the drum, to divest himself of this sacred character, to go without resisting, often even with a certain excitement, which also has its peculiar character, to cut to pieces on the battle-field his brother who has never injured him, and who advances on his side to make him suffer the same fate, if he can.

This strange phenomenon, de Maistre quite rightly insists, cries out for an explanation. But before embarking upon possible explanations, there is another strangely paradoxical element associated with the phenomenon of war, to which he draws our attention in striking fashion.

Suppose, he says, a visitor from outer space came to earth to be told that the human vices and corruption of which he was the spectator necessitated the killing of man by man. Killing is accordingly not accounted a crime by human beings, provided that this 'necessity' is undertaken either by the soldier or the executioner. The executioner, he is told, dispenses death only to those found guilty after judicial conviction and sentence; and there are relatively so few thus convicted and sentenced that one public executioner per province is normally adequate to the demand for his services. The soldier on the other hand is always in short supply, and there are never enough of them, because there is no limit to the numbers they are required to kill, and so far from their victims being confined to the ranks of the guilty, the contrary is true; they are permitted to kill only honest people. The man from Mars is further told that of these two professional killers, one is and always has been honoured among all nations, while the other is as universally execrated. He is then asked to guess on whom the anathema falls. He would not hesitate a moment, suggests de Maistre. The soldier, of course. For the executioner is the extirpator of crime, 'a sublime being', the main pillar of order, 'the corner-stone of society', whereas the soldier, on the other hand, is the instrument of injustice and a minister of cruelty. 'Would that not be the rational reply?' he asks; and yet the Martian would be quite wrong, for we esteem them in quite the reverse order.

How then are we to explain this extraordinary paradox? Why does war occur? Or in the striking phrase which de Maistre puts into the mouth of the Senator: 'Explain why it is that what is most honourable in the world, in the judgement of the whole of humanity without exception, is the right to shed in innocence blood'.

Perhaps the explanation is that rulers decide on war for their own purposes, and the subjects blindly obey. This explanation de Maistre rejects as false, the reasons for which I will return to later in view of the crucial nature of the discussion. Perhaps wars are caused by nationalism. This hypothesis rather surprisingly is dismissed as not worth discussing. 'How many national wars are there?' he asks rhetorically; and answers: 'One in a thousand years perhaps.' Perhaps the desire for glory explains it all. But this is rejected (*a*) because the glory goes only to the commanders and (*b*) because this explanation begs the essential question which consists precisely of why human beings should ever have associated glory with anything so bestial as the carnage of war.

In effect de Maistre gives no rational explanation for this extraordinary and dreadful phenomenon. Instead he leans very heavily on its ubiquity both in Nature and in human affairs. It requires no explanation, he seems to believe, because it is a fact of nature, a fact of life, universal, eternal, a rule from which there is no escaping. The argument from Nature relies heavily on rhetoric, of which the following is only a sample. There is, he says, manifest throughout Nature 'a kind of prescribed rage', 'a decree of violent death'.

> Already, in the vegetable kingdom, you begin to experience the law: from the immense catalpa down to the humblest *graminée,* how many plants *die,* and how many are *killed!* but as soon as you enter the animal kingdom, the law is suddenly terribly in evidence. . . . In each great division of the animal species, it [a hidden force] has selected a certain number of animals charged with the task of devouring the others: thus, there are insects of prey, reptiles of prey, birds of prey, fish of prey, and quadrupeds of prey. There is not a moment when a living creature is not being devoured by another. Above these numerous animal species is placed man, whose destructive hand spares nothing of all that lives. He kills to feed himself, he kills to clothe himself, he kills to ward off others, he kills to attack, he kills to defend himself, he kills to teach himself, he kills to amuse himself, he kills to kill. Superb and terrible king, he has need of everything and nothing resists him. He knows how many barrels of oil the head of the shark or whale will furnish him with; his sharp pin pricks . . . the elegant butterfly . . . ; he stuffs the crocodile, he embalms the humming bird . . . Man demands all at one and the same time: of the lamb its entrails to make the harp sound, of the whale its bones to support the young girl's corset; of the wolf its most murderous fang to polish light works of art; of the elephant its defences to fashion the toy of a child: his tables are covered with corpses.

It is a graphic picture. To a sensitive man it is a horrifying picture. De Maistre did not find it so. It was enough for him that it was so. And logic compels him to ask: 'Is there any reason to suppose that this law so evident in nature and in man will stop at man?' Why should it? Why indeed? 'Which being will exterminate that which exterminates them all?' And the answer is as remorseless as it is obvious. 'He himself. It is man who is charged with slaughtering man.' Thus the original question with which we started out, 'how man is capable of waging war on his fellows, is neatly stood on its head. Man, it appears, is required by Nature's law to slaughter his fellows. The problem that then presents itself is how, given the fact that man is a moral and compassionate being, who weeps over the calamities of others as over his own, how is such a being to overcome his natural sensibilities in order to fulfil what Nature requires of him? War alone makes this possible. The earth whose thirst for blood is unsated by the slaughter of beasts and of the guilty demands also the slaughter of the innocent. For this, war is indispensable. This and this alone explains the enigma of men, contrary to their nature, advancing on the battlefield without the slightest understanding of why or to what end, doing that which inspires in them a natural horror.

> Have you never noticed that on the field of death, man never disobeys? He can massacre easily enough a Nerva or Henry IV. But on the battle-field the most abominable tyrant, the most insolent butcher of human flesh will never hear: 'We are no longer willing to serve you.' A revolt there, an agreement to embrace one another in repudiation of a tyrant, is a phenomenon outside my recollection.

Moreover, if we look at the actual history of mankind, we find that this *a priori* law of violent destruction is empirically fulfilled. History demonstrates that war is the normal condition of mankind, that peace is no more than a respite, that blood is always flowing somewhere or other. He casts a rapid illustrative eye over his own century in confirmation of his claim, and concludes that France alone has been at war for forty out of the ninety-six years under scrutiny, and if some nations have been more fortunate, others have been less so.

> The century which is ending started for France with a bloody war which ended only in 1714 with the Treaty of Rastadt. In 1719, France declared war on Spain; the Treaty of Paris put an end to it in 1727. The election to the Polish throne rekindled war in 1733; peace came in 1736. Four years later, the terrible war of the Austrian Succession broke out and lasted without break until 1748. Eight years of peace started to heal the wounds of eight years of war, when English ambition forced France to take up arms. The Seven Years' War is only too well known. After fifteen years' respite, the American Revolution dragged France once more into a war whose consequences no human wisdom could have foreseen. Peace was signed in 1782; seven years later, the Revolution started; it has lasted to this day and has so far cost France three million men. [*Considerations on France*]

War, he concludes, is a chronic, constant attribute of the human condition, 'a persistent fever marked by terrifying crises'. Sometimes the shedding of blood is sporadic over a wide area, at other times more narrowly confined but more intensive, and at yet other periods the spilling of blood reaches frenzied proportions, as for example in the Punic Wars, the period of the Triumvirates, Caesar's wars, the barbarian invasions, the Crusades, the wars of religion, the war of the Spanish Succession, the French Revolution. Meterologists draw up weather charts to enable us to forecast the direction from which the next squall or hurricane is expected to blow up. Is it not time we had parallel war charts? 'If tables of massacre were available like meteorological tables, who knows if some law might not be discovered after centuries of observation?' [*Considerations*].

As we read the highly relevant evidence, marshalled so vividly and compellingly by de Maistre, we naturally feel profoundly disturbed as we wonder where this is all leading to. The author occasionally concedes that the picture he is delineating is 'unfortunate'; at other times the conviction seems irresistible that the author's intent must be ironic. But no! The purpose is to demonstrate not merely that violent destruction is not in general 'as great an evil as is believed', but that war is above all divinely ordained. He succeeds in finding ten or more reasons for this perverted conclusion.

It is 'divine' because it represents a law of the world. It has supernatural consequences in that it is a great privilege to die in battle, and the dead may never be said to have died in vain. There is universally attached to war a glory which has an inexplicable fascination for us. Its divinity is manifest in the protection it affords the great captains in the face of all hazards, preserving their lives at least until their renown has been fully accomplished. Its divinity is seen in the way in which its declaration is the result of silent, remorseless forces which over-ride the petty wills of the sovereigns who ostensibly declare it. The results of war transcend human reasoning powers, degrading some nations, exalting others, irrespectively of which side is the conqueror and which the conquered. Success in battle is itself determined by an indefinable force, which is entirely independent of the size of the respective battalions. Humanity may be likened unto a tree that is constantly being pruned by an invisible hand. Loss of resilience and indolence, the successes of civilization, eat like gangrene into the human spirit, which can be retempered only in blood.

So far from the arts and sciences flourishing as a result of peace, together with other great human enterprises, noble ideas and manly virtues, they take their rise from war. Supreme genius and the pinnacles of civilization are manured in the blood spilled in war. The apex of Greek civilization was coterminous with the terrible Peloponnesian war, the Age of Augustus followed hard upon the civil war and the proscriptions, the peculiar glory of the French genius itself was nurtured in the wars of the League and brought to maturity in the wars of the Fronde. The great ages of civilization, the epochs of Alexander, Pericles, Augustus, Leo X and Francis I, Louis XIV and Queen Anne were not in the least peaceful. Finally, let it not be objected that war is cruel and unjust. For the principle that the innocent must suffer for the benefit of the guilty is a universal dogma which has moreover been consecrated by Christianity itself.

In short, de Maistre's 'God', so far from being the God of the Evangel, is Mars, the god of war, of Jehovah and the Old Testament, in whose honour he celebrates a veritable hymn of praise to carnage.

> The entire earth, continually soaked in blood, is only an immense altar where everything that lives must be immolated without end, without limit, without relaxation, until the consummation of things, until the extinction of evil, until the death of death.

Horrible and blasphemous as all this is, it has not in any way tarnished de Maistre's reputation. He is not only a highly respected figure in the history of European thought, he was one of the authors most widely read in the intellectual circles of his day, and he has continued to exert considerable influence. It is not fashionable to express overtly and so unambiguously what de Maistre has to say on the subject of war, but that does not mean that his dicta do not correspond to very widely held and correspondingly powerful beliefs. They do not of course exhaust the content of popular belief, which is highly ambivalent, but they represent an important element, which it is salutary to bring out into the open and not repress.

War, then, and the causes of war, are according to de Maistre, natural, inevitable and 'divine'. There remain to discuss two other important topics in the context of his view of war: firstly, his theory as to how battles are won and lost; secondly, and related to this, his view of the nature of sovereign power.

De Maistre is concerned to refute the well-known saying that 'God is always on the side of the big battalions'. He makes the obvious point that numbers are not everything: that armies in a physical ratio to one another of two to three may well stand in a very different ratio in matters of courage, experience and discipline, so that a simple prediction of who will vanquish whom on the basis of that purely physical ratio may very well be falsified in the event. Moreover, he believes that so far as the physical ratio is concerned, rival forces will normally be fairly evenly balanced, for if this were not so, war would be unlikely to break out in the first instance. De Maistre, like other balance-of-power theorists, who believe in a natural equilibrium which always reasserts itself, never succeeds in explaining a central contradiction in the theory. In one context, we are assured that no small power would ever be so foolish as to take on a great power, since that would be to invite its own destruction. Yet the best way apparently to insure against the threat of war from the ambitions of great powers is to balance their power with an effective counter-power. In fact, both sets of circumstances have time and time again served as the circumstances out of which war has emerged; as, for instance, (*a*) Austria swallowing the Serbs in 1908; and (*b*) World War I erupting in August 1914 at a time when the balance of power had never before reached such a peak of perfection.

However, to be fair to de Maistre, he is theorizing not in order to prevent war, since it is a 'divine' phenomenon. His point is that there is a natural tendency for the equilibrium of power forces always to reassert itself in the sphere of international relations. If an over-mighty power threatens the balance of forces, sometimes the giant cuts his own throat, and at other times a much weaker power initially throws itself into the path of the giant and gradually and mysteriously grows until it constitutes itself an insurmountable obstacle. Thus the equilibrium, which is divinely sustained, is restored. The equilibrium depends for its maintenance not on human prudence or skill. Divine Providence may use as its instrument even geese to save the capitol. In short, extra-human, supernatural forces are at work which effectively remove ultimate human destinies out of merely human hands, ensuring that wars always and regularly take place, that they are normally between physically well-matched contenders, and that the ultimate outcome is determined by the divine wisdom, expressed sometimes through the seemingly trivial instruments of geese or hares, but more commonly through the factor of the *morale* and courage displayed by the soldiers on either side. Battles are the least predictable of phenom-

ena; nowhere is the hand of Providence—de Maistre suggests that a special department of Providence must be necessitated—more in evidence. 'Never is he warned more frequently and more sharply than in war of his own nullity and of the inevitable power which rules everything. It is opinion which loses battles, and it is opinion which wins them.' Hence the anxiety displayed by all 'great' commanders to prevent their ranks being weakened or decimated by fear or panic.

De Maistre relates how he asked an eminent military figure to tell him what is 'a battle lost', and received the candid reply that he did not know. To which was added after further reflection that a battle lost is a battle believed to be lost. 'To conquer is to advance' is Frederick II's aphorism, but what determines who does it? De Maistre speaks significantly of 'that solemn moment when, without knowing why, an army feels itself carried forward, as if it were slipping on an inclined plane'. 'And the soldier who *slips forward*,' he asks rhetorically, 'has he counted the dead?' Everything depends upon the moral factor. The same physical events are construed quite differently by the contending sides. If A's force comes between two of B's forces, A will claim: 'I have cut him off. He is lost.' While B will claim: 'He has placed himself between two lines of fire. He is lost.' The one who in fact loses is the one who first loses his nerve, capitulates to fear and feels himself to be defeated.

In view of the fame subsequently to be achieved by Stendhal's description of the battle of Waterloo in *The Charterhouse of Parma* (*La Chartreuse de Parme*), to which Tolstoy particularly expressed his indebtedness, it is worth quoting verbatim de Maistre's description in 1821 of the nature of a battlefield. After observing that frequently no one knows who won and who lost until several days after the battle is over, he goes on to correct the popular notion of what a battle looks like.

> People talk a lot about battles in society without knowing what one is. People are particularly prone to consider them as points, whereas they cover two or three leagues of country. People say to you in all seriousness: How is it that you don't know what took place in this battle, since you were there? Whereas often enough it is precisely the opposite that could be said. Does he who is on the right know what is happening on the left? Does he even know what is happening two paces from him? I easily imagine to myself one of those terrible scenes: on a vast landscape, covered with all the preparations for the slaughter, which seems to shake under the feet of men and horses; amidst fire and whirlwinds of smoke, dazed, carried away by the resounding din of firearms and military machines and voices which command, shout or die away; surrounded by dead and dying and mutilated corpses; possessed in turn by fear, by hope, by rage, by five or six different forms of intoxication, what becomes of a man? What does he see? What does he know after a few hours? What is his power over himself and over the others? Among this crowd of fighting men who have fought all day, there is often not a single man, not even the general, who knows where is the victor.

Both Stendhal and Tolstoy had more first-hand knowledge of warfare than de Maistre—Stendhal at Borodino, Moscow and Bautzen, Tolstoy in the Caucasus and in the Crimea—each could depict it unforgettably in detail and depth in fiction, but the stage directions in a nutshell for their battle-scenes are contained completely in the graphic passage just quoted from the *Soirées de Saint-Petersbourg.*

If, as we have seen, de Maistre believed that wars occur and are won or lost as a result of the decrees of divine Providence, this belief has obvious implications for the significance of what men see fit to refer to as State sovereignty. If history is shaped by Providence, what is the real nature of the power of those earthly sovereigns who, men at any rate imagine, command the obedience of their subjects? On the field of battle, as we saw, de Maistre asserts that he knows of no instance of men disobeying their sovereign commanders by refusing to bear arms and to kill. At the same time, however, he acknowledges that the outcome of a battle has little or nothing to do with the will of the commander. How about the decision to embark upon war in the first place, since this is an even more significant event historically speaking for humanity at large than is the issue of victory or defeat for any particular side? However devoutly we may believe A rather than B to be on the side of the angels, the fact of their warring against one another is of much greater significance for humanity, since whoever wins, the battle for peace has certainly been lost. Here again de Maistre is consistent. Whether we are destined to have war or peace is determined not by sovereign rulers but by Providence, an invisible hand remorselessly shaping the destiny of whole nations. The power which a Napoleon or Alexander wields in reality is illusory—although de Maistre is of course not so lost to all sense of political discretion as to cite examples so near to hand. De Maistre was after all a professional diplomat; the subject is one of some delicacy: he strikes a light, almost jocular note in introducing it, by recalling the popular joke about a nation which enjoyed an academy of sciences, an astronomer royal and Observatory, and at the same time a false calendar. The implication is made explicit. There are occasions when the most powerful of sovereigns is impotent against the forces of conservatism and prejudice. Even a Peter the Great had to bring his whole invincible might to bear in order to cut off men's beards and shorten their suits. 'Sovereigns effectively command on a stable basis', he wrote, 'only within the circle of things admitted by opinion; and it is not they who trace this circle.'

There is a slight element of ambiguity here, since in the case of the great autocrats whom de Maistre admires, like Peter the Great, he insists that when it comes to raising and leading their legions into war, even into defeat, their unquestioned authority is matched only by the submissiveness of their subjects. When he tells us that 'God has warned us that he has reserved the formation of sovereignties to himself by never entrusting the choice of their masters to the masses' [*Considerations*], his intent is to emphasize 'the divinity that doth hedge a king', not to stress that the authority of the sovereign dissolves in the presence of firmly antagonistic opinion.

De Maistre tends to confuse two different propositions: (i) 'sovereigns' are powerless to defy firmly entrenched opinion or prejudice, and (ii) the power of sovereigns is illusory because it is directed by a superior supernatural power of divine Providence. More commonly he means the latter, especially when construing the French Revolution, the events of which he sees as a divine punishment for the sins of men, quite independently of the wills or designs of the actual 'villains' who appear to be directing events.

> The very villains, who appear to guide the Revolution take part in it only as simple instruments; and as soon as they aspire to dominate it, they fall ingloriously. Those who established the Republic did so without wishing it and without realizing what they were creating; they have been led by events: no plan has achieved its intended end. . . . It cannot be too often repeated that men do not at all guide the Revolution; it is the Revolution that uses men. [*Considerations*]

It is interesting to compare and contrast with this reactionary theological view of the Revolution the radical republican view of Michelet, who is similarly convinced that the power of the leaders is an illusory power, but who sees the limits to this power arising not from the invisible hand of Providence, but from the force of public opinion—a view towards which de Maistre is sometimes sympathetically inclined but never where the opinion in question is radical or stemming from the masses. Michelet, the historian of the French Revolution, has this to say in his Introduction to that massive work:

> Another thing which this History will clearly establish and which holds true in every connection is that the people were usually more important than the leaders. The deeper I have excavated, the more surely I have satisfied myself that the best was underneath, in the obscure depths. And I have realized that it is quite wrong to take these brilliant and powerful talkers who expressed the thought of the masses, for the sole actors in the drama. They were given the impulse by others much more than they gave it themselves. The principal actor is the people. To find the people again and put it back in its proper role, I have been obliged to reduce to their proportions the ambitious marionettes whose strings it manipulated and in whom hitherto we have looked for and thought to see the secret play of history. [*La Révolution Française*, 1847]

Tolstoy certainly read and admired Michelet, although I know of no evidence that he knew this particular work; but the above passage expresses powerfully and unambiguously the spirit which animated the author of *War and Peace* in the creation and direction of the novel. In Michelet as in Tolstoy the emphasis falls on the 'marionette' status of the ostensible leaders as contrasted with the substantive role exercised by the ordinary people. In de Maistre, on the other hand, the emphasis is on the passive and submissive role of the people to their sovereign ruler, himself subject to the will of Providence but not to the will of the people. The mass of men in de Maistre's universe play no part in political events, and this is as it should be. The people know only two words: submission and belief. Let there be no talk of scrutiny, choice, discussion. The people get the government they deserve. 'In politics, we *know* that it is necessary to respect those powers established we know not how or by whom' [***Study on Sovereignty***].

In so far as the people may be said to participate directly in the historical process at all, we must have recourse to such metaphors as 'wood and rope used by a workman' to give a real idea of the subordinate, not to say passive nature of their contribution, according to de Maistre. But the power of the leaders themselves only appears to be such to the inexperienced eye. In reality, the tyrant is usually himself subject to the will of a still more powerful tyrant, and if we approach close to the tyrant who is lord over all and would learn the secret of his Sphinx-like soul, we would find that he is as ignorant as the rest of us as to the source of his mysterious power. He simply does not know how it came to descend upon him. For 'circumstances he was unable either to foresee or bring about have done everything for him and without him' [***Considerations***].

To conclude this summary of de Maistre's contribution, it can be said that for all his obscurantist theology and acceptance of things and conditions that are morally indefensible, he brought a new and vividly incisive element of realism into the discussion of the nature of power in the context of modern warfare. If the reasoning is often confused, if he lapses into rhetoric, if his conclusions are sometimes pernicious, he nevertheless throws light into dark places, even when he least intended it. De Maistre has only contempt for the projects of eternal peace which emanated from the most humane of the figures of the eighteenth-century Enlightenment, the Abbé de St. Pierre, Rousseau, Condorcet, Kant. These men sincerely struggled to promote and strengthen the prospects for peace among men. De Maistre certainly did not. If in one passage he says that we must still thunder against war, it is only to denounce in the next sentence the naïveté of the would-be abolitionists. For all that, de Maistre is more helpful to a realistic abolitionist of today than the precursors of League of Nations projects for the simple reason that he is not deceived by the illusion that sovereign nations in command of big battalions will ever voluntarily yield their sovereignty to any international tribunal not capable of enforcing its will. Free from this illusion, notwithstanding his ultimate contempt for humanity, he has much to say that is highly relevant to the student of power, with all its dire consequences for those who strive to preserve or rather to discover and create the conditions necessary for peace. (pp. 8-23)

> *R. V. Sampson, "Joseph de Maistre," in his*
> The Discovery of Peace, *Pantheon Books,*
> *1973, pp. 8-23.*

Charles M. Lombard   (essay date 1977)

[*In the following excerpt, Lombard discusses de Maistre's position on the Spanish Inquisition.*]

The ***Letters on the Spanish Inquisition*** were composed by Count Joseph de Maistre during the summer of 1815 in Russia and published posthumously in 1822 at Paris by Mequignon. The subject lent itself readily to the energetic and contentious pen of the Count. Spain was a prime example of a traditionally strong Catholic country and the Inquisition was an institution attacked by Protestants and freethinkers alike as an atrocious period in the history of intolerance in Europe. Not one to balk at a difficult task Maistre plunged into the topic with characteristic gusto and applied his absolutist and Catholic principles unsparingly. Undaunted by the prospect of fierce challenges from opponents, Maistre seemed to take delight in writing a tract that would precipitate a heated debate. Ultimately the ***Letters*** formed part of his overall defense of legitimate authority exercised by altar and throne. To Maistre Spain was a paragon of this principle put to practice.

As he often does, the Count adopts the epistolary form to allow himself a more intimate tone in addressing the reader who is presumably a willing disciple in complete accord with Maidstrean principles. It would be a mistake however to dismiss the ***Letters*** as just another inconsequential piece of propaganda. Maistre was anathema to liberal spokemen but they did not take him lightly. Religious and political conservatives throughout the nineteenth century regarded him as their champion. For that reason the opposition, like it or not, had to deal with him seriously. Inwardly many of them undoubtedly derived considerable pleasure from the Count's stylistic verve even though outwardly vexed by the belligerent presentation of his ideas.

In approaching his subject Maistre assumes a tone of complete confidence. To him the Inquisition was a great institution and the sole objective in his mind is merely to prove the extent of its fame and grandeur. In Maistre's estimation, no greater tribute could have been paid to the Inquisition than its abolition in 1812 by the Cortes whose members were impregnated with the philosophy of the Enlightenment. Another proof, in Maistre's mind, of its efficacy was Protestant criticism of the Inquisition, in particular the verbal barbs directed against St. Dominic. The Count insists that the founder of the Dominican order never took an active role as an inquisitor. Maistre follows a similar line of reasoning throughout the ***Letters*** in slanting historical facts to play down the Church's part in the Inquisition. His general attitude is that Protestants were especially ungrateful in rejecting a Church that in their hearts they knew to be the sole repository of Christian truth.

Any moves made by the Inquisition are vindicated by Maistre without compunction. By nature, "good, mild, and preservative," it carried out its charge to protect the faithful from the inroads of heresy. If Judaism came under the inquisitor's purview in fifteenth-century Spain the subsequent developments under the circumstances were entirely understandable. Through their wealth and power Spanish Jews were a menace to the "national plant." Conformity to the general will is Maistre's position here, an odd stance for a writer so violently opposed to Rousseau's *Social Contract*. Since both Jews and Muslims threatened the fiber of the Spanish nation, the kings of Spain had no recourse but to establish the Inquisition to protect the nation from the threat within. A firm believer in the divine right of kings, Maistre seldom questioned the justice of a royal decision any more than he would entertain serious doubts about the judgment of high ecclesiastical authorities. In the view Maistre takes of the situation in Spain he judges Jews and Muslims to be security risks to the state and defends what seems the bigotry and intolerance of Spanish inquisitors as in reality patriotic concern and devotion to religion. The Count further denies that the tribunal of the Inquisition consisted solely of clerics who sentenced persons to death and that people were declared guilty for expressing opinions contrary to the established civil and religious order.

Torquemada is pictured by Maistre as a conscientious prelate acting in concert with the king to assure the smooth functioning of the Inquisition. Voltaire who dares to assail this honorable institution is, to Maistre's way of thinking, a pernicious infidel who, were he born in Spain, would be instantly silenced. With obvious relish the Count suggests that Europe would have fared far better in the eighteenth century if the Church had had inquisitors in various countries with the power to curtail the dissemination of anti-Catholic notions and scurrilous attacks on Rome. No member of the Enlightenment could plead ignorance of the enormity of his crimes when it was common knowledge that Catholicism alone possessed the religious truths essential to man's salvation. As for the notion that deism and other non-Catholic beliefs rendered one guilty in the inquisitor's eyes, Maistre summarily dismissed all such charges as a pack of lies. To ward off any accusation of anti-Semitism the Count points proudly to the privileges enjoyed by Jews in Rome under the Pope's kindly rule. If the Church can be a force for tolerance and justice in Rome, a fact admitted on occasion even by Voltaire (according to Maistre's interpretation), there is little cause to conclude that a kind and just authority would almost capriciously and inexplicably countenance injustice in Spain, the Count triumphantly concludes.

In the matter of the periods when the Inquisition was most severely criticized for its cruelty Maistre inquires in amazement why such false notions prevail. The tribunal confined itself to the confiscation of property and even that sentence could be reversed if the "criminal" acknowledged the error of his ways. Should the accused be found guilty of heresy he was handed over to the state by the ecclesiastical Court. What process, Maistre asks, could be more direct and impartial? The Dominican presence in the Inquisition is viewed by the Count as a privilege bestowed on the order by Rome. Moreover, the friars on the tribunal were in the minority so they could hardly be accused of determining the outcome of any deliberations by the inquisitors.

Maistre goes to great lengths to defend the integrity of Spanish justice. On the basis of the evidence at his disposal he finds it inconceivable that any court in Spain, civil or clerical, would coldly sentence innocent parties to death. According to Spanish law, if such an abomination did transpire, the judges themselves would be liable to prosecution. Horrendous tales of hopeless victims of the Inquisition being hauled off to prison in the dead of night were unspeakable calumnies against a great nation. Always persuaded that an absolute monarchy invariably guaranteed

equity and justice, Maistre is at a loss to explain the unfounded charges of Protestant and rationalist critics.

Turning to the Enlightenment Maistre chuckles in amusement at Montesquieu's outburst in the *Spirit of the Laws* about the case of a Jewish girl burnt at the stake by the Spanish Inquisition. Scornfully the Count denies the possibility of such outrages taking place in a Catholic country and, above all, in Spain. No responsible representatives of Catholicism would burn an innocent girl simply because she was Jewish. In the final analysis it is unthinkable to Maistre that foreign critics would presume to sit in judgment on Spanish institutions. His Catholic Majesty of Spain knows best the needs of his country. A concept of a transcendent international law here has little meaning in the Count's thinking.

Severe punishment for religious and civil offenses was after all common to European countries from the Middle Ages up to modern times. Why single out Spain for criticism, argues Maistre, when Protestant countries exceeded the Spanish courts in the severity and harshness of their penalties? Only recently was the rack abolished in England and elsewhere. In general, sacrilege and treason were punished by fire. Unlike many Protestant tribunals Spanish inquisitors were willing to release a prisoner once he repented. "Dissuasive" measures affected the common good by protecting the status quo and assuring law and order. The Golden Age of Spanish literature flourished when the Inquisition was in full swing, thus giving the lie to those that accused it of having a deleterious effect on artistic and intellectual life.

Maistre particularly enjoys roasting English critics of Spain for their ignorance of the country and its customs. By no means an anglophobe the Count was fond of British traditions and had nothing but praise for Shakespeare and Milton. Although an anglophile in several respects Maistre could not abide unrestrained English denunciations of Spain. To him it was the height of arrogance. In refutation of skeptical English critics Maistre cites a case where, thanks to the alertness of an honest judge, two clerics were dismissed by the court when their innocence was brought to light.

Protestant writers in general never cease, Maistre notes, to excoriate the Church, especially Spain, for repression and persecution of opposing religious beliefs. Yet far greater abuses took place in England and Germany, St. Bartholomew's Day notwithstanding. English Quakers and German Mennonites had a different view of the respective blessings of Anglicanism and Lutheranism. Queen Elizabeth and Luther perpetrated many of the atrocities of which the Inquisition was falsely accused. With all due respect for the integrity and salutary features of British law and government Maistre perceives glaring inconsistencies in the English constitution. On one hand religion is treated indifferently under the theory all honest beliefs are of equal value; yet on the other hand England does not hesitate to assail Spain for intolerance. By comparison Spanish Catholicism represents a position more intellectually respectable than that of English Protestantism. To the Spanish mind there is logically only one source of theological truth, the Catholic Church founded by Jesus Christ.

For all its preaching on the virtues of tolerance England forgot its altruistic principles in suppressing the Catholic Church in Ireland. The cruelty of Henry VIII and Elizabeth was a matter of record. Spain was never guilty of such ruthlessness. In fact ridiculous in the extreme was the ambiguous position of Anglicans who claimed to be both Catholic and Protestant. But then Maistre was accustomed to such self-contradictory statements, examples of which were abundant among English leaders of the Enlightenment. With a careless disregard of logic they endeavored to be deistic and Christian in the same breath. England lacked the benefit of the Inquisition which proved "a terrific and an impenetrable barrier" to the spread of heresy in Spain. Its absence in France and Germany clearly aided the dissemination of untruth. In England, the leading Protestant nation, the encouragement of heretical groups led to the eventual rise of anti-Christian ideas. Hume was a worse threat to faith and morals than Voltaire. The Sixth Letter closes on this note as Maistre delivers a forthright denunciation of the foes of legitimate religion and political authority.

Maistre's one-sided approach to a complex historical question must be understood in view of the intellectual climate in which he was reared. Driven from his home in Sardinia by the tatterdemalion regiments of revolutionary France he came to associate all opponents with the forces of irreligion and Jacobinism. His tirades against critics of the Spanish Inquisition were essentially a rebuttal of all adversaries who dared to question his position. Since Maistre was personally a kind-hearted man with many Protestant friends on a social level there is reason to believe he did not have all the facts concerning the Inquisition at his disposal. Today there are Catholic authorities who concede the Spanish Inquisition was a dark chapter in Church history. Even a conservative estimate of the number of persons who died under Torquemada's administration, places the number of victims during his reign at 2,000. Pope Alexander VI was sufficiently alarmed by Torquemada's tactics to appoint four inquisitors for the sole purpose of restraining his activities. Jewish and Protestant authorities concede that some officials within the Church had from time to time the courage to oppose openly the Inquisition. If Maistre were to rewrite the *Letters* on the basis of current knowledge and research, he would be compelled, despite innate reactionary tendencies, to reassess substantially his position. Under any circumstances, however, Maistre would never have changed the fiery and lucid style so much a part of the creative and artistic side of his temperament.

On firmer ground when defending Spain from the unqualified criticism of English writers unwilling to admit the Spanish capable of any intellectual achievements, Maistre did provide a unique contribution to European thought. Very few writers of the time outside Spain, Catholic or Protestant, gave the Iberian spirit credit for any measure of accomplishment. If nothing else Maistre sternly challenged this benighted attitude by treating Spanish civilization in terms of moral integrity, artistic traditions, and in-

tellectual institutions. By consistently taking an unpopular position Maistre not infrequently championed the cause of the underdog and effectively counteracted injustice. (pp. v-xi)

> *Charles M. Lombard, in an introduction to*
> Letters on the Spanish Inquisition *by Count*
> *Joseph de Maistre, Scholars' Facsimiles & Reprints, 1977, pp. v-xii.*

FURTHER READING

Berlin, Isaiah. "V." In his *The Hedgehog and the Fox: An Essay on Tolstoy's View of History*, pp. 75-95. New York: The New American Library of World Literature, Inc., 1957.
    Notes the parallels between Tolstoy's *War and Peace* and many of de Maistre's doctrines.

———. "Joseph de Maistre and the Origins of Fascism." *The New York Review of Books* XXXVII, Nos. 14-16 (27 September; 11 October; 25 October 1990): 57-64, 54-8, 61-5.
    A series of three essays exploring de Maistre's ideology as a possible forerunner to modern fascist philosophy.

Boas, George. "Philosophies of History." In his *Dominant Themes of Modern Philosophy: A History*, pp. 577-91. New York: The Ronald Press Co., 1957.
    Compares de Maistre's Catholic philosophy of history with that of Vicomte de Bonald.

Review of *Essay on the Generative Principle of Political Constitutions*, by Joseph de Maistre. *Brownson's Quarterly Review* n.s. I, No. IV (July 1847): 458-85.
    Discusses de Maistre's thought on political constitutions.

Cecil, Algernon. "Joseph de Maistre: I and II." *The Dublin Review* 203, Nos. 407, 408 (October 1938; January 1939) 286-301, 20-31.
    Examines de Maistre's later life and principal works.

Edwards, David W. "Count Joseph Marie de Maistre and Russian Educational Policy, 1803-1828." *Slavic Review* 36, No. 1 (March 1977): 54-75.
    Attempts to interpret early nineteenth-century Russian educational policy trends by studying de Maistre's works on the subject.

Ewing, Cortez. "De Maistre and Marx in the Modern World." *The Southwestern Social Science Quarterly* XXIX, No. 1 (June 1948): 1-14.
    Assesses the similarities between the authoritarian and anti-democratic doctrines of de Maistre and Marx.

Gans, Eric. "Maistre and Chateaubriand: Counter-Revolution and Anthropology." *Studies in Romanticism* 28, No. 4 (Winter 1989): 559-75.
    Contends that de Maistre's theories of social order and conflict resulted from his contempt for the French Revolution.

Gay, Peter. "Order Was His Goal." *The New York Times Book Review* (14 March 1965): 14-20.

Mixed review of an edition of de Maistre's works, offering generally unfavorable commentary on his anti-revolutionary theories.

Gianturco, Elio. "Juridical Culture and Politico-Historical Judgement in Joseph de Maistre." *The Romanic Review* XXVII, Nos. 3, 4 (July-December 1936): 254-62.
Identifies de Maistre's juridicial knowledge as a major influence on his works.

Jamieson, T. John. "Conservatism's Metaphysical Vision: Barbey d'Aurevilly on Joseph de Maistre." *Modern Age* 29, No. 1 (Winter 1985): 28-37.
Appraises de Maistre's influence on nineteenth-century metaphysical and theological thought, particularly focusing on the theories of Charles Baudelaire and Barbey d'Aurevilly.

LeBrun, Richard Allen. *Throne and Altar: The Political and Religious Thought of Joseph de Maistre.* Ottawa: University of Ottawa Press, 1965, 170 p.
Examines what LeBrun describes as the paradoxical relationship between de Maistre's political and religious thought.

Lichtheim, George. "Rousseau and de Maistre." *New Statesman* 72, No. 1853 (16 September 1966): 398-99.
Comparative study of the political thought of Jean-Jacques Rousseau and de Maistre.

Lombard, Charles M. Introduction to *Essay on the Generative Principle of Political Constitutions,* by Joseph de Maistre, pp. v-xiii. 1847. Reprint. Delmar, N.Y.: Scholars' Facsimiles & Reprints, Inc., 1977.
Analyzes the thematic and stylistic elements of de Maistre's *Essay on the Generative Principle of Political Constitutions* and describes the work as "a handy compendium of Maistre's fundamental notions in the field of philosophy and political science."

"De Maistre and Romanism." *The North American Review* LXXIX, No. CLXV (October 1854): 371-406.
Detailed examination of de Maistre's proponency of Roman Catholicism.

Watt, E. D. " 'Locked In': De Maistre's Critique of French Lockeanism." *Journal of the History of Ideas* XXXII, No. 1 (January-March 1971): 129-32.
Discusses de Maistre's critique of John Locke and eighteenth-century French Lockeanism in the *Soirées de Saint-Petersbourg.*

————. "The English Image of Joseph de Maistre: Some Unfinished Business." *European Studies Review* 4, No. 3 (July 1974): 239-59.
Contends that de Maistre's works have been generally neglected by English-language scholars.

G. W. M. Reynolds

1814-1879

(Full name George William MacArthur Reynolds) English novelist, journalist, and critic.

INTRODUCTION

The most prolific and widely read author in nineteenth-century England, Reynolds achieved unparalleled popularity with his melodramatic fiction for the British magazines of the 1840s and 1850s. A journalist and editor as well as the founder of such publications as *Reynolds's Miscellany* and *Reynolds's Weekly Newspaper,* he played an influential role in the development of the popular press, but during his lifetime he was best known for his sensational tales of crime, horror, and passion that appealed to England's increasingly literate working class. While Reynolds's readership surpassed even that of his contemporary Charles Dickens, literary critics, including Dickens himself, dismissed Reynolds's works along with the other so-called "penny bloods" or "penny dreadfuls" of the day. Nonetheless, Reynolds's florid prose style, his radical political slant, and his comparatively complex characterization transcended the typical cheap serial fiction of the era to provide not only a detailed portrait of urban life but a critique of the capitalist system. Social commentary remained secondary to entertainment in Reynolds's fiction, and his novels, with their shocking subject matter and crude opposition of vice and virtue, have been recognized as an important barometer of audience tastes in the Victorian Age.

Reynolds was born in 1814 at Sandwich, Kent. The son of a distinguished captain in the Royal Navy, he entered the Royal Military Academy at Sandhurst in 1828 with the intention of pursuing a naval career. However, two years later the sixteen-year-old Reynolds inherited a considerable fortune from his parents and promptly left Sandhurst for Paris. There, Reynolds associated himself with radical political groups and immersed himself in French literature. Biographers surmise that he became a French citizen for a time, since he served in the National Guard for two years before taking a position with the Librarie des Étrangers in Paris. During this period he married Susanna Frances Pearson and began his literary career, working as an editor for the *Paris Literary Gazette* while completing his first novel, *The Youthful Imposter,* which was published in 1835. Subsequently, his involvement with several English-language newspapers resulted in financial ruin, and by 1836 Reynolds had lost the bulk of his fortune.

Bankrupt, he returned to London, where he continued to pursue his journalistic and literary endeavors. In 1837 he became the editor of *Monthly Magazine,* which published the first of his novels to achieve popular success, *Pickwick Abroad; or, The Tour in France,* an unauthorized continu-

ation of Dickens's *Pickwick Papers* (1837). He also translated the works of several French authors and completed a series of critical articles on contemporary French fiction; these were collected and published in 1839 as *Modern Literature of France.* After leaving the *Monthly,* Reynolds edited the *Teetotaler* and the *Weekly Dispatch* before becoming the first editor of the *London Journal* in 1845. Conceived as an inexpensive weekly mass publication, the *London Journal* was designed to take advantage of technological advances in printing to meet the literary demands of the burgeoning working class. The publishers hoped to appeal to this new market with an assortment of adventure fiction, short stories, and educational pieces. Reynolds was instrumental in determining this format, and his own contributions soon became the publication's most celebrated features. The year 1845 marked the first installment of *The Mysteries of London,* Reynolds's long-running serial based on Eugène Sue's *Les Mysteres des Paris. The Mysteries of London* was perhaps the most popular work of its day; as Reynolds's tales of urban intrigue reached their climax, sales of the *Journal* routinely surpassed three hundred thousand copies per week. After a dispute with the publisher in 1846, however, Reynolds left the *Journal* to found his own competing weekly, *Rey-*

nolds's Miscellany. While running the *Miscellany,* he continued to fulfill his contract to his former employer by providing installments of *The Mysteries of London* to the *Journal* for the next two years, at which point the series was taken over by another writer.

Reynolds declared bankruptcy a second time in 1848, but he managed to keep his *Miscellany* afloat, and continued to edit it until 1869. The *Miscellany* followed the same basic formula as the *London Journal,* relying primarily on Reynolds's sensationalistic fiction—with the most shocking scenes usually illustrated on the cover—to attract readers. Typical works written for the *Miscellany* include *Wagner the Wehr-Wolf,* a Gothic horror tale which ran in 1846 and 1847, and, after his commitment to the *Journal* was complete, *The Mysteries of the Court of London,* his retitled urban serial format which ran from 1848 to 1856. The *Miscellany*'s primary difference from the *Journal* lay in its increased emphasis on Reynolds's radical political articles and replies to readers' inquiries in which he stressed his republican views and voiced his outrage at the oppression of the poor. His active participation in politics began in 1848, when he presided over an outlawed meeting of the Chartists, a working-class movement for political reform; he remained active in the movement for the next four years. Reynolds found another outlet for his anti-aristocratic, anti-clerical message by establishing *Reynolds's Political Instructor* in 1849. He converted this into *Reynolds's Weekly Newspaper* a year later, and it quickly became England's leading working-class radical publication. Although his output of fiction decreased markedly after 1860, he remained active as an editor until his death in 1879, and his *Weekly Newspaper* continued to be published until 1967.

Reynolds's vast literary output has been estimated at fifty-eight novels, but numerous piracies, false attributions, and reissues leave the exact number open to debate. This achievement, critics point out, is even more remarkable when Reynolds's full-time career as a journalist is taken into account, as well as the size of his works; *The Mysteries of the Court of London* alone—comprised of eight volumes and estimated at four million words—is the equivalent of some fifty modern novels. The tremendous increase in literacy among the poor and lower-middle-class British brought a demand for both political information and escapist fantasy, and Reynolds provided the ideal formula with his inexpensive periodicals. The two popular *Mysteries* series typify his approach to fiction, in which a convoluted and improbable plot and a plethora of characters provide a loose framework for an interrelated series of shocking scenes. Some critics claim that Reynolds's melodramatic stories are simply a steady stream of lurid and horrifying depictions of torture, oppression, crime, and illicit passion. Others, however, assert that Reynolds's assured, robust style and his moralizing tone separated him from the hack writers and plagiarists that typified the genre of penny fiction. Furthermore, scholars maintain that Reynolds's unrelenting exploration of the theme of crime often mirrored contemporary events to convey the complexity and terror of urban life. It was Reynolds's moral tone—his outright sympathy with the poor and his pleas for reform—that solidified his hold on the masses,

for his novels primarily depicted the virtuous poor pitted against the corrupt rich in an implicit critique of the capitalist system. Critics observe that the very elements that made Reynolds a best-seller in his own day doomed his literary reputation. The penny serials did not generally reach the middle and upper classes, and when they did, critics dismissed them as political propaganda or worthless pornography. Many recent commentators have maintained that Reynolds simply sought to fulfill a particular need for a particular audience, and some have characterized Reynolds as a cynic interested solely in increasing the sales of his periodicals. Despite such critical arguments over his motives, it is clear that no one writer in Victorian England reached as many people as G. W. M. Reynolds, whom the *Bookseller* hailed as "the most popular writer of our time."

PRINCIPAL WORKS

The Youthful Imposter (novel) 1835; also published as *The Parricide; or, A Youth's Life of Crime,* 1847
Pickwick Abroad; or, The Tour in France (novel) 1837-38
Alfred; or, The Adventures of a French Gentleman (novel) 1839
Grace Darling; or, The Heroine of the Fern Islands: A Tale Founded on Recent Facts (novel) 1839
Modern Literature of France (criticism) 1839
Robert Macaire in England (novel) 1840
The Drunkard's Progress (novel) 1841
Master Timothy's Bookcase (novel) 1842
The Mysteries of London. 4 vols. (novel) 1845-48
Wagner, the Wehr-Wolf (novel) 1846-47
Faust: A Romance of the Secret Tribunals (novel) 1847
The Mysteries of the Court of London. 8 vols. (novel) 1848-56
The Bronze Statue; or, The Virgin's Kiss (novel) 1850
The Seamstress: A Domestic Tale (novel) 1850; also published as *The Seamstress; or, The White Slaves of England,* 1853
Mary Price; or, The Memoirs of a Servant-Maid (novel) 1851-52
The Necromancer (novel) 1851-52
The Soldier's Wife (novel) 1853
Joseph Wilmot; or, The Memoirs of a Man-Servant (novel) 1853-54
Rosa Lambert; or, The Memoirs of an Unfortunate Woman (novel) 1853-54; also published as *Rosa Lambert; or, The Memoirs of a Clergyman's Daughter,* 1862
The Rye House Plot; or, Ruth the Conspirator's Daughter (novel) 1853-54
Agnes; or, Beauty and Pleasure (novel) 1854-55
Ellen Percy; or, The Memoirs of an Actress (novel) 1854-55
The Loves of the Harem: A Tale of Constantinople (novel) 1855
Margaret; or, The Discarded Queen (novel) 1856-57
Canonbury House; or, The Queen's Prophecy (novel) 1857-58
The Empress Eugenie's Boudoir (novel) 1858-59

J. V. B. Stewart Hunter　(essay date 1947)

[*In the following excerpt, Hunter offers an overview of Reynolds's life and career, describing his publishing methods and surveying the critical response to his novels.*]

The sixth of March, 1848. The illegal meeting in Trafalgar Square had broken up. Sweeping aside the few top-hatted Victorian policemen, the crowd was pouring along the Strand, carrying triumphantly shoulder high to his house in Wellington Street, the youngish man with the bushy side-whiskers and steel-rimmed spectacles whom they had acclaimed as a new leader of Chartism—the gospel of revolution that was sweeping the country.

It was typical of the pugnacious courage that George Reynolds displayed in his life and writings that, after the original promoters had discreetly "faded out" at the hint of legal action, he had been willing to become the chairman of the meeting. Not only that, but under his chairmanship the meeting had transformed the original rather innocuous resolution demanding the repeal of the Income Tax into one favouring the revolution in Paris!

A full day for most people. But when the curtains had been drawn and the lamps lit; when the last excited supporters had drifted away, the real work of the day had yet to be done. "Best-seller" Reynolds sat down to write his weekly instalment of that amazing serial which had commenced three years earlier and was to run for another nine years before its author could write in his Postscript: "For twelve years, therefore, I have hebdomadally issued to the world a fragmentary portion of that which, as one vast whole, may be termed an Encyclopedia of Tales. This Encyclopedia consists of twelve volumes, comprising six hundred and twenty-four weekly numbers." The stirring events of the day faded and Reynolds was lost in the struggles of his poor—but virtuous—heroes and heroines against the tyrannies of the rich and powerful.

Yet George William Macarthur Reynolds was no "child of the people". His father Sir George Reynolds, was a distinguished captain in the Royal Navy, who had intended his son for a military career, entering him at Sandhurst when he was fourteen years old. But two years later both his parents were dead, and, with a six-figure fortune, he had gladly left Sandhurst for a Grand Tour of the Continent.

His twenty-first birthday in 1835 found him settled in Paris, the proprietor of a bookselling and publishing business, busily engaged in issuing a daily paper in English. The Paris of that time was alive with the revolutionary spirit—"Liberty, Equality, Fraternity" was no old catchphrase, but the shining beacon of every advanced thinker throughout the world. It is not surprising that in this atmosphere Reynolds developed that sympathy for the "under dog" that was to dominate his life—and, incidentally, to build his fortune.

That it did so was only simple justice, for when Reynolds returned to London two years later there was very little of the original fortune left, and it needed all of his literary gifts and personal thrust to force his way to the front in the struggling literary London of his day. With his fluent French it was fairly easy to obtain work translating the writings of the modern French novelists, the editorship of an obscure magazine was obtained, and he also acted as political correspondent for one of the leading journals.

He had earlier written an immature novel, but his first real essay in fiction came with the publication of *Pickwick Abroad.* Charles Dickens was rapidly becoming famous, and numerous plagiarisms of his work were being written by hack writers anxious to "cash in" on his popularity.

Plagiarism and literary piracy were not then considered—except, perhaps, by the original author—such heinous sins as they are to-day, and Reynolds's apology is contained in a single sentence of preface: "Allow me to remark that if the talented 'Boz' have not chosen to enact the part of Mr. Pickwick's biographer in his continental tour, it is not my fault: the field was open to him who had so well and so successfully traced the progress of that great man during his travels in England." His publishers went even further in suggesting that, while the story was as good as the original *Pickwick,* it had the added advantage that it could be used as a guide-book to Paris!

Dickens lovers will question that opinion, and perhaps the quality of Reynolds's humour can be assessed from his genuine astonishment that Dickens should resent this "continuation" of the immortal *Pickwick,* although shortly after, he himself was to denounce American pirates of his work as "unprincipled scoundrels . . . infinitely worse than mere pirates, they are downright rogues, imposters, and forgers."

Nevertheless, *Pickwick Abroad* was a distinct success, and its weekly penny numbers were purchased avidly by readers to whom the "three-decker" novels of the day were unattainable, and even the shilling parts of the Dickens novels far too dear.

Its success dictated to Reynolds both his clientele and his publishing methods. He would appeal to that great mass of the working people, who were just emerging from illiteracy and clamouring for mental fodder—and finding so much that was specially prepared for them dull and stodgy, designed entirely to "elevate and instruct". He also would elevate and instruct, but the dish he would set before his clients would be highly seasoned with melodrama, and spiced with scandal. He would publish, too, in weekly penny numbers so that even the poorest could buy. Under this system the first two numbers were issued in an illustrated paper wraper, subsequent numbers consisting simply of an eight-page double-column instalment of the story, each number embellished with an exciting wood-cut illustration. The numbers appeared every week until the story ended, and the purchaser could then, if he wished, have the parts bound up to make the complete novel.

Meantime, Reynolds had become editor of the *London Journal,* and it was under its auspices that Reynolds commenced his massive work. Under its original title of *The Mysteries of London,* and later—when he broke away from the *London Journal*—as *Mysteries of the Court of*

London, it was to run for twelve years, the complete work amounting to the terrific total of nearly four and a half million words—the equivalent of fifty full-length modern novels!

A rather disgruntled contemporary critic gives an idea of the contents: ". . . as we turn over the pages," he says,

> looking at the drawings, we very quickly discover into what sort of scenes we are likely to be conducted. Here we see men dogging each other on dark nights, lurking behind trees and looking round corners; gipsies in woods are entering into mysterious compacts with gentlemen disguised in huge cloaks; burglars with dark lanterns are prowling in houses; assassins are aiming blows at the backs of unconscious victims; murderers steal into the chambers of sick men; women wake up startled in their beds and listen; ladies listen at doors; young girls are seen flying on the tops of houses from highly-impassioned pursuers; ladies elope with lovers in the dead of night; post-chaises are driven at the gallop in thunder, lightning, and rain over lonely moors; women are stabbing women and offering to shoot men; men hurl each other down trap doors; dead men are carried to the doctor; ladies are oppressed with awful secrets, and faint before the altar at the sight of gentlemen; houses are on fire; duels are a standing institution; mask balls are the order of the day and night; ladies are carried away by force; horses are ever in readiness; there is much drinking, eternal embraces, and ever and everywhere we see hair flying wild and dishevelled in the wind.

True, yet Reynolds's novels really have a closely-knit, complicated plot, and he is very adroit in the administering of the powder of instruction in the jam of the story. Does the movement of his story demand a coal-mine—there is a carefully documented account of the condition of the miners; the conspirators meet in a churchyard—and there is a spirited description of the terrible condition of the London burying grounds of the day; a pot-boy sneaks into Buckingham Palace—and, lying concealed, listens to a long conversation on working-class conditions between Queen Victoria and the Prince Consort!

The writing of this work would be sufficient for most men, but at the same time Reynolds was writing new romances for *Reynolds's Miscellany,* the magazine he had commenced on leaving the *London Journal;* he was revising and issuing his *French Self-Instructor,* assisting in compiling a volume of *Practical Receipts,* had commenced a new journal, *Reynolds's Political Instructor,* and was deeply engaged in the party councils of the Chartists.

It was too much, and soon we find a notice in his journals addressed to "My late Constituents of Derby", in which he declines the honour of representing them in the National Assembly, because "the fact is that my literary avocations occupy nearly the whole of my time; and as my works are all weekly serials, any interruption to the issue of which on the appointed days would prove ruinous to them and most detrimental to my reputation as an author, I felt that if I sate in the National Assembly I must either

neglect the interests of my constituents or the pursuits whereby I obtain a livelihood for myself and family."

This however, was only a partial explanation of his withdrawal from active political work. He was impatient of slow progress, always advocating the extreme measure, and galled by the restrictions and manœuvring of party politics. Gradually he withdrew from the Chartist movement, and finally severed his connection with it in 1856. But with the founding of *Reynolds's Weekly News,* a "journal of democratic progress" which maintains its working-class viewpoint up to the present day, and indeed, throughout his life, he redeemed his promise "with my pen I shall continue to labour arduously and enthusiastically in the good cause."

Meanwhile, romance after romance poured from his pen until his position as the "best-seller" of his day was unchallenged. Historical stories such as *The Rye House Plot* alternated with stories of the "industrious classes" of his own time—*The Seamstress, or The White Slaves of England* with *Faust*; *Mary Price, The Memoirs of a Servant Maid,* with *The Necromancer,* and over thirty others.

Needless to say, in those hard-hitting literary days, such success did not pass uncriticized, and all his life this criticism was to pursue him. Even so late as 1876—three years before his death—a critic could write:

> It is now nearly a quarter of a century since the *Mysteries of the Court* and similar works from the same talented pen appeared to poison the minds of boys and girls; and at the present writing I have before me a "penny number" by the author of the *Mysteries of the Court,* and I am bound to state that a cursory glance though it convinces me that it lacks none of the ancient fire—and brimstone.

But if G. W. M. R. had to "take it" he was capable of "giving it" as well! His wife, Susannah Frances, was also an author, and the *Daily News* foolhardily ventured a criticism. Reynolds's reply flayed the unfortunate proprietors of the *Daily News* and all their publications:

> . . . there is Charles Dickens's *Dombey and Son,* a clever work whose only defect is that it will not sell well . . . Mr. Thackeray's *Vanity Fair,* a publication of extraordinary talent and great originality, but each number of which falls almost still-born from the press . . . *Punch,* which is going down as rapidly as possible . . . the *Daily News,* which is notoriously an awful abortion.

For the last twenty years of his life Reynolds was little seen in public. His long series of romances came to an end, and he devoted his energies to his political newspaper. He died, a wealthy man, in 1879 at the age of sixty-five.

To-day his works, so immensely popular in their time, are almost forgotten. It is this generation's loss, for, with their fascinating, if highly-coloured, pictures of Victorian England, they are all eminently readable, and a guinea or so spent on the 104 numbers which make up one of the six series of the *Mysteries* would ensure entertainment for many a winter evening. (pp. 225-36)

J. V. B. Stewart Hunter, "George Reynolds, Sensational Novelist and Agitator," in Book Handbook, *No. 3, 1947, pp. 225-36.*

Margaret Dalziel   (essay date 1957)

[*In the excerpt below, Dalziel contrasts Reynolds's novels with the typical popular serial fiction of his era, asserting that his florid prose style, his vivid depictions of torture and sexual passion, and his political radicalism differentiated him from his contemporaries.*]

There is . . . one writer whose works form an interesting exception to the general run of stories in the most popular penny periodicals of the eighteen-forties and fifties. . . . G. W. M. Reynolds [was] the first editor of the *London Journal.* Reynolds had an interesting life. As a young man he travelled widely on the Continent, where he gained some knowledge of French life and literature, and became an admirer both of the novels of Eugene Sue and of the principles of the revolution of 1789. Between 1848 and 1851 he took a leading part in Chartist agitation, but most of his life was devoted to journalism of one kind or another. He left the *London Journal* to found his own penny weekly, *Reynolds's Miscellany,* at the end of 1846. In 1850 he established a newspaper, which under the title *Reynolds' News* runs to this day. And from 1845 for many years he wrote long novels, which appeared either in penny weekly parts, or else as serials, first in the *London Journal* and later in his *Miscellany.* It is these stories, or rather those written between 1845 and about 1850, that form so strong a contrast with the stories in the other penny periodicals at the time.

Reynolds was an almost unbelievably voluminous writer. A serial, *Mysteries of the Inquisition,* appeared in the first volume of the *London Journal,* to be followed by *Faust;* during 1845 and 1846 there appeared quite independently in penny numbers his very long novel, the *Mysteries of London.* The influence of Sue is at once apparent in the titles. From 1846 his *Miscellany* printed an instalment of one of his serials every week. His *Mysteries of the Court of London* was another huge novel, or rather series of novels, issued between 1849 and 1856. Other works by him continued to appear, but these are the most important and interesting.

All of his stories were long, and all of them were popular. Mayhew tells us that the street-folk regarded Reynolds as 'a trump'; Thackeray, in his lecture 'Comedy and Humour', first delivered in 1852, describes an interview with a bookseller at the Brighton station who attributed Reynolds's unique popularity to the fact that the *Mysteries of the Court of London* lashed the aristocracy. The *Bookseller* in 1868 stated that Reynolds had written more and sold in far greater numbers than Dickens, and in an obituary notice after his death in 1879 the same journal described him as 'the most popular writer of our time'. The notice also describes him as a 'notorious writer'.

Unlike Lloyd, who employed other writers to fill the pages of his publications, and who abandoned penny dreadfuls as soon as his newspaper began to pay, Reynolds kept up his penny weekly and wrote for it during many years. It continued till 1869. As a general rule, writers who make a real success of bad fiction do so because they both enjoy and, in some sense, believe in it. And this was probably the case with Reynolds. What makes his penny stories so interesting to the modern student of popular literature is the detail and gusto with which the early ones describe pain, torture and sexual passion. This kind of writing is a perennial problem to those concerned with public taste and morals, and the control of popular literature today is chiefly designed to eliminate what borders on sadism and pornography. Alone of those who were writing or publishing cheap periodicals in the mid-nineteenth century Reynolds deliberately exploited the market for such literature.

When it is added that some of these earlier stories also reflect his radicalism, the contrast between Reynolds and contemporary writers of cheap fiction is complete.

An excellent example of his work is a serial called *Wagner: the Wehr-Wolf,* which appeared in the first volume of his *Miscellany.* At first sight it might appear merely another tale of love, intrigue and violence, both natural and supernatural, set in sixteenth-century Italy. But, though readers of *The Monk* will be aware of the literary sources of much in the story, it was something very new in penny fiction.

The plot is fundamentally the story of the lovely Nisida, daughter of a noble Italian family, and her love for Wagner, who is compelled in return for the gift of youth to become on one day of every month a dangerous wolf and to roam the country doing harm. Nisida is jealous by disposition, and commits several crimes in order to be certain of her lover. Episodes include a description of a convent where influential people send young females to be disciplined, sea voyages, wrecks, life on a desert island, scenes in the life of an apostate Christian in the service of the Sultan, and the activities of the Inquisition. The story ends with the transformation of Wagner back to his proper form as a very old man, and his immediate death, followed by that of Nisida.

The first distinction which we notice between this work and the usual run of things in cheap periodicals is the skill with which it is written. Reynolds has a fluent, luscious, polysyllabic style which never fails him. Not only is he never ungrammatical, but he is almost never awkward or clumsy.

Secondly, the strain of the sensuous of which the *Bookseller* complained in Reynolds's obituary is indescribably startling. There is a general tendency in this cheap fiction, as in most popular fiction, to describe feminine beauty in considerable detail. But this is a typical description, taken from the *Family Herald* of 1850:

> Alice was one of those tall, aristocratic-looking creatures, who notwithstanding a certain slimness, realise, perhaps, the highest ideal of female beauty. Her figure was of the lordly Norman type, and perfect in its proportions; while every movement was graceful, yet dignified. Her face was of that almost divine beauty we see in the Beatrice Cenci of Guido. The same dazzling complexion, the same blue eyes, the same golden hair. . . . Her countenance, always lovely, was

now transcendently beautiful, for it glowed with enthusiasm.

The usual run of penny weeklies is thick with these beauties, and the last sentence is very important. Intellectual and spiritual qualities were paramount in determining physical beauty.

Now consider this description of Nisida:

> She was attired in deep black; her luxuriant raven hair, no longer depending in shining curls, was gathered up in massy bands at the sides, and in a knot behind, whence hung a rich veil *that meandered over her body's splendidly symmetrical length of limb in such a manner as to aid her attire in shaping rather than hiding the contours of that matchless form.* The voluptuous development of her bust was shrouded, not concealed, by the stomacher of black velvet which she wore, and which set off in strong relief the dazzling whiteness of her neck.

When Nisida goes to visit Wagner, who is immured in a dungeon on suspicion of a murder she has herself committed, she disguises herself as a man. This literary device is little used in fiction at this period, but Reynolds avails himself of it often. Nisida's appearance in male attire is fully described:

> Though tall, majestic, and of rich proportions for a woman, yet in the attire of the opposite sex she seemed slight, short, and eminently graceful. The velvet cloak sate so jauntily on her sloping shoulder;—the doublet became her symmetry so well;—and the rich lace-collar was so arranged as to disguise the prominence of the chest—that voluptuous fullness which could not be compressed!

Still later, Nisida is carried away by banditti and then wrecked on a Mediterranean isle. This is a great opportunity for the exercise of Reynolds's peculiar talents. The island is exquisitely beautiful, and productive of every tropical fruit and flower. Nisida roams about it, half-clad and wreathed in flowers, or swims, allowing 'the little wavelets to kiss her snowy bosoms'.

But there is more than the element of the voluptuous (to use a favourite word of Reynolds's) to astonish the reader. By a curious chance, Wagner the Wehr-Wolf is wrecked on the same island as Nisida, and the two become lovers. Illicit love is by no means unusual in nineteenth-century literature, but its treatment by Reynolds is at this date unique. His lovers, the women as well as the men, *enjoy* themselves. They may not escape punishment (though often they do) but neither do they drag out a miserable existence, tormented by the reproaches of conscience and each other, ostracized by society, cut off from family and friends, and at length, the females at any rate, sinking into an early grave, a prey to remorse. The exemplar of such stories is *East Lynne.* So clear is the conscience of the mistress of Nisida's father (who was of course a Count) that she attended mass regularly throughout their amour. No special point is made of this, and it does not seem to be a part of Reynolds's anti-clericalism, merely an indication

of ideas with which his travels and reading had doubtless made him familiar.

This elastic attitude to immorality in the narrow sense of the word extends at times to its wider aspects. It is true that on the whole Reynolds's murderers, swindlers, robbers, seducers, and criminals generally, come to a bad end, but they have a wonderful run for their money first, and sometimes retribution is brief. Nisida, after committing two murders and plotting mercilessly against the girl who is loved by her brother, not to mention the love-affair with Wagner, repents only on her death-bed, when we are assured by the mysterious Rosicrucian who attends her that all is well. Even a single case of such lenience in a world of rigid and clear-cut moral distinctions is remarkable.

Reynolds's taste for the voluptuous is reasonably restrained in the serials published in the *Miscellany.* In the *Mysteries of London,* however, and still more in the earlier volumes of the *Mysteries of the Court of London,* both of which first appeared in penny numbers, there is a good deal of the semi-pornographic. Examples are to be found in the numerous scenes in the *Mysteries of the Court of London* which take place in the superior brothel disguised as the establishment of a fashionable milliner. Here most of the work-women are enchanting prostitutes, while others are innocent victims about to be enticed to their doom. George IV pursues many of his amours in these surroundings, and scenes of seduction and passion abound. Some of these have their amusing side, as when a chapter ends as follows: 'And as he glued his lips, hot and parched with the fever of burning lust, to her delicious mouth, her senses abandoned her—and she remained powerless and inanimate in his arms!' The next chapter, part of the same instalment, begins: 'Grieved as we are to leave the reader in a state of suspense relative to the issue of the adventure of Pauline Clarendon and the Prince of Wales, we must nevertheless break the thread of that episode for a short space and return to Covent Garden Theatre.'

Another characteristic of Reynolds's work which comes as a shock after even the most lurid of the penny dreadfuls is the description of cruelty. The first instalment of the *Mysteries of the Inquisition* gave a detailed account of half-naked victims of the Holy Office being scourged, and of the application of torture by water to a young woman whose offence is that her sister has become a Lutheran. We are carefully told that the victim has just had a baby. The details include the description of the 'wooden horse', the special couch on which she was laid, the tightening of cords binding her so that they disappeared, embedded in flesh, and the actual torture (this is followed immediately by an article decrying the early penny dreadfuls as 'appealing exclusively to the passions, or, rather, the excitabilities of men', and proclaiming that the *London Journal* will be subjected to the wholesome restraints of reason and the moral principle). In *Wagner* the inquisition appears again, and a good deal is made of the torture and death of one, fair but frail, stretched naked on the rack before the eyes of her captive lover and her exulting husband. At times also there are in the *Miscellany* articles giving information on subjects which we would prefer not to know about, as one with a detailed illustration and a full account of guillo-

The cover of an issue of Reynolds's Miscellany.

tining, and another describing instruments of torture. The translation of Sue's *Mysteries of the People* in the 1850 volume contains some scenes of torture, also illustrated. Reynolds's serials in later volumes of the *Miscellany* are inoffensive enough in this respect, but the *Mysteries of London,* also one of his earlier works, is full of cruelty. In Volume I we find, among other things, horrible descriptions of the ill-treatment of children, including blinding them to make them useful beggars; a detailed account of a hanging; and an account of the slow and systematic murder of a child for the sake of 'burial money'. Reynolds's very skill as a writer makes this kind of thing peculiarly disagreeable. That such things happened is only too true, but we can bear to read them only if they are described with compassion. Reynolds may have felt this, but his florid and declamatory style does not convey it.

His hostility to the clergy extends from the dissenting parson who gets so drunk that he has to be conveyed home in a wheel-barrow, is voted a piece of plate by his congregation, and increases its numbers to the extent of three children by three different servant girls, to the gaol chaplain who is seen through the eyes of the hangman:

> 'Last time there was an execution, the Chaplain says to me, says he, "Smithers, I don't think you

had your hand nicely in this morning"?— "Don't you, sir?" says I.—"No," says he: "I've seen you do it more genteel than that."—"Well, Sir," says I, "I'll do my best to please you next time."—"Ah! do, there's a good fellow, Smithers," says the Chaplain; and off he goes to breakfast with the Sheriffs and governor, a-smacking his lips at the idea of the cold fowl and ham that he meant to pitch into.'

A major part in the plot of the *Mysteries of London* is played by a fashionable clergyman named Reginald Tracy, who is seduced by a fashionable lady. He thereupon becomes a complete libertine, not confining his attentions to any one woman. His meeting with one of the less consistently respectable female characters in the book gives rise to the following:

> At a glance his eyes scanned the fair form of Ellen from head to foot; and his imagination was instantly fired with the thoughts of her soft and swelling charms—those graceful undulations which were all her own, and needed no artificial aids to improve the originals of nature!

Later the same gentleman peers at Ellen through the keyhole of the 'bathing-room', but he is interrupted before she is completely undressed. We are not surprised when he comes to a bad end.

Similar attacks on the clergy are found throughout the eight volumes of the *Mysteries of the Court of London,* the events of which vary in date from the late eighteenth century to more or less the time of writing. The grossest avarice and lust are thinly disguised, while the threat of exposure reduces the reverend gentlemen to pulp. A more rational indictment assails the indifference of the clergy to the condition of the common people:

> Oh! what have the myriad fat and bloated pastors done for the population that swarms in those frightful neighbourhoods? . . . If a missionary of Religion be ever encountered in such places, be well assured that he belongs not to the Established Church, which is so extravagantly paid by compulsion, but to the sphere of Dissent, which is sustained by voluntary contributions.

Finally, Reynolds's radicalism. This is shown in the *Miscellany,* in articles at first and later more frequently in answers to correspondents. In a serial like *Wagner: the Wehr-Wolf,* with setting and events as remote as possible from those of daily life, there is no scope for it, but one like *The Slaves of England. No. 1. The Seamstress* (published in the *Miscellany* in 1850) is a good vehicle for the expression of social and political ideas. Reynolds is very disturbed about the wrongs of seamstresses—his blood boils repeatedly as he chronicles the sufferings of 'Virginia' and her colleagues. (It is a pity that the undoubted righteousness of his cause, a cause taken up by people like Shaftesbury, should be obscured by Reynolds's artificial and declamatory style, so that it is hard to avoid suspicions about his sincerity.)

When Virginia goes to sew in private houses, she is said seldom or never to receive considerate treatment, but to be hurried on with her work when she is feeling ill and to be exposed to the insulting attentions of the young men in the families. She dies at last of overwork. The Duke of Belmont, the weak and wicked father of her faithful suitor, commits suicide; the suitor, having announced that 'Hope is to me like a withered flower—and despair spreads its vampyre-like wings over my heart!' engages in a duel with the man who has contrived his father's downfall, both parties are killed, and the Duchess dies of grief and shock. Thus are demonstrated the general perfidy of the aristocracy (the honest lover always excepted) and the nobility of the poor.

Like Reynolds's *Miscellany,* the *Mysteries of London* and the *Mysteries of the Court of London* are active in the onslaught on the aristocracy which Mayhew's costermonger and Thackeray's bookseller saw as the secret of Reynolds's popularity. The attack in the *Mysteries of London* is on constituted authority of every kind, and not only members of the governing classes but all government institutions are represented as corrupt. For example, there occurs a minute description of the illegal censorship of letters carried on from 'The Black Chamber' in the main post office of St. Martin-le-Grand; horror of the workhouse is consistently instilled and the whole system of justice is attacked. The Home Secretary's charge to a newly appointed magistrate runs as follows: 'You must always shield the upper classes as much as possible; and . . . bring out the misdeeds of the lower orders in the boldest relief.'

But if government is an organized conspiracy of the rich against the poor, the poor as individuals in these books are not idealized, in spite of Reynolds's outbursts of glowing sentiment on their behalf as a class. They are in most cases represented as miserably debased, venal and corrupt, rather than as sublime, generous and noble-hearted. Reynolds's whole view of human nature and society is fundamentally cynical. It is impossible, in reading him, to avoid the conviction that he relishes the description of vice and crime. But he freely proclaims a high moral purpose. Towards the end of the second volume of the *Mysteries of London* he asks: 'And shall we be charged with vanity, if we declare that never until now has the veil been so rudely torn aside, nor the corruptions of London been so boldly laid bare?' The epilogue of the same volume forestalls objections to the sordidness of this revelation by claiming that the good as well as the bad has been described, and the bad only that it may be condemned. 'In exposing the hideous deformity of vice, have we not studied to develop the witching beauty of virtue?' he cries. In other words, he muckrakes only to reform.

Yet it is with a certain regret that the modern reader sees the qualities which make his work so strongly individual disappear from Reynolds's work, which in his later years was not much different from that of other writers of penny fiction. In his earlier days he was at least original. The reason why it has been necessary to discuss in such detail his luscious style, his descriptions of the sensuous and the cruel, his strong radical and anti-clerical attitude, is just that they are unique. Considering their enormous success, the fact that they were not imitated speaks volumes for either the moral standards or the incompetence of other writers of popular fiction at the time. Were they deterred

from attempting the imitation, and was Reynolds himself induced to change his style by the attack on popular literature that began somewhere about 1847? It is certain that the later volumes of the *Mysteries of the Court of London* abandon the dramatic exposure of the dishonesty, profligacy and intemperance of George IV for sensational stories involving fictitious characters in more conventional courses of embezzlement, murder, abduction and the rest. And the later volumes of the *Miscellany* differ much from the earlier ones. Reynolds himself contributed mild historical serials, such as *Margaret: or, the Discarded Queen,* and *Mary Stuart, Queen of Scots.* Gone are the voluptuous houris who lend such life to his earlier works, and in their place we meet niminy-piminy little creatures like the two girls who are described respectively as 'a sweet fair-haired young creature of seventeen, and whose beauty was of the most interesting and exquisite description', and 'a superbly handsome, fine-grown, dark-haired damsel of about eighteen'. Even when his heroines are up to their old tricks and disguise themselves in male attire, it is no longer the same thing, as is shown by the following:

> We must nevertheless pause for a moment to remark how well that page's apparel became the slight, lithe, and elegant figure which it invested. The redundant ebon tresses were gathered up in such a way that the greater portion of their mass was concealed by the black velvet cap; while the plume, as above stated, served to shade the countenance. Gualdi could not help thinking that the lady looked as interesting and attractive in male apparel as she was ravishing in her own more appropriate garb.

Scenes of cruelty, debauchery and vice seldom occur, and if they do they are described in a conventional and colourless style. It seems possible that Reynolds was influenced in making these changes by the increasingly frequent attacks on the morality of cheap literature, and by the example of a better class of cheap periodical. (pp. 35-45)

> *Margaret Dalziel, "The Most Popular Writer of Our Time," in her* Popular Fiction 100 Years Ago: An Unexplored Tract of Literary History, *Cohen & West, 1957, pp. 35-45.*

Richard C. Maxwell, Jr.   (essay date 1977)

[*In the following excerpt, Maxwell explores Reynolds's use of the motif of "the Gothic secret" in* The Mysteries of London, *asserting that Reynolds depicted relationships hinging on hidden information to convey the complexity and terror of city life.*]

> Thus compelled to bear within her own mind the whole horror of the secret that oppressed it, her reason seemed to totter under the intolerable weight.
> Ann Radcliffe, *The Mysteries of Udolpho,*
> chapter 27

Between *The Mysteries of Udolpho* (1794) and *The Mysteries of London* (1845-1848), secrets became entangled with an idea of city life. It is possible to observe this trend in process, emerging during the 1840's in the tales of George W. M. Reynolds, authoritatively present shortly

---

> **An excerpt from** *The Mysteries of the Court of London*
>
> Like two demons did the murderers appear as they did their awful work,—one keeping the victim down, despite of his desperate struggles and agonised writhings—the other throttling him in his savage gripe,—the former gnashing his teeth and foaming at the mouth with the ferocious excitement of the deed—the latter with compressed lips and corrugated brows indicating all the tremendous power of the muscular energy which his entire frame furnished to accomplish the task of strangulation.
>
> And in the meantime the roar of the tempest had recommenced; and the terrors of the storm were added to the horrors of that foul iniquity.
>
> 'Twas done: and the captain lay lifeless on the cabin-floor—his countenance livid and blue—his eyes starting from their bloody sockets.
>
> *G. W. M. Reynolds, in his* Mysteries of the Court of London, *John Dicks, 1850-56.*

after 1850 in [Charles Dickens's] *Bleak House.* Reynolds began to experiment with the Gothic secret; he perceived how this "intolerable weight" could express the terrors of the city. Dickens's adaptation of the convention, while in the same spirit, has a new sophistication. The urban intriguer, the incriminating document—essential motifs in *The Mysteries of London*—are used to suggest the contradictory movements of society. London can be perceived as the center of progress, the place where rationalized techniques of government and business gradually evolve. *Household Words* often adopts such a perspective. Yet the means of rationalization (above all, writing) push the city back towards Gothic "mysteries." *Bleak House* is an account of this terrifying and unexpected regression.

One pleasure of Ann Radcliffe's novels is that secrets are always changing status. First they are carefully guarded, then they begin to get out, then they are no longer secrets. What starts as a "mystery" is divested of exclusiveness, shared among author, reader, protagonist, villain, and the rather scanty supporting cast that an isolated castle, for example, affords. The dissolution of secrets is terrifying but finally reassuring. The heroine walks into danger ignorantly, then realizes that she must discover the true nature of her situation. Eventually she is in danger because she knows too much. At this point there is no going back; she must try to find out yet more. Her inquisitiveness will ultimately save her. At the end, when the secrets of Udolpho are exhausted, the world is restored to normal and the survivors can move on.

Cities afford a much wider field for the cultivation of secrets, but it was well into the nineteenth century before novelists took advantage of this fact. The first of the great experimenters was Victor Hugo, whose *Notre Dame de Paris* (1831) describes Paris at a moment of transition. The ordered scholastic Gothicism which formed the medieval city is on the point of breaking down; Paris at the end of the fifteenth century is about to become Gothic in a modern sense. Among those profiting from Hugo's account of this change was Eugène Sue, author of *The Mysteries of Paris* (1842-43). For Sue, Paris is a murky labyrinth, a setting for intricate conspiracies and terrible, secret deeds permeating the whole of society. No memory of the ordered city survives in his account; but Hugo's feeling for the grotesque, the obscure, the complexity of intrigue and counterintrigue in an urban setting, are exploited to the full. Urban Gothic had found its popular incarnation. By the middle of the 1840's, the "Mysteries" formula was spreading to many parts of Europe.

The great English imitator of Hugo and Sue was G. M. Reynolds, who, after much immersion in French fiction—he published an enthusiastic book on the subject—put pen to paper and brought forth *The Mysteries of London.* The first series of *Mysteries* (October 1844-September 1846) is the story of two brothers, Richard and Eugene Markham. Eugene goes off to seek his fortune in the city, having been too stubborn to settle a quarrel with his father. He promises to meet Richard again twelve years from the day of their parting, at which time the brothers will compare their respective fortunes. The narrative then follows alternately the careers of Richard and Eugene. Richard, after being duped by a gang of forgers and imprisoned for two years in the Old Bailey, leads a revolution in an Italian state and wins the hand of a princess. Eugene, under the name Montague Greenwood, becomes an accomplished financial swindler and a member of Parliament. Eventually Greenwood is driven to moral and financial desperation, dying repentantly a few moments after he is reunited with Richard. Meanwhile, the reader has made his way through the huge maze of characters who have gathered around these two: gypsies, faithful and unfaithful retainers, criminals, victimized working girls, men of fashion, politicians, bankers, and many others. Reynolds constantly expands the world he is writing about, taking care, every few chapters, to describe new characters and scenes. "Haply the reader may begin to imagine that our subject is well-nigh exhausted—that the mysteries of London are nearly all unveiled?" The answer, of course, is that London is inexhaustible; so many strange people and institutions thrive there that its mysteries can never be fully unveiled. Thus the reassuring tale of the good brother and the bad becomes the framework for a more elaborate and elusive narrative: fifty or sixty interlocking stories, presenting "all that is most refined in elegance, or most strange in barbarism." The novel depicts the enigmatic complexity of a great city; London is perceived as a gigantic web of secrets.

At first the secrets accumulate gradually. A London bank that seems wealthy has little or no money within its coffers, and its officers must organize their lives around this uncomfortable fact. The wife of an aristocrat is having an affair with a financier, a matter likely to be of interest to others besides the lovers. The bond between a young man aspiring to respectability and a desperate criminal is the latter's knowledge of the former's prison record. A potboy is drawn back repeatedly to Buckingham Palace to eavesdrop on ladies-in-waiting who are gossiping about madness and marital problems in the Hanoverian dynasty. By the time the serial reaches its halfway point, these situations and many others have accumulated; they weigh on the mind all at once. " 'Lord, sir!' said the constable, 'if we took up all persons that we know to be imposters, we should have half London in custody.' " More than half of Reynolds's characters are imposters, and so one falsehood constantly confronts or creates another. The Reverend Reginald Tracy is reputedly pure and upright but has lusted after women and fallen. Ellen Monroe is reputedly a chaste young woman but has had an illegitimate child by Montague Greenwood. When Reginald and Ellen meet, the relationship immediately centers on secrets guessed at or known. A balance of power is temporarily established: " 'Yes—go,' said Ellen: 'you are punished sufficiently. You possess the secret of my frailty—I possess the secret of your hypocrisy: beware of the use you make of your knowledge of me, lest I retaliate by exposing you.' " This kind of deadlock often punctuates the action in *The Mysteries of London.* Situations never become completely static, however. Reginald and Ellen may have maneuvered themselves into a brief equilibrium; on the other hand, they have managed in the course of a few pages to reveal important secrets to other characters. In this way, further plans are set in motion; there is a gradual piling up of motives and perceptions among a widening circle of plotters.

The lower classes devoured *The Mysteries of London;* they made it the most widely read novel of its time. Here was a wonderfully accessible version of Gothic literature, set in familiar London locales but unveiling lurid conspiracies which took place just behind the scenes. The central character of *The Mysteries* is Montague Greenwood. Greenwood has directed his whole career towards learning the ways of power, first as a kind of Pierce Egan character—"A few years ago, when I first entered on a London life, I determined to make myself acquainted with all the ways of the metropolis, high or low"—then, like Trollope's Melmotte or Dickens's Merdle, as an apparently respectable financier. In the latter role, he achieves real finesse in juggling secrets. Chapter forty-eight shows him working at the height of his powers, negotiating with one and then another visitor to his West End quarters, always attempting to extract, use or create secrets. He inquires after the whereabouts of an Italian prince in hiding: " 'That remains a secret,' answered the count." The impending resignation of an M.P. from Rottenborough, though also a "profound secret," is known both to Greenwood and to the idiotic Lord Tremordyn. Greenwood makes it clear to Tremordyn that he wants the seat. Soon after, he consults with Lady Cecilia Harborough and then seduces her; there follows immediately a financial discussion with Sir Rupert, her impecunious husband. " 'I shall hold him in iron chains,' said Greenwood to himself, when he was again alone. 'This bill will hang constantly over his head. Should he detect my intrigue with his wife, he will not dare open his mouth.' "

Greenwood's mode of behavior, as Reynolds argues a chapter later, belongs particularly to a type of modern criminal:

> The more civilization progresses, and the more refined becomes the human intellect, so does human iniquity increase.
>
> It is true that heinous and appalling crimes are less frequent;—but every kind of social, domestic, political, and commercial intrigue grows more into vogue . . . hypocrisy is the cloak which conceals modern acts of turpitude, as dark nights were trusted to for the concealment of the bloody deeds of old; mere brute force is now less frequently resorted to; but the refinements of education or the exercise of duplicity are the engines chiefly used for purposes of plunder. The steel engraver's art, and the skill of the calligrapher, are mighty implements of modern misdeed . . . he who gambles at a gaming-table is a scamp, and he who propagates a lie upon the Exchange and gambles accordingly, and with success, is a respectable financier.

This passage defines much of what goes on in *The Mysteries of London.* Reynolds displays "every kind of social, domestic, political, and commercial intrigue." There are also "heinous and appalling crimes," the "bloody deeds" of proletarian malefactors. The emphasis, however, is on a new kind of villainy characteristic of an advanced age and of the middle classes. In the Black Chamber of the Post Office, one of Reynolds's favorite places, industrious servants of the Crown steam open the correspondence of suspected persons; the Spanish Inquisition of the Gothic novelist has here its modern equivalent, except that letters rather than people are being violated. This transgression of social decency alarms the narrator greatly, prompting him to remark of the chief Examiner: "Can we be astonished if he gloated, like the boa-constrictor over the victim that it retains in its deadly folds, over the mighty secrets stored in his memory?"

The Mysteries of London is one of those books which works only when one has read too much, when situations have been repeated so that they echo painfully in the head. Reynolds creates a city filled with and controlled by manipulators of Greenwood's type. One understands that they are significant because there are so many of them. Similarly with the materials to hand, the secrets: their sheer plenitude is absurdly improbable but also expressive of a social condition. London is built on intrigue, a fact brought conspicuously to the reader's attention by a miraculous materialization. How often secrets become objects—letters to be opened surreptitiously, scribbled messages dropped accidentally by the road, certificates of insanity covering evil intentions. Even at the very end of the serial, when Greenwood is dying, Reynolds fixes the reader's attention on a tree covered with inscriptions. Greenwood tells Richard who he is and so do the inscriptions, if only they are interpreted properly. Intrigue, typically, is a visible fact as well as a state of mind. Hear George Saintsbury on the Mysteries novel: "When you have got an ivory casket supposed to be full of all sorts of compromising documents, somebody produces another, exactly like it, but containing documents more compromising still" [*A History of the French Novel*, 1917-19]. *The Mysteries of Constantinople,* Edward Gorey's pastiche-parody, makes a similar point: "The ambassador is compulsively going over some documents with his secretary when a bogus message is brought by an urchin mute." The mystique of the document is the final, excessive flowering of the Gothic secret. Secrets have become commodities.

They are traded, hoarded, stolen, and in these ways bring about arrangements of power or status.

These are fairly deep waters. Since one can't accuse Reynolds of being a systematic thinker, it might be well to see what a social philosopher can do with the phenomenon of urban secrets. The corrupting presence of entrepreneurial manipulators is a motif in complaints about city life as far back as the Renaissance. The first analyst of the urban scene to discuss secrets at length, however, is Georg Simmel. His *Soziologie* (1908) presents a theory of secrets and modern life which originates in observations about mass society. Democratic government, as it began to develop in nineteenth-century Europe, established new possibilities for individual fulfillment while also prompting an extension of the public domain. The result of these trends was a complex interaction between secrecy and publicity:

> Politics, administration, and jurisdiction . . . have lost their secrecy and inaccessibility in the same measure in which the individual has gained the possibility of ever more complete withdrawal, and in the same measure in which modern life has developed, in the midst of metropolitan crowdedness, a technique for making and keeping private matters secret, such as earlier could be attained only by means of spatial isolation.

In brief, "what is public becomes ever more public, and what is private becomes ever more private." Simmel is describing a highly charged situation. Publicity and secrecy both acquire new momentum; society's dependence on information and the desire for a private existence flourish simultaneously. This seems to be a case of complete polarization. Under pressure, however, polarization can produce some surprising reversals. The secret becomes the public and vice-versa.

Simmel explains in detail the nature of this double transformation, which he traces in each direction. On the one hand, great quantities of information are becoming accessible or significant for the first time. A good way to achieve power is to discover methods for reversing this trend, for shrouding, once again, public affairs in secrecy. There are two advantages thus gained. If one can act secretly in a society which is presumed to operate publicly, all kinds of illicit opportunities open up. Money, above all, has an "abstractness and qualitylessness, through which transactions, acquisitions, and changes in ownership can be rendered hidden and unrecognizable in a way impossible where values are owned only in the form of extensive, unambiguously tangible objects." Even more important, secrecy within an expected context of public action creates a special aura of prestige. What the ordinary man cannot understand, cannot even gain access to, he respects. "Formally secretive behavior"—above and beyond the mere shielding of a secret content—is a way for elite groups to affirm their eliteness.

As public institutions can turn to secrecy, so, on the other hand, can private life be exposed or annihilated. This danger is wrapped up with the function of the personal letter. Not only is the letter "subjective, momentary, solely-personal," but it asserts the importance of these categories; transient states of feeling are put down in permanent form and thus given a new significance. The letter embodies an affirmation of subjective life and its rewards. There is unfortunately a major weakness involved in the affirmation. A letter will tend to betray itself, for it is among the most vulnerable forms of communication: it can, for instance, be opened by the wrong person. When Simmel studies this fact, he approaches a favorite theme: "the difficulty of asserting [one's] own personality within the dimensions of metropolitan life." The individual "can cope less and less with the overgrowth of objective culture," and "it is the function of the metropolis to provide the arena for this struggle and its reconciliation." Given the context of the city, letters suggest perfectly both the need for privacy and the constant difficulties in trying to keep it. Betrayal is implicit in this effort to maintain a separate space for one's mind—and those of one's friends—away from the "overgrowth of objective culture" which typifies the urban scene.

It is a striking quality of Simmel's work that intimations of progress are often cancelled by a sense of despair. Every "good" trend—good according to Enlightenment values—creates a kind of backlash, a fearful regression. Under these circumstances, Simmel can hardly emphasize definitive solutions or results. Instead, he isolates a common ground, an "arena" where opposing forces can be observed to mingle. Broadly speaking, the common ground of public and private is the city. Narrowly speaking, it is the written word, at once "opposed to all secrecy" and the embodiment of the secret. The reader is presented with what seems to be a drastic gulf between the massive recorded data of bureaucracies and the fragile message of the letter. Yet these phenomena are not so far removed from one another after all. Both play a role in urban life; both clash and combine in the realm of writing. For all that Simmel begins with demarcated categories, these categories soon shift like quicksand. The *Sociology* suggests an eerie continuity between individual consciousness and what is now called the "information explosion." Ego and information move in a limbo of documents, each poised between concealment and revelation.

Simmel's discussion provides emblems—points of focus—for the sociologist and the novelist alike. It has, in the first place, more than a passing relation to the Mysteries novel, a genre in which Gothic conventions have become the vehicle of social commentary, in which the secret and its manipulator have become crucial to city life. Even the document plays a part in this wonderfully elaborate scheme. The point is not, however, that Reynolds is a systematic thinker after all—far from it. He ignores what, to Simmel, is of central importance: the paradoxical give-and-take between secrets and information. These two opposing forces—the one subjective and surreptitious, the other demystifying and rational—could be shown as interrelated only in a narrative of great sophistication. How could this perception be expressed or activated in fiction? Suppose that a novelist were to depict [as Dickens does in *Bleak House*] some great London institution which had retreated from general accessibility back towards mystery and at the same time to depict the buried love affair of a great lady hovering on the edge of exposure. Suppose, furthermore, that these two stories were to twine inextricably, each in some peculiar way seeming to precipitate or comment on the other. An accomplishment of this virtuosity might suggest what a strange mental labyrinth the city has become, and thus rival the kind of analysis in which Simmel is engaged. (pp. 188-97)

> *Richard C. Maxwell, Jr., "G. M. Reynolds, Dickens, and the Mysteries of London," in* Nineteenth-Century Fiction, *Vol. 32, No. 2, September, 1977, pp. 188-213.*

Daniel S. Burt   (essay date 1980)

[*In the excerpt below, Burt examines the depiction of lurid and shocking incidents in* The Mysteries of London *to characterize Reynolds's use of the melodramatic form to convey his social message.*]

Early in the course of G. W. M. Reynolds's melodramatic serial, *The Mysteries of London,* the narrator comments: "Shakespeare said, 'All the world is a *stage*'; we say, 'All the world is an *omnibus.*' " Despite the pun, Reynolds's conception of the world as an omnibus provides an accurate description of his dramatic method as well as his fictional vehicle, which ran through a change of publisher and title from 1844 to 1855 in weekly penny numbers, monthly sixpenny parts, and a reissue of twelve volumes of approximately four-and-one-half-million words. The world that Reynolds dramatized is one in which, as on an omnibus, "The old and the young—the virtuous and wicked—the rich and the poor, are invariably thrown and mixed together." Accordingly, the passengers of *The Mysteries of London* include prostitutes, thieves, murderers, paupers, body snatchers, bankers, members of Parliament, clergymen, and even Victoria and Albert. With a cast ever growing and changing, brought together by the contrivance of an exciting, if improbable, plot, the hair-raising ride of the omnibus is underway, resulting in an omnibus of a different sort: an encyclopedia of Victorian thrills, sensation, and sentiment.

By the 1830s and 1840s, melodrama as adapted by novelists in Gothic romances had changed. The Gothic novel was largely subsumed by other popular literary forms for a new working-class readership who demanded more realistic and recognizable sensation. As Michael Sadleir points out [in his *Things Past,* 1944], "The Gothic novel crashed and became the vulgar blood." The popular press was quick to offer a dizzying assault of shocks and thrills in cheap periodicals, penny numbers, and multiple volumes. Tales of horror, crime, and villainy were elaborated and expanded weekly by a large complement of hack writers. Like the Gothic novel or the stage melodrama, the penny bloods rapidly became a formula fiction with stock characters and incidents and with excitement created by the simple dramatic situation of virtue threatened by villainy. Among writers who catered to the Victorian readers' appetites for the sensational and the melodramatic, G. W. M. Reynolds was by far the most popular and the most successful. *The Mysteries of London* sold an estimated 40,000 copies a week, and, when Reynolds died in 1879, *The Bookseller* reported that "Dickens and Thackeray and Lever had their thousands of readers, but Mr.

Reynolds's were numbered in the hundreds of thousands, perhaps millions." Reynolds's success stemmed from his mastery of the art of fictional melodrama in concocting rousing stories to horrify, instruct, and morally uplift a massive popular audience.

Modeled on Eugène Sue's *The Mysteries of Paris,* Reynolds's series of novels, *The Mysteries of London* and its sequel *The Mysteries of the Court of London,* dramatize the secrets and thrills of London high and low life. His scope is panoramic, and his subject is crime and villainy:

> The visitor to the Polytechnic Institution or the Adelaide Gallery has doubtless seen the exhibition of the microscope. A drop of the purest water, magnified by that instrument some thousands of times, appears filled with horrible reptiles and monsters of revolting forms.
>
> Such is London.
>
> Fair and attractive as the mighty metropolis may appear to the superior observer, it swarms with disgusting, loathsome, and venomous objects, wearing human shapes.
>
> Oh! London is a city of strange contrasts!

Reynolds's multivolume serial provides such a sensational magnification that the entire urban panorama may be studied to reveal its perfidy and wickedness. The narrative is a series of strange contrasts, and a summary of the plot of *The Mysteries of London* would be exceedingly complicated and beside the point. The interest in Reynolds's serial comes not from the working out of its tangled narrative but from its separate episodes, on a multitude of sensational vignettes and short melodramatic stories. To get a sense of Reynolds's fiction it is better to examine representative scenes and characters to illustrate his fictional method and material.

A prime ingredient in any installment of *The Mysteries of London* is its shock value. Reynolds's work is strongly laced with horror guaranteed to cause a shiver or chill in even the most phlegmatic or hardened reader. For his sensation Reynolds resorted to the relatively new subject of the horrors of the modern city and dramatized what Henry Mayhew in *London Labour and the London Poor* examined with statistics, eyewitness accounts, interviews, and a sociologist's eye. Reynolds, like Mayhew, was concerned with the various strata and social groups in London, but he presented his findings with the eye of a sensationalist, taking his readers firsthand into the city's "Den of Horrors":

> Some of the houses have small back yards, in which the inhabitants keep pigs. A short time ago, an infant belonging to a poor widow, who occupied a back room on the ground-floor of one of those hovels, died, and was laid upon the sacking of the bed while the mother went to make arrangements for its interment. During her absence a pig entered the room from the yard, and feasted upon the dead child's face!
>
> In that densely populated neighbourhood that we are describing, hundreds of families each live and sleep in one room. When a member of one

of these families happens to die, the corpse is kept in the close room where the rest still continue to live and sleep. Poverty frequently compels the unhappy relatives to keep the body for days—aye, and weeks. Rapid decomposition takes place;—animal life generates quickly; and in four-and-twenty hours myriads of loathsome animaculae are seen crawling about. The very undertaker's men fall sick at these disgusting—these revolting spectacles.

The horror of such scenes is drawn out to extract the maximum in shock and macabre thrills. Comparing Reynolds's account of the slum of Saffron Hills and Smithfield with Mayhew's study of similar material, the reader senses not so much Reynolds's exaggeration (nothing in fact is more sensational or horrifying than some of Mayhew's interviews and statistics) but his absolute relish for sensational details such as the child's mutiliated face and the close-up view of a corpse's decomposition. Reynolds updated Gothic horror by casting it in modern dress and setting it in scenes of London city life that highlighted its monstrousness. In one particularly graphic passage, the narrator describes the activities of a gravedigger that demonstrates Reynolds's unflinching realism and his zest for shock effects:

> The man returned to the grave, and was about to resume his labour, when his eyes caught the sight of a black object, almost embedded in the damp clay heaped up by the side. He turned it over with his spade: it was the upper part of the skull, with the long, dark hair of a woman still remaining attached to it. The grave-digger coolly took up the relic by that long hair which perhaps had once been a valued ornament; and, carrying it in this manner into the Bone-House, threw it upon the fire. The hair hissed a moment as it burnt, for it was damp and clogged with clay; then the voracious flames licked up the thin coat of blackened flesh which had still remained on the skull; and lastly devoured the bone itself.

Cemeteries are favorite settings, and corpses are favorite characters in Reynolds's fiction. One of the novel's main villains is a resurrection man or body snatcher. Although the profession was in decline after 1829 and the notorious trial of the Scottish resurrection men and murderers Burke and Hare, which resulted in legislation to make cadavers legally available to doctors, Reynolds employs a body snatcher who still plies his grisly trade as an all-purpose bogeyman in the novel. Reynolds includes in his presentation "A Body-Snatcher's Song" that illustrates the horrifying thrills in which the novel delights:

> In the churchyard the body is laid,
> There they inter the beautiful maid:
>   "Earth to earth" is the solemn sound!
> Over the sod where their daughter sleeps,
> The father prays, and the mother weeps:
>   "Ashes to ashes" echoes around!
>
> Come with the axe, and come with the spade;
> Come where the beautiful virgin's laid:
>   Earth from earth must we take back now!
> The sod is damp, and the grave is cold:
> Lay the white corpse on the dark black mould,
>   That the pale moonbeam may kiss its brow!

> Throw back the earth, and heap up the clay;
> This cold white corpse we will bear away,
>   Now that the moonlight waxes dim;
> For the student doth his knife prepare
> To hack all over this form so fair,
>   And sever the virgin limb from limb!
>
> At morn the mother will come to pray
> Over the grave where her child she lay,
>   And freshest flowers thereon will spread:
> And on that spot will she kneel and weep,
> Nor dream that we have disturbed the sleep
>   Of her who lay in that narrow bed.

Like his famous Scottish predecessors, Reynolds's resurrection man frequently does not wait for nature to take its course before procuring a new cadaver. Often as many victims are sent to their graves as he takes out. Reynolds gives a description of the method used in preparing a new corpse for sale, in the words of the resurrection man: by " 'holding him with his head downwards in a tub of water . . . till he was drowned. That way don't tell no tales;—no wound on the skin—no poison in the stomach; and there ain't too much water inside neither, cos the poor devils don't swallow with their heads downwards.' " In one scene the resurrection man retrieves from a pond the body of a murdered girl to torment his fellow murderer, Lady Adeline Ravensworth:

> Then, holding the light in such a manner that its beams fell upon the floor, and withdrawing his arms from Adeline's waist, he exclaimed in a tone of ferocious triumph, "Behold the remains of the murdered Lydia Hutchinson!"

> Lady Ravensworth threw one horrid glance upon the putrid corpse; and uttering a terrific scream expressive of the most intense agony, she fell upon the floor—her face touching the feet of the dead body.

> Tidkins raised her: but the blood gushed out of her mouth.

> "Perdition! I have gone too far," cried the Resurrection Man.

Most readers will no doubt strongly agree.

The horror portrayed by Reynolds at times verges on the sadistic, showing a delight in graphic scenes of violence. The domestic life of Bill Bolter will serve as an example. Bolter is a kind of Bill Sikes as a family man. His two children are almost continuously beaten and brutalized, but the violence done to them is nothing compared to that contemplated by their mother. Planning their children's future, the parents decide that young Henry can go into his father's business and will be "so handy to shove through a window, or to sneak down an area and hide himself all day in a cellar to open the door at night,—or a thousand things." Fanny's vocation, however, remains a problem until her mother suggests blinding her to increase her potential as a beggar. As she remarks, "There's nothing like a blind child to exact compassion." As if this were not enough, Reynolds offers a description how the blinding might be accomplished. Fanny's mother has heard of another woman who covered her child's eyes "with cockle shells, the eye-lids, recollect, being wide open; and in each shell there was a huge black beetle. A bandage tied tight round the head kept the shells in their place; and the shells kept the eye-lids open. In a few days the eyes got quite blind, and the pupils had a dull white appearance." The horror of such a torture suggested by the child's mother is revolting enough even, one imagines, for the strongest stomachs. Mrs. Bolter's friend could have been Mary Arnold, the Female Monster, celebrated in a popular Victorian street ballad:

Of all the tales was ever told,
I now will you impart,
That cannot fail to terror strike,
To every human heart.
The deeds of Mary Arnold,
Who does in a jail deplore,
Oh! such a dreadful tale as this,
Was never told before.

Chorus
This wretched woman's dreadful deed,
Does every one affright.
With black beetles in walnut shells,
She deprived her child of sight.

Now think you tender parents,
What must this monster feel,
The heart within her breast must ten
Times harder be than steel.
The dreadful crime she did commit,
Does all the world surprise,
Black beetles placed in walnut shells,
Bound round her infant's eyes.

The beetles in a walnut shell,
This monster she did place,
This dreadful deed, as you may read,
All history does disgrace,
The walnut shell, and beetles,
With a bandage she bound tight,
Around her infant's tender eyes,
To take away its sight.

A lady saw this monster,
In the street when passing by,
And she was struck with terror,
For to hear the infant cry.
The infant's face she swore to see,
Which filled her with surprise,
To see the fatal bandage,
Tied round the infant's eyes.

With speed she called an officer,
Oh! shocking to relate,
Who beheld the deed, and took the wretch,
Before the Magistrate.
Who committed her for trial,
Which did the wretch displease,
And she's now transported ten long years,
Across the briny seas.

Is there another in the world,
Could plan such wicked deed,
No one upon this earth before,
Of such did ever see.
To take away her infant's sight,
'Tis horrible to tell,
Binding black beetles round its eyes,
Placed in walnut shells.

Reynolds answered the ballad's last stanza with his own female monster.

After Mrs. Bolter contemplates blinding her daughter, Reynolds in characteristic fashion pulls back from the scene to moralize on its hideousness and then arranges a fitting punishment for such an unnatural mother. She is interrupted while beating her children by Bolter who is unexpectedly moved by the children's suffering:

The poor lad screamed piteously: the hand of his mother had fallen with the weight of a sledge hammer upon his naked flesh.

But that ferocious blow was echoed by another, at scarcely a moment's interval. The latter was dealt by the fist of Bill Bolter, and fell upon the back part of the ruthless mother's head with a stunning force.

The woman fell forward, and struck her face violently against the corner of the deal table.

Her left eye came in contact with the angle of the board, and was literally crushed in its socket— an awful retribution upon her who only a few hours before was planning how to plunge her innocent and helpless daughter into the eternal night of blindness.

Reynolds here demonstrates his chilling orchestration of shocking and sensational scenes with moral commentary, melodramatically staging the punishment for the villainy and violence he has so lavishly depicted.

In addition to scenes of horror and violence, a staple in Reynolds's melodramatic fare is a kind of semipornographic and titillating depiction of sex. The unfortunate history of the Reverend Reginald Tracy offers a characteristic example. Tracy is seduced by a temptress, and the stages of his moral decline are described at some length. In one scene, Tracy, revolted by his recent lapse into the arms of his lover (discreetly presented in the text by two lines of asterisks), tries to avoid any further temptation. He is, however, called on parish business to the garret of a sculptor where he sees what he takes to be a statue resembling his lover. The scene recalls the *tableau vivant* popular on the Victorian stage where nudity might be presented if it involved classical subjects. Here the subject is Pygmalion: "It was naked to the middle; the arms were gracefully rounded; and one hand sustained the falling drapery which, being also coloured, produced upon the mind of the beholder the effect of real garments." The statue to Tracy's amazement comes rather markedly to life: "the statue burst from chill marble into warmth and life; it was indeed the beauteous but wily Cecilia—who returned his embrace and hung around his neck;—and the rector was again subdued—again enslaved!" Such a theatrical way for Cecilia to reclaim her lover is typical in Reynolds's presentation of sex.

Tracy's fall into lust is further dramatized in a scene that is a kind of Victorian peep show. Tracy is attracted to one of the novel's heroines, Ellen Monroe, and Reynolds allows Tracy and the reader a provocative glimpse of her before bathing with her child:

When the rector beheld her descend in that be-witching *negligee,* her hair unconfined, and floating at will—her small round, polished ankles glancing between the white drapery and the little slippers—and the child, with merely a thick shawl thrown about it, in her arms . . . without a moment's hesitation he stole softly from the recess where he concealed himself, and approached the door of the bath-room.

His greedy eyes were applied to the key-hole; and his licentious glance plunged into the depths of that sacred privacy.

The narrator gives a moral commentary and condemnation of the reverend's actions in no uncertain terms, yet the reader still finds himself with Tracy at the keyhole. Reynolds, therefore, has it both ways—moral correctness and titillation at the same time:

The fires of gross sensuality raged madly in his breast.

Ellen's preparations were now completed.

With her charming white hand she put back her hair from her forehead.

Then, as she still retained the child on her left arm, with her right hand she loosened the strings which closed her dressing gown round the neck and the band which confined it at the waist.

While thus occupied, she was partly turned towards the door; and all the treasures of her bosom were revealed to the ardent gaze of the rector.

His desires were now inflamed to that pitch when they almost became ungovernable. He felt that could he possess that charming creature, he would care not what the result—even though he forced her to compliance with his wishes, and murder and suicide followed,—the murder of her and the suicide of himself!

He was about to grasp the handle of the door when he remembered that he had heard the key turn in the lock immediately after she had entered the room.

He gnashed his teeth with rage.

And now the drapery had fallen from her shoulders, and the whole of her voluptuous form, naked to the waist, was exposed to his view.

He could have broken down the door, had he not feared to alarm the other inmates of the house.

He literally trembled under the influence of his fierce desires.

How he envied—Oh! how he envied the innocent babe which the fond mother pressed to that bosom—swelling, warm, and glowing!

And now she prepared to step into the bath: but, while he was waiting with fervent avidity for the moment when the whole of the drapery should fall from her form, a step suddenly resounded upon the stairs.

Ellen's striptease is stopped at the last possible moment with her modesty barely preserved but not before Reynolds has extracted as many thrills as possible from the scene. The reader should note his stage directions as Tracy gnashes his teeth with rage like a melodramatic stage villain. The image of the mother and child with its sacred, madonnalike associations, perversely made so profane by Tracy's monstrous lust, is a further twist or element to heighten and intensify the scene which grotesquely mixes lewdness and morality. The reader can both sin with Tracy and be saved by adopting the narrator's perspective and tone of righteous indignation at such infamy.

If the history of Reginald Tracy shows the reader the early stages in the making of a voluptuary, the depiction of the final moments of the aged Marquis of Holmesford offers a glimpse of the last stage and in the process shows the reader the private bedchambers and excesses of the wealthy. We learn that the Marquis has established a harem at Holmesford House:

There was the Scotch charmer, with her brilliant complexion, her auburn hair, and her red cherry lips:—there was the English girl—the pride of Lancashire—with her brown hair, and her robust but exquisitely modelled proportions:—and next to her, on the same ottoman, sate the Irish beauty whose sparkling black eyes denoted all the fervour of sensuality.

On the sofa facing these three women, sate the French wanton, her taper fingers playing with the gold chain which, in the true spirit of coquetry, she had thrown negligently round her neck, and the massive links of which made not the least indentation upon the plump fullness of her bosom. By her side was the Spanish houri, her long black ringlets flowing on the white drapery which set off her transparent olive skin to such exquisite advantage.

This group formed an assemblage of charms which would have raised palpitations and excited mysterious fires in the heart of the most heaven-devoted anchorite that ever vowed a life of virgin-purity.

Such excitement has no doubt contributed to the Marquis' failing health, and, although close to death, he seeks the company of his harem for one last time:

"Consider that I am going on a long journey, my dear girls," he exclaimed, with a smile; "and do not let our party be sorrowful. Kathleen, my sweet one, come nearer: there—place yourself so that I may recline my head on your bosom—and now throw that warm, plump, naked arm over my shoulder. Oh! this is paradise!"

And for a few minutes the hoary voluptuary, whose licentious passions were dominant even in death, closed his eyes and seemed to enjoy with intense gratification all the luxury of his position.

Reynolds does not neglect the opportunity to note the scene's strange, not to say grotesque, contrast and its moral lesson:

> It was a painful and disgusting sight to behold the shrivelled, haggard, and attenuated countenance of the dying sensualist, pressing upon that full and alabaster globe so warm with health, life, and glowing passions;—painful and disgusting, too, to see that thin, emaciated, and worn-out frame reclining in the arms of a lovely girl in the vigour and strength of youth:—hideous—hideous to view that contiguity of a sapless, withered trunk and a robust and verdant tree!

Chastened by the narrator, the Marquis nevertheless continues to enjoy his sensual pleasure (as does the reader), and dies, fulfilling his dream to go "with his head pillowed on the naked—heaving bosom of beauty, and with a glass of sparkling champagne in his hand."

After several hundred pages such sensational and shocking scenes start to be repeated with fairly tedious regularity. If there is one scene in a graveyard, one hero who falls to what seems to be certain death, one virgin who *almost* loses her honor, there are several such scenes and situations. Incidents displaying the monstrous underside of city life and the formula of villainy's assault on virtue are played out again and again in newer and stranger episodes as Reynolds tries to find fresher stimulants to shock and thrill his audience. Whatever Reynolds concocted to electrify each installment, the outcome is not long in doubt. His moral is as inescapable as the shocks and the blood. " 'Tis done," the narrator proclaims at the end of the first series of *The Mysteries of London,* "VIRTUE is rewarded—VICE has received its punishment." After a litany of sensation, Reynolds ends with a homily: "If, then, the preceding pages be calculated to engender one useful thought—awaken one beneficial statement,—the work is not without its value." Like the stage melodrama that is part thrilling adventure and part morality play, Reynolds's fiction is also a kind of all-purpose entertainment: a guided tour through brothels, lady's boudoirs, elegant drawing rooms, and gin shops, in which the reader can get his full penny's worth of practical advice, sentiment, and terror that combines the tabloid and the tract.

It may be argued that, in Reynolds's fiction, terror and sentimentality have finally found their proper level among undiscriminating readers, beginning a long underground history in subliterary forms that surface today in detective fiction, thrillers, Victoria Holt and Barbara Cartland romances, soap operas, and comic books. Such fictional entertainment, though immensely popular, is critically ignored, recognized as not the sort of fiction from which great art is made. Yet the gap separating popular and serious literature—highbrow and lowbrow art—was not as wide nor as difficult to bridge in the Victorian period as it is in our own. The audience for the best Victorian fiction overlapped in part with the audience for the worst. Reynolds, for example, began his novel-writing career with an imitation of *The Pickwick Papers,* and Dickens's *Household Words* and *All the Year Round* competed for a portion of the same audience as the more lurid *London Journal* and *Reynolds's Miscellany.* The mode of publication for many of the classic Victorian novels in installments was the same as that for the lowest fictional hack work, and it is hard to imagine that a novelist like Dickens who

The frontispiece for Reynolds's Pickwick Abroad; or, The Tour in France, *published in book form in 1838.*

was so conscious of the tastes of the marketplace was not also aware of his competitors in the popular press and their readers' craving for strong scenes full of suffering and sentiment with as many thrills as laughter and tears. Reynolds's novels and the other penny bloods are important, therefore, in giving the modern reader a clear indication of what a majority of the age demanded in popular entertainment—an audience whose taste the major Victorian novelists had to contend with—to cater to, react against, or modify.

Reynolds's popularity and career curiously parallels Dickens's. Both men were the age's bestsellers, though by most accounts Reynolds's sales far outdistanced those of Dickens. And, although Dickens expressed nothing but contempt for Reynolds's novels, which he called "a national reproach," both writers have certain interesting similarities in their melodramatic methods. Reynolds was a passionate reformer, drawn to the temperance movement and the Chartists, and his moral and political concerns crept into even the most extravagantly sensational of his tales. Reynolds used his sensational and melodramatic stories as a vehicle for a certain degree of propagandizing and social satire, much in the same manner as did Dickens. In *The Mysteries of London,* for example, though the incidents verge on the pornographic and the luridly sensational, Reynolds makes it clear that

> We have a grand moral lesson to work out—a great lesson to teach every class of society; a moral and lesson whose themes are
> Wealth. | Poverty.

Reynolds's social theme and panorama are not far removed from Dickens's in novels like *Dombey and Son, Bleak House, Little Dorrit,* and *Our Mutual Friend.* Both novelists use the melodramatic and the sensational to dramatize a social message; both attempt to show the connection between the lowest members of society and the highest. Reynolds writes:

> Crime is abundant in this city: the lazar-house, the prison, the brothel, the dark alley, are rife with all kinds of enormity; in the same way as the palace, the mansion, the club-house, the parliament, and the parsonage, are each and all characterised by their different degrees and shades of vice. . . . Crimes borrow their comparative shades of enormity from the people who perpetrate them: thus it is that the wealthy may commit all social offenses with impunity; while the poor are cast into dungeons and coerced with chains, for only following at a humble distance in the pathway of their lordly precedents.

Reynolds's diagnosis of the connection between vice and social class resembles Dickens's analysis of society and particularly of the urban slums in *Dombey and Son:*

> Those who study the physical sciences, and bring them to bear upon the health of Man, tell us that if the noxious particles that rise from vitiated air were palpable to the sight, we should see them lowering in a dense cloud above such haunts, and rolling slowly on to corrupt the better portions of a town. But if the moral pestilence that rises with them, and, in the eternal law of outraged Nature, is inseparable from them, could be made discernable too, how terrible the revelation! Then should we see depravity, impiety, drunkenness, theft, murder, and a long train of nameless sins against the natural affections and repulsions of mankind, overhanging the devoted spots, and creeping among the poor.

Like Reynolds's microscope, Dickens uses the instrument of his melodramatic plot to reveal the moral climate of his society: the connection, as in Reynolds's omnibus, of rich and poor, the wicked and the virtuous.

Without asserting that Reynolds's novels provided a direct model for Dickens, it is possible to claim a kindred quality in both novelists, as it is between the penny bloods and the work of the major Victorian novelists. Reynolds opened new territory for the novelist in his scenes of city life and perfected the form for the successful melodramat-

ic serial while also developing ways in which a sensational narrative might be extended to encompass other themes and purposes. If Reynolds largely succumbs to the melodramatic and sensational excesses that Dickens and novelists like Wilkie Collins and Thomas Hardy were often able to transcend and develop in more challenging and interesting ways, Reynolds's fiction remains a useful collection of fictional melodrama: a wild assortment of stories, character types, gruesome details, and sentimentality that were the stock elements on the Victorian stage and in the novel. (pp. 141-56)

> *Daniel S. Burt, "A Victorian Gothic: G. W. M. Reynolds's 'Mysteries of London'," in* New York Literary Forum, *v. 7, 1980, pp. 141-58.*

An excerpt from *The Mysteries of the Court of London*

O Almighty God! how long must these things last?—how long are the millions to remain the slaves of the few?—how long wilt thou suffer the fruits of the earth to be monopolised by a tyrant oligarchy? Do thy thunders sleep, thou Creator of all?—or hast thou abandoned the world to chance and its proceedings to the wild will of those who rule by violence, by oppressive laws, by cruelty, and by blood?

For four days did the wife of the working man drag her weary limbs through the streets, and squares, and alleys of this vast metropolis—seeking her husband,—and vainly seeking! For four days did her children train at her heels, enduring the poignant anguish of famine, the brutality of constables, the insults of pampered flunkeys, and the frowns of the rich and great.

Stately equipages swept past, splashing them with mud—and no compassionate look was thrown upon that wretched family—no pence proffered from the hand of wealth and beauty. If they sank down, fainting and exhausted, upon the door step of a West End palace, a hall-porter, flaming with scarlet and yellow and bedizened with gold-lace, would drive them away as if they had just emerged from a lazar-house and their breath was fraught with pestilence. If they wandered forth into the suburbs with the hope of meeting a husband and a father there, a signboard with a painted notice to the effect that "all vagrants found loitering about near those premises would be prosecuted according to law," scared them away. If they entered a churchyard and sate down to rest in the porch of the house of God, a burly beadle or a stern overseer would drive them roughly off. If they sought to enter the parks—*the people's parks*—those parks which belong to the nation, and consequently to all the individuals constituting this nation,—if they hoped to pass the gates of these enclosures, there was a harsh voice raised to warn them off and perhaps a cane wherewith to drive away the children? And wherefore?—because they were in rags—and your aristocratic folks, who frequent those parks, lolling listlessly in their splendid carriages, cannot bear the sight of rags!

> *G. W. M. Reynolds, in his* Mysteries of the Court of London, *John Dicks, 1850-56*

Louis James (essay date 1981)

[*In the excerpt below, James examines* The Mysteries of London *as representative of working-class literature of the early Victorian era. Contrasting the work with other fiction of the period, the critic asserts that Reynolds transcended conventional melodrama to provide a detailed critique of the capitalist system.*]

Although crude penny-issue novels had followed on the popularity of such plagiarisms as [Edward Lloyd's] *Oliver Twiss,* by 1844 they were coming into competition with a more sophisticated type of popular journalism and a rapid expansion in the field of newspapers and magazines. In terms of working-class social life, the 'hungry forties' opened with bad harvests and a slump in industry. In 1841 one Englishman in eleven was a pauper. In the Yorkshire mills, hands averaged less than half-a-crown a week. Riots and disturbances occurred throughout the manufacturing districts. But the wide dissemination of cheap papers, the beginnings of trade-unionism, and the educating activities of the Chartist Movement, formed in 1838 from the London Working Men's Association, meant that the working population as a whole was more informed and politically aware than in the thirties. The popularity of Reynolds's romances was made possible by a readership concerned not just about poverty but with the economic structure of society that lay behind it.

Reynolds himself was well educated, the son of a post-captain in the navy, and the product of Ashford Grammar School and Sandhurst. He had edited the middle-class *Monthly Magazine* (1837-38), and contributed to it pioneering introductions to literary extracts collected as **The Modern Literature of France** (1839). He had also written a work derivative of Dickens, **Pickwick Abroad, or the Tour in France** (1837-38), but it was very different from Lloyd's plagiarisms, a middle-class 'continuation' of Dickens's work. With **The Mysteries of London** he became, in the considered judgement of *The Bookseller,* the most popular writer of his time: his readership was probably wider even than that of Dickens. Only social ostracism as a Radical and a novelist purveying 'hellish wares' denied him a more prominent place in mid-Victorian history.

One unexpected champion of Reynolds was Thackeray. The association started during Thackeray's Paris days in the early thirties, where he met Reynolds and contributed to his magazine, the *Paris Literary Gazette,* the first writing for which he received payment. Thackeray reported objectively Reynolds's Chartist speech on Kennington Common, 13 March 1848 and, replying for 'the novelists of England' at the 1848 Royal Literary Fund dinner, spoke warmly of Reynolds as 'a great Novelist, a member of my own profession' [cited in Lewis Melville's *William Makepeace Thackeray,* 1910]. In his consistent attacks on the 'Newgate Novel' Thackeray notably omitted works by Reynolds. This sympathy between active Radical and political conservative, between sensational writer and sophisticated ironist, requires some explanation. Some of the issues are illuminated by comparing *Vanity Fair* with **The Mysteries of London.**

If Thackeray's novel has outlived its place in the controversy about criminal and 'high life' romance, the debate helped give it its form. Thackeray saw novels such as Bulwer's *Paul Clifford* (1830) and Ainsworth's *Rookwood* (1834) as a sensationalizing of crime which, like public executions, drew on a morbid fascination with violence. His classical temperament took particular exception to the romantic glamour such works gave to criminals, who are 'not dandy, poetical rose-water thieves; but downright scoundrels, leading scoundrelly lives, drunken, profligate, dissolute, low; as scoundrels will be' [Thackeray's *Catherine: A Tale,* 1838-39]. Here even Dickens in *Oliver Twist* failed; prostitutes do not 'die whitewashed saints, like poor "Biss Dadsy" in *Oliver Twist*'. In *Catherine* Thackeray attempted to attack the genre by sardonically giving the public 'what it wanted'. In *Vanity Fair* Thackeray showed how such subjects might appear in real life.

Aristocratic life was shown as inhabited not by dashing young bucks, but by vulgar baronets such as Sir Pitt Crawley, or the cool calculating Lord Steyne. Instead of criminals like the seductive husband-poisoner of Bulwer's *Lucretia* (1846) we are shown Becky Sharp, who plays out her charade of Clytemnestra when she murders Rawdon for the insurance. (' "By —, she'd do it too", Lord Steyne had muttered' (Chapter 41)). If villainy is revalued in Becky, the heroine is equally scrutinized in the limp, sweet, but ultimately selfish Amelia. Thackeray appeals from general principles to acts taking place in a particular time and place. 'I think I could be a good woman if I had five thousand a year', muses Becky (Chapter 51). In turn, therefore, the novel's characters offer criticism of the structure of upper middle-class society. Politically, Thackeray allied himself with the right wing; in terms of his fictional analysis of society, as Barbara Hardy has pointed out in *The Exposure of Luxury: Radical Themes in Thackeray* (1972), he is closer to the reformers.

Where Thackeray, looking back to the good sense of Fielding's world, was critical of nineteenth-century bourgeois society, Reynolds rejected it for economic and political reasons. The Victorian age had brought not a better era, but one of increased heartlessness and hypocrisy: 'The more civilization progresses, the more refined becomes the human intellect, so does iniquity increase . . . mere brute force is now less frequently resorted to; but the refinements of education or the exercise of duplicity are the engines chiefly used for the purposes of plunder' [Reynolds's **The Mysteries of London**]. Reynolds's criminals are never romantic, but the product of an exploitative society, and perfectly answer Thackeray's description of 'leading scoundrelly lives, drunken, dissolute, low'. Neither Thackeray nor Reynolds saw an answer to social problems in the simple benevolence of a Pickwick, a Fezziwig, or the Cheeryble brothers.

Thackeray and Reynolds were also united in their sympathy for French culture and literature. Reynolds's work was inspired directly by the French 'mysteries' literature. This can be traced back to England, for Pierce Egan's pioneering novel of life in the city, *Life in London* (1821-22), influenced Eugene Sue's *Les Mystères de Paris* (1842-43), which in turn invoked Paul Feval's rival *Les Mystères de Londres* (1842-43) and a host of city 'mysteries' set in Europe and America. Victor Hugo's *Notre Dame de Paris*

(1831), which influenced Sue, was set at the end of the fifteenth century, at a time when the medieval society was breaking down, and introduced a picture of the traditional city resolving into a web of conspiracies and sinister secrets. Sue and Feval brought the genre up to date with nineteenth-century town life networked by criminal organizations and concealed identities. In 1844 Thackeray was working on his own translation of *Les Mystères de Paris,* although he also satirized it in passages of *Vanity Fair,* later omitted. 'Mysteries' literature combined the interest of the Gothic romance of the Mrs Radcliffe tradition with the fashion for 'life as it is', and the beginnings of the detective thriller. It dramatized the town-dweller's sense of menacing urban confusion. Further, because the mysteries prompted the question 'why?', the genre lent itself to Radical sentiments: by identifying crime as caused by the corrupt effect of the modern city, the way was open for attacks on the capitalist system.

Reynolds opens *The Mysteries of London* with a panoramic view of the city, ambitiously set in the history of mankind.

> Between the 10th. and 13th. centuries Civilization withdrew from Egypt and Syria, rested for a little space at Constantinople and then passed away to the western climes of Europe . . . For centuries has Civilization established, and for centuries will it maintain, its headquarters in the great cities of Western Europe: and with Civilization does Vice go hand-in-hand.

> Amongst these cities there is one in which contrasts of a strange nature exist. The most unbounded wealth is the neighbour of the most hideous poverty; the most gorgeous pomp is placed in strong relief by the most deplorable squalor; the most seducing luxury is only separated by a narrow wall from the most appalling misery.

London is seen under the eye of history; it becomes an allegorical landscape like that of Langland or Bunyan, politicized. 'From this city of strange contrasts branch off two roads, leading to two points totally distinct from each other' [Series 1, Volume 1, Chapter 1]. From Feval's *Les Mystères de Londres* Reynolds took the theme of the two brothers, one brother, with power in both upper-class and lower-class London, attempting to destroy the other. Eugene is an unscrupulous capitalist who works his way up the rungs of London society, helped by various members of the criminal underworld, until he becomes Member of Parliament for Rottenborough. The virtuous Richard is several times ensnared by his brother, who twice changes his name and remains unknown to Richard. Periodically, however, he shows his presence by leaving his name and date on a particular tree. When the two brothers confront each other at the end, Eugene has been ruined, and is dying of a wound given by Lafleur, his French valet and criminal accomplice. Richard, recovering from his misfortunes, has become a Prince for fighting for the freedom of the Duchy of Castelcicala, also winning the hand of Isabel Montoni.

Reynolds follows the form of melodrama noticed in *Oliver Twiss,* juxtaposing highly ritualized sensational passages with realism. He creates scenes of extreme debauchery to attack the Church in Reginald Tracy, the Rector of St David's (1, 1, Chapters 126-31), and the aristocracy in the obscene Duke of Holmesford, who dies in the middle of a debauch. Yet the capitalist Eugene, the most destructive figure, is far from the stereotypes of the capitalist shown, for example, in Eisenstein's *Strike* (1924). He is amoral rather than villainous, working out a role created by a corrupt society. He proposes to blackmail Lady Cecilia Harborough into sleeping with him, only to be taken aback by the alacrity with which she accepts (1, 1, Chapter 48). He is a born manipulator. If he seduces a girl, he skilfully arranges for the illegitimate child to be cared for in a way which protects both himself and the mother (1, 1, Chapter 82). His ability to manage the stock exchange, however evil its ends, inspires respect (1, 1, Chapters 53, 84). Like Becky Sharp, he is the inevitable product of a system that rewards the unscrupulous and the ambitious. Richard is no Amelia, but his innocence makes him, until the end, the constant victim: he prospers only when he leaves England for the political-liberation movements of Europe.

Reynolds's insight into character is particularly evident in his portrayal of women. Here he enjoyed freedom from many of the moral restraints imposed on Dickens and Thackeray. Reynolds's female characters have sexual and emotional lives comparable to or more intense than those of his men. Eliza Sydney's inner conflict when she discovers that Stephen, whom she likes, has planned to rape her, or Ellen Munroe's emotions when her position in society forces her to conceal her illegitimate child (1, 1, Chapters 21, 62), are more than sensationalism; they explore areas which no middle-class writer in the forties could handle.

Reynolds's criminals, also, are more than stereotypes of villainy. If we wish to see Fagin as the victim of society we have to impose this on the novel that Dickens gives us. Almost all of Reynolds's criminals have been driven into crime by the evils of society, and Reynolds gives us biographies to show how this occurred. This is true even of Anthony Tidkins, the Resurrection Man, who digs up corpses or creates them with equal alacrity, and who, we will see, comes to portray more than simple criminality. Several criminals reform and live respectable lives. Reynolds gives us detailed accounts of the criminals' backgrounds that suggest first-hand research. Indeed, Cyril Pearl considers Reynolds's documentary passages are 'as penetrating and painstaking as his contemporary, Mayhew' [*Victorian Patchwork,* 1972]. It is difficult to believe that the work of the two men was not related in some way. Mayhew's characters are more balanced than those of Reynolds; Reynolds's have a sharper edge of social indignation. Mayhew wrote for an interested audience; Reynolds for an angry one.

The same is true if we compare Dickens and Reynolds. Dickens gives us a powerful picture of the dark streets and alleys of Saffron Hill. By comparison, Reynolds's account of Upper Union Court, Holborn, the home of the criminal Bolter, is flat and distracted by detail.

> The dwellings are chiefly let out in lodgings, and through the open windows upon the ground-floor may occasionally be seen the half-starved

mechanics crowding around the scantily-supplied table. A few of the lower casements are filled with children's books, pictures of actors and highwaymen glaringly coloured, and lucifer-matches, twine, sweet-stuff, cotton, etc. At one door there stands an oyster-stall, when the comestible itself is in season: over another hangs a small board with a mangle painted upon it. (1, 1, Chapter 17).

This is far from the urban Gothic of the world Dickens gives us, but it leads in to a significant discussion of the problems of living in these overcrowded poverty-stricken tenements, such as the difficulty of disposing of bodies after a death, or the sexual problems of a family sleeping in one bed. Dickens uses the slums as a setting, and they have little causal connexion with Sikes's murder of Nancy. When Bolter kills his woman (1, 1, Chapter 19) it is a direct consequence of overcrowding and of ugly joyless lives.

The murder takes place as the mother is planning to make her children better beggars by binding black beetles over their eyes to blind them. This practice was used in Dublin up to the beginning of the present century, and there is no reason to believe that the scene was not drawn from Reynolds's observation. Before the mother can act, however, her drunken husband knocks her eye out against the corner of a table, and kills her. The scene is described with the style of a newspaper report, from which it may well have been taken, and the realism is continued when the hardened Bolter shows little grief at what he has done, only terror at being caught by the police. While he is hiding he overhears the avidity with which the public enjoy the details of the crime (1, 1, Chapter 27), a point which would have pleased Thackeray. Bolter is captured and sentenced to death. Instead of approving the death penalty, which panders to the public's lust for blood and prevents any possibility of reforming the criminal, Reynolds launches into an appeal for penal reform (1, 1, Chapter 36).

Reynolds develops his theme that society creates criminals into the very structure of the book. In portraying a panorama of society he is again close to Thackeray's *Vanity Fair,* although Thackeray stops short of showing the lowest orders, and he looks forward to Dickens's *Bleak House,* which George Brimley in 1853 considered 'disagreeably reminiscent of that vilest of modern books, Reynolds's **Mysteries of London**' [in the *Spectator,* 24 September 1853]. Where in Thackeray the organizing image is the puppet show, and in Dickens's novel the disease that links Lady Dedlock to Jo, in Reynolds it is crime. The inhumanity of the capitalist system expresses itself in the criminal classes that carry out the predatory desires of the rich.

To work out this design, Reynolds uses not only the mixed form of melodrama already noticed but also the content of the newspaper, with its crime columns, its court news, its editorial comment, and even in some cases serialized fiction. Many of the sections are written like newspaper reports, and some of them are adapted fact. Thus he shows Edward Holcroft breaking into the Palace, where he glimpses a moment of courtship between Victoria and Albert (a society-column scoop ahead of its time) and later overhears Victoria explaining to Albert that newspaper reports of starvation and hardship among the working classes are 'greatly exaggerated': the result of journalists trying to improve their copy (1, 1, Chapter 59; 1, 2, Chapters 193-94). Bizarre as such episodes may seem, Holcroft would have been recognized as a thinly disguised portrait of Edward Oxford, who made an assassination attempt on Queen Victoria and who, like Holcroft, was first confined to Bethlehem asylum and then deported. Some of the most sensational scenes concern the degenerate Duke of Holmesford, yet Holmesford is modelled on the third Marquis of Hertford, whose obituaries had appeared in 1842 and who served Thackeray as a model for Lord Steyne in *Vanity Fair.* By taking some of the format of the newspaper, which as a journalist he knew well, Reynolds was able to unite different subjects and kinds of writing, from statistical accounts of poverty to 'human interest' dramas. He was also able to draw on some of the authenticity of the newspaper.

Thackeray's *Vanity Fair* examines society distanced in history; Reynolds achieves a sense of near-contemporaneity. Reynolds wrote for an audience that, suffering the hardships of the 'hungry forties', could not afford Thackeray's urbane balance. His picture is not 'fair', and would not serve its purpose if it were. The strategies of Radical propaganda lead him to write, not the balanced study of social problems we find, for example, in Mrs Gaskell's *Mary Barton,* but social melodrama. When Ellen Munroe has fallen down the ladder of economic exploitation she sensationally sells her likeness to an artist, her bust to a sculptor, her whole form to a photographer, and her virtue to Greenwood (1, 1, Chapters 56, 57, 70). The story could be criticized as going from objective reportage to the clichés of the stage; in terms of arousing the audience the theatrical format of Ellen's seduction was something they could recognize and which reinforced the theme in ways an objective account could not.

Another important example is the 'Resurrection Man'. Anthony Tidkins is turned to crime as a boy by the social injustice he suffers, but through the book he becomes an increasingly monstrous figure of gratuitous cruelty. He is finally murdered by an ex-accomplice, walled up in a cellar, and blinded by the gunpowder with which he tries to force an exit. The episode is immediately contemporaneous with Poe's *The Cask of Amontillado,* but whether or not Reynolds took the episode from Poe, he followed Poe's purpose of using the tale of terror to explore the psychology of sadism and motiveless violence. In James Walker's melodrama, *The Factory Lad* (1832), the main figure, Rushton, is a poacher who earlier had been driven out of society by poverty and now leads a machine-wrecking riot occasioned by the lay-off of the workers. The play is entirely sympathetic to the workers, but Rushton grows from a victim into a demonic figure who evokes not only pity, but also horror at the consequences of social disorder. Reynolds's Resurrection Man, placed in a novel hostile to the rich, nevertheless presents also an image of the violent anarchy latent in the poor.

The crime and even murder in *Vanity Fair* is not shown in its grim detail; it is only implied. 'Has [the author] once forgotten the laws of politeness', asked Thackeray, 'and shown the monster's hideous tail above water?'. A middle-class reader of Reynolds might complain that the tail was all that was shown. But the contrast between the two books is not only due to the respective writer, or to political viewpoints. Each book reflects the audience for which it was intended, a style, a set of conventions, a way of structuring a social awareness of the world. (pp. 94-101)

> Louis James, "The View from Brick Lane: Contrasting Perspectives in Working-Class and Middle-Class Fiction of the Early Victorian Period," in The Yearbook of English Studies, Vol. 11, 1981, pp. 87-101.

Anne Humpherys (lecture date 1982)

[*In the following excerpt, first presented as a lecture in 1982, Humpherys provides an overview of Reynolds's career as a writer and editor, outlining the format of his weekly publications and emphasizing their often contradictory combination of popular literature and radical politics.*]

G. W. M. Reynolds has been called "the most popular writer in England" [*Bookseller*, 1 July 1868], and indeed in a decade of issue and reissue and simultaneous issue, his mammoth novel *The Mysteries of London* sold over a million copies. He was also an important editor of several journals in the 1840s and 1850s which played a significant role in the development of the popular press. The nature of his life and work in fact make him a critical figure to our understanding of how the radical weeklies of Cobbett, Hetherington, and others modulated into the commercially successful mass market newspaper.

Reynolds—as a person, as an editor, and as a politician—was full of contradictions; this piece might very well be titled "The Mysteries of G. W. M. Reynolds". For example, he was an upper-middle-class Englishman who was violently republican in his sentiments. Most interesting in this context, however, is the paradoxical mixture in his fiction and journals of politics and pornography, sentiment and sensationalism, rules of behaviour and calls to political action. These mysterious contradictions were also elements in Victorian popular culture, and so, by looking at Reynolds' work, we may be able to understand further that partially charted sea of readership as well.

Despite his enormous popularity in his own time, Reynolds has suffered the fate of many best-seller writers: he is now almost totally unknown to many modern Victorianists. Therefore, some pertinent biographical information may be helpful in studying his work. George William MacArthur Reynolds was born in 1814, the son of a post-captain in the Royal Navy. He was educated at Ashford Grammar School and at the Royal Military College, Sandhurst, but in 1830, on the death of his mother (his father died in 1822), he inherited £12,000. At that point he left Sandhurst and went to Paris, where he encountered the revolutionary politics that shaped his political consciousness for the rest of his life, and where he gained his lasting interest in French literature. Not much is known about his years in Paris; according to Louis James and John Saville [in their *Dictionary of Labour Biography*, 1976], he "temporarily" became a French citizen and served in the National Guard. About 1833 he married an Englishwoman, Susanna Frances Pearson, in France. During the next few years he was involved with various English language newspapers, through which, he later said, he lost most of his fortune. In 1836, bankrupt, he returned to England. There he moved into the world of London journalism, and during the next ten years established a pattern of interchange between his fiction and his journalism. Over half of his novels first appeared as serials in journals he was editing, while the first series of his grand novel *The Mysteries of London* was published in weekly parts by the publishers of *The London Journal* which he was editing at the time. In the twenty years between 1840 and 1860, Reynolds wrote some thirty-five or forty million words, published fifty-eight novels, eleven works of translation, plus many political pieces.

As editor his career was equally varied. While in France he edited *The London and Paris Courier* (1835) and was literary editor for *The Paris Literary Gazette*, where he published the first pieces by Thackeray for which the novelist ever received payment. After Reynolds returned to England, for over a year (1837-1838) he edited the old *Monthly Magazine* in which he published his first big literary success—*Pickwick Abroad* (a continuation of Dickens' novel as a sort of travel guide to France)—and his critical work *Modern Literature of France.* In 1840 he began an association with the radical *Weekly Dispatch*, for whom he acted as foreign intelligence editor, and began a short-lived, somewhat breathlessly polemical, journal *The Teetotaller*, which ran for about a year. One of the more startling contradictions in Reynolds' career is associated with this otherwise predictable journal. A fortnight before he began publishing *The Teetotaller* Reynolds "had become Director-General of the United Kingdom Anti-Teetotal Society", and under this hat had "published one or more issues of an anti-teetotal magazine" [James and Saville].

Not until Reynolds took the editorship of the new *London Journal* in 1845, however, was his career as editor of the popular press really launched. *The London Journal* was one of the first "mass market" publications, and its initiation was made possible by technological advances, such as high-speed presses and cheaper paper, and by an increasingly literate working class. There was also a shift in the economic assumptions of publishers like John Vickers, the publisher of *The London Journal*, as Sally Mitchell has pointed out, when they "recognized that the same profit could be made by selling a magazine to thirty thousand people at a penny each instead of to three thousand at sixpence and that a lot more people could afford to spend a penny than could part with a larger sum" [Sally Mitchell, "The Forgotten Woman of the Period: Penny Weekly Magazines of the 1840's and 1850's," in *A Widening Sphere: Changing Roles of Victorian Women*, edited by Martha Vicinus, 1977]. Two journals soon controlled most of this market, *The Family Herald* and *The London Journal*, the latter generally considered the more low brow and sensational of the two. A decade after the founding of these two journals in the mid-forties, their "combined sale was at least three quarters of a million copies per week".

Though Reynolds' association with *The London Journal* was brief, lasting only from its start in March of 1845 to November of 1846, he played a decisive role in establishing the pattern that made this magazine so successful. Basically the formula was simple: appeal to every taste represented by an audience of lower-middle-class and working-class readers. So each issue contained an adventure serial, some short fiction, occasionally a 'true-life' adventure story, and a page of answers to correspondents. The editors also liked to include an educational piece, one on history, or a biography of a model figure. Nor were the editors shy of including discussions of contemporary problems, and like the daily newspapers, the magazines filled out their columns with household hints, recipes, and cases of odd events.

After a year Reynolds and Vickers had some sort of disagreement, and Reynolds left *The London Journal.* (Vickers involvement with the publishing of **The Mysteries of London** is probably the reason Reynolds changed the name of that serial to **The Mysteries of the Court of London** after he and *The London Journal* parted ways.) Reynolds' affairs were in disarray again, and he had to sell off his assets and declare bankruptcy in 1848 for a second time. Probably in 1847, however, he had made a business association with John Dicks, a clerk in his office, that eventually gave him financial security, even wealth. Dicks acted as publisher and Reyolds as editor for all Reynolds' subsequent journalism; out of this association finally came their greatest success, *Reynolds's Weekly Newspaper,* which was founded in 1850 and lasted until 1967.

The first enterprise Dicks and Reynolds began, however, was modelled on *The London Journal* and was meant to compete with it for the new mass readership. *Reynolds's Miscellany* (1846-69) underwent some modifications in format in its early years—increasing both page size and the number of pages—but the nature and quality of contents remained fairly consistent. Like *The London Journal, Reynolds's Miscellany* combined escapist fantasy and improving lessons. The *Miscellany* differed from *The London Journal,* however, in at least two important ways, both of which reflected Reynolds' personal tastes and enthusiasms. First the serialized novel which began each number and from which the cover engraving was taken, tended to be somewhat more sensational than even those in *The London Journal,* particularly when these serials were written by Reynolds himself. The first such serial, for example, was a horrific Gothic tale by Reynolds, **Wagner the Wehr-Wolf.**

Second, Reynolds' politics were much more in evidence in this 'family' magazine than in *The London Journal.* For example, in the first volume, Reynolds contributed a series of **"Letters to the Industrious Classes"** in which he tried to educate cotton spinners and needlewomen, schoolmasters and governesses, to the ways in which an aristocratic hierarchy oppressed them. In later volumes the popular "Notices to Correspondents", in which the editor answered all kinds of questions, provided additional opportunity for Reynolds to propagandize his readers. This

seeming paradox of an increased sensationalism and a more overt radical political content in *Reynolds's Miscellany* is an emblem of Reynolds' peculiar place in the history of the popular press.

In any case, the formula for *Reynolds's Miscellany* was immediately successful. Within a year the weekly *Miscellany* had reached what Sally Mitchell and others consider the economically crucial circulation number of 30,000, a number which allowed a penny weekly to meet fixed expenses. This success soon recouped Reynolds' financial losses, gave him an outlet for his literary productions, and assured him a place in the history of the popular press.

In 1848, however, something happened to him that redirected some of his energies. Reynolds became an active Chartist. Though an outspoken republican from his youthful days in France, in 1848 he was catapulted into active politics by his apparently spontaneous speech at the Chartist demonstration at Trafalgar Square on 6 March. His performance there led to him being carried home on the shoulders of a cheering crowd and subsequently to an intense involvement in the Chartist movement as speaker and writer. This period of activism lasted only four years, however, and ended in acrimony and libel suits against other Chartist leaders, particularly Ernest Jones, whom Reynolds found too soft and accommodating. It was during those years of his political activism that *Reynolds's Weekly* was founded, a journal which is important not only in the history of the press, but also, as James and Saville say, significant in the development of the working-class movement itself.

The story of *Reynolds's Weekly* has been told, not finally but generally, and is not my focus here. Instead, I would like to look at Reynolds' career just before that final endeavour, for *Reynolds's Weekly Newspaper* grew out of another weekly Reynolds tried in the first flush of success of his *Miscellany* and his new career as a political activist, namely *Reynolds's Political Instructor* (November 1849-May 1850).

In the title of this weekly political journal, one of whose purposes was to propagandize for the Charter, lies another emblem for the contradictory nature of Reynolds' career as editor. The *Political Instructor* clearly echoes, if it does not repeat exactly, the name of one of the most important radical newspapers of the 1820s, William Cobbett's *Political Register.* I think this echo is more significant than the slightly condescending implications of being an 'Instructor' to the working classes. It called attention to the politically serious nature of the work. However, by also prefixing his own name to that echoing the earlier journal, Reynolds was in addition connecting his political journal to his widely read family magazine, *Reynolds's Miscellany,* often referred to simply as *Reynolds's,* with its successful blend of sensational fiction, frequent woodcuts of full-bosomed ladies, improving lessons, and practical advice. In the connection between these two essentially working-class journals lies the problem of G. W. M. Reynolds and the popular press in general. The elements of popular literature and those of popular politics do not always mix very comfortably. The often prurient fascination with the private lives of the high and mighty, the normative values of melodrama, the escapism of romance and fantasy undercut the realism and call to action of practical politics. That Reynolds linked the two raises questions about intent. To what degree was his invocation of the association with Cobbett's newspaper a courageous reflection of political belief and to what degree was it a cynical exploitation to gain sales? This is the central question about Reynolds' work as editor. It was asked, and answered variously, in his own day and continues to perplex modern commentators.

Let me outline the problem another way. From the very beginning of his career as a successful editor, that is from 1844 and the publication of *The Mysteries of London,* to the end of his life, the expressed opinion about Reynolds seems strangely at odds with his enormous popularity among lower-middle- and lower-class readers. 'Respectable' commentators abhorred him for his sensationalism as much as for his espousal of republican sentiments. Dickens indirectly referred to Reynolds as one of the "Bastards of the Mountain, draggled fringe on the Red Cap, Panders to the basest passions of the lowest natures" in the opening number of *Household Words.* Another reviewer scorned his work as "poison", full of "fire and brimstone" with "terrific" views [*Bookseller,* 1 July 1868]. At the same time important elements of the working classes also rejected him. Many Chartists did not credit his role in the movement. W. E. Adams wrote of him later [in his *Memoirs of a Social Atom,* 1903] that "it was rather as a charlatan and a trader than as a genuine politician that G. W. M. was regarded by the rank and file of Chartism". Marx called him a "scoundrel", at the same time acknowledging the special role *Reynolds's Weekly* played in the consciousness of the working class [letter to Ferdinand Lasalles, 28 April 1862, in *The Letters of Karl Marx,* edited by Saul K. Padover, 1979]. Marx did not trust Reynolds; in a letter to Engels in 1858 he said that Reynolds was a "rich and an able speculator. The mere fact that he has turned into a Chartist shows that this position must still be a 'bearable' one . . . " [cited in Virginia Berridge's "Popular Sunday Papers and Mid-Victorian Society," in *Newspaper History,* edited by George Boyce, et al., 1978]. Meanwhile the working classes bought Reynolds' serialized novels and weekly publications by the hundreds of thousands.

Marx was referring to Reynolds in his role as political agitator both on the hustings and in the pages of the *Weekly* and not to his role as editor of the *Miscellany* or as author of *Wagner, the Wehr-Wolf,* but surely Reynolds' career as writer of slightly salacious tales of adventure and romance made him as suspect in the eyes of the more radical elements of the working class, as did the financial success these fictions brought him. Though the anonymous reviewer who called his work "poison" was referring primarily to his sensational stories, he probably found Reynolds' virulent republican sentiments just as revolting. I think all these critics were talking about the same element, that all were reacting—from quite opposed positions—to the same thing in Reynolds' work: his coming to rest, as it were, on the fine point in the popular mind where escapism and activism touch. Reynolds' work and life was, to change the comparison, like a print by the artist M. C. Es-

cher, in which distinct forms are imperceptibly transformed into each other. As in an Escher print, where it is not possible to point to the exact place that a bird becomes a fish (and vice versa), it is hard to separate sincere political expressions from clever careerism in Reynolds' work. In the interchange between these two aspects the significance of his success lies, a significance that has importance not only for the study of the press but also for an understanding of the nature of popular culture itself and, not incidently, for the course of many broad-based political movements.

We can see this 'problem' most clearly at one particular moment in Reynolds' early career as editor, the seven months when he was active in Chartist politics and editing both the *Political Register* and the *Miscellany.* The difficulties of coming to terms with Reynolds at this time have been eloquently expressed by Raymond Williams [in his "Radical and/or Respectable," in *The Press We Deserve,* edited by Richard Boston, 1970]. He has argued that the early nineteenth-century radical journals like the *Political Register* or *The Black Dwarf* were popular in a good sense in that they were truly "for the people" with a "style of genuine arousal". Running counter to these political journals however was the "established popular reading" of the lower classes, the chapbooks, last dying speeches, and other "street literature" as Henry Mayhew referred to it, material which served up crime, scandal, romance, and sport in crude and, from one point of view, politically irresponsible ways.

As Williams pointed out, when the political climate changed, the nature of the popular journals did, too. Reduced official opposition lessened the intense focus and tone, and the introduction of a profit motive into the popular press, when the technological developments in printing and distribution became practical, aborted any expansion of those early radical journals. Instead a new kind of popular press emerged at mid-century, the Sunday newspaper, which combined "general political attitudes" with the more sensational elements of popular reading, particularly, as it developed, sports news. This movement culminated in a popular press that was not "for the people" but for the money—amoral and apolitical, that used, in Williams' words, "apparent arousal as a cover for an eventual if temporary satisfaction". He wrote of *The Daily Mail;* we can think of *The Daily News* or perhaps even more poignantly, *The New York Post.* Williams saw *Reynolds's Weekly* as one of the journals in which the shift took place, and in his gentle censure of the commercialism of the *Weekly,* came down on the side of Marx about Reynolds.

I see it a little differently. In Reynolds' work, we do indeed see limned the point at which the ingredients for the shift Williams deplored have been brought together but not perfectly mixed—in fact, not mixed at all. Further, Reynolds' very ability not to try to blend the various elements of the popular mind into a unified position is what made his work successful both as fiction writer and as editor. To borrow a term from an earlier English poet, I think Reynolds as editor possessed a kind of 'negative capability'— an ability to absorb the contradictory impulses and desires of the populace without any 'irritable' effort at resolution.

His instinct for doing so may have been at bottom commercial—one group of his critics certainly thinks so—but the result was the creation of a form that was popular in the best sense of the word because it was inclusive.

We can see signs of this 'negative capability' in Reynolds' first important editorial enterprise, *The London Journal.* In its first year Reynolds contributed a few characteristic tales, either uplifting or romantic, but his major contribution as a writer was a seventeen part series on **"Etiquette for the Millions"**. The various topics covered included proper table manners, dress, correct forms of address, and hints on proper behavior in different social situations. In all of these pieces Reynolds took the most conventional line; as he said in the introductory piece: "No man has a right to consider himself entitled, as a unity in the millions which constitute a society, to act entirely for himself and by himself. He must pay deference to the interests of others" [*London Journal,* No. 7, 12 April 1845]. While this sentiment out of context could receive a nod of approval from the most devoted socialist, in context it was used to justify adherence to the most restrictive of surface behavior.

Reynolds' series on etiquette fit right in with the general tone of *The London Journal* with its appeal to a "mass readership . . . made up of people with aspirations for respectability" as Sally Mitchell put it, but it strikes an odd note coming as it did simultaneously with Reynolds' calls for revolutionary political changes in the columns of *The Weekly Dispatch.* We can charge him with hypocrisy, a willingness to do anything that paid, or we can see in this juxtaposition a straightforward, perhaps unconscious, expression of two paradoxical elements in the popular mind: the desire for a better life, defined predominantly by what the populace perceived as better in the lives of those 'above' them, and a contradictory tendency to want to destroy that very desired life because those who had it were seen as exploiting those who didn't.

A similar series of paradoxes is reflected in the contrasting pages of *Reynolds's Political Instructor* and *Reynolds's Miscellany.* The two journals were issued simultaneously over a period of seven months, after which time Reynolds abandoned the *Political Instructor* for *Reynolds's Weekly Newspaper.* The *Political Instructor* itself was an outgrowth of his personal involvement in Chartist politics. Eight months after his triumphal appearance at the Trafalgar Square demonstration, Reynolds issued the first weekly number of the *Instructor.* Though a political platform for Chartism, it took its formal aspects from the *Miscellany.* For example, each issue began with a handsome woodcut, though in the *Instructor* these were of "eminent Political Characters" while in the *Miscellany* they were of exciting scenes from the current sensational serial. The two journals also advertised the same things, including each other.

The contents of the two were, of course, different in tone, but surprisingly not very much in content. The *Political Instructor* ran articles which addressed current social and economic issues; the *Miscellany* frequently referred to the same events. In the *Instructor,* Edwin Roberts, a minor journalist of the period, was contributing a "New History

of England" while in the *Miscellany* the same author was represented by romanticized historical fiction. The Stamp Act prohibited overtly political articles in journals like the *Miscellany,* but in the "Notices to Correspondents" there were many short "essays" on political economy and politics. There was, however, frequently a real difference in attitude in these articles. Take, for example, the different approaches to the aristocracy. In the *Political Instructor* attacks on the aristocracy were the fundamental statement of Reynolds' politics after his assertion of the Chartist program, with its added demand for the elimination of primogeniture. At the same time that he was running a series on "The Aristocracy: Its Origins, Progress and Decay" in the *Political Instructor,* in the *Miscellany* he was featuring a series on famous aristocratic ladies, presenting large numbers of titillating tales of intrigue, scandal, and sometimes, selfless sacrifice. Thus the aristocracy provided for his readers, as it always has, the target for abuse and the source of escapist fantasy.

A juxtaposition of one simultaneous issue of the two journals will further demonstrate the contradictions of popular literature and politics. The December 1849 *Political Instructor* ran a woodcut of Thomas Cooper, the poet-shoemaker, plus articles on Manchester, a segment of the series on the aristocracy, an article "The Cry of the Poor", and short items on "The People" (anti-oligarchy) and "The Colonies" (anti-imperialist). The corresponding issue of the *Miscellany* for 8 December 1849, featured a very exciting woodcut showing a diaphanously clothed maiden about to be subjected to some machine of torture, an illustration for Reynolds' romantic historical novel **The Bronze Statue; or, the Virgin's Kiss,** derived ultimately from the notorious eighteenth-century Gothic novel *The Monk* by Matthew Lewis. There was another serial on "The Beauties of the Court of Charles the Second", while the featured article on social conditions was entitled "The Evil Consequences of Tight Lacing". The reader who took both the *Instructor* and the *Miscellany* could have it any way he wanted it: he could blame the aristocracy for every social ill and feed on the imagined pleasures their money and position brought them; he could be shocked by living conditions in Manchester or soothed into thinking that tight lacing was a major cause of ill health among women.

While editing both journals and attending Chartist meetings and rallies, Reynolds' own contributions to the *Miscellany* diminished in number, but two of his novels were serialized after February 1850, and they, too, demonstrate Reynolds' ability to take the popular pulse. The first was **The Pixy; or, The Unbaptized Child,** a tale with much folklore and superstition in it. The other was a politically relevant piece called in the first installment, **The Slaves of England,** but which became in one of the next installments **The Seamstress: A Domestic Tale.** In the quick change of title we see again that frustrating blend of calculation and politics that marks his work. **The Slaves of England** as a title must have seemed a bit strong for the readers of the *Miscellany,* though presumably many of them were reading at the exact same time in the *Political Instructor* a famous series by Bronterre O'Brien on "The Rise, Progress and Phases of Human Slavery". James and Saville think Reynolds was closest in his political attitudes to O'Brien.

So Reynolds changed his title to emphasize that sentimental and safe iconography of the early Victorian period, the victimized seamstress.

To me Reynolds' 'negative capability' as editor is most interesting in his "Notices to Correspondents", a department in the *Miscellany* that served the readers of both the *Political Instructor* and the *Miscellany* since there was no room in the *Instructor* for a "notices" column. He announced in the *Instructor* that queries sent to that journal would be answered in the *Miscellany*.

A "Notices to Correspondents" column was a very popular department in the family periodicals of the 1840s and 1850s. *Lloyd's* had one as did *The London Journal*. The readers of these journals asked similar questions. In *Reynolds's Miscellany* they wanted to know about etiquette, and medical and legal matters. The answers to their queries about political and historical concerns became a hallmark of all of Reynolds' journals. There were also many questions regarding jobs as clerks and ways to emigrate. Almost every issue of *Reynolds's Miscellany* included the answer to one or more requests for Reynolds to evaluate the correspondent's handwriting.

There seems little room for doubt that Reynolds, albeit with help, wrote most of the responses, and maintained his role as respondent even when he did not have time for other writing for the *Miscellany*. There are several reasons for his devotion to this department, which grew from a couple of columns when the journal started in 1846 to several pages in 1849. For one thing, the "Notices" was one place politics could be addressed without calling too obvious attention to them. More important, I think, was the intimacy of the relationship that developed between Reynolds and his readers through the personal nature of many of the requests. They wrote to ask him about specific doctors; Reynolds in turn recommended various medical men by name. He gave advice on love and legal matters, and in these concerns no question seemed too personal. For example, a characteristic response to a personal question was: "To Robert—the young lady is perhaps only a little inclined to flirtation, and you must not judge her too severely. It is out of our power, being unacquainted personally with the party, to determine whether you are suited to each other. Study the lady's character and watch her disposition closely; after six months have elapsed let us know the result, that is to say, if our advice is then required" [*Reynolds's Miscellany*, n.s. III, No. 72, 24 November 1849]. The next week's "Notices" began with an essay decrying the exploitation of needlewomen, followed by short pieces of medical and legal advice, and some job counselling: "Your handwriting is very good, but if you had read our Notices in previous numbers, you would have had your mind disabused of the fallacious idea, that a clerk's situation is to be got for the mere asking, whereas, in point of fact, it is most difficult to obtain" and (to a dyer) "there will soon be a good opening for your trade in Australia, but at present we could hardly recommend you to emigrate" [*Reynolds's Miscellany*, n.s. III, No. 73, 30 November 1849].

The harshness in Reynolds' response to the query about getting a clerk's job was a frequent tone in the "Notices":

for example, "E.H.B. You cannot claim any relationship: your mother was not married: your father's wife being still alive, he committed bigamy, and you are consequently illegitimate". He could, however, be encouraging as well: "There is no need ever to apologize for the looseness of the writing, we are always happy on hearing from our friends from the working classes, and never scrutinize, unless asked, their style of penmanship" [both from *Reynolds's Miscellany*, n.s. III, No. 74, 8 December 1849]. In addition to these sorts of responses, Reynolds gave advice about proper behavior—when to wear white gloves—and hundreds of recipes for making everything from hearty soup to silver paint. These recipes, which he published with the aid of his wife, were so popular, that when he indexed the volume, he included "Useful and Practical Receipts in the Notices to Correspondents", which was the longest single section in the index. His wife subsequently published under her own name a collection entitled *The Household Book of Practical Receipts*. (She also wrote a number of popular romances such as *Gretna-Green; or, All for Love*, with "a high moral purpose", according to the advertisements for it in the *Miscellany*.)

We cannot know which queries were originally sent to the *Instructor* as opposed to the *Miscellany*. There are a few direct references to the *Instructor* and some of the longer "essays" that appeared in the "Notices" on social questions are likely to have been in response to questions addressed to the political journal. The audience for both journals, though, seems fairly consistent: for the most part an upwardly mobile working class concerned, even obsessed, with respectability.

The complex relationship between Reynolds and his readers—he being in turn stern adviser, knowledgeable informant, avuncular domestic manager—was surely one of the reasons for the *Miscellany*'s success; by 1855 it had a circulation of 300,000. Yet in the "Notices" we can see the same contradictory mixture of social conformism and political radicalism in evidence elsewhere in Reynolds' work. Although he was nearly always hard-nosed about careers in the respectable trade of clerking, he never challenged the desires of his readers to fit into the established order of things by getting these jobs and hence moving up the class scale. The political inclusiveness of the "Notices" in fact raises the same questions about Reynolds' seriousness as a political radical. Some critics have charged that he was unthinking and just repeated the old-fashioned republicanism he had learned in Paris in the 1830s. It is true that he usually blamed all social and economic injustice on the aristocracy's control of land; he seemed to believe that elimination of that class plus achievement of the Charter would usher in a political Utopia. Yet every now and again, Reynolds wrote something which suggested that he knew as well as Marx did that feudalism had already been replaced by industrial capitalism. For example, in the conventional little essay in the "Notices" on the "contrasts of London", Reynolds substituted the labels "labour and capital" for the more clichéd "rich and poor", and remarked that "land was at first the capital that swept everything before it, then came capital, and now must come labour—the only real and permanent capital—the only currency upon which society can with safety calculate for its endurance, and, which must before long assert its supremacy and independence" [*Reynolds's Miscellany,* n.s. III, No. 72, 24 November 1849].

Reynolds' political understanding was more complicated than he has been given credit for by later critics like Raymond Williams who criticized him for his out-dated views and the role they played in misdirecting the political energies of the working class. Reynolds' politics as well as his editorial stance and the contents of his fiction reflected the inclusiveness of popular culture. His contradictions were the contradictions of the audience he was writing for. Social and literary historians have the same difficulty in coming to terms with the one as with the other. Each time Virginia Berridge, in her study of *Lloyd's* and *Reynolds's Weekly,* attacked these Sunday papers for their commercialism and their dissipating of working-class radicalism, she qualified her censure when it came to *Reynolds's Weekly.* Nevertheless her final judgment of G. W. M. Reynolds as insincere and politically expedient is harsh. This contradiction in her own text remains unresolved as does my own disconcerted reaction to seeing advertisements for Chartist meetings cheek by jowl in the *Weekly* with others promising to make the buyer more respectable with a patent medicine to grow more luxuriant whiskers. Unless we take into account these contradictions in the popular mind, unless we are able to exercise our own negative capabilities as literary historians, we will not be able to understand fully either popular literature or popular politics. G. W. M. Reynolds as editor and writer is a good place to begin our task. (pp. 79-88)

Anne Humpherys, "G. W. M. Reynolds: Popular Literature & Popular Politics," in Victorian Periodicals Review, *Vol. XVI, Nos. 3 & 4, Fall-Winter, 1983, pp. 79-89.*

FURTHER READING

Berridge, Virginia. "Popular Sunday Papers and Mid-Victorian Society." In *Newspaper History: From the Seven-teenth Century to the Present Day,* edited by George Boyce; James Curran; and Pauline Wingate, pp. 247-64. London: Constable and Co., 1978.

In-depth study of the weekly periodicals popular in the Victorian era. Berridge discusses the circulation, content, and impact of *Reynolds's Weekly Newspaper.*

Grierson, Francis D. "G. W. M. Reynolds." *The Bookman* LXVII, No. 401 (February 1925): 251-52.

Overview of Reynolds's life and works.

James, Louis. *Fiction for the Working Man.* London: Oxford University Press, 1963, 226 p.

Examines *Pickwick Abroad* and *The Mysteries of London* as part of a comprehensive analysis of working-class fiction of the early Victorian era.

Lucas, E. V. "The Parasites." In his *Only the Other Day: A Volume of Essays,* pp. 11-15. 1937. Reprint. Freeport, N. Y.: Books for Libraries Press, 1967.

Censures *Pickwick Abroad* as an egregious and humorless plagiarism of Dickens, calling it "the worst book I have ever read."

MacKenzie, Norman. "Socialist Pioneer." *The New Statesman and Nation* XXXIX, No. 1000 (6 May 1950): 508-09.

Overview of Reynolds's life and career, centering on his political affiliations.

Summers, Montague. "George William MacArthur Reynolds." In his *A Gothic Bibliography,* pp. 146-59. London: The Fortune Press, n.d.

Offers a comprehensive bibliography of Reynolds's works.

———. "Bibliography: G. W. M. Reynolds." *The Times Literary Supplement,* No. 2109 (4 July 1942): 336.

Details the problems determining the authorship and publication date of several works attributed to Reynolds.

"Notes on Sales: G. W. M. Reynolds and Penny Fiction." *The Times Literary Supplement,* No. 1149 (24 January 1924): 56.

Surveys Reynolds's literary output, noting that despite his tremendous popularity, "copies of his original editions are quite scarce" and have therefore become collectors' items.

Additional coverage of Reynolds's life and career is contained in the following source published by Gale Research: *Dictionary of Literary Biography,* Vol. 21.

Ivan Turgenev

Fathers and Sons

(Full name Ivan Sergeyevich Turgenev; also transliterated as Toorgenef, Tourghenief, Tourguénief, Turgeneff, Turgenieff, and Turgéniew) Russian novelist, short fiction writer, dramatist, poet, and essayist.

The following entry presents criticism of Turgenev's novel *Ottsy i deti* (1862; *Fathers and Sons;* also translated as *Fathers and Children*). For discussion of Turgenev's complete career, see *NCLC,* Volume 21.

INTRODUCTION

Praised as Turgenev's greatest work, *Fathers and Sons* has been called one of the most brilliant novels of the nineteenth century and is credited with giving the concept of "nihilism" wide currency in the political discourse of the era. By contrasting Russian characters representative of liberals of the 1840s with young radicals of the 1860s, *Fathers and Sons* comments on the eternal clash between generations and the political and social turmoil of mid-nineteenth-century Russia. However, according to René Wellek, *Fathers and Sons* "is neither an anti-nihilist novel nor a glorification of the coming revolution. Its beauty is in the detachment, the objectivity, and even the ambivalence with which Turgenev treats his hero and his opinions and presents the conflict between his crude, arrogant, youthful nihilism and the conservative romanticism of his elders."

Fathers and Sons was written in the early 1860s, when Russia was a politically troubled country, divided among conservatives, radicals who called for economic communism and a complete restructuring of society, and liberals who favored free enterprise and slow, peaceful reform. The publication of *Fathers and Sons* in the journal *Russian Messenger* in 1862 intensified the heated political atmosphere, generating an unprecedented literary and social controversy in which the work received both accolades and condemnations from all parties. Some conservatives praised Turgenev's novel, claiming that it appropriately derided Russia's left-wing youth, while others charged that, in its sympathetic portrayal of the radical Bazarov, it flattered lawless fanatics. Similarly, the radical intelligentsia both censured and lauded the work, some members complaining that the author had slandered them by portraying Bazarov as a man who indiscriminately repudiates institutions of which he has no knowledge, and others extolling the thoughtful, sensitive depiction of a political partisan. In his 1869 essay "A Propos of *Fathers and Sons*," Turgenev denied the presence of a specific political agenda in his depiction of Bazarov, claiming that he was simply attempting to create an accurate, realistic portrait of contemporary youth, and noting that the inspiration for the character came from a conversation with a young pro-

vincial doctor he had met on a train: "In depicting Bazarov's personality, I excluded everything artistic from the range of his sympathies, I made him express himself in harsh and unceremonious tones, not out of an absurd desire to insult the younger generation (!!!), but simply as a result of my observations of my acquaintance, Dr. D., and people like him." Disillusioned by the furor and by widespread misinterpretation of his work, Turgenev left Russia, living in self-imposed exile, except for short visits to his homeland, until his death in 1883.

Fathers and Sons begins as the university student Arkady Nikolaevich Kirsanov returns home from St. Petersburg after three years at school, accompanied by his friend Evgeny Vassilyev Bazarov, a medical student with markedly radical political views and a brusque, opinionated manner. Arkady's widowed father, the provincial aristocrat Nikolai Petrovich Kirsanov, is a member of the liberal generation of the 1840s who holds progressive views but has proven ineffectual in his attempts to implement reforms at Marino, his country estate. In addition, he and his peasant mistress Fenitchka have produced a son, a condition he is reluctant to admit to Arkady. Nikolai's brother Pavel Petrovich is a dandy who, disappointed in love, has secluded himself at Marino. Pavel Petrovich can barely disguise his hatred for Bazarov, who, Arkady explains, is "a nihilist": "a man who does not bow down before any authority, who does not take any principle on faith, whatever reverence that principle may be enshrined in." In keeping with these views, Bazarov rejects every aspect of political, social, and cultural life, but retains a belief in empirical science. He spends his days at Marino talking to the peasants and hunting frogs to dissect, while Arkady, who admires his friend's skepticism and confrontational attitude, suggests that his father modernize his thought by substituting his reading of Alexander Pushkin's poetry with the latest in German philosophy.

The two friends grow tired of Marino and decide to visit a nearby town, where they meet the beautiful young widow Anna Sergeyevna Odintsova. Intrigued by Bazarov's ideas, she invites them to Nikolskoe, her estate. Odintsova unknowingly begins to inspire Bazarov's affections through her continual attention. Although Bazarov would normally deny romantic emotions as useless nonsense, he succumbs to his strong feelings and declares his love to her. Odintsova gently rejects her suitor, intent on continuing her sheltered and static life at Nikolskoe. Arkady, meanwhile, falls in love with Anna Sergeyevna's younger sister Katya, but after Odintsova's rebuff of Bazarov, the two young men quickly leave the estate.

After a visit with Bazarov's parents—his mother is a minor aristocrat and his father a doctor from the peasant class—they return to Marino. In his eagerness to see Katya, Arkady departs for Nikolskoe almost immediately, leaving Bazarov behind. Hoping to avoid a confrontation with Pavel Petrovich, Bazarov busies himself with scientific experiments. However, he is caught by Arkady's uncle as he steals a kiss from Fenitchka, to whom he is attracted. Pavel Petrovich challenges him to a duel, during which the elder man is wounded in the leg. Bazarov returns to his parents' home and, in an attempt to forget his love for Odintsova, immerses himself in work by assisting his father in his medical practice among the peasants. While performing an autopsy on a patient infected with typhus, Bazarov contracts the disease and soon dies. In an epilogue it is revealed that Arkady and Katya have married, as have Nikolai Petrovich and Fenitchka. Pavel Petrovich, however, has left Marino for self-imposed exile abroad, and Odintsova has acceded to a marriage of convenience.

Examinations of the character Bazarov have pervaded criticism of *Fathers and Sons.* Critics long regarded the great diversity of conflicting interpretations of Bazarov as evidence of the author's ambivalent attitude toward his main character or, worse, as confusion and ineptitude in the delineation of Bazarov. Some even accused Turgenev of simply "killing off" Bazarov because he was incapable of resolving the contradictions in his creation. Most commentators now extol the intricacy of the characterization and cite the importance of Bazarov to the work's structure, asserting that the novel's development hinges on the slow revelation of his personality. Turgenev presents his hero from a variety of perspectives by pairing him with different characters in a series of locations in order to re-

veal the essence of who he is and what he represents. While early commentators—including Turgenev himself—have described this structure as merely episodic, recent critics have detected an underlying unity in the close interweaving of characters and themes. Contrasts and balances between Bazarov and the other figures, scholars note, are carefully developed, resulting in a complex elucidation of a tumultuous society. In this view, Odintsova, Pavel Petrovich, and the other characters are important not just for the light they shed on Bazarov, but as vivid depictions of isolationists, Westernizers affecting European manners and fashion, well-meaning but ineffectual liberals and other segments of Russian society. Critics have applauded Turgenev's ability to create multifaceted personalities even in these secondary characters.

Aside from considering *Fathers and Sons* as political commentary, scholars have also interpreted the novel as a love story, a tragedy designed along classical lines, and as a philosophical work of considerable depth and insight. Wellek for example, has asserted that *Fathers and Sons* conveys the message that there is "no personal immortality, no God who cares for man; nature is indifferent, fate is blind and cruel, love is an affliction, even a disease beyond reason." With such studies has come an increased emphasis on Turgenev's artistry, particularly his simple, detached style and his evocative use of nature imagery. Modern commentators cite *Fathers and Sons* as a successful fusion of art and politics which, according to Richard Freeborn, creates "a remarkable organic unity. The result is the most artistically perfect, structurally unified and ideologically compelling of Turgenev's novels."

N. N. Strakhov   (essay date 1862)

[*In the following excerpt from an essay first published in Russian in 1862, Strakhov appraises Turgenev's portrayal of Bazarov in* Fathers and Sons, *noting that the author's purpose in the novel was to support neither progressive nor reactionary ideologies, but rather to demonstrate "the eternal principles of human life."*]

In order to be completely consistent to the very end, Bazarov refrains from preaching, as another form of empty chatter. And in reality, preaching would be nothing other than the admission of the rights of thought and the force of ideas. Preaching would be that justification which, as we have seen, was superfluous for Bazarov. To attach importance to preaching would mean to admit intellectual activity, to admit that men are ruled not by the senses and need, but also by thought and the words in which it is vested. To start preaching would mean to start going into abstractions, would mean calling logic and history to one's aid, would mean to concern oneself with those things already admitted to be trifles in their very essence. That is why Bazarov is not fond of arguments, disputation, and does not attach great value to them. He sees that one cannot gain much by logic; he tries instead to act through his personal example, and is sure that Bazarovs will spring up by themselves in abundance, as certain plants spring up where their seeds are. Pisarev understands that position very well. He says, for example: "Indignation at stupidity and baseness in general is understandable, though it is for that matter as fruitful as indignation at autumn dampness or winter cold." He judges Bazarov's tendency in the same way: "If Bazarovism is a disease, then it is a disease of our time, and must be endured to the end, no matter what palliatives and amputations are employed. Treat Bazarovism however you please—that is your business; but you will not be able to put a stop to it; it is just the same as Cholera."

Therefore it is clear that all the chatterer-Bazarovs, the preacher-Bazarovs, the Bazarovs occupied only with their Bazarovism rather than with deeds are on the wrong road, which will lead them to endless contradictions and stupidities, that they are far less consistent and stand much lower than Bazarov.

Such is the stern cast of mind, the solid store of thoughts Turgenev embodied in Bazarov. He clothed that mind with flesh and blood, and fulfilled that task with amazing mastery. Bazarov emerged as a simple man, free of all affectation, and at the same time firm and powerful in soul and body. Everything in him fits his strong character unusually well. It is quite noteworthy that he is *more Russian,* so to speak, than all the rest of the characters in the novel. His speech is distinguished by its simplicity, appropriateness mockery, and completely Russian cast. In the same way he approaches the common people more easily than any other character in the novel and knows better than they how to behave with them.

Nothing could correspond so well as this to the simplicity and straight forwardness of the view Bazarov professes. A man who is profoundly imbued with certain convictions, who is their complete embodiment, must without fail also turn out natural and therefore close to his native traditions and at the same time a strong man. That is why Turgenev, who up to this point had created divided characters, so to speak, for example, the Hamlet of the Shchigry District, Rudin, and Lavretsky [in *Nest of Noblemen*], finally attained the type of an undivided personality in Bazarov. Bazarov is the first strong character, the first whole character, to appear in Russian literature from the sphere of so called educated society. Whoever fails to value that, whoever fails to understand the importance of that phenomenon, had best not judge our literature. Even Antonovich noticed it, as one may see by the following strange sentence: "Apparently Turgenev wanted to portray in his hero what is called a *demonic or Byronic character, something on the order of Hamlet.*" Hamlet—a demonic character! That indicated a confused notion of Byron and Shakespeare. Yet actually *something of a demonic order* does emerge in Turgenev's work, that is, a figure rich in force, though that force is not pure.

In what does the action of the novel really consist?

Bazarov together with his friend Arkady Kirsanov arrives in the provinces from Petersburg. Both are students who have just completed their courses, one in the medical academy, the other at the university. Bazarov is no longer a man in his first youth; he has already acquired a certain

reputation, has managed to present his mode of thought; while Arkady is still completely a youth. The entire action of the novel takes place during one vacation, perhaps for both the first vacation after completing their courses. For the most part the friends visit together, in the Kirsanov family, in the Bazarov family, in the provincial capital, in the village of the widow Odintsov. They meet many people, whom they either meet for the first time or have not seen for many years. To be precise, Bazarov had not gone home in three years. Therefore there occurs a variegated collision of their new views, brought from Petersburg, with the views of the people they meet. The entire interest of the novel is contained in these collisions. There are very few events and little action in it. Toward the end of the vacation Bazarov dies, almost by accident, becoming infected from a decomposing body, and Kirsanov marries, having fallen in love with Odintsov's sister. With that the entire novel ends.

In this Bazarov appears completely the hero, despite the fact that there is apparently nothing brilliant or striking in him. The reader's attention is focused on him from the first, and all the other characters begin to turn about him as around the main center of gravity. He is least of all interested in other characters, but the others are all the more interested in him. He does not try to attach anyone to himself and does not force himself on them, and yet wherever he appears he arouses the greatest attention and becomes the main object of feelings and thoughts, love and hatred.

In setting off to spend time with his parents and with friends Bazarov had no particular aim in mind. He does not seek anything and does not expect anything from that trip. He simply wants to rest and travel. At the most he sometimes wants to *look at people.* But with that superiority he has over those around him and as a result of their all feeling his strength, these characters themselves seek closer relations with him and involve him in a drama he did not at all want and did not even anticipate.

He had hardly appeared in the Kirsanov family when he immediately arouses irritation and hatred in Pavel Petrovich, respect mixed with fear in Nikolai Petrovich, the friendly disposition of Fenichka, Dunyasha, the servants' children, even of the baby Mitya, and the contempt of Prokofich. Later on, things reach the stage that he is himself carried away for a moment and kisses Fenichka, and Pavel Petrovich challenges him to a duel. "What a piece of foolery!" Bazarov repeats, not at all having expected such *events.*

The trip to town, its purpose to *look at people,* also is not without consequences for him. Various characters begin to mill around him. Sitnikov and Kukshin, masterfully depicted characters of the false progressive and the false emancipated woman, begin to court him. Of course they do not disconcert him; he treats them with contempt and they only serve as a contrast, from which his mind and force, his total integrity emerge still more sharply and in greater relief. But here the stumbling block, Anna Sergeyevna Odintsov, is also met. Despite his coolness Bazarov begins to waver. To the great amazement of his worshipper Arkady he is even embarrassed once, and on another occasion blushes. Without suspecting any danger, however, firmly confident of himself, Bazarov goes to visit Odintsov, at Nikolskoe. And he really does control himself splendidly. And Odintsov, like all the other characters, becomes interested in him, as she probably had not become interested in anyone else in her whole life. The matter ends badly, however. Too great a passion is aroused in Bazarov, while Odintsov's inclination does not rise to real love. Bazarov leaves almost completely rejected and again begins to be amazed at himself and to upbraid himself. "The devil knows what nonsense it is! Every man hangs on a thread, the abyss may open under his feet any minute, and yet he must go and invent all sorts of discomforts for himself, and spoil his life."

But despite these wise comments, Bazarov continues involuntarily to spoil his life just the same. Even after that lesson, even during his second visit to the Kirsanovs, he is carried away with Fenichka and is forced to fight a duel with Pavel Petrovich.

Apparently Bazarov does not at all desire and does not expect a love affair, but the love affair takes place against his iron will; life, which he had thought he would rule, catches him in its huge wave.

Near the end of the story, when Bazarov visits his father and mother, he apparently is somewhat bewildered after all the shocks he had undergone. He was not so bewildered that he could not be cured, that he would not rise again in full force after a short while. But nevertheless the shadow of sorrow which lay over that iron man even at the beginning becomes deeper toward the end. He loses the desire to work, loses weight, begins to make fun of the peasants no longer in a friendly way but rather sardonically. As a result, it turns out that this time he and the peasant fail to understand each other, while formerly mutual understanding was possible up to a point. Finally, Bazarov begins to improve and becomes interested in medical practice. The infection of which he dies nevertheless seems to testify to inadequate attention and agility, to a momentary diversion of his spiritual forces.

Death is the last test of life, the last accident that Bazarov did not expect. He dies, but to the very last moment he remains foreign to that life with which he came into conflict so strangely, which bothered him with such *trifles,* made him commit such *fooleries* and, finally killed him as result of such an *insignificant* cause.

Bazarov dies altogether the hero and his death creates a shattering impression. To the very end, to the last flash of conscience, he does not betray himself by a single word nor by a single sign of cowardice. He is broken, but not conquered.

Thus despite the short time of action in the novel and despite his quick death, Bazarov was able to express himself completely and completely show his force. Life did not destroy him—one cannot possibly draw that conclusion from the novel—but only gave him occasions to disclose his energy. In the readers' eyes Bazarov emerges the victor from his trials. Everyone will say that people like Bazarov can do much, and that with such strength one may expect much from them.

Strictly speaking, Bazarov is shown only in a narrow frame and not with all the sweep of human life. The author says practically nothing about his hero's development, how such a character could have been formed. In precisely the same way, the novel's rapid ending leaves the question "would Bazarov have remained the same Bazarov, or in general what development awaited him in the future" as a complete puzzle. And yet silence on the first as on the second question has, it seems to me, its reason in realistic basis. If the hero's gradual development is not shown, it is unquestionably because Bazarov did not become educated through the gradual accumulation of influences but, on the contrary, by a rapid, sharp break. Bazarov had not been home for three years. During that time he studied, and now suddenly he appears before us imbued with everything he has managed to learn. The morning after his arrival he already goes forth after frogs and in general he continues his *educational* life at every convenient opportunity. He is a man of theory, and theory created him, created him imperceptibly, without events, without anything that one might have related, created him with a single intellectual turnabout.

Bazarov soon dies. That was necessary to the artist in order to make the picture simple and clear. Bazarov could not long remain in his present tense mood. Sooner or later he would have to change and stop being Bazarov. We have no right to complain to the author that he did not choose a broader task and limited himself to the narrower one. He decided to stop at a single step in his hero's development. Nonetheless the *whole man,* not fragmentary traits, appear at that step of his development, as generally happens in development. In relation to the fullness of character the author's task is splendidly fulfilled.

A living, whole man is caught by the author in each of Bazarov's actions and movements. Here is the great merit of the novel, which contains its main idea, and which our hurried moralizers did not notice. Bazarov is a theoretician; he is a strange and sharply one-sided person; he preaches unusual things; he acts eccentrically; he is a schoolboy in whom the coarsest *affectation* is united with profound sincerity; as we said before, he is a man foreign to life; that is, he himself avoids life. But a warm stream of life courses beneath all these external forms. With all his sharpness and the artificiality of his actions Bazarov is a completely live person, not a phantom, not an invention but real flesh and blood. He rejects life yet at the same time lives profoundly and strongly.

After one of the most wonderful scenes in the novel, namely, after the conversation in which Pavel Kirsanov challenges Bazarov to a duel and the latter accepts the challenge and agrees on its terms, Bazarov, amazed by the unexpected turn of events and the strangeness of the conversation, exclaims: "Well, I'll be damned! How fine, and how foolish! A pretty farce we've been through! Like trained dogs dancing on their hind paws." It would be difficult to make a more caustic remark. And yet the reader feels that the conversation Bazarov so characterizes was in reality a completely live and serious conversation; that despite all the deformity and artificiality of its form, the conflict of two energetic characters has been accurately expressed in it.

The poet shows us the same thing with unusual clarity through the whole novel. It may constantly be seen that the characters and particularly Bazarov *put on a farce* and that like trained dogs they *dance on their hind legs.* Yet beneath this appearance, as beneath a transparent veil, the reader clearly discerns that the feelings and actions underlying it are not at all canine but purely and profoundly human.

That is the point of view from which the action and events of the novel may best be evaluated. Beneath the rough, deformed, artificial, and affected forms, the profound vitality of all the phenomena and characters brought to the scene is heard. If Bazarov, for example, possesses the reader's attention and sympathy, he does so because in reality all these words and actions flow out of a living soul, not because each of his words is sacred and each action fair. Apparently Bazarov is a proud man, terribly egoistic and offending others by his egoism. But the reader makes his peace with that pride because simultaneously Bazarov lacks all smugness and self-satisfaction; pride brings him no joy. Bazarov treats his parents carelessly and curtly. But no one could suspect him, in that instance, of pleasure in the feeling of his personal superiority or the feeling of his power over them. Still less can he be reproached for abusing that superiority and that power. He simply refuses tender relationship with his parent and refuses it incompletely. Something strange emerges: he is uncommunicative with his father, laughs at him, sharply accuses him either of ignorance or tenderness. And yet the father is not only not offended but rather happy and satisfied. "Bazarov's jeers did not in the least perturb Vassily Ivanovich; they were positively a comfort to him. Holding his greasy dressing-gown across his stomach with two fingers, and smoking his pipe, he used to listen with enjoyment to Bazarov; and the more malicious his sallies, the more goodnaturedly did his delighted father chuckle, showing every one of his black teeth." Such are the wonders of love. Soft and goodnatured Arkady could never *delight* his father as Bazarov does his. Bazarov himself, of course, feels and understands that very well. Why should he be tender with his father and betray his inexorable consistency!

Bazarov is not at all so dry a man as his external actions and the cast of his thoughts might lead one to believe. In life, in his relations to people, Bazarov is not consistent (with himself); but in that very thing his vitality is disclosed. He likes people. "Man is a strange being," he says, noticing the presence of that liking in himself, "he wants to be with people, just to curse them, so long as he can be with them." Bazarov is not an abstract theoretician who solves all problems and is completely calmed by that solution. In such a case he would be a monstrous phenomenon, a caricature, not a man. That is why Bazarov is easily excited, why everything vexes him, everything has an effect on him, despite all his firmness and consistency in words and actions. This excitement does not betray his view and his intentions at all; for the most part it only arouses his bile and vexes him. Once he says the following to his friend Arkady: "You said, for instance, to-day as we passed our bailiff Philip's cottage—it's the one that's so nice and clean—well, you said Russia will attain perfection when the poorest peasant has a house like that, and every one of us ought to work to bring it about. And I felt such a hatred for this poorest peasant, this Philip or Sidor, for whom I'm to be ready to jump out of my skin, and . . . what do I need his thanks for? Why, suppose he does live in a clean hut, while the nettles are growing out of me,— well, what comes after that?" What a terrible, shocking speech, isn't it?

A few minutes later Bazarov does still worse: he discloses a longing to choke his tender friend Arkady, to choke him for no particular reason and in the guise of a pleasant trial already spreads wide his long and hard fingers.

Why does all this not arm the reader against Bazarov? What could be worse than that? And yet the impression created by these incidents does not serve to harm Bazarov. So much so that even Antonovich (striking proof!) who with extreme diligence explains everything in Bazarov on the bad side in order to prove Turgenev's sly intention to blacken Bazarov—completely left that incident out!

What does this mean? Apparently Bazarov, who so easily meets people, takes such lively interest in them, and so easily begins to feel rancor toward them, suffers more from that rancor than those for whom it is destined. That rancor is not the expression of destroyed egoism or insulted self-esteem, it is the expression of suffering, and oppression created by the absence of love. Despite all his views, Bazarov eagerly seeks love for people. If that desire appears as rancor, that rancor only represents the reverse of love. Bazarov cannot be a cold, abstract man. His heart demands fullness and demands feeling. And so he rages at others but feels that he should really rage at himself more than at them.

From all this it at least becomes apparent what a difficult task Turgenev undertook in his latest novel and how successfully in our view he carried it out. He depicted life under the deadening influence of theory; he gave us a living being, though that man apparently embodied himself in an abstract formula without leaving a remnant behind. Through this, if one were to judge the novel superficially, it is not very comprehensible, presents little that is appealing, and seems to consist entirely of an obscure logical construction. But in reality, it is actually marvelously clear, unusually attractive, and throbs with warm life.

There is practically no need to explain why Bazarov turned out and had to turn out a theoretician. Everyone knows that our *real* representatives, that the "carriers of thought" in our generation, have long ago renounced being *practical,* that active participation in the life around them had long ago become impossible. From that point of view Bazarov is a direct and immediate imitator of Onegin, Pechorin, Rudin, and Lavretsky. Exactly like them he lives in the mental sphere for the time being and spends his spiritual forces on it. But the thirst for activity has reached the final, extreme point in him. His entire theory consists in the direct demand for action. His mood is such that he inevitably would come to grips with that action at the first convenient possibility.

The characters surrounding Bazarov unconsciously feel the living man in him. That is why so many attachments turn upon him, far more than on any other character in the novel. Not only do his father and mother remember him and pray for him with infinite and inexpressible tenderness; in other characters too the memory of Bazarov is accompanied by love; in a moment of happiness Katya and Arkady drink "to Bazarov's memory."

Such is Bazarov's image for us, too. He is not a hateful being who repels through his shortcomings; on the contrary, his gloomy figure is grandiose and attractive.

"What then is the idea of the novel?" Lovers of bare and exact conclusions will ask. Does Bazarov present a subject for imitation according to you? Or should his failure and roughness on the contrary teach the Bazarovs not to fall into the errors and extremes of the real Bazarov? In short, is the novel written *for* the young generation or *against* it? Is it progressive or reactionary?

If the question so insistently concerns the author's intentions, what he wanted to teach and what he wanted to have unlearned, then it seems these questions would have to be answered as follows: Turgenev does in fact want to be instructive, but he chooses tasks far higher and more difficult than you suppose. It is not a difficult thing to write a novel with a progressive or reactionary tendency. But Turgenev had the pretension and daring to create a novel that had *all possible* tendencies. The worshipper of eternal truth and eternal beauty, he had the proud aim of showing the eternal in the temporary and to write a novel neither progressive nor reactionary but, so to speak, *constant.* In this instance he may be compared to a mathematician who tries to find some important theorem. Let us assume that he has finally found that theorem. Would he not be terribly amazed and disconcerted if he were suddenly approached with the question whether his theorem was progressive or reactionary? Does it conform to the *modern* spirit or does it obey the *old?*

He could only answer such questions thus: your questions make no sense and have no bearing on my findings: my theorem is an *eternal truth.*

> Alas! In life's furrows
> By Providence's secret will
> Generations are the fleeting harvest
> They rise, ripen and fall;
> Others come in their wake . . .

The change of generations is the outward theme of the novel. If Turgenev did not depict all fathers and sons, or not *those* fathers and sons who would like to be different, he splendidly described fathers *in general* and children *in general* and the relationship between those two generations. Perhaps the difference between generations has never been as great as it is at the present, and therefore their relationship too appears to be particularly acute. However that may be, in order to measure the difference between objects the same measure must be used for both; in order to draw a picture all objects must be described from a point of view common to all of them.

That single measure, that general point of view for Turgenev is *human life* in its broadest and fullest meaning. The reader of his novel feels that behind the mirage of external actions and scenes there flows such a profound, such an inexhaustible current of life, that all these actions and scenes, all the characters and events are insignificant in comparison to that current.

If we understand Turgenev's novel that way, then, perhaps the moral we are seeking will also be disclosed to us more clearly. There is a moral, even a very important one, for truth and poetry are very instructive.

If we look at the picture presented by the novel more calmly and at some distance, we note easily that though Bazarov stands head and shoulders above all the other characters, though he majestically passes over the scene, triumphant, bowed down to, respected, loved, and lamented, there is nevertheless something that taken as a whole stands above Bazarov. What is that? If we examine it attentively, we will find that that higher something is not a character but that *life* which inspires them. Above Bazarov stands that fear, that love, those tears he inspires. Above Bazarov is that scene he passes through. The enchantment of nature, the charm of art, feminine love, family love, parents' love, *even* religion, all that—living, full, powerful—is the background against which Bazarov is drawn. That background is so clear and sparkling that Bazarov's huge figure stands out clearly but at the same time gloomily against it. Those who think that for sake of a supposed condemnation of Bazarov the author contrasts to him one of his characters, say Pavel Petrovich, or Arkady, or Odintsov, are terribly wrong. All these characters are insignificant in comparison to Bazarov. And yet their life, the human element in their feelings is not insignificant.

We will not discuss here the description of nature, of Russian nature, which is so difficult to describe and in describing which Turgenev is such a master. It is the same in this as in previous novels. The sky, air, fields, trees, even horses, even chicks—everything is caught graphically and exactly.

Let's simply take people. What could be weaker or more insignificant than Bazarov's young friend Arkady? He apparently submits to every passing influence; he is the most ordinary of mortals. And yet he is extremely nice. The magnanimous agitation of his young feelings, his nobility and purity are emphasized by the author with great finesse and are clearly depicted. Nikolai Petrovich, as is proper, is the real father of his son. There is not a single clear trait in him and the only good thing is that he is a man, though a very simple man. Further, what could be emptier than Fenichka? The author writes "The expression of her eyes was charming, particularly when she seemed to gaze up from beneath her brow and smiled kindly and a little stupidly." Pavel Petrovich himself calls her an *empty creature.* And yet that silly Fenichka attracts almost more adorers than the clever Odintsov. Not only does Nikolai Petrovich love her, but in part Pavel Petrovich falls in love with her as does Bazarov himself. And yet that love and falling in love are real and valuable human feelings. Finally, what is Pavel Petrovich—a dandy, a fop with gray hair, completely taken up with his concern for his toilette? But even in him, despite the apparent distortion there are living and even energetic vibrations of the heartstrings.

The farther we go in the novel, the nearer to the end of the drama, the more gloomy and tense does Bazarov's figure become, while the background becomes clearer and clearer. The creation of such figures as Bazarov's mother and father is a real triumph of talent. Apparently nothing could be less significant and useless than these people who have lived out their time and who become decrepit and disfigured in the new life with all their prejudices of old. And yet what richness of *simple* human feeling! What depth and breadth of spiritual life among the most ordinary life that does not rise a jot above the lowest level.

When Bazarov becomes ill, when he rots alive and inexorably undergoes the cruel battle with illness, life around him becomes more tense and clear in proportion to his becoming gloomier. Odintsov comes to say farewell to Bazarov! She had probably done nothing generous in her life and will not do so again all her life. So far as the father and mother are concerned, it would be difficult to find anything more touching. Their love bursts forth like some sort of lightning, for a moment striking the reader. From their simple hearts there seem to be torn infinitely sad hymns, some sort of limitlessly deep and tender outcries that irresistibly touch the soul.

Bazarov dies amidst that light and that warmth. For a moment a storm flares up in his father's soul. It is harder to imagine anything more fearful. But it soon dies down and everything again becomes bright. Bazarov's very grave is illuminated by light and peace. Birds sing over it and tears are poured on it.

So there it is, there is that secret moral which Turgenev put in his work. Bazarov turns away from nature; Turgenev does not reproach him for it; he only depicts nature in all its beauty. Bazarov does not value friendship and rejects romantic love; the author does not reproach him for it; he only describes Arkady's friendship toward Bazarov and his happy love for Katya. Bazarov denies close bonds between parents and children; the author does not reproach him for it; he only develops a picture of parental love before us. Bazarov shuns life; the author does not present him as a villain for it; he only shows us life in all its beauty. Bazarov repudiates poetry; Turgenev does not make him a fool for it; he only depicts him with all the fullness and penetration of poetry.

In short, Turgenev stands for the eternal principles of human life; for those fundamental elements which can endlessly change their forms but actually always remain unchangeable. But what have we said? It turns out that Turgenev stands for those things all poets stand for, that every real poet must stand for. And, consequently, in this case Turgenev put himself above any reproach for ulterior motives; whatever the particular circumstances he chose for his work may be, he examines them from the most general and highest point of view.

All his attention is concentrated on the general forces of life. He has shown us how these forces are embodied in Bazarov, in that same Bazarov who denies them. He has shown us if not a more powerful then a more apparent, clearer embodiment of those forces in those simple people who surround Bazarov. Bazarov is a titan, rising against

mother earth; no matter how great his force it only testifies to the greatness of the forces that begot him and fed him, but it does not come up to mother earth's force.

However it may be, Bazarov is defeated all the same. He is not defeated by the characters and occurrences of life but by the very idea of that life. Such an ideal victory over him is only possible if he is done all justice, if he is exalted to his appropriate grandeur. Otherwise the victory would have no force or meaning.

In his *Government Inspector* Gogol said there was a single honorable character in the play—laughter. One might say similarly about **Fathers and Sons** that it contains one character who stands higher than the others and even higher than Bazarov—*life*. That life that rises above Bazarov would apparently be smaller and lower to the extent that the main hero of the novel, Bazarov, would be portrayed smaller and lower. (pp. 218-29)

> *N. N. Strakhov, in a review of "Fathers and Sons," in* Fathers and Sons *by Ivan Turgenev, edited and translated by Ralph E. Matlaw, second edition, W. W. Norton & Company, 1989, pp. 218-29.*

Dmitry I. Pisarev   (essay date 1862)

[*In the excerpt below from an essay first printed in Russian shortly after the publication of* Fathers and Sons, *Pisarev considers Bazarov's powerful personality as representative of Russian radicals of the 1860s.*]

Turgenev's new novel affords us all those pleasures which we have learned to expect from his works. The artistic finish is irreproachably good: the characters and situations, the episodes and scenes are rendered so graphically and yet so unobtrusively, that the most arrant repudiator of art will feel on reading the novel a kind of incomprehensible delight which can be explained neither by the inherent interest of the narrated events, nor by the striking truth of the fundamental idea. The fact is that the events are not particularly entertaining and that the idea is not startlingly true. The novel has neither plot nor denouement, nor a particularly well-considered structure; it has types and characters, it has episodes and scenes, and above all through the fabric of the narration we see the personal, deeply felt involvement of the author with the phenomena he has portrayed. And these phenomena are very close to us, so close that our whole younger generation with its aspirations and ideas can recognize itself in the characters of this novel. By this I do not mean to say that in Turgenev's novel the ideas and aspirations of the younger generation are depicted just as the younger generation itself understands them: Turgenev regards these ideas and aspirations from his own point of view, and age and youth almost never share the same convictions and sympathies. But if you go up to a mirror which while reflecting objects also changes their color a little bit, then you recognize your own physiognomy in spite of the distortions of the mirror. We see in Turgenev's novel contemporary types and at the same time we are aware of the changes which the phenomena of reality have undergone while passing through the consciousness of the artist. It is interesting to observe the effects on a man like Turgenev of the ideas and aspirations stirring in our younger generation and manifesting themselves, as do all living things, in the most diverse forms, seldom attractive, often original, sometimes misshapen.

Such an investigation may have profound significance. Turgenev is one of the best men of the last generation; to determine how he looks at us and why he looks at us thus and not otherwise is to find the reason for that conflict which is apparent everywhere in our private family life; this same conflict which so often leads to the destruction of young lives and which causes the continual moaning and groaning of our old men and women, who have not been able to fit the deeds and ideas of their sons and daughters to their own mold. As you can see, this is a task of vital importance, substantial and complex; I probably will not be able to cope with it but I am willing to try.

Turgenev's novel, in addition to its artistic beauty, is remarkable for the fact that it stirs the mind, leads to reflection, although, it does not solve a single problem itself and clearly illuminates not so much the phenomena depicted by the author as his own attitudes toward these phenomena. It leads to reflection precisely because everything is permeated with the most complete and most touching sincerity. Every last line in Turgenev's latest novel is deeply felt; this feeling breaks through against the will and realization of the author himself and suffuses the objective narration, instead of merely expressing itself in lyric digressions. The author himself is not clearly aware of his feelings; he does not subject them to analysis, nor does he assume a critical attitude toward them. This circumstance gives us the opportunity to see these feelings in all their unspoiled spontaneity. We see what shines through and not just what the author wants to show us or prove. Turgenev's opinions and judgments do not change our view of the younger generation or the ideas of our time by one iota; we do not even take them into consideration, we will not even argue with them; these opinions, judgments, and feelings, expressed in inimitably lifelike images, merely afford us material for a characterization of the older generation, in the person of one of its best representatives. I shall endeavor to organize this material and, if I succeed, I shall explain why our old people will not come to terms with us, why they shake their heads and, depending on the individual and the mood, are angry, bewildered, or quietly melancholy on account of our deeds and ideas.

The action of the novel takes place in the summer of 1859. A young university graduate, Arkady Nikolaevich Kirsanov, comes to the country to visit his father, accompanied by his friend, Evgeny Vassilyich Bazarov, who, evidently, exerts a strong influence on his young comrade's mode of thought. This Bazarov, a man of strong mind and character, occupies the center of the novel. He is the representative of our young generation; he possesses those personality traits which are distributed among the masses in small quantities; and the image of this man clearly and distinctly stands out in the reader's imagination.

Bazarov is the son of a poor district doctor; Turgenev says nothing about his life as a student, but it must be surmised that this life was poor, laborious, and difficult; Bazarov's father says of his son that he never in his life took an extra kopeck from them; to tell the truth, it would have been impossible to take very much even if he had wanted to; consequently, if the elder Bazarov says this in praise of his son, it means that Evgeny Vassilyich supported himself at the university by his own labor, eking out a living by giving cheap lessons and at the same time finding it possible to prepare himself ably for his future occupation. Bazarov emerged from this school of labor and deprivation a strong and stern man; the course of studies in natural and medical sciences which he pursued developed his innate intelligence and taught him never to accept any idea and conviction whatsoever on faith; he became a pure empiricist; experience became for him the sole source of knowledge, his own sensations—the sole and ultimate proof. "I maintain a negative attitude," he says, "by virtue of my sensations; I like to deny—my brain's made on that plan, and that's all! Why do I like chemistry? Why do you like apples?— also by virtue of our sensations. It's all the same thing. Men will never penetrate deeper than that. Not everyone will tell you that, and, in fact, I won't tell you so another time." As an empiricist, Bazarov acknowledges only what can be felt with the hands, seen with the eyes, tasted by the tongue, in a word, only what can be examined with one of the five senses. All other human feelings he reduces to the activity of the nervous system; consequently, the enjoyment of the beauty of nature, of music, painting, poetry, the love of a woman do not seem to him to be any loftier or purer than the enjoyment of a copious dinner or a bottle of good wine. What rapturous youths call an ideal does not exist for Bazarov; he calls all this "romanticism," and sometimes instead of the word "romanticism" he uses the word "nonsense." In spite of all this, Bazarov does not steal other people's handkerchiefs, he does not extract money from his parents, he works assiduously and is even not unwilling to do something useful in life. I have a presentiment that many of my readers will ask themselves: what restrains Bazarov from foul deeds and what motivates him to do anything useful? This question leads to the following doubt: is not Bazarov pretending to himself and to others? Is he not showing off? Perhaps in the depths of his soul he acknowledges much of what he repudiates aloud, and perhaps it is precisely what he thus acknowledges which secretly saves him from moral degradation and moral worthlessness. Although Bazarov is nothing to me, although I, perhaps, feel no sympathy for him, for the sake of abstract justice, I shall endeavor to answer this question and refute this silly doubt.

You can be as indignant as you please with people like Bazarov, but you absolutely must acknowledge their sincerity. These people can be honorable or dishonorable, civic stalwarts or inveterate swindlers, depending on circumstances and their personal tastes. Nothing but personal taste prevents them from killing or stealing and nothing but personal taste motivates such people to make discoveries in the realms of science and social life. Bazarov would not steal a handkerchief for the same reason that he would not eat a piece of putrid beef. If Bazarov were starving to death, then he probably would do both. The agonizing feeling of an unsatisfied physical need would conquer his aversion to the smell of rotting meat and to the secret encroachment on other people's property. In addition to direct inclination, Bazarov has one other guiding principle in life—calculation. When he is sick, he takes medicine, although he feels no direct inclination to swallow castor oil or assafetida. He acts thus through calculation: he pays the price of a minor unpleasantness in order to secure greater comfort in the future or deliverance from a greater unpleasantness. In a word, he chooses the lesser of two evils, although he feels no attraction even to the lesser evil. This sort of calculation generally proves useless to average people; they are calculatingly cunning and mean, they steal, become entangled and wind up being made fools of anyway. Very clever people act differently; they understand that being honorable is very advantageous and that every crime, from a simple lie to murder, is dangerous and consequently inconvenient. Thus very clever people can be honorable through calculation and act openly where limited people would equivocate and lay snares. By working tirelessly, Bazarov is following his direct inclination and taste, and, furthermore, acts according to the truest calculation. If he had sought patronage, bowed and scraped, acted meanly instead of working and conducting himself proudly and independently, he would have been acting against his best interests. Careers forged through one's own work are always more secure and broader than a career built with low bows or the intercession of an important uncle. By the two latter means, it is possible to wind up as a provincial or even a metropolitan bigwig, but since the world began, no one has ever succeeded in becoming a Washington, Copernicus, Garibaldi, or Heinrich Heine through such means. Even Herostratus built his career by his own efforts and did not find his way into history through patronage. As for Bazarov, he does not aspire to become a provincial bigwig: if his imagination sometimes pictures the future, then this future is somehow indefinitely broad; he works without a goal, in order to earn his crust of bread or from love of the process of work, but, nevertheless, he vaguely feels that given the caliber of his mind his work will not pass without a trace and will lead to something. Bazarov is exceedingly full of self-esteem, but this self-esteem is unnoticeable as a direct consequence of his vastness. He is not interested in the trifles of which commonplace human relationships are composed; it would be impossible to insult him with obvious disdain or to make him happy with signs of respect; he is so full of himself and stands so unshakably high in his own eyes that he is almost completely indifferent to other people's opinions. Kirsanov's uncle, who closely resembles Bazarov in his cast of mind and character, calls his self-esteem "satanic pride." This expression is well-chosen and characterizes our hero perfectly. In truth, it would take nothing short of a whole eternity of constantly expanding activity and constantly increasing pleasures to satisfy Bazarov, but to his misfortune, Bazarov does not believe in the eternal existence of the human personality. "You said, for instance," he says to his friend Arkady,

> "to-day as we passed our bailiff Philip's cottage—it's the one that's so nice and clean—well, you said Russia will attain perfection when the poorest peasant has a hut like that, and every one of us ought to work to bring it about. . . . And I felt such a hatred for this poorest peasant, this Philip or Sidor, for whom I'm to be ready

> to jump out of my skin, and who won't even thank me for it . . . and what do I need his thanks for? Why, suppose he does live in a clean hut, while I am pushing up daisies,—well, what comes after that?"

Thus Bazarov, everywhere and in everything, does only what he wishes or what seems to him to be advantageous or convenient. He is ruled only by his whims or his personal calculations. Neither over himself, nor outside himself, nor within himself does he recognize a moderator, a moral law or principle; ahead—no exalted goal; in his mind—no high design, and yet he has such great capacities.—But this is an immoral man! A villain, a monster!—I hear the exclamations of indignant readers on all sides. Well, all right, a villain and a monster; abuse him further; abuse him more, persecute him with satire and epigrams, indignant lyricism and aroused public opinion, the fires of the Inquisition and the executioners' axes—and you will neither rout him out nor kill this monster, nor preserve him in alcohol for the edification of the respectable public. If Bazarovism is a disease, then it is a disease of our time, and must be endured to the end, no matter what palliatives and amputations are employed. Treat Bazarovism however you please—that is your business; but you will not be able to put a stop to it; it is just the same as cholera.

The disease of an age first infects the people who by virtue of their mental powers stand higher than the common level. Bazarov, who is possessed by this disease, is distinguished by his remarkable mind and consequently produces a strong impression on people who come into contact with him. "A real man," he says, "is one whom it's no use thinking about, whom one must either obey or hate." This definition of a real man precisely fits Bazarov himself: he continually seizes the attention of the people surrounding him at once; some he frightens and antagonizes; others he conquers, not so much with arguments as with the direct force, simplicity, and integrity of his ideas. As a remarkably intelligent man, he has never yet met his equal. " 'When I meet a man who can hold his own beside me,' he said, dwelling on every syllable, 'then I'll change my opinion of myself.' "

He looks down on people and rarely even takes the trouble to conceal his half-disdainful, half-patronizing attitude toward those who hate him and those who obey him. He loves no one; although he does not break existing ties and relationships, he does not move a muscle to renew or maintain these relationships, nor does he soften one note in his harsh voice or sacrifice one cutting joke or witty remark.

He acts thus not in the name of a principle, not in order to be completely frank at every moment, but simply because he considers it completely unnecessary to lay any restraint whatsoever on himself; for the same motive from which Americans throw their legs over the backs of chairs and spit tobacco juice on the parquet floors of elegant hotels. Bazarov needs no one, fears no one, loves no one and consequently spares no one. Like Diogenes he is almost ready to live in a barrel and because of this grants himself the right to tell people to their faces the harsh truth, simply because it pleases him to do so. We can distinguish two sides to Bazarov's cynicism—an internal and an external one; a cynicism of thought and feeling and a cynicism of manner and expression. An ironic attitude toward emotion of any sort, toward dreaminess, lyrical transports and effusions, is the essence of the internal cynicism. The rude expression of this irony, and a causeless and purposeless harshness in the treatment of others relates to external cynicism. The first depends on the cast of mind and general world view; the second is conditioned by purely external conditions of development; the traits of the society in which the subject under consideration lived. Bazarov's derisive attitude toward the softhearted Kirsanov follows from the basic characteristic of the general Bazarov type. His rude clashes with Kirsanov and his uncle arise from his individual traits. Bazarov is not only an empiricist, he is also an uncouth rowdy, who has known no life other than the homeless, laborious, sometimes wildly dissipated life of the poor student. In the ranks of Bazarov's admirers there will undoubtedly be those who will be enraptured by his coarse manners, the vestiges of student life, who will imitate these manners, which are, in any case, a shortcoming and not a virtue, who will perhaps even exaggerate his harshness, gracelessness, and abruptness. In the ranks of Bazarov's enemies there will undoubtedly be those who will pay particular attention to these ugly features of his personality and will use them to reproach the general type. Both of these groups would be mistaken and would only be displaying their profound incomprehension of the real matter. We may remind them of Pushkin's lines:

> One may be a man of sense
> Yet consider the beauty of his fingernails.

It is possible to be an extreme materialist, a complete empiricist and at the same time look after your toilet, treat your acquaintances politely, be amiable in conversation and a perfect gentleman. I say this for the benefit of those readers who attribute great significance to refined manners, who look with aversion on Bazarov, as on a man who is *mal élevé* and *mauvais ton*. He really is *mal élevé* and *mauvais ton,* but this really has no relevance to the essence of the type and speaks neither against it nor in its favor. Turgenev decided to choose as a representative of the Bazarov type an uncouth man; of course as he delineated his hero, he did not conceal or try to gloss over his awkwardness. Turgenev's choice can be explained by two motives: first, the character's personality, the tendency to deny ruthlessly and with complete conviction everything which others consider exalted and beautiful, is most often engendered by the drab conditions of a life of labor; from hard labor the hands coarsen, so do the manners and emotions; the man grows stronger and banishes youthful dreaminess, rids himself of lachrymose sensitivity; it is not possible to daydream at work, the attention is directed on the business at hand, and after work one must rest and really satisfy one's physical needs and one has no time for dreams. This man has become used to looking on dreams as on a whim, peculiar to idleness and aristocratic pampering; he has begun to consider moral sufferings to be products of daydreams; moral aspirations and actions as imagined and ridiculous. For him, the laboring man, there exists only one, eternally recurring care: today he must think about how not to starve tomorrow. This simple care, terri-

ble in its simplicity, overshadows everything else for him, secondary anxieties, the petty troubles and cares of life; in comparison with this care the artificial products of various unsolved problems, unresolved doubts, indefinite relations which poison the lives of secure, idle people seem to him to be trivial and insignificant.

Thus the proletarian laborer, by the very process of his life, independently of the process of reflection, arrives at practical realism; from lack of leisure he forgets how to dream, to pursue an ideal, to aspire to an unattainably lofty goal. By developing the laborer's energy, labor teaches him to unite thought and deed, an act of will with an act of the mind. The man who has learned to rely on himself and on his own capacities, who has become used to accomplishing today what he conceived yesterday, begins to look with more or less obvious disdain on people who dream of love, of useful activity, of the happiness of the whole human race, and yet are not capable of lifting a finger to improve even a little whether he be doctor, artisan, pedagogue, or even a writer (it is possible to be a writer and at the same time a man of action), feels a natural, indefinable aversion to phrase making, to waste of words, to sweet thoughts, to sentimental aspirations, and in general to all pretensions not based on real tangible forces. This aversion to everything estranged from life and everything that has turned into empty phrases is the fundamental characteristic of the Bazarov type. This fundamental characteristic is engendered in precisely those various workshops where man, sharpening his mind and straining his muscles, struggles with nature for the right to live in the wide world. On these grounds, Turgenev had the right to take his hero from one of these workshops and to bring him into the society of cavaliers and ladies, in a work apron, with dirty hands, and a gloomy and preoccupied gaze. But justice forces me to put forward the proposition that the author of **Fathers and Sons** acted thus not without an insidious intention. This insidious intention is the second motive to which I referred earlier. The fact is that Turgenev, evidently, looks with no great favor on his hero. His soft, loving nature, striving for faith and sympathy, is jarred by corrosive realism; his delicate esthetic sensibility, not devoid of a large dose of aristocratism, takes offense at the faintest glimmer of cynicism; he is too weak and sensitive to bear dismal repudiations; he must become reconciled with existence, if not in the realm of life, at least in the realm of thought, or, more precisely, dreams. Like a nervous woman or the plant "touch-me not," Turgenev shrinks from the slightest contact with the bouquet of Bazarovism.

This feeling, an involuntary antipathy toward this tenor of thought, he presented to the reading public in a specimen as ungraceful as possible. He knows very well that there are very many fashionable readers in our public and, counting on the refinement of their aristocratic tastes, he did not spare the coarse details, with the evident desire of debasing and vulgarizing not only his hero but the cast of ideas which form the defining characteristic of the type. He knows very well that the majority of his readers will say of Bazarov that he is badly brought up and that it would be impossible to have him in a respectable drawing room; they will go no further or deeper; but speaking with such people, a talented artist and honorable man must be extremely careful out of respect for himself and the idea which he is upholding or refuting. Here one must hold one's personal antipathy in check since under some conditions it can turn into the involuntary slander of people who do not have the opportunity to defend themselves with the same weapons. . . .

Arkady's uncle, Pavel Petrovich, might be called a small-scale Pechorin; he sowed some wild oats in his time and played the fool but finally began to tire of it all; he never succeeded in settling down, it just was not in his character; when he reached the time of life when, as Turgenev puts it, regrets resemble hopes and hopes resemble regrets, the former lion moved in with his brother in the country, surrounded himself with elegant comfort and turned his life into a peaceful vegetation. The outstanding memory of Pavel Petrovich's noisy and brilliant life was his strong feeling for a woman of high society, a feeling which had afforded him much pleasure, and afterward, as is almost always the case, much suffering. When Pavel Petrovich's relations with this woman were severed, his life became perfectly empty.

"He wandered from place to place like a man possessed;" Turgenev writes,

> he still went into society; he still retained the habits of a man of the world; he could boast of two or three fresh conquests; but he no longer expected anything special of himself or of others, and he undertook nothing. He aged and his hair turned grey; to spend his evenings at the club in jaded boredom, and to argue in bachelor society became a necessity for him—a bad sign as we all know. He did not even think of marriage, of course. Ten years passed in this way. They passed by colorless and fruitless—and quickly, fearfully quickly. Nowhere does time fly past as in Russia; in prison they say it flies even faster.

An acrimonious and passionate man, endowed with a versatile mind and a strong will, Pavel Petrovich is sharply distinguished from his brother and from his nephew. He does not succumb to the influence of other people; he himself dominates the people around him and he hates those people from whom he suffers a rebuff. He has no convictions, truth to tell, but he has habits by which he sets great store. From habit he speaks of the rights and duties of the aristocracy, and from habit proves in arguments the necessity for *principles*. He is used to the ideas which are held by society and he stands up for these ideas, just as he stands up for his comfort. He cannot bear it when someone refutes his ideas, although, at bottom, he has no heartfelt attachment to them. He argues with Bazarov much more energetically than does his brother, and yet Nikolai Petrovich suffers much more from his merciless repudiations. In the depths of his soul, Pavel Petrovich is just as much of a skeptic and empiricist as Bazarov himself; in practical life he always acted and acts as he sees fit, but in the realm of thought he is not able to admit this to himself and thus he adheres in words to doctrines which his actions continually contradict. It would be well if uncle and nephew were to exchange convictions, since the first mistakenly ascribes to himself a belief in *principles* and the

second just as mistakenly imagines himself to be an extreme skeptic and a daring rationalist. Pavel Petrovich begins to feel a strong antipathy toward Bazarov from their first meeting. Bazarov's plebeian manners rouse the indignation of the outdated dandy; his self-confidence and unceremoniousness irritate Pavel Petrovich as a lack of respect for his elegant person. Pavel Petrovich sees that Bazarov does not allow him to predominate over himself and this arouses in him a feeling of vexation on which he seizes as a diversion amidst the profound boredom of country life. Hating Bazarov himself, Pavel Petrovich is outraged by all his opinions, he carps at him, forces him into arguments, and argues with the zealous enthusiasm which is displayed by people who are idle and easily bored.

And what does Bazarov do amidst these three personalities? First of all, he endeavors to pay them as little attention as possible and spends the greater part of his time at work; he roams about the neighborhood, collects plants and insects, dissects frogs, and occupies himself with his microscope; he regards Arkady as a child, Nikolai Petrovich as a good-natured old man or, as he puts it, an old romantic. His feeling toward Pavel Petrovich is not exactly amicable; he is annoyed by the element of haughtiness in him, but he involuntarily tries to conceal his irritation under the guise of disdainful indifference. He does not want to admit to himself that he can be angered by a "provincial aristocrat," yet his passionate nature outs, frequently he replies vehemently to Pavel Petrovich's tirades and does not immediately succeed in gaining control over himself and once more shutting himself up in his derisive coldness. Bazarov does not like to argue or, in general, to express his opinions and only Pavel Petrovich is sometimes able to draw him into a significant discussion. These two strong characters react with hostility to each other; seeing these two men face to face it is easy to be reminded of the struggle between two successive generations. Nikolai Petrovich, of course, is not capable of being an oppressor: Arkady Nikolaevich, of course, is incapable of struggling against familial despotism; but Pavel Petrovich and Bazarov could, under certain conditions, be clear representatives: the former of the congealing, hardening forces to the past, the latter of the liberating, destructive forces of the present.

On whose side are the artist's feelings? This vitally important question may be answered definitely: Turgenev does not fully sympathize with any of his characters; his analysis does not miss one weak or ridiculous trait; we see how Bazarov senselessly repudiates everything, how Arkady revels in his enlightenment, how Nikolai Petrovich is as timid as a fifteen-year-old boy, and how Pavel Petrovich shows off and is angry that he has not won the admiration of Bazarov, the only man whom he respects, despite his hatred of him.

Bazarov talks nonsense—this is unfortunately true. He bluntly repudiates things which he does not know or understand: poetry, in his opinion is rubbish; reading Pushkin is a waste of time; to be interested in music is ludicrous; to enjoy nature is absurd. It is very possible that he, a man stifled by a life of labor, lost or never had time to develop the capacity to enjoy the pleasant stimulation of the visual and auditory nerves, but it does not follow from this that he has a rational basis for repudiating or ridiculing this capacity in others. To cut other people down to fit your own measure is to fall into narrow-minded intellectual despotism. To deny completely arbitrarily one or another natural and real human need is to break with pure empiricism.

Bazarov's tendency to get carried away is very natural; it can be explained, first by the one-sidedness of his development, and secondly by the general character of the time in which we live. Bazarov knows natural and medical sciences thoroughly: with their assistance he has rid himself of all prejudices; however, he has remained an extremely uneducated man; he has heard something or other about poetry, something or other about art, and not troubling to think, he passed abrupt sentence on these subjects which were unknown to him. This arrogance is generally a characteristic of ours; it has its good sides such as intellectual courage, but on the other hand, of course, it leads at times to flagrant errors. The general character of the time is practicality: we all want to live by the rule that fine words butter no parsnips. Very energetic people often exaggerate the prevailing tendency; on these grounds, Bazarov's overly indiscriminate repudiations and the very one-sidedness of his development are tied directly to the prevailing striving for tangible benefits. We have become tired of the phrases of the Hegelians, our heads have begun to spin from soaring around in the clouds, and many of us, having sobered up and come down to earth, have gone to the other extreme and while banishing dreaminess have started to persecute simple feelings and even purely physical sensations, like the enjoyment of music. There is no great harm in this extremity, but it will not hurt to point it out; and to call it ludicrous does not mean to join the ranks of the obscurantists and old romantics. Many of our realists are up in arms against Turgenev because he does not sympathize with Bazarov and does not conceal his hero's blunders from the reader; many express the desire that Bazarov had been presented as an irreproachable man, a knight of thought without fear and reproach, and that thereby the superiority of realism to all other schools of thought would thus have been proved to the reading public. In my opinion, realism is indeed a fine thing; but let us not, in the name of this very realism, idealize either ourselves or our movement. We coldly and soberly regard all that surrounds us; let us regard ourselves just as coldly and soberly; all around us is nonsense and backwardness, but, God knows, we are far from perfect. What we repudiate is ridiculous but the repudiators have also been known, at times, to commit colossal follies; all the same, they stand higher than what they repudiate, but this is no great honor; to stand higher than flagrant absurdity does not yet mean to become a great thinker. But we, the speaking and writing realists, are now too carried away by the mental struggle of the moment, by this fiery skirmish with backward idealists, with whom it is not even worthwhile to argue; we, in my view, have gotten too carried away to maintain a skeptical attitude toward ourselves and to submit to rigorous analysis the possibility that we might have fallen into the dust of the dialectic battles which go on in journalistic pamphlets and in everyday life. Our children will regard us skeptically, or, perhaps, we ourselves will learn our real value and will begin to look *à vol d'oiseau* on our present beloved ideas. Then we will regard the past from the height of the present; Turgenev is now regarding the present from the height of the past. He does not follow us, but tranquilly gazes after us and describes our gait, telling us how we quicken our pace, how we jump across ditches, how now and then we stumble over rough places in the road.

There is no irritation in the tone of his description; he has simply grown tired of moving on; the development of his own world view has come to an end, but his capacity to observe the movement of another person's thought process, to understand and reproduce all its windings, has remained in all its fullness and freshness. Turgenev himself will never be a Bazarov, but he has pondered this type and gained an understanding of it so true that not one of our young realists has yet achieved it. There is no apotheosis of the past in Turgenev's novel. The author of **Rudin** and **"Asya,"** who laid bare the weaknesses of his generation and who revealed in **A Hunter's Sketches** a whole world of wonders which had been taking place right in front of the eyes of this very generation, has remained true to himself and has not acted against his conscience in his latest work. The representatives of the past, the "fathers," are depicted with ruthless fidelity; they are good people, but Russia will not regret these good people; there is not one element in them which would be worth saving from the grave and oblivion, but still there are moments when one can sympathize more fully with these fathers than with Bazarov himself. When Nikolai Petrovich admires the evening landscape he appears more human than Bazarov who groundlessly denies the beauty of nature to every unprejudiced reader.

> "And is nature nonsense?" said Arkady, looking pensively at the bright-colored fields in the distance, in the beautiful soft light of the sun, which was no longer high in the sky.
>
> "Nature, too, is nonsense in the sense you understand it. Nature's not a temple, but a workshop, and man's the workman in it."

In these words, Bazarov's repudiation has turned into something artificial and has even ceased to be consistent. Nature is a workshop and man is a worker in it—with this idea I am ready to agree; but when I carry this idea further, I by no means arrive at the conclusion which Bazarov draws. A worker needs rest and rest does not only mean heavy sleep after exhausting labor. A man must refresh himself with pleasant sensations; life without pleasant sensations, even if all the vital needs are satisfied, turns into unbearable suffering. The consistent materialists, like Karl Vogt, Moleschotte, and Büchner do not deny a day-laborer his glass of vodka, nor the well-to-do classes the use of narcotics. They indulgently regard even the excessive use of such substances, although they acknowledge that such excesses are harmful to the health. If a worker found pleasure in spending his free time lying on his back and gazing at the walls and ceiling of his workshop, then every sensible man would say to him: gaze on, dear friend, stare as much as you please, it won't harm your health but don't you spend your working hours staring or you will make mistakes. Why then, if we permit the use of vodka and narcotics, should we not tolerate the enjoyment of beautiful scenery, mild air, fresh verdure, the gentle play of form and color? Bazarov, in his persecution of romanticism, with incredible suspiciousness seeks it in places where it never has existed. Taking arms against idealism and destroying its castles in the air, he himself, at times, becomes an idealist, that is, he begins to prescribe to man how he should enjoy himself and how he should regulate his own sensations. Telling a man not to enjoy nature is like telling him to mortify his flesh. The more harmless sources of pleasure there are, the easier it is to live in the world, and the whole task of our generation is precisely to decrease the sum of suffering and increase the strength and amount of pleasure. Many will retort that we live in such a difficult time that it is out of the question to think about pleasure; our job, they will say, is to work, to eradicate evil, disseminate good, to clear a site for the great building where our remote descendants will feast. All right, I agree that we are compelled to work for the future, since the fruit we have sown can ripen only after several centuries; let us suppose that our goal is very lofty, still this loftiness of goal affords very little comfort in everyday unpleasantnesses. It is doubtful whether an exhausted and worn-out man will become gay and contented from the thought that his great-great-grandson will enjoy his life. Comforting oneself in the hard moments of life with a lofty goal is, if you will, just the same as drinking unsweetened tea while gazing on a piece of sugar hung from the ceiling. For people without exceedingly vivid imaginations, these wistful upward looks do not make the tea any tastier. In precisely the same way, a life consisting exclusively of work is not to the taste and beyond the powers of contemporary man. Thus, with whatever viewpoint you regard life, you will still be brought up against the fact that pleasure is absolutely indispensable. Some regard pleasure as a final goal; others are compelled to acknowledge pleasure as a very important source of the strength necessary for work. This is the sole difference between the epicureans and stoics of our day.

Thus, Turgenev does not fully sympathize with anyone or anything in his novel. If you were to say to him: ' "Ivan Sergeevich, you do not like Bazarov, but what would you prefer?" he would not answer the question. He would not wish the younger generation to share their fathers' ideas and enthusiasms. Neither the fathers nor the sons satisfy him, and in this case, his repudiation is more profound and more serious than the repudiations of those people, who, having destroyed everything that existed before them, imagine that they are the salt of the earth and the purest expression of total humanity. These people are perhaps right in their destruction, but in their naïve self-adoration or in their adoration of the type which they consider that represents, lies their limitation and one-sidedness. The forms and types with which we can be contented and feel no need to look further have not yet been and perhaps never will be created by life. People who give up their intellectual independence and substitute servile worship for criticism, by giving themselves over completely to one or another prevailing theory, reveal that they are narrow, impotent, and often harmful people. Arkady is capable of acting in this way, but it would be completely im-

possible for Bazarov, and it is precisely this trait of mind and character which produces the captivating power of Turgenev's hero. The author understands and acknowledges this captivating power, despite the fact that neither in temperament nor in the conditions of his development does he resemble his nihilist. Furthermore, Turgenev's general attitudes toward the phenomena of life which make up his novel are so calm and disinterested, so devoid of slavish worship of one or another theory, that Bazarov himself would not have found anything timid or false in these attitudes. Turgenev does not like ruthless negations, but, nevertheless, the personality of the ruthless negator appears as a powerful one—and commands the involuntary respect of every reader. Turgenev has a propensity for idealism, but, nevertheless, not one of the idealists in his novel can be compared to Bazarov either in strength of mind or in strength of character. I am certain that many of our journalistic critics will want, at all costs, to find in Turgenev's novel a repressed urge to debase the younger generation and prove that the children are worse than their parents, but I am just as certain that the readers' spontaneous feelings, unfettered by the necessity of supporting a theory, will approve Turgenev and will find in his work not a dissertation on a particular theme, but a true, deeply felt picture of contemporary life drawn without the slightest attempt at concealment of anything. If a writer belonging to our younger generation and profoundly sympathizing with the "Bazarov school" had happened upon Turgenev's theme, then, of course, the picture would have been drawn otherwise and the colors would have been applied differently. Bazarov would not have been portrayed as an awkward student dominating the people around him through the natural strength of his healthy mind; he, perhaps, would have been turned into the embodiment of the ideas which make up the essence of this type; he, perhaps, would have manifested in his personality the clear expression of the author's tendencies, but it is doubtful whether he would have been Bazarov's equal in faithfulness to life and roundness of characterization. My young artist would have said to his contemporaries of his work: "This, my friends, is what a fully developed man must be like! This is the final goal of our efforts!" But Turgenev just says calmly and simply: "This is the sort of young people there are nowadays!" and does not even try to conceal the fact that such young people are not completely to his taste. "How can this be?" many of our contemporary journalists and publicists will cry. "This is obscurantism!" Gentlemen, we could answer, why should Turgenev's personal sensations concern you? Whether he likes such people or does not like them is a matter of taste; if, for instance, feeling no sympathy for the type, he were to slander it, then every honorable man would have the right to unmask him, but you will not find such slander in the novel: even Bazarov's awkwardnesses, to which I already alluded, are perfectly satisfactorily explained by the circumstances of his life and constitute, if not an essential requirement, at least a very frequently encountered trait of people of the Bazarov type. It would, of course, have been much more pleasant for us, the young people, if Turgenev had concealed and glossed over the graceless rough places in Bazarov, but I do not think that an artist who indulged our capricious desires could better capture the phenomena of reality. Both virtues and shortcomings are more clearly apparent when regarded from a detached point of view, and, for this reason, a detached, severely critical view of Bazarov proves, at present, to be much more fruitful than indiscriminate admiration or slavish worship. By regarding Bazarov detachedly as is possible only for a man who is "behind the times" and not involved in the contemporary movement of ideas; by examining him with the cold, probing gaze which is only engendered by long experience of life, Turgenev has justified his hero and valued him at his true worth. Bazarov has emerged from this examination as a pure and a strong man. Turgenev did not find one essential indictment against this type, and thus his voice, the voice of a man who finds himself in a camp which is inconsistent with his age and his views of life, has an especially important and decisive meaning. Turgenev did not grow fond of Bazarov, but he acknowledged his strength and his superiority and offered him a full tribute of respect.

This is more than sufficient to absolve Turgenev's novel from the powerful charge of being behind the times; it is even sufficient to compel us to acknowledge his novel as practically useful for the present age. (pp. 195-211)

> *Dmitry I. Pisarev, "Bazarov," translated by Lydia Hooke, in "Fathers and Sons" by Ivan Turgenev: The Author on the Novel, Contemporary Reactions, Essays in Criticism, edited and translated by Ralph E. Matlaw, second edition, W. W. Norton & Company, Inc., 1989, pp. 195-218.*

Ivan Turgenev   (essay date 1869)

[*In the following excerpt from an essay first published in 1869, Turgenev defends his decision to present an objective portrait of a young radical through the character of Bazarov. He adds that it was not his intent to insult the younger generation with the portrayal but to present contemporary life and thought as he saw it.*]

I was sea-bathing at Ventnor, a small town on the Isle of Wight—it was in August, 1860—when the first idea occurred to me of **Fathers and Sons,** the novel which deprived me, forever I believe, of the good opinion of the Russian younger generation. I have heard it said and read it in critical articles not once but many times that in my works I always "started with an idea" or "developed an idea." Some people praised me for it, others, on the contrary, censured me; for my part, I must confess that I never attempted to "create a character" unless I had for my departing point not an idea but a living person to whom the appropriate elements were later on gradually attached and added. Not possessing a great amount of free inventive powers, I always felt the need of some firm ground on which I could plant my feet. The same thing happened with **Fathers and Sons;** as the basis of its chief character, Bazarov, lay the personality of a young provincial doctor I had been greatly struck by. (He died shortly before 1860.) In that remarkable man I could watch the embodiment of that principle which had scarcely come to life but was just beginning to stir at the time, the principle which later received the name of nihilism. Though very

---

An excerpt from *Fathers and Sons* (1862)

'What is Bazarov?' Arkady smiled. 'Would you like me, uncle, to tell you what he really is?'

'If you will be so good, nephew.'

'He's a nihilist.'

'Eh?' inquired Nikolai Petrovitch, while Pavel Petrovitch lifted a knife in the air with a small piece of butter on its tip, and remained motionless.

'He's a nihilist,' repeated Arkady.

'A nihilist,' said Nikolai Petrovitch. 'That's from the Latin, *nihil, nothing,* as far as I can judge; the word must mean a man who . . . who accepts nothing?'

'Say, "who respects nothing," ' put in Pavel Petrovitch, and he set to work on the butter again.

'Who regards everything from the critical point of view,' observed Arkady.

'Isn't that just the same thing?' inquired Pavel Petrovitch.

'No, it's not the same thing. A nihilist is a man who does not bow down before any authority, who does not take any principle on faith, whatever reverence that principle may be enshrined in.'

'Well, and is that good?' interrupted Pavel Petrovitch.

'That depends, uncle. Some people it will do good to, but some people will suffer for it.'

> *Ivan Turgenev, in his* Fathers and Sons, *translated by Constance Garnett, William Heinemann, 1895.*

---

powerful, the impression that man left on me was still rather vague. At first I could not quite make him out myself, and I kept observing and listening intently to everything around me, as though wishing to check the truth of my own impressions. I was worried by the following fact: not in one work of our literature did I ever find as much as a hint at what I seemed to see everywhere; I could not help wondering whether I was not chasing after a phantom. On the Isle of Wight, I remember, there lived with me at the time a Russian who was endowed with excellent taste and a remarkable "nose" for everything which the late Apollon Grigoryev called "the ideas" of an epoch. I told him what I was thinking of and what interested me so much and was astonished to hear the following remark: "Haven't you created such a character already in— Rudin?" I said nothing. Rudin and Bazarov—one and the same character!

Those words produced such an effect on me that for several weeks I tried not to think of the work I had in mind. However, on my return to Paris, I sat down to it again— the *plot* gradually matured in my head; in the course of the winter I wrote the first chapters, but I finished the novel in Russia, on my estate, in July [1861]. In the autumn I read it to a few friends, revised something, added something, and in March, 1862, *Fathers and Sons* was published in *The Russian Herald*.

I shall not enlarge on the impression this novel has created. I shall merely say that when I returned to Petersburg, on the very day of the notorious fires in the Apraksin Palace, the word "nihilist" had been caught up by thousands of people, and the first exclamation that escaped from the lips of the first acquaintance I met on Nevsky Avenue was: "Look, what *your* nihilists are doing! They are setting Petersburg on fire!" My impressions at that time, though different in kind, were equally painful. I became conscious of a coldness bordering on indignation among many friends whose ideas I shared; I received congratulations, and almost kisses, from people belonging to a camp I loathed, from enemies. It embarrassed and—grieved me. But my conscience was clear; I knew very well that my attitude towards the character I had created was honest and that far from being prejudiced against him, I even sympathized with him. I have too great a respect for the vocation of an artist, a writer, to act against my conscience in such a matter. The word "respect" is hardly the right one here; I simply could not, and knew not how to, work otherwise; and, after all, there was no reason why I should do that. My critics described my novel as a "lampoon" and spoke of my "exasperated" and "wounded" vanity; but why should I write a lampoon on Dobrolyubov, whom I had hardly met, but whom I thought highly of as a man and as a talented writer? However little I might think of my own talent as a writer, I always have been, and still am, of the opinion that the writing of a lampoon, a "squib," is unworthy of it. . . .

The critics, generally speaking, have not got quite the right idea of what is taking place in the mind of an author or of what exactly his joys and sorrows, his aims, successes and failures are. They do not, for instance, even suspect the pleasure which Gogol mentions and which consists of castigating oneself and one's faults in the imaginary characters one depicts; they are quite sure that all an author does is to "develop his ideas"; they refuse to believe that to reproduce truth and the reality of life correctly and powerfully is the greatest happiness for an author, even if this truth does not coincide with his own sympathies. Let me illustrate my meaning by a small example. I am an inveterate and incorrigible Westerner. I have never concealed it and I am not concealing it now. And yet in spite of that it has given me great pleasure to show up in the person of Panshin (in *A Nobleman's Home*) all the common and vulgar sides of the Westerners; I made the Slavophil Lavretsky "crush him utterly." Why did I do it, I who consider the Slavophil doctrine false and futile? Because *in the given case life, according to my ideas, happened to be like that,* and what I wanted above all was to be sincere and truthful. In depicting Bazarov's personality, I excluded everything artistic from the range of his sympathies, I made him express himself in harsh and unceremonious tones, not out of an absurd desire to insult the younger generation (!!!), but simply as a result of my observations of my acquaintance, Dr. D., and people like him. "Life happened to be *like that,*" my experience told me once

more, perhaps mistakenly, but, I repeat, not dishonestly. There was no need for me to be too clever about it; I just had to depict his character *like that*. My personal predilections had nothing to do with it. But I expect many of my readers will be surprised if I tell them that with the exception of Bazarov's views on art, I share almost all his convictions. And I am assured that I am on the side of the "Fathers"—I, who in the person of Pavel Kirsanov have even "sinned" against artistic truth and gone too far, to the point of caricaturing his faults and making him look ridiculous!

The cause of all the misunderstandings, the whole, so to speak "trouble," arose from the fact that the Bazarov type created by me has not yet had time to go through the gradual phases through which literary types usually go. Unlike Onegin and Pechorin, he had not been through a period of idealization and sympathetic, starry-eyed adoration. At the very moment the *new* man—Bazarov—appeared, the author took up a critical, objective attitude towards him. That confused many people and—who knows?—that was, if not a mistake, an injustice. The Bazarov type had at least as much right to be idealized as the literary types that preceded it. I have just said that the author's attitude towards the character he had created confused the reader: the reader always feels ill at ease, he is easily bewildered and even aggrieved if an author treats his imaginary character like a living person, that is to say, if he sees and displays his good as well as his bad sides, and, above all, if he does not show unmistakable signs of sympathy or antipathy with his own child. The reader feels like getting angry: he is asked not to follow a well-beaten path, but to pave his own path. "Why should I take the trouble?" he can't help thinking. "Books exist for entertainment and not for racking one's brains. And, besides, would it have been too much to ask the author to tell me what to think of such and such a character or what he thinks of him himself?" But it is even worse if the author's attitude towards that character is itself rather vague and undefined, if the author himself does not know whether or not he loves the character he has created (as it happened to me in my attitude towards Bazarov, for "the involuntary attraction" I mentioned in my diary is not love). The reader is ready to ascribe to the author all sorts of non-existent sympathies or antipathies, provided he can escape from the feeling of unpleasant "vagueness."

"Neither fathers nor sons," said a witty lady to me after reading my book, "that should be the real title of your novel and—you are yourself a nihilist." A similar view was expressed with even greater force on the publication of *Smoke.* I am afraid I do not feel like raising objections: perhaps, that lady was right. In the business of fiction writing everyone (I am judging by myself) does what he can and not what he wants, and—as much as he can. I suppose that a work of fiction has to be judged *en gros* and while insisting on conscientiousness on the part of the author, the other *sides* of his activity must be regarded, I would not say, with indifference, but with calmness. And, much as I should like to please my critics, I cannot plead guilty to any absence of conscientiousness on my part.

I have a very curious collection of letters and other documents in connection with *Fathers and Sons.* It is rather interesting to compare them. While some of my correspondents accuse me of insulting the younger generation, of being behind the times and a reactionary, and inform me that they "are burning my photographs with a contemptuous laugh," others, on the contrary, reproach me with pandering to the same younger generation. "You are crawling at the feet of Bazarov!" one correspondent exclaims. "You are just pretending to condemn him; in effect, you are fawning upon him and waiting as a favour for one casual smile from him!" One critic, I remember, addressing me directly in strong and eloquent words, depicted Mr. Katkov and me as two conspirators who in the peaceful atmosphere of my secluded study, are hatching our despicable plot, our libellous attack, against the young Russian forces. . . . It made an effective picture! Actually, that is how this *plot* came about. When Mr. Katkov received my manuscript of *Fathers and Sons,* of whose contents he had not even a rough idea, he was utterly bewildered. The Bazarov type seemed to him "almost an apotheosis of *The Contemporary Review,*" and I should not have been surprised if he had refused to publish my novel in his journal. "*Et voilà comme on écrit l'histoire!*" one could have exclaimed, but—is it permissible to give such a high-sounding name to such small matters?

On the other hand, I quite understand the reasons for the anger aroused by my book among the members of a certain party. They are not entirely groundless and I accept—without false humility—part of the reproaches levelled against me. The word "nihilist" I had used in my novel was taken advantage of by a great many people who were only waiting for an excuse, a pretext, to put a stop to the movement which had taken possession of Russian society. But I never used that word as a pejorative term or with any offensive aim, but as an exact and appropriate expression of a fact, an historic fact, that had made its appearance among us; it was transformed into a means of denunciation, unhesitating condemnation and almost a brand of infamy. Certain unfortunate events that occurred at that time increased the suspicions that were just beginning to arise and seemed to confirm the widespread misgivings and justified the worries and efforts of the "saviors of our motherland," for in Russia such "saviors of the motherland" had made their appearance just then. The tide of public opinion, which is still so indeterminate in our country, turned back. . . . But a shadow fell over my name. I do not deceive myself; I know that that shadow will not disappear. But why did not others—people before whom I feel so deeply my own insignificance—utter the great words: *Perissent nos noms, pourvu que la chose publique soit sauvée* . . . i.e. may our names perish so long as the general cause is saved! Following them, I too can console myself with the thought that my book has been of some benefit. This thought compensates me for the unpleasantness of undeserved reproaches. And, indeed, what does it matter? Who twenty or thirty years hence will remember all these storms in a teacup? Or my name—with or without a shadow over it. (pp. 265-70)

Ivan Turgenev, "Apropos of 'Fathers and Sons'," in Partisan Review, *Vol. XXV, No. 2, Spring, 1958, pp. 265-73.*

Henry James   (essay date 1883)

[*James was an American-born novelist, short story writer, critic, and essayist of the late nineteenth and early twentieth centuries. He is regarded as one of the greatest novelists of the English language and is also admired as a lucid and insightful critic. In addition, James was a frequent contributor to many prominent American journals, including the* North American Review, *the* Nation, *and the* Atlantic Monthly. *Here, he praises Turgenev's detailed and accurate characterizations, noting, however, inherent pessimism in his ironical portraits.*]

M. Turgénieff's themes are all Russian; here and there the scene of a tale is laid in another country, but the actors are genuine Muscovites. It is the Russian type of human nature that he depicts; this perplexes, fascinates, inspires him. His works savour strongly of his native soil, like those of all great novelists, and give one who has read them all a strange sense of having had a prolonged experience of Russia. We seem to have travelled there in dreams, to have dwelt there in another state of being. M. Turgénieff gives us a peculiar sense of being out of harmony with his native land—of his having what one may call a poet's quarrel with it. He loves the old, and he is unable to see where the new is drifting. American readers will peculiarly appreciate this state of mind; if they had a native novelist of a large pattern, it would probably be, in a degree, his own. Our author *feels* the Russian character intensely, and cherishes, in fancy, all its old manifestations—the unemancipated peasants, the ignorant, absolute, half-barbarous proprietors, the quaint provincial society, the local types and customs of every kind. But Russian society, like our own, is in process of formation, the Russian character is in solution, in a sea of change, and the modified, modernized Russian, with his old limitations and his new pretensions, is not, to an imagination fond of caressing the old, fixed contours, an especially grateful phenomenon. A satirist at all points, . . . M. Turgénieff is particularly unsparing of the new intellectual fashions prevailing among his countrymen. The express purpose of one of his novels, *Fathers and Sons,* is to contrast them with the old; and in most of his recent works, notably *Smoke,* they have been embodied in various grotesque figures. (pp. 220-21)

Fathers and Sons, . . . dates from ten years ago, and was the first of M. Turgénieff's tales to be translated in America. In none of them is the subject of wider scope or capable of having more of the author's insidious melancholy expressed from it; for the figures with which he has filled his foreground are, with their personal interests and adventures, but the symbols of the shadowy forces that are fighting for ever a larger battle—the battle of the old and the new, the past and the future, of the ideas that arrive with the ideas that linger. Half the tragedies in human history are born of this conflict; and in all that poets and philosophers tell us of it the clearest fact is still its perpetual necessity. The opposing forces in M. Turgénieff's novel are an elder and a younger generation; the drama can indeed never have a more poignant interest than when we see the young world, as it grows to a sense of its strength and its desires, turning to smite the old world which has brought it forth with a mother's tears and a mother's hopes. The young world, in *Fathers and Sons,* is the fiercer combatant; and the old world in fact is simply for ever the *victa causa* that even stoics pity. And yet with M. Turgénieff, characteristically, the gaining cause itself is purely relative, and victors and vanquished are commingled in a common assent to fate. Here, as always, his rare discretion serves him, and rescues him from the danger of exaggerating his representative types. Few figures in his pages are more intelligibly human than Pavel Petrovitsch and Eugene Bazaroff—human each of them in his indefeasible weakness; the one in spite of his small allowances, the other in spite of his brutal claims. In the elder Kirsanoff the author has imaged certain things he instinctively values—the hundred fading traditions of which the now vulgarized idea of the "gentleman" is the epitome. He loves him, of course, as a romancer must, but he has done the most impartial justice to the ridiculous aspect of his position. Bazaroff is a so-called "nihilist"—a red-handed radical, fresh from the shambles of criticism, with Büchner's *Stoff und Kraft* as a text-book, and everything in nature and history for his prey. He is young, strong, and clever, and strides about, rejoicing in his scepticism, sparing nothing, human or divine, and proposing to have demolished the universe before he runs his course. But he finds there is something stronger, cleverer, longer-lived than himself, and that death is a fiercer nihilist than even Dr. Büchner. The tale traces the course of the summer vacation that he comes to spend in the country with a college-friend, and is chiefly occupied with the record of the various trials to which, in this short period, experience subjects his philosophy. They all foreshadow, of course, the supreme dramatic test. He falls in love, and tries to deny his love as he denies everything else, but the best he can do is only to express it in a coarse formula. Mr. Turgénieff is always fond of contrasts, and he has not failed to give Bazaroff a foil in his young comrade, Arcadi Kirsanoff, who represents the merely impermanent and imitative element that clings to the skirts of every great movement. Bazaroff is silenced by death, but it takes a very small dose of life to silence Arcadi. The latter belongs to the nobility, and Bazaroff's exploits in his tranquil, conventional home are those of a lusty young bull in a cabinet of rococo china. Exquisitely imagined is the whole attitude and demeanour of Pavel Petrovitsch, Arcadi's uncle, and a peculiarly happy invention the duel which this perfumed conservative considers it his manifest duty to fight in behalf of gentlemanly opinions. The deeper interest of the tale, however, begins when the young Büchnerite repairs to his own provincial home and turns to a pinch of dust the tender superstitions of the poor old parental couple who live only in their pride in their great learned son and have not even a genteel prejudice, of any consequence, to oppose to his terrible positivism. M. Turgénieff has written nothing finer than this last half of his story; every touch is masterly, every detail is eloquent. In Vassili Ivanovitsch and Arina Vlassievna he has shown us the sentient heart that still may throb in disused forms and not be too proud to subsist a while yet by the charity of science. Their timid devotion to their son, their roundabout caresses, their longings and hopes and fears, and their deeply pathetic stupefaction when it begins to be plain that the world can spare him, all form a picture which, in spite of its dealing with small things in a small style, carries us to the utter-most limits of the tragical. A very noticeable stroke of art, also, is Bazaroff's ever-growing discontentment—a chronic moral irritation, provoked not by the pangs of an old-fashioned conscience, but, naturally enough, by the absence of the agreeable in a world that he has subjected to such exhaustive disintegration. We especially recommend to the reader his long talk with Arcadi as they lie on the grass in the midsummer shade, and Bazaroff kicks out viciously at everything suggested by his ingenuous companion. Toward him too he feels vicious, and we quite understand the impulse, identical with that which in a nervous woman would find expression in a fit of hysterics, through which the overwrought young rationalist, turning to Arcadi with an alarming appearance of real gusto, proposes to fight with him, "to the extinction of animal heat." . . . (pp. 232-36)

Not a single person in the novel of *Fathers and Sons* but has, in some degree, a lurking ironical meaning. Every one is a more or less ludicrous parody on what he ought to have been, or an ineffectual regret at what he might have been. The only person who compasses a reasonable share of happiness is Arcadi, and even his happiness is a thing for strenuous minds to smile at—a happiness based on the *pot au feu,* the prospect of innumerable babies and the sacrifice of "views." Arcadi's father is a vulgar failure; Pavel Petrovitsch is a poetic failure; Bazaroff is a tragic failure; Anna Sergheievna misses happiness from an ungenerous fear of sacrificing her luxurious quietude; the elder Bazaroff and his wife seem a couple of ingeniously grotesque manikins, prepared by a melancholy *fantoccinista* to illustrate the mocking vanity of parental hopes. We lay down the book, and we repeat that, with all the charity in the world, it is impossible to pronounce M. Turgénieff anything better than a pessimist.

The judgment is just, but it needs qualifications, and it finds them in a larger look at the author's position. M. Turgénieff strikes us, as we have said, as a man disappointed, for good reasons or for poor ones, in the land that is dear to him. Harsh critics will say for poor ones, reflecting that a fastidious imagination has not been unconcerned in his discontentment. To the old Muscovite virtues, and especially the old Muscovite *naïveté,* his imagination filially clings, but he finds these things, especially in the fact that his country turns to the outer world, melting more and more every day into the dimness of tradition. The Russians are clever, and clever people are ambitious. Those with whom M. Turgénieff has seen himself surrounded are consumed with the desire to pass for intellectual cosmopolites, to know, or seem to know, everything that can be known, to be astoundingly modern and progressive and European. Madame Kukshin, the poor little literary lady with a red nose, in *Fathers and Sons,* gives up George Sand as "nowhere" for her want of knowledge of embryology, and, when asked why she proposes to remove to Heidelberg, replies with "Bunsen, you know." The fermentation of social change has thrown to the surface in Russia a deluge of hollow pretensions and vicious presumptions, amid which the love either of old virtues or of new achievements finds very little gratification. It is not simply that people flounder laughably in deeper waters than they can breast, but that in this discord of crude ambitions the integrity of character itself is compromised and men and women make, morally, a very ugly appearance. (pp. 247-48)

Henry James, "Ivan Turgénieff," in his French Poets and Novelists, *Bernhard Tauchnitz, 1883, pp. 211-52.*

Edward Garnett (essay date 1895)

[*Garnett was a prominent editor for several London publishing houses, and discovered or greatly influenced the work of many important English writers, including Joseph Conrad, John Galsworthy, and D. H. Lawrence. He also published several volumes of criticism, all of which are characterized by thorough research and sound critical judgments. In the excerpt below, Garnett explores Bazarov's personality in* Fathers and Sons, *suggesting that the character represents "the bare mind of Science first applied to Politics."*]

Fathers and Children was published in the spring of 1862 in Katkoff's paper, *The Russian Messenger,* the organ of 'the Younger Generation,' and the stormy controversy that the novel immediately provoked, was so bitter, deep, and lasting, that the episode forms one of the most interesting chapters in literary history. Rarely has so great an artist so thoroughly drawn public attention to a scrutiny of the new ideas rising in its midst; rarely has so great an artist come into such violent collision with his own party thereby; never perhaps has there been so striking an illustration of the incapacity of the public, swayed by party passion, to understand a pure work of art. The effect of the publication was widespread excitement in both political camps. Everybody was, at the time, on the alert to see what would be the next move on the political board. The recent Emancipation of the Serfs was looked upon by young Russia as only a prelude to many democratic measures, while the Reactionists professed to see in that measure the ruin of the country and the beginning of the end. The fast increasing antipathy between the Old Order and the New, like a fire, required only a puff of wind to set it ablaze. And Bazarov's character and aims came as a godsend to the Reactionists, who hailed in it the portrait of the insidious revolutionary Ideas current in young Russia; and they hastened to crowd round Turgenev, ironically congratulating the former champion of Liberalism on his penetration and honesty in unmasking the Nihilist. (pp. vi-vii)

The Younger Generation, irritated by the public capital made out of Bazarov and his Nihilism by 'the Fathers,' flew into the other extreme, and refused to see in Bazarov anything other than a *caricature* of itself. It denied Bazarov was of its number, or represented its views in any way; and to this day surviving Nihilists will demonstrate warmly that the creation of his sombre figure is 'a mistake from beginning to end.' The reason for this wholesale rejection of Bazarov is easy to account for; and Turgenev, whose clear-sightedness about his works was unaffected either by vanity, diffidence, or the ignorant onslaughts of the whole tribe of minor critics, penetrates at once to the heart of the matter:—

The whole ground of the misunderstanding lay in the fact that the type of Bazarov had not time to pass through the usual phases. At the very moment of his appearance the author attacked him. It was a new method as well as a new type I introduced—that of Realising instead of Idealising. . . . The reader is easily thrown into perplexity when the author does not show clear sympathy or antipathy to his own child. The reader readily gets angry. . . . After all, books exist to entertain.

An excellent piece of analysis and a quiet piece of irony this! The character of Bazarov was in fact such an epitome of the depths of a great movement, that the mass of commonplace educated minds, the future tools of the movement, looked on it with alarm, dislike, and dread. The average man will only recognise his own qualities in his fellows, and endow a man with his own littlenesses. So Bazarov's depth excited the superficiality of the eternally omnipresent average mind. The Idealists in the Younger Generation were morally grieved to see that Bazarov was not wholly inspired by their dreams; he went deeper, and the average man received a shock of surprise that hurt his vanity. So the hue and cry was raised around Turgenev, and raised only too well. Bazarov is the most dominating of Turgenev's creations, yet it brought upon him secret distrust and calumny, undermined his influence with those he was with at heart, and went far to damage his position as the leading novelist of his day. The lesson is significant. No generation ever understands itself; its members welcome eagerly their portraits drawn by their friends, and the caricatures drawn of their adversaries; but to the new type no mercy is shown, and everybody hastens to misunderstand, to abuse, to destroy.

So widely indeed was Bazarov misunderstood, that Turgenev once asserted, 'At this very moment there are only two people who have understood my intentions—Dostoievsky and Botkin.'

And Dostoievsky was of the opposite camp—a Slavophil.

What, then, is Bazarov?

Time after time Turgenev took the opportunity, now in an article, now in a private or a public letter, to repel the attacks made upon his favourite character. Thus in a letter to a Russian lady, he says—

What, you too say that in drawing Bazarov I wished to make a caricature of the young generation. You repeat this—pardon my plain speaking—idiotic reproach. Bazarov, my favourite child, on whose account I quarrelled with Katkoff; Bazarov, on whom I lavished all the colours at my disposal; Bazarov, this man of intellect, this hero, a caricature! But I see it is useless for me to protest.

And in a letter addressed to the Russian students at Heidelberg, he reiterates:—

Flatter comme un caniche, I did not wish; although in this way I could no doubt have all the young men at once on my side; but I was unwilling to buy popularity by concessions of this kind. It is better to lose the campaign (and I believe

I have lost it) than win by this subterfuge. I dreamed of a sombre, savage, and great figure, only half emerged from barbarism, strong, *méchant,* and honest, and nevertheless doomed to perish because it is always in advance of the future. I dreamed of a strange parallel to Pugatchev. And my young contemporaries shake their heads and tell me, "*Vous êtes foutu,* old fellow. You have insulted us. Your Arkady is far better. It's a pity you haven't worked him out a little more." There is nothing left for me but, in the words of the gipsy song, "to take off my hat with a very low bow."

What, then, is Bazarov?

Various writers have agreed in seeing in him only 'criticism, pitiless, barren, and overwhelming analysis, and the spirit of absolute negation,' but this is an error. Representing the creed which has produced the militant type of Revolutionist in every capital of Europe, *he is the bare mind of Science first applied to Politics.* His own immediate origin is German Science interpreted by that spirit of logical intensity, Russian fanaticism, or devotion to the Idea, which is perhaps the distinguishing genius of the Slav. But he represents the roots of the modern Revolutionary movements in thought as well as in politics, rather than the branches springing from those roots. Inasmuch as the early work of the pure scientific spirit, knowing itself to be fettered by the superstitions, the confusions, the sentimentalities of the Past, was necessarily destructive, Bazarov's primary duty was to Destroy. In his essence, however, he stands for *the sceptical conscience of modern Science.* His watchword is *Reality,* and not Negation, as everybody in pious horror hastened to assert. Turgenev, whose first and last advice to young writers was, 'You need truth, remorseless truth, as regards your own sensations,' was indeed moved to declare, 'Except Bazarov's views on Art, I share almost all his convictions.' The crude materialism of the sixties was not the basis of the scientific spirit, it was merely its passing expression; and the early Nihilists who denounced Art, the Family, and Social Institutions were simply freeing themselves from traditions preparatory to a struggle that was inevitable. Again, though Bazarov is a Democrat, perhaps his kinship with the people is best proved by the contempt he feels for them. He stands forward essentially as an Individual, with the 'isms' that can aid him, mere tools in his hand; Socialist, Communist, or Individualist, in his necessary phases he fought this century against the tyranny of centralised Governments, and next century he will be fighting against the stupid tyranny of the Mass. Looking at Bazarov, however, as a type that has played its part and vanished with its generation, as a man he is a new departure in history. His appearance marks the dividing line between two religions, that of the Past—Faith, and that growing religion of to-day—Science. His is the duty of breaking away from all things that men call Sacred, and his savage egoism is essential to that duty. He is subject to neither Custom nor Law. He is his own law, and is occupied simply with the fact he is studying. He has thrown aside the ties of love and duty that cripple the advance of the strongest men. He typifies Mind grappling with Nature, seeking out her inexorable laws, Mind in pure devotion to the What Is, in startling contrast to the minds that follow their self-created kingdom of What Appears, and Ought to Be. He is therefore a foe to the poetry and art that help to increase Nature's glamour over man by alluring him to yield to her; for Bazarov's great aim is to see Nature at work behind the countless veils of illusions and ideals, and all the special functions of belief which she develops in the minds of the masses to get them unquestioning to do her bidding. Finally, Bazarov, in whom the comfortable compromising English mind sees only a man of bad form, bad taste, bad manners, and overwhelming conceit; finally, Bazarov stands for Humanity awakened from century-old superstitions, and the long dragging oppressive dream of tradition. Naked he stands under a deaf, indifferent sky, but he feels and knows that he has the strong brown earth beneath his feet.

> [Bazarov] represents the roots of the modern Revolutionary movements in thought as well as in politics, rather than the branches springing from those roots. Inasmuch as the early work of the pure scientific spirit, knowing itself to be fettered by the superstitions, the confusions, the sentimentalities of the Past, was necessarily destructive, Bazarov's primary duty was to Destroy. In his essence, however, he stands for *the sceptical conscience of modern Science.*
>
> —Edward Garnett

This type, though it has developed into a network of special branches to-day, it is not difficult for us to trace as it has appeared and disappeared in the stormy periods of the last thirty years. Probably the genius and energy of the type was chiefly devoted to positive Science, and not to Politics; but it is sufficient to glance at the Revolutionary History, in theory and action, of the Continent to see that every movement was inspired by the ideas of the Bazarovs, though led by a variety of leaders. Just as the popular movements for Liberty fifty years earlier found sentimental and *romantic* expression in Byronism, so the popular movements of our time have been realistic in idea, and have looked to Science for their justification. Proudhon, Bakunin, Karl Marx, the Internationals, the Russian Terrorists, the Communists, all have a certain relation to Bazarov, but his nearest kinsmen in these and other movements we believe have worked, and have remained, obscure. It was a stroke of genius on Turgenev's part to make Bazarov die on the threshold unrecognised. He is Aggression, destroyed in his destroying. And there are many reasons in life for the Bazarovs remaining obscure. For one thing, their few disciples, the Arkadys, do not understand them; for another, the whole swarm of little interested persons who make up a movement are more or less engaged in personal interests, and they rarely take for a leader a man who works for his own set of Truths, scornful of all cliques, penalties, and rewards. Necessarily, too, the Bazarovs work alone, and are given the most dangerous tasks to accomplish unaided. Further, they are men whose brutal and breaking force attracts ten men where it repels a thousand. The average man is too afraid of Bazarov to come into contact with him. Again, the Bazarovs, as Iconoclasts, are always unpopular in their own circles. Yesterday in political life they were suppressed or exiled, and even in science they were the men who were supplanted before their real claim was recognised, and to-day when order reigns for a time, the academic circles and the popular critics will demonstrate that Bazarov's existence was a mistake, and the crowd could have got on much better without him.

The Crowd, the ungrateful Crowd, though for it Bazarov has wrested much from effete or corrupt hands, and has fought and weakened despotic and bureaucratic power, what has its opinion or memory to do with his brave heroic figure? Yes, heroic, as Turgenev, in indignation with Bazarov's shallow accusers, was betrayed into defining his own creation, Bazarov, whose very atmosphere is difficulty and danger, who cannot move without hostility, carrying as he does destruction to the old wornout truths, contemptuous of censure, still more contemptuous of praise, he goes his way against wind and tide. Brave man, given up to his cause, whatever it be, it is his joy *to stand alone,* watching the crowd as it races wherever reward is and danger is not. It is Bazarov's life to despise honours, success, opinion, and to let nothing, not love itself, come between him and his inevitable course, and, when death comes, to turn his face to the wall, while in the street below he can hear the voices of men cheering the popular hero who has last arrived. The Crowd! Bazarov is the antithesis of the cowardice of the Crowd. That is the secret why we love him.

As a piece of art *Fathers and Children* is the most powerful of all Turgenev's works. The figure of Bazarov is not only the political centre of the book, against which the other characters show up in their respective significance, but a figure in which the eternal tragedy of man's impo-

The Turgenev estate at Spasskoye.

tence and insignificance is realised in scenes of a most ironical human drama. How admirably this figure dominates everything and everybody. Everything falls away before this man's biting sincerity. In turn the figure-heads of Culture and Birth, Nikolai and Pavel representing the Past; Arkady the sentimentalist representing the Present; the father and mother representing the ties of family that hinder a man's life-work; Madame Odintsov embodying the fascination of a beautiful woman—all fall into their respective places. But the particular power of *Fathers and Children,* of epic force almost, arises from the way in which Turgenev makes us feel the individual human tragedy of Bazarov in relation to the perpetual tragedy everywhere in indifferent Nature. In *On the Eve,* Turgenev cast his figures against a poetic background by creating an atmosphere of War and Patriotism. But in *Fathers and Children* this poetic background is Nature herself, Nature who sows, with the same fling of her hand, life and death springing each from each, in the same rhythmical cast of fate. And with Nature for the background, there comes the wonderful sense conveyed to the reader throughout the novel, of the generations with their fresh vigorous blood passing away quickly, a sense of the coming generations, whose works, too will be hurried away into the background, a sense of the silence of Earth while her children disappear into the shadows, and are whelmed in turn by the inexorable night. While everything in the novel is expressed in the realistic terms of daily commonplace life, the characters appear now close to us as companions, and now they seem like distant figures walking under an immense sky; and the effect of Turgenev's simply and subtly drawn landscapes is to give us a glimpse of men and women in their actual relation to their mother earth and the sky over their heads. This effect is rarely conveyed in the modern Western novel, which deals so much with purely indoor life; but the Russian novelist gained artistic force for his tragedies by the vague sense ever present with him of the enormous distances of the vast steppes, bearing on their bosom the peasants' lives, which serve as a sombre background to the life of the isolated individual figures with which he is dealing. Turgenev has availed himself of this hidden note of tragedy, and with the greatest art he has made Bazarov, with all his ambition opening out before him, and his triumph awaited, the eternal type of man's conquering egoism conquered by the pin-prick of Death. Bazarov, who looks neither to the right hand nor the left, who delays no longer in his life-work of throwing off the mind-forged manacles; Bazarov, who trusts not to Nature, but would track the course of her most obscure laws; Bazarov, in his keen pursuit of knowledge, is laid low by the weapon he has selected to wield. His own tool, the dissecting knife, brings death to him, and his body is stretched beside the peasant who had gone before. Of the death-scene, the great culmination of this great novel, it is impossible to speak without emotion. The voice of the reader, whosoever he be, must break when he comes to those passages of infinite pathos where the father, Vassily Ivanovitch, is seen peeping from behind the door at his dying son, where he cries, 'Still living, my Yevgeny is still living, and now he will be saved. Wife, wife!' and where, when death has come, he cries, 'I said I should rebel. I rebel, I rebel!' What art, what genius, we can only repeat, our spirit humbled to the dust by the exquisite solemnity of that undying simple scene of the old parents at the grave, the scene where Turgenev epitomises in one stroke the infinite aspiration, the eternal insignificance of the life of man.

Let us end here with a repetition of a simple passage, that echoing through the last pages of *Fathers and Children* must find an echo in the hearts of Turgenev's readers: ' "To the memory of Bazarov," ' Katya whispered in her husband's ear, . . . but Arkady did not venture to propose the toast aloud.' We, at all events, can drink the toast today as a poor tribute in recompense for those days when Turgenev in life proposed it, and his comrades looked on him with distrust, with coldness, and with anger. (pp. ix-xxi)

> *Edward Garnett, in an introduction to* Fathers and Children: A Novel *by Ivan Turgenev, translated by Constance Garnett, 1895. Reprint by AMS Press, 1970, pp. v-xxi.*

Avrahm Yarmolinsky   (essay date 1926)

[*Yarmolinsky was a Russian-born American translator, biographer, social historian, and critic who wrote extensively on Russian literature and edited numerous anthologies of Russian literature as well as works by Fyodor Dostoevsky, Anton Chekov, and Alexander Pushkin. Below, Yarmolinsky traces Turgenev's creative process in developing the character Bazarov, claiming that though the author professed to a lack of imagination, he proved his skill as a novelist by turning his observations of living people into believable characters.*]

Always ill at ease when it came to traffic with abstract ideas, principles, opinions, Turgenev felt sure of himself only when he was dealing with what is visible, audible, tangible. Such matters as division of fractions or the mechanism of a watch were, he confessed, quite beyond him. "When I don't have to do with concrete figures," he wrote, "I am entirely lost and I don't know where to turn. It always seems to me that exactly the opposite of what I say could be asserted with equal justice. But if I am speaking of a red nose and blonde hair, then the hair is blonde and the nose red; no amount of reflection will change that."

Belinsky had said at the outset of Turgenev's career that while he was extremely observant, he had no imagination. The young author had agreed with this judgment wholeheartedly. To the end he was possessed by a self-distrust which would not allow him to rely upon his inner consciousness and led him to lean heavily upon the world. George Moore went to the root of the matter when he said that Turgenev had the illuminative rather than the creative imagination and that he "borrowed" his stories, leaving them, as far as structure went, much as he found them.

Turgenev confessed that he envied the English their secret of making a successful plot, an ability which he found lacking in himself as in so many Russian writers. He had a prodigious memory, which served him well. He liked to insist that his characters were not invented, but discovered. He stalked them with the patience, the eagerness, and the skill with which he pursued his woodcock and his partridge. Indeed, it appears that he almost invariably drew from living models and that his fictions were fathered by experience rather than by fancy. He told a friend that it was his custom, after meeting a stranger, to set down in his note-book any peculiarities he had observed. He studied Lavater's work on physiognomy from cover to cover. Drawing-rooms, railway carriages, and reading-rooms were his favorite observatories. He did not hesitate to incorporate verbatim in his story, **"The Brigadier,"** a private letter which he found among his mother's papers. If he had had his choice, he once remarked, he would have been a writer like Gibbon. The novelist had the historian's need for documentation. He proved his artistry by digesting his documents and turning them into flesh and blood.

In the case of *Fathers and Children,* as in most of his writings, the germ came to Turgenev not in the form of a situation or an idea, but in that of a person. Chancing to meet in a railway train a provincial doctor who, talking shop, had something to say on the subject of anthrax, Turgenev was struck by the man's rough, matter-of-fact, candid manner. It flashed upon him that here was a representative of an emerging and significant type. He relates in his Reminiscences how he began to look about him for other signs pointing to the rise of this type. He could find no effigy of his traveling companion in any work of fiction. But as he attended literary dinners in Moscow and read the Petersburg reviews, it seemed to him that he was always just on the edge of tracking down his quarry. And yet the traces were so faint and unfamiliar that he sometimes thought he was "chasing a ghost."

The notion of building a novel around this figure occurred to him during his stay at Ventnor, where he had gone in August, 1860, for the sake of the bathing. When he confided his project to one of his literary friends there, he met only discouragement, and with his usual suggestibility dropped the idea forthwith. Later in the summer when he was back in Paris again, the thought returned to him with renewed strength, and he found himself increasingly absorbed in it. In October he was writing to Countess Lambert that the stuff for his new novel was all in his head, but that "the spark which must kindle everything had not yet blazed up."

It was presumably about this time that he began to get up for his characters the *"dossiers"* without which he could not begin work on a novel. He was in the habit, as he told Henry James among others, of setting down "a sort of biography of each of his characters, and everything that they had done and that had happened to them up to the opening of the story." As in the case of *On the Eve,* he kept a diary for one of the characters, but this time it was not the journal of a minor figure, but of the protagonist, Bazarov, whom he was modeling partly on his railway companion, partly on another man who was later exiled to Siberia. He was drawing his people, by his own account, as he might have sketched "mushrooms, leaves, trees," things that he had seen until, in the Russian phrase, they had "calloused his eyes." In the winter he was at work on the first chapters and by July 19 of the next year he was telling Countess Lambert that in about two weeks he expected to taste his "only joy in life," that is, "writing the last line." The next six months were given over to revision. In later years he asserted that he had written the novel seemingly without volition, almost surprised at what came from his pen.

In September the manuscript went to the judicative Annenkov for a first reading. He swallowed it in two days. Then it went the rounds. Turgenev, who at first had been buoyed up with confidence in his book, became more and more doubtful of it as he received his friends' comments. Katkov, the editor of *The Russian Herald,* in which it was to make its first appearance, disliked it for what he considered its outrageous adulation of the radicals. Others condemned it as an attack upon the younger generation. Countess Lambert had nothing good to say for it. In the distress and confusion that seized him, Turgenev had an impulse, which he did not obey, to feed the manuscript to the flames. What increased his perplexities was the news of student riots in Petersburg. Should he, in such circumstances, allow a work which had a bearing, however remote, upon the political situation, to appear in type? Turgenev's hemmings and hawings went on until the exasperated Annenkov, who as usual had taken it upon himself to see the manuscript through the press, was ready to wash his hands of it. The author wrote to Countess Lambert that he finally published the book only because Katkov insisted on having it and because he himself needed the money.

When that delightful period was over during which the figures for his novel floated like nebulæ through his mind, and he once had a good grasp of his characters, Turgenev's final move, according to James, was the arduous business of devising the action which would lead them to reveal their inner natures. In *Fathers and Children* the novelist put Bazarov through his paces by taking this brusque commoner on a visit to a house of gentlefolk; by leading him into arguments with his two middle-aged, cultivated hosts; by making him fall in love with a beautiful, ineffectual, frigid lady; by involving him in a stupid, almost comical duel with one of his hosts, because he had been caught kissing the mistress of the other; by engaging him in talk with his earnest, apish, pliant disciple; by sending him home to see his pathetic old parents; by bringing upon him an untimely death, the result of an infection contracted at a rural post-mortem.

One might perhaps wish that the author had seen fit to show Bazarov in the urban setting in which a man of his type was more likely to be found, rather than against the manorial background with its lax, gracious, somnolent atmosphere. Then, too, the modern reader is inclined to resent Turgenev's awkwardness in dealing with the natural sciences, to which his hero is devoted. But these are only minor flaws. Turgenev gave to this work all that was in him: the fruit of his contacts with men and women, his knowledge of Russian social history, his lyric sensitiveness to the natural scene and to the fine vibrations of the human mood, his penchant for satire, his little faith overlaid by a composed despair.

From the moment when we first see Bazarov taking his time about offering his bare red hand to his host, and turning down the collar of his nondescript coat to show his long, thin face, with its sandy side-whiskers and cool green eyes, to the moment, a few months later, when the dying agnostic raises one eyelid in horror as the priest administers the last sacrament, we are in the presence of a torso modeled, if not quite with the elemental energy, yet with all the sure skill of a Rodin. Turgenev believed that to be a novelist was to be "objective." He meant that novel-writing was an art which could be practised only by one who was concerned with representing the world about him, rather than in rendering its effect upon him; an art which required an interest in and a cumulative knowledge of other people's lives, as well as an understanding of the hidden forces that shaped them. He himself did not quite answer to this description of a novelist. Alert as he was to every aspect of the sensible world, his mind nevertheless was a mind that was turned inward. He lived, like a character in one of his early works, in a room walled with mirrors, and created most of his heroes in his own image. Bazarov would seem to be the magnificent exception to this rule. This hard-headed medic, with his plebeian pride, his contempt for the finicky gentry, his scorn of the fine arts, his disgust with all accepted values, this cynic, this barbarian, this "Nihilist" is at once an extraordinary example of what objective insight can achieve, and in some respects a fulfilment of Turgenev's day-dream of the self he vainly longed to be.

An hour and a half after finishing the novel, he noted in his diary (July 30, 1861) that while writing the book he had felt "an involuntary attraction" toward his hero. A few months after the book appeared, he wrote to Foeth that he didn't know whether he liked Bazarov or not. Seven years later he stated publicly that he agreed with all of Bazarov's views, except for his ideas on art. On the other hand, we have the author's word for it that Nikolai Petrovich Kirsanov was something of a self-portrait, and Nikolai Petrovich is one of the two men who symbolize the older generation where Bazarov is the epitome of the younger. It is certain that the admiration he felt for his hero went hand in hand with regret for the traditions the man was bent on smashing.

One of Bazarov's sentiments was undoubtedly shared by his creator—dislike of the gentry. Indeed, Turgenev's treatment of them in this novel afforded him the strange satisfaction of the flagellant. He spoke of the book, shortly after it was published, as having been directed against the class into which he was born. Look at these gently nurtured Kirsanovs, both young and old, and what do you find? "Weakness, flabbiness, inadequacy." And these were gentlefolk of the better sort. "If the cream is bad, what can the milk be like?" How well he knew these people—their good intentions, their feeble achievements, their sensibilities, so readily touched by the glow of a setting sun which makes the aspens look like pines, or by enchanted memories of a dead love, or by a line of verse, or by a point of honor! But the knowledge which made him contemptuous of them, stirred his pity, too, and Nikolai Petrovich, at least, is a lovable fellow. When it came to the drawing of Bazarov's parents, Turgenev bathed them in an atmosphere of such tenderness and burdened them with so cruel a tragedy, that these passages are among the most moving in literature. As he wrote the last lines, in which the old couple are shown visiting the grave of their only son, Turgenev had to turn away his head, so that his tears would not blot the manuscript, and even in such a dry-eyed age as ours, few readers will finish the paragraph without blinking.

Throughout the novel, the writing is on an extraordinarily high plane. What is not perfectly expressed, is perfectly suggested. The description of Bazarov's illness gave Chekhov, a physician as well as an artist, the sensation of having "caught the infection from him." It is true that the plot, while plausible enough, has not the strength of inevitability. But, without question, Turgenev achieved his intention. The method used here is his habitual one—realization of the characters not by analysis of their consciousness, but by exhibition of their behavior. Like so many of his fellow-craftsmen, he exalted into a dogma his way of working. When he was brooding over the plan for *Fathers and Children* he set down for a literary protégé one of the few precepts that should be weighed by every practitioner of the novelist's art: "The writer must be a psychologist, but a secret one: he must sense and know the roots of phenomena, but offer only the phenomena themselves,—as they blossom or wither." Ten years earlier he had said, in the course of a critique, much the same thing in other words: "The psychologist must disappear in the artist, as the skeleton is concealed within the warm and living body, for which it serves as a firm but invisible support."

Fathers and Children made its appearance in the second number of *The Russian Herald* for 1862, and shortly afterward was published as a separate volume. When Turgenev returned to Petersburg from Paris, in the spring of the year, he found the capital excited by a number of conflagrations, which rumor put at the door of revolutionary incendiaries, students and Poles. An acquaintance, meeting him on the Nevsky, exclaimed: "See what *your* 'Nihilists' are doing! They're setting Petersburg on fire!" Turgenev had not invented the term, any more than he had invented the type, but his employment of the word and the character alike made for the vogue of both. A girl wanting a new frock was likely to face her parents with the threat of becoming a Nihilist, if they didn't come round. Where, as in Russia of the sixties, literature has great prestige, the novelist is peculiarly able to become the arbiter of fashion in personality. Besides, the novel was read by everybody, from the empress down to people who hadn't opened a book since their school-days, and before long one discovered at least a dash of Bazarov in nearly every young man of independent spirit.

Not that the general public understood Turgenev's intention in the novel. The conservatives applauded him for having "caricatured" and shown up these dreadful Nihilists. The radical youth, placing the author's sympathies where the conservatives did, was ready to burn him in effigy. Some few recognized themselves in Bazarov, and acknowledged the book to be an honest objective study of "the children," by a fair-minded representative of the older generation. Most of them, however, saw in it a slanderous attack. Some of his young compatriots in Heidelberg, he said, wrote to him threatening to descend upon

him in Baden to settle accounts. It was a disconcerting reception. Turgenev wrote bitterly to a friend: "I was struck by hands I wanted to clasp, and caressed by hands from whose touch I wanted to fly to the ends of the earth." Fortunately for his peace of mind he never knew the worst: a secret police report for 1862, which only came to light recently, commended the author for a novel which shook the doctrine of materialism and "branded our revolutionists with the biting name of Nihilist."

It was the greater blow to him to find that he was at odds with the younger generation because, aside from the disagreeable business of being considered an old fogey, if he hadn't made his public see that he admired Bazarov, then he was a failure as a novelist. "If the reader doesn't love Bazarov," he wrote to a friend soon after the book appeared, "with all his coarseness, heartlessness, pitiless dryness, and brusqueness, it's my fault. I haven't achieved my purpose. . . . I envisaged a somber figure, savage, huge, half-imbedded in the soil, strong, honest, a man of wrath, and yet for all that doomed to perish, because he was only on the threshold of the future." This giant a caricature! And yet Turgenev could find only two men who knew at what he was aiming: Botkin and Dostoyevsky, a strange pair. And perhaps a third, the poet Maikov, to whom he wrote: "Now I can say to myself that I couldn't have written something altogether absurd if such people as you and Dostoyevsky pat me on the head, and say, Very good, my boy, I'll give you eighty per cent. on that!" For his own part, he was as nearly content with his book as he ever could be. He told Annenkov as much, saying that he was "for the first time . . . seriously satisfied" with his work, although sometimes he felt as though it had been written by a stranger.

Some half a dozen years after the appearance of the book, a German friend, Ludwig Pietsch, being about to write a critique on it, was urged by Turgenev to express astonishment at the attitude of the Russians toward it. Certainly Pietsch as a clear-sighted outsider could see the absurdity of taking Bazarov as a vicious lampoon against the younger generation. Turgenev went on:

> Do rather show that I conceived the fellow entirely too heroically, too ideally (which is true), and that the Russian youth is altogether too thin-skinned. Because of Bazarov I was (and for that matter, still am) so spattered with muck and filth; so much abuse and opprobrium, so many curses, have been heaped upon my head (Vidocq, Judas, lout, ass, poisonous toad, spittoon—this was the least that was said of me) that it would be a satisfaction to me to prove that other nations look at the matter in a different light.

What kept the young people from accepting Bazarov as a portrait of themselves was the fact that, aside from his lack of a political program, he had no interest in bettering the lot of the masses, which became, as the years passed, their fundamental concern. On a hot afternoon Bazarov and the young Kirsanov are lying in the shadow of a haystack and philosophizing. The Nihilist is in a mood for metaphysical speculation. Talk turns upon Russia, and he observes to his companion in a deliberate tone:

Here, for instance, you said to-day, as we passed the cottage of your steward, Philip,—it's such a fine, white one,—you said that Russia would attain perfection when the last peasant would have such a house, and every one of us ought to help to bring this about. . . . But as you spoke I hated this last peasant, Philip or Sidor, for whom I am to wear myself out, and who won't even say thanks to me. . . . And what do I want with his thanks, anyway? He'll live in a white cottage, and burdocks will be growing out of me. Well, and what next?

To the advanced youth such unsocial ideas were simply abominable. And yet it was not out of character for Bazarov to speak in this fashion, because what Turgenev was representing was not so much a revolutionist as the stuff out of which revolutionists came to be made. It is conceivable that he meted out to his hero a premature death precisely because his denying and denouncing was merely preliminary to a more constructive phase of social criticism. In saying that Bazarov was "doomed to perish because he was only on the threshold of the future," he may have meant just this. But looking at the novel in the light of the author's personality, it seems more likely that he killed off his hero in obedience less to a law of that man's nature than to a law of his own nature. Turgenev was inclined to accept the idea of an ironic fate, smiting the strong with the weapons of chance, and passing over the nullities, and moreover, he could never quite bring himself to crown the work of his characters with success, or to grant them that sense of accomplishment which he had never fully tasted, himself. (pp. 189-97)

> *Avrahm Yarmolinsky, in his* Turgenev: The Man—His Art—and His Age, *The Century Co., 1926, 386 p.*

Irving Howe (essay date 1957)

[*A longtime editor of the leftist magazine* Dissent *and a regular contributor to the* New Republic, *Howe is one of America's most highly respected literary critics and social historians. His criticism is frequently informed by a liberal social viewpoint. In the following excerpt, Howe considers Bazarov one of Turgenev's "superfluous men," and, like other such characters, "essentially good."*]

If Rudin has partly been created in Turgenev's own image, Bazarov, the hero of **Fathers and Sons,** is a figure in opposition to that image. The one rambles idealistic poetry, the other grumbles his faith in the dissection of frogs; the one is all too obviously weak, the other seems spectacularly strong. Yet between the two there is a parallel of social position. Both stand outside the manor-house that is Russia, peering in through a window; Rudin makes speeches and Bazarov would like to throw stones but no one pays attention, no one is disturbed. The two together might, like Dostoevsky's Shatov and Kirillov, come to a whole man; but they are not together, they alternate in Russian life, as in Russian literature, each testifying to the social impotence that has made the other possible.

Like all of Turgenev's superfluous men, Bazarov is essentially good. Among our more cultivated critics, those who

insist that the heroes of novels be as high-minded as themselves, it has been fashionable to look with contempt upon Bazarov's nihilism, to see him as a specimen of Russian boorishness. Such a reading is not merely imperceptive, it is humorless. Would it really be better if Bazarov, instead of devoting himself to frogs and viscera, were to proclaim about Poetry and the Soul? Would it be better if he were a metaphysician juggling the shells of Matter and Mind instead of a coarse materialist talking nonsense about the irrelevance of Pushkin?

For all that Bazarov's nihilism accurately reflects a phase of Russian and European history, it must be taken more as a symptom of political desperation than as a formal intellectual system. Bazarov is a man ready for life, and cannot find it. Bazarov is a man of the most intense emotions, but without confidence in his capacity to realize them. Bazarov is a revolutionary personality, but without revolutionary ideas or commitments. He is all potentiality and no possibility. The more his ideas seem outmoded, the more does he himself seem our contemporary.

No wonder Bazarov feels so desperate a need to be rude. There are times when society is so impervious to the kicks of criticism, when intellectual life softens so completely into the blur of gentility, that the rebellious man, who can tolerate everything but not being taken seriously, has no alternative to rudeness. How else is Bazarov to pierce the elegant composure of Pavel Petrovich, a typically "enlightened" member of the previous generation who combines the manners of a Parisian literateur with an income derived from the labor of serfs. Bazarov does not really succeed, for Pavel Petrovich forces him to a duel, a romantic ceremony that is the very opposite of everything in which Bazarov believes. During the course of the duel, it is true, Pavel Petrovich must yield to Bazarov, but the mere fact that it takes place is a triumph for the old, not the new. Bazarov may regard Pavel Petrovich as an "archaic phenomenon," but the "archaic phenomenon" retains social power.

The formal components of Bazarov's nihilism are neither unfamiliar nor remarkable: 19th century scientism, utilitarianism, a crude materialism, a rejection of the esthetic, a belief in the powers of the free individual, a straining for tough-mindedness and a deliberate provocative rudeness. These ideas and attitudes can gain point only if Bazarov brings them to political coherence, and the book charts Bazarov's journey, as an uprooted plebeian, in search of a means of expression, a task, an obligation. On the face of it, Bazarov's ideas have little to do with politics, yet he is acute enough to think of them in political terms; he recognizes that they are functions of his frustrated political passion. "Your sort," he says to his mild young friend Arkady, "can never get beyond refined submission or refined indignation, and that's no good. You won't fight—and yet you fancy yourselves gallant chaps—but we mean to fight . . . We want to smash other people! You're a capital fellow: But you're a sugary liberal snob for all that . . ." This is the language of politics; it might almost be Lenin talking to a liberal parliamentarian. But even as Bazarov wants to "smash other people" he senses his own helplessness: he has no weapons for smashing anything. "A harmless person," he calls himself, and a little later, "A tame cat."

In the society of his day, as Turgenev fills it in with a few quick strokes, Bazarov is as superfluous as Rudin. His young disciple Arkady cannot keep pace with him; Arkady will marry, have a houseful of children and remember to be decent to his peasants. The older generation does not understand Bazarov and for that very reason fears him: Arkady's father, a soft slothful landowner, is acute enough, however, to remark that Bazarov is different: he has "fewer traces of the slaveowner." Bazarov's brief meeting with the radicals is a fine bit of horseplay, their emptyheaded chatter being matched only by his declaration, as preposterous as it is pathetic: "I don't adopt anyone's ideas; I have my own." At which one of them, in a transport of defiance, shouts: "Down with all authorities!" and Bazarov realizes that among a pack of fools it is hard not to play the fool. He is tempted, finally, by Madame Odnitzov, the country-house Delilah; suddenly he finds his awkward callow tongue, admitting to her his inability to speak freely of everything in his heart. But again he is rejected, and humiliated too, almost like a servant who has been used by his mistress and then sent packing. Nothing remains but to go home, to his good sweet uncomprehending mother and father, those remnants of old Russia; and to die.

Turgenev himself saw Bazarov in his political aspect:

> If he [Bazarov] calls himself a nihilist, one ought to read—a revolutionary . . . I dreamed of a figure that should be gloomy, wild, great, growing one half of him out of the soil, strong, angry, honorable, and yet doomed to destruction—because as yet he still stands on the threshold of the future. I dreamed of a strange parallel to Pugatchev. And my young contemporaries shake their heads and tell me, "You have insulted us . . . It's a pity you haven't worked him out a little more." There is nothing left for me but, in the words of the gipsy song, "to take off my hat with a very low bow."

Seldom has a writer given a better clue to the meaning of his work, and most of all in the comparison between Bazarov and Pugatchev, the leader of an 18th century peasant rebellion who was hanged by a Tzar. Pugatchev, however, had his peasant followers, while Bazarov . . . what is Bazarov but a Pugatchev without the peasants?

It is at the end of *Fathers and Sons* that Turgenev reaches his highest point as an artist. The last twenty-five pages are of an incomparable elevation and intensity, worthy of Tolstoy and Dostoevsky, and in some respects, particularly in their blend of tragic power and a mute underlying sweetness, superior to them. When Bazarov, writhing in delirium, cries out, "Take ten from eight, what's left over?" we are close to the lucidity of Lear in the night. It is the lucidity of final self-confrontation, Bazarov's lament over his lost, his unused powers: "I was needed by Russia . . . No, it's clear, I wasn't needed . . ." Nothing so thoroughly undercuts his earlier protestations of self-sufficiency as this last outcry.

This ending too has failed to satisfy many critics, even one

so perceptive as Prince Mirsky, who complains that there is something arbitrary in Bazarov's death. But given Russia, given Bazarov, how else *could* the novel end? Too strong to survive in Russia, what else is possible to Bazarov but death? The accident of fate that kills him comes only after he has been defeated in every possible social and personal encounter; it is the summation of those encounters. The "arbitrariness" of Bazarov's death comes as a bitterly ironic turning of his own expectations. Lying lonely and ignored in a corner of Russia, this man who was to change and destroy everything ends in pitiful helplessness. Political and not political, the ending is the only one that was available to Turgenev at the time he wrote. (pp. 132-35)

Irving Howe, "Turgenev: The Politics of Hesitation," in his Politics and the Novel, *1957. Reprint by Fawcett Publications, Inc., 1967, pp. 117-42.*

Nabokov on Bazarov and romantic love:

Fathers and Sons is not only the best of Turgenev's novels, it is one of the most brilliant novels of the nineteenth century. Turgenev managed to do what he intended to do, to create a male character, a young Russian, who would affirm his—that character's—absence of introspection and at the same time would not be a journalist's dummy of a socialistic type. Bazarov is a strong man, no doubt—and very possibly had he lived beyond his twenties (he is a graduate student when we meet him), he might have become, beyond the horizon of the novel, a great social thinker, a prominent physician, or an active revolutionary. But there was a common debility about Turgenev's nature and art; he was incapable of making his masculine characters triumph within the existence he invents for them. Moreover, in Bazarov's character there is behind the brashness and the will-power, and the violence of cold thought, a stream of natural youthful ardency which Bazarov finds difficult to blend with the harshness of a would-be nihilist. This nihilism sets out to denounce and deny everything, but it fails to dismiss passionate love—or to reconcile this love with his opinions regarding the simple animal character of love. Love turns out to be something more than man's biological pastime. The romantic fire that suddenly envelops his soul shocks him; but it satisfies the requirements of true art, since it stresses in Bazarov the logic of universal youth which transcends the logic of a local system of thought—of, in the present case, nihilism.

Vladimir Nabokov, in his Lectures on Russian Literature, *edited by Fredson Bowers, Harcourt Brace Jovanovich, 1981.*

P. G. Pustovoyt   (essay date 1960)

[*In the following excerpt from an essay originally published in 1960, Pustovoyt describes how Turgenev uses detailed description, satire, and contradictions in personality to develop the characters in* Fathers and Sons.]

Dialogue plays so large a role in Turgenev's novels that it would be incorrect to consider it simply as a technical device of the writer's. The increasing role of dialogue is determined by the themes and the intellectual content of his works. In general, dialogue is the most appropriate form in the sociological novel to raise philosophical arguments on the large questions preoccupying the author's contemporary society. It makes it possible to develop actual political problems, and to cast light on them from various points of view. Finally, in dialogue characters are disclosed and discovered and appear as active agents and participants in ideological conflict.

In the novel **Fathers and Sons** dialogues are above all passionate political and philosophical arguments. Unlike his opponents, Bazarov is brief and lapidary in arguments. He does not conquer and overwhelm his opponents through long arguments and philosophical tirades as Rudin did but in laconic, pregnant replies, apt, full of meaning, appropriately expressed in aphorisms. Bazarov does not attempt to speak beautifully, he does not try "to pin down words like butterflies." And yet Bazarov emerges the victor in almost all the arguments, since his replies, thrown off almost as if in passing, are jammed full of profound thoughts and testify to the hero's colossal erudition, his knowledge of life, his resourcefulness and cleverness. Bazarov's replies may be turned into a complete system of opinions. A definite democratic scheme underlies every reply. For example, the replies "peasants are glad to rob even themselves to get dead drunk at the pot-house" or "when it thunders the common folk think Elijah the Prophet is riding through the heavens in a chariot" clearly express the educational plans formulated in Chernyshevsky's and Dobrolyubov's articles in *The Contemporary* at the end of the 1850's, and embodied in many of N. Uspensky's stories about common folk, which usually appeared in the opening pages of that periodical. Bazarov's reply "The art of making money or 'Shrink Hemorrhoids' " has been explained by N. K. Brodsky as a reference by Bazarov for polemical purposes to two works by a writer of the 1860's, I. T. Kokorev, reviewed by Chernyshevsky and Dobrolyubov. It is easy to prove that the main hero's other replies ("Raphael isn't worth a plugged nickel," "a good chemist is twenty times more useful than any poet") are based on the rich real material of the epoch.

In order to make Bazarov's speech in the dialogues broad and to make it express the hero's ideas in concentrated form, Turgenev makes Bazarov use proverbs and sayings, idiomatic expressions, and other forms of phraseology more frequently than other characters ("a scalded cat fears cold water," "that's not the whole story," "as the ale is drawn it must be drunk"). And yet it would be incorrect to consider the aphoristic and idiomatic quality of Bazarov's speech in argumentation as its only characteristic feature. Turgenev endowed his main hero with the capacity for oratorical speech in addition to these very real and characteristic marks of Bazarov's speech, which reveal in him the genuine democrat who tries to make himself understood by common folk. Thus, in Chapter Ten of the novel, in the argument with Pavel Petrovich, Bazarov does not limit himself to the brief and devastatingly apt replies ("We've heard that song a good many times," that is, he criticizes Pavel Petrovich's discussion of the English aristocracy; or "The ground has to be cleared first"), but

he also delivers a fairly long critical tirade against liberal phrasemongering:

> Then we figured out that talk, perpetual talk, and nothing but talk about our social sores was not worthwhile, that it all led to nothing but banality and doctrinairism. We saw that even our clever ones, so-called advanced people and accusers, were no good; that we were occupied by nonsense, talked about some sort of art, unconscious creativeness, parliamentarism, the legal profession, and the devil knows what all, while it's a question of daily bread, while we're stifling under the grossest superstition, while all our corporations come to grief simply because there aren't enough honest men to carry them on . . .

The syntactical construction of that sentence is itself enough to prove that before us is not an ordinary district doctor but an orator, a tribune, a leader of a certain party (that is, the presence of parallel constructions: "We figured out," "we saw," and before that "we said"; repeated conjunctions "that" and "while"). If we examine the content of Bazarov's angry tirade it becomes clear that Turgenev did not shut his hero's lips, did not limit his participation in arguments to witticisms, but permitted him to express himself "at the top of his voice," that is, as he might have expressed himself before a large mass of his partisans.

Bazarov knows how to ridicule and parry Pavel Petrovich's country squire's drawing-room manner of speech with its countless formulas of servile-courtier politeness and ingratiation like "I haven't the honor of knowing," "permit me to be so curious as to ask," "will you be so kind as." Thus, for example, when Pavel Petrovich in his usual elegant manner, which he considered a mark of special chic, offers Bazarov with solemn grandioseness to "be so good as to choose (pistols)" Bazarov answers him calmly but with deadly irony "I will be so good." Such are some of the characteristics of dialogue in Turgenev's **Fathers and Sons**.

The portraits of characters play a vital, though not the most important, role in Turgenev's novels in general and in **Fathers and Sons** in particular. Turgenev very carefully studies a character's bearing, his exterior, and his gestures before engraving it on the artistic work. Turgenev wrote "I define characters as for a play: so and so, aged such and such, dresses this way, bears himself this way. Sometimes a certain gesture occurs to me and I immediately put down: passes his hand over his hair or pulls at his moustache. And I do not start to write until he becomes an old acquaintance for me, until I see him and hear his voice. And so with all the characters." In Turgenev's works, the characters are portrayed in many different ways. Upon close examination at least three types of portraits emerge from the variety offered.

The first is a detailed portrait with a description of the height, hair, face, and eyes of the hero and also several characteristic individual traits designed for the reader's visual impression. As a rule this sort of portrait is accompanied in Turgenev by little commentaries by the author, which distinguishes Turgenev's manner from, say, Goncharov's. This type of portrait appears as early as **The**

Hunter's Sketches, for example the portrait of Yashka the Turk in **"The Singers"**:

> a lean and well-built man of twenty-three, dressed in a long-skirted blue nankeen coat. He looked like a dashing factory worker and, it seems, could hardly boast of good health. His sunken cheeks, large, restless gray eyes, straight nose with fine moving nostrils, a white, sloping brow, with flaxen curls pushed back from it, large but handsome and expressive lips—*his entire face revealed an impressionable and passionate man.*

Natalia Lasunsky in **Rudin,** Lavretsky in *A Nest of Noblemen,* Shubin in *On the Eve* are other examples. . . . In *Fathers and Sons* the portraits of Bazarov and Odintsov are executed in a similar way. Here, for example, is the portrait of Bazarov in the second chapter:

> Nikolai Petrovich turned around quickly and going up to a *tall* man in a *long,* loose, rough coat with tassels, who had only just got out of the carriage, he warmly pressed the *bare red* hand, which the latter did not at once hold out to him. . . . answered Bazarov, in a *lazy* but *manly* voice; and turning back the collar of his rough coat, he showed Nikolai Petrovich his whole face. It was *long* and *lean,* with a *broad* forehead, a nose flat at the base and *sharp* at the tip, *large greenish* eyes, and *drooping* side whiskers of a *sandy* color.

Then the author's explanations occur: "It was animated by a tranquil smile, and showed self-confidence and intelligence."

It is easy to note that dominant psychological trait of the hero is in the present case already defined through the portrait. With the aid of numerous precise details and commentary on the general impression given, Turgenev really creates that "physical and moral union" noted by Prosper Mérimée. The further description of the hero's exterior may continue even after the definition of the dominant psychological traits: the following details are added to the basic portrait of Bazarov: "his *long, thick, dark-blond* hair did not hide the prominent bumps of his *large skull.*"

The portrait of Odintsov in the fourteenth chapter is presented in the same kind of relief and in the same clear images:

> Arkady looked round, and saw a tall woman in a *black* dress standing at the door of the room. He was struck by the dignity of her carriage. Her *bare* arms lay gracefully beside her *slender* waist; gracefully some *light* sprays of fuchsia drooped from her *shining* hair on to her *sloping* shoulders; her *clear* eyes looked out from under a somewhat *protruding white* brow, with a tranquil and intelligent expression—tranquil it was precisely, not pensive—and on her lips was a *scarcely perceptible* smile. A kind of *gracious* and *gentle* force emanated from her face.

Here too, after explaining what sort of impression the figure of Odintsov should produce on the reader, Turgenev does not stop describing the exterior of his heroine; he goes on to remark that

her nose—like almost all Russian noses—was a little thick; and her complexion was not perfectly clear; Arkady made up his mind, for all that, that he had never before met such an attractive woman.

Second. In Turgenev's novels we encounter satirical portraits in some respects similar to Gogol's manner. These consist of portraits with extensive use of the background, characterizing the figure by oblique means. The author's commentary on the satirical portrait sometimes does not limit itself to a simple indication of one quality or another in the figure, but develops into a whole picture. . . .

In *Fathers and Sons,* the clearest satiric portraits approximating Gogol's manner, gradually disclosing the essence of character by oblique means, are those of Kukshin and Sitnikov. The portrait of Kukshin is created against a broad background, consisting of several concentric circles that increasingly strengthen the satiric element. Turgenev begins Chapter Thirteen, devoted to Kukshin, by describing the city, then discusses the city's streets, then the little house "in the Moscow style" where Madame Kukshin lives, then adduces details like the "visiting card nailed on askew," the "bell-handle," the "some one who was not exactly a servant nor exactly a companion, in a cap—unmistakable tokens of the progressive tendencies of the mistress." It is perfectly clear that the background heralds to the reader nothing great and grandiose but testifies to some sort of unfounded pretense on the part of the inhabitant of this place; while the author's comment on "the progressive tendencies of the mistress" clearly has an ironic ring.

Continuing to develop the device of oblique characterization, Turgenev moves to a narrower concentric circle of observation and presents a detailed description of Kukshin's room: "Papers, letters, thick issues of Russian journals, for the most part uncut [a very characteristic detail!], lay at random on the dusty tables; cigarette ends lay scattered everywhere." It suffices to remember how in *Dead Souls* Gogol gradually discloses the image of Manilov by means of the furnishings (the exposed house, the abandoned pond, the room, the book with a bookmark on page 14), to become convinced that Turgenev successfully uses Gogol's device of oblique characterization.

The figure Turgenev chooses as the object of his satire usually appears in the novel, as in Gogol, after a distinctive descriptive overture, after the corresponding background has been drawn and when the reader has already formed a definite impression about him or her on the basis of the preceding description of setting an environment around the figure. Turgenev draws Kukshin's portrait only after discussing the city, its streets, the house, and the room in which she lives:

> On a leather-covered sofa a lady, still young, was reclining. Her fair hair was rather dishevelled; she wore a silk gown, not altogether tidy, heavy bracelets on her short arms, and a lace handkerchief on her head. She got up from the sofa, and carelessly drawing over her shoulders a velvet cape trimmed with yellowish ermine, she said languidly, "good-morning, *Victor.*"

Underlining a series of incongruities in Kukshin's external appearance (young—rather dishevelled; in a silk gown—not altogether tidy; bracelets—on short arms), a series of deprecatory details ("round eyes, between which was a forlorn little turned-up red nose," "when she laughed, the gum showed above her upper teeth," "fingers brown with tobacco stains," etc.), Turgenev adds force to the author's comments to the portrait. In this case it is no longer a casual author's remark or a reply as, for example, the one about Bazarov's face "It was animated by a tranquil smile and expressed self-confidence and intelligence."

In describing Kukshin the commentaries grow into an extensive satirical characterization which is presented as it were not only through the author but also through another character, in this instance Bazarov. The author and Bazarov seem to fuse into a single character to convey the satiric judgment on Kukshin: "Bazarov frowned. There was nothing repulsive in the little plain person of the emancipated woman; but the expression of her face produced a disagreeable effect on the spectator. One felt impelled [it is hard to say who was impelled: the author or Bazarov, or everyone, including the reader] to ask her, 'What's the matter; are you hungry? Or bored? Or shy? What are you fidgeting about?' Both she and Sitnikov always had the same uneasy air. She was extremely unconstrained and at the same time awkward; she obviously regarded herself a good-natured, simple creature, and all the while, whatever she did, it always struck one that it was just what she did not want to do; everything with her seemed, as children say, done on purpose, that's to say, not simply, not naturally." We note that the satiric portrait of the imitative nihilist is presented before the dialogue in which her negative essence is disclosed.

Sitnikov's portrait is created through separate satirical brush strokes and subtle details that characterize him accurately. He is a man of small stature, he doesn't get out of the carriage but *leaps* out, *dashes* toward Bazarov like a shot although there is no reason either for shouting or for hurrying, immediately starts to *fidget* around Bazarov, *hops* over the ditch, runs now at the right of Bazarov, now at the left, advances somehow sideways, laughs *shrilly,* smiles *subserviently,* etc. "An expression of *worry* and *tension,*" Turgenev writes in Chapter Twelve, was "imprinted on the *small* but *pleasant* features of his *well-groomed* face; his small eyes, that seemed *squeezed in,* had a fixed and uneasy look, and his laugh, too, was uneasy—a sort of short, wooden laugh." The words "but pleasant" are neutralized to such an extent by the preceding "worry and tension" and subsequent "well-groomed face" that they must be taken as the author's malicious irony toward his character. Sitnikov's portrait is concluded with the following stroke: in Kukshin's room Sitnikov "by now was lolling in an armchair, one leg in the air."

When a definite impression of these caricature-like nihilists has been created through their portraits, an impression Shchedrin later so aptly called one of "flap-ears playing the fool," Turgenev discloses their foolishness in detail through dialogue and action.

In the *third place,* a portrait that contradicts the inner content of the person is very characteristic for Turgenev. The variations of that kind of portrait are determined by the nature of the contrast between that which the author emphasizes in the exterior of the person and what he later discloses his essence to be. . . . The exterior [of Pavel Petrovich] emphasizes his aristocracy and European polish, satirical traits creep into the description of the character's external anglomania, while the essence of Pavel Petrovich is not disclosed by satiric means. . . .

Several critics of Turgenev's work are inclined to consider the figure of Pavel Petrovich satirical in general, relying upon Turgenev's own words "I raised his faults to the point of making them a caricature, I made him laughable." Actually, of course, the matter is not quite so. Turgenev criticises very sharply but not by satirical means Pavel Petrovich's principles and convictions with the exception of his views on dueling and the duel itself. The bankruptcy of Pavel Petrovich's pompous speeches about reforms, government steps, committees, and deputies is exposed with "the thunder of indignation." Turgenev notes his character's complete inactivity without satire. But Turgenev permits obvious satirical strokes to appear in depicting Pavel Pavlovich's anglomania and external aristocracy. This was clearly expressed in his portrait and gave various satirical journals an opportunity to parody precisely that part of the character.

Pretensions to something special and original are seen in the figure's dress and in his manners: the English *suit,* the stylish cravate, various fezzes, his custom of speaking while gently rocking, moving his shoulders, his European "shake-hands," etc.

Actually Pavel Petrovich did not create and could not create anything new and original, since the social force he represented was disappearing from the historical arena in the 1860's, yielding its place to the progressively developing democratic forces that were gathering strength. Turgenev understood that both Pavel Petrovich and Nikolay Petrovich became outmoded people, and even had his Bazarov say that their song had been sung. However, this could not please Turgenev who was a moderate liberal and therefore in dismissing the principles of liberals of the 1860's, the author avoided satire. . . .

Bazarov's parents may serve as clear examples of transitional or mixed portraits. The portrait of Bazarov's father appears in Chapter Twenty as follows:

> Bazarov leaned out of the carriage, while Arkady thrust his head out behind his companion's back, and caught sight on the small porch of the little manor-house of a *tall, gaunt* man with *dishevelled* hair, and a *thin aquiline* nose, dressed in an *old military* frock coat not buttoned up. He was standing, his legs wide apart, smoking a *long* pipe and squinting his eyes to keep the sun out of them.

Here everything reminds one of the manner in which the first type of portrait is drawn (that of Bazarov, for example), but there are no author's comments in the portrait of the father. On the other hand, Turgenev later pays considerable attention to the device of oblique characterization—he presents a detailed description of Vassily Ivanovich's study:

A thick-legged table, littered over with papers black with the accumulation of ancient dust as though they had been smoked, occupied the entire space between two windows; on the walls hung Turkish firearms, whips, swords, two maps, anatomical charts of some sort, a portrait of Hufeland, a monogram woven in hair in a black frame, and a glass-framed diploma; a leather sofa, torn and worn into hollows here and there was placed between two enormous cupboards of Karelian birchwood; books, boxes, stuffed birds, jars, and phials were huddled together in confusion on the shelves; in one corner stood a broken galvanic battery.

Speaking more accurately, the reader sees a museum of an ancient Aesculapius, whose archaic exhibits testify to former enthusiasm in equal degree for medicine and hunting, rather than the study of a contemporary scholar and practitioner, keeping up with recent discoveries in science. Even more, it testifies to the desolation and backwardness reigning in Vassily Ivanovich's house. After such a description of Bazarov's father's study, it is clear that such details as "dishevelled hair," "old military frock coat not buttoned up," "legs wide apart" are not amassed accidentally in the portrait.

Before turning to the portrait of Arina Valasyevna, Bazarov's mother, Turgenev traces a distinctive background in Gogol's style: "at last, on the slope of a gently rising knoll, appeared the *tiny village* where Bazarov's parents lived. Beside it, in a *small copse* of young birch, could be seen a *tiny* house with a thatched roof."

One should draw attention to the use of diminutives, through which the author creates in the reader an impression of something pitiful and insignificant. In the same way and with the help of similar diminutives, the author paints a portrait "of a real Russian little gentlewoman of the former, ancient days"; "the door was flung open, *plump, short, little old woman in white cap and a short little striped jacket* appeared on the threshold. She oh'd, swayed, and would certainly have fallen had not Bazarov supported her. Her *small plump hands* were instantly entwined around his neck."

Later on, details in the external appearance of the sentimental old woman that lower the portrait are increased ("crumpled and adoring face," "blissful and comic-looking eyes") and the author seems, as it were, to create a second portrait (but now no longer in full), at which he himself looks with good-natured, kindly irony: "leaning, on her little closed fist, her *round* face, to which the *full, cherry-colored lips and the little moles* on the cheeks and over the eyebrows gave a very simple, good-natured expression, she did not take her eyes off her son, and kept sighing."

Other forms of characterization do not play a primary role in Turgenev's novels and are not distinguished from the specific traits that strike one. Thus, characterization of a figure in action is almost identical in Turgenev with Goncharov's procedure. A. Mazon correctly writes that Turgenev "conceived a novel as a succession of scenes, connected one to the other by means of a simple plot." Therefore there are no extravagances and unexpected situations in Turgenev's novels. Thereby Turgenev distinguishes himself, among others, from Dostoevsky, in whose novels the actions and behavior of characters is given before they are characterized, and therefore at times seem strange and unexpected (for instance in *The Possessed* and *The Idiot*).

The conflict of "fathers" and "sons," the characters of each of the groups, to a certain extent of course are disclosed in their actions: Bazarov's duel with Pavel Petrovich, his behavior toward Odintsov, his clash and break with Arkady, Arkady's marriage to Katya. Finally Bazarov's infection and death is presented by the author as the result of selfless, noble, but unconsidered action by the hero.

As a rule the action of Turgenev's characters is not accompanied by such long and at times tormenting reflections as frequently occurs in Dostoevsky (it suffices to mention Raskol'nikov). Nor do Turgenev's novels contain extensive "interior monologues" characteristic of Tolstoy's heroes. This fact is explained by Turgenev's special view of the role and place of psychology in the artist's creative process. As early as 1852 Turgenev published in *The Contemporary* a review, **"A few Words on Ostrovsky's New Play *The Poor Bride*."** Firmly protesting against the dramatist's excessive fragmentation of characters, Turgenev wrote: "In our view Mr. Ostrovsky creeps, so to speak, into the soul of every character he creates; but we permit ourselves to remark to him that this unquestionably useful operation should be completed by the author as a preliminary step. His characters must be in his complete power when he presents them to us. We will be told that that is psychology; very well, but the psychologist must disappear in the artist, as the skeleton disappears beneath the living body, which it serves as a solid but invisible support." This Turgenev affirmed before he wrote his novels. But even later, in a letter to A. A. Fet apropos of Tolstoy's *War and Peace* Turgenev didn't change his view of psychological analysis in an artistic work. He wrote,

> The second part of *The Year 1805* is also weak: how petty and sly that all is, and is Tolstoy really not fed up with those eternal reflections, 'Am I coward, or not' . . . And the historical additions . . . is a puppet show and charlatanism while the psychology—all those sharply pointed boots of Alexander, Speransky's laugh—are nonsense. . . . these delicate reflections, meditations and observations on one's own feeling are boring. . . .

From what has been said several conclusions may be made concerning Turgenev's principles of psychological analysis of characters.

In the first place, in order not to destroy the unity of the created figures, not to fragment characters and not to harm the artistry of the work, the writer must not carry on the analysis of the character psychology before the reader's eyes. All that is accomplished earlier by the writer, who offers the reader only the psychological results. We note that the psychological picture of Bazarov is presented precisely that way in *Fathers and Sons.* Odintsov evaluates Arkady's qualities in accordance with the same psychological principles after the falling out with Bazarov.

In the second place, the device of presenting the psychological process itself ("the dialectic of the soul") a characteristic feature of Tolstoy's art, is completely unacceptable and foreign to Turgenev's heart.

In the third place, opposing the fragmentation of psychological characterization into particularities, Turgenev fights for the wholeness and clarity of the general psychological portrait of the hero, for the careful choice and artistic filtering of the fundamental, primary psychological traits of the character.

All these conclusions find support in the writer's artistic practice. In the psychological tales and socio-psychological novels, where the psychological characterization plays a corresponding role, Turgenev made use of internal monologues, as well as diaries and letters and reminiscences and dreams and indirect speech—that is, all the existing components of psychological characterization, as an artistic device. He artfully alternated that artistic device with others—characterization by portrait, speech, and dialogue.

In those novels, like *Fathers and Sons,* that clearly express the dominating importance of the political, there was no great need for psychological characterization. Therefore it does not occupy so large a place in the novel *Fathers and Sons* as it does, for example, in *A Nest of Noblemen* or *First Love.* This permits us to limit ourselves to general observations on this artistic device. (pp. 302-12)

> *P. G. Pustovoyt, "Some Features of Composition in 'Fathers and Sons',*" in "Fathers and Sons" by Ivan Turgenev: The Author on the Novel, Contemporary Reactions, Essays in Criticism, *edited and translated by Ralph E. Matlaw, second edition, W. W. Norton & Company, Inc., 1989, pp. 302-12.*

Richard Freeborn (essay date 1960)

[*Freeborn is a Welsh critic, educator, and translator who has written and edited numerous studies of Russian history, literature, and literary figures. In the excerpt below, he comments on the structure of* Fathers and Sons. *By avoiding conventional narrative devices such as diary extracts, letters, or commentators, Freeborn contends, the author gives the novel the impression of naturalness and objectivity.*]

Turgenev has said that he was first prompted to write about a hero of the type of Bazarov by the example of a young provincial doctor of his acquaintance who had died, presumably, about the year 1859. When he mentioned his intention to a friend whom he met on the Isle of Wight in August 1860, he was amazed to hear this gentleman reply: 'But surely you have already presented a similar type in—Rudin?' Turgenev adds: 'I was speechless: what was there to say? Rudin and Bazarov—one and the same type? . . . These words had such an effect on me that for several weeks I avoided all thought of the work on which I had embarked. . . .' The gentleman's remark, however, is not so extraordinary as it may appear at first sight. It simply serves to underline the fact that Bazarov, like Rudin, was conceived as a hero designed to have more intellectual in-

terest than Lavretsky, for instance, or Yelena. Like Rudin, he was intended to dominate the fiction, although—unlike the Rudin of the original version—he was conceived as a tragic figure whose tragedy would be climaxed by his death.

Fathers and Children tells the story of Bazarov's return from the university in the company of his young friend, Arkady Kirsanov. They both stay for a while on the Kirsanovs' estate, where the contrast between the Fathers and the Children is initiated in the arguments between Pavel Petrovich Kirsanov and the hero, and later they visit the local town, where Bazarov meets the heroine, Odintsova. This meeting initiates the major love theme of the novel, but the action is by no means devoted exclusively to the development of it. Subsequently Bazarov visits his parents, spends a short while with them and then, to their understandable dismay, returns to the Kirsanovs' estate where the argument between Fathers and Children is concluded by the duel between him and Pavel Petrovich. Later Bazarov returns to his parents, where he decides to help his father, a retired army doctor, in his practice. Here he contracts typhus after performing an autopsy on a peasant killed by the disease and finally succumbs to it himself. As can be seen, there is more story content in *Fathers and Children* than in the previous novels, but this does not alter the fact that it is the characterization of the central figure which provides the interest of the fiction.

The objectivity of the work is remarkable on two counts. Firstly, in portraying Bazarov Turgenev has achieved a masterly portrait of a type—the type of the 'new man' of the sixties, the *raznochinets* intellectual or 'nihilist'—with whose political and social views he was manifestly out of sympathy. Secondly, the novel possesses an organic unity, in which there are no narrative devices that obtrude into the fiction to distort, however slightly, the final impression of naturalness. This is not to say that *Fathers and Children* is merely a factual document or chronicle, unenlivened by the author's technique as an artist. It simply means that the technique has been perfected to the point where such devices as the use of commentator (in *Rudin* and *A Nest of the Gentry*) or devices such as diary extracts and letters (as in *On the Eve*) are no longer necessary in the delineation of character. The emphasis now falls squarely on the scenic, pictorial objectivity of the narrative and the artistic composition of the work, leaving the impression that the novel is 'telling itself', as it were, almost without the author's agency or participation.

In every respect this is more obviously 'a novel of ideas' than *On the Eve,* although the ideological independence of each minor character is linked, without being in any sense compromised or diminished, to the development of the central figure, Bazarov, in a more compelling manner than were Shubin and Bersenev to Yelena. This is due to the fact that in *Fathers and Children* the minor characters are not only spokesmen or embodiments of ideas or ideological attitudes, but they are also representatives of a particular social class with specific class attitudes; and Bazarov, opposed to them, is not only an opponent of their ideas, but a spokesman for a new, emergent social class which is to usurp the political and social authority of the older generation. In his previous novels Turgenev had not delineated class distinctions so clearly, but in *Fathers and Children* he carefully welds the social and political issues, the ideological and class attitudes, into the structure of his novel, creating a remarkable organic unity. The result is the most artistically perfect, structurally unified and ideologically compelling of Turgenev's novels.

Arkady Kirsanov and his father, Nikolay Petrovich Kirsanov, are introduced in detail to the reader at the very beginning of the novel. All the other characters—Pavel Petrovich Kirsanov, Odintsova, Bazarov's parents and such lesser characters as Fenichka (the peasant girl who has borne Nikolay Petrovich an illegitimate son), Kukshina and Sitnikov, the talkative representatives of the younger generation—are introduced into the fiction to the accompaniment of biographical and other information sufficient to explain their significance. The exception is again the unknown quantity, the hero, whose characterization is to provide the interest of the novel. Bazarov is not introduced to the reader by means of any biographical excerpt which might set his character in perspective; he is introduced, and his background lightly sketched in, by the remarks made about him by the other characters (particularly during the conversation between Arkady and Pavel Petrovich in Chapter V). While these remarks serve to provide information about Bazarov without which the reader might not be able to understand his significance for the fiction, they also serve to illustrate the contrasting nature of Bazarov, arising from his different social background. There are, of course, intimations in the fiction that Bazarov is 'different' from the other characters, but Turgenev does not rely on his omniscient position as author of the fiction to emphasize this 'difference'. On the contrary, he allows it to be made clear by the natural contrast that arises initially from the fact that Bazarov enters the fiction unexplained and by the more definite contrast which is provided through Bazarov's contact with the other characters.

Bazarov is further highlighted in the fiction by the fact that the novel is so constructed as to isolate him from the other characters. This is achieved by giving the other characters not only biographical backgrounds or information sufficient to make their backgrounds comprehensible, but also specific 'places' in the fiction. Each character, with the exception of Bazarov, has his or her own 'place' or situation in the fiction: Nikolay, Arkady, Pavel—the poverty-stricken Mar'ino; Odintsova, Katya—the luxurious Nikol'skoye; the elderly Bazarovs—their humble estate; Sitnikov, Kukshina—the background of the town. With the exception of Bazarov and Arkady, all these characters remain in their own particular 'places' and are only comprehensible in relation to their 'places' (Odintsova and Sitnikov, admittedly, can be said to abandon their 'places' for short episodes—Odintsova to the town and to visit Bazarov on his death-bed, Sitnikov to Nikol'skoye (Chapter XIX)—but it is still true that they are only comprehensible in relation to their own 'places'). Moreover, each 'place' in the fiction and its occupants has the purpose of illuminating, by contrast, an aspect of the hero. Pavel Petrovich in Mar'ino illuminates the ideological aspect of Bazarov's significance for the fiction, the problem of the socio-political conflict between the generations; Sitnikov and Kukshina in the town illuminate the superiority of Bazarov by comparison with other members of the younger generation; Odintsova in Nikol'skoye illuminates the essential personality of the hero as a man, the duality in his nature; Bazarov's parents illuminate his egoism, the personal, as distinct from the ideological, barrier dividing the generations, and his individual insignificance as a human being, for their adoration of him is carefully offset by his own pessimistic musings on his destiny. Each 'place' in the fiction can therefore be seen as a stage in the process of the hero's characterization, and the stages are graded to elaborate and deepen the hero's portrait. Finally, Arkady ceases to play an active part in the fiction (after becoming involved in his love-story with Katya), and Bazarov is isolated as the central figure of the novel's action. In this way it can be seen that Turgenev emphasizes the tragedy of Bazarov's isolation, both as a social type and as a human being, by emphasizing his isolation within the fiction itself.

The process of characterization is also structurally integrated with the pattern of love-stories which, loosely speaking, supplies the plot of the novel and illustrates the ideological issues at stake. There are, in all, four different love-stories: (*a*) Nikolay-Fenichka; (*b*) Pavel-Fenichka, involving Bazarov; (*c*) Bazarov-Odintsova; (*d*) Arkady-Katya. All these love-stories express in one way or another an aspect of the conflict between the Fathers and the Children. The first love-story, between the land-owner and the peasant girl, implies at once the underlying social problem of the day: the relationship between land-owner and peasant on the eve of the Emancipation in 1861 (the action of the novel, it may be noted, occurs in 1859). The nature of this particular relationship between Nikolay and Fenichka also illustrates the moral failure of the older generation, of the Fathers, and it is a point at issue, in the early stages of the novel, between Nikolay and his son. The second love-story (it scarcely obtrudes as a love-story, but it must not be overlooked) is of considerably greater importance for the structure of the novel. So far as the external action of the novel is concerned, the fact that Pavel Petrovich sees Bazarov kissing Fenichka (Chapter XXIII) simply supplies him with grounds for challenging Bazarov to a duel. But the inner meaning of this episode must also be noted. The ideological conflict has already occurred (Chapters VI and X); the contrast with the members of the younger generation has been made (Chapters XII and XIII); the relationship with Odintsova has already been explored and has reached a climax (Chapters XV-XVIII), though it has not yet been abandoned; Bazarov's awareness of his own significance as a human being and his tragic destiny, despite the great future hoped for by his parents, has been made explicit in his conversation with Arkady on his parents' estate (Chapter XXI). Bazarov is now ready to reject the ideological and social precepts of the *dvoryanstvo*, the gentry; his desire to provoke a fight with Arkady in Chapter XXI foreshadows his readiness to accept the challenge that Pavel Petrovich offers him in Chapter XXIV. Yet the fact that they fight the duel ostensibly over Fenichka, the peasant girl, shows the way in which the ideological issues are welded into the structure of the novel. For Bazarov's readiness to fight the duel must be understood in the light of the fact that he is prepared not only to reject the *dvoryanstvo,* but also to devote his life to working for the peasants. His interest in Fenichka may be purely personal, but it is also given ideological significance. Similarly, Pavel Petrovich's readiness to offer the challenge must be understood in relation to the fact that for him Fenichka bears a resemblance to a certain Princess R. . . . out of passion for whom he had ruined his career and had been obliged to retire to the splendid isolation of Mar'ino (the predicament of the 'superfluous man' *par excellence*), and in relation to the fact that the crux of his earlier argument with Bazarov (Chapter X) had been the problem of the peasantry, whom he had claimed to understand better than Bazarov. His interest in Fenichka is also a mixture of the personal and the ideological. The subsequent duel represents the climax in the personal and ideological conflict between the two generations; and the defeat of Pavel Petrovich is not simply the defeat of the older generation by the younger, it is also the defeat of the gentry, the *dvoryanstvo,* by the new class of the *raznochintsy.*

The third love-story, between Odintsova and Bazarov, is clearly the most interesting, both because it concerns two people of widely differing social status and because it serves, like all the major love-stories in Turgenev's fiction, as a means of illustrating the differing personalities of the two characters. It is, however, Bazarov who emerges more successfully from this contrast. Odintsova is almost as passive a participant in the relationship as was Insarov in *On the Eve.* But, unlike the Yelena-Insarov relationship, the relationship between Odintsova and Bazarov does not absorb the whole of the fiction. There is no definite continuity to it and it is allowed to languish, in contrast to the fourth love-story, between Arkady and Katya, which is both the most conventional in the sense that it is between two young people of similar social status and the most conventional in the sense that it has a happy outcome.

It is in the different relationships involved in these love-stories that an enlargement of both structure and content in *Fathers and Children* as compared with [Turgenev's] previous novels is to be discerned. . . .

[In] *Fathers and Children* there is a multiplication of love-stories in the structure of the novel, and all the love-stories, with the exception of the Arkady-Katya relationship, involve social inequalities. Inevitably this means that the novel embraces an enlarged view of Russian society, for all classes in Russian society are exemplified by this means: the gentry (*dvoryanstvo*), the new men (*raznochintsy*), and the peasantry. The single love-story in the earlier novels, standing at the centre of the fiction and absorbing the greater part of its interest, had not permitted such an enlarged view.

Yet, in structural terms, the main feature of *Fathers and Children* is the figure of Bazarov. The action of the novel hinges upon him almost exclusively. He is present in practically every scene of the novel, and it is his movement within the fiction that serves to link together the different 'places' or foci of interest which comprise the setting of the novel. Simultaneously, these 'places' and their occupants contribute, stage by stage, to the process of his character-

ization. A natural unity of form and content is thus achieved, which is the most striking development in Turgenev's exploration of the novel-form. The portrait of Bazarov that finally emerges from the novel is one that transcends all other issues in the fiction. Beginning on May 20th 1859, the action of the novel portrays Bazarov during approximately the last three or four months of his life. His portrait acquires finally a tragic grandeur, culminating in his death which is a moment unequalled in Turgenev's fiction. (pp. 68-74)

> *Richard Freeborn, in his* Turgenev: The Novelist's Novelist, a Study, *Oxford University Press, London, 1960, 201 p.*

Bernard Guilbert Guerney (essay date 1961)

[*Guerney was a Russian-born editor and translator best known for his* Treasury of Russian Literature *(1943). In the following excerpt, he examines some of the effects of the harsh initial reception of* Fathers and Sons.]

Were the question put: Which work of Turgenev's created the greatest sensation—it seems inconceivable that any other title could be named in answer save *Fathers and Sons.* To put it baldly: even the *succès de fou* of *Doctor Zhivago* did not come within an ocean's breadth of the *succès de scandale* of *Fathers and Sons,* which not only awakened more interest than any previous or subsequent work of Turgenev's but aroused more controversies than any other Russian novel of the nineteenth century, controversies the heat of which persisted literally for decades and which has not died out in certain quarters to this day. *Fathers and Sons,* we are assured by a contemporary witness, was read (and even bought) by those who had never opened a book since their school days and whose souls were taken up only with the price fluctuations of axle-grease in Astrakhan. What sort of book was it—progressive or retrograde? Whom was the author glorifying, both critics and readers wanted to know, and whom was he denigrating?

Indubitably, the author is by no means tongue-tied about his book, but, after all, we do have the advantage of a century's wisdom-after-the-event. I am under the persistent impression that no archaeological dredging up of pictographs, hieroglyphs, cuneiform inscriptions, scrolls has ever failed (or ever will fail) in restating (or antedating) all previous puttings-forth of the proposition that Crabbed Age and Youth cannot live together, and at first glance *Fathers and Sons* may seem to have congealed into a classic on that theme.

Yet the book was very much more than that in its beginnings; the conflict it dealt with was more than merely intratribal, merely regional. All of Russia (literate Russia, that is) was split into two camps: Slavophiles and Westernizers. The Slavophiles may be described, not too uncharitably, as 100 percent Russians, professed and professional, as patriots who made both heads of the Imperial Eagle scream—"for such Saviors of the Fatherland had at that time cropped up even in our Russia"; they put up villas that were grandiose takeoffs on the log huts of the peasants; got themselves up in long shirts of Irish linen, worn outside balloon-pantaloons of British broadcloth tucked into high boots of French kid, and, by way of coats, sleeveless garments of Italian velour reaching to below the knees (which outfits had, of course, to be sent to London or Paris to be properly laundered and cleaned); they ate their truffles and *pâté de foie gras* off peasantish earthenware and drank champagne out of mouzhikian wooden cups—the Slavophiles were, in short, all those who were perfectly willing to do anything on earth for the dear little mouzhik except get off his back. The Westernizers, on the other hand, were fighting to spread enlightenment; believing that the future and progress of Russia lay toward the West, they wanted to emulate Peter the Great by breaching a few more windows into Europe and letting the light and fresh air of civilization into benighted and stifling Russia.

Despite Hertzen's witticism to the effect that Ivan Sergheievich never went in for politics, "except for a fortnight on the Isle of Wight, when he discussed the alphabet with Robinson Crusoe," Turgenev had always (and justly) prided himself on his awareness of current history and political trends, and on his sensitiveness to the possible reaction of his readers. Among the very numerous and conflicting counsels he had received from sundry friends had been the advice of one well-wisher that he should waste no time in burning the new novel while it was still only a manuscript; Turgenev himself had wanted to postpone publication, owing to a number of unfavorable circumstances, mostly political: the book was decidedly topical, filled with references and details that were fraught with the utmost significance to the public of that day. Even when the reader was informed that certain actions were *not* performed, such information was not pointless. Why was he told, for instance, in the opening sentence of Chapter 4, that "no throng of domestics trooped out onto the front steps to welcome the masters"? Because not the least of the shadows cast by coming events was that of 'mancipation, as that flunky-soul Feerss shapes the word in *The Cherry Orchard.*

"The only good trait about a Russian," to quote none other than Bazarov, "is that he has a most atrocious opinion of himself." And, coupled with this pejorative pride (or mania) there is, not altogether illogically, something very like xenophily, a naïve admiration for non-Slavs: "There, see how clever them Germans are—they even invented monkeys!"

Could anybody but a Russian, then, be the laziest man in the world? And whom else could Goncharov choose as a foil to Oblomov except an impossibly energetic and enterprising German? Could anybody but a Russian hit upon so droll a swindle as trading in so whimsical a commodity as dead souls? And whom did Gogol pick to be a guide and a shining light unto his Chichikov? Why, an incredibly upright and knowledgeable businessman but, of all things, a Turk!

No such all-Russian monoliths of vice as Oblomov, Chichikov, old Karamazov, Little Judas are to be found in Turgenev's magnificent gallery of characterizations; but, somehow, he did not escape the pitfall of xenophily: when he needed a positive, strong revolutionary as a hero

for *On the Eve* he produced Insarov, who decidedly filled the bill but who was a Bulgarian. Wasn't an all-Russian *hero* possible (the critics sniggered)—just for a change?

The master obliged by creating Bazarov, whose all-Russian status was as indisputable as his positive nature. Early in 1861 he had written P. V. Annenkov concerning *Fathers and Sons:* "I have worked long, assiduously, conscientiously. . . . The goal I had set myself was a true one, but whether I have attained it, God knows." Every seasoned artist takes both brickbats and bouquets in his stride; the hurtful, the shocking thing is to have the bouquets tendered by life-long enemies and the brickbats flung by old friends. Turgenev had held a true mirror up to Russia and was bewildered to hear so many voices berating both him and the mirror for what they saw therein. Only two men, according to Turgenev himself, grasped his intentions, and one of them was Dostoevsky—but Dostoevsky was the leading cantor of the congregation of Slavophiles. And one of the very few who perceived the true image of Bazarov was Pisarev, whose authoritative tone in due time persuaded the younger generation actually to accept Bazarov proudly as their authentic prototype.

Not the least important effect of the harsh reception of *Fathers and Sons* was that which it had upon the author himself. Not being as tough-skinned as Leskov, he left Russia and did not revisit it except for stays of short duration, and died in his self-imposed exile. That he could not forget the hurt inflicted by the misunderstanding on the part of the youth of Russia of his motives in writing this book is attested to by the embitterment evident in *" 'Thou Shalt Hear the Judgment of the Fool' "*—a poem in prose written sixteen years after the publication of *Fathers and Sons* and brought out in print twenty years after that publication: in 1882, less than a year before his death.

One indisputable contribution of *Fathers and Sons* was the currency it gave to *nihilist* and *nihilism,* at first in Russia and subsequently throughout the world. The *Encyclopaedia Britannica* (1956) devotes exactly five lines to NI-HILISM, of which no more than three are misinformative: *nihilism* was *not* "first used by Ivan Turgenev"; neither was *nihilist:* both words, as political terms, were first launched in print as far back as 1829 by N. E. Nadezhdin, who in his turn had borrowed them from the muzzy terminologies of philosophy and theology, and who, according to a contemporary, defined nihilists as "people who know nothing, who do not base themselves upon anything in art or life." As used by Turgenev *nihilist* meant *materialist, realist, extreme skeptic, atheist,* and he suggested, specifically, that whenever it was used as a term of abuse it ought to be read, properly, as *revolutionary.* It was not long before *nihilist* was bandied about by the penny-a-liners as loosely as *anarchist* was at the turn of the twentieth century and as *communist* is today, while Leskov, Goncharov and Pisemsky in their novels shortly reduced the honest image of Bazarov the Nihilist to the stock-caricature of the popeyed, bushy-haired bomb-thrower, until in the popular so-called mind *nihilist* became synonymous with *terrorist,* and was used in that sense even by such skilled wordsmen as Wilde (*circa* 1880) and by France, who lumped *nihilists* and *anarchists* together as late as the eve of World War I. In current Russian-English dictionarese *nihilist* is equated with *negationist, negativist* and even *negator,* but not *terrorist.*

Turgenev's fears have proven groundless: his name, free of any shadow, has not been forgotten nor is likely to be—at least until such time as the ultimate model in atomic bombs is unleashed, while his Bazarov has not only stepped over the threshold of the future but will, *strontium volens,* go on striding through the further future as one of the major heroic and tragic figures of all literature. For *Fathers and Sons,* even in our fissionable day, is still something more than a presentment of the ever-recurring conflict between the Wise Old Ones of the Cave and the Young Hotheads of the Tribe. After all, imprudent as it may be to point it out at this febrile moment of a shift in literary fashions, with fiction headed for the scrap-heap, this masterwork remains, and will indefinitely remain, an engrossing tale, superbly told by one of whom George Moore, himself no mean teller of tales, has said: "The best storytellers are the Russians, and the best among them was Turgenev." (pp. viii-xiii)

> *Bernard Guilbert Guerney, in a foreword to*
> Fathers and Sons *by Ivan S. Turgenev, translated by Bernard Guilbert Guerney, The Modern Library, 1961, pp. vii-xvi.*

James H. Justus   (essay date 1961)

[*In the following excerpt from an essay originally published in 1961, Justus claims that the sons of* Fathers and Sons *are each reconciled to the traditional world of their fathers—Arkady through marriage and Bazarov through death—resulting in their "reunion with and reconciliation to the mainstream of humanity."*]

One of the most striking successes of *Fathers and Sons* is not its rather reluctant political statement, which at best reveals the division of Turgenev's mind, but the unambiguous theme of the "goodness" of nature. In a day when the concept has become philosophically banal, this achievement is all the more remarkable. However positively Bazarov preaches his nihilism, however influentially he sways disciples, however rabidly he hints of the Advent, he remains a powerless, unused talent. Arguing that he remains so because "the time is not yet at hand" is to beg the question. Moreover, Turgenev drops sufficient clues to suggest that Bazarov's fault is not in the "when" of Russia's destiny but in the "how" of his own nature.

By the time he seeks out Anna Sergyevna, observing what a "tame cat" he is becoming, the threat (or promise) of any significant influence he may have on society at large is passed; and with that passing goes the political interest Bazarov may have whipped up earlier in the reader. Yet structurally the novel gains, not loses, interest after this climax at Nikolskoe. Obviously, Turgenev's story of a young revolutionary is concerned with a more comprehensive and at the same time more personal rebellion than that which a single-dimensioned political reading can give. What we face is nothing less than the very life, the focus, of the novel: the search for self-definition.

That which sets in relief the world view of the Fathers and records, both explicitly and implicitly, the progress of the world view of the Sons is external nature, a symbolic system observable in the varying degrees to which the two opposing world views conflict and reconcile. To see nature serving a more artistic purpose than mere scene-painting is not to deny the politics in the novel; rather, the methods by which Turgenev uses nature (particularly the suggestion of the mystic "Mother Russia" or "native soil" idea) enhance the tragedy which he foresees—the loss of communication between the generations and the ultimate rupture in revolution.

Throughout *Fathers and Sons* there is greater emphasis on the conflict between generations than between bourgeoisie and proletariat. Conflict of the latter type, inevitable though it is, is less explicit, that is, it has less ideological affection, sorrow, or even concern for the peasant who will be caught up in it than, say, Conrad's *Under Western Eyes* or even James's *Princess Casamassima.* In Turgenev's novel the hurt is both something less and something more—families dissolved by ideological postulates. Intellectually powerful as the political issues are, they are vapid compared with the moral-emotional episodes in the homes of the Fathers. These scenes are memorable not because of their vigor—as Dostoyevsky's memorable scenes are apt to be—but because of quiet, undertoned pathos. And much of this pathos is created by the repetitive use of nature symbols.

Superficially the great world of nature is associated with the Fathers, the guardians and lovers of the land, which includes the recognizable objects of an agrarian society: aspens, swallows, bees, lilac blossoms, gardens of roses, sunsets. This is the natural milieu of both Arkady and Bazarov, an environment from which they have wrenched themselves but to which they return. Though it is a harsh land with its satisfactions dearly earned, it is also a gentle land, which supports a society of individuals who show mutual respect and love and abide by the canons of traditional manners and faith.

Almost mournfully Turgenev seems to permit the naturalistic, scientific Sons to better their Fathers in argument and in their vision of a new Russia—mournfully because his heart-felt sympathy is attached to the dying class in spite of its "vanity, dandy habits, fatuity . . . perpetual talk . . . about art, unconscious creativeness, parliamentarism, trial by jury" and its sometimes hollow adherence to the principle of man's dignity.

Perhaps the single most affecting scene occurs immediately after the explosive dinner argument between Bazarov and Pavel Petrovitch. After the arrogant young nihilist challenges Pavel to take two days to think of an institution that "does not call for complete and unqualified destruction," Nikolai, overtaken by melancholy, retires in the dying day to his favorite arbor to reflect on the chasm that separates him from his son. Not even the violence of Bazarov's gibes when they are pertinent nor the shallow discipleship of Arkady when it is most excusable can overshadow the dramatic force of this scene in which Nikolai comprehends the nature of the tension. He wants to agree with his son and up to a point applauds his world view:

. . . I feel there is something behind them we have not got, some superiority over us. . . . Is it youth? No; not only youth. Doesn't their superiority consist in there being fewer traces of the slave-owner in them than in us?

But how far must he go to bridge the widening chasm? He is already known as a "Red Radical" over the province for his soft policies toward the peasants; he reads and studies, trying to keep abreast of developments. But all this is not enough. His methods smack of reform, when the young men have little patience with anything short of revolution.

But even the image of revolution, of sheer energy unleashed, is not so hateful to Nikolai as the Sons' underlying assumption that a chemist is "twenty times as useful as any poet," a materialism that ignores and even denounces the values of poetry, art, and nature:

> And he looked round, as though trying to understand how it was possible to have no feeling for nature. . . . The sun's rays from the farther side fell full on the copse, and piercing through its thickets, threw such a warm light on the aspen trunks that they looked like pines, and their leaves were almost a dark blue, while above them rose a pale blue sky, faintly tinged by the glow of sunset. . . . "How beautiful, my God!" thought Nikolai Petrovitch, and his favorite verses were almost on his lips . . . but still he sat there, still he gave himself up to the sorrowful consolation of solitary thought. He was fond of dreaming; his country life had developed the tendency in him.

Here is more than scene-painting. Couched in even more religious terms than the references to religion itself, this episode is Turgenev's most explicit use of nature as a symbolic system embodying the deepest values of the Fathers. Despite the depressing presence of streams with hollow banks, hovels with tumble-down roofs, barns with gaping doorways and neglected threshing-floors, and tattered peasants, these values are stubbornly insisted on and equated with the Fathers' native soil. At such times the scenes take on an almost sacramental cast.

Vassily Ivanovitch, even though a provincial doctor, is also identified with the Russian soil and landscape. He reads authorities in order to keep up with advances in healing, and though he understands the fad of discarding idols for more advanced ones, he cannot understand his son's concept of laughing at medicine altogether. With obvious relief he turns to Bazarov's comment on the growth of his birch trees.

> And you must see what a little garden I've got now! I planted every tree myself. I've fruit, and raspberries, and all kinds of medicinal herbs.

After tea Vassily takes them to his garden "to admire the beauty of the evening" and whispers to Arkady,

> At this spot I love to meditate, as I watch the sunset; it suits a recluse like me. And there, a little farther off, I have planted some of the trees beloved of Horace.

This initial impression of Bazarov's father is reinforced time and time again; Arkady sees him garbed in an Oriental dressing gown industriously digging in the garden, regaling his visitor with his plans for late turnips, and citing Rousseau's philosophy of the necessity for man's obtaining "his sustenance with his own hands." And later, when he unknowingly interrupts a hostile fight between Arkady and Bazarov in the shade of a haystack, he can see only a Castor-and-Pollux pair "excellently employed," with a special "significance" in their lying on the earth and gazing up to heaven.

But the Fathers' orientation to the natural world, a source of both their strength and inefficacy, does not constitute a simple opposition to the crude scientism and anti-esthetic pragmatism of the Sons. Ultimately the Sons' ideology is fuzzy and narrow, separated as it is from the deceptively simple agrarian world view. Paradoxically, it is this simple orientation that proves multidimensional, capable of absorbing both Bazarov's aggressive and Arkady's passive revolutionary airs. Both Sons consistently underrate their Fathers' world. Bazarov cannot channel his arrogance, rudeness, and frustration into political coherence (Arkady hardly tries) and so cannot overcome the settled, all-encompassing, and pervading social coherence of the Fathers. With considerable skill Turgenev traces the Sons' progress from the stages of rebellion against this social coherence to at least a partial reconciliation with it, and his methods are enhanced by the framework of nature which gives authority to this agrarian world view. Significant or not, the Sons' references to objects of nature outnumber those of the Fathers. Some are, of course, openly negative: a flourishing denial of the symbols means a denial of the entire system, which must be destroyed and built anew, presumably in an image yet to be found. On the night before the duel Bazarov has a dream in which Pavel Petrovitch takes "the shape of a great wood, with which he had yet to fight." And the same dark image recurs on his deathbed, where after his fitful siege of self-confronting, he sees the final struggle: "There's a forest here. . . ."

But the negative responses to nature—or those which take the form of "disordered dreams"—are surely no less indicative of the massive strength of the Fathers' world (and indeed of the Sons' unconscious involvement in it) than the more obvious garden scenes with the Fathers. The battle lines are not simply Sons versus Fathers but, more importantly, Sons versus Themselves. They possess too much of their Fathers' world to dismiss it successfully, even though it is a dying world, for to dismiss it outright is to deny themselves the self-definition they both crave. It is this tension that ideologically tilts the outcome to the Fathers and dramatically signifies Turgenev's theme. Without this inner tension, the story would be simply another tale of young ideals clashing against old ones. As it is, this novel is essentially a modification of the traditional story of the young hero who sets out in search of his fortune, which (according to Lionel Trilling in his essay on *The Princess Casamassima*) is "What the folktale says when it means that the hero is seeking himself." In *Fathers and Sons* it is a painful progress, and the opposing forces are not a series of physical obstacles but the ponderous irrationality of an entire social system. The irony in such a modern modification is that this society into which

Arkady and Bazarov are plunged is not new to their experience. They have not only been there before; it is part of themselves. In one sense of their return, they do battle with themselves to attain a fully satisfactory self-definition.

Arkady, prone as he is to accept all premises and conclusions of Bazarov, still permits himself to recognize the symbols of the land; and in spite of that land's "endless, comfortless winter, with its storms, and frosts, and snows," he feels swayed by a familiar spring:

> All around was golden green, all—trees, bushes, grass—shone and stirred gently in wide waves under the soft breath of the warm wind; from all sides flooded the endless trilling music of the larks; . . . the rooks strutted among the half-grown short spring-corn . . . only from time to time their heads peeped out amid its grey waves.

This is the natural attraction of the land—dramatically juxtaposed against Arkady's own denial that it is his birthplace which creates this special feeling. (In the same connection he can exclaim: "What air . . . ! How delicious it smells! Really I fancy there's nowhere such fragrance . . . !") Later, countering Bazarov's declaration that "two and two make four, and the rest is all foolery," Arkady asks, "And is nature foolery?" and notes the "bright-colored fields in the distance, in the beautiful soft light of the sun. . . ."

Once back under the family roof, influence of the old order increases as Bazarov's declines. Finally, as a gesture, he offers to help his father with the difficult problems of the farm; doubtless the involvement would have been deeper immediately but for his preoccupation with Katya. At Nikolskoe the major scenes occur out-of-doors, primarily in various parts of the garden. Here under ash trees he and Katya feed sparrows and relax into a "confidential intimacy" where they admit that Bazarov's influence on them and Anna has passed. In the same garden but hidden "in the very thickest part," he loses himself in meditation and "at once wondering and rejoicing" he resolves to marry Katya. It is a significant scene, for it constitutes his final break with what is essentially an alien spirit; his alliance with Katya ushers in a domestic period of acceptance. It discards revolution, but not reform.

Bazarov, on the other hand, is the strong character but simultaneously the most decisively divided. His pastime is natural history, psychologically a more acceptable deference to the old order than the more esthetic, wasteful nature-observing of the others. His frog-cutting contributes to his scientific-medical knowledge. Only occasionally he permits himself observations, and then often from a pragmatic impulse. He explains to Arkady that poplars and spruce firs do better than oaks. To assure Anna that studying a single human specimen is enough to judge the entire race he makes an analogy quite in character: "People are like trees in a forest; no botanist would think of studying each individual birchtree." His walks more often take him to the forest, and he naps regularly in the barn's hayloft. And in a rare self-revealing speech to Arkady he says:

> That aspen-tree . . . reminds me of my childhood; it grows at the edge of the clay-pits where

the bricks were dug, and in those days I believed firmly that that clay-pit and aspen-tree possessed a peculiar talismanic power; I never felt dull near them. I did not understand then that I was not dull, because I was a child. Well, now I'm grown up, the talisman's lost its power.

Unusually loquacious, Bazarov broods on his "loathsome pettiness." Contrasting himself to his parents, who "don't trouble themselves about their own nothingness; it doesn't sicken them," he mutters: "I feel nothing but weariness and anger." Part of his frustration derives from his unfortunate, unrealized love for Anna, and in self-pity he advises an ant dragging off a half-dead fly,

> Take her, brother, take her! Don't pay attention to her resistance; it's your privilege as an animal to be free from the sentiment of pity—make the most of it—not like us conscientious self-destructive animals!

His conversation with Fenichka, which culminates in their kissing, takes place in the lilac arbor; and the duel which Pavel instigates as a result of it occurs at dawn on a fresh morning, when the most salient part of the picture is the singing of the larks. Hearing of Arkady's coming marriage, he calls his friend a jackdaw, "a most respectable family bird," and later advises him with more gravity:

> And you get married as soon as you can; and build your nest, and get children to your heart's content. They'll have the wit to be born in a better time than you and me.

Despite Bazarov's death-bed pledge to himself and to Anna ("Never mind; I'm not going to turn tail"), he realizes that any number of men are more important to Russia than he. He solves his last problem of "how to die decently," but Turgenev makes it clear that the giant succumbs in the end to the same natural processes as the pygmy Fathers and in fact on the Fathers' own terms. However wretched the graveyard with its rotting wooden crosses and scrubby shade trees, birds perch on Bazarov's tomb and sing while his parents pray. And conventional as Turgenev's personal conclusion to the tale may be, it underscores the rebellious principle quite apart from political considerations. Here is one whose self was not only divided but at war and whose reconciliation and submission to the basic pattern, the natural life, come inexorably:

> However passionate, sinning, and rebellious the heart hidden in the tomb, the flowers growing over it peep serenely at us with their innocent eyes; they tell us not of eternal peace alone, of that great peace of "indifferent" nature; they tell us, too, of eternal reconciliation and of life without end.

It is not correct to say that Bazarov's reconciliation is entirely unsought, a matter of physical necessity. Long before his death he deliberately returns, giving up dissection of frogs for the healing of humans, pleasing his parents in his perverse manner, and indulging them in their "toys," which are part of the old order.

That Turgenev as a conscious craftsman intends his novel to bear its theme partly through external nature as a referent can be deduced from his many pertinent allusions to

Rousseau, Emerson, Pushkin, and even Fenimore Cooper's Natty Bumpo. But, more important, he communicates the stature of Nikolai and Vassily through identification with the land that can produce stability, affection, and even growth, as well as tradition-bound inadequacies in social and political matters. For Arkady and Bazarov, their radical notions at first dispossess them from such a heritage; but despite this open rejection, the reader can follow consistently their alliance to it through a patterned thematic thread of nature references, an alliance that the two characters recognize and admit only sporadically. The movement is reunion with and reconciliation to the mainstream of humanity, and with all its faults, that mainstream is the world of the Fathers. (pp. 295-302)

> James H. Justus, " 'Fathers and Sons': The Novel as Idyll," in "Fathers and Sons" by Ivan Turgenev, The Author on the Novel, Contemporary Reactions, Essays in Criticism, *edited and translated by Ralph E. Matlaw, second edition, W. W. Norton & Company, Inc., 1989, pp. 295-302.*

V. S. Pritchett on the power of Turgenev's prose:

The scene of Bazarov's death is famous. It is one of the most moving and beautifully observed things that the great observer ever wrote—Chekhov admired it as a doctor and as an artist who himself was a master of recording human sorrow. The power of this narrative owes something to the hypochondria and sense of the presence of death which Turgenev felt so continuously in his own life; and in this the writing is one of those cleansings which a great artist achieves in his maturity. If the death, by such a small misadventure, may strike one as trivial and therefore not tragic—the point made by hostile critics—it has its own ironic logic: for Bazarov the Nihilist cannot object to accident or the random hostility of nature. When the death occurs, Turgenev writes, the experience of life on earth is not altogether in our hands. The last lines that describe the visit of the parents to Bazarov's grave are devastating:

Vassily Ivanych was seized by a sudden frenzy. "I said I would rebel," he shouted hoarsely, his face inflamed and distorted, waving his clenched fist in the air as though threatening someone— "And I will rebel, I will!" But Arina Vlassyevna, suffused in tears, hung her arms round his neck and both fell prone together. "And so," as Anfisushka related afterwards in the servants' rooms, "side by side they bowed their poor heads like lambs in the heat of noonday . . ."

> *V. S. Pritchett, in his* The Gentle Barbarian: The Life and Work of Ivan Turgenev, *Vintage Books, 1977.*

Henry Gifford (essay date 1964)

[*Gifford is an English critic specializing in Russian literature. His works include* The Hero of His Time: A Theme in Russian Literature *(1950) and* The Novel in

Russia: From Pushkin to Pasternak. *In the following excerpt from the latter work, Gifford asserts that though* Fathers and Sons *falls short of the greatness of works by Leo Tolstoy or Fyodor Dostoevsky, it nevertheless reflects the author's honest objectivity and keen eye for details.*]

[*Fathers and Children*] is constructed around Bazarov—medical student, brutal positivist, radical. To elicit what he is Turgenev sends him to the small manor of Arkady his college friend; involves him there in a quarrel with Arkady's fastidious uncle; then in a love affair which humiliates him; in a final dispute with Arkady at the house of Bazarov's parents; and in the sudden catastrophe of death from typhus. The other people serve to bring Bazarov variously to the test; in death, the ultimate test, he reveals all the strength and bitterness of his nature. Properly speaking there are three *events* in the story: the first when Bazarov invades the tranquility of Odintsova with his violent declaration; the second his duel with Pavel Petrovich (the uncle); and the third his death agony. With Pavel Petrovich—and eventually with his nephew—the quarrel is ideological; and the duel over Fenichka merely carries on their dispute of the tenth chapter by other means. With Odintsova—a grand lady though once she had been poor—the quarrel is in part ideological, but mainly Bazarov protests against the despotism of sexual love. And in his quarrel with death he meets a reality still more insulting. So he has three problems: that of the outsider in a society which he judges effete; that of the lover in spite of himself who is rejected (and here he retains some dignity); and that of a young man murdered by fate, which he resists to his dying breath. The novel, though it describes the ordeal of Bazarov, is rightly called *Fathers and Children:* Turgenev presents through this ordeal a familiar conflict.

Many years later he wrote to Saltykov-Shchedrin about the 'enigma' of Bazarov:

I can't very well make out how I described him. Here was—and please don't laugh—a kind of fate, something stronger than the author himself, and independent of him. I do know one thing: I had no preconceived thought, no tendency . . . (January 1876)

Bazarov he explained in [a letter to K. K. Sluchevsky on 4 April] 1862 came to him as

a gloomy, wild, grand figure, half emerging from the soil powerful, enraged, honourable and yet doomed to destruction, because it stands as yet on the threshold of the future . . . I imagined a sort of strange pendant to Pugachov . . .

There are moments when Bazarov (like Stavrogin in Dostoevsky's *Devils*) seems to derive from Gothic romance:

Bazarov splayed out his long cruel fingers . . . Arkady turned and got ready, in play, to resist him . . . But his friend's face looked to him so ominous, and such a far from playful menace appeared in the wry sneer of his lips, and in the blazing eyes, that against his will he felt timid . . . (xxi)

Bazarov is Satanic perhaps in his 'fathomless' pride. Arkady asks

> 'Have you a high opinion of yourself?' For a moment Bazarov was silent. 'When I meet the man who doesn't get out of the way for me,' he said deliberately, 'then I shall change my opinion about myself.' (*Ib.*)

This pride sustains him in the last hours. Yet despite the Gothic affinities Bazarov has nothing to do with Cain. Nor was he forsaken in childhood. He suffers from no oppression, apart from the discouragement facing all able but poor young men in Russia. The only exceptional thing about Bazarov is that he belongs to the future.

Arkady's father and that liberal ghost his uncle, like Bazarov's own parents, are reconciled to the existing order; and that means to serfdom. Bazarov believes that his 'tendency'—the destructive principle—will have popular sentiment behind it: that you must 'clear a space' for others to build. The work of levelling must go on, and many things dear to Turgenev—the pieties and the pretences together—are flung down. In Arkady's father (with the symbolic lameness) he chose a peculiarly weak country gentleman; in the uncle a very ineffectual champion of the ideas current in Turgenev's own class; in Odintsova a *grande dame* apathetic almost beyond belief. So much for benevolence, liberalism and fashion: Bazarov wants no 'civilization' of that kind: he is what Arnold would have termed an 'acrid dissolvent'.

Turgenev professed to share all Bazarov's views, except over art. (Bazarov holds it ridiculous for Arkady's father to play the cello, and wants him to read a textbook on materialism instead of Pushkin). But what Turgenev said afterwards as apologist—the novel was attacked from all sides—may even confuse what he affirms as author in the story itself. The insensibility, the churlish dogmatism and one might add the provincial arrogance of Bazarov—these annoy and they are surely meant to annoy. Herzen refused to accept them as more than adolescent defiance. But though Turgenev's 'nihilist' (a name that stuck) discomfits the reader, his bad manners are not meant to obscure his good cause. ('Of course he had to crush "the man with perfumed whiskers" and the rest! This is the triumph of democratic principle over aristocracy,' Turgenev explained [in a letter to Herzen dated 28 April 1862].) The author himself is facing a dilemma which comes to a head in **Virgin Soil.** There Nezhdanov recognizes that his poetry makes him a poor revolutionary, and commits suicide. Turgenev lets Bazarov expel Pushkin, and it is doubtful whether Pushkin comes back at all convincingly, when Arkady sits with Katya on a bench under the tall aspen. Turgenev was prepared to suppress his own doubts in the name of democracy. He respected that crude energy in Bazarov's nihilism.

His projection of Bazarov—the most original thing in **Fathers and Children**—yet differs strikingly from that of Dostoevsky's nihilists. Turgenev, we know, always began with

> the vision of some person, or persons, who hovered before him, soliciting him . . . He . . . saw

them vividly, but then had to find for them the right relations, those that would most bring them out . . . [H. James in his Preface to *The Portrait of a Lady*].

First, the hint of a new 'type': in this case, a young provincial doctor met briefly and by chance. Then, having noted the figure, to work out the situations and courses that seemed likely for him. With Dostoevsky the character experiences an idea which drives him along in a terrifying dialectic. Turgenev had to confess, in the year he began **Fathers and Children:** 'Whatever I write, the result is a series of sketches'; not, as with Dostoevsky, scenes in a necessary drama. Bazarov's death, though finely imagined, has no reason unlike Kirillov's death, or Stavrogin's. Herzen was probably right in thinking that Turgenev got rid of Bazarov by typhus because he could settle with him in no other way. In Turgenev's eyes this death 'put the last touch' to a 'tragic figure', and yet, he added, 'the young people find it fortuitous'. The 'young people' saw that his natural pessimism (it could not be called here a tragic sense) had cut short the story. 'Russia needs me . . . No, clearly she doesn't.' So Bazarov speaks his own epitaph. He has 'fallen under the wheel'. Not, like Anna Karenina, because his way of life had become unbearable, but because all is vanity, and the strength and pride of Bazarov mean nothing to nature.

Fathers and Children falls short of greatness if the standard is taken from Tolstoy or Dostoevsky. It has the merit of complete honesty: Turgenev seems to have written the story almost in spite of himself; and except perhaps for the pious hopes in the conclusion he has checked sentiment firmly throughout. This was the occasion for him to concentrate all his powers on a theme of peculiar interest: the essential work for which his talents had been maturing. The first of these is the ability to connect: Turgenev possesses the entire scene and has placed it in history. He is expert in relations, whether between individuals—take for instance Arkady's indulgence and his father's mixed shame and relief when they discuss Fenichka—or between the individual and society at large. He notes a careless pronunciation whereby Pavel Petrovich in his dispute with Bazarov assumes the negligence of 'the quality' in Alexander's reign; he catches the old-fashioned pedantry and rustic rigmarole of Bazarov's father, as Scott had done with the Baron of Bradwardine; and he devotes to Bazarov's mother a careful paragraph (too long to quote in full) which makes her a part of history:

> Arina Vlasevna was the genuine Russian gentlewoman of an earlier time; she ought to have lived two hundred years ago, in the old Muscovite days. She was very devout and impressionable, she believed in all sorts of signs, auguries, spells and dreams . . . she believed that if on Easter day the candles at mass do not go out, the buckwheat will come on well, and that a mushroom will not grow once the eye of man has looked on it . . . she would not eat . . . watermelons because a carved water-melon recalls the head of John the Baptist . . . she read no book at all except for *Alexis, or the Cabin in the Forest* . . . she knew that in the world there are gentlefolk who have to give orders and the com-

mon people who have to obey them, and therefore didn't dislike timidity on their side, or bowing to the ground; but she was very gentle and mild with her subordinates, she never let a beggar go without giving him something, and she censured nobody though she was inclined to gossip. In youth she had been very charming, played the clavichord and could make herself more or less understood in French; but in the course of many years' travelling with her husband, whom she had married against her will, she grew ampler and forgot both music and the French language . . . (xx)

This kind of perception might not have been possible without the stanzas on Tatyana's mother in *Onegin;* but Turgenev can also net fish unknown to Pushkin, for example Kukshina the emancipated woman (who may have helped Henry James to visualize his Bostonian feminists):

On the leather divan half reclined a lady, still young, fair-headed, a little dishevelled, in a silk dress not altogether clean, with heavy bracelets on her short arms and a lace kerchief upon her head. She rose from the divan and carelessly drawing on to her shoulders a glossy pelisse of yellowed ermine, she drawled:

'Hallo, Victor,' and pressed Sitnikov's hand.

'Bazarov, Kirsanov,' he announced abruptly, in imitation of Bazarov.

'Please be welcome,' answered Kukshina, and turning upon Bazarov her round eyes, between which her little snub nose looked red and orphaned, she added 'I know you' and pressed his hand too.

Bazarov frowned. In the small and insignificant figure of the emancipated woman there was nothing ugly, and yet the expression of her face had an unpleasant effect on the beholder. It was difficult not to ask her: 'What's wrong, are you hungry? or bored? or frightened? Why are you all strung up?' She like Sitnikov was always on edge. She spoke and moved very unconstrainedly and at the same time awkwardly: it was clear she counted herself a good-natured and simple being, and yet whatever she did you kept thinking she hadn't precisely meant to do that; everything with her was done, as children say, 'on purpose', and not simply and naturally. (xiii)

And like Pushkin—like all novelists who concern themselves with 'the meaning of aspects'—Turgenev notes carefully her surroundings:

The room in which they found themselves was more like a working study than a drawing-room. Papers, letters, thick copies of Russian journals, mostly uncut, were scattered on dusty tables; everywhere was a white litter of cigarette ends.

Contrast with this Fenichka's sweet-smelling room with its lyre-backed chairs, the china egg hung from the halo on an ikon of Nicholas the Miracle-worker, and the caged siskin (viii); or the jumbled 'study' of old Bazarov (xx). These are all forms where a hare has lain.

Turgenev may be compared with Thackeray in his general

attitudes: an early radicalism modified with the years; a certain hauteur; and a deep-seated pessimism. Both respond to the spectacle of this world, its brightness and variety, the grain on the social surface; they observe keenly and feel humanely. And both write with the same effortless grace and sensitivity to all the nuances of the spoken word. Turgenev is not free from sentimentality, though (unless in *Smoke*) he can hardly be accused of cynicism. The deep difference between them shows in Turgenev's superior moral courage. He never conceded anything to the public, but braved misunderstanding and even fury; his ideal of truthfulness puts him nearer to Mill than to Thackeray. Being a Russian, with a well-known Decembrist in the family, and the keenest consciences of the time among his personal friends, Turgenev learned a civic fortitude which did not issue in politics but in his practice as an artist. Liberalism was to become under the ridicule of Saltykov-Shehedrin an old, shabby word denoting the show but not the substance of democratic principle. But liberalism in the sense of free play for the humane, secular mind never had a more faithful adherent than Turgenev. He was in the 1850's what he had called Belinsky, 'the right man in the right place'. But after 1861, when liberal politics gave way to revolutionary, his place had gone. (pp. 68-74)

Henry Gifford, "Turgenev in 'Fathers and Children'," in his The Novel in Russia: From Pushkin to Pasternak, *Hutchinson University Library, 1964, pp. 65-74.*

René Wellek (essay date 1965)

[*Wellek's* A History of Modern Criticism *(1955-86) is a major, comprehensive study of the literary critics of the last three centuries. His critical method, as demonstrated in* A History *and outlined in his* Theory of Literature *(1949), is one of describing, analyzing, and evaluating a work solely in terms of the problems it poses for itself and how the writer solves them. In the following excerpt Wellek praises Turgenev's objective narrative style and perceptive characterizations in* Fathers and Sons.]

Fathers and Sons (1861) stands out among Turgenev's novels for many good reasons. It is free from the sentimentality and vague melancholy of several of the other books. Unobtrusively it achieves a balanced composition, while some of the later books seem to fall apart. It shows Turgenev's power of characterization at its best. He not only draws men and women vividly but he presents an ideological conflict in human terms, succeeding in that most difficult task of dramatizing ideas and social issues, while avoiding didacticism, preaching, and treatise-writing—succeeding, in short, in making a work of art.

In Russia *Fathers and Sons* stirred up an immense and acrimonious debate which centered around the figure of Bazarov, the nihilist who is the hero of the novel. Turgenev did not invent the word "nihilism": it was used in Germany early in the century in philosophical contexts and was imported into Russia by a satirical novelist, Vasily Narezhny (1780-1825). But Turgenev's novel gave it currency as a name for the young generation which did not recognize any authority. In reading the book we must dismiss from our minds the later connotation of the term, when it was affixed to the bomb-throwing revolutionaries who, in 1881, succeeded in killing the tsar. As Turgenev uses the word, however, and as Bazarov and his pupil Arkady explain it, "nihilism" means materialism, positivism, utilitarianism. It implies a rejection of religion and of the Russian class system of the time; it implies a trust in the spread of enlightenment and in science, conceived rather naively as purely empirical observation and investigation, symbolized by Bazarov's collecting of frogs and peering through the microscope at insects and infusoria. It implies a contempt for the conventions of society and romantic illusions, which for Bazarov include poetry and all art. But Bazarov is only potentially a revolutionary; he has no plan, no opportunity, and no time for political action. In debate he tells us that he wants to "make a clean sweep," that he wants to "change society," but he has no allies or even friends, except the doubtful Arkady. Although Bazarov comes from the people and gets along easily with them when he wants to do so, he despises their ignorance and at the end taunts the peasants for their superstition and subservience to their masters. Bazarov is entirely unattached; he is and remains an individualist, even though he tells us that all people are alike.

The figure of this rugged, uncouth, and even rude young man aroused at first the violent anger of the Russian radical intelligentsia. M. A. Antonovich, the critic of the main opposition journal, *The Contemporary,* denounced Bazarov as a "scarecrow" and "demon" and Turgenev for having written a panegyric of the fathers and a diatribe against the sons. A secret-police report ascribed to the novel "a beneficent influence on the public mind" because it "branded our underage revolutionaries with the biting name 'Nihilist' and shook the doctrine of materialism and its representatives." Turgenev was abused by the opposition, to which he himself belonged, and became so disgusted with the misinterpretation of the book that he defended and explained himself in letters and finally, in 1869, in a long article, **"A propos of *Fathers and Sons*"**. . . . Turgenev puts forth two arguments. He did not write about ideas, but he simply described an actual person whom he had met: a young doctor who had impressed him. And besides, "many of my readers will be surprised if I tell them that with the exception of Bazarov's views on art, I shared almost all his convictions." He put this even more strongly in an earlier letter (April 26, 1862, to Sluchevsky): "Bazarov dominates all the other characters of the novel . . . I wished to make a tragic figure of him. . . . He is honest, truthful, and a democrat to the marrow of his bones. If he is called a 'nihilist,' you must read 'revolutionary.' My entire story is directed against the gentry as a leading class." Turgenev's defense was, surprisingly enough, accepted by the radicals: at least Dmitri Pisarev (1840-1868), who wrote a paper, "The Destruction of Aesthetics" (1865) and actually thought that a cobbler is more important than Pushkin (or pretended to believe it), hailed Bazarov as the true image of the "new man" and elevated, in a genuine act of self-recognition, a fictional figure to a symbol quite independently of the intentions of the author. Soviet Russian criticism accepts this interpretation and consistently hails the novel as a forecast of the Revolution.

> Though the eternal conflict between the old and young is one of the main themes of the book, *Fathers and Sons* is not exhaustively described by the title. Even the preoccupation with nihilism is deceptive. The book goes beyond the temporal issues and enacts a far greater drama: man's deliverance to fate and chance, the defeat of man's calculating reason by the greater powers of love, honor, and death.
>
> —*René Wellek*

But surely this is a gross oversimplification, to which the critics and Turgenev himself were driven in the polemical situation of the time. The book is neither an anti-nihilist novel nor a glorification of the coming revolution. Its beauty is in the detachment, the objectivity, and even the ambivalence with which Turgenev treats his hero and his opinions and presents the conflict between his crude, arrogant, youthful nihilism and the conservative romanticism of his elders. We can delight in the delicate balance which Turgenev keeps and can admire the concrete social picture he presents: the very ancient provincials, father and mother Bazarov, devout, superstitious, kindhearted, intellectually belonging to a dead world; the finicky, aristocratic Pavel Kirsanov and his weak brother Nikolay, who represent the romantic 1840's; the sloppy, name-dropping, cigarette-smoking emancipated woman, Mme. Kukshin; and the elegant, frigid, landowning widow Mme. Odintsov.

Though the eternal conflict between the old and young is one of the main themes of the book, *Fathers and Sons* is not exhaustively described by the title. Even the preoccupation with nihilism is deceptive. The book goes beyond the temporal issues and enacts a far greater drama: man's deliverance to fate and chance, the defeat of man's calculating reason by the greater powers of love, honor, and death. It seems peculiarly imperceptive of some critics to dismiss Bazarov's death by complaining that Turgenev got weary of his hero. His accidental death is the necessary and logical conclusion: Bazarov, the man of reason, the man of hope, is defeated throughout the book. His pupil Arkady becomes unfaithful and reveals his commonplace mind. Bazarov had dismissed love as a matter of mere physiology, but fell in love himself. He is furiously angry at himself when he discovers what he feels to be an inexplicable weakness; he becomes depressed, tries to forget his love by work, and almost commits suicide when he neglects his wound. Bazarov is defeated even in the duel with Pavel, though he was the victor; he had jeered at chivalry as out of date and considered hatred irrational, but he did fight the duel after all. It was ridiculous and even grotesque, but he could not suffer humiliation or stand the charge of cowardice. He did love his parents, though he was embarrassed by their old-fashioned ways. He even consented to receive extreme unction. When death came,

Turgenev at age 12.

he took it as a cruel jest which he had to bear with Stoic endurance. He died like a man, though he knew that it made no difference to anyone how he died. He was not needed, as no individual is needed. We may feel that the moving deathbed scene is slightly marred by the rhetoric of his request to Mme. Odintsov, "Breathe on the dying lamp," and surely the very last paragraph of the book contradicts or tones down its main theme. Turgenev's reference to the "flowers" on the grave (when Bazarov himself had spoken of "weeds" before) and to "eternal reconciliation and life without end" seems a concession to the public, a gesture of vague piety which is refuted by all his other writings. Turgenev puts here "indifferent nature" in quotation marks, but as early as in *Sportsman's Sketches* he had said: "From the depths of the age-old forests, from the everlasting bosom of waters the same voice is heard: 'You are no concern of mine,' says nature to man." In the remarkable scene with Arkady on the haystack—the two friends almost come to blows—Bazarov had pronounced his disgust with "man's pettiness and insignificance beside the eternity where he has not been and will not be." There is no personal immortality, no God who cares for man; nature is indifferent, fate is blind and cruel, love is an affliction, even a disease beyond reason—this seems the message Turgenev wants to convey.

But *Fathers and Sons* is not a mere lesson or fable. It is a narrative, which with very simple means allows the author to move quietly from one location to the other—from the decaying farm of the Kirsanovs, to the provincial town, to the elegant estate of Mme. Odintsov, and from there to the small estate of the old Bazarovs, and back again—firmly situating each scene in its appropriate setting, building up each character by simple gestures, actions, or dialogue so clearly and vividly that we cannot forget him. Only rarely do we feel some lapse into satire, as in Mme. Kukshin's silly conversation. But on the whole, with little comment from the author, a unity of tone is achieved which links the Russian of 1859 with the eternally human and thus vindicates the universalizing power of all great art. (pp. 658-62)

> *René Wellek, in an introduction to* World Masterpieces Vol. 2, *edited by René Wellek, W. W. Norton & Company, Inc., 1965, pp. 645-84.*

Ralph E. Matlaw   (essay date 1966)

[*Matlaw was an American authority on nineteenth-century Russian literature and a professor of Slavic languages. He edited the works of Turgenev, Anton Chekhov, Leo Tolstoy, Fyodor Dostoevsky, and Appolon Grigor'ev. In the excerpt below, he explains two fundamental aspects of Bazarov's character in* Fathers and Sons: *"his immaturity and his position as an outsider in 'a world he never made'."*]

Perhaps the most suggestive insight ever made into *Fathers and Sons* was V. E. Meyerhold's attempt to cast the poet Vladimir Mayakovsky in the role of Bazarov for a film version contemplated in 1929. Among those who remember the young Mayakovsky's early appearances in films, Yuri Olesha described his face as "sad, passionate, evoking infinite pity, the face of a strong and suffering man." It is a little hard to imagine Mayakovsky with sidewhiskers (Bazarov, after all, presumably wears these to resemble more closely his intellectual prototype, the studious and sickly N. A. Dobrolyubov), but apart from that one could not conceive of a better reincarnation of Bazarov than Mayakovsky. For Mayakovsky, in his flamboyant and tragic life, and frequently in his verse, was or would have been if Bazarov had not already staked out a claim to that title, the arch example of the phenomenon we now call "the angry young man."

The term, with due allowance for the changes of a century and of cultures, points to two fundamental aspects of Bazarov that underlie both his attractive and repulsive traits for most readers—his immaturity and his position as an outsider in "a world he never made." And these, in turn, point to the psychological and social verities that secure so high a place for *Fathers and Sons* in modern literature. The second of these has a specific historical context and prototype, V. G. Belinsky, to whom the novel is dedicated. Bazarov's portrait, like Belinsky's career, is associated with and typifies two important notions in Russian intellectual history. The first is the rise of the "intelligentsia," a term, apparently of Russian invention, that designates intellectuals of all persuasions dedicated in one form or another to the improvement of life in Russia, and so carries far greater ethical implications than the mere word "intellectual." The second is that of the *raznochintsy,* literally "persons of various classes," a term applied to those members of classes other than the gentry, usually the clergy or the minor and provincial professional and bureaucratic classes, who sought to pursue a career other than the one their background would normally indicate. Frequently they became members of the intelligentsia, usually after considerable privation. Unlike members of the gentry like Herzen or Turgenev, who could always turn to other sources if necessary, they were entirely dependent upon their intellectual labors, whether as tutors, journalists, writers, or in other pursuits, and from their difficult position derived no small part of their exaltation and indefatigability. While there were factions and enmities within the intelligentsia, all its members were in principle agreed on one point: opposition to the conditions of life around them. Clearly connected with these conditions is the intrusion of the *raznochintsy* into literature, until 1830 or so the exclusive purview of the gentry, who were all too eager to avoid the imputation of professionalism. In style and in tone a sharp shift may be observed, and no one better exemplifies this change in real life than Belinsky or in literature than Bazarov.

Intellectual equality, unfortunately, offered no social prerogatives. Beyond his intellectual circles and his normal habitat, the major cities, even in the rapidly changing society of the mid-nineteenth century, the *raznochinets* was an outsider, if not an upstart. Bazarov, with his enormous sensitivity and vanity, feels out of place at the Governor's Ball and at Odintsov's estate (the wording of his request for vodka amazes the butler). He frequently and deliberately emphasizes his plebeian origin, as in the ironic reference to his similarity to the great Speransky, his sharp reaction to his father's apologies, his feelings about Pavel Kirsanov, and in numerous turns of speech that the English translation cannot convey completely. As for Pavel Kirsanov, we need only think of Prince André's disdain for Speransky in *War and Peace* to judge the gulf that in Pavel's mind separates Bazarov from him. To the aristocrat who has cultivated and refined his privileged position, the democratic virtue of being a self-made man does not appear so laudable. And from this point of view Bazarov's contempt for Pavel Petrovich, "snobism in reverse," to adapt Bazarov's witticism, is another manifestation of his discomfort when out of his class. Still, as Bazarov makes clear, his prospects are very meager, and it leads to great bitterness. Outside the "establishment," which he cannot tolerate, there is no opposition party, not even a real hierarchy, and the consciousness of insuperable obstacles leads to Bazarov's great "anger." As Turgenev chose to present the matter it appears more as a social than political theme, but its motive force is just as operative. The point may profitably be compared to a similar one in *The Red and The Black* where, in Stendhal's happier imagination, Julien Sorel rises to the top, only to insist perversely at his trial on his peasant origin and to accuse his jury of seeking "to punish in me and to discourage forever that class of young men who, born in an inferior station and in a sense burdened with poverty, have the good fortune to secure a sound education, and the audacity to mingle with what the pride of rich people calls society."

The second component is more directly implied in the novel's title as the conflict between generations, apparently an inherent problem in human nature, though manifesting itself in different forms and in different degrees. *Fathers and Sons* presents it in particularly sharp form. Nikolai Kirsanov tells his brother of the remark he made to his mother, "Of course you can't understand me. We belong to different generations," and is now resigned to his turn having come to "swallow the pill." Bazarov's father similarly remembers how he scoffed at the earlier generation, accepts Bazarov's ridiculing his outdated notions, but as a matter of course indicates that in twenty years Bazarov's idols too will be replaced. The intensity of rejection, however, does differ and is a sign of the times. For Bazarov replies "For your consolation I will tell you that nowadays we laugh at medicine altogether, and don't bow down to anyone," which his father simply cannot comprehend. Normally, the problem of generations is resolved by time: the sons gradually move toward their permanent positions, give over being "angry young men," and become husbands and fathers, angry or not. It is perhaps the hardest subject of all to handle, as the reaction to the end of *War and Peace* with its assertion of domestic permanence, and, in *Fathers and Sons,* the quick taming of Arkady Kirsanov prove: the world of struggle and aspiration is more interesting to contemplate that that of fixity and acceptance. The "angry young man" cannot remain so, and is something of an anomaly if not of outright ridicule, when he maintains that view as paterfamilias. Bazarov denies the values of normal human behavior, but when his theory is put to a single test it collapses. Bazarov falls in love and can no longer return to his former mode. Turgenev permits him to maintain his character by shifting the problem of generations to its ultimate form, that of death. This condition, at least, Bazarov must accept: "An old man at least has time to be weaned from life, but I . . . Well, go and try to disprove death. Death will disprove you, and that's all!" And in his illness Bazarov compresses into a brief period that acceptance of traditional values—family, love, life itself—that otherwise would accrue slowly and undramatically, in the process to some extent attenuating the strident expression of his former views.

But this only occurs at the end. Throughout the novel the high-mindedness, dedication, and energy that make Bazarov tower over the other characters are occasionally expressed with an immaturity bordering on adolescent revolt. The ideas themselves thus in part express the temperament of the "sons." Superficially the state may seem to apply more readily to Arkady, but it is far more ingrained in Bazarov. There are such remarks as "Bazarov drew himself up haughtily. 'I don't share anyone's ideas: I have my own,'" and "When I meet a man who can hold his own beside me, then I'll change my opinion of myself," his deliberately offensive manners, his sponging on and abuse of Kukshin and Sitnikov, his trifling with Fenichka and his jejune declaration to Odintsov. In short, the attempt to impose his own image on the world and to reshape the world accordingly. It is a point Turgenev made quite explicit in his draft for *Virgin Soil:*

> There are *Romantics of Realism*. . . . They long for a reality and strive toward it, as former Romantics did toward the ideal. In reality they seek not poetry—that is ludicrous for them—but

something grand and meaningful; and that's nonsense: real life is prosaic and should be so. They are unhappy, distorted, and torment themselves with this very distortion as something completely inappropriate to their work. Moreover, their appearance—possible only in Russia, always with a *sermonizing* or educational aspect—is necessary and useful: they are preachers and prophets in their own way, but complete prophets, contained and defined in themselves. Preaching is an illness, a hunger, a desire; a healthy person cannot be a prophet or even a preacher. Therefore I put something of *that* romanticism in Bazarov too, but only Pisarev noticed it.

The two problems of youth and anger, or maturity and acceptance, come to a head in Bazarov's involvement with Odintsov, the central episode in the novel, which also serves as a kind of structural dividing line between the political (or social) and the psychological. The discussions of nihilism and contemporary politics, that phase of the battle between the generations dominates the opening of the novel but is practically concluded when Bazarov and Arkady leave Odintsov in Chapter Nineteen. From this point on an opposite movement assumes primary importance: Bazarov's and Arkady's liberation from involvement with theories and the turn toward life itself, that is, toward those people and things in the characters' immediate existence. It entails a shift from scenes and formulations essentially intellectual to others that are more ruminative, inwardly speculative, communicating psychological states and feelings rather than ideas. With it, Bazarov's views and behavior assume a different cast, far more personal, more indicative of his real needs and dissatisfactions. His speeches about necessary reforms now turn into expressions of personal desire ("I felt such a hatred for this poorest peasant, this Philip or Sidor, for whom I'm to be ready to jump out of my skin, and who won't even thank me for it"), his rigorous materialism into the purely Pascalian speech on man's insignificance as a point in time and space. His brusqueness and former contempt for decorum now are so tempered that he accepts a challenge to a duel, has a frock coat easily accessible as he returns to Odintsov, and practices elaborate politeness as she visits him on his deathbed. The end with Bazarov's disquisition on strength, life, and necessity strikes the reader as rather mawkish and hollow, for the words now have if not a false, at least a commonplace ring. Indeed, the great effect of the ending is achieved not through Bazarov's speeches but communicating the despair of his parents.

In the final analysis Turgenev could neither condemn nor yet wholly redeem Bazarov without falsifying or diminishing the portrait. On the last page of the novel he instead implies the reconciliation of the character with a larger, permanent order of things, expressed in terms of the touchstone and overriding image of the novel—nature. The concluding words "[the flowers] tell us, too, of eternal reconciliation and of life without end" do not at all tend toward mysticism, as Herzen claimed and Turgenev denied, but affirm that "the passionate, sinning, and rebellious heart" buried beneath the ground has finally come to terms with permanent reality. The passage is secular rather than religious: life is "without end" not "eternal"; it is life on earth, not in the hereafter. (pp. 274-78)

> *Ralph E. Matlaw, "Turgenev's Novels and 'Fathers and Sons'," in* "Fathers and Sons" by Ivan Turgenev: The Author on the Novel, Contemporary Reactions, Essays in Criticism, *edited and translated by Ralph E. Matlaw, W. W. Norton & Company, Inc., 1966, pp. 261-78.*

Yarmolinsky on Bazarov as hero:

Bazarov exhibits to the full Turgenev's power to give body and breath to his characters. The budding medico's impulses and convictions are made as real to us as his long face with its sandy sideburns and his cool green eyes. From the moment when he is first seen in no haste to offer his red hand to his host to the moment, several months later, when this atheist lifts an eyelid in horror as he is made to receive the last sacrament, he is the center and pivot of the tale, literally its hero. Tough-minded and hard-fisted, a model of steadfastness, he is unique among Turgenev's male characters, dominating the action and throwing the other *dramatis personae,* all of them marvels of portraiture, into the shade. If he is brash, arrogant, boorish, it is perhaps because he finds himself among people who are incapable of understanding his ideas, who are out of sympathy with them, and who, worst of all, do not take them seriously. The reader fancies that he behaves differently when he is among those who share his views. The indication is that such a congenial group does exist. His is not a lone voice crying in the wilderness.

Avrahm Yarmolinsky, in his The Russian Literary Imagination, *Funk & Wagnalls, 1969.*

Charles R. Bachman   (essay date 1968)

[*In the essay below, Bachman describes how the false self-images of Bazarov, Pavel Petrovich, and Anna Sergeyevna Odintsova contribute to the tragedy of* Fathers and Sons.]

Though Ivan Turgenev dealt with self-deception in a number of his works, nowhere is the theme more pervasive, or more subtly or convincingly handled, than in *Fathers and Sons.* Here false self-images are crucial to the tragic view which the action of the novel seems to demand, a view which in turn helps make it probably Turgenev's greatest work. This self-deception is most obvious in the case of certain minor characters. Peter (Piotr), Nikolai Kirsanov's "progressive" servant, is "a man whose whole merit consisted in the fact that he looked civil," and he obviously believes himself so, even though his civility is little more than an appearance. The progressive dandy, Sitnikov, is a sycophant who believes himself brave and definite when he feels the support of his idol, Bazarov, Madame Kukshin compensates for feminine plainness and frustration with the self-image of a woman of "advanced" views, and Matvey Ilyich Kolyazin, Arkady's relative who is sent to the town of X—to investigate the governor, is a "progressive" who "had the highest opinion of himself," whose slogan was *"l'énergie est la première qualité d'un homme d'état;* and for all that, he was usually taken in, and any moderately experienced official could turn him round his finger."

These characters help exemplify Turgenev's satire on a society which wished to believe itself progressive; but they also reflect, in miniature as it were, the basic problem of self-identity of the three strong characters of the novel: Evgeny Vassilyich Bazarov, Pavel Petrovich Kirsanov and Anna Sergeyevna Odintsov. Turgenev distinguishes them as strong by giving them poise and self-confidence. They seem to feel superior to those around them, and have enough pride to trust their own personalities and judgements in social intercourse. By contrast Arkady, his father Nikolai, Bazarov's parents and Sitnikov are more typical of Turgenev's male figures: pliant and anxious to please. Arkady, for example, like Sitnikov, appears strong mainly when he senses Bazarov's support, and Turgenev implies that he will always be a follower.

In the novel strength of personality causes both attraction and repulsion, so that the points of greatest tension occur when the strong characters interact: the debate over nihilism, Bazarov's infatuation for Anna and the duel. These provide the major occasions through which Bazarov, Pavel and Anna each discover that the self-identity which formed the basis for their inner poise had been an illusion.

The chief encounter is that of Bazarov and Pavel, who at first appear to be opposite in several significant ways. The former is young, plain-featured, gruff and rude in manner, disrespectful of tradition and the humanities, and unconcerned with form, social and otherwise. Pavel is past middle-age, strikingly handsome, sensitive and careful in manner, strongly in favor of tradition and the humanities and over-concerned with form in dress, speech and behavior. While Arkady echoes Bazarov and Nikolai tries to be polite, the two main antagonists clash over the arts, tradition and nihilism. Their seemingly opposite attitudes and temperaments, however, and their contemptuous references to each other as "An antique survival" and "That unkept creature" can become the occasion for open conflict only because they are depicted as so similar in their egoism and their strength of personality. Both are accustomed to being deferred to, and cannot tolerate a lack of respect for themselves. Pavel is especially defensive. He " . . . had grown to detest Bazarov with all the strength of his soul; he regarded him as stuck-up, impudent, cynical and plebian; he suspected that Bazarov had no respect for him, that he had all but contempt for him—him. Pavel Kirsanov!"

The most basic reason for Pavel's antagonism, however, lies deeper, and concerns his self-image. The great love affair of his life had been with the Princess R—, the glance of whose eyes was "swift and deep." Her reply to Pavel's statement that she was a sphinx indicated her intelligence: " 'I?' she queried, and slowly raising her enigmatical glance upon him. 'Do you know that's awfully flattering?' she added with a meaningless smile, while her eyes still kept the same strange look."

In becoming infatuated with the Princess, Pavel had fallen in love with stupidity unconsciously masking itself as depth, and his tragedy in this affair had a conscious and an unconscious aspect. His whole personality was so bound up with her love that when she lost interest he became disillusioned with life. But a major reason for his being attracted to her in the first place would seem to have been that, like the Princess, Pavel himself had grown accustomed to depending for his sense of identity upon the esteem and expectations of others—an esteem based upon his impressive mask of manners and physical appearance. His response to the Princess had a quality of desperation. Thrust by handsome looks and a dashing manner into the role of a romantic, Pavel came to believe the role himself. His pride grasped at it as a self-identity which seemed as impressive as was his appearance. "Much admired in society," he "had read in all five or six French books." " . . . a brilliant career awaited him. Suddenly everything changed." The most ironic aspect of this change was that in becoming ensnared in the deep but "meaningless" gaze of the Princess' eyes, Pavel had, not unnaturally, fallen victim to the same kind of deception as had the society which admired him. While he had perhaps read "five or six" more French books than the Princess, his statement that she was a sphinx was almost as unperceptive as her inane but pretentious reply.

After being deserted, and unaware of the irony implicit in his love, Pavel settled at Marion, where "he arranged his whole life in the English style." Of course Turgenev is satirizing in this "man with the fragrant mustache" the snobbishness and artificiality of the Russian gentry. But the satire is mixed with sympathy, since Pavel's artificiality and need for a style of life are largely unconscious attempts to retain in a new setting the romantic self-image with which he has so long identified himself. While Pavel and his brother are standing outside at night, however, and Nikolai "had not the force to tear himself away from the darkness, the garden, the sense of the fresh air in his face, from that melancholy, that restless craving," Pavel's feelings are similar to what would have been expected from Bazarov: " . . . he too raised his eyes towards the heavens. But nothing was reflected in his beautiful dark eyes except the light of the stars. He was not born a romantic, and his fastidiously dry and sensuous soul, with its French tinge of misanthropy was not capable of dreaming . . . ."

Pavel's view of himself as a romantic, then, is quite obviously a self-deceptive illusion. In view of this, the underlying motive for his resentment of Bazarov would seem to be that he sensed in the younger man a rather complete image of his own genuine temperament: not only his egoism and pride, but his misanthropy and lack of romanticism as well. During the first argument (Chs. V and VI), his defense of nature, art and poetry against Bazarov, who refuses to acknowledge their value and is even "indifferent to the beauties of nature," actually conceal an insensitiveness to the things Pavel is defending. His staunch support of "the traditions accepted in human conduct," and of "personal dignity" and firmness of character as the "foundation for . . . the social fabric" are an overcompensation for the fear that in his encounter with Bazarov he is losing the basis for his own firmness of character—the image of self which he had so carefully though unconsciously created.

The duel not only forces the two antagonists into a grudging respect for each other's courage, but also reveals that they seem to hold similar attitudes toward Nikolai and the peasants. Pavel believes that Bazarov "behaved honorably," and they have a similar estimate of Nikolai's character:

> "There's no deceiving my brother; we shall have to tell him we quarreled over politics."
>
> "Very good," assented Bazarov. "You can say I insulted all Anglomaniacs."
>
> "That will do splendidly."

Pavel is surprised at Bazarov's statement that the Russian peasant does not understand himself, because he obviously shares this belief: "Ah! so that's your idea! . . . Look what your fool of a Peter has done!"

These similarities, however, only further convince Pavel of the extent to which his self-image has been an illusion, and his joking with Bazarov is probably a cloak for this realization. What is even more significant is the major cause of the duel itself: Pavel's feelings for Fenichka. Before the duel, Fenichka had become "more afraid of Pavel Petrovich than ever; for some time he had begun to watch her and would suddenly make his appearance as though he sprang out of the earth behind her back, in his English suit, with his immovable vigilant face . . . ." After the duel, while mildly delirious, Pavel states that he sees a physical resemblance between the Princess R—and Fenichka, thus acknowledging that the latter has replaced the former as the symbol of his romantic illusion. The exclamation, "Ah, how I love that light-headed creature!" seems to refer to the Princess, but the object of Pavel's subsequent threat is omitted by Turgenev: "I can't bear any insolent upstart to dare to touch . . . ." Both the Princess and Fenichka are meant, just as whatever rival had robbed Pavel of the Princess seems to be identified with Bazarov. By threatening the object toward which Pavel felt himself romantically inclined, both rivals have also threatened his careful illusion that he has a romantic temperament. His reaction in both cases is similarly desperate: in the first, disillusionment and exile from the Princess' scene of activity; in the second, the challenge to a duel and subsequent disillusionment and exile from Fenichka's scene of activity. After Bazarov's departure, Pavel tries to convince Nikolai that he should marry Fenichka: "I begin to think Bazarov was right in accusing me of being an aristocrat. No, dear brother, don't let us worry ourselves about appearances and the world's opinion any more; we are old folks and resigned; it's time we laid aside vanity of all kind." In laying aside "appearances and the world's opinion," Pavel is acknowledging the falseness of the only self-identity he has consciously known, and the tear that rolls down his cheek as he exhorts Fenichka to love Nikolai is partly one of regret that the waste caused by this false self-identity is irrevocable. His suggestion that Nikolai marry Fenichka is really an act of despair. It is after the marriage that Pavel goes abroad, spiritually "a dead man."

The most ironic aspect of Bazarov's effect on Pavel is that the former's anti-romanticism and cynicism, which have made Pavel aware of these qualities at the heart of his own personality, are also an appearance concealing a different kind of person than Pavel ever realizes. Bazarov's profession of physician and his intense faith in the validity of experimental research are in direct contradiction to his statements that as a nihilist he believes "in nothing." But his infatuation with Anna is the chief event which reveals the romantic and at times lyrical sensibility beneath the gruff exterior. This is an ironic reversal for one who has characterized love as "romanticism, nonsense, rot, artiness." His overt scorn of poetry rings false when he quotes a line of "Der Wanderer" to Anna, and in his lyrical recollection of childhood in his later conversation with Arkady:

> "That aspen," began Bazarov, "reminds me of my childhood; it grows at the edge of the clay-pits where the brick-shed used to be, and in those days I believed firmly that that clay-pit possessed a peculiar talismanic power . . . ."

When alone, Bazarov "recognized the romantic in himself." One probable reason for his resentment of Pavel, then, is also an insecurity with his own self-image—a fear that his real temperament contains some of the romantic idealism which Pavel avows.

A further irony is that Bazarov has criticized Pavel for allowing his whole life to become dependent upon his passion for the Princess: "Still, I must say that a man who stakes his whole life on one card—a woman's love—and when that card fails, turns sour, and lets himself go till he's fit for nothing, is not a man, but a male." Yet after being rejected by Anna Sergeyevna, Bazarov himself loses most of his own drive and sense of direction. He visits his parents, but feels dissatisfied and bored. After three days he impulsively visits Anna again and returns to Marino, where he conceals his romanticism from all but Arkady and Fenichka.

The source of Bazarov's disillusionment, however, is not only his discovery that his own self-image was an illusion. Anna's poise and serenity, which had attracted him and seemed to suggest genuine emotional depth, were actually manifestations of an emotional lethargy, an inability to feel deep passion. After Bazarov departs she begins to realize that there is something false about her conception of herself: "Under the influence of various vague emotions, the sense of life passing by, the desire of novelty, she had forced herself to go up to a certain point, forced herself to glance behind it, and had seen behind it not even an abyss, but a void . . . or something hideous."

Bazarov realizes that, like Pavel, he has become infatuated with a deceptive appearance. He turns to Fenichka partly because he senses that in her there is no illusion of self, and therefore no false mask. His declaration to her that "I live alone, a poor wretch," indicates the extent of both his trust in her and his disillusionment. The duel severs both him and Pavel from Fenichka, and Bazarov also becomes virtually a dead man, telling Arkady that "there seems to be an empty space in the box, and I am putting hay in; that's how it is in the box of our life; we would stuff it up with anything rather than have a void." He pays Anna one last visit, and the attempted casualness of their conversations cannot conceal the fact that they both feel ill at ease and empty. Feeling again "dreary boredom or vague restlessness," Bazarov finally returns home, and his death by typhus, like the demise of several of Thomas Hardy's heroes, is no artistic flaw in the novel, but an anticipated symbol of the death of his spirit which has already taken place.

Bazarov's tragic dilemma approaches the perspective which Turgenev invites the reader to share. The social class in the novel which suffers least from self-deception is the one to which Bazarov, in a last fruitless attempt to reestablish an identity, instinctively returns: that of the peasants and small rural landowners. The aristocracy, on the other hand, which wishes to believe itself progressive, is the class which as a whole suffers most from self-deception. In spite of disclaimers of didacticism Turgenev stated in a letter [dated 14 April 1862] to the poet K. K. Sluchevsky that "My entire tale is directed against the nobility as a leading class." Bazarov, however, like the reader, has seen that not only "aristocrats" such as Pavel and Anna, but also all pseudo and genuine intellectual sophisticates, including himself, have been deceived as to their identity. Even Arkady, before his relationship with Katya, has had such illusions. As in Thomas Hardy, the gain of awareness has brought an inevitable loss of a sense of integrity—a dilemma which foreshadows the questioning of the very possibility of self-identity so prevalent in post-Freudian literature and society. But *Fathers and Sons,* though lacking the detailed psychological penetration present in the greater works of Tolstoy and Dostoevsky, nonetheless moves beyond the depiction of a pathetic paradox toward genuine tragedy; and perhaps the most fruitful method of discussing the tragic quality of this novel is by comparison with tragic drama.

As in Sophoclean tragedy, pride in Turgenev's novel is both a source of greatness and a tragic flaw. Because their pride is their own responsibility it becomes the main source of our admiration for Anna, Pavel and Bazarov, helping to give them magnitude and significance. Yet in contributing most to their perseverance in believing in and sustaining illusions of the self, their pride is also the major reason for their fall. Their own proud reserve and the modern universe in which they live prevent them from railing at the gods as did Lear, or examining the fatefulness of life as did Oedipus, Hamlet or Phèdre. But the questioning of the justice of fate, and the violent fall or destruction usually demanded by Sophoclean, Shakespearean and Racinian tragedy has become in *Fathers and Sons* the loss of self-identity: a paradox and a catastrophe which may well be as potentially tragic for modern man. This loss of self-identity, however, can be tragic rather than pathetic only if it involves a genuine, forceful and courageous internal and external struggle to maintain a sense of self. Necessary are both awareness and sheer stubbornness—which is presented rather than analyzed away. Though it would be foolish to argue equivalencies, this dilemma, which characterizes Bazarov and Pavel, and to a lesser degree Anna, is also that of Oedipus. The pride with which Bazarov and Pavel assert themselves so forcefully as compensation for an unconscious insecurity is unexplained; the forcefulness does not depend on the insecurity. Sitnikov is also insecure, but weak. This unexplained

but human dignity of pride which "goeth before a fall," combined with the seeming injustice—but not absurdity—of the fall, make it valid to classify *Fathers and Sons* as a basically tragic novel. The view of society and fate invited by the novel depends not upon Turgenev's final phrases concerning "eternal reconciliation," but upon the fact that for the strongest characters there has been no earthly reconciliation. In typical Turgenev fashion, the most assertive figure is killed off. The probability that the novelist's compulsion to destroy such heroes was motivated by his own pliant personality is only relevent to Turgenev's psychology, however. It does not affect the essential tragedy of *Fathers and Sons,* which lies in the fact that not only Bazarov, but all three strong characters in the novel have had self-images so dangerously false that, when uncovered, their personalities have been left shattered, dead of vitality or genuine hope. (pp. 269-76)

> *Charles R. Bachman, "Tragedy and Self-Deception in Turgenev's 'Fathers and Sons',"* in Revue des langues vivantes, *Vol. XXXIV, No. 3, 1968, pp. 269-76.*

Isaiah Berlin   (lecture date 1970)

[*In the excerpt below from a lecture first delivered in 1970, Berlin considers the confrontation between old and young, conservative and liberal in* Fathers and Sons, *and discusses the conflicting interpretations of Bazarov.*]

> Young Man to Middle-Aged Man: 'You had content but no force.' Middle-Aged Man to Young Man: 'And you have force but no content.'
>
> From a contemporary conversation

This is the topic of Turgenev's most famous, and politically most interesting, novel *Fathers and Children.* It was an attempt to give flesh and substance to his image of the new men, whose mysterious, implacable presence, he declared, he felt about him everywhere, and who inspired in him feelings that he found difficult to analyse. 'There was', he wrote many years later to a friend [Saltykov–Shehedrin, in a letter dated 15 January 1876], '—please don't laugh—some sort of *fatum,* something stronger than the author himself, something independent of him. I know one thing: I started with no preconceived idea, no "tendency"; I wrote naïvely, as if myself astonished at what was emerging.' He said that the central figure of the novel, Bazarov, was mainly modelled on a Russian doctor whom he met in a train in Russia. But Bazarov has some of the characteristics of Belinsky too. Like him, he is the son of a poor army doctor, and he possesses some of Belinsky's brusqueness, his directness, his intolerance, his liability to explode at any sign of hypocrisy, of solemnity, of pompous conservative, or evasive liberal, cant. And there is, despite Turgenev's denials, something of the ferocious, militant, anti-aestheticism of Dobrolyubov too. The central topic of the novel is the confrontation of the old and the young, of liberals and radicals, traditional civilization and the new, harsh positivism which has no use for anything except what is needed by a rational man. Bazarov, a young medical researcher, is invited by his fellow student and disciple,

Arkady Kirsanov, to stay at his father's house in the country. Nicolai Kirsanov, the father, is a gentle, kindly, modest country gentleman, who adores poetry and nature, and greets his son's brilliant friend with touching courtesy. Also in the house is Nicolai Kirsanov's brother, Paul, a retired army officer, a carefully dressed, vain, pompous, old-fashioned dandy, who had once been a minor lion in the *salons* of the capital, and is now living out his life in elegant and irritated boredom. Bazarov scents an enemy, and takes deliberate pleasure in describing himself and his allies as 'nihilists', by which he means no more than that he, and those who think like him, reject everything that cannot be established by the rational methods of natural science. Truth alone matters: what cannot be established by observation and experiment is useless or harmful ballast—'romantic rubbish'—which an intelligent man will ruthlessly eliminate. In this heap of irrational nonsense Bazarov includes all that is impalpable, that cannot be reduced to quantitative measurement—literature and philosophy, the beauty of art and the beauty of nature, tradition and authority, religion and intuition, the uncriticized assumptions of conservatives and liberals, of populists and socialists, of landowners and serfs. He believes in strength, will-power, energy, utility, work, in ruthless criticism of all that exists. He wishes to tear off masks, blow up all revered principles and norms. Only irrefutable facts, only useful knowledge, matter. He clashes almost immediately with the touchy, conventional Paul Kirsanov: 'At present', he tells him, 'the most useful thing is to deny. So we deny.' 'Everything?' asks Paul Kirsanov. 'Everything.' 'What? Not only art, poetry . . . but even . . . too horrible to utter . . . ' 'Everything.' 'So you destroy everything . . . but surely one must build, too?' 'That's not our business . . . First one must clear the ground.' The fiery revolutionary agitator Bakunin, who had just then escaped from Siberia to London, was saying something of this kind: the entire rotten structure, the corrupt old world, must be razed to the ground, before something new can be built upon it; what this is to be is not for us to say; we are revolutionaries, our business is to demolish. The new men, purified from the infection of the world of idlers and exploiters and its bogus values—these men will know what to do. The French anarchist Georges Sorel once quoted Marx as saying 'Anyone who makes plans for after the revolution is a reactionary.' This went beyond the position of Turgenev's radical critics of the *Contemporary Review;* they did have a programme of sorts: they were democratic populists. But faith in the people seems just as irrational to Bazarov as the rest of the 'romantic rubbish'. 'Peasants?' he says, 'They are prepared to rob themselves in order to drink themselves blind at the inn.' A man's first duty is to develop his own powers, to be strong and rational, to create a society in which other rational men can breathe and live and learn. His mild disciple Arkady suggests to him that it would be ideal if all peasants lived in a pleasant, whitewashed hut, like the head man of their village. 'I have conceived a loathing for this . . . peasant,' Bazarov says, 'I have to work the skin off my hands for him, and he won't so much as thank me for it; anyway, what do I need his thanks for? He'll go on living in his whitewashed hut, while weeds grow out of me.' Arkady is shocked by such talk; but it is the voice of the new, hard-

boiled, unashamed materialism. Nevertheless Bazarov is at his ease with peasants, they are not self-conscious with him even if they think him an odd sort of member of the gentry. Bazarov spends his afternoon in dissecting frogs. 'A decent chemist', he tells his shaken host, 'is twenty times more use than any poet.' Arkady, after consulting Bazarov, gently draws a volume of Pushkin out of his father's hands, and slips into them Büchner's *Kraft und Stoff,* the latest popular exposition of materialism. Turgenev describes the older Kirsanov walking in his garden: 'Nikolai Petrovich dropped his head, and passed his hand over his face. "But to reject poetry," he thought again, "not to have a feeling for art, for nature . . ." and he cast about him, as if trying to understand how it was possible not to have a feeling for nature.' All principles, Bazarov declares, are reducible to mere sensations. Arkady asks whether, in that case, honesty is only a sensation. 'You find this hard to swallow?' says Bazarov. 'No, friend, if you have decided to knock everything down, you must knock yourself down, too! . . . ' This is the voice of Bakunin and Dobrolyubov: 'one must clear the ground.' The new culture must be founded on real, that is materialist, scientific values: socialism is just as unreal and abstract as any other of the 'isms' imported from abroad. As for the old aesthetic, literary culture, it will crumble before the realists, the new, tough-minded men who can look the brutal truth in the face. 'Aristocracy, liberalism, progress, principles . . . what a lot of foreign . . . and useless words. A Russian would not want them as a gift.' Paul Kirsanov rejects this contemptuously; but his nephew Arkady cannot, in the end, accept it either. 'You aren't made for our harsh, bitter, solitary kind of life,' Bazarov tells him, 'you aren't insolent, you aren't nasty, all you have is the audacity, the impulsiveness of youth, and that is of no use in our business. Your type, the gentry, cannot get beyond noble humility, noble indignation, and that is nonsense. You won't, for instance, fight, and yet you think yourselves terrific. We want to fight . . . Our dust will eat out your eyes, our dirt will spoil your clothes, you haven't risen to our level yet, you still can't help admiring yourselves, you like castigating yourselves, and that bores us. Hand us others—it is them we want to break. You are a good fellow, but, all the same, you are nothing but a soft, beautifully bred, liberal boy . . . '

Bazarov, someone once said, is the first Bolshevik; even though he is not a socialist, there is some truth in this. He wants radical change and does not shrink from brute force. The old dandy, Paul Kirsanov, protests against this: 'Force? There is force in savage Kalmucks and Mongols, too . . . What do we want it for? . . . Civilization, its fruits, are dear to us. And don't tell me they are worthless. The most miserable dauber . . . the pianist who taps on the keys in a restaurant . . . they are more useful than you are, because they represent civilization and not brute Mongol force. You imagine that you are progressive; you should be sitting in a Kalmuck wagon!' In the end, Bazarov, against all his principles, falls in love with a cold, clever, well-born society beauty, is rejected by her, suffers deeply, and not long after dies as a result of an infection caught while dissecting a corpse in a village autopsy. He dies stoically, wondering whether his country had any real need of him and men like him; and his death is bitterly lamented by his old, humble, loving parents. Bazarov falls because he is broken by fate, not through failure of will or intellect. 'I conceived him', Turgenev later wrote to a young student [K. K. Sluchevsky, in a letter dated 26 April 1862], 'as a sombre figure, wild, huge, half-grown out of the soil, powerful, nasty, honest, but doomed to destruction because he still stands only in the gateway to the future . . . ' This brutal, fanatical, dedicated figure, with his unused powers, is represented as an avenger for insulted human reason; yet, in the end, he is incurably wounded by a love, by a human passion that he suppresses and denies within himself. In the end, he is crushed by heartless nature, by what the author calls the cold-eyed goddess Isis who does not care for good or evil, or art or beauty, still less for man, the creature of an hour; he struggles to assert himself; but she is indifferent; she obeys her own inexorable laws.

Fathers and Children was published in the spring of 1862 and caused the greatest storm among its Russian readers of any novel before or, indeed, since. What was Bazarov? How was he to be taken? Was he a positive or a negative figure? A hero or a devil? He is young, bold, intelligent, strong, he has thrown off the burden of the past, the melancholy impotence of the 'superfluous men' beating vainly against the bars of the prison house of Russian society. The critic Strakhov in his review spoke of him as a character conceived on a heroic scale. Many years later Lunacharsky described him as the first 'positive' hero in Russian literature. Does he then symbolize progress? Freedom? Yet his hatred of art and culture, of the entire world of liberal values, his cynical asides—does the author mean to hold these up for admiration? Even before the novel was published his editor, Mikhail Katkov, protested to Turgenev. This glorification of nihilism, he complained, was nothing but grovelling at the feet of the young radicals. 'Turgenev', he said to the novelist's friend Annenkov, 'should be ashamed of lowering the flag before a radical, or saluting him as an honourable soldier.' Katkov declared that he was not deceived by the author's apparent objectivity: 'There is concealed approval lurking here . . . this fellow, Bazarov, definitely dominates the others and does not encounter proper resistance,' and he concluded that what Turgenev had done was politically dangerous. Strakhov was more sympathetic. He wrote that Turgenev, with his devotion to timeless truth and beauty, only wanted to describe reality, not to judge it. He too, however, spoke of Bazarov as towering over the other characters, and declared that Turgenev might claim to be drawn to him by an irresistible attraction, but it would be truer to say that he feared him. Katkov echoes this [in a letter to Turgenev]: 'One gets the impression of a kind of embarrassment in the author's attitude to the hero of his story . . . It is as if the author didn't like him, felt lost before him, and, more than this, was terrified of him!'

The attack from the Left was a good deal more virulent. Dobrolyubov's successor, Antonovich, accused Turgenev in the *Contemporary* of perpetrating a hideous and disgusting caricature of the young. Bazarov was a brutish, cynical sensualist, hankering after wine and women, unconcerned with the fate of the people; his creator, whatever his views in the past, had evidently crossed over to the blackest reactionaries and oppressors. And, indeed, there were conservatives who congratulated Turgenev for exposing the horrors of the new, destructive nihilism, and thereby rendering a public service for which all men of decent feeling must be grateful. But it was the attack from the Left that hurt Turgenev most. Seven years later he wrote to a friend [L. Pietsch, in a letter dated 3 June 1869] that 'mud and filth' had been flung at him by the young. He had been called fool, donkey, reptile, Judas, police agent. And again, 'While some accused me of . . . backwardness, black obscurantism, and informed me that "my photographs were being burnt amid contemptuous laughter", yet others indignantly reproached me with kowtowing to the . . . young. "You are crawling at Bazarov's feet!" cried one of my correspondents. "You are only pretending to condemn him. Actually you scrape and bow to him, you wait obsequiously for the favour of a casual smile." . . . A shadow has fallen upon my name.' At least one of his liberal friends who had read the manuscript of *Fathers and Children* told him to burn it, since it would compromise him for ever with the progressives. Hostile caricatures appeared in the left-wing press, in which Turgenev was represented as pandering to the fathers, with Bazarov as a leering Mephistopheles, mocking his disciple Arkady's love for his father. At best, the author was drawn as a bewildered figure simultaneously attacked by frantic democrats from the Left and threatened by armed fathers from the Right, as he stood helplessly between them. But the Left was not unanimous. The radical critic Pisarev came to Turgenev's aid. He boldly identified himself with Bazarov and his position. Turgenev, Pisarev wrote, might be too soft or tired to accompany us, the men of the future; but he knows that true progress is to be found not in men tied to tradition, but in active, self-emancipated, independent men, like Bazarov, free from fantasies, from romantic or religious nonsense. The author does not bully us, he does not tell us to accept the values of the 'fathers'. Bazarov is in revolt; he is the prisoner of no theory; that is his attractive strength; that is what makes for progress and freedom. Turgenev may wish to tell us that we are on a false path, but in fact he is a kind of Balaam: he has become deeply attached to the hero of his novel through the very process of creation, and pins all his hopes to him. 'Nature is a workshop, not a temple' and we are workers in it; not melancholy daydreams, but will, strength, intelligence, realism—these, Pisarev declares, speaking through Bazarov, these will find the road. Bazarov, he adds, is what parents today see emerging in their sons and daughters, sisters in their brothers. They may be frightened by it, they may be puzzled, but that is where the road to the future lies.

Turgenev's familiar friend, Annenkov, to whom he submitted all his novels for criticism before he published them, saw Bazarov as a Mongol, a Genghiz Khan, a wild beast symptomatic of the savage condition of Russia, only 'thinly concealed by books from the Leipzig Fair' [Letter to Turgenev, 26 September 1861]. Was Turgenev aiming to become the leader of a political movement? 'The author himself . . . does not know how to take him,' he wrote, 'as a fruitful force for the future, or as a disgusting boil on the body of a hollow civilization, to be removed as rapidly as possible.' Yet he cannot be both, 'he is a Janus with two faces, each party will see only what it wants to see or can understand.' Katkov, in an unsigned review in his own journal (in which the novel had appeared), went a good deal further. After mocking the confusion on the Left as a result of being unexpectedly faced with its own image in nihilism, which pleased some and horrified others, he reproaches the author for being altogether too anxious not to be unjust to Bazarov, and consequently of representing him always in the best possible light. There is such a thing, he says, as being too fair: this leads to its own brand of distortion of the truth. As for the hero, he is represented as being brutally candid: that is good, very good; he believes in telling the whole truth, however upsetting to the poor, gentle Kirsanovs, father and son, with no respect for persons or circumstances: most admirable; he attacks art, riches, luxurious living; yes, but in the name of what? Of science and knowledge? But, Katkov declares, this is simply not true. Bazarov's purpose is not the discovery of scientific truth, else he would not peddle cheap popular tracts—Büchner and the rest—which are not science at all, but journalism, materialist propaganda. Bazarov (he goes on to say) is not a scientist; this species scarcely exists in Russia in our time. Bazarov and his fellow nihilists are merely preachers: they denounce phrases, rhetoric, inflated language—Bazarov tells Arkady not to talk so 'beautifully'—but only in order to substitute for this their own political propaganda; they offer not hard scientific facts, in which they are not interested, with which, indeed, they are not acquainted, but slogans, diatribes, radical cant. Bazarov's dissection of frogs is not genuine pursuit of the truth, it is only an occasion for rejecting civilized and traditional values which Paul Kirsanov, who in a better-ordered society—say England—would have done useful work, rightly defends. Bazarov and his friends will discover nothing; they are not researchers; they are mere ranters, men who declaim in the name of a science which they do not trouble to master; in the end they are no better than the ignorant, benighted Russian priesthood from whose ranks they mostly spring, and far more dangerous.

Herzen, as always, was both penetrating and amusing. 'Turgenev was more of an artist in his novel than people think, and for this reason lost his way, and, in my opinion, did very well. He wanted to go to one room, but ended up in another and a better one.' The author clearly started by wanting to do something for the fathers, but they turned out to be such nonentities that he 'became carried away by Bazarov's very extremism; with the result that instead of flogging the son, he whipped the fathers.' Nature sometimes follows art: Bazarov affected the young as Werther, in the previous century, influenced them, like Schiller's *The Robbers,* like Byron's Laras and Giaours and Childe Harolds in their day. Yet these new men, Herzen added in a later essay, are so dogmatic, doctrinaire, jargon-ridden, as to exhibit the least attractive aspect of the Russian character, the policeman's—the martinet's—side of it, the brutal bureaucratic jackboot; they want to break the yoke of the old despotism, but only in order to replace it with one of their own. The 'generation of the forties', his own and Turgenev's, may have been fatuous and weak, but does it follow that their successors—the brutally rude, loveless, cynical, philistine young men of the sixties, who sneer and mock and push and jostle and don't apologize—

are necessarily superior beings? What new principles, what new constructive answers have they provided? Destruction is destruction. It is not creation.

In the violent babel of voices aroused by the novel, at least five attitudes can be distinguished. There was the angry right wing which thought that Bazarov represented the apotheosis of the new nihilists, and sprang from Turgenev's unworthy desire to flatter and be accepted by the young. There were those who congratulated him on successfully exposing barbarism and subversion. There were those who denounced him for his wicked travesty of the radicals, for providing reactionaries with ammunition and playing into the hands of the police; by them he was called renegade and traitor. Still others, like Dimitri Pisarev, proudly nailed Bazarov's colours to their mast and expressed gratitude to Turgenev for his honesty and sympathy with all that was most living and fearless in the growing party of the future. Finally there were some who detected that the author himself was not wholly sure of what he wanted to do, that his attitude was genuinely ambivalent, that he was an artist and not a pamphleteer, that he told the truth as he saw it, without a clear partisan purpose.

This controversy continued in full strength after Turgenev's death. It says something for the vitality of his creation that the debate did not die even in the following century, neither before nor after the Russian Revolution. Indeed, as lately as ten years ago the battle was still raging amongst Soviet critics. Was Turgenev for us or against us? Was he a Hamlet blinded by the pessimism of his declining class, or did he, like Balzac or Tolstoy, see beyond it? Is Bazarov a forerunner of the politically committed, militant Soviet intellectual, or a malicious caricature of the fathers of Russian communism? The debate is not over yet. (pp. 26-37)

Isaiah Berlin, in his Fathers and Children: The Romanes Lecture, *Oxford at the Clarendon Press, 1972, 295 p.*

Alexander F. Boyd   (essay date 1972)

[*In the following excerpt, Boyd considers the conflicting progressive and conservative themes in* Fathers and Sons, *explaining how Turgenev incorporated these ideas into the main characters of his work.*]

The appearance of the novel **Fathers and Sons** in 1862 caused a storm which is difficult for use, as it was for Turgenev's Western contemporaries, to understand. A young man of rather radical outspoken views spends a few months in the country with a friend during which time a declaration of love is rejected and he fights a rather comical duel with his friend's uncle; shortly after he dies of typhus. There is apparently not a great deal here, no dynamic clash of good and evil, of nation against nation, and yet Turgenev found himself and his novel at the very centre of a critical storm whose cause can be traced back to Turgenev's earlier **Sketches from a Hunter's Album.** These stories had been originally published separately, but their appearance as a collection in 1852 offended the censorship and brought about the arrest of their author and his temporary exile to his mother's Spasskoe estate. The penetrating sketches, allegedly drawn from the memoirs of a hunter as he roamed in search of game over the countryside of central Russia, apparently centred round nothing more substantial than depictions of personalities and customs. But their cumulative effect was to show the peasantry as abused and long-suffering and the gentry who owned them as ineffectual and self-obsessed. Turgenev's commitment to the cause of serf emancipation and rural reform seemed clear-cut. The authorities noted him down as a potentially dangerous literary agitator and the liberals cheered him as a man obviously belonging to their camp.

Sketches from a Hunter's Album and Turgenev's novels of the mid-1850s, *Rudin,* and *A Nest of Gentlefolk,* all appeared in *The Contemporary,* a literary journal founded by Pushkin and purchased in 1846 by Turgenev's friend, the poet Nekrasov, who made *The Contemporary* the leading literary journal of the day in Russia. As elsewhere in Europe, it was the custom of literary journals to serialise novels prior to their publication in book form, and Nekrasov was able to secure the works of Turgenev and of the young Leo Tolstoy. In 1854, however, a young radical, Chernyshevsky, took over the editorship of the journal, and its comment soon took on a radical, utilitarian note. Chernyshevsky's dictum that 'Art must exist for Life's sake; not Life for Art's' made Turgenev admire the young radical's earnestness but at the same time feel apprehensive of what the full application of the precept might entail. When, two years later, a second young radical, Dobrolyubov, also joined the editorial board of *The Contemporary,* Turgenev began to have real cause for concern. *The Contemporary*'s editorial view of literature as only of value as social comment and of the writer's significance solely as social commentator were ones with which Turgenev could not agree. Turgenev's open break with *The Contemporary* came when Turgenev chose to submit his latest novel *On The Eve* to the rival journal *Russian Herald* in 1859.

In response to this, Dobrolyubov, writing about Turgenev's new novel in *The Contemporary,* chose to make his 'review' a tribune for his own radical interpretation of what Turgenev 'intended' in his novel. In his article, entitled 'When Will the Real Day Come?' Dobrolyubov justified his action by proclaiming—'The important thing for us is not so much what the author intended to say, as what he did say, even unintentionally, simply in the act of faithfully reproducing the facts of life.' Thus, the publication of Turgenev's subsequent novel *Fathers and Sons* in 1862 took place against Turgenev's recent and apparently petulant break with the platform of the young Russian progressive camp. Turgenev had been presented with the choice of meekly accepting its 'interpretations' of what he said or making an open break with it. He chose to make the break.

No wonder then that the character of the radical Bazarov created such a furore; the radicals accused him of caricaturing the new generation of radicals, while at the same time the conservatives construed Turgenev's attitude to his hero as one of sympathy, some even welcoming Bazarov as a figure deliberately contrived 'to include all the reprehensible characteristics of modern youth'. Turgenev's exasperation and irritation were more than justified. Writing about the reception of *Fathers and Sons* in his literary memoirs, Turgenev cites the following pointed example of radical reaction to Bazarov:

> Among the many proofs of my 'malice for our youth' one critic used the fact that I had made Bazarov lose his game of cards to Father Aleksey. 'He doesn't know how to hurt and humiliate him enough! He can't even play cards!' There is no doubt that if I had made Bazarov win the game the same critic would have triumphantly exclaimed, 'Isn't it evident? The author wants us to understand that Bazarov cheats at cards!'

The airy figure of Bazarov caused as much havoc in Turgenev's personal life as it had ever done at Marino. Turgenev, of course, had never intended Bazarov to be the hero of a *roman à thèse;* the very idea of the *roman à thèse* was abhorrent to him and was rapidly to cool him in his later reception of the French Naturalists. Nor was it, as was also claimed, to caricature Dobrolyubov personally that Bazarov was created. Turgenev later wrote about his first meeting with the 'Bazarov type', a purely casual meeting in a train taking him from Petersburg to Moscow. In the same second-class compartment as Turgenev sat a country doctor, Dimitriev, whose opinions and mannerisms he noted. Struck by this new forthright dedication, Turgenev began looking for its manifestations elsewhere. Gradually, the core of a character was formed and the idea of Bazarov was born. Candour, dedication, contempt for the cultural heritage, all these impressed Turgenev as he searched out the attributes of his new hero, so different from those of Rudin and of Lavretsky, the hero of *A Nest of Gentlefolk.* Here there was no vacillation, no rhetoric, none of the abstractions of a foreign education. Bazarov was of the people and with the people. He is no Rudin, a *neudachnik*—a failure, who has intelligence, education, charm—and yet, is simply conquered by the task of being himself. 'Yes,' says Rudin, 'Nature endowed me with a great deal, but I shall die without doing anything worthy of my talents, without leaving anything worthwhile behind me.' In depicting Rudin, Turgenev had drawn on memories of his own student days, the student circles who met to discuss romantic philosophy with heated enthusiasm deep into the night, who settled the problems of mankind round the samovar, but who did nothing.

In one of the stories from *Sketches from a Hunter's Album,* 'The Hamlet of the Shchigrovsky District',* Turgenev describes a meeting with what might have been a fellow student—a man now forgotten, overlooked, living from day to day the same dreary existence on his provincial estate, driven to seek the company of his fellow gentry at stultifying house-parties where he is ignored and snubbed. Yet he protests that he is not without intelligence or talent, and looks bitterly backwards to the wasted years of his youth.

> You would get up in the morning and the day would pass by as if you were shooting downhill on a toboggan. You would look round and there it was speeding to a close, evening already, and your sleepy valet would help you pull on your frock-coat; you got dressed, and off you would

go to see a friend, smoke your pipe, drink glass after glass of weak tea, and talk away about German philosophy, love, the eternal sun of the spirit, and various other remote things.

What a contrast Bazarov is to all this! He is the shabby, down-at-heel scholar who wants to sweep away the old order, although not clear about what he wants to replace it with. He is at war with all about him, his pride and aggressive polemic the only weapons he holds against all he challenges. As a student of the natural sciences, he compels himself to interpret everything in their light and in the process of doing so he confines himself just as much as the young gentlemen of Rudin's day did with their romantic philosophy. His creed of materialism, too, makes him dogmatic, the very thing a true scientist should not be, and his own vanity obliges him to refute everything in his country's past, especially the values of the previous generation—the 'fathers'.

When we first see Bazarov at Marino he strikes us as deliberately ill-mannered, belligerent, a mere pose of boorishness; it is only when the action moves to the provincial town which he and Arkady visit and we meet other examples of Russia's 'progressives', the fop Sitnikov and the absurd Madame Kukushkina, that we take a second look at Bazarov and find sincerity, devotion, and true idealism. Like Insarov, the Bulgarian hero of *On The Eve,* Bazarov dies without accomplishing anything, although it is unlikely that he could have been anything more than a country doctor like Dimitriev, his prototype. But, like Insarov, it is what he is and what he stands for that are important. It is his tragedy that Russia has no place for him, no way of harnessing his energies—he exists in a vacuum. He meets his death at the services of his science, a science directly related to the practical needs of his fellow men and one motivated by a burning desire to serve them. Thus is he distinguished from the passivity of the fathers and the pompous vanity of the 'progressive' intellectuals. Pavel Petrovich brands Bazarov as a 'nihilist', a man who believes in nothing, an atheist, an amoralist. But Bazarov's nihilism is more a refusal to accept and revere, he will not take the *status quo* on trust and sees the hypocrisy, the arrogance, and the ineptitude of the order bequeathed by the fathers' generation. He feels that without active committed intervention things will not turn out to be 'the best of all possible worlds'.

The word 'nihilist' was first used in the 1820s to denote a man who was ignorant and lacking in principle. Dobrolyubov revived it in 1858 to signify 'sceptic'. For Turgenev it meant 'empiricist', a refusal to accept any precept or principle on trust. By the middle of the 1860s it was used freely in Russia to refer to any radical trait, from free love to female emancipation, and by the end of the decade 'nihilist' was firmly equated with 'revolutionary'. The new nihilist of that age took Bazarov's ideas further; if the old order must go, it must be destroyed since it showed a remarkable tenacity in clinging to power, it must be destroyed by violence which as a means is justified by its ends. The embodiment of 'nihilism' in the late 1860s was a young disciple of the anarchist Bakunin, a student named Nechaev.

He believed in revolution as a tenet valid and sufficient in itself . . . he had no romantic faith in human nature or democracy. He did not merely proclaim, he acted on the hypothesis that morality does not exist, and, in the interests of revolution (of which he set himself up as the sole judge), every crime in the calendar from murder to petty larceny was legitimate and laudable [E. H. Carr, *The Romantic Exiles*].

In 1869 Nechaev carried out the cold-blooded murder of a fellow student, a student who belonged to the same revolutionary group as Nechaev and whom Nechaev suspected of being a police informer. The crime shocked Russia and announced the beginning of an age of violence and terrorism as the war between revolutionaries and police grew increasingly ruthless. The Nechaev affair inspired Dostoevsky's novel, *The Possessed* (also translated as *The Devils*), which was published in 1871 and 1872 in the same literary journal, *Russian Herald,* in which **Fathers and Sons** had appeared ten years before. The portrait of Stefan Trofimich in Dostoevsky's novel was partly derived from his view of Turgenev—an honourable, quixotic figure who has unwittingly given birth to a new race of bloodthirsty revolutionaries.

Bazarov shares with his adversary, Pavel Petrovich, the characteristics of pride, heroism, vanity, and contempt for the peasantry—although Pavel Petrovich's contempt is that of a master for his slaves while Bazarov is exasperated by their indolence and apathy. The conflict between Pavel Petrovich and Bazarov is a clash of pride, the pride of the rebel and the pride of the aristocrat. Bazarov is at heart fond of Arkady but he cannot forget their difference in 'class'; he is attracted by and yet jealous of Arkady's generosity and warmth. He takes a malicious pleasure in goading Arkady about his father and his uncle, and Arkady's ability to forgive this arouses both his respect and his envy. Bazarov's love for Anna Odintsova shows us some of the hollowness of his pretensions. The critic Pisarev wrote that Bazarov was the self-assured revolutionary up to Chapter 19, his rejection by Anna, after which he gives way to the despairing rebel. His rejection by her is indeed a triple blow; he is compelled to acknowledge the despised phenomenon of love, the woman he loves is of a type his doctrines most deride, and her refusal of him deals a grievous wound to his vanity. His love for Anna tells us what kind of person he is; without it we might merely have learned what he stood for.

In 1860 Turgenev delivered his famous lecture, **Hamlet and Don Quixote.** Speaking of Don Quixote, Turgenev said

What does Don Quixote stand for? Before all else faith, faith in something eternal, unchanging—truth. In one word, truth. A truth not lightly yielding to him, demanding devotion and sacrifice, but accessible through the constancy of devotion and the magnitude of his sacrifice. He lives outside himself, for others, for his brother men, to destroy evil and oppose all forces hostile to men's well-being.

Bazarov must have been in his mind as he spoke, and if his hero fails to meet all the ideals which Turgenev sets here, if he falters, appears ludicrous or brutish in his struggle, then perhaps the sacrifice of his happiness and peace of mind, and ultimately his life, atone a little.

Bazarov's opponent, Arkady's Uncle Pavel Petrovich, is almost fifty. His student days would have been spent in the social round so scathingly described by "The Hamlet of the Shchigrovsky District." He is the ageing dandy who, after his self-imposed exile to Marino, has made a cult of maintaining the role of aristocrat among provincial 'vulgarity'. A sense of form dominates his values; he is outraged at Bazarov's lack of respect for him, his class, and the high principles for which he believes he stands. Pavel is the relic of a bygone age, and although not given to any degree of penetrating self-criticism, he feels this at heart and it makes him the more tenacious in the defence of his values. He prides himself on his devotion to his country—but it is a country he hardly knows, his ideas and standards are all imported from Europe and only include those which serve to consolidate his views on the worth and necessity of his class. Our last picture of him in Dresden, with his silver ashtray in the shape of a peasant's bast shoe, exemplify him with gentle sarcasm. Bazarov is quite right when he says that Pavel Petrovich has no roots in Russia and has done nothing to further the interests of either his country or its people. Like his brother, Nikolai, Pavel is not a practical man. But with Pavel it is by inclination; he feels that his mere existence is a sufficient contribution to the general good. And yet, in spite of all this, he is not just a cardboard figure into which Bazarov can plunge his sword. He has courage, he adheres to his strict code of honour, and he has a certain ability to see his own failings—'I am beginning to think that Bazarov was right after all in accusing me of being a snob.' His conflict with Bazarov shows both of them new aspects of themselves and others. With their duel they reach a kind of understanding even if the differences between them can never be reconciled.

Arkady's father, Nikolai Petrovich, is a more sympathetic portrait of the fathers' generation. He is a kindly man and means well by everyone. He tries to do his best by his serfs, but they take advantage of him and as a result the estate fares badly. Unlike his brother, Nikolai makes an effort to understand his son's generation, and he tries to come to terms with Bazarov in spite of the rebuffs he earns in the process. He remains a romantic dreamer at heart; his fundamental weakness, fear of criticism, led initially to his abandoning his career in Petersburg for the life of a recluse in the country and is still present in his apprehension of what Arkady might think about his relationship with his serf mistress—Fenichka. Turgenev put much of himself into Nikolai and he was not afraid to portray the failings he saw within himself.

If Nikolai Petrovich contains the gentler faults of the fathers' generation, Arkady embodies many of the gentler virtues of the sons' and there is a great deal in him with which Turgenev is openly in sympathy. Arkady's affectation of nihilism is a flimsy one, and is obviously the result of his admiration for Bazarov. He sheds it as soon as he finds something more compatible with his own nature, his love for Katya and his feeling for the land. Sensing that

Bazarov has something in him which transcends his shortcomings, he maintains his loyalty in the face of his friend's biting criticism of all that he secretly loves. Bazarov is indeed correct in diagnosing him as a liberal landowner. Arkady has much in common with his father, for whom he feels a constant and warm affection. While Bazarov and Pavel Petrovich represent the extremes of their generations' attitudes, the inevitable friction between thesis and antithesis, Arkady and his father find mutual ground in their shared attachments to people rather than ideas and their feelings for Russia, not as an abstraction, but as a physical presence. They are both romantics, but Arkady manifests that redeeming streak of practicality which suggests that Marino may yet prosper with him as its master.

Fathers and Sons is singular among Turgenev's novels for its lack of the central heroine, the Liza, Natalya, and Elena who had played such a central part in the previous novels. But although *Fathers and Sons* is more directly concerned with social issues than the earlier novels, its female characters still have important, if less obtrusive, roles to play. The love stories of Bazarov and Anna, and of Arkady and Katya, illuminate and deepen our understanding not only of what Bazarov and Arkady stand for but of what they are. Turgenev uses every relationship in the novel to telling effect and it is his genius here which gives the novel its peculiar concentration and power.

Anna Odintsova is an attractive, intelligent widow of twenty-nine. The insecurity of her childhood and the dilemma she faced on the death of her improvident father have had a great effect on the shaping of her personality. Her self-centred materialism contrasts nicely with Bazarov's idealistic materialism; his is born of a dissatisfaction with the social order he finds around him, hers of a personal struggle to find the life of sheltered ease she guards so zealously. Her first loveless marriage, the need to realise herself emotionally, the unreasoning attraction she feels for Bazarov, almost tempt her to relinquish these priorities, but she can no longer change what has become almost instinct. It comes as no surprise to us that she eventually marries the man she does, a man who will provide her every need and make few demands on her other than to provide an adornment for his life and his career.

And yet the questions posed by that fateful evening which she and Bazarov spend together are far from clear-cut. Does his ability to show passion without affection frighten her? Does she understand fully the cruel game she is playing with him? Perhaps she must act out the play, hear one confession of real love to complete her self-esteem as a woman; or is she fascinated purely by the forces she has unleashed within him? Is she really in love, as the final visit to the dying Bazarov might suggest, and trying to surrender herself before reason can return? 'She was filled with fear and at the same time felt pity for him'; his passion was, 'not unlike fury and perhaps close to it'. His attraction is that of the stormy sea or the mountain chasm. She knows that she has led him to betray himself, she is aware that such rejection after her apparent encouragement will affect him deeply. Like Valentina in Turgenev's later novel *Virgin Soil,* Anna is 'intelligent, good rather than ill-natured', and like Valentina virtue comes easily to her since, as Turgenev says of such women, 'their temperaments are placid but they have a constant desire to command, to attract, and to please which gives them nobility and brilliance'.

Anna's capable handling of the situation on her father's death, her astute marriage, her success in educating herself and her sister, her ability to run her estate at Nikolskoe, a striking contrast with the inefficient and poorly managed Marion, testify to her intelligence. Her visit to Bazarov as he lies dying and her parting kiss are motivated by a part of her which has remained dormant—Turgenev's final mention of her is to remark that love may not be denied her after all. For Turgenev, love is a malaise, a moment of divine, ecstatic madness with which compromise or reason cannot co-exist. Above all it requires surrender of self. Anna cannot surrender her life of independence, and Bazarov cannot deal with love as a breach in his defences. It alarms him, he must cast off his pride and step down from the gods. Once he is forced to admit an experience not valid in his creed he cannot come to terms with his defeat; like his rival, Pavel Petrovich, he is vanquished by a passion he cannot suppress.

The love of Arkady and Katya gives a healthy, optimistic balance to the novel. Both understand, humble creatures that they are, that love is of prime importance in their lives. They are not inhibited by fear or pride. Katya is not of the noble stature of the previous girl-heroines in Turgenev, her attachments are primarily to people not to ideals. She is charming, 'simple, single-minded, pure and passionate'. Her exact age is not certain, as Turgenev tells us that she is eight years younger than her sister in Chapter Fifteen, and then calmly mentions that she is eighteen in the next, but eighteen or twenty-one, it matters little with her dark hair, her olive complexion, her round but pleasing face, her small, dark eyes, and her smile at once bashful and candid. She is pretty but not beautiful, for beauty in Turgenev's novels, like power, corrupts. She seems rather characterless when we first meet her, like someone invited along to dinner because there are odd numbers. As such a person often does, she becomes the star of the evening. She is quite unlike her elder sister. Anna is intelligent but does not understand people well, whereas Katya is sensible and very shrewd in her assessment of others. She merely raises her eyebrows when Bazarov states that people are as alike as trees in a forest; Anna may be intrigued by the novelty of such a concept, but Katya indicates by this slight gesture what she thinks of such a poor philosophy although she does not think it her place to say so here. Anna is happy to argue with men, Katya is not. She reveals little of what she really thinks, but when she does her observations are acute and to the point. Her handling of Arkady would be artful in a less ingenuous young woman. She is too sincere for aimless flirtation, but once she sees that Arkady is the man for her she has no hesitation in using every weapon in her gentle armoury.

When we first meet Katya, she is still content to be treated as a child by her sister, who appears not to have noticed that she is no longer twelve. By Chapter Twenty-five she knows enough about Arkady's feelings for her to assure herself that she is no longer a child, and does not hesitate to point this out gently to her sister. 'Anna Sergeevna took Katya under the chin and raised her face. "You have not quarrelled, I hope?" "No," said Katya, gently removing her sister's hand.' We can feel sure that she will be able to handle Arkady, with his tendencies to dreaminess, in the same gentle but firm manner.

There are, of course, many other minor portraits in the novel. Fenichka, Nikolai's serf mistress whom he marries, perhaps retrospective compensation by Turgenev for his own conduct, is a shadowy figure, pretty, gentle, and submissive. Her simplicity is perhaps her greatest asset and makes her attractive to men who may see in her what they wish—Nikolai, his late wife, Pavel, his long dead princess, and Bazarov, a place of tranquility, someone who accepts him as a man without ideas or a mission, simply someone for whom her baby smiles. Even the baby finds something new in Bazarov, perhaps a tenderness we had not suspected and which Bazarov would never have thought of revealing.

Bazarov's parents, too, are fine minor portraits. They are not here for relief from the stories of love or the jousting of temperaments, they have been living long before we meet them and they will go on living long afterwards. If all that remained of the novel was Chapter Twenty-one, when Bazarov takes his leave of his parents, it would be enough to make Turgenev a master:

> When Bazarov, after repeated promises to return before a month at the most was out, had finally torn himself free of the embraces which sought to detain him and seated himself on the tarantas; when the horses had moved off and the wheels had turned to the sound of the bell and there was nothing to look back at and the dust had settled, and Timofeyich, bent and walking with difficulty had reached his little room; when the old people remained alone in their ramshackle home which seemed to have aged as abruptly as they had—Vasily Ivanovich, who had kept on jauntily waving his handkerchief from the porch, sank into a chair and dropped his head on his chest. 'They've left us, left us,' he muttered, 'gone. They got bored here with us. I'm left alone, like this finger' and he repeatedly thrust his hand forward with the forefinger upraised. Then Anna Vlasevna came up to him and, laying her grey head against his, said "There's nothing we can do about it, Vasya. A son goes off on his own. He's like a falcon who flies to see you and then flies away when the fancy takes him, while you and I go on sitting here side by side like two mushrooms on a tree. I'm the only one who will always be the same for you and you will be the only one for me.' Vasily Ivanovich took his hands from his face and embraced his wife, his friend, as closely as ever he had held her in the days of their youth. She consoled him in his sorrow.

This scene might have happened yesterday, it will probably happen tomorrow and go on happening until the end of time. There is no sentimentality here, this is Turgenev and the poetry of life. If we find it a sad poetry, it is because so often Turgenev is in tune with the underlying rhythm of life, the flowering and the fading, of love, ideals, and of ourselves. But in all this, as in the flowers which cover Bazarov's grave, there is a constant faith in the continuity and the purpose of ordinary human life—and wonder at its perpetual mystery. (pp. 73-86)

> Alexander F. Boyd, "A Landscape with Figures: Ivan Turgenev and 'Fathers and Sons'," in his Aspects of the Russian Novel, *Rowman and Littlefield, 1972, pp. 68-86.*

Turgenev responds to Russian students' reactions to Bazarov:

The qualities attributed to [Bazarov] are not accidental. I wanted to make a tragic character out of him—there was no room in this case for gentleness. He is honest, truthful, and a democrat through and through—and you don't find any *good* sides to him? He recommends *Stoff und Kraft* precisely because it is a *popular,* i.e., an empty book; the duel with Pavel Petrovich is introduced specifically as a visual demonstration of the emptiness of elegant gentry chivalry— it is presented in an almost exaggeratedly comic way; and how could he decline it; after all, Pavel Petrovich would have clubbed him. It seems to me that Bazarov constantly crushes Pavel Petrovich, and not vice versa; and if he is called a nihilist, then that ought to read as a "revolutionary."

[If] the reader doesn't come to love Bazarov, with all his coarseness, callousness, pitiless dryness and harshness—I repeat—if he doesn't come to love him, then I'm at fault and have missed the mark. But I didn't want to "oversweeten things," to use his words, though by doing so I would probably have had the young people on my side immediately. I didn't want to solicit popularity with concessions of that sort. It's better to lose a battle (and I seem to have lost it) than to win it by a ruse. I imagined a gloomy, wild, large figure, half grown out of the soil, strong, spiteful, honest— and one all the same doomed to perish—because that figure is nonetheless still in the anteroom of the future, I imagined a sort of strange pendant [counterpart] to Pugachov—and so on—but my young contemporaries shake their heads and tell me: "Hey, brother, you made a boo-boo and even offended us: Arkady came off better—too bad you didn't work on him a little more even." All that I can do is "remove my cap and make a low bow," as in the gypsy song.

> Ivan Turgenev, in a letter to K. K. Sluchevsky, dated April 14, 1862, in his Turgenev: Letters, Volume I, *edited and translated by David Lowe, Ardis, 1983.*

Alexander Fischler   (essay date 1976)

[*In the excerpt below, Fischler examines the structure of* Fathers and Sons *in terms of Turgenev's use of the garden motif.*]

It has taken the better part of a century to shift the focus of critical attention from the *raznochintsy* and assorted contemporaries whom Turgenev was alleged to have satirized in **Fathers and Sons** to the characters of the novel itself, notably to Bazarov as fictional hero. In recent years, it has even been possible to argue that the oft analyzed death of Bazarov was less a commentary on the character or the times than the culminating point of a tragic plot, carefully devised along the lines of classical tragedy; that, once politics are set aside, the novel turns out to be centered on love; and that the natural environment is far more significant than the political in allowing us to understand the characters. It ought to be possible by now to ignore, if not to challenge, a tacit assumption which runs throughout Turgenev criticism, namely, that his plots are scarcely worth studying since, by his own admission—recorded and consecrated by no less an authority than Henry James—the works are dominated by character and lacking in *architecture* (plot, story or, as James puts it, "composition").

Just as Turgenev was misleading at home in defending his Bazarov against political attacks "from the left and the right," so he was misleading abroad in slighting his own interest in composition before his Western novelist friends who, as he knew and told James, had made composition their main stock in trade. He was obviously much less concerned with form than either James or Flaubert, and he indeed had much less respect for story than Stendhal and Balzac. He took broad license in the genre from Gogol, the English novelists of the eighteenth century, and, of course, Cervantes, with the result that his plots did not quite conform to the realistic canons in vogue by the middle of the nineteenth century. However, and this in fact is the gist of his remarks to James, the very presentation which he allowed to seem archaic brought out the contemporaneity of his characters and their problems. Stylization calls attention to itself: this, of course, is one of the foundations of rhetoric. Besides, Turgenev's stylization tolerated a great range of ironic devices and could give characters a mythic dimension not readily available to a James or a Flaubert. The *manque d'architecture* in his works, which Turgenev confessed, is at the most an apology for frequent reliance on structural devices and conventions. Obviously, it did not always serve him well, but, obviously also, **Fathers and Sons** is a notable exception: here, the uneasy coexistence of the old and the new, the artificial and the "natural" was in perfect accord with the main themes the author had chosen.

The narrative technique of the novel underlines the fact that the problems raised are insoluble, that rifts revealed can be mended "only by time"; indeed, the entire novel culminates in this old adage. And the progression is just as unoriginal: it is insured by the horse-and-carriage method, with an explicitly omniscient narrator holding the reins. The pauses are carefully and obviously contrived. On the very first page, the author invites us to leave Nikolai Kirsanov, "his feet tucked under him," at the posting station of S—. so that he may explain his background and why he is anxiously awaiting the return of his son. On the road between the station and Marino, a few pages later, he stops the horses in scarcely more subtle fashion to provide, in one cart, a match to light Bazarov's pipe and, in the other, relief for Arkady from the lyric effusions of his father. Throughout the novel, Turgenev does not miss an opportunity to create fortuitous interruptions and fortunate intrusions at moments of high drama.

The drama prepared at every changing of the horses and crossing of the roads must be transformed, so the author himself will suggest in the epilogue, into *prostodushnaia komediia,* "artless comedy"—life itself or a play in which the author's strings no longer matter. In such comedy, the naive pursuit of happiness by the characters remaining on stage blends with timeless designs, overwhelming what momentarily stood out and was disturbing because of its alien, fortuitous or fateful appearance. Architecture, indeed, almost in its "real-estate sense," fixes the fathers in time and place within this novel; but *architecture* of a subtle, literary kind fixes the sons as well: within a few chapters, they are reduced to shuttling back and forth between their "estates," and even the detours to the bedlam of the city or to its antipode, the ordered realm of Nikolskoe, merely confirm their confinement to native grounds, two points "in the same district." Turgenev obviously enjoyed and meant for his readers to enjoy every twist and turn along a road which, in the end, had to become the straight and narrow: he measured out every segment in versts as well as in days, counting pauses for drink, noting the landmarks, especially the human landmarks along the way, and he took up as often as possible the challenge of animating them for the measured moment. What could be more contrived and yet more full of life than, at the end of Chapter XX, the portrait-presentation of Arina Vlasyevna, Bazarov's mother, ruling over her household?

Far from allowing "composition" to be secondary to character, as he claimed he had done throughout his works, and far from sacrificing character in this novel to political considerations, as he was accused of doing, Turgenev sacrificed character to literary tradition following established guidelines. From the Western handbook of composition, he had chosen one of the oldest rhetorical *topoi,* the *locus amoenus,* using its variants to evolve his plot, and using its traditional thematic associations to suggest an answer to the contemporary problems he had raised as well as to determine the stature of his main protagonist. An examination of the garden pattern in **Fathers and Sons** shows that Turgenev performed the sacrifice of his characters as ritualistically as possible. At the same time that he was anchoring the novel in reality, ending the action and the composition in "August 1861," he gave the characters mythic dimensions, thus sparing himself the task of passing judgment upon them. The fact that we can nonetheless look upon the novel as a monument of nineteenth-century realism suggests classical guidelines may indeed facilitate passage through the "gate of horn."

One must first note that Bazarov belongs to a special category of protagonists, the tragic protagonist or even the nature hero. He fits there less because of his famous assertion that nature is his "workshop," than because of his repeatedly underlined mysterious bonds with the natural surroundings. He is associated with nature not only by brute strength and passion, but by vaguer, though not necessarily less awesome bonds of sympathy: the world responds to him, follows him, at least so long as he chooses to practice and accept association, that is, throughout the first part of the novel. He is born with a gift for harmony with the creation, yet, as he himself points out to Arkady, it is a gift of limited usefulness: one may derive strength from

nature so long as one yields to it through naïve faith, so long as one is willing to believe in the talismanic virtue of an aspen tree by a clay pit; but, when the magic is lost, one must drift to the inevitable end. Nonetheless, even when Bazarov's bond to nature ceases being a means for coping with the world, his fate remains associated with it by the structure of the novel. He is a nature hero, and, by ironic extension, he is even a nature "god": he appears on the stage in spring (May 1859) to offer the traditional challenge to an existing order already undermined by inner and outer turmoil; he is defeated (except perhaps in the duel with Pavel Kirsanov, the living-dead representative of the old order who, in many respects, is a projection of himself); then, largely through his own acquiescence and even complicity, he dies in August, at the height of summer, a traditional time for the death of gods; in midwinter, six months later, the living celebrate their own survival in a double marriage ceremony that unites the young with the young as well as the "old" with the young, and this is followed by a farewell dinner for the erstwhile antagonist, Pavel Kirsanov, which culminates in a libation offered "To the memory of Bazarov"; finally, in the last lines of the novel which close two full revolutions of the cycle bringing things to the "present," August 1861, it is suggested to us that Bazarov's spirit has passed into the flowers on his grave which tell "of eternal reconciliation and of life without end"—evidently, the irony associated with him throughout the novel, Romantic or circumstantial, has exhausted itself here, on the edge of timelessness where everything is necessarily antithetical to what the living, vital Bazarov had stood for.

Such a glance at Bazarov's career stresses merely one aspect of his presentation, the one most clearly relevant to the current investigation. Other aspects, no less stylized and no less ironic, can be identified to cast him in a Romantic hero role: the dark rebel (with "pride almost Satanic," as Pavel Petrovich points out), the spirit of negation whose deathbed is visited by an ineffectual "angel." The roles are complementary. Just as Turgenev's realism (using the term in an extremely narrow sense of "contemporaneity," with a tingle of "relevance") must emerge from fusion of the traditional and the actual, so the stature of his protagonist is enhanced by triumph over the personal inconsistencies, the social inadequacies, the more-or-less tragic flaws, and the seemingly overwhelming figures with which the novelist associates him and with which he must struggle to seem great. (pp. 243-46)

It might well be argued that if the main goal of Turgenev's stylization was to create god-like heroes for his time, he most nearly reached it in **On the Eve,** with Insarov and Elena. In **Fathers and Sons,** the attempt to reconcile the scientist with the restless seeker, the reformer with the spirit of negation and to reincarnate them in "a figure that was gloomy, wild, huge, half grown out of the ground, powerful, sardonic, honest" could only yield an all too human creature of inconsistencies, a Bazarov [Turgenev in a letter to K. K. Sluchevsky dated 14 April 1862]. The contemporaries were understandably disturbed by him, for they were personally concerned with the issues raised and generally partisan with respect to the solutions proposed; they could ill afford aesthetic distance. Elena, as a

Russian Proserpine who follows a Bulgarian hero into the dark side of spring, was obviously easier to accept than a promising returning native who comes to an ambiguous, yet unquestionably inglorious end in the "study" of a country doctor, his father.

Distance in time, for us, makes it possible to marvel at the attempt and, in particular, at the sustained artistic effort evident in the creation of Bazarov. Not only his career, but the entire plot of the novel is linked with the seasons. Bazarov himself governs only the tragic segment, spring to mid-summer; he is survived, however, by young and old who complete the cycle. The old are forced to resign themselves to tragedy ("Side by side," says the one-eyed Anfisuchka, "they drooped their heads like lambs at noonday"); they have almost nothing left beyond a graveyard plot to tend. But the young inherit the land to be fruitful and to multiply. If one reads the novel without expecting to find a political oracle in its pages, the concluding "cultivate your garden" seems not only an appropriate message, but the only one possible, the only one which the death-transcending cyclical view would tolerate.

Turgenev evidently sought to insure the palatability of the message by structuring the novel in large part on a garden motif urbanely, at times even ironically, presented to his readers. Though Russian soil is considered implicitly, Marino is the garden whose cultivation is topical throughout the novel, the only reasonable gauge of progress and adjustment in the world opened for the readers. Of course, to see a beautiful garden here at all required a sympathetic or proprietary interest, preferably supplemented, as in the case of Nikolai Petrovich and his son Arkady, by a good deal of sentimentality. One notes besides, already in the initial presentation, that both are a little dazzled by the May sun. An objective viewer, like Bazarov, immediately notes that Marino is a very sorry estate, an originally poor design, poorly executed and poorly kept up. Yet there is at the heart of Marino a garden in the conventional sense, a place where nature was not frustrated and hence produced an arbor of acacias and lilacs which, particularly in the spring, is indeed an approximation of paradise. Here Nikolai Petrovich can come to seek release from an overwhelming sense of disjointedness in time, brought home to him by the acrimonious debate between Arkady and Bazarov on the one hand and by his brother Pavel on the other. Here he can review things in what seems like a proper perspective, accommodate uncertain hopes for the future with present sympathies and even friendly shades that rise out of the past. The arbor, in fact, enhances everything that had always appeared to him intrinsically and unquestionably beautiful and good, notably poetry and nature. The setting sun not only creates beauty, but confirms its permanence (through the cycles again); here the past reaches out reassuringly to the present, love conquers time, Nikolai Petrovich's late, beloved Marya waits in the shadow to come to his aid. But the promise of the dark turns out to be Fenichka, paradigm of flesh and blood, "the present" come to inquire about him. At a time of less storm and stress, the sight would have brought Nikolai Petrovich back into the house; in this instance however, it merely seems to prevent absolute communion with nature, leaving him to his uncertainties.

Though unconfirmed, Nikolai Petrovich's view of nature as foundation of permanence and source of beauty is allowed to stand. From the very beginnings of Western literature, the *locus amoenus* and the related myths of Golden Age and Paradise had been the means for expressing precisely this view, not the ground for testing it. The garden is a privileged ground, a place for escape, and we should not be surprised that even Bazarov, for whom it is a mere *locus,* "a workshop," and for whom testing and challenging are a way of life, will turn instinctively (and ironically) to the same arbor for distraction. As a geomorphological concept, the garden is a microcosm of nature, foreshortening its laws to uphold *what ought to be:* the perpetual spring that reigns within does not threaten the full cycle beyond. And yet, as James Justus pointed out [in *"Fathers and Sons:* The Novel as Idyll," *Western Humanities Review,* XV (1961)] in commenting on this scene, even in the realm of *what is,* nature is viewed as idyllic, "as a symbolic system embodying the deepest values of the Fathers."

For Nikolai Petrovich, the Marino arbor is the Romantic version of the *locus amoenus,* a setting where a recalcitrant but sympathetic Nature (the flowers around, the stars above) is called to witness vague fears and longings, and where at the age of forty-four a man may yet shed "causeless tears" in the dark. The setting is equally sympathetic to all. Pavel Petrovich appears, and, having learned the reason for his brother's ghost-like appearance, he "went to the end of the garden, and he too grew thoughtful, and he too raised his eyes towards the heavens. But nothing was reflected in his beautiful dark eyes except the light of the stars. He was not born a romantic, and his fastidiously dry and sensual soul, with its French tinge of misanthropy, was not capable of dreaming. . . ." Pavel Petrovich, Turgenev explained a few pages earlier, is at home in his elegant study, not in the garden, though in the study he cannot conjure up sympathetic influences from the dark either.

On a more general plane, a garden is defined by contrast with the town. Appropriately, the next stage of the journey leads the two friends to the town of X. Yet almost as soon as they arrive, it becomes evident that unlike the idyllic realm of nature, the city in this novel permits no definition of relative positions, offers no basis for valuation. It is a mad world of sham and distortion, a combination of witches' kitchen and *Walpurgisnacht,* in which the seemingly crucial mentor-disciple bond between Arkady and Bazarov, already strained in Marino over Nikolai Petrovich's cello playing, is further undermined by the appearance of two more disciples, Sitnikov and Eudoxia Kukshina, in relation to whom learning as well as instruction appear futile and absurd endeavors. The friendship barely survives, yet out of the mad whirl emerges the alluring figure of Odintsova, and a new purpose is given to the journey, as well as a new stop on their itinerary, Nikolskoe.

It is another garden, the world of order and perfection to which Baudelaire invites in his refrain:

> *Là tout n'est qu'ordre et beauté*
> *Luxe, calme et volupté.*

It is a peculiar kind of voluptuousness though. Nikolskoe is an extension of its mistress, Odintsova, a world in which time has not been escaped or forgotten, but mastered: routines enforced and adhered to by all have made the many seem like one, and, as Turgenev suggests at the beginning of Chapter XII, inability to tell the passage of time is, for man, akin to happiness. (Odintsova's name is probably relevant in this context; in any case, she unites the "dominant twin characteristics" of the enchanted earthly garden: desirability and inaccessibility.) Bazarov, although he is no ordinary mortal and although he raises an occasionally critical question about the place and its occupants, is charmed by Anna Sergeevna and submits to her routines. His father's bailiff, Timofeich, must break into the magic circle like the messenger of the gods to remind him of duties in the real, imperfect world, represented in this case by the aging father and mother longing for his return, rather than by the empire awaiting foundation or the island that must be ruled again. But the bailiff elicits from Bazarov only an assurance that he will return to the main road eventually; his appearance, although it confirms the spell that binds the visitors to Nikolskoe, hardly disturbs the existing routines: at ten o'clock, instead of the normal end of activities for the day, a window is opened in Odintsova's room, but the fresh air that enters stirs little; even when, the next day, Bazarov confesses his passion, the sight of his "almost bestial face" only brings the mistress of Nikolskoe to take firmer hold of herself: she realizes that, "under the influence of various vague emotions, the sense of life passing by, the desire of novelty, she had forced herself to go up to a certain point, forced herself to glance behind it, and had seen behind it not even an abyss, but a void . . . or something hideous." Anna Sergeevna's only human foible is curiosity: it can lead her to play with fire, but not to burn herself. Though she is associated with a long line of enchantresses, beginning with Pavel Kirsanov's sphinx-like princess and ending, no doubt, with Circe, there is ultimately no mystery behind her reserve: she is frigid and too fond of peace and comfort to allow an intruder into her circle for long. It is best suited to heraldic figures like Fifi the wolfhound, Princess Kh——, the dragon aunt, and Porfiri Platonovich: its sterility suggests lifelessness, its opulence is characterized by lack of taste. Those who would live and love here must, like Katya, discover a natural garden within the artificial paradise and draw a private circle about themselves. Those who, like Bazarov, cannot build gardens and do not have the *molü* antidote or a goal beyond, find that even after they "escape" they are unsuited for any other world. Nikolskoe is the garden that reveals the idyll's other side: death.

The classical tradition is by no means exhausted here. About the same distance from Marino, opposite the timeless realm of perfection, Turgenev next takes his protagonists to "a tiny house with a thatched roof," surrounded by a young birch copse, with a "little garden" in the midst of which stands an exiled (retired) Adam, Laertes, or, as he says himself, Cincinnatus (classical figures are very much at home here!), wearing "an Oriental dressing-gown girt round the waist with a pocket-handkerchief," and tilling the soil. Here is the idyll of the good and simple, the *rus amoenum,* the Horation country garden, with even a bench for the old man to philosophize upon at sunset. "I planted every tree myself," he says, "I've fruit, and rasp-

berries, and all kinds of medicinal herbs. However clever you young gentlemen may be, old Paracelsus spoke the holy truth: *in herbis, verbis et lapidibus.* . . ." Within a few hours, on another part of the family estate, Bazarov, for whom this circle is far more constricting than the last one, will argue the opposite philosophy. For his argument, the open field at high noon is better suited than the garden at dawn or dusk. Bazarov has little faith in the virtues of herbs, words, and minerals, and he admits to Arkady that he has lost his faith in the talismanic virtues of the aspen tree growing by the clay pit which had warded off boredom during his childhood. Then, as if to insure that the disciple understands what happens when one no longer believes in a cosmos held together by a tree, he makes a rather elaborate and desperate attempt to rationalize his present inability to generate anything other than "weariness and malice," blending Pascalian isolation, Romantic ennui, Hamletian melancholy, positivist arrogance, and just plain misanthropy. Only his father's timely intrusion upon the scene prevents him from confirming the lesson upon Arkady by force. The truth at midday has obviously little more pedagogic impact and practical value than musings and philosophizings at dawn or dusk in the garden. Before Vassily Ivanovich has a chance to cast the two friends in the roles of Castor and Pollux (apparently just recalling the setting of the Dioscuri hymn of Theocritus, but striking a foreboding note nonetheless), the author himself offers an editorial assessment to mark this turning point in his narrative: "no friendship can long survive such collisions."

Indeed, the initial impetus for a common journey by two friends has been exhausted, and the mentor-disciple bond holds no longer. They remain together just long enough to backtrack to Marino with a very ill-timed detour and unwelcome visit to Nikolskoe. From now on, only Arkady, who still has hope of finding true love in the Nikolskoe garden, will sally forth "before ten days had passed . . . like a young officer riding to battle"; he is delayed by a driver with a taste for liquor, but, at last, the bridge groans under his carriage, an avenue of green ("pruned pines") opens before him onto a vision of pink, Katya; and Anna Sergeevena too is obviously pleased to have him back in her fold.

"Having seen Arkady off with ironical compassion, and given him to understand that he was not in the least deceived as to the real object of his journey, Bazarov shut himself up in complete solitude; he was overtaken by a fever for work." It is, however, a fever that does not keep his mind on frogs for very long. Turgenev returns the irony on him by casting him in an even more conventionally heroic role than that of Arkady. The man who had claimed nature as a mere workshop receives his final humiliation in the garden. Once again it is the arbor at Marino, but this time, in the absence of the imaginative Nikolai Petrovich, the author must supply the trappings himself. We are past the lilac season. The arbor has become the Garden of the Rose; Fenichka is seated in the middle, beside "a whole heap of red and white roses still wet with dew. He said good morning to her." Turgenev spares Bazarov nothing, underlining by means of Fenichka's artlessness the conventionality of each of his "arguments" or ploys. The Lover asks for a rose. "Which will you have—a red or white one?" "Red—and not too large." There is a slight suspense, a sense of danger nearby; then the tryst goes on. The Lover bends down to pick the rose. "A dry cough was heard behind the lilac bushes." Pavel Petrovich or, rather, Envie, "Qui ne rit onques en sa vie / N'onques por riens ne s'esjoi," had stood outside the arbor all along.

Unlike Fenichka, Bazarov can afford no illusions about the role he played; so he "ironically congratulated himself 'on his formal assumption of the part of the gay Lothario,' and went off to his own room." The duel is *de rigueur:* it pits him against a "rival" who is an alter-ego and forces him to play to the end a role he had ridiculed mercilessly. In fact, Turgenev makes him play it even subconsciously, by night; as he tossed in his bed before the duel, "he was harassed by disordered dreams . . . Odintsova kept appearing in them, now she was his mother, and she was followed by a kitten with black whiskers, and this kitten seemed to be Fenichka; then Pavel Petrovich took the shape of a big forest with which he had to fight anyway." *De rigueur* no less is that the duel take place in a *locus amoenus.* Romance has defeated its detractor once again.

In Nikolskoe, on the Arkady side of the now conveniently divided plot, Turgenev has reserved a garden scene in which the various strands of the tradition he employed are brought together. Though high seriousness is being prepared (continuity, hope), irony is not banished; it presides in fact over the allegorization necessary to transmit the traditional message in this contemporary setting, a message contained in fragments of dialogue that pass through a niche reserved for Silence. The stage could not have been more carefully prepared:

> The deceased Odintsov had not liked innovations, but he had tolerated "a certain play of ennobled taste," and had in consequence put up in his garden, between the hothouse and the lake, something like a Greek portico, made of Russian brick. Along the dark wall at the back of this portico or gallery were six niches for statues, which Odintsov had proceeded to order from abroad. These statues were to represent Solitude, Silence, Meditation, Melancholy, Modesty, and Sensibility. One of them, the goddess of Silence, with her finger on her lip, had been sent and put up; but on the very same day some boys on the farm had broken her nose; and though a plasterer of the neighborhood undertook to make her a new nose "twice as good as the old one," Odintsov ordered her to be taken away, and she was still to be seen in the corner of the threshing barn, where she had stood many long years, a source of superstitious terror to the peasant women. The front part of the portico had long been overgrown with thick bushes; only the pediments of the columns could be seen above the dense green. In the portico itself it was cool even at midday. Anna Sergeevna did not like to visit the place ever since she had seen a snake there; but Katya often came and sat on the wide stone seat under one of the niches. Here, in the midst of the shade and coolness, she used to read and work, or to give herself up to that sensation of perfect peace, doubtless known to each of us, the

charm of which consists in the half-unconscious, silent listening to the vast current of life that flows forever both around us and within us.

This meticulous staging carries over into the ensuing episode: in every detail almost there is departure from the preceding garden scenes suggesting a contrast with them. The hour is near noon; we will not be getting absolute truth here, but a fragmentary, unexplained, yet nonetheless crucial message for Arkady and Katya, the representatives of the future, to take out into the real world with them but not to discuss. Truth from beyond, of course, does tend to come garbled, ambiguous, or fragmented. Moreover, in contrast to the dramatic but unequivocal action we just witnessed on the stage of the Marino garden, the portico at Nikolskoe creates two stages and two actions with lacunae due to the topography of the *locus* and to the fact that two of the main actors are moving about while the other two act out of instinctive and unexplained fears. Indeed, if there is a shadowy allegorical presence in this arbor with them, it is Dangier.

The scene originates in convention. Arkady has asked Katya to meet him by the portico, so that he may present to her his new, mature self which no longer seeks ideals beyond reach. The author caps this part of the action with the song of a chaffinch "above his head." Then, as Arkady runs out of words, the voices of Anna Sergeevna and Bazarov come from the other side of the portico. They, of course, are unaware of the presence of the young couple and are trying to explain their former attraction to one another—"curiosity" turned stale. The cause of their misunderstanding, she says, and Bazarov agrees, is that they "had no need of one another," they were too much alike. On the other hand, the love of Arkady for her, just disclosed to Odintsova by Bazarov, intrigues Odintsova. "In such youthful, fresh feeling there is a special charm. . . ." She then offers her interpretation of the young couple's interest in one another ("He is just like a brother with Katya") and her own feelings for Bazarov (". . . I trust you, because in reality you are so good"; which, after appropriate denial, he describes as "laying a wreath of flowers on the head of a corpse"). Obviously, since we could not suspect Odintsova of either lying or deceiving herself, we must conclude from this that the spell of the garden affects even her.

We now return to the main action by the portico. The silence left after the older pair retreated is broken with a fervent declaration of love from Arkady, met with consent and "guileless" tears by Katya. United in the garden they must, of course, marry outside, in the real world.

Were Bazarov a romantic comedy figure, this would be the point to reintegrate him in the "world" of the novel. He is not. So the paths divide once more, the friends part formally to fulfill their respective destinies: the one to become an alien on his native ground and to die from blood poisoning caused by careless dissection; the other, now seconded by a practical wife, to cultivate his garden, Marino, which, by the time of the epilogue, "yields a fairly good income."

The message that came through the portico of Silence and that accompanied the couple on their remaining journey speaks thus vaguely of the threat to young life and the need for commitment and true love to put in the place of idle curiosity or fascination. The epilogues offer more clues and pointers. Complete versions of the message were of course already available to Turgenev's readers in earlier works, notably in Shubin's reflections at the beginning and at the end of *On the Eve,* in Lavretsky's summing-up on the garden bench, and in the author's conclusions about the dragon-fly on the edge of the Forest Belt. In *Fathers and Sons,* Turgenev evidently chose not to be explicit because he had used the oracular mode, words from beyond the portico of silence, but probably also because Bazarov's defeat, which had confirmed the great, permanent laws of nature and society, had made submission to them seem much harder and much less glorious.

Turgenev was obviously sensitive to the traditions he had adopted as bases for his novel. If anything, the action performed against the garden background had demonstrated how easy it is to defeat a nihilist who, by definition, sides with the dark, seeks what is not, and reaches for what lies beyond reach (we recall that the dying Bazarov's main worry is that he will enter "darkness" unconscious). Born for the garden, he cannot rest there, and yet he has no attainable goal beyond it. We are not surprised to find his greatest temptation in Nikolskoe, the enchanted garden, where the show or the promise of ideals fulfilled arrests him for a while and subjects him to the dominion of a power other than his own. All and nothing blend in the enchanted garden: Bazarov is in his own element. But there is a clue here also to the uses of the garden tradition for a mid-nineteenth-century Russian novelist. The tradition offered two clearly distinct strains which we may call in context the "arkadian" and the "bazarian": where the one led to the message and morality of cultivation and to cyclical permanence, the other led to a tragic ending after utter inability to fit the unsorted and overabundant supply to a yet unformulated demand (to rephrase Turgenev's own, correct assessment of his hero's failure with his contemporaries). A. Bartlett Giamatti has told us [in his *The Earthly Paradise and Renaissance Epic,* 1966] that the enchanted garden assumed prominence in the Renaissance because it represented ambiguity and allowed conflicting forces to stand facing each other with no possibility for a reconciliation: it would have been out of place. The conflicts Giamatti situates in the great garden poems of the Renaissance can be made parallel to those which were the contemporary background in Turgenev's novels. Thus, "the conflict between classical heritage and Christian culture" has its counterpart in the conflict between Westernizers and Slavophiles; the conflict "between Love and Duty" persists; for Bazarov, the rival pair "woman and God" would have to be adapted, perhaps by substituting Science for God; the conflict between "illusion and reality" persists as well, tending in this novel to define itself more narrowly in terms of "Romanticism and realism," without much precision in either category.

Finally, it can of course be argued that Turgenev had a personal affinity for the ambiguous, enchanted garden, for exile, and for contempt, one that was to become even stronger in the years following publication of *Fathers and Sons,* allegedly because of its reception. This particular affinity suggests that he spoke the truth when he repeatedly asserted his sympathy for Bazarov. But the sympathy of the author evidently could not save the character from either his fate or his critics. The left and the right had good grounds for condemning the novel from a political point of view, since, by using the garden motif as key to its structure, Turgenev had fallen back upon a device that precluded political commitment, demanded ambiguity, focused hopes and aspirations, but, at the same time, frustrated them with inaccessibility. It was, nonetheless, a device that enhanced the presentation of themes and characters; indeed, when we consider the artistic achievement in *Fathers and Sons,* we must concur with what [Ernst R. Curtius says in his *European Literature and the Latin Middle Ages,* 1963] to sum up the merits of the garden motif: "The finest fruit ripens on espaliers." (pp. 247-55)

> *Alexander Fischler, "The Garden Motif and the Structure of Turgenev's 'Fathers and Sons',"* in Novel: A Forum on Fiction, *Vol. 9, No. 3, Spring, 1976, pp. 243-55.*

Gary R. Jahn   (essay date 1977)

[*In the following essay, Jahn compares pairs of characters in* Fathers and Sons *to illuminate the theme of opposing intellectual and emotional natures. He suggests that the novel begins by assuming generations are in conflict and ends by suggesting the essential similarities between generations.*]

When I. S. Turgenev's *Fathers and Sons* was first published in 1862, Russian intellectual life was marked by open antagonism between generations. Not unnaturally, the majority of those who first read the novel understood its title to be suggestive of that antagonism. Readers of our own time and place, having recently passed through a period of similar bitterness between the generations, easily reach the same conclusion, supported by the sharpness of the polemic between Bazarov and Pavel Petrovich Kirsanov which the novel contains.

The impression that the work concerns a younger generation presenting a united front of opposition to its predecessor becomes, however, weakened and confused as the novel develops. The careful reader will, therefore, be aware of the possibility that the theme of the novel is, instead of being implied at the beginning and confirmed by what follows, developed gradually throughout the work as a whole and made completely apparent only at the end.

The purpose of the present paper is to offer an analysis of the novel's characters and organization in order to illuminate the thematic development which they represent.

Just as the title of the novel suggests its theme, so it also suggests the artistic method by which the theme is to be realized, a comparison between the fathers and the children. Taking the title literally, the reader is confronted with two primary character pairs: the fathers in Nikolay Petrovich Kirsanov and old Bazarov and the sons in Arkady Nikolaevich and Bazarov. By taking the title in the broader sense as indicating a generational rather than a parental and filial comparison, Pavel Petrovich, the uncle of Arkady, may be added to the group of the "fathers." This is clearly justifiable since it is in the relationship between Pavel Petrovich and the younger generation that the antagonism between the generations is most evident.

If we begin with these two groups of characters, the following specific comparisons are immediately suggested: Pavel Petrovich to Bazarov and Arkady, Nikolay Petrovich to Bazarov and Arkady, and old Bazarov to Bazarov and Arkady.

Beyond these comparisons a large group of supplemental comparisons are offered in the novel. These are of two sorts: comparison of the fathers and the sons within rather than across generations and comparison with other characters in the novel, most importantly Mme. Odintsova, Katya, Sitnikov, Kukshina, and the Princess R. (with whom Pavel Petrovich in his youth carried on a destructive love affair). Thus many new comparisons are introduced into the novel: Arkady is compared to Bazarov and Nikolay Petrovich to Pavel Petrovich; Bazarov and Arkady are matched to Mme. Odintsova, Katya, and Sitnikov; Pavel Petrovich is compared to the Princess R., Nikolay Petrovich to Mme. Odintsova, and Mme. Odintsova to Kukshina.

The presentation of these comparisons is effected in such a way that Arkady and Bazarov are the organizational focus of the novel. The novel falls into two main parts; the first is roughly twice the length of the second. In the first part of the novel Arkady and Bazarov journey together to the four main settings of the novel; chapters 1-11 find them at Marino, the estate of Nikolay Petrovich; chapters 12-15 describe their stay in a provincial town; chapters 16-19 are set at Nikolskoe, the estate of Mme. Odintsova; and chapters 20 & 21 cover the visit of the two young men to the home of Bazarov's parents. It is through these visits that comparisons among the characters are made possible. In fact, since the development of action in the traditional sense is almost non-existent in the novel, one may justifiably conclude that the traveling of the two young men from place to place occurs chiefly to provide action and the interaction that make these comparisons possible.

In a transitional chapter (22) Arkady and Bazarov are separated and then throughout the remainder of the novel are studied individually against the same backgrounds before which the reader has already seen them standing together. Chapters 23-24 show Bazarov at Marino, chapters 25-26 present Arkady at Nikolskoe, and chapter 27 describes the last days of Bazarov at home with his mother and father. The novel ends with an epilog (chapter 28) in which the fates of the main characters are described.

In exploring the thematic development of the novel, this paper will be limited to consideration of a restricted number of the character pairs which might be discussed. I have selected the relationships between Nikolay Petrovich and Arkady, Pavel Petrovich and Nikolay Petrovich, Pavel Petrovich and Bazarov, and Arkady and Bazarov for detailed investigation, for two reasons. First, they are the character pairs with the most direct thematic relevance to the title of the novel. Second, they are the four characters who, together with Mme. Odintsova, receive the greatest

amount of attention in the novel (and the role of Mme. Odintsova will be seen to play an important part in the understanding of the relations among them).

The fact about the relationships represented by the four major pairs of characters which is most immediately evident is that the nature of the relationship has in each case reversed itself, by the end of the novel, from what it was in the beginning.

As the novel opens, the relationship between Nikolay Petrovich and Arkady contains elements of strain and uneasiness which are occasioned by Nikolay Petrovich's concern that communication and affection between his son and himself have been impaired by their belonging to generations which are contending against one another. On the other hand, the affection which Arkady feels for his father is blunted by his resolve to follow his mentor Bazarov in the rejection of the sentimental and by an attitude of gratifying condescension toward his father as a representative of the older generation. By the end of the novel this strain in their relations has been completely removed, as shown by their portrayal in the epilog.

The relations between Nikolay Petrovich and his brother Pavel are extremely close at the beginning of the novel. They have resided together at Marino for many years in harmony. In the epilog, however, it is learned that Pavel Petrovich, despite Nikolay's request to the contrary, has departed from Marino to live abroad, thus severing the close relations between them.

The relationship between Pavel Petrovich and Bazarov is cool from their first meeting and rapidly develops into open hostility. By the end of the novel, however, they have come to share what may well be regarded as the same fate in that both have been withdrawn from the action of the novel, Pavel Petrovich in his removal to Germany and Bazarov in death.

Arkady and Bazarov are first presented as fast friends and intellectual comrades, but by the end of the novel they have been separated, not alone by the death of Bazarov but previously by Arkady's rejection of Bazarov as a model.

Thus the relations existing among Bazarov, Arkady, Pavel Petrovich, and Nikolay Petrovich are developed from a position of solidarity within generations to a position of solidarity, for Arkady and Nikolay Petrovich, and of similarity, for Pavel Petrovich and Bazarov, between generations. This reversal of positions has important consequences for understanding the way in which the them of "fathers and sons" is developed in the novel.

The pattern of development by which each of these four relationships is reversed in the novel remains identical. They begin in clarity, elements of ambiguity are introduced, the ambiguities are resolved, and they end in new clarification. The first two stages of the pattern are recounted in chapters 1-21, which recount the travels of Arkady and Bazarov together to the four major settings of the novel. The third stage is accomplished as Arkady and Bazarov revisit separately and respectively Nikolskoe and Marino, and the last stage is reached in chapter 27 (Bazarov's death) and the epilog. This pattern is evident in summaries of the relations among the four main characters.

Nikolay and Arkady. The relations between them are shown to be uneasy during the first visit of Arkady and Bazarov to Marino. The uneasiness is the result of Arkady's attitude of condescension toward his father as portrayed in his disdain of his father's reluctance to reveal the true position of Fenichka in the household, the existence of a half-brother to Arkady, and in the scene where Arkady removes the copy of Pushkin's works from his father's hands and replaces it with Büchner's "Stoff und Kraft" [*sic*]. Nikolay compounds the strain between the two by the temerity of his conduct. Fearing to widen the gap which he detects between his own thoughts and ideals and those of his son, he retreats into a state of passivity from which he emerges only to intervene to prevent the quarrel between Pavel and Bazarov from reaching ugly proportions. Nikolay fears that the close relationship between his son and himself, which he so fervently desires, has become impossible because of the differences inevitably dividing the generations. This fear is clearly expressed in conversation with Pavel:

> "So it seems," Nikolai Petrovich said the same day after dinner to his brother, as he sat in his study, "you and I are behind the times, our days over. Well, well. Perhaps Bazarov is right; but one thing hurts, I confess; I did hope, precisely now, to get on close, intimate terms with Arkady, and it turns out I'm left behind, and he has gone forward, and we can't understand one another."

Turgenev at age 25.

At the same time, elements of ambiguity are present. The first meeting between Nikolay and Arkady brings forth a burst of natural affection and similarity of sentiments between them which suggest the presence of a unifying bond beneath the superficial uneasiness of their relations. These moments are twice repeated, once in the carriage on the way from the station to the manor house and later in the manor house itself. Significantly, each of these scenes is brought to an embarrassed conclusion, in the first instance by Bazarov and in the second by Pavel. In the first instance Arkady's exclamations to his father about the fineness of the air and scenery of his native place are cut short by "a stealthy look behind him" where Bazarov is following in a separate conveyance. Later we read the following:

> Nikolai Petrovich tried to articulate something, tried to get up and open his arms. Arkady flung himself on his neck.
>
> "What's this, embracing again?" sounded the voice of Pavel Petrovich behind them.

The cause of the uneasiness in the relations between Nikolay and Arkady is evidently the result of their consciousness of their membership in different generations interfering with an underlying sense of closeness and affection. The ambiguity is finally resolved when Arkady visits Nikolskoe by himself and, under the influence of his growing affection for Katya, it is implied that he has abandoned his desire to view himself as a replica of Bazarov.

> "My sister was under his influence then, just as you were."
>
> "As I was? Do you find that I've shaken off his influence now?" Katya did not speak.

Later, the rift between the two young men is openly acknowledged by both.

This renunciation of the priority of solidarity among the younger generation clears the way for the ultimate portrait of Nikolay and Arkady as having given way to the sense of affection which unites them. They settle down to live and work together at Marino following the ceremony in which Arkady has married Katya and Nikolay has married Fenichka. The uneasiness between them has disappeared and they have been united in their mutually shared capability of entering into happy, successful, and permanent love relationships.

Pavel and Nikolay. The close bond which unites them at the beginning of the novel is implied to be the result of their common membership in the older generation. Underlying this closeness, however, are differences of several kinds. From the biographical sketches of the two brothers we learn that from their youth they had been of quite different natures: Pavel extroverted and successful, Nikolay retiring and introspective. While Pavel makes a brilliant career in the capital, Nikolay marries beneath himself and retires to a life of contentment in the country. While Pavel fails abjectly in his love for Princess R., Nikolay enjoys exceptional success in his marriage. Furthermore, during their life together in the country Nikolay comes to adopt toward his brother the attitude of pupil to master, attaching great weight to Pavel's advice, striving to conduct himself in a way which Pavel will find acceptable, and feeling guilty when he does not succeed, as in his relationship with Fenichka.

This ambiguity is resolved by Nikolay's forced withdrawal into the concerns of his estate, and by Pavel's withdrawal into himself, especially following the duel with Bazarov. This is symbolized by the hours which he spends lying on the divan in his room with his face turned to its back and culminates in his departure from Marino to live out his life in a self-imposed European exile. Thus, a relationship which began in closeness is disrupted and ends in distance. The closeness with which it began is in the process shown to have been artificial, the result perhaps of a sense of shared misfortune rather than genuine attraction. When genuine and open affection again becomes possible for Nikolay, it is as though there is no longer a place for Pavel at Marino and so he departs.

Pavel and Bazarov. The relations between these two characters seem to be exceptionally clear in the early stages of the novel. Besides the open animosity of their intellectual views, they are separated by their styles of life, their social conduct, and even their manners of speech. Yet, these apparent dissimilarities are themselves ambiguous. The intellectual debate between them is wrongly perceived by Pavel as a contest between an insistence upon a set of principles and an insistence upon a lack of principle (the nihilism of Bazarov). What is in fact the crux of the dispute is the contest between two different sets of principles, each supported by a character fully convinced of the absolute validity of the principles which he holds. In manners, also, they are diametrically opposed: Pavel's reserved formality and icy politeness are contrasted to Bazarov's off-hand and even coarse casualness; Pavel's daintiness at table contrasts with Bazarov's robust appetite. Yet, here too we are dealing with a certain similarity between them in that they both hold to their somewhat exaggerated forms of conduct absolutely. In short, the proverbial similarity between opposites is obliquely suggested. Several other details support this suggestion. Both Bazarov and Pavel Petrovich are marked by a pride which reveals itself in a reluctance to shake hands, for instance. At their arrival at the way station near Marino Arkady and Bazarov are greeted by Nikolay Petrovich and we read:

> Nikolai Petrovich turned around quickly, and going up to a tall man [Bazarov] in a long, loose, rough coat with tassels, who had only just got out of the carriage, he warmly pressed the bared hand, which the latter did not at once hold out to him.

Later we read "Nikolay Petrovich presented him [Pavel Petrovich] to Bazarov; Pavel Petrovich greeted him with a slight inclination of his supple figure, and a slight smile, but he did not give him his hand, and even put it back into his pocket."

However, it is too much to say that the first part of the novel suggests that they are more like than unlike. So far it is clear only that they are similar in the degree to which they uphold their dissimilarity. The resolution of the ambiguity must wait upon further evidence to show that the dissimilarities between them are merely conventional or

accidental and that underlying them is a similarity which is essential.

This evidence is forthcoming in the first visit of Arkady and Bazarov to Nikolskoe and in Bazarov's second visit to Marino. At Nikolskoe Bazarov, to his surprise and chagrin, falls in love with Mme. Odintsova. The mockery which he had earlier heaped upon Pavel for "staking everything on a single card" when "there were so many other fish in the sea," after hearing from Arkady about Pavel's unhappy love affair with the Princess R., now turns upon himself with bitter irony. Indeed, in the materialism of Bazarov and the social brilliance and Casanovian expertise of Pavel there is little room for genuine emotional attraction. Yet both fall victim to love. The circumstances are nearly identical. Both encounter a woman of checkered reputation, both are encouraged by them, fall in love, and then are ultimately rejected by them. Following the termination of the relationship both strive to return to what they had been before (Pavel makes a few new conquests, Bazarov throws himself into feverish scientific work at Marino) and both fail. Pavel accepts his brother's invitation to retire to the country and Bazarov returns to the home of his father, where he dies. In their inability to succeed in love and the effect which this has upon them, the underlying identity between them begins for the first time to supercede their superficial dissimilarities.

The central scene of Bazarov's second visit to Marino is the duel which he fights with Pavel. It has been pointed out that the duel represents the triumph of the younger generation over the older, and this is certainly true. It is doubtful, however, that in the pattern of disintegrating solidarity within generations and increasing similarity between generations which is being developed in the novel that such a resolution of the theme of fathers and sons is here primarily at issue. Other points of significance in the duel are not far to seek.

Bazarov's participation in the duel is in itself exceedingly strange. With his initially consistent rejection of what he terms "romanticism" nothing could be more surprising than his agreeing to submit himself to that epitome of the romantic, the code of the duel. His very participation suggests a weakening of his principles and implies that he has come to regard himself as something other than the self-assured materialist to whom we were introduced at the beginning of the novel.

Pavel's challenge is also surprising, for the main function of the duel was to provide a means of settling disputes between equals. Since he views himself as an aristocrat and Bazarov as a low-born upstart, it would be more in accord with his principles to have beaten Bazarov with the cane, which he carried for precisely that purpose should Bazarov refuse the challenge.

It would seem, in fact, that the challenge is more pertinent to the development of the relations between them than the duel itself and its outcome. In effect, Pavel, in issuing the challenge, implicitly recognizes Bazarov as his equal, and Bazarov in accepting recognizes Pavel as his. Since this equality between them is achieved at the expense of the principles both have previously adhered to so absolutely, it is justifiable to conclude that at this point the dissimilarities between them have to be regarded as accidental and the similarity between them as essential. This conclusion is, of course, reinforced by the ending of the novel where both Pavel and Bazarov have departed, each in his own way, from the sphere of the novel.

Arkady and Bazarov. Like the relations between Pavel and Bazarov, those between Arkady and Bazarov seem eminently clear in the first portion of the novel, but where the relation is one of animosity between Pavel and Bazarov, that between Arkady and Bazarov is one of solidarity. As with the other relationships here discussed, however, ambiguities soon appear.

The first is that the relation between Arkady and Bazarov is not wholly one of identity, for it soon becomes clear that Arkady regards himself as the pupil and Bazarov the master. This is reminiscent of Nikolay's attitude to Pavel and a further similarity is to be seen in Arkady's sense of guilt at not always living up to the example which Bazarov has set for him.

Second, Arkady and Bazarov disagree as to the attitude which it is proper to adopt to the story of Pavel's love affair with Princess R. Arkady cannot bring himself to feel the harshness and scorn which Bazarov expresses, and already here he differs from his "teacher" without the guilt which would seem to be a logical consequence of what is manifestly a compromise from principle in favor of sentiment. Third, the statement which Arkady offers of the principles of the "nihilists" does not meet with the full approval of Bazarov.

> "Allow me, though," began Nikolay Petrovich. "You deny everything, or speaking more precisely, you destroy everything . . . But one must construct too, you know."
>
> "That's not our business now . . . The ground has to be cleared first."
>
> "The present condition of the people requires it," added Arkady with dignity; "we are bound to carry out these requirements, we have no right to yield to the satisfaction of our personal egoism."
>
> This last phrase apparently displeased Bazarov; there was a flavor of philosophy, that is to say, romanticism, about it, for Bazarov called philosophy, too, romanticism, but he did not think it necessary to correct his young disciple.

Despite his displeasure, Bazarov says nothing, leaving the reader to speculate as to why this should be. Perhaps even Bazarov needs an idealistic defense, such as that offered by Arkady, for his materialism, even though it smacks rather strongly of that vague romanticism which he opposes.

The lack of solidarity between Arkady and Bazarov grows stronger as they visit Nikolskoe and compete for the affections of Mme. Odintsova. This phase culminates on the estate of Bazarov's father, where it is only the old man's chance arrival that prevents their coming to blows.

When Arkady visits Nikolskoe alone he abandons himself to his love for Katya and in so doing implicitly abandons also the teaching of his master Katya then leads him to an implied forswearing of the character he had tried to assume in the imitation of his former mentor.

Bazarov, too, comes more and more clearly to recognize the gulf between himself and Arkady. Mme. Odintsova tells him that the two of them are old by comparison with Arkady and Katy and by his silence he seems to agree. He tells Arkady straight out his view of those who follow the leader and of the essential selfishness and lack of idealism of the true materialist, whereas at an earlier opportunity he had refrained.

> Bazarov at first stirred a little in his bed, then pronounced the following: "You're still a fool, my boy, I see. Sitnikovs are indispensable. I—do you understand? I need dolts like him. It's not for the gods to bake bricks, in fact."
>
> "Oho!" Arkady thought to himself, and then in a flash all the fathomless depths of Bazarov's conceit dawned upon him. "Are you and I gods then? At least, you're a god; am not I a dolt then?"
>
> "Yes," repeated Bazarov gloomily; "you're still a fool."

Finally, at his death, Bazarov sends not for Arkady, who began the novel as his closest friend and comrade, but for Mme. Odintsova.

The epilog confirms the break between Arkady and Bazarov. Arkady has abandoned all pretensions to the life of the scientist and social critic and has taken his place beside his father without much thought for Bazarov or his former ideals.

The analysis of the relations among Arkady, Bazarov, Pavel, and Nikolay uniformly suggests that insofar as these relations are the medium through which the theme represented by the title is developed, the reader's perception of the significance of the title is guided through two phases. The reader is first offered what he may, in fact, quite probably be expecting, "fathers and sons" in the sense of "fathers against sons." This initial impression is rendered ambiguous as the novel develops and the work concludes having guided the reader to the opposite, probably unexpected, perception of the meaning of the title: "fathers and sons" in the sense of "fathers united with sons." The novel begins with the assumption that generations are essentially in conflict and ends with the conclusion that generations are essentially the same.

This conclusion opens the way to a yet deeper thematic line in the novel. While the work has proved to be an illustration of the error in dividing human beings arbitrarily by age, it does not suggest that all divisions of people into categories are erroneous. The novel may be approached as material for meditation on the proper categorization of basic human types, a system which is implicitly justified by its being unaffected by the succession of the generations. In short, "fathers and sons" may be taken broadly to include mankind as a whole.

This suggested meaning of the title transfers the attention

of the reader from concern with the process of man's development through time (shown in the novel to be of secondary importance) to concentration on the essential qualities of the human character which, in appearing in successive generations, are suggested to be an essential part of the human condition.

The novel offers a view of humanity as arranged along a linear continuum extending between antinomical extremes. The qualities represented by each of the extremes are various but consistently associated, and the characters in the novel may be thought of as occupying positions along a scale stretching between the extremes.

One of the extremes seems to have collected around it such concepts as will and intellect, the systematic, that which changes; the other is represented by the emotional or sentimental (in a non-pejorative sense), the random, and that which remains the same. All of these are, of course, positive human characteristics and it is typical of Turgenev's pessimism with regard to the achievement of human felicity that the extremes are incompatible with one another. Thus true happiness, represented by a union of all of the positive human characteristics in full degree, is shown to be logically impossible. It is an impossibility that a person could, for instance, possess a full measure of man's potential emotional and intellectual strength simultaneously. As the level of will and intellect is high, that of emotion and sentiment will be low.

The characters of *Fathers and Sons* fit with exquisite balance into the continuum described above. Using just one set of antinomies, intellect and will opposed to emotion and sentiment, the novel shows us in Mme. Odintsova, a character perfectly representative of the intellect and will, the self subordinated completely to an abstraction, in her case a desire for physical comfort, which is, in effect, the same as the materialism espoused by Bazarov. All her arrangements, including her decision not to fall in love with Bazarov, are designed to insure an unbroken state of material comfort. And she succeeds! One need only compare the smooth efficiency and material comfort of Nikolskoe with the ramshackle Marino. Yet, she confesses herself piqued by a desire to look behind the screen which intellect and will have erected before her emotions. She goes so far as to visit the dying Bazarov, at his request, but does not neglect to wear her white gloves.

At the other extreme are Bazarov's parents—especially his mother—characters with no sort of pretensions to intellect, but seeming to be endlessly capable of emotional attachment. Thus, their life after the death of their son is suggested in the epilog, to be spent at his graveside.

Moving toward the intellect from the extreme of emotion the characters of Arkady and his father are encountered. Both of them prove in the course of the novel to be genuinely capable of experiencing emotion in their respective affairs of the heart: Nikolay with his beloved wife Mariya and later with Fenichka, and Arkady with Katya. Yet both are attracted also by the intellect. The reader notes in them a respect for the intellect and a desire to form themselves according to the dictates of the progressive intellectualism of the day. Thus Nikolay's desire to keep

abreast of the intellectual development of his son, his institution of modern reforms on his estate, and his respect for the counsel of his brother. So too Arkady's admiration for Bazarov and his evident desire to pattern his own life after that of this mentor. The novel, however, shows that Arkady and Nikolay really have no place in the sphere to which they aspire. Nikolay's reforms are ineptly carried through and do not bring the desired results, while Arkady ultimately renounces Bazarov and his ways to become involved in just such a life as he had at first opposed. The reason for this failure of aspiration is the same in both cases; neither of them is able to sacrifice the emotional sufficiently to allow them to achieve their intellectual goals. Nikolay lacks the firmness of will to contend with the recalcitrance of his peasants. Arkady falls in love with Katya and, facing a choice between Katya and Bazarov, must choose love over intellect.

Bazarov himself finds a place on the scale of human types which is primarily intellectual but marred by uncontrollable vestige of the emotional. His aspirations to the intellectual extreme are both very clear and nearly realized in the novel. His failure to meet the mark is shown most clearly by his inability to control his emotional response to Mme. Odintsova. It is clearly indicated in the text that this response is something other than acute physical desire.

> His [Bazarov's] blood was on fire as soon as he thought of her; he could easily have mastered his blood, but something else was taking root in him, something he had never admitted, at which he had always jeered, at which all his pride revolted. In his conversations with Anna Sergeyevna he expressed more strongly than ever his calm contempt for everything romantic; but when he was alone, with indignation he recognized the romantic in himself.

Bazarov the materialist considers himself able to control the physical aspect of his response, but he is unable to control that which underlies it, a genuine emotion which is at the same time impermissibly "romantic."

Thus, like Arkady, Bazarov is faced with a choice between his intellectual aspirations and the presence of genuine emotions in his nature. Unlike Arkady, however, he is not able to make a decision. He is close enough to the intellectual extreme that he cannot renounce his aspirations, indeed he considers himself to have achieved his goal rather than to be aspiring to it. At the same time, his emotional response to Mme. Odintsova is so strong that it cannot be denied. He is left in a position from which the only exits are a harmonization of antitheses or death. He is unable to achieve the former, possibly even unaware of the true nature of his difficulty, and so he falls willing victim to the latter. His death, while not perhaps self-inflicted is clearly permitted by him to occur, and the reason that the formerly assured materialist allows himself to suffer this worst of material calamities is best explained in terms of the irresolvable mixture of opposites inherent in the character assigned to him by the author. (pp. 80-90)

Gary R. Jahn, "Character and Theme in 'Fathers and Sons'," in College Literature, *Vol. IV, No. 1, Winter, 1977, pp. 80-91.*

Peter Henry   (essay date 1978)

[*Henry is a Scottish critic and professor of Slavic languages and literature. In the excerpt below, he praises Turgenev as a Realist writer, concluding that, despite its flaws as a historical and social record,* Fathers and Sons *remains "one of the great works of Realism."*]

In his novels and stories Turgenev describes ordinary people who are typical of their times and social class. This stress on normalcy and the subsequent absence of the heroic, the melodramatic, and the exceptional . . . is, of course, a characteristic of all Realist fiction. It is not invalidated by the fact that Turgenev focuses on 'new' men like Rudin, Insarov, and Bazarov, who as representatives of new social types are perfectly credible in the context of their times; they are 'exceptional' in a relative sense only.

Prosper Mérimée [in *Études de Littérature Russe,* 1932] said aptly that Turgenev 'excludes from his works the themes of great crimes, you will find no tragic scenes in them. There are few events in his novels. Their plots are very simple, there is nothing in them that diverges from normal life and this is a consequence of his love of Truth.' As regards *Fathers and Sons* the only point here that has to be refuted is the 'absence of tragic scenes'. The death of Bazarov, described in terms of controlled intensity, is not only deeply moving, but tragic in the precise, Greek sense of the word.

Stated in crude, skeletal form, the typical Turgenevian novel is a short, compact work of some 200 pages, it covers a short time span, involves a small number of characters, and operates within a restricted location. Basically, it is 'a month in the country', where the main action takes place, followed by some sort of epilogue. The narrative is in strict chronological order, with some explanatory biographical digressions. The setting is a Russian country estate, 'a nest of the gentry', and into this static aristocratic microcosm movement is injected by the intrusion of an Outsider—Rudin, Insarov, Bazarov. The Outsider exerts a powerful impact on what is an uncongenial and even hostile social environment, like some bacillus suspended in an alien culture, with the author standing by to observe and record the reactions it sets off. The conflicts and tensions that arise normally include a love relationship between the Outsider and the young heroine, the daughter of the aristocratic household, e.g. Rudin and Natalya. The hero arouses in her a resolve to escape from her idle, claustrophobic world and involve herself in some worthwhile Cause in the outside world, and she sees him as her saviour. The crisis occurs in a confrontation between them, when his inspiring words have to be transformed into decisive action. He fails the test and is exposed as her moral inferior, a fraud and a weakling, and disappears from the scene to wander through life to a futile death. The heroine is left with a legacy of disillusionment and shattered hopes, while for the others life goes on along its pre-ordained course.

Fathers and Sons is a more complex and at the same time more refined variant on this formula. Bazarov is a strong man—perhaps the only successful one in all of Turgenev's novels—who is exposed to the destructive power of love, or rather, the unexpected and unwelcome confrontation with his own sexuality, which disrupts his inner balance and threatens to transform him into a creature of self-doubt. And he comes close to losing control of his life and to losing faith in his mission. It is true that the disturbance of his self-assuredness was set off by an encounter with an intriguing woman, but Odintsova at twenty-eight and widowed is no young Turgenevian virgin on the threshold of life. That role, in diluted form, is shared by secondary characters—Fenichka, Nikolai Petrovich's mistress, and Odintsova's younger sister Katya, whose aspirations are significantly more prosaic and attainable than those of Natalya, Elena, and Liza in the earlier novels. Nonetheless, those who insist that all of Turgenev's novels are love stories are entitled to include *Fathers and Sons* in their list. The love theme is undeniably there, in triplicate even: [Nikolai Petrovich and Fenichka], Arkady and Katya, Bazarov and Odintsova—one could even add Pavel Petrovich with his nostalgic memories of 'Countess R.' and his ambiguous relationship with Fenichka. Thus, at one level, this, too, is a love story. The Russian critic Yu. Aikhenval'd had a point when he described Turgenev's novels as 'parthenocentric.'

But *Fathers and Sons* is more than that. It is an important political novel recording a crucial stage in Russian social history, the emergence of the militant, revolutionary wing of the Russian Intelligentsia. What fascinated the social historian in Turgenev was the appearance of new men and new attitudes in contemporary Russian Society. He had a unique gift for observing and recording these subtle shifts at the very beginning of their occurrence. As a Realist he therefore asks and deserves to be judged on the historical validity, as well as the aesthetic merits, of his portrayal of the succeeding waves of 'new' men: Rudin, the compulsive and eloquent idealist of the 1840s who died on the barricades of Paris of 1848; Lavretsky, the Westerner disillusioned by the failure of that Year of Revolution and returning to the native soil of Russia and the nostalgic dreams of the Slavophile; Insarov, a first attempt at portraying a revolutionary, whom Turgenev felt compelled to make a Bulgarian patriot, precisely because he could not yet detect a Russian prototype and would not rely on imagination alone; and Bazarov, the Russian Nihilist, drawn from contemporary life in the most real sense, about whose veracity Turgenev had doubts, because 'no one else had yet portrayed this type, and I was afraid I was chasing a phantom.' Yet he went ahead, because his intuition convinced him of the crucial importance of the Nihilists and because he had met at least one real-life Nihilist himself. He admitted that he saw Bazarov 'powerfully but not very clearly.' Later, in *Virgin Soil,* he portrayed, less successfully, the Russian Populists of the 1870s. One reason for the relative failure of this novel was that at the time of writing Turgenev had been living abroad for many years and was out of touch with Russian life. This contributed both to the lack of credibility of his Populists as fictional characters and to their rejection by his Russian readers as representatives of the movement. For Turgenev, historical veracity seemed to be a pre-condition for achieving artistic truth.

Turgenev's Realism consists in a picture of reality severely subordinated to his own artistic principles. Real life was not given free rein, there is no rambling documentary narrative, that *bytovaya literatura* that was being poured out in quantity about this time, whether in long descriptive chronicles in the manner of the Natural School, or the factual sketch (*ocherk*) by Gleb Uspensky or other Populists. With him, the principle of selection had a high priority. There is no round-the-clock diary, no indiscriminate camera technique. While his novel has the air of simple and straightforward narrative, he manipulates his material in a number of significant ways that will be discussed below.

The overriding priority in Turgenev's artistic credo was loyalty to his personal vision of reality. Out of his raw material he created a subtly balanced and aesthetically satisfying work of art, subordinated to exacting standards of artistic design and control. This fitted him more closely into the European literary tradition than his greater contemporaries, Tolstoy and Dostoyevsky. A penetrating observer of the human dilemma, he describes his characters with sympathy, understanding, and benevolent irony. But with regard to form, it has been objected that in his hands the novel became too elegantly shaped, too well controlled, too well rounded, that he imposed an impossibly well ordered patterning on the amorphous chaos of real life, his raw material. But his enduring achievement is that, at least in his best works, his conscious artistry has not resulted in artificiality. The illusion of life as conjured up in his novels generally succeeds; when it does, it has an uncontrived, three-dimensional quality and his characters are alive and psychologically convincing within the studied elegance of his artistic form. (pp. 43-6)

It was Turgenev's method to focus on a particular character, sometimes, arguably, on two—Rudin, Liza–Lavretzky, Elena–Insarov, Bazarov. *Fathers and Sons* is not so much a novel about Nihilism, but about a Nihilist, and Bazarov is no mere mouthpiece for an ideology, but a person of flesh and blood, capable of self-contradiction and error. Turgenev's concept of man caused him to endow the 'strong' Bazarov, his 'favourite child', with weaknesses that were seriously to affect his capacity for decisive action and for fulfilling his life purpose.

As in most of his novels, the action grew out of the personalities and interplay of his characters. Turgenev's method was first to develop his main character, then add others, writing out their biographies on separate sheets of paper. Only then did he write a brief summary of the action. In order to get 'inside' his main character, he made up Bazarov's diary and notebook, containing his probable experiences and views. It is therefore very much a planned novel and his characters did not take on an independent existence during the writing—which is important when considering the view that the 'break' in Bazarov in the middle of the novel, as well as his death, are both unexpected and inappropriate, that, as Hertsen had suggested, Turgenev killed off his hero because he did not know what to do with him. Richard Freeborn persuasively argues [in 'Turgenev at Ventnor', *Slavonic and East European Review*, li (1973)] that he may well have started from the death of Bazarov. Turgenev was satisfied that his portrayal of Bazarov was psychologically valid; that the contemporary Radicals refused to see themselves mirrored in him is another matter.

Turgenev once said of his novels that they lacked 'architecture'. The structural pattern of *Fathers and Sons* would cause one to disagree with him. The story is told in strict chronological sequence, with the addition of several biographical digressions. It opens with the arrival of two young men, Arkady and his friend Bazarov, at Maryino, the estate of Arkady's father, Nikolai Petrovich Kirsanov. They have newly graduated from St. Petersburg University and now stay at Maryino for about a fortnight. During this time a personal and ideological antagonism develops between the 'Fathers', represented primarily by Pavel Petrovich, Arkady's uncle who is also living on the estate, and the 'Sons', represented by the radical Bazarov and, to a sharply decreasing extent, by Arkady. Another important member of the Kirsanov household is Fenichka, a former peasant girl who is Nikolai Petrovich's mistress and mother of his baby son. The two young friends pay a visit to the provincial town, where, at the Governor's ball, they meet Anna Sergeyevna Odintsova, the young widow of a rich landowner, who is the heroine of the novel. From here, Arkady and Bazarov visit Odintsova at her estate at Nikolskoye, where they spend another fortnight and Bazarov to his own astonishment and dismay falls in love with Odintsova, while Arkady is attracted to her younger sister Katya. Next they visit the small estate of Bazarov's parents, where they stay only three days and abruptly return to Maryino, calling briefly at Nikolskoye on the way. At Maryino, during Arkady's absence—he has gone to woo his Katya—the conflict between Bazarov and Pavel Petrovich culminates in a duel, in which the latter is slightly injured. Bazarov departs, calls again at Nikolskoye, takes his leave of Odintsova, and returns to his parents. Here he helps his father, a retired army surgeon, in his medical practice. While working in a typhus epidemic among the peasants, Bazarov performs an autopsy, is himself infected and dies.

In all, the action extends over no more than two months. There is an Epilogue, set six months after Bazarov's death, which contains a description of a double wedding (Nikolai Petrovich and Fenichka, Arkady and Katya). The further lives of the other surviving characters are briefly filled in—Pavel Petrovich has emigrated and lives the life of an aristocratic exile in Dresden. Odintsova has married again, this time an able lawyer, 'kind-hearted and as cold as ice', thereby putting the seal on her emotional and social adventures. The final paragraph shows Bazarov's aged parents visiting their son's grave.

Thus the events are confined to four places, each with its own unmistakable identity. The action is broken up into more or less self-contained sections by the travels of Bazarov and Arkady between these places. These provide a simple and convenient device for achieving movement and change in the narrative, while preserving unity and continuity. What further emerges is that the action is not a steady flow of events, but rather a skilfully linked series of episodic 'scenes'.

One is immediately struck by the wonderfully visual quality of Turgenev's work. He describes carefully the natural surroundings of his action, though there are few nature descriptions for their own sakes, few set pieces, such as occur frequently in his other works. The physical setting is done with a fine selective eye for the telling detail, which sometimes distracts attention from the fact that a total picture has in fact not been provided. Such descriptions are regularly broken up and placed strategically in the action at the psychologically right moment, rather than being delivered *in toto* at the first available opportunity. The drive to Maryino in Chapter 3 is a good example of how such a description is built up gradually in small appropriate amounts, without unduly holding up the narrative. Similarly, the description of Nikolskoye is given in several stages, and that of Arkady's and Katya's 'special' place— 'the Grecian portico made in Russian brick'—is delayed until Chapter 26, when it has become emotionally relevant.

The same is true of the characters. One sees them clearly and fully described—their clothing, their facial expression, their stance, their gesturing and the way they move about. Here Turgenev reveals his great powers of observation, or rather his skill in conveying visually the fiction he is creating. He had the ability, so vital for the Realist with his concern with the commonplace, to make the most ordinary and ephemeral character fascinating. This is the possibly over-elaborate description of the steward of Bazarov's parents: 'This Timofeich, a seasoned and astute old man with faded yellow hair, a red weather-beaten face and tiny teardrops in his shrunken eyes had unexpectedly confronted Bazarov, wearing a short coat of greyish-blue cloth belted with a leather thong, and tarred boots'. This person has a temporary importance in that his arrival at Nikolskoye caused a forward movement in the action and he is a visual reminder to Bazarov that he had forgotten about his purpose of going straight to his parents. Timofeich is engaged in conversation long enough for the reader to take in his appearance. At the end of the scene he is seen pulling his cap over his eyes with both hands and getting into his rickety *drozhky*. Timofeich is a minor character, but his image is fixed in the reader's mind and he will recognize him at his next appearance.

Henry James [in *Theory of Fiction*, ed. James E. Miller, Jr., 1972] was the first to draw attention to the visual and dramatic qualities of Turgenev's novels.

> Turgenev might often be a vain demonstrator and a very dull novelist if he were not so constantly careful to be a dramatist. Everything, with him, takes the dramatic form; he is apparently unable to conceive anything independently of it, he has no recognition of unembodied ideas; an idea, with him, is such and such an individual, with such and such a nose and chin, such and such a hat and waistcoat . . . In this way, as we read, we are always looking and listening.

Fathers and Sons is an excellent example of this. It has a basically dramatic, i.e. scenic, structure, consisting, as stated, of a series of visually effective episodes. It has to be admitted that, in making such extensive use of dramatic devices, Turgenev reaches the outer limits of Realist technique. This aspect of Turgenev's art is convincingly discussed in Richard Freeborn's classic study of Turgenev

[*Turgenev: The Novelist's Novelist. A Study,* 1962]. The novel's restricted number of 'foci', as Freeborn puts it, are Maryino, struggling to retain its standing and economic viability, the provincial town, the neat and prosperous Nikolskoye, and the modest, homely, and old-Russian estate of Bazarov's parents. The characters are psychologically and practically related to their location, from which they do not move; if they do, there is an artistic reason for making them appear out of place, like Sitnikov's unwarranted and unwelcome visit to Nikolskoye in Chapter 19.

Frequently Turgenev places his characters in specific settings where their encounters are enacted, occasionally in a group situation, as in the vital discussion over dinner in Chapter 10, the Governor's ball in Chapter 14, or the double wedding in the Epilogue; more commonly in a one-to-one situation, as in the several duologues between Arkady and Bazarov, the conversations between the brothers Kirsanov, Bazarov and Odintsova, Arkady and Katya, etc.

Hence the structural importance of dialogue in the novel, in particular duologues, which mark vital stages in the narrative. In them important ideological and social attitudes are expounded, often in the manner of the Socratic dialogue. Several chapters consist entirely of conversation. But such conversations are not allowed to develop into extended and independent elements divorced from their proper place in the novel. Their content is never allowed to break the overall artistic form. They are generally kept down to manageable proportions and tend not to exceed the confines of a brief chapter. If they do become too long, they are broken off and resumed at a later stage.

Turgenev was at pains to integrate much of his material into such dialogues, even when this created new structural problems. Thus in Chapter 6 Arkady, while talking to Bazarov, prepares to give his uncle's biography, 'which the reader will find in the following chapter'. The action is stopped and the author takes over from Arkady, with an attempt at the end of the chapter to reintegrate this information into the conversation of the two characters: 'So you see, Eugene,' said Arkady, *ending his account* [my italics; the words are omitted in the Signet translation], 'how unfair you were in judging my uncle!' Similarly, the biography of Nikolai Petrovich, already referred to, is inserted into the opening scene of the novel.

Conversations, like most episodes in the novel, do not take place in some visual vacuum. However significant, they never lose their concrete setting and one hears the characters speak—each has his own distinctive vocabulary and intonation—even more, one *sees* them speak. For example, on hearing the word Nihilism for the first time, Pavel Petrovich has a typically melodramatic response: 'he poised his knife in the air with a piece of butter on the tip of the blade and froze into immobility', and only resumed his buttering later, when he had commented that a Nihilist must be 'somebody who respects nothing'. His slightly comical frozen gesture is more eloquent of his distaste for Bazarov and his Nihilism than the actual words he uttered.

Monologues, as distinct from thoughts and emotions briefly summarized by the author, are almost totally absent, although on occasion they are used in the nature of humorous 'asides'. When during his visit to Fenichka in Chapter 8 Pavel Petrovich makes the inevitable comparison between his young nephew and his brother, ' "Whom else should he be like?" Fenichka thought.' Such 'asides' are used to brilliant effect during the duel between Bazarov and Pavel Petrovich. The entire action is seen through Bazarov's eyes and his amused, down-to-earth remarks to himself enhance the ludicrous effect of the confrontation of the two socially very disparate adversaries. Previously, after being detected kissing Fenichka, he had congratulated himself on 'joining the ranks of the gay Lotharios'. Similarly, in a simultaneous aside both Arkady and Katya try to dismiss Odintsova from their minds: 'The thought flashed through his mind: "What's she got to do with it?"—"What's she got to do with it?" [was the thought that] also flashed through her mind'.

The absence of other literary devices like letters and diary entries, beloved of most novelists and dramatists, enhances the illusion that events occur entirely in the present and in the presence of author–narrator and reader. Dispensing with such devices gives the work a compact and severely controlled form.

Yet the analogy with the theatre may be taken further. Turgenev the novelist provides stage directions in the manner of playwright and producer. Not only every 'speaking' character, but even some of the 'walk-on' characters are accorded full visual description, though the method varies according to the standing of the character in the hierarchy of the cast. In addition to the description of Timofeich (above), the beginning of Chapter 4 provides a good example of the description of minor characters. As Nikolai Petrovich, his son and Bazarov arrive at the estate, they are greeted only by a girl of about twelve, followed by a 'lad, very like Peter [who has already been described], wearing a grey livery jacket with white crested buttons'. If the girl is nameless and does not exist visually, the young boy, also nameless, is described entirely in terms of his clothes, emphasizing perhaps that he is not an independent individual, but is the property of Pavel Petrovich.

Essential information about a major character like Pavel Petrovich is provided in a more complex way, being distributed within the narrative in a seemingly random manner. He was mentioned twice in the biography of his brother; Arkady's first question is about his uncle; he is referred to when his servant appears on the porch. He makes a suitably delayed appearance, unnamed at first, and described in terms of his elegant clothes—his dark English suit, fashionable low cravat and patent leather shoes, which emphasize his incongruity on an estate deep in the Russian countryside. His good looks and aristocratic bearing are stressed throughout and even visually he makes a striking contrast with Bazarov, illustrating this latent antipathy between the two ideological and social antagonists that is present from the start. Later, an entire chapter is devoted to his biography (Chapter 8).

These descriptions are remarkable for the amount of detail they provide—there is nothing here resembling a visual cliché. Turgenev is at pains to convey the uniqueness of his character, described in an almost Dickensian manner of emphasizing the odd and the unusual; a few degrees further in this direction would give us a caricature, a danger from which Turgenev's sense of moderation usually saves him. A minor character is given the full visual treatment in one go, as he comes on stage. The staggered method of releasing information, reserved for his important characters, achieves a full portrait without unduly retarding the action. In a similar, apparently casual manner, we are provided with essential socio-economic information during the drive to Maryino.

That nothing whatever is said about Bazarov's past makes him unique in Turgenev's novels, and this is another method of stressing his 'strangeness'. He exists entirely in the present, his personality being gradually revealed in his impact on virtually all other characters, not only his aristocratic opponents, but Fenichka, his parents, peasants, village boys, his briefly loyal acolyte Arkady, and Sitnikov and Kukshina, his spurious sympathizers.

A typically Turgenevan device for heightening the dramatic tension is to create a mood of expectancy, where a character, expected to occupy the centre of the stage, fails to appear or does not have attention focused on him; instead, the 'wrong' person arrives and takes his place. *Fathers and Sons* opens with the father waiting for his son, while it is his unexpected and unknown plebeian companion who is to dominate and disrupt life at Maryino. A further echo of this device occurs in Chapter II. Nikolai Petrovich sits late at night absorbed in loving memories of his dead wife, when he hears the voice of Fenichka, her substitute in the present. The result is an emotional turmoil, the elegaic mood is broken and the normally liberal and gentle Nikolai Petrovich curtly dismisses his mistress, aware of the traces of the feudal lord welling up in him. A similar deception is worked in that initially it had been Arkady and not Bazarov who felt drawn towards Odintsova.

Another dramatic device that Turgenev used in this novel was later to be made famous by Chekhov, that of 'strophe' and 'anti-strophe'. Two separate groups of characters are on stage simultaneously and among one of these a lyrical mood of hopefulness, make-believe, or intimacy builds up. This mood is then rudely, though, it seems, inadvertently, shattered by the other group, their intrusion being timed to occur as the mood reaches its high point. The obvious but by no means only example in *Fathers and Sons* of this device occurs during the drive home in Chapter 3. Arkady and his father are in an intimate, sentimental mood, and as the latter is reciting Pushkin—' "Arkady!", Bazarov shouted from the tarantass. "Will you send some matches over? I've none left to light my pipe with." Nikolai Petrovich fell silent.' Arkady, in imitation of his friend and mentor, also starts smoking a pipe and the acrid smell of cheap tobacco obliterates the mood of intimacy between father and son.

The pairing of characters forms an important element in the structure of *Fathers and Sons*—Arkady and Bazarov, [Nikolai] and Pavel Petrovich, Odintsova and Katya, Bazarov's parents, Sitnikov and Kukshina. In this way he is able to make the characters reveal themselves and render their attitudes and actions comprehensible without having to resort to authorial statements or to use the inner monologue or other literary conventions. By this method he is also able to fix their position within the hierarchy of his characters. The consequent increase in the use of dialogue maintains the dramatic movement of the narrative.

Turgenev develops the simple scheme of pairing by making a number of permutations, as persons basically paired with their 'proper' partner are brought into temporary one-to-one relationships with members of other pairs. An obvious example is Fenichka. Most typically she is shown with her baby son and Dunyasha. But a number of emotional currents emanate from her, and at some stage she attracts all the males in turn and thus is 'paired' with Arkady, Bazarov, and Pavel Petrovich. Each of these encounters is important for the novel: for Arkady the legalization of her status is of primary concern; the antagonism between Bazarov and the Kirsanovs is brought into relief by the trust Fenichka instinctively feels for him, while his amorous impulse towards her provokes the duel between him and Pavel Petrovich; Pavel Petrovich's visits embarrass her, while for him she is a surrogate for his beloved 'Countess R.'—after the duel he says that Fenichka has something in common with her, 'especially the upper part of her face. C'est de la même famille'.

It is a brilliant stroke of irony on Turgenev's part that Bazarov and Pavel Petrovich, so sharply contrasted in every way, are endowed with an essential identity as unsuccessful lovers as they face each other in the duel, consumed by emotions of hopeless love, each aware that he is fighting over a substitute for his real love. In the night before the duel, Bazarov had dreamt of Odintsova, who suggestively enough assumed 'the likeness of his mother and was followed by a kitten with black whiskers; the kitten turned out to be Fenichka'. When Bazarov had injured his opponent, they both felt embarrassed and 'both were aware that they understood each other'.

Here the parallelism is taken further, with the scales weighted in favour of Bazarov. His opponent is described as increasingly absurd, hypocritical, and irrelevant, and this is conveyed partly by the author and more importantly by Fenichka's response to the two men. Both had kissed her—Bazarov on a happy sunny morning in an idyllic setting, and Pavel Petrovich as he lay recovering from his trivial wound. Bazarov had implanted a protracted kiss on her lips, the latter pressed her hand to his lips without kissing it, only sighing feverishly. She had not resented Bazarov's kiss beyond the required display of outraged modesty; Pavel Petrovich's action is feebly disguised as growing out of concern that she love and never leave his brother. She cannot accept his attempt as anything but incredible and abnormal ('Good God, is he having a fit or something?'). Though her role is not as important as Odintsova's, she is both a focal character around whom much of the action revolves and an authority who in a feminine way passes judgement on the three dominant males of the novel—Bazarov, Nikolai Petrovich, and Pavel Petrovich.

If Turgenev wrote his novels in dramatic form—he was, after all, a dramatist, too—it has to be conceded that on occasion he abused the rights of the producer, as when he has sets of characters overhearing each other so that crucial or embarrassing information is passed on 'by accident'. An example of this occurs in Chapter 26 where Arkady is telling Katya of his love for her and they overhear Bazarov and Odintsova discussing them; they also learn that Bazarov and Odintsova agree to terminate their relationship—emotional climax and anti-climax coinciding in too contrived a manner. Several other episodes have a 'stagey' quality, as for example the scene between Bazarov and Fenichka in Chapter 23, with Pavel Petrovich as it were appearing at the back of the stage the very moment Bazarov implants the fatal kiss upon her lips. He appears almost in the manner of the Victorian villain and less as the instrument of retribution.

Other devices that contribute to the structural patterning of the novel include the foreshadowing of events and characters, and the repetition of situations with new meaning and emotional content. Thus Nihilism is expounded on two major occasions, once by Arkady and once by Bazarov. The duel between Pavel Petrovich and Bazarov is preceded by a narrowly avoided duel between Arkady and Bazarov, which is meaningful at both the personal and the ideological levels. It is stressed that Bazarov takes leave of Odintsova in the very room in which he had declared his love for her. There are numerous other examples of this technique.

One can also detect a number of symbols in the novel, generally too well concealed to obtrude unduly. One is the symbol of the crossroads, illustrating the agonizing problem of choice as in Chapter 22, where one road leads to Maryino, and the other to Nikolskoye—Bazarov makes the mistake of choosing the latter; and the parting of the ways of the two friends in Chapter 26. Another, conceivably, is that of the caged bird in Fenichka's room; and, explicitly, that of Pavel Petrovich on his bed after the duel. 'He moistened his brow with eau-de-Cologne and closed his eyes. . . . His handsome, emaciated head lay on the white pillow, like the head of a corpse. . . . Indeed, he was a corpse'. His 'death' represents the dying of his class and his fake agony contrasts with the poignant death of his adversary.

Turgenev employs a sleight-of-hand technique to achieve an easy transition from authorial narrative to dramatic action, changing both tone and direction at the same time. Thus, during his unsuccessful card game with the priest in Chapter 21, Bazarov feels particularly frustrated and when his doting mother offers him yet another drink of wholesome blackcurrant juice, 'Bazarov merely shrugged his shoulders. "No," he said;' but this 'No', while appearing to be addressed to his mother, is addressed to Arkady on the following day. This transition terminates a stagnant emotional situation and replaces it by a vigorous and energetic mood, a prelude to action.

On occasion, he conveys the illusion that the author is a mere observer, as [in Chapter 26]: ' "Of course you are free", Bazarov was heard to say after a while. But the rest was lost, the steps faded away . . . and silence supervened.' He denies himself any authorial omniscience and only rarely gives us definitive statements on his characters' inner motivations. In emotionally crucial situations, his sense of discretion causes him to tread delicately, as when Bazarov and Odintsova take leave of each other. 'Thus spoke Bazarov, and thus spoke Anna Sergeyevna; they both believed they were speaking the truth. Was there truth, the whole truth, in their words? They themselves didn't know, still less does the author' (pp. 48-58).

Fathers and Sons is essentially the story of Bazarov. As a literary hero, he was a new departure among the many 'Superfluous Men' in nineteenth-century Russian fiction—Pushkin's Onegin, Lermontov's Pechorin, Herzen's Beltov, and virtually all of Turgenev's own major characters. The new hero was no attractive, if weak-willed and ineffective young aristocrat, no frustrated and introspective army officer, but a medical student, a Son of the People and committed revolutionary. He dominates the action throughout and is 'on stage' for the greater part of the novel. By the sheer force of his personality, his intellectual power and the cogency of his opinions he exercises an authority over all other characters, who do not exist in a genuinely independent sense outside their reaction to Bazarov. If Odintsova is a magnet, he is a chemical agent that generates strong reactions, with equal powers to repel and to attract.

Turgenev went out of his way to make the antithesis as stark as possible. There is an arresting sense of reality about Bazarov; one is aware of his presence in a more palpable sense than the other characters who, successful, life-like creations though they are, do not live on in the reader's mind to the same extent that he does. Generally he is shown engaged in some physical activity, frequently incongruous in his aristocratic environment. He is out of the house early in the morning, tramps around the countryside collecting frogs, and returns to the house fresh and vigorous as the gentry are just assembling for breakfast. In his room he is cutting up his frogs, peering through his microscope, consulting a scientific manual, making notes. He emanates the smell of cheap tobacco and medicine. As he makes his farewell speech to Arkady in Chapter 26, he is engaged in the prosaic and bizarre activity of stuffing tufts of hay into his suitcase. He is fully alive, self-reliant, tough and firm in his convictions, energetic and active. For him, living is doing, and he embodies the concept of Man, the Worker. He sees the life of the gentry as a pointless charade, and is aware of the absurdity of himself participating in it on their terms, as in the duel, or by falling in love. For him, life is harsh and offers no rewards. As he says to Arkady,

> you were not made for our bitter, harsh, lonely existence. There's no audacity in you, no venom; you've the fire and energy of youth, but that's of no use for our job. Your sort, the gentry, can't get much further than well-bred resignation and well-bred indignation, and that's nothing. The likes of you won't stand up and fight . . . but we insist on fighting. Yes, that's the trouble! Our dust would sting your eyes, our dirt would soil you, . . . unconsciously you admire yourself, you enjoy finding fault with yourself. We're fed up with that.

Here there is an abrupt shift in Bazarov's attitude to his former disciple: 'Let's have some fresh opponents! It's oth-

ers we have to break! You're a nice lad; but you're too soft, a good little liberal gentleman—*et voilà tout,* as my parent would say'. Here, ironically echoing Arkady's words as spokesman for Nihilism earlier in the novel ('We break because we are a force'), Bazarov prophetically sees his former friend as his future enemy, if an insignificant one. 'We want to fight'—but only with an enemy strong and important enough.

Here Bazarov states explicitly the antithesis between himself and the well-bred and self-regarding aristocrats, the revolutionary who fights on aware that he is doomed, both by external circumstances and weaknesses within himself. He perishes 'on the threshold of the future', as Turgenev said of him, while they fade quietly into irrelevance. Both in his life and his death he is physically more real and more vital than those who survive him.

In Bazarov, Turgenev illustrated with remarkable accuracy the essential features of the *Raznochintsy.* 'My grandfather,' he says with pride, 'ploughed the soil.' He flouts the conventions of his aristocratic hosts, horrifying them by the scorn he pours on their life-style and cherished ideals. Turgenev describes his scientific preoccupations with a tinge of irony or incredulity—'he doesn't believe in principles, but does believe in frogs' as Pavel Petrovich sneers. He is impatient of fine talk, of everything he labels 'Romanticism'—Beauty, Art, Love, Sentiment. He does not see the point of explaining his views; when forced to do so, he states his case with a shrug of indifference. He speaks in a series of abrasive, down-to-earth and often incredibly naive aphorisms. For him, Nature is not a temple, but a workshop and man is a workman in it; he looks at the sky only when he sneezes—a tidied-up version of a coarse Russian saying; Raphael's Madonna isn't worth a brass farthing; Pushkin and Schubert are worthless, and so is Logic—you don't need Logic to put a piece of bread in your mouth. The main thing is that two and two makes four ('answered' by Dostoyevsky's Underground Man: 'twice-two-makes-five is also a very nice little thing on occasion'). A decent chemist is worth twenty poets any time. He denies the sanctity and uniqueness of the Individual—people are like trees, there's no sense in studying each one separately. The beautiful Odintsova has such a fine body that he can't wait to get her on the dissecting table.

More important than his anti-romanticism is his rejection of all accepted authority and all general principles, and this includes 'Science as such'. He is self-reliant and filled with arrogance—'the day I meet the man who can hold his own with me, I'll change my opinion of myself'. As he appears in the alien milieu of Maryino, he is strong and defiant and, if his behaviour is put on in part 'pour épater les aristocrates', Turgenev was evidently fascinated, horrified, and puzzled by his literary offspring.

Bazarov attempts to iron out the complexities of human nature—including his own—and is resolved to live by the simplistic formulae of the fanatic, who allows nothing about him, apart from his Cause and his work for it, to be of any consequence. He is 'himself' only as long as he fully identifies with and lives out the role he has created for himself. Therefore, he is initially shown as accepting the inevitability of 'progress' and his own role in promoting it. His views were not unduly sophisticated. Social ills—crimes etc.—could be cured once the diagnosis had been correctly stated; change Society and the distinction between a good man and an evil one will disappear. He is not moved by compassion or any other soft emotion for the Russian peasant; in fact, he is offhand with those he meets and certainly does not take their views seriously. Nor does he expect any gratitude from them. He is even sceptical about the ultimate value of working to improve their conditions. He says to Arkady: 'You said that Russia will reach perfection when every peasant will own a house like that one, and each of us must help towards that end . . . But I've developed a hatred for that 'every peasant', that Philip or Sidor, for whose sake I'm to wear myself to the bone and who won't even thank me for it . . . And why do I need his thanks? All right, so he's going to live in a white cottage and I'll be pushing up daisies. And what happens then?' Here there emerges a strain of the author's own introspective pessimism, which was certainly not typical of the real-life Radicals.

Bazarov, the *Raznochinets,* is at the same time the embodiment of Russian Nihilism. The word was not new. If 'Nihilism' is now defined as 'total negation of everything, total scepticism,' Turgenev popularized it to describe the spirited attitude and ideas of the young generation of the 1860s. As such, the term was badly chosen and one may agree with Venturi [in his *Roots of Revolution,* 1966] and others that it indicates Turgenev's latent disapproval of the 'Sons', whatever he may have said to the contrary. The young radicals believed fanatically in their ideals and were anything but sceptical or apathetic. But the label stuck and throughout the world it became the charismatic synonym for the Russian revolutionary. Turgenev even went to the extent of having one of the characters in the novel give the etymological origin of the word: ' "A Nihilist," said Nikolai Petrovich. "That comes from the Latin *nihil—nothing,* I imagine. The term must signify a man . . . who recognizes nothing?" ' His brother suggests that it is a man 'who respects nothing', which Arkady corrects: 'someone who looks at everything critically. A Nihilist is a person who admits no established authorities, who takes no principle for granted, however much that principle may be revered'.

The historical veracity of Turgenev's hero and the whole social picture he created is of crucial importance when establishing his novel as a work of Realism. His own words are pertinent: 'to reproduce the truth, the reality of life, is the greatest happiness for a writer, even if that truth does not coincide with his own sympathies.'

In deciding how valid Turgenev's portrait of the Nihilist generation is, one may compare Bazarov with D. I. Pisarev, the radical extremist and outstanding representative of Russian Nihilism. Indeed, Pisarev's pronouncements come remarkably close to Bazarov's. In his article 'Realists', with its detailed analysis of Bazarov, Pisarev asserted that Turgenev had come closer to understanding the Nihilists than any of the young Realists had.

Pisarev shared Bazarov's exaggerated expectations of Science as providing the solution to social problems, and shared his rejection of all absolutes ('In the natural sciences, everything is in the fact'). His concept of Revolution was élitist: the 'People' were to him mere 'passive material' and he asserted that the Intelligentsia 'could extract nothing of importance from popular wisdom.' It was a case not of mobilizing the peasants, but of extending the influence of the Intelligentsia—this was 'the alpha and omega of social development'. For Pisarev, the truly historic figure was the 'Exceptional Individual', foreshadowing the men and women of 'The People's Will' of the late 1870s. Bazarov's 'negation' was to him no mere form of iconoclasm, but became the heroic deed, the exposure of falsehood. Like Bazarov, he denied the importance of the Russian tradition and its cultural heritage; he was contemptuous of his own country and argued that Russia must learn from the superior nations of the West.

He was close to Bazarov not only *in re,* but *in modo,* and some of their statements have a similar ring about them. Pisarev said he would rather be a Russian cobbler than a Russian Raphael; the 'temples' of culture were to become 'workshops of human thought.' He could see no difference between 'the great Beethoven,' 'the great Raphael,' and 'the great chef Dussault.' According to Pisarev, 'we are wrong to enter into pathetic relations with Nature, we lose time in wonder, we obfuscate our minds with all sorts of illusory images, in which some claim to discover beauty, others consolation, still others even meaning and logic.'

However, the main body of Russian left-wing opinion angrily denounced Turgenev's work. Turgenev's own ambiguous attitude to his hero did not go unnoticed. Yet, even if some of the details are arguable, he did succeed in defining this new social type, and Bazarov has been perceived as the prototype of the Bolshevik, became the cult figure for generations of young revolutionaries, who adopted his outlook, behaviour, manner of speech and even his type of clothing; and outstanding Russian scientists, like K. A. Timiryazev and I. I. Mechnikov, acknowledged that they modelled themselves on Bazarov. Thus even his dubious scientific method has found vindication.

Turgenev has Bazarov claim that 'there are quite a few of them', and Sitnikov and Kukshina have apparently known him previously and regard him as one of the leaders of the 'movement'. But this does not compensate for the overall impression that Bazarov has no contact with any other Nihilists, is totally isolated, and, as such, is doomed. Turgenev either did not know or did not want to reveal any information about the activities of the radical student circles in St. Petersburg. From the point of historical credibility, this is a major flaw in the portrait of Bazarov. So, too, is his great emotional crisis after his encounter with Odintsova and the resultant break in his character. These are some of the reasons why the Radicals refused to see themselves in Bazarov. But some of their indignation seems to be misplaced; it was even objected that Turgenev's hero loses the game of cards with Father Alexei in Chapter 21.

Although he recommends Büchner's *Stoff und Kraft* to his host, as a mouthpiece for Materialism Bazarov is less than adequate. One reason for this must be Turgenev's uncommitted political outlook; another, his distaste for Chernyshevsky's 'Peasant Socialism'; a third, his artistic restraint that prevented him from indulging in political pamphleteering. Moreover, the editor of *The Russian Messenger* insisted on reducing the 'apotheosis' of the New Men, and major cuts were made in the text as a result. This is why Pavel Petrovich's statement: 'This Materialism you are preaching . . .' is left suspended in a vacuum—nowhere does Bazarov preach Materialism in a comprehensive way. He does not go beyond uttering a number of telling aphorisms.

These are some of the aspects in which Bazarov is deficient as a portrait of the 'Sons'. But there is another dimension to his personality. In the company of the ordinary men and women around him he is a brooding, alien presence, mocking their trivial deeds and aspirations. Turgenev visualized him as 'a large figure, gloomy and savage, only half-emerging from the soil, powerful, enraged and honest, and yet doomed.' This is a prose equivalent of Milton's Satan, Lermontov's Demon, the Spirit of Negation and Defiance, the Destroyer. As Maurice Baring, somewhat overstating his case [in his *Landmarks in Russian Literature,* 1910], had put it: 'Bazarov is the Lucifer type that recurs again and again in Russian history and fiction. . . . He is the man who denies; . . . he believes in nothing; he bows to nothing; he can break, but cannot bend; he does break, and that is the tragedy, but, breaking, he retains his invincible pride.' Odintsova senses this 'strangeness' in him, is fascinated and frightened by it, as when he declared his love for her and the passion that was struggling within him was 'not unlike rage and perhaps akin to it'; or when she recalled with a shudder the 'almost animal-like expression on his face' as he had advanced on her. She is incredulous when he describes himself as 'a future provincial doctor'—so very different from Turgenev's other young lovers, and closer perhaps to the 'Possessed' in Dostoevsky's novel. We see this demonic aspect in him when, aware of the passion arising in him, 'he went into the forest and prowled around with large strides, breaking branches that barred his way and cursing her and himself under his breath'.

Even while fully committed to the Cause he was serving he was also aware of the vanity of human existence and aspirations, including his own, and this can go some way to serve as a link between the two aspects of his personality—Bazarov the purposeful Nihilist and Bazarov who realizes that he, too, is doomed to oblivion, having achieved nothing; that he, too, is the 'insignificant creature of a single day' [Freeborn, *Turgenev: The Novelist's Novelist*]. And the revolutionary with his programme for social change gives way to the human being, infinitesimal in the vast perspective of eternity, indistinguishable from his fellow men, as he, too, completes his pre-ordained cycle and becomes subject to eternal, unalterable laws. Those whom the gods love, die young, and this Angry Young Man is spared the humiliation of the steady decline of ageing (or is it maturing?), the inevitable betrayal, as Turgenev viewed it, of the ideals of youth. Bazarov's early death is therefore an act of mercy, an attempt to preserve his image undamaged by forces that have already sent out their warning shots.

This appears to be Turgenev's view of the tragic destiny of men who sacrifice themselves in the service of humanity. And his way of stating his ultimate affection for, and compassion with, his hero, 'the passionate, sinful and rebellious heart' is shown in the closing lines of the novel, a moving, if incongruous, requiem in terms of 'all-embracing peace, the vast repose of "indifferent" Nature, of everlasting reconciliation and life without end.'

After Bazarov, the person of whom Turgenev gave the most complete inner picture is Odintsova. She emerges as a mature, but complex and enigmatic woman, radiant and triumphant in her femininity, the type of woman that intrigued Turgenev, though she does not fully belong in the gallery of dangerous and strong-willed *femmes fatales,* like Polozova in **Torrents of Spring** or Ratmirova in **Smoke** who destroyed the amorous bliss of young lovers by force of personality and their overwhelming sexuality. There are several extensive character studies of Odintsova, notably in Chapters 15 and 16, in terms of her biography and social identity—her first marriage, her wealth, and success as mistress of a prosperous estate; her personality is also conveyed in the several descriptions of her estate, that veritable 'Calypso's Island'. She is the only person to measure up to Bazarov and understand him in depth, and she alone could destroy him. She relishes her power over men, but also over her younger sister—the latent tensions between the two women are conveyed with much insight and humour. But her love of calm and order triumphs over the curiosity that Bazarov had aroused in her. 'Bazarov is evidently right—curiosity, mere curiosity, love for peace and quiet, and egoism'. Earlier, the author had explained that her conflicting emotions had brought her to the brink; 'and as she peered beyond it, she saw no abyss but only a void . . . a shapeless chaos'. Thus she reveals herself as a 'necrophile', to use E. Fromm's term for describing those who need to impose a pattern of order and tidiness upon the chaotic variety of life, which the 'biophile' readily accepts. Turgenev referred to her as representing 'those idle, dreamy, curious and cold epicurean lady aristocrats' and after her flirtation with a dangerous relationship ('stroking a wolf's fur, hoping it won't bite') she returns to 'lying on velvet, washed and dainty' [Turgenev, in a letter to K. K. Sluchevsky dated 14 April 1862]. If she is a social and psychological type she is no stereotype, but a successful portrait of a lady who loses none of her mystery for being revealed. Odintsova is a minor masterpiece of Turgenev's discreet, controlled technique of psychological realism.

A Realist writer is commonly expected to produce 'objective' pictures of reality, with his own bias reduced to a minimum, and Turgenev is no exception. But no writer could wholly surrender his interpretation of the reality he views, or his attitude to the characters he has created. While in this novel, Turgenev does stay outside the action to a remarkable degree, his bias is unmistakable, for example, in his portrayal of Pavel Petrovich, whom he treats with more than a touch of satire. He admitted [in his letter to Sluchevsky] that he had 'sinned against artistic truth' by endowing him with those more extravagant absurdities—his anglomania, the fez he wears deep in the Russian countryside, the cocoa he drinks, his perfumed whiskers, his affected rhetoric, his life as a *poseur,* his pathetic behaviour during and after the duel, the travesty of a deathbed benediction, the ashtray shaped like a peasant's bast shoe on his desk in Dresden. Yet he did not go so far as to make him grotesque. 'My aesthetic sense caused me to take *good* representatives of the gentry, in order to prove my point: if the cream is bad, what would the milk be like?' He does not seem to dislike Pavel Petrovich. Kukshina and Sitnikov, however, emerge as caricatures of the emancipated progressives, camp-followers that bring noble causes into disrepute. There is a strong sense of distaste both in Bazarov and the author for this 'new woman' with her unsavoury habits and her borrowed and vulgarized 'ideas'. Sitnikov is the incarnation of *poshlost'*, that untranslatable Russian vice that includes ostentatious vulgarity, lack of ideals, preoccupation with material things (Nabokov's rendering as 'Poshlust' [in his *Nikolay Gogol*, 1944] comes close to conveying this). Turgenev does not spare the 'young progressive' and reintroduces him almost gratuitously in Chapter 19 as the 'appearance of *poshlost'*' merely to pour all his sarcasm on him.

He clearly sympathizes with Nikolai Petrovich and Arkady, whereas his attitude to his hero is ambiguous, as shown above. Though he asserted that Bazarov was his 'favourite child' he was clearly upset by his uncouth manners and his contempt for art, which he dwells on with a dismayed fascination and bewilderment. He watches and listens to him, disagrees with and disapproves of him but is incapable of pronouncing judgement on him. At the same time he is aware that he had created a titan, sensing that this is 'some strange pendant to Pugachov'. Critics have asserted that he only began to feel for Bazarov when he had him fall victim to love. This is an oversimplification, and yet the change in Bazarov from then onwards— his growing self-doubt, his pessimism and his futile death—illustrates the author's ambivalent attitude to him. Turgenev was more at home with failures, idealists who have lost faith in their ideals and Bazarov comes dangerously close to ending his life as another 'superfluous man'. This may have been Turgenev's way of redeeming his hero and he was dismayed to find that his readers appeared to deny Bazarov 'the right to idealization'.

The publication of **Fathers and Sons** produced what was probably the greatest *skandal* in the history of Russian literature. The Radical Left was outraged by the figure of Bazarov, whom they regarded as a spiteful caricature of themselves and denounced Turgenev in unambiguous terms as a traitor to the cause of freedom and progress. A long review of the novel [by M. A. Antonovich] appeared in *The Contemporary,* entitled 'Asmodeus of Our Times' which 'passed a sort of legally reasoned sentence on the author for having falsified reality' [Venturi, *Roots of Revolution*]. In official quarters the work was received with smug satisfaction: Turgenev had poured ridicule on the 'Sons' in this unflattering portrait and had, moreover, coined a useful label to brand them with. Turgenev was bewildered and dismayed by this reception of his novel, forgetting that in Russia in the heat of literary and ideological controversy views expressed by the fictional characters are too often taken as those of the author, and objectivity and neutrality may be regarded as reactionary.

The action of Turgenev's novel takes place in the agree-

able surroundings of a Russian estate; his characters are attractive and likeable persons, except for Kukshina and Sitnikov. The social picture is confined to landowners, though the contrast between the Kirsanovs and the Bazarovs shows how wide and varied the range of that class was. One gets a picture of the household, including the domestic staff, but the action only once moves into the servants' quarters, significantly in the Bazarov home. There is no full picture of the village, the peasants are only encountered in the open, as animated figures in the landscape or as representing problems that Nikolai Petrovich has to cope with. Only Bazarov has any personal encounters with them. The rural setting is a backcloth to the human action and, apart from the *rapport* between Nature and the moods of a few of the characters, especially Arkady's and his cello-playing father, it is not integrated with their lives in any practical sense; again the Bazarov family is the exception. Turgenev's social background and artistic temperament prevented him from writing broad panoramic chronicles of country life, and the absence of the ugly, the sordid, and low-class life necessarily reduces the stature of his novel as a social document of the times.

Yet what in social terms endows the novel with tragic dimensions is not merely Bazarov's death and instant oblivion, but the fact that this parasitical life-style will go on essentially unaltered, regardless of Alexander II's 'Great Reforms'. Turgenev implies that the old order continues, its adherents, like Pavel Petrovich, being driven to disguise their corroding boredom by indulging in futile pursuits and ludicrous poses, while Arkady, the young enthusiast, gradually lapses into the social attitudes of the 'Fathers'. And their 'liberalism' is shown in neat little touches to be little more than skin-deep.

The long-overdue Emancipation of the Serfs—four-fifths of the population—finally took place in March 1861. But this did not relieve social tension. On the contrary, in 1861-2 the political situation became acute. There was mounting unrest both in the countryside and in the major cities. Some of the peasant disturbances were put down by force of arms. In St. Petersburg a number of revolutionary proclamations were published and student activity intensified; some 200 were imprisoned in the Peter and Paul Fortress and elsewhere. In 1862 Chernyshevsky and Pisarev were arrested and their journals, *The Contemporary* and *The Russian Word,* were temporarily closed down (they were finally suppressed in 1866); censorship became more severe than ever. The government had succeeded in gaining some public support by attributing to the Radicals, probably falsely, responsibility for several major fires that had broken out mysteriously in the capital. Within a few years, a number of 'anti-Nihilist' novels had appeared, culminating in Dostoyevsky's *The Possessed* (1871) and the real-life Bazarovs were more and more discredited.

This wider political dimension is signally absent from Turgenev's work. The Act of Emancipation is barely referred to, and barely affects the lives of his characters: in the Epilogue, we are told that Nikolai Petrovich became very busy, travelling around the countryside delivering speeches, but this and a steady improvement in the affairs of his estate is about all, nothing seems to have changed. This despite the fact that Turgenev was working on the novel both during and after March 1861.

In spite of such limitations, the novel is an important historical record. In the Soviet Union *Fathers and Sons* is firmly established as one of the great classics, read and discussed by every schoolchild. Elsewhere, commentators will have us believe, Turgenev's novels are being forgotten. How true is this? It has been asserted that the ideological aspect of the novel has long ceased to interest the modern reader. Such views are unduly complacent, for Bazarov, far from being dead and forgotten, has his descendants today, not only in the Soviet Union but among the Dissident Left in Western Europe and America, in whose statements many of his blunt and aggressive aphorisms are echoed with impressive accuracy. As the controversial Soviet Jewish poet Naum Korzhavin told a Western audience with some feeling: 'Don't tell us again that Russia is always behind the West, is always learning from it. Your young people are now "discovering" some social ideals and are fighting to realize them in life, and you think this is new and original. Here in Russia we went through all this a hundred years ago. Go and read *Fathers and Sons*— it's all there. Bazarov, you know.' This was in 1969, the year after the student revolts in France and elsewhere.

The Nihilist programme was stated more fully and more accurately by Chernyshevsky and others, but it was Turgenev who made it available in palatable and accessible form. The current revival of interest in *Fathers and Sons* has been amply demonstrated. . . . Is it only read by aesthetic highbrows for the beauty of the language and lyrical evocations of the Russian countryside? The ideological battles have not died down. Turgenev may have considered the matter closed, but there have been and will continue to be groups of Angry Young Men determined to pull down the existing edifice and clear the ground for a transformed Society. History proved Turgenev's scepticism wrong. The Russian Radicals, far from being doomed to oblivion, were the spearhead of the movement that culminated in the October Revolution. As Isaiah Berlin persuasively argues [in his *Fathers and Children*, 1972], 'it's the Bazarovs who have won'.

Radical criticism holds that every literary work is ultimately a political statement; every novel is a political novel. Even Turgenev, liberal gradualist that he was, stated [in his letter to Sluchevsky] that 'the entire novel [*Fathers and Sons*] was directed against the gentry as the leading class.' Indeed, *Fathers and Sons* is a political novel written by a political sceptic of scrupulous integrity who was only too aware of the complexity of the saving truth and the inefficacy of simple solutions. The most important and most painful lesson that Turgenev has demonstrated—he was experiencing it in his own life—is that the most bitter fight is not between the extreme Right and the extreme Left, but between political cousins; and in this sense the parting of the two young friends is a moment of greater historical symbolism than the duel between Bazarov and Pavel Petrovich. It is the turning in upon each other of Young Liberal and Young Socialist and foreshadows the bitter strife between Populist and Marxist, Menshevik and Bolshevik, Social Democrat and Communist—

all claiming equally to champion the causes of Freedom, Equality, and Justice.

This is but one indication that *Fathers and Sons* is a statement of enduring universal force. What Turgenev has shown in this human drama is at some point true of all mankind—the clash of generations, the power of love, the transience of friendships, the pull of social origin and convention, 'the triumph,' as Eugène-Melchior de Vogüé, the first serious Western student of the Russian novel, had put it [in his *Le Roman russe,* 1886], 'of the group over the individual, of the crowd over the hero'; and the intervention in our lives of indefinable and uncontrollable forces. If Turgenev's novel is technically not 'a slice of life', it is much more than 'a summer in the country'; and his characters come alive as unique individuals, while also being recognizable both as perennial human types and as representatives of a particular period in Russian history. As such, they are 'realistic' in the full sense of the term. The fact that Turgenev manipulated his material according to his own artistic principles, that he kept faith with his own vision of reality and political outlook, and that his work is not without its defects and limitations as a historical and social record, in no way reduces its standing as one of the great works of Realism. (pp. 60-72)

Peter Henry, "I. S. Turgenev: 'Fathers and Sons' (1862)," in The Monster in the Mirror: Studies in Nineteenth-Century Realism, *edited by D. A. Williams, Oxford University Press, 1978, pp. 40-74.*

D. S. Mirsky on *Fathers and Sons* and Bazarov:

The best of the novels and ultimately the most important of Turgénev's works is *Fathers and Sons,* one of the greatest novels of the nineteenth century. Here Turgénev triumphantly solved two tasks that he had been attempting to solve: to create a living masculine character not based on introspection, and to overcome the contradiction between the imaginative and the social theme. *Fathers and Sons* is Turgénev's only novel where the social problem is distilled without residue into art, and leaves no bits of undigested journalism sticking out. Here the delicate and poetic narrative art of Turgénev reaches its perfection, and Bazárov is the only one of Turgénev's men who is worthy to stand by the side of his women. But nowhere perhaps does the essential debility and feminineness of his genius come out more clearly than in this, the best of his novels. Bazárov is a strong man, but he is painted with admiration and wonder by one to whom a strong man is something abnormal. Turgénev is incapable of making his hero triumph, and to spare him the inadequate treatment that would have been his lot in the case of success, he lets him die, not from any natural development of the nature of the subject, but by the blind decree of fate. For fate, blind chance, crass casualty, presides over Turgénev's universe as it does over Hardy's, but Turgénev's people submit to it with passive resignation. Even the heroic Bazárov dies as resigned as a flower in the field, with silent courage but without protest.

D. S. Mirsky, in his A History of Russian Literature from Its Beginnings to 1900, *edited by Francis J. Whitfield, Vintage Books, 1958.*

Victor Ripp (essay date 1980)

[*In the excerpt below, Ripp examines* Fathers and Sons *in the context of the nineteenth-century Russian social reform movement.*]

The Emancipation Act was signed by Alexander II on February 19, 1861, a little less than five years after he had openly declared his support for the abolition of serfdom. The publication of the new act was delayed until March 5, which was an ecclesiastical holiday, in the hope that religious feeling would temper any anger or disappointment. In the event, the public was mainly confused. That was partly because the Editing Committee that wrote the final version had allowed the Metropolitan of Moscow to introduce inspirational language into some of the passages, obscuring the legal issues without making anyone feel better. But understanding the act would have been difficult in any case. In its effort to please all factions, the Editing Committee produced an immensely complicated document. The rules governing land settlements and the continued obligations of the peasantry varied from region to region, depending on local conditions. More important, the Editing Committee had to meet the contradictory purposes of the government: a liberalized economic system, which meant a mobile labor force, and a restrictive political system, which meant that the labor force should not be allowed to develop into a rootless proletariat.

Despite the many confusing resolutions, some of which were not cleared up for decades, one thing about the Emancipation Act was clear: it was not the momentous document that had been dreamed of five years before. Though it abolished personal ownership of the peasant by the landlord, the act perpetuated the less visible injustices of the old system, using both economic leverage and administrative control to keep the peasant oppressed. Existing social arrangements were pushed about a bit but not significantly altered. (pp. 187-88)

Turgenev wrote **Fathers and Sons,** his greatest novel, while directly under the influence of the crisis caused by the Emancipation Act. His first reference to the project that became the novel was in the summer of 1860, and he finished writing in July or August 1861. When the book appeared, it immediately provoked bitter controversy. Because Turgenev had created characters that could be placed on a recognizable political spectrum, every one of their false steps seems an ideological judgment. What is remarkable, however, is that **Fathers and Sons** was attacked from all sides. Liberals, radicals, and conservatives alike found the book politically deficient, not merely in a few details but at its heart.

Contemporaries mainly argued about one question, ending with widely divergent conclusions: was Turgenev too respectful or too scornful of his hero, the radical medical student Bazarov? Several years after the height of the controversy, Turgenev stated that he endorsed his character's views on all matters except art, which Bazarov disdains. It is certain that even if Turgenev had declared his position earlier, debate would not have cooled; the proof is that the effort to define Turgenev's attitude toward Bazarov persists to the present day.

It should be obvious that the degree of sympathy that Turgenev feels for his hero was always an irrelevant issue. If that were all that was at stake, radicals who disliked the book could have dismissed Turgenev's treatment as prejudiced, while dissatisfied liberals could have declared that what they perceived as an overly respectful characterization of Bazarov was Turgenev's attempt to curry favor with the younger generation. And that would have been the end of it. But even after such judgments were made, the controversy continued. In fact, the fascination of **Fathers and Sons** is the result of Turgenev's having made his hero more than a spokesman—or even a vivid exemplar—of a narrow ideological position. On the most important level of the book, Bazarov represents all of *obshchestvo,* liberals as well as radicals. [In his Preface, Ripp defines *obshchestvo* (literally, "society,") as "an alliance of individuals holding diverse political beliefs but united in their resistance to the encroaching influence of the central government."] What made **Fathers and Sons** a scandal is that Turgenev shows that Bazarov's very virtues contain the seeds of his destruction. **Fathers and Sons** is simultaneously an endorsement of some of *obshchestvo's* most cherished beliefs and a proof of their illogicality.

The opening scene, which depicts Arkadii Kirsanov returning home from the university, bringing his friend and mentor Bazarov with him, shows that Turgenev intends to use the same narrative structure as in his previous novels. The main action is set on a provincial estate; contemporary social and political forces will be only implied, not directly described. In **Fathers and Sons,** however, these forces clearly threaten the stability of the enclave as never before. The time is announced in the second sentence of the book: it is the spring of 1859, and the emancipation of the serfs, with all its uncertain consequences, is only two years ahead. In the short space that it takes to describe how Arkadii's father meets the two young men at the posting station and escorts them back to the manor house, Turgenev manages to suggest a world on the brink of extreme change. Even the seemingly prosaic exchange between Nikolai Kirsanov and his valet, as they await the arrival of the coach, becomes permeated by ambiguity. The valet, like all the other characters, moves in a society where traditional relationships have been put into question:

> The valet, in whom everything—his single turquoise earring, his pomaded hair of various shades and his studied gestures—announced him as a representative of a modern and more perfect age, stared superciliously down the road and deigned to reply, "No sir, there's no sign of them."

One social order is dying, but a new one has not yet been born. Nikolai thinks of himself as a progressive and liberal, and he has granted his peasants improved working and financial conditions before the emancipation would require it. Nevertheless old attitudes and interests die hard. Nikolai's tone when he speaks of the peasants does not altogether hide his sense of superiority, and he is not above assuring himself of a profit at their expense: he has astutely sold off in advance the timber from land that will shortly pass to the peasants' possession. For their part, the peasants regard their new lot with great uncertainty. They treat all the concessions Nikolai has made them, both altruistic and self-serving ones, with suspicion. At times they seem on the verge of open rebellion: horses are being stolen, ploughs sabotaged, rents left unpaid.

Bazarov is a political animal, highly sensitive to shifting balances of power, and he is eager to channel the peasants' resentment; but he is not a blind ideologue. Turgenev immediately establishes his shrewdness about human relations. When Arkadii's father begins to insinuate traditional values by reciting Pushkin's poetry and rhapsodizing about nature, Bazarov breaks the sentimental mood by abruptly asking for cigarettes; he does not itemize an abstract program but rather shows its correlatives in everyday life.

Throughout the book Bazarov absorbs politics into psychology. He relies on the aura of his presence to persuade others; his politics are an overflow of who he is. He says to Arkadii, "As to the times, why should I depend on them? Much better that they should depend on me." In fact, Bazarov's imperious claim of self-sufficiency is indisputable; but it proves to be the very quality that leads to disaster. Turgenev neatly illustrates the ambiguous consequences of self-sufficiency by contrasting two of Bazarov's encounters.

Bazarov's argument with Arkadii's uncle Pavel—a "battle royal," Turgenev calls it—range over a wide variety of subjects, from art to philosophy to politics. While Pavel argues for an ameliorative humanism, Bazarov accepts only practical activity. He even believes that science is an abstract category that makes no sense until filled by precise experiments. For all the ideological points that get made, however, the argument is primarily a psychological confrontation. It is Bazarov's ability fully to comprehend Pavel's attitude that gives him the upper hand. He never bothers to refute Pavel point-by-point; indeed, he always appears on the verge of giving up the argument altogether in order to pursue tasks he insinuates are infinitely more rewarding, such as dissecting frogs. Pavel, who guesses Bazarov's opinion of him, can only sputter angrily, like a punctilious duelist who finds his opponent has abruptly decided rules governing the confrontation are ridiculous.

Pavel insults Bazarov, calling him a Mongol who does not understand civilization, but the charge is inaccurate. It is significant that Bazarov always leaves it to others to describe his position as "nihilism." Though he favors the destruction of much of contemporary Russian life, he is no unthinking destroyer: he has a precise knowledge of the attitudes he wants to abolish. At one point, Bazarov observes to Arkadii, "Nature is not a temple, but a workshop, and man is a worker in it." The remark expresses an extreme form of positivism, a disdain of beauty in favor of science. But its epigrammatic style—and Bazarov talks in epigrams continually—has the gracefulness of poetry. Indeed, no character in *Fathers and Sons* except Bazarov could have made the point so neatly. In general, Bazarov has worked through the positions he opposes and comes

out the other side. He resolves the dilemmas that hobbled Russians in the middle of the nineteenth century by the sheer force of his personality.

By the end of the book, Bazarov has fallen from the lofty position he occupied in his confrontation with Pavel, brought low by his love for the beautiful widow Anna Sergeevna Odintsova. But, as in *On the Eve,* Turgenev does not portray love as a blank, elemental force: the relationship between Bazarov and Odintsova is a vehicle for exposing the traps that lie in wait for someone who believes in the philosophy that self-sufficiency will carry the day. They become acquainted when Bazarov visits Odintsova's estate. The "excellent, wonderfully furnished house, with a lovely garden and conservatories," "not far from a yellow stone church with a green roof, white columns and a fresco above the main entrance representing the Resurrection, painted in the 'Italian' manner" provides a luxurious and idyllic setting for their conversation. As always in Turgenev's novels, however, bucolic peacefulness is mixed with a sense of practical urgency. The great world threatens to intrude, and men and women feel compelled to define their basic beliefs. Odintsova soon asks Bazarov, in tones insistent enough to appear inquisitorial, "What goal do you wish to attain? Where are you headed? What is your aim? In a word, who are you?" These are the questions put to all Turgenev's heroes, the demand that they prove themselves by displaying their inner as well as their outer lives.

Bazarov replies, "I have already informed you that I am a future district doctor." The terseness of Bazarov's remark reflects an important tacit assumption: an extreme focusing of energy must inform all activity. Since Russian reality offers no occupation commensurate with great individual talent, Bazarov will take up a constricting role, hoping to stretch it to fit his extravagant spirit. Odintsova grasps Bazarov's meaning and reinforces it. She declares that "district doctor" is too paltry a job, even temporarily, for someone like Bazarov. His great capacities (which she assumes without evidence) guarantee him a significant future. He should insist on the importance of his inner qualities. Though Bazarov remonstrates, "I am not in the habit of speaking freely about myself" Odintsova insists: "I do not see why one cannot express everything in his soul." She persuades him to behave in such a way that "your tension (*napriazhennost'*), your restraint will vanish."

Bazarov is easily persuaded. A view of personality that privileges the inner self is one he already holds, though he has never made it explicit. His superior attitude toward Pavel sprang from his high esteem of his own potential, his belief that his inner qualities would shortly flower into significant action. But what was effective in that antagonistic encounter proves disastrous in love. Judgment that is based on what men and women *are,* on the merits of their essential selves, instead of on what they *do,* makes union unlikely. There is no way to bridge any gap that may exist between individuals; love is either instantaneous or impossible. As Odintsova defines her ideal, "A life for a life. You take mine and give me yours, without regrets and with no turning back. Or else it is not worth it."

Bazarov declares his love in a form that he hopes will meet

Odintsova's expectations. "Well, let me tell you then. I love you foolishly, senselessly. There, that is what you have forced out of me." He agrees that his truest qualities must be "forced" to the surface. He comes before Odintsova not as man with political beliefs and plans for social activity, but as a bundle of suddenly exposed instincts. Of course, once he has revealed his inner self, he has exhausted his suit. He can only stand silently, awaiting Odintsova's reply. Unfortunately for him, his revelation of his essential self has reminded Odintsova of her own. She decides she must live alone, nourishing purely personal desires and interests. "No," she says to herself after rejecting Bazarov, "God knows where that might have led, it's no joking matter. A quiet life is better than anything else in the world." Though he knows that Odintsova is attracted to him, Bazarov grumpily leaves her estate on the following morning. There is no way even to begin to overcome the impasse that the principle of individualism has created.

Ironically, Odintsova has both admitted that Bazarov possesses an impressive strength of personality and proven how easily that strength can be ignored. That is a poisonous judgment, since the dismissiveness is wrapped in praise that Bazarov cherishes. To counter the ill effects of his visit to Odintsova, Bazarov decides to refuse to play any role that is not clearly commensurate with the grandeur of spirit he believes is his. Whereas before he believed that any occupation could be stretched to fit his personality, now he needs something that brings immediate acknowledgement of his inner qualities. Politics, which in Russia entailed dealing with peasants who traditionally refused to recognize an intellectual's good intentions, seems an especially poor prospect. Resting on a haystack with Arkadii on his parents' farm, Bazarov provides a striking image to justify his new lethargy: "But I've developed a hatred for that 'every peasant,' that Philip or Sidor, for whom I must crawl out of my skin."

Bazarov's great glory is that he refuses meekly to acquiesce in his lethargy, though he sees its logical necessity. He accepts the principle of individualism, describing himself to Arkadii as "This atom of myself, this mathematical point where blood flows." But he still wants to get beyond himself, to make contact with others. "One wants to deal with other people," he says, "if only to swear at them, or to be bothered by them." From this deadlock arises the most striking moment in Turgenev's novels—because it is dramatic in itself, but also because it marks a logical conclusion of Turgenev's intellectual development. Disdaining all social roles as a diminishment of his inner self, Bazarov tries to find a pure representation of his being: he lunges into behavior of a different, almost metaphysical, dimension. Signaling his state of high anxiety by a surprising and abrupt playfulness of tone, he suggests to Arkadii that they wrestle, and quickly puts his hands around Arkadii's throat:

> Bazarov spread his long and wiry fingers . . . Arkadii turned and prepared, as it were in jest, to defend himself. . . . But the face of his friend appeared to him so sinister, he sensed such an unjoking menace in the crooked smile of the lips,

in the enflamed eyes, that he experienced an intuitive fear.

Only the unexpected appearance of Bazarov's father deflects his murderous impulses. Arkadii has in fact done nothing to merit such treatment, but that is just the point: Bazarov hardly cares about the object of his hatred. Lashing out against the threat of inertia and isolation but lacking the means for sustained and purposeful activity, he indulges a blind and unbridled aggression, ready to inflict pain with the sole aim of imposing himself on the world.

Much of the rest of the book is a record of Bazarov's aghast reaction to what he has found himself capable of. He adopts a style of great restraint, keeps himself in check by assuming postures that will not call his essential nature into play. When he returns to the Kirsanov estate, he immerses himself in his scientific work and stays in his laboratory as if it were a haven. When he chances to encounter Pavel, he is always correct, giving no offense, provoking no arguments. Altogether, he puts himself on a short leash.

The one occasion when he does permit his personality to assert itself as of old is when he flirts with Nikolai's mistress, Fenochka, whom he comes upon in the garden. The result is disastrous, and drives him back immediately to his strategy of a purposeful neglect of natural inclinations. Bazarov's flirtation appears to be only an innocent exuberance in the presence of fresh beauty, and even the kiss with which the scene ends has no lascivious intent; nevertheless, Bazarov concludes that his impulses have again carried him in a direction he did not want to go: "He felt both ashamed and contemptuously annoyed. But he immediately shook his head, ironically congratulated himself 'on his formal entry into the ranks of woman-chasers' and marked off to his room."

The self-stylization that is expressed in this passage reflects a mind at bay. Seemingly, only an escape from who he is can bring Bazarov any relief. His path, so logically curved toward despair, signals the end of an ideal: the reliance by *obshchestvo* on the inner self apparently leads to the isolation of man from man, to a constraint on activity and finally to a loss of self-confidence.

But this is only one aspect of *Fathers and Sons.* From the beginning, alongside Bazarov's compelling drama, Turgenev has drawn another line of development: the theme of a home apart from the corrupting world. When Odintsova rejects Bazarov's love, hers is simultaneously a decision to remain within the confines of a sustaining domesticity, the strategy that Turgenev endorses time and again in his novels. In almost acceding to Bazarov's overtures, she "had brought herself to a certain limit, had forced herself to look beyond—and saw there not merely an abyss but a void . . . or shapeless chaos." The theme of the family is embodied in the actions of Nikolai Kirsanov, Fenochka, Odintsova, and, most tellingly, Arkadii and Odintsova's younger sister Katia. The family ideal they all strive for is presented as a form of tacit rebuttal to Bazarov's emphasis on individualism, and as a way to avoid the "shapeless chaos" his actions invite.

But, ever skeptical, Turgenev also shows that the family

ideal entails difficulties of its own. Almost as soon as Arkadii and Katia discover their love, they elaborate a set of guiding rules. The rules are not insisted upon—to have done so would have been to transform marriage vows into a declaration of armed truce—but they bind nevertheless. Sitting in a bower, walking through a lush garden, or enjoying the weather, Arkadii and Katia urgently test each other's willingness to make sacrifices, and each other's determination to insist on individual needs. They fix to their mutual satisfaction the rights and limits of the parties in a matrimonial union. Arkadii happily learns that Katia has no money of her own and lives off her sister's generosity, for that means she will have less right to threaten his domination. Katia smugly notes to herself that she will soon have Arkadii at her feet. On the other hand, alongside their willfulness, both Arkadii and Katia indicate a readiness to yield control to the other. Katia sums up the delicate arrangement when she says to Arkadii, "I am prepared to submit, it is only inequality that is hard to bear." Katia envisions a curious situation where submission does not weaken self-assertion.

Underlying that illogical formulation is the desperate need of *obshchestvo*. The individual's strength should not be curtailed, since it is needed to fight existing corruption; but individuals giving free vent to their impulses can never blend into true harmony. A social entity is required that will acknowledge diversity while keeping it in check. The family seemed an especially attractive possibility: within the family there are fewer diverse urges to consider, fewer egos to confront at one time. In truth that is no logical resolution of the problem, only a scaling down of it, much like hoping to weaken the laws of mechanics by removing some of the colliding atoms. Nevertheless to *obshchestvo* it seemed that if the members of a family were all equally eager to avoid strife, the worst problems of individualism would be solved.

To such an intricate mutuality Bazarov is alien. Though the achievement of Arkadii and Katia suggests an answer to his overriding problem, he must reject it: as Katia says of him at one point, Bazarov is "undomesticated." The family ideal goes counter to his most enduring quality. Though he has forced himself to explore a variety of artificial roles, he has done so in full self-consciousness; in the family, as represented by Arkadii and Katia, the participants cannot look too closely at what they have fashioned, for it is a structure kept in place very largely by wishful thinking.

One other character shares Bazarov's disdain for domesticity, though he arrives at the attitude along a totally different path. That is Pavel Kirsanov. The most important experience in Pavel's life, one that still consumes his thoughts after more than twenty years, is his love for the Princess R———. Her name is never given in full; that detail accurately reflects the mystery and extravagance of the relationship in general. "Pavel met her at a ball, danced a mazurka with her, during which she did not say a single sensible word, and fell passionately in love with her." From her deathbed, after years of brief frenzied meetings and abrupt departures, the Princess sends to Pavel the ring with a sphinx depicted on it which he had given her. "She

had scratched in the image of a cross over the sphinx and had ordered that he be told that the cross was—the answer to the riddle." In fact, the gesture solves no riddles; it only intensifies the overtones of mystery and extravagance. Such attitudes, which Pavel still cultivates, cannot fit into a domestic structure.

When Pavel challenges Bazarov to a duel after he sees the flirtation with Fenochka, he is only superficially attempting to defend his brother's honor; nor does the resemblance that Pavel sees between Fenochka and Princess R——— fully explain his action. The duel, ethically grotesque and historically anachronistic, is Pavel's effort to create a structure that will contain his feelings, since the world he lives in does not offer one. Indeed, for Pavel the duel is totally satisfying. It answers his needs so exactly as to leave in doubt whether the delirium he falls into after being wounded is not actually an ecstasy of spiritual fulfillment. The surge of friendship he feels for Bazarov as he lies bleeding in his arms, though unexpected, makes sense, for Pavel is experiencing finally the great pleasure of a release in concrete ritual for feelings that have long been pent up, and he is grateful to the man who has helped to make this release possible.

For Bazarov the duel solves nothing. He sees it as an empty charade. The example of Pavel's fatuous joy only confirms him in his deadlock more fully than before: he, Bazarov, is a man who requires a structure to contain and check his errant impulses, but who refuses the only structures that seem available. His return to his parents' house after the duel, his efforts to continue his scientific experiments, his desultory participation in his father's medical practice—these are the actions of a man going through the motions. Even Bazarov's death, as Turgenev depicts it, is not so much a biological event as an illustration of how even this ultimate act loses all meaning for a man lacking any abiding confidence in who he is. Though the death is caused by a typhus infection contracted during an autopsy, it is the utter carelessness with which Bazarov tends to his disease which guarantees his fate. He is a man totally unable to focus on his own best interests. The final words he speaks are to Odintsova, who has been summoned to his bedside: "Blow on the dying light and let it go out," he says, and in their extravagant Romanticism, they are very far from the sort of words that came from Bazarov at the beginning of the book: they are the words of a man crammed into a mode of expression not his own, and for that reason—rather than for their immediate purport, which is melodramatic—they attain a certain pathos.

The last chapter of **Fathers and Sons** presents a culminating image for each of the two main lines of narrative development—Bazarov's and that of the family theme—and the two images are mutually illuminating. They illuminate as well Turgenev's intellectual and creative progress. These last words in the last novel that Turgenev wrote during the period before emancipation stand forth with the power of a logical conclusion, though it is a logic informed by great feeling. The process that Turgenev began with *Notes of a Hunter* here finds an end, a tense balance of real hope and pessimism.

At the beginning of this chapter Turgenev describes the double wedding of the Kirsanovs, father and son:

> A week ago, in the small parish church, quietly and almost without witnesses, there took place two weddings, Arkadii to Katia and Nikolai Petrovich to Fenochka; and on the same day Nikolai Petrovich gave a farewell dinner for his brother, who was going to Moscow on business. . . .
>
> Exactly at three o'clock everyone gathered at the table. Mitia [the son of Nikolai and Fenochka] was also brought in and seated; he had already acquired a nanny in a brocaded headdress. Pavel Petrovich enthroned himself between Katia and Fenochka. "The husbands" arranged themselves next to their wives.

The last paragraph of the book describes Bazarov's grave.

> In one of the far corners of Russia stands a small village graveyard. Like most of our graveyards it appears dismal: the ditches surrounding it have long been overgrown by weeds, the drab wooden crosses sag and rot beneath their once freshly painted gables. . . . But in their midst stands a grave untouched by any man, untrampled upon by any animal: only the birds at dawn perch and sing on it. An iron railing fences it in, two fir trees have been planted there, one at each end; in that grave Evgenii Bazarov lies buried. Often from the nearby village a tottering old couple, man and wife, make their way here. Supporting each other, they walk with heavy steps; on reaching the railing they fall down upon their knees and weep long and bitterly, and yearningly they gaze at the mute tombstone beneath which their son is lying; exchanging a brief word they brush the dust from the stone, set straight a branch of the fir tree and then resume their prayers, unable to tear themselves away from the spot where they feel themselves so close to their son and their memories of him. . . . Can it be that love, sacred and devoted, is not omnipotent? Oh no! However, passionate, sinful, and rebellious the heart hidden away in that grave, the flowers that blossom there look at us unrebelliously with their innocent eyes: not only about eternal tranquility do they tell us, about that great peace of "indifferent" nature; they speak as well about eternal reconciliation and of life without end.

In the one scene there is conviviality and joy, in the other bleakness and breavement. But the contrast between the two passages is in fact less than straightforward. Thus the reference to Pavel's departure at once introduces a slight dissonant note into the celebratory proceedings. It is as if the transformation of the place the peasants call "Bachelor's Farm" ("*Bobylii khutor*") into a site of domestic bliss were too delicate a process to withstand the presence of a single disharmonious element. Pavel must be ejected, albeit with ceremony and honor. The narrative style suggests the fragility of the community that is being formed. The remarkable attention to seating arrangements and the precision of schedules suggests a constraining formality, as if the feelings of the participants were being held in check by proprieties. When Turgenev stresses the word

"husbands," he seems to confirm that forms and labels are crucial here, a necessary adhesive to individuals not naturally inclined to band together. Turgenev omits any reference to states of mind. All evidence of diverse urges has been muffled. We are shown things as in a tableau, a careful grouping that suggests affection but offers no hint of emotional complexity. And as in a tableau our attention is precisely focused, all extraneous confusion screened out or put into abeyance. Turgenev refers to the world beyond ("going to Moscow") in order to dismiss it, so that we can concentrate fully on the representation of the properly cultivated family.

The bleak characterization of Bazarov's grave suggests the ultimate futility of his life. Unmourned and unremembered except by his parents, Bazarov seems to have made no lasting effect on the world. But just as Turgenev had managed to insinuate the limitations of a domesticity that seemed at first glance altogether idyllic, he manages now to recapitulate a logic to Bazarov's failure which in part redeems him. In death Bazarov regains some of his original power, which the events of his life after meeting Odintseva had undercut. Significantly, though Turgenev describes a most emphatically circumscribed area, he manages to suggest considerable movement, and especially in comparison with the scene of the double wedding. The main characters in the first passage were free to move, but the scene was static; the main character is here fixed, but the scene is fluid. The narrative focus shifts rapidly and energetically, from the graveyard to the path and to a suggestion of a nearby village, and then finally to Bazarov's grave. There is an acknowledgement of the world beyond the immediate setting ("Like most of our graveyards") which suggests that Bazarov's fate may have wider meaning. In general, the space referred to in the second passage seems more expandable than in the first.

By the same token, time in the second passage seems more repeatable. The description of the family dinner suggests a snapshot, as if only an instantaneous rendering could capture the diverse impulses of the subjects. The description of Bazarov's grave shows an occasion that will be duplicated many times. The demands of the plot have something to do with the differences between the two passages, but the crucial influence is the different emotions in each. That pathetic moment when Bazarov's parents kneel in prayer indicates a grief that will extend and enrich itself for a long time to come. The happiness of the Kirsanovs, on the other hand, requires a finely adjusted context not likely to be easily secured again. In all, though he is dead and his grave isolated, it is Bazarov who projects the possibilities of greatest energy and purpose.

In the very last lines of the novel, the narrator is swept along by the pathos of Bazarov's fate, His style overflows with great feeling: the syntax careens out of control and meanings are blurred. That, in fact is a duplication of Bazarov's dilemma during much of the book. Feelings too powerful to find an embodying structure become dissipated. Bazarov's spirit, the narrator remarks, escapes the bleak grave and mingles with the universe; but the universe is "indifferent." Bazarov's strength has led him to renounce the supports that those more timid than he cling to, but the consequence is utter failure. In the indifferent universe, Turgenev more than once made clear, every atom pursues its own goal, so that individual purpose is inconsequential and success both accidental and unlikely. The last chapter of **Fathers and Sons** presents an uneasy choice: to be a strong individual, who is necessarily homeless and thus lacks the support that would allow him to impress his values on the world at large; or to be a part of a community that sustains its members, but at the cost of forcing them to restrain their natural impulses.

The ending to **Fathers and Sons** raises a major question about Turgenev's political achievement. Did he help Russians to conceive of their world more efficaciously or was the vision he offered merely one of elaborate stalemate, helplessness disguised by a complexity of emotions? (pp. 190-203)

To most of his Soviet critics, Turgenev is a representative of the liberal tradition that failed to comprehend the country's needs. Most of his Western critics place him in the same tradition, but voice regret that the country failed to understand the merits of liberalism. Whether a misguided fool or an unheeded prophet, Turgenev appears as a voice crying in the wilderness. From this point of view, it makes sense to ignore his politics altogether, which indeed is not an uncommon approach.

But I believe there is no need either to stigmatize or to fantasize about Turgenev's political position, for it was in fact very much in the mainstream of Russian history. It is true that Russia had no room for ameliorist dreams: that some individuals achieve contentment is not a reason to assume, as Turgenev often did, that contentment will spread. In omitting a description of the mechanism for social improvement, he exhibited a distressing political tentativeness. Russian life clearly required a more purposeful wrench than he cared to contemplate. Nevertheless, in conceiving of an area apart from government hegemony where individuals could control their own destinies, Turgenev established the basis for much of the progressive political activity of the late nineteenth century.

In his novels Turgenev proceeded with hesitation, with constant self-correction. Ideas and social forms that are endorsed are also fiercely scrutinized. Even if his contemporaries had read him with perfect sympathy and understanding, they would not have learned of a program for changing Russia; his novels raise more questions than they answer. Nevertheless, the novels did strikingly define the political landscape, which had the effect of making questions purposeful. He showed Russians that they lived in a comprehensible world. Considering the national psychology before he came on the scene, that was a very great achievement. (p. 211)

> *Victor Ripp, in his* Turgenev's Russia from 'Notes of a Hunter' to 'Fathers and Sons', *Cornell University Press, 1980, 218 p.*

David Lowe   (essay date 1983)

[*An American professor of Russian literature, Lowe has edited and translated Turgenev's* Letters *(1983) and is the author of* Turgenev's "Fathers and Sons." *In the following excerpt from the latter work, he traces elements of both comedy and tragedy in* Fathers and Sons.]

Sometime during the first months of 1862 Afanasy Fet sent Turgenev his reactions to **Fathers and Sons.** Fet's letter is not extant, but we do have Turgenev's reply, and it reinforces the often expressed conviction that one ought not to pay too much attention to what writers have to say about their own works. In the letter of April 6/18, 1862, Turgenev writes: "You also mention parallelism; but where is it, allow me to ask, and where are these pairs, believing and unbelieving?" . . . [In] spite of Turgenev's protests parallelism is one of the two basic principles at work in the novel. The other is contrast. No doubt there are few works in world literature that do not depend to some extent on parallels and contrasts for the building blocks that hold them together and give them coherence. In **Fathers and Sons,** however, their significance is all-inclusive and extends to matters of composition, characterization, and thematics. In **Fathers and Sons,** a novel whose very title both links and contrasts the generations, form and content are one. That pronouncement is not the pious repetition of a Formalist cliché. As the examination proceeds it should become increasingly apparent that in **Fathers and Sons** thematics determine form. As the first step in proving the validity of that contention, let us turn our attention to matters of composition and their relation to the novel's thematic concerns.

One way to look at the novel's structure is as a series of trips: Arkady and Bazarov are thus examined and illuminated in a variety of environments. At Marino Arkady is at home and Bazarov is the stranger. In town and at Nikolskoe, both Arkady and Bazarov are thrown into an unfamiliar environment, while at Bazarov's parents' estate Arkady is the stranger (though, paradoxically, he is less an outsider there than is Bazarov). Parallelism and contrast are immediately evident in such a scheme: Bazarov is the newcomer in one milieu, Arkady in another. But even within the series of trips we can establish cycles. [T. G.] Brazhe writes of two cycles of trips from Marino to Bazarov's home [in *Tselostnoe izuchenie epichekogo proizvedeniia*, 1964]. Such a calculation takes into account only Bazarov's point of view. It would be more accurate to identify three cycles of trips. The interesting structural note here is that Arkady's and Bazarov's travels consistently dovetail with each other, even when the two protagonists are not together. In the first cycle, Arkady and Bazarov go from Marino to town to Nikolskoe to Bazarov's home and back through Nikolskoe to Marino. In the second cycle, Arkady goes to Nikolskoe on his own. In a later and parallel development, Bazarov arrives at Nikolskoe on his own. Finally, in the last cycle, Bazarov goes home alone, as does Arkady. Implicit in this view of the novel's structure is one of the novel's major themes: children cannot turn their backs on the world of their fathers. Imperfect as it may be, it represents the mainstream of humanity. Children ultimately do go "home" again, and willingly or grudgingly, they are reconciled to the family hearth. At that point, as Joel Blair notes [in "The Architecture of Turgenev's *Fathers and Sons*," *Modern Fiction Studies* 19,

No. 4 (Winter 1973-74)], "the lives of the fathers become patterns for understanding the lives of the children."

A second way of viewing the structure is as a series of confrontations. Such an interpretation is particularly widespread, since it provides abundant opportunities to discuss the ideological battles of the 1860s. Thus, we can map out the structure of *Fathers and Sons* as a series of ideological duels between Bazarov and Pavel, the ideological duels then capped by a real duel in which politics and social issues are as much at stake as personalities. Doubling the ideological skirmishes is Bazarov's series of erotic clashes with Odintsova. All discussions of the structure of *Fathers and Sons* in terms of confrontations are ultimately spinoffs from [Vasilii] Gippius' Formalist analysis of composition in Turgenev's novels [in "O kompozitsii turgenevskikh romanov," in *Venok Turgenevu,* 1919]. (Rarely are they acknowledged as such.) Gippius' analysis is quite sophisticated, and there will be a need to return to it in some detail. It is nonetheless limited because, like most analyses of *Fathers and Sons,* it proceeds from the assumption that the novel is a tragedy and that Bazarov is the novel's only significant protagonist. These assumptions lead critics to attempt to identify a single, all-embracing structural pattern in the novel, whether it be trips, confrontations, love stories, or whatever. But the assumption needs to be reexamined. *Fathers and Sons* is a novel wholly dependent upon parallels and contrasts for its composition, and its structure is dualistic: it involves two parallel but contrasting patterns. The first is that of tragedy, while the second is comedy.

Since many will probably find controversial the notion that *Fathers and Sons* is in any way comedic, let us begin with this, the less obvious structural pattern in the novel. In using the word comedy, what it intended is not comedy in the popular sense (a funny play with a happy ending), but in the Aristotelian sense, specifically in its modern formulation by Northrop Frye [in his *Anatomy of Criticism,* 1957] Frye uses comedy as a term denoting a literary mode, as he calls it, not a genre. Thus, as defined by Frye, the term is equally applicable to drama and narrative prose.

Basing his treatise on Aristotle's *Poetics,* Frye suggests that comedies deal with the integration of society. The standard comedic formula involves a young couple—the technical hero and heroine—whose marriage is blocked by other members of the cast (society). In realistic fiction employing the comedic mode, the hero and heroine tend to be dull but decent people, while the blocking characters are the truly interesting ones. The blocking characters are normally, but not necessarily, parental figures. They are consumed by a single passion (usually absurdly so), and they are in control of the society into which the hero and heroine seek entrance. The blocking characters are likely to be impostors, as Frye calls them, people who lack self-knowledge. At the conclusion of comedy the blocking characters are either incorporated into or expelled from the society, as a result of which the hero and heroine are free to wed. Thus, comedies often conclude with a wedding and the birth of babies, and have a rural setting (an escape to a simpler, less corrupt society). At the conclu-

Turgenev at age 44.

sion of comedy the audience feels that justice has triumphed, that the people who should have been united have been, and that everyone will live happily ever after in a freer, more flexible society.

This is a rather bald reduction of Frye's Aristotelian description of comedy, but it should be sufficient to demonstrate that in *Fathers and Sons* we are dealing in part with the comedic mode. However, Turgenev spins some fascinating variations around the age-old comedic pattern.

Arkady is the technical hero about whom the comedic plot revolves. This is not to say that he is the novel's central hero. He is the *technical* hero of the comedic plot. Significantly, Gary Jahn notes [in "Character and Theme in *Fathers and Sons,*" College Literature 4 (1977)] that "Arkady *and* Bazarov are the organizational focus of the novel [Italics mine-DL]." And true to comedic type, Arkady is a rather bland but not unattractive personality. As in Roman comedy, we have not a single hero, but a pair of heroes. Instead of the typical pair of young heroes, however, Turgenev gives us a father and son, both of whose marriages are blocked, as is a genuine reconciliation between father and son. The blocking characters are Pavel and Bazarov, and consistent with the traditions of fictional comedy, both of them are considerably more interesting than the technical heroes and heroines, and both of them are removed from the stage at the culmination of the comedic plot line.

Bazarov's negative influence on Arkady forestalls an accomodation between him and his father, and it temporarily blocks Arkady and Katya's marriage, largely because Bazarov's attitudes, which Arkady attempts in vain to adopt, prevent the latter from coming to terms with himself and his true nature. In this connection, James Justus points out [in "*Fathers and Sons:* The Novel as *Idyll,*" *Western Humanities Review* XV (1961)] that "the battle [in *Fathers and Sons*] is not just fathers against sons, but sons against themselves." Bazarov's obstructing influence is apparent as early as the third chapter. Arkady, riding along in a carriage with his father, waxes lyrical, thus betraying his "unnihilistic" enthusiasm for the beauties of nature. He abruptly breaks off in mid-sentence. "Arkady suddenly paused, glanced back obliquely [at Bazarov, who is riding along behind] and lapsed into silence." Bazarov's presence prevents Arkady from being himself, and as a result the relations between father and son are strained. Bazarov is a blocker, and his status as an obstacle to reconciliation between father and son is emphasized in several of the novel's passages. Just after the scene in which Bazarov suggests that Arkady wean his father away from Pushkin by giving him more adult food for thought, i.e., Büchner's *Stoff und Kraft* (sic), we discover Pavel and Nikolay in conversation:

> "Well, you and I," Nikolay Petrovich, sitting in his brother's room the same day after dinner, said to Pavel, "have fallen into the ranks of the retired, our song is sung. What's to be done? Perhaps Bazarov is right; but I confess that one thing pains me: I was hoping just now to become close friends with Arkady; but it turns out that I have lagged behind, he has gone forward, and we cannot understand each other."

By the end of the novel there is no doubt that it is precisely Bazarov's sway over Arkady that temporarily thwarts mutual understanding between father and son. Furthermore, Arkady's distorted image of himself as a fire-breathing, militant disciple of Bazarov's impedes his progress toward the realization that his love is not for Odintsova, as he imagines, but for her sister Katya. It is Katya who articulates what the reader has sensed all along—Arkady has been under Bazarov's thumb. "My sister was under his [Bazarov's] influence then, just as you were," Katya tells Arkady. She goes on to inform Arkady that he has nothing in common with Bazarov. When Arkady protests, saying that he wants to be strong and energetic like his friend, Katya lectures him: "You can't just wish that . . . Your friend does not wish for it, it's just there in him." Here Katya sounds another of the novel's major themes: one cannot be what one is not. That Arkady's attempt to play the nihilist causes him to be untrue to himself is made explicit when Bazarov suggests that they go to town:

> " . . . Well, what do you think? Shall we go?"
>
> "I guess so," Arkady answered lazily.
>
> In his soul he rejoiced at his friend's suggestion, but felt obliged to hide his feeling. Not for nothing was he a nihilist!

Arkady's transition from his false role as Bazarov's prote-

gé and a rival for Odintsova to his true status as his father's son and claimant for Katya's hand is signalled in a scene at Nikolskoe:

> They did not find him [Arkady] soon: he had taken himself off to the most remote part of the garden where, resting his chin on his folded hands, he sat, sunk in thought. [Cf. Nikolay's penchant for garden meditation.] They were profound and important, these thoughts, but not sad. He knew that Anna Sergeievna was sitting alone with Bazarov, and he did not feel jealousy, as had happened in the past; on the contrary, his face shone quietly; it seemed that he was surprised at something and gladdened, and that he was deciding on something.

It is appropriate that Arkady should come to such self-knowledge in the garden. Alexander Fischler has noted [in "The Garden Motif and the Structure of *Fathers and Sons,*" *Novel* 9 (1976)] that the architecture of ***Fathers and Sons*** is linked to a garden motif, and that "the garden is a microcosm of nature, foreshortening its laws to uphold *what ought to be.*" Arkady's post-garden proposal to Katya is a symbolic declaration of what he must be—independent from Bazarov: Arkady is now free to be himself, to express his true feelings. Bazarov's dramatic farewell and rejection of Arkady are really no more than a recognition on the former's part that he no longer has any influence over Arkady. Bazarov then retires to his father's house, removing himself from the comedic plot line and freeing Arkady to marry Katya and to be reconciled with his father.

Pavel is a blocking character vis-à-vis Nikolay and Fenechka. His presumed hostility to the idea of their marriage dissuades Nikolay from regularizing his liaison with Fenechka. Note Nikolay's reaction when Pavel asks him to marry Fenechka:

> Nikolay Petrovich took a step back and threw up his hands. "Is that you saying this, Pavel? You, whom I have always considered an implacable foe of such marriages? . . . But don't you know that it was only out of respect for you that I haven't fulfilled what you so rightly call my duty!"

So Pavel encourages Nikolay to marry Fenechka—an act that will assuage Nikolay's guilty conscience and allow him to feel more at ease with his son.

Then, at the culmination of the comedic plot line the blocking characters have been expelled (or have expelled themselves): Pavel prepares to spend the rest of his days in Europe, where he will continue his superfluous existence, while Bazarov retires to his father's home, and the pairs who belonged together all along are at last united.

Some critics have noted the importance of couplings, uncouplings, and recouplings in the novel. [F. R. Reeve in his *The Russian Novel,* 1966] writes:

> Characters in pairs . . . relate each to the other through a succession of still other people, each relationship forming a temporary triangle, each triangle imperfect. . . . The third person's action always in some sense splits the original pair.

Or, as Blair formulates it:

> The principle of composition operating in the novel is the grouping and regrouping of characters; our understanding of the novel develops as we observe the initial groups of characters dissolve and perceive the formation of new pairs. Eventually, those characters who seemed most unalike are aligned; their similarities become more important than their differences.

This general movement toward the final, "inevitable" pairings is the stuff of comedy. The double wedding noted in the epilogue underscores the emergence of a new, pragmatically freer society, a salient feature of comedy. The crystallization of this less rigid society is underlined by Pavel when he urges Nikolay to marry Fenechka: "No, dear brother, enough of high-mindedness and thinking about society: we're already old and peaceful people; it's time we put aside empty pretense." The new society, though not earthshakingly different from the old, is a little less rigid, a little more spontaneous: Nikolay, a member of the gentry, has become free to take Fenechka, a peasant, as his lawfully wedded wife. In this respect [Viktor Shklovsky, in his *Zametki o proze russkikh klassikov*, 1955] overstates the case in arguing that "What is new in Turgenev's novel was that he understood the love story as the confrontation of new people with a world built on old principles." It is really Nikolay and Fenechka who confront old social values with new ones, Arkady and Katya's thoroughly conventional marriage with their own socially "progressive" one. Shklovsky's assessment nonetheless shows that he perceives a comedic base in the novel. Fischler, who emphasizes the classical bases of *Fathers and Sons,* also sees comedy at work here. He writes of the epilogue as "*prostodushnaia komediia,* 'artless comedy'—life itself or a play in which the author's strings no longer matter. In such comedy, the naive pursuit of happiness by the characters remaining on the stage blends with the timeless designs, overwhelming what momentarily stood out and was disturbing because of its alien, fortuitous or fateful appearance."

What are the implications of the novel's comedic structure? One, obviously, is that the comedic mode is extraordinarily hardy and adaptive. But, more importantly, an analysis of *Fathers and Sons* in terms of comedy explains in generic terms why many critics read the novel as an affirmative one—one that celebrates life and nature (or, more accurately, Life and Nature). [N. N.] Strakhov, for instance, argues [in "Ottsy i deti," in *O Turgeneve,* 1918]: "Although Bazarov stands above everyone in the novel, life stands above him."

But what kind of life stands above Bazarov? Some critics dismiss the life led by Katya, Arkady, Nikolay, and Fenechka as banal, mediocre, *poshly.* [D. I.] Pisarev, for one, suggests [in "Bazarov," in *Bazarov, Realisty,* 1974]: "The life of a limited person always flows more evenly and pleasantly than the life of a genius or even just an intelligent person." [G. A. Byaly, in his *Romana Turgeneva "Ottsy i deti,"* 1963] asserts that Pavel and Nikolay are "finished" (*konchenye liudi*), that "life is passing them by." . . . Thus, for Byaly, Nikolay is not even involved in life.

Do Nikolay and Arkady and their wives represent mediocrity? Yes, but not in a negative sense. Their mediocrity is that of the middle way, the golden mean. Arkady and Nikolay may be ordinary, but, as Paul Bourget suggested, nearly a century ago [in "Ivan Tourguéniev," in his *Nouveaux essais de psychologie contemporaine,* 1894], there is something fresh and appealing about Turgenev's average man. Turgenev himself spoke of Goethe's Faust as the defender of "the individual, passionate, limited man" who still has the right and the opportunity to be happy and not be ashamed of his happiness." Boyd writes: "The love of Arkady and Katya gives a healthy, optimistic balance to the novel. [A. Batyutor, in *Turgenev-romantist,* 1972] calls the novel's love scenes life affirming. And [I. A.] Vinogradov writes [in *Bor'ba za stil'. Sbornik statei,* 1937]:

> The novel in essence is a battle of "cerebral" negative theories with the mighty power of love, with the inexpressible beauty of nature, with all the intermix of human feelings which, though "old," are alive and warm—a battle that ends with the triumph of "humanness," "nature," "beauty," over "nihilism."

The comedic couples may be limited, but they are hardly vegetables, nor is their existence gray. Arkady is a competent estate manager, and all the Kirsanovs' lives, ordinary as they may be, are enriched by an instinctual and profound attraction to nature, art, and their fellow man. They represent an ideal that Turgenev himself was unable to attain. While working on *Fathers and Sons,* he wrote a letter to K. N. Leontiev in which he confessed:

> And that I, as you write, have lately become gloomy, there's nothing surprising in that: I will soon be 42 years old, but I haven't made a nest for myself, haven't secured any spot for myself on earth: there is little cause for joy in that.

It must be admitted, however, that Turgenev claimed (*post-facto*) that in *Fathers and Sons* he had taken a contemptuous, despairing attitude toward bourgeois domesticity. In a letter of April 14/26, 1862, to Sluchevsky, Turgenev responds to what seems to have been Sluchevsky's summary of the reactions of Russian students in Heidelberg to *Fathers and Sons* (no letters from Sluchevsky are extant). The students' reactions are indicative, as is Turgenev's reply:

> What was said about Arkady, about the rehabilitation of the fathers, etc., only shows—forgive me!—that I haven't been understood. *All my povest* [short novel] *is directed against the gentry as a progressive class.* Examine closely Nikolay Petrovich, Pavel Petrovich, Arkady. Weakness, flabbiness (*vialost*), or limitedness (*organichennost*).

Later in the same letter Turgenev expresses bewilderment at the Heidelberg students' having found Arkady "a more successful type [than Bazarov]." Thus we have Turgenev's own testimony that he did not intend to portray Arkady or Nikolay in a positive light. But an author's intentions are one thing, the reader's perceptions quite another. In spite of scornful depictions of "blissful" marriages in other Turgenev works, such as **"Andrey Kolosov," "Two Friends,"** and **"The Country Doctor,"** and Turgenev's protestations to the contrary, Nikolay, Arkady, and their wives add a healthy, optimistic note to *Fathers and Sons.* In this connection Gippius, discussing groups of *poshlye* characters in *Smoke* and *Nest of Gentlefolk,* points out that these characters are "portrayed with exaggerated distortion, not at all as in *Fathers and Sons,* where the corresponding characters are presented in a significantly muted (*smiagchenny*) form, almost idealized, no matter how much Turgenev himself denied it."

Arkady and Nikolay are not men of great stature, they are not great thinkers, but Turgenev's having infused them with love of Schubert, Pushkin, evening sunsets, their families, and their fellow man makes it difficult to conceive of them and the life they lead as *poshly.* Turgenev portrays the Kirsanovs in a positive, if subdued light. And he does so within the context of a comedic structure, one that invariably leads the audience at the conclusion to recognize that "this is how things ought to be." Bazarov's death is quite another matter, of course. That is the culmination of the novel's tragedic structure. But in the first part of the novel's epilogue, where life and love are celebrated at Pavel's farewell dinner, with its exaltation of marriage and family [as Strakhov writes] "Turgenev stands for the eternal foundations of human life, for those basic elements which may perpetually change their forms, but in essence always remain unchanged."

But of course not all critics find such positive notes in *Fathers and Sons.* Most would probably argue that the novel is a tragedy. Such an analysis should surprise no one—it is a bromide of Turgenev criticism. But how and why *Fathers and Sons* is a tragedy—these are questions that until recently have remained largely unexplored. Once again Northrop Frye provides useful tools for analysis. The basic movement of tragedy, according to Frye, is toward the exclusion of a hero from a given society, with an emphasis on the hero's tragic isolation. It is in this connection that Gippius' analysis of the structure of *Fathers and Sons* is particularly apt. He perceives the novel's "dynamic highway" in this way: "Having cast himself off from the elements of his milieu, the obviously hostile ones as well as the pseudo-friendly ones, the hero remains tragically alone." Yury Mann sees a similar pattern, which he calls "one against all" ["Bazarov i drugie," *Novyi mir* 44, No. x (1968)].

According to Frye, the tragic hero must be of heroic proportions: "The tragic hero is very great as compared with us, but there is something else, something on the side of him opposite the audience, compared to which he is small." Surely this is the case with Bazarov, whose greatness (implied, rather than shown) is, as Strakhov argues, less than the sum of life forces represented by the Kirsanovs and their spouses.

In addition, Frye conceives of the tragic hero as an impostor, someone who is deceived about himself, who plays a role that is not his to play. Significantly, Charles Bachman writes of "tragedy and self-deception" in *Fathers and Sons* [in "Tragedy and Self–Deception in Turgenev's *Fathers and Sons,*" *Revue des Langues Vivantes* (Brussels) 34, No. 3 (1968)], pointing out that "false self-images are crucial to the tragic view which the action of the novel seems to

demand. . . . " Most of the characters in the novel suffer from identity crises: this is true not just in the case of the strong characters, as Bachman suggests, but also of such a person as Arkady. But Bazarov's self-deception is the most extreme and his journey toward self-discovery the most painful and tragic. He dismisses the laws governing human life; his fatal infection, leading him to summon Odintsova for a last meeting in which he confesses that he is not the giant he had imagined himself to be, demonstrates that finally he understands the extent of his self-delusion.

The movement toward tragedy is generally toward a revelation of natural law, "that which is and must be," so that the audience's reaction to the hero's fall is paradoxical: we feel a sense of rightness (the tragic hero represents an imbalance in nature and thus must fall) and horrible wrongness (how sad that this man must fall). Such indeed is our reaction to Bazarov's death. Poignant as it may be, we nevertheless perceive, as Richard Freeborn formulates it, that Bazarov is a

> usurper of divine right, whose arrogant self-will proclaims for itself a self-sufficiency in life which contravenes the limits of human experience and gives rise to a dilemma which is only to be resolved in death.

Fischler's approach to the question of Bazarov throws additional light on Turgenev's reliance on classical tragedic models:

> One must first note that Bazarov belongs to a special category of protagonists, the tragic protagonist or even the nature hero. He fits there less because of his famous assertion that nature is his "workshop," than because of his repeatedly underlined mysterious bonds with his natural surroundings. He is associated with nature not only by brute strength and passion, but by vaguer, though not necessarily less awesome bonds of sympathy: the world responds to him, follows him, at least so long as he chooses to practice and accept association, that is, throughout the first part of the novel. He is born with a gift for harmony with the creation, yet, as he himself points out to Arkady, it is a gift of limited usefulness: one may derive strength from nature so long as one yields to it through naive faith, so long as one is willing to believe in the talismanic virtue of an aspen tree by a clay pit; but, when the magic is lost, one must drift to the inevitable end. Nonetheless, even when Bazarov's bond to nature ceases being a means for coping with the world, his fate remains associated with it by the structure of the novel. He is a nature hero, and, by ironic extension, he is even a nature "god"; he appears on the stage in spring (May 1859) to offer the traditional challenge to an existing order already undermined by inner and outer turmoil; he is defeated (expect perhaps in the duel with Pavel Kirsanov, the living-dead representative of the older order who, in many respects, is a projection of himself); then, largely through his own acquiescence and even complicity, he dies in August, at the height of summer, a traditional time for the death of gods. . . .

Comedy and tragedy coexist in *Fathers and Sons.* It is of course the novel's tragic side that impresses us most deeply. Such is human nature. Moreover, Turgenev takes pains to reinforce the novel's tragic overtones by placing the description of Bazarov's aged parents weeping inconsolably at their son's grave as the last element in the novel, the final chord of a tragic symphony, as it were. And yet, if we look closely at the very last lines of *Fathers and Sons,* we see that the narrator holds out a certain note of optimism, ambivalent as it may be:

> Can it really be that their prayers and their tears are fruitless? Can it really be that love, sacred, devoted love is not all-powerful? Oh no! No matter what a passionate, sinful, rebellious heart may be hidden in the grave, the flowers that grow on it look at us serenely with their innocent eyes; they speak to us not only of eternal peace, of that great peace of "indifferent" nature; they speak as well of eternal reconciliation and of life eternal. . . .

But what does Turgenev mean by "life everlasting"? The life of nature, which renews itself annually? The life of humanity, which is everlasting inasmuch as a new generation always takes the place of the dying one? Does the narrator really have in mind the Christian notion of the immortality of the soul? He is purposely vague in this quasi-pantheistic, quasi-Orthodox formulation. What is clear is that life goes on. Bazarov is dead, but Nikolay and Fenechka, along with Arkady and Katya, are multiplying and bringing forth much fruit.

The novel's tragic side predominates, but it does not overwhelm. Significantly, critics who write of *Fathers and Sons* as a tragedy often stop short of calling it a tragedy, pure and simple. Charles Bachman calls it "a basically tragic novel." Helen Muchnic describes the novel as "tragic in its implications, but not in its tone" [*An Introduction to Russian Literature,* 1942]. Such hesitation can be accounted for on the formal level by the recognition of coexisting comedic and tragic modes within the novel. Observing this relationship helps us to understand—in formal terms—the initial and continuing furor created by *Fathers and Sons.* In "Apropos of *Fathers and Sons*" Turgenev writes that he has an interesting collection of documents and letters from readers who accuse him of doing totally contradictory things in his novel. This is hardly surprising, since Turgenev *is* doing what seem to be contradictory things within the work. By combining the tragedic and comedic modes he seems to stand behind two diametrically opposed views of life at one and the same time. If we take the novel's comedic structure out of context, we conclude that life is triumphant, rewarding, and meaningful. Such is the conclusion that any comedy forces upon us. And in *Fathers and Sons* the portraits of the Kirsanovs, their babies, their joyful participation in the natural cycle, all lead the audience to infer that all's right with the world. On the other hand, if we take the novel's tragedic side out of context, we are led to the view that life, which is ruled by fate and the irrational, is essentially meaningless: death is triumphant. Where does Turgenev stand? "Where is the truth, on which side?" We may ask, as does Arkady. And Bazarov's answer is most appropri-

ate: "Where? I'll answer you like an echo: where?" An analysis of the novel's dualistic structure shows that the truth is on both sides. Or, as Fischler argues, the problems raised in *Fathers and Sons* are insoluble and the rifts revealed can be mended only by time. This conclusion is supported by one of Turgenev's letters to Annenkov, in which he writes: "I know that in nature and in life everything is reconciled one way or another. . . . If life cannot [do the reconciling], death will reconcile." Thus Turgenev's own view of life is dualistic, but not contradictory, and this dualism lies at the heart of *Fathers and Sons:* as we have seen in this [essay], it accounts for the novel's structure. (pp. 15-27)

> *David Lowe, in his* Turgenev's "Fathers and Sons," *Ardis, 1983, 165 p.*

Kathryn Feuer (essay date 1983)

> [*Feuer is an American professor of Slavic languages and literature. In the excerpt below, she suggests that* Fathers and Sons *explores not only the debate between Russian liberals and radicals, but, more importantly, themes involving love, death, and "continuity between generations."*]

That *Fathers and Sons (Ottsy i deti)* is a novel about the conflict between Russia's liberal, idealistic "men of the 1840s" and the radical, materialist "men of the 1860s" hardly needs demonstration. Most impressive in this respect is the delicacy and subtlety with which Turgenev has introduced many of the key signata of that debate into his fiction: the Pushkin—Gogol quarrel is there because Kirsanov senior loves to read Pushkin; Büchner's *Kraft und Stoff* is there as a "popularization" which Bazarov recommends for the elder Kirsanov's first step toward enlightenment (though nothing that we hear from Bazarov suggests that his own scientific sophistication extends beyond Büchner); even the seminarists are there—Bazarov's grandfather, we learn in a side remark, was a sexton, while Pavel Kirsanov refers to Bazarov as a "dirty seminarist." Many more instances could be cited of beautifully integrated specific references to Russian intellectual life in the late 1850s and anticipatory of the early sixties. As D. S. Mirsky has observed [in his *A History of Russian Literature: From Its Beginnings to 1900,* 1958], "*Fathers and Sons* is Turgenev's only novel where the social problem is distilled without residue into art. . . . " It is even prophetic, in its clash between the force of nihilistic destruction (Bazarov) and reverence for created beauty (Nikolai and Pavel Kirsanov), of three great future novels of revolution: Dostoevsky's *The Possessed (Besy),* Joseph Conrad's *Under Western Eyes,* and Henry James's *The Princess Casamassima.* Perhaps the most decisive argument for the novel's topicality, if any is needed, can be derived from the characters not included in its cast. In *Fathers and Sons* there are no reactionaries, not even any conservatives (except Nikolai Kirsanov's coachman, "who didn't share the latest views"); in a novel set in 1859, on the eve of the emancipation of the serfs, there is not one landowner who regrets, let alone opposes, this measure which, as Tolstoy wrote at the time, "deprived them of half their property." Here then is no panorama or even slice of Russian country gentry life but rather a selective representation of one small part.

The social-political interpretation of *Fathers and Sons* has been widespread. It was most recently articulated by Isaiah Berlin in his Romanes Lectures, published as *Fathers and Children,* where he calls the "central topic of the novel . . . the confrontation of the old and the young, of liberals and radicals, traditional civilization and the new, harsh positivism which has no use for anything except what is needed by a rational man." Ralph Matlaw, in his preface to the valuable Norton Critical Edition, explains that he has chosen the widely used English title "Fathers and Sons" rather than the literal "Fathers and Children" because " 'Sons' in English better implies the notions of spiritual and intellectual generations conveyed by the Russian *deti.*" Matlaw, with the majority of non-Soviet critics, sees Turgenev as having drawn on the specific details and data of the debate between Russian liberals and radicals for the portrayal of a not merely political but universal theme, the eternal conflict of generations.

Yet can our interpretation of the novel stop here? Only, I believe, at the cost of ignoring its deepest layer of meaning and thus missing its consummate achievement. The most perceptive discussion of *Fathers and Sons* that I have read is also, regrettably, very brief, an "introduction" to the novel by René Wellek [in *World Masterpieces,* vol. 2, ed. Maynard Mack, 1956]. Wellek begins by explaining and paying tribute to the admirable "concrete social picture" of an era and its disputes which Turgenev presents. Calling "the eternal conflict between the old and the young . . . one of the main themes of the book," nevertheless, he asserts, *Fathers and Sons* "goes beyond the temporal issues and enacts a far greater drama: man's deliverance to fate and chance, the defeat of man's calculating reason by the greater powers of love, honor, and death." "Man's deliverance to fate and chance" is indeed, I would submit, one central theme of the novel, but to see this clearly we must go a step further in the rejection of traditional interpretations. We must dispense with the notion that the novel portrays the conflict of generations and recognize that instead it portrays love between generations, the triumph of love over tension and conflict; that its essential core is the intertwining of two great themes, affectionate continuity from parent to child and child to parent and "man's deliverance to fate and chance," that is, man's knowledge of his own mortality. It is to this novel that Turgenev gave the title *Fathers and Children,* which is, moreover, a novel far more profound in its political implications than we have heretofore realized.

This reading of the book can best be elucidated by beginning at its conclusion, at the almost unbearable closing picture of Bazarov's aged parents kneeling and weeping at his grave. Waste, futility, and anguish are overwhelming, but then comes a dramatic reversal, and the novel ends with a declaration of hope:

> Can it be that their prayers, their tears, will be fruitless? Can it be that love, sacred, dedicated love will not be all-powerful? Oh no! However passionate, guilty, rebellious the heart concealed in the grave, the flowers growing over it gaze at

us serenely with their innocent eyes: not only of eternal peace do they speak to us, of that great peace of "indifferent" nature; they speak also of eternal reconciliation and of life without end. . . . [chap. 28]

This passage is remarkable, almost incomprehensible as a conclusion to all that has gone before it in the novel; the incongruity has been described best by Wellek: "Turgenev puts here 'indifferent nature' in quotation marks, but as early as in *A Sportsman's Sketches* (*Zapiski okhotnika*) he had said: 'From the depths of the age-old forests, from the everlasting bosom of waters the same voice is heard: "You are no concern of mine," says Nature to Man.' " And he adds, with reference to *Fathers and Sons:* "There is no personal immortality, no God who cares for man; nature is even a disease beyond reason—this seems the message Turgenev wants to convey." The contradictory quality of the last sentence of the novel has been noted by many readers, yet Wellek alone has commented on the particular peculiarity of Turgenev's having written " 'indifferent' nature" with the adjective in quotation marks, seeming to imply rejection of the idea of nature's indifference, an implication almost insulting to the reader, so opposite is it to the text of *Fathers and Sons* and to the major body of Turgenev's writings over the preceding quarter of a century.

The quotation marks can be read another way, however, as meaning not "so called" or "not really" but denoting— literally—a quotation, in this case a quotation from Pushkin, from the last lines of one of his bestknown poems, "Whether I wander along noisy streets" ("Brozhu li Ya vdol ulits shumnykh"):

> And let indifferent nature
> Shine in her eternal beauty.

That Turgenev could have had the poem in mind is not difficult to suppose. For most writers there are other writers whose lines, paragraphs, works, exist as part of their consciousness, touchstones which may only occasionally be specified but whose presence is constant. For Turgenev, Pushkin was such a writer. The last stanza of the poem, indeed, is a major passage in the conclusion of one of Turgenev's most important early works, **"Diary of a Superfluous Man"** (**"Dnevnik lishnego cheloveka"**). Moreover, Pushkin's poetry is an important presence in *Fathers and Sons:* as a thematic element, as an emotional vector, as an emblem for the existence of beauty.

The significance for the novel of the proposed allusion to "Whether I wander . . ." emerges only from the entire poem:

> Whether I wander along noisy streets,
> Or go into a crowded temple,
> Or sit among carefree young men,
> I give myself up to revery.
>
> I say: the years will pass,
> And though so many of us are here today,
> We shall all reassemble beneath the
> Eternal vaults—And for some one
> Of us the hour is already near.
>
> If I gaze at a solitary oak tree

I think: this patriarch of the forest
Will outlive my transitory age,
As it has outlived that of my fathers.

As I caress a sweet little child,
Already I think: farewell!
I yield place to you:
It's time for me to decay, for you to flower.

Every day, every season
It's become my habit to accompany with the
    thought
Of the anniversary of my approaching death
Trying to guess what day it will be.

And where will fate send death to me?
In battle? On the road? On the sea?
Or will a near-by valley
Receive my cold ashes?

And although to my lifeless body
It can make no difference where it will molder,
Still I would wish to rest
Close to a dear familiar place.

And at the entrance to my tomb
Let there be young life at play.
And let indifferent nature
Shine in her eternal beauty.

Pushkin's poem is about death and about the poet's morbidly haunted awareness of the random uncertainty of the time when it will come and the utter certainty of its coming. What we find in **Fathers and Sons,** I suggest, is the onset of Pushkin's malady in Bazarov, as a direct consequence of his love for Odintsova. Once this love has infected him, he becomes haunted by the knowledge of his own mortality. It has always been recognized that Bazarov's love crippled him, although some readers see Odintsova's rejection as the decisive event. I am proposing here that the effect of love on Bazarov was not some sort of general demoralization coming from a recognition that his nature does not correspond with his ideology, but a specific effect, the one I have called Pushkin's malady: an obsession with the knowledge of his own mortality.

Throughout the first fourteen chapters of the novel Bazarov is a triumphant expression of the life-force, a man exuberantly intelligent and supremely self-confident, caring for no one's good opinion but his own. He is liked by the peasants, works assiduously, takes pride in being Russian, exhibits a zest for life in a variety of ways: his pleasure in Fenichka's "splendid" baby, his eagerness for a visit to town, his appreciation of pretty women. His serious concerns are positive. He scorns upbringing or the "age we live in" as excuses for weakness: "As for our times—why should I depend on that? Let my times depend on me" (chap. 7).

In chapter 15 the crucial transition occurs. When Bazarov and Arkadi first call on Odintsova, Arkadi sees that "contrary to his habit Bazarov was talking a good deal and obviously trying to interest" Odintsova. Then, as they leave, when Odintsova expresses the polite hope that they may visit her estate: "Bazarov only bowed and—a last surprise for Arkadi; he noticed that his friend was blushing." Shortly after, when Arkadi comments on Odintsova's beauty, Bazarov agrees: "A splendid body! Perfect for the

dissection table." And three days later, as the friends are driving to Odintsova's estate: " 'Congratulate me,' Bazarov suddenly exclaimed, 'today is June 22nd, my guardian angel's day. Well, we'll see how he'll take care of me.' "

What has happened here? Bazarov has called on his "guardian angel"; whether he realizes it or not he is aware for the first time of his vulnerability to death; he is subconsciously asking Pushkin's question: "Is the hour already near?" He will continue to ask the question until he dies, and his preoccupation, usually just below the surface though sometimes bursting forth in bitter outrage, will be expressed in the imagery of disease or death, which first enters his consciousness and conversation in the moment we have witnessed: "A splendid body! Perfect for the dissection table."

In chapter 16 he illustrates a nonmedical argument to Odintsova by an analogy with "the lungs of a consumptive." In chapter 17, when he has acknowledged his passion to himself, this love "tortured and possessed him," for he regarded such feelings "as something like deformity or disease." In chapter 18, when Odintsova asks whether happiness exists, Bazarov can answer only: "You know the proverb: it's always better where we don't exist." A little later, when she tries to question him about his plans and ambitions, he answers ominously: "What's the point of talking or thinking about the future, which for the most part doesn't depend on us?"

Immediately after this exchange come Bazarov's declaration of his love and Odintsova's refusal. Now the images of disease increase: in Bazarov's speech there is a movement from the sense of vulnerability to that of fatality. Moreover, new motifs appear: insecure megalomania supersedes self-confidence, hostility to Arkadi replaces condescending but genuine friendship. In chapter 19 he agrees to Arkadi's accusation of elitism: " 'Is it that *you're* a god while I'm just one of the blockheads?' 'Yes,' Bazarov repeated weightily, 'you're still stupid.' " Besides increasing in number, Bazarov's images of disease and death are now applied to himself: "The machine's become unstuck." Then, still in chapter 19, Bazarov articulates the first unequivocal statement of his intimation: "Every man hangs on a thread; the abyss can open up beneath him at any moment. . . . "

Soon after, his preoccupation with his "approaching . . . anniversary" breaks forth more explicitly:

> "I think, here I am, lying under a haystack . . .
> the tiny, cramped spot I occupy is so minute in
> comparison with the rest of the universe, where
> I don't exist and where I don't matter; and the
> space of time allotted for me to live in is a mere
> moment in that eternity of time where I was not
> and will not be . . . And in this atom, in this
> mathematical dot, the blood circulates, the brain
> works, there's even a desire for something. . . .
> How outrageous it is! How petty!" [chap. 21]

Bazarov now gives way to impotent fury, vindictiveness, malice:

> "Ha! There's a fine fellow of an ant, dragging off
> a half-dead fly. Take her, brother, take her. It

doesn't matter that she resists, make use of her as you will."

When Bazarov lauds hatred, "How strange!" Arkadi observes, "why I don't hate anyone." "And I hate so many," Bazarov replies:

> "Hatred! Well, for example take yesterday—as we were passing our bailiff, Phillip's cottage—and you said that Russia will attain perfection when every last muzhik has such a place to live, and that every one of us ought to work to bring that about. . . . And I felt such a hatred for your every last muzhik. . . . Yes, he'll be living in a white cottage, while the nettles are growing out of me. . . ."

> "Ah, Arkadi, do me a favor, let's have a fight, a real fight, till we're laid out in our coffins, till we destroy each other."

This attack on Arkadi has been triggered by his comment on a dead leaf falling to earth, fluttering like a butterfly: "Gloom and death," he remarks, "and at the same time gaiety and life!" What seems to enrage Bazarov is that Arkadi can accept the unity of life and death, can see death as a part of life rather than as its negation.

Bazarov's bravery during the duel with Pavel Kirsanov only underlines the depth and inner intensity of his preoccupation with death. It is not the concrete incident in which his life is endangered which obsesses the death-haunted man; it is the subliminal question, when and where, which accompanies him whether wandering noisy streets or lounging beneath a haystack.

After his departure from the Kirsanovs Bazarov pays a brief visit to Odintsova; once again the imagery of death is related to himself. When Odintsova tells him that he is a "good man," he replies: "That's the same as laying a wreath of flowers on the head of a corpse" (chap. 26). Is there also a presentiment of fatality in Bazarov's parting words to her? When she tells him she is sure they will meet again (as of course they do, at Bazarov's deathbed), he answers: "In this world, anything may happen!" Such an interpretation of his words is prepared by the grim pun with which he has just before informed Arkadi that he is stopping by at Odintsova's on his way home: "Well, so I've set off 'to the fathers.' " As Matlaw points out, Bazarov here "mockingly (and ominously) recalls the *'ad patres'* used by Bazarov's father earlier [in chap. 20] as an expression for death."

Bazarov goes home for six weeks to settle down to work. Are the lethargy and melancholy that soon overtake him further evidence of his morbid preoccupation? It hardly matters. Soon, whether by accident or suicide, he *is* dying and, as when he faced death in the duel, his behavior is calm and courageous. The fear has dissolved, once it has become recognized reality. On one occasion he does rebel: he takes hold of a heavy table and manages to swing it around: " 'Strength, real strength,' he murmured. 'It's all still here, and yet I must die! . . . Well, go and try to refute death. She'll refute you, and that's that!' " (chap. 27). Bazarov is no longer haunted by wondering: the question of the date of the "approaching . . . anniversary" has been

answered and we have come to the scene of Bazarov's grave, to the grieving parents, to Turgenev's assertion that the flowers speak of eternal reconciliation and not just of " 'indifferent' nature," and so back to Pushkin's poem.

The poet is haunted by the question of when death will come and then proceeds to a corollary question; *where* will it come? But this question is not obsessive; rather it provides a transition to the one consideration which can make the question of "when" bearable, for it allows him to imagine the grave in which—since there must be one—he would choose to lie. He has spoken of "moldering" or "decaying," but now he writes of "the place where I shall rest." It is, he hopes, a nearby valley, radiant with the beauty of "indifferent nature" but also alive with "young life at play." Death is bearable because life goes on. Pushkin has prepared this final statement in stanza 4: "As I caress a sweet little child." He speaks, moreover, of the continuity of generations not only for the future but from the past; in stanza 3 he writes of the oak tree which will outlive his age as it has outlived those of his fathers. (The force of the juxtaposition is vitiated in translation; in the original, "fathers" is the last word of stanza 3 and "child" is the first word of stanza 4.)

Once again the poem sheds light on *Fathers and Sons.* At Bazarov's grave are only his aged parents, grieving for the worst thing that can happen to parents, for the most unnatural pain which Nature can inflict, to outlive one's own child. Despite the birds and flowers and young pine trees there is no "young life at play;" Bazarov has been denied the single solace Pushkin offers to the man beset by the knowledge of his own mortality. This solace not only sheds light on the novel's closing scene but also states its second, inextricably related theme: love and continuity between generations.

Sharp conflict in the novel there is, but it is not between fathers and sons: it is between two men who dislike each other because they are fundamentally so much alike, Pavel Kirsanov and Bazarov. Were they contemporaries they might find different things to quarrel and duel over, but quarrel and duel they would. The father-son and son-father relationships are, on the other hand, respectful, affectionate, and deeply loving, despite the faint note of menace at the very outset, on the ride home after Arkadi's father has met him and Bazarov at the station. Arkadi and his father, riding together in the carriage, are renewing their acquaintance with affectionate sympathy when Bazarov, from the other coach, interrupts to give Arkadi a cigar. Arkadi lights the cigar, and it emits "such a strong and sour smell of stale tobacco that Nikolai Petrovich . . . could not avoid averting his face, though he did so stealthily so as not to offend his son" (chap. 3). But the threat of estrangement dissipates; it is never more substantial than cigar smoke in the breeze.

Arkadi's father defers to him on occasion after occasion and tries hard to adopt his attitudes and opinions. When he cannot, it is himself he considers inferior, as, when musing in the garden, he reflects:

> "My brother says that we are right, and putting aside any element of vanity, it does seem to me that they are farther from the truth than we are,

but at the same time I feel that behind them there is something that we don't possess, a kind of superiority over us. . . . Is it youth? No, it's not just youth. That's not the source of their superiority; isn't it that in them there are fewer traces of the slave owner than in us?" [chap. 11]

At the end of this remarkable scene Kirsanov is called by Fenichka, and he answers her more offhandedly than he would a woman of his own class: "I'm coming—run along!" And yet throughout the novel, although she is the housekeeper's daughter, both Nikolai and his brother treat her with perfect courtesy: Pavel Kirsanov, for example, always addresses her formally. It is only Bazarov who, having no right to do so, uses the familiar form of her name. And it is only Bazarov who flirts with her as with a servant girl, who behaves as he does not and would not behave with Odintsova. It is only Bazarov, in fact, who displays "the slave owner's mentality."

Bazarov's mother beatifically adores him, while his father does not merely defer to his son's views, he suppresses some of his own deepest feelings. The love of the fathers for the sons, however, hardly needs demonstration; instances can be found in every scene in which they appear together. The interpretation of the novel as a depiction of the conflict of generations rests rather on the attitudes of the sons toward the fathers. Where are these conflicts to be found? In a few moments of condescension or irritation or even unkindness by the sons, in Nikolai Kirsanov's hour of melancholy in the garden, in the disappointment of Bazarov's parents that his visit is so short. One can apply the term *conflict* to such moments only under the assumption that gentle condescension, slight irritation, unkindness, sorrow, and disappointment are not normal components of all human relations, under the assumption that we are living on the planet of Dostoevsky's Ridiculous Man before he visited it.

From the outset Arkadi is glad to be hugged and kissed by his father and hugs and kisses him in return, calling him "daddy" (*papasha*); even Bazarov's presence is only faintly inhibiting. The one feeling Arkadi has toward his father that could be called critical is that of condescension; it occurs on three occasions. First, when Arkadi, smiling "affectionately," tells him that his shame at his relationship with Fenichka is "nonsense" . . . "and his heart was filled with a feeling of condescending tenderness toward his good and soft-hearted father, combined with a sense of a certain secret superiority" (chap. 3). Second, when he displays conscious magnanimity in paying a formal call on Fenichka. Third, when Arkadi agrees to give his father *Kraft und Stoff* to read, approving this choice because it is a "popularization" (chap. 10). Not only does Arkadi never once manifest hostility or irritation toward his father, there is even no friction between them. On the three occasions when he condescends to him he does so tenderly, with affectionate respect, with embraces, with loving compassion and gentleness.

Perhaps even more significant is Arkadi's behavior to his uncle. Their mutual affection is open, and for a man of Pavel Petrovich's deep reserve, even demonstrative. When Pavel criticizes Bazarov (and on this occasion unjustly)

Arkadi's response is the one with which we are acquainted—a silent look of compassion for his uncle's noncomprehension. When Bazarov criticizes Pavel (both wittily and aptly) Arkadi attempts a weak rejoinder, then deflects the attack: "Maybe so, only truly, he's a fine, good person" (chap. 4). Most important is that, despite his imitation of Bazarov's opinions, awe of his powers, and fear of his disapproval, despite, in short, Arkadi's schoolboy crush on Bazarov, he never wavers in his defense of his uncle.

Bazarov can be brusque to his parents but never treats them with the rudeness with which he treats everyone else. He submits to their repeated embraces ("Just let me hug you once more, Yenyushechka"), and he willingly kisses his mother (chap. 20). He is perfectly good-humored about having the priest to dinner, understanding what this means to his mother and father. When he decides to leave—abruptly and even cruelly after a visit home of only three days—part of his motivation is, in fact, love for his parents:

> "While I'm here my father keeps assuring me: 'My study is all yours; no one will bother you there'; and he can't keep a foot away from me. And it makes me feel guilty to shut myself away from him. And it's the same with mother. I hear through the wall how she's sighing—and so I go out to her—and then I have nothing to say to her." [chap. 21]

Though he tells himself, "never mind, they will get over it," all the same it takes Bazarov a whole day to bring himself to inform his parents that he is leaving, and having gone: "Bazarov was not altogether satisfied with himself" (chap. 22). At the one place in the novel where he exposes his inner feelings with ruthless honesty, the scene beneath the haystack, there is the following solemn exchange:

> "Do you love them, Yevgeni?"
>
> "I love them, Arkadi."

The supreme expression of Bazarov's love for his parents comes with his ultimate sacrifice for their sake. He is willing to receive extreme unction, though "at the sight of the priest in his robes, of the smoking censer and the candles before the icon something like a shudder of horror passed for a moment over the death-stricken face" (chap. 27). This is for him a final negation of all that his life has meant to him.

May it not even be said that Bazarov, who loves his parents and understands their love for him, has intimations not only of his mortality but also of the despair that will surround his grave, where there will be no "young life at play"? Consider his final parting with Arkadi:

> "There is, Arkadi, there is something else I want to say, only I won't say it because it's romanticism—and that means soggy sentiments. You get married, as soon as you can, and you build your nest, and you have lots of children. . . ." [chap. 26]

(pp. 67-77)

Kathryn Feuer, "High Noon: 'Fathers and Sons', Fathers and Children," in The Russian Novel from Pushkin to Pasternak, *edited by*

John Garrard, Yale University Press, 1983, pp. 67-80.

Maurice Baring on Bazarov's nihilism:

In *Fathers and Sons,* Tourgeniev drew a portrait of the 'Lucifer' type, of an unbending and inflexible will, namely, Bazarov. There is no character in the whole of his work which is more alive; and nothing that he wrote ever aroused so much controversy and censure as this figure. Tourgeniev invented the type of the intellectual Nihilist in fiction. If he was not the first to invent the word, he was the first to apply it and to give it currency. The type remains, and will remain, of the man who believes in nothing, bows to nothing, bends to nothing, and who retains his invincible pride until death strikes him down.

Maurice Baring, in his Landmarks in Russian Literature, *Methuen, 1910.*

James B. Woodward   (essay date 1986)

[*Woodward is a British educator and the author of several works on Russian writers. In the following excerpt, he explores how* Fathers and Sons *is fundamentally a depiction of various "wars of wills," and as such expresses Turgenev's philosophical belief that life is a continuous struggle.*]

'In order to produce an artistic result', Turgenev wrote in **"Po povodu Ottsov i detey"** (1868-69), 'the combined action of many *factors*—to use modern terminology—is necessary'. It is the 'combined action', of course, of 'many factors' in his most famous novel that has produced an 'artistic result' of such absorbing complexity. The continuing debate on the novel's meaning and on the significance of its hero has centred thus far on four 'factors' in particular, on the nature, interaction and relative importance of the four major sources of conflict between the characters: the differences of generation, class, ideology and personality. The two contrasting views of the work that have emerged from this debate are well known. Some commentators, citing in support the statement of Turgenev's personal views in his letter to K. K. Sluchevsky of 14 April 1862, have attached an overriding importance to the first three sources of conflict and have acclaimed Bazarov as an unequivocally heroic figure, as an uncompromising rebel against the existing order tragically born before his time and as a personified exposé of the limitations of the other characters. Others have placed the emphasis on the fourth source of conflict, arguing that 'the grouping of characters illustrating the conflict of generations gives way to one of personality and experience that cuts across differences of age or ideology' [J. Blair, in his "The Architecture of Turgenev's *Fathers and Sons*," *Modern Fiction Studies* XIX, No. A (1973-74)]. According to this reading, it is the limitations of Bazarov that are exposed and Nikolay and Arkady are 'the true heroes of the novel'. Various attempts have been made to reconcile these views, among which the recent monograph of D. Lowe [*Turgenev's "Fathers and*

Sons," 1983] deserves special mention, but in each case one view has tended to prevail at the expense of the other. The purpose of this article is to suggest a different approach to the problem by switching the emphasis to an additional 'factor' in the novel which dictates a notably different attitude to the relationships and conflicts depicted. This fifth 'factor' is the conception of life that is dramatized in the novel—a conception, it will be argued, which is chiefly associated with the figure of Bazarov but which lies at the basis of the work as a whole. It is proposed to examine the nature of this conception and some of the more striking ways in which it receives expression.

Bazarov's nihilistic theories are usually characterized as essentially a reformulation of the views of the radicals or 'enlighteners' of the 1860s. The argument is based, of course, on substantial evidence. The materialistic doctrines of Chernyshevsky and Dobrolyubov and the aggressively critical style of the movement they represented are clearly reflected in Bazarov's statements and attitudes. At the same time it is generally conceded that his views cannot be wholly explained by reference to these sources. Indeed, some commentators have insisted that the differences are so significant that the traditional view is untenable. Thus V. M. Markovich writes [in *I. S. Turgenev i russkiy realistichesky roman XIX veka,* 1982]: 'We have before us a view of the world which is unlike any that is known (though it is comparable to many) and which has its own special aims and reference points. The revolutionary character of the figure before us is in essence and in principle quite different from that of the democrats of the 'sixties'. Three features, in particular, of Turgenev's hero have prompted this judgement. They are the absolute self-affirmation of the individual ego to which Bazarov gives such vigorous expression; the 'maximalism', the 'rejection of everything', that results from this elevation of the self above all authorities; and the limitation of his aims to simple 'destruction'. This combination of features, it is argued, finds no parallel in the theories and personalities of Bazarov's alleged prototypes and must therefore be regarded as indicating the author's intention to convey something more than simply an aspect of the 'body and pressure' of the time in question. The latter part of this argument is accepted in this article, but not to the exclusion of the more usual view. The view taken is that the indicated characteristics of Bazarov should be seen as reflecting Turgenev's attempt to combine in the portrait of his hero certain aspects of the 'new man' proclaimed by Chernyshevsky and Dobrolyubov with the general understanding of life to which he came increasingly to subscribe from the late 'fifties onward. This was the conception of life as a 'struggle for existence' to which a number of influences clearly contributed.

The source of influence that immediately suggests itself, of course, is Darwin's *The Origin of Species* which appeared in 1859—the year in which Turgenev completed **Nakanune** and in which the action of **Ottsy i deti** takes place. Both novels, as A. Batyuto has argued [in *Turgenev-romanist,* 1967], provide grounds for the inference that he was familiar with the work. The most obvious are Shubin's observations in **Nakanune** on the 'centripetal' law of nature and the reflections of this law in the personality and conduct of Bazarov—for example, his pride in his strength and self-sufficiency, his conception of himself as a superior being (as a 'god' or 'giant'), his contempt for his fellow men, the pleasure that he derives from the sight of an ant dragging off its prey, and the uncontrollable urge inspired by this spectacle to assert his own authority physically over the unfortunate Arkady. 'Everywhere there is the same Darwinian "battle for life" ', Turgenev wrote in a letter to Ya. P. Polonsky of 1 March 1878, and the evidence of his art is that he had reached this conclusion much earlier. Even so, it must be judged highly questionable whether he had reached it under Darwin's influence in the period 1860-62 when he was working on *Ottsy i deti*. The most obvious reason for doubt is the complete absence of explicit references to Darwin from his works and correspondence of this period. Only three references to Darwin, in fact, are encountered in the whole of his correspondence, the earliest in a letter [to A. A. Fet dated 26 September 1871], while references in the fiction are confined to Paklin's invocation of 'Darwinism' in the last chapter of *Nov'* (1877). In addition, there are clear indications that the notion of life as a 'struggle for existence' had already taken root in Turgenev's thinking even before *The Origin of Species* appeared. The evidence suggests, in short, that Darwin's work served him less as a source of enlightenment than as a confirmation of conclusions that he had reached already. The actual development of these conclusions can more plausibly be linked with an influence which he more readily acknowledged—that of Schopenhauer's *Die Welt als Wille und Vorstellung*.

The influence of Schopenhauer on Turgenev's thought has frequently been noted and is now generally accepted. It can be dated, in Batyuto's judgement, from 1855. Hitherto, however, it has been considered a factor of importance only in relation to the changed vision of nature which is first attested in Turgenev's works in *Poyezdka v Poles' ye* (1857) and to the pessimism of *Prizraki* (1863), *Dovol'no* (1865) and *Senilia* (1882). Rather surprisingly discussion of the subject has rarely been broadened to incorporate the three novels that appeared between 1857 and 1863, and on the few occasions on which it has been raised in connection with *Ottsy i deti* it has been considered only in relation to the deepening pessimism of Bazarov in the latter half of the novel. Yet in *Die Welt als Wille und Vorstellung* Turgenev encountered a conception of life which anticipated that of Darwin in a number of significant respects. Here [in Schopenhauer's *The World as Will and Idea*, translated by R. B. Haldane and J. Kemp, 1907-09], for example, he would have read:

> Everywhere in nature we see strife, conflict and alternation of victory, and in it we shall come to recognize more distinctly that variance with itself which is essential to the will. Every grade of the objectification of will fights for the matter, the space and the time of the others. . . . Thus the will to live everywhere preys upon itself, and in different forms is its own nourishment, till finally the human race, because it subdues all the others, regards nature as a manufactory for its use. Yet even the human race . . . reveals in itself with most terrible distinctness this conflict,

this variance with itself of the will, and we find *homo homini lupus*.

For Schopenhauer too, therefore, life is a struggle for existence, a 'war of wills', and on at least two occasions in the passage we are again reminded of Bazarov. The statement that the human race 'regards nature as a manufactory for its use' is reminiscent of his well known description of nature as 'no temple but merely a workshop', while the concluding characterization of human relations is echoed in Turgenev's reference to him as 'a wolf' in his letter to Sluchevsky of 14 April 1862. 'Only the life of the individual has unity, connection and true significance', wrote Schopenhauer, and with his rejection of all supra-individualistic abstractions and general principles Bazarov presents himself as the embodiment of this belief. Turgenev's description of his hero in his letter to Sluchevsky as 'a gloomy figure, wild, huge, half-grown out of the earth, powerful, malicious and honest' suggests strongly that he conceived of him as the very incarnation of that crude, elemental, 'ferocious' force of nature which Schopenhauer termed the 'will to live'.

The passage quoted, however, introduces only one aspect of Schopenhauer's philosophy—his conception of nature from the point of view of self-consciousness, according to which nature has her centre in every individual and therefore announces: 'I alone am all in all: in my maintenance everything is involved; the rest may perish, it is really nothing'. This aspect is complemented by his conception of nature from the universal point of view which he summarizes as follows:

> From the *universal* point of view—which is that of the *consciousness of other things,* that of objective knowledge, which for the moment looks away from the individual with whom the knowledge is connected,—from without then, from the periphery, nature speaks thus: 'The individual is nothing, and less than nothing. I destroy millions of individuals every day, for sport and pastime: I abandon their fate to the most capricious and willful of my children, chance, who harasses them at pleasure. I produce millions of new individuals every day, without any diminution of my productive power; just as little as the power of a mirror is exhausted by the number of reflections of the sun which it casts on the wall one after another. The individual is nothing'.

Such, according to Schopenhauer, is the objectively viewed position of the individual who sees himself as everything, and reflections of this view, as *Poyezdka v Poles'ye* most obviously testifies, are clearly apparent in Turgenev's works of the late 'fifties. This is the view of the human condition that he commended to Herzen when he wrote to him [in a letter dated 23 October 1862] one month after the serialization of *Ottsy i deti* began in *Russkiy vestnik:* 'Schopenhauer, my friend, you should read Schopenhauer a little more diligently.' And he must surely have been struck by Herzen's response [in a 10 November 1862 letter]: 'Have you noticed that with your Schopenhauer . . . you are becoming a nihilist?' Endorsing Schopenhauer's view of the individual as 'nothing', he was himself branded with the term which he had used in his novel to denote the precise opposite—the individual who is 'everything', who recognizes nothing except the dictates of his own will and sensations. The same term was employed to denote the two contrasting conceptions of the human condition which coincided with the contrasting views of nature that Turgenev had encountered in his reading of Schopenhauer.

In *Ottsy i deti* these two forms of nihilism—that of Bazarov and that of Turgenev—coexist and collide with tragic consequences for the hero. The fictional apostle of nihilism is ironically sacrificed on the altar of the nihilism of his creator. The hero who recognizes no authority above himself is ultimately obliged to acknowledge his human impotence. Morover, the irony extends further, for the transition results from the natural scientist's defeat in the world of nature as he himself apprehends it, in the 'war of wills' which the novel depicts. In accordance with Schopenhauer's 'objective' view of nature, Turgenev remarked to Valentina Delessert in a letter of 16 July 1864: 'Des mouches qui se heurtent sans relâche contre une vitre— c'est, je crois, notre plus parfait symbole.' The symbol is anticipated in *Ottsy i deti* in the scene that depicts Bazarov's defeat—his first confrontation with a will that resists his attempts at conquest. Having declared his love for Odintsova, whose name is itself an obvious symbol of self-sufficiency, he 'leaned with his forehead', we read, 'against the window-pane. He was gasping for breath; his whole body was visibly trembling'. From this moment onward the power of his will is seen in its gradual decline. 'The machine has fallen apart', he declares to Arkady as they drive away from Nikol'skoye, and the second half of the novel records his agonizing experience of the mental, and ultimately physical, paralysis induced by the revelation of his limited powers and by his deepening awareness of the 'objective' truth of the human condition.

Bazarov's eventual acknowledgement of this truth is clearly one of the major differences between him and Insarov in *Nakanune.* It is this, perhaps above all, that makes him such an incomparably more interesting figure. In both novels Turgenev portrays men distinguished by their strength of will and preaches the futility of the will's striving by condemning them both to a premature death. The difference is that Bazarov is prepared for the futility of death by the knowledge that he acquires of the futility of life, so that in the end death comes to him as much from within as from without. In other respects the two heroes plainly have much in common, and the motto of Cesare Borgia 'Aut Caesar aut nihil' with which the doctor in *Nakanune* defines the two possible futures that he foresees for the stricken Insarov succinctly foreshadows also the two contrasting faces of Bazarov. In one sense, of course, the prediction expressed by the motto misrepresents the fates of both heroes, for the two possibilities indicated by the doctor turn out in reality to be not alternatives but the two sequential stages of their common experience. Both begin as 'Caesars', as 'strong men' who see themselves as the centre of the universe, and end as 'nothing'. But again the difference must be stressed. Although both novels end with the hero's death, the transition from 'Caesar' to 'nihil' in the case of Bazarov is effected, as stated, not by death's brutal intervention, as it is in the story of Insarov, but by the defeat that he experiences in the 'war of wills'

in which the characters of *Ottsy i deti* are almost uniformly engaged. In this celebrated novel of conflict this 'war of wills' or 'war of Caesars' is Turgenev's primary subject, forming the basis on which he erects the complex superstructure of ideological, class and generational differences, and consideration must now be given to some of the reflections of its presence and to some aspects of the manner in which the participants are portrayed.

The phrase 'Aut Caesar aut nihil' may itself be taken to introduce one of the more significant of these aspects, and it is in this connection that account should be taken of a third influence on Turgenev's thinking in the late 'fifties— that of the works of the Roman historians, especially Suetonius's *De vita Caesarum,* in which he displayed a profound interest during this period. The coordinating theme of Suetonius's portraits of the twelve Caesars is the power of the individual and its abuse, and in the light of Turgenev's philosophical interests at this time and his increasing preoccupation with the topical problem of the 'strong man' it is not difficult to understand why he became so absorbed in these portraits and why he professed to find Suetonius and the other major Roman historians 'extremely modern' writers. 'You will ask', he wrote to Herzen [on 24 November 1856] 'what is this "Latinomania" that has seized me. I don't know. Perhaps it is induced by the times in which we live'. Considered against this background, the relative frequency with which Latin words and phrases appear in *Ottsy i deti* cannot be regarded as coincidental. Excluding the two technical terms used by Bazarov (the name of a beetle and that of a muscle), there are twelve in all, compared with one in *Rudin,* one in *Dvoryanskoye gnezdo,* two in *Nakanune,* three in *Dym* (two of which are merely linguistic indicators of Potugin's Westernism), and four in *Nov'* (all of which form satirical elements in the portraits of Sipyagin and Kislyakov); and with the exception of Nikolay Petrovich's comment on the Latin source of the term 'nihilist' they are all encountered in statements by Bazarov (five) and his father Vasily Ivanovich (six), who is described by his son as having been 'a mighty Latinist in his time' and whose 'Latinomania' reveals itself also in his familiarity with the poetry of Horace, in his reference to himself as 'a kind of Cincinnatus' and in his comparison of his son and Arkady to Castor and Pollux. The view is usually taken, therefore, that these words and phrases are interpolated as reflections of the kind of education received by such *raznochintsy* as Bazarov *père* and *fils* in seminaries and *gimnazii*, and Bazarov's disclosure that his paternal grandfather was a sacristan would seem to support this view. There is substantial evidence, however, that the primary function of these words and phrases is symbolic, that they form part of the symbolic representation of the self-sufficient individual in the novel as an 'emperor' or 'Caesar'. Ostensibly, of course, this would seem a rather curious claim to make in reference to the portrait and personality of Bazarov's father, and it will be necessary to substantiate it in some detail. But one general observation must first be made. It is that the Latin words and phrases used by Bazarov and his father are neither quotations (with the one exception of Vasily Ivanovich's quotation from Paracelsus) nor (with the two indicated exceptions) technical terms reflecting their common professional interests, but on the contrary conspicuously ordinary words and phrases which enter their conversation freely in places where Russian words and phrases would in almost every case have been equally appropriate. Thus Bazarov responds 'bene' (instead of 'khorosho') when informed by Arkady that Fenechka's patronymic is Nikolayevna and 'optime' (instead of 'prevoskhodno') when Arkady confirms that Odintsova's estate Nikol'skoye is on the way to his parents' village. Similarly his father prefers 'suum cuique' to 'vsyakomu svoyo', 'ad patres' to 'k praottsam' and 'gratis' to 'darom', and in general shows little sign, when using these words, of that straining for effect which is apparent in his attempts to convince Arkady that he is no rural primitive. The impression conveyed, in short, is that for both father and son the Latin language is just as natural a mode of self-expression as is the French language for Pavel Petrovich, and it is interesting to note in this connection the 'duel' between these second languages of Pavel Petrovich and Bazarov which precedes their pistol duel. Responding to Pavel Petrovich's complaint about his persistent joking—a complaint which ends with the admonition 'A bon entendeur, salut!'—Basarov remarks: 'Why shouldn't we laugh and combine *utile dulci?*', adding: 'You address me in French, and I address you in Latin. The duel itself is thus prefigured. In the exchange of shots, as in the verbal exchange, the adherent of Latin, the language of Caesar, fires last and duly conquers.

In the light of these remarks the mistaken rendering of Arkady's surname by the governor of the town in chapter 12 clearly acquires a certain interest. Mistaking Arkady and Bazarov for brothers, he addresses them in apparent confusion not as Kirsanovs but as Kaysarovs ('Caesarovs'). As the most explicit allusion in the novel to the symbolic 'idea of Caesar' with which the notion of the powerful individual is associated, the name explains, in effect, Bazarov's 'Latinomania'. And the extension of the symbolism to Arkady is entirely appropriate, for at this stage in the novel's development, of course, he is still wholly under the influence of his mentor, subscribing unreservedly to his views on the prerogatives and obligations of the individual and having no compunction about confiscating his father's copy of Pushkin's *Tsygany* and replacing it with Büchner's *Stoff und Kraft* (*Matter and Power*). The 'mistake', however, not only provides an explicit indication of a symbolic theme that pervades the work; it also illuminates two additional points of general significance. In the first place, it confirms, like the name 'Odintsova', that ***Ottsy i deti*** is one of the numerous works by Turgenev which reflect his predilection for characteronyms. And secondly, as a substitution for 'Kirsanov', the name 'Kaysarov' indirectly informs the reader that the various reflections in the novel of Turgenev's 'Latinomania' form merely a part of the more generally *classical* element that he enlists to express the idea of the self-sufficient or 'imperial' individual. For the name is not only a substitution for 'Kirsanov'; it is also a gloss on it, a pointer to the Greek source of its first syllable—the noun *kurios* meaning 'lord' or 'master' which is combined with the root of the Russian *sanovnik* ('dignitary') to express the same idea. But it is not only the significance of the name 'Kirsanov' that the 'mistake' illuminates in this manner, for it is equally informative about the name 'Bazarov'. Naturally enough, though quite inappropriately, the name of the novel's central figure has often been connected with the noun *bazar* ('bazaar, market') and has accordingly been interpreted as suggesting the notion of a hotch-potch of ideas and attitudes or, in the words of one commentator, an 'unsorted and overabundant supply' [A. Fischler, "The Garden Motif and the Structure Of Turgenev's *Fathers and Sons,*" (*Novel: a Forum on Fiction* IX, No. 3, 1976)]. The bestowal on the hero of the name 'Kaysarov' suggests as a far more likely and appropriate source the first and second syllables respectively of the Greek and Latin words for 'emperor' *Basileus* and *Caesar* (in Russian *Tsezar'*). And this suggestion becomes all the more plausible in the light of the fact that *Basileus* is also the source of his father's Christian name Vasily and thus of Bazarov's patronymic, while the Greek sources of the hero's Christian name Yevgeny convey the related idea of 'well born'. In the name 'Bazarov', therefore, if this hypothesis is correct, expressive elements derived from the two classical languages are not simply juxtaposed, as in the names 'Kirsanov' and 'Kaysarov', but are uniquely combined to give fittingly consummate expression to the idea of the individual as 'emperor'.

The symbolic portrayal of Bazarov in the novel as a conquering 'emperor' or 'lord' is conveyed, of course, in many other ways—by such passing statements, for example, as the narrator's remark that in his discussions with him 'Arkady usually remained vanquished', by his exclamation to Arkady: 'Give us fresh victims! For us the breaking of other men is a need!' and by Pavel Petrovich's contemptuous reference to him as 'that *signor,* that nihilist', which expresses succinctly the view of the individual on which Bazarov's nihilism rests. But particularly noteworthy in this connection is his father's tendency to associate him with the figures of Napoleon I and Napoleon III. Thus when Father Aleksey expresses surprise in chapter 21 at the risks taken by Bazarov in a card game, Vasily Ivanovich remarks: 'It's the Napoleonic rule, father, the Napoleonic rule', to which Father Aleksey aptly responds with the oblique prediction: 'It was this that brought him to the island of St Helena.' And again, when congratulating a peasant woman in chapter 27 on her good fortune in having his son to treat her, Vasily Ivanovich exclaims: 'The Emperor of the French, Napoleon himself, has no better doctor.' These remarks of Bazarov's father acquire particular interest in the light of Turgenev's comments on Napoleon I in a letter to Pauline Viardot of July 1849: 'Quelle grande et forte organisation que ce Napoléon, quelle force de caractère, quelle suite et quelle unité dans la volonté! . . . Il a organisé l'autorité, le gouvernement, ce hideux fantôme, qui, impuissant à produire, vide et bête avec le mot *Ordre* à la bouche . . . nous écrase tous sous ses pieds de fer.' The theme of 'order' (*poryadok*)—or, more precisely, that of the imposition of order by the powerful personality—is one that recurs in ***Ottsy i deti,*** though it is linked with Bazarov only to the extent that the 'order' of nature is of concern to him as a natural scientist. It is mainly developed in the portraits of the novel's female characters, especially that of Odintsova, where it is significantly associated with the Latin language. Thus when she is asked by Bazarov why she is anxious to learn from him the Latin names of wild plants, she replies: 'There must be order in everything.' But before the implications of this point are more fully considered, the question must be asked: why is the task of establishing the connection between Bazarov and the two Napoleons entrusted specifically to the hero's father?

It has rightly been observed [by J. Blair] in connection with *Ottsy i deti* that 'the lives of the fathers become patterns for understanding the lives of the children'. Hitherto, however, the argument has been based almost exclusively on the obvious similarities between Arkady and Nikolay Petrovich. The comparable similarities between Bazarov and his father have received much less attention, presumably because they are not so immediately apparent. Three links between them have already been noted: the symbolism of their names, their 'Latinomania' and their professional interests. In addition, they bear a strong facial resemblance to one another; they both possess a strong sense of pride; and both insist on the need for self-sufficiency. Yet another link between them is established by Vasily Ivanovich's references to the two Napoleons, for they reveal that he not only sees his son as the embodiment of Napoleonic power, skill and daring but also has an intense personal interest in these French emperors. The evidence is his remark to Bazarov and Arkady soon after their arrival about 'the grave fears roused in him by Napoleon's policy and the complications of the Italian question'. The statement may be seen, at least in part, as reinforcing the development of the 'imperial' motif in the portrait of Vasily Ivanovich himself. But the most important similarity between father and son has yet to be mentioned. It is the conflict which they both experience between the aspirations symbolized in their portraits by the 'imperial' motif and the uncontrollable reality of life. In the case of Vasily Ivanovich this conflict is symbolically conveyed by two brief statements—by his description of himself to Arkady as 'a plebeian, a *homo novus*' and by his comparison of himself to Cincinnatus, the Roman dictator and persistent enemy of the plebeians who voluntarily surrendered power in order to work his small farm. The two statements disclose the tension that lies at the basis of Vasily Ivanovich's portrait between the plebeian and the aspiring 'dictator'. In both cases the reflections of his 'Latinomania' convey his 'imperial' aspirations, while the word 'plebeian' expresses the conflicting reality. Like his son, the 'giant' or 'Napoleon' whose only task in the end is 'to die a decent death' and who significantly returns for this purpose to the house of his father, Vasily Ivanovich is thus exposed as a frustrated 'dictator', obliged by his status to renounce his aspirations and, like Cincinnatus, to work his farm. Herein lies the significance of his nervousness about 'Napoleon's policies' and of Bazarov's remark that his father was 'a mighty Latinist *in his time*'. Yet the tension, the sense of restriction, is still in evidence and is even apparent in Vasily Ivanovich's physical portrait—in the reference, for example, to his perpetual restlessness and his habit of 'continually shrugging his shoulders as if his clothes were too tight under the armpits', and the face of the would-be 'dictator' still shows itself in glimpses—in the flogging, for example, of a peasant that he orders, in his pride and nostalgia when describing his travels and meetings with eminent personalities as a doctor in the army, and in the envy that he betrays for Arkady's grandfather, the commander of his brigade. 'My job', he says to Arkady, 'was of little consequence: to be proficient with the lancet and nothing more! But your grandfather was a very honourable man, a real soldier!' For Vasily Ivanovich, the would-be 'Caesar', whose drawing-room wall is adorned with a portrait of Suvorov and who hastens to point out to Arkady: 'I live the simple life of a soldier here', there could plainly be no higher praise.

Vasily Ivanovich's attitude to his son is dictated precisely by this conflict in his portrait between 'imperial' ambition and 'plebeian' reality. His insistence on comparing Bazarov to the military 'giant' Napoleon I is indicative of the fact that he sees him as a kind of substitute for himself, as the means of realizing his own failed ambition. The many indirect indications of this attitude include his confession to Arkady that he 'deifies' his son, his impatience to ascertain Arkady's opinion of him, the subservient manner in which he 'curled himself up on the sofa at his son's feet', and his cherished wish to see written in his son's biography: 'The son of a simple army doctor who nevertheless was able to understand him early in life and spared nothing for his education. . . .' And it may now be understood why the effect of Bazarov's illness and death on his parents is conveyed more through the reactions of Vasily Ivanovich than through those of his wife. His panic is the response not simply of a father but of a man who is himself faced with death, with the second 'death' of the aspiration expressed by his 'imperial' name. And the irony of the situation should not be overlooked. It lies in the fact that the two 'deaths' are attributable to a common cause, to an identical weakness unwittingly bequeathed by the father to the son. For the information is obliquely conveyed to the reader that Vasily Ivanovich's failure to realize his life's ambition is explained not only by his lack of status and his sense of social inferiority. The cause lies ultimately, it is suggested, in the depths of his personality—in the romantic strain, the weakness for women, that his son inherits. Not for nothing, we may assume, does Turgenev insert among the weapons, maps and anatomical drawings on the walls of Vasily Ivanovich's study 'a monogram woven from hair in a black frame'. It is no coincidence that the conversation between Bazarov and Arkady on their journey to the village—a conversation into which even the coachman is drawn—is dominated by the subject of how women should be treated. Bazarov declares:

> In my opinion it's better to break paving-stones than to allow a woman to possess as much as the tip of your finger. . . . You won't believe me now, but I tell you: we have been drawn into a feminine society and have found it agreeable; but to give up such a society is like pouring cold water over yourself on a hot day. A man has no time to engage in such trifles. As the excellent Spanish proverb says: 'A man must be ferocious'.

These sentiments, of course, express his reaction to his experiences at Nikol'skoye, the domain of Odintsova, from which the two heroes are travelling, but they are equally relevant to the new domain which they are about to enter. Indeed, their relevance is signalled at once, at the very entrance to the village, by an exchange of abuse between two peasants in which the charge is levelled: 'Your wife's a witch.' Nine pages later the significance of the charge becomes apparent for it is there revealed to be a prefigurative comment on Bazarov's mother. Arina Vlas'yevna, we learn, is not only her husband's social superior and the actual owner of the estate; by her striking idiosyncrasies and numerous superstitions, by her belief in 'all kinds of omens, fortune-telling, spells and dreams', she is herself identified as a 'witch'. Hence, perhaps, the narrator's concluding comment on her: 'Nowadays women like her are becoming extinct. God knows whether that is a matter for rejoicing.' Here, as later in the portrait of Arina's namesake Irina in *Dym,* the theme of witchcraft is introduced to convey the power of woman over man. 'She has no wiles', Bazarov says of his mother, and this is true. It is clear that the once 'pretty' (*milovidnaya*) girl who had 'played the clavichord and could express herself a little in French' had not consciously enticed her husband into marriage. She married him, we are told, 'against her will'. But his insistence on the marriage denotes the power of her spell, reflecting the state of bewitchment in which he forsook his ambitions and, like Cincinnatus, retired to his farm.

It is possible, therefore, to appreciate now the force of Vasily Ivanovich's interruption when his wife remarks on Bazarov's handsome appearance: 'Handsome or not, he is a man—an *homme fait,* as they say.' He sees his son as the 'man' that he failed to be himself, as the embodiment of the 'ferocity' which he himself lacked. But the irony is, of course, that his son has already undergone his own experience, that he has himself succumbed to a similar spell and, likewise bewitched by a beautiful aristocrat, is similarly fated to retire to the farm. And the parallel suggests that we are perhaps meant to see in the figure of Arina Vlas'yevna the fate that would have befallen Odintsova, had she yielded to Bazarov's ardour. But Arina's experience is not repeated. Whereas she surrendered and thus acquired her 'plebeian' name, the will of the 'cold, reserved' Odintsova, whom Bazarov describes as 'veritably a duchess' and who greets him on his death-bed as a gracious queen', proves equal to the challenge of the 'ferocious emperor' and by her victory she condemns him to his premature death.

The victory of Odintsova is clearly the most important event in the novel. It marks the culmination of the 'war of wills' which is dramatized in her relationship with Bazarov from the very beginning. Even before she is introduced to him at the ball, we note, she has marked him out—not because of his 'fine face', as Arkady naively assumes, for his physical portrait has already disclosed that his face is not particularly 'fine' at all, but because she recognizes in him at once, as Irina in *Dym* recognizes in Litvinov, an intriguing challenge to her considerable powers. 'She detected in him', we read, 'something new, something she had never encountered before, and her curiosity was aroused.' And five pages later the narrator observes: 'It seemed as if she wished both to test him and to explore her own depths.' The alternations of warmth and reserve in her attitude towards him, her impatience to know his innermost thoughts, her probing questions which seem to

him to have no purpose, her ordered routine to which he reluctantly submits—all are indicative of the 'test' to which she subjects him, and an appropriate image of insidious pressure is subtly introduced by the 'hiss' that accompanies her elegant movements and by the reference to her hair 'uncoiling itself like some dark snake'. As the narrator makes clear, the test is equally a test of Odintsova herself, a searching process of self-examination, the outcome of which she cannot foresee. Hence her surprise at the effect on her victim, at the violence that accompanies his despairing confession. But the confession is the mark of his final submission—the submission foretold once more by a game. Inviting him in chapter 16 to join her neighbour and herself in a game of preference, she had warned him: 'Take care, Porfiry Platonych and I will rout you', and after doing so in the game, she does so in life. While the second game, as noted, is a prediction of his death, the first at Nikol'skoye predicts its cause.

The importance, however, of the relationship that culminates in Odintsova's victory lies not only in the fact that it determines Bazarov's fate. It lies equally in the consummate expression that it gives to the major form assumed in the novel by the struggle of 'warring wills'. This is the form of sexual conflict, which plays a more central and extensive role in the work than any of the other kinds of conflict on which criticism has traditionally focussed its attention. Bazarov's infatuation with Odintsova, of course, does not contradict this definition of the essential nature of the conflict between them, for it is made abundantly clear that the attraction which she holds for him is predominantly physical and that physical beauty is, in general, the only attribute of a woman that can excite his interest. His attitude to the female otherwise is summed up in his remark: 'It's a good sign if a woman can keep up a conversation for half an hour.' The sexual prejudice of Odintsova is equally strong. The entire domain of Nikol'skoye over which she presides epitomizes the misanthropy which the Schopenhauerian conception of life implies. It is evident in the instinctive hostility to everyone of Princess Kh., Odintsova's aunt—'a small, thin woman with a clenched fist of a face and motionless, spiteful eyes under a grey wig'—in the contempt of Odintsova's father for his neighbours, In the 'unfriendly manner' in which the deceased Odintsov gazes out from his portrait, in the repeatedly sensed tension between Odintsova and her sister Katya. All these reflections of a uniform state of mind convey the unappealing reality beneath the beauty of Nikol'skoye and its regal mistress who, the narrator informs us, 'was not liked in the province'. But Odintsova's particular scorn, like that of Bazarov, is reserved for the opposite sex. 'She could hardly bear', we read, 'the deceased Odintsov (whom she had married for practical reasons . . .) and had developed a secret revulsion for all men, regarding them as nothing more than untidy, clumsy, limp and impotently tiresome creatures.' The male exists for her, it seems, for two purposes only—either, like her two wealthy husbands, to be exploited or, like Bazarov (and probably the 'handsome young Swede with a chivalrous face' who had once powerfully affected her on a journey abroad, to be used as a means of confirming her strength and to be ultimately vanquished in the 'war of wills'. Such is the purpose that is vividly announced by the fresco over the entrance to the Nikol'skoye church: the picture of 'a swarthy warrior in a helmet lying prostrate in the foreground'.

The representation of the 'war of wills' in the Bazarov— Odintsova relationship as a struggle for sexual supremacy is mirrored in the novel in every other relationship between the sexes. Appropriately the theme of sexual conflict is first introduced by the 'parodic doubles' of the two principal figures—the fawning Sitnikov, who 'made a particular point', we read, 'of attacking women, not suspecting that a few months later he would have to crawl before his wife for no other reason than that she was born a Princess Durdoleosova', and the 'emancipated' Kukshina, who accuses Sitnikov of being 'an upholder of the *Domostroy*' and swears 'to defend the rights of women to the last drop of my blood'. It is plainly significant that their conversation with Bazarov and Arkady in chapter 13 embraces the pertinent questions of 'whether people are born equal or not' and 'the essence of individuality'. And the social positions of the antagonists should also be noted. Like Bazarov *père* and *fils,* Sitnikov is the social inferior of the woman he pursues, for Kukshina, like Arina Vlas'yevna and Odintsova, is a landowner. The point is of general significance, for with one exception (the relationship between Arkady and Katya) every conflict in the novel between the sexes is also a conflict between individuals of different social status. Not that the woman, of course, is the social superior in every case, but in one sense this is unimportant, for whether she is or is not, it is her will that prevails. Again there is only one exception—the relationship between Bazarov's parents in which the will of the socially inferior male proves uniquely the stronger for the reasons, and with the consequences, that have been discussed. In every other case the female triumphs, and it is tempting to relate this recurrent outcome of the 'war of wills' to the personal experience of Turgenev himself—to his life-long experience of female power in the formidable person of his tyrannical mother and the beguiling figure of Pauline Viardot. But there is also a sense in which social status does directly affect the outcome of the sexual conflicts. The triumph of the female expresses itself in one of two ways, and which of the two obtains in each case depends on whether or not she is the social superior. If she is, the result is death for the male; if she is not, the result is the marriage which represents her objective. The former result is the outcome of two relationships, one of which, of course, is the relationship between Bazarov and Odintsova; the latter is illustrated in three.

The relationship in which the development and outcome of the principal relationship in the novel are duplicated is the affair between Pavel Petrovich Kirsanov and Princess R. which Arkady recalls for Bazarov's benefit in chapter 7. In recent scholarship the similarities of temperament and attitude which underlie the ideological differences between Bazarov and Pavel Petrovich have been well enough documented to obviate the need for further substantiation. It will suffice to remark that they are endowed in equal measure with the 'imperial' attributes (self-sufficiency, pride, aggressiveness, misanthropy) denoted by their surnames—qualities which in Pavel Petrovich's case are additionally symbolized by his 'aristocratism' and military

background. The similar roles which Princess R. and Odintsova play in the lives of the two heroes have also been recognized. It is true, of course, that the personalities of these two female characters are strikingly dissimilar— so dissimilar, in fact, that some commentators have questioned whether a parallel was intended. But the differences between them are certainly no greater than those that coexist with the noted affinities between Pavel Petrovich and Bazarov. They are likewise far outweighed in importance by the similarities between them—by the totally 'bewitching' and ultimately paralysing effect which they both have on men distinguished by their powerful wills and by the 'deaths' which they both inflict by their refusal to submit. Thus chapter 24 ends with the narrator's comment on Pavel Petrovich: 'In the bright daylight his handsome, emaciated head lay on the white pillow like the head of a corpse. . . . Indeed, he was a corpse.' Such is the conclusion of the process which begins with the symbolic act of the resignation of his commission, and perhaps his Christian name Pavel, derived from the Latin *paulus* ('small'), may be taken as a symbol of his defeat, of his forfeiture, to which Bazarov refers, of his right to be called 'a man, a male'. Princess R., we read, 'seemed to be in the power of mysterious forces unknown even to herself'. Again the idea of the 'witch' is evoked and is combined with the image of the sphinx, of a lion with the head of a Pharoah, which is engraved on the ring given to her by Pavel Petrovich, to endow her with the formidable attributes of mystery, 'ferocity' and royalty.

The three relationships in which the triumph of the female is expressed in the form of marriage are those that involve the other two Kirsanovs, Arkady and his father, and it is appropriate to consider in this connection the question of the names that Turgenev chose for the two estates between which he distributes his principal characters. In both cases there is a striking contradiction between their names and their inhabitants. Thus Mar'ino, the estate of the Kirsanovs, is named after a woman, Nikolay Petrovich's first wife Masha, but is the home of three men—moreover, three unmarried men—and is even referred to by the peasants as 'the solitary man's farm' (*Bobyliy khutor*). Nikol'skoye, in contrast, is named after a man, presumably the deceased Odintsov or one of his ancestors, but is the home of three women, who are likewise single. The contrast is so clearly expressed that to ascribe it to coincidence would again seem unreasonable. The contradictions are susceptible, in fact, of at least two interpretations which essentially complement each other: as denoting a reversal of conventional sexual roles and as implying the existence of female control over both estates. Thus while the name 'Nikol'skoye', the source of which, the masculine name Nikolay, is derived from Greek roots meaning 'conqueror of peoples', may be taken to reflect the masculine role of 'conqueror' which Odintsova plays in her relationship with Bazarov and which she had probably usurped from her 'hypochrondriac' husband even before his death, the name 'Mar'ino' might be interpreted as alluding both to that lingering presence on the estate of the dead Masha's spirit to which Nikolay Petrovich is so sensitive and, more generally, to that peculiar dependence on women which the three 'lordly' Kirsanovs alike display and which may be viewed in retrospect as their common birthright. In the light of the obvious importance in the novel of the theme of heredity, the inclusion of brief portraits of Arkady's paternal grandparents cannot be regarded as gratuitous. Through the portrait of Major-General Kirsanov, who even signs himself as such in his letters to his sons, the 'military motif' is first introduced into the work as a symbolic expression of the 'idea of Caesar', of the powerful individual will. But the general, we observe, also exhibits a curious fallibility, which is most notably reflected in the 'unsuccessful inspection' for which he is obliged to retire and which is followed abruptly by his death from a stroke. It is this fallibility that he bequeaths to his sons, whose subsequent experiences seem to define its nature and to explain, in effect, the brief references to their mother. The formidable Agafokleya Kuz' minishna Kirsanova, we read, 'belonged to the species of "commanding matrons"' and 'lived as she pleased'. Authority is stamped on her every action, and under its shadow the two brothers grew up. Herein, we may infer, lies the source of their dependence on women.

The consequences for Pavel Petrovich of this inherited trait have already been noted, but the theme of fallibility, in both the general sense and the particular sense ascribed to it, receives its major development in the portrait of his brother Nikolay. From the beginning of his mature life Nikolay Petrovich displays a proneness to error and misfortune which is strikingly at odds with the attributes conveyed by his name, and the contradiction is symbolically mirrored in the episode of the broken leg which puts an end to his military career before it has even begun. He presents himself, in short, as the principal embodiment of that weakness of the Kirsanovs which is chiefly apparent in their relationships with women. Between his name and his actions there is the kind of contradiction between word and deed that is definitive of such men of the 'forties as Rudin and Potugin. He is a 'conqueror of peoples' who liberates his house-serfs, cannot manage his estate and displays throughout his dependence on women. The overwhelming effect on him of Masha's death, like that of Bazarov's death on Vasily Ivanovich, is not only an expression of love; it is also a mark of this dependence which is indicated at the very beginning of their relationship by the reversal of sexual roles denoted by his amusing 'mistake' in addressing her at their first meeting as 'monsieur'. And support for this reading is obtained from Masha's portrait, the few details of which suffice to illuminate her character and also her affinities with the novel's other female figures. Thus like Bazarov's mother, we are told, she was 'pretty' (*milovidnaya*); the description of her as an 'intellectually mature girl' (*razvitaya devitsa*) recalls the phrase 'advanced woman' (*peredovaya zhenshchina*) applied to the 'emancipated' Kukshina; and her habit of reading the 'Science' sections of 'serious journals' anticipates the interest displayed by both Kukshina and Odintsova, not to mention Bazarov, in chemistry. In addition, the regime of cleanliness, order and 'chilliness' which this 'good, thrifty housewife' installed foreshadows the more detailed description of the same regime in Turgenev's portrait of Nikol'skoye. The parallel, it seems, was fully intended, for in chapter 16 the connection is strengthened by Odintsova's disclosure that her mother, the sister of the venomous Princess Kh., 'had known Arkady's mother and had

even been her confidante when the latter had fallen in love with Nikolay Petrovich'. Both directly and indirectly, therefore, Masha is linked with Odintsova (and her 'parodic double') and with Nikol'skoye in its role as a symbol of the masculine will of the female. Considered in relation to these links and parallels, her marriage to Nikolay Petrovich may consequently be viewed as representing the first invasion of 'the solitary man's farm' by the powerful force which Nikol'skoye symbolizes, and the name 'Mar'ino' is the symbol of her success.

Nikol'skoye's second victory over the Kirsanovs is Katya's 'conquest' of Nikolay's son Arkady. Once more the fate of the father is experienced by the son. Arkady, whose Christian name, like his surname, is yet another characternym of Greek derivation, is his father's heir in every sense, having inherited from him, together with his love of music and the love of nature to which his Christian name alludes, the Kirsanov legacy of dependence on others. The entire story of Arkady, in fact, is the record of his dependence on three competing influences—those of Bazarov, Odintsova and Katya—and Katya's victory in this contest duplicates her sister's triumph over the novel's hero. Hence the toast that she proposes to Arkady at the end of the novel: 'To Bazarov's memory.' At the same time Katya's methods are notably different from those of her sister. The abrupt confrontation in which the 'war of wills' between Odintsova and Bazarov culminates during the latter's first visit to Nikol'skoye is replaced by a process of gradual subordination which requires two visits by Arkady to be completed. The reasons for the difference are entirely self-evident. They are the problem that faces Katya of seducing Arkady from the two competing influences to which he is subject and her inability, which distinguishes her from her sister, to make an immediate impact. Of necessity, therefore, guile and attrition are her principal tactics, as her recourse to music most clearly demonstrates. For music is employed by Katya, as it was, we may perhaps deduce, by Masha and as it was to be later by the resourceful Mutsy in Turgenev's tale **"Pesn' torzhestvuyushchey lyubvi"** (1881), both as an expression of her own will and as a means of subduing that of her victim. Here there is reason once more to suspect the influence of Schopenhauer—of his conception of music as a 'direct copy' of the striving will and of his interpretation of its effect on the enraptured listener. He writes:

> Music is distinguished from all the other arts by the fact that it is not a copy of the phenomenon, or, more accurately, the adequate objectivity of will, but is the direct copy of the will itself, and therefore exhibits itself as the metaphysical to everything physical in the world, and as the thing-in-itself to every phenomenon. We might, therefore, just as well call the world embodied music as embodied will. . . . Aesthetic pleasure in the beautiful consists in great measure in the fact that in entering the state of pure contemplation we are lifted for the moment above all willing.

Such is the state which Katya's tactics induce, and Arkady's proposal confirms their success. Moreover, the proposal is secured, it should be noted, at the precise moment when Odintsova, as Arkady himself discovers from the overheard conversation in the garden, is turning her attention increasingly towards him. The conclusion to be drawn is that in the final reckoning the will of Katya is even stronger than that of her sister, and unlike Bazarov, her principal rival, who is hopelessly deceived by her subtle guile, Arkady becomes ultimately aware of this truth. 'You are just as clever,' he says to her, 'you have just as much character as she, if not more . . .'. In her conversation with Arkady two pages earlier Katya refers to Bazarov as 'a predatory beast' and adds: 'But you and I are domestic animals.' The contrast is justified both by her less violent methods of imposing her will and by the consistent objective that dictates her actions—the delights of marriage and domesticity. But again guile and deceit are plainly in evidence, as they are in her statement that she aspires in marriage to a position of equality, not of domination. The truth is disclosed by the glimpses provided of her hidden 'ferocity'. 'Just you wait,' she jokes to Arkady, 'we shall transform you', and after her sister has praised the beauty of her feet, she says to herself as she climbs to the terrace: 'The time will come when he will be sitting at them.' The novel's conclusion bears out her prediction.

The third of the three major relationships in the novel in which the triumph of the female will expresses itself in marriage is the relationship between Nikolay Petrovich and the peasant girl Fenechka. Fenechka is in many ways the most intriguing and complex female character in the work and certainly the most misjudged. In all appearance, of course, she is the soul of modesty, submissiveness and self-effacement—in Nabokov's phrase, 'one of the passive types of Turgenev's young women' [*Lectures on Russian Literature*, 1982]. The colour 'white' recurs in her portrait—ostensibly as a symbol of innocence and purity. The blackness of her hair, however, which is similarly emphasized, establishes a contrast which suggests from the beginning the possibility of a discord between appearance and reality, and this suspicion is later reinforced by the repetition of the contrast in the portrait of Odintsova. Still more disconcerting are the allusive indications of her significant affinities with the black-haired Katya, to whom she becomes particularly devoted in the novel's concluding pages. 'Next to her husband and Mitya', we read, 'Fenechka adored no one so much as her daughter-in-law.' Especially striking is the habit they share of looking up 'from under their eyelids' which reflects their common reluctance to look people squarely in the face. Thus Pavel Petrovich remarks to Fenechka: 'You never look at me. It's as if your conscience is not clear', and the narrator recalls an episode from the early days of her relationship with Nikolay Petrovich in which she had fled into a field of rye 'to avoid meeting him face to face'. And we may infer that it is to this less obvious aspect of Fenechka's self-effacement that the photograph of her in her 'very clean and tidy' room is meant to allude—a photograph of 'a kind of eyeless face straining to smile in a dark room'. By means of such details the impression is progressively reinforced that Fenechka, like the secretive, calculating Katya, has something to conceal.

The reference to the 'tidiness' of Fenechka's room is an indication of the concern for order which is another characteristic that she shares with Odintsova. Here again Turge-

nev introduces the theme of heredity, for the source of the characteristic is explicitly disclosed by the information provided about her mother whom Nikolay Petrovich, we are told, had appointed his 'chief housekeeper' and who had 'installed order in his home'. The theme performs its usual function. Just as the experiences of Bazarov and Arkady are anticipated in the biographies of their fathers, so these references to Fenechka's mother define her own ambition—that of replacing her mother and Masha as the mistress of Mar'ino. They provide, in effect, an illuminating gloss on the intriguing episode in chapter 11 in which Nikolay Petrovich immerses himself in the garden in nostalgic dreams about his life with Masha only to have his reverie abruptly dispelled by Fenechka's intervention at the precise moment when the spirit of Masha becomes so tangible that he even senses 'her warmth and breath'. The episode adds notably to the gradual exposure of Fenechka as yet another aspiring 'conqueror' in the 'war of wills' between the sexes and thus explains the recurrence in her portrait of the familiar symbols by which this 'war' is conveyed. It explains, for example, why the portrait in her room of General Yermolov, another military symbol of male authority, is positioned beneath a pin-cushion and why she is associated with the name 'Nikolay' both by the icon of St Nicholas the Miracle-worker in her room and by her patronymic 'Nikolayevna' which Bazarov, we note, is strangely intent on ascertaining. It also explains, at least in part, why Pavel Petrovich compares her to Prince R., why she is paired with Odintsova in Bazarov's dream on the eve of the duel, and why the 'imperial' motif is developed in her portrait from the very beginning.

The motif is first introduced by another attribute that Fenechka inherits from her mother, her 'dignified manner' (*stepennost'*)—an attribute confirmed by Bazarov's approving reference to her habit of 'not showing too much embarrassment' for which, he adds, 'some people might criticize her'. But the most noteworthy symbols of her 'imperial' authority are the kisses which both Nikolay Petrovich and Pavel Petrovich feel impelled to bestow on her milk-white hand. The kisses are testimony to the peasant girl's skill, and the second represents her final triumph. It denotes the removal of the main obstacle to the achievement of her goal. Throughout the novel the 'war of wills' in which Fenechka is engaged is primarily a war with Pavel Petrovich, whose sense of properties is affronted by the thought of her elevation to the position of his sister-in-law. She fears him not because of the difference of class, but precisely because of his objections to the formalized union with his brother that she craves. These objections are her *casus belli,* and she fights her war with unparalleled 'ferocity'. Allusions to this aspect of her character are again woven into her portrait from the beginning. Thus in the episode in which she flees from Nikolay Petrovich into the field of rye she is portrayed peering out at him 'like a wild animal' from 'her ambush (*zasady*)'. 'Hello, Fenechka', he calls to her, 'I do not bite.' But Fenechka, we learn later, does 'bite', and the narrator's reference in chapter 8 to the 'moist glitter of her pearl-like teeth in the sun' may be viewed as heralding the proof provided in chapter 24. Not for nothing, it seems, is a copy of K. P. Masal'sky's historical novel *Strel'tsy* noted among her personal possessions. For the bullet from Bazarov's pistol by which Pavel Petrovich is felled in the duel is indeed the 'bite' that Fenechka inflicts. Bazarov becomes, in effect, her teeth, displaying yet again a serious misjudgement of a female. In the figure of the conqueror of Pavel Petrovich in the battle of ideologies Fenechka recognizes at once a weapon to be used in her personal battle, and with the aid of the 'imperial' motif Bazarov's unconscious acceptance of this role is anticipated as early as their first meeting. Doffing his cap and bowing to her, he announces himself as 'a humble person' (*chelovek smirnyy*). 'Fenechka', we read, 'half-rose from the bench and stared at him in silence', and from this time forth she smiles upon him, preparing him for the part that he is to play. Recalling his argument with Pavel Petrovich, she says to him: 'I had no idea what your argument was about, but I saw that you were twisting him round your little finger. . . . No one could get the better of you.' It is in this belief that she propels him into battle in the scene in the garden that precipitates the duel. Seduced once more by female beauty, Bazarov says to her: 'I know a hand that could knock me over with a finger if it wished to', not realizing that this is precisely what Fenechka's hand is doing. Now it is Bazarov's turn to be twisted round a little finger. Fully aware that Pavel Petrovich is near, Fenechka lures him on to the decisive act which, we read, 'she resisted feebly, and he was able to renew and prolong his kiss'. Shortly before she had offered him the choice between a red rose and a white one, and he had chosen the former. The episode serves to remind us that the colour 'red' is combined in Fenechka's portrait with 'black' and 'white' from the beginning and on its first appearance is significantly associated with 'blood'. She is described in chapter 5 as 'a young woman of about twenty-three, all white and soft, with dark hair and dark eyes, red, childishly pouting lips and delicate hands. . . . The hot blood spread in a crimson wave beneath the fine skin of her pretty (*milovidnogo*) face.' Bazarov's choice of the red rose may be interpreted as signalling his final submission to the power of Fenechka's will, as foreshadowing the blood, the mark of her 'bite', which eight pages later begins to flow down the immaculate white breeches of her vanquished opponent. And the effects of the 'bite' are immediately reflected within the same chapter: in Pavel Petrovich's renunciation of his 'aristocratic airs', in Fenechka's uncharacteristically public display in his presence of her feelings for Nikolay Petrovich, and in the withdrawal by Pavel Petrovich of his objections to the marriage. This is the chapter in which with his concluding word the narrator aptly describes him as an emaciated 'corpse', and three chapters later is joined in death by his conqueror in the duel. Having been linked by both combatants with their *femmes fatales,* Odintsova and Princess R., Fenechka completes the destruction already inflicted and thus, like Katya, achieves her aim. And the concluding symbols of their similar triumphs are the names under which they last appear—no longer Fenechka and Katya, but Fedos'ya Nikolayevna and Katerina Sergeyevna.

Having noted, therefore, the two different ways in which the triumph of the female will is expressed in the novel, we must finally consider why the distinction is made. Why, we must ask, is the result of this triumph sterility and death in the cases of Bazarov and Pavel Petrovich and marital bliss in the cases of Nikolay Petrovich and Arkady? The simple answer, of course, is that the difference of effect results from the indicated differences between the two types of personality involved. For Bazarov and Pavel Petrovich with their boundless pride in their self-sufficiency defeat is a blow which undermines their entire conception of themselves and leaves them permanently disfigured. The defeats of Nikolay Petrovich and Arkady, in contrast, are hardly recognized as such, so naturally do they follow from their need for dependence. Here defeat takes the form of willing submission which duly gives birth to happy and productive relationships. This difference of personality, however, still does not explain why Turgenev makes the distinction, why he does not confine himself to simply portraying his two 'strong men'. The thought of Schopenhauer again suggests a possible answer. Presenting his views on the manner in which the will ensures its self-perpetuation, Schopenhauer writes:

> What draws two individuals of different sex exclusively to each other with such power is the will to live, which exhibits itself in the whole species, and which here anticipates in the individual which these two can produce an objectification of its nature answering to its aims.

He refers to the manner in which each individual, in obedience to the will of the species of which he is an objectification, 'endeavours to neutralize by means of the other his weaknesses, defects and deviations from the type, so that they will not perpetuate themselves, or even develop into complete abnormalities in the child which is to be produced. The weaker a man is . . . , the more he will seek for strong women'. And he continues:

> Marriages from love are made in the interest of the species, not of the individuals. Certainly the persons concerned imagine they are advancing their own happiness; but their real end is one which is foreign to themselves, for it lies in the production of an individual which is only possible through them.

Not only, therefore, is the individual will, according to this conception, engaged in ceaseless strife; its struggles and 'conquests' are also the means by which the will of the species ensures its continuing existence, the 'life without end' to which the last words of the novel refer. It is this particular aspect of the 'war of wills', it is suggested, which explains the presence in the novel of the relationships which end in marriage and the production of children. Imparting a new level of meaning to the novel's title, it explains the inclusion in the work of the infants Mitya and Kolya, the sons of Fenechka and Katya, the overtly sexual nature of Bazarov's attitude to women, and the emphatically physical character of Fenechka's impact on the three males (Nikolay Petrovich, Pavel Petrovich and Bazarov) who are drawn to her.

The conclusion, therefore, that follows from this reading is that in the two forms of female triumph which the novel depicts Turgenev is intent on representing two contrasting aspects of Schopenhauer's 'war of wills'. These aspects might be termed the destructive and the productive, and each of them is illustrated by three relationships—by those involving Princess R., Odintsova and Kukshina, whose relationships with men are either trials of strength or merely unions of convenience and therefore barren, and by those involving Masha, Katya, and Fenechka which are happy and fruitful. This conclusion has been reached on the basis of reinterpretations of the roles of the major characters which have implicitly ascribed a much more important role to symbolism in the Turgenevan novel than is generally recognized. Yet the object of this article has been not so much to challenge the more familiar views of the novel as to suggest that they relate to the superstructure which Turgenev erected on a conceptual or philosophical basis which has thus far escaped notice. The aim has been to illuminate this basis, to examine the forms in which its presence is revealed, and show that without reference to this level of meaning there is much in the novel that defies understanding. (pp. 161-88)

> *James B. Woodward, "Aut Caesar 'aut nihil': The 'War of Wills' in Turgenev's 'Ottsy i deti',"* in The Slavonic and East European Review, *Vol. 64, No. 2, April, 1986, pp. 161-88.*

FURTHER READING

Chamberlin, Vernon A., and Weiner, Jack. "Galdós' *Doña Perfecta* and Turgenev's *Fathers and Sons:* Two Interpretations of the Conflict between Generations." *PMLA* 86, No. 1 (January 1971): 19-24.

Suggests that *Fathers and Sons* is a prime source for Galdós' novel, while contrasting their individual treatments of the theme of conflict between generations.

Freeborn, Richard. "Turgenev at Ventnor." *Slavonic and East European Review* LI, No. 124 (July 1973): 387-412.

Examines how Turgenev's three-week sojourn at Ventnor on the Isle of Wight in the summer of 1860 may have led to the creation of Bazarov, "his greatest hero."

———. "Egoistic Nihilism and Revolutionary Nihilism." In his *The Russian Revolutionary Novel: Turgenev to Pasternak*, pp. 4-38. Cambridge: Cambridge University Press, 1982.

In-depth discussion of Russia's social upheaval at the time Turgenev wrote *Fathers and Sons*.

Matlaw, Ralph E., ed. *Fathers and Sons* by Ivan Turgenev. Translated by Ralph E. Matlaw. Norton Critical Edition. New York: W. W. Norton & Company, 1989, 345 p.

Includes a selection of Turgenev's letters describing the critical controversy following the work's initial publication, contemporary reactions to the novel, and modern essays in criticism. Contains the essays by Matlaw, Dmitry I. Pisarev, N. N. Strakhov, P. G. Pustovoyt, and James H. Justus excerpted above.

Moser, Charles A. *Ivan Turgenev.* New York: Columbia University Press, 1972, 48 p.

Introductory monograph. Moser briefly describes the questions raised by radical literary critics who discussed the novel when it first appeared.

Reeve, F. D. "*Fathers and Children* (Turgenev)." In his *The Russian Novel*, pp. 119-58. London: Frederick Muller, 1967.

Examines the social and political circumstances surrounding the writing of *Fathers and Sons* as well as the power of the work itself. Reeve writes: "Turgenev wrote from affection for life and its values with a deep, quiet talent which expressed the inside through the forms of the outside."

Additional coverage of Turgenev's life and career is contained in the following sources published by Gale Research: *Nineteenth-Century Literature Criticism,* Vol. 21 and *Short Story Criticism,* Vol. 7.

Nineteenth-Century Literature Criticism

Cumulative Indexes
Volumes 1-37

This Index Includes References to Entries in These Gale Series

Children's Literature Review includes excerpts from reviews, criticism, and commentary on works of authors and illustrators who create books for children.

Classical and Medieval Literature Criticism offers excerpts of criticism on the works of world authors from classical antiquity through the fourteenth century.

Contemporary Authors Series encompasses five related series. *Contemporary Authors* provides biographical and bibliographical information on more than 97,000 writers of fiction and nonfiction. *Contemporary Authors New Revision Series* provides completely updated information on authors covered in *CA*. *Contemporary Authors Permanent Series* consists of listings for deceased and inactive authors. *Contemporary Authors Autobiography Series* presents specially commissioned autobiographies by leading contemporary writers. *Contemporary Authors Bibliographical Series* contains primary and secondary bibliographies as well as analytical bibliographical essays by authorities on major modern authors.

Contemporary Literary Criticism presents excerpts of criticism on the works of novelists, poets, dramatists, short story writers, scriptwriters, and other creative writers who are now living or who have died since 1960.

Dictionary of Literary Biography encompasses four related series. *Dictionary of Literary Biography* furnishes illustrated overviews of authors' lives and works. *Dictionary of Literary Biography Documentary Series* illuminates the careers of major figures through a selection of literary documents, including letters, interviews, and photographs. *Dictionary of Literary Biography Yearbook* summarizes the past year's literary activity and includes updated entries on individual authors. *Concise Dictionary of American Literary Biography*, a six-volume series, collects revised and updated sketches on major American authors that were originally presented in *Dictionary of Literary Biography*.

Drama Criticism provides excerpts of criticism on the works of playwrights of all nationalities and periods of literary history.

Literature Criticism from 1400 to 1800 compiles significant passages from the most noteworthy criticism on authors of the fifteenth through eighteenth centuries.

Nineteenth-Century Literature Criticism offers significant passages from criticism on authors who died between 1800 and 1899.

Poetry Criticism presents excerpts of criticism on the works of poets from all eras, movements, and nationalities.

Short Story Criticism compiles excerpts of criticism on short fiction written by authors of all eras and nationalities.

Something about the Author Series encompasses three related series. *Something about the Author* contains well-illustrated biographical sketches on juvenile and young adult authors and illustrators from all eras. *Something about the Author Autobiography Series* presents specially commissioned autobiographies by prominent authors and illustrators of books for children and young adults. *Authors & Artists for Young Adults* provides high school and junior high school students with profiles of their favorite creative artists.

Twentieth-Century Literary Criticism contains critical excerpts by the most significant commentators on poets, novelists, short story writers, dramatists, and philosophers who died between 1900 and 1960.

Yesterday's Authors of Books for Children contains heavily illustrated entries on children's writers who died before 1961. Complete in two volumes.

Literary Criticism Series
Cumulative Author Index

This index lists all author entries in the Gale Literary Criticism Series and includes cross-references to other Gale sources. References in the index are identified as follows:

AAYA: *Authors & Artists for Young Adults,* Volumes 1-8
BLC: *Black Literature Criticism,* Volumes 1-3
CA: *Contemporary Authors* (original series), Volumes 1-136
CAAS: *Contemporary Authors Autobiography Series,* Volumes 1-15
CABS: *Contemporary Authors Bibliographical Series,* Volumes 1-3
CANR: *Contemporary Authors New Revision Series,* Volumes 1-37
CAP: *Contemporary Authors Permanent Series,* Volumes 1-2
CA-R: *Contemporary Authors* (first revision), Volumes 1-44
CDALB: *Concise Dictionary of American Literary Biography,* Volumes 1-6
CLC: *Contemporary Literary Criticism,* Volumes 1-73
CLR: *Children's Literature Review,* Volumes 1-26
CMLC: *Classical and Medieval Literature Criticism,* Volumes 1-9
DC: *Drama Criticism,* Volumes 1-2
DLB: *Dictionary of Literary Biography,* Volumes 1-114
DLB-DS: *Dictionary of Literary Biography Documentary Series,* Volumes 1-9
DLB-Y: *Dictionary of Literary Biography Yearbook,* Volumes 1980-1990
LC: *Literature Criticism from 1400 to 1800,* Volumes 1-20
NCLC: *Nineteenth-Century Literature Criticism* Volumes 1-37
PC: *Poetry Criticism,* Volumes 1-5
SAAS: *Something about the Author Autobiography Series,* Volumes 1-14
SATA: *Something about the Author,* Volumes 1-69
SSC: *Short Story Criticism,* Volumes 1-10
TCLC: *Twentieth-Century Literary Criticism,* Volumes 1-46
WLC: *World Literature Criticism, 1500 to the Present,* Volumes 1-6
YABC: *Yesterday's Authors of Books for Children,* Volumes 1-2

A. E. 1867-1935 .... TCLC 3, 10
See also Russell, George William
See also DLB 19

Abbey, Edward 1927-1989 ...... CLC 36, 59
See also CANR 2; CA 45-48;
obituary CA 128

Abbott, Lee K., Jr. 19??- .... CLC 48

Abe, Kobo 1924- .... CLC 8, 22, 53
See also CANR 24; CA 65-68

Abell, Kjeld 1901-1961 .... CLC 15
See also obituary CA 111

Abish, Walter 1931- .... CLC 22
See also CA 101

Abrahams, Peter (Henry) 1919- ..... CLC 4
See also CA 57-60

Abrams, M(eyer) H(oward) 1912- ... CLC 24
See also CANR 13; CA 57-60; DLB 67

Abse, Dannie 1923- .... CLC 7, 29
See also CAAS 1; CANR 4; CA 53-56;
DLB 27

Achebe, (Albert) Chinua(lumogu)
1930- .... CLC 1, 3, 5, 7, 11, 26, 51
See also BLC 1; CLR 20; WLC 1; CANR 6,
26; CA 1-4R; SATA 38, 40

Acker, Kathy 1948- .... CLC 45
See also CA 117, 122

Ackroyd, Peter 1949- .... CLC 34, 52
See also CA 123, 127

Acorn, Milton 1923- .... CLC 15
See also CA 103; DLB 53

Adamov, Arthur 1908-1970 ...... CLC 4, 25
See also CAP 2; CA 17-18;
obituary CA 25-28R

Adams, Alice (Boyd) 1926- ... CLC 6, 13, 46
See also CANR 26; CA 81-84; DLB-Y 86

Adams, Douglas (Noel) 1952- ... CLC 27, 60
See also CA 106; DLB-Y 83

Adams, Francis 1862-1893 .... NCLC 33

Adams, Henry (Brooks)
1838-1918 .... TCLC 4
See also CA 104; DLB 12, 47

Adams, Richard (George)
1920- .... CLC 4, 5, 18
See also CLR 20; CANR 3; CA 49-52;
SATA 7

Adamson, Joy(-Friederike Victoria)
1910-1980 .... CLC 17
See also CANR 22; CA 69-72;
obituary CA 93-96; SATA 11;
obituary SATA 22

Adcock, (Kareen) Fleur 1934- ...... CLC 41
See also CANR 11; CA 25-28R; DLB 40

Addams, Charles (Samuel)
1912-1988 .... CLC 30
See also CANR 12; CA 61-64;
obituary CA 126

Addison, Joseph 1672-1719 .... LC 18
See also DLB 101

Adler, C(arole) S(chwerdtfeger)
1932- .... CLC 35
See also CANR 19; CA 89-92; SATA 26

Adler, Renata 1938- .... CLC 8, 31
See also CANR 5, 22; CA 49-52

Ady, Endre 1877-1919 .... TCLC 11
See also CA 107

Afton, Effie 1825-1911
See Harper, Francis Ellen Watkins

Agee, James 1909-1955 . . . . **TCLC 1, 19**
See also CA 108; DLB 2, 26;
CDALB 1941-1968

Agnon, S(hmuel) Y(osef Halevi)
1888-1970 . . . . **CLC 4, 8, 14**
See also CAP 2; CA 17-18;
obituary CA 25-28R

Ai 1947- . . . . **CLC 4, 14, 69**
See also CAAS 13; CA 85-88

Aickman, Robert (Fordyce)
1914-1981 . . . . **CLC 57**
See also CANR 3; CA 7-8R

Aiken, Conrad (Potter)
1889-1973 . . . **CLC 1, 3, 5, 10, 52; SSC 9**
See also CANR 4; CA 5-8R;
obituary CA 45-48; SATA 3, 30; DLB 9,
45, 102; CDALB 1929-1941

Aiken, Joan (Delano) 1924- . . . . **CLC 35**
See also CLR 1, 19; CANR 4; CA 9-12R;
SAAS 1; SATA 2, 30

Ainsworth, William Harrison
1805-1882 . . . . **NCLC 13**
See also SATA 24; DLB 21

Aitmatov, Chingiz 1928- . . . . **CLC 71**
See also CA 103; SATA 56

Ajar, Emile 1914-1980
See Gary, Romain

Akhmadulina, Bella (Akhatovna)
1937- . . . . **CLC 53**
See also CA 65-68

Akhmatova, Anna
1888-1966 . . . . **CLC 11, 25, 64; PC 2**
See also CAP 1; CA 19-20;
obituary CA 25-28R

Aksakov, Sergei Timofeyvich
1791-1859 . . . . **NCLC 2**

Aksenov, Vassily (Pavlovich) 1932-
See Aksyonov, Vasily (Pavlovich)

Aksyonov, Vasily (Pavlovich)
1932- . . . . **CLC 22, 37**
See also CANR 12; CA 53-56

Akutagawa Ryunosuke
1892-1927 . . . . **TCLC 16**
See also CA 117

Alain 1868-1951 . . . . **TCLC 41**
See also Chartier, Emile-Auguste

Alain-Fournier 1886-1914 . . . . **TCLC 6**
See also Fournier, Henri Alban
See also DLB 65

Al-Amin, Jamil Abdullah 1943-
See also BLC 1; CA 112, 125

Alarcon, Pedro Antonio de
1833-1891 . . . . **NCLC 1**

Alas (y Urena), Leopoldo (Enrique Garcia)
1852-1901 . . . . **TCLC 29**
See also CA 113

Albee, Edward (Franklin III)
1928- . . . **CLC 1, 2, 3, 5, 9, 11, 13, 25, 53**
See also WLC 1; CANR 8; CA 5-8R;
DLB 7; CDALB 1941-1968

Alberti, Rafael 1902- . . . . **CLC 7**
See also CA 85-88

Alcott, Amos Bronson 1799-1888 . . **NCLC 1**
See also DLB 1

Alcott, Louisa May 1832-1888 . . . . **NCLC 6**
See also CLR 1; WLC 1; YABC 1; DLB 1,
42, 79; CDALB 1865-1917

Aldanov, Mark 1887-1957 . . . . **TCLC 23**
See also CA 118

Aldington, Richard 1892-1962 . . . . . . **CLC 49**
See also CA 85-88; DLB 20, 36

Aldiss, Brian W(ilson)
1925- . . . . **CLC 5, 14, 40**
See also CAAS 2; CANR 5; CA 5-8R;
SATA 34; DLB 14

Alegria, Fernando 1918- . . . . **CLC 57**
See also CANR 5; CA 11-12R

Aleixandre, Vicente 1898-1984 . . . **CLC 9, 36**
See also CANR 26; CA 85-88;
obituary CA 114

Alepoudelis, Odysseus 1911-
See Elytis, Odysseus

Aleshkovsky, Yuz 1929- . . . . **CLC 44**
See also CA 121, 128

Alexander, Lloyd (Chudley) 1924- . . **CLC 35**
See also CLR 1, 5; CANR 1; CA 1-4R;
SATA 3, 49; DLB 52

Alexander, Margaret Abigail Walker 1915-
See Walker, Margaret

Alfau, Felipe 1902- . . . . **CLC 66**

Alger, Horatio, Jr. 1832-1899 . . . . . **NCLC 8**
See also SATA 16; DLB 42

Algren, Nelson 1909-1981 . . . . **CLC 4, 10, 33**
See also CANR 20; CA 13-16R;
obituary CA 103; DLB 9; DLB-Y 81, 82;
CDALB 1941-1968

Ali, Ahmed 1910- . . . . **CLC 69**
See also CANR 15, 34; CA 25-28R

Alighieri, Dante 1265-1321 . . . . **CMLC 3**

Allard, Janet 1975- . . . . **CLC 59**

Allen, Edward 1948- . . . . **CLC 59**

Allen, Roland 1939-
See Ayckbourn, Alan

Allen, Sarah A. 1859-1930
See Hopkins, Pauline Elizabeth

Allen, Woody 1935- . . . . **CLC 16, 52**
See also CANR 27; CA 33-36R; DLB 44

Allende, Isabel 1942- . . . . **CLC 39, 57**
See also CA 125

Alleyne, Carla D. 1975?- . . . . **CLC 65**

Allingham, Margery (Louise)
1904-1966 . . . . **CLC 19**
See also CANR 4; CA 5-8R;
obituary CA 25-28R; DLB 77

Allingham, William 1824-1889 . . . **NCLC 25**
See also DLB 35

Allston, Washington 1779-1843 . . . . **NCLC 2**
See also DLB 1

Almedingen, E. M. 1898-1971 . . . . . . **CLC 12**
See also Almedingen, Martha Edith von
See also SATA 3

Almedingen, Martha Edith von 1898-1971
See Almedingen, E. M.
See also CANR 1; CA 1-4R

Alonso, Damaso 1898- . . . . **CLC 14**
See also CA 110; obituary CA 130

Alta 1942- . . . . **CLC 19**
See also CA 57-60

Alter, Robert B(ernard) 1935- . . . . . . **CLC 34**
See also CANR 1; CA 49-52

Alther, Lisa 1944- . . . . **CLC 7, 41**
See also CANR 12; CA 65-68

Altman, Robert 1925- . . . . **CLC 16**
See also CA 73-76

Alvarez, A(lfred) 1929- . . . . **CLC 5, 13**
See also CANR 3; CA 1-4R; DLB 14, 40

Alvarez, Alejandro Rodriguez 1903-1965
See Casona, Alejandro
See also obituary CA 93-96

Amado, Jorge 1912- . . . . **CLC 13, 40**
See also CA 77-80

Ambler, Eric 1909- . . . . **CLC 4, 6, 9**
See also CANR 7; CA 9-12R; DLB 77

Amichai, Yehuda 1924- . . . . . . **CLC 9, 22, 57**
See also CA 85-88

Amiel, Henri Frederic 1821-1881 . . **NCLC 4**

Amis, Kingsley (William)
1922- . . . . . . **CLC 1, 2, 3, 5, 8, 13, 40, 44**
See also CANR 8; CA 9-12R; DLB 15, 27

Amis, Martin 1949- . . . . **CLC 4, 9, 38, 62**
See also CANR 8, 27; CA 65-68; DLB 14

Ammons, A(rchie) R(andolph)
1926- . . . . **CLC 2, 3, 5, 8, 9, 25, 57**
See also CANR 6; CA 9-12R; DLB 5

Anand, Mulk Raj 1905- . . . . **CLC 23**
See also CA 65-68

Anaya, Rudolfo A(lfonso) 1937- . . . . **CLC 23**
See also CAAS 4; CANR 1; CA 45-48;
DLB 82

Andersen, Hans Christian
1805-1875 . . . . **NCLC 7; SSC 6**
See also CLR 6; WLC 1; YABC 1

Anderson, Jessica (Margaret Queale)
19??- . . . . **CLC 37**
See also CANR 4; CA 9-12R

Anderson, Jon (Victor) 1940- . . . . **CLC 9**
See also CANR 20; CA 25-28R

Anderson, Lindsay 1923- . . . . **CLC 20**
See also CA 125

Anderson, Maxwell 1888-1959 . . . . . **TCLC 2**
See also CA 105; DLB 7

Anderson, Poul (William) 1926- . . . . **CLC 15**
See also CAAS 2; CANR 2, 15; CA 1-4R;
SATA 39; DLB 8

Anderson, Robert (Woodruff)
1917- . . . . **CLC 23**
See also CA 21-24R; DLB 7

Anderson, Roberta Joan 1943-
See Mitchell, Joni

Anderson, Sherwood
1876-1941 . . . . . . **TCLC 1, 10, 24; SSC 1**
See also WLC 1; CAAS 3; CA 104, 121;
DLB 4, 9; DLB-DS 1

Andrade, Carlos Drummond de
1902-1987 . . . . **CLC 18**
See also CA 123

Andrade, Mario de 1892-1945 . . . . . **TCLC 43**

Andrewes, Lancelot 1555-1626 . . . . **LC 5**

Andrews, Cicily Fairfield 1892-1983
    See West, Rebecca

Andreyev, Leonid (Nikolaevich)
    1871-1919 . . . . **TCLC 3**
    See also CA 104

Andrezel, Pierre 1885-1962
    See Dinesen, Isak; Blixen, Karen
    (Christentze Dinesen)

Andric, Ivo 1892-1975 . . . . **CLC 8**
    See also CA 81-84; obituary CA 57-60

Angelique, Pierre 1897-1962
    See Bataille, Georges

Angell, Roger 1920- . . . . **CLC 26**
    See also CANR 13; CA 57-60

Angelou, Maya 1928- . . . . **CLC 12, 35, 64**
    See also BLC 1; CANR 19; CA 65-68;
    SATA 49; DLB 38

Annensky, Innokenty 1856-1909 . . . **TCLC 14**
    See also CA 110

Anouilh, Jean (Marie Lucien Pierre)
    1910-1987 . . . . . . **CLC 1, 3, 8, 13, 40, 50**
    See also CA 17-20R; obituary CA 123

Anthony, Florence 1947-
    See Ai

Anthony (Jacob), Piers 1934- . . . . . . **CLC 35**
    See also Jacob, Piers A(nthony)
    D(illingham)
    See also DLB 8

Antoninus, Brother 1912-
    See Everson, William (Oliver)

Antonioni, Michelangelo 1912- . . . . . **CLC 20**
    See also CA 73-76

Antschel, Paul 1920-1970 . . . . . . **CLC 10, 19**
    See also Celan, Paul
    See also CA 85-88

Anwar, Chairil 1922-1949 . . . . **TCLC 22**
    See also CA 121

Apollinaire, Guillaume
    1880-1918 . . . . **TCLC 3, 8**
    See also Kostrowitzki, Wilhelm Apollinaris
    de

Appelfeld, Aharon 1932- . . . . **CLC 23, 47**
    See also CA 112

Apple, Max (Isaac) 1941- . . . . **CLC 9, 33**
    See also CANR 19; CA 81-84

Appleman, Philip (Dean) 1926- . . . . . **CLC 51**
    See also CANR 6; CA 13-16R

Apuleius, (Lucius) (Madaurensis)
    125?-175? . . . . **CMLC 1**

Aquin, Hubert 1929-1977 . . . . **CLC 15**
    See also CA 105; DLB 53

Aragon, Louis 1897-1982 . . . . **CLC 3, 22**
    See also CA 69-72; obituary CA 108;
    DLB 72

Arany, Janos 1817-1882 . . . . **NCLC 34**

Arbuthnot, John 1667-1735 . . . . **LC 1**

Archer, Jeffrey (Howard) 1940- . . . . **CLC 28**
    See also CANR 22; CA 77-80

Archer, Jules 1915- . . . . **CLC 12**
    See also CANR 6; CA 9-12R; SAAS 5;
    SATA 4

Arden, John 1930- . . . . **CLC 6, 13, 15**
    See also CAAS 4; CA 13-16R; DLB 13

Arenas, Reinaldo 1943- . . . . **CLC 41**
    See also CA 124, 128

Arendt, Hannah 1906-1975 . . . . **CLC 66**
    See also CA 19-20R; obituary CA 61-64

Aretino, Pietro 1492-1556 . . . . **LC 12**

Arguedas, Jose Maria
    1911-1969 . . . . **CLC 10, 18**
    See also CA 89-92

Argueta, Manlio 1936- . . . . **CLC 31**

Ariosto, Ludovico 1474-1533 . . . . **LC 6**

Aristophanes
    c. 450 B. C.-c. 385 B. C. . . . . . **CMLC 4;**
                                              DC 2

Arlt, Roberto 1900-1942 . . . . **TCLC 29**
    See also CA 123

Armah, Ayi Kwei 1939- . . . . **CLC 5, 33**
    See also BLC 1; CANR 21; CA 61-64

Armatrading, Joan 1950- . . . . **CLC 17**
    See also CA 114

Arnim, Achim von (Ludwig Joachim von
    Arnim) 1781-1831 . . . . **NCLC 5**
    See also DLB 90

Arnold, Matthew
    1822-1888 . . . . **NCLC 6, 29; PC 5**
    See also WLC 1; DLB 32, 57;
    CDALB 1832-1890

Arnold, Thomas 1795-1842 . . . . . . **NCLC 18**
    See also DLB 55

Arnow, Harriette (Louisa Simpson)
    1908-1986 . . . . **CLC 2, 7, 18**
    See also CANR 14; CA 9-12R;
    obituary CA 118; SATA 42, 47; DLB 6

Arp, Jean 1887-1966 . . . . **CLC 5**
    See also CA 81-84; obituary CA 25-28R

Arquette, Lois S(teinmetz) 1934-
    See Duncan (Steinmetz Arquette), Lois
    See also SATA 1

Arrabal, Fernando 1932- . . . **CLC 2, 9, 18, 58**
    See also CANR 15; CA 9-12R

Arrick, Fran 19??- . . . . **CLC 30**

Artaud, Antonin 1896-1948 . . . . . **TCLC 3, 36**
    See also CA 104

Arthur, Ruth M(abel) 1905-1979 . . . . **CLC 12**
    See also CANR 4; CA 9-12R;
    obituary CA 85-88; SATA 7;
    obituary SATA 26

Artsybashev, Mikhail Petrarch
    1878-1927 . . . . **TCLC 31**

Arundel, Honor (Morfydd)
    1919-1973 . . . . **CLC 17**
    See also CAP 2; CA 21-22;
    obituary CA 41-44R; SATA 4;
    obituary SATA 24

Asch, Sholem 1880-1957 . . . . **TCLC 3**
    See also CA 105

Ashbery, John (Lawrence)
    1927- . . . **CLC 2, 3, 4, 6, 9, 13, 15, 25, 41**
    See also CANR 9; CA 5-8R; DLB 5;
    DLB-Y 81

Ashton-Warner, Sylvia (Constance)
    1908-1984 . . . . **CLC 19**
    See also CA 69-72; obituary CA 112

Asimov, Isaac 1920- . . . . **CLC 1, 3, 9, 19, 26**
    See also CLR 12; CANR 2, 19; CA 1-4R;
    SATA 1, 26; DLB 8

Astley, Thea (Beatrice May)
    1925- . . . . **CLC 41**
    See also CANR 11; CA 65-68

Astley, William 1855-1911
    See Warung, Price

Aston, James 1906-1964
    See White, T(erence) H(anbury)

Asturias, Miguel Angel
    1899-1974 . . . . **CLC 3, 8, 13**
    See also CAP 2; CA 25-28;
    obituary CA 49-52

Atheling, William, Jr. 1921-1975
    See Blish, James (Benjamin)

Atherton, Gertrude (Franklin Horn)
    1857-1948 . . . . **TCLC 2**
    See also CA 104; DLB 9, 78

Attaway, William 1911?-1986
    See also BLC 1; DLB 76

Atwood, Margaret (Eleanor)
    1939- . . . . **CLC 2, 3, 4, 8, 13, 15, 25, 44;**
                                              SSC 2
    See also WLC 1; CANR 3, 24; CA 49-52;
    SATA 50; DLB 53

Aubin, Penelope 1685-1731? . . . . **LC 9**
    See also DLB 39

Auchincloss, Louis (Stanton)
    1917- . . . . **CLC 4, 6, 9, 18, 45**
    See also CANR 6; CA 1-4R; DLB 2;
    DLB-Y 80

Auden, W(ystan) H(ugh)
    1907-1973 . . . . . **CLC 1, 2, 3, 4, 6, 9, 11,**
                                   14, 43; PC 1
    See also WLC 1; CANR 5; CA 9-12R;
    obituary CA 45-48; DLB 10, 20

Audiberti, Jacques 1899-1965 . . . . . . **CLC 38**
    See also obituary CA 25-28R

Auel, Jean M(arie) 1936- . . . . **CLC 31**
    See also CANR 21; CA 103

Auerbach, Erich 1892-1957 . . . . **TCLC 43**
    See also CA 118

Augier, Emile 1820-1889 . . . . **NCLC 31**

Augustine, St. 354-430 . . . . **CMLC 6**

Austen, Jane
    1775-1817 . . . . **NCLC 1, 13, 19, 33**
    See also WLC 1

Auster, Paul 1947- . . . . **CLC 47**
    See also CANR 23; CA 69-72

Austin, Mary (Hunter)
    1868-1934 . . . . **TCLC 25**
    See also CA 109; DLB 9

Averroes 1126-1198 . . . . **CMLC 7**

Avison, Margaret 1918- . . . . **CLC 2, 4**
    See also CA 17-20R; DLB 53

Ayckbourn, Alan 1939- . . . . **CLC 5, 8, 18, 33**
    See also CA 21-24R; DLB 13

Aydy, Catherine 1937-
    See Tennant, Emma

Ayme, Marcel (Andre) 1902-1967 . . . **CLC 11**
    See also CA 89-92; DLB 72

Beard, Charles A(ustin)
    1874-1948 .... **TCLC 15**
    See also CA 115; SATA 18; DLB 17

Beardsley, Aubrey 1872-1898 ..... **NCLC 6**

Beattie, Ann 1947- ... **CLC 8, 13, 18, 40, 63**
    See also CA 81-84; DLB-Y 82

Beattie, James 1735-1803 .... **NCLC 25**

Beauvoir, Simone (Lucie Ernestine Marie
    Bertrand) de
    1908-1986 ... **CLC 1, 2, 4, 8, 14, 31, 44,**
                         50, 71
    See also WLC 1; CANR 28; CA 9-12R;
    obituary CA 118; DLB 72; DLB-Y 86

Becker, Jurek 1937- .... **CLC 7, 19**
    See also CA 85-88; DLB 75

Becker, Walter 1950- .... **CLC 26**

Beckett, Samuel (Barclay)
    1906-1989 ..... **CLC 1, 2, 3, 4, 6, 9, 10,**
           11, 14, 18, 29, 57, 59
    See also WLC 1; CA 5-8R; DLB 13, 15

Beckford, William 1760-1844 .... **NCLC 16**
    See also DLB 39

Beckham, Barry 1944-
    See also BLC 1; CANR 26; CA 29-32R;
    DLB 33

Beckman, Gunnel 1910- .... **CLC 26**
    See also CANR 15; CA 33-36R; SATA 6

Becque, Henri 1837-1899 .... **NCLC 3**

Beddoes, Thomas Lovell
    1803-1849 .... **NCLC 3**

Beecher, Catharine Esther
    1800-1878 .... **NCLC 30**
    See also DLB 1

Beecher, John 1904-1980 .... **CLC 6**
    See also CANR 8; CA 5-8R;
    obituary CA 105

Beer, Johann 1655-1700 .... **LC 5**

Beer, Patricia 1919?- .... **CLC 58**
    See also CANR 13; CA 61-64; DLB 40

Beerbohm, (Sir Henry) Max(imilian)
    1872-1956 .... **TCLC 1, 24**
    See also CA 104; DLB 34

Begiebing, Robert J. 1946- .... **CLC 70**
    See also CA 122

Behan, Brendan
    1923-1964 .... **CLC 1, 8, 11, 15**
    See also CA 73-76; DLB 13

Behn, Aphra 1640?-1689 .... **LC 1**
    See also WLC 1; DLB 39, 80

Behrman, S(amuel) N(athaniel)
    1893-1973 .... **CLC 40**
    See also CAP 1; CA 15-16;
    obituary CA 45-48; DLB 7, 44

Beiswanger, George Edwin 1931-
    See Starbuck, George (Edwin)

Belasco, David 1853-1931 .... **TCLC 3**
    See also CA 104; DLB 7

Belcheva, Elisaveta 1893-
    See Bagryana, Elisaveta

Belinski, Vissarion Grigoryevich
    1811-1848 .... **NCLC 5**

Belitt, Ben 1911- .... **CLC 22**
    See also CAAS 4; CANR 7; CA 13-16R;
    DLB 5

Bell, Acton 1820-1849
    See Bronte, Anne

Bell, Currer 1816-1855
    See Bronte, Charlotte

Bell, James Madison 1826-1902 ... **TCLC 43**
    See also BLC 1; CA 122, 124; DLB 50

Bell, Madison Smartt 1957- .... **CLC 41**
    See also CA 111

Bell, Marvin (Hartley) 1937- ..... **CLC 8, 31**
    See also CA 21-24R; DLB 5

Bellamy, Edward 1850-1898 ...... **NCLC 4**
    See also DLB 12

Belloc, (Joseph) Hilaire (Pierre Sebastien
    Rene Swanton)
    1870-1953 .... **TCLC 7, 18**
    See also YABC 1; CA 106; DLB 19

Bellow, Saul
    1915- ..... **CLC 1, 2, 3, 6, 8, 10, 13, 15,**
                25, 33, 34, 63
    See also WLC 1; CA 5-8R; CABS 1;
    DLB 2, 28; DLB-Y 82; DLB-DS 3;
    CDALB 1941-1968

Belser, Reimond Karel Maria de 1929-
    See Ruyslinck, Ward

Bely, Andrey 1880-1934 .... **TCLC 7**
    See also CA 104

Benary-Isbert, Margot 1889-1979 ... **CLC 12**
    See also CLR 12; CANR 4; CA 5-8R;
    obituary CA 89-92; SATA 2;
    obituary SATA 21

Benavente (y Martinez), Jacinto
    1866-1954 .... **TCLC 3**
    See also CA 106

Benchley, Peter (Bradford)
    1940- .... **CLC 4, 8**
    See also CANR 12; CA 17-20R; SATA 3

Benchley, Robert 1889-1945 .... **TCLC 1**
    See also CA 105; DLB 11

Benedikt, Michael 1935- .... **CLC 4, 14**
    See also CANR 7; CA 13-16R; DLB 5

Benet, Juan 1927- .... **CLC 28**

Benet, Stephen Vincent
    1898-1943 .... **TCLC 7; SSC 10**
    See also YABC 1; CA 104; DLB 4, 48

Benet, William Rose 1886-1950 ... **TCLC 28**
    See also CA 118; DLB 45

Benford, Gregory (Albert) 1941- .... **CLC 52**
    See also CANR 12, 24; CA 69-72;
    DLB-Y 82

Benjamin, Walter 1892-1940 ..... **TCLC 39**

Benn, Gottfried 1886-1956 .... **TCLC 3**
    See also CA 106; DLB 56

Bennett, Alan 1934- .... **CLC 45**
    See also CA 103

Bennett, (Enoch) Arnold
    1867-1931 .... **TCLC 5, 20**
    See also CA 106; DLB 10, 34

Bennett, George Harold 1930-
    See Bennett, Hal
    See also CA 97-100

Bennett, Hal 1930- .... **CLC 5**
    See also Bennett, George Harold
    See also DLB 33

Bennett, Jay 1912- .... **CLC 35**
    See also CANR 11; CA 69-72; SAAS 4;
    SATA 27, 41

Bennett, Louise (Simone) 1919- ..... **CLC 28**
    See also Bennett-Coverly, Louise Simone
    See also BLC 1

Bennett-Coverly, Louise Simone 1919-
    See Bennett, Louise (Simone)
    See also CA 97-100

Benson, E(dward) F(rederic)
    1867-1940 .... **TCLC 27**
    See also CA 114

Benson, Jackson J. 1930- .... **CLC 34**
    See also CA 25-28R

Benson, Sally 1900-1972 .... **CLC 17**
    See also CAP 1; CA 19-20;
    obituary CA 37-40R; SATA 1, 35;
    obituary SATA 27

Benson, Stella 1892-1933 .... **TCLC 17**
    See also CA 117; DLB 36

Bentley, E(dmund) C(lerihew)
    1875-1956 .... **TCLC 12**
    See also CA 108; DLB 70

Bentley, Eric (Russell) 1916- .... **CLC 24**
    See also CANR 6; CA 5-8R

Beranger, Pierre Jean de
    1780-1857 .... **NCLC 34**

Berger, John (Peter) 1926- ...... **CLC 2, 19**
    See also CA 81-84; DLB 14

Berger, Melvin (H.) 1927- .... **CLC 12**
    See also CANR 4; CA 5-8R; SAAS 2;
    SATA 5

Berger, Thomas (Louis)
    1924- .... **CLC 3, 5, 8, 11, 18, 38**
    See also CANR 5; CA 1-4R; DLB 2;
    DLB-Y 80

Bergman, (Ernst) Ingmar
    1918- .... **CLC 16, 72**
    See also CANR 33; CA 81-84

Bergson, Henri 1859-1941 .... **TCLC 32**

Bergstein, Eleanor 1938- .... **CLC 4**
    See also CANR 5; CA 53-56

Berkoff, Steven 1937- .... **CLC 56**
    See also CA 104

Bermant, Chaim 1929- .... **CLC 40**
    See also CANR 6; CA 57-60

Bernanos, (Paul Louis) Georges
    1888-1948 .... **TCLC 3**
    See also CA 104; DLB 72

Bernard, April 19??- .... **CLC 59**

Bernhard, Thomas
    1931-1989 .... **CLC 3, 32, 61**
    See also CA 85-88,; obituary CA 127;
    DLB 85

Berriault, Gina 1926- .... **CLC 54**
    See also CA 116

Berrigan, Daniel J. 1921- .... **CLC 4**
    See also CAAS 1; CANR 11; CA 33-36R;
    DLB 5

Berrigan, Edmund Joseph Michael, Jr.
    1934-1983
    See Berrigan, Ted
    See also CANR 14; CA 61-64;
    obituary CA 110

Booth, Martin 1944-............. **CLC 13**
See also CAAS 2; CA 93-96

Booth, Philip 1925-............... **CLC 23**
See also CANR 5; CA 5-8R; DLB-Y 82

Booth, Wayne C(layson) 1921-..... **CLC 24**
See also CAAS 5; CANR 3; CA 1-4R;
DLB 67

Borchert, Wolfgang 1921-1947 ..... **TCLC 5**
See also CA 104; DLB 69

Borges, Jorge Luis
1899-1986 ... **CLC 1, 2, 3, 4, 6, 8, 9, 10,
13, 19, 44, 48; SSC 4**
See also WLC 1; CANR 19; CA 21-24R;
DLB-Y 86

Borowski, Tadeusz 1922-1951 ...... **TCLC 9**
See also CA 106

Borrow, George (Henry)
1803-1881 .... **NCLC 9**
See also DLB 21, 55

Bosschere, Jean de 1878-1953..... **TCLC 19**
See also CA 115

Boswell, James 1740-1795 .... **LC 4**
See also WLC 1

Boto, Eza 1932-
See Beti, Mongo

Bottoms, David 1949-............. **CLC 53**
See also CANR 22; CA 105; DLB-Y 83

Boucolon, Maryse 1937-
See Conde, Maryse
See also CA 110

Bourget, Paul (Charles Joseph)
1852-1935 .... **TCLC 12**
See also CA 107

Bourjaily, Vance (Nye) 1922- .... **CLC 8, 62**
See also CAAS 1; CANR 2; CA 1-4R;
DLB 2

Bourne, Randolph S(illiman)
1886-1918 .... **TCLC 16**
See also CA 117; DLB 63

Bova, Ben(jamin William) 1932-.... **CLC 45**
See also CLR 3; CANR 11; CA 5-8R;
SATA 6; DLB-Y 81

Bowen, Elizabeth (Dorothea Cole)
1899-1973 ..... **CLC 1, 3, 6, 11, 15, 22;
SSC 3**
See also CAP 2; CA 17-18;
obituary CA 41-44R; DLB 15

Bowering, George 1935-........ **CLC 15, 47**
See also CANR 10; CA 21-24R; DLB 53

Bowering, Marilyn R(uthe) 1949-... **CLC 32**
See also CA 101

Bowers, Edgar 1924- .... **CLC 9**
See also CANR 24; CA 5-8R; DLB 5

Bowie, David 1947- .... **CLC 17**
See also Jones, David Robert

Bowles, Jane (Sydney)
1917-1973 .... **CLC 3, 68**
See also CAP 2; CA 19-20;
obituary CA 41-44R

Bowles, Paul (Frederick)
1910- .... **CLC 1, 2, 19, 53; SSC 3**
See also CAAS 1; CANR 1, 19; CA 1-4R;
DLB 5, 6

Box, Edgar 1925-
See Vidal, Gore

Boyd, William 1952-........ **CLC 28, 53, 70**
See also CA 114, 120

Boyle, Kay 1903- ... **CLC 1, 5, 19, 58; SSC 5**
See also CAAS 1; CA 13-16R; DLB 4, 9, 48

Boyle, Patrick 19??-.............. **CLC 19**

Boyle, Thomas Coraghessan
1948-................... **CLC 36, 55**
See also CA 120; DLB-Y 86

Brackenridge, Hugh Henry
1748-1816 .... **NCLC 7**
See also DLB 11, 37

Bradbury, Edward P. 1939-
See Moorcock, Michael

Bradbury, Malcolm (Stanley)
1932-..................... **CLC 32, 61**
See also CANR 1; CA 1-4R; DLB 14

Bradbury, Ray(mond Douglas)
1920- .... **CLC 1, 3, 10, 15, 42**
See also WLC 1; CANR 2, 30; CA 1-4R;
SATA 11, 64; DLB 2, 8;
CDALB 1968-1988

Bradford, Gamaliel 1863-1932..... **TCLC 36**
See also DLB 17

Bradley, David (Henry), Jr. 1950- .. **CLC 23**
See also BLC 1; CANR 26; CA 104;
DLB 33

Bradley, John Ed 1959-........... **CLC 55**

Bradley, Katherine Harris 1846-1914
See Field, Michael

Bradley, Marion Zimmer 1930-..... **CLC 30**
See also CANR 7; CA 57-60; DLB 8

Bradstreet, Anne 1612-1672......... **LC 4**
See also DLB 24; CDALB 1640-1865

Bragg, Melvyn 1939- .... **CLC 10**
See also CANR 10; CA 57-60; DLB 14

Braine, John (Gerard)
1922-1986.............. **CLC 1, 3, 41**
See also CANR 1; CA 1-4R;
obituary CA 120; DLB 15; DLB-Y 86

Braithwaite, William Stanley 1878-1962
See also BLC 1; CA 125; DLB 50, 54

Brammer, Billy Lee 1930?-1978
See Brammer, William

Brammer, William 1930?-1978 ..... **CLC 31**
See also obituary CA 77-80

Brancati, Vitaliano 1907-1954..... **TCLC 12**
See also CA 109

Brancato, Robin F(idler) 1936-..... **CLC 35**
See also CANR 11; CA 69-72; SATA 23

Brand, Millen 1906-1980.......... **CLC 7**
See also CA 21-24R; obituary CA 97-100

Branden, Barbara 19??-........... **CLC 44**

Brandes, Georg (Morris Cohen)
1842-1927 .... **TCLC 10**
See also CA 105

Brandys, Kazimierz 1916-........ **CLC 62**

Branley, Franklyn M(ansfield)
1915-..................... **CLC 21**
See also CLR 13; CANR 14; CA 33-36R;
SATA 4

Brathwaite, Edward 1930-........ **CLC 11**
See also CANR 11; CA 25-28R; DLB 53

Brautigan, Richard (Gary)
1935-1984 .... **CLC 1, 3, 5, 9, 12, 34, 42**
See also CA 53-56; obituary CA 113;
SATA 56; DLB 2, 5; DLB-Y 80, 84

Braverman, Kate 1950- .... **CLC 67**
See also CA 89-92

Brecht, (Eugen) Bertolt (Friedrich)
1898-1956 .... **TCLC 1, 6, 13, 35**
See also WLC 1; CA 133;
brief entry CA 104; DLB 56

Bremer, Fredrika 1801-1865 ..... **NCLC 11**

Brennan, Christopher John
1870-1932 .... **TCLC 17**
See also CA 117

Brennan, Maeve 1917-............. **CLC 5**
See also CA 81-84

Brentano, Clemens (Maria)
1778-1842 .... **NCLC 1**
See also DLB 90

Brenton, Howard 1942-........... **CLC 31**
See also CA 69-72; DLB 13

Breslin, James 1930-
See Breslin, Jimmy
See also CA 73-76

Breslin, Jimmy 1930-........... **CLC 4, 43**
See also Breslin, James

Bresson, Robert 1907-............. **CLC 16**
See also CA 110

Breton, Andre 1896-1966... **CLC 2, 9, 15, 54**
See also CAP 2; CA 19-20;
obituary CA 25-28R; DLB 65

Breytenbach, Breyten 1939-..... **CLC 23, 37**
See also CA 113, 129

Bridgers, Sue Ellen 1942- .... **CLC 26**
See also CANR 11; CA 65-68; SAAS 1;
SATA 22; DLB 52

Bridges, Robert 1844-1930........ **TCLC 1**
See also CA 104; DLB 19

Bridie, James 1888-1951 .... **TCLC 3**
See also Mavor, Osborne Henry
See also DLB 10

Brin, David 1950-................ **CLC 34**
See also CANR 24; CA 102

Brink, Andre (Philippus)
1935-..................... **CLC 18, 36**
See also CA 104

Brinsmead, H(esba) F(ay) 1922- .... **CLC 21**
See also CANR 10; CA 21-24R; SAAS 5;
SATA 18

Brittain, Vera (Mary) 1893?-1970... **CLC 23**
See also CAP 1; CA 15-16;
obituary CA 25-28R

Broch, Hermann 1886-1951....... **TCLC 20**
See also CA 117; DLB 85

Brock, Rose 1923-
See Hansen, Joseph

Brodkey, Harold 1930-............ **CLC 56**
See also CA 111

Brodsky, Iosif Alexandrovich 1940-
See Brodsky, Joseph (Alexandrovich)
See also CA 41-44R

Brodsky, Joseph (Alexandrovich)
1940- .... **CLC 4, 6, 13, 36, 50**
See also Brodsky, Iosif Alexandrovich

Brodsky, Michael (Mark) 1948- .... CLC 19
See also CANR 18; CA 102

Bromell, Henry 1947- .... CLC 5
See also CANR 9; CA 53-56

Bromfield, Louis (Brucker)
1896-1956 .... TCLC 11
See also CA 107; DLB 4, 9

Broner, E(sther) M(asserman)
1930- .... CLC 19
See also CANR 8, 25; CA 17-20R; DLB 28

Bronk, William 1918- .... CLC 10
See also CANR 23; CA 89-92

Bronte, Anne 1820-1849 .... NCLC 4
See also DLB 21

Bronte, Charlotte
1816-1855 .... NCLC 3, 8, 33
See also WLC 1; DLB 21

Bronte, (Jane) Emily
1818-1848 .... NCLC 16, 35
See also WLC 1; DLB 21, 32

Brooke, Frances 1724-1789 .... LC 6
See also DLB 39

Brooke, Henry 1703?-1783 .... LC 1
See also DLB 39

Brooke, Rupert (Chawner)
1887-1915 .... TCLC 2, 7
See also WLC 1; CA 104; DLB 19

Brooke-Rose, Christine 1926- ...... CLC 40
See also CA 13-16R; DLB 14

Brookner, Anita 1928- ...... CLC 32, 34, 51
See also CA 114, 120; DLB-Y 87

Brooks, Cleanth 1906- .... CLC 24
See also CA 17-20R; DLB 63

Brooks, Gwendolyn
1917- .... CLC 1, 2, 4, 5, 15, 49
See also BLC 1; WLC 1; CANR 1, 27;
CA 1-4R; SATA 6; DLB 5, 76;
CDALB 1941-1968

Brooks, Mel 1926- .... CLC 12
See also Kaminsky, Melvin
See also CA 65-68; DLB 26

Brooks, Peter 1938- .... CLC 34
See also CANR 1; CA 45-48

Brooks, Van Wyck 1886-1963 ...... CLC 29
See also CANR 6; CA 1-4R; DLB 45, 63

Brophy, Brigid (Antonia)
1929- .... CLC 6, 11, 29
See also CAAS 4; CANR 25; CA 5-8R;
DLB 14

Brosman, Catharine Savage 1934- .... CLC 9
See also CANR 21; CA 61-64

Broughton, T(homas) Alan 1936- ... CLC 19
See also CANR 2, 23; CA 45-48

Broumas, Olga 1949- .... CLC 10, 73
See also CANR 20; CA 85-88

Brown, Charles Brockden
1771-1810 .... NCLC 22
See also DLB 37, 59, 73;
CDALB 1640-1865

Brown, Christy 1932-1981 .... CLC 63
See also CA 105; obituary CA 104

Brown, Claude 1937- .... CLC 30
See also BLC 1; CA 73-76

Brown, Dee (Alexander) 1908- .. CLC 18, 47
See also CAAS 6; CANR 11; CA 13-16R;
SATA 5; DLB-Y 80

Brown, George Douglas 1869-1902
See Douglas, George

Brown, George Mackay 1921- .... CLC 5, 28
See also CAAS 6; CANR 12; CA 21-24R;
SATA 35; DLB 14, 27

Brown, H. Rap 1943-
See Al-Amin, Jamil Abdullah

Brown, Hubert Gerold 1943-
See Al-Amin, Jamil Abdullah

Brown, (William) Larry 1951- ..... CLC 73
See also CA 134; brief entry CA 130

Brown, Rita Mae 1944- .... CLC 18, 43
See also CANR 2, 11; CA 45-48

Brown, Rosellen 1939- .... CLC 32
See also CANR 14; CA 77-80

Brown, Sterling A(llen)
1901-1989 .... CLC 1, 23, 59
See also BLC 1; CANR 26; CA 85-88;
obituary CA 127; DLB 48, 51, 63

Brown, William Wells
1816?-1884 .... NCLC 2; DC 1
See also BLC 1; DLB 3, 50

Browne, Charles Farrar
1834-1867 .... NCLC 37
See also DLB 11

Browne, Jackson 1950- .... CLC 21
See also CA 120

Browning, Elizabeth Barrett
1806-1861 .... NCLC 1, 16
See also WLC 1; DLB 32

Browning, Robert
1812-1889 .... NCLC 19; PC 2
See also YABC 1; DLB 32

Browning, Tod 1882-1962 .... CLC 16
See also obituary CA 117

Bruccoli, Matthew J(oseph) 1931- .. CLC 34
See also CANR 7; CA 9-12R

Bruce, Lenny 1925-1966 .... CLC 21
See also Schneider, Leonard Alfred

Bruin, John 1924-
See Brutus, Dennis

Brunner, John (Kilian Houston)
1934- .... CLC 8, 10
See also CAAS 8; CANR 2; CA 1-4R

Brutus, Dennis 1924- .... CLC 43
See also BLC 1; CANR 2, 27; CA 49-52

Bryan, C(ourtlandt) D(ixon) B(arnes)
1936- .... CLC 29
See also CANR 13; CA 73-76

Bryant, William Cullen
1794-1878 .... NCLC 6
See also DLB 3, 43, 59; CDALB 1640-1865

Bryusov, Valery (Yakovlevich)
1873-1924 .... TCLC 10
See also CA 107

Buchan, John 1875-1940 .... TCLC 41
See also YABC 2; brief entry CA 108;
DLB 34, 70

Buchanan, George 1506-1582 .... LC 4

Buchheim, Lothar-Gunther 1918- .... CLC 6
See also CA 85-88

Buchner, (Karl) Georg
1813-1837 .... NCLC 26

Buchwald, Art(hur) 1925- .... CLC 33
See also CANR 21; CA 5-8R; SATA 10

Buck, Pearl S(ydenstricker)
1892-1973 .... CLC 7, 11, 18
See also CANR 1; CA 1-4R;
obituary CA 41-44R; SATA 1, 25; DLB 9

Buckler, Ernest 1908-1984 .... CLC 13
See also CAP 1; CA 11-12;
obituary CA 114; SATA 47

Buckley, Vincent (Thomas)
1925-1988 .... CLC 57
See also CA 101

Buckley, William F(rank), Jr.
1925- .... CLC 7, 18, 37
See also CANR 1, 24; CA 1-4R; DLB-Y 80

Buechner, (Carl) Frederick
1926- .... CLC 2, 4, 6, 9
See also CANR 11; CA 13-16R; DLB-Y 80

Buell, John (Edward) 1927- .... CLC 10
See also CA 1-4R; DLB 53

Buero Vallejo, Antonio 1916- ... CLC 15, 46
See also CANR 24; CA 106

Bukowski, Charles 1920- .... CLC 2, 5, 9, 41
See also CA 17-20R; DLB 5

Bulgakov, Mikhail (Afanas'evich)
1891-1940 .... TCLC 2, 16
See also CA 105

Bullins, Ed 1935- .... CLC 1, 5, 7
See also BLC 1; CANR 24; CA 49-52;
DLB 7, 38

Bulwer-Lytton, (Lord) Edward (George Earle
Lytton) 1803-1873 .... NCLC 1
See also Lytton, Edward Bulwer
See also DLB 21

Bunin, Ivan (Alexeyevich)
1870-1953 .... TCLC 6; SSC 5
See also CA 104

Bunting, Basil 1900-1985 .... CLC 10, 39, 47
See also CANR 7; CA 53-56;
obituary CA 115; DLB 20

Bunuel, Luis 1900-1983 .... CLC 16
See also CA 101; obituary CA 110

Bunyan, John 1628-1688 .... LC 4
See also WLC 1; DLB 39

Burgess (Wilson, John) Anthony
1917- ..... CLC 1, 2, 4, 5, 8, 10, 13, 15,
                                      22, 40, 62
See also Wilson, John (Anthony) Burgess
See also DLB 14

Burke, Edmund 1729-1797 .... LC 7
See also WLC 1

Burke, Kenneth (Duva) 1897- .... CLC 2, 24
See also CA 5-8R; DLB 45, 63

Burney, Fanny 1752-1840 .... NCLC 12
See also DLB 39

Burns, Robert 1759-1796 .... LC 3
See also WLC 1

Burns, Tex 1908?-
See L'Amour, Louis (Dearborn)

Burnshaw, Stanley 1906- ..... CLC 3, 13, 44
See also CA 9-12R; DLB 48

Burr, Anne 1937- .... CLC 6
  See also CA 25-28R

Burroughs, Edgar Rice
  1875-1950 .... TCLC 2, 32
  See also CA 104; SATA 41; DLB 8

Burroughs, William S(eward)
  1914- .... CLC 1, 2, 5, 15, 22, 42
  See also WLC 1; CANR 20; CA 9-12R;
  DLB 2, 8, 16; DLB-Y 81

Busch, Frederick 1941- ... CLC 7, 10, 18, 47
  See also CAAS 1; CA 33-36R; DLB 6

Bush, Ronald 19??-............... CLC 34

Butler, Octavia E(stelle) 1947- ..... CLC 38
  See also CANR 12, 24; CA 73-76; DLB 33

Butler, Samuel 1612-1680 .... LC 16
  See also DLB 101

Butler, Samuel 1835-1902 ..... TCLC 1, 33
  See also WLC 1; CA 104; DLB 18, 57

Butor, Michel (Marie Francois)
  1926- .... CLC 1, 3, 8, 11, 15
  See also CA 9-12R

Buzo, Alexander 1944-........... CLC 61
  See also CANR 17; CA 97-100

Buzzati, Dino 1906-1972 .... CLC 36
  See also obituary CA 33-36R

Byars, Betsy 1928-............... CLC 35
  See also CLR 1, 16; CANR 18; CA 33-36R;
  SAAS 1; SATA 4, 46; DLB 52

Byatt, A(ntonia) S(usan Drabble)
  1936-.................... CLC 19, 65
  See also CANR 13, 33; CA 13-16R;
  DLB 14

Byrne, David 1953?-............... CLC 26

Byrne, John Keyes 1926-
  See Leonard, Hugh
  See also CA 102

Byron, George Gordon (Noel), Lord Byron
  1788-1824 .... NCLC 2, 12
  See also WLC 1

Caballero, Fernan 1796-1877..... NCLC 10

Cabell, James Branch 1879-1958 ... TCLC 6
  See also CA 105; DLB 9, 78

Cable, George Washington
  1844-1925 .... TCLC 4; SSC 4
  See also CA 104; DLB 12, 74

Cabrera Infante, G(uillermo)
  1929- .... CLC 5, 25, 45
  See also CANR 29; CA 85-88

Cade, Toni 1939-
  See Bambara, Toni Cade

CAEdmon fl. 658-680........... CMLC 7

Cage, John (Milton, Jr.) 1912- ..... CLC 41
  See also CANR 9; CA 13-16R

Cain, G. 1929-
  See Cabrera Infante, G(uillermo)

Cain, James M(allahan)
  1892-1977 .... CLC 3, 11, 28
  See also CANR 8; CA 17-20R;
  obituary CA 73-76

Caldwell, Erskine (Preston)
  1903-1987 .... CLC 1, 8, 14, 50, 60
  See also CAAS 1; CANR 2; CA 1-4R;
  obituary CA 121; DLB 9, 86

Caldwell, (Janet Miriam) Taylor (Holland)
  1900-1985 .... CLC 2, 28, 39
  See also CANR 5; CA 5-8R;
  obituary CA 116

Calhoun, John Caldwell
  1782-1850 .... NCLC 15
  See also DLB 3

Calisher, Hortense 1911-.... CLC 2, 4, 8, 38
  See also CANR 1, 22; CA 1-4R; DLB 2

Callaghan, Morley (Edward)
  1903-1990 .... CLC 3, 14, 41, 65
  See also CANR 33; CA 9-12R;
  obituary CA 132; DLB 68

Calvino, Italo
  1923-1985 .... CLC 5, 8, 11, 22, 33, 39,
               73; SSC 3
  See also CANR 23; CA 85-88;
  obituary CA 116

Cameron, Carey 1952-........... CLC 59

Cameron, Peter 1959-............. CLC 44
  See also CA 125

Campana, Dino 1885-1932....... TCLC 20
  See also CA 117

Campbell, John W(ood), Jr.
  1910-1971 .... CLC 32
  See also CAP 2; CA 21-22;
  obituary CA 29-32R; DLB 8

Campbell, Joseph 1904-1987 .... CLC 69
  See also CANR 3, 28; CA 4R;
  obituary CA 124; AAYA 3

Campbell, (John) Ramsey 1946- .... CLC 42
  See also CANR 7; CA 57-60

Campbell, (Ignatius) Roy (Dunnachie)
  1901-1957 .... TCLC 5
  See also CA 104; DLB 20

Campbell, Thomas 1777-1844 .... NCLC 19

Campbell, (William) Wilfred
  1861-1918 .... TCLC 9
  See also CA 106

Camus, Albert
  1913-1960 ... CLC 1, 2, 4, 9, 11, 14, 32,
         63, 69; DC 2; SSC 9
  See also WLC 1; CA 89-92; DLB 72

Canby, Vincent 1924-............. CLC 13
  See also CA 81-84

Canetti, Elias 1905- .... CLC 3, 14, 25
  See also CANR 23; CA 21-24R; DLB 85

Canin, Ethan 1960-............... CLC 55

Cape, Judith 1916-
  See Page, P(atricia) K(athleen)

Capek, Karel
  1890-1938 .... TCLC 6, 37; DC 1
  See also WLC 1; CA 104

Capote, Truman
  1924-1984 ..... CLC 1, 3, 8, 13, 19, 34,
         38, 58; SSC 2
  See also WLC 1; CANR 18; CA 5-8R;
  obituary CA 113; DLB 2; DLB-Y 80, 84;
  CDALB 1941-1968

Capra, Frank 1897-.............. CLC 16
  See also CA 61-64

Caputo, Philip 1941-............. CLC 32
  See also CA 73-76

Card, Orson Scott 1951- .... CLC 44, 47, 50
  See also CA 102

Cardenal, Ernesto 1925-........... CLC 31
  See also CANR 2; CA 49-52

Carducci, Giosue 1835-1907...... TCLC 32

Carew, Thomas 1595?-1640 .... LC 13

Carey, Ernestine Gilbreth 1908-.... CLC 17
  See also CA 5-8R; SATA 2

Carey, Peter 1943-............. CLC 40, 55
  See also CA 123, 127

Carleton, William 1794-1869...... NCLC 3

Carlisle, Henry (Coffin) 1926-..... CLC 33
  See also CANR 15; CA 13-16R

Carlson, Ron(ald F.) 1947-........ CLC 54
  See also CA 105

Carlyle, Thomas 1795-1881...... NCLC 22
  See also DLB 55

Carman, (William) Bliss
  1861-1929 .... TCLC 7
  See also CA 104

Carpenter, Don(ald Richard)
  1931- .... CLC 41
  See also CANR 1; CA 45-48

Carpentier (y Valmont), Alejo
  1904-1980 .... CLC 8, 11, 38
  See also CANR 11; CA 65-68;
  obituary CA 97-100

Carr, Emily 1871-1945........... TCLC 32
  See also DLB 68

Carr, John Dickson 1906-1977 ...... CLC 3
  See also CANR 3; CA 49-52;
  obituary CA 69-72

Carr, Virginia Spencer 1929-....... CLC 34
  See also CA 61-64

Carrier, Roch 1937-............. CLC 13
  See also DLB 53

Carroll, James (P.) 1943-.......... CLC 38
  See also CA 81-84

Carroll, Jim 1951- .... CLC 35
  See also CA 45-48

Carroll, Lewis 1832-1898......... NCLC 2
  See also Dodgson, Charles Lutwidge
  See also CLR 2; WLC 1; DLB 18

Carroll, Paul Vincent 1900-1968.... CLC 10
  See also CA 9-12R; obituary CA 25-28R;
  DLB 10

Carruth, Hayden 1921- .... CLC 4, 7, 10, 18
  See also CANR 4; CA 9-12R; SATA 47;
  DLB 5

Carson, Rachel 1907-1964 .... CLC 71
  See also CANR 35; CA 77-80; SATA 23

Carter, Angela (Olive) 1940-..... CLC 5, 41
  See also CANR 12; CA 53-56; DLB 14

Carver, Raymond
  1938-1988 ... CLC 22, 36, 53, 55; SSC 8
  See also CANR 17; CA 33-36R;
  obituary CA 126; DLB-Y 84, 88

Cary, (Arthur) Joyce (Lunel)
  1888-1957 .... TCLC 1, 29
  See also CA 104; DLB 15

Casanova de Seingalt, Giovanni Jacopo
  1725-1798 .... LC 13

Casares, Adolfo Bioy 1914-
  See Bioy Casares, Adolfo

Conner, Ralph 1860-1937........ TCLC 31

Conrad, Joseph
     1857-1924 ...... TCLC 1, 6, 13, 25, 43;
                                          SSC 9
     See also WLC 2; CA 104, 131; SATA 27;
          DLB 10, 34, 98

Conrad, Robert Arnold 1904-1961
     See Hart, Moss

Conroy, Pat 1945-................ CLC 30
     See also CANR 24; CA 85-88; DLB 6

Constant (de Rebecque), (Henri) Benjamin
     1767-1830 .... NCLC 6

Cook, Michael 1933- .... CLC 58
     See also CA 93-96; DLB 53

Cook, Robin 1940- .... CLC 14
     See also CA 108, 111

Cooke, Elizabeth 1948- .... CLC 55

Cooke, John Esten 1830-1886..... NCLC 5
     See also DLB 3

Cooney, Ray 19??- .... CLC 62

Cooper, Edith Emma 1862-1913
     See Field, Michael

Cooper, J. California 19??- .... CLC 56
     See also CA 125

Cooper, James Fenimore
     1789-1851 .... NCLC 1, 27
     See also SATA 19; DLB 3;
          CDALB 1640-1865

Coover, Robert (Lowell)
     1932- .... CLC 3, 7, 15, 32, 46
     See also CANR 3; CA 45-48; DLB 2;
          DLB-Y 81

Copeland, Stewart (Armstrong)
     1952- .... CLC 26
     See also The Police

Coppard, A(lfred) E(dgar)
     1878-1957 .... TCLC 5
     See also YABC 1; CA 114

Coppee, Francois 1842-1908 ...... TCLC 25

Coppola, Francis Ford 1939-....... CLC 16
     See also CA 77-80; DLB 44

Corcoran, Barbara 1911-.......... CLC 17
     See also CAAS 2; CANR 11; CA 21-24R;
          SATA 3; DLB 52

Corman, Cid 1924-................ CLC 9
     See also Corman, Sidney
     See also CAAS 2; DLB 5

Corman, Sidney 1924-
     See Corman, Cid
     See also CA 85-88

Cormier, Robert (Edmund)
     1925-.................... CLC 12, 30
     See also CLR 12; CANR 5, 23; CA 1-4R;
          SATA 10, 45; DLB 52

Corn, Alfred (Dewitt III) 1943-..... CLC 33
     See also CA 104; DLB-Y 80

Cornwell, David (John Moore)
     1931-.................... CLC 9, 15
     See also le Carre, John
     See also CANR 13; CA 5-8R

Corso, (Nunzio) Gregory 1930-... CLC 1, 11
     See also CA 5-8R; DLB 5, 16

Cortazar, Julio
     1914-1984 ..... CLC 2, 3, 5, 10, 13, 15,
                                    33, 34; SSC 7
     See also CANR 12; CA 21-24R

Corvo, Baron 1860-1913
     See Rolfe, Frederick (William Serafino
          Austin Lewis Mary)

Cosic, Dobrica 1921- .... CLC 14
     See also CA 122

Costain, Thomas B(ertram)
     1885-1965 .... CLC 30
     See also CA 5-8R; obituary CA 25-28R;
          DLB 9

Costantini, Humberto 1924?-1987... CLC 49
     See also obituary CA 122

Costello, Elvis 1955-.............. CLC 21

Cotter, Joseph Seamon, Sr.
     1861-1949 .... TCLC 28
     See also BLC 1; CA 124; DLB 50

Couperus, Louis (Marie Anne)
     1863-1923 .... TCLC 15
     See also CA 115

Courtenay, Bryce 1933-........... CLC 59

Cousteau, Jacques-Yves 1910-...... CLC 30
     See also CANR 15; CA 65-68; SATA 38

Coward, (Sir) Noel (Pierce)
     1899-1973 .... CLC 1, 9, 29, 51
     See also CAP 2; CA 17-18;
          obituary CA 41-44R; DLB 10

Cowley, Malcolm 1898-1989 .... CLC 39
     See also CANR 3; CA 5-6R;
          obituary CA 128; DLB 4, 48; DLB-Y 81

Cowper, William 1731-1800...... NCLC 8

Cox, William Trevor 1928-... CLC 9, 14, 71
     See also Trevor, William
     See also CANR 4; CA 9-12R; DLB 14

Cozzens, James Gould
     1903-1978 .... CLC 1, 4, 11
     See also CANR 19; CA 9-12R;
          obituary CA 81-84; DLB 9; DLB-Y 84;
          DLB-DS 2; CDALB 1941-1968

Crabbe, George 1754-1832....... NCLC 26

Crace, Douglas 1944-............. CLC 58

Cram, Ralph Adams 1863-1942.... TCLC 45

Crane, (Harold) Hart
     1899-1932 .... TCLC 2, 5; PC 3
     See also WLC 2; CA 127;
          brief entry CA 104; DLB 4, 48;
          CDALB 1917-1929

Crane, R(onald) S(almon)
     1886-1967 .... CLC 27
     See also CA 85-88; DLB 63

Crane, Stephen
     1871-1900 ..... TCLC 11, 17, 32; SSC 7
     See also WLC 2; YABC 2; CA 109;
          DLB 12, 54, 78; CDALB 1865-1917

Craven, Margaret 1901-1980....... CLC 17
     See also CA 103

Crawford, F(rancis) Marion
     1854-1909 .... TCLC 10
     See also CA 107; DLB 71

Crawford, Isabella Valancy
     1850-1887 .... NCLC 12
     See also DLB 92

Crayencour, Marguerite de 1903-1987
     See Yourcenar, Marguerite

Creasey, John 1908-1973.......... CLC 11
     See also CANR 8; CA 5-8R;
          obituary CA 41-44R; DLB 77

Crebillon, Claude Prosper Jolyot de (fils)
     1707-1777 .... LC 1

Creeley, Robert (White)
     1926- .... CLC 1, 2, 4, 8, 11, 15, 36
     See also CANR 23; CA 1-4R; DLB 5, 16

Crews, Harry (Eugene)
     1935- ....CLC 6, 23, 49
     See also CANR 20; CA 25-28R; DLB 6

Crichton, (John) Michael
     1942-....................CLC 2, 6, 54
     See also CANR 13; CA 25-28R; SATA 9;
          DLB-Y 81

Crispin, Edmund 1921-1978........ CLC 22
     See also Montgomery, Robert Bruce
     See also DLB 87

Cristofer, Michael 1946- .... CLC 28
     See also CA 110; DLB 7

Croce, Benedetto 1866-1952 ...... TCLC 37
     See also CA 120

Crockett, David (Davy)
     1786-1836 .... NCLC 8
     See also DLB 3, 11

Croker, John Wilson 1780-1857 .. NCLC 10

Cronin, A(rchibald) J(oseph)
     1896-1981 .... CLC 32
     See also CANR 5; CA 1-4R;
          obituary CA 102; obituary SATA 25, 47

Cross, Amanda 1926-
     See Heilbrun, Carolyn G(old)

Crothers, Rachel 1878-1953....... TCLC 19
     See also CA 113; DLB 7

Crowley, Aleister 1875-1947 .... TCLC 7
     See also CA 104

Crowley, John 1942-
     See also CA 61-64; DLB-Y 82

Crumb, Robert 1943- .... CLC 17
     See also CA 106

Cryer, Gretchen 1936?- .... CLC 21
     See also CA 114, 123

Csath, Geza 1887-1919.......... TCLC 13
     See also CA 111

Cudlip, David 1933-.............. CLC 34

Cullen, Countee 1903-1946 ..... TCLC 4, 37
     See also BLC 1; CA 108, 124; SATA 18;
          DLB 4, 48, 51; CDALB 1917-1929

Cummings, E(dward) E(stlin)
     1894-1962 ..... CLC 1, 3, 8, 12, 15, 68;
                                          PC 5
     See also WLC 2; CANR 31; CA 73-76;
          DLB 4, 48; CDALB 1929-1941

Cunha, Euclides (Rodrigues) da
     1866-1909 .... TCLC 24
     See also CA 123

Cunningham, J(ames) V(incent)
     1911-1985 .... CLC 3, 31
     See also CANR 1; CA 1-4R;
          obituary CA 115; DLB 5

Cunningham, Julia (Woolfolk)
    1916- . . . . **CLC 12**
    See also CANR 4, 19; CA 9-12R; SAAS 2;
    SATA 1, 26

Cunningham, Michael 1952- . . . . **CLC 34**

Currie, Ellen 19??- . . . . **CLC 44**

Dabrowska, Maria (Szumska)
    1889-1965 . . . . **CLC 15**
    See also CA 106

Dabydeen, David 1956?- . . . . **CLC 34**
    See also CA 106

Dacey, Philip 1939- . . . . **CLC 51**
    See also CANR 14; CA 37-40R

Dagerman, Stig (Halvard)
    1923-1954 . . . . **TCLC 17**
    See also CA 117

Dahl, Roald 1916- . . . . **CLC 1, 6, 18**
    See also CLR 1, 7; CANR 6; CA 1-4R;
    SATA 1, 26

Dahlberg, Edward 1900-1977. . . **CLC 1, 7, 14**
    See also CA 9-12R; obituary CA 69-72;
    DLB 48

Daly, Elizabeth 1878-1967. . . . . **CLC 52**
    See also CAP 2; CA 23-24;
    obituary CA 25-28R

Daly, Maureen 1921- . . . . **CLC 17**
    See McGivern, Maureen Daly
    See also SAAS 1; SATA 2

Daniken, Erich von 1935-
    See Von Daniken, Erich

Dannay, Frederic 1905-1982
    See Queen, Ellery
    See also CANR 1; CA 1-4R;
    obituary CA 107

D'Annunzio, Gabriele
    1863-1938 . . . . **TCLC 6, 40**
    See also CA 104

Dante (Alighieri)
    See Alighieri, Dante

Danvers, Dennis 1947- . . . . **CLC 70**

Danziger, Paula 1944- . . . . **CLC 21**
    See also CLR 20; CA 112, 115; SATA 30,
    36

Dario, Ruben 1867-1916 . . . . **TCLC 4**
    See also Sarmiento, Felix Ruben Garcia
    See also CA 104

Darley, George 1795-1846. . . . . . . **NCLC 2**

Daryush, Elizabeth 1887-1977. . . . **CLC 6, 19**
    See also CANR 3; CA 49-52; DLB 20

Daudet, (Louis Marie) Alphonse
    1840-1897 . . . . **NCLC 1**

Daumal, Rene 1908-1944. . . . . **TCLC 14**
    See also CA 114

Davenport, Guy (Mattison, Jr.)
    1927- . . . . **CLC 6, 14, 38**
    See also CANR 23; CA 33-36R

Davidson, Donald (Grady)
    1893-1968 . . . . **CLC 2, 13, 19**
    See also CANR 4; CA 5-8R;
    obituary CA 25-28R; DLB 45

Davidson, John 1857-1909. . . . . . . **TCLC 24**
    See also CA 118; DLB 19

Davidson, Sara 1943- . . . . **CLC 9**
    See also CA 81-84

Davie, Donald (Alfred)
    1922- . . . . **CLC 5, 8, 10, 31**
    See also CAAS 3; CANR 1; CA 1-4R;
    DLB 27

Davies, Ray(mond Douglas) 1944- . . **CLC 21**
    See also CA 116

Davies, Rhys 1903-1978. . . . . **CLC 23**
    See also CANR 4; CA 9-12R;
    obituary CA 81-84

Davies, (William) Robertson
    1913- . . . . **CLC 2, 7, 13, 25, 42**
    See also WLC 2; CANR 17; CA 33-36R;
    DLB 68

Davies, W(illiam) H(enry)
    1871-1940 . . . . **TCLC 5**
    See also CA 104; DLB 19

Davis, Frank Marshall 1905-1987
    See also BLC 1; CA 123, 125; DLB 51

Davis, H(arold) L(enoir)
    1896-1960 . . . . **CLC 49**
    See also obituary CA 89-92; DLB 9

Davis, Rebecca (Blaine) Harding
    1831-1910 . . . . **TCLC 6**
    See also CA 104; DLB 74

Davis, Richard Harding
    1864-1916 . . . . **TCLC 24**
    See also CA 114; DLB 12, 23, 78, 79

Davison, Frank Dalby 1893-1970 . . . **CLC 15**
    See also obituary CA 116

Davison, Peter 1928- . . . . **CLC 28**
    See also CAAS 4; CANR 3; CA 9-12R;
    DLB 5

Davys, Mary 1674-1732. . . . . **LC 1**
    See also DLB 39

Dawson, Fielding 1930- . . . . **CLC 6**
    See also CA 85-88

Day, Clarence (Shepard, Jr.)
    1874-1935 . . . . **TCLC 25**
    See also CA 108; DLB 11

Day, Thomas 1748-1789. . . . . **LC 1**
    See also YABC 1; DLB 39

Day Lewis, C(ecil)
    1904-1972 . . . . **CLC 1, 6, 10**
    See also CAP 1; CA 15-16;
    obituary CA 33-36R; DLB 15, 20

Dazai Osamu 1909-1948 . . . . **TCLC 11**
    See also Tsushima Shuji

De Crayencour, Marguerite 1903-1987
    See Yourcenar, Marguerite

Dee, John 1527-1608 . . . . **LC 20**

Deer, Sandra 1940- . . . . **CLC 45**

De Ferrari, Gabriella 19??- . . . . **CLC 65**

Defoe, Daniel 1660?-1731 . . . . **LC 1**
    See also WLC 2; SATA 22; DLB 39

De Hartog, Jan 1914- . . . . **CLC 19**
    See also CANR 1; CA 1-4R

Deighton, Len 1929- . . . . . . **CLC 4, 7, 22, 46**
    See also Deighton, Leonard Cyril
    See also DLB 87

Deighton, Leonard Cyril 1929-
    See Deighton, Len
    See also CANR 19; CA 9-12R

De la Mare, Walter (John)
    1873-1956 . . . . **TCLC 4**
    See also CLR 23; WLC 2; CA 110;
    SATA 16; DLB 19

Delaney, Shelagh 1939- . . . . **CLC 29**
    See also CA 17-20R; DLB 13

Delany, Mary (Granville Pendarves)
    1700-1788 . . . . **LC 12**

Delany, Samuel R(ay, Jr.)
    1942- . . . . **CLC 8, 14, 38**
    See also BLC 1; CANR 27; CA 81-84;
    DLB 8, 33

de la Ramee, Marie Louise 1839-1908
    See Ouida
    See also SATA 20

De la Roche, Mazo 1885-1961 . . . . . **CLC 14**
    See also CA 85-88; DLB 68

Delbanco, Nicholas (Franklin)
    1942- . . . . **CLC 6, 13**
    See also CAAS 2; CA 17-20R; DLB 6

del Castillo, Michel 1933- . . . . **CLC 38**
    See also CA 109

Deledda, Grazia 1871-1936 . . . . **TCLC 23**
    See also CA 123

Delibes (Setien), Miguel 1920- . . . **CLC 8, 18**
    See also CANR 1; CA 45-48

DeLillo, Don
    1936- . . . . **CLC 8, 10, 13, 27, 39, 54**
    See also CANR 21; CA 81-84; DLB 6

De Lisser, H(erbert) G(eorge)
    1878-1944 . . . . **TCLC 12**
    See also CA 109

Deloria, Vine (Victor), Jr. 1933- . . . . **CLC 21**
    See also CANR 5, 20; CA 53-56; SATA 21

Del Vecchio, John M(ichael)
    1947- . . . . **CLC 29**
    See also CA 110

de Man, Paul 1919-1983 . . . . **CLC 55**
    See also obituary CA 111; DLB 67

De Marinis, Rick 1934- . . . . **CLC 54**
    See also CANR 9, 25; CA 57-60

Demby, William 1922- . . . . **CLC 53**
    See also BLC 1; CA 81-84; DLB 33

Denby, Edwin (Orr) 1903-1983 . . . . . **CLC 48**
    See also obituary CA 110

Dennis, John 1657-1734. . . . . **LC 11**

Dennis, Nigel (Forbes) 1912- . . . . **CLC 8**
    See also CA 25-28R; obituary CA 129;
    DLB 13, 15

De Palma, Brian 1940- . . . . **CLC 20**
    See also CA 109

De Quincey, Thomas 1785-1859 . . . **NCLC 4**

Deren, Eleanora 1908-1961
    See Deren, Maya
    See also obituary CA 111

Deren, Maya 1908-1961. . . . . **CLC 16**
    See also Deren, Eleanora

Derleth, August (William)
    1909-1971 . . . . **CLC 31**
    See also CANR 4; CA 1-4R;
    obituary CA 29-32R; SATA 5; DLB 9

Derrida, Jacques 1930- . . . . **CLC 24**
    See also CA 124, 127

Hellman, Lillian (Florence)
1905?-1984.....   **CLC 2, 4, 8, 14, 18, 34, 44, 52; DC 1**
See also CA 13-16R; obituary CA 112;
DLB 7; DLB-Y 84

Helprin, Mark   1947- ..... **CLC 7, 10, 22, 32**
See also CA 81-84; DLB-Y 85

Hemans, Felicia   1793-1835 ...... **NCLC 29**

Hemingway, Ernest (Miller)
1899-1961 ...   **CLC 1, 3, 6, 8, 10, 13, 19, 30, 34, 39, 41, 44, 50, 61; SSC 1**
See also CA 77-80; DLB 4, 9; DLB-Y 81, 87; DLB-DS 1; CDALB 1917-1929

Hempel, Amy   1951- .... **CLC 39**
See also CA 118

Henley, Beth   1952- .... **CLC 23**
See also Henley, Elizabeth Becker
See also CABS 3; DLB-Y 86

Henley, Elizabeth Becker   1952-
See Henley, Beth
See also CA 107

Henley, William Ernest
1849-1903 .... **TCLC 8**
See also CA 105; DLB 19

Hennissart, Martha
See Lathen, Emma
See also CA 85-88

Henry, O.   1862-1910 ... **TCLC 1, 19; SSC 5**
See also Porter, William Sydney
See also YABC 2; CA 104; DLB 12, 78, 79;
CDALB 1865-1917

Henryson, Robert   1430?-1506? ...... **LC 20**

Henry VIII   1491-1547 .... **LC 10**

Henschke, Alfred   1890-1928
See Klabund

Hentoff, Nat(han Irving)   1925- ..... **CLC 26**
See also CLR 1; CAAS 6; CANR 5, 25;
CA 1-4R; SATA 27, 42; AAYA 4

Heppenstall, (John) Rayner
1911-1981 .... **CLC 10**
See also CANR 29; CA 1-4R;
obituary CA 103

Herbert, Frank (Patrick)
1920-1986 .... **CLC 12, 23, 35, 44**
See also CANR 5; CA 53-56;
obituary CA 118; SATA 9, 37, 47; DLB 8

Herbert, George   1593-1633 .... **PC 4**

Herbert, Zbigniew   1924- .... **CLC 9, 43**
See also CA 89-92

Herbst, Josephine   1897-1969..... **CLC 34**
See also CA 5-8R; obituary CA 25-28R;
DLB 9

Herder, Johann Gottfried von
1744-1803 .... **NCLC 8**

Hergesheimer, Joseph
1880-1954 .... **TCLC 11**
See also CA 109; DLB 9

Herlagnez, Pablo de   1844-1896
See Verlaine, Paul (Marie)

Herlihy, James Leo   1927- .... **CLC 6**
See also CANR 2; CA 1-4R

Hermogenes   fl.c. 175- .... **CMLC 6**

Hernandez, Jose   1834-1886 ...... **NCLC 17**

Herrick, Robert   1591-1674 .... **LC 13**

Herriot, James   1916- .... **CLC 12**
See also Wight, James Alfred
See also AAYA 1

Herrmann, Dorothy   1941- .... **CLC 44**
See also CA 107

Hersey, John (Richard)
1914- .... **CLC 1, 2, 7, 9, 40**
See also CA 17-20R; SATA 25; DLB 6

Herzen, Aleksandr Ivanovich
1812-1870 .... **NCLC 10**

Herzl, Theodor   1860-1904...... **TCLC 36**

Herzog, Werner   1942- .... **CLC 16**
See also CA 89-92

Hesiod   c. 8th Century B.C.- ...... **CMLC 5**

Hesse, Hermann
1877-1962 ... **CLC 1, 2, 3, 6, 11, 17, 25, 69; SSC 9**
See also CAP 2; CA 17-18; SATA 50;
DLB 66

Heyen, William   1940- .... **CLC 13, 18**
See also CAAS 9; CA 33-36R; DLB 5

Heyerdahl, Thor   1914- .... **CLC 26**
See also CANR 5, 22; CA 5-8R; SATA 2, 52

Heym, Georg (Theodor Franz Arthur)
1887-1912 .... **TCLC 9**
See also CA 106

Heym, Stefan   1913- .... **CLC 41**
See also CANR 4; CA 9-12R; DLB 69

Heyse, Paul (Johann Ludwig von)
1830-1914 .... **TCLC 8**
See also CA 104

Hibbert, Eleanor (Burford)   1906- .... **CLC 7**
See also CANR 9, 28; CA 17-20R; SATA 2

Higgins, George V(incent)
1939- .... **CLC 4, 7, 10, 18**
See also CAAS 5; CANR 17; CA 77-80;
DLB 2; DLB-Y 81

Higginson, Thomas Wentworth
1823-1911 .... **TCLC 36**
See also DLB 1, 64

Highsmith, (Mary) Patricia
1921- .... **CLC 2, 4, 14, 42**
See also CANR 1, 20; CA 1-4R

Highwater, Jamake   1942- .... **CLC 12**
See also CLR 17; CAAS 7; CANR 10;
CA 65-68; SATA 30, 32; DLB 52;
DLB-Y 85

Hijuelos, Oscar   1951- .... **CLC 65**
See also CA 123

Hikmet (Ran), Nazim   1902-1963.... **CLC 40**
See also obituary CA 93-96

Hildesheimer, Wolfgang   1916- ..... **CLC 49**
See also CA 101; DLB 69

Hill, Geoffrey (William)
1932- .... **CLC 5, 8, 18, 45**
See also CANR 21; CA 81-84; DLB 40

Hill, George Roy   1922- .... **CLC 26**
See also CA 110, 122

Hill, Susan B.   1942- .... **CLC 4**
See also CANR 29; CA 33-36R; DLB 14

Hillerman, Tony   1925- .... **CLC 62**
See also CANR 21; CA 29-32R; SATA 6

Hilliard, Noel (Harvey)   1929- ...... **CLC 15**
See also CANR 7; CA 9-12R

Hillis, Richard Lyle   1956-
See Hillis, Rick

Hillis, Rick   1956- .... **CLC 66**
See also Hillis, Richard Lyle

Hilton, James   1900-1954........ **TCLC 21**
See also CA 108; SATA 34; DLB 34, 77

Himes, Chester (Bomar)
1909-1984 .... **CLC 2, 4, 7, 18, 58**
See also BLC 2; CANR 22; CA 25-28R;
obituary CA 114; DLB 2, 76

Hinde, Thomas   1926- .... **CLC 6, 11**
See also Chitty, (Sir) Thomas Willes

Hine, (William) Daryl   1936- .... **CLC 15**
See also CANR 1, 20; CA 1-4R; DLB 60

Hinton, S(usan) E(loise)   1950- .... **CLC 30**
See also CLR 3, 23; CA 81-84; SATA 19, 58; AAYA 2

Hippius (Merezhkovsky), Zinaida (Nikolayevna)   1869-1945...... **TCLC 9**
See also Gippius, Zinaida (Nikolayevna)

Hiraoka, Kimitake   1925-1970
See Mishima, Yukio
See also CA 97-100; obituary CA 29-32R

Hirsch, Edward (Mark)   1950-... **CLC 31, 50**
See also CANR 20; CA 104

Hitchcock, (Sir) Alfred (Joseph)
1899-1980 .... **CLC 16**
See also obituary CA 97-100; SATA 27;
obituary SATA 24

Hoagland, Edward   1932- .... **CLC 28**
See also CANR 2; CA 1-4R; SATA 51;
DLB 6

Hoban, Russell C(onwell)   1925- .. **CLC 7, 25**
See also CLR 3; CANR 23; CA 5-8R;
SATA 1, 40; DLB 52

Hobson, Laura Z(ametkin)
1900-1986 .... **CLC 7, 25**
See also CA 17-20R; obituary CA 118;
SATA 52; DLB 28

Hochhuth, Rolf   1931- .... **CLC 4, 11, 18**
See also CA 5-8R

Hochman, Sandra   1936- .... **CLC 3, 8**
See also CA 5-8R; DLB 5

Hochwalder, Fritz   1911-1986 ...... **CLC 36**
See also CA 29-32R; obituary CA 120

Hocking, Mary (Eunice)   1921- ..... **CLC 13**
See also CANR 18; CA 101

Hodgins, Jack   1938- .... **CLC 23**
See also CA 93-96; DLB 60

Hodgson, William Hope
1877-1918 .... **TCLC 13**
See also CA 111; DLB 70

Hoffman, Alice   1952- .... **CLC 51**
See also CA 77-80

Hoffman, Daniel (Gerard)
1923- .... **CLC 6, 13, 23**
See also CANR 4; CA 1-4R; DLB 5

Hoffman, Stanley   1944- .... **CLC 5**
See also CA 77-80

Hoffman, William M(oses)   1939- ... **CLC 40**
See also CANR 11; CA 57-60

Jhabvala, Ruth Prawer
1927- . . . . CLC 4, 8, 29
See also CANR 2, 29; CA 1-4R

Jiles, Paulette 1943- . . . . CLC 13, 58
See also CA 101

Jimenez (Mantecon), Juan Ramon
1881-1958 . . . . TCLC 4
See also CA 104

Joel, Billy 1949- . . . . CLC 26
See also Joel, William Martin

Joel, William Martin 1949-
See Joel, Billy
See also CA 108

John of the Cross, St. 1542-1591 . . . . LC 18

Johnson, B(ryan) S(tanley William)
1933-1973 . . . . CLC 6, 9
See also CANR 9; CA 9-12R;
obituary CA 53-56; DLB 14, 40

Johnson, Charles (Richard)
1948- . . . . CLC 7, 51, 65
See also BLC 2; CA 116; DLB 33

Johnson, Denis 1949- . . . . CLC 52
See also CA 117, 121

Johnson, Diane 1934- . . . . CLC 5, 13, 48
See also CANR 17; CA 41-44R; DLB-Y 80

Johnson, Eyvind (Olof Verner)
1900-1976 . . . . CLC 14
See also CA 73-76; obituary CA 69-72

Johnson, Fenton 1888-1958
See also BLC 2; CA 124;
brief entry CA 118; DLB 45, 50

Johnson, James Weldon
1871-1938 . . . . TCLC 3, 19
See also Johnson, James William
See also BLC 2; CA 125;
brief entry CA 104; SATA 31; DLB 51;
CDALB 1917-1929

Johnson, James William 1871-1938
See Johnson, James Weldon
See also SATA 31

Johnson, Joyce 1935- . . . . CLC 58
See also CA 125, 129

Johnson, Lionel (Pigot)
1867-1902 . . . . TCLC 19
See also CA 117; DLB 19

Johnson, Marguerita 1928-
See Angelou, Maya

Johnson, Pamela Hansford
1912-1981 . . . . CLC 1, 7, 27
See also CANR 2, 28; CA 1-4R;
obituary CA 104; DLB 15

Johnson, Samuel 1709-1784 . . . . LC 15
See also DLB 39, 95

Johnson, Uwe
1934-1984 . . . . CLC 5, 10, 15, 40
See also CANR 1; CA 1-4R;
obituary CA 112; DLB 75

Johnston, George (Benson) 1913- . . . CLC 51
See also CANR 5, 20; CA 1-4R; DLB 88

Johnston, Jennifer 1930- . . . . CLC 7
See also CA 85-88; DLB 14

Jolley, Elizabeth 1923- . . . . CLC 46
See also CA 127

Jones, D(ouglas) G(ordon) 1929- . . . . CLC 10
See also CANR 13; CA 29-32R, 113;
DLB 53

Jones, David
1895-1974 . . . . CLC 2, 4, 7, 13, 42
See also CANR 28; CA 9-12R;
obituary CA 53-56; DLB 20

Jones, David Robert 1947-
See Bowie, David
See also CA 103

Jones, Diana Wynne 1934- . . . . CLC 26
See also CLR 23; CANR 4, 26; CA 49-52;
SAAS 7; SATA 9

Jones, Gayl 1949- . . . . CLC 6, 9
See also BLC 2; CANR 27; CA 77-80;
DLB 33

Jones, James 1921-1977 . . . . CLC 1, 3, 10, 39
See also CANR 6; CA 1-4R;
obituary CA 69-72; DLB 2

Jones, (Everett) LeRoi
1934- . . . . CLC 1, 2, 3, 5, 10, 14, 33
See also Baraka, Amiri; Baraka, Imamu
Amiri
See also CA 21-24R

Jones, Louis B. 19??- . . . . CLC 65

Jones, Madison (Percy, Jr.) 1925- . . . CLC 4
See also CAAS 11; CANR 7; CA 13-16R

Jones, Mervyn 1922- . . . . CLC 10, 52
See also CAAS 5; CANR 1; CA 45-48

Jones, Mick 1956?- . . . . CLC 30
See also The Clash

Jones, Nettie 19??- . . . . CLC 34

Jones, Preston 1936-1979 . . . . CLC 10
See also CA 73-76; obituary CA 89-92;
DLB 7

Jones, Robert F(rancis) 1934- . . . . CLC 7
See also CANR 2; CA 49-52

Jones, Rod 1953- . . . . CLC 50
See also CA 128

Jones, Terry 1942?- . . . . CLC 21
See also Monty Python
See also CA 112, 116; SATA 51

Jong, Erica 1942- . . . . CLC 4, 6, 8, 18
See also CANR 26; CA 73-76; DLB 2, 5, 28

Jonson, Ben(jamin) 1572(?)-1637 . . . . . . LC 6
See also DLB 62

Jordan, June 1936- . . . . CLC 5, 11, 23
See also CLR 10; CANR 25; CA 33-36R;
SATA 4; DLB 38; AAYA 2

Jordan, Pat(rick M.) 1941- . . . . CLC 37
See also CANR 25; CA 33-36R

Josipovici, Gabriel (David)
1940- . . . . CLC 6, 43
See also CAAS 8; CA 37-40R; DLB 14

Joubert, Joseph 1754-1824 . . . . NCLC 9

Jouve, Pierre Jean 1887-1976 . . . . . . CLC 47
See also obituary CA 65-68

Joyce, James (Augustine Aloysius)
1882-1941 . . . . . . TCLC 3, 8, 16, 26, 35;
SSC 3
See also CA 104, 126; DLB 10, 19, 36

Jozsef, Attila 1905-1937 . . . . TCLC 22
See also CA 116

Juana Ines de la Cruz 1651?-1695 . . . . LC 5

Julian of Norwich 1342?-1416? . . . . LC 6

Jung Chang 1952- . . . . CLC 71

Just, Ward S(wift) 1935- . . . . CLC 4, 27
See also CA 25-28R

Justice, Donald (Rodney) 1925- . . CLC 6, 19
See also CANR 26; CA 5-8R; DLB-Y 83

Juvenal c. 55-c. 127 . . . . CMLC 8

Kacew, Romain 1914-1980
See Gary, Romain
See also CA 108; obituary CA 102

Kacewgary, Romain 1914-1980
See Gary, Romain

Kadare, Ismail 1936- . . . . CLC 52

Kadohata, Cynthia 19??- . . . . CLC 59

Kafka, Franz
1883-1924 . . . . TCLC 2, 6, 13, 29; SSC 5
See also CA 105, 126; DLB 81

Kahn, Roger 1927- . . . . CLC 30
See also CA 25-28R; SATA 37

Kaiser, (Friedrich Karl) Georg
1878-1945 . . . . TCLC 9
See also CA 106

Kaletski, Alexander 1946- . . . . CLC 39
See also CA 118

Kalidasa fl. c. 400- . . . . CMLC 9

Kallman, Chester (Simon)
1921-1975 . . . . CLC 2
See also CANR 3; CA 45-48;
obituary CA 53-56

Kaminsky, Melvin 1926-
See Brooks, Mel
See also CANR 16; CA 65-68

Kaminsky, Stuart 1934- . . . . CLC 59
See also CANR 29; CA 73-76

Kane, Paul 1941-
See Simon, Paul

Kanin, Garson 1912- . . . . CLC 22
See also CANR 7; CA 5-8R; DLB 7

Kaniuk, Yoram 1930- . . . . CLC 19

Kant, Immanuel 1724-1804 . . . . . . NCLC 27

Kantor, MacKinlay 1904-1977 . . . . . . CLC 7
See also CA 61-64; obituary CA 73-76;
DLB 9

Kaplan, David Michael 1946- . . . . . . CLC 50

Kaplan, James 19??- . . . . CLC 59

Karamzin, Nikolai Mikhailovich
1766-1826 . . . . NCLC 3

Karapanou, Margarita 1946- . . . . CLC 13
See also CA 101

Karl, Frederick R(obert) 1927- . . . . . CLC 34
See also CANR 3; CA 5-8R

Kassef, Romain 1914-1980
See Gary, Romain

Katz, Steve 1935- . . . . CLC 47
See also CANR 12; CA 25-28R; DLB-Y 83

Kauffman, Janet 1945- . . . . CLC 42
See also CA 117; DLB-Y 86

Kaufman, Bob (Garnell)
1925-1986 . . . . CLC 49
See also CANR 22; CA 41-44R;
obituary CA 118; DLB 16, 41

Lennon, John (Ono)
1940-1980 . . . . CLC 12, 35
See also CA 102

Lennon, John Winston   1940-1980
See Lennon, John (Ono)

Lennox, Charlotte Ramsay
1729?-1804. . . . . NCLC 23
See also DLB 39

Lentricchia, Frank (Jr.)   1940- . . . . . . CLC 34
See also CANR 19; CA 25-28R

Lenz, Siegfried   1926- . . . . CLC 27
See also CA 89-92; DLB 75

Leonard, Elmore   1925- . . . . . . CLC 28, 34, 71
See also CANR 12, 28; CA 81-84

Leonard, Hugh   1926- . . . . CLC 19
See also Byrne, John Keyes
See also DLB 13

Leopardi, (Conte) Giacomo (Talegardo
Francesco di Sales Saverio Pietro)
1798-1837 . . . . NCLC 22

Lerman, Eleanor   1952- . . . . CLC 9
See also CA 85-88

Lerman, Rhoda   1936- . . . . CLC 56
See also CA 49-52

Lermontov, Mikhail Yuryevich
1814-1841 . . . . NCLC 5

Leroux, Gaston   1868-1927. . . . . . . TCLC 25
See also CA 108

Lesage, Alain-Rene   1668-1747. . . . . . . LC 2

Leskov, Nikolai (Semyonovich)
1831-1895 . . . . NCLC 25

Lessing, Doris (May)
1919- . . . . CLC 1, 2, 3, 6, 10, 15, 22, 40;
SSC 6
See also CA 9-12R; DLB 15; DLB-Y 85

Lessing, Gotthold Ephraim
1729-1781 . . . . LC 8

Lester, Richard   1932- . . . . CLC 20

Lever, Charles (James)
1806-1872 . . . . NCLC 23
See also DLB 21

Leverson, Ada   1865-1936. . . . . TCLC 18
See also CA 117

Levertov, Denise
1923- . . . . . . CLC 1, 2, 3, 5, 8, 15, 28, 66
See also CANR 3, 29; CA 1-4R; DLB 5

Levi, Peter (Chad Tiger)   1931- . . . . . CLC 41
See also CA 5-8R; DLB 40

Levi, Primo   1919-1987. . . . . CLC 37, 50
See also CANR 12; CA 13-16R;
obituary CA 122

Levin, Ira   1929- . . . . CLC 3, 6
See also CANR 17; CA 21-24R

Levin, Meyer   1905-1981 . . . . CLC 7
See also CANR 15; CA 9-12R;
obituary CA 104; SATA 21;
obituary SATA 27; DLB 9, 28; DLB-Y 81

Levine, Norman   1924- . . . . CLC 54
See also CANR 14; CA 73-76; DLB 88

Levine, Philip   1928- . . CLC 2, 4, 5, 9, 14, 33
See also CANR 9; CA 9-12R; DLB 5

Levinson, Deirdre   1931- . . . . CLC 49
See also CA 73-76

Levi-Strauss, Claude   1908- . . . . CLC 38
See also CANR 6; CA 1-4R

Levitin, Sonia   1934- . . . . CLC 17
See also CANR 14; CA 29-32R; SAAS 2;
SATA 4

Lewes, George Henry
1817-1878 . . . . NCLC 25
See also DLB 55

Lewis, Alun   1915-1944. . . . . TCLC 3
See also CA 104; DLB 20

Lewis, C(ecil) Day   1904-1972
See Day Lewis, C(ecil)

Lewis, C(live) S(taples)
1898-1963 . . . . CLC 1, 3, 6, 14, 27
See also CLR 3; CA 81-84; SATA 13;
DLB 15

Lewis (Winters), Janet   1899- . . . . CLC 41
See also Winters, Janet Lewis
See also CANR 29; CAP 1; CA 9-10R;
DLB-Y 87

Lewis, Matthew Gregory
1775-1818 . . . . NCLC 11
See also DLB 39

Lewis, (Harry) Sinclair
1885-1951 . . . . TCLC 4, 13, 23, 39
See also CA 104; DLB 9; DLB-DS 1;
CDALB 1917-1929

Lewis, (Percy) Wyndham
1882?-1957. . . . . TCLC 2, 9
See also CA 104; DLB 15

Lewisohn, Ludwig   1883-1955. . . . . . TCLC 19
See also CA 73-76, 107;
obituary CA 29-32R; DLB 4, 9, 28

L'Heureux, John (Clarke)   1934- . . . . . CLC 52
See also CANR 23; CA 15-16R

Lieber, Stanley Martin   1922-
See Lee, Stan

Lieberman, Laurence (James)
1935- . . . . CLC 4, 36
See also CANR 8; CA 17-20R

Li Fei-kan   1904- . . . . CLC 18
See also Pa Chin
See also CA 105

Lifton, Robert Jay   1926- . . . . CLC 67
See also CANR 27; CA 17-18R

Lightfoot, Gordon (Meredith)
1938- . . . . CLC 26
See also CA 109

Ligotti, Thomas   1953- . . . . CLC 44
See also CA 123

Liliencron, Detlev von
1844-1909 . . . . TCLC 18
See also CA 117

Lima, Jose Lezama   1910-1976
See Lezama Lima, Jose

Lima Barreto, (Alfonso Henriques de)
1881-1922 . . . . TCLC 23
See also CA 117

Limonov, Eduard   1943- . . . . CLC 67

Lincoln, Abraham   1809-1865. . . . . NCLC 18

Lind, Jakov   1927- . . . . CLC 1, 2, 4, 27
See also Landwirth, Heinz
See also CAAS 4; CA 9-12R

Lindsay, David   1876-1945 . . . . TCLC 15
See also CA 113

Lindsay, (Nicholas) Vachel
1879-1931 . . . . TCLC 17
See also CA 114; SATA 40; DLB 54;
CDALB 1865-1917

Linney, Romulus   1930- . . . . CLC 51
See also CA 1-4R

Li Po   701-763 . . . . CMLC 2

Lipsius, Justus   1547-1606 . . . . LC 16

Lipsyte, Robert (Michael)   1938- . . . . CLC 21
See also CLR 23; CANR 8; CA 17-20R;
SATA 5

Lish, Gordon (Jay)   1934- . . . . CLC 45
See also CA 113, 117

Lispector, Clarice   1925-1977. . . . . . CLC 43
See also obituary CA 116

Littell, Robert   1935?- . . . . CLC 42
See also CA 109, 112

Little, Malcolm   1925-1965
See also BLC 2; CA 125; obituary CA 111

Liu E   1857-1909. . . . . TCLC 15
See also CA 115

Lively, Penelope   1933- . . . . CLC 32, 50
See also CLR 7; CANR 29; CA 41-44R;
SATA 7; DLB 14

Livesay, Dorothy   1909- . . . . CLC 4, 15
See also CAAS 8; CA 25-28R; DLB 68

Lizardi, Jose Joaquin Fernandez de
1776-1827 . . . . NCLC 30

Llewellyn, Richard   1906-1983. . . . . . . CLC 7
See also Llewellyn Lloyd, Richard (Dafydd
Vyvyan)
See also DLB 15

Llewellyn Lloyd, Richard (Dafydd Vyvyan)
1906-1983
See Llewellyn, Richard
See also CANR 7; CA 53-56;
obituary CA 111; SATA 11, 37

Llosa, Mario Vargas   1936-
See Vargas Llosa, Mario

Lloyd, Richard Llewellyn   1906-
See Llewellyn, Richard

Locke, Alain   1886-1954 . . . . TCLC 43
See also CA 124, 106; DLB 51

Locke, John   1632-1704 . . . . LC 7
See also DLB 31

Lockhart, John Gibson
1794-1854 . . . . NCLC 6

Lodge, David (John)   1935- . . . . CLC 36
See also CANR 19; CA 17-20R; DLB 14

Loewinsohn, Ron(ald William)
1937- . . . . CLC 52
See also CA 25-28R

Logan, John   1923- . . . . CLC 5
See also CA 77-80; obituary CA 124; DLB 5

Lo Kuan-chung   1330?-1400? . . . . LC 12

Lombino, S. A.   1926-
See Hunter, Evan

London, Jack
1876-1916 . . . . . . TCLC 9, 15, 39; SSC 4
See also London, John Griffith
See also SATA 18; DLB 8, 12, 78;
CDALB 1865-1917

London, John Griffith 1876-1916
See London, Jack
See also CA 110, 119

Long, Emmett 1925-
See Leonard, Elmore

Longbaugh, Harry 1931-
See Goldman, William (W.)

Longfellow, Henry Wadsworth
1807-1882 . . . . NCLC 2
See also SATA 19; DLB 1, 59;
CDALB 1640-1865

Longley, Michael 1939- . . . . CLC 29
See also CA 102; DLB 40

Longus fl. c. 2nd century- . . . . CMLC 7

Lopate, Phillip 1943- . . . . CLC 29
See also CA 97-100; DLB-Y 80

Lopez Portillo (y Pacheco), Jose
1920- . . . . CLC 46
See also CA 129

Lopez y Fuentes, Gregorio
1897-1966 . . . . CLC 32

Lord, Bette Bao 1938- . . . . CLC 23
See also CA 107; SATA 58

Lorde, Audre (Geraldine) 1934- . . . . . CLC 18
See also BLC 2; CANR 16, 26; CA 25-28R;
DLB 41

Loti, Pierre 1850-1923 . . . . TCLC 11
See also Viaud, (Louis Marie) Julien

Louie, David Wong 1954- . . . . CLC 70

Lovecraft, H(oward) P(hillips)
1890-1937 . . . . TCLC 4, 22; SSC 3
See also CA 104

Lovelace, Earl 1935- . . . . CLC 51
See also CA 77-80

Lowell, Amy 1874-1925 . . . . TCLC 1, 8
See also CA 104; DLB 54

Lowell, James Russell 1819-1891 . . NCLC 2
See also DLB 1, 11, 64, 79;
CDALB 1640-1865

Lowell, Robert (Traill Spence, Jr.)
1917-1977 . . . CLC 1, 2, 3, 4, 5, 8, 9, 11,
15, 37; PC 3
See also CANR 26; CA 9-10R;
obituary CA 73-76; CABS 2; DLB 5

Lowndes, Marie (Adelaide) Belloc
1868-1947 . . . . TCLC 12
See also CA 107; DLB 70

Lowry, (Clarence) Malcolm
1909-1957 . . . . TCLC 6, 40
See also CA 105, 131; DLB 15

Loy, Mina 1882-1966 . . . . CLC 28
See also CA 113; DLB 4, 54

Lucas, Craig . . . . CLC 64

Lucas, George 1944- . . . . CLC 16
See also CANR 30; CA 77-80; SATA 56;
AAYA 1

Lucas, Victoria 1932-1963
See Plath, Sylvia

Ludlam, Charles 1943-1987 . . . . . CLC 46, 50
See also CA 85-88; obituary CA 122

Ludlum, Robert 1927- . . . . CLC 22, 43
See also CANR 25; CA 33-36R; DLB-Y 82

Ludwig, Ken 19??- . . . . CLC 60

Ludwig, Otto 1813-1865 . . . . NCLC 4

Lugones, Leopoldo 1874-1938 . . . . . TCLC 15
See also CA 116

Lu Hsun 1881-1936 . . . . TCLC 3

Lukacs, Georg 1885-1971 . . . . CLC 24
See also Lukacs, Gyorgy

Lukacs, Gyorgy 1885-1971
See Lukacs, Georg
See also CA 101; obituary CA 29-32R

Luke, Peter (Ambrose Cyprian)
1919- . . . . CLC 38
See also CA 81-84; DLB 13

Lurie (Bishop), Alison
1926- . . . . CLC 4, 5, 18, 39
See also CANR 2, 17; CA 1-4R; SATA 46;
DLB 2

Lustig, Arnost 1926- . . . . CLC 56
See also CA 69-72; SATA 56; AAYA 3

Luther, Martin 1483-1546 . . . . LC 9

Luzi, Mario 1914- . . . . CLC 13
See also CANR 9; CA 61-64

Lynch, David 1946- . . . . CLC 66
See also CA 129; brief entry CA 124

Lyndsay, Sir David 1490-1555 . . . . . . LC 20

Lynn, Kenneth S(chuyler) 1923- . . . . CLC 50
See also CANR 3, 27; CA 1-4R

Lytle, Andrew (Nelson) 1902- . . . . . . CLC 22
See also CA 9-12R; DLB 6

Lyttelton, George 1709-1773 . . . . LC 10

Lytton, Edward Bulwer 1803-1873
See Bulwer-Lytton, (Lord) Edward (George
Earle Lytton)
See also SATA 23

Maas, Peter 1929- . . . . CLC 29
See also CA 93-96

Macaulay, (Dame Emilie) Rose
1881-1958 . . . . TCLC 7, 44
See also CA 104; DLB 36

MacBeth, George (Mann)
1932- . . . . CLC 2, 5, 9
See also CA 25-28R; SATA 4; DLB 40

MacCaig, Norman (Alexander)
1910- . . . . CLC 36
See also CANR 3; CA 9-12R; DLB 27

MacCarthy, Desmond 1877-1952 . . TCLC 36

MacDermot, Thomas H. 1870-1933
See Redcam, Tom

MacDiarmid, Hugh
1892-1978 . . . . CLC 2, 4, 11, 19, 63
See also Grieve, C(hristopher) M(urray)
See also DLB 20

Macdonald, Cynthia 1928- . . . . . . CLC 13, 19
See also CANR 4; CA 49-52

MacDonald, George 1824-1905 . . . . . TCLC 9
See also CA 106; SATA 33; DLB 18

MacDonald, John D(ann)
1916-1986 . . . . CLC 3, 27, 44
See also CANR 1, 19; CA 1-4R;
obituary CA 121; DLB 8; DLB-Y 86

Macdonald, (John) Ross
1915-1983 . . . . . . CLC 1, 2, 3, 14, 34, 41
See also Millar, Kenneth
See also DLB-DS 6

MacEwen, Gwendolyn (Margaret)
1941-1987 . . . . CLC 13, 55
See also CANR 7, 22; CA 9-12R;
obituary CA 124; SATA 50, 55; DLB 53

Machado (y Ruiz), Antonio
1875-1939 . . . . TCLC 3
See also CA 104

Machado de Assis, (Joaquim Maria)
1839-1908 . . . . TCLC 10
See also BLC 2; brief entry CA 107

Machen, Arthur (Llewellyn Jones)
1863-1947 . . . . TCLC 4
See also CA 104; DLB 36

Machiavelli, Niccolo 1469-1527 . . . . . . LC 8

MacInnes, Colin 1914-1976 . . . . . . CLC 4, 23
See also CANR 21; CA 69-72;
obituary CA 65-68; DLB 14

MacInnes, Helen (Clark)
1907-1985 . . . . CLC 27, 39
See also CANR 1, 28; CA 1-4R;
obituary CA 65-68, 117; SATA 22, 44;
DLB 87

Macintosh, Elizabeth 1897-1952
See Tey, Josephine
See also CA 110

Mackenzie, (Edward Montague) Compton
1883-1972 . . . . CLC 18
See also CAP 2; CA 21-22;
obituary CA 37-40R; DLB 34

Mac Laverty, Bernard 1942- . . . . CLC 31
See also CA 116, 118

MacLean, Alistair (Stuart)
1922-1987 . . . . CLC 3, 13, 50, 63
See also CANR 28; CA 57-60;
obituary CA 121; SATA 23, 50

MacLeish, Archibald
1892-1982 . . . . CLC 3, 8, 14, 68
See also CANR 33; CA 9-12R;
obituary CA 106; DLB 4, 7, 45;
DLB-Y 82

MacLennan, (John) Hugh
1907- . . . . CLC 2, 14
See also CA 5-8R; DLB 68

MacLeod, Alistair 1936- . . . . CLC 56
See also CA 123; DLB 60

Macleod, Fiona 1855-1905
See Sharp, William

MacNeice, (Frederick) Louis
1907-1963 . . . . CLC 1, 4, 10, 53
See also CA 85-88; DLB 10, 20

Macpherson, (Jean) Jay 1931- . . . . . . CLC 14
See also CA 5-8R; DLB 53

MacShane, Frank 1927- . . . . CLC 39
See also CANR 3; CA 11-12R

Macumber, Mari 1896-1966
See Sandoz, Mari (Susette)

Madach, Imre 1823-1864 . . . . NCLC 19

Madden, (Jerry) David 1933- . . . . CLC 5, 15
See also CAAS 3; CANR 4; CA 1-4R;
DLB 6

Madhubuti, Haki R.
1942- . . . . CLC 6, 73; PC 5
See also Lee, Don L.
See also BLC 2; CANR 24; CA 73-76;
DLB 5, 41; DLB-DS 8

Mason, Bobbie Ann
1940- . . . . CLC 28, 43; SSC 4
See also CANR 11; CA 53-56; SAAS 1;
DLB-Y 87

Mason, Nick 1945- . . . . CLC 35
See also Pink Floyd

Mason, Tally 1909-1971
See Derleth, August (William)

Masters, Edgar Lee
1868?-1950. . . . . TCLC 2, 25; PC 1
See also CA 104; DLB 54;
CDALB 1865-1917

Masters, Hilary 1928- . . . . CLC 48
See also CANR 13; CA 25-28R

Mastrosimone, William 19??- . . . . . . CLC 36

Matheson, Richard (Burton)
1926- . . . . CLC 37
See also CA 97-100; DLB 8, 44

Mathews, Harry 1930- . . . . CLC 6, 52
See also CAAS 6; CANR 18; CA 21-24R

Mathias, Roland (Glyn) 1915- . . . . . . CLC 45
See also CANR 19; CA 97-100; DLB 27

Matthews, Greg 1949- . . . . CLC 45

Matthews, William 1942- . . . . CLC 40
See also CANR 12; CA 29-32R; DLB 5

Matthias, John (Edward) 1941- . . . . . . CLC 9
See also CA 33-36R

Matthiessen, Peter
1927- . . . . CLC 5, 7, 11, 32, 64
See also CANR 21; CA 9-12R; SATA 27;
DLB 6

Maturin, Charles Robert
1780?-1824. . . . . NCLC 6

Matute, Ana Maria 1925- . . . . CLC 11
See also CA 89-92

Maugham, W(illiam) Somerset
1874-1965 . . . . CLC 1, 11, 15, 67; SSC 8
See also CA 5-8R; obituary CA 25-28R;
SATA 54; DLB 10, 36, 77, 100

Maupassant, (Henri Rene Albert) Guy de
1850-1893 . . . . NCLC 1; SSC 1

Mauriac, Claude 1914- . . . . CLC 9
See also CA 89-92; DLB 83

Mauriac, Francois (Charles)
1885-1970 . . . . CLC 4, 9, 56
See also CAP 2; CA 25-28; DLB 65

Mavor, Osborne Henry 1888-1951
See Bridie, James
See also CA 104

Maxwell, William (Keepers, Jr.)
1908- . . . . CLC 19
See also CA 93-96; DLB-Y 80

May, Elaine 1932- . . . . CLC 16
See also CA 124; DLB 44

Mayakovsky, Vladimir (Vladimirovich)
1893-1930 . . . . TCLC 4, 18
See also CA 104

Mayhew, Henry 1812-1887 . . . . . . NCLC 31
See also DLB 18, 55

Maynard, Joyce 1953- . . . . CLC 23
See also CA 111, 129

Mayne, William (James Carter)
1928- . . . . CLC 12
See also CA 9-12R; SATA 6

Mayo, Jim 1908?-
See L'Amour, Louis (Dearborn)

Maysles, Albert 1926- and **Maysles, David**
1926- . . . . CLC 16
See also CA 29-32R

Maysles, Albert 1926- . . . . CLC 16
See also Maysles, Albert and Maysles,
David
See also CA 29-32R

Maysles, David 1932- . . . . CLC 16
See also Maysles, Albert and Maysles,
David

Mazer, Norma Fox 1931- . . . . CLC 26
See also CLR 23; CANR 12; CA 69-72;
SAAS 1; SATA 24

Mazzini, Guiseppe 1805-1872 . . . . NCLC 34

McAuley, James (Phillip)
1917-1976 . . . . CLC 45
See also CA 97-100

McBain, Ed 1926-
See Hunter, Evan

McBrien, William 1930- . . . . CLC 44
See also CA 107

McCaffrey, Anne 1926- . . . . CLC 17
See also CANR 15; CA 25-28R; SATA 8;
DLB 8

McCarthy, Cormac 1933- . . . . CLC 4, 57
See also CANR 10; CA 13-16R; DLB 6

McCarthy, Mary (Therese)
1912-1989- . . . CLC 1, 3, 5, 14, 24, 39, 59
See also CANR 16; CA 5-8R;
obituary CA 129; DLB 2; DLB-Y 81

McCartney, (James) Paul
1942- . . . . CLC 12, 35

McCauley, Stephen 19??- . . . . CLC 50

McClure, Michael 1932- . . . . CLC 6, 10
See also CANR 17; CA 21-24R; DLB 16

McCorkle, Jill (Collins) 1958- . . . . . . CLC 51
See also CA 121; DLB-Y 87

McCourt, James 1941- . . . . CLC 5
See also CA 57-60

McCoy, Horace 1897-1955 . . . . TCLC 28
See also CA 108; DLB 9

McCrae, John 1872-1918. . . . . TCLC 12
See also CA 109; DLB 92

McCullers, (Lula) Carson (Smith)
1917-1967 . . CLC 1, 4, 10, 12, 48; SSC 9
See also CANR 18; CA 5-8R;
obituary CA 25-28R; CABS 1; SATA 27;
DLB 2, 7; CDALB 1941-1968

McCullough, Colleen 1938?- . . . . CLC 27
See also CANR 17; CA 81-84

McElroy, Joseph (Prince)
1930- . . . . CLC 5, 47
See also CA 17-20R

McEwan, Ian (Russell) 1948- . . . CLC 13, 66
See also CANR 14; CA 61-64; DLB 14

McFadden, David 1940- . . . . CLC 48
See also CA 104; DLB 60

McFarland, Dennis 1956- . . . . CLC 65

McGahern, John 1934- . . . . CLC 5, 9, 48
See also CANR 29; CA 17-20R; DLB 14

McGinley, Patrick 1937- . . . . CLC 41
See also CA 120, 127

McGinley, Phyllis 1905-1978 . . . . . . CLC 14
See also CANR 19; CA 9-12R;
obituary CA 77-80; SATA 2, 44;
obituary SATA 24; DLB 11, 48

McGinniss, Joe 1942- . . . . CLC 32
See also CANR 26; CA 25-28R

McGivern, Maureen Daly 1921-
See Daly, Maureen
See also CA 9-12R

McGrath, Patrick 1950- . . . . CLC 55

McGrath, Thomas 1916- . . . . CLC 28, 59
See also CANR 6; CA 9-12R, 130;
SATA 41

McGuane, Thomas (Francis III)
1939- . . . . CLC 3, 7, 18, 45
See also CANR 5, 24; CA 49-52; DLB 2;
DLB-Y 80

McGuckian, Medbh 1950- . . . . CLC 48
See also DLB 40

McHale, Tom 1941-1982 . . . . CLC 3, 5
See also CA 77-80; obituary CA 106

McIlvanney, William 1936- . . . . CLC 42
See also CA 25-28R; DLB 14

McIlwraith, Maureen Mollie Hunter 1922-
See Hunter, Mollie
See also CA 29-32R; SATA 2

McInerney, Jay 1955- . . . . CLC 34
See also CA 116, 123

McIntyre, Vonda N(eel) 1948- . . . . . CLC 18
See also CANR 17; CA 81-84

McKay, Claude
1889-1948 . . . . TCLC 7, 41; PC 2
See also BLC 3; CA 104, 124; DLB 4, 45,
51

McKay, Claude 1889-1948
See McKay, Festus Claudius

McKay, Festus Claudius 1889-1948
See also BLC 2; CA 124; brief entry CA 104

McKuen, Rod 1933- . . . . CLC 1, 3
See also CA 41-44R

McLuhan, (Herbert) Marshall
1911-1980 . . . . CLC 37
See also CANR 12; CA 9-12R;
obituary CA 102; DLB 88

McManus, Declan Patrick 1955-
See Costello, Elvis

McMillan, Terry 1951- . . . . CLC 50, 61

McMurtry, Larry (Jeff)
1936- . . . . CLC 2, 3, 7, 11, 27, 44
See also CANR 19; CA 5-8R; DLB 2;
DLB-Y 80, 87; CDALB 1968-1987

McNally, Terrence 1939- . . . . . . CLC 4, 7, 41
See also CANR 2; CA 45-48; DLB 7

McNamer, Deirdre 1950- . . . . CLC 70

McNeile, Herman Cyril 1888-1937
See Sapper
See also DLB 77

McPhee, John 1931- . . . . CLC 36
See also CANR 20; CA 65-68

McPherson, James Alan 1943- . . . . . CLC 19
See also CANR 24; CA 25-28R; DLB 38

McPherson, William 1939- . . . . CLC 34
See also CA 57-60

McSweeney, Kerry 19??- . . . . CLC 34

Author Index

Prichard, Katharine Susannah
          1883-1969 .... CLC 46
     See also CAP 1; CA 11-12

Priestley, J(ohn) B(oynton)
          1894-1984 .... CLC 2, 5, 9, 34
     See also CA 9-12R; obituary CA 113;
          DLB 10, 34, 77; DLB-Y 84

Prince (Rogers Nelson) 1958?- ..... CLC 35

Prince, F(rank) T(empleton) 1912- .. CLC 22
     See also CA 101; DLB 20

Prior, Matthew 1664-1721.......... LC 4

Pritchard, William H(arrison)
          1932- .... CLC 34
     See also CANR 23; CA 65-68

Pritchett, V(ictor) S(awdon)
          1900- .... CLC 5, 13, 15, 41
     See also CA 61-64; DLB 15

Probst, Mark 1925- .... CLC 59
     See also CA 130

Procaccino, Michael 1946-
     See Cristofer, Michael

Prokosch, Frederic 1908-1989.... CLC 4, 48
     See also CA 73-76; obituary CA 128;
          DLB 48

Prose, Francine 1947-............. CLC 45
     See also CA 109, 112

Proust, Marcel 1871-1922 .. TCLC 7, 13, 33
     See also CA 104, 120; DLB 65

Pryor, Richard 1940- .... CLC 26
     See also CA 122

Przybyszewski, Stanislaw
          1868-1927 .... TCLC 36
     See also DLB 66

Puig, Manuel
          1932-1990 .... CLC 3, 5, 10, 28, 65
     See also CANR 2, 32; CA 45-48

Purdy, A(lfred) W(ellington)
          1918- .... CLC 3, 6, 14, 50
     See also CA 81-84

Purdy, James (Amos)
          1923- .... CLC 2, 4, 10, 28, 52
     See also CAAS 1; CANR 19; CA 33-36R;
          DLB 2

Pushkin, Alexander (Sergeyevich)
          1799-1837 .... NCLC 3, 27

P'u Sung-ling 1640-1715 .... LC 3

Puzo, Mario 1920-......... CLC 1, 2, 6, 36
     See also CANR 4; CA 65-68; DLB 6

Pym, Barbara (Mary Crampton)
          1913-1980 .... CLC 13, 19, 37
     See also CANR 13; CAP 1; CA 13-14;
          obituary CA 97-100; DLB 14; DLB-Y 87

Pynchon, Thomas (Ruggles, Jr.)
          1937- .. CLC 2, 3, 6, 9, 11, 18, 33, 62, 72
     See also CANR 22; CA 17-20R; DLB 2

Quarrington, Paul 1954?-......... CLC 65
     See also CA 129

Quasimodo, Salvatore 1901-1968 ... CLC 10
     See also CAP 1; CA 15-16;
          obituary CA 25-28R

Queen, Ellery 1905-1982........ CLC 3, 11
     See also Dannay, Frederic; Lee, Manfred
          B(ennington)

Queneau, Raymond
          1903-1976 .... CLC 2, 5, 10, 42
     See also CA 77-80; obituary CA 69-72;
          DLB 72

Quin, Ann (Marie) 1936-1973 .... CLC 6
     See also CA 9-12R; obituary CA 45-48;
          DLB 14

Quinn, Simon 1942-
     See Smith, Martin Cruz
     See also CANR 6, 23; CA 85-88

Quiroga, Horacio (Sylvestre)
          1878-1937 .... TCLC 20
     See also CA 117

Quoirez, Francoise 1935-
     See Sagan, Francoise
     See also CANR 6; CA 49-52

Raabe, Wilhelm 1831-1910 .... TCLC 45

Rabe, David (William) 1940-... CLC 4, 8, 33
     See also CA 85-88; CABS 3; DLB 7

Rabelais, Francois 1494?-1553........ LC 5

Rabinovitch, Sholem 1859-1916
     See Aleichem, Sholom
     See also CA 104

Rachen, Kurt von 1911-1986
     See Hubbard, L(afayette) Ron(ald)

Radcliffe, Ann (Ward) 1764-1823 .. NCLC 6
     See also DLB 39

Radiguet, Raymond 1903-1923 .... TCLC 29
     See also DLB 65

Radnoti, Miklos 1909-1944 ...... TCLC 16
     See also CA 118

Rado, James 1939-.............. CLC 17
     See also CA 105

Radomski, James 1932-
     See Rado, James

Radvanyi, Netty Reiling 1900-1983
     See Seghers, Anna
     See also CA 85-88; obituary CA 110

Rae, Ben 1935-
     See Griffiths, Trevor

Raeburn, John 1941- .... CLC 34
     See also CA 57-60

Ragni, Gerome 1942-.............. CLC 17
     See also CA 105

Rahv, Philip 1908-1973 .... CLC 24
     See also Greenberg, Ivan

Raine, Craig 1944-................ CLC 32
     See also CANR 29; CA 108; DLB 40

Raine, Kathleen (Jessie) 1908- ... CLC 7, 45
     See also CA 85-88; DLB 20

Rainis, Janis 1865-1929.......... TCLC 29

Rakosi, Carl 1903-.............. CLC 47
     See also Rawley, Callman
     See also CAAS 5

Ramos, Graciliano 1892-1953 ..... TCLC 32

Rampersad, Arnold 19??-........... CLC 44

Ramuz, Charles-Ferdinand
          1878-1947 .... TCLC 33

Rand, Ayn 1905-1982........ CLC 3, 30, 44
     See also CANR 27; CA 13-16R;
          obituary CA 105

Randall, Dudley (Felker) 1914-...... CLC 1
     See also BLC 3; CANR 23; CA 25-28R;
          DLB 41

Ransom, John Crowe
          1888-1974 .... CLC 2, 4, 5, 11, 24
     See also CANR 6; CA 5-8R;
          obituary CA 49-52; DLB 45, 63

Rao, Raja 1909-.............. CLC 25, 56
     See also CA 73-76

Raphael, Frederic (Michael)
          1931-..................... CLC 2, 14
     See also CANR 1; CA 1-4R; DLB 14

Rathbone, Julian 1935- .... CLC 41
     See also CA 101

Rattigan, Terence (Mervyn)
          1911-1977 .... CLC 7
     See also CA 85-88; obituary CA 73-76;
          DLB 13

Ratushinskaya, Irina 1954- .... CLC 54
     See also CA 129

Raven, Simon (Arthur Noel)
          1927-..................... CLC 14
     See also CA 81-84

Rawley, Callman 1903-
     See Rakosi, Carl
     See also CANR 12; CA 21-24R

Rawlings, Marjorie Kinnan
          1896-1953 .... TCLC 4
     See also YABC 1; CA 104; DLB 9, 22

Ray, Satyajit 1921-............... CLC 16
     See also CA 114

Read, Herbert (Edward) 1893-1968 .. CLC 4
     See also CA 85-88; obituary CA 25-28R;
          DLB 20

Read, Piers Paul 1941- ...... CLC 4, 10, 25
     See also CA 21-24R; SATA 21; DLB 14

Reade, Charles 1814-1884 .... NCLC 2
     See also DLB 21

Reade, Hamish 1936-
     See Gray, Simon (James Holliday)

Reading, Peter 1946- .... CLC 47
     See also CA 103; DLB 40

Reaney, James 1926- .... CLC 13
     See also CA 41-44R; SATA 43; DLB 68

Rebreanu, Liviu 1885-1944 .... TCLC 28

Rechy, John (Francisco)
          1934-..................CLC 1, 7, 14, 18
     See also CAAS 4; CANR 6; CA 5-8R;
          DLB-Y 82

Redcam, Tom 1870-1933 .... TCLC 25

Reddin, Keith 1956?- .... CLC 67

Redgrove, Peter (William)
          1932-..................... CLC 6, 41
     See also CANR 3; CA 1-4R; DLB 40

Redmon (Nightingale), Anne
          1943-...................... CLC 22
     See also Nightingale, Anne Redmon
     See also DLB-Y 86

Reed, Ishmael
          1938-........ CLC 2, 3, 5, 6, 13, 32, 60
     See also BLC 3; CANR 25; CA 21-24R;
          DLB 2, 5, 33; DLB-DS 8

Reed, John (Silas) 1887-1920 ...... TCLC 9
     See also CA 106

Rodgers, Mary   1931- . . . .   **CLC 12**
See also CLR 20; CANR 8; CA 49-52;
SATA 8

Rodgers, W(illiam) R(obert)
1909-1969 . . . .   **CLC 7**
See also CA 85-88; DLB 20

Rodman, Howard   19??- . . . .   **CLC 65**

Rodriguez, Claudio   1934- . . . .   **CLC 10**

Roethke, Theodore (Huebner)
1908-1963 . . . . . .   **CLC 1, 3, 8, 11, 19, 46**
See also CA 81-84; CABS 2; SAAS 1;
DLB 5; CDALB 1941-1968

Rogers, Sam   1943-
See Shepard, Sam

Rogers, Thomas (Hunton)   1931- . . . .   **CLC 57**
See also CA 89-92

Rogers, Will(iam Penn Adair)
1879-1935 . . . .   **TCLC 8**
See also CA 105; DLB 11

Rogin, Gilbert   1929- . . . .   **CLC 18**
See also CANR 15; CA 65-68

Rohan, Koda   1867-1947 . . . .   **TCLC 22**
See also CA 121

Rohmer, Eric   1920- . . . .   **CLC 16**
See also Scherer, Jean-Marie Maurice

Rohmer, Sax   1883-1959 . . . .   **TCLC 28**
See also Ward, Arthur Henry Sarsfield
See also CA 108; DLB 70

Roiphe, Anne (Richardson)
1935- . . . .   **CLC 3, 9**
See also CA 89-92; DLB-Y 80

Rolfe, Frederick (William Serafino Austin
Lewis Mary)   1860-1913 . . . . .   **TCLC 12**
See also CA 107; DLB 34

Rolland, Romain   1866-1944 . . . .   **TCLC 23**
See also CA 118; DLB 65

Rolvaag, O(le) E(dvart)
1876-1931 . . . .   **TCLC 17**
See also CA 117; DLB 9

Romains, Jules   1885-1972 . . . .   **CLC 7**
See also CA 85-88

Romero, Jose Ruben   1890-1952 . . .   **TCLC 14**
See also CA 114

Ronsard, Pierre de   1524-1585 . . . .   **LC 6**

Rooke, Leon   1934- . . . .   **CLC 25, 34**
See also CANR 23; CA 25-28R

Roper, William   1498-1578 . . . .   **LC 10**

Rosa, Joao Guimaraes   1908-1967 . . .   **CLC 23**
See also obituary CA 89-92

Rosen, Richard (Dean)   1949- . . . .   **CLC 39**
See also CA 77-80

Rosenberg, Isaac   1890-1918 . . . .   **TCLC 12**
See also CA 107; DLB 20

Rosenblatt, Joe   1933- . . . .   **CLC 15**
See also Rosenblatt, Joseph

Rosenblatt, Joseph   1933-
See Rosenblatt, Joe
See also CA 89-92

Rosenfeld, Samuel   1896-1963
See Tzara, Tristan
See also obituary CA 89-92

Rosenthal, M(acha) L(ouis)   1917- . . .   **CLC 28**
See also CAAS 6; CANR 4; CA 1-4R;
SATA 59; DLB 5

Ross, (James) Sinclair   1908- . . . .   **CLC 13**
See also CA 73-76; DLB 88

Rossetti, Christina Georgina
1830-1894 . . . .   **NCLC 2**
See also SATA 20; DLB 35

Rossetti, Dante Gabriel
1828-1882 . . . .   **NCLC 4**
See also DLB 35

Rossetti, Gabriel Charles Dante   1828-1882
See Rossetti, Dante Gabriel

Rossner, Judith (Perelman)
1935- . . . .   **CLC 6, 9, 29**
See also CANR 18; CA 17-20R; DLB 6

Rostand, Edmond (Eugene Alexis)
1868-1918 . . . .   **TCLC 6, 37**
See also CA 104, 126

Roth, Henry   1906- . . . .   **CLC 2, 6, 11**
See also CAP 1; CA 11-12; DLB 28

Roth, Joseph   1894-1939 . . . .   **TCLC 33**
See also DLB 85

Roth, Philip (Milton)
1933- . . . . . .   **CLC 1, 2, 3, 4, 6, 9, 15, 22,
31, 47, 66**
See also CANR 1, 22; CA 1-4R; DLB 2, 28;
DLB-Y 82; CDALB 1968-1988

Rothenberg, James   1931- . . . .   **CLC 57**

Rothenberg, Jerome   1931- . . . .   **CLC 6, 57**
See also CANR 1; CA 45-48; DLB 5

Roumain, Jacques   1907-1944 . . . . . .   **TCLC 19**
See also BLC 3; CA 117, 125

Rourke, Constance (Mayfield)
1885-1941 . . . .   **TCLC 12**
See also YABC 1; CA 107

Rousseau, Jean-Baptiste   1671-1741 . . .   **LC 9**

Rousseau, Jean-Jacques   1712-1778 . . .   **LC 14**

Roussel, Raymond   1877-1933 . . . . .   **TCLC 20**
See also CA 117

Rovit, Earl (Herbert)   1927- . . . .   **CLC 7**
See also CANR 12; CA 5-8R

Rowe, Nicholas   1674-1718 . . . .   **LC 8**

Rowson, Susanna Haswell
1762-1824 . . . .   **NCLC 5**
See also DLB 37

Roy, Gabrielle   1909-1983 . . . .   **CLC 10, 14**
See also CANR 5; CA 53-56;
obituary CA 110; DLB 68

Rozewicz, Tadeusz   1921- . . . .   **CLC 9, 23**
See also CA 108

Ruark, Gibbons   1941- . . . .   **CLC 3**
See also CANR 14; CA 33-36R

Rubens, Bernice   192?- . . . .   **CLC 19, 31**
See also CA 25-28R; DLB 14

Rubenstein, Gladys   1934-
See Swan, Gladys

Rudkin, (James) David   1936- . . . . . .   **CLC 14**
See also CA 89-92; DLB 13

Rudnik, Raphael   1933- . . . .   **CLC 7**
See also CA 29-32R

Ruiz, Jose Martinez   1874-1967
See Azorin

Rukeyser, Muriel
1913-1980 . . . .   **CLC 6, 10, 15, 27**
See also CANR 26; CA 5-8R;
obituary CA 93-96; obituary SATA 22;
DLB 48

Rule, Jane (Vance)   1931- . . . .   **CLC 27**
See also CANR 12; CA 25-28R; DLB 60

Rulfo, Juan   1918-1986 . . . .   **CLC 8**
See also CANR 26; CA 85-88;
obituary CA 118

Runyon, (Alfred) Damon
1880-1946 . . . .   **TCLC 10**
See also CA 107; DLB 11

Rush, Norman   1933- . . . .   **CLC 44**
See also CA 121, 126

Rushdie, (Ahmed) Salman
1947- . . . .   **CLC 23, 31, 55, 59**
See also CA 108, 111

Rushforth, Peter (Scott)   1945- . . . . .   **CLC 19**
See also CA 101

Ruskin, John   1819-1900 . . . .   **TCLC 20**
See also CA 114; SATA 24; DLB 55

Russ, Joanna   1937- . . . .   **CLC 15**
See also CANR 11; CA 25-28R; DLB 8

Russell, George William   1867-1935
See A. E.
See also CA 104

Russell, (Henry) Ken(neth Alfred)
1927- . . . .   **CLC 16**
See also CA 105

Russell, Mary Annette Beauchamp   1866-1941
See Elizabeth

Russell, Willy   1947- . . . .   **CLC 60**

Rutherford, Mark   1831-1913 . . . . . .   **TCLC 25**
See also CA 121; DLB 18

Ruyslinck, Ward   1929- . . . .   **CLC 14**

Ryan, Cornelius (John)   1920-1974 . . .   **CLC 7**
See also CA 69-72; obituary CA 53-56

Ryan, Michael   1946- . . . .   **CLC 65**
See also CA 49-52; DLB-Y 82

Rybakov, Anatoli   1911?- . . . .   **CLC 23, 53**
See also CA 126

Ryder, Jonathan   1927-
See Ludlum, Robert

Ryga, George   1932- . . . .   **CLC 14**
See also CA 101; obituary CA 124; DLB 60

Séviné, Marquise de Marie de
Rabutin-Chantal   1626-1696 . . . . .   **LC 11**

Saba, Umberto   1883-1957 . . . .   **TCLC 33**

Sabato, Ernesto   1911- . . . .   **CLC 10, 23**
See also CA 97-100

Sacher-Masoch, Leopold von
1836?-1895 . . . .   **NCLC 31**

Sachs, Marilyn (Stickle)   1927- . . . . .   **CLC 35**
See also CLR 2; CANR 13; CA 17-20R;
SAAS 2; SATA 3, 52

Sachs, Nelly   1891-1970 . . . .   **CLC 14**
See also CAP 2; CA 17-18;
obituary CA 25-28R

Sackler, Howard (Oliver)
1929-1982 . . . .   **CLC 14**
See also CA 61-64; obituary CA 108; DLB 7

Author Index

Schulberg, Budd (Wilson)
   1914- .... CLC 7, 48
   See also CANR 19; CA 25-28R; DLB 6, 26,
   28; DLB-Y 81

Schulz, Bruno   1892-1942 .... TCLC 5
   See also CA 115, 123

Schulz, Charles M(onroe)   1922- .... CLC 12
   See also CANR 6; CA 9-12R; SATA 10

Schuyler, James (Marcus)
   1923- .... CLC 5, 23
   See also CA 101; DLB 5

Schwartz, Delmore
   1913-1966 .... CLC 2, 4, 10, 45
   See also CAP 2; CA 17-18;
   obituary CA 25-28R; DLB 28, 48

Schwartz, John Burnham   1925- .... CLC 59

Schwartz, Lynne Sharon   1939- ..... CLC 31
   See also CA 103

Schwarz-Bart, Andre   1928- .... CLC 2, 4
   See also CA 89-92

Schwarz-Bart, Simone   1938? .... CLC 7
   See also CA 97-100

Schwob, (Mayer Andre) Marcel
   1867-1905 .... TCLC 20
   See also CA 117

Sciascia, Leonardo
   1921-1989 .... CLC 8, 9, 41
   See also CA 85-88

Scoppettone, Sandra   1936- .... CLC 26
   See also CA 5-8R; SATA 9

Scorsese, Martin   1942- .... CLC 20
   See also CA 110, 114

Scotland, Jay   1932-
   See Jakes, John (William)

Scott, Duncan Campbell
   1862-1947 .... TCLC 6
   See also CA 104; DLB 92

Scott, Evelyn   1893-1963 .... CLC 43
   See also CA 104; obituary CA 112; DLB 9,
   48

Scott, F(rancis) R(eginald)
   1899-1985 .... CLC 22
   See also CA 101; obituary CA 114; DLB 88

Scott, Joanna   19??- .... CLC 50
   See also CA 126

Scott, Paul (Mark)   1920-1978 .... CLC 9, 60
   See also CA 81-84; obituary CA 77-80;
   DLB 14

Scott, Sir Walter   1771-1832 ..... NCLC 15
   See also YABC 2

Scribe, (Augustin) Eugene
   1791-1861 .... NCLC 16

Scudery, Madeleine de   1607-1701 ..... LC 2

Sealy, I. Allan   1951- .... CLC 55

Seare, Nicholas   1925-
   See Trevanian; Whitaker, Rodney

Sebestyen, Igen   1924-
   See Sebestyen, Ouida

Sebestyen, Ouida   1924- .... CLC 30
   See also CLR 17; CA 107; SATA 39

Sedgwick, Catharine Maria
   1789-1867 .... NCLC 19
   See also DLB 1, 74

Seelye, John   1931- .... CLC 7
   See also CA 97-100

Seferiades, Giorgos Stylianou   1900-1971
   See Seferis, George
   See also CANR 5; CA 5-8R;
   obituary CA 33-36R

Seferis, George   1900-1971 .... CLC 5, 11
   See also Seferiades, Giorgos Stylianou

Segal, Erich (Wolf)   1937- .... CLC 3, 10
   See also CANR 20; CA 25-28R; DLB-Y 86

Seger, Bob   1945- .... CLC 35

Seger, Robert Clark   1945-
   See Seger, Bob

Seghers, Anna   1900-1983 .... CLC 7, 110
   See also Radvanyi, Netty Reiling
   See also DLB 69

Seidel, Frederick (Lewis)   1936- ..... CLC 18
   See also CANR 8; CA 13-16R; DLB-Y 84

Seifert, Jaroslav   1901-1986 ..... CLC 34, 44
   See also CA 127

Sei Shonagon   c. 966-1017? .... CMLC 6

Selby, Hubert, Jr.   1928- ..... CLC 1, 2, 4, 8
   See also CA 13-16R; DLB 2

Sembene, Ousmane   1923-
   See Ousmane, Sembene

Sembene, Ousmane   1923-
   See Ousmane, Sembene

Senacour, Etienne Pivert de
   1770-1846 .... NCLC 16

Sender, Ramon (Jose)   1902-1982 .... CLC 8
   See also CANR 8; CA 5-8R;
   obituary CA 105

Seneca, Lucius Annaeus
   4 B.C.-65 A.D. .... CMLC 6

Senghor, Leopold Sedar   1906- ...... CLC 54
   See also BLC 3; CA 116, 125

Serling, (Edward) Rod(man)
   1924-1975 .... CLC 30
   See also CA 65-68; obituary CA 57-60;
   DLB 26

Serpieres   1907-
   See Guillevic, (Eugene)

Service, Robert W(illiam)
   1874-1958 .... TCLC 15
   See also CA 115; SATA 20

Seth, Vikram   1952- .... CLC 43
   See also CA 121, 127

Seton, Cynthia Propper
   1926-1982 .... CLC 27
   See also CANR 7; CA 5-8R;
   obituary CA 108

Seton, Ernest (Evan) Thompson
   1860-1946 .... TCLC 31
   See also CA 109; SATA 18; DLB 92

Settle, Mary Lee   1918- .... CLC 19, 61
   See also CAAS 1; CA 89-92; DLB 6

Sevine, Marquise de Marie de
   Rabutin-Chantal   1626-1696 ..... LC 11

Sexton, Anne (Harvey)
   1928-1974 ... CLC 2, 4, 6, 8, 10, 15, 53;
                                       PC 2
   See also CANR 3; CA 1-4R;
   obituary CA 53-56; CABS 2; SATA 10;
   DLB 5; CDALB 1941-1968

Shaara, Michael (Joseph)   1929- .... CLC 15
   See also CA 102; obituary CA 125;
   DLB-Y 83

Shackleton, C. C.   1925-
   See Aldiss, Brian W(ilson)

Shacochis, Bob   1951- .... CLC 39
   See also CA 119, 124

Shaffer, Anthony   1926- .... CLC 19
   See also CA 110, 116; DLB 13

Shaffer, Peter (Levin)
   1926- .... CLC 5, 14, 18, 37, 60
   See also CANR 25; CA 25-28R; DLB 13

Shalamov, Varlam (Tikhonovich)
   1907?-1982 .... CLC 18
   See also obituary CA 105

Shamlu, Ahmad   1925- .... CLC 10

Shammas, Anton   1951- .... CLC 55

Shange, Ntozake   1948- .... CLC 8, 25, 38
   See also BLC 3; CANR 27; CA 85-88;
   CABS 3; DLB 38

Shapcott, Thomas W(illiam)   1935- .. CLC 38
   See also CA 69-72

Shapiro, Karl (Jay)   1913- .. CLC 4, 8, 15, 53
   See also CAAS 6; CANR 1; CA 1-4R;
   DLB 48

Sharp, William   1855-1905 .... TCLC 39

Sharpe, Tom   1928- .... CLC 36
   See also CA 114; DLB 14

Shaw, (George) Bernard
   1856-1950 .... TCLC 3, 9, 21, 45
   See also CA 128; brief entry CA 104;
   DLB 10, 57

Shaw, Henry Wheeler
   1818-1885 .... NCLC 15
   See also DLB 11

Shaw, Irwin   1913-1984 .... CLC 7, 23, 34
   See also CANR 21; CA 13-16R;
   obituary CA 112; DLB 6; DLB-Y 84;
   CDALB 1941-1968

Shaw, Robert   1927-1978 .... CLC 5
   See also CANR 4; CA 1-4R;
   obituary CA 81-84; DLB 13, 14

Shawn, Wallace   1943- .... CLC 41
   See also CA 112

Sheed, Wilfrid (John Joseph)
   1930- .... CLC 2, 4, 10, 53
   See also CA 65-68; DLB 6

Sheffey, Asa   1913-1980
   See Hayden, Robert (Earl)

Sheldon, Alice (Hastings) B(radley)
   1915-1987
   See Tiptree, James, Jr.
   See also CA 108; obituary CA 122

Shelley, Mary Wollstonecraft Godwin
   1797-1851 .... NCLC 14
   See also SATA 29

Shelley, Percy Bysshe
   1792-1822 .... NCLC 18

Shepard, Jim   19??- .... CLC 36

Shepard, Lucius   19??- .... CLC 34
   See also CA 128

Shepard, Sam
   1943- .... CLC 4, 6, 17, 34, 41, 44
   See also CANR 22; CA 69-72; DLB 7

Slavitt, David (R.) 1935- . . . . CLC **5, 14**
See also CAAS 3; CA 21-24R; DLB 5, 6

Slesinger, Tess 1905-1945 . . . . TCLC **10**
See also CA 107

Slessor, Kenneth 1901-1971 . . . . CLC **14**
See also CA 102; obituary CA 89-92

Slowacki, Juliusz 1809-1849 . . . . . NCLC **15**

Smart, Christopher 1722-1771 . . . . LC **3**

Smart, Elizabeth 1913-1986 . . . . CLC **54**
See also CA 81-84; obituary CA 118;
DLB 88

Smiley, Jane (Graves) 1949- . . . . . . CLC **53**
See also CA 104

Smith, A(rthur) J(ames) M(arshall)
1902-1980 . . . . CLC **15**
See also CANR 4; CA 1-4R;
obituary CA 102; DLB 88

Smith, Betty (Wehner) 1896-1972 . . . CLC **19**
See also CA 5-8R; obituary CA 33-36R;
SATA 6; DLB-Y 82

Smith, Cecil Lewis Troughton 1899-1966
See Forester, C(ecil) S(cott)

Smith, Charlotte (Turner)
1749-1806 . . . . NCLC **23**
See also DLB 39

Smith, Clark Ashton 1893-1961 . . . . CLC **43**

Smith, Dave 1942- . . . . CLC **22, 42**
See also Smith, David (Jeddie)
See also CAAS 7; CANR 1; DLB 5

Smith, David (Jeddie) 1942-
See Smith, Dave
See also CANR 1; CA 49-52

Smith, Florence Margaret 1902-1971
See Smith, Stevie
See also CAP 2; CA 17-18;
obituary CA 29-32R

Smith, Iain Crichton 1928- . . . . CLC **64**
See also DLB 40

Smith, John 1580?-1631 . . . . LC **9**
See also DLB 24, 30

Smith, Lee 1944- . . . . CLC **25, 73**
See also CA 119; brief entry CA 114;
DLB-Y 83

Smith, Martin Cruz 1942- . . . . CLC **25**
See also CANR 6; CA 85-88

Smith, Martin William 1942-
See Smith, Martin Cruz

Smith, Mary-Ann Tirone 1944- . . . . . CLC **39**
See also CA 118

Smith, Patti 1946- . . . . CLC **12**
See also CA 93-96

Smith, Pauline (Urmson)
1882-1959 . . . . TCLC **25**
See also CA 29-32R; SATA 27

Smith, Rosamond 1938-
See Oates, Joyce Carol

Smith, Sara Mahala Redway 1900-1972
See Benson, Sally

Smith, Stevie 1902-1971 . . . . CLC **3, 8, 25, 44**
See also Smith, Florence Margaret
See also DLB 20

Smith, Wilbur (Addison) 1933- . . . . . CLC **33**
See also CANR 7; CA 13-16R

Smith, William Jay 1918- . . . . CLC **6**
See also CA 5-8R; SATA 2; DLB 5

Smolenskin, Peretz 1842-1885 . . . . NCLC **30**

Smollett, Tobias (George) 1721-1771 . . LC **2**
See also DLB 39

Snodgrass, W(illiam) D(e Witt)
1926- . . . . CLC **2, 6, 10, 18, 68**
See also CANR 6; CA 1-4R; DLB 5

Snow, C(harles) P(ercy)
1905-1980 . . . . CLC **1, 4, 6, 9, 13, 19**
See also CA 5-8R; obituary CA 101;
DLB 15, 77

Snyder, Gary (Sherman)
1930- . . . . CLC **1, 2, 5, 9, 32**
See also CANR 30; CA 17-20R; DLB 5, 16

Snyder, Zilpha Keatley 1927- . . . . . . CLC **17**
See also CA 9-12R; SAAS 2; SATA 1, 28

Sobol, Joshua 19??- . . . . CLC **60**

Soderberg, Hjalmar 1869-1941 . . . . TCLC **39**

Sodergran, Edith 1892-1923 . . . . . . TCLC **31**

Sokolov, Raymond 1941- . . . . CLC **7**
See also CA 85-88

Sologub, Fyodor 1863-1927 . . . . TCLC **9**
See also Teternikov, Fyodor Kuzmich
See also CA 104

Solomos, Dionysios 1798-1857 . . . NCLC **15**

Solwoska, Mara 1929-
See French, Marilyn
See also CANR 3; CA 69-72

Solzhenitsyn, Aleksandr I(sayevich)
1918- . . . CLC **1, 2, 4, 7, 9, 10, 18, 26, 34**
See also CA 69-72

Somers, Jane 1919-
See Lessing, Doris (May)

Sommer, Scott 1951- . . . . CLC **25**
See also CA 106

Sondheim, Stephen (Joshua)
1930- . . . . CLC **30, 39**
See also CA 103

Sontag, Susan 1933- . . . CLC **1, 2, 10, 13, 31**
See also CA 17-20R; DLB 2, 67

Sophocles
c. 496? B.C.-c. 406? B.C. . . . . . . CMLC **2**;
DC **1**

Sorrentino, Gilbert
1929- . . . . CLC **3, 7, 14, 22, 40**
See also CANR 14; CA 77-80; DLB 5;
DLB-Y 80

Soto, Gary 1952- . . . . CLC **32**
See also CA 119, 125; DLB 82

Soupault, Philippe 1897-1990 . . . . . . CLC **68**
See also CA 116; obituary CA 131

Souster, (Holmes) Raymond
1921- . . . . CLC **5, 14**
See also CANR 13; CA 13-16R; DLB 88

Southern, Terry 1926- . . . . CLC **7**
See also CANR 1; CA 1-4R; DLB 2

Southey, Robert 1774-1843 . . . . NCLC **8**
See also SATA 54

Southworth, Emma Dorothy Eliza Nevitte
1819-1899 . . . . NCLC **26**

Soyinka, Wole
1934- . . . . . . CLC **3, 5, 14, 36, 44**; DC **2**
See also BLC 3; CANR 27; CA 13-16R;
DLB-Y 86

Spackman, W(illiam) M(ode)
1905-1990 . . . . CLC **46**
See also CA 81-84

Spacks, Barry 1931- . . . . CLC **14**
See also CA 29-32R

Spanidou, Irini 1946- . . . . CLC **44**

Spark, Muriel (Sarah)
1918- . . . . CLC **2, 3, 5, 8, 13, 18, 40**;
SSC **10**
See also CANR 12; CA 5-8R; DLB 15

Spencer, Elizabeth 1921- . . . . CLC **22**
See also CA 13-16R; SATA 14; DLB 6

Spencer, Scott 1945- . . . . CLC **30**
See also CA 113; DLB-Y 86

Spender, Stephen (Harold)
1909- . . . . CLC **1, 2, 5, 10, 41**
See also CA 9-12R; DLB 20

Spengler, Oswald 1880-1936 . . . . . . TCLC **25**
See also CA 118

Spenser, Edmund 1552?-1599 . . . . LC **5**

Spicer, Jack 1925-1965 . . . . . . CLC **8, 18, 72**
See also CA 85-88; DLB 5, 16

Spielberg, Peter 1929- . . . . CLC **6**
See also CANR 4; CA 5-8R; DLB-Y 81

Spielberg, Steven 1947- . . . . CLC **20**
See also CA 77-80; SATA 32

Spillane, Frank Morrison 1918-
See Spillane, Mickey
See also CA 25-28R

Spillane, Mickey 1918- . . . . CLC **3, 13**
See also Spillane, Frank Morrison

Spinoza, Benedictus de 1632-1677 . . . . LC **9**

Spinrad, Norman (Richard) 1940- . . . CLC **46**
See also CANR 20; CA 37-40R; DLB 8

Spitteler, Carl (Friedrich Georg)
1845-1924 . . . . TCLC **12**
See also CA 109

Spivack, Kathleen (Romola Drucker)
1938- . . . . CLC **6**
See also CA 49-52

Spoto, Donald 1941- . . . . CLC **39**
See also CANR 11; CA 65-68

Springsteen, Bruce 1949- . . . . CLC **17**
See also CA 111

Spurling, Hilary 1940- . . . . CLC **34**
See also CANR 25; CA 104

Squires, (James) Radcliffe 1917- . . . . CLC **51**
See also CANR 6, 21; CA 1-4R

Stael-Holstein, Anne Louise Germaine Necker,
Baronne de 1766-1817 . . . . NCLC **3**

Stafford, Jean 1915-1979 . . . CLC **4, 7, 19, 68**
See also CANR 3; CA 1-4R;
obituary CA 85-88; obituary SATA 22;
DLB 2

Stafford, William (Edgar)
1914- . . . . CLC **4, 7, 29**
See also CAAS 3; CANR 5, 22; CA 5-8R;
DLB 5

Stannard, Martin 1947- . . . . CLC **44**

Weir, Peter 1944-................ CLC 20
See also CA 113, 123

Weiss, Peter (Ulrich)
1916-1982 .... CLC 3, 15, 51
See also CANR 3; CA 45-48;
obituary CA 106; DLB 69

Weiss, Theodore (Russell)
1916- .... CLC 3, 8, 14
See also CAAS 2; CA 9-12R; DLB 5

Welch, (Maurice) Denton
1915-1948 .... TCLC 22
See also CA 121

Welch, James 1940-......... CLC 6, 14, 52
See also CA 85-88

Weldon, Fay
1933-......... CLC 6, 9, 11, 19, 36, 59
See also CANR 16; CA 21-24R; DLB 14

Wellek, Rene 1903- .... CLC 28
See also CAAS 7; CANR 8; CA 5-8R;
DLB 63

Weller, Michael 1942-......... CLC 10, 53
See also CA 85-88

Weller, Paul 1958-.............. CLC 26

Wellershoff, Dieter 1925-.......... CLC 46
See also CANR 16; CA 89-92

Welles, (George) Orson
1915-1985 .... CLC 20
See also CA 93-96; obituary CA 117

Wellman, Mac 1945- .... CLC 65

Wellman, Manly Wade 1903-1986 .. CLC 49
See also CANR 6, 16; CA 1-4R;
obituary CA 118; SATA 6, 47

Wells, Carolyn 1862-1942 .... TCLC 35
See also CA 113; DLB 11

Wells, H(erbert) G(eorge)
1866-1946 ...... TCLC 6, 12, 19; SSC 6
See also CA 110, 121; SATA 20; DLB 34,
70

Wells, Rosemary 1943-............ CLC 12
See also CLR 16; CA 85-88; SAAS 1;
SATA 18

Welty, Eudora (Alice)
1909-.... CLC 1, 2, 5, 14, 22, 33; SSC 1
See also CA 9-12R; CABS 1; DLB 2;
DLB-Y 87; CDALB 1941-1968

Wen I-to 1899-1946 .... TCLC 28

Werfel, Franz (V.) 1890-1945 ...... TCLC 8
See also CA 104; DLB 81

Wergeland, Henrik Arnold
1808-1845 .... NCLC 5

Wersba, Barbara 1932-............ CLC 30
See also CLR 3; CANR 16; CA 29-32R;
SAAS 2; SATA 1, 58; DLB 52

Wertmuller, Lina 1928- .... CLC 16
See also CA 97-100

Wescott, Glenway 1901-1987....... CLC 13
See also CANR 23; CA 13-16R;
obituary CA 121; DLB 4, 9

Wesker, Arnold 1932- .... CLC 3, 5, 42
See also CAAS 7; CANR 1; CA 1-4R;
DLB 13

Wesley, Richard (Errol) 1945-....... CLC 7
See also CA 57-60; DLB 38

Wessel, Johan Herman 1742-1785 .... LC 7

West, Anthony (Panther)
1914-1987 .... CLC 50
See also CANR 3, 19; CA 45-48; DLB 15

West, Jessamyn 1907-1984 ...... CLC 7, 17
See also CA 9-12R; obituary CA 112;
obituary SATA 37; DLB 6; DLB-Y 84

West, Morris L(anglo) 1916-..... CLC 6, 33
See also CA 5-8R; obituary CA 124

West, Nathanael
1903-1940 .... TCLC 1, 14, 44
See also CA 104, 125; DLB 4, 9, 28;
CDALB 1929-1941

West, Paul 1930- .... CLC 7, 14
See also CAAS 7; CANR 22; CA 13-16R;
DLB 14

West, Rebecca 1892-1983 .. CLC 7, 9, 31, 50
See also CANR 19; CA 5-8R;
obituary CA 109; DLB 36; DLB-Y 83

Westall, Robert (Atkinson) 1929-... CLC 17
See also CLR 13; CANR 18; CA 69-72;
SAAS 2; SATA 23

Westlake, Donald E(dwin)
1933- .... CLC 7, 33
See also CANR 16; CA 17-20R

Westmacott, Mary 1890-1976
See Christie, (Dame) Agatha (Mary
Clarissa)

Whalen, Philip 1923- .... CLC 6, 29
See also CANR 5; CA 9-12R; DLB 16

Wharton, Edith (Newbold Jones)
1862-1937 .... TCLC 3, 9, 27; SSC 6
See also CA 104; DLB 4, 9, 12, 78;
CDALB 1865-1917

Wharton, William 1925-......... CLC 18, 37
See also CA 93-96; DLB-Y 80

Wheatley (Peters), Phillis
1753?-1784. .... LC 3; PC 3
See also BLC 3; DLB 31, 50;
CDALB 1640-1865

Wheelock, John Hall 1886-1978 .... CLC 14
See also CANR 14; CA 13-16R;
obituary CA 77-80; DLB 45

Whelan, John 1900-
See O'Faolain, Sean

Whitaker, Rodney 1925-
See Trevanian

White, E(lwyn) B(rooks)
1899-1985 .... CLC 10, 34, 39
See also CLR 1; CANR 16; CA 13-16R;
obituary CA 116; SATA 2, 29, 44;
obituary SATA 44; DLB 11, 22

White, Edmund III 1940-......... CLC 27
See also CANR 3, 19; CA 45-48

White, Patrick (Victor Martindale)
1912-1990 .. CLC 3, 4, 5, 7, 9, 18, 65, 69
See also CA 81-84; obituary CA 132

White, T(erence) H(anbury)
1906-1964 .... CLC 30
See also CA 73-76; SATA 12

White, Terence de Vere 1912-...... CLC 49
See also CANR 3; CA 49-52

White, Walter (Francis)
1893-1955 .... TCLC 15
See also BLC 3; CA 115, 124; DLB 51

White, William Hale 1831-1913
See Rutherford, Mark
See also CA 121

Whitehead, E(dward) A(nthony)
1933-....................... CLC 5
See also CA 65-68

Whitemore, Hugh 1936-.......... CLC 37

Whitman, Sarah Helen
1803-1878 .... NCLC 19
See also DLB 1

Whitman, Walt
1819-1892 .... NCLC 4, 31; PC 3
See also SATA 20; DLB 3, 64;
CDALB 1640-1865

Whitney, Phyllis A(yame) 1903-.... CLC 42
See also CANR 3, 25; CA 1-4R; SATA 1,
30

Whittemore, (Edward) Reed (Jr.)
1919-....................... CLC 4
See also CAAS 8; CANR 4; CA 9-12R;
DLB 5

Whittier, John Greenleaf
1807-1892 .... NCLC 8
See also DLB 1; CDALB 1640-1865

Wicker, Thomas Grey 1926-
See Wicker, Tom
See also CANR 21; CA 65-68

Wicker, Tom 1926-.............. CLC 7
See also Wicker, Thomas Grey

Wideman, John Edgar
1941-............. CLC 5, 34, 36, 67
See also BLC 3; CANR 14; CA 85-88;
DLB 33

Wiebe, Rudy (H.) 1934-...... CLC 6, 11, 14
See also CA 37-40R; DLB 60

Wieland, Christoph Martin
1733-1813 .... NCLC 17

Wieners, John 1934-.............. CLC 7
See also CA 13-16R; DLB 16

Wiesel, Elie(zer) 1928-..... CLC 3, 5, 11, 37
See also CAAS 4; CANR 8; CA 5-8R;
SATA 56; DLB 83; DLB-Y 87

Wiggins, Marianne 1948-.......... CLC 57

Wight, James Alfred 1916-
See Herriot, James
See also CA 77-80; SATA 44

Wilbur, Richard (Purdy)
1921-............. CLC 3, 6, 9, 14, 53
See also CANR 2; CA 1-4R; CABS 2;
SATA 9; DLB 5

Wild, Peter 1940-................ CLC 14
See also CA 37-40R; DLB 5

Wilde, Oscar (Fingal O'Flahertie Wills)
1854-1900 .... TCLC 1, 8, 23, 41
See also CA 119; brief entry CA 104;
SATA 24; DLB 10, 19, 34, 57

Wilder, Billy 1906-.............. CLC 20
See also Wilder, Samuel
See also DLB 26

Wilder, Samuel 1906-
See Wilder, Billy
See also CA 89-92

Wilder, Thornton (Niven)
     1897-1975 . . . . . **CLC 1, 5, 6, 10, 15, 35;**
                                                     DC 1
     See also CA 13-16R; obituary CA 61-64;
     DLB 4, 7, 9

Wilding, Michael 1942- . . . . **CLC 73**
     See also CANR 24; CA 104

Wiley, Richard 1944- . . . . **CLC 44**
     See also CA 121, 129

Wilhelm, Kate 1928- . . . . **CLC 7**
     See also CAAS 5; CANR 17; CA 37-40R;
     DLB 8

Willard, Nancy 1936- . . . . **CLC 7, 37**
     See also CLR 5; CANR 10; CA 89-92;
     SATA 30, 37; DLB 5, 52

Williams, C(harles) K(enneth)
     1936- . . . . **CLC 33, 56**
     See also CA 37-40R; DLB 5

Williams, Charles (Walter Stansby)
     1886-1945 . . . . **TCLC 1, 11**
     See also CA 104

Williams, Ella Gwendolen Rees 1890-1979
     See Rhys, Jean

Williams, (George) Emlyn
     1905-1987 . . . . **CLC 15**
     See also CA 104, 123; DLB 10, 77

Williams, Hugo 1942- . . . . **CLC 42**
     See also CA 17-20R; DLB 40

Williams, John A(lfred) 1925- . . . . **CLC 5, 13**
     See also BLC 3; CAAS 3; CANR 6, 26;
     CA 53-56; DLB 2, 33

Williams, Jonathan (Chamberlain)
     1929- . . . . **CLC 13**
     See also CANR 8; CA 9-12R; DLB 5

Williams, Joy 1944- . . . . **CLC 31**
     See also CANR 22; CA 41-44R

Williams, Norman 1952- . . . . **CLC 39**
     See also CA 118

Williams, Paulette 1948-
     See Shange, Ntozake

Williams, Sherley Anne 1944-
     See also BLC 3; CANR 25; CA 73-76;
     DLB 41

Williams, Shirley 1944-
     See Williams, Sherley Anne

Williams, Tennessee
     1911-1983 . . . . **CLC 1, 2, 5, 7, 8, 11, 15,**
                                     19, 30, 39, 45, 71
     See also CANR 31; CA 5-8R;
     obituary CA 108; CABS 3; DLB 7;
     DLB-Y 83; DLB-DS 4;
     CDALB 1941-1968

Williams, Thomas (Alonzo) 1926- . . . **CLC 14**
     See also CANR 2; CA 1-4R

Williams, Thomas Lanier 1911-1983
     See Williams, Tennessee

Williams, William Carlos
     1883-1963 . . . **CLC 1, 2, 5, 9, 13, 22, 42,**
                                                                     67
     See also CA 89-92; DLB 4, 16, 54, 86;
     CDALB 1917-1929

Williamson, David 1932- . . . . **CLC 56**

Williamson, Jack 1908- . . . . **CLC 29**
     See also Williamson, John Stewart
     See also DLB 8

Williamson, John Stewart 1908-
     See Williamson, Jack
     See also CANR 123; CA 17-20R

Willingham, Calder (Baynard, Jr.)
     1922- . . . . **CLC 5, 51**
     See also CANR 3; CA 5-8R; DLB 2, 44

Wilson, A(ndrew) N(orman) 1950- . . **CLC 33**
     See also CA 112, 122; DLB 14

Wilson, Andrew 1948-
     See Wilson, Snoo

Wilson, Angus (Frank Johnstone)
     1913- . . . . **CLC 2, 3, 5, 25, 34**
     See also CANR 21; CA 5-8R; DLB 15

Wilson, August
     1945- . . . . **CLC 39, 50, 63; DC 2**
     See also BLC 3; CA 115, 122

Wilson, Brian 1942- . . . . **CLC 12**

Wilson, Colin 1931- . . . . **CLC 3, 14**
     See also CAAS 5; CANR 1, 122; CA 1-4R;
     DLB 14

Wilson, Edmund
     1895-1972 . . . . **CLC 1, 2, 3, 8, 24**
     See also CANR 1; CA 1-4R;
     obituary CA 37-40R; DLB 63

Wilson, Ethel Davis (Bryant)
     1888-1980 . . . . **CLC 13**
     See also CA 102; DLB 68

Wilson, Harriet 1827?-?
     See also BLC 3; DLB 50

Wilson, John 1785-1854 . . . . **NCLC 5**

Wilson, John (Anthony) Burgess 1917-
     See Burgess, Anthony
     See also CANR 2; CA 1-4R

Wilson, Lanford 1937- . . . . **CLC 7, 14, 36**
     See also CA 17-20R; DLB 7

Wilson, Robert (M.) 1944- . . . . **CLC 7, 9**
     See also CANR 2; CA 49-52

Wilson, Sloan 1920- . . . . **CLC 32**
     See also CANR 1; CA 1-4R

Wilson, Snoo 1948- . . . . **CLC 33**
     See also CA 69-72

Wilson, William S(mith) 1932- . . . . . **CLC 49**
     See also CA 81-84

Winchilsea, Anne (Kingsmill) Finch, Countess
     of 1661-1720 . . . . **LC 3**

Wingrove, David 1954- . . . . **CLC 68**
     See also CA 133

Winters, Janet Lewis 1899-
     See Lewis (Winters), Janet
     See also CAP 1; CA 9-10

Winters, (Arthur) Yvor
     1900-1968 . . . . **CLC 4, 8, 32**
     See also CAP 1; CA 11-12;
     obituary CA 25-28R; DLB 48

Winterson, Jeannette 1959- . . . . **CLC 64**

Wiseman, Frederick 1930- . . . . **CLC 20**

Wister, Owen 1860-1938 . . . . **TCLC 21**
     See also CA 108; DLB 9, 78

Witkiewicz, Stanislaw Ignacy
     1885-1939 . . . . **TCLC 8**
     See also CA 105; DLB 83

Wittig, Monique 1935?- . . . . **CLC 22**
     See also CA 116; DLB 83

Wittlin, Joseph 1896-1976 . . . . **CLC 25**
     See also Wittlin, Jozef

Wittlin, Jozef 1896-1976
     See Wittlin, Joseph
     See also CANR 3; CA 49-52;
     obituary CA 65-68

Wodehouse, (Sir) P(elham) G(renville)
     1881-1975 . . . **CLC 1, 2, 5, 10, 22; SSC 2**
     See also CANR 3; CA 45-48;
     obituary CA 57-60; SATA 22; DLB 34

Woiwode, Larry (Alfred) 1941- . . . . **CLC 6, 10**
     See also CANR 16; CA 73-76; DLB 6

Wojciechowska, Maia (Teresa)
     1927- . . . . **CLC 26**
     See also CLR 1; CANR 4; CA 9-12R;
     SAAS 1; SATA 1, 28

Wolf, Christa 1929- . . . . **CLC 14, 29, 58**
     See also CA 85-88; DLB 75

Wolfe, Gene (Rodman) 1931- . . . . **CLC 25**
     See also CAAS 9; CANR 6; CA 57-60;
     DLB 8

Wolfe, George C. 1954- . . . . **CLC 49**

Wolfe, Thomas (Clayton)
     1900-1938 . . . . **TCLC 4, 13, 29**
     See also CA 104; DLB 9; DLB-Y 85;
     DLB-DS 2

Wolfe, Thomas Kennerly, Jr. 1931-
     See Wolfe, Tom
     See also CANR 9; CA 13-16R

Wolfe, Tom 1931- . . . **CLC 1, 2, 9, 15, 35, 51**
     See also Wolfe, Thomas Kennerly, Jr.

Wolff, Geoffrey (Ansell) 1937- . . . . . **CLC 41**
     See also CA 29-32R

Wolff, Tobias (Jonathan Ansell)
     1945- . . . . **CLC 39, 64**
     See also CA 114, 117

Wolfram von Eschenbach
     c. 1170-c. 1220 . . . . **CMLC 5**

Wolitzer, Hilma 1930- . . . . **CLC 17**
     See also CANR 18; CA 65-68; SATA 31

Wollstonecraft Godwin, Mary
     1759-1797 . . . . **LC 5**
     See also DLB 39

Wonder, Stevie 1950- . . . . **CLC 12**
     See also Morris, Steveland Judkins

Wong, Jade Snow 1922- . . . . **CLC 17**
     See also CA 109

Woodcott, Keith 1934-
     See Brunner, John (Kilian Houston)

Woolf, (Adeline) Virginia
     1882-1941 . . . . **TCLC 1, 5, 20, 43; SSC 7**
     See also CA 130; brief entry CA 104;
     DLB 36, 100

Woollcott, Alexander (Humphreys)
     1887-1943 . . . . **TCLC 5**
     See also CA 105; DLB 29

Wordsworth, Dorothy
     1771-1855 . . . . **NCLC 25**

Wordsworth, William
     1770-1850 . . . . **NCLC 12; PC 4**
     See also DLB 93, 107

Wouk, Herman 1915- . . . . **CLC 1, 9, 38**
     See also CANR 6; CA 5-8R; DLB-Y 82

Literary Criticism Series
Cumulative Topic Index

This index lists all topic entries in the Gale Literary Criticism Series *Contemporary Literary Criticism, Literature Criticism from 1400 to 1800, Nineteenth-Century Literature Criticism,* and *Twentieth-Century Literary Criticism.*

Topic Index

NCLC Cumulative Nationality Index

POLISH
Fredro, Aleksander 8
Krasicki, Ignacy 8
Krasiński, Zygmunt 4
Mickiewicz, Adam 3
Norwid, Cyprian Kamil 17
Słowacki, Juliusz 15

ROMANIAN
Eminescu, Mihail 33

RUSSIAN
Aksakov, Sergei Timofeyvich 2
Bakunin, Mikhail Alexandrovich 25
Bashkirtseff, Marie 27
Belinski, Vissarion Grigoryevich 5
Chernyshevsky, Nikolay Gavrilovich 1
Dobrolyubov, Nikolai Alexandrovich 5
Dostoevsky, Fyodor 2, 7, 21, 33
Gogol, Nikolai 5, 15, 31
Goncharov, Ivan Alexandrovich 1
Herzen, Aleksandr Ivanovich 10
Karamzin, Nikolai Mikhailovich 3
Krylov, Ivan Andreevich 1
Lermontov, Mikhail Yuryevich 5
Leskov, Nikolai Semyonovich 25
Nekrasov, Nikolai 11
Ostrovsky, Alexander 30
Pisarev, Dmitry Ivanovich 25
Pushkin, Alexander 3, 27
Saltykov, Mikhail Evgrafovich 16
Smolenskin, Peretz 30
Turgenev, Ivan 21, 37
Tyutchev, Fyodor 34
Zhukovsky, Vasily 35

SCOTTISH
Baillie, Joanna 2
Beattie, James 25
Campbell, Thomas 19
Ferrier, Susan 8
Galt, John 1
Hogg, James 4
Jeffrey, Francis 33
Lockhart, John Gibson 6
Oliphant, Margaret 11
Scott, Sir Walter 15
Stevenson, Robert Louis 5, 14
Thomson, James 18
Wilson, John 5

SPANISH
Alarcón, Pedro Antonio de 1
Caballero, Fernán 10
Castro, Rosalía de 3
Larra, Mariano José de 17
Tamayo y Baus, Manuel 1
Zorrilla y Moral, José 6

SWEDISH
Bremer, Fredrika 11
Tegnér, Esias 2

SWISS
Amiel, Henri Frédéric 4
Keller, Gottfried 2
Wyss, Johann David 10

Nationality Index

Title Index to Volume 37

ISBN 0-8103-7976-7